Italy possesses one of the richest and most influential literatures of Europe, stretching back to the thirteenth century. This first substantial history of Italian literature to appear in the English language for forty years provides a comprehensive survey of Italian writing from its earliest origins up to the present day. Leading scholars describe and assess the work of writers who have contributed to the Italian literary tradition, including Dante, Petrarch and Boccaccio, the Renaissance humanists, Machiavelli, Ariosto and Tasso, pioneers and practitioners of opera and drama from *commedia dell'arte* to Pirandello and Dario Fo, the nineteenth- and twentieth-century poets from Leopardi to Montale, and the novelists from Manzoni to Calvino and Eco. *The Cambridge History of Italian Literature* is accessible to the general reader as well as to students and scholars: translations are provided, along with a map, chronological charts, and up-to-date and substantial bibliographies.

The Cambridge History of Italian Literature

The Cambridge History of
Italian Literature

Edited by

PETER BRAND
University of Edinburgh

and

LINO PERTILE
Harvard University

Revised Edition

CAMBRIDGE
UNIVERSITY PRESS

CAMBRIDGE UNIVERSITY PRESS
Cambridge, New York, Melbourne, Madrid, Cape Town, Singapore, São Paulo

Cambridge University Press
The Edinburgh Building, Cambridge CB2 8RU, UK

Published in the United States of America by Cambridge University Press, New York

www.cambridge.org
Information on this title: www.cambridge.org/9780521434928

First published 1996
First paperback edition (revised) 1999
Reprinted 2001, 2003, 2004

A catalogue record for this publication is available from the British Library

ISBN 978-0-521-43492-8 hardback
ISBN 978-0-521-66622-0 paperback

Transferred to digital printing 2007

Contents

List of contributors   xvii

Preface   xix

Acknowledgements   xxi

Map   xxii

Chronology   xxiii

Origins and Duecento
JONATHAN USHER

1 The earliest evidence   3

2 Poetry   5
   Francis of Assisi   5
   Popular and didactic poetry   6
   Provençal influence   8
   Sicilian school   9
   Tuscan imitators   14
   Guittone d'Arezzo   15
   Bonagiunta da Lucca   17
   Guido Guinizzelli   19
   Guido Cavalcanti   22
   Cavalcantian circle   25
   Cino da Pistoia   25
   Stilnovo   26

3 Prose   28
   Non-fictional works   28
   Vernacular translations   31
   From *exemplum* to *novella*   33
   The *Novellino*   34

Contents

The Trecento

4 Dante   39
LINO PERTILE
  Early life   40
  Vita Nuova   41
  Rime   44
  Florentine politics   46
  Convivio and *De vulgari eloquentia*   46
  The last *Rime*   50
  Monarchia   50
  The political letters   51
  The amnesty   54
  The *Commedia*   54
    Birth of a 'comedy'   55
    Composition and early diffusion   57
    Formal organisation and language   58
    Allegory and realism   59
    Dante's journey   60
    Myth and history   62
    The *contrapasso*   63
    Dante-the-character among the dead   64
    Politics and society   66
  The last years   68
  Dante today   68

5 Boccaccio   70
PAMELA D. STEWART
  Early years   70
  Caccia di Diana and *Rime*   72
  Filocolo   73
  Filostrato, Teseida and other works of the 1340s   74
  The *Decameron*   76
    Setting and structure   76
    Thematic patterns   78
    The storytellers   80
    The 'author'   82
  Later life and works   85

6 Petrarch   89
JOHN TOOK
  Life   89
  Cultural and moral context   91

The *Canzoniere* 92
  Petrarch's originality 92
  Composition and structure 94
  First part 97
  Second part 99
  Technical virtuosity 101
The *Trionfi* 104
Latin works 106

7 Minor writers 108
STEVEN BOTTERILL
  The literary culture of the Trecento 108
  Verse 114
    Poesia aulica 114
    Poesia giocosa 115
    The *perugini* 116
    Political poetry 117
    Devotional poetry 118
    Narrative poetry 119
    Poetry as entertainment 119
  Prose 120
    Vernacular translations 120
    Historical writing 121
    The *novelle* 123
    Devotional prose 123
    Commentaries on Dante 125

The Quattrocento
LETIZIA PANIZZA

8 Humanism 131
  Petrarch's legacy 132
  Education, libraries and translations from Greek 135
  Humanist profiles 137
    Leonardo Bruni and civic humanism 137
    L. B. Alberti: polyglot and polymath 138
    Lorenzo Valla: language in the service of ethics 140
    Women humanists 142

9 Power, patronage and literary associations 144
  Florence 144
  Rome 145
  Venice 147
  Naples 149
  Ferrara 150

10 Literature in the vernacular   152

   Latin and the vernacular   152

   Prose   154

     The *novella*   154

     Novels and other prose writings   158

     Arcadia   159

   Poetry   161

     The forms of poetry   161

     Lorenzo and Poliziano   164

     Narrative poetry   167

     PETER MARINELLI

       Pulci and the narrative tradition   167

       Boiardo   172

   Theatre   175

The Cinquecento

11 Prose   181

   BRIAN RICHARDSON

   The forms of literary prose   181

     The expansion of the vernacular   181

     Rhetoric and form   185

     Publishing and censorship   187

   Statecraft and history   188

     Politics and historiography in Florence   188

     Machiavelli   188

     Guicciardini   193

     Other Florentine writers on history and politics   196

     Politics and historiography in other states   200

     Ideal states   202

   The individual and society   203

     Court life and advice on behaviour: Castiglione   203

     Other writers on court life and behaviour   208

     Society and morality   212

     Women in society; love and marriage   214

   Literature and art   220

   Narrative fiction   223

     The *novella*   223

     The *romanzo*   231

12 Narrative poetry   233

   PETER MARINELLI

   From Boiardo to Ariosto   233

   Ariosto   234

From Ariosto to Tasso   240
Tasso   243

13 Lyric poetry   251
ANTHONY OLDCORN
    'Classicism' and 'anti-classicism'   251
    Bembo and the classicist tradition   252
        The inheritance of Sannazaro   255
        The classicising Petrarchism of Bernardo Tasso 256
        The georgic and didactic poem   257
        Ariosto's realistic non-alignment   258
        Michelangelo   260
        Della Casa and Magno   262
        Women poets   264
        Torquato Tasso   266
    The anti-classicist tradition: parody, satire, burlesque 268
        Ariosto and other satirists   268
        Berni and the *Berneschi*   270
        Aretino   271
        Macaronic and Fidentian verse   273

14 Theatre   277
RICHARD ANDREWS
    Scripted comedy to 1550   278
    Commedia dell'arte   284
    Scripted comedy after 1550   286
    Classical tragedy and tragi-comedy   288
    Pastoral drama   292

The Seicento
Poetry, Philosophy and Science
PAOLO CHERCHI

15 The Baroque   301

16 Lyric poetry   303
    Chiabrera and the melic trend   303
    The Baroque vanguard   304
    Marino and his followers   305
    Classicists   308

17 Mock-epic poetry and satire   310
    Heroi-comic poems   310
    Satiric poetry   311

18 Treatises   312
   Treatises on aesthetics   312
   Writers on politics, history and morals   313
   Science writers   316

Narrative prose and theatre
ALBERT N. MANCINI

19 Narrative prose   318
   The novel   318
   The *novella*   322
   Travel literature and autobiography   324

20 Theatre   326
   Commedia dell'arte   327
   Regular comedy   329
   Tragedy   331
   Pastoral plays   334

21 Opera   336
   DAVID KIMBELL
   The beginnings of opera   336
   Opera for the public theatre   338

The Settecento
FRANCO FIDO

22 The first half of the Settecento   343
   Muratori and historiography   344
   Venice: polygraphs, journalists and dramatists   345
   Intellectual life in Naples: Giannone, Vico, Genovesi   347
   Arcadia   350

23 The theatre from Metastasio to Goldoni   353
   Metastasio and melodrama   353
   Goldoni and comedy   355
   Gozzi and the *Fiabe*   361

24 Opera   363
   DAVID KIMBELL
   Dramma per musica and *opera buffa*   363
   After Metastasio   367

25 The Enlightenment and Parini 371
    The Enlightenment in Naples 371
    The Enlightenment in the north 373
    The dissident Baretti 376
    Milan: *Il Caffè*, the Verri brothers, Beccaria 378
    Parini: from Sensism to neo-classicism 380

26 Alfieri and pre-Romanticism 387
    Alfieri 387
    Between neo-classicism and pre-Romanticism 393
    The late Settecento autobiographies 395

The Age of Romanticism (1800–1870)
GIOVANNI CARSANIGA

27 The Romantic controversy 399
    Writers and cultural policy 399
    The controversy over translations 401
    Did Italian Romanticism exist? 402
    Women writers and the literary canon 403

28 Monti 406
    Changing sides: the Bassville affair 406
    The language of classicism 408
    The uses of mythology 409

29 Foscolo 412
    Love and politics: *Ultime lettere di Jacopo Ortis* 412
    A new mythology: *Le Grazie* 413
    Dei sepolcri: a 'smoky enigma' 415
    Exile 416

30 Leopardi 418
    'Mad and desperate study' 418
    Science and the idea of Nature: the evolution of the
        Canti 421
    Nature and society 423
    Leopardi and his readers 425

31 Manzoni and the novel 427
    Early life and works 427
    The novel 431
    The ideological programme 432
    From *Fermo e Lucia* to *I promessi sposi* 434

The *questione della lingua*   435
Room to dissent   437

32 Other novelists and poets of the Risorgimento   440
Novelists   440
Nievo   441
Political literature and literary criticism   444
'Popular' poetry   445
Tommaseo   447

33 Opera since 1800   450
DAVID KIMBELL
Romantic opera   450
Opera since unification   453

The Literature of United Italy (1870–1910)

34 Writer and society in the new Italy   459
ROBERT DOMBROSKI
Carducci and classicism   461
Naturalism and *verismo*   463
Capuana   463
Verga   464
De Roberto and other *veristi*   469
The borders of naturalism   470
Cuore and *Pinocchio*   471
Fogazzaro and Deledda   471
D'Annunzio   473
Pascoli   476
Popular fiction   479

35 Pirandello   480
FELICITY FIRTH
Early essays and novels   481
Short stories   483
Theatre   484

The Rise and Fall of Fascism (1910–45)
ROBERT DOMBROSKI

36 Poetry and the avant-garde   493
Futurism   495
Poetry   497
The *crepuscolari*   497
Campana   498

Saba 499
Ungaretti 502
Quasimodo 504
Montale 505

37 Philosophy and literature from Croce to Gramsci 509
Croce 510
Gentile 511
Gramsci 513
Fascism and culture 514

38 The novel 515
Svevo 515
Borgese 519
Tozzi 520
Bontempelli and Alvaro 521
Savinio and Buzzati 523
Solaria 524
Bilenchi 525
Vittorini 526
Gadda 527

The Aftermath of the Second World War (1945–56)
JOHN GATT-RUTTER

39 After the Liberation 533

40 Neo-realism 535
Peasant novels 537
Pavese 539
Vittorini 543
Naples and the urban south 545
The death camps 546
The female subject 547
Beyond the fringe of neorealism 549

41 History and the poets 553
Pasolini 556

Contemporary Italy (since 1956)
MICHAEL CAESAR

42 The late 1950s and the 1960s 561
The older poets 561

Novels of memory	563
Reviews	564
'Industrial' novels	568
Poets of the neo-avant-garde	570
Experimental novels	575

43 The 1970s — **581**

Poetry	581
Feminism and poetry	583
Problems of the self and language	584
Theatre	587
Fiction	588
Morante and other women writers	588
Primo Levi	590
Sciascia and other Sicilian writers	590
Other 'regional' writers	593
Calvino	594
Morselli, Volponi and others	595
Celati and Vassalli	596
Eco	598

44 The 1980s — **599**

Women writers	600
Tabucchi	602
A new generation of writers	603

Bibliography   607

General	607
Origins and Duecento	609
Trecento	612
Quattrocento	622
Cinquecento	627
Seicento	641
Settecento	646
The Age of Romanticism (1800–1870)	652
Opera	657
Literature of United Italy	659
Novecento (since 1910)	663

Index   674

Contributors

RICHARD ANDREWS, University of Leeds
STEVEN BOTTERILL, University of California, Berkeley
MICHAEL CAESAR, University of Birmingham
GIOVANNI CARSANIGA, University of Sydney
PAOLO CHERCHI, University of Chicago
ROBERT DOMBROSKI, City University of New York
FRANCO FIDO, Harvard University
FELICITY FIRTH, University of Bristol
JOHN GATT RUTTER, La Trobe University
DAVID KIMBELL, University of Edinburgh
ALBERT N. MANCINI, Ohio State University
† PETER MARINELLI, University of Toronto
ANTHONY OLDCORN, Brown University
LETIZIA PANIZZA, Royal Holloway University of London
LINO PERTILE, Harvard University
BRIAN RICHARDSON, University of Leeds
PAMELA STEWART, McGill University
JOHN TOOK, University College, London
JONATHAN USHER, University of Edinburgh

Preface

The *Cambridge History of Italian Literature* is intended to provide a comprehensive survey of Italian literature from its origins to the present day within the scope of a single volume. This obviously presents significant problems of selection and compression given the magnitude of the subject – a literary tradition of more than 700 years – and the considerable expansion of scholarly and critical studies in recent years. We believe however that this concentration helps to bring into focus features and issues which may be obscured by a more diffuse treatment. The volume also represents an act of faith in literary history as such and a belief that tradition, perhaps more in Italy than in some other cultures, is an important determining factor in literary creativity.

Italian literature is here taken generally to mean literature in the Italian vernacular: it has been possible, in a volume of this size, to mention only briefly a considerable output of dialect works which, however vibrant and illustrative of Italian genius, are nevertheless accessible to only a limited section of the Italian people. Similarly, works in Latin by Italian writers have received only brief mention, except in the case of the humanists of the fifteenth century when Latin came to dominate the vernacular as the principal vehicle for all serious writing.

Because of the size and complexity of the undertaking a multi-author approach seemed desirable and the responsibility for writing this volume has been shared among nineteen scholars, each of whom is a specialist in the appropriate field and able to give an authoritative assessment of the current state of research and criticism in that area. The editors have reduced as far as possible discrepancies and overlaps, but they have not sought to impose uniformity of approach or style on the different contributors – in the belief that variations between the sections of this volume are themselves reflective of a healthy diversity of research in the discipline as a whole.

The volume is aimed at the general reader rather than at specialists in the subject, and while it is assumed that most readers will have some knowledge of the Italian language an attempt has been made to cater for those who do not by providing translations of the longer passages of Italian and clarifying shorter passages (including titles) which might prove obscure. The translations are normally those cited in the bibliographies; where no published translations exist the author has provided one. Quotations of verse are given in both English and Italian, quotations of prose normally in English only. English versions of titles are provided in parenthesis after the Italian (in italics to indicate known published translations, in Roman where they have been supplied by the author), followed by the date of the first Italian edition.

The structure is broadly traditional in acknowledging *centuries* as convenient landmarks while recognising the significant overlaps in all periods; and within the period-divisions *genre* distinctions are generally paramount. For authors mentioned in more than one section of the volume the reader is referred to the cross-references in the text and to the Index, which provides a guide to all the significant mentions of writers and major subjects. Special features of this volume are the inclusion of sections on Italian opera, believed to be important for Italian literary history at various stages, and the attempt to bring the history as close as possible up to the present day.

For reasons of space footnotes have been reduced to a minimum, and bibliographies are very selective. For the reader's convenience they are structured to match as closely as possible the format of the relevant chapters, even though this causes some variations in layout.

While there has not been room to provide detailed contextual information on political, social or broadly cultural matters attention is drawn to the charts setting the main literary figures and works in a framework of contemporary political and artistic events.

Finally the editors would like to record their sorrow at the death of one of the contributors, Peter Marinelli, only days after completing his account of Renaissance epic, and their appreciation of his scholarly contribution to his subject.

P.B., L.P.

Preface to the paperback edition

The present paperback edition of the *Cambridge History of Italian Literature* is a revised version of the hardback published in 1996. Authors and editors were much encouraged by the response of reviewers and other readers and have tried in the new edition to take account of the comments and suggestions for improvement that have been made. Misprints and various other errors have been corrected and a number of omissions rectified; the index has been substantially recast and revised.

Acknowledgements

The following material has been reproduced from existing publications: passages from Dante, *Dantis Alagherii Epistolae, The Letters of Dante*, ed. and trans. Paget Toynbee, 2nd edn (1966), and *Dante's Lyric Poetry*, trans. K. Foster and P. Boyde (1967), by permission of Oxford University Press; passages from *Il Filocolo*, trans. David Cheaney and Thomas G. Bergin (1985), by permission of Garland Publishing Inc.; passages from Petrarch by permission of the publisher, from *Petrarch's Lyric Poems*, trans. and ed. R. M. Durling, Cambridge, Mass.: Harvard University Press, copyright © 1976 by Robert M. Durling; passages from Dante, *Vita Nuova*, trans. Barbara Reynolds (1969), by permission of Penguin Books Ltd and David Higham Associates; passages from Boccaccio, *Decameron*, trans. G. H. McWilliam (1995), by permission of Penguin Books Ltd. The editors would like to thank the publishers concerned for allowing the material to be reproduced.

They would also like to record their thanks to numerous colleagues for their assistance on various occasions: to Zygmunt Barański, Patrick Boyde, Michael Bury, Martin Clark, Richard Mackenny, Brian Moloney, Onofrio Speciale, Roger Tarr, and to members of the Italian Department of Edinburgh University which has housed and supported the project, notably to Carmine Mezzacappa, Federica Pedriali, Perry Wilson, and particularly to Jonathan Usher for his valuable editorial assistance and advice, and to Marie Dalgety, Secretary of the Department, who has cheerfully endured long hours at the keyboard.

MODERN ITALY

Chronology

Origins and Trecento

Political events

- 1209 Franciscan Order founded
- 1215 Dominican Order founded
- 1250 Death of Emperor Frederick II
- 1260 Ghibelline triumph at battle of Montaperti
- 1266 Guelfs victorious at battle of Benevento
- 1267 Guelfs rule in Florence
- 1300 First Jubilee
- 1303 Boniface VIII prisoner at Anagni
  Death of Boniface VIII
- 1305 Clement V detained in Avignon
- 1309 Holy See transferred to Avignon
- 1310 Emperor Henry VII in Italy
- 1311 Matteo Visconti becomes lord of Milan
- 1312 Siege of Florence by Henry VII
- 1313 Henry VII dies near Siena
- 1313– Castruccio Castracani takes over Lucca, Pistoia and Pisa (–1328)

Literature

- c. 1225 St Francis, *Cantico di Frate Sole*
- 1230– Sicilian School of Poetry (–1250)
  Guittone, 'Or è la stagion ...'
- 1260– Brunetto Latini, *Trésor* and *Tesoretto* (–1266)
- –1276 Guido Guinizzelli, 'Al cor gentil rempaira sempre Amore'
- c. 1281 Anon, *Il Novellino*
- 1293– Dante, *Vita Nuova* (–1295)
- c. 1298 Marco Polo, *Milione*
- c. 1300 Guido Cavalcanti, 'Perché non spero ...'
- 1303– Dante, *De vulgari eloquentia* and *Convivio* (–c. 1307)
- c. 1307 Dante, *Commedia* (–1321)
- 1310 Dante, *Letter to Lords and Peoples of Italy*
- 1310 Dino Compagni, *Cronica*
- 1316? Dante, *Monarchia*
- c. 1320 Giovanni Villani, *Cronica*
- 1322 Iacopo Alighieri, *Chiose all'Inferno di Dante*

Other arts

- c. 1050 New musical notation by Guido d'Arezzo
- 1050– St Mark's, Venice (–1071)
- 1063– Cathedral, Pisa (–1118)
- 1088 University of Bologna founded
- 1222 University of Padua founded
- 1228– Church of St Francis, Assisi
- –1260 Nicola Pisano, Baptistry pulpit, Pisa
- 1259– Aquinas, *Summa theologiae*
- 1279– Santa Maria Novella, Florence, rebuilt
- 1293 Arnolfo di Cambio, *Ciborium*
- 1295– Santa Croce, Florence, refounded
- c. 1295 Cimabue, St Francis frescoes, Assisi
- 1296– Santa Maria del Fiore, Florence
- 1299– Palazzo Vecchio, Florence
- 1302 Giovanni Pisano, pulpit, Pisa
- 1304– Giotto, Scrovegni chapel frescoes, Padua (–1308)
- 1308 Duccio, *Maestà*
- 1309– Palace of the Doges, Venice
- 1330 Andrea Pisano, Baptistry south door, Florence (–1336)

Political events		Literature		Other arts	
1337	Start of Hundred Years' War	1335–	Petrarch, *Canzoniere* (–1374)	1333	Simone Martini, *Annunciation*
				1334–	Giotto, Campanile, Florence
		1336–	Boccaccio, *Filocolo, Filostrato,* etc. (–1338)	1337–	Lorenzetti, *Allegories of Good and Bad Government*, Siena (–1339)
1343	Death of Robert and end of Anjou dynasty in Naples	1338–	Petrarch, *Africa* (–1342)	c. 1340	Italian *Ars nova*
1347	Cola di Rienzo leaves Rome				
1347–8	The Black Death	1348–	Boccaccio, *Decameron* (–1353)		
		1350–	Petrarch, *Trionfi* (–1374)		
1355	Charles IV crowned Emperor	c. 1354	Jacopo Passavanti, *Specchio di vera penitenzia*		
1355–	Expansion of territory of Savoy				
1358	Peace of Milan (between Venice and the Visconti)			1357	Orcagna, *Christ in Majesty*
		1362–	Sacchetti, *Rime*		
		1373	Boccaccio, *Esposizioni sopra la Comedia di Dante*		
1375	Tuscany, Milan and Naples allies against papal expansionism				
1377	Holy See returns to Rome	c. 1378	Giovanni Fiorentino, *Pecorone*	1379	F. Landino, Organist of SS. Annunziata, Florence
1378–	The Great Schism in Papacy (–1420) Florence: the Ciompi riots		Catherine of Siena, *Dialogo della divina provvidenza*	1385	Schifanoia Palace, Ferrara
1378–	Gian Galeazzo Visconti occupies Verona, Pavia, Pisa, Siena (–1399)	c. 1385	Benvenuto da Imola, Commentary on Dante	1386	Cathedral, Milan
		c. 1392–	Sacchetti, *Trecentonovelle* (–c. 1397)	1390	Church of S. Petronio, Bologna
				1396	Certosa, Pavia

1400–1600

Political events		Literature		Other arts	
1412–	Filippo Maria Visconti Duke of Milan (–1447)	1429	Matteo Palmieri, *Della vita civile*	c. 1415	Donatello, *St George* (–1417)
1420	End of Great Schism in Papacy			1427/8	Masaccio, *Trinity* (S.Maria Novella)

Politics and History

1434–	Cosimo de' Medici dominant in Florence (–1464)
1442–	Alfonso of Aragon King of Naples (–1458)
1447–	Nicholas V Pope (–1455)
1447	Ambrosian republic (Milan)
1450–	Francesco Sforza Duke of Milan (–1466)
1453	Turks capture Constantinople
1454	Peace of Lodi – Italian states ally against Turks
1469–	Lorenzo de' Medici dominant in Florence (–1492)
1479–	Ludovico Sforza (il Moro) Duke of Milan (–1500)
1492–	Alexander VI Pope (–1503)
1494	Invasion of Italy by Charles VIII of France
1494–	Medici exiled from Florence
1499	Invasion by Louis XII of France
1500	Treaty of Granada – France and Spain partition Kingdom of Naples
1503–	Julius II Pope (–1513)
1508	League of Cambrai (Emperor, France, Spain) against Venice
1511	Holy League (Pope, Spain, Venice) against France
1512	Battle of Ravenna, French withdrawal Medici restored to Florence

Literature

1437–	Alberti, *Della famiglia* (–1441)
1441	'Certame coronario' organised by Alberti
1475–	Poliziano, *Le stanze* (–1478)
1476	Masuccio Salernitano, *Novellino*
1477	*Raccolta aragonese* compiled by Poliziano
1480	Poliziano, *Orfeo*
1483	Luigi Pulci, *Morgante*
1486–	Sannazaro, *Arcadia* (–1504)
–1492	Lorenzo de' Medici, *Comento de' miei sonetti*
1494	Boiardo, *Orlando Innamorato*
1508	Ariosto, *La cassaria*

Art and Music

c. 1432–	Ghiberti, *Porta del Paradiso*, Florence (–1452)
1433–	Brunelleschi, Pazzi Chapel, Florence
1436	Alberti, *Della pittura*
1438–	Fra Angelico, *Annunciation* (–1445)
1450	Alberti, Malatesta Temple, Rimini
1454–	Piero della Francesca, Arezzo frescoes (–1458)
1459–	Josquin des Prés settles in Milan (–1479)
c. 1465–	Mantegna, *L. Gonzaga and family* (–1474)
c. 1476	Bellini, *S. Giobbe Altarpiece*, Venice
c. 1482	Botticelli, *Primavera*
1485–	Giuliano da Sangallo, Villa Poggio a Caiano
c. 1495–	Leonardo, *Last Supper* (–1498)
1501	Michelangelo, *David* (–1504)
c. 1502–	Bramante, Tempietto, Rome (–1503)
1503	Josquin des Prés moves to Ferrara
1508	Raphael, *Stanze*, Vatican (–1509)
1508–	Michelangelo, Sistine ceiling (–1512)

Political events

1513–	Leo X Pope (–1521)
1515	Invasion of Italy by Francis I of France
1523–	Clement VII Pope (–1534)
1525	French defeated by Charles V at Pavia
1526	League of Cognac (Pope, France, Florence, Venice, Milan) against Charles V
1527	Sack of Rome by Imperial troops
1529	Treaty of Barcelona – Charles V dominant in Italy
1542	Inquisition revived
1545–	Council of Trent – Counter-Reformation reinforced
1559	Treaty of Cateau-Cambrésis – Spanish hegemony in Italy
1571	Naval battle of Lepanto – Holy League defeats Turks
1598	Ferrara annexed to Papacy

Literature

c. 1513–	Machiavelli, *Principe, Discorsi* (–c. 1517)
1516	Ariosto, *Orlando Furioso* 1st edn
c. 1518	Machiavelli, *Mandragola*
1525	Bembo, *Prose della volgar lingua*
1528	Castiglione, *Cortegiano*
1530	Bembo, *Rime*
1532	Ariosto, *Orlando Furioso*, 3rd edn Anon. *Gli ingannati*
1535–	Guicciardini, *Storia d'Italia* (–1540)
1537–	Aretino, *Lettere* (–1557)
1538	Colonna, *Rime*
1554	Bandello, *Novelle*
1558–	Cellini, *Vita* (–1566)
1558	Della Casa, *Rime e prose* (inc. *Il Galateo*)
1564	Index of Proscribed Books published by Council of Trent
1573	Tasso, *Aminta*
1581	Tasso, *Gerusalemme liberata*
1590	Guarini, *Il pastor fido*

Other arts

1516–	Titian, *Assumption of the Virgin* (–1518)
1519–	Michelangelo, Medici Chapel, Florence (–1534)
1526–	Giulio Romano, Palazzo del Te, Mantua (–1534)
1527–	Adrian Willaert settles in Venice
c. 1531	Correggio, *Danae*
1544–	Orlandus Lassus settles in Italy (–1555)
1546	Titian, *Pope Paul III*
1546–	Michelangelo, St Peter's (–1564)
1550–	Palladio, Villa Rotonda
1554	Palestrina, 1st Book of Masses
1559	Willaert, *Musica nova*
1565	Tintoretto, *Crucifixion*
1573	Palestrina, *Missa Papae Marcelli* Veronese, *Feast in House of Levi*
1585	A. Gabrieli, *Edipo tiranno*, Vicenza
1598	G. Gabrieli, *Symphoniae sacrae I*

1600–1800

Political events	Literature	Other arts
1601 Savoy (C. Emmanuel I) regains Saluzzo		1600 Peri, *Euridice*, Florence
		c. 1600 Caravaggio, *Conversion of St Paul*
		1602 Caccini, *Nuove musiche*
1606 Venice (P. Sarpi) defies papal interdict	1605 Chiabrera, *Vendemmie del Parnaso*	c. 1604 A. Caracci, *Flight into Egypt*
		1607 Monteverdi, *Orfeo*, Mantua
	1612 Boccalini, *Ragguagli di Parnaso*	1613– Reni, *Aurora* (–1614)
		1614 Domenichino, *St Jerome*
1618– Thirty Years' War (–1648)	1619 Sarpi, *Istoria del Concilio Tridentino*	
	1622 Tassoni, *Secchia rapita*	1622– Bernini, *Apollo e Dafne* (–1623)
	1623 Marino, *Adone*; Campanella, *Città del sole*; Galileo, *Il Saggiatore*	
1628 Mantua sacked by Imperial troops	1627– Della Valle, *Judith*, *Esther* (–1628)	
1631 Urbino devolved to Papacy	1632 Galileo, *Dialogo sopra i due sistemi*	1631– Longhena, Church of S. Maria della Salute, Venice
1638– Charles Emmanuel II, King of Savoy (–1675)	1634– Basile, *Cunto de li cunti* (–1636)	1637 First public opera house, Venice
		1638– Borromini, Church of S. Carlo alle 4 Fontane, Rome (–1641)
1643 Masaniello rising in Naples		1642 Monteverdi, *Incoronazione di Poppea*
1647– Anti-Spanish revolts in Sicily and Naples (–1648)		1649 Cavalli, *Giasone*
		c. 1650 Rosa, *Finding of Moses*
		1656– Bernini, Colonnade of St Peter's (–1665)
1669 Venice loses Crete to Turks		
1675– V. Amedeus King of Savoy (–1730)		1681 Corelli, *Trio Sonatas I*
1683 Venice joins Holy League against Turks	1687– Frugoni, *Cane di Diogene* (–1689)	
	1690 Arcadian Academy founded	
	1694 Rosa, *Satire* (posth.)	
1700– War of Spanish Succession (–1713)		1706– Handel in Italy (–1710)
1713 Peace of Utrecht (Milan, Mantua, Naples to Austria; Sicily to Savoy)	1713 Maffei, *Merope*	1707 Scarlatti, *Mitridate Eupatore*, Venice
		1711 Vivaldi, *Estro armonico* concertos
1720 Treaty of The Hague (Sicily to Austria, Sardinia to Savoy – V. Amedeus II)		1717– Juvara, Basilica of Superga, Turin (–1731)

Political events	Literature	Other arts
	1723 Giannone, *Istoria civile di Napoli*	1723– De Sanctis and Specchi, Spanish Steps, Rome (–1726)
	1724 Metastasio, *Didone abbandonata*	
	1725 Vico, *Principi di una scienza nuova*	1732– Salvi, Trevi Fountain, Rome (–1762)
1733– War of Polish Succession (–1738)	1733– Muratori, *Rerum italicarum scriptores* (–1751); Metastasio, *L'Olimpiade*	1733 Pergolesi, *La serva padrona*
1738 Treaty of Vienna (Naples, Sicily to Spain, Tuscany to Francis of Lorraine)		1737– Tiepolo, ceiling of Gesuati Church, Venice (–1739)
1740– War of Austrian Succession (–1748)	1745 Goldoni, *Il servitore di due padroni* (scenario)	
1748 Treaty of Aix-la-Chapelle (Kingdom of Sardinia enlarged)		1749 Galuppi and Goldoni, *L'Arcadia in Brenta*
	1753 Goldoni, *La Locandiera*	1752– Vanvitelli, Royal Palace, Caserta
	1763 Parini, *Il mattino* (1765 *Giorno*)	1760 Piccinni, *La buona figliuola*, Rome
	1763– Baretti, *Frusta letteraria* (–1765)	c. 1760 Canaletto, *Piazza S. Marco*
	1763– Cesarotti, *Ossian* (–1772)	
	1764 Beccaria, *Dei delitti e delle pene*	
	1764– P. Verri, *Il Caffè* (–1766)	
1768 France purchases Corsica from Genoa		
1773– V. Amedeus III King of Sardinia (–1796)		
1775 Pope dissolves Order of Jesus (Jesuits)		
	1782 Alfieri, *Saul*	1782 Paisiello, *Barbiere di Siviglia*, St Petersburg
	1786 Alfieri, *Del principe e delle lettere*	1786 Mozart and Da Ponte, *Nozze di Figaro*, Vienna
		1787– Canova, *Cupid and Psyche* (–1793)
		1790 Guardi, *View of Lagoon*
		1792 Cimarosa, *Il Matrimonio segreto*, Vienna
1796– Napoleonic campaigns in Italy (–1797)		
1797 Treaty of Campoformio (Venice to Austria)		
1798– Republic in Naples (–1799)		
1799 French defeats; collapse of Naples republic		
1800 New Napoleonic invasion of Italy		

Since 1800

Political events	Literature	Other arts (P = periodical, C = cinema)
1800 Napoleon defeats Austrians at Marengo		
1802 Proclamation of the Italian Republic	1802 Foscolo, *Ultime lettere di Jacopo Ortis* (2nd edn)	
1805 Proclamation of Kingdom of Italy under Napoleon	1806 Manzoni, *In morte di Carlo Imbonati*	
1806 French occupy Naples	1807 Foscolo, *Dei sepolcri*	
1808 French occupy Rome	1810 Monti, *L'Iliade* (trans.)	1808 Canova, *Pauline Borghese as Venus Victrix*
	Cesari, *Sullo stato presente della lingua italiana*	'Conservatorio di Musica', Milan, founded
1814 Austria regains Lombardy and Veneto	1812– Foscolo, *Le Grazie*	
1815 Congress of Vienna. Restoration of pre-Napoleonic Italy	1812– Manzoni, *Inni sacri*	1816 Rossini, *Barbiere di Siviglia* (Rome)
	1816 Mme de Staël, *Sulla maniera e l'utilità delle traduzioni*	1817 Jappelli, Caffè Pedrocchi, Padua
	Berchet, *Lettera semiseria di Grisostomo*	1818–19 (P) *Il Conciliatore*
1820 'Carbonari' conspirators arrested in Milan	1819– Leopardi, 'Primi idilli' and 'Canzoni'	
1820–1 Insurrections in Naples and Turin	1820– Manzoni, *Conte di Carmagnola, Marzo 1821, 5 maggio, Adelchi* (–1822)	
	1821 Porta, *Poesie in dialetto milanese*	
	1821– Manzoni, *Fermo e Lucia* (–1823)	
	1822 Pindemonte, *L'Odissea* (trans.)	
	1827 Leopardi, *Operette morali*	
	Manzoni, *I Promessi sposi* (1st edn)	
	1828– Leopardi, 'Grandi idilli'	1829 Rossini, *Guglielmo Tell* (Paris)
	1830– Belli, 2000 Roman Sonnets (–1836)	
1831– Carlo Alberto King of Savoy (–1849)	1831 Leopardi, *Canti* (1st edn)	1831 Bellini, *Sonnambula* and *Norma* (Milan)
1831–4 Insurrections in Modena, Parma, Papal States, Piedmont, Genoa	1832 Pellico, *Le mie prigioni*	
	1833 D'Azeglio, *Ettore Fieramosca*	1835 Donizetti, *Lucia di Lammermoor* (Naples)
	1834 Grossi, *Marco Visconti*	
	1835 Leopardi, *Canti* (2nd edn)	1836 Mazzini, *Filosofia della musica*
1839 First Italian railway opened Naples–Portici	1840 Manzoni, *Promessi sposi* (2nd edn)	1842 Verdi, *Nabucco* (Milan)
1844 Insurrection in Calabria		

Political events

- 1846 Pius IX elected Pope
- 1848–9 Insurrections and first War of Independence. Roman Republic established. Austrian intervention and repression
- 1855 Piedmont joins France in Crimean War
- 1857 Pisacane's insurrectionary landing near Salerno fails
- 1859 Second War of Independence
- 1860 Garibaldi's Expedition to Sicily ('the Thousand')
- 1861– Vittorio Emanuele II King of united Italy (–1878)
- 1866 Third War of Independence: the Veneto joined to Italian Kingdom
- 1870 Italian troops enter Rome
- 1871 Rome proclaimed capital of Italy
- 1874 Pius IX's denunciation of Italian state
- 1882 The Triple Alliance (Italy, Germany, Austria)
- 1885 Italian troops occupy Massawa (Eritrea)
- 1890 Eritrea becomes Italian colony
- 1892 Italian Workers Party founded (banned 1894)
- 1895 Workers Party named Socialist Party (PSI)
- 1899 FIAT founded

Literature

- 1847 Mameli, *Fratelli d'Italia*
- 1850– Carducci, *Juvenilia* (–1860)
- 1852 Mastriani, *La cieca di Sorrento*
- 1853 Guerrazzi, *Beatrice Cenci*
- 1853– Ruffini, *Lorenzo Benoni* and *Il dottor Antonio* (–1855)
- 1857– Rovani, *Cento anni* (–1858)
- 1861– Carducci, *Levia gravia* (–1871)
- 1862 Arrighi, *La scapigliatura*
- 1864 Aleardi, *Canti*
- 1866 Verga, *Una peccatrice*
- 1867 Nievo, *Confessioni di un italiano*
- 1870–1 De Sanctis, *Storia della letteratura italiana*
- 1877– Carducci, *Odi barbare* (–1879)
- 1880– Collodi, *Pinocchio* (–1883)
- 1881 Verga, *I Malavoglia*
- 1886 De Amicis, *Cuore*
- 1888 D'Annunzio, *Il piacere*
- 1889 Verga, *Mastro don Gesualdo*
- 1891 Pascoli, *Myricae*
- 1892 Svevo, *Una vita*
- 1894 De Roberto, *I viceré*
- 1895 Fogazzaro, *Piccolo mondo antico*
- 1898 Svevo, *Senilità*
- 1900– D'Annunzio, *Il fuoco, Laudi, La figlia di Iorio, Fedra*, etc. (–1910)

Other arts (P = perodical, C = cinema)

- 1846 Hayez, *Sicilian Vespers*
- c. 1850– D'Ancona, Signorini, Banti, 'Macchiaioli' paintings (–c. 1870)
- 1851 Verdi, *Rigoletto* (Venice)
- 1853 Verdi, *Traviata* (Venice)
- 1859 Hayez, *Il bacio*
- 1863 Antonelli, 'Mole antonelliana', Turin
- 1868 Boito, *Mefistofele* (Milan)
- 1871 Verdi, *Aida* (Cairo)
- 1876 Ponchielli, *La Gioconda* (Milan)
- 1877 Mengoni, 'Galleria Vittorio Emanuele', Milan
- 1887 Verdi, *Otello* (Milan)
- 1890 Mascagni, *Cavalleria rusticana* (Rome)
- 1892 Leoncavallo, *Pagliacci* (Milan)
- 1893 Puccini, *Manon Lescaut* (Turin); Verdi, *Falstaff* (Milan)
- 1896 Giordano, *Andrea Chenier* (Milan)
- 1900 Puccini, *Bohème* (Turin); Puccini, *Tosca* (Rome)

	Literature	Arts
	1901 Capuana, *Il marchese di Roccaverdina*	
	1903 Pascoli, *Canti di Castelvecchio*	
	1904 Pirandello, *Il fu Mattia Pascal*	
	1906 Aleramo, *Una donna*	
	1909 Marinetti, *Manifesto del futurismo*	**1908** (P) *La Voce*
		1909 Marinetti, Futurist Manifesto published, Paris
	1911 Gozzano, *I colloqui*	**1910–12** Pratella, Three Manifestos of Futurist music
	1914 Campana, *Canti orfici*	**1913** Balla, *Abstract Speed*; Boccioni, *Unique Forms of Continuity in Space*
		1914 De Chirico, *The Enigma of a Day*
		1915 Modigliani, *Portrait of Juan Gris*
	1917 Deledda, *Canne al vento*	
		1918 Morandi, *Flowers*
	1919 Ungaretti, *Allegria di naufragi*	**1919** (P) *La Ronda* (–1923)
	1921 Borgese, *Rubè*	**1920** Malipiero, *Sette canzoni*, Paris
	1921–2 Pirandello, *Sei personaggi*, *Enrico IV*	
	1923 Croce, *Poesia e non poesia*; Svevo, *La coscienza di Zeno*	
	1925 Montale, *Ossi di seppia*	**1924–** (P) *Il selvaggio*
		1926 Puccini, *Turandot* (Milan); (P) *Solaria*
	1929 Moravia, *Gli indifferenti*	**1929** Sironi, *Urban Landscape*
	1930 Silone, *Fontamara*	**1932** (C) First cinema festival, Venice

1912 Italy occupies Libya, Rhodes and Dodecanese. Suffrage extended for literate male adults

1913 Engineering workers' right to organise recognised

1915 Italy declares war on Austro-Hungarian Empire

1917 October: Italians defeated at Caporetto

1918 October: Italian offensive. Armistice

1919 First 'fascio di combattimento' founded in Milan. D'Annunzio occupies Fiume (–1920)

1920 Strikes and occupation of factories

1921 Communist Party of Italy (PCI) formed as breakaway from PSI. Fascist National Party formed

1922 October: Fascist march on Rome. Mussolini head of government

1924 General elections. Social-Democrat Deputy Matteoti murdered

1925 *Manifesto of Fascist Intellectuals* issued

1926 Opposition parties and non-Fascist unions suppressed

1928 Gramsci sentenced to 20 years by Special Tribunal

1929 Concordat between Church and State

Political events

1935–6	Invasion of Ethiopia. Empire proclaimed. Rome–Berlin Axis
1937	Anti-Fascist Rosselli brothers assassinated in France
1938	Racial Laws promulgated
1939	Italy occupies Albania. Pact of Steel with Germany
1940	Italy enters Second World War
1943	25 July: Mussolini removed from power. 8 Sept.: Armistice declared. Committees of National Liberation (CLN) formed. 11–23 Sept: Mussolini, freed by Germans, creates the Italian Social Republic
1944	4 June: Allied forces enter Rome
1945	28 April: Mussolini executed by partisans. 20 June: Parri government with Committee of National Liberation. 10 Dec.: First De Gasperi Christian Democrat (DC) government
1945	Women's suffrage granted
1946	2 June: Referendum. Italy becomes a republic
1947	De Gasperi evicts PCI and PSI from government
1948	Constitution of Italian Republic comes into effect. Attempted assassination of Togliatti, leader of PCI
1949	Italy enters NATO. Church excommunicates Communists

Literature

1934	Palazzeschi, *Sorelle Materassi*
1936	Pavese, *Lavorare stanca*
1938–	Vittorini, *Conversazione in Sicilia*; Gadda, *La cognizione del dolore*
1939	Montale, *Le occasioni*
1940	Quasimodo, *Lirici greci* (trans.)
1941	Pavese, *Paesi tuoi*
1945	Levi, Carlo, *Cristo si è fermato a Eboli*; Saba, *Il canzoniere* (1900–1945)
1947	Pratolini, *Cronache di poveri amanti*; Ungaretti, *Il dolore*; Sereni, *Diario d'Algeria*; Levi, Primo, *Se questo è un uomo*
1948	Morante, *Menzogna e sortilegio*; Pavese, *Prima che il gallo canti*

Other arts (P = periodical, C = cinema)

1933	'Maggio musicale' established, Florence
1937	(P) *Letteratura*
1938	(P) *Campo di Marte*
1941	Guttuso, *Crocifissione*
1942	(C) Visconti, *Ossessione*
1945	(C) Rossellini, *Rome, Open City*
1946	(C) Rossellini, *Paisà*
1948	(C) De Sica, *Bicycle Thieves*
1948–9	Nervi, Exhibition Hall, Turin
1949	Dallapiccola, *Il prigioniero*

1950	Pavese, *La luna e i falò*	1950–	Capogrossi, Art exhibition, Rome; Burri, First *Sacco*, Rome
		1950–	Studio BBPR (Ludovico Barbiano etc.), Torre velasca, Milan
		1951	Fontana, *Manifesto spazialismo*, Milan
1954	Fenoglio, *La malora*	1954	(C) Fellini, *La strada*
		1954–5	Colla, First metal sculptures, Rome
1955	Moravia, *Racconti romani*; Pasolini, *Ragazzi di vita*; Pratolini, *Metello*	1955	Berio and Maderna, 'Studio di fonologia' established, Milan
1956	Caproni, *Il passaggio di Enea*; Montale, *La bufera e altro*; Pasolini, *Le ceneri di Gramsci*	1956	Scarpa, 'Museo di Castelvecchio', Verona
1957	Calvino, *Il barone rampante*		
1958	Tomasi di Lampedusa, *Il gattopardo*; Pasolini, *Una vita violenta*	1958–	Manzù, Doors of St Peter's (–1964)
1959	Cassola, *La ragazza di Bube*	1960	(C) Fellini, *La dolce vita*; (C) Visconti, *Rocco e i suoi fratelli*; (C) Antonioni, *Avventura*
1961	Sciascia, *Il giorno della civetta*	1961	(C) Pasolini, *Accattone*; Nono, *Intolleranza* (Venice); Manzoni, *Socle du monde. Omaggio a Galileo*
1962	Bassani, *Il giardino dei Finzi-Contini*		
1963	Ginzburg, *Lessico famigliare*; Levi, Primo, *La tregua*; Meneghello, *Libera nos a malo*; Luzi, *Nel magma*	1963	(C) Fellini, *8 1/2*
1965	Calvino, *Cosmicomiche*; Sereni, *Strumenti umani*	1967	Boetti and others, 'Arte povera' exhibition, Genoa
1968	Fenoglio, *Il partigiano Johnny*	1968	(C) Leone, *C'era una volta il West*; Fo, *Mistero buffo*
		1970	(C) De Sica, *Il giardino dei Finzi Contini*
1971	Montale, *Satura*	1970	Fo, *Morte accidentale di un anarchico*
1974	Morante, *La storia*	1973	(C) Fellini, *Amarcord*
1975	D'Arrigo, *Horcynus Orca*	1975–	Piano, 'Centre Georges Pompidou', Paris

1950	*Cassa per il Mezzogiorno* (Development Fund for the South) created
1951	Fiscal reform
1953	Electoral reform ('legge truffa') approved
1955	Ente Nazionale Idrocarburi (ENI) founded; Italy enters UNO
1963	Moro heads centre–left government; Compulsory schooling extended to 14-year-olds
1968	Students' occupation of universities
1969	Terrorist attack in Piazza Fontana, Milan
1974	Terrorist attacks in Brescia and on 'Italicus' train. Referendum confirms divorce law of 1970

Political events		Literature		Other arts (P = periodical, C = cinema)	
1976	Lockheed bribery scandal	1976	Consolo, *Il sorriso dell'ignoto marinaio*	1976	(C) Bertolucci, *Novecento*
				1977	(C) Taviani brothers, *Padre, padrone*
1978	Moro kidnapped and murdered by Red Brigades	1978	Sciascia, *L'affaire Moro*		
1980	Terrorist bombing of Bologna railway station	1979	Calvino, *Se una notte d'inverno*		
		1980	Eco, *Il nome della rosa*		
			Sanvitale, *Madre e figlia*		
1981	Masonic P2 Lodge uncovered. Abortion referendum. Abortion law passed	1981	Bufalino, *Diceria dell'untore*	1981–	Clemente, Chia, Cucchi, 'Transavanguardia' paintings
			De Carlo, *Treno di panna*		
		1983	Calvino, *Palomar*		
			Benni, *Terra!*		
		1984	Tabucchi, *Notturno indiano*	1984	Berio, *Un re in ascolto* (Salzburg)
		1985	Celati, *Narratori delle pianure*	1985	(C) Moretti, *La messa è finita*
			Del Giudice, *Atlante occidentale*	1988	Clemente, *Brotherhood* (painting)
		1989	Sciascia, *Una storia semplice*		(C) Tornatore, *Nuovo cinema paradiso*
1990	The Gladio arms-cache exposure	1990	Vassalli, *La chimera*		
1991	Communist Party dissolved – refounded as PDS (Democratic Party of Left)		Maraini, *La lunga vita di Marianna Ucria*		
1992	'Tangentopoli' bribery scandal begins. Collapse of DC at general election				
1993	Referendum leads to new electoral law				
1994	Parliamentary election won by coalition of 'Forza Italia' and allies				
	Dec.: Coalition collapses				

Origins and Duecento

Jonathan Usher

The earliest evidence

Looking back from the beginning of the Trecento, Dante surveyed the relative literary achievements of French, Provençal and Italian vernaculars up to his day:

French boasts that, because of its greater ease and pleasantness of use, anything set down or composed in vernacular prose belongs to it: for instance the biblical compilation with the deeds of the Trojans and Romans, and the exquisite adventures of King Arthur, and many other stories and learning. Provençal claims that vernacular writers wrote poetry in it first, as in a more perfect and sweeter language: think of Peire d'Alvernhe and other learned men of older times. The third language, of the Italians, has two claims to preeminence: the first is that those who have more sweetly and subtly written vernacular poetry were from its household; Cino da Pistoia and his friend are examples: and the second is that it is seen to rely more on Latin, which is universal.

(*De vulgari eloquentia* [henceforth *DVE*] I, 10 (?1304))

What is striking about this summary is that both French and Provençal have well-defined traditions behind them: the examples Dante cites go back generations (Peire d'Alvernhe wrote between 1150 and 1180; Chrétien de Troyes and Thomas, authors of the most important French romances, were writing around 1170). Significantly, Dante extends the references to French and Provençal writers by mentioning unspecified 'plures' and 'alii' (numerous others). For Italian, however, the examples could hardly be more solitary or recent: Cino da Pistoia was in his early thirties and his friend – Dante is referring to himself – was nearing forty: no other 'vulgares eloquentes' are mentioned. Indeed, much of the *DVE* is a fruitless search for writing in Italian vernaculars which rises above the municipal or the uncouth. A similar picture of the relative juniority of Italian is painted, protestingly, in *Vita Nuova* (henceforth *VN*) xxv, and in *Convivio* I, 10. Nevertheless, Dante believed the new poetry just emerging from Italy at the end of the Duecento could hold its own with the best. Where did this new-found, superior sweetness and subtlety suddenly come from?

The political fragmentation of early medieval Italy, its poor communications hampered by difficult geography, and the localisation resulting from the economic implosion of the Dark Ages left their mark on the culture and language of the peninsula. Local dialects, still a marked feature of Italy today, restricted expression to a cramped territorial radius. Everywhere Latin remained the language of administration, learning and thought, not just for reasons of cultural prestige but because there was no other *lingua franca*. When the new literary language of Italy finally developed, it was to do so in those limited cultural spaces where Latin offered no predominant tradition, and where nevertheless cohesive patterns of expression could be established. In short, Italy would have to wait for other vernacular cultures to come of age. 'Italian', from the origins to at least the end of the *Duecento*, is a construction *post-factum* because of an unbroken cultural rather than a linguistic tradition.

Such was the monopoly of Latin as a written medium in the early Middle Ages that the first evidence of Italian *volgare* is fragmentary, amounting to a few scattered lines, and very late (early ninth century) in comparison with French or English. The fragments are not literary, and the Latinity of the scribes has made evaluation problematic. The so-called *Indovinello veronese* (early ninth century) is a riddle about writing, which can be read either as Latin influenced by the emerging vernacular, or as the new language deformed by scribal familiarity with Latin.

Similar doubts pertain to a series of *placiti*, or sworn statements, preserved in the archives of Montecassino. The documents, referring to land disputes around Capua, Teano and Sessa between 960 and 963, are set out in Latin, but the oral testimony is recorded in the vernacular. The presence of Latinisms and of dialectally unexpected verb forms suggests that the testimonies are really 'legalese' and not a reliable record of tenth-century Campanian dialect.

More extensive, though still non-literary, evidence has to wait till the late eleventh century. To eliminate blank spaces in a deed of covenant of 1087 (blank spaces facilitated surreptitious codicils), a notary by the name of Rainerio from Monte Amiata near Siena scribbled a ribald tercet about a client Caputcoctu (Capocotto, or 'Hothead'). The earthy colloquialisms can still be half heard through the scribe's latinate spelling.

The first lengthy document is a confessional formula from Norcia in Umbria, again from the late eleventh century. The vernacular character (Umbrian dialect) is unmistakable, even though the doctrinal context ensures that Latin is predominant, in both lexis and sentence structure.

Despite the increasing length of such documents, consciously artistic and linguistically autonomous use of the vernacular would have to wait till the second half of the twelfth century, when an unknown *giullare* (minstrel) composed, in eastern Tuscany, the *Ritmo laurenziano*, a poem praising a bishop and brazenly begging for a horse. The octosyllabic metre, along with the obsequious content, displays affinities with models north of the Alps. Other poems displaying the same *giullaresco* characteristics are the *Ritmo cassinese* and the *Ritmo di S. Alessio* (both late twelfth or early thirteenth century), the latter a substantial but incomplete hagiography in 27 irregular stanzas.

2

Poetry

Francis of Assisi

None of the documents mentioned so far indicates conscious cultural accumulation or progressive literary development, and this unsophisticated localised production was to carry on for centuries in its geographical and linguistic isolation, long after literary standards had been established. Piety and humour were to be its staples, and genre and metrical forms were to remain closely linked to the oral humus from which it spontaneously germinated. This hidden dimension (hidden, that is, from the history of 'high' literature) could occasionally throw surprises, such as the impressive religious outpourings of Umbria, starting with St Francis (1182–1226) himself. The saint, whose very name indicates how fashionable French culture was, and who sang in French when jolly, who liked to name his companions after the characters in the Round Table, and whose followers were nicknamed *ioculatores domini* (minstrels of the Lord), was able, even in the discomfort of his last illness (c. 1225), to compose a hymn of astounding freshness and innocence. The *Laudes Creaturarum*, also known as the *Cantico delle creature* ('Praise of God's Creation'), starts by singing the praises of God for creating the sun, moon and stars, then, after thanking Him for the four elements, concludes in gratitude for patience in suffering and for Death itself. Here, in the stanzas in praise of water and fire, the character of St Francis, a cross between extraordinarily heightened directness and a simplicity verging on the simple-minded, comes across in all its exaltation:

> Laudato si', mi' Signore, per sor'aqua,
> la quale è multo utile, et humile, et pretiosa et casta.
> Laudato si', mi' Signore, per frate focu,
> per lo quale ennallumini la nocte:
> ed ello è bello, et iocundo, et robustoso et forte.

(Be thou praised my Lord for Sister Water, which is very useful, humble, precious and chaste. Be thou praised my Lord for Brother Fire, by which you light up the night, and which is fair and jolly, strapping and strong.)

Francis's pantheistic celebration is written in assonantal prose, with what was an originally marked Umbrian timbre ennobled by biblical turns of phrase and notions of Latin rhetoric. The use of the vernacular was, of course, linked to the essentially *popular* nature of this new piety, in contrast to the Latinity of the regular Church. The spreading of religious enthusiasm, unimpeded by barriers of language or learning, meant that the Franciscan tradition was to produce many other *laudes*, some of the most dramatic, even terrifying, being written by Iacopone da Todi (1230–1306), who is also tentatively credited with composing the famous *Stabat Mater*, Mary's lament on the crucified Christ, later set to music by Palestrina, Haydn, Rossini and others. In *O Segnor, per cortesia, manname la malsanía*, Iacopone catalogues a ghastly checklist of deformities, suppurations and illnesses, ending up with a gruesome wish: to be devoured by a wolf and defecated among briars. The sufferings, however horrible, could not compare with the poet's sin against God: 'ché me creasti en tua diletta / e io t'ho morto a villania' (for you created me in your charity / and I killed you basely). The dramatic distance between these late outpourings from Todi and the original simplicity of St Francis's welcome of 'Our Sister Bodily Death' could hardly be wider.

Popular and didactic poetry

Important as St Francis is (and many take the composition of the *Cantico delle creature* as the starting-point of Italian literature), the religious poetry of Umbria was, like its counterparts in the north of the peninsula, a cultural blind alley, incapable of fomenting a lay artistic tradition. Amongst the northern writers, most of whom stuck to edifying or devotional subjects, Girard Pateg (fl. 1228) from Cremona rendered parts of Ecclesiastes into a *Splanamento* or dialect explanation in alexandrines. Pietro da Bescapè's *Sermoni* (1274) crudely paraphrased in a variety of metres large chunks of the Gospels and other parts of the Old and New Testaments. The least grey of these northern moralists was Bonvesin da la Riva (d. ?1315), a schoolteacher whose *De quinquaginta curialitatibus ad mensam* ('Concerning Fifty Courtesies at Table'), despite its Latin title, furnishes copious and doubtless much-needed vernacular advice. More importantly, Bonvesin's substantial *Libro delle tre scritture* ('Book of the Three Scriptures') catalogues Hell, Christ's passion, and the joys of Heaven in a Milanese dialect already beginning to show tentative ambitions to refinement.

  Whilst popular poetry (both humorous and didactic) was also to appear in Tuscany, its later appearance meant that it was created in a more sophisticated context, reacting to, as well as adopting, values and forms (e.g. the sonnet) from the 'high' literature which was beginning to assert itself. Rustico di Filippo (b. ?1235) is typical, in that his extant production of nearly sixty sonnets divides almost exactly into two halves: one uninspiringly in the new literary style and the other more enjoyably in a mordant, 'street-wise' popular idiom. Cecco Angiolieri (?1260–1312) embraced a costermongerish delight in ribald vituperation which belied his well-bred upbringing in Siena. Forese Donati (d. 1296) would exploit this burlesque vein in his *tenzone* (poetic exchange) possibly with Dante, whose replies were no less caustic.

Tuscan didactic poetry also distanced itself from its more pedestrian forebears elsewhere in the peninsula. Brunetto Latini (?1220–1294) composed his major work, *Li livres dou Trésor* (mid 1260s), in French, claiming that the language was 'plus delitable e plus commune' (pleasanter and more widely known). The *Trésor* is part of a wider medieval phenomenon of encyclopaedic works, the most famous being Vincent of Beauvais's *Speculum Maius*, but it is the first scientific text in any of the vernacular languages. Though Brunetto consciously chose French as the vehicle for his most ambitious work, he nevertheless produced in his *Rettorica* a vernacular translation and commentary for the first seventeen chapters of Cicero's *De inventione*, and also began to compose an allegorical poem in Tuscan in rhyming heptasyllables, the *Tesoretto*, in which the protagonist loses himself in a dark wood (Roncesvals of the *Chanson de Roland!*), only to be conducted on an educational tour of Virtue and Knowledge. The problem with the *Tesoretto* lies in the heptasyllables which impose a breathless rhythm on a naturally august subject matter. The intention is serious, but the effect is doggerel. The author himself was aware of the limitations of this format, complaining that the dictates of rhyme 'hide the precept and change the meaning' (*Tesoretto* 411ff.). When Dante came to the *Commedia*, though he drew inspiration from the *Tesoretto*, he took good care to write his own poem in more spacious hendecasyllables.

The allegorical-dramatic approach à la *Roman de la rose*,[1] clearly the result of Brunetto's long stay in France, is also much in evidence in anonymous poems from the end of the Duecento. The *Fiore* is a remarkable paraphrase in 232 sonnets of the more 'novellistic' parts of the French poem, more Jean de Meung than Guillaume de Lorris, enthusiastically concentrating on the erotic or voyeuristic message. The lively but cynical tone is faithfully conveyed by these lines from sonnet LX, advocating 'firm' action:

> E quando tu ssarai co llei soletto,
> Prendila tra lle braccia e fa 'l sicuro,
> Mostrando allor se ttu sse' forte e duro,
> E 'mantenente le metti il gambetto.

(When you find yourself alone with her take her in your arms, confidently, showing then how strong and hard you are, then shove the peg in.)

The *Fiore* has received a lot of attention because some have identified its author as the young Dante (the name *Durante* crops up, but this may be just another phallic pun). A further work based on the *Roman de la rose* is the *Detto d'amore* (it too now attributed to Dante), a pedestrian paraphrase, but notable for its transfer of attention from the Lover (male) to the Beloved (female), a refocusing occasioned by new emphasis on the Lady in the Tuscan love lyric.

---

[1] A long French poem by Guillaume de Lorris, c. 1230, completed by Jean de Meung c. 1275, in which Eros stands as the desire for knowledge.

Provençal influence

The development of an Italian literary tradition, whether in poetry or in prose, would take place, as the more travelled Tuscans like Brunetto Latini sensed, through the mediation of Provençal, French and Latin models. Provençal acted as a catalyst to the development of the lyric, French offered models of prose and of epic or allegorical verse, and Latin provided a constant challenge to both the syntactic and the rhetorical ambitions of the language.

Provençal verse, with its technical sophistication, its lyrical approach to the poetry of passions, and its conversion of chivalry from warfare to wooing, was well known in Italy, particularly in the north where linguistic similarity meant few problems of comprehension. Whilst Provençal poets found work easily in Italy (too easily, judging by Aimeric de Peguilhan's complaint about unfair competition in *Li fol e.il put e.il filol*, 'Fools and sodomites'), their views on the poetic backwardness of the Italians were implicitly harsh: Raimbautz de Vaqueiras (fl. 1180–1207) wrote, in addition to a large number of poems in his own language, two pieces making use of Italian dialect for comic effect. In the *Descort* (Discord) he uses five languages (Provençal, Italian dialect, French, Gascon and Galician) to symbolise the strife and confusion of love's ferment. Paradoxically, Raimbautz's Italianising is far more refined and 'Italian' than any native production of his time. In the *Contrasto bilingue* a suave Provençal's elegant courtship, complete with request for 'merces' (favour) meets with indelicate refusal from a Genoese-speaking woman, who calls her wooer 'sozo, mozo, escalvao' (filthy, stupid and cropped like a thief). The *Contrasto* humorously exploits the dramatic and linguistic possibilities suggested by the seduction dialogues in Andreas Capellanus' Latin treatise *De amore*, where lovers of different classes are pitted against one another.

The traffic between Provence and Italy was not one way: some Italians were so enamoured of the expressive possibilities of Provençal that they composed exclusively in it. The Bolognese Lambertino Buvalelli (d. 1221) probably learned to write in Provençal from reading anthologies of Occitanic (written in *langue d'oc*) poetry circulating in northern Italy, rather than from direct contact. But the next generation, which included Lanfranco Cigala from Genoa (d. 1278) and Sordello da Goito (d. 1260), was sufficiently respected as to compete on its own terms with Provençal poets. Sordello was famous in his day for a lament on the death of Ser Blacatz, in which the cream of European chivalry is invited to partake of the dead hero's heart as a cure for cowardice: 'Premiers manje del cor, per so que grans ops l'es, / l'emperaire de Roma ... ' (May the first to eat of the heart be the Emperor of Rome, whose need of it is very great ...). Our image of the poet is now coloured by Dante's emotion-charged portrayal in *Purgatorio* VI–VII, and Robert Browning's philosophising *Sordello* (1840).

Interesting as they are, these early importers and exporters were few and lacked influence. For real change, there needed to be a context where imported values, conceits and techniques could be acclimatised in such a way as to provoke not only imitation but also emulation.

The poets of Provence had flourished in a fragile environment of small courts and an impecunious nobility. Feudal hierarchy and etiquette, which governed the approach to patrons, became a metaphor in their verse for amorous frustrations, for the search for recognition, and for a sense of exclusion. The resultant poetry of *fin'amors* (true love as opposed to *fol amors*, mere sensual instinct) is one where passion meets hindrance, longing meets indifference, and feelings of inferiority are sublimated into conceptual sophistication (*trobar clus*) or verbal ostentation (*trobar ric*); it proved internationally attractive because of its romantic courtly milieu and its artistic panache.

Sicilian school

Social organisation in most of Italy was different from that in Provence. Whereas in parts of the north there were small courts (and Provençal models were able to penetrate directly), in central Italy the political, cultural and economic centres of gravity were the towns, already acquiring independence and evolving post-feudal forms of government. The closest approximation to Occitanic conditions existed in the south, where the Hohenstaufen Emperors had inherited a state shaped by Norman occupation. The Emperor Frederick II, who reigned from 1220 to 1250, epitomised this strange amalgam of northern and southern European cultures: his father was German and his mother Norman, but his interests were decidedly Mediterranean. His relations with Arab and Greek subjects were often better than those with western counterparts. Frederick's court, the Magna curia or Great Court, was filled with officials and supplicants from all over Europe, and its taste in culture was catholic. Though the court was in many ways more bureaucratic than chivalrous, the lure of the love poetry of Provence was strong, but only as one amongst many competing forms of expression. The narrow concentration on love in the vernacular production of the Magna curia compared with its Provençal source is explained by the fact that the Frederician court was also hyperactive in Latin, and many of the themes (political invective, reference to historical events) missing from the Sicilian poets can be found transposed into this other language. Guido delle Colonne, for instance, an important lyric poet in the *volgare*, produced an elegant and very influential translation into Latin, not Sicilian, of the French poet Benoît de Ste Maure's *Roman de Troie* (Romance of Troy).

From reading the verse of the Magna curia, the impression one gets – an impression reinforced by the high percentage of lawyers and imperial functionaries to whom the surviving examples of Sicilian poetry can be ascribed – is of a civil-service mentality with an educated élite indulging in an esoteric amateur pastime, a *nomenklatura* concerned with mutual recognition amongst fellow hobbyists, rather than full-time troubadours playing to the public as in Provence. One unwitting consequence of this private, non-professional context was that the link between poetry and music (which still survives in the terminology of forms, *sonetto*, *canzone*, *ballata* etc.) was undermined. Much Provençal poetry was written down together with its musical notation, and the *Vidas* (accompanying biographies) state whether the poets were gifted with a good singing voice or instrumental technique. The poetry of the Magna curia bears no melodic indications, and some of the phrasing, indeed, would be unrewarding to set to music. Poetry amongst equal amateurs could now be *read*, privately and silently, and not *sung* for patronage, and was therefore freed from aedic disciplines. The poet's task would now be deemed to be *dittare* (to set in writing) not *cantare* (to sing).

The golden age of the Frederician court was shortlived, and the collapse of the Swabian house in the years after Frederick's death in 1250 meant that the structures which had permitted a compact and intercommunicative 'school' of poets to thrive were quickly dismembered. Effectively the first generation of Sicilian poets started writing around 1230, and the second generation were contemporaries with the more vigorous poets of Tuscany. Indeed, nearly all the evidence we now possess of the Sicilians comes from anthologies and imitations made in Tuscany, whose political and economic ascent paralleled the decline in Swabian fortunes.

This foreclosed timespan means that, except for accidental survivals such as Stefano Protonotaro's *Pir meu cori alligrari* ('To liven my heart', late Frederician period), we are unable to read the works of the Sicilians in their original linguistic garb. Medieval copyists saw it as their job not to transmit a text passively, orthographic difficulties and linguistic incomprehensions included, but rather to interpret it, so as actively to facilitate its transmission. The anthologies of Sicilian poetry transmitted by Tuscan copyists are heavily Tuscanised: in particular, the differences in the vowel systems of the two languages were marked, and produced unintended changes in rhyme in the Tuscanised versions. Sicilian has five tonic vowels, whereas Tuscan has seven, plus two diphthongs. Sicilian rhyme was perfect, that is to say there was a complete correspondence between the vowels of both the penultimate and the final syllables of lines. In 'translating' Sicilian into Tuscan, the copyists found that originally perfect rhymes could not be respected. Key words such as *placiri* (pleasure) and *sospiri* (sighs), for instance, which rhyme in Sicilian, would give *piacere* and *sospiri* in Tuscan. Likewise, the distinction between 'open' and 'closed' *e* and *o* (separate phonemes in Tuscan) ran counter to the single forms in Sicilian. The tonic diphthongs, too, a marked feature of Tuscan, do not occur in Sicilian. The cultural impact of the poetry of the Magna curia meant that these unavoidable compromises of transmission became naturalised, even sought after, in straight Tuscan writers: 'open' and 'closed' vowels could be allowed to rhyme; non-diphthongised Sicilian variants (such as *core* for *cuore*) would be considered more 'poetic' than the common Tuscan forms

(Dante would consistently use *core* in the verse sections of *VN* and *Convivio*, and *cuore* for the prose). In certain instances, the glaring conflicts of rhyme (and their solutions) acquired legitimacy: *sospiri* and *dire* could pass muster, and *voi* could be Sicilianised to *vui* to avoid awkward problems of rhyme with *altrui* (the 'other person', a key word in love lyric). In addition, some grammatical forms (the future in -*aggio*, the conditional in -*ia*, *aggio/ave* for *ho/ha* and *saccio/saccente* instead of *so/sapiente*) provided convenient 'doubles' to Tuscan forms. Opportunistic as they were, the Tuscan poets do not seem to have exploited these possibilities to the hilt, and only adopted authentic Sicilianisms, never making up new ones by analogy.

The difference between the actual language of the poets of the Magna curia and the Tuscanised versions of the copyists can still be seen in the canzone *S'eo trovasse pietanza* ('If I could find pity') by 'Re Enzo' (1224–72) – Henry of Sardinia, the illegitimate son of Frederick II, who languished for most of his adult life in a Bolognese prison. By an accident of transmission, parts of the poem have come down to us in two different versions: one is still in its original Sicilian form, the other has been Tuscanised.

Such was the early diffusion of the Tuscanised copies of Sicilian poetry that Dante was firmly convinced that they were the 'real thing' and that verse which remained genuinely Sicilian was mere barbarism: in the *DVE* (i, 12) he quotes disapprovingly a line from Cielo d'Alcamo's delightfully humorous *Rosa fresca aulentissima* ('Fresh, fragrant rose') as an example of what issues from 'mediocre natives', not realising that Cielo was indulging in an elaborate joke almost on a par with Raimbautz de Vaqueiras's *Contrasto*. But Dante's error was commonly held, and moreover productive: it was to be the modified Sicilian material rather than the original which was to serve as the model for subsequent poetry in Italy.

The importance of the Sicilian school resides in its role as a filter. There is little direct quotation of individual Provençal poets, as there was to be in Tuscany later. Whereas elsewhere Occitan poetry had been directly read or imitated in its own language, at the Magna curia the material was transposed into local speech, only the technical terms showing the debt to Provençal: *gioia*, *amanza*, *fin'amore*, *caunoscenza*, *tristanza*. This vocabulary would be transmitted to the standard language in due course, with borrowings such as 'speranza' all but replacing the former 'speme'. In addition to the technical terms for rendering *fin'amors*, the Sicilians also took over many of the verse forms, the Provençal *cobla* (stanza) becoming the *cobbola*, the *canso* becoming the *canzone*, the *tenso* or poetic exchange becoming the *tenzone*. The troubadours of Provence had conducted such exchanges by means of single stanzas (*coblas esparsas*) of the *canso* form, which normally required multiple stanzas. It is probably from the high-art *cobla esparsa*, rather than from the popular Sicilian *strambotto* (eight-line stanza of alternate rhyme), that the sonnet was to develop.

The invention of the sonnet is generally attributed to Giacomo (or Iacopo)

da Lentini, an imperial notary (fl. 1233–c. 1245), of whom we possess about
forty poems, more than of any other poet of the Magna curia. Giacomo's
poetry is characterised by a constant questioning about the nature of Love,
rather than a concern for the erotic vicissitudes of the poet or his beloved, who
often seem mere pretexts for philosophical soul-searching. His rationalising,
almost syllogistic approach demanded a formal structure which contained
within one stanzaic unit both the premiss and the conclusion. The sonnet, with
its two quatrains sufficiently capacious to accept the development of an
exposition, whilst the closely enchained tercets rammed home a tightly argued
conclusion, was just the vehicle for the Notary's almost forensic inspiration.

Though Giacomo still maintains some of the feudal metaphorics of the
troubadours (one of his most famous poems, *Madonna dir vi voglio* – 'My
lady, I wish to tell you' – is a loose re-working of a poem by Folquet de
Marselha), these are often only opening gambits, and the discussion of Love
proceeds rather by a series of daring analogies or comparisons: the failure of
paintings, like poems, to do justice to their subject, the value versus the virtue
of magic stones, etc. One of the most interesting compositions is a *canzone*,
Amor non vole ch'io clami ('Love does not wish me to declaim'), in which
Giacomo claims that his protestations of love are something new – not the
tired old verbal formulae of *fin'amors*. Here is the second stanza in which he
ridicules the by-now ritual request for the Lady's *mercede* (favour):

> Per zo l'amore mi 'nsigna
> ch'io non guardi a l'autra gente:
> non vuole ch'io resembri a signa,
> c'ogni viso tene mente.
> E per zo, madonna mia,
> a voi non dimanderìa
> merzede, né pietanza,
> ché tanti son li amatori,
> ch'este scinta di savori
> merzede per troppa usanza.

(Thus Love teaches me not to imitate others: it does not want me to resemble the
monkey who imitates everything it sees. And for that reason, my lady, I would not
crave your favour, nor your pity, because lovers are so plentiful that favour, overused,
has lost all its savour.)

Though Giacomo is remembered chiefly as an innovator, both in content
and form (apart from inventing the sonnet, he was instrumental in stabilising
the metrical characteristics of the *canzone*),[2] his ability to reproduce the
highest levels of Provençal-style *trobar ric* can be seen in the sonnet *Eo viso – e
son diviso – da lo viso* ('I see and yet am separated from what I see'), where

2 A pluristanzaic composition using symmetrical verses, much favoured for its capacity to convey
  developed argument.

convoluted semantic games with etymologically related words (*replicatio* and *rima equivoca*) rival the pyrotechnics of the great troubadour Arnaut Daniel.

By the standards of Giacomo da Lentini, the other poets of the Magna curia are lesser figures. Guido delle Colonne (b. ?1210), the translator of the *Roman de Troie*, who was active in the same years as Giacomo, came from Messina, a key city in an empire which straddled both Sicily and the 'continente'. The five poems extant show him to have been particularly successful in marrying lyrical thematics with a rigorous rhetorical framework. Dante was so impressed that he repeatedly quotes Guido's *Ancor che l'aigua per lo foco lassi* ('Though water loses its coolness through fire') and *Amor che lungiamente m'hai menato* ('Love, you who have long led me') as examples of prestigious verse. The first of these, with its use of natural similes – fire, water, ice, magnets and iron – was later to act as a model for Guinizzelli's famous programme canzone *Al cor gentil rempaira sempre amore* (see below p. 20).

Rinaldo d'Aquino (fl. 1240s), traditionally if insecurely identified as the brother of Thomas Aquinas, was less original than either Giacomo or Guido. His *Per fin'amore vao sí allegramente* ('True love makes me go lightly'), quoted approvingly by Dante as one of the *cantiones illustres*, is an elegant sampler of much of the Provençal repertoire of motifs – worth, joy, vassal service and courtesy. His best-known poem, *Già mai non mi conforto* ('Never am I cheered'), a lady's lament for the departure of her lover to the crusades, is written in a much more accessible, popular style, even to the point of seeming ingenuous. Its notoriety derives principally from the romantic circumstances of the heroine's abandonment (reminiscent of Ovid's *Heroides*), rather than from any literary merit: as a crusading song it is unique in the *volgare*. Giacomino Pugliese, about whom almost nothing is known, wrote, like Rinaldo, in both a high and a popular style. The serious poetry is mostly sterile rhetorical posing, as in the bombastic *Morte, perché m'hai fatta sí gran guerra* ('Death, why have you warred against me so'). His most famous composition in the popular idiom, *Donna, di voi mi lamento* ('Lady, it is of you I complain'), is a *contrasto* between a man who jealously accuses his lover of inconstancy, and his lady who replies protesting her innocence and complaining of the suffering he causes her.

Pier della Vigna (?1180–1249), now remembered chiefly as a magniloquent suicide in *Inferno* XIII, was a judge, and later 'logotheta' (imperial secretary) to Frederick II. His principal output, as was to be expected of one of his profession, consisted of Latin letters employing all the artifices of *dictamen*, or ornamented prose. His vernacular poetic production is exiguous, amounting to two, possibly three *canzoni*. Even the opening lines of the two *canzoni* securely attributed to him resemble each other: *Amore, in cui disio ed ho speranza* and *Amando con fin core e con speranza* ('Love, in whom I desire and hope'; 'Loving with true heart and hope'). Piero's language is replete with Latinisms and Provençalisms, and he is not averse to classical allusions (e.g. Pyramus and Thisbe). The word-play which is so conspicuous in Dante's treatment of him in the *Inferno* is hardly a parody: *Amando con fin core* is held together not so much by a lyric impulse as by a crossword-puzzler's delight in verbal ingenuity.

Though few in number, and shortlived in timespan, the Sicilians were important for two main reasons. Firstly, they acted as a vector for a sophisticated, imported art-poetry, whilst incidentally filtering out those elements of Provençal thematics and language which were unassimilable in Italy. As a result, the concepts, metrical forms and verbal conceits of nearly all subsequent Italian poetry are already established in the lyric output of the Magna curia. And secondly, they served as an inspirational example, dignified by imperial prestige, of a clear self-referential group, the first compact 'school' of poets in an Italian vernacular able to promote a consciously artistic expression. Dante was clearly aware of the psychological impact of such group-consciousness, which he acknowledged with a mixture of Ghibelline[3] pride and genuine literary recognition in the *DVE* (I, 122, 2ff.).

Tuscan imitators

The decline in Swabian fortunes coincided with an upturn in the economic, political and cultural position of central Italy. Riding on a remarkable upsurge in trade, particularly in textiles, the central Italian communes began to assert themselves politically, a role made sensitive by their location on the fault-line between Guelf and Ghibelline zones of influence. Confident, perhaps even brash, the cities began to have cultural ambitions, expressed in architecture and the visual arts, but also in less material forms of expression. The concentration of literate, lay intelligentsia which had facilitated the development of a school of poetry in Frederick's Magna curia now began to be reproduced, albeit in a more fragmented and localised way, in Tuscany and the Romagna. As in Sicily, it was the professional class, the lawyers, notaries and secretaries, who were in the forefront of both the political and the cultural developments. Many of them had spent time at Bologna university, a cultural melting-pot which attracted students from the south as well as from north-central Italy.

Traditionally, an effort has been made to distinguish between a first group of imitators, the so-called Siculo-Tuscans, and a second group of more self-confident, autonomous poets, the fully fledged Tuscans. Whilst there is indeed evidence to show that some, particularly of the later poets, were more adept at finding their own idiom while others were cruder borrowers, the chronology of this period in the development of the Italian lyric is so restricted, and the character and inspiration of the individual poets so markedly varied, that the

---

[3] *Ghibellines* were supporters of imperial rule in Italy, as opposed to *Guelfs* who favoured papal claims.

distinctions have to be treated warily. To all intents and purposes they were contemporaries, frequently joined by correspondence through letters and verse, and separated only by talent, taste and reciprocal vituperation.

Guittone d'Arezzo

Amongst the earlier poets, Guittone d'Arezzo (?1230–94) and Bonagiunta da Lucca (?1220–1296) represent very different reactions to the challenge of imported models. Guittone's father had been chamberlain to the commune of Arezzo, and the early life of the poet followed this Guelf political tradition, despite the momentary decline of the papal party. Voluntarily exiled towards 1260 (for reasons expounded in the canzone *Gente noiosa e villana*, 'Persons unpleasant and boorish'), Guittone underwent a religious conversion, and in about 1265 abandoned a wife and three children to enter the lay Franciscan order of the *Milites Beatae Virginis Mariae* (Knights of the Blessed Virgin Mary), popularly nicknamed the 'Frati gaudenti' (Jovial Friars). The order's religious calling was overlaid with a political programme of arbitration between warring civic factions, and much of Guittone's spiritual exhortation can be read as conservative reaction to changes in the ruling coalitions within the communes. Guittone's literary output (some three hundred poems and an important epistolary) tends to be classified according to this watershed in his life, with one half conventionally lyrical (*Guittone*), and the other moralistic and spiritual (*Fra Guittone*). He would himself allude to this abrupt change in the direction of his poetry in the palinodic canzone *Ora parrà s'eo saverò cantare* ('Now you'll see if I can sing'). Despite the changes in inspiration and subject-matter, there is substantial literary continuity: his serious poems are as full of Sicilianisms and Provençal keywords as his earlier love poetry.

Guittone's love poetry is a meeting place for competing influences, a diversity whose persistence was no doubt encouraged by the poet's autodidacticism. The recent lesson of the Sicilians (and of Giacomo da Lentini in particular) in assimilating Provençal forms and thematics prompted a new look at the Provençal repertoire itself. Guittone shows signs of a direct knowledge of some thirty Provençal poets, as well as of the Italians writing in Provençal such as Lanfranco and Sordello. There is in Guittone a fascinating rivalry between direct and indirect troubadour influence, which shows in his oscillation between already digested motifs and crude borrowings, such as *ciauzire* for 'to choose'. Some clauses even contain juxtaposed Provençal and Sicilian lexis – *enante creo* (I would *rather* [Prov.] *believe* [Sicil.]). His re-reading of the troubadours also led him to reintroduce some of the metrical and formal devices of Provence which the Sicilians had largely dispensed with, such as the *commiato* or leave-taking signature (Provençal *tornada*) at the end of the poem. Guittone's favourite metrical form, however, was of Sicilian origin, the sonnet. Even here, however, he was not content to remain within

the parameters of the primitive sonnet form, and experimented with augmented sonnets, intercalating various extra seven-syllable lines between the
hendecasyllables (*sonetto doppio* and *rinterzato*), or adding lines to the two
quatrains to make a sixteen-line poem (*sonetto con fronte di dieci versi*).

Guittone's penchant for ambitious intellectualising led him to an enthusiastic
use of *trobar ric* (see *Tuttor, s'eo veglio o dormo* and *Tuttor ch'eo dirò 'gioi',
gioiva cosa*, 'Always whether awake or asleep' and 'Always if I say "joy",
there was real enjoyment'), or judged less generously, to tormented contor-
tions, an involuntary *trobar clus*: indeed he himself admitted that his verse was
'hard and harsh to taste' and that he 'squashed words in' (an admission of
obscurity can be found in lines 159–70 of *Altra fiata aggio già, donne, parlato*,
'Ladies, I spoke another time'). Studies of Guittone point out that rhetorical
organisation has a primary role in the genesis of his poetry, whilst the sonnet
or *canzone* structures struggle to accommodate the dynamics of discourse.
Whatever the artistic merits of his poetry (and critics are much divided),
Guittone's ambitions for the medium were crucial in raising the intellectual
status and territory of vernacular verse. One device which was to be taken up
by others, including Petrarch, was the idea of programmed sequences of
poems, linked by thematic and prosodic continuity. Five cycles, or *corone*, of
sonnets can be discerned, three of them conventional narratives of enamour-
ment, one of them a *tenzone* with a 'villana donna' and one an exposition of
love doctrine or *ars amandi*; in addition he composed a short cycle glossing a
love-emblem which has not survived, sometimes referred to as the *Trattato
d'amore*. Though in many respects rebarbative, the *corone* show a dazzling
ingenuity of formal variation and reprise, an intellectual if not an inspirational
stamina of the first order.

The political and moral poetry Guittone wrote could find no models
amongst the Sicilians with their rarefied concentration on love phenomenology, and instead it took up the other traditions of the troubadours: the *planh*
(complaint), the *plazer* (enumeration of satisfactions), the *sirventes* (politico-
moral diatribe), and the poetry of separation (used to great if novel effect in
Gente noiosa ...). The two most famous political canzoni are *Ahi lasso, or è
stagion de doler tanto* ('Now is the time for grief') and *O dolce terra aretina*
('O sweet land of Arezzo'). The first is a stunning indictment of the Florentine
Guelfs for their pusillanimity at the battle of Montaperti (1260). Playing with
toponymic etymologies, he calls Florence a 'deflowered flower'. The second is
an impassioned complaint, probably written shortly before the battle of
Campaldino (1289), for the degeneracy of his home town, moving adroitly
from a *plazer* detailing past (Guelf) amenity to an *enueg* (a poetic catalogue of
dissatisfactions) criticising present (Ghibelline) vice. Both poems prefigure
Dante's violent denunciations of Florence in the *Commedia*.

But Guittone's best verse is that dealing with religious themes, perhaps
because his inspiration was more direct and less dependent on concepts
lyrically formulated by others. Though some of the religious *canzoni* are

outpourings of spiritual fervour similar to Iacopone da Todi's *laude*, others are best understood in a tight dialectic with his previous love poetry. Guittone's favourite figure was antithesis, and his religious work can be seen to simultaneously condemn secular love and exalt its divine counterpart. The *canzone O tu, de nome Amor, guerra de fatto* ('You, by name Love, but in fact war'), attacks profane passion, whilst its companion piece, *O vera vertù, vero amore* ('O true virtue, true love'), outlines true spiritual devotion. Guittone's Christian zeal occasionally transcends sententiousness to reach a genuine *élan*, as in the delightful *ballata Vegna, vegna chi vole giocundare* ('Come, come if you wish to be merry'), where the rhythms and sentiment of a popular Provençal dance-song are infused with a joyous and unaffected piety and driven by a catchy chorus which prefigures Lorenzo de' Medici's secular *Canzona di Bacco* ('Song of Bacchus') two centuries later.

Guittone's letters, written in the vernacular, are likewise closely linked with his verse output: not only are a number of them metrical (some in sonnet form), but they often deal with themes, and use language, similar to specific poems. Thus, for instance, the letter *Infatuati, miseri fiorentini* ('Wretched Florentines') takes up the same material as the *canzone Ahi lasso, or è stagion de doler tanto*. If Giacomo da Lentini had been important for importing rhetoric into the lyric, and Pier della Vigna had brought *dictamen* in his baggage, Guittone is a key figure for introducing into prose the new inflections and mannerisms of vernacular poetry.

Guittone's place in the history of Italian verse is an important one, if only because his attempts to force the language and imagery of conventional poetry into conveying serious or difficult messages were only partially successful, and prompted both criticism and changes of direction in the next generation of poets. Dante in particular was to be uncharitable, but the very space (*DVE* I, xiii, 1 and II, vi, 8; *Purg.* XXIV, 56 and XXVI, 124–6) devoted to undermining him shows how large the Guittonian lesson loomed.

Bonagiunta da Lucca

The other major figure of this transitional period was Bonagiunta Orbicciani of Lucca. From his title of 'ser' we can deduce that he was a notary. His output, not quite thirty compositions, is less than a tenth of Guittone's. Bonagiunta was primarily interested in sound and form: in content he tamely followed the thematics of *fin'amors* already established by the Sicilians. One of Guittone's followers, possibly Chiaro Davanzati (b. ?1235), even accused him in a vituperative sonnet (*Di penne di paone*, 'Peacock's feathers') of shamelessly plagiarising Giacomo da Lentini. Like Guittone, however, Bonagiunta was fascinated by the troubadours of Provence, especially Peire Vidal and Folquet de Marselha, and his work contains much more direct quotation from

these poets than do the poems of the Magna curia, which followed a more
generic style of emulation.

Bonagiunta's life was long enough to encompass the extraordinarily swift
metamorphosis of vernacular poetry from the Sicilians to the *dolce stil novo*.
Though he corresponded with Guinizzelli (see his sonnet *Voi ch'avete mutata la
mainera* 'You who have changed the manner', objecting to Guinizzelli's
philosophical terminology) and Cavalcanti (*Con sicurtà dirò, po' ch'i' son
vosso* ('I shall say confidently, now I am with you'), a sonnet objecting to
Cavalcanti's *malvagi spiriti*, is ascribed to Bonagiunta), he stayed aloof from
the intellectual changes these writers were promoting, concerned as he was
merely to naturalise the poetic idiom of the Frederician court in western
Tuscany. Guittone had looked to Sicily and Provence as competing suppliers of
raw material for his restless self-questioning. Bonagiunta saw no conflict
between the Sicilian and Provençal models. Taking poets of the Magna curia,
especially Giacomo da Lentini, Guido delle Colonne and Mazzeo di Ricco, he
re-injected the accessible accent of melody which he sensed in the troubadours,
and which the Sicilians, wrapped up in their hieratic exclusiveness, had
neglected. Bonagiunta may not say very much that is new (indeed he purveys
the poetic equivalent of reproduction antiques: *Quando appar l'aulente fiore*
('When the fragrant flower appears') seems a pastiche of Provençal springtime
motifs, including birds twittering in 'Latin'), but his verse reads easily aloud,
presenting a standard of euphony that Guittone's tortured language could not
provide. Our appreciation of him is now coloured by Dante's choice of
Bonagiunta as a spokesman for the old-fashioned kind of verse which had been
rendered obsolete by the poets of Dante's generation. In the *Divine Comedy*
Dante had fictionally introduced himself to Bonagiunta saying that he was one
of the new poets who transcribed love *directly*. Bonagiunta in his reply
recognises that he and his fellow poets had been unable to make that leap:

> 'O frate, issa vegg'io,' diss'elli, 'il nodo
> che 'l Notaro e Guittone e me ritenne
> di qua dal dolce stil novo ch'i' odo!'

('Oh brother, now I see,' he said, 'the knot which held back the Notary, Guittone and
me from reaching the sweet new style which I hear!')

(Purg. XXIV, 55–7)

The remaining figures of the transitional period are minor, and mostly
swayed by the example of Guittone: it is only worth mentioning a few, on a
geographical basis, to emphasise the localised nature of the phenomenon.
Apart from Arezzo and Lucca, the centres where Sicilian poetry took root
include Pisa (Panuccio dal Bagno), Pistoia (Meo Abbracciavacca) Siena
(Bartolomeo Mocati and Mico da Siena), Bologna (despite overt Guittonian
tendencies, Onesto da Bologna is treated kindly by Dante, *DVE* I, xv, 6) and
Florence (Monte Andrea enthusiastically takes up Guittone's challenge of
trobar clus and verbal invention; Chiaro Davanzati, whose production of

poems was second only to Guittone's, has sunk into deserved oblivion; the so-called 'Compiuta Donzella' has intrigued more for her gender than her exiguous poetic output, and even her gender is now questioned).

Guido Guinizzelli

The first poet to write in the 'modern usage' was Guido Guinizzelli (?1230–76), whom Dante calls 'maximus Guido' (*DVE* I, xv, 6) and, echoing Bonagiunta's own praise of Guittone (see below): 'il padre / mio e de li altri miei miglior che mai / rime d'amor usar dolci e leggiadre' (father to me and to my betters who ever composed sweet, graceful rhymes of love), (*Purg.* XXVI, 97–9). A judge in Bologna, he was exiled in 1274 along with the Ghibelline faction of the Lambertazzi, a misfortune which may have hastened his early death. The importance of his poetic output is out of all proportion to its size (twenty-two poems of reliable attribution). To begin with, Guido was under the spell of Guittone, as can be seen in *Lo fin pregi' avanzato* ('The complete worth'). Indeed, in a sonnet (probably 'humbly' presenting this poem for correction) he addressed Guittone as 'my dear father', an affection returned by the Aretine, who, quoting Matthew 3:17, called him 'my beloved son'. The subsequent cooling of relations can be seen in Guittone's sonnet *S'eo tale fosse ch'io potesse stare* ('If only I could be such as to stay'), where umbrage is taken at Guinizzelli's two sonnets *Io voglio del ver la mia donna laudare* ('I wish truly to praise my lady') and *Vedut'ho la lucente stella diana* ('I have seen the shining morning star'). In these exquisite sonnets, Guinizzelli had daringly reversed the trite comparisons of previous poets, and compared natural marvels to his lady instead of the other way round. Guittone sourly saw this as *lèse-majesté* against nature and the Creator.

Guinizzelli's poetry makes abundant use of visual images: flowers, precious stones and metals, sunshine, clear air and stars. The concept of luminosity is central, for the emanation, reflection and perception of light are metaphors for the psychological effect of the lady on her lover. Though *luce* and *splendore* were already motifs in Giacomo da Lentini, here they acquire an epiphanic quality, and the tremulous amazement of the poet seems unfeigned. Guido Cavalcanti would subsequently take this poetry of reverberation even further. Here is a stanza from *Tegno de folle 'mpres', a lo ver dire* ('I regard it as foolhardy, to tell the truth') which is characteristic of Guinizzelli's shimmering optics:

> Ben è eletta gioia da vedere
> quand'apare 'nfra l'altre più adorna,
> ché tutta la rivera fa lucere
> e ciò che l'è d'incerchio allegro torna;
> la notte, s'aparisce,
> come lo sol di giorno dà splendore,

così l'aere sclarisce:
onde 'l giorno ne porta grande 'nveggia,
ch'ei solo avea clarore,
ora la notte igualmente 'l pareggia.

(A singular joy she is to behold, when she appears, amidst others, more comely she
makes the surroundings gleam and what is around her becomes happier once more; at
night if she appears she gives forth light like the daytime sun the air itself does
brighten so: hence the day feels great envy, since it alone once dispensed brightness,
and now the night is its equal.)

The most complete manifesto of Guinizzelli's concept of love is to be found
in *Al cor gentil rempaira sempre amore* ('Love always repairs to the noble
heart'), a *canzone* whose impact was to echo through the vernacular lyric for
generations. Dante's homage to this poem was explicit: in *Amor e 'l cor gentil
sono una cosa* ('Love and the noble heart are but one') in *VN* xx, he is referring
to Guinizzelli *per antonomasia*: 'Love and the noble heart are but one, / as the
wise poet says in his verse'. Likewise, in the *DVE* (i, ix, 3) the vernacular poem
used to illustrate the relatedness of French, Provençal and 'Italian' by means of
the key word *amor* is none other than *Al cor gentil rempaira sempre amore*.

Developing the naturalistic analogies used by Guido delle Colonne in *Ancor
che l'aigua per lo foco lassi* ('Though water loses its coldness through fire'),
Guinizzelli sets out a programme of maxims, each developing out of the one
before, and linked by sophisticated verbal and metrical reprises. If Guittone
worked by antithesis, Guinizzelli works by analogy, in the manner of Giacomo
da Lentini. As a result, the suggestions are strong, but the precise logical
progressions are tenuous. Guinizzelli's is the elegant poetry of suggestive
parallels rather than the dour *distinguos* of Guittone.

In its six stanzas *Al cor gentil* first defines love and the noble heart as
concomitant co-creations, with the noble heart as natural abode for love. The
heart's potential for loving is like a precious stone, whose ability to attract
magic power from the stars is dependent on the stone's prior purification by
the sun. Noble heart and love go together like torch and flame, but base
natures and love react violently like fire and water: love and the noble heart
interact like magnets and iron. The sun can beat down on mud all day, but the
sun will remain sun, and mud mud. In the same way, the heart can receive love
from the lady only if it has been made noble by nature: mere lineage is like
water, through which light-rays pass leaving nothing behind. True nobility is
not through lineage, but through an inclination to virtue. The reflection of God
in the eyes of the angels is brighter than the reflection of the sun in Man's eyes.
Angels in comprehending their Maker cause the cosmos to rotate in obedience
to Him, and receive immediate fulfilment: the lady should offer similar
blessedness, since her lover's eyes are filled with a desire which never departs
from obeying her. God will object to the bold comparison of the lady with
Himself and the Virgin, but the poet will counter that the lady possessed the
likeness of an angel, so it was no sin to love her.

The analogies (fire, precious stones and stellar magic, magnets and iron, sun, mud and water, water and fire) can all be found individually in previous poets. Indeed, Giacomo da Lentini uses nearly all of them in separate sonnets. What is special about *Al cor gentil* is the way in which it acts as a kind of 'catalogue raisonné' collecting together all these motifs, and employing them in a consistent programme.

The discussion on true nobility is not new either: in the late twelfth century Andreas Capellanus, in his *De amore* I, 10, 12, had insisted that 'morum probitas' (virtuous character) was the 'only way to make a man blessed with nobility'. The motif had surfaced in Sicily (even in Frederick II himself, in his sonnet *Misura, providenzia e meritanza*, 'Balance, foresight and merit'), and had reappeared in Guittone's *Comune perta fa comun dolore* ('Common loss makes common grief'): 'Non ver lignaggio fa sangue, ma core' (The heart, not breeding, makes for true nobility). Guinizzelli's definition of nobility is not that of static virtue but rather a precondition for further elevation, a potential for promotion.

Similarly, the comparison of the lady to an angel can be traced back through Guittone's letters (*Soprapiacente donna*, 'Most pleasing lady') and his poetry (*Gentile ed amorosa criatura*, but see also *Altra fiata aggio già, donne, parlato* 'Another time, ladies, I spoke'). It can also be found in Giacomo da Lentini's *Angelica figura e comprobata* ('Angelic figure demonstrably') and Mazzeo di Ricco's *Lo gran valore e lo presio amoroso* ('Great worth and loving esteem'), just two of a number of Sicilian poems to use the topos. But, here again, Guinizzelli's 'angelic appearance' is no tired reprise, but a *conscious* reference, through a chain of analogies, to the lady's intercessionary status.

What makes Guinizzelli's poem important is the immediate juxtaposition of these key motifs in an ideologically connected sequence. From having been, in earlier poets, separate opportunistic images, the heart's nobility and the lady's angelic nature have come to be implicit stages in a traffic of spiritual ascension. A receptive soul, through the intermediary influence of a lady, might aspire to higher levels of contemplation. The process is implicit only, for Guinizzelli's rather evasive last stanza does not go all the way, and refrains from following the logic of the situation, a logic which could have led him to posit the lady as a means for indirectly contemplating divine beauty itself. Dante was to be far bolder in *Donne ch'avete intelletto d'amore* ('Ladies who know by insight what love is') (the *canzone* immediately preceding *Amor e il cor gentil* in *VN*), where lady and angel are fused, and he would later take up Guinizzelli's implicit challenge of divine contemplation when he made Beatrice his intercessor and guide in the *Comedy*.

Dante called Guinizzelli his father, but pointedly did not place him amongst the poets who had achieved the 'sweet new style' so envied by Bonagiunta. Indeed, in the *Commedia* he has Oderisi da Gubbio predict that Guido Cavalcanti will eclipse the other Guido (Guinizzelli) (*Purg.* XI, 97–8). Guinizzelli's importance lies in his distillation of Sicilian and Provençal motifs and images into a concentrated sampler, clearly labelled as love doctrine. The issues are profoundly serious, but there is no hint of questioning or debate in Guinizzelli as there was in Guittone, and the psychology of passion remains at a superficial level. It is almost as if Guinizzelli had accidentally discovered something of shattering potential, but not found a way of exploiting it. The real *stilnovisti* can be distinguished from Guinizzelli by their willingness to accept the philosophical and intellectual consequences of the metaphors and analogies they inherit.

Guido Cavalcanti

The most significant poet of the new grouping was Guido Cavalcanti (?1259–1300). A Guelf, born into 'one of the most powerful families, in retainers, riches and property, in Florence' (according to the chronicler Giovanni Villani), he led an eventful life. Banished in childhood with his family after the Ghibelline victory of Montaperti (1260), he returned after the battle of Benevento (1266). Married off, as a gesture of political reconciliation, to the daughter of the Ghibelline leader Farinata degli Uberti, he joined the Cerchi in factional fighting against the Donati.[4] He was nearly assassinated by Corso Donati during a pilgrimage to Santiago de Compostela (Guido's revenge attack in Florence with a flechette also failed), and was among the ringleaders exiled in June 1300 by the Florentine government whilst Dante was one of the Priors (see below p. 46), after street-fighting occasioned by the assassination of the imprisoned Cerchi by means of a poisoned black pudding. By late August Guido was dead, possibly from malaria contracted during his exile in the swampy Tuscan Maremma.

Despite this eventful life, Cavalcanti found time to become a prolific poet (fifty-two compositions survive), and also to engage in serious philosophical speculation. He is the first poet, apart perhaps from St Francis, whose personality attracted intense interest and comment from fellow citizens and near contemporaries. Dino Compagni, who knew him, called him 'courteous and brave, but haughty, a loner and absorbed in study'. Villani praised his intellect, but thought his character 'touchy and irascible'. Many of the verbal portraits we have of him have been influenced by Dante's indirect treatment of him in *Inferno* x, where there is a strong suggestion that he was tainted with Averroism, or potentially atheistic Aristotelianism, though the primary targets in the burning tomb of the Epicureans are Guido's father and his father-in-law Farinata. Boccaccio, following Dante, embroidered a wry anecdote about how Cavalcanti's philosophical bent intrigued and mystified fellow Florentines (*Decameron* IV, 9).

---

[4] After the decline of the Ghibellines following the battle of Benevento, the Guelfs split into two factions, the Whites (led by the Cerchi) and the Blacks (led by the Donati), which inherited the old imperial–papal rivalry of the Ghibellines and Guelfs.

In keeping with Italian precedent, Cavalcanti's verse is almost exclusively about love, but the way he perceives and describes it is far from the mechanical torments and predictable joys of previous poets. Five general topics animate groups of poems, though it would be wrong to assume too deliberate a pattern. They are: a traditional Sicilian/Guinizzellian discussion of love; an examination of 'sbigottimento' (stupefaction caused by contemplation of the beloved); self-commiseration or choral anguish; analysis of the mental processes involved in the imagining of the beloved; introspection and grief.

The sight of his lady can render Cavalcanti dumbstruck: the 'sbigottimento' is at once both terrifying and miraculous, and can lead the poet to admit his own inability to describe her effects. In *Chi è questa che vèn* ('Who is she who comes'), a sonnet partly derived from the Song of Songs, all who come into contact with his lady and her shimmering grace are rendered speechless and reduced to sighs. Occasionally Cavalcanti can come out with wonderfully carefree ballads like the almost Bonagiuntian *Fresca rosa novella* ('Fresh new rose'), or guiltless sexual celebrations in the French tradition like *In un boschetto trova' pasturella* ('In a glade I found a shepherdess'). More typically his poems dramatise anguish, with the poet's passions the subject of interventions from various personified emotions: in *S'io prego questa donna* ('If I ask this lady'), the poet embarrassedly asks his lady for pity which is refused, whereupon pity itself comes to witness his ensuing death. In *Io temo che la mia disaventura* ('I fear my misfortune') the poet is visited by fear, who warns him he would mismanage an appeal to his lady for *mercede*; so, sensing his spirits fleeing him, he seeks consolation elsewhere. Cavalcanti's desire to dramatise inner processes leads him to elevate the term *spirit*, scholastic terminology for nerve-impulses, into a veritable dramatis persona of *hypostases*, or materialised formulations of abstract concepts. The Cavalcantian lover is possessed by unruly *spiritelli* (Cavalcanti loved diminutives) coming and going, commanding and conflicting. A fine self-parody can be seen in *Pegli occhi fere un spirito sottile* ('Through the eyes penetrates a subtle spirit').

Cavalcanti's account of love is characterised by an extraordinarily precise differentiation of its chronological and psychological components. It is the crisis of transition from one state or realisation to another. At its best, it resembles self-vivisection without anaesthetic, as the vital functions are probed and ruthlessly laid bare: a poetry of pathology. Central to this analysis is the belief that love is an imbalance, an illness which disturbed the working relationship between senses and reason. This pessimistic evaluation is much closer to Fra Guittone's strictures than to Guinizzelli's easy-going celebration, and it explains the predominance of grief, anguish and death in Cavalcanti's verse.

The fullest account of Cavalcanti's love theory is to be found in the *canzone Donna me prega*, a virtuoso reply to a banal sonnet by Guido Orlandi asking what love was. Technically *Donna me prega* ('A lady asks me') is a tour de force: using an exceptionally demanding internal/external rhyme scheme, fifty-two out of the 154 syllables of each stanza are predetermined. Despite this out-Guittoning of Guittone, the main interest of the *canzone* is the 'natural dimostramento' (scientific demonstration) of the metabolism of passion. This is achieved not through colourful analogies as in Guinizzelli, but through the harnessing of scholastic discourse to lyric purpose. These necessarily elliptic references to a vast system of knowledge have meant that the poem has attracted a tradition of far from unanimous commentary ever since.

Love, Cavalcanti declares, is, in Aristotelian terms, an accident, not a substance, occasioned in the sensitive rather than rational soul by a malign influence of Mars combined with a visual form. The visual form becomes an abstraction and lodges in the possible intellect (the part of the mind beyond the immediate senses) as an ideal incapable of arousing passion. Love is not rational, but rather an event of the senses, which are the highest perfection of Man. But this event can lead to obfuscation, not because it is against nature, but because it crowds out rational operations. Love is a temporary state, with pronounced physical effects, awakening the irascible appetite in an energetic struggle against the obstacles to fulfilment. Pleasure can be found only by discovering a similar temperament, even though the primary manifestations of love are invisible.

What Cavalcanti is saying in his intellectual shorthand is that through early experience and psychological disposition we acquire sensual notions of ideal beauty which stay in our memory and exercise a dormant fascination. These notions are subsequently challenged by the contemplation of real-life attractions. The pent-up force of the ideal, coupled with the mismatch of the real, leads to major psychological instability. Occasionally, however, when there is a reciprocal match of sensual ideals between partners, difficult to ascertain because love is invisible, the experience can be beneficial.

Despite the Aristotelian terminology and largely negative stance, the theoretical position is not so far removed from Guinizzelli's ideas on predisposition to love (*gentilezza*), with the passage from potency to act triggered by contemplation of someone of similar temperament. The pairing of the influence of Mars (one might have expected Venus) and the visual form, which together occasion love's lodging in memory, is the most difficult concept in the poem. Whereas the rational soul directly receives its intellectual light pure and undiminished, the sensitive soul receives its input imperfectly through the senses, senses which are conditioned by the stars. The potential lover sees feminine beauty through a glass darkly; his complexion is one susceptible to strong emotions and violent conflict (the attributes of Mars).

The cerebrality of such discussion can easily obscure the fantastic verbal dynamics underpinning the argument: 'da Marte' (from Mars) could also be read 'd'amar te' (loving you), and repeated anagrams of *amare* are woven effortlessly into the poem. Critics still disagree on whether Cavalcanti's insistence on the primacy of the *sensitive* as opposed to the *rational* soul is a sign of radical Averroism. For the Averroists, the rational intellect was universal, not specific to individuals, whereas the sensitive soul was the highest *individual* faculty. Love in such circumstances would be resolutely secular, and part of our mortal attributes, completely separate from the incorruptible rational soul, and far from the vaguely Neoplatonic ascensional love of Guinizzelli. Cavalcanti's linking of *eros* and *thanatos*, then, is no shallowly inherited metaphor: love is the operation of those parts of us which are destined to die.

If the technical bravura of *Donna me prega* impressed poets (right up to Ezra Pound), the investigation of erotic metabolism intrigued doctors and philosophers. Dino del Garbo (1280–1327), a celebrated Florentine physician, wrote a major commentary concentrating on the psychological and physiological assumptions behind the poem, a commentary which Boccaccio was to read assiduously. Even well into the Renaissance, Marsilio Ficino (1433–99) commenting on Plato's *Symposium*, was to refer copiously to Cavalcanti's love theory, though in a Neoplatonic rather than an Aristotelian context.

Cavalcantian circle

Dante called Cavalcanti his 'first friend', celebrating their first poetic contact in *VN* III, where he claims that Guido was one of those who responded to his poem *A ciascun'alma presa* ('To each captured soul'). Dante and Guido were to exchange a number of poems, one of which, Dante's charming sonnet *Guido, i' vorrei che tu e Lapo e io* ('Guido, I wish that you, Lapo and I'), imagines the small group of like-minded poets idyllically marooned on a magic ship with their lady-loves. This element of *sodalitas* (personal friendship) is an important factor in the development of *stilnovismo*, where close social contact meant that influences were swiftly felt and ideas supplanted each other rapidly. Dante's early poetry was to feature fear and trembling straight out of Guido's catalogue. Soon, however, gentler motifs from Guinizzelli, such as praise of the lady, began to overlay the stern poetry of distress. The *VN* can be read almost as a diary of changing influences, as Dante heeds Guittone, Cavalcanti, Guinizzelli and finally his own voice.

The other figures in Dante and Guido's circle are relatively minor. Lapo Gianni, Dino Frescobaldi and Gianni Alfani were active around the turn of the century, and ingenuously reproduced Cavalcantian motifs along with allusions to older Guittonian and Sicilian themes.

Cino da Pistoia

The only other poet of some note, whose professional (if not lyric) career was to be prolonged with distinction into the Trecento, was Cino da Pistoia (?1265–1337). A jurist of international repute (his *Lectura in Codicem* was a milestone in Roman Law), his poetic inspiration petered out shortly after the turn of the century. Dante had already named him as one of the two poets who had salvaged the reputation of Italian vernaculars in the face of French and Provençal primacy (*DVE* I, 10), rendering urbane the 'rustic accents' of the *volgare* (*DVE* I, 17). Dante would refer to him again (*DVE* II, 2) as a distinguished poet of love, whilst keeping for himself the laurels for 'singing rectitude'. Very much in the shadow of Cavalcanti and Dante, Cino's poetry is characterised by an attenuation of the more intense aspects of his mentors. Both Cavalcanti's anguished drama and Dante's propensity to worship, manifestations of the uncompromising zeal of the converted, give way to a concern for balance and elegance, for a melodious accommodation of ideas which have finished by becoming uncontroversial. In *Una gentil piacevol giovanella* ('A nice young noble girl'), the miraculous lady whose apparition brings Cavalcanti to a juddering halt is replaced by a reassuringly 'nice' young girl who infuses the poet with simple celebratory joy. In *La dolce vista e 'l bel guardo soave* ('Sweet sight and beautiful, elegant gaze'), the grief at separation is rehearsed with calibrated stylishness rather than tongue-tied desperation. Both Petrarch and Boccaccio were to admire and cite this poem, and Cino can be seen as a transitional figure, halfway between the emotional discoveries of Cavalcanti and Dante and the mature connoisseurship of Petrarch. The latter would write a moving sonnet on hearing of Cino's death.

Stilnovo

'Dolce' and 'soave' are key words in Cino's sound-palette, and there has been much critical speculation about Bonagiunta's naming of the '*sweet* new style' (*Purg.* XXIV, 57) from which the poet from Lucca was excluded, and about Dante's preceding definition of the new poetics as 'what love inspires, I note, and what he dictates within, I express'. The statements are indeed finely balanced between the powerfully enigmatic and the possibly banal. More perhaps than any ideological feature, the fact that the *stilnovo* poets were predominantly Florentine, and came from a similar upper middle-class background, contributed to a sense of group cohesion, and also to a conscious differentiation from other poets (who often vented their disapproval in verse). That the *stilnovisti* spoke the same dialect with the same vowel qualities must also have made agreement on the aesthetic criteria of verse easier. Dante's comments on lexis in *DVE* II, 7, dividing words by sound, are clearly a rationalisation of an implicit standard, with the ideologically loaded terms like 'donna', 'disio', 'amore' singled out for special praise.

Although, seen in retrospect, there is little new in the *stilnovisti*, the important thing is that they felt themselves to be such. Cavalcanti's dismissal of Guittone in *Da più a uno face un sollegismo* ('From the many to the one makes a syllogism'), which pokes fun at the older poet's logical deficiencies whilst cruelly parodying Guittone's involved syntax, displays all the arrogance of the young Turk. The perceived novelty of the *stilnovisti* was in turn debunked by outsiders: Onesto da Bologna wrote a telling complaint to Cino da Pistoia, *Mente ed umile e più di mille sporte* (' "Mind" and "humble" and more than a thousand basketsfull'), in which he pokes fun at *stilnovisti* debating in a daze with hordes of hypostatic spirits, and spouting trendy buzz-words like 'umile' with the stress indulgently moved *à la française* to the penultimate syllable (to rhyme with 'gentile'). Cino replied in kind, saying that at least the new poets didn't use tired old clichés like the Sicilians and Guittonians.

If there is real novelty it is psychological: the *stilnovisti* feel they are expressing love directly, and not through stale convention. Having found in the coincidence of love and the noble heart an ideal fusion between inspiration (love) and expression (noble heart), they are convinced that the role of the poet is to accept the pre-verbal *flatus* and voice it *per verba*. Dante's reply to Bonagiunta makes this clear: 'quando / Amor mi spira, noto, e a quel modo / ch'e' ditta dentro vo significando' (when love inspires, I note, and what he dictates within, I express). Superficially this sounds like nothing more than a protestation of veracity: the writer constrained by truth is a common topos in all medieval literature. But the *stilnovisti* believe they have made a break-through: they have discovered what love actually is, as opposed to merely observing its indirect effects, for it is love itself which initiates the literary act ('dittare' is the technical term for writing poetry), whereas the poet's function is to find appropriate verbal expression. Cavalcanti, taking up a conceit of Arnaut Daniel, expresses the same idea when he says in *Di vil matera mi conven parlare* ('I must talk of a lowly subject') 'Amore ha fabbricato ciò ch'io limo' (Love has fashioned what I finish). One consequence of this conviction is that love as a *noun* predominates in *stilnovo* lyric, whereas the *verb* is rare. Poetry has turned its attention from the lover to love itself.

At a textual level, the poets of the *stilnovo* seem to have discovered, wide-eyed, the full meaning of terms and images used with uncritical abandon by previous writers. The same vocabulary is used, but the significance and consequences are reverently gauged. There is an almost audible frisson when they draw out the possibilities of 'apparere' (to appear), 'vertute' (essential quality), 'salute' (salvation). One senses an evolving code, with stratifications of added meaning excitedly superimposed on a previously unappreciated lexis. This semantic revolution is the real legacy of the *stilnovo*. By the time Petrarch started writing, the vocabulary of the lyric had acquired a redolent, allusive, self-conscious quality which was ripe for secondary manipulation and indulgent retrospection.

3
Prose

Non-fictional works

While the language, thematics and culture of vernacular poetry developed rapidly through competing attempts to come to terms with the powerfully suggestive, relatively unified courtly lyric of Provence, vernacular prose literature evolved much less uniformly and easily. Culturally, there was no single body of material demanding attention and admiration: instead there were many different potential models, each with its own traditions and readership. Linguistically, the situation was no more clear-cut. If French prose literature was a precocious phenomenon, it was nevertheless dwarfed by its Latin parent, even in France; Latinity in Italy was in an even more predominant position. Many of the dialects indeed had no tradition of writing at all. Learning to use Latin as a written medium was, however, a major investment in time and money, not undertaken lightly. For lawyers and clerics, the pay-off could be justified by professional opportunities and efficiency. Changing patterns of economic and political activity in the expanding communes meant that other groups, hitherto illiterate, were beginning to require records of transactions. For the unlettered who merely needed occasional written corroboration, it was better to use a notary, who could provide an instant technical translation. Increasingly, though, merchants, bankers and politicians sought regular, confidential records. There was an incentive for them to acquire the skills themselves: fragments of a Florentine bank ledger dating from 1211 clearly show a developing utilitarian jargon in the vernacular entries. The progress of mercantile literacy from book-keeping to book-writing would reach its culmination in the Trecento, when Boccaccio, a banker himself, would make his mark in both prose and epic poetry. But to begin with, the only group with the wherewithal for linguistic transfer was the lawyers.

Acting as mediators between vernacular tractation and Latin transcription placed notaries in a unique position. Such was the importance of this activity in the commercial life of the communes that already in 1246 the statutes of the guild of notaries of Bologna required candidates to pass an examination in oral and written translation to and from the vernacular. It was no accident that this profession not only produced many pioneers of vernacular poetry (where feelings had to be accurately accommodated to form), but was also instrumental in extending the Latin prose tradition into Italian.

Guido Faba (fl. 1220–48) studied law at Bologna, taught rhetoric briefly, then, after a serious illness, became a notary. Author of a number of Latin works on rhetoric and *dictamen* (ornamented official prose), he is remembered for two works which demonstrate the possibilities of transposing stylistic devices from Latin to the vulgar tongue. The *Gemma purpurea* is a handbook on the art of letter-writing. Though the instructions are in Latin, Guido illustrates his precepts indifferently in both languages. The formulas, whether in Latin or the vernacular, are generic and mechanical, like 'personalised' junk-mail, but they reveal a fascinating hunger for cultural advancement even amongst the supposedly uncultivated. Though predominantly aimed at practical, prosaic situations, there are moments, such as here in formula 6, when the heady attractions of the new love lyric seep into the stilted epistolary recipes:

Quando eo vego la vostra splendiente persona, per grande alegrança me pare ch'eo scia in paradiso; sì me prende lo vostro amore, donna çençore, sovra onne bella.

(When I see your splendid person, the resultant happiness makes me think I am in Paradise; so much does your love take me, noble Lady, beautiful above all others.)

Faba's *Parlamenta et epistole*, written somewhat later, are an 'exercice de style' in the manner of Raymond Queneau. A vernacular letter responding to a particular situation is followed by three Latin versions of decreasing complexity, *major, minor,* and *minima*. The intent was to teach *amplificatio* (stylistic elaboration) and other forms of rhetorical enhancement via the Latin texts. The vernacular passages were a linguistically neutral, 'invisible' way of presenting the content before concentrating on the style in the Latin versions. Even so, the vernacular texts exhibit clear signs of oratorical design, employing figures of speech and thought and mimicking the solemn accentuation of Latin *cursus* (rhythmic end-patterns). Here is the beginning of a form-letter, *De filio ad patrem pro pecunia*, in which a student asks his father for further financial support, employing newly learnt rhetorical colours in a directly relevant exercise of persuasion:

Andato sono al prato de la Filosofia bello, delectevele e glorioso, e volsi cogliere flore de diversi colori, açò ch'eo facesse una corona de merevegliosa belleça [...] Ma lo guardiano del çardino contradisse, s'eo non li facessi doni placeveli et onesti.

(I have been to the beautiful meadow of Philosophy [university], both delightful and glorious, and I wished to gather flowers of many colours [enrol for courses], so that I could make a crown of marvellous beauty [get a degree] [...] But the guardian of the garden [the dean] said no, unless I presented him with pleasant and honourable gifts [paid my fees]).

Commercial ascendancy and increasingly complex financial structures were not the only spur to literacy. The emergent communes offered opportunities for political activity to groups hitherto excluded. There was now a market for practical advice on political oratory. Some was distinctly down-to-earth and primitive, such as Giovanni da Vignano's *Flore de parlare* ('Flower of Speech'), whose sub-title hopefully declares it 'ad utilità de coloro che desidrano sapere arengare' (useful for those who desire to know how to speak in public). Access to an ideologically appropriate past became an urgent necessity for politicians. The protagonists' culture was, however, largely limited to the vernacular, and translations of works relevant to civic politics, the history and oratory of republican Rome in particular, were amongst the first to appear.

Brunetto Latini's partial translation of Cicero's *De inventione*, and Guidotto da Bologna's *Fiore di rettorica* (?1260), a free adaptation of the pseudo-Ciceronian *Rhetorica ad Herennium*, were responses to this need for a more informed, political use of Italian prose. Brunetto's foreword to the *Rettorica* eloquently voices this desire to develop a reliable form of vernacular persuasion:

Sovente e molto ho io pensato in me medesimo se la copia del dicere e lo sommo studio della eloquenzia hae fatto più bene o più male agli uomini e alle cittadi; però che quando io considero li dannaggi del nostro Comune, e raccolgo nell'animo l'antiche aversitadi delle grandissime cittadi, veggio che non picciola parte di danni v'è messa per uomini molto parlanti sanza sapienza.

(Often and deeply have I pondered whether a way with words and the lofty pursuit of eloquence have done more good or harm to individuals and cities; for that reason when I consider the misfortunes of our Commune, and I call to mind the ancient tribulations of the greatest cities, I see that no small part of the misfortunes can be attributed to men speaking overmuch but without knowledge.)

In the glosses to the Ciceronian passages, glosses in a markedly plainer style than the translated excerpts from the *De inventione*, Brunetto's explanations abound not only with examples from ancient Rome, but also with the homespun politics and deputations of Tuscan political life. This link between rhetoric and politics was keenly felt: Giovanni Villani would subsequently write, with gratitude, that Brunetto was the 'initiator and teacher in removing the rough edges of the Florentines, and making them aware of how to speak properly, and how to direct and rule our republic according to [Aristotle's] *Politics*' (*Cronica* VIII, 10).

If political and social eloquence were both in demand, so was the knowledge-base that went with it. Scientific and moral doctrine began to cross the boundaries of language. In medieval encyclopaedism, Brunetto Latini's *Trésor* had made the leap from Latin to the vernacular, but the language he wrote in had been French. Ristoro (or Restoro) d'Arezzo wrote his *Composizione del mondo* ('The making of the world') in the 1280s in a rhetorically artless Aretine dialect, far removed from the studied periods of Brunetto. Ristoro believed that Creation was ruled by the Aristotelian principle of opposites (what is white, except by reference to black?) and his review of the world and the cosmos proceeds by a kind of lexical dialectic, a rich dictionary of antonyms, particularly adjectives. The effect is relentless. Here in the second chapter of the sixth 'particula', he is distinguishing the qualities of plants:

tale trovamo grande e tale piccola, a respetto l'una a l'altra, e tale è grossa e tale sottile, e tale è longa e tale corta, e tale è armata, come quelle c'hano le spine acute, e tale so' sciarmate, e tale odorifera e tale fetida ...

(we find one large and another small, in relation to one another, and one thick and another thin, one long and another short, one armed, like those which bear sharp thorns, and another unarmed, and one scented and another foul-smelling ...)

If Ristoro is amongst the first to deal scientifically with the cosmos in an Italian vernacular, then the Florentine judge Bono Giamboni is one of the initiators of ethico-doctrinal writing in Tuscan. In his *Della miseria dell'uomo* ('On the Wretchedness of Man'), Bono produced a free vernacular re-working of Innocent III's well-known *De miseria humane conditionis*, in which the original text became encased in a narrative framework reminiscent of Boethius' *De consolatione Philosophiae*. Innocent's purpose had been contemplative, whereas the Florentine's version stressed the didactic element. Bono's most original work, however, is the slightly later *Libro de' vizi e delle virtudi* ('Book of Vices and Virtues'). Taking again the Boethian situation of a visitation by an allegorical personage at a time of crisis, he dramatises the struggle in the soul between good and evil. The emulation of Boethius is anything but mechanical. Lady Philosophy may graciously converse with the anguished Boethius, but for the practical Bono she offers the hem of her garment to cleanse the author's clogged eyes of their 'crosta di sozzura puzzolente di cose terrene' (scab of stinking filth of earthly things). While Boethius remained firmly in his cell mulling over the transience of the world, Bono will be invited on a journey to discover the virtues, and during his travels will be told of the epic struggle of the Christian faith against paganism (Islam). The theology of the *Libro de' vizi e delle virtudi* may be embedded in earlier medieval models, but the language and narrative verve are distinctly original, endowed with an authentic voice, and already prefigure the vigour of Dante and Boccaccio in the Trecento.

Vernacular translations

The desire of the new middle class to acquire culture, to parade modestly appropriate quotations from the classics, lies behind the various *volgarizza-menti* (vernacular translations) of the *Disticha Catonis*, a second-century collection of Latin *sententiae* which enjoyed enormous popularity in the Middle Ages. Apart from a number of Tuscan versions, Duecento translations into Venetian and Neapolitan have been found, and Bonvesin de la Riva was not alone in producing a *volgarizzamento* into Lombard. A similar desire to parade cultural baggage underlies the multiple translations (predominantly Tuscan, but also Venetian) of Albertano da Brescia's *Liber consolationis et consilii* (1246), a work of moral improvement which was to influence Chaucer, in which the long-suffering Meliboeus is taught patience through a surfeit of maxims and biblical examples.

The translations of Latin material are crucial to our understanding of the period on two counts. The first is that they show the cultural aspirations of an emerging lay middle class, no longer subservient to legal or ecclesiastic hierarchies. The second is that the very process of translation forced the pace of linguistic development. The accretion of centuries of rhetorical tradition, the civilised patina of allusivity, and the sophistication of syntactic devices, all these Latin assets were hard to reproduce in a language more fitting for the cut-and-thrust of the street. It was inevitable that the struggling target language should absorb characteristics from the confident source language. During the Duecento, the *volgarizzamenti* were to introduce a progressive Latinisation of vernacular vocabulary and a marked tendency away from parataxis (sequences of undifferentiated main clauses) towards complex sentences with involved subordination (hypotaxis).

The choice of written language in the late Middle Ages was to a large extent sectorially determined, that is to say subject-specific. If Latin was the vehicle for the history of the Greeks and Romans, French was the medium for contemporary record. Brunetto's remarks about the universality of French were to find an echo in Martino da Canale, a Venetian whose *Chronique des Veniciens* (1275) proudly presents the virtues and achievements of his city, 'the most beautiful and pleasing in this our earthly existence', in the vernacular language most likely to have universal readership. What seems like luke-warm linguistic patriotism is in fact a hard-headed calculation of impact. In 1298, another Venetian, Marco Polo, would dictate from a Genoese prison cell his *Divisament dou monde*, commonly known as the *Milione* (from *Emilione*, his family nickname), the account of a quarter of a century of eventful travels in the Orient. The language would again be an Italianate French, though whether this was the choice of Polo himself or his amanuensis, Rustichello da Pisa, is unclear. Paradoxical proof that the linguistic choice had been opportune can be seen in the almost immediate separate translations into Tuscan (pre-1309) and Latin (1320), a sign that, beyond French, readers could still not be reached by a single Italian dialect.

Rustichello was no mere scribe, however, and he is remembered for having composed one of the classics of the chivalrous tradition. The *Meliadus* (?1270), written in French, is an imaginative and voluminous reworking of offshoots of the Tristan and Lancelot material (Meliadus is Tristan's wayward father) whose fortune spread across Europe in the wake of the French romancers Chrétien, Thomas and Béroul. The passion of Tristan and Iseult the Blonde, like that of Lancelot and Guinevere, was to be popular in Italy, where the intrigues of the heart seem to have had more pulling power than the vicissitudes of the battlefield. As in Germany, versions in the local vernacular were to play an influential role in subsequent culture. The *Tristano Riccardiano* (late Duecento), named after the Florentine library where the manuscript is preserved, is a fluent semi-independent derivative of the French prose versions, written in Tusco-Umbrian dialect. Though dealing with a fantasy world, the storytelling is careful rather than imaginative, and the repetitive use of narratorial interventions ('here the story says . . .', 'if anybody asks who the knight was, I will say his name is . . .') gives a primitive, pseudo-oral feel, a feature which would be exploited to ironic antiquarian effect in the romance epics of the late Renaissance.

Outside Tuscany, the *Tristano Veneto* and *Tristano Corsiniano* (both late Duecento) are written in Venetian dialect: the Veneto was to be a prime importer of Arthurian and Carolingian epic, and much of it was to circulate in a hybrid language, Franco-Venetian, haphazardly composed, but nonetheless vital and above all *popular*. The common herd were now trespassing on the preserve of an aristocratic élite. An anonymous intellectual set his scorn for such vulgarity in Latin metre:

> Karoleas acies et gallica gesta boantem
> cantorem aspicio; pendet plebecula circum
> auribus arrectis . . .
> . . . Francorum dedita lingue
> carmina barbarico passim deformat hiatu.

(I see the minstrel booming out . . . Charlemagne's battle-host and French derring-do; the wretched plebs hang round with their ears pricked . . . and persistently he deforms with his barbaric phrasing verses set in the language of the Franks.)

(Text in Francesco Novati, *Attraverso il medioevo*, Bari, 1905, p. 298.)

In Italy, then, chivalrous epic finally left its aristocratic readership behind, and embarked on a fascinating adventure at the popular end of the market, losing belligerence and gaining humour on the way, and preparing for the great nostalgic achievements of Pulci, Boiardo, Ariosto and Tasso in the Renaissance.

From *exemplum* to *novella*

Though Arthurian material pandered to the taste for romance and adventure, its organisation and scope were rambling and long-winded. Other briefer forms from a different tradition were to occupy the niche of snappy narration. One spur for such a development was the growing importance of sermons and preaching in the wake of the evangelism of the Franciscans and Dominicans. Moral points would be illustrated by appropriate narrative examples, or *exempla*. In effect, the *exemplum* was a short story embedded in a religious discourse and rounded off with a homily. Vincent of Beauvais's *Speculum historiale* was a widely diffused compilation of such *exempla*, furnished with suitable moralising tailpieces. Some time after 1264 it was partially translated into Tuscan as the *Fiori e vita di filosafi ed altri savi ed imperadori* ('Life and

Sayings of Philosophers and other Sages and Emperors'). What is interesting about the *volgarizzamento* is that the anonymous translator kept very much to a literal, almost pedantic rendition of the moralising sequences, but put a great deal of narrative enthusiasm into the *exempla* themselves. A similar interest in what was to become the classic short-story form can be seen in the late-Duecento *Fatti di Cesare* ('Deeds of Caesar'), *Conti di antichi cavalieri* ('Tales of Knights of Old') and *Libro dei sette savi* ('Book of the Seven Sages'). The first is a free translation of *Li fet des Romains*, an early thirteenth-century compilation from Lucan, Sallust and Suetonius outlining events and personalities connected with the career of Julius Caesar. Its episodic character was clearly attractive to a public seeking short, autonomous narrations. The *Conti di antichi cavalieri* is a curious assembly of twenty anecdotes about rulers: Saladin takes pride of place, followed by Henry II of England, various Roman heroes such as Scipio, Pompey and Caesar, and the entirely fictional Tristan. The *Libro dei sette savi* translates, sometimes indirectly through French, the *Dolopathos*, a Latin version of a collection of short stories originating in India and popular in both the Middle East and Europe. A prince is unjustly accused by his stepmother of rape: over a week, the stepmother and the boy's seven tutors compete in telling stories to prove his guilt or innocence. The 'frame plus intercalation' structure anticipates Boccaccio's *Decameron* (1350s).

The *Novellino*

The aforementioned compilations all provided material for the *Novellino*, or *Cento novelle antiche* ('Hundred Old Tales', post ?1280) the most successful and original example of vernacular prose literature of the Duecento. The edificatory tone which still coloured the earlier anthologies is now conspicuously absent. Instead, there is a simple appeal to social promotion through culture, as can be seen in the opening passage:

Since the nobility is in its words and deeds like a mirror to lesser mortals, since their speech is more pleasant, issuing from a more delicate instrument, let us record here a few flowers of speaking, of elegant manners, elegant replies, elegant accomplishments, elegant generosity and elegant loves, as took place in olden times. And whoever has a noble heart and subtle intelligence will be able to imitate them in the future, and reason and speak and recount wherever he finds himself.

The hundred tales (it is thought the now-lost original may have had more than a score more) are loosely arranged by theme, location or protagonist. Whilst the written sources of the older material can frequently be identified, and point to a 'middle-brow' culture with gross misattributions and elementary anachronisms, the stories relating to the Duecento have all the sureness of oral currency. Studies of the *Novellino* hint at the possibility of more than one author, but suggest only one compiler. Whoever he was he had a soft spot for

Frederick II: the first story (II) concerns the Emperor's well-known contacts with the oriental world, and even quotes indirectly one of Frederick's sonnets (*Misura, providenzia e meritanza*). This enthusiasm has led some commentators to assume the compiler was a Ghibelline. But given similarly warm treatment of Saladin and Richard the Lionheart, it might be safer to imagine a naive hankering for a heroic age of chivalry in net contrast to contemporary venality.

Though the protagonists of the *novelle* are typically emperors, kings, prelates or philosophers, what is striking is that they are portrayed not at their moments of historical or fictional triumph – battles, theological or forensic victories, moments of pomp and splendour. Instead, the *Novellino* places us in the interstices of great events and relates fleeting incidents when the famous come into contact with common experience. In the middle of the crusades, Saladin breaks off battle, curious to observe the eating habits of his Christian foes; unimpressed with their hospitality, he invites them to dinner, where they show their lack of manners by spitting on the carpets specially embroidered with crosses in their honour (xxv). Out hunting one day Frederick II feels thirsty and, without revealing his identity, asks a picnicking commoner for some wine: the commoner refuses to let a stranger sully his clean goblet. Frederick humbly asks for the use of his water-bottle, promising it will not touch his lips: but instead of giving it back, he rides away with it. The commoner traces the perpetrator of this theft and confronts the Emperor, much to the latter's amusement. As a reward for his frankness the commoner leaves with liberal gifts (xxiii).

Stylistically, the *Novellino* is economical to the point of curtness. Initially, critics took this pared-down quality for a desire to furnish only a bare outline, as if the stories were mere aide-mémoires, and amplification would take place orally. Subsequent studies have identified quite sophisticated levels of rhetorical organisation, and conclude that the leanness of the *Novellino* is a conscious attempt at *sermo brevis* (desirable briefness). One of the main reasons *sermo brevis* was an attractive gambit is that the *novelle* are predominantly vehicles for coming to a quick climax, *bel motto* (quip) or *belli risposi* (ripostes). Here in the *Novellino*, the moral conclusion of the *exemplum*, outside the story, has been superseded by the narrative justification of the punch-line, placed within it. The displacement of the centre of gravity was not to stop there, however. By the time of Boccaccio's *Decameron*, though the taste for such quick-wittedness was undiminished, and 'leggiadri motti' (amusing remarks) are the theme for Day Six, narrative interest would find itself transferred from the moment of climax to the circumstances leading up to it. In this context, it is clear that the *Novellino* is a crucial step in the development of modern narrative.

Perhaps the lasting importance of the *Novellino* lies in the fact that it has escaped from the world of *volgarizzamenti* and has acquired narrative autonomy. The shape of the work and the choice of *novelle* is its own. The aesthetic criteria are sometimes even advertised in the rubrics – 'Here is recounted a *fine* judgement . . . ' (x); 'Here is recounted a *most beautiful novella* . . . ' (XLII). The humorous dialectic of many of the *novelle* also points to another major advance: direct speech itself is handled with great confidence, even if the ancillary devices identifying the changeover of interlocutors are rather primitive. The postmodern *novella* of the courtier who starts a *novella* which goes on and on, for lack an ending (LXXXIX), is an example of wonderfully cutting repartee articulated by insecure 'he replieds':

Brigata di cavalieri cenavano una sera in una gran casa fiorentina, e avevavi uno uomo di corte, il quale era grandissimo favellatore. Quando ebbero cenato, cominciò una novella che non venìa meno. Uno donzello della casa che servia, e forse non era troppo satollo, lo chiamò per nome, e disse: – Quelli che t'insegnò cotesta novella, non la t'insegnò tutta. – Ed elli rispuose: – Perché no? – Ed elli rispuose: – Perché non t'insegnò la restata.

(A band of knights were dining one evening in a great Florentine house, and there was a courtier who was a great talker. When they had finished eating, he began a story which went on and on. A young man of the house who was serving, and perhaps not had his fill, called out to him by name and said, 'Whoever told you this story didn't tell you the whole of it.' And he replied, 'Why not?' And he replied, 'Because he didn't tell you the ending.')

These discoveries of narrative autonomy and of direct speech were to be major lessons for Boccaccio, whose *Decameron* would incorporate a number of the *novelle*. Indeed this knight's tale of the *Novellino* was to end up reworked as the first *novella* of Day Six.

By the end of the Duecento, then, prose was just beginning to acquire that independence which verse had already manifested. The earlier maturation of verse was not just a historical fact, but also confirmation of a cultural precedence already claimed for Latin and Greek, in which poetry had come before prose. But when Dante, following Isidore of Seville (*Etymologies* I, 38), wrote in *DVE* II, I 'it is the prose-writers who receive the illustrious vernacular from verse-writers . . ., and not vice-versa', he was a mite premature. If one looks at most of the prose of the Duecento, the lyric barely impinges on a medium nourished more by rhetoric, history and *sententiae*. But the interdependence of the two media would be convincingly demonstrated by Dante himself in *VN* xxv, where the formal alternation of prose and poetry reveals poems as vehicles for narration, and plain text as poetry: 'it would be shame indeed for a poet writing beneath the cloak of figures and colours of rhetoric to be unable, if asked, to bare his words to reveal the true meaning'. By the end of the Duecento, the language was ready: it was merely awaiting writers, the real guarantee of an 'illustrious vernacular'. It would not wait for long.

The Trecento

Lino Pertile, Pamela Stewart, John Took,
Steven Botterill

4

Dante

Lino Pertile

When in 1313–14 it began to circulate in Italy, the *Inferno* must have taken its first Tuscan readers by surprise. Dante Alighieri was a Florentine exile, a sophisticated poet and intellectual who, some twenty years earlier, had published a slim volume, a love story in vernacular verse and prose, entitled *Vita Nuova*. He was also known as the author of many other poems in the vernacular (sonnets, *canzoni*, ballads) which had placed him at the forefront of a small group of young poets active in Tuscany in the 1290s. However, his main claim to fame was probably of a different nature: in the year 1300 he had been one of Florence's six Priors, the highest public officers in the Commune. But his political career had been dramatically interrupted in 1301, when as a White Guelf[1] he had been banished from his native city. Since that year he had been living in exile, mainly in Northern Italy, producing the occasional *canzone* but apparently involving himself more with philosophy and politics than with poetry. In fact, in the previous two to three years he had written various open letters advocating the restoration of the Holy Roman Empire under the rule of a German monarch, Henry VII of Luxembourg – the same Henry who had vainly besieged Florence in the autumn of 1312 and had died ten months later, near Siena, without having achieved much for himself or the Empire.

This is, more or less, all that was likely to have been common knowledge around 1313 about Dante Alighieri: hardly enough to forewarn his readers of what was to come. The *Inferno* was the first instalment of a three-part account in which the author claimed to have been on a journey among the dead, where he had met and talked to, among others, many of his friends and foes, especially from Florence. Even apart from the question of credibility, the work broke all the rules: literary, political, religious. Its subject was deeply serious, but its language vernacular; its stylistic range was unprecedented, mixing the low and base with the lofty and abstract, the comic with the tragic, the lyric with the epic, the Christian with the pagan. Politically, it condemned to eternal damnation Guelfs (both Black and White) as well as Ghibellines, ecclesiastical as well as secular rulers. Though it favoured Florence as the target of its indignation and sarcasm, it spared no city in Tuscany or beyond. Above all, it displayed a profound aversion for the new class of entrepreneurs and self-

---

[1] See above, p. 22, note.

39

made men who had transformed Florence into a major international centre of trade and industry, and now exercised power over its civil, social and cultural institutions, its customs and laws, its internal and foreign affairs. Finally, although its theology appeared to be broadly orthodox, the poem was in many ways a veritable scandal: it denounced the Popes and the customs of the Holy Roman Church, calling for the surrender of all the wealth and power accumulated over a thousand years. What was worse, indeed intolerable, its author claimed to speak with the voice of God, to be a new Christian prophet, sent to reform the world before its impending end. How could a decent, intelligent, cultivated Florentine have written anything as subversive as the *Inferno*?

To begin to answer this question it is natural to turn to Dante's life and times. Unfortunately, we know very little indeed of Dante's life. Very few dates and facts are documented. We have nothing in his own hand, not even a signature. What we know is what he chose to tell us in his poetry. He almost totally identified his life with his art, blurring all distinctions between one and the other, and it is largely a vain effort to try to disentangle them. Conversely, the few facts about his life which are independently documented – mainly concerning his marriage and his children – are completely excluded from his writings, no part of which can be relied upon to convey anything historically certain about him. With this important caveat in mind, we may begin to look at Dante's early years.

Early life

Dante Alighieri was born in Florence into a modest Guelf family towards the end of May 1265. After receiving an ordinary secular education, based on the standard classical and medieval Latin texts, he began to write poetry in the Siculo-Tuscan manner and came into contact with some of the most influential Florentine poets and intellectuals of the period, such as Brunetto Latini and Guido Cavalcanti. It was probably the latter, five years his elder and a member of one of Florence's noblest Guelf families, who offered Dante the example of a poetry worth emulating.

It is at this early stage of Dante's life that historical events, poetic auto-biography and reflection on poetry begin to be inextricably interwoven. From its very inception, his poetry appears to be a self-conscious elaboration of personal experiences, where the lines between dreams, imaginings and real events are blurred and crossed. At first there seems to be nothing remarkable about this procedure, which was largely conventional among Dante's circle of friends and correspondents. What is unique to him is the coherence and originality with which he developed it.

The modern reader will be struck by the absolute silence in which Dante leaves some major facts of his life. In 1285, aged twenty, he married Gemma

Donati. Two years later he was father to a son, Pietro, who was soon to be followed by two siblings, Jacopo and Antonia; the existence of a fourth child, Giovanni, is still disputed. None of them gains entrance into any of Dante's works; it is as if they, and their mother, never existed. The opposite is true of Beatrice, the love of his life, with whom he hardly had any contact at all. If she actually existed, she is likely to have been Bice, the daughter of Folco Portinari, who was born in 1266, married Simone de' Bardi in 1287, and died in 1290.

In any case, it is assumed that neither Dante's domestic life nor his extramarital interests kept him from pursuing his poetical training and experimentation. Some scholars believe that around 1286 he wrote the 232 sonnets of *Il fiore*, a bawdy and brilliant Tuscan adaptation of the *Roman de la rose* (see above, p. 7), and the 480 *settenari* of the *Detto d'Amore*. In 1287 he spent a period of up to six months in Bologna, where he came into contact with the poetry of Guido Guinizzelli whom he was later to acknowledge as the father of the *stilnovo* (*Purg.* XXVI, 97–9; see above, p. 19). Two years later he was involved as a cavalry officer in the battle of Campaldino and in the siege of the Pisan castle of Caprona, both episodes later remembered in the *Commedia*. In 1290 Beatrice died, a crucial event in Dante's life, which at first, as he tells us in his *Convivio*, drew him to theology and philosophy. Nothing else is known about the years 1290–5; but all circumstantial evidence indicates that in this period he wrote his first book, the *Vita Nuova*. In ten years Dante had become a leading practitioner of Italian poetry. The *Vita Nuova* was to prove his technical and intellectual mastery, and at the same time demonstrate that he was far from satisfied with his achievement.

Vita Nuova

The *Vita Nuova* is a 'little book' (a *libello*) in which Dante transcribes from 'the book of his memory' the story of his love for Beatrice. The nature of the project is eminently literary. The poet-protagonist selects thirty-one poems (twenty-five sonnets, five *canzoni* and one ballad) out of all those he has written in the past ten years or so, and sets them within the frame of a prose commentary: forty-two chapters in all, according to the standard modern editions. This alternation of poetry and prose (*prosimetron*) had influential models, notably Boethius' *Consolatio*, the Provençal *razos* and the glossed manuscripts of the Song of Songs, as well as of classical poets, especially Ovid. Dante's anthology aims to be both a sophisticated autobiography and a treatise on poetry: the exemplary story of a spiritual education coinciding with the development of a poetic career. As such it was not, and could not be, intended for the ordinary reader, but for a select circle of fellow poets who would be able to understand its complex nature. Among these was Guido Cavalcanti, Dante's 'first friend', who had advised him to write his commentary in Italian rather than Latin. Having been in existence for about one and a half centuries, Italian poetry had developed rules and conventions; but an Italian prose scarcely existed. Dante took up the challenge and dedicated the *Vita Nuova* to Cavalcanti.

Taken by themselves, the lyrics of the *Vita Nuova*, at least up to the crucial chapter 19, can be viewed as exercises and experiments in the disparate literary traditions of love poetry prevalent at the time of their composition; they are mainly in the courtly style of the Sicilian school and of Guittone d'Arezzo, or they are inspired by the more recent *stilnovo* examples of Guinizzelli and Cavalcanti. However, from the outset of the *libello*, Dante's prose narrative lends them much more weight than they originally had, anchoring them firmly to the figure of Beatrice. The prose brings to the surface the secret order, the meanings and the inner connections intuited by the poet when he started writing. Revealing the universal, exemplary value of an otherwise fragmented itinerary, it gives the *libello* a coherent, unified and progressive structure which the actual experiences, if and when they occurred, did not have. The *Vita Nuova* thus bears witness to that 'editing' of the self which was to become one of Dante's obsessions.

The agent inspiring Dante's revisitation and revision of his own past is, simply, Beatrice. It is impossible to establish the extent to which this figure corresponds to the real Bice de' Bardi. For, paradoxically, though the *Vita Nuova* suggests that she is a real woman, Beatrice hardly has any life outside Dante's mind. Her effects on him are physical enough: she makes him sigh, tremble, weep; she overwhelms him. Yet she has neither body nor character of her own; she is a vision, an angel, a divine messenger. Dante does not even try to approach or speak to her; indeed, as the story develops, he becomes incapable of withstanding her presence or her gaze. Once ignited, his passion is totally internalised; it is a desire that feeds on itself, a desire of desire.

These are not uncommon ingredients in the theory and practice of courtly love poetry. However, the myth of Beatrice rests on original elements which Dante drew from another, indigenous and exceptionally rich source: the 'popular', hagiographic tradition which, itself feeding on a vast body of writings surrounding the Song of Songs, created the Lives of the Saints. The mystic atmosphere of miracles and revelations, of dreams and ecstasies, of visions and prophecies which pervades the *Vita Nuova*; the structure, fabric and rhythm of its prose narrative; its allusions to biblical language and the liturgy of the Church: all this is a personal, exquisitely literary elaboration – it is impossible to determine whether religious or aesthetic – of oral and written, 'low-brow' material that was circulating in central Italy towards the end of the thirteenth century. The transformation of Beatrice from courtly lady to saint represents the most mature literary fruit of this relatively humble tradition, just as the Madonnas of the Italian churches of the time are its first artistic expression.

The *Vita Nuova* is not a story of events and characters, but of gazes from afar, desires, imaginings and dreams. Dante is nine years old when he first sets eyes on Beatrice; the second time he sees her he is eighteen. These numerical correspondences emphasise Beatrice's providential role in the renewal of Dante's life. She enters into it as a divine agent whose greeting causes the poet to feel profound joy but also immense anguish. When she later refuses him her greeting, he decides he will place all his hopes of future happiness in words of praise for his lady, something which cannot fail him. At first, however, this theme proves too lofty for his writing, until one day his tongue speaks, 'almost as though moved of its own accord', and he begins:

> Donne ch'avete intelletto d'amore,
> i' vo' con voi de la mia donna dire,
> non perch'io creda sua laude finire,
> ma ragionar per isfogar la mente.

(Ladies who know by insight what love is, With you about my Lady I would treat, Not that I think her praises I'll complete, But seeking by my words to ease my mind.)

This (chapter 19) is the heart of the *Vita Nuova* and the start of its most original section. From now on, the poet is driven by a superior force to sing the praises of his lady and expect nothing in return from her: *Donne ch'avete intelletto d'amore* is the *canzone*-manifesto of this new style. Gone is Cavalcanti's idea of love as a disruptive, utterly negative power which Dante had espoused at the beginning of his *libello*. But even Guinizzelli's vision of the lady as beatifier is surpassed. Now Beatrice is a manifest 'miracle', she is 'gentleness' and 'grace' personified, the source of every 'salvation'; her beauty delivers the world from everything negative and unworthy; in short, she is a saint, a mirror of Christ.

But the signs of her imminent death are by now unmistakable. Her father dies, then the poet is struck for nine days by a painful sickness. On the ninth day he has a vision in which his own death is announced, and that of his lady, too, at which, as at Christ's death, the sun grows dark, air-borne birds fall down dead, and the earth trembles violently. Soon afterwards Beatrice actually dies, summoned to Heaven by God Himself. The *libello* has become, paradoxically, the story not of the conjoining of two lovers, but of their progressive parting. Beatrice's death, after the withdrawal of her greeting and presence, is the indispensable step in Dante's sublimation of his love for her; by making even her body redundant, the poet proves the ultimate autonomy of his love.

Dante mourns Beatrice's departure for one year. Then, as one day his thoughts are full of sorrows, he sees 'una gentile donna', young and very beautiful, who is looking at him from a window so compassionately that pity seems to be epitomised in her appearance. A conflict develops within the poet's mind between the memory of Beatrice and the feelings the gentle lady inspires in him, until one day Beatrice reappears to him as young as when he first saw her and clothed in the same crimson garments. Overcome by bitter remorse, the poet recognises the vanity of every consolation that does not stem from the memory of his beloved. His thought becomes a 'sigh', 'a pilgrim spirit' which longs to be reunited with her *Oltre la spera che più larga gira*, 'beyond the sphere that circles widest'. This is the last poem of the *Vita Nuova*. There follows a mysterious 'marvellous vision' in which the poet sees 'things' which make him decide to write no more of the blessed Beatrice until he can do so more worthily:

And to this end I apply myself as much as I can, as she indeed knows. Thus, if it shall please Him by whom all things live that my life continue for a few years, I hope to compose concerning her what has never been written in rhyme of any woman. And then may it please Him who is the Lord of courtesy that my soul may go to see the glory of my lady, that is of the blessed Beatrice, who now in glory beholds the face of Him *qui est per omnia secula benedictus* [who is blessed forever].

What is the meaning of this ending which promises, or rather searches for, a new beginning? Had Dante not written the *Commedia*, it could be read as a sublime *praeteritio* – after all, the *Vita Nuova* had gone so far as to speak of Beatrice in terms that had never been used for any woman. But the fact that Dante did write the *Commedia* makes the temptation to link the end of the *libello* with the beginning of the *poema sacro* almost irresistible, even if nothing else in either text justifies such speculation, except the finale of the *Vita Nuova*. The question must be: was that 'marvellous vision' already present in the original *libello*, or was it added later by the poet, when the idea of the *Commedia* took shape in his mind, in order to connect his first and his last book, through the name of Beatrice, even if at the expense of all he wrote in between?

Be this as it may, the conclusion of the *Vita Nuova* forces us to assume that at a certain point Dante began to see 'things' for which his old poetics were inadequate. Thus the *Vita Nuova* marks the triumph, and simultaneously uncovers the limitations, of the *stilnovo*. When some fifteen years later he publicly resumes his writing for Beatrice, Dante does so on the basis of a much wider and more ambitious perspective.

Rime

Dante's lyric production spans twenty-five years, from the early 1280s to 1306–7, when he undertook the composition of his major poem. This production, excluding the poems which he used for the *Vita Nuova*, make up what is traditionally known as his *Rime*, his collected verse as arranged posthumously and variously by successive generations of editors. One of the major problems concerning the *Rime* is their chronological ordering. What is beyond any doubt is the extraordinary richness of their experimental vein.

The first lyrics are in the styles already exemplified in the *Vita Nuova*, but they include poems dedicated to women other than Beatrice, such as Fioretta and Lisetta; and poems such as *Guido, i' vorrei che tu e Lapo ed io* ('Guido, I wish that you, Lapo and I'), that capture, as a pendant of courtly love and ideals, the exclusive atmosphere of intellectual refinement and male friendship typical of Florentine *stilnovo*.

Yet the influence of Cavalcanti at his most dark and dolorous is plainly visible in a *canzone* like *E' m'incresce di me sì duramente* ('I pity myself so intensely'), which records the destructive power of a fierce lady – perhaps Beatrice herself – or in another early *canzone*, *Lo doloroso amor che mi conduce* ('The sorrowful love that leads me'), where Beatrice – this time mentioned explicitly – is the merciless carrier of death, as in the best Provençal and courtly tradition. It is only when we compare these poems with those in praise of Beatrice included in the *Vita Nuova* that we begin to appreciate the ideological significance of Dante's selection for the *libello*, and the chasm this opened between its author and its dedicatee.

What distinguishes Dante's lyric production after the *Vita Nuova* is, together with its variety and experimentation, a move towards more complex forms and increasingly demanding subject-matter. This is particularly noticeable in the *rime* he composed after his exile from Florence, which we shall consider below.

Meanwhile, as a direct result of the philosophical studies undertaken after the death of Beatrice, Dante composed throughout the 1290s a series of poems in which philosophical and theological subjects were articulated in the language of love poetry. Among these poems are the three *canzoni* on which Dante comments in detail in the *Convivio*. The Lady who inspired them was possiby a real woman, perhaps the 'gentle and compassionate lady' of the *Vita Nuova*, but in the *Convivio* Dante identifies her allegorically as Lady Philosophy. The critical problem is whether the allegorical meanings which Dante attributes to these poems were originally present (as the poet would have us believe), or whether they were written into them retrospectively by the author of the *Convivio*. The difference between the two hypotheses is substantial: in the first case the feminine object of his lyrics is a symbol of Dante's emotional life; in the second that same feminine object is a symbol of his philosophical fervour and of the moral virtues he aims to achieve by means of his rational faculties. The question is a thorny one and remains largely unresolved.

During the same period the poet was experimenting also in other directions. The *tenzone* (poetic exchange) with Forese Donati, a friend of Dante's who died in 1296, is an exchange of sonnets so scurrilous, base and harsh that they can hardly be accommodated even within the conventions of the burlesque genre; indeed their paternity is keenly contested. Significantly, Dante will later remember this episode with regret (*Purg.* XXIII, 115–17).

Another group of lyrics articulates the theme of love not in *stilnovo* terms as a beneficent, saving force, but as a disturbing, invincible reality. For instance, even though she comes from Heaven, love does not touch the young girl of the ballad *I' mi son pargoletta bella e nova* ('I am a young girl, lovely and marvellous'). Much more hard-hearted and insensitive, the 'donna petra' (stony lady) of the *rime petrose* (stony poems) pushes the poet to experiment in the difficult style, hitherto untried in Italian, of the troubadour Arnaut Daniel. The *canzone Così nel mio parlar voglio esser aspro* ('I want to be as harsh in my speech') is shocking for the harshness of its sounds and the violence of its imagery; it is a style to which the poet will return, especially in his *Inferno*.

Florentine politics

In 1295, having joined the Guild of Doctors and Apothecaries, Dante became involved in politics. His progress was rapid. In 1300 he was elected to Florence's highest office, the Priory, for the period June to August. This was a particularly critical moment in the conflict between the Guelf factions of the Blacks and the Whites. The former was headed by Corso Donati, intransigently opposed to any popular participation in public life; the latter, with whom Dante sided, was led by Vieri de' Cerchi, more open to cooperation with the lower classes. In an attempt to quell the violence Dante and his colleagues decided to banish the leaders of both warring factions, including Guido Cavalcanti, who was to die in exile that summer. However, this move failed to pacify the city. In October 1301 the intervention at the Pope's request of Charles of Valois, brother of Philip, King of France, put Corso Donati back in control. Dante, who at the time was on a peace mission to Rome, was charged with barratry (misuse of public funds) and sentenced to a huge fine, two years of exile, and a permanent ban from public office. As he refused to pay, his property was confiscated and the sentence changed to perpetual exile from Florence. It was the end of the poet's political life and the opening of a wound which bled for the remainder of his life. For two further years the poet persisted with the Whites in their attempt to regain control of Florence. But they were finally defeated at La Lastra, near Florence, on 20 July 1304, by which time Dante had left them. Utterly disillusioned, he had 'made a party unto himself'.

For the rest of his life Dante wandered from court to court, visiting Bartolomeo della Scala in Verona before 1303–4. After 1304 few details of his movements are known for certain, and these are clouded by the many legends that grew across the centuries around the figure of the lonely exile. What is surely remarkable is that, despite his precarious circumstances, he quickly found the determination necessary to begin and considerably advance the *De vulgari eloquentia* and the *Convivio*, and, probably in 1307, having interrupted these works, the *Commedia*.

Convivio and De vulgari eloquentia

Seen retrospectively from the vantage point of the *Commedia*, the *Convivio* and the *De vulgari eloquentia* inevitably appear as 'minor' works that record

Dante's efforts to 'find himself' during the transitional years following his exile from Florence. But such a view ignores the facts that with these works Dante intended to assert his authority far beyond the field of love poetry, and that, even in their unfinished form, nothing quite like them exists in any European language at the beginning of the fourteenth century. What, therefore, may seem like a slow and hesitant transition, was in fact a period of intense activity and of rapid, almost irresistible, intellectual evolution for the poet.

After his recent misfortune, Dante was radically reviewing his past, seeking to restore his battered self-confidence and reputation, and to find new and more solid grounds upon which to base his future. In this enterprise he was aided by his extraordinary ability to assimilate and synthesise all sources of knowledge, transforming them into his own coherent ideas. Besides Cicero and Boethius, he read St Augustine's *Confessions* and re-read Virgil's *Aeneid*, but now with a new sense of purpose. He studied the scholastic philosophy and theology of Thomas Aquinas, Albert the Great and St Bonaventure, but also the mystics and, perhaps, such heterodox thinkers as Siger of Brabant and the speculative grammarians.

When he undertook his two projects, Dante consciously aimed as high as he could: the *Convivio* was to bring his philosophical *canzoni* within reach of a wide Italian audience; the *De vulgari* was to demonstrate in Latin the formal dignity of his vernacular poetry in the context of a universal theory and history of language and literature. Dante hoped that works of such significance would compel Florence to recognise his merits and revoke his exile.

Like the *Vita Nuova*, the *Convivio* is retrospective, but its stake is now the status and value of Dante's poetry as purveyor of philosophical truths. There are other, equally substantive differences. The 'donna gentile' of the *Vita Nuova* now becomes Lady Philosophy, and in this guise she replaces Beatrice as the force that motivates the poet's new quest. Dante no longer addresses himself to a small circle of 'fedeli d'Amore', but to all who seek knowledge. This is why he writes in the vernacular. His *Convivio* will indeed be a 'banquet' in which the food of knowledge will be offered to all.

The project was extremely ambitious. As an Italian 'encyclopaedia', the fifteen treatises of the *Convivio* were intended to bridge the enormous gulf between academic and 'popular' culture. The first treatise was to serve as general introduction; the following fourteen were to be critical commentaries on as many philosophical *canzoni*. In the event, only four were completed, the introductory one plus three commentaries on three *canzoni* written in the 1290s: *Voi che 'ntendendo il terzo ciel movete*, *Amor che ne la mente mi ragiona*, and *Le dolci rime d'amor ch'i' solia*. ('O you who move the heavens by intellection'; 'Love, speaking fervently in my mind'; 'The sweet love poetry I was accustomed'.) The four treatises contain a vast array of arguments whose relevance to the text of the poems is often only superficial. Dante's defence of his poetry and of himself as *exul immeritus* produces pages of great intensity and resonance. What constantly fires his enthusiasm, however, often producing blatant digressions, is his desire to communicate knowledge, to convey to all his faith in reason and human intelligence.

The *Convivio* proves the depth and range of Dante's familiarity with the main currents of thought in thirteenth-century Europe. Central to philosophical debate in the universities was the question (which had endless ramifications in all human sciences) of how to reconcile Aristotelian authority with biblical doctrine – in other terms, philosophy and theology, reason and Revelation. Different thinkers offered different solutions. Recognising and simultaneously undermining canonical authority, Dante eclectically echoes now Thomas Aquinas, now Albert the Great and now even the Averroist current to which his friend Cavalcanti had subscribed. His observations range from literary criticism to ethics, metaphysics, cosmology and politics. The *Convivio* is a work which bursts with ideas, but ideas still in a state of fluctuation, confusion and even contradiction: this is both its strength and its weakness. What Dante fails to resolve is the tension he set out to overcome for himself and his potential readers, between a rational, humanist, Aristotelian world view and an idealist, Christian, Neoplatonist one.

The *Convivio* fully reflects the richness and complexity of Dante's philosophical quest in the early years of his exile. In terms of language and style, it is a veritable tour de force, proving that one could treat in Italian, effectively and beautifully, even the most arduous philosophical arguments, traditionally believed to be the preserve of Latin.

The digression on the vernacular in the first treatise of the *Convivio* was developed, probably in 1303–4, into the *De vulgari eloquentia*, a thoroughly original work, planned to include at least four books and to deal with the origins and history of language and the complete range of styles and forms used in vernacular literature. To convince even the most conservative among the literati of the worth of the vernacular, and at the same time to pay it the ultimate accolade, the analysis is conducted in Latin. The treatise remained unfinished and unpublished, probably overshadowed, like the *Convivio*, by the dawning of the *Commedia*. Nevertheless, it is of fundamental importance both for the history of the 'questione della lingua' (see below, pp. 181–5) and for what it reveals of Dante's perspectives on language and style.

The first book begins, astonishingly, by asserting the superiority of the vernacular over Latin (known also as *gramatica*). To justify his radically unconventional view – the opposite of what he had stated in the *Convivio* – Dante traces a brief history of human language from the first word ever spoken by Adam (rather than by Eve, as the Bible states) to the building of the Tower of Babel and the ensuing gradual division, subdivision, and finally atomisation of idioms which characterise present usage. Dante shows an unprecedented grasp of the historical character of language as a living organism in continuous evolution through time and space. Of the three closely related, Latin-derived languages in Southern Europe (the languages of *oc*, *oïl* and *sì*), Italian (the language of *sì*) presents the greatest variety. However, none of its many (at least fourteen) dialects is in itself dignified enough to become the literary language of Italy. Such a language already exists, not as an immanent presence but as a transcendent paradigm to which the best Italian poets strive to conform. It is the 'illustrious vernacular', a literary language free from, and superior to, all municipalisms, and already as fixed as Latin within the ever changing flux of local idioms: effectively, a new *gramatica*.

The second book is Dante's *ars poetica*. The illustrious vernacular, he writes, is no mere form but the only language capable of reflecting the writer's moral and intellectual personality. Therefore, it is suitable only for the most excellent poets seeking to express the noblest subjects: arms, love and rectitude. As to metrical forms, the highest and most convenient for such lofty subjects, and especially for rectitude, is the *canzone*. The illustrious vernacular and the *canzone* are essential components of the superior 'tragic' style.

The major logical contradiction of the *De vulgari* lies in its presentation of the illustrious vernacular as both a historical reality and a transcendent ideal. In his search for a morally and expressively mature model of vernacular eloquence Dante is obliged to repudiate the spoken language in favour of the literary variety employed by the few writers – namely, the Sicilians and the *stilnovisti*, himself included – who had excelled in the tragic style. He is seeking to find one integrated solution to two discrete orders of problems concerning language as a historical phenomenon, and language in terms of salvation history. More specifically, Dante interprets the episode of Babel as the crucial second Fall through which humanity irreparably lost its linguistic paradise. After Babel, all the vernaculars became themselves fallen, corrupt and incapable of fulfilling the primary function of language – universal communication. *Gramatica*, first as Latin and now as illustrious vernacular, represents the only morally valid response to post-Babelic confusion: an attempt to move back from fragmentation to unity, from the hell of individuality and incommunicability to the paradise of universality and communion. Though intellectually exciting and morally uplifting, this idea was a linguistic dead-end. The *De vulgari* was interrupted in mid-sentence. More significantly, the illustrious vernacular and the tragic style turned out to be totally inadequate when Dante set out to write his salvation poem. It is an instance, one of many, of how Dante's mind was always ahead of his own experimentation – at least until he successfully attempted that all-inclusive enterprise towards which all his experiments tended and beyond which no further experiment was possible.

The *Convivio* and the *De vulgari eloquentia* contain a store of information of the utmost importance for our understanding of Dante's intellectual evolution. Yet they are works which Dante never completed, revised or published. In Dante's mind, they may well have been entirely superseded by the *Commedia* in which we find them substantially and repeatedly contradicted. The great poem was like an earthquake in Dante's life. It caused his own final revision of his past: principally, the rejection of the double project *Convivio/ De vulgari*, and probably the writing of a new ending for the *Vita Nuova*. The cluster of critical problems surrounding the sequence *Vita Nuova–Convivio/ De vulgari–Commedia* is likely to be the result of Dante's attempt to rewrite his past in order to endow his public figure with a unified sense of purpose, a teleology which would prove the extraordinary nature of his artistic calling.

The last *Rime*

During the first years of his exile, Dante also composed some important lyrics characterised by a strong moral content. The language remains that of love poetry, but is now used to convey the poet's ideals of public justice and morality. Dante presents himself as the poet of rectitude, contrasting his own scornful solitude with the disorder, violence and corruption that prevail in society. In *Tre donne intorno al cor mi son venute* ('Three women have come round my heart') – a *canzone* which was to be commented on in the last, never-written, treatise of the *Convivio* – the three women personifying divine justice, human justice and the law are exiled from a world that has banned all virtue, and the poet, listening to their 'divine speech', 'counts as an honour the exile imposed on him' ('l'essilio che m'è dato, onor mi tegno'). Clearly, Dante begins here to view his personal predicament as both emblematic and symptomatic of a crisis affecting the whole world.

Monarchia

The relationship between Church and Empire was a major problem in Italian history, and one very acutely felt from the eleventh century onwards. Though it gave rise to many polemical tracts, the question was far from academic, having often involved the two institutions, more or less directly, in open warfare. In the overlapping of temporal and spiritual powers Dante saw one of the principal roots of the social and moral degeneration which afflicted contemporary life. He keenly opposed the Church holding or exercising any temporal power at all – something which had become prevalent, especially after the death of the Emperor Frederick II in 1250. Hence his siding with the White Guelfs against the interference of Pope Boniface VIII.

Dante elaborated his views on politics in a Latin treatise entitled *Monarchia*, though when exactly is a crucial and much-debated question that affects the interpretation of the work itself. There are at least three proposed dates: 1308, 1311–13, and post-1316, the third being philologically the most likely.

The treatise is in three books. Book 1 argues on philosophical grounds the necessity of a universal monarchy for the fulfilment of all human potentialities in the fields of both action and contemplation. This fulfilment is the supreme purpose of civilisation, and can be achieved on the sole condition that the entire world lives in peace: a peace which only a supreme all-powerful monarch can guarantee by impartially administering justice, favouring harmony, and allowing the exercise of individual freedom. Book II seeks to prove historically that the Roman people are the legitimate holders of universal power and Rome this power's proper, divinely ordained seat (accordingly, this is also the book where the classics are most often quoted, especially Virgil as the poet of justice). The events of Roman history are treated by Dante in the same way as the events of the Old Testament, that is, as the expression of God's will. The unification of the ancient world under Rome, he argues, was providentially willed so that the sacrifice of Christ should be undertaken by a universal authority, and its fruits benefit the whole of humanity.

Book III deals with the question of the relationship between Church and Empire, a theological minefield which one crossed only at great personal risk. Dante did not flinch or compromise, systematically demolishing all arguments in favour of ecclesiastical property and jurisdiction. He particularly refuted the idea that God wanted imperial authority to be subordinated to papal, and challenged the Donation of Constantine, a document forged between the eighth and ninth century - as Lorenzo Valla later showed (see below, pp. 140–2) - claiming to be the official act by which the Emperor Constantine granted imperial power to the Pope. Dante did not doubt its authenticity, but he denied it juridical validity: on the one hand, he argued, the Emperor could not give away or divide the Empire, for he had been ordained by God in order to preserve its integrity; on the other, the Pope could not receive it, for Christ had ordered him to live in total poverty. For Dante, both imperial and papal authorities derived directly from God. The former's proper function was to lead humanity to earthly happiness through philosophical teaching; the latter's was to lead it to heavenly glory through the teaching of Revelation. The two authorities, and their respective jurisdictions, were complementary but entirely discrete.

The *Monarchia* is sustained throughout by Dante's firm belief in the unity of society and creation; though based on a scholastic approach and mode of argumentation, it is fired by a genuine political and religious passion. The critical problem is whether or not it is to be interpreted as an early example of a modern, lay conception of the State. The question concerns Dante's intentions, and neither the *Monarchia* nor the *Commedia*, with its impassioned treatment of politics, can elucidate them. However, there are some documents which unambiguously illustrate Dante's ideological stance between 1310 and 1314. These are the letters which he wrote on the occasion of Henry VII's descent into Italy and for the election of Pope Clement's successor.

The political letters

In 1310 Dante's hopes of returning to Florence were abruptly rekindled. Henry VII of Luxembourg was on his way to Rome, invited by the Gascon Pope Clement V to be crowned Holy Roman Emperor, take possession of his

Italian lands, and put a stop to the peninsula's endemic factionalism. For Dante, this represented the only possible solution to both the Italian crisis and his personal predicament. But Henry was indecisive, and although such Ghibelline cities as Milan and Verona welcomed him, others, especially Florence, fiercely resisted the prospect of losing their autonomy.

Dante entered the fray by writing public letters to the Princes of Italy and to the Florentines, urging them to welcome Henry as God's envoy, and to the Emperor exhorting him to strike at Florence, the heart of the enemy camp. While Henry hesitated, the Pope switched sides, allying himself with Robert of Anjou, King of Naples, and with the Black Guelfs. When it was finally mounted, the siege of Florence (September 1312) was a fiasco for Henry and the imperial cause. Dante left Tuscany before it ended, and once again found refuge at the court of the Della Scala in Verona, now ruled by the young Cangrande. The following year, the Emperor died of malaria at Buonconvento, near Siena (24 August 1313). Dante was left bitterly disappointed and without a glimmer of hope for his own future return to Florence. His only consolation was later to assign Henry a seat in the Rose of the Blessed (*Par.* xxx, 133–8), and predict eternal damnation for the Gascon Pope who had 'betrayed' him (*Inf.* xix, 82–4).

The four letters just mentioned (*Epistole* v–vii and xi) are documents of extraordinary interest, and not only as a powerful witness to the bitterness of Dante's exile. Written at a time when he was almost certainly composing his *Commedia*, they enable us to observe Dante as he engages directly with a historical situation involving Florence, the Church and the Empire; they exemplify how he responds in real life to the moral and intellectual dilemmas which he so compellingly and obsessively feeds into his poetry.

The ideas which Dante foregrounds in his letters are not substantially different from those of the *Monarchia*. Yet here Dante abandons any attempt to argue logically for the dualism of Church and Empire, using instead Virgil's writings and the Bible as sacred texts for political persuasion. From the time of the struggles between Pope Gregory VII and Emperor Henry IV, the Church had been invoking the authority of the Bible against all those who, like the Emperor, attempted to check its power. Now, apparently making common cause with the Spiritual Franciscans, the 'apocalyptic' agitators and other 'heretical' sects, Dante turned the Bible against the Church and its acolytes. More significantly, in doing so he affirmed that the State was not a lay but a sacred institution, and that all history, not only biblical and Roman, was sacred history. Henry VII was the rightful owner of everything on earth, 'the shepherd descended from Hector' (v, 17), a new Messiah, another Moses 'who shall deliver his people from the oppression of the Egyptians' (v, 4). He was Italy's bridegroom, 'hastening to the wedding' (v, 5); a new Augustus who 'shall take vengeance for the evil deeds of the backsliders, and pursue them even unto Thessaly, the Thessaly of utter annihilation' (v, 10).

And what of Florence? Dante identified the city that had exiled him as the root of all evil and rebellion, a new Babylon, the arrogant slave of cupidity:

She is the viper that turns against the vitals of her own mother; she is the sick sheep that infects the flock of her lord with her contagion; she is the abandoned and unnatural Myrrha, inflamed with passion for the embraces of her father Cinyras; she is the passionate Amata, who, rejecting the fated marriage, did not shrink from claiming for herself a son-in-law whom the fates denied her, but in her madness urged him to battle, and at the last, in expiation for her evil designs, hanged herself in the noose.

(VII, 24; Toynbee, VII, 7)

Nor did Henry's failure and death temper the poet's wholehearted faith in his Utopia. When, in the spring of 1314, the Cardinals gathered in conclave at Carpentras to elect a successor to the defunct Clement, Dante wrote yet another letter pleading for the speedy election of an Italian Pope. This letter, too, was steeped in biblical allusions. It started with the opening verse of the *Lamentations* which, significantly, the poet had used twenty years earlier to describe Florence after the death of Beatrice. Now it was Rome which, like Jerusalem after her fall, sat solitary, 'a widow that was great among the nations'. Deprived of her two luminaries (both the Emperor and the Pope were dead, and in any case the Holy See had been transferred to Avignon under Clement V), she moved to pity even the infidels who believed that her fate was decreed by the heavens. On the contrary, it was the result of choices which the Cardinals themselves had made out of sheer greed. 'You', Dante writes directly addressing them,

who are as it were the centurions of the front rank of the Church militant, neglecting to guide the chariot of the Spouse of the Crucified along the track which lay before you, have gone astray from the track, no otherwise than as the false charioteer Phaëthon. And you, whose duty it was to enlighten the flock that follows you through the forest on its pilgrimage here below, have brought it along with yourselves to the verge of the precipice.

(XI, 5; Toynbee, VIII, 4)

Dante concluded urging the Cardinals to return to the right track and fight manfully for the Spouse of Christ, for Rome, for Italy and for the whole world in pilgrimage on earth. But again his pleas were not heeded. The Carpentras conclave lasted two more years and produced a new French Pope, John XXII, while the Papal See remained at Avignon until 1377. The irony of it all is that this was happening in the context of France's successful drive towards national independence from both Rome and the Empire, a development which Dante vehemently opposed, for it frustrated his hope of seeing universal monarchy restored. And here lies what may be the major contradiction inherent in Dante's Christian fundamentalism: the separation of temporal from spiritual power, which he greatly desired for the benefit of all humanity, was possible only on condition that the State asserted its own lay nature, precisely as

Florence and France were doing, an assertion totally alien to Dante's world
view.

The amnesty

The period which Dante spent at the court of Cangrande della Scala between
late 1312 and (probably) 1318 was the longest and quietest he enjoyed
anywhere during his twenty years of exile. Verona was the most congenial
environment Dante could find in Italy, and Cangrande a staunch Ghibelline
and Imperial Vicar, a title which he refused to relinquish even after Henry's
death – thus gaining for himself excommunication by Pope John XXII. This
situation perhaps strengthened Dante's resolve when, in 1315, he refused to
take advantage of the amnesty which Florence offered him on condition that
he pay a light fine and acknowledge his guilt. Writing to a friend in Florence,
who had probably worked hard to obtain his recall, the poet explained his
decision in fiery words:

This, then, is the gracious recall of Dante Alighieri to his native city, after the miseries
of well-nigh fifteen years of exile! This is the reward of innocence manifest to all the
world, and of the sweat and toil of unremitting study! Far be from a familiar of
philosophy such a senseless act of abasement [...]! Far be it from the preacher of
justice, after suffering wrong, to pay of his money to those that wronged him [...]!
  No! [...] not by this path will I return to my native city. If some other can be found,
in the first place by yourself and thereafter by others, which does not derogate from
the fame and honour of Dante, that will I tread with no lagging steps. But if by no
such path Florence may be entered, then will I enter Florence never. What! can I not
anywhere gaze upon the face of the sun and the stars? can I not under any sky
contemplate the most precious truths, without I first return to Florence, disgraced, nay
dishonoured, in the eyes of my fellow-citizens? Assuredly bread will not fail me!

(*Ep.* XII, 5–9; Toynbee, IX, 3–4)

Behind these words is the poet of justice and rectitude, the poet who, in those
very years, was completing the *Purgatorio* and setting out on the waters 'never
sailed before' of the *Paradiso*. How could he submit to the indignity of the
Florentine 'pardon' without making a mockery of his *poema sacro*, that is, of
everything he believed in and stood for?

The *Commedia*

We do not and probably never will know what was the spark which ignited
the fire of the great poem. Behind it lie undoubtedly Dante's encyclopaedic
knowledge and his personal experiences of love, politics and exile. But there is
more. The *Commedia* is a *summa* of medieval culture, a synthesis of all facets
of reality as an integral whole – earthly and heavenly, physical and spiritual,

natural and historical, cultural and ethical. This synthesis was conceived and achieved just as, and because, the ideological and historical premises that underpinned it were manifestly failing, and the unity of the medieval world was irreversibly breaking up under the pressure of historical forces superior to any individual will. Dante perhaps dreamed that his poem would somehow reverse this irresistible process of disintegration; we assume he did not see that such a poem was possible only because the battle it waged was already lost. Such untimely vision is not uncommon among great thinkers. What is unique to Dante is that it was achieved by means of a poetry which may claim to be unrivalled in the history of Western literature.

Dante confronted in the *Commedia* a knot of problems which deeply affected European civilisation at the end of the Middle Ages: the relation between sensual and spiritual love, between reason and faith, between morality and politics, between the individual and society, between God's will and human freedom, between this life and the life beyond. These are problems which, albeit in different forms, belong to any age. The solutions that the *Commedia* offers to each and all of them may not seem of pressing concern to us today; however, the vigour and lucidity with which it identifies and illuminates them, exposing their effects in the concrete experience of individuals and communities, has preserved their significance intact across the ages.

Birth of a 'comedy'

The *Commedia* claims to be the true account of a journey through Hell, Purgatory and Paradise which the poet Dante undertook, by the explicit will of God and through the intercession of his beloved Beatrice, when he was thirty-five years of age in the year 1300 – a year of crucial significance not only in marking the beginning of a new century and the first Holy Year declared by Pope Boniface VIII, but also a year when, for Dante, humanity was deprived of its two leaders, the Pope and the Emperor. The journey starts on the night of Good Friday and ends a week later, coinciding thus with the liturgical recurrence of Christ's passion, death and resurrection. It leads to the salvation of its protagonist and to the making of a 'sacred poem' whose purpose is the salvation of the whole world.

The story begins abruptly, with a directness that is the hallmark of its author. Having reached the middle point in the journey of our life (traditionally said to last seventy years), Dante finds himself in a dark forest. We are not told how he got there, nor does he seem to know. Yet the situation is real enough; the forest so 'selvaggia e aspra e forte' (savage and harsh and dense), that the mere thought of it still terrifies him. From its very beginning, the poem forces us to visualise simultaneously, and as equally true, two separate stages in Dante's life, two kinds of 'present': the stage of the journey, or the present of the narrative; and the stage of its account, or the present of the narrator who has accomplished the journey.

As he recounts his extraordinary experience, the narrator often interjects, reflecting and commenting on it and on his present efforts to equate his words with it. Indeed, one of the most striking features of the *Commedia* is that it not only narrates a story, but contains within itself the story of its making. The point where it comes closest to releasing the secret of its origin is perhaps in the Earthly Paradise when Dante meets Beatrice at the centre of a symbolic pageant representing the history of the world, past, present and future (*Purg.* XXIX–XXXIII). This Beatrice is the same miraculous woman of the *Vita Nuova*, but with a major difference. She is no longer a symbol, but the reality of herself ten years after her death in Florence. She is a Beatrice who has now grown through Dante's experiences to the point that she has become his active conscience. This is why she can trace Dante's itinerary from the times of the *Vita Nuova* to the present; she can shed light on that dark hole from which he emerges at the beginning of the poem. Beatrice says that after she died, Dante forgot her, sinking into such moral and intellectual dissipation that it brought him to the brink of spiritual death. The only way to save him was to send him on the journey which he is now making.

The story of Dante's salvation, as told by Beatrice, is a *mise en abîme* of Dante's journey in the *Commedia* and of the story of universal salvation as synthesised in the pageant. There are no loose ends to this knot. Dante's reunion with Beatrice at Easter time 1300 re-enacts the union of Christ with his Church as represented in the pageant by the Griffin who draws the chariot to the great tree. The pattern of these events is provided by the biblical narrative of the Song of Songs. It is this timeless pattern that gives meaning both to the individual life of Dante and to the history of humanity as a whole. As a result of his meeting with Beatrice, Dante's life is renewed, just as the dead tree is revived by the touch of the Griffin. Paradise is now opened to him, as it was opened to humanity by the sacrifice of Jesus Christ, and is ritually opened again now at Easter time 1300. Suddenly, the pattern of Dante's life, like that of historical man on earth, is transformed from tragedy to comedy.

The title *Commedia* – the adjective *divina*, employed by Boccaccio, was added to the title only in 1555 – puzzled and shocked many of Dante's Trecento readers; it is indeed so original that its motivation and meaning are still a matter of controversy. The most widely held opinion is that it was meant to refer to the composite nature of the poem, which mixes different and traditionally incompatible themes and registers, the basest and loftiest subjects, imagery and language. No doubt this is correct. However, its original motivation may not only be of a rhetorical nature. The title given in the manuscript tradition and in the Epistle to Cangrande is *Comedia Dantis Alagherii, florentini natione sed non moribus* ('Comedy of Dante Alighieri, a Florentine by Birth not by Conduct'), a title which blends the reality of objective experience with that of its narration, Dante the character with Dante the narrator and the man. Quite simply, the poem is called a 'comedy' because it narrates Dante's salvation – an experience which is 'comic' in the medieval sense that it leads to a happy conclusion. Hell and Paradise, the beginning and the end of the poem, are thus already included in the title itself.

Around 1306–7, just as he seems to be overwhelmed by his vicissitudes, Dante discovers that he is, after all, a winner – otherwise, his all-encompassing Christian view of the world would make no sense. But if it has sense, then it applies to everyone. Dante's crisis is the crisis of the whole world around him; if he found himself lost in the dark forest, it is because the whole world, deprived of its leaders, has, like him, gone astray. But if he can be saved, the whole world can, too. When Christ dies on the cross, His defeat is His victory; the cross becomes the sign of His triumph. After that event no Christian soul need fear misfortune or even death; no destiny need be tragic. This intuition is so overwhelming that Dante abandons all his previous literary projects: what is at stake now is the salvation of the world.

Composition and early diffusion

When did Dante begin his masterpiece? The consensus among modern scholars is that composition began in 1306–8. There is evidence that the three *cantiche* were released separately, one after the other, as they were completed: the *Inferno* after 1309, the *Purgatorio* after 1313, and the *Paradiso* in the last two or three years of the poet's life. Between the 'publication' of the *Inferno* and that of the *Paradiso* there was a gap of eight to ten years.

There are no signs that the poet ever modified or rewrote any parts of his poem after their initial release, though he might well have revised them previously. This is a most remarkable fact, given the range, complexity, internal cross-referencing, and near total consistency of the narrative as a whole. The entire poem, from beginning to end, must have been in Dante's mind as he set down in writing each canto. If we accept his fundamental claim, what was at stake in the poem was nothing less than the eternal destiny of his fellow men and women: real people, some of whom he had met, known and loved, or heard about from those who had. Yet every line was written once and forever, and so was every destiny. Dante never changed his mind. As a judge, he knew neither doubt nor second thoughts; he conceded no appeal.

The poem was widely read as soon as it, or parts of it, became available to the public. After the poet died, it became the object of learned glosses and commentaries, in Latin as well as Italian (see below, p. 125), receiving the sort of attention normally reserved for Scripture and a few classics. Dante himself probably inaugurated this tradition by writing in 1316, or soon thereafter, the Epistle to Cangrande della Scala. This is a letter in Latin – whose authenticity is still disputed – with which the poet elucidates important aspects of the whole poem, and dedicates the *Paradiso* to his illustrious patron and host, the Lord of Verona.

Formal organisation and language

The metrical and narrative structure of the *Commedia* is based on numerical symmetries which are meant to mirror the unity and symmetry of the universe itself. The poem is divided into three *cantiche* (the term itself is probably a reminiscence of the Song of Songs) which are in turn subdivided in *canti*. As there are thirty-four *canti* in the *Inferno* (the first serves as general prologue) and thirty-three each in *Purgatorio* and *Paradiso*, their total is one hundred, a perfect number. The *canti* are made up on average of just under fifty stanzas of three hendecasyllables each, called *terzine*. In this metrical form the first and third hendecasyllable rhyme with each other and the second introduces a new rhyme which in turn frames the following *terzina* with a forward movement that halts only at the end of each *canto*. In creating this original triadic structure, the poet was not only devising a powerful narrative machine, but imitating God's way of writing.

The nature of Dante's new work dictated the language in which it was to be written. As a Christian epic and a serious eschatological poem, it would have been normal, if not mandatory at the time, to write it in Latin. However, for Dante, the *Commedia* was itself inherently 'vernacular', just as the *sermo* of Scripture was inherently *humilis*. The choice was ideologically, rather than rhetorically, determined. As a poem of salvation, his *Comedìa* would surpass Virgil's 'alta tragedìa' which, lacking the message and model of Scripture, could never be a 'sacred poem'. It would also achieve by itself what the *Vita Nuova* and the *Convivio*, with their mixture of verse and prose, and the *De vulgari eloquentia*, with its highly wrought Latin, had together failed to deliver: the discovery and revelation of a universal and timeless system of truths.

The language of the *Commedia* still impresses the reader as prodigious in range, energy and sophistication. Breaking all conventions, Dante extends enormously the 'comic' register, borrowing freely, even inventing, according to his expressive needs. His experimental vein now reaches full maturity without losing any freshness and originality. The vocabulary is gathered from a wide variety of sources, both written and spoken: Latin, Tuscan, Provençal, French, as well as Northern Italian dialects. The language of science (astronomy, physics, geometry, optics, medicine, philosophy, theology, etc.) coexists with that of the street, the kitchen and the stable; the sophisticated dispute of the university classroom with the quick repartee of the *piazza*; the sweet sounds of the *stilnovo* with the harsh and grating syllables of the *rime petrose*. This extraordinary linguistic eclecticism is constantly kept in check by Dante's rhetorical consciousness.

With the *Commedia*, the Italian vernacular comes of age, and simultaneously surpasses all other Romance languages, establishing a supremacy that will remain unchallenged at least until the Cinquecento.

Allegory and realism

The *Commedia*'s claim to truth radically distinguishes it from the medieval genre of visions and allegorical journeys to which it superficially belongs. But above all it guarantees its absolute exemplarity, for the truer the individual experience, the more effective it must be as an *exemplum*. This applies not only to Dante, the poet-protagonist, but also, with a few clearly signposted exceptions, to all the events he witnesses and the characters he meets in the course of his journey, starting from his three guides: Virgil, the Roman poet of the *Aeneid*, who leads him through Hell and Purgatory; Beatrice, who accompanies him through the nine heavens of Paradise; and St Bernard of Clairvaux, the writer and mystic (1091–1153), who leads him to the final vision of God in the Empyrean.

For Dante, as indeed for any Christian believer, death is not the end of life, but the beginning of a new immortal life in which every individual soul (immediately in Hell and Paradise, and at the end of purgation in Purgatory) achieves its ultimate reality, its definitive state of being. It is this ultimate and unchanging reality, in which all the souls are fixed forever in the contemporaneity of eternity, that Dante claims to have visited and to be describing.

There is therefore little in the *Commedia* that can be read as conventional allegory, where the literal meaning is no more than a beautiful lie, and the 'real' meaning is other, to be discovered only by decoding the text according to its in-built cultural code. Dante does occasionally employ this type of allegory. For instance, the three beasts which, at the beginning of the poem, prevent him from climbing the hill are not meant to have a reality of their own, but to be symbols of lust, pride and greed. But this is *allegoria in verbis* or 'allegory of the poets', no more than a rhetorical device and a literary technique, while the basic allegory of the *Commedia* is the *allegoria in factis* or 'allegory of the theologians', which is nothing less than a way of understanding reality in all its interconnected multiple meanings. Such allegory is based on the Christian notion – a commonplace in medieval thought – that all objects, people and events in space and time, besides signifying themselves in their objective reality, are also signs of the providential design that has created them. 'The world is a book written by the finger of God', wrote Hugh of St Victor in the twelfth century. And as he gazes through 'the eternal light' in the Empyrean, Dante sees the truth of this analogy (*Par.* XXXIII, 85–7):

> Nel suo profondo vidi che s'interna,
> legato con amore in un volume,
> ciò che per l'universo si squaderna

(In its depth I saw that it contains, bound by love in one volume, that which is scattered in leaves through the universe.)

But God is also the author of another book, the book *par excellence* that is the Bible, the book which reveals His working in the history of humanity. According to the Fathers of the Church, the events of the Old Testament were real, they had actually occurred, while at the same time they prefigured (they were 'figures' or 'types of') events which were to occur later in the New Testament. The subsequent events gave meaning and substance to the former, they were their fulfilment. Thus Adam and Eve were seen as 'figures' of Christ and the Church, and Abraham and Isaac as 'figures' of God and Christ. In their turn, certain events, characters and even parables of the New Testament were figurally related to the foundation and life of the Church, as Militant in this world and Triumphant in the next. The historical event which motivated and verified this conception of history was the incarnation of Jesus Christ, the son of God. That single, essential event gave a rationale to everything that had happened before and was to happen later, including Christ's second coming. Thanks to it, nothing in history appeared meaningless; history was the temporal fulfilment of God's extratemporal design.

Figural allegory teaches the hidden network of relations that exists between apparently unrelated events. In Dante's hands, this approach to reality preserves the irreducible individuality of persons while revealing their position in the divine scheme. Thanks to it, reality becomes more, not less, meaningful, and this applies especially to the reality of the afterlife. The state of the souls after death is the fulfilment of their lives on earth. Virgil is not Reason, and Beatrice is not Theology: they are both the final fulfilment of their historical selves; not personifications of abstract qualities, but what they have become at the end of their journeys, one in Limbo and the other in Heaven. The same is generally true of the many characters whom Dante meets in the three realms of the afterlife. Nevertheless, there is much that can be learned from the journeys, now completed, of these characters. Like Dante the character, they are examples which can guide the readers of the poem who are still *in via*, and can thereby determine their eternal destinies in a kind of moral allegory which coexists in the *Commedia* along with figural allegory.

Dante's journey

Adam and Eve were created to replace the fallen angels. Placed originally in the Earthly Paradise, they were driven out after the Fall and forced to live and suffer all the consequences of mortality on earth. History began then, as an effort on the part of humanity to recapture its original Paradise, to wind time back – something which only Christ's incarnation made actually possible. The *Commedia* shows how this can be done, and what awaits us if we fail in this effort.

Dante's universe is a moral, as much as a physical, reality. At its centre stands, motionless, the earth. All the land is in the northern hemisphere between the delta of the Ganges and the Pillars of Hercules (Straits of Gibraltar); the mid-point between these two boundaries is Jerusalem. The southern hemisphere is completely covered by water, except for the mountain of Purgatory.

Dante's Hell is in the shape of a huge funnel, located below the surface of the northern hemisphere and extending to the centre of the earth. It is divided into the Antinferno and nine concentric circles, sloping down towards the bottom. Here, most remote from God, is Lucifer. His fall from the Empyrean caused the earth to recoil in horror, making the chasm of Hell and, in the southern hemisphere, the mountain of Purgatory which stands in the shape of a cone at the antipodes of Jerusalem. This, topographically Dante's original creation, is divided into seven terraces, preceded by the Ante-Purgatory and followed, at the top, by the Earthly Paradise. Nine concentric, diaphanous spheres rotate around the earth, one for each of the seven planets (Moon, Mercury, Venus, Sun, Mars, Jupiter, Saturn) plus one for the Fixed Stars and one for the Primum Mobile, the invisible heaven which, taking its motion directly from the Love of God, communicates it to the planets below. Beyond the Primum Mobile is the Empyrean, the space of absolute rest, which contains everything and is contained by nothing. Dante's journey, therefore, takes him across the entire universe, from the centre of the earth to the Empyrean. But it also takes him back to where time began.

The structural correspondence between the three realms of the afterlife allows the poet to organise his three *cantiche* with a high degree of symmetry. This symmetry, however, is not presented as an arbitrary choice on his part, but as an objective necessity of the subject-matter itself, a mirror of the reality of the afterlife. The topography of the three realms appears to Dante-the-character as the objective manifestation of the ethical system according to which they are inhabited.

The moral system of Dante's *Inferno* is based on a broadly Aristotelian-Ciceronian scheme, but with variations that depend on other traditions. After the Neutrals, who are rejected by both Satan and God, and the Virtuous Pagans who inhabit the first circle (Limbo), the damned are distributed from the top to the bottom of the funnel in precise relation to the increasing gravity of their sins, beginning with the Incontinent who were unable to control their instincts, and proceeding through the Heretics, the Violent and the Fraudulent to the worst sinners of all, the Traitors. At the bottom of the pit, Lucifer chews in his three mouths the worst traitors ever known to humankind: Judas who betrayed Christ, and Brutus and Cassius who betrayed the Empire in the person of Julius Caesar.

In the *Purgatorio* the excommunicate, the lethargic, the late repentants, and the negligent rulers wait at the foot of the mountain until they may begin their purification. Purgatory proper is structured on the traditional ordering of the seven capital sins. When the penitents reach it, they are made to progress through its seven terraces, spending more or less time in each one of them according to the degree of their guilt in respect of each sinful disposition. The seven faults are therefore rectified from the bottom to the top of the mountain according to their decreasing weight. The first three (pride, envy and wrath) are a perversion of love; the fourth (sloth) is a sign of defective love; the last three (avarice, gluttony, and lust) represent excessive love. On the top of the mountain, as we have seen, is Earthly Paradise where human history began.

In the *Paradiso*, though they all reside in the Empyrean, the blessed appear to Dante, from sphere to sphere, gradually closer to God according to their capacity to see Him and partake of His bliss. In the Moon are those who were forced to break their vows, in Mercury the seekers of glory, in Venus the lovers, in the Sun the theologians, in Mars the martyrs and crusaders, in Jupiter the righteous rulers, and in Saturn the contemplatives. In the Fixed Stars Dante sees the Church Triumphant, and in the Primum Mobile the Angelic Orders. This distribution is reflected in the Mystical Rose in the Empyrean, where the blessed sit beyond space and time, yet paradoxically still more or less close to God. This is also where Dante's journey ends.

Myth and history

The landscape of Dante's Hell is extremely varied. Natural obstacles separate its major divisions, often doubling up as penal places: the river Acheron; the marshes of the Styx; the walls of the City of Dis; the river Phlegethon; the sheer, precipitous bank of the eighth circle, known as Malebolge (evil moats), etc. All circles have guardians and torturers – mythological monsters which embody in essence the moral features of the sinners they rule over and torment: Charon ferries the souls across the Acheron; Minos assigns them to their proper places; Cerberus flays and rends the Gluttonous; the Gorgon and the Furies guard the walls of the City of Dis, and so forth. Only the devils of the fifth moat of Malebolge, collectively called 'Malebranche', belong to the Christian tradition. Most of the other demons, like the topography of Hell generally, are derived from classical sources, especially Virgil's *Aeneid*. Nevertheless, they are no mere ornamental device. Dante transforms the fables of the classical past into organic components of the Christian afterlife revealing the full meanings of old forms by realising and fulfilling them in the new.

The same holds for the classical figures who appear in *Inferno*. By and large, Dante's characters belong to his own times; most of them are Florentine or Tuscan. However, he also discusses Aeneas and St Paul as though both were historical personages. Next to Francesca da Rimini (murdered by her husband c. 1285) he places Dido and Helen of Troy; next to the modern *condottiere*, Guido da Montefeltro (1220?–98), he places Ulysses and Diomedes. All events and characters – mythological, legendary, historical – become equally real and contemporary in Dante's afterlife. And the reason for this is not his lack of historical perspective, but his belief in an eschatology to which history itself is subservient.

The souls Dante meets in Purgatory are almost exclusively drawn from recent history. They are friends of his like Casella, Belacqua and Forese Donati; poets like Bonagiunta, Guido Guinizzelli and Arnaut Daniel; kings like Hugh Capet and Manfred, and Popes like Hadrian V. The major exception to this rule is Cato, the ancient Roman who, rather than submit to Caesar and lose republican freedom, chose suicide in Utica. His love of freedom, greater even than his love of life, made him guardian of that Christian freedom which now Dante, like all the purging souls, seeks in Purgatory.

In the *Paradiso*, in the gigantic, luminous cross suspended in the Heaven of Mars, Dante sees congregated Charlemagne, Roland, Count William of Orange and Renouard, a legendary Saracen (*Par.* XVIII, 43–8); and in the eye of the Eagle in the Heaven of Jupiter, together with the Emperor Constantine and the King of Sicily William the Good, he is shown a Trojan warrior by the name of Ripheus (*Par.* XX, 67–9), whom Virgil barely mentions in *Aeneid* II. Nothing and no one escapes the all-inclusive Christian myth of Dante's *Commedia*.

Dante greatly admires the ancient world: in the Roman Empire he sees a model of reason and justice, the indispensable vehicle of God's redemptive plan. Yet that world cannot be saved, for it lacked divine Grace. The character of Virgil is the best illustration of this tragic destiny.

For Dante, as for his contemporaries, Virgil's *Aeneid* foreshadowed the Christian message, and his fourth eclogue prophesied the coming of Christ. In the *Commedia*, the Latin poet is appointed to guide Dante through Hell and Purgatory, leading him, like a father, through all the hurdles of the journey and, like a master, through all the problems that human reason can solve. However, once they reach Earthly Paradise, Virgil must go back to Limbo: he is not, and never will be, allowed to reach beyond. Virgil's tragic destiny is underlined by Statius, the other Latin poet who, on his way to Paradise, declares that he owes both his art and his salvation to Virgil's poetry ('Per te poeta fui, per te cristiano' (Through you I was a poet, through you a Christian, *Purg.* XXII, 73). Like one who goes by night carrying the light behind him, Virgil lit the way for those who followed him, but he walked in the dark. His figure is a memorable and moving symbol of a humanity in every respect perfect, but deprived of Grace: Dante's Christianisation of history and mythology entails their subjection to the rigours, and the unfathomable ways, of Christian justice.

The contrapasso

Christian justice operates throughout Dante's afterlife ensuring that nothing in it is gratuitous or arbitrary. Assigning every soul to its appropriate place is the rigorous law of *contrapasso* (*Inf.* XXVIII, 142), a retributive principle whereby everyone must suffer in the afterlife according to the sin he or she has committed on earth. This suffering is retributive and eternal in Hell, whilst in Purgatory it is remedial and temporary. In Paradise, too, the situation of the blessed is closely related to their earthly behaviour: by appearing in different spheres, they are shown to receive the quality and measure of reward appropriate to each of them. Thus God's justice is done, and is seen to be done, in all three realms of the afterlife.

The *contrapasso* is not Dante's invention. What distinguishes its appearance in the *Commedia* is that it functions not merely as a form of divine revenge, but rather as the fulfilment of a destiny freely chosen by each soul during his or her life. Thus, in Dante's afterlife, far from being cancelled, diminished or even altered, the historical identity of each soul is revealed in its very essence and so is intensified. Each individual is fixed in the other world as he or she really was, beneath all appearances, in this. In Hell the damned are forever petrified in the particular act, thought or attitude that defined them in life. In Purgatory the penitent continue and fulfil the process of repentance they began on earth. In Paradise the blessed enjoy the measure of happiness appropriate to the merits and capacity which characterised them while living. Thus, in Dante's hands, the *contrapasso* works simultaneously as an instrument of justice and a powerful narrative device.

Dante-the-character among the dead

The *Commedia* is no mere catalogue of crimes and punishments, virtues and rewards. It is a poem of ever-changing human emotions, a poem in which human actions are explored in the infinite complexity of their public and private, social and psychological motivations. In the darkness of Hell the damned are whipped, bitten, crucified, burned, butchered, deformed by repulsive diseases; they are transformed into shrubs and snakes; buried alive in flaming graves and fixed head-first into rocky ground; immersed in mud, in excrement, in boiling blood and pitch; frozen in ice and chewed in the mouth of Satan. The sounds and signs of physical pain are present everywhere. What is deeply disturbing is the relentlessness of the attitudes in which victims and tormentors are caught by the eye of the passing visitor: the notion that the Harpies will always bite and feed on the leaves that are the limbs of Pier della Vigna; that Ulysses and Diomedes will never get out of their envelope of fire; that Count Ugolino will always gnaw at the skull of Archbishop Ruggieri. It is this implacability of God's justice that makes the dead plead in vain for a second, definitive death.

Nevertheless, despite their atrocious suffering, brutish nastiness and disgusting cruelty, the damned remain quintessentially human, and it is with that humanity, albeit distorted and perverted, that Dante-the-character time after time engages. As he descends deeper in Hell, his reactions range from horror to compassion, from terror to indignation, from pity to pitilessness. He swoons at the tale of Francesca's fatal love but, by will or chance, he kicks Bocca degli Abati in the face; he delights at the torments inflicted on Filippo Argenti and Vanni Fucci, but feels filial affection for the disfigured Brunetto Latini; he weeps at the sight of the Diviners, but is in awe before Farinata and Ulysses. *Inferno* is a Christian exploration of the effects of sin, but also a descent into the darkest recesses of the human soul.

In *Purgatorio*, as the physical and human landscapes change, the poetic register changes, too. Like earth, Purgatory is in time, it has dawns and sunsets, days and nights, visions and dreams. The penitents are not frozen in their earthly individuality; they move on together, in peace with God and with themselves, listening intently, or gazing at, or themselves voicing, examples of virtues and vices. They suffer physical pain, of course: for example, the Proud walk on their knees under the crushing weight of huge stones; the Envious have their eyelids sewn up with wire; and the Wrathful walk blinded by thick smoke. Yet their pain is internalised; its very existence ensures that it will end, giving way to the joy of Paradise. This is why they are so eager to undertake their purification. What they feel with much greater intensity is their distance from God. Like a reversed nostalgia, this sense of separation and exile characterises their ascent, transforming it into a pilgrimage towards the heavenly home. Dante climbs the mountain with them; a pilgrim among pilgrims, he understands and shares their memories of the past and their longings for the future. His encounters in Purgatory often become dialogues about art and poetry, but the thought of the earth with its horrors and injustices is never allowed to slip too far away.

With the *Paradiso* Dante is proudly aware of 'sailing waters never sailed before'. Having placed Paradise beyond the confines of human memory and language, what he describes is not the reality of perfect bliss, but his experience of approaching it, the desire which propels him from the Heaven of the Moon to the Empyrean – for the fulfilment that lies beyond that desire is also beyond the limits of poetry. The desire for God becomes in the *Paradiso* the pilgrim's fundamental impulse and the poet's central thematic nucleus. The narrative devices employed in the *cantica* have the function of anticipating and simultaneously delaying the final vision. In this sense Dante's ascent is not – not at least until its very end – an appeasement, but a constant intellectual and emotional challenge, a struggle to reach beyond, for God's desirability lies in His transcendence, His power of attraction in His distance and His absence. Conversely, it is only by deferring for thirty-three cantos the full satisfaction of desire that the poet creates a space within which the poem may be completed in line with the formal requirements of its overall structure.

The blessed, too, are depicted in a state of desire, but an irreducible gap separates the visitor from the residents of this Paradise. The desire of the blessed is constantly satisfied and constantly rekindled; they always have what they desire, and always desire what they have. Moreover, each desires God according to his or her own capacity to enjoy Him, thus preserving and fulfilling in Paradise their individual earthly identity.

There are no landscapes to be described in Dante's Heaven, only ever-changing lights, colours, sounds, emblems and geometric figures. Nor are there complex characters to be explored: only blessed spirits, all absolutely happy and fulfilled. There are disquisitions on science, ethics and theology – a hard banquet for the inexperienced reader. *Paradiso* brings to fruition Dante's enthusiasm for philosophy, and simultaneously sets the limits beyond which reason and intelligence cannot venture. The pilgrim's – and the reader's – ascent is therefore meant to be not only emotional and spiritual, but intellectual, too; Paradise is not just a mystical experience, but a process of enlightenment. Light is indeed the external manifestation of this internal process. Occasionally, the pilgrim feels blinded by it, until, time after time, strengthened by the gift of ever-increasing Grace, he surpasses his own capacity to see. This is the long and dramatic 'battaglia de' debili cigli' (struggle of the feeble eyelids, *Par.* XXIII, 78) that mirrors the internal, psychological drama of ever-increasing desire.

All this does not mean that earth is forgotten in the *Paradiso*. Beatrice, Justinian, St Thomas Aquinas, St Bonaventure, Cacciaguida, St Peter deplore in the strongest terms possible the corruption of Church and Empire, of religious orders and civil society, of individuals and communities. Indeed, it is in the *Paradiso* that Dante's journey receives its final legitimation, and that the prophetic nature of the poem is fully claimed and sanctioned from within the poem itself.

Politics and society

The totalising, all-encompassing nature of Dante's world view entails that the reality of this life is constantly recalled in and by the other, and vice versa. Life on earth is a pilgrimage, an exile at the end of which we reach our true destination. Whether this will be Hell or Heaven depends on the choices we freely make while we are on our way. The vision of life beyond death is, therefore, the key that reveals the definitive truth about the world of the living. The souls whom Dante meets along his journey carry their memories of well-known historical facts, or of legends and myths, or of quite private events. But as the journey is set in 1300 and the *Commedia* was written later, they can also 'prophesy' Dante's future as well as many events which had already occurred when the poet was writing. The result is a dramatic and 'truthful' picture of Dante's world and times.

The profound ideological crisis that shook the thirteenth century had given rise to a diffused feeling and fear that the end of the world was near. Many people believed that the degeneration of humanity had reached its nadir, and were therefore eagerly awaiting a spectacular and definitive reaffirmation of God's justice over the evil forces of the Antichrist. This belief gripped not only the naive, the uncultured and the fanatics, but also mystics, like Joachim of Fiore, and intellectuals, like the Franciscan Pietro di Giovanni Olivi who taught at Santa Croce in Florence between 1287 and 1289. Even apart from apocalyptic expectations, a longing for peace and justice was especially widespread in Italy, a country torn by internal struggles and in the throes of social upheaval. As he begins his journey, Dante is lost, a victim of these troubled times; but by the end of it he is enlightened and saved. What is more, he is authorised, indeed instructed, to don the garb of a prophet and offer in the *Commedia* a fully integrated answer to all the questions and fears of his contemporaries.

As we have seen, for Dante the conflict of temporal interests between Church and Empire had deprived humanity of both guides, essential to its well-being on earth and its fulfilment in Heaven. As a consequence *cupiditas*, the root of all evil, had triumphed everywhere. Possessed by an insatiable craving for material goods and power, contemporary society had become utterly corrupt: Popes, bishops, monks, kings, princes, barons, ordinary men and women, communes and republics – everyone was fighting for individual advantage and gratification. Nowhere was this more the case than in Florence, which had become for Dante the true kingdom of *cupiditas*, where only the 'accursed florin' ruled. The depth of her depravation is hammered home in his encounters with countless Florentines who inhabit Hell – which indeed seems to be a province, or a penal colony, of Dante's native city.

The political theme surfaces everywhere in the *Commedia*, but there are certain strategically positioned cantos in which Dante focuses on it with particular vehemence. It is in the central cantos of *Paradiso* that, using as his mouthpiece his own ancestor Cacciaguida, Dante dissects Florentine society. Echoing Dante's fierce indictment of 'la gente nova e i sùbiti guadagni' (the new people and their sudden gains, *Inf.* XVI, 73), Cacciaguida identifies in the 'confusion de le persone' (the mixture of peoples, *Par.* XVI, 67) and in individual enterprise – essentially, people's geographical and social mobility, brought about by a rapidly evolving economic situation – the roots of the city's moral degeneration. This he contrasts with the social stability, the sobriety and purity of twelfth-century Florence into which he was born. That same old Florence is, for Dante, the ideal of a well-ordered and balanced society in which private and public morality coincide, and all citizens, free of greed, live and die as good men and women, in peace with their neighbours and with God.

Cacciaguida's Florence never existed outside Dante's imagination: it was his personal Utopia. However, faced with profound social and political change, which he considered utterly negative for this and the next life alike, Dante reacted by pointing to the past as the only possible model for the future. He never envisaged that the present conflicts and contradictions could pave the way for a new, more just society, nor that any movement, individual or collective, could be good which aimed for earthly well-being independently of humanity's eternal destiny. In short, he could and would not contemplate the notion of a lay society. Dante's Christian fundamentalism was, to use a modern term, reactionary. But it was the only answer, consistent with his Christian beliefs, which he could give to the real suffering, the collapse of values and the contradictions engulfing contemporary society, while 'progress' was inching its way forward.

Unable to see what political forces would actually be capable of enabling a return to the past, Dante resorts to prophecy. Many encounters with the shades of the dead reveal God's wrath, and prophesy His imminent revenge. Not surprisingly, the most terrifying threats are directed at Florence, particularly at Florentine women whose degenerate customs are for Dante the most telling symptom of the present decadence (*Purg.* XXIII, 106–11). At the same time, however, other voices answer his yearning for universal peace and justice. At the beginning and the end of the earthly part of Dante's journey, Virgil and Beatrice prophesy the coming of a Saviour, possibly a new Emperor, who will soon deliver the world from all evil. God's Providence, which ensures the happy ending of Dante's journey, will ultimately bring about the happy ending of the world, too. Despite its remorseless catalogue of human wickedness, the *Commedia*, as its title implies, remains a poem of hope.

The last years

In 1318 – though again the date and the motivation behind this move are uncertain – Dante left Verona and settled in Ravenna as a guest of Guido Novello da Polenta. Here his family joined him, and he completed the *Paradiso*; between 1319 and 1320 he wrote the *Egloge* to Giovanni del Virgilio and a short scientific treatise, the *Questio de aqua et terra*. The *Egloge* are two compositions in Latin hexameters, based on the model of Virgil's *Eclogues*, in which Dante reaffirms the dignity of vernacular poetry and politely refuses the invitation, by the Bolognese teacher Giovanni del Virgilio, to seek glory in Latin poetry and leave Ravenna for Bologna. The *Questio* is the text of a Latin lecture, given on 20 January 1320 during a brief visit to Verona, in which he considers the relationship between the spheres of land and water, arguing that, due to the pull of the stars over the land, they are not concentric.

In 1321 Dante went on a mission to Venice on behalf of Guido Novello, charged with the task of negotiating a reduction of hostilities between the Republic and Ravenna. On his way back he caught malaria, like his friend Cavalcanti and his Emperor Henry, and died on 13 September 1321 in Ravenna, where he was buried.

Dante today

Dante's *oeuvre* is almost seven hundred years old, but it has never been read and investigated with more interest and enthusiasm than in our own time by students and scholars worldwide. The questions surrounding it are as numerous as ever, even if the quantity of scholarly papers, articles and books devoted to them is now increasing at an alarming rate. The eventual goal of this activity is to provide a single coherent system capable of describing the whole universe that is Dante. But, as with the universe in which we live, the acquisition of new knowledge seems to complicate, rather than clarify, the overall picture. The approach today is to focus on partial aspects of Dante's world: his language, style and poetics; his ideas on religion, morality, society, politics, literature; his life, sources and culture; his relation to classical and medieval literatures and to other art-forms. But perhaps even this approach is mistaken. 'If everything in the universe', a physicist has said recently, 'depends on everything else in a fundamental way, it might be impossible to get close to a full solution by investigating parts of the problem in isolation.' No doubt this is true of Dante, too. It is a measure of his genius that he apprehended and reproduced so closely the 'book' of the universe, as consciously to construct a body of work as tantalising and baffling as that book itself.

5

Boccaccio

Pamela D. Stewart

Giovanni Boccaccio entertained a lifelong friendship with his contemporary Francesco Petrarca, which became particularly close after their meeting in 1350. His admiration for Dante was sparked very early on and lasted to the end of his life. Unlike his two mentors, however, Boccaccio does not place his *persona* at the centre of his work but rather, somewhat slyly, at the periphery. At times he takes on the role of *voyeur*, as in the *Caccia di Diana*, and above all in the *Comedia delle ninfe fiorentine* in which the author turns up unexpectedly at the very end (XLIX, 1–6), crouching in the thick greenery where, hidden from view, he has watched the beautiful nymphs and listened to the tales of their joyful and charming loves. At other times, poking fun at his envious detractors, apparently all too solicitous of his reputation and well-being, he takes on a tone of amused self-effacement and feigned humility: 'In the course of my lifelong efforts to escape the fierce onslaught of those turbulent winds [of envy], I have always made a point of going quietly and unseen about my affairs, not only keeping to the lowlands but occasionally directing my steps through the deepest of deep valleys' (*Dec.* IV, Intr.). More often Boccaccio's ubiquitous, elusive presence is entrusted to a subtle play of allusions scattered here and there among his fictional characters, notably Idalogo, Caleon, Fileno in *Filocolo*, Ibrida, Caleon in *Comedia delle ninfe*, Dioneo in the *Decameron*, and possibly even Fiammetta (reversing the gender roles) in *Elegia di Madonna Fiammetta*. Among the recurring elements of the suggested self-portrait are birth out of wedlock to a French mother – either a king's daughter (*Filocolo*) or a widowed Parisian noblewoman (*Comedia delle ninfe*) – subsequently abandoned by her lover. Thus came into being the legend of his highborn French mother and the myth of Paris as his birthplace.

Early years

Giovanni Boccaccio was born in Tuscany between June and July of the year 1313, most probably in Florence rather than in nearby Certaldo as sometimes suggested. His father, Boccaccino di Chelino, was a prosperous and respected Florentine merchant, his mother a local woman, probably of humble origins, but about whom nothing is known. Shortly before marrying Margherita de' Mardoli around 1320, Boccaccino legally recognised his illegitimate son ('he himself who, freely and happily, had so kindly raised me like a son, and I had called him and still call him my parent', *Amorosa visione* XIV, 42–5) and made sure he received a good education. He had him instructed in Latin by Giovanni di Domenico Mazzuoli da Strada (whose son Zanobi was later to be Boccaccio's successful rival for the post of official poet at the Angevin court in Naples), and, with a future business career for his son in mind, saw to it that he acquired the appropriate accounting skills. Boccaccio's education was continued in Naples, where, at about age thirteen, he was apprenticed to the Bardi banking house, a Florentine firm whose Neapolitan branch had a flourishing business lending money to King Robert. Around 1327 his father joined him, having been appointed chamberlain to the king and one of the three financial consultants of the Realm of Naples. The prestige and trust his father enjoyed at court gave Boccaccio access to the charmed company of the rich and the aristocratic.

The port city, besides being a thriving commercial centre at the crossroads of Mediterranean trade, was also culturally important, the university as well as the court attracting scholars, scientists, men of letters and artists from other parts. Over thirty years later Boccaccio was to remember, in the pages of the *Genealogie deorum gentilium* ('Genealogies of the Pagan Gods', XIV, 8 and XV, 6), some of the intellectuals who stimulated his youthful mind: the Venetian scholar Paolino Minorita; the astrologist Andalò del Negro; the scientist Paolo dell'Abaco; the erudite director of the King's Library, Paolo da Perugia (the library, frequented by Boccaccio, was well stocked with French works of poetry and narrative); and the Calabrian monk Barlaam, consultant to the royal librarian in matters pertaining to Greek and Hellenistic texts. (Boccaccio's partiality for Greek-sounding names and titles goes back to his contacts with Barlaam. Later, in 1360, he had Barlaam's disciple, Leonzio Pilato, installed at the University of Florence, in the first Western chair of Greek, and housed him while the unpleasant fellow was translating the *Iliad*.)

The great jurist and poet, Cino da Pistoia, close friend of both Dante and Petrarch, must have held a particular fascination for Boccaccio, who in 1330–1 attended his lectures on the Justinian Code at the University of Naples. Another Tuscan, also a friend of Petrarch's, was to exercise a spiritual influence on him: the Augustinian friar Dionigi da Borgo San Sepolcro, who was present in Naples from the end of the 1330s until his death in 1342, called there by King Robert for his expertise as a theologian and astrologer trained at the Sorbonne. Even Giotto was in Naples around this time (from 1329 to c. 1333), and Boccaccio, a great admirer of his, was probably familiar with the famous Castel Nuovo frescoes (*Amorosa visione* IV, 7–24).

It soon became apparent that Boccaccio was not cut out for a career in banking. His father was persuaded to release him from his commercial pursuits on condition he study canon law – a lawyer after all would be able to earn as good a living as a merchant. But even here Boccaccio fretted at the precious time irremediably stolen from his true vocation, poetry. His repugnance to moneymaking, and in particular to the idea of reaping profit from learning, is echoed in the description in *Decameron* VIII, 7 of the scholar Rinieri who had gone to study in Paris 'with the purpose, not of selling his knowledge for gain as many people do, but of learning the reasons and causes of things' (VIII, 7, 5). After his father's departure for France in 1332, Boccaccio dedicated himself increasingly to humanistic studies, indulging his eclectic tastes and reading with the consuming enthusiasm of the self-taught.

Caccia di Diana and *Rime*

His first fiction, *Caccia di Diana* (1333–4, Branca's dating), bears the signs of his early interests – classical mythology as well as Christian allegory – and his veneration for Dante. It also reflects his fascination with the elegant society in which he moved at the time. The eighteen-canto poem in *terza rima* takes its lead from Dante's lost catalogue of the sixty most beautiful women in Florence (*Vita Nuova* VI, 2). Combining the *serventese* with the *caccia* genre,[1] it pays homage to fifty-eight young ladies of prominent Neapolitan families and indirectly celebrates their relatives; a fifty-ninth lady, 'whom Love honours more than any other for her lofty virtue' (I, 46–7), remains unnamed and is the one from whom the narrator hopes for salvation (XVIII, 58). The narrator, from his vantage point in the springtime greenery, gives an account of the hunting exploits of the energetic and purposeful young girls directed by the goddess Diana. At the end the virginal Diana gives way to Venus who, alighting from a hovering cloud, transforms the slain quarry (the conquered vices), burning on a huge bonfire, from animals into men; each young man is bathed in the cleansing waters of the stream (the rite of baptism) then clothed in vermilion and assigned to a young lady. Surprisingly, it turns out that the narrator too is an animal, a stag, and he too now undergoes the same transformation as the others and is then offered to his lady: 'and I saw myself offered to the Fair Lady, changed beyond doubt from a stag into a human being and a rational creature' (XVIII, 10–12). The theme of the miraculous power of love and beauty will return again and again in Boccaccio's subsequent works and is central, for instance, to the *Comedia delle ninfe*. But even more significant, in the *Caccia di Diana*, is the first evidence of Boccaccio's flair for mingling various literary genres and cultural traditions – a key factor in his renewal of a whole range of literary forms.

Much of Boccaccio's extant lyric output, his *Rime*, belongs to the Neapolitan period and bears the unmistakable traces of his debt to Dante and the *stilnovisti*. Boccaccio never set about making an ordered collection of his scattered poems. Indeed, in a letter to Pietro Piccolo (1373), he says he had

---

[1] The *serventese* was a metrical form in which successive stanzas were linked with a single rhyme; the *caccia* was normally a musical composition, in canonic form and of irregular metre.

burned his youthful verses, convinced he could never attain first place in these endeavours, obviously because of the unparallelled perfection of Petrarch's lyric poetry. Whatever we may wish to make of this statement (questions have been raised about the actual extent of the fiery destruction), Boccaccio's vocation is not that of a lyric poet but rather of a narrator, a vocation already very much in evidence in the lively verse account of Diana's hunt and amply confirmed in the prose narrative of his *Filocolo*.

Filocolo

The *Filocolo* (1336–8, Quaglio's dating) retells the love story of Florio and Biancifiore (Floire and Blancheflor), retrieving it from the idle chatter of the ignorant, the 'fabulosi parlari degli ignoranti' (I, 1, 25). The narrator is commanded by his lady, Fiammetta, to record in a little book ('picciolo libretto', 1, 1, 26), using the vernacular, 'the birth, the falling in love and the adventures' of this exemplary pair. The work, divided into five books, turns out to be anything but 'little', at least in size, with the account of the pair's trials and tribulations liberally interspersed with digressions (the justification of the takeover by the foreign Angevins of the Realm of Naples, the founding of Certaldo, the history of the Christian church, and so on). The fourth book is the best known. Florio – or Filocolo as he calls himself upon setting out on his wanderings to find Biancifiore, sold by his parents to Eastern merchants – is in Naples where he joins a select group of young people who are entertaining themselves, in a pleasant garden, by telling stories that give rise to spirited debates on Questions of Love: a situation foreshadowing the happy brigade of Florentine storytellers in the frame-tale of the *Decameron*. Indeed, tales x, 4 (Messer Gentile de' Carisendi) and x, 5 (Madonna Dianora) of the *Decameron* are taken, with some changes, from the eleventh and fourth 'questions' respectively (*Filocolo* IV, 67 and 31). However, Boccaccio in the *Decameron* seems implicitly to mark the difference in the purpose of the storytelling by comparison with the earlier work by having Fiammetta, at the beginning of the sixth tale, distance herself from the kind of debates the previous two tales (derived from the *Filocolo*) had provoked: 'I have always been of the opinion that in a gathering such as ours, we should talk in such general terms that the meaning of what we say should never give rise to argument among us' (*Dec.* x, 6, 3).

The attempt, organised by Duke Ferramonte, to distract Florio from his love for Biancifiore (III, 11), is one of the most lively and amusing episodes in the *Filocolo*. The duke enlists the help of two young girls of marvellous beauty, instructing them to wait for Florio in the palace garden dressed as provocatively as possible, and promising that whichever of them succeeds in pleasing him most will be given to him in marriage. Attired in sheer gowns with tight-fitting bodices designed to reveal the shape of their pretty breasts, they wait expectantly. Florio, attracted by the strains of their angelic singing, is over-whelmed by their beauty. After a certain amount of erotic foreplay, just as the young ladies think they are about to succeed in their intent, they are suddenly repulsed and summarily invited to leave. In tears, one of them even resorts to tearing open her bodice, but to no avail. Humiliated, without saying a word, as the sun is setting, they return to the palace, put back on their usual clothes and report to the duke what had happened. Then, generously rewarded by him with gifts, they take leave and, their hopes dashed, sadly return home. Reminiscences of this episode – almost a self-contained *novella* – are to be found in the tale of King Charles the Old and Messer Neri's two beautiful teenage daughters (*Decameron* x, 6), where the deliberate and unsuccessful attempt to seduce Florio, with its ironic overtones, is replaced by a refined scene of unwitting and more subtle seduction to which the Old King, unlike Florio, falls pathetically victim.

Florio and Biancifiore are finally reunited and married. Through the good offices of the priest Ilario (who is of Greek extraction), Florio is converted to Christianity, the religion of his beloved, along with his friends and family. At the death of his newly converted father, Florio and Biancifiore are crowned king and queen of Spain and live happily ever after. In the Envoy the author addresses his 'libretto'. Assuming a posture of humility (as we have seen, a rhetorical device Boccaccio was to use over and again), he warns against vying with the great epic poets of antiquity – Virgil, Lucan, Statius – and then continues: 'whoever loves with great purpose, let him follow Ovid of Sulmona, of whose works you are a supporter. And do not be concerned to aspire to be where the measured verses of the Florentine Dante are sung, whom you ought to follow very reverently as a minor servant' (v, 97, 5–6). The 'little' book is for his lady's eyes only. Should others see it and voice objections, they are to be referred to the authoritative Ilario (the same Ilario responsible for Florio's conversion), the first to write the story down. Thus, as the work comes to a close, we learn that our narrator's story is only the transcription of another's account: 'in a systematic way he [Ilario] wrote down in the Greek language the story of the young king' (v, 96, 3).

The *Filocolo* is the longest and most ambitious literary project of Boccaccio's years in Naples, and in some respects already announces the *Decameron*. It is a mixture of classical lore, Christian doctrine and history, French romance and medieval knowledge, and precisely because of this daring *contaminatio*, has been regarded as the 'first great example of the modern European novel'.

Filostrato, Teseida and other works of the 1340s

The *Filostrato* (c. 1335, Branca's dating), and the *Teseida delle nozze d'Emilia* (1339–41?, Limentani's dating), are the other main works of the Neapolitan period. Both were composed in octave rhyme (*ottava rima*):

stanzas of eight hendecasyllables (*endecasillabi*) rhyming ABABABCC, the invention of which is attributed to Boccaccio and which was henceforth to become the standard form of Italian narrative poetry. Against the backdrop of the siege of Troy, the *Filostrato*, a nine-book poem, tells the story of the unhappy love of Troilo for Criseida (the title in Boccaccio's shaky Greek etymology is meant to signify 'the man vanquished and struck down by love'). The work shows traces of the oral tradition of the Italian *cantari*, but is mainly indebted to the French romance tradition for its subject-matter, drawn directly or indirectly from Benoît de Sainte-Maure's *Roman de Troie* and also probably from its abbreviated adaptation in the *Historia destructionis Troiae* by Guido delle Colonne. Boccaccio, however, breathes new life into the old romance genre by shaping a narrative which, differently from his sources, focuses on the emotional effect on Troilo of separation from his beloved, and his despair when he discovers Criseida's betrayal.

The *Teseida*, an epic poem in the prescribed twelve books, shows reliance on classical works: Virgil's *Aeneid*, but above all Statius' *Thebaid*. Perhaps spurred on by Dante's declaration in the *De vulgari eloquentia* (II, 2) that Italian literature had as yet no epic, Boccaccio intended with his *Teseida* to fill that gap. But on to the epic theme of arms he grafted a love story. Two Theban warriors, Arcita and Palemone, taken prisoner during the war of Theseus against Thebes, compete for the affections of Emilia, Theseus' sister-in-law. Arcita, although the victor against Palemone in a tournament to decide who should marry Emilia, dies of his wounds, and the poem ends with the wedding of Emilia and Palemone. The close interweaving of the themes of arms and love makes the work an important forerunner of the great narrative poems of the Italian Renaissance. At a later date, Boccaccio added to the text a scholarly commentary. Many of his glosses turn out to be elegant miniature narratives on mythological subjects. Chaucer drew on the plot of the *Teseida* for the 'Knight's Tale', and on the *Filostrato* for *Troilus and Criseyde*, as did Shakespeare for his *Troilus and Cressida*.

The winter of 1340–1 marks the beginning of a new phase in Boccaccio's life. The increasing difficulties experienced by the principal Florentine merchant bankers, whose royal borrowers were defaulting on their loans, had negative repercussions on the general economy of Florence and the personal finances of Boccaccino, to the extent that he was obliged to recall his son from Naples where he could no longer afford to support him. Boccaccio found adjusting to the austere, culturally deprived life of Florence, with its essentially business-oriented society, extremely hard. The depressing pall of financial failure hanging over the paternal household did not of course help. Furthermore, the Florentines struck him as an avaricious and factious lot. In spite of everything, he continued to dedicate himself to his writing, beginning the Latin eclogues he eventually organised into the *Bucolicum carmen* and composing in rapid succession the *Comedia delle ninfe fiorentine* (1341–2); the *Amorosa visione* (1342, second redaction 1355?), a fifty-canto poem in *terza rima*, largely taken up (IV–XXX) by a guided tour of the frescoed hall of a castle where the triumphs of learning, glory and love are depicted; the *Elegia di Madonna Fiammetta* (1343–4), generally considered to be modern literature's first psychological novel; and the *Ninfale fiesolano* (1344–6), a work considerably less trammelled with literary and allegorical baggage than the others, which gives an account in octaves of the love story of the shepherd Africo and the nymph Mensola, and concludes with the founding of Fiesole. The *Comedia delle ninfe fiorentine* is in some respects the work closest to the *Decameron* – in the sixteenth century it was even tagged the 'little *Decameron*', perhaps a bookseller's publicity ploy – since it has a group of seven nymphs who, in a country setting, tell the story of their lives and loves, each ending with a song. But in another sense it is the most distant from Boccaccio's major work, because of the wealth of erudite references, the curious combination of classical mythology, Christian allegory and religious moralising, and the lengthy descriptions (repetitive in spite of the subtle variations in aspect and meaning) of each nymph, that follow meticulously the prescribed order, from the top of the head right down to the tip of the toes. The *Comedia* is indeed an exercise in sophisticated elegance, an example of the most scrupulous observance of the precepts – usually neglected in the *Decameron* – to be found in twelfth-century treatises on Poetics for the description of feminine beauty.

The *Decameron*

Setting and structure

At the end of the decade, Boccaccio started writing the *Decameron*. The Black Death had for centuries been endemic in Europe. Paul the Deacon, for instance, recorded an eighth-century episode in his *Historia gentis Langobardorum*, well known to Boccaccio. The 1348 outbreak in Florence was particularly severe, decimating the population and causing the death of several of Boccaccio's close friends, as well as of his father and stepmother. Depictions of the devastation remain in many contemporary frescoes in the city's public buildings. A sombre description of its terrible effects on Florentine society provides the setting for the formation of the brigade of ten young people who will tell the *Decameron*'s one hundred tales. The seven noblewomen and their three gentlemen friends, who make up the group, meet in the Church of Santa Maria Novella and decide to retreat to a villa in the nearby hills to escape not only the disease, rampant in the city, but also the moral corruption and civic decay it has engendered. Boccaccio shows himself at pains to protect the good reputation of his young ladies so that they will not 'feel embarrassed, at any time in the future, on account of the ensuing stories, all of which they either listened to or narrated themselves' (I, Intr., 50). He therefore does not reveal their 'true' names, but gives them 'names which are either wholly or partially appropriate to the qualities of each' (I, Intr., 51). He chooses names he had already used in previous works (Filomena, Fiammetta, Emilia, Pampinea) or names that allude to other literary characters (Elissa – Virgil; Neifile – *dolce stil novo*, Dante; Lauretta – Petrarch). Even the young men's names (Dioneo, Filostrato, Panfilo) hark back to his previous works. Boccaccio's cautious strategy in introducing his fictitious lady narrators has given rise to much speculation on two fronts: on the one hand there have been attempts to link the ladies to real-life contemporaries of the writer; on the other, to see them as a reincarnation of the nymphs in the *Comedia delle ninfe fiorentine*, who are explicitly identified at the end with the seven virtues.

On Wednesday, the day after their meeting in the church, the members of the group settle into their country quarters and immediately plan to put their sorrows behind them and to spend their time pleasantly and in an orderly fashion (' "nothing", says Pampinea, "will last very long unless it has a definite form" ', I, Intr., 95): they will all gather once a day to participate in a common activity, storytelling. They will elect from among themselves a leader to supervise the activities of the day and to establish the theme for the tales; following each day's ten tales there will be music, dancing and songs. The storytelling will be interrupted on Friday to observe the day of Christ's Passion and on Saturday to carry out the week's ablutions ('it is customary on that day for the ladies to wash their hair and rinse away the dust and grime that may have settled on their persons in the course of their week's endeavours', II, Concl., 6), and will resume on Sunday. After a fortnight in the country, the group returns to Florence. Thus, the one hundred tales are distributed over two symmetrical sets of five days, each set starting on Wednesday and each interrupted on Friday and Saturday.

This structural division in two parts is signalled in the almost verbatim repetition by Filomena, as she introduces the first tale of the Sixth Day, of the beginning of Pampinea's introduction to the last tale of the First Day. The subject is the art of social conversation and well-placed repartee, an art particularly becoming to women but which has recently suffered a decline. Pampinea with her tale (I, 10) illustrates the shaming of the beautiful widow Malgherida dei Ghisolieri, who had thought to make fun of her elderly suitor, the celebrated physician Master Alberto, and was instead elegantly silenced by him. Conversely, Filomena's tale (VI, 1) provides proof that the women of previous generations talked well and to the point. The gentlewoman Madonna Oretta (who actually lived in Florence at the beginning of the fourteenth century) adroitly intervenes to stop a knight, travelling on foot in her company, from continuing a tale he is telling. The unwary fellow had offered to take her (metaphorically) on horseback a good part of the way by telling her 'one of the finest tales in the world' (VI, 1, 9). The inept storyteller commits every possible error in both organisation and delivery, seemingly unable to extricate himself from the mess until Madonna Oretta can stand it no longer and, picking up on the knight's metaphor, says to him: 'Sir, you have taken me

riding on a horse that trots very jerkily. Pray be good enough to set me down'
(VI, I, II). Pampinea has capped a day of tales which, although there has been
no announced theme, are related in one way or another to verbal dexterity:
half-way through the day Fiammetta notes, in preparing to tell of the
Marchioness of Monferrato's well-chosen words that put the King of France in
his place: 'For this reason and also because of the pleasure I feel at our having,
through our stories, begun to demonstrate the power of good repartee, I have
been prompted to show you ...' (I, 5, 4). While the clever use of words was
the *undeclared* theme of the First Day, it is the *declared* theme of the Sixth. If
we then look at the first tale of the First Day and the last tale of the Sixth Day,
a chiastic relationship between the four tales becomes evident. The protagonists of I, I and VI, 10, Ciappelletto and Friar Cipolla, present similarities,
though Ciappelletto has something sinister about him while Cipolla is a
sociable, merry fellow. Both are wizards with words (the friar is said to be so
excellent a speaker that he might pass for 'Cicero or perhaps Quintilian', VI,
10, 7) and masters of the art of lying; both tales end with the faithful being
gulled.

Thematic patterns

Any attempt, however, at establishing an obvious homogeneity of theme in
each of the two halves of the *Decameron* is doomed to failure. Boccaccio's
compository scheme is much more subtle and unpredictable, continually
eluding the neat patterns critics try to impose. At the most, it can be said that
in the first half, Days II, III and V tell of undertakings or adventures (some
centred on love, some not) with a happy ending, and Day IV of unhappy love
affairs; the second half tells, in Days VII and VIII, of pranks and practical jokes,
and in Day X of quite the opposite, namely, acts of great generosity in the
'cause of love or otherwise' (X, I, I). In each of the two parts there can thus be
discerned a dominant theme and in each a day dedicated to that theme's
opposite. The Third Day takes up the general theme of the Second – the
capricious workings of Fortune – restricting it 'to a single aspect of the many
facets of Fortune' (II, Concl., 8), while the corresponding Days in the second
part, VII and VIII, present a similar restriction of the chosen theme reversing
mirrorlike the order. The Seventh Day is dedicated to tricks women play on
their menfolk, the Eighth Day to 'the tricks that people in general, men and
women alike, are forever playing upon one another' (VIII, I, I).

The best-known butt of practical jokes in the *Decameron* is the stingy,
foolish Calandrino. He figures in tales three and five of the Eighth Day, and
also in tales three and six of the Ninth Day. To the end he remains totally
unaware of providing ever new opportunities for fun to his fellow painters,
Bruno and Buffalmacco, both consummate pranksters. They make him believe
he has found the famous heliotrope, the stone that renders invisible or, to be
more exact, 'has the miraculous power of making people invisible when they

are out of sight, provided they are carrying it on their person' (VIII, 3, 20). They get him drunk, steal his pig, then set up an elaborate lie-detecting test (paid for by the victim) to prove he himself is responsible for the theft (VIII, 6). They convince him he is pregnant and make him spend all of a recent inheritance to procure an abortion (IX, 3); and finally they get him into hot water with his wife, Tessa, by having her find him in a haystack with a young girl (IX, 5). Calandrino and the practical jokes played on him, the *beffe*, inspired many of the comic situations and characters in Italian Renaissance comedy. The most famous of his descendants is Calandro, the foolish protagonist of Bibbiena's *Calandra* (1513).

Changes of location, which add some variety to the brigade's repetitive daily routine, are effected in both the first and second parts of the *Decameron*: the transfer from one villa to another at the end of Day II 'to avoid being joined by others' (II, Concl., 7) and the transfer to the enchantingly beautiful 'Valley of the Ladies' for the whole of Day VII. As we have already seen, Day VI returns to the theme of the clever use of words and witty repartee implicitly present in Day I, but the absence of a set theme in Day I can also link it to Day IX, during which the narrators are freed by the queen from the constraints of a prescribed theme. Boccaccio seems to enjoy playing a tantalising game of hide-and-seek with his readers, since nothing ever really fits pat. The symmetries are never perfect.

The members of the brigade will tell their stories in no special order. In Day I the queen, Pampinea, invites all the others to tell their tales before telling her own. At the end of the Day Dioneo – the non-conformist of the group, always stretching boundaries and debunking polite conventionality – asks the new queen, Filomena, to allow him from then on always to tell the last tale (displacing the group leader to the penultimate position) and to be exempted from having to stick to the stated theme should he so wish:

> The queen, knowing what a jovial and entertaining fellow he was and clearly perceiving that he was only asking this favour so that, if the company should grow weary of hearing people talk, he could enliven the proceedings with some story that would move them to laughter, cheerfully granted his request.
>
> (I, Concl., 14)

The last of the one hundred tales is thus his, while the opening one is Panfilo's.

Decameron I, I concerns Ciappelletto, a thoroughly wicked Tuscan tax-collector operating in France, and his false deathbed confession; *Decameron* X, 10 is about the extraordinarily submissive and patient Griselda. It has been pointed out that Boccaccio's vast 'human comedy' starts out with a Judas figure, 'the worst man ever born' (I, I, 15) and ends with the Virgin-Mary-like Griselda. The opposition of initial vice to final virtue suggests an ascensional progression that is not, however, evident in the intervening ninety-eight stories. Furthermore, if we consider the way the first and last tales are presented by their narrators, we will notice a sharp contrast between presentation and tale.

Panfilo declares his story will illustrate the compassion and generosity of God in answering the prayers of the faithful, even though they unwittingly resort to sinful intercessors. After this pious introduction, we are treated to an exhilarating account of how a holy friar is hoodwinked into taking Ciappelletto's mocking confession seriously, thus preparing the way for the unholy sinner, upon his giving up the ghost, to be declared a saint. Dioneo introduces the tenth tale of the Tenth Day not as an illustration of Griselda's exemplary obedience (the interpretation given by Petrarch in his Latin translation of the tale, shorn of course of the narrator's introduction and concluding remarks), but as a cautionary tale about the 'senseless brutality' of her marquis husband Gualtieri – an exact reversal of the 'liberal and munificent deeds' of the prescribed theme. When he has finished, Dioneo muses on the fact that 'celestial spirits may sometimes descend even into the houses of the poor, whilst there are those in royal palaces who would be better employed as swineherds than as rulers of men' (x, 10, 68). But his final lewd remarks, on how Gualtieri sent the swineherd's daughter Griselda back to her humble home in nothing but a shift, irreverently deflate the tale's atmosphere of exalted virtue: 'For perhaps it would have served him right if he had chanced upon a wife, who, being driven from the house in her shift, had found some other man to shake her skin-coat for her, earning herself a fine new dress in the process' (x, 10, 69).

The storytellers

The comments made by Panfilo and Dioneo raise the general question as to the function of what the storytellers say about their tales. More often than not their comments serve to justify the tale's particular place in the series, to establish a link with previous or subsequent stories, to stress the relationship with the chosen theme of the Day, or to allow for some playful remarks on the part of the storyteller, the other members of the brigade and, on occasion, even the author. Those features of a tale best suited to further one or more of these specific purposes are, therefore, the ones singled out. Filomena, in preparing her listeners for the story of the rich Jew Melchizedek and how he told a parable of three rings to avoid Saladin's trick question, announced that 'since we have heard such fine things said concerning God and the truth of our religion, it will not seem inappropriate to descend at this juncture to the deeds and adventures of men' (1, 3, 3). She intends to show with her tale that wisdom brings great rewards, while folly may lead to great misery, and to make the ladies in the company more wary when answering questions. Her tale, however, does concern religion (four centuries later Lessing used it as the basis for his play *Nathan the Wise*, a kind of manifesto for religious tolerance), since Saladin asks Melchizedek to tell him 'which of the three laws whether the Jewish, the Saracen, or the Christian' he deems 'to be truly authentic' (1, 3.8). Filomena's preamble is clearly intended to build a bridge from the declared religious intent of the previous tales. (1, 1 and 1, 2) to the tales that follow, centred as they are on prompt and apt replies, and to give Dioneo the opportunity of pointing out the parallels between the bawdy tale (I, 4) he is about to tell and the previous two (I, 2, I, 3), thus waggishly exonerating himself from the anticipated disapproval of the ladies.

On the Second Day, the denunciation of female vanity – a recurring topic in Boccaccio, most insistently developed in his later work, the *Corbaccio* – is prominent in Panfilo's lengthy preface (II, 7, 3–7) to his story of the extraordinarily beautiful Saracen princess Alatiel. The tale he proposes to tell is designed to persuade his lady listeners of the dangers and sorrow great beauty can bring. But the fair Alatiel does not appear overly distressed at passing 'through the hands of nine men in various places within the space of four years' (II, 7), and at the end she even manages, 'having been returned to her father as a virgin' (II, 7, I), to marry the king to whom she had originally been promised. The edifying intent seems contradicted by the tale and by the proverb that brings it to a close: 'A kissed mouth doesn't lose its freshness, for like the moon it always renews itself' (II, 7, 122). As for the ladies in the company, they react to Alatiel's adventures with sighs but, as the author slyly remarks, perhaps not so much from pity for the beautiful princess as from envy, 'because they longed to be married no less often than she was' (II, 8, 2).

The tale of Giletta of Narbonne (III, 9), told by Neifile, satisfies not only one but both the alternative requirements of the theme set by her as queen of the Third Day. The topic concerns 'people who by dint of their own efforts have achieved an object they greatly desired, or recovered a thing previously lost' (III, I, I). The perfect fitting of her story to the twofold topic is elegantly implied in Neifile's casual introduction to her tale: 'for what it is worth, I am going to tell you the story that occurs to me as relevant to the topic we proposed' (III, 9, 3). Giletta, a physician's daughter, wins the hand (though not the heart) of a count, Bertrand of Roussillon; he leaves her right after the wedding, but in the end she succeeds in winning him once again and is solemnly received as his beloved wife. Criticism of the tale and the topic it so perfectly exemplifies is ironically implied in the introduction to the next tale, that of Alibech (easily the most risqué of the entire collection), told by Dioneo, who having listened *diligently* to the queen's tale presents his own as not straying from the *true subject* of the Day's storytelling. All the other tales of the Third Day, in fact, emphasise the satisfaction of sexual desire, also the subject of Dioneo's tale. The Giletta story told by Neifile is the only exception. (Shakespeare was to rewrite the story for the stage in *All's Well That Ends Well*; he also derived the plot of his romance *Cymbeline* from another of Boccaccio's tales, the one told by the queen of the Second Day, Filomena, about the courageous and highly accomplished Zinevra who, unjustly accused of infidelity, manages to escape death disguising herself and living undetected as a man until finally able to prove her innocence. Shakespeare probably read both tales in Painter's sixteenth-century English translation in *The Palace of Pleasure*.)

The summary presentation by Fiammetta of the Fourth Day's opening tale –

the woeful account of Prince Tancredi's murder of his daughter Ghismonda's lover – as 'an occurrence that was not only pitiful, but calamitous, and fully worthy of our tears' (IV, 1, 2), is simply a particularly apt reminder of the Day's chosen theme of tragic love affairs, coming as it does after the author's lengthy intervention in defence of his work against real or imagined detractors who had accused him of frivolity. In introducing the tale of Federigo degli Alberighi (V, 9), the narrator, Fiammetta, only refers to the resistance of Monna Giovanna to the amorous attentions of Federigo so as to emphasise the connection with the preceding tale, which tells of the reluctance of the disdainful young lady from Ravenna wooed by Nastagio degli Onesti. The tale of Federigo and Monna Giovanna is best remembered for Federigo's generous gesture in sacrificing his prized hunting falcon to honour his lady at table, only to learn she had come to request of him this very falcon, to satisfy the wish of her ailing son. The list of examples could go on. The point is that the comments of the storytellers are not mainly intended to provide an interpretation – more or less moralising – of the tales, but to contribute to the order and unity of the work and to the playful atmosphere that prevails in it. They could hardly be taken as reflecting Boccaccio's view of the tales and of the lesson to be learned from them.

In any case, whatever paradigmatic significance one might be tempted to attribute to the tales would be undermined by their complexity – the detailed description of the characters and their milieu, the minute analysis of their actions and motivations, the careful justification of each tale's conclusion: in a word, by what constitutes the originality and artistry of the tales. This complexity is mirrored in the prose style of the *Decameron*. The Latinisms, inversions and lengthy sentences that abound in the earlier works are here reserved for occasions when solemnity is appropriate (in the Proem, in certain of the narrators' preambles, in Ghismonda's speech to her father in IV, 1, etc.), leaving ample room for a lively, rapid style. Direct speech occupies a good part of a number of tales and is interspersed with words from different regional dialects, professional or underworld jargons, and popular expressions, which all serve to characterise the speakers and place them in a precise social setting. An amazing display of verbal virtuosity and inventiveness (Branca speaks of 'expressivism') enhances the comic effect of certain of the most memorable tales (e.g. VI, 10, VIII, 2, VIII, 9), and perhaps best exemplifies Boccaccio's sophisticated, daring use of the language. This language, the 'Florentine vernacular', and 'the most homely and unassuming style' (*Decameron* IV, Intr., 3) in which he wrote his masterpiece came to be considered, in the sixteenth century, as the sole model for Italian prose.

The 'author'

Boccaccio, or rather, the fictionalised author of the *Decameron*, speaks at some length of himself and his work: at the outset, in the Proem and in the initial part of the general introduction; at the very end, in the 'Author's Epilogue'; and a third of the way through, at the beginning of the Fourth Day. In the Proem he presents himself as a man no longer subject to the anguish of an unhappy love, which is now fortunately extinguished, and as eager to be of assistance to those who still suffer. He singles out as the most in need of his help the idle lovelorn ladies – of Ovidian memory – who, 'cooped up within the narrow confines of their rooms', lack the freedom and the many distractions that engage the minds of their male counterparts: 'fowling, hunting, fishing, riding and gambling', or attending to 'their business affairs' (Proemio, 12). The remedy proposed is storytelling: 'I shall narrate a hundred stories [*novelle*] or fables or parables or histories or whatever you choose to call them' (Proemio, 13). Throughout the *Decameron* Boccaccio consistently uses the term 'novella' when referring to his tales (the sole exception is in x, 9, 4, where 'istoria' is used for the tale of Messer Torello, set in the time of the Third Crusade and involving an historical character, Saladin.) It is clear that 'novella' is intended as an inclusive term, covering 'fables', 'parables' and 'histories' and thus indicating the scope of the genre.

Once he has defined his audience, the author sets about his task. He addresses his gentle ladies, warning them that the going will initially be rough (the account of the plague), but then infinitely more pleasant (the merry brigade's storytelling), so they must not despair. To the rapport established here is added a sense of complicity when the author, at the beginning of the Fourth Day before proceeding further on the 'established course', seeks his ladies' sympathy and support in defending himself from his detractors, who have grown 'so numerous and presumptuous' (IV, Intr., 10) that they must be rebutted without further delay. The assumption is that at least some of the tales had circulated in uncollected form and had provoked the reactions Boccaccio records. (No trace whatsoever of these adverse reactions has survived and they are probably simply a pretext to address in advance certain issues the work might raise.) The detractors' criticisms – mostly to do with the author's overweening interest in women and their consolation – are treated with irony and dismissed one by one, their target (Boccaccio) assuming, as we have previously noted, an attitude of playful humility. The mainstay of the defence is the tale of the hermit Filippo Balducci and his adolescent son. After a secluded childhood in their mountain retreat, the boy accompanies his father on an outing to Florence, where he sees a host of things unknown to him and asks his father what they are called. When they come across a party of elegant young ladies the devout Filippo refuses to name them, saying only that they are evil. But his son insists, so 'not wishing to arouse any idle longings in the young man's breast, his father avoided calling them by their real name, and instead of telling him that they were women, he said: "They are called goslings"' (IV, Intr., 23). But the damage has been done. The young man will talk of nothing else and begs his father to get him one of the goslings to take home, promising 'to pop things into its bill'. ' "Certainly not", replied his father. "Their bills are not where you think, and require a special sort of diet." ' Filippo immediately realises that 'his wits are no match for Nature, and regretted having brought the boy to Florence in the first place' (IV, Intr., 28–9). On the pretext of not wishing to enter into competition with the members of the brigade with a full-blown tale of his own, the author insists his tale is incomplete. It has been suggested that in reality the only thing missing is the epilogue, which, with a stroke of mischievous irony, is left to the imagination.

In his conclusion to the whole work the author gives thanks to God for His assistance and to the chosen female audience for their help, proposing to deal briefly with 'certain trifling objections, which, though remaining unspoken' ('Conclusione dell'autore', 2) may possibly have arisen in the minds of his readers. The most substantive of the issues is the obscenity question, the unseemliness of the subject-matter of some of the tales and the use of language considered improper in polite company. A discussion within the brigade had arisen at the end of the Sixth Day about the suitability of telling racy tales. Dioneo had successfully argued that such topics should not be off-limits if the purpose was to amuse and entertain. Furthermore, given the irreproachable behaviour of the group, such pleasurable discourse could not possibly reflect badly on the good reputation of the women. In the 'Author's Epilogue' the matter is similarly disposed of, and in conclusion readers are reminded that among the tales they are 'free to ignore the ones that give offence, and read only those that are pleasing. For in order that none of you may be misled, each of the stories bears on its brow the gist of that which it hides in its bosom' ('Conclusione dell'autore', 19). The reference is to the summary prefaced to each tale. Many of these summaries show consummate narrative skill and form tiny tales in themselves, often giving a different emphasis to the narrative material from that in the tale (see I, 1, II, 5, II, 7, III, 2, III, 3, III, 8, IV, 3, IV, 7, IV, 9, etc.). They brilliantly exemplify the technique of *abbreviatio* as opposed to the technique of *amplificatio* evident in the tales themselves. Thus the summaries, the tales, and the narrators' comments provide slightly different perspectives, all designed to coexist and not to be mutually exclusive.

In deflecting the criticism that he might have done well to skip some of the tales he has included, the author archly replies that he could only write down the stories actually told:

> But even if one could assume that I was the inventor as well as the scribe of these stories (which was not the case), I still insist that I would not feel ashamed if some fell short of perfection, for there is no craftsman other than God whose work is whole and faultless in every respect.
>
> ('Conclusione dell'autore', 16–17)

So once again we have Boccaccio shunning the limelight, slyly hiding behind his fictitious narrators, and demurely taking the role of scribe. The humble role in which he casts himself cannot but remind us of the role he actually played. In writing his masterpieces, he raised storytelling to the dignity of a literary genre. As we have seen, he defined the scope of the *novella* and firmly established it in European literature. He certainly was not unaware of the importance of the *Decameron*, as is obvious from the time and care he took, towards the end of his life, to revise and copy the text. The manuscript (Berlin codex Hamilton 90), besides being the only extant holograph, has the added interest of containing small portraits of some of the characters and narrators drawn in the margins, probably by Boccaccio himself.

Later life and works

Boccaccio's last work of fiction is his *Corbaccio*, variously dated as early as 1354/55 and as late as 1365/66. In it he returns to the dream-vision formula he had used in the *Amorosa visione*. This time, however, the narrator's guide is not an unidentified lady but a spirit come from Purgatory, at the behest of the Virgin Mary, to persuade him of the error of his carnal love for a cruel widow. The spirit, none other than the shade of the woman's dead husband, is well placed to explode the myth of the lady's beauty, by providing an inside view of the deception that went into improving on God's handiwork when the woman was young and of the measures needed, as she aged, to repair the ravages of time. The spirit marshalls arguments that range over the vast body of misogynist literature from Juvenal and Theophrastus to Jerome, from the *fabliaux* to the anti-feminist digressions in the *Roman de la rose* and to the many rambling treatises on the dangers women pose to the physical and spiritual well-being of men. Boccaccio's interest in anti-feminist writings is documented by the texts and passages he copied, some time before 1350, into one of his notebooks, the *Zibaldone laurenziano*. But the vehement misogyny of the *Corbaccio* may come as a surprise (and indeed has caused much discussion), following as it does the celebration of so many accomplished and intelligent women in the *Decameron*. The truth is that misogynist *topoi* are by no means absent from the *Decameron*, or even from such earlier works as the *Filocolo* and the *Filostrato*. At the beginning of the *Decameron*'s frame story, Filomena unflatteringly characterises her sex as 'fickle, quarrelsome, suspicious, cowardly and easily frightened' (I, Intr., 75). According to her, women are not 'the most rational of creatures' (I, Intr., 74) and are quite incapable of getting along without male supervision. A wide selection of anti-feminist argumentation is present in the sadistic and vengeful Rinieri's tirade in VIII, 7 against Elena, a flirtatious but unwary young widow. Tedaldo's somewhat specious reasoning in favour of women yielding to the desires of men in III, 7 rests on man's God-given superiority over women: 'If they would only consider their own natures, and stop to think of how much more nobility God has conceded to man than to any of the other animals, they would undoubtedly be proud of a man's love and hold him in high esteem and do everything in their power to please him' (III, 7, 51). The narrator in the *Corbaccio* is told that 'a woman is an imperfect creature' and reproached for not remembering what his studies must surely have taught him, namely 'that you are a man made in the image and semblance of God, a perfect creature, born to govern and not to be governed'.

Though at times tiresome, the 'humble treatise' is often funny, lusty and lively, containing some brilliant vignettes on the widow's wiles and exasperating ways: the midnight chase of the entire household for the offending mosquito that had dared to land on madam's make-up; the scene of her veiling, with the help of a much-maligned servant girl, ending with the lady wetting her fingers with her tongue to smooth in place a few last stray hairs, just like a cat at its toilette.

Boccaccio's commitment to his studies and writing did not exclude his involvement in the affairs of Florence. Except during the early 1360s, after the ruling party had savagely crushed an anti-government conspiracy in which some of Boccaccio's close friends were implicated, he filled a number of civic offices and undertook various missions on behalf of the Republic. One such mission took him in 1350 to a convent near Ravenna to deliver ten gold florins to Sister Beatrice, Dante's daughter. In 1362, in search of a post that would afford much-needed financial security to himself and his half-brother Iacopo, he accepted an invitation from his childhood friend Niccolò Acciaiuoli, now grand seneschal to Queen Giovanna, to settle permanently in Naples. The details of Boccaccio's unhappy and humiliating experience at the hands of Acciaiuoli, and the depth of his bitterness and disappointment, are clear from the letter he wrote to Francesco Nelli, the friend who had helped arrange the invitation. Abandoning the hope of a stable position and the dream of recapturing the happy times of his youth, he left the city, returning north to retire to a small family property in Certaldo, which was to be his base for the rest of his life. He refused all subsequent offers of patronage and all invitations to move elsewhere. He died in Certaldo in 1375, one year after Petrarch.

In the years following the composition of the *Decameron*, Boccaccio devoted himself to intense scholarly activities. To this period belong, for the most part, the works inspired by his lifelong veneration for Dante. The biography in praise of Dante (generally known under its short title, *Trattatello in laude di Dante*) has come down to us in an early lengthy redaction (1351, Ricci's dating) and in two later shorter versions (1360, 1365, Ricci's dating). In spite of evident traces of rhetorical schemata appropriate to the laudatory purpose, and in spite of Boccaccio's efforts to fit the life of his subject into the mould of Virgil's life as told by Servius and Donatus, the *Trattatello* remains, together with Leonardo Bruni's, the most important biography of Dante. The *Esposizioni sopra la Comedia* are an expansion, in commentary form, of notes Boccaccio had made in preparation for his public readings of the *Divine Comedy* – the first ever *Lectura Dantis* – commissioned by the Florentine government and held in the church of Santo Stefano di Badia between

23 October 1373 and the beginning of 1374. The commentary breaks off at the beginning of Inferno XVII.

Around 1355 he compiled an encyclopaedia of geographical information (*De montibus, silvis, fontibus, lacubus, fluminibus, stagnis seu paludibus et de nominibus maris*, 'Concerning Mountains, Woods, Springs, Lakes, Rivers, Swamps or Marshes and the Names of the Sea') designed to elucidate references in classical and modern literature. In 1361 he started putting together a collection of biographies of women (*De mulieribus claris*) famous not only for their virtue but also for their intelligence, courage, generosity of spirit and even for their literary and artistic accomplishments. The 104 women treated are taken from ancient myths, fiction and history, and are ordered more or less chronologically, starting with Eve and ending with Queen Giovanna of Naples. The enterprise, as Boccaccio himself points out, was novel and proved to be highly successful. It was widely consulted, drawn upon, translated, and imitated down through the centuries. (Chaucer used the biography of Zenobia in 'The Monk's Tale' and John Parker translated the entire work for Henry VIII.) Another collection of biographies had been started by Boccaccio somewhat earlier (1355) and underwent continuous revisions until shortly before his death. *The Fates of Illustrious Men (De casibus virorum illustrium)* furnish proof of the capricious workings of Fortune, who raises men and women high on her wheel only to dash them down. The famous victims of Fortune appear before the author to plead their case for inclusion in his book. At the end there is still a long queue of petitioners, but the author has decided it is time to rest. He begs those wiser than himself to make the necessary corrections and additions to his 'little book', especially calling upon 'one who in these times is the brightest and most vivid beacon of impeccable life and praiseworthy erudition, Francesco Petrarca, poet laureate and my honoured master' ('Conclusio'). This too proved to be an immensely popular reference work throughout Europe for several centuries (it was drawn upon, for instance, by Chaucer in 'The Monk's Tale' and paraphrased by John Lydgate).

The major undertaking of Boccaccio's scholarly career was another work in Latin, the *Genealogie deorum gentilium* (started in 1363), widely known for the defence of poetry contained in Book XIV. Boccaccio traces the genealogy of the pagan deities, piecing together in an organic whole (as he says in the Proem) the scattered fragments of the ancient shipwreck of classical mythology, tracing the genealogy of the pagan deities and elucidating their hidden meanings and moral message. He justifies this recovery operation by insisting on the inherent and lasting truth of ancient mythology. The vehicle of truth, then as now, is poetry, and essential to the poet is learning. Thus the *Genealogie*, like the other scholarly works, is conceived as a useful tool for cultivated persons in general and poets in particular.

The influence of Petrarch on Boccaccio's humanistic undertakings is undeniable, and was recognised time and again by Boccaccio himself. But although he embraced Petrarch's historical perspective – the exaltation of classical antiquity coupled with the condemnation of the centuries that followed – Boccaccio did not subscribe to his friend's pessimistic view of the present and, in particular, did not share his reservations concerning Dante and literature in the vernacular. He strongly believed that a revival was already under way, but not restricted to the field of literature and not necessarily dependent on the use of Latin. In the figurative arts, he says, Giotto 'brought back to light an art which had been buried for centuries beneath the blunders of those who, in their paintings, aimed to bring visual delight to the ignorant rather than intellectual satisfaction to the wise' (*Decameron* IV, 5, 6). As for literature, in a letter written in 1371 to his friend Iacopo Pizzinga, Boccaccio assigns a distinct place to each of the two great men of his time who had revived 'the lost Italian glory': Dante, taking a new route, 'dared to make the Muses sing in his mother tongue, neither vulgar, nor rustic, as some would have it', while Petrarch followed 'the route of the Ancients'. To these two, posterity has added the 'humble psalmist', Giovanni Boccaccio: reformer and innovator of the European literary tradition, classical and modern scholar of encyclopaedic erudition, poet and prose writer always ready to attempt new subjects and new forms, and above all great narrator and author of one of the most enduring masterpieces of world literature.

6

Petrarch

John Took

Petrarch, the most committed of the great *trecentisti* to the revitalisation of a Latin literary culture in Italy, was at the same time the most decisive of them for the development of the vernacular tradition. Dante, it is true, had his followers – not least among them Boccaccio in the *Amorosa visione* and Petrarch himself in the *Trionfi* – in respect of a certain kind of visionary literature in the vernacular, and Boccaccio was to remain for generations a point of reference in respect of the *novella* tradition in Italian. But neither was as decisive for the development of literary good taste in Europe, in and beyond the Renaissance period, as the Petrarch of the *Rime*. And here there is an irony, for of all the great *trecentisti*, Petrarch, a poet of well-nigh unerring tact in the management of form, is psychologically the least settled of them, the least at one with himself in respect of the conflicting forces of personality and of moral sensibility. At every point in the *Canzoniere* (the traditional title of his collected *Rime*), the technical assurance flowing from his extraordinarily developed sense of formal propriety contrasts with – even as it gives expression to – a sustained sense of spiritual uncertainty, a state of mind characterised at every turn by a sense of restlessness and irresolution.

Life

The formal circumstances of Petrarch's life, with its endless oscillation between the courtly patronage of popes, priests and princes and the stillness of his country retreats, are themselves a metaphor of his spiritual existence. Born in Arezzo in 1304 of a Florentine lawyer exiled (like Dante) from his native city as a White Guelf, his early years were spent in Pisa, in Avignon (where his father came to work in 1312) and at Carpentras in Provence, where he was schooled in grammar and rhetoric by another exiled spirit, Convenevole da Prato. In 1316, in Montpellier, he began his legal studies, which for a time, though with less than complete commitment, he continued in Bologna. With the death of his father in 1326, Petrarch abandoned law and returned to Avignon, where in 1330, thanks to Cardinal Giovanni Colonna, he enjoyed his first ecclesiastical appointment as household chaplain. It was here, on 6 April 1327, in the church of St Clare, that he first caught sight of Laura, a figure who thereafter stood both materially and symbolically at the centre of his complex

spirituality. It was during this period too that, in the course of his travels to
northern Europe (1333), he discovered at Liège the lost *Pro Archia* oration of
Cicero, important for his own conception of the public responsibilities of the
literary man, and that he was appointed, on the recommendation of Giovanni
Colonna, to a canonry (the first of several he was to receive) in Lombez
cathedral. In 1337 he returned to Avignon, where he acquired a house at
Vaucluse on the banks of the Sorgue.

These, for Petrarch, were years of intense humanist ambition, and the late
1330s saw the start of his Latin epic, the *Africa*, conceived along the lines of
the *Aeneid* as a celebration of Scipio Africanus, and of the *De viris illustribus*
('On Famous Men'), a celebration of great men in the manner of the Roman
historian Livy. They were years which culminated in his examination for, and
coronation as, poet laureate (Rome, 1341), an occasion largely engineered by
Petrarch himself, which confirmed him in his vocation as the prototypical
representative of a new order of humanist scholarship and literary enterprise.
But the doubts always present in Petrarch's mind as to the moral legitimacy of
his humanist aspirations began at once to surface. Though the following years
(spent between the peace of Vaucluse and the diplomatic busyness of Naples,
Rome and various cities in the north of Italy) saw the continuation of the
Rerum memorandarum libri ('Books of Things to be Remembered') and the
inception of the *Bucolicum Carmen* or *Eclogues* (1346), they saw too the more
meditative undertaking represented by the *De vita solitaria* ('On the Solitary
Life') and the *De otio religioso* ('On Religious Ease') (Lent, 1346 and 1347
respectively). The same period (1342-53), which witnessed the catastrophic
plague of 1348 responsible for the deaths of some of Petrarch's closest friends
and, above all, of Laura, saw also the drafting and finalisation (possibly as late
as 1352 or 1353) of the *Secretum* ('My Secret'), a sustained act of self-
interrogation on the part of one repeatedly inclined to call into question the
principles of his moral and intellectual existence. The year 1350 saw, too,
Petrarch's first initiative – probably in response to the example of Cicero (in
1345 he had discovered Cicero's letters to Atticus, Quintus and Brutus in the
cathedral library at Verona) – in the collecting and ordering of his now ample
private and public correspondence, and of his *Rime* or *Rerum vulgarium
fragmenta*, or fragments in the vernacular as he came to call them, a process
which continued to the end of his life.

Following his final departure from Vaucluse in 1353, Petrarch established
himself at the court of Archbishop Giovanni Visconti in Milan, whence, often
on diplomatic business, he visited, among other places, Venice, Mantua,
Prague and Paris. This period saw the conception of his other main vernacular
work, the *Trionfi* ('Triumphs'), which occupied him until the final year of his
life. From 1362 to 1367, he lived principally in Venice, where in 1363 he
entertained Boccaccio as his guest. This is the period of the *Familiares*
('Familial') and *Seniles* ('Of Advanced Years') collections of letters (begun

before 1353), of the morally encyclopaedic *De remediis utriusque fortune* ('Remedies for Fortune both Good and Ill', 1354–65), and of the *De sui ipsius et aliorum multorum ignorantia* ('On his Own Ignorance and That of Many Besides', 1367), a work especially important for Petrarch's self-affirmation as a poet-philosopher in the classical and humanist tradition over and against the scholastic, and particularly the Averroist, tradition of the thirteenth and early fourteenth centuries. In 1370, he settled definitively at Arquà near Padua (he had a house built there on land given to him by Francesco da Carrara), where he continued working on his edition of the *Rime* and where he composed his autobiographical and confessional 'Letter to Posterity' ('Posteritati', *Seniles* XVIII, 1). He died on the night of 18 July 1374, and was buried at Arquà.

Cultural and moral context

Petrarch is the most monothematic of the great *trecentisti* in that, notwithstanding the varied occasion and inspiration of his successive works, each of them, from the discrete letters and poems which flow into the *Familiares*, *Seniles* and *Canzoniere* to the more extensive meditations on the moral and religious life, bears on the nucleus of concerns which dominated his existence as a whole. Petrarch himself was inclined to define and analyse these concerns in terms of the legitimacy or otherwise of his ambitions as a poet and lover – as a poet in the tradition of the great Latin *auctores* of antiquity, and as a lover of Laura inasmuch as she came to symbolise for him every kind of worldly desire and happiness, poetic and philological as well as erotic. More precisely he was inclined to define and analyse them in terms of the kind of psychological conflict engendered by a Neoplatonising metaphysic apt to cast doubt on the nobility of the flesh, by a Stoicising Christianity apt to question the worthiness of irrational passion and impetuosity and by a Pauline and Augustinian sense of the soul as divided against itself. Conscious of the call to be in God as the final cause of its activity as a creature of understanding and love, the wayward spirit nonetheless settles for a merely proximate end, for an idolatrous delight in the possibilities of the moment. Called, as Dante had put it in the *Paradiso* (I, 70), to a species of transhumanisation or spiritual self-surpassing, the recalcitrant soul settles instead for a tragic dissipation of spiritual energy. Thus, for example, the *Secretum*, having diagnosed the author's basic problem as a failure of the will, goes on to explore in terms of the seven deadly sins plus, in the third book, his inordinate love for Laura and his extravagant thirst for glory, each alike a trap for the indisciplined spirit – so too in the moral treatises, any number of his letters, and, in a melancholy vein at times shading off into the contrite, many of his *Rime*.

But the moral situation in Petrarch is more complicated than his own account of it suggests; for Petrarch, endowed certainly with a remarkable volatility and restlessness of character, witnessed, and indeed acted out at first hand, a cultural transition apt inevitably to bring him into conflict with himself. Quite apart from the data of personality, his circumstances were in themselves sufficient to ensure a crisis of self-interpretation. On the one hand, then, there is the Pauline and Augustinian part of his culture and formation which at every point calls into question the integrity of the will, which encourages a sense of the impossibility of justification short of a movement of grace, and which summons the soul to a systematic relegation of every mortal concern to the soul's eternal well-being. This aspect of Petrarch's temperament, greatly stimulated by his brother's enrolment as a Carthusian monk in 1343 and by the solitude of Vaucluse, emerges even in moments of the greatest humanist enthusiasm to challenge the legitimacy of his scholarly, poetic and amorous initiatives and, in doing so, to precipitate a mood of spiritual concern. On the other hand, there is the summons and the companionship of the classical poets and moralists (especially, among the latter, of Cicero and Seneca) calling the uncertain spirit to an act of self-affirmation – intellectual, moral and affective – here and now, this side of death. And the result of this counter-summons from antiquity to an act of self-affirmation here and now – of this impossible juxtaposition, within one and the same consciousness, of conflicting and ultimately irreducible world views – is a crisis of being everywhere discernible in Petrarch, a state of spiritual affliction apparent even in the most apparently assured of his literary formulas.

The *Canzoniere*

Petrarch's originality

Petrarch's poetry – and for the moment we are thinking primarily of the *Canzoniere* – is the poetry of ceaseless self-qualification. It is poetry marked at every point, both formally and substantially, by the subtlest – as well as, at times, by the most violent – forms of conceptual and expressive gradation and opposition. Thus the rising intensity and linear progression of the *stilnovo* sonnet give way in Petrarch to a species of reflexivity whereby the leading emphases of the poem are at once – in the very moment of their formulation – subject to interrogation and revision. The sustained momentum and insistent resolution of thought frequently characteristic of the Cavalcantian and Dantean *stilnovo* give way to a kind of critical self-reprise which vastly complicates the psychological texture of the poem and introduces into it a new rhythm and periodicity. Take, for example, the following poem from the mature phase of Dante's activity as a *stilnovista* (*Tanto gentile e tanto onesta pare* from Chapter XXVI of the *Vita Nuova*) and compare it with Petrarch's *In qual parte del ciel, in quale ydea* (*Canz.* CLIX):

Tanto gentile e tanto onesta pare
la donna mia quand'ella altrui saluta,
ch'ogne lingua deven tremando muta,
e li occhi no l'ardiscon di guardare.

Ella si va, sentendosi laudare,
benignamente d'umiltà vestuta;
e par che sia una cosa venuta
da cielo in terra a miracol mostrare.

Mostrasi sì piacente a chi la mira,
che dà per li occhi una dolcezza al core,
che 'ntender no la può chi no la prova:

e par che de la sua labbia si mova
un spirito soave pien d'amore,
che va dicendo a l'anima: Sospira.

(So noble and full of dignity my lady appears when she greets anyone that all tongues tremble and fall silent and eyes dare not look at her. She goes on her way, hearing herself praised, graciously clothed with humility; and seems a creature come down from heaven to earth to make the miraculous known.

She appears so beautiful to those who gaze at her that through the eyes she sends a sweetness into the heart such as none can understand but he who experiences it; and from her lips seems to come a spirit, gentle and full of love, that says to the soul: 'Sigh.')

In qual parte del ciel, in quale ydea
era l'exempio, onde Natura tolse
quel bel viso leggiadro, in ch'ella volse
mostrar qua giù quanto lassù potea?

Qual nimpha in fonti, in selve mai qual dea,
chiome d'oro sì fino a l'aura sciolse?
quando un cor tante in sé vertuti accolse?
benché la somma è di mia morte rea.

Per divina bellezza indarno mira
chi gli occhi de costei già mai non vide
come soavemente ella gli gira;

non sa come Amor sana, et come ancide,
chi non sa come dolce ella sospira,
et come dolce parla, et dolce ride.

(In what part of heaven, in what Idea was the pattern from which Nature copied that lovely face, in which she has shown down here all that she is capable of doing up there? What nymph in a fountain, in the woods what goddess ever loosed to the breeze locks of such fine gold? Whenever did a heart contain so many virtues? Though the sum of them is guilty of my death.

He looks in vain for divine beauty who never saw her eyes, how sweetly she turns them; he does not know how Love heals and how he kills, who does not know how sweetly she sighs and how sweetly she speaks and sweetly laughs.)

Thematically, technically, but above all in terms of psychological structure, the transition is absolute. On the one hand, there is the rapturous transcendentalism of the Dantean *stilnovo*, where the object of the poet's celebration is a *new* (in the sense of a miraculous, even messianic) presence in the historical order. On the other hand, there is the fraught psychologism of the Petrarchan sonnet, where the intuition of an ideal precipitates in one and the same moment a state of spiritual confusion and a sense of imminent demise. The uninterrupted progression of the Dantean sonnet from appearance ('tanto onesta pare') to the unspeakable bliss of disinterested celebration ('che va dicendo a l'anima: Sospira'), a progression which subsumes each successive emphasis in the rhythm and continuity of the whole, gives way in Petrarch to a sharp and even brutal reversal of thought and sensation as the poet registers the spiritual consequences of his own, no less rapturous intuition ('benché la somma è di mia morte rea'). And what follows, far from being an ecstatic resolution of the 'ideal' motif with which the poem begins (Laura as the perfect manifestation of an original Idea), takes the form of a circular meditation ('dolce ... dolce ... dolce') on the irony of love as a principle both of affirmation and of destruction, of being and of non-being ('come Amor sana, et come ancide'). Assurance, as the mood of the poet's utterance, gives way to uncertainty, and progression gives way to a more or less desperate sense of repetition, of unending sameness.

Composition and structure

Petrarch worked on the ordering of his poems in the *Canzoniere* right up until his death in July 1374, and there is no reason to suppose that the shape of the collection as contained in the Vatican Library manuscript V.L. 3195 (which witnesses to the state of the *Canzoniere* as Petrarch left it at his death and of which about a third is autograph) would have been definitive. Certain structural principles are evident in its composition – the poems divide into those composed before and after Laura's death, there are several anniversary poems pointing to a chronological interest in the overall arrangement, and there is a beginning and an end to the collection suggesting a process of moral evolution – but it is probable that Petrarch inserted and arranged poems according to his ever-changing perception of checks and balances in the work, of its thematic clusters and contrasts. The American scholar E. H. Wilkins has provided a painstaking, but even so still largely conjectural, account of the development of the collection based on manuscript evidence. An early grouping of the poems, contained in another Vatican Library manuscript (Chigi L.V. 176, which dates from 1359–62 and which has 215 of the final 366 poems making up the *Canzoniere* in its final form), suggests a process of organisation originating in the 1340s and based on chronological, thematic and metrical considerations. But, for all the available evidence (and a third manuscript, V.L. 3196, consists of fair copies and annotations in Petrarch's own hand dating from the mid-1330s), the earliest phases in the creation of the collection remain obscure. The later phases are more certain. In 1366 Petrarch engaged a copyist, Giovanni Malpaghini, to begin transcribing his poems into what is now Vatican Library V.L. 3195, and by April 1367, when Malpaghini resigned this task, he (Malpaghini) had copied out 244 poems, whereupon Petrarch himself continued the work right up until the last months of his life. By this time, indeed by the time of Malpaghini's departure, Petrarch had settled on the title *Francisci Petrarche laureati poete Rerum vulgarium fragmenta* for his collection ('Occasional Pieces in the Vernacular by Francis Petrarch Poet Laureate'), and here again indications in the manuscripts confirm details of chronology and intended organisation. Even so, several issues – such as the date of the prologue poem *Voi ch'ascoltate in rime sparse il suono* ('You who hear in scattered rhymes the sound') or when exactly Petrarch settled on the primary twofold division of the poems before and after the death of Laura – remain a matter for conjecture, a situation only complicated, in the absence of firm manuscript evidence, by recourse (useful as it sometimes is) to parallel texts outside the *Canzoniere*.

The *Canzoniere* consists of 366 poems made up of sonnets (317), *canzoni* (29), *sestine* (9), ballads (7) and madrigals (4). The vast majority of these poems concern Laura and the vicissitudes of Petrarch's love for her. Prominent among the poems of other than amorous inspiration is the political *canzone Italia mia* ('My Italy', CXXVIII), an indictment of Bavarian (i.e. mercenary) treachery ('bavarico inganno', line 66) in respect of Italy's 'fair land' (line 18). With this may be grouped the *canzone* addressed to Giacomo Colonna on the occasion of the 1333 crusade against Islam (XXVIII) and Petrarch's hymn to Rome as the city most favoured by Fortune but, alas, the most destitute now of modern champions (LIII), which probably belongs to the occasion of his first visit there in 1337. Another group of poems, including most conspicuously *Una donna più bella assai che 'l sole* ('A lady more beautiful by far than the sun', CXIX), conceived in the wake of Petrarch's crowning as poet laureate in April 1341), concerns poets and poetry. Notable here is the sonnet *S'i' fussi stato fermo a la spelunca* ('If I had stayed in the cave', CLXVI), with its expression of the aridity of Petrarch's inspiration in the vernacular, together with XCII (on the death of Cino da Pistoia in 1336) and CCLXXXVII (on the death of Sennuccio del Bene, another poet friend of Petrarch's, in 1349), each an act of literary acknowledgement. Other poems in the non-amorous sector of the *Canzoniere* include the moral meditation of VII on the exile of philosophy in Petrarch's generation, and a number of correspondence poems, including a sonnet addressed (probably) to the Carthusians of Montrieux in the wake of a visit there (CXXXIX).

But by far the majority of the poems in the *Canzoniere* are erotic in inspiration. They set out to explore the patterns of thought and emotion generated by Petrarch's love for Laura, the subjective or psychological aspect of this love figuring, within the economy of the whole, altogether more prominently than its objective or descriptive aspect, than the figure of Laura herself. This main body of amorous poems both does and does not have a formal structure and development. It *does* have a formal structure in the sense, first, that the collection as a whole is prefaced by an introductory sonnet which, in the manner of an epilogue rather than of a proemium proper, sets the experience of the whole within the perspective of age and of maturity; and secondly, it has a conclusion which appears to mark the resolution of its accumulated uncertainty and anguish. Straightaway, then, in the opening poem, the reader is called into an attitude of understanding and compassion in respect of an order of experience now superseded in its vanity and plaintiveness by wisdom, repentance, and a sense of the illusive character of mortal joy:

> Voi ch'ascoltate in rime sparse il suono
> di quei sospiri ond'io nudriva 'l core
> in sul mio primo giovenile errore
> quand'era in parte altr'uom da quel ch'i' sono,
>
> del vario stile in ch'io piango et ragiono
> fra le vane speranze e 'l van dolore,
> ove sia chi per prova intenda amore,
> spero trovar pietà, non che perdono.
>
> Ma ben veggio or sì come al popol tutto
> favola fui gran tempo, onde sovente
> di me medesmo meco mi vergogno;
>
> et del mio vaneggiar vergogna è 'l frutto,
> e 'l pentersi, e 'l conoscer chiaramente
> che quanto piace al mondo è breve sogno.

(1)

(You who hear in scattered rhymes the sound of those sighs with which I nourished my heart during my first youthful error, when I was in part another man from what I am now; for the varied style in which I weep and speak between vain hopes and vain sorrow, where there is anyone who understands love through experience, I hope to find, not only pardon, but pity.

But now I see well how for a long time I was the talk of the crowd, for which I am often ashamed of myself within; and of my raving shame is the fruit, and repentance, and the clear knowledge that whatever pleases in the world is a brief dream.)

And these – vanity, repentance and the sense of an obsession lived out over the years in an attitude of perverse wilfulness – are the leading emphases of the concluding plea to the Virgin, now at last established at the centre of the soul's desire:

> Vergine, in cui ò tutta mia speranza
> che possi et vogli al gran bisogno aitarme,
> non mi lasciare in su l'extremo passo.

Non guardar me, ma Chi degnò crearme;
no 'l mio valor, ma l'altra Sua sembianza,
ch'è in me, ti mova a curar d'uom sì basso.
Medusa et l'error mio m'àn fatto un sasso
d'umor vano stillante:
Vergine, tu di sante
lagrime et pie adempi 'l meo cor lasso,
ch'almen l'ultimo pianto sia devoto,
senza terrestro limo,
come fu 'l primo non d'insania voto.

(CCCLXVI, 105–17)

(Virgin in whom I have put all my hopes that you will be able, and will wish to help me in my great need; do not leave me at the last pass; do not consider me, but Him who deigned to create me; let not my worth but His high likeness that is in me move you to help one so low. Medusa and my error have made me a stone dripping vain moisture. Virgin, fill my weary heart with holy, repentant tears; let at least my last weeping be devout and without earthly mud, as was my first vow, before my insania.)

First part

Thus the whole experience of the *Canzoniere* is circumscribed, in Petrarch's presentation of it, by his first infatuation with Laura on Good Friday, 1327 (III) – its *terminus a quo* – and by the redirection of spiritual energy represented by his turning to the Virgin in the twilight of his years, its *terminus ad quem*. Between these two points, and constituting the next most important principle as far as the structure of the *Canzoniere* is concerned, comes the division of the collection into before and after her death, with its implications for the substance and psychology of the love song. Of the poems in the first part of the *Canzoniere*, the first six are in the nature of an exposition. Petrarch establishes the time, the place and the mood of his first encounter with Laura. In what follows, each aspect of this experience – its joy, pain, hope and disappointment – is developed in terms of a dialectical relationship with its opposite, pleasure shading off into pain, anticipation into remorse, hope into disillusionment and exultation into guilt. Among the many recurrent themes and psychological motifs to emerge more or less insistently in this part of the collection are those of Petrarch's sense of captivity and yearning for deliverance, his deepening sense of isolation and wretchedness, and an increasingly desperate sense of the passage of time and of his own ebbing, but unfulfilled, mortality, all qualified (at times simultaneously) by intuitions of bliss, by the fluctuations of sensuousness and even, occasionally, by a kind of humorous self-mockery. This, above all, is the poetry of restlessness, of a progressively urgent search for the kind of peace contingent on the freeing of the soul from its obsessive concern with Laura. Exemplary in this respect is the opening stanza from the exquisite canzone *Di pensier in pensier, di monte in monte* ('From thought to thought, from mountain to mountain', CXXIX), where a sense of the soul's victimisation by love – in truth, of its amorous *self*-victimisation – issues in an unclouded expression of existential confusion ('this man is burning and of his state is uncertain'):

> Di pensier in pensier, di monte in monte
> mi guida Amor, ch'ogni segnato calle
> provo contrario a la tranquilla vita.
> Se 'n solitaria piaggia, rivo o fonte,
> se 'nfra duo poggi siede ombrosa valle,
> ivi s'acqueta l'alma sbigottita;
> et come Amor l'envita,
> or ride, or piange, or teme, or s'assecura;
> e 'l volto che lei segue ov'ella il mena
> si turba et rasserena,
> et in un esser picciol tempo dura;
> onde a la vista huom di tal vita experto
> diria: Questo arde, et di suo stato è incerto.

(CXXIX, 1–13)

(From thought to thought, from mountain to mountain, Love guides me; for I find every trodden path to be contrary to a tranquil life. If there is on some solitary slope a river or spring, or between two peaks a shady valley, there my frightened soul is quieted; and, as Love leads it on, now it laughs, now weeps, now fears, now is confident; and my face, which follows wherever my soul leads, is clouded and made clear again, and remains but a short time in any one state; and at the sight anyone who had experienced such a life would say: 'This man is burning [with love] and of his state is uncertain.')

By this time, the penitential element lurking beneath the surface of Petrarch's discourse, and emerging explicitly in poems such as the sonnet *Padre del ciel* ('Father in heaven', LXII), has itself become a dominant theme of the collection, and confirms in its prominence the parallel meditation of the famous Mont Ventoux letter (self-dated April 1336 but finalised possibly as late as 1352), with its sense of misdirected spiritual energy. Even so, from this point on in Petrarch's celebration of Laura as the historical manifestation of the proto-typical Idea (see again CLIX, quoted above), there is a growing sense of the spirit as suffering and as standing in need of redemption. And with this, the psychological analysis becomes ever more searching and acute. Torn as he is between loving and non-loving, between existing for Laura and struggling to be free from her, Petrarch stands somehow over and against himself, in a state of self-estrangement characterised alternately by rebellion and by resignation. Some poems, it is true, maintain the celebratory mood, but the general drift of Petrarch's argument, or rather its deep but progressively explicit state of mind, is that of conflict and self-interrogation.

Second part

Conflict and self-interrogation are again leading features of the second part of the *Canzoniere*, inaugurated by the sustained confessionalism – of recognisably Pauline and Augustinian provenance – of the *canzone I' vo pensando* ('I go thinking', CCLXIV). This is a study in the divided self, in the predicament of the one who both wills and does not will his own well-being. The final line of the poem, which neatly fuses classical and Christian motifs – the Ovidian 'I see and approve the better but follow the worse' (*Metam.* VII, 20–1) and the Pauline 'for what I would do, that I do not, but what I hate, that I do' (Romans 7:15) – expresses precisely the situation of the soul lost to itself and powerless to embrace its own highest good: 'et veggio 'l meglio, et al peggior m'appiglio' ('I see the better and embrace the worse'). But Laura's death, though by no means resolving the existential conflict at the root of his being, at least engenders a new possibility, that of seeing her henceforth as a principle of salvation, as a means of lifting the soul from its carnality. Bit by bit, then – though the process is by no means linear or uninterrupted – Laura is perceived by Petrarch as being at work redemptively in his experience. Miraculously present to him (and there are several visitation or apparition poems in this second part of the *Canzoniere*), she is at work as one who admonishes and guides, as one who identifies with the suffering spirit in its struggle for liberation and decisiveness. An example is CCLXXXV, where Laura's companionship as a lover is at the same time that of a mother and a wife:

> Né mai pietosa madre al caro figlio
> né donna accesa al suo sposo dilecto
> die' con tanti sospir, con tal sospetto
> in dubbio stato sì fedel consiglio,
>
> come a me quella che 'l mio grave exiglio
> mirando dal suo eterno alto ricetto,
> spesso a me torna co l'usato affecto,
> et di doppia pietate ornata il ciglio:
>
> or di madre, or d'amante; or teme, or arde
> d'onesto foco; et nel parlar mi mostra
> quel che 'n questo viaggio fugga o segua,
>
> contando i casi de la vita nostra,
> pregando ch'a levar l'alma non tarde:
> et sol quant'ella parla, ò pace e tregua.

(Never did a pitying mother to her dear son or a loving wife to her beloved husband give with so many sighs, with such anxiety, such faithful counsel in a perilous time, as she gives to me, who, seeing from her eternal home my heavy exile, often returns to me with her usual affection and with her brow adorned with double pity, now that of a mother, now that of a lover. Now she fears, now she burns with virtuous fire; and in her speech she shows me what in this journey I must avoid or pursue, telling over the events of our life, begging me not to delay in lifting up my soul. And only while she speaks do I have peace, or at least a truce.)

Other poems too (CCCLIX, for example, or CCCLXII) confirm the notion of Laura, in death, as a guide and intercessor for the lost and perplexed spirit, but the problem of Petrarch's love for her – to be interpreted, as we have said, in terms not simply of a conflict between the rational and the sensitive soul, but of a clash of two world views, of the Stoic sense of affirmation in and through self and the Christian sense of affirmation in and through God – is not itself open to solution in terms simply of a redefinition of Laura and of her function in the experience of Petrarch as her lover. The situation is too complex for this, and the ambiguities of the Laura theme too stubborn and deeply rooted. The final phase of the *Canzoniere*, therefore, offers an altogether more drastic solution as Petrarch confesses the guilt of his obsession with Laura and turns repentantly, in a mood of specifically Christian piety, to the Virgin. The final poem of the collection, *Vergine bella* ('Beautiful Virgin'), is a plea for com-passion on the part of a spirit hopelessly lost in the twisted byways ('torta via') of its sorrowful existence. Liturgical in its repetitive, almost formulaic structure and at times psalmic in imagery, the *canzone* is as fiercely self-critical as anything Petrarch ever wrote. From the beginning, he says, he has been waylaid by his own folly, and has brought upon himself his own wretchedness. Laura, recast now as Medusa (line 111), has been a principle, not of renewal and elevation, but of spiritual paralysis. His mood is contrite, and in the face of a mortal span now quickly nearing its end, Petrarch bids the Virgin intercede in favour of a peaceful homecoming:

> Il dì s'appressa, et non pote esser lunge,
> sì corre il tempo et vola,
> Vergine unica et sola,
> e 'l cor or conscientia or morte punge.
> Raccomandami al tuo figliuol, verace
> homo et verace Dio,
> ch'accolga 'l mio spirito ultimo in pace.

(CCCLXVI, 131–7)

(The day draws near and cannot be far, time so runs and flies, single, sole Virgin; and now conscience, now death pierces my heart; commend me to your Son, true man and true God, that He may receive my last breath in peace.)

But if the *Canzoniere* does in this sense have a 'story' – a more or less discernible spiritual progression culminating in an act of Christian confession – it is a story all but subsumed in the circularity of its leading emphases. The 'twisted byways' and 'prayer to the Virgin' motifs of the final *canzone* recall clearly enough the infernal–paradisal progression of the *Commedia*; but where the 'story' of the *Commedia* is one of progressive self-transcendence through a simultaneous presence in the pilgrim spirit of human and divine willing, the *Canzoniere*, for all its final turning of the soul to Mary, is a study in the psychology of obsession, a psychology not so much resolved as confirmed by its closing formula. In both parts of the collection, both before and after the death of Laura, each successive proposition is qualified by its opposite, and each successive emphasis shades off into, or else is starkly countered by, its antithesis.

Technical virtuosity

It is here, in relation to the endless process of spiritual self-qualification in Petrarch, that we discern most clearly the leading features of his craftsmanship as a poet, for Petrarch's is the art, precisely, of technical graduation and contrast, of spiritual articulation in and through the reflexiveness of form. Metrically, he exploits the essentially binary structure of the *canzone* stanza and of the sonnet for the purposes of a more or less drastic, and frequently ironic, inflection of the argument. The principal division generated by the *canzone*-stanza and sonnet form occurs between the *frons* (in the sonnet, the quatrains) and the *sirima* (in the sonnet, the tercets), and it is at this point that, in keeping with the reader's expectation, Petrarch will frequently introduce his leading discursive inflection; so, for example, the first sonnet (*Voi ch'ascoltate in rime sparse il suono*, quoted above), with its adversative 'Ma' ('But') at line 9. Quite as often, however, he will counter expectation, and thus reinforce the change of direction, by advancing or retarding the antithetical moment of his argument, as, for example, in the sonnet *In qual parte del ciel*, also quoted above, where the about-turn of line 8 ('benché la somma è di mia morte rea', 'though the sum of them is guilty of my death') unexpectedly disrupts the more normal discursive pattern of the sonnet. Elsewhere, as, for example, in xxxv (*Solo et pensoso i più deserti campi*, 'Alone and filled with care the most deserted fields'), the antithetical inflection is delayed until the last tercet. In each case, form, far from constraining thought or imposing upon it aesthetically, confirms it in its basic angularity, its tendency to proceed in terms of thematic shifts and polarities.

The same responsiveness of form to the endlessly shifting patterns of thought and emotion is evident at the metrical level of the poem, where the hendecasyllable (*endecasillabo*) in particular – the *superbissimum carmen*, as Dante had called it (*DVE* ii, v, 8), of Italian vernacular verse – is subject to constant rhythmic variation. The main stresses in the hendecasyllable fall on the sixth and the tenth (or penultimate) syllable of the line. A caesura after the fourth syllable produces a hendecasyllable *a minore* (the first block is smaller than the second), while a caesura after the sixth syllable gives a hendecasyllable *a maiore* (the first block is larger than the second). Thus the first line of the sonnet *Voi ch'ascoltate*, quoted above, is a regular hendecasyllable *a minore* ('Voi ch'ascoltate / in ríme sparse il suóno'), while the last line is a regular hendecasyllable *a maiore* ('che quanto piace al móndo / è breve sógno'). Also, an additional stress falls on one or other of the even syllables in the line (in *Voi*

ch'ascoltate on the eighth syllable of line 1 – 'spárse' – and on the fourth
syllable of line 14 – 'piáce'), or else on the seventh syllable of an *a minore* line
('del vario stile / in ch'io piángo et ragiono') or the third syllable of an *a maiore*
line ('fra le váne speranze / e 'l van dolore'). But these basic provisions are
subject in Petrarch to infinite experimentation in pursuit of rhythmic variety, a
variety achieved sometimes by simply multiplying the number of words in the
line (a practice which militates against the notion of three canonical stresses),
sometimes through synaeresis (the metrical elision of contiguous vowels within
a word) and sometimes through synaloephe (the metrical elision of vowels
between words) – a feature which, as in the case of the opening line of
Voi ch'ascoltate, can diminish the force of the caesura ('Voi ch'ascoltáte^in
ríme spárse il suóno'). Indeed, a truer metrical representation of this line,
taking into account the secondary stress on syllable 1, the synaloepha which
interrupts the primary caesura at syllable 5 and the secondary caesura which
interrupts the synaloepha at syllable 9, would be as follows: 'Vói ch'ascoltáte
/ ^in ríme spárse / ^il suóno' – something which, on the very threshold of the
Canzoniere, points up the freedom and accomplishment with which Petrarch
handles rhythm within the established patterns of the hendecasyllable.

Lexically and acoustically, Petrarch develops the selective vocabulary of the
stilnovo in keeping both with his more ample appeal to the lexicon of the
Provençal poets (and, as far as Dante is concerned, the *rime petrose*, for which
see above, p. 46), and also with his heightened sense of contrastive sound
texture. For example, in *Voi ch'ascoltate* we have 'Voi', 'ascoltate', 'core',
'errore', 'dolore', 'vergogno', 'sogno' and '*v*ane', '*v*an', '*o*ve', 'pro*v*a', '*v*eggio',
'*v*aneggiar'). Near-synonyms or semantic clusters designed to give expression
to the endless inflection of his leading emphases abound: 'affanni' (distress),
'doglia' and 'dolore' (pain), 'fatiche' (labours), 'stanchezza' (tiredness); and
alliteration at every point reinforces the semantic substance and the mutual
invocation of terms (in *Voi ch'ascoltate* at line 12: 'et del mio *v*aneggiar
*v*ergogna è 'l frutto'). At the same time, a certain exclusiveness and tendency
towards the generic in respect of vocabulary confirms the fundamental
atemporality and abstraction of Petrarch's meditation in the *Canzoniere*,
preserving it – except on rare and calculated occasions – from the merely
anecdotal.

Syntactically, Petrarch pursues the thought and mood of the poem as a
whole by means of a (for the most part) gentle linguistic 'consequentialism' –
the kind of consequentialism secured by such connectives as 'onde' ('whence'),
'quando' ('when'), 'ove', ('where'), 'come' ('as'), 'overo' ('or else'), 'ché'
('because'), 'però' (in the sense of 'therefore') and 'se non che' ('except that') as
well as by the frequently concatenated 'e' ('and'). True, dramatic reversals are
not lacking, both within poems and between them. But especially persuasive in
Petrarch is the kind of technical and expressive chromaticism in which one
emphasis shades off well-nigh imperceptibly into another, modifying it as
much tonally as substantially; so, for example, in *Voi ch'ascoltate*, the move-

ment from apostrophe (line 1) to apothegm (line 14) by way of a discreet linking of clauses designed to elucidate the complexities of Petrarch's situation in a manner entirely unfussed by syntactical difficulty. Syntactical difficulty, as cultivated at key points in his tradition by Arnaut Daniel, Guittone and Dante in the *petrose* is, again with the occasional calculated exception, resolved in a gracious flow of delicately subversive periods.

Rhetorically, Petrarch deploys, with the greatest finesse and sense of responsibility, the figures of speech and thought most apt to guarantee the subtleties of his discourse. Of these, particularly prominent are the contrastive devices of oxymoron and antithesis, and the repetitive devices of synonym and polysyndeton. Each in its way serves to differentiate and to intensify the leading propositions of Petrarch's argument; so, for example, the oxymoron of CCV, the exasperated 'dolci ire', 'dolci sdegni', 'dolce mal', 'dolce affanno' and 'dolce amaro' ('sweet angers', 'sweet disdains', 'sweet evil', 'sweet grief' and 'sweet bitterness'), and the antithesis of the first quatrain of CCXV with its play on the polarities of nobility and humility, sophistication and purity, age and youth, and gravity and joy ('nobil sangue ... vita humile', 'alto intellecto ... puro core', 'frutto senile ... giovenil fiore', 'aspetto pensoso ... anima lieta'). Notable too is the polysyndeton of LXI with its feverish 'and ... and ... and': 'Benedetto sia 'l giorno, e 'l mese, et l'anno, / et la stagione, e 'l tempo, et l'ora, e 'l punto ...' ('Blessed be the day, and the month, and the year, / and the season, and the time, and the hour, and the moment ...'), as well as the synecdoche, the metonymy and (especially) the metaphor which throughout confirm and maintain the complexity of Petrarch's moral and emotional sensibility, the firmness, and yet at the same time the elusiveness, of the meanings he seeks to establish.

Characteristic too of Petrarch's style in the *Canzoniere* is its ample recourse to the texts central to his humanistic and vernacular-literary culture. Throughout the collection, motifs derived from the classical sector of his learning – from (among others) Virgil's *Eclogues*, *Georgics* and *Aeneid*, Ovid's *Metamorphoses* and *Ars amatoria*, Horace's *Odes*, and Statius' *Thebaid* and *Achilleid* – are interwoven, often with the subtlest kind of allusion and rhythmic dexterity, with scriptural motifs and reminiscences of Petrarch's Provençal, Siculo-Tuscan and *stilnovo* tradition. His poetry testifies in this sense not only to a secure possession both of the classical and of the vernacular literary traditions in which he stands, but also, as far as the classical tradition in particular is concerned, to a characteristically humanist, and theologically unprejudiced, delight in the encounter in and for itself. But – and this is where the formalities of the *Canzoniere* refer back, as they always do in Petrarch, to its thematic concerns – the humanist encounter with antiquity is for him a matter not primarily of aesthetic concern (though it is that too), but of existential concern. It is in and through the text, as subject to a kind of re-enactment in conscience, that he seeks to define the shape and substance of his own problematic being. This process of self-definition in and through the text is everywhere discernible in his work. At every stage of his experience as a poet and moralist, the authors and texts he takes most to heart are there as companions in the search for a properly structured and intelligible humanity: Cicero's letters, orations and *De officiis* and Seneca's *Epistolae* as models of public self-affirmation; the *Aeneid* as a model of Roman epic grandeur and magnanimity; the *Metamorphoses* as an exploration (especially in the myth of Daphne and Apollo) of changeability and elusiveness; Augustine's *Confessions* as a model of anxious spiritual pilgrimage. These especially are ever present to him as an invitation and guide to self-elucidation, all of which lends to the drama of the *Canzoniere* an exquisitely literary patina, an unmistakable (but not on this account disingenuous) *letterarietà*.

The *Trionfi*

The *Trionfi*, Petrarch's other main work in the vernacular, is problematic in a different sense, for here it is a question not merely of the basic, and basically unresolved, existential crisis at the root of Petrarch's experience as a lover and poet, but of the adequacy of his text, in its precise imaginative and technical conception, significantly to meet this crisis. This, certainly, was Petrarch's aim in the work: to resolve the recurrent questions of his troubled conscience (questions of time and eternity, mortality and immortality, and human glory) in a fresh form, by means of an alternative poetic structure. Like the *Rime*, but more systematically, the *Trionfi* (which Petrarch began probably in the early 1350s and with which he was still occupied as late as January 1374) was to be an exercise in moral elucidation, an attempt to integrate one with another the various, and for the most part conflicting, forces at work within him. But implicit in the project from the outset were the seeds of its non-viability, of its insufficiency to solve the kinds of problem it was called upon to solve; for Petrarch's genius lay not so much in systematic resolution as in the projection of discrete states of mind and dispositions, a state of affairs to which the *Canzoniere* answered with perfect precision, but to which the *Trionfi*, with its eminently Dantean structure (but lack of Dantean economy), remains indifferent. The result is an order of poetry which, while bearing about it a characteristically Petrarchan sense of moral commitment, betrays in its formal conception the most authentic features of the poet's analytical and expressive temperament.

The structure and narrative line of the poem are straightforward enough. Caught up in a vision in which he enjoys the services of an unidentified guide, Petrarch witnesses a series of triumphs or victorious pageants. The first is that of Love, in the course of which he sees and speaks with the endless victims of amorous obsession, including at one point (I, iv, 31ff.) Dante, Cino, Guittone and other representatives of the Sicilian, Tuscan and *stilnovo* schools of lyric poetry. Then, in more or less quick succession, come the triumphs of Chastity,

Death, Fame, Time and Eternity, where again the Petrarch character at the centre of the *Trionfi*, like the Dante character at the centre of the *Commedia*, hears and interrogates those he meets along the way. Throughout Laura is celebrated as a model of purity in love, as one transfigured by death and as a principle of the poet's salvation. Some of the *Trionfi* are divided, like the *Commedia*, into cantos (the 'Triumph of Love' is in four parts, the 'Triumph of Death' in two, and the 'Triumph of Fame' in three); and, like the *Canzoniere*, the work as a whole reflects Petrarch's humanist learning as well as his responsiveness to a number of vernacular sources (possibly including, in addition to Dante's *Commedia*, the *Amorosa visione* of Boccaccio and the *Roman de la rose* of Guillaume de Lorris and Jean de Meung). Only a small part of the work (passages from the Triumphs of Love and Eternity) has come down in autograph manuscript (V.L. 3196 in the Vatican Library).

The characteristic strategies and sonorities of the Petrarchan line are everywhere in evidence in the *Trionfi*, and the metrical form of the poem (Dantean *terza rima*), however much of a constraint in other respects, encourages in its cyclic structure the use of anaphora and other kinds of repetitive device. The lexis and tonality of the poem is frequently, and at times exquisitely, Petrarchan; so, for example, this tercet from the Triumph of Love:

> le chiome accolte in oro e sparse al vento,
> gli occhi, ch'accesi d'un celeste lume
> m'infiamman sì ch' i' son d'arder contento!

> (I, iii, 136–8)

(her tresses gathered in gold and loosed to the wind, and her eyes which, lit up with a heavenly light, enflame me such that I am content to burn!)

Or this from the 'Triumph of Death':

> che' vostri dolci sdegni e le dolci ire,
> le dolci paci ne' belli occhi scritte,
> tenner molti anni in dubbio il mio desire.

> (III, ii, 82–4)

(for the sweet disdain, the sweet reproaches and the sweet peace written in your beautiful eyes held my desire for many years in uncertainty.)

But the need to maintain a narrative line and to sustain the forward momentum of the *terza rima* in which it is developed, not to mention the poem's self-consciously Dantean sense of eschatological drama, impinge throughout the *Trionfi* to disturb, and in the end to destroy, the non-progressive form of the properly Petrarchan meditation. The reiterative pattern of thought and expression discernible in the more reflective moments of the work is by and large taken up in a kind of argumentative relentlessness apt to drown the meditative in the moral; so, for example, these lines from the 'Triumph of Death':

> O ciechi, e 'l tanto affaticar che giova?
> Tutti tornate a la gran madre antica,
> e 'l vostro nome a pena si ritrova.
>   Pur de le mill'è un'utile fatica,
> che non sian tutte vanità palesi?
> Chi intende a' vostri studii sì mel dica.

(III, i, 88–93)

(O blind souls, what is the point of all this labouring? You all return to the great mother of old and your names are hardly remembered. Is there one profitable labour among your thousand such that all are not overt vanity? Let the one all-intent on your business thus confess himself to me.)

This does not mean that the moralism of the *Trionfi* is not itself authentically Petrarchan. On the contrary, arising as it does from the perpetual crisis at the centre of Petrarch's existence, it represents yet a further, heroic attempt to assuage that crisis and to enable the poet to discover an inner peace. Rather, it fatally upsets the meditative stillness, the constant recapitulation and the delicate inflection of mood and emphasis, which mark the most characteristic and the most compelling of Petrarch's utterances. The 'horizontal' movement of thought and argumentation which in Dante complements the 'verticality' or depth of his intuition is, in Petrarch, achieved at the expense of this verticality – for which reason the *Trionfi*, for all the grandeur of its general conception, remains marginal to his poetic production in the vernacular.

Latin works

Petrarch's Latin works (see also below pp. 132–5) enter into the history of Italian literature in two ways. First, they help to develop and sustain the kind of classicism (verifiable especially on the imaginative and lexical plane) which renders the poetic language of the *stilnovisti* subject, in the *Canzoniere*, to renewal; and secondly, they elaborate, in a kind of parallel meditation, the central concerns of the *Rime*, exploring and unfolding them sometimes in the quietist manner of the Christian recluse and sometimes in the domestic-epistolary (but always self-consciously literary) manner of the Stoic moralist and confidant. Especially important, for the first of these, are the incomplete *Africa*, begun probably in 1338 and published posthumously in nine books (but with a number of lacunae) in 1396 by Pier Paulo Vergerio; the *Epistolae metricae*, a collection of sixty-six letters in hexameters dating from 1331 onwards and dedicated to Petrarch's friend Marco Barbato di Sulmona; and the *Bucolicum carmen*, a collection of twelve Latin eclogues conceived in 1346. Each of these works testifies to the strength of Petrarch's ambition as a humanist scholar and poet in the years up until 1350 or thereabouts, and each witnesses to the extraordinary depth and tenacity of his apprenticeship as a literary technician in the manner of (especially) Virgil. But it is their confessional aspect which links them with the other main group of texts most obviously representative of Petrarch as a Latinist: the *Secretum*, the *De vita solitaria* and the *De otio religioso*, and with the various collections of Petrarch's letters. Each of these constitutes in its way an interpretative key to the *Canzoniere*, for each explores, more or less systematically, one or other of Petrarch's concerns in the vernacular poems: the idea of an existence uncluttered by ambition and by irrational passion, a life of spiritual calm dedicated to the pursuit of classical and Christian wisdom; and an ideal unity of understanding and willing in respect of the diverse possibilities for human beings in time and eternity. This, at any rate, is the ideal proposed by the *De vita solitaria* and by the *De otio religioso*, while the *Secretum* and the letters explore the same kind of themes in the more dramatic context of moral self-confrontation and – as far as many of the *Familiares* are concerned – in the more domestic context of Petrarch's minutely documented day-to-day existence.

Other works of importance in this sector include two historical compilations (the *De viris illustribus*, begun in the late 1330s, and the *Rerum memorandarum libri* of the mid 1340s); a vast moral compendium, conceived in the form of a series of dialogues, on prosperity and adversity (*De remediis utriusque fortune*, dating from the mid 1350s); a series of invectives and polemical pieces, including especially the *De sui ipsius et aliorum multorum ignorantia* (1367), an act of self-vindication in respect of the – as far as Petrarch was concerned – alien and hostile spirituality of late medieval radical Aristotelianism; and the *Posteritati* or *Letter to Posterity* (c. 1370), grouped by Petrarch with the *Seniles* collection of letters (XVIII, 1) but constituting in an altogether unique fashion, and in a manner designed to engage the sympathy of generations to come, a final *apologia pro vita sua*.

7

Minor writers

Steven Botterill

The literary culture of the Trecento

The glittering light of the *tre corone* has traditionally left the rest of Trecento literature in its shadow. Few of the scholars who have pored so minutely over the voluminous texts of Dante, Petrarch and Boccaccio have spared more than a glance for the work of the canonical threesome's contemporaries. Even Natalino Sapegno's magisterial *Storia letteraria del Trecento* – still the best short introduction, though sadly never translated into English – is typical in devoting barely sixty (of over four hundred) pages to 'la letteratura dei minori'. Minor the other writers of the Trecento may be in comparison with the three great Florentines – most writers are – but, for all that, their work offers a richly varied range of literary responses to a historical and cultural situation, that of the Italian peninsula between about 1300 and about 1400, which is itself of unusual interest.

The approach to Italian literature in terms of the relationship between history and geography, pioneered by Carlo Dionisotti, is especially valuable for students of the fourteenth century. In this period none of the convenient shorthand of literary and cultural history – 'Italy', 'Italian', 'author', 'text', even 'literature' – has enough validity to pass unchallenged. The Italian peninsula in the Trecento, as Dante, Petrarch, and others lamented, enjoyed neither political nor linguistic unity; instead, many relatively small and congenitally hostile administrative units, practising disparate political systems and speaking numerous related but often mutually incomprehensible languages, occupied the region that, centuries later and through processes unthinkable to late medieval intellectuals, was to become the united nation with its standardised national language that we know today. When dealing with the fourteenth century, it often makes more sense to think of both Italy's language and its literature in the plural: to see distinct but equally valid forms of what was later to become *the* Italian language generating, in different social settings and geographical locations, texts of many kinds, some of which would qualify as 'literature' in later definitions, but many, perhaps most, of which would not.

Even at this early stage, however, some familiar cultural developments are prefigured in Trecento Italy. Several perennially active centres of literary and artistic production are already recognisable: Florence above all, but also

Rome, Naples, Milan and (though scarcely yet making an important contribution to specifically *literary* history) Venice. Some kinds of writing – lyric poetry, spiritual and devotional prose – are practised on a level of achievement that is the equal of any attested since; others – historical writing, literary criticism, narrative verse, prose fiction – are only beginning to appear in the vernacular, laying the foundations on which later texts will build. Perhaps most significant, the literary activity of the Italian Trecento is already characterised by a lively interest in the theory and practice of the language which is its medium. Trecento texts are often marked by a sense of audacious linguistic experimentation, and they are, by and large, highly self-conscious of their own historical status as belonging to an almost entirely new branch of discursive practice: writing in Italian.

The whole century, in fact, is pervaded by the urgent debate – started by Dante's *De vulgari eloquentia* – on the origins, nature, and usage of the Italian language(s); on the role and status of the vernacular (vis-à-vis the Latin that continued to be employed and accorded greater prestige in government, education and the Church); on the relative status of Tuscan and other brands of 'Italian' (in 1332 the Paduan judge Antonio da Tempo's *Summa artis rithimici* already concedes that 'the Tuscan language is better suited to letters and literature than any other', but many Trecento writers disagreed); and on the obligations and opportunities that devolved upon individual writers faced with the practices and conventions of a fundamentally bilingual – or multilingual – culture. To write in 'Italian' is never, in the fourteenth century, a straightforward or uninflected option, and vernacular texts must always be seen in their relations (which vary, of course, according to factors like authorship, genre and audiences actual and implied) with a long-standing, internationally practised, institutionally supported, and culturally dominant tradition of writing in Latin.

It may be true that the anxieties and ambiguities inherent in this linguistic climate presented themselves with the greatest acuity to the greatest writers – Dante, Petrarch, and Boccaccio were all haunted by questions of the definition of literary language and its appropriateness to particular styles and genres, and each dealt with them in his own more or less idiosyncratic way – but it should never be forgotten that the simple fact of a text's existence in some form of the vernacular always implies, in the Italian Trecento, its emergence from a complicated situation in which issues of linguistic practice, authorial intention, readers' expectations, social standing, institutional affiliation, generic convention, educational background, and even writers' and readers' gender are inextricably intertwined. It follows that any attempt to provide an adequate overview of the literary history of this fascinating century will fail, if *literary* history is all that it provides.

Even the Trecento itself, as a historiographical concept in the study of Italian culture, is open to challenge. Like many another century, it refuses to conform to the tyranny of the calendar and begin exactly on time, or indeed to wrap itself neatly up at the chronologically suitable moment for the next century to begin. Authors who seem, with hindsight, overwhelmingly representative of the Duecento cheerfully survive into the fourteenth century without significantly changing their approach: Cino da Pistoia, for example, carries the *dolce stil novo* into the 1330s, where he hands it on unsullied to Petrarch, and much Trecento lyric poetry follows, by its overt acceptance and conscious refinement of poetic convention, doggedly in the footsteps of its thirteenth-century predecessor. Conversely, as late as 1417 Giovanni Bertoldi da Serravalle could complete a commentary on Dante's *Commedia* whose technical method and intellectual underpinnings are identical with those of similar texts written half a century before; while the scholarly and political labours of the group of intellectuals who surrounded the Florentine chancellor Coluccio Salutati from the 1370s onwards embody concerns and practices that already seem more representative – again with the perfect vision of hindsight – of the Quattrocento. In some ways, or in some places, or for some individuals, the (cultural) Trecento begins in the 1320s and is over by 1375; in others it begins in the thirteenth century and lasts well beyond 1400.

Yet, for all that, the calendrical Trecento has a unity that still makes it a useful notion for the student of literature. The Italian cultural panorama in 1300 exhibits many features that we think of as 'medieval' and that are no longer present so forcibly, or at all, in the Italy of a hundred years later. The history of Italian literature in the Trecento is, in part, the history of that change. Indeed, there is more than a grain of truth in the hackneyed idea of the fourteenth century as a time of transition from 'Middle Ages' to 'Renaissance'. As long as it is recognised that these terms are modern interpretative instruments rather than unproblematic, naturally occurring categories, it can sometimes be helpful to see the Trecento as the crucible in which the linguistic and intellectual structures of the Middle Ages begin to be melted down to produce the raw material for the Renaissance. The vernacular begins to be taken seriously by writers and is admitted even to the most intellectually prestigious and morally authoritative of genres; the philosophical climate loosely called scholasticism is consciously challenged by thinkers whose work lays the basis of the movement equally loosely called humanism. New classes of readers and writers begin to form, as literacy and (at least) basic education spread in the wake of commercial prosperity. Authority of many kinds – political, social, religious, moral, intellectual, literary – increasingly becomes itself the subject of debate. None of these elementary formulations is adequate in itself to characterise the cultural processes at work in fourteenth-century Italy; but they will serve as a starting-point. Above all, they place the necessary stress on the interaction between the realm of culture and contemporary social and economic forces.

The single most important socio-economic reality connected with literature in the Trecento is the fact that texts, as material objects, played no part whatever in the lives of the huge majority of the population. The number of those who could read and write remained almost inconceivably tiny, by modern Western standards, throughout Italy and throughout the century – though some cities, especially Florence, enjoyed above-average rates of literacy (and numeracy, important in a commercially oriented polity), and seem to have made serious efforts to extend access to education beyond the narrow social and ideological circles to which it was confined in most of late medieval Europe. But the result was still that contact with written texts, even vernacular ones, was restricted to a very small and unrepresentative segment of the population as a whole – those who could read; and the vexed relationship between traditions of reading and writing and traditions of oral practice, further complicated by questions of social hierarchy (to what extent does the written/oral distinction coincide with one between 'highbrow' and 'popular' content, or with perhaps anachronistic notions of 'aristocracy', 'middle class', and 'proletariat'?), is another basic issue that cannot be ignored by the reader of Trecento Italian literature. The textual material we have, which is often taken as exemplary of deep-seated general truths about intellectual, social and even personal life in the late Middle Ages, in fact emerges from a stratum of society that is very narrowly defined in terms of prestige, education and gender – consisting, with few (though immensely significant) exceptions, of relatively well educated, relatively prosperous men – and its universal validity is thus often questionable. Generalisations about 'Trecento culture' or 'the medieval mind' based on such flimsy foundations are always risky – even when they are inevitable – and the modern reader should never lose sight of the risks.

Furthermore, even for that tiny minority which could read and write, the possibility of actually using the concrete objects in which literature was preserved and transmitted – manuscripts – was further affected by their sheer expensiveness and scarcity. The creation of even an ordinary workaday manuscript of any text was a skilled and laborious task that required considerable expenditure of time and money from both producer and consumer; most Trecento readers and writers can have had access to only a very few books, and those few, if the evidence of contemporary wills, inventories and catalogues is any guide, will mostly have belonged to the sphere of popular devotion rather than to the category thought of today as 'literature in the vernacular'. Quite simply, what we read and value in Trecento Italian writing seldom corresponds (especially once Dante, Petrarch and Boccaccio are removed from the equation) with what Trecento Italian readers themselves read and valued – let alone with what the vast majority of the population did in its (non-literate) use of language.

Finally, it should not be forgotten that our view of fourteenth-century Italian literature is also affected, and not for the better, by unmistakable but probably irrecoverable gaps in our objective knowledge. We do not have copies of every text that was written in the Trecento – many failed to overcome the ravages of time or the material fragility of manuscripts – and even the survivors are often textually unstable, in the sense that divergent traditions of copying and transmission have generated differing versions of what still seems to be 'one and the same' text. For all these reasons, none of which is 'literary' in the strict sense but all of which are vital to the proper understanding of Trecento Italian (and all medieval) literature, modern readers constantly need to bear in mind the fragmentary state of our knowledge, the elusiveness, for us, of Trecento readers' and writers' own understanding of these matters, and the finally provisional nature of all twentieth-century judgements and interpretations of fourteenth-century writing.

It is impossible, not to say pointless, to avoid referring to Dante, Petrarch and Boccaccio when discussing the 'minor' literature of the Trecento. All three were instantly recognised, by the very contemporaries who composed that literature, as having changed forever the terms in which vernacular writing in Italy could be conceived, and the ways in which literary and linguistic practice could develop among users of the various varieties of Italian. Inevitably, therefore, many of their Trecento readers, when they became writers in their turn, responded directly (though not always positively) to the models offered by the work of the three great Tuscans. Some caution is necessary here. The influence of Petrarch's vernacular lyrics, for example, which became so massive as to be inescapable in the Quattrocento and beyond, was restrained in the fourteenth century by the comparatively limited diffusion of the poems: only after Petrarch's death in 1374 – by which time, thanks in part to Petrarch himself, a shift back towards a preference for Latin as an expressive medium was well under way among Italian writers in general – did the *Canzoniere* begin to penetrate into the collective literary consciousness, and thence into vernacular culture throughout the peninsula. Many of the lexical, thematic and stylistic elements in Trecento poetry that look (or sound) 'Petrarchan' to us are much more likely, in fact, to derive from Duecento models – which is, of course, also where Petrarch himself found them.

Moreover, the massive presence of Dante – the Dante of the *Commedia* at least, since the minor works find little echo in Trecento culture beyond the ecclesiastical attempt to proscribe the *Monarchia* in the late 1320s – inspired both extensive commentary and a critical debate as acrid as any seen during the half-dozen centuries of later scholarship, but surprisingly little creative response. Outside the tradition of doctrinal and didactic poetry represented by the *Dottrinale* of Dante's own son Jacopo (c. 1290–1348), the unfinished *Dittamondo* of Fazio degli Uberti (1301–67), and Federico Frezzi's *Quadriregio* (begun c. 1394; Frezzi died in 1416), and notwithstanding the frequent Dantean allusions and use of *terza rima* in the work of Antonio da Ferrara (1315–71/74), it is unusual to find any Trecento text that is directly inspired by either the narrative, the thematics or the poetic form of the *Commedia*. On some poets, indeed, Dante's work acted chiefly as an irritant: the most celebrated case is that of Cecco d'Ascoli (c. 1269–1327), whose lengthy didactic poem *L'Acerba*, a storehouse of late medieval learning in the natural sciences, reaches its climax in a bitter polemic against not only Dante but poetry itself – although, since its composition was interrupted by the author's execution for heresy, it is not clear whether this was indeed the note on which the poem was meant to end.

In strictly literary terms, in fact, the most fruitful model left by the *tre corone* seems to have been Boccaccio's *Decameron*. Both the *Trecentonovelle* ('Three Hundred *Novelle*', c. 1392– c. 1397) of Franco Sacchetti (c. 1332–1400) and the *Novelle* of Giovanni Sercambi (1347–1424) start from the desire to compete with, or at least re-envision, the acknowledged prose masterpiece of the preceding generation. But whether they responded with approbation or disdain, there can be no doubt that every writer who took up the pen in fourteenth-century Italy was aware of the precedents set by Dante, Petrarch and Boccaccio – in Latin as well as in the (Tuscan) vernacular – just as many Trecento texts, especially in highly developed genres such as serious love poetry, are steeped in a language and thematics devised as early as the thirteenth century. Vernacular writing – and reading – in Trecento Italy was already a complex, self-conscious, intellectually demanding activity carried on by a dedicated minority that shared both a strong sense of tradition and a commitment to exploring the resources offered by their recently coined expressive idiom, for the benefit of a public that can never have been more than minuscule and often may have consisted entirely of other writers. At the same time, it marks the point at which Italian, in its various forms, takes the decisive step, in both theory and practice, from being a despised offshoot of a hegemonic Latin to becoming a universally acknowledged linguistic system in which anything and everything could be conveyed, from a merchant's bill of sale to a scientific treatise to Dante's *Paradiso*. This sense of witnessing the creation of a wholly new cultural paradigm helps to make the fourteenth century perhaps the most intensely interesting period in Italian literary history.

Although authorial presence in texts, like the role of the author as a historically active individual, need not and should not be altogether discounted in the study of Trecento literature, there is ample justification for considering the abundant material primarily from the viewpoint of genre. It is well known that medieval writing tended to be highly conventional, in the sense of being based on respect for an elaborate system of preconceived ideas about such topics as form, structure, style, image and theme, the relations among them, and the appropriate use of language in given communicative circumstances. This kind of thinking governed the activity of even those writers who seem most radically original or individually self-assertive to us, and it is all too easy, in the aftermath of Romanticism, to forget that medieval readers generally accorded greater esteem to the author (or text) who perpetuated or refined convention than to the one who broke with it. Central to the whole system of medieval culture was a subtly developed notion of textual genres and the hierarchy of value among them; and it is probably more useful to survey the 'minor' literature of the Trecento from this angle, rather than setting off in pursuit of the countless individual authors whose individuality fails to emerge clearly from either the historical record or their own writings.

Verse

The Trecento's most basic principle of genre is the formal distinction between poetry and prose. Fourteenth-century Italian writers and readers, like their descendants at least until the Ottocento, prized the former more than the latter, devoted more attention to the composition and analysis of poetry, and entrusted to it a range of topics that can still surprise modern readers accustomed to a much less vibrantly ambitious poetic culture. Trecento poetry deals with every imaginable subject, in every conceivable stylistic register: from political rivalry to mystical experience, from popular narratives of knights and damsels to learned treatises on philosophy, from bawdy songs to exquisite evocations of the agonies of unrequited love. At work throughout is the principle of matching the poem's language and form to its subject-matter, and classifying types of poem on the basis of these combinations: the principle of genre. A serious love poem, a poem of religious devotion, a comic vignette of everyday life, a political satire, a historical narrative, can be defined and distinguished one from another on the basis of the linguistic and formal features manifest in the text. Likewise, a poem's intended audience, both social and geographical, can often be deduced from objective elements of its text. And, above all, language and form are used to call attention to existing works in the same (or a related) genre; to identify, that is, the tradition to which the new text is destined to belong, both through overt or indirect allusion and through the redeployment of established formal and/or thematic conventions.

Poesia aulica

Pre-eminent among the poetic genres practised in the Trecento is the thematically serious and linguistically refined love poetry often called *poesia aulica*, and associated with many Duecento authors – the Sicilian school, Guinizzelli, the *stilnovisti* – as well, of course, as with Petrarch. Indeed, what is most obvious about the innumerable fourteenth-century instances of this genre is the extent of their dependence on precedent: language and themes borrowed wholesale from the *dolce stil novo*, above all, occur everywhere, either with endlessly elegant variation or with stale and unprofitable repetition, but without developing textual features that would help to define a specifically Trecento version of the genre. The very timelessness of *poesia aulica*, its normative reliance on convention and refusal to engage with the historically concrete, gives it a homogeneity that transcends chronological boundaries. It was, in the Trecento, very much what it had been in the previous century; and its many exponents – notably Matteo Frescobaldi (d. 1348), Sennuccio del Bene (c. 1275–1349), Francesco di Vannozzo (c. 1340– after 1389), and Cino Rinuccini (c. 1350–1417) – were, for the most part, content to work within limits laid down by their predecessors. Perhaps the most interesting aspect of Trecento *poesia aulica*, in fact, is the evidence of its geographical spread, in the many texts resulting from the interaction of Tuscan – which the combined efforts of Florentine poets and 'Tuscanising' scribes had already established as this poetry's canonical language during the Duecento – with other linguistic systems. The work of Giovanni and Niccolò Quirini, for instance (both active in the first few decades of the century), reveals the impact of literary Tuscan on the language of Venice; while Antonio da Ferrara and Francesco di Vannozzo (from Padua) both tried to integrate a tradition stemming from Tuscan linguistic practice with their own northern forms of the vernacular. Meanwhile, Florentines like Frescobaldi (whose father Dino had been a celebrated *stilnovista*), Rinuccini and Antonio degli Alberti (c. 1360–1415) maintained the tradition in its original linguistic guise, aided, towards the end of the century, by the increasing availability of the impeccably Tuscan lyrics of Petrarch.

Poesia giocosa

Alongside the intellectually elevated and linguistically austere tradition of *poesia aulica*, the thirteenth century had already produced a parodic counter-image of that tradition in the so-called *poesia giocosa* (or *comico-realistica*), which also continued to flourish in the Trecento. In language and theme, *poesia giocosa* is everything that *poesia aulica* is not: it shrinks from no subject-matter, however scabrous, and excludes no feature of language, however inelegant. As a genre it had quickly become associated with the colourful and (at least ostensibly) realistic evocation of everyday life, a representation of lived experience laying claim to a plausibility that the self-consciously idealised narrative world of *poesia aulica* could not – and did not seek to – attain. It had also come to embody an exuberant vivacity in the use of language that differs sharply from the intensely charged but narrowly circumscribed diction of *poesia aulica*. Its vocabulary is not limited by concepts of tastefulness or scruples about euphony; it freely admits colloquialisms, regionalisms and obscenities; it depicts everyday human experience (especially the body and its functions) without recourse to idealisation or euphemism; it makes frequent use of direct speech and dialogue; and, most subversively of all, it gives voice to the female protagonists whom *poesia aulica* had so consistently and so effectively silenced. In short, *poesia giocosa* cocks a snook at the dominant and most highly valued poetic genre of its time – much of which, however, was written by the same poets who also practised the *giocoso* genre, which fact has led to the abandonment of the formerly widespread notion that *poesia giocosa* could often be read as an autobiographical document springing unmediated from the lives of the individuals who wrote it. It is now clear that this was a complex, intriguing and supremely (inter)textual genre, in which elements of individual experience or social observation, if they exist at all, never fail to be modified by the author's conscious manipulation of a particular set of literary conventions.

The perugini

Some leading exponents of *poesia giocosa* already active in the Duecento – including the most famous, Cecco Angiolieri (see p. 6) – continued to work in the genre well into the fourteenth century; and this is another case where Trecento poets, by and large, happily conform to generic requirements laid down by earlier generations. But the genre also produces some interesting and specifically fourteenth-century offshoots. Foremost among these is the work of a small group of poets who seem to have formed a kind of school – perhaps an early instance of the creative-writing seminar – in Umbria in the middle of the century. This group, whose leading members were Cecco Nuccoli (c. 1290–c. 1350) and Marino Ceccoli (died c. 1371), apparently both notaries and distinguished citizens of Perugia, produced a substantial corpus of lyric poetry preserved in only one manuscript. In their work the *perugini* show themselves to be accomplished and well-read versifiers in several lyric modes, producing sonnets (especially *sonetti caudati*)[1] and *canzoni* on various themes – love, politics, spirituality – and frequently engaging in *tenzoni*, the poetic exchanges (fictive or otherwise) that had been a staple of vernacular lyric output since the time of the Provençals. What makes the Perugians unique in the Trecento is that the love they invoke is for other men; whether in the serious vein of *poesia aulica* or its humorous counterpart in *poesia giocosa*, the feelings and experiences represented in their poetry are almost always homoerotic. The nature of their subject-matter made their work a controversial topic in criticism for a long time – many scholars were convinced that fourteenth-century writing on this theme could only be a 'literary exercise', generated entirely by its authors' study of other texts – but the undeniable power and elegance of this poetry at its best continues to demand a more sensitive reading, one that acknowledges the consistent ambiguity of the relationship between lived experience and its representation in language within the context of a given poetic tradition. As an example, here is one of a dozen sonnets which Nuccoli wrote to Trebaldino Manfredini:

> Po' che nel dolce aspetto abbandonai
> e legai l'alma nei vostre costume,
> o signor, de mia vita guida e lume,
> prima ch'io mòra vederovv'io mai?

---

[1] *Sonetti caudati* were sonnets with a 'tail' of three lines, consisting of a *settenario* (seven-syllable line) and two *endecasillabi* (eleven-syllable lines).

Io me partie da voi e 'l cor lassai,
   onde convèn che sempre io me consume;
   e ben ch'io sparga de lagreme fiume,
   pianger non posso, che me paia assai.
Non serà mai piager che mi contente,
   né ch'ai dogliose spirte dona pace,
   fin ch'io non veggio voi, signor verace.
Ma questa angossa che così mi sface,
   signore, or ve ricorda il cor servente:
   che, poi ch'è vostro, non v'esca de mente.

(Since I delivered my soul to your sweet face and bound it to your gentle ways, o my lord, guide and light of my life, shall I ever see you again before I die? I parted from you and left behind my heart, so I must forever waste away, and even though I shed a flood of tears I cannot weep enough. No pleasure now will ever satisfy me or bring peace to my grieving spirit until I see you once more, my true lord. But of the anguish that so destroys me let this be a reminder to you, my lord, from a faithful heart which you should not forget since it belongs to you.)

As this sonnet shows, the *perugini* deserve recognition as some of the most technically resourceful and thematically innovative 'minor' lyric poets of the Trecento.

Political poetry

Whatever its object and whatever the register in which it was treated, love was by no means the only theme dear to Trecento lyric poets, even if it never ceased to be the most profoundly engaged or the most widely appealing. Lyric forms were frequently used for purposes of political propaganda or controversy – as, for example, in the fervently pro-Guelf sonnets composed by Pietro dei Faitinelli (d. 1349) after his exile from Lucca by political rivals in 1310. Indeed, the interplay between the interests of individual writers and the political (and economic) circumstances in which they found themselves is often startlingly evident in their work. The Trecento was marked by the gradual entrenchment, especially in northern and central Italy, of the court as a political institution, and poetry duly reflects this, both on a thematic level (as with Faitinelli) and in the careers of many fourteenth-century writers – the *tre corone* not excepted – for whom the prospect of courtly employment or patronage carried with it, at the very least, an obligation to bear in mind, when writing, the requirements of employer or patron. To a much greater extent than in the previous century, Trecento writers were able – or compelled – to become 'professionalised', to live by and through their writing, and the impact of this development should not be disregarded.

Devotional poetry

While the political lyric attends chiefly to the immediate present and the world
at hand, its religious counterpart claims to deal with the prospect of eternity
and the world to come. There is no shortage of devotional poetry in the Italian
Trecento – although, by critical consensus, it fails to match its Duecento
predecessor in quality, since it lacks a figure of the stature of Francis of Assisi
or Jacopone da Todi – and much of it is interesting in ways that go beyond the
details of its content or its power to strike a chord in the reader's spiritual
nature. In particular, fourteenth-century religious poetry occupies a formal
and authorial space quite distinct from that of the poetry considered so far.
Secular lyric, whatever its language or subject-matter, derived from a single,
cohesive tradition, practised almost exclusively by identifiable authors belonging to a socially privileged group that was sharply and narrowly defined
in terms of gender, education and social standing. It also emphasised
particular poetic forms – pre-eminently the sonnet, but also the *canzone* and
others – that it inherited from the Duecento. When it comes to religious
poetry, however, there is a clear shift from the individual towards the
collective, from the lyric towards the narrative and dramatic, and from
(socially and intellectually) 'high' culture in at least the general direction of the
popular. Much of this writing is anonymous, though we have a sketchy
knowledge of some authors, like Bianco da Siena (d. 1417), a late Trecento
admirer of Jacopone. Much of it is highly formulaic; much of it seems to have
arisen in the context of communal devotional practice or from the day-to-day
activities of particular religious groups or institutions; and most of it eschews
the forms prevalent in secular lyric, preferring looser and more flexible
structures, suitable for a public untrained in the complexities of poetic
technique, which also lend themselves, in many cases, to some kind of
(musical? theatrical?) performance.

Especially noteworthy in this context is the *lauda drammatica*, a widely
diffused genre which renders biblical and hagiographical narratives in simple
but often very effective dramatic structures, using language that shows every
sign of being very close to that which a comparatively uneducated (and
certainly non-Latinate) audience would have known. Probably the most
famous *laude drammatiche* are those preserved in several collections from
Umbria, where they were composed and circulated among religious confrater-
nities in such towns as Perugia, Orvieto and Gubbio; but the phenomenon
extended well beyond that region, assuming distinct local linguistic and
expressive features wherever it went. It would be simplistic to assume that the
lauda drammatica represents genuine fourteenth-century 'popular culture' –
both its doctrinal substance and its formal elaboration (starting with the fact
that it was written down in the first place) argue for the involvement of trained
intellectuals in its composition – but it is legitimate to conclude that it provides
evidence of a literature destined for a non-learned and perhaps even non-

literate public, and therefore that it offers some degree of potential access to that public's mentality.

Narrative poetry

Nor is devotional poetry the only Trecento genre that fits this description. The century produced a large number of narrative poems (*cantari*), usually in the eight-line stanza form known as *ottava rima*, which recount, in unpretentious language and relatively unsophisticated formal structures, traditional tales from mythology, epic and medieval legend, not to mention contemporary history, *fabliaux* and the Bible. A rich and varied cast of characters populates this literature: all the usual subjects of late medieval narrative are there, from Tristan to Charlemagne to Pyramus and Thisbe, along with re-tellings of the fall of Troy, the campaigns of Julius Caesar, and the valiant deeds of the knights of the Round Table. Here are the origins of the chivalric romances of the Quattrocento (see below, pp. 167ff). Perhaps less predictable are the narrative commentaries on recent events – Antonio Pucci's *Cantari della guerra di Pisa*, for example, on the war of 1362–4, or the anonymous *Morte di Giovanni Aguto*, a tribute to the great English *condottiere* John Hawkwood (d. 1394). (A related but less elaborate genre, the *serventese*, also treats contemporary topics, but in a wider variety of metres and at much shorter length than the *cantari*.)

Antonio Pucci (c. 1310–88) is exceptional in being an identifiable author in the *cantare* genre. Most of these texts, once again, are both anonymous and highly formulaic, and they have earned little but disdain from literary critics on grounds of aesthetic poverty; but, even in the often confused and fragmentary manuscript traditions in which they have survived, the outstanding examples of this genre, like Pucci's, have a verve and a narrative dexterity that make them more than mere witnesses to the existence of a literature aimed at the less educated, perhaps even non-literate, elements of the Trecento population.

Poetry as entertainment

This literature forms part of what Natalino Sapegno calls 'cultura semipopolare'; and his notion, of a culture that is written (and therefore by definition not truly popular, since the *popolo* in the fourteenth century was not literate), but not intellectually, formally or linguistically on a par with the most complex textual artefacts of the period (especially *poesia aulica*), is also useful in approaching another significant body of Trecento poetry, the many surviving texts that seem to have been intended as accompaniment to musical performance or dancing. Here too their written nature prevents these from being seen as unmediated witnesses to popular tradition; but their generally colloquial language and uncomplicated forms – *madrigale*, *ballata*, *caccia*, *canzone a ballo*, *strambotto* – make it clear that they do not belong to a 'high' cultural register or an academic or professional context. In the most tangible of senses, this is poetry as entertainment. It is sometimes possible to identify the audiences whom this poetry sets out to entertain. Some representative texts of the genre seem to have emerged from either the nascent court culture of northern Italy or, like those of Niccolò Soldanieri (d. 1385), from the Florentine bourgeoisie, and may thus suggest the image of a prosperous and educated public letting its hair down; others, particularly the many anonymous texts in which themes and language familiar from *giocoso* poetry are prominent, may be more closely attuned to a genuinely popular register. As always, any attempt at classification in such terms is fraught with difficulties of a documentary, philological and socio-historical nature. One interesting detail, which may serve to highlight the essentially functional (and perhaps subsidiary) nature of much of this writing, is the fact that in manuscripts where words and music appear together, the name of the composer is almost always recorded, while that of the poet usually is not.

Prose

The idea of 'cultura semipopolare' can also be usefully applied to fourteenth-century vernacular prose. It is axiomatic in late medieval Italy, as elsewhere, that prose is less technically demanding than poetry, and therefore less highly valued in aesthetic terms; but also that it is more readily accessible to the reader – particularly the reader with no, or at best an inadequate, knowledge of Latin. Trecento vernacular prose frequently served the purpose of opening up the previously inaccessible resources of Latinate culture to a new public, one that had not benefited from the possibilities traditionally offered by Church-based education – except perhaps in rudimentary form – but which was interested in acquiring some elements of that culture in a more 'user-friendly' linguistic guise, as well, perhaps (at least in certain times and places, such as mid-Trecento Florence), as beguiling the extra leisure time provided by increasing economic well-being and social status. In a word, prose (especially, but not exclusively, fictional narrative) becomes the literary medium *par excellence* of the emergent bourgeois and mercantile classes.

Vernacular translations

Crucial to this process is the *volgarizzamento* (see above pp. 31ff.). Offering its author far greater freedom and flexibility than a 'translation' in the twentieth-century sense – strict fidelity to the letter of the original text is seldom a prerequisite, though it is by no means unknown – a *volgarizzamento* can become an occasion for innovation and experimentation in the target language, for radical editing and re-ordering of the material to suit the perceived requirements of the non-Latinate reader, or even for a more or less wholly new meditation on the given subject-matter, through which the actual words of the original show from time to time as in a palimpsest. By such means the canonical works of the Christian Latin tradition, from the Bible through numerous patristic and spiritual writings to saints' lives, extracts from the liturgy, and collections of moral *exempla* or aphorisms (like the hugely popular *Ammaestramenti degli antichi* of the Dominican friar Bartolomeo da San Concordio, who died in 1347), were gradually made available to a far larger segment of the population than could ever have read them in Latin. Original texts in other (especially French) vernaculars were assimilated in the same way. The Arthurian and Carolingian cycles found their way into Italian prose (*La storia di Merlino*, *La Tavola Ritonda*, *Il viaggio di Carlomagno*) during the Trecento, along with a mass of epic, legendary, romance and quasi-historical material originating outside the Italian peninsula. In subject-matter, stylistic register, intellectual level and implicit assumptions about audience (non-Latinate, relatively uneducated, 'semipopolare'), these works form an obvious prose counterpart to the verse *cantari* mentioned above. Nor was classical Latin culture excluded from the process. Historical works were especially popular among *volgarizzatori* (Livy, Sallust, Valerius Maximus), but the prose of Cicero, Seneca, and even Boethius was also turned into Italian, along with much of Ovid (*Metamorphoses*, *Heroides*, *Ars amandi*, *Remedia amoris*) and most of Virgil (Ciampolo degli Ugurgieri's Sienese version of the *Aeneid* enjoyed particular renown in both complete and anthological format).

Even if it was still only a minority of the population of Trecento Italy that was able to profit from *volgarizzamenti* – for the illiterate majority remained debarred from reading texts in any language – that minority grew steadily throughout the century, and the stimulating effect of *volgarizzamenti* on the growth and diffusion of literate culture, in whatever language, should not be underestimated. Indeed, it is *volgarizzamenti*, especially religious and devotional ones, that constitute the bulk of the recorded personal libraries of which we have evidence from the fourteenth century, far outweighing the presence of original vernacular works on any cultural level.

Yet such original vernacular works do exist in fourteenth-century prose, as in poetry, and form a substantial contribution in at least four genres: history and chronicle; narrative fiction; the (often autobiographical) expression of religious feeling and experience; and the didactic tradition of commentary on authoritative literary and philosophical writings. Each of these will now be examined in turn.

Historical writing

The prose literature of the Italian Trecento is dominated by history. Not just in the sense that imaginative writings in poetry and prose frequently depend on or respond to historical processes and events, but because so many texts of the period are themselves serious and self-conscious attempts to record or interpret the ebb and flow of history. By far the best-known of the fourteenth-century historians are two Florentine chroniclers of the first half of the century, Dino Compagni (1255/60–1324), author of a *Cronica delle cose occorrenti ne' tempi suoi* (1310–12), and Giovanni Villani (c. 1276–1348), whose *Cronica* was probably begun in the 1320s and was continued after his death by his brother Matteo (c. 1285–1363); Matteo's son Filippo (c. 1325–c. 1405) later brought the annals as far as 1364. Their fame, however – which owes almost as much to a deep-rooted historiographical tradition of concentration on Florence, at the expense of other cities and regions, as it does to the intrinsic interest of the events and personalities they describe – has had the unfortunate effect of obscuring the sheer scale of historical writing in the Trecento, and the extent of its geographical and linguistic diversity. Quite apart from the many Latin texts that narrate the contemporary experiences of individual cities – Milan, Faenza, Bologna, Ferrara and especially Venice, where Andrea Dandolo, Doge from 1343 to 1354, wrote not only a history of his native city but also one of the whole world from the Creation to 1280 – historical writing in the vernacular began to flourish, especially in Tuscany. Less well-known Florentines like Marchionne di Coppo di Stefano di Buonaiuti (1336–85) tried their hand at the genre, as did the unknown Pistoian author of the *Storie pistoresi* (presumably written after 1348, date of the last event they record), and at least one fairly obscure citizen of Siena, Andrea Dei. Outside Tuscany, there are vernacular historical texts from Sicily, Naples and Rome, this last being an account of the period 1327–54 that concentrates on the colourful career of Cola di Rienzo.

Naturally, these works vary widely in substance and appeal. Compagni's history of his own times is very much a history of the (considerable) part he himself played in those times, and its autobiographical vivacity and sharp focus on the immediately contemporary help to explain its lasting success. Villani's work has a broader scope and a more abstract, even theoretical, concern with the nature of its own enterprise. Villani was interested in what writing history might actually imply, beyond the level of straightforward chronicle, and alongside numerous variably reliable statistics and concrete details that have been grist to the mill of Florentine historians ever since, he provides an interpretation of Florence's history in terms of universally opera-tive processes of sin and retribution. (Both authors, like their colleagues from other cities, are also a precious resource for historians of language.) Most of the other historical writers of the period were less ambitious, even when they set out to write – as do both Dandolo and Marchionne – a history that begins with the Creation: the recording of notable events was their principal purpose, and the degree of their attentiveness to detail and avoidance of formula generally increases the nearer they come to their own times. (It should also be remembered that the boundary between 'history' and 'fiction' was much less clearly drawn in the Middle Ages than today, and that, accordingly, to judge these writers by twentieth-century historiographical standards of accuracy and plausibility is usually inappropriate; conversely, familiarity with the 'literary' conventions and techniques of medieval narrative is often invaluable when dealing with Trecento historians.)

The novelle

Fictional narrative itself is particularly characteristic of the second half of the Trecento, and, as noted above, was placed firmly under the seal of Boccaccio's *Decameron* – whether as positive or as negative response. One of the two extant versions of Giovanni Sercambi's *Novelle*, for example, begins from the pretext of a group of storytellers fleeing a plague-stricken city (Lucca rather than Florence), and reproduces the earlier work's structure, down to the arrangement of its hundred tales in *cornice* and *giornate*. (The other, consisting of 155 stories, is more loosely organised, with the *giornate* disappearing and the *cornice* [frame] being significantly reduced.) None of the stories achieves the degree of stylistic or formal elaboration characteristic of the *Decameron*, and Sercambi also dispenses with Boccaccio's multiple narrators and the possibilities for patterning and contrast that they provide; but the comparison is perhaps inherently unfair. Sercambi's work is interesting in its own right as further evidence of an active literary (and oral) culture among the late Trecento bourgeoisie.

The same is true of Franco Sacchetti's *Trecentonovelle*, written in his old age after a long career as author of *cantari* (the intriguingly entitled *La battaglia delle belle donne di Firenze con le vecchie*, 'Battle of the beautiful ladies of Florence with the old women', 1352–4), lyric poetry (*Il libro delle rime*, begun c. 1362), and devotional prose (*Sposizioni di Vangeli*, 'Commentaries on the Gospels', 1381). The *Trecentonovelle* (only 223 of which have come down to us) dispense with the narrative trappings of the *Decameron* – gone are the plague, the storytellers and the *cornice/giornate* structure – and generally remain faithful to the tradition of the moral *exemplum*, familiar in the Duecento vernacular text known as the *Novellino*. Most of these brief anecdotes end with an obvious pointing of their moral; and in general, even though Sacchetti certainly knew the work of Boccaccio (and Petrarch), he seems to have made a deliberate decision – perhaps on ethical grounds, perhaps in modesty, perhaps in order to simplify his message for a larger public – to distance himself from it. A similarly ambivalent response to precedent is visible in the *Pecorone* of Ser Giovanni Fiorentino (c. 1378), in which fifty stories are told over twenty-five days by a nun and a chaplain in a convent; the structure and the amorous subject-matter recall Boccaccio, the rudimentary narrative technique and poverty of language and characterisation are more reminiscent of his Duecento predecessors.

Devotional prose

The real-life counterparts of the *Pecorone*'s love-sick nun and chaplain no doubt existed, but Trecento literature is also rich in spiritual and devotional prose in the vernacular, emanating from both clerical and lay circles, and taking the form of both *volgarizzamenti* and original texts. One writer active in both fields was the Dominican friar Domenico Cavalca (c. 1270–1342), author of vernacular renderings of the Acts of the Apostles, biographies of various Church Fathers, and, most famously, Gregory the Great's *Dialogues*. He also composed several devotional treatises (including *Trattato della pazienza*, *Specchio di Croce*, *Pungilingua* and *Disciplina degli spirituali*) which, though still heavily dependent on earlier works, go far enough beyond *volgarizzamento* or anthologising to achieve a degree of originality that makes it legitimate to see Cavalca as their author in the full sense. Another Dominican, Jacopo Passavanti (c. 1302–57), prior of Santa Maria Novella in Florence, turned his Lenten sermons of 1354 into a popular treatise, *Specchio di vera penitenza*. The Order of Preachers, as is only fitting, also produced the other most highly influential author of vernacular sermons in the Trecento, Giordano da Pisa (d. 1311), as well as the great *volgarizzatore* Bartolomeo da San Concordio, mentioned above, who also wrote a Latin *Summa casuum conscientiae* (1338), which itself soon appeared in innumerable *volgarizzamenti*.

The Dominicans' great rival Order, the Franciscans, is less vitally present in Trecento than in Duecento literature. Though individuals like Ugo Panziera (died c. 1330) and Simone da Cascia (c. 1295–1348) wrote letters and mystical treatises, and the aggressively puritanical writings of Angelo Clareno (1255–1337) circulated widely in *volgarizzamenti*, the most significant Franciscan work to appear in the fourteenth century was the hugely popular compilation of deeds and sayings of St Francis known as the *Fioretti di san Francesco*, whose fifty-three lucid, entertaining and very readable chapters owe a good deal to the Latin *Actus beati Francisci et sociorum eius* and may thus also be seen as, to some extent, a *volgarizzamento*. But the most consistently rewarding body of spiritual prose in the Italian Trecento is probably that connected with three outstanding figures in mid-century Siena: Giovanni Colombini (1304–67), Girolamo da Siena (1335/40–1420) and Caterina Benincasa (1347–80), better known as St Catherine of Siena.

Colombini, whose traditional biography shows striking parallels (unless they are hagiographical stereotypes) with that of St Francis – he was a wealthy merchant who saw the light and gave his possessions away – was an active preacher who gathered about him a group of followers that eventually became the Order of Gesuati. His many vernacular letters abound in both mystical fervour and points of linguistic interest. Girolamo, also a famous preacher and spiritual director, was among Colombini's (and Catherine's) correspondents, and himself wrote devotional and meditational handbooks in the vernacular. But the most remarkable individual in this group is, beyond question, Catherine, for reasons that are of immense interest to both literary and social historians.

The fascinating story of Catherine's brief life cannot detain us here, except in so far as her precocious reputation for sanctity, personal and epistolary relations with popes, prelates, monarchs, statesmen and artists, wide-ranging travels to preach and fulfil diplomatic missions, and frantic efforts to resolve the Great Schism that began in 1378, are reflected in her writings. These consist of nearly four hundred letters, addressed to most of the principal figures in the ecclesiastical and political worlds of her day, and a passionate mystical treatise, the *Dialogo della divina Provvidenza* (1378), also known as the *Libro della divina dottrina*.

In all these writings Catherine handles the vernacular with subtlety and force, commanding a wide range of tonal registers and using her expressive medium with a supple ease and pithy eloquence that make her letters, in particular, one of the monuments of epistolary tradition. But the very idea of Catherine as 'author' of her own texts brings with it several extra-literary problems that affect interpretation. Born and raised in working-class poverty, and subject, like nearly all women of her century, to virtually complete exclusion from the realm of education and literate culture, she learned to read and write only near the end of her life. Most if not all of her 'writings' were thus orally dictated to (male) secretaries, foremost among them the famous friar Raimondo da Capua. It is by no means clear exactly what role these secretaries played in editing, revising or otherwise preparing Catherine's dictated texts for circulation in manuscript; and any conception of Catherine as a woman writer of the Trecento – a *rara avis* indeed – needs to be modified by attention to the individual and social realities that govern her work, and which include substantial involvement by men in the preservation of that work in written form.

Catherine was a remarkable woman by any standards, and her career, for a woman in the fourteenth century, was truly extraordinary; but to think of her as a woman *writer* – let alone to attribute to her, on the basis of her texts, a consciousness or an approach to writing that is claimed to be characteristic of women writers in our own day – is dangerously simplistic, unless her literary activity is seen in its precise late medieval context. Even though female literacy was not unknown in the Trecento, it would be the Quattrocento before learned women began to play an active role in any branch of literary culture outside the strictly religious, and the century after that before they began to be taken seriously by male (and even other female) readers as writers in the vernacular.

Commentaries on Dante

The fourth major corpus of Trecento vernacular prose is one in which the reader's role and experience is of paramount importance – is, in fact, the point of departure for writing: that of commentary on, and analysis of, authoritative (Latin and vernacular) writings. The idea of commentary itself was, of course, universally familiar in the late Middle Ages from its application to the Bible and the major classical authors; but in late Duecento and early Trecento Italy the practice spread to vernacular texts as well. Dante's *Vita Nuova* and *Convivio* are both, essentially, commentaries on vernacular lyrics; Francesco da Barberino (1264–1348), author of love lyrics and two important didactic works, the *Documenti d'Amore* (c. 1310) and the *Reggimenti e costumi di donna* ('Rules and Customs of Ladies', c. 1318–20), commented (in Latin) on his own poetry, as did the pro-Guelf political sonneteer Niccolò de' Rossi (c. 1285–c. 1348); and a physician, Dino del Garbo, wrote a Latin scientific commentary (soon *volgarizzato*), on Guido Cavalcanti's notoriously elusive *canzone* 'Donna me prega'. But by far the largest body of writing in this area is connected with the poetic presence looming inescapably over all Trecento writers: Dante's *Commedia*.

The fourteenth century produced a score of commentaries, complete and partial, on Dante's poem, and large-scale dependence on methods and critical axioms current in the Trecento is still visible in the early fifteenth-century commentaries of Giovanni da Serravalle and Guiniforte Barzizza. Many of these are in Latin, including perhaps the most intellectually impressive and stylistically polished, that of Benvenuto da Imola (c. 1338–90; final version of the commentary c. 1385), as well as that of Dante's son Pietro (c. 1290–1364; final version c. 1355); but from its earliest beginnings the tradition also produced vernacular commentaries on this eminently vernacular text. Dante's other son Jacopo, exiled at Verona, began a set of vernacular glosses (*chiose*) on *Inferno* within a year of his father's death in 1321; it was complete by 1324. Between 1324 and 1328, in Venice, the Bolognese scholar Jacopo della Lana composed the first vernacular commentary on the whole *Commedia*, inventing in the process an analytical technique (introductory essay on each canto followed by detailed glosses on single lines or words) that has survived unchanged to the present day. Lana's work swiftly became popular and influential on later commentators, and even enjoyed *volgarizzamento* in reverse, so to speak, being translated at least twice into Latin.

Other major vernacular commentaries in the Trecento came, ironically enough, from Dante's own loved and hated Florence. The so-called *Ottimo commento*, usually attributed nowadays to the notary Andrea Lancia (who died c. 1360), went through at least three (distinctly different) versions in the 1330s. In 1373–4 Giovanni Boccaccio gave a series of public lectures on *Inferno* which subsequently became his *Esposizioni sopra la Comedia di Dante* (see above p. 86). At about the same time, an anonymous Florentine wrote a mediocre set of glosses that early editors wrongly attributed to Boccaccio himself, earning both author and text the sobriquet 'Falso Boccaccio' (c. 1375).

Elsewhere in Tuscany an unknown commentator, probably (to judge by his language) from Siena, compiled, in 1337, the glosses on *Inferno* now called (after their modern editors) the *Chiose Selmiane* or *Marciane*; in Arezzo, some time after 1345, another glossator wrote the so-called *Chiose Cagliaritane* on the whole poem; and in Pisa, from the mid 1380s onwards, Francesco da Buti

(1324–1405) delivered the *lecturae* on the entire *Commedia* that eventually (c. 1395) became his published commentary. Finally, in about 1400, another anonymous scholar, possibly a Florentine and therefore known as the 'Anonimo fiorentino', stitched together much of Buti's commentary on *Inferno* and *Purgatorio* and all of Lana's on *Paradiso*, along with some material of his own, to produce a new if heavily derivative analysis of the poem. Thereafter the pressure of early Quattrocento humanism seems to have stifled attempts at producing vernacular commentary – with the relatively unimportant exception of Guiniforte Barzizza – until Cristoforo Landino came along in 1481 with a commentary that made a point (in its long introductory *proemio*) of expounding a Tuscan author in the Tuscan language.

Vast, unwieldy and almost infinitely variegated though this body of critical writing is, it demonstrates several central truths about the literary activity of the Italian Trecento. Its linguistic and geographical diversity; its broad and searching range of intellectual and critical interests; the combination of ease and self-awareness with which it moves between Latin and vernacular elements in contemporary culture; the high value it places on poetry (even – especially – poetry *in volgare*); and, above all, the constant sense that reading and writing in the vernacular is a worthwhile, prestigious, complex, demanding, vital, innovative, exciting and supremely *necessary* enterprise, are threads that run throughout the often disparaged 'minor' writing of the Trecento. Here as elsewhere in the century's literature, the dazzling light shed by the *tre corone* is steadily reflected back with – almost – equal splendour.

The Quattrocento

Letizia Panizza

8

Humanism

In modern Italian literary studies, the Quattrocento often appears like Petrarch's personified Philosophy, 'povera e nuda': a neglected century compared to her attractive sisters, the Trecento on one side and the Cinquecento on the other. Some of the reasons have to do with the cultural phenomena of the century itself; others with interpretations of the phenomena. To critics for whom a national literature in Italian was and is a top priority, the Quattrocento leaves much to be desired. With the deaths of Petrarch and Boccaccio in 1374 and 1375 respectively, and no one of equal stature to replace them, the ensuing century – roughly 1375 to 1475 – has been seen as a period of literary desolation, a 'secolo senza poesia' (a century without poetry), with 'poetry' meaning imaginative literature in the vernacular.

According to this view, blame lay in excessive adulation of classical Latin language, letters and values. Poets were replaced by scholars who gave themselves over to imitating a dead literature instead of carrying forwards the newly founded and vigorous one in their own spoken mother-tongue. The educated élite in the Italian peninsula lost confidence in their own culture, and only the invasions of Italy – first by the French in the 1490s and later by Charles V's troops in the 1520s – brought the decadent classicisers to their senses.

On the other hand, the cultural territory of the Quattrocento has been to a large extent carved up by historians: cultural historians, intellectual historians, art historians, historians of philosophy and neo-classical scholars. While they have identified the Quattrocento as the core period of the Renaissance in Italy, their focus has not been specifically on literature, whose achievements have not been fully recognised; or even when recognised, undervalued. Those critics interested in the vernacular see the cult of the classics as culturally regressive, élitist, unoriginal and predominantly didactic. Historians of philosophy, on the other hand, sometimes regard humanists as intellectually inferior to 'proper' philosophers precisely because they used literary genres, even poetry. This chapter on the Quattrocento will rest on less antagonistic premisses. First of all, Italian literature will be taken in a geographical sense as literature written just in the Italian peninsula, whether Latin or vernacular, rather than literature written in the Italian language. Many authors, after all, wrote in both, and in Greek as well, and even in hybrid, invented 'macaronic' languages. Secondly, writing in languages other than the vernacular will not be taken as a regrettable episode, but on the contrary as a phenomenon that ultimately enriched what came to be known as 'Italian' language and literature. Furthermore, the study of Latin will not be seen as leading to atrophy in vernacular literature even if, in the short term, exclusive attention was drawn away from the latter. Latin and Greek literature afforded a wider canon of authors which an educated person could study and draw on for his or her own compositions. As a result, new genres were added, like the dialogue, the literary letter and satirical literary parody. The intensive study of classical Latin and Greek also led to a new critical awareness of language itself, and of the need for definition and precision in vocabulary that would standardise correct usage. This need, in turn, led to the compiling of dictionaries, grammars and manuals of style. A deeper understanding of Latin and Greek rhetoric and dialectic promoted greater sensitivity in general to different kinds of styles or linguistic registers for different genres.

All the above activities may be 'élitist' in that only a few, highly educated people could engage in them, but they were far from 'élitist' in their intent and effect. Humanists brought about a dissemination of texts, and of learning and literacy, greater than at any previous time. The number of translations in the Quattrocento far surpassed that of any other century. The skills of turning a text from Greek into Latin and Latin into the vernacular were seen as a means of acquiring an entire patrimony in all the disciplines, and therefore of spreading the available store of knowledge to an ever-wider public. Many of the basic tools of literacy and of literary study on an organised scale were produced by humanists: grammars, dictionaries, textbooks, reference works, lists of canonical authors, syllabuses for schools. These went a long way down the road of popularising high literary culture, generating methods for studying language and literature which would be applied to all European tongues, and could be used by all who wanted to read, write and interpret texts more effectively. They made written texts more legible, and therefore more accessible, by their reforms of handwriting and the layout of text on the manuscript page. These techniques determined the way books look up to the present, because they were taken over by printers later in the Quattrocento. The present book makes use of two basic founts in typography, roman and italic, developed by Italian humanists.

Petrarch's legacy

Although Petrarch died in 1374, he dominates the end of the Trecento and – at least – the first half of the Quattrocento, shaping the development of classical literary studies. A quick look at Petrarch's *œuvre* shows that his many volumes are nearly all in Latin. There is not a single prose work, not one of his several hundred letters, in the vernacular; and most of his poetry is in Latin too. The portrait of the melancholy lyric poet assailed by conflicting desires, by passion and reason, by pleasure and virtue, characteristic of the *Canzoniere* and to a lesser extent of the allegorical *Trionfi*, Petrarch's only two works in Tuscan, was not the dominant one in the century after his death.

The three or four generations immediately following looked up to Petrarch as a moral philosopher who shared much in common with the Roman Stoic letter-writer and essayist Seneca; as a prose writer like Cicero; a Latin poet to rival Virgil; a scholar utterly dedicated to the pursuit of classical learning; a scourge of contemporary academics obsessed with dialectic and the natural sciences; a devout Christian who cared more for inner piety than institutional religion, more for St Augustine's introspective *Confessions*, than for Franciscan or Dominican devotional manuals; and even a mentor to princes on how they should conduct themselves. Petrarch's ambition to write as well as his Latin literary ancestors had fuelled his search to recover and study as wide a classical library as possible. In service for many years to Cardinal Giovanni Colonna in the papal city of Avignon – the Trecento crossroads of European culture – Petrarch was ideally situated to gather intelligence about classical manuscripts, often lying unrecognised in richly endowed monastic and cathedral libraries. He found Cicero's letters to Atticus, and a number of speeches, including *Pro Archia*, defending the poet's role in a republic. He also acquired most of Cicero's philosophical and rhetorical works. Cicero's letters and Seneca's letters to Lucilius also provided Petrarch with models for his own, and set a vogue for the literary letter/moral essay in the Quattrocento. Another of his scholarly achievements was to put together different sections of Livy's history of republican Rome to make the most complete copy of the *Decades* yet seen. Petrarch annotated and corrected the text, pioneering skills that later humanists would carry further. Lorenzo Valla, for example, and afterwards Poliziano, owned Petrarch's Livy and added their emendations.

Petrarch's combination of literary talents with classical scholarship fired Quattrocento humanists, but not unreservedly. His moral treatises aligned the poet/philosopher/scholar with the contemplative life of solitude and reflection, and equated this life with Christian virtue. This is the tenor of Petrarch's *Secretum*, *De vita solitaria*, *De otio religioso* and *De remediis utriusque fortunae* (see above, pp. 106–7), and it is one that not all humanists could accept. As we shall see, Leonardo Bruni valued the active life of the citizen/ scholar; and Lorenzo Valla utterly condemned Petrarch's Stoic aloofness as un-Christian.

Petrarch's more durable contribution to later humanism lay in his letters and invectives. The former established the poet's true community, a 'république des lettres' as seventeenth-century savants termed it, in which Petrarch was the acknowledged leader. The literary letter suited him perfectly. It allowed him to express intimate thoughts on matters large and small in a lively, relaxed style – direct address to a friend – which could nevertheless drip with classical allusions at every turn of phrase. By means of his letters he fashioned his own persona, and some became miniature literary masterpieces – his account of a climb of

nearby Mount Ventoux with his younger brother (*Familiares* IV, I, 26 April
1336), for example. The various stages and frustrations of the upward journey
are followed by Petrarch's commentary on his own – and mankind's – stages
and frustrations in a spiritual journey. And Petrarch's opening up of his copy of
St Augustine's *Confessions*, which he was carrying with him, recalls the
example of two earlier models, St Augustine himself and St Anthony, the desert
hermit. In all three cases opening a book at random and reading the first words
that appeared signifies a moment of conversion. By embedding text within text
Petrarch creates a series of parallels that authoritatively validate and add
meaning to his own experience. Petrarch also set an example to humanists of
rhetorical invective. This, like the letter, involved the dramatic qualities of
direct address, plus erudite virtuoso vituperation with no holds barred.
Invective lost its appeal as a literary genre only at the end of the fifteenth
century – replaced in part, perhaps, by the mocking, satirical dialogue.
Petrarch's *Invectiva contra medicum*, completed in 1357, pulverised an
Avignon doctor's accusation that poets – unlike doctors of course – were
socially useless, ignorant parasites, and rightfully banished by Plato for their
lying fictions.

De sui ipsius et multorum aliorum ignorantia ('On his Own Ignorance and
That of Many Besides'), dated 1370, could be considered the manifesto of
Quattrocento humanism. Petrarch's wide-ranging invective rejects a stagnant
and stultifying scholastic university curriculum, and sets up Ciceronian *studia
humanitatis* and Augustinian piety in its stead. The autograph copy was
owned by Bernardo Bembo and then by his more illustrious son Pietro, and
was known to Poliziano. Nicholas of Cusa, too, owned a copy. In the treatise
Petrarch, dismissed by four young intellectuals as a good man but ignorant
because not truly versed in Aristotelian logic and natural philosophy, quickly
turns the tables. Some very great and good men like Socrates, Augustine and St
Paul himself, he says, boasted of their ignorance because, unlike Petrarch's
attackers, they understood how little the human mind can know. Adopting the
paradoxical Christian position of *docta ignorantia*, Petrarch champions a new
educational programme of reading philosophical texts in the original Latin or
Greek, not in bad translations or reductionist manuals.

On the authority of Augustine Petrarch insists that Plato is more compatible
with Christianity than Aristotle, and he promotes Cicero as a better natural
philosopher: Cicero's *De natura deorum*, with its exposition of Stoic divine
providence and benevolent ordering of the universe, is closer to Christian
teaching than is Aristotle. He also points an accusing finger at the numerous
heresies Aristotelians have disseminated – especially regarding the soul's
mortality, the most disputed issue in medieval philosophy. He has read
Aristotle's *Ethics* – presumably in poor Latin translations – but this did not
move him to embrace a good life. On the other hand, eloquent Latin writers
like Cicero, Seneca and Horace stir his emotions, move his will, and do what
the scholastics have never done: make him morally better.

Petrarch, who remained independent of institutional academic life, had nevertheless touched on a number of festering sore points. The crucial one was the unintelligibility, if not impenetrability, of scholastic writings to all but a few adepts, followed by the failure of medieval universities to communicate with an intelligent but not specialist audience. Seen from this perspective, Petrarch's alternative, a wide classical curriculum in poetry and prose, represented a refreshing change. Petrarch, furthermore, exploited Cicero's arguments that all the great ancient philosophers were eloquent, and that effective expression cannot be separated from profound thought. Finally, Petrarch touched on the deficiencies of medieval devotional literature as well as scholastic theology. Here, too, his preference for early Christian Latin writers like Lactantius, Jerome and Augustine started another enduring trend that stretched well beyond the Quattrocento.

Education, libraries and translations from Greek

If we take 'humanist' in the widest possible sense of someone who could read classical Latin texts and write a Latin beyond the medieval formulae of the Latin-based professions (especially law and medicine), we find, not surprisingly, that the largest professional group was made up of schoolmasters or tutors. Only a sprinkling taught in the universities, usually occupying Chairs of Rhetoric. By the end of the Quattrocento, the word *umanista* was used to refer to such a teacher. Especially in the early Quattrocento, some famous humanists started and ran boarding schools frequented by the sons of the middle, professional and upper classes: Vittorino da Feltre (1378–1446) at Padua and later Mantua; Gasparino Barzizza (1360–1431) at Padua; Guarino Veronese (1374–1460) at Ferrara. Barzizza was one of the first to study and diffuse the recently discovered (1421) oratorical works of Cicero; he also wrote commentaries on Seneca's letters to Lucilius, and ended his career in the Chair of Rhetoric at the University of Milan. Guarino, an avid collector of Greek manuscripts which he brought back to Italy from frequent trips to Constantinople, was himself an outstanding humanist scholar and translator from Greek; his school trained a whole generation of translators. He and his son, Battista Guarino, tutored the household of the ruling d'Este family at Ferrara.

Emphasis in these schools lay on learning the Latin language, and memorising long passages of Latin poetry (Virgil, Ovid and Lucan) as well as prose (Cicero, Valerius Maximus, Caesar and Livy). Vittorino, and especially Guarino, made their students learn Greek, following Cicero's own counsel that Greek should be studied as an aid to Latin. None of these schools, it should be noted, studied vernacular authors, not even Dante – an attitude which did not mean contempt. The assumption was that you did not have to be taught in secondary school how to read works in the vernacular; that was done in an elementary school or at home. On the other hand, these schools, in contrast to medieval monastic ones, and in contrast with Petrarch's ideal of the solitary life of scholarship, aimed at preparing laymen for an active role in society. In a widely read treatise by Pier Paolo Vergerio (1370–1444), written in 1403, new importance is given to history and moral philosophy in forming a pupil's values, the sources for which are classical (and therefore secular) writers.

The unifying term given to the new programme was *studia humanitatis*, a phrase borrowed from Cicero, who used it to mean the scope of an orator's training in all the skills to do with verbal persuasion: composition, figures of speech and thought, probable argument. Educators translated these into what are now known as liberal arts, with the accent on Latin grammar, rhetoric, poetry, history and moral philosophy. They regarded literary texts which proclaimed human values, private and public, as referring to themselves. The natural sciences, metaphysics, theology and the mechanical arts were usually excluded from the school curriculum, mainly because they were studied elsewhere: the first three at university, and the last in apprenticeships. While it is obvious that humanists encouraged language and letters, it should not be thought that they were by definition opposed to other disciplines. In fact, they often showed themselves better trained in areas prized by scholastic academics like philosophy, theology and law.

The importance of building up large private libraries and searching out unavailable works, established by Petrarch, was not lost on these scholars. The recognised successor to Petrarch in Florence was Coluccio Salutati (1331–1406), a layman and Chancellor of the city-state, who also collected a distinguished personal library. While Petrarch had discovered Cicero's letters to Atticus, Salutati brought to light Cicero's *Ad familiares*, a completely unknown collection. With both sets of letters presenting a Cicero deeply involved in politics, Salutati and later humanists found further encouragement for overcoming prejudices against a life of study blended with public service.

The court also became a centre of study, as imaginative, wealthy patrons sought to attract first-rate humanists by promising them libraries they could enrich and use. Duke Federigo da Montefeltro at Urbino, Alfonso of Aragon in Naples, the Medici in Florence spring to mind; but Popes, too, became splendid patrons of libraries. Nicholas V appointed the distinguished historian Platina as papal librarian, and Raphael painted his portrait. For the first time, a private citizen could have a library made to order. Vespasiano da Bisticci (1421–98), an enterprising Florentine who wrote lives of famous contemporaries (particularly those who bought his books, like Federigo da Montefeltro), organised teams of scribes who could produce up to forty manuscript copies at a time if required.

The Quattrocento was also a pioneering century for translations. In no previous century had so many Greek works of all kinds been turned into Latin. The impact of Greek studies can be charted from the end of the fourteenth century, when Manuel Chrysoloras was formally invited to Florence to give lessons, to the death in Venice, in 1515, of Aldo Manuzio, who systematically published Greek texts for the first time ever. In just over a century, in fact, the Italian humanists succeeded in preserving almost all the Greek texts that had survived the Sack of Constantinople during the Fourth Crusade of 1204. What was saved by Italian ingenuity were texts we take for granted as part of our cultural legacy: Homer's epic poems, the *Iliad* and the *Odyssey*; the Greek tragedies and comedies; the lyric poets; the historians Herodotus and Thucydides; nearly all of Plato, and his systematiser Plotinus; Aristotle in the original Greek, plus his early Greek commentators; medical authorities like Hippocrates and Galen; and household names in mathematics and astronomy like Euclid, Archimedes and Ptolemy. The Byzantines also possessed a vast library of early Greek Christian writers like Basil, Origen and Chrysostom, known for their expertise in biblical interpretation, and their exhortations to ethical living. Humanists often found the Greek Church's approach to religion more in tune with their own scholarly, literary and rhetorical training than medieval scholasticism. Lorenzo Valla criticised the Latin Vulgate New Testament in the light of the original Greek, and turned philology into the foundation of a new theology.

Humanist profiles

Leonardo Bruni and civic humanism

The wide range of scholarly and literary interests that humanists displayed can perhaps be best illustrated by looking at a few very different writers. Out of a long list of remarkable scholars and men of letters three are singled out below to demonstrate some characteristic humanist goals and achievements which were to have striking repercussions on the culture not only of Italy, but of Western Europe generally, in the next century.

In some respects, Leonardo Bruni (1370–1444) turned his back on Petrarch's recommendations of a life of detachment and isolation for the man of letters. He championed what has been termed 'civic humanism', a union of classical studies and writing in the service of the 'common good' – in Bruni's case, the good of the Florentine republic, and the cause of republicanism. Bruni detested clerical pretensions, served his city-state as Chancellor, married, and enjoyed a comfortable life. In many other ways he followed in Petrarch's footsteps. He started translating Aristotle directly from the Greek, and chose works neglected in the universities but central to moral philosophy: the *Ethics* (1416) and *Politics* (1435–7) – an initiative which led to Aristotle being studied in greater depth outside the university precincts than within. But Bruni realised, as Petrarch had not, that Aristotle could be used to further the aims of the secular city-states. According to Aristotle, asceticism and poverty have no value in an ethical system; some material goods are necessary in order to be happy, and one could not even practise a virtue like magnanimity without wealth,

including property, and a desire for public recognition. The *Politics*, furthermore, makes it clear that we are political animals who find our highest
fulfilment in performing the offices of a citizen. Bruni drew together his
readings from Cicero about republicanism and liberty, blended them with
Aristotle, and found he had a recipe that mirrored the aspirations of Quattrocento Florence.

Bringing together what he had learned from these writers, Bruni composed
the first ideological panegyric promoting Florentine civic ideals, *Laudatio
florentinae urbis* (1403–4). The immediate occasion was the successful defeat
by Florence of Milanese claims to domination in northern Italy, similar, Bruni
persuaded his readers, to Athens defending Greek liberty against the Persians,
and Romans defending the liberty of Italy against invaders. His main thesis
was that liberty, equality before the law, and economic prosperity were greater
in republics than in tyrannies; and that precisely because of liberty, all the arts
flourished there more abundantly. In *Historiae florentini populi*, the Florentine
people were seen as keeping alive a long tradition of republican struggles
against tyranny stretching back to Roman and Etruscan antiquity (note that
Bruni repudiated links with the Roman Empire). The History was translated
into the vernacular by another Florentine, Donato Acciaiuoli, at the request of
the Signoria, and printed in 1476. Bruni did not disdain vernacular literature;
he composed a *Vita di Dante*, whom he praised, together with Petrarch and
Boccaccio, on the grounds that Florentine authors who wrote in the vernacular
were further proof of the city's cultural hegemony. Matteo Palmieri, a
Florentine disciple of Bruni, popularised Bruni's republicanism further by
composing *Della vita civile* in Italian in 1429.

Bruni's *Dialogi*, dedicated to Pier Paolo Vergerio (1401–2), favoured the
dialogue (rather than formalised debating questions in the scholastic manner)
as the appropriate vehicle for argumentative (that is, philosophical) prose
about serious contemporary issues: a choice that was to be reinforced by Valla
and Alberti, who brought the Latin prose dialogue in the Renaissance to new
heights. Taking his cue from Cicero, Bruni represents actual contemporaries
arguing in a normal Florentine setting: Coluccio Salutati's house the first day,
and Roberto Rossi's the second. The topics introduced are relevant to the
group's interests; the speakers put forward differing views which are not
reconciled, and readers, therefore, do not have their minds made up for them.
The dialogue, in fact, is an example of how to dispute according to renovated
classical, mainly Ciceronian, precepts.

Leon Battista Alberti: polyglot and polymath

Leon Battista Alberti (1404–72), more versatile than Bruni, is often considered
the archetype of the Renaissance polymath. He wrote fluently in both Latin
and the vernacular, producing a comedy, moral treatises, biographies, fables,
love poetry and eclogues, a massive survey of architecture in ten books,

treatises on painting, a manual of practical mathematics, and another one on devising codes used in diplomatic correspondence. He excelled in the argumentative Ciceronian dialogues as well as brief satirical ones in the manner of Lucian. As an illegitimate child, he was disadvantaged in matters of inheritance; when, in 1432, Pope Eugene IV lifted the ban which prevented him from being appointed to lucrative benefices, his income came from the Church. Like Petrarch, he was a cleric only of convenience, and suffered from incurable melancholia. Yet he could be fiercely anti-clerical if not anti-religious, and was also unusual in combining his humanist studies with the mechanical arts, for which he always expressed the greatest respect. He was a practising architect, and his theoretical writings on art and architecture are of fundamental importance.

Alberti's written Latin has been judged more fluent than his Italian, perhaps because he grew up outside Florence when his wealthy and powerful family was in exile. Given that he spent barely a decade of his life in Florence, mainly between 1434 and 1443, it is remarkable that he threw himself into the cause of the *volgare* with such enthusiasm. Even before arriving in Florence, he had drafted his most sustained vernacular prose piece, the dialogue *Della famiglia*, in which three generations of the Alberti family discuss their mercantile, civic values. In 1441 he helped to organise a contest, the *Certame Coronario*, to promote the study and composition of poetry in the vernacular; the theme, set by Alberti himself, was 'Friendship'.

The dialogue *Della famiglia* served a public and personal aim: it vindicated the Alberti family against their enemies, also Florentine, who had brought about their exile; and it also vindicated Leon Battista, who, though disinherited and a cleric, showed himself to be the Alberti family's most outstanding defender. A glance at *Della famiglia* will make clear that Alberti 'ennobled' the vernacular by bringing to it Greek and Latin learning. The discussions about the education of children (Book I), and married life (Book II) owe more to Aristotle's and Xenophon's *Economics* (in antiquity, economics meant household management) than to his own experience; put into the mouths of his illustrious relatives, the ancient norms appear as native Florentine ideals and practice. Book IV is about friendship, a bond more enduring than marital and family ones. Book III, the most radical, owes more to experience, to *pratica*, than book-learning – as the main speaker, the elderly Giannozzo, affirms. He makes everything to do with money – saving and spending, investing, profit-making, merchant banking – respectable and ethical, a duty of the family if it is not to become a parasite on society. Wealth and profit are good in themselves if earned by hard work and *masserizia*, meaning careful management of the family's possessions and income. Such a startling re-evaluation of money overturned first the classical Greek and Roman view (for Aristotle, while barter was acceptable, trading for money, which implies profit, was base, and usury was condemned; for Cicero, private property constituted wealth); secondly the Christian view (the Bible says: 'Money is the root of all evil', and

Christ commanded his followers to sell all they had and give to the poor; usury
was universally condemned); and thirdly the feudal aristocratic view (the ideal
is to spend lavishly from wealth gained from the land; trading is base). By
using the dialogue form, Alberti could distance himself, a cleric and scholar,
from such views while celebrating Florentine mercantile republicanism, especially his own family's. Book III, understandably popular with the merchant
class, was detached from the rest of the work, expanded here and there, and
attributed to a different author, Agnolo Pandolfini. It was printed under that
name in the eighteenth and nineteenth centuries.

In Alberti's case, the choice of Latin or Italian was often tied to the social
level he was writing for, and the nature of the subject-matter. Latin could reach
a wider audience geographically, but a small number within any area – clergy,
professionals and those who had been to secondary school. The reverse was
true of the vernacular. Alberti, for example, first wrote *De pictura* in Latin, a
choice dictated by the technical vocabulary he needed to employ. But interested
painters and architects could not read Latin, so Alberti wrote a version in the
vernacular, in which, however, he struggled to find equivalents for precise
Latin terms. Among Alberti's other contributions we should perhaps mention
his Latin *Intercenales*, a collection of short satirical dialogues in the style of
Lucian which introduced a new note into Renaissance literature of *serio
ludere*, or 'playful seriousness' – mocking, witty attacks on contemporary
mores put into the mouths of gods and goddesses, personified abstractions and
other fictional characters with little regard for setting, time, and other conventions of verisimilitude.

Lorenzo Valla: language in the service of ethics

If Alberti's stern Stoic ethics owe little to Christianity, Lorenzo Valla (1407–
57) swings in a diametrically opposed direction, reforming Christian ethics in a
way that he claims owes nothing to pagan philosophy, especially the Stoics.
Valla's reforms are more radical than any of his contemporaries'. They extend
to literacy and learning; grammar, rhetoric and dialectic; textual criticism and
biblical scholarship; and he dismantles the entire scholastic curriculum by
means of relentless argument. He displayed no interest in the vernacular. On
the other hand, he was convinced that Latin had been and could be the perfect
instrument of communication for educated speech and writing, and to that end
composed a dictionary of correct Latin usage based on a staggering range of
sources, *Elegantiae linguae latinae* (completed 1441, but published 1448).
Grammatical and lexical questions absorbed him: concluding his analysis of
logical fallacies, Valla laments that the 'greatest thinkers have made mistakes
in reasoning because of carelessness in their use of words'. Whether they like it
or not, philosophers are concerned with the meanings of terms; yet 'they never
descend to grammar; and failing to become engaged with the very heart of
their subject-matter, they never support their edifices by means of columns',

that is, words correctly used. The *Dialecticae disputationes* which he worked on up to his death, in three successive versions, were nothing less than a stripping down of Aristotle's *Organon* (his books on reasoning) as taught in the medieval universities, and a verbatim substitution of sections of Book v of Quintilian's *Institutes of Oratory*, which Valla deemed more useful, as instruction on the art of reasoning, than Aristotle's, because Quintilian was more practical. Valla exploited the new finds of Cicero's mature oratorical works (1421), and the complete Quintilian (1421); and to the horror of scholastics, he declared that rhetoric (or oratory as the Romans called it), understood in its richer sense, was the queen of the liberal arts. He judged that neither the philosopher nor the theologian could exercise his discipline competently without it.

Valla chose the dialogue as the perfect vehicle for displaying his reformed eloquence, arguing for and against all views (identified by the Ciceronian phrase *in utramque partem*) in order to arrive at the closest approximation to the truth. His very first, and clearly the new model of the genre, was *De vero falsoque bono* (in three versions of 1431, 1433, 1444–9), on true and false ethical goals. Here he shows how to dismantle ancient moral philosophies, particularly Stoic, Epicurean and Peripatetic; how to arrive at a better understanding of the New Testament by unravelling the Latin Vulgate translation and restoring the meaning of the Greek words; how to integrate parts of ancient moral teaching into a coherent whole; and how to use literary techniques of vivid description to paint an attractive, moving picture of a community bound by charity as the ultimate moral 'good'.

If Valla undermined ancient philosophy – and many humanist values in the process – he did likewise to scholastic theology and canon law. The dialogue *De libero arbitrio* asserts a deep conviction in choice as the foundation of ethics, but it relentlessly questions facile 'solutions' to the problem of free will and predestination: our minds are not privy to God's, and we cannot use language about what we cannot experience. Another dialogue denounces religious vows, by which members of religious orders set themselves apart as spiritually 'superior' to lay Christians. An active life of service to the community is proposed as an alternative Christian ideal. While not formally a dialogue, *De falso credita et ementita Constantini donatione declamatio* is dialogic with its series of direct and indirect speeches representing diverse voices of Constantine's contemporaries, all reminding him of his loyalties to Rome and Roman citizens, and his duty to preserve the Empire and its sovereignty. Only then does Valla, as a prosecuting attorney, compel the forger to read his forgery of Constantine's 'donation', after which he performs a devastating textual analysis, paragraph by paragraph, revealing its anachronisms, contradictions and mistakes in grammar and vocabulary. The Church has no claim to temporal rule whatsoever, and should be reduced to a group of preachers earning their living in the community.

Not surprisingly, contemporary clerics loathed Valla, while later Protestants went to the other extreme. Erasmus, more than any other writer, borrowed from Valla, printing the latter's notes on the New Testament for the first time.

Women humanists

While women played no part in discovering manuscripts, editing books, running schools, negotiating in chanceries or public disputing, their achievements as humanists were nonetheless considerable. Many obstacles lay in their path, above all, getting an education beyond the elementary 'vernacular' school. Women were not allowed to leave the home and attend a public school with boys. Their classical studies had to be carried on indoors, with a private tutor or under the guidance of brothers and fathers, and with the alleged primary purpose of personal moral improvement and nothing beyond. Furthermore, since intellectual excellence was considered a male virtue, learned women ran the risk of being labelled 'unnatural', and had to defend their studies as enhancing, not undoing, their 'female nature'. Finally, writing itself was morally suspect: a public advertisement of the self, which for women was associated with immodesty. Women writers continually justify the act of writing, assuring disapproving male (but also female) readers that their learning has not put immoral thoughts into their heads, nor caused them to question or disobey (male) authority.

Characteristic genres for Quattrocento women were literary letters and orations. Battista da Montefeltro Malatesta (1383–1450), the widow of an assassinated despot, delivered an oration pleading for the restoration of Pesaro to herself and her family. She tutored her own grand-daughter, Costanza Varano, who as a young woman composed Latin letters, orations and poems. Once married, her studies ceased, and she died in 1447, at the age of nineteen, shortly after giving birth to her second child. Outstanding in this early part of the century was Isotta Nogarola (1418–66), proficient in Latin and Greek, who was taught by humanists of Guarino Veronese's circle along with her two sisters, Ginevra and Angela. Isotta corresponded with educated men in Latin – the way of establishing a literary circle of one's own. But when she wrote to Guarino himself, he snubbed her by first not answering, and then answering only at others' insistence. Isotta was also the object of defamatory letters circulated in 1438, accusing her of incest with her brother. Her learning was to blame, for 'an eloquent woman is never chaste'. Going even more against social expectations, she refused both marriage and life in a convent.

Isotta distinguished herself by formally debating with a Venetian, Lodovico Foscarini, on a by no means idle theological issue: whether Adam or Eve sinned the most in the Garden of Eden. At stake was the nature of male and female as God had created them, and the natural relationship of male to female in marriage as God, the supreme law-giver, had decreed. Isotta had carefully read Genesis, and the commentaries of Augustine, among others, as well as Aristotle; she knew that theologians and philosophers agreed in declaring woman morally infirm and less rational than men. Her chosen debating tactic was therefore to point out contradictions (in which she could succeed), rather than confront higher authorities (in which she could not).

At the end of the Quattrocento, Cassandra Fedele (1465–1558) and Laura Cereta (1469–1499) both came from professional families in Venice and Padua respectively, where their fathers encouraged and even directed their Latin and Greek studies. Fedele delivered orations before the Venetian Doge, the Venetian citizens, and even at the University of Padua, where she praised the philosophical studies of a (male) relative. No woman was permitted to study or obtain a degree from a university at the time. She was even extolled by Poliziano. After marriage in 1497, her literary studies petered out. Laura Cereta wrote several collections of letters, some published in Padua in 1460. She is perhaps the most rounded woman writer of the Quattrocento, studying Petrarch as well as classical Latin and Greek authors, composing pastoral eclogues, and entering the male preserves of astrology, invective and polemics. Yet she encountered hostility, and had to defend herself against carping women resentful of her 'unwomanly' attainments, as well as against men who denied that she could have written such polished Latin letters. Her defence of women's education (1488) presents for the first time a canon of women writers (poets and philosophers) through the ages, set forth by a woman writer herself. Isotta Nogarola and Cassandra Fedele conclude her proof that men and women share in one human nature, which imparts to both sexes equally the same freedom to learn; the comparative lack of exceptional women has to do not so much with nature as with the fact that the sexes fulfil divergent roles.

None of these women had their works printed in the Quattrocento. Women writers come into their own in the next century, when they achieved eminence principally as vernacular poets, and along with men, could publish without need of classical learning.

9
Power, patronage and literary associations

The literary map of Quattrocento Italy is one of geographical centres, and within these, of various kinds of structured social groups in the form of organisations: either religious (the Church or a religious order), educational (university, school, academy) or political, especially the court. In all cases, patronage was a determining factor for the author, for the kind of work written, the language it is written in, the arguments put forward, and the intended public. Even then, authors also depended on teachers, friends, professional colleagues, scribes (Pico della Mirandola dictated so fast that he needed two at a time!), librarians and booksellers. After the invention of printing, they needed in addition publishers and further patrons to cover printing expenses, and yet more friends in high places to write letters (often printed with the book) persuading the readers that they would not be dissatisfied after parting with a considerable amount of money. The courts were the obvious centres, with their traditions of patronage – not always happy – attracting large numbers – not always talented – of cultural and social climbers. Naples and Ferrara became flourishing centres of literary activity in the Quattrocento, each in very different ways. The diversification of activity needed to sustain a wide range of literary activity and printed book production favoured urban centres with a strong economy or guaranteed income. Florence and Venice fit the former requisite, and Rome the latter. This chapter will look at the ways in which different geographical centres in Italy produced the kinds of literature they did, whether Latin or vernacular, and try to identify the features particular to each centre. Only Florence, Venice, Rome, Naples and Ferrara can be considered in this brief survey, but these give some indication of the nature of patronage and literary activity across the Italian centres as a whole.

Florence

Florence under the Medici affords a cogent example of a republic in which patronage, which had hitherto been scattered in the hands of prominent citizen families, was consolidated, largely by a leading family, for both public and private purposes. Latin literature promoting republicanism naturally found expression in Florence, as we have seen; and it was also true that the promotion of the vernacular was linked to Florentine historical awareness of two centuries of prose and poetry that had boasted Dante, Petrarch and Boccaccio.

Two dates stand out. The first is 1434, the year of the return of the Medici from exile, and the beginning of their rise under Cosimo, his son Piero, and his illustrious grandson Lorenzo 'il Magnifico' as the leading family within an oligarchy. The other is 1454, the date of the Peace of Lodi, Cosimo's diplomatic triumph, which ushered in a half-century of comparative peace in the Italian peninsula, and concomitantly, a surge of literary activity that came to a close with Lorenzo's death in 1492, followed by the French invasions of 1494.

Cosimo energetically promoted Greek and Latin studies, especially translations of classical authors: his success in bringing to Florence the famous Council of Greek and Latin Churches, held in 1439, brought not only business opportunities for Florentine merchants and bankers but also Greek scholars and precious Greek texts. His initiative in commissioning Marsilio Ficino to make the first complete translation of Plato into Latin was enormously important in diffusing a new Platonic culture which was to influence the poetry and art of the next generation. Cosimo also brought the Greek Giovanni Argyropoulos to lecture at the Florentine *studium* (university) on Aristotle and his Greek commentators, and to translate Aristotle anew.

Medici patronage of the vernacular also had important consequences: not least, it was a means of disarming anti-Medici factions and promoting a sense of Florentine identity. Biographies of Dante, Petrarch and Boccaccio by humanist authors such as Leonardo Bruni and Giannozzo Manetti turned them into embodiments of national values. Cosimo's patronage, carried on by Lorenzo, gave a new impetus to vernacular poetry, and Lorenzo, himself a poet of distinction, allied himself with outstanding classical scholars such as Angelo Poliziano and Pico della Mirandola and relaunched the Tuscan lyric. Lorenzo's circle undertook to give literary expression to a range of popular forms, from bawdy carnival songs to sacred plays and hymns and narrative poems: and Luigi Pulci, at the urging of Lorenzo's mother, Lucrezia Tornabuoni, produced the first of the great Italian chivalric epics.

Rome

Rome provides a striking contrast to the lay courts and to thriving commercial republics. Because of the papal 'Captivity' in Avignon, which lasted for most of the Trecento and was followed by the election of rival Popes in rival seats during the Great Schism, the Papacy did not return permanently to Rome until the 1440s. Rome came only eighth in size of population of Italian cities, yet humanists flocked there in increasing numbers in the second half of the Quattrocento, with the result that the city stood on a par with Florence and

Venice in attracting educated men. Literary and artistic life lay overwhelmingly with the Church, not with local inhabitants; and the language of Rome was Latin – of necessity, as Latin was the *lingua franca* of the Church, the largest international institution in Europe. But while Rome's literary production lay mainly in the service of religion, it succeeded in wedding religion to the pagan culture of the ancient world.

Compared to that of secular courts, with their sudden dynastic shifts, the patronage of Rome appeared financially secure and long-lasting. It was bestowed not only by the Pope, but also by wealthy and powerful cardinals, who were princes in their own right, with their numerous households, called *familiae*. The centre of ecclesiastical bureaucracy, the Curia, needed an ever-greater supply of educated civil servants to write good Latin and take care of diplomatic correspondence and the preparation of official documents. Rome also boasted a university (established in 1406, with the help of Leonardo Bruni), academies, and a magnificent library. All of these social structures promoted learning, debate and writing.

But Rome, a city of nominally celibate clergy, lacked the wives, mothers, sisters and daughters to demand a vernacular literature with a large element of entertainment; it also lacked a large, native, lay, professional and commercial class to support and supply that demand, or at least combine humanist and vernacular interests. Rome did not produce its own humanists, like Florence or Venice. It relied on 'immigrants', who at the beginning of the century were predominantly Florentine and often laymen (Leonardo Bruni, Poggio Braccio-lini); but there were also Germans (Nicholas of Cusa) and Greeks (Cardinal Bessarion, Theodore Gaza, George of Trebizond). The only outstanding humanist born in Rome, in fact, was Lorenzo Valla.

The result of humanists working for the papal court, and Quattrocento Popes blessing humanism, was to make the leaders of the Catholic Church the heirs and propagators of the language and learning of the Roman Empire in particular, and of classical Greek and Latin in general. Pius II, the Sienese Aeneas Sylvius Piccolomini (1405–64), was a prolific writer, a worldly humanist before his conversion – author of an obscene comedy set in a brothel, *Chrysis*, as well as a volume of *Commentaries*, or memoirs written in the third person about his prominent roles at the Council of Basel on the side of the Conciliarists and the anti-Pope.

Three aspects of Roman humanism deserve notice. Firstly, the Roman Curia, which included the chancery proper and the papal secretaries, and was the largest and most advanced bureaucracy of its day, became the major seat for the reform, along humanist lines, of the Latin language and its oral and written practice. Secondly, humanist historical and political literature explicitly linked the Popes to secular monarchs, projecting their image as new Roman Emperors with courts to match. In addition theocracy, rampant in the Middle Ages, found a new lease of life dressed in classical garb: biographies of the Popes, and histories of Rome and the Papacy as a civilising force, magnified the Papal court. Thirdly, with the collapse of Constantinople under Turkish invasion in 1453, Greek orthodox prelates and scholars came to Italy for refuge and Rome, no less than Florence and Venice, took the opportunity to become a new Athens. One of the outstanding figures was Giovanni (later Basilio) Bessarion, created a cardinal in 1439, who resided in the city from 1443 to his death in 1472 and made his house a meeting place for the study of all things Greek.

In the climate of purist classicism that dominated Rome in the Quattrocento, there was little place for Italian. But to Rome came printers from Germany, in 1466–7, to set up a press. Leon Battista Alberti documented the event; what amazed him was the speed of reproduction: in 100 days more than 200 copies of a substantial book by three men only! One whole page of type at a time! Although Venice had outstripped Rome by the end of the century, Rome kept its second place in printing, producing both classical and early Christian writers.

Venice

In Venice the outstanding features of the literary scene were the role of the schools and of the governing patrician class, and the strong emphasis on Greek studies. As in Florence works of scholarship and literature came from the pens of native Venetians, but in the reproduction and diffusion of literature Venice and its printing presses were at the centre of a thriving international culture. It could be said that the Venetian state engaged in the biggest act of collective patronage of classical and vernacular literature in Italy through its subsidies to printing presses. An enlightened policy of patronage in Venice took it for granted that learning and literature were good for commerce and for the prestige of the state. As in Florence, there was a vaunting of republican *libertas*; but in respect of freedom of the press, Venice, a city with twice the population of Florence, and more resident immigrant communities, made Florentine book production look provincial. This hard-headed side of the Venetian literary scene was exemplified by Venetian merchant-travellers who developed a genre of their own, the travel book (harking back, however, to the Trecento and Marco Polo).

Venetian scholarship revolved around the schools, which stimulated the development of libraries, the publication of text books and philosophical commentaries, and the study of Greek. The alliance of these schools with the University of Padua resulted in the involvement of patrician families in Aristotelian philosophical studies and writings. Early in the Quattrocento, Venice produced two great teachers who ran their own schools, Gasparino Barzizza and Guarino Veronese; both subsequently moved to the mainland, to Padua and Ferrara respectively. Guarino emphasised Greek, and taught young patricians. But the main humanist schools were in Venice, and aimed to train their young citizens for public office and the diplomatic service. The principal ones, the Scuola di Rialto and the Scuola di San Marco, assumed a role similar to the academy in Florence, the Curia in Rome, and the court in Naples or Ferrara.

Even more marked than in Florence was the presence of families with generations of powerful, wealthy and highly literate individuals dedicated to public service: the Barbaro, Bembo, Contarini, Donà, Foscarini, Giustinian families and others. For example, the most famous Venetian humanist of the Quattrocento, Ermolao Barbaro the younger (1453/4–92), a close friend of Poliziano and Pico della Mirandola in Florence, reformed the teaching of Aristotle in the University of Padua, using Greek texts and early Greek commentaries. One of his goals was to produce clear, readable Latin translations of Greek scientific works; another was to edit and annotate difficult Latin scientific authors such as Pliny.

Another characteristic feature of Venetian literature in the Quattrocento was the travel accounts which Venetian merchants, patrician and middle class, monopolised, just as they monopolised tourism to the East, whether for sacred or profane purposes. Merchants were true explorers, and needed to gather economic intelligence for Venice if their trading was to prosper. Giosaphat Barbaro, Ambrosio Contarini and Nicolò di Conti all held public office, and were sent out to spy. Nicolò dictated an account of his journey to India to Poggio Bracciolini, who turned it into Latin. Markets, foods, raw materials and manufacturing are looked at with the calculating merchant's eye. The Venetian state also organised regular pilgrimages to the Holy Land and other shrines; pilgrims' safety was guaranteed. Guide books by Gabriele Capodilista (1458), Santo Brasca (1480) and Francesco Suriano (1475) gave details of places to go, prayers to say, and indulgences granted.

Printing remains, however, Venice's outstanding contribution to Renaissance culture. Of all the printers, and of all the books printed in Italy, Venice had already cornered about half of the market by the end of the Quattrocento. A landmark was the setting up of a press by the Greek scholar and humanist Aldo Manuzio in 1488. At first, classical texts dominated, but gradually vernacular ones came to the fore. Editions of Dante, Petrarch and Boccaccio signalled what has been called the 'Tuscanisation' of the literary vernacular. But in plurilingual Venice and its adjacent territories, there was acceptance not only of the Venetian dialect in print, as with the travel books and poetry, but also of 'invented' languages. The *Hypnerotomachia Poliphili* of the Venetian Dominican Francesco Colonna, a unique hybrid blend of Latin and vernacular, was the first non-classical text printed by Aldo Manuzio, in 1499. In Padua, in university circles, Tifi Odasi and his brother Corrado (friends of Ermolao Barbaro the Younger) composed parodic mock-epics in equally parodic plurilingual styles. Tifi bequeathed the word 'macaronic' to literary vocabulary: it derives from the title of his *Macaronea*, printed in the late Quattrocento, later emulated by Teofilo Folengo (see below pp. 273–4).

Naples

In Naples, literature was almost exclusively dependent on court patronage – more precisely, on two Spanish Kings originating from Aragon: Alfonso, called 'the Magnanimous' (1443–58), and his only, illegitimate, son, Ferdinand or Ferrante (1458–94). While Naples and Venice were the cities with the largest population in Italy, and both depended on commerce, Naples did not have a highly educated middle class like its rival. In their day, the Spanish Aragonese dynasty constituted ideal models of patron-princes who recognised merit and rewarded it. Alfonso was the generous benefactor of an illustrious group of humanists and vernacular scholars and writers – as well as artists and architects – from all over Italy and outside, who with few exceptions spoke of him with admiration and affection. Conscious that he might be looked down on as an unsophisticated foreigner who spoke Castilian, Alfonso strove to spread the image of a civilised triumphant monarch bringing peace and prosperity to southern Italy, and his enthusiasm about books and learning made it possible for Panormita, Facio, Valla, Pontano, Sannazaro, Manetti and Biondo to produce some, if not most, of their best work. While his court has been called 'imported' in that none of the above, with the exception of Sannazaro, was a native Neapolitan, Alfonso did succeed in creating a literary community that lasted until the end of the century; his son Ferrante also re-launched the university at Naples as a centre of learning in 1465, establishing four chairs in the humanities, one of which was in Greek. Alfonso's ambitions as a patron took shape when he brought Antonio Beccadelli, 'il Panormita' (1394–1471), to his court in 1434 and entrusted him with a range of administrative posts within and without the Kingdom, and, most importantly of all, gave him free rein to build up the King's library and bring illustrious writers to the Neapolitan court. The meetings in Alfonso's library at Castel Capuano were the origin of the famous Accademia Pontaniana, which, under Pontano's leadership, gathered together an impressive group of intellectuals – civil servants, military men, political exiles and scientists.

In the favourable climate promoted by the Aragonese rulers, Neapolitan letters developed a number of characteristic features. Firstly, neo-Latin prose and poetry of high quality flourished in abundance, rivalling, if not at times surpassing, that of Florence and Venice. Secondly, humanists at Naples combined without conflict active lives in administration with literary pursuits. Alfonso trusted humanists more than local barons to run the Kingdom, which led to a proliferation of political and historical writings: for once humanists felt their talents were being used to the full. Thirdly, the Aragonese, partly because of wars against papal claims to disputed territory, were self-consciously secular, resistant to clerical interference in their affairs, and unsympathetic not just to superstitious rituals allowed by the Church, but to dogma itself. Valla spent thirteen of his most productive years in the service of Alfonso, receiving much support for his polemical treatise against papal claims to sovereignty (see above, p. 141), which was dedicated to the king. Naples was later to become a centre of the reform movement in Italy.

Three of the outstanding figures at the Neapolitan court give some idea of the strength and diversity of its literary culture: Giovanni Pontano (1426/29–1503), 'poet and prime minister' as his latest biographer hails him; Jacopo Sannazaro (1458–1530) and Masuccio Salernitano (1410–75). The last is famed for his *novelle* in the vernacular (see below, p. 155). Pontano was probably the most versatile and prolific Latin poet and prose writer of the Italian Renaissance. His Latin love lyrics, while reminiscent of Catullus, Propertius and Ovid, still convey the vividness and freshness of immediate experience, and are unusual in including a collection of poems about the joys of married love and family life (*De amore coniugali*). His prose dialogues bear comparison with Alberti's 'dinner-pieces' for their social satire and sense of 'serious playfulness'. Sannazaro is best known for his pastoral romance, *Arcadia*, discussed below (p. 159), but he was equally gifted in Latin and vernacular poetry. In the former he followed Pontano's love of the eclogue, but transformed it by substituting fishermen and dramatic marine events such as storms and shipwrecks, set around the Bay of Naples, for more conventional shepherds and woodlands (*Eclogae piscatorie*, composed before 1500). He also wrote a major epic poem in Virgilian hexameters on the triumphant birth of the world's saviour (*De partu virginis*), turning the Christian salvation story into an Ovidian myth about metamorphosis. Evangelicals like Erasmus were appalled: for them the gospel accounts were sacred and should not be contaminated by pagan values.

Ferrara

The court of Ferrara is an example of a small northern principality (like Mantua and Urbino) which was able to achieve high cultural distinction in art, architecture and letters, both classical and – especially – vernacular. The prominence of the latter is undoubtedly linked to the existence of a number of distinguished women patrons who had the power and resources to commission specific works and attract some of the best poets and artists of the time.

For most of the Quattrocento Ferrara was ruled by successive members of the d'Este family. Leonello, who was in control from 1441 to 1450, was a scholar in his own right, having been tutored by Guarino da Verona, with whom, as with other court humanists, he regularly engaged in learned discussions. He suggested to Leon Battista Alberti that he should write his monumental treatise on architecture, and Alberti in turn encouraged Leonello's taste for medals with subtle Greek and Latin inscriptions. Borso d'Este, who ruled from 1450 to 1471, commissioned lavishly illuminated manuscripts, spending a fortune on a Bible with over a thousand miniatures. His love of spectacle was carried to new heights by his brother Ercole, in power from 1471 to 1505. Brought up at Naples, he married Eleonora of Aragon, who bore him three distinguished children: Beatrice, who married Ludovico Sforza ('il Moro') of Milan; Isabella, wife of Francesco Gonzaga of Mantua; and Alfonso, who married Lucrezia Borgia. All these women played prominent parts in the cultural lives of their respective courts.

The sympathetic attitude to women of the Ferrarese court is exemplified in numerous works by Antonio Cornazzano (c. 1432–84) such as *Del modo di reggere e di regnare* written in 1478 for the Duchess (Eleonora of Aragon Este), and, on Boccaccio's model, a celebration of famous women, *De mulieribus admirandis* (1466–7).

Under Ercole the comedies of Terence and Plautus were given full-scale productions, and contemporary drama of classical inspiration was encouraged. He built up a chapel choir, and interest in sung music extended to the staging of *intermezzi* for religious and secular plays. Classical mythology was much exploited in all the arts, as for example the story of Cupid and Psyche from Apuleius' *Golden Ass*, on which Niccolò da Correggio based a poem in *ottave*, *L'Innamoramento di Cupido e di Psyche* (dedicated to Isabella d'Este), and to which Giulio Romano devoted a whole room of frescoes at Mantua. Boiardo, whose fame is based on the long chivalric poem *Orlando innamorato*, written for the Estense court, translated the whole of Apuleius' novel.

Isabella d'Este and Beatrice were both tutored by the humanist Battista Guarino, and Isabella was taught Latin by another famous scholar, Mario Equicola. She was a great patron of dramatic spectacles both in Mantua and Ferrara: one of the earliest vernacular plays on a secular subject, Ovid's story of Cephalus and Procris, also by Niccolò, was presented before her in 1487. At Mantua she promoted plays based on *novelle* by Boccaccio: in 1499, for example, Antonio Cammelli ('il Pistoia'), a prolific poet, sent her a tragedy based on the tale of Tancred and Ghismonda (*Decameron* IV, 1). Isabella engaged a distinguished poet, Antonio Tebaldeo (1463–1537), to tutor her in vernacular poetry, and she favoured another talented poet at Mantua, Serafino Aquilano. The esteem in which these cultured women were held, and the influence they exerted, were repeatedly acknowledged by the leading writers and artists of their day. Isabella d'Este was known in her circle as 'la prima donna del mondo'.

10

Literature in the vernacular

Latin and the vernacular

Language was the object of keener scrutiny in the Quattrocento than it had ever been before. Contributing to the intensity of the debates was the enhanced study of rhetoric, and the consequent appreciation of language as an instrument of communication used to enlighten, move and delight its hearers. Italian humanists assumed a disparity between spoken vernaculars, seen as inferior, and written Latin (*grammatica*), deemed superior because it was 'fixed' by rules. But they also grew aware that Latin itself was not 'fixed', and that medieval Latin, termed 'barbaric' since Petrarch, differed substantially from classical Latin, both lexically and syntactically. Some humanists then distinguished between a *volgare illustre*, a prestigious written vernacular to be used by poets and scholars, and the Babel of spoken regional dialects that existed in Italy – a situation now called diglossia.

In ancient Rome, humanists asked, what had been the relationship between the language spoken by Romans and the written language of, say, Cicero? Acrimonious exchanges began in 1435, when Flavio Biondo wrote to Leonardo Bruni that, unlike modern Italians, the ancient Romans both spoke and wrote fundamentally the same language. Guarino Veronese was surprised to observe how well modern, even unlettered Greeks spoke the same language that scholars wrote, and believed that this monolingualism also held for ancient Rome. Bruni himself differed: bilingualism reigned in ancient Rome, with one language for the uneducated (like the vernacular in contemporary Italy), and another used by educated writers like Cicero. Lorenzo Valla raised the stakes in a series of mid-century disputes with Bartolomeo Facio and Poggio Bracciolini. While accepting a distinction between an informal spoken Latin and a more 'literary' style, Valla denied that Latin was an artificial language taught according to grammatical rules. He followed the orator Quintilian's view that one learned how to speak and write correctly and idiomatically by following the principle of usage, *consuetudo*. For Valla, the vernacular was reserved merely for domestic use, and had no value whatsoever in the public sphere. Valla also insisted that *romana lingua* was a synonym for *latina lingua*, against Poggio, who reserved the former for the vernacular spoken by contemporary Quattrocento Romans.

A key participant, Leon Battista Alberti, strongly defended monolingualism both for ancient Latin and modern vernacular (*Della famiglia*, Bk III, *Proem*), differing with Valla on the worth of the vernacular, and with Bruni on bilingualism in Rome. Alberti even wrote the first Florentine grammar, showing that the vernacular had rules just like Latin. This 'separate but equal' status for Latin and the vernacular was championed particularly by Florentines, from Dante and Boccaccio to Bruni, Matteo Palmieri, Cristoforo Landino and Lorenzo de' Medici. Alberti fully understood the social importance of the vernacular, which one needed if one wanted to be understood by all one's fellow citizens. But how had the vernaculars arisen in territory that was once Roman? Metaphors of corruption, implying contempt for the vernacular, were often used to explain the transition from one to the other. For Biondo and Alberti, however, while Latin had fallen from its 'purity', it had been transformed into spoken and written vernaculars wherever the Roman Empire had extended. Regarding the change from classical to medieval Latin, corruption metaphors were also used in abundance. For Valla, the Latin language and Latin letters had perished; his task was to bring about their restoration. 'Bad' scholastic Latin had come about through centuries of carelessness. But as the vernacular gained ascendancy in the age of Lorenzo, disputes centred around which vernacular was the best.

Prose and poetry in the *volgare*, or the vernacular, do not divide into easily distinguishable categories in the Quattrocento; nor are there obvious alignments of subject-matter within prose or metric genres. Other distinctions come into play: the literary tradition, written and oral; the level of decorum; and the audience to be addressed. Dante and Boccaccio were already models for a formal vernacular prose and poetry, and Petrarch for an especially refined and classicising poetry; but an author could draw on vibrant oral sources – 'popular' culture – and transform them.

For both prose and poetry, decorum prescribed that the style or linguistic register had to be 'fitting' for the subject-matter. A lowly subject, with ordinary people and domestic situations, required plain language with little or no artifice – that is, with none of the rhetorical 'adornments' such as figures of speech and thought, rare or imported words and the like. A high subject like a hymn to nature or to a divinity, epics with heroic exploits or tragedy, required an unusual vocabulary and was expected to be rich in 'adornments'. To mismatch style and subject-matter deliberately was to enter the territory of parody (as in the mock-epic). The transposition of the content of Latin poetry into vernacular genres almost word for word, as was done by Poliziano, was the kind of parody we now call pastiche. Decorum was frequently brought into attacks on vernacular works by rigid classicists, who felt the subject-matter of Latin and the vernacular should be kept within watertight compartments. (Their assumption was that the vernacular was only for 'lowly' subjects.) Dante had been the path-breaker, proving in his *Divina Commedia* that the *volgare* had enough lexical *copia* or abundance for 'high' subject-matters with specialist vocabularies like philosophy, astronomy and theology. Nevertheless, Quattrocento vernacular writers were continually struggling against the prejudice that the vernacular was an 'ignoble' language, so much so that using it could be a daring act of defiance.

By choosing the vernacular, an author – especially after the invention of printing – could reach a wider public which had no knowledge of 'grammar' (that is, Latin), and above all women, who could not be reached otherwise. Love poetry, chivalric romances and fiction sometimes explicitly included them. But there was still the question of choosing between a vernacular that had a literary tradition and one that did not; and then choosing from among many different spoken vernaculars; or even inventing a hybrid tongue. The latter choice might limit one's audience more than Latin. Sticking to literary models allowed a writer to reach a wider audience geographically (as was the case with imitators of Petrarch's lyrics), to the detriment of a wider one socially in a given linguistically homogeneous area like Naples.

In a famous rebuttal about the 'right' kind of Latin vocabulary and syntax, Poliziano accused the Roman humanist Paolo Cortese of slavishly imitating only Cicero: 'Writers who merely copy others, in my opinion are like parrots who pronounce words without understanding. The compositions of such people are lifeless, they lack force. ... "You do not write like Cicero", someone objects. So what? I am not Cicero; what I say, however, is my own."' (*Pros. lat.*, p. 902). Cortese, on the other hand, felt that most people needed to be told what was the 'best' style, and to learn from that.

Poliziano's and Cortese's positions represent two poles which are also relevant for vernacular poetry. Cortese feared that going too far in Poliziano's direction would lead to linguistic anarchy, to some sort of incomprehensible 'macaronic' language that would spell the end of clear communication. Poliziano, on the other hand, feared that following one author too closely would lead to the fossilisation of language lexically and syntactically. Throughout the Quattrocento, there was tension between the two views, but also tolerance as vernacular poets often veered from one to the other, from close adherence to Petrarch to a profusion of poetic models. By the end of the century, Lorenzo and (most of all) Poliziano were at one pole, the champions of *varietas* and versatility, the grand experimenters; at the other pole, Bembo would soon plant the flag of imitation with his *Prose della volgar lingua*: Petrarch for poetry and Boccaccio for prose.

Prose

The novella

Inevitably, Quattrocento *novelle*, whether in collections or singly, were written in the shadow of Boccaccio's towering masterpiece, both within Tuscany and without. Those presenting collections respond in varying ways to the need for a structure, either by arranging their material according to criteria like themes or genres, or by a frame narrative of sorts. *Novella* writers often specialise in particular kinds like collections of jokes and *beffe* (practical jokes). Very few could ever match Boccaccio's narrative genius: his sense of verbal economy, his ear for graphic dialogue and witty repartee, and above all his love of comic double meanings and ambiguities.

Gentile Sermini's *Novelle*, put together after 1426, stylistically are some rungs down the ladder compared to Boccaccio and even Sercambi. In the absence of a frame-story, a unitary feature is provided by a common setting for the forty tales, which include sonnets and *canzoni*: the public baths in Siena, an appropriate place for scandalous gossip and picaresque (if not obscene) stories of low life. The subject-matter is matched by a coarse linguistic texture full of popular idiomatic expressions typical of the oral tradition. One tale includes a motif later incorporated into the Romeo and Juliet story. The beautiful Montanina, married to a bestial husband, laboriously contrives her own death and burial with the aid of a drug in order to escape from Perugia to Milan with her dashing young lover Vannino. She plans for rapacious friars to rob her tomb and let her out unawares, by giving them to understand that she would be buried with her jewels. Tales told in baths being for enjoyment, these two lovers are so successful they actually return to live in Perugia.

Outside Tuscany, Masuccio Salernitano (Tommaso Guardati of Salerno, 1410–75) overtly praised Boccaccio and his 'beautifully adorned language and style', but his tales have little of Boccaccio's sparkling wit and less of his irony. Masuccio groups his fifty *novelle* thematically into five Parts, ten to a Part, like Boccaccio's Days: I against the clergy, invariably venal, lascivious and corrupt; II against jealous husbands; III against women's sexual wickedness; IV a more entertaining mixed bag of tragic and comic tales; and V in praise of noble and magnificent rulers (like his patrons). From exposing vice, the *novelle* thus progress to illustrating virtue. Masuccio departs from Boccaccio in dedicating each *novella* to a different patron or friend, mainly Aragonese nobility, courtiers like Giovanni Pontano, and visiting diplomats like the Venetian Zaccaria Barbaro. Each *novella* is also preceded by a short prologue, and followed by Masuccio's own heavy moralising commentary. There are no narrators to provide stylistic variety and diverse perspectives. Parts I and II follow Boccaccio closely. A scoundrel Dominican, for example, artfully seduces a pious wealthy nun, persuading her that God wants her to conceive and bear the Fifth Evangelist (shades of Frate Alberto). He disappears when she is about to give birth. Part III adopts the virulent misogyny of Boccaccio's *Corbaccio*, and Juvenal too, with tales of savage revenge, nearly always against erring wives, and nearly always in praise of vindictive husbands. Masuccio exposes the 'insatiable lust' that drives the 'more bestial than human actions of the depraved and utterly degenerate female sex'. In III, 28, a debauched wife prefers a monstrously deformed dwarf; the husband spies on them, and runs through both of them in bed with a spear used for hunting wild pigs, leaving their bodies on a mountain top for animals and birds of prey to devour. Ariosto overturns these offensive tales in Canto 28 of *Orlando furioso*, where an innkeeper like Masuccio tells a *novella* about depraved wives of model husbands to a Rodomonte who also speaks like Masuccio. A wise listener remarks that such tales have no truth in them at all, and those who tell them are liars.

On a gentler note, Masuccio also has a Romeo and Juliet story (Part IV, 34): Mariotto and Gannozza fall in love and bribe a monk to marry them secretly. Then Mariotto has to flee because of his involvement in a brawl and Gannozza, pressed by her parents to marry another man, takes a potion, is thought to be dead and is buried, but flees secretly to search for her lover. The despairing Mariotto returns and is beheaded, and when Gannozza learns of this, she dies of grief.

In northern Italy, Giovanni Sabadino degli Arienti (c. 1445–1510) courtier at Bologna, and then from 1491 at the court of Ercole d'Este at Ferrara, completed *Le porretane* in 1468. It was printed at Bologna in 1483. The sixty-one tales have a frame-story that promises light-hearted, pleasant entertainment: ladies and gentlemen from the Bologna court spend five days telling tales at the baths of Porretta – giving this collection a resemblance to Gentile Sermini's. The settings and characters are mainly Bolognese, the dialogue is colloquial, and there are numerous anecdotes of historical and social interest.

The *novella* was rooted so firmly in Quattrocento literary consciousness that humanists tried their hand at composing individual *novelle* in Latin, and even translating Boccaccio's vernacular ones into Latin. Petrarch had set an example, Latinising the tale of patient Griselda (X, 10) to 'preserve' and ennoble it. Leonardo Bruni translated the tragic story of Ghismonda, whose royal father Tancredi kills her lover (IV, 1), and counterpointed it with another one of his own about a Greek king who behaved nobly rather than cruelly in a parallel case. Filippo Beroaldo (and others) translated the tale about the friendship and self-sacrifice of Tito and Gisippo (X, 8).

In the vernacular, *L'Istorietta amorosa fra Leonora de' Bardi e Ippolito Bondelmonti*, attributed to Leon Battista Alberti and dated somewhere in the 1430s, tells of (historically authenticated) lovers who marry for love in opposition to their parents' wishes. But the single most famous Florentine tale of the Quattrocento was *La novella del grasso legnaiuolo*, about an elaborate, unusual *beffa* devised in 1409 by Filippo Brunelleschi, the architect of the dome of Florence's cathedral, and his circle of artists, architects and artisans. The author is unknown. The 'fat cabinet-maker' of the title was Manetto Ammannatini. The *beffa* consisted in persuading Ammannatini that he was somebody else, called Matteo (who was in on the joke), and instructing all friends and acquaintances to keep up the pretence. 'Il grasso' was so shaken that he began to doubt his sanity, and left Florence for Hungary. (Others in Florence doubted Brunelleschi's.) Only after years abroad did 'Il grasso' return to Florence and reconciliation. *Beffe*, of course, had formed a large part of Boccaccio's *Decameron*: Days VII and VIII were given over exclusively to them.

Boccaccio had also given over all of Day VI to verbal wit, *motti e facezie*, in which the Florentines again excelled. Little wonder, then, that one finds collections of jokes and humorous anecdotes, usually shorter than *novelle* but sometimes overlapping them in length. Poggio Bracciolini's largely porno-graphic *Liber facetiarum* enjoyed wide diffusion, although it was in Latin. Its justification was the need for relaxation and laughter in solemn all-male environments like the Roman Curia; later Lodovico Carbone and Antonio Cornazzano called their collections *Facezie* and *Proverbi in facezie* respectively. Poliziano too composed a collection of jokes or *Detti piacevoli*. But the masterpiece is *Motti e facezie del Piovano Arlotto*, by an anonymous admirer of Arlotto Mainardi (1396–1484), a Florentine parish priest who never wrote anything down himself except for his own epitaph, where he declares that he had built his tomb for himself and 'for anyone else who cared to join him inside'! Piovano Arlotto is presented as a Florentine folk hero, beloved by men and women of all social classes for his shrewd quick-wittedness. Through him, the author presents old republican values – the same ones Dante praises, sobriety, hard work, and fraternity – which have all but disappeared in a grasping, competitive society in which money measures worth. For the Piovano, religion and virtue mean practical works of mercy for the desperately poor people of Florence, and first of all his own parishioners. The *motti* and *facezie* are ways of puncturing arrogance and pomposity from whatever quarter. In one anecdote, Leonardo Bruni (who had a reputation for having amassed enormous wealth) visits the Piovano after death, urging him to tell the Florentines that 'You can't take it with you': wealth should be enjoyed, not hoarded in life, and also shared with others. To the mother of Lorenzo, Lucrezia Tornabuoni, he tells a story about a better form of charity than giving dowries to daughters of the poor, which she favours: not to oppress them in the first place. And to an *arriviste* Roman Cardinal who has invited Piovano Arlotto to dine, then mocks his shabby dress, the Piovano explains that he is much more content with what he has than the Cardinal, who, the Piovano reveals, now wants to hide his own humble origins.

Leonardo da Vinci (1452–1519), *uomo universale*, spent most of his life in Florence and Milan. He used a private vernacular to assert his defiance of a culture based on mere book-learning, and of language and content overly deferential to the authority of the ancients rather than to direct experience. In this spirit, he defined himself *omo sanza lettere*, 'a man without Latin learning' – to be taken in irony! He wrote riddles which parody biblical-sounding oracles: 'Those who give light for divine services will be destroyed.' Answer? Bees. His moral anecdotes, little *novelle*, bear no resemblance to Boccaccio or Piovano Arlotto, however. They bring to mind Aesop's fables, and the lessons inculcated are based on close observation of an unsentimental nature. Thus a bell-tower agrees to shelter an eloquent nut in a tiny hole in its walls. Growing into a tree, the nut spreads its roots, causing the wall to crack and finally collapse. The lesson? Do not be hospitable even to those in danger, for you may foolishly bring about your own destruction.

Novels and other prose writings

Boccaccio was also the dynamic force behind the novel, or longer fictional narrative, in the Quattrocento. Two prose love stories gave impetus to the romantic novel. *Filocolo*, based on the medieval French romance of Florio and Blanchefleur, tells of young lovers brought together only after a long series of misadventures and misunderstandings. *L'Elegia di Madonna Fiammetta* is, as the title suggests, a sad tale of an abandoned woman in which the attention is on her psychological sufferings (see further above, pp. 73, 76).

Some remarkable novels were written at the very end of the Quattrocento, although two of them were printed only at the beginning of the Cinquecento. The first is the mysterious *Hypnerotomachia Poliphili*, written by the Dominican friar Francesco Colonna (1433/34–1527) in a decidedly Latinate vernacular, and exquisitely illustrated by an unknown master. It was the first vernacular book printed by Aldo Manuzio in 1499. The protagonist, Polyphilo, falls asleep at dawn, and dreams of beginning a journey on a solitary shore. He enters a dark wood, and passes through a series of extraordinary classical ruins, described with an antiquarian architect's precision. Most of them are adorned with Latin, Greek and Arabic inscriptions, and even hieroglyphs, seen as a sacred secret language in the Renaissance. Polyphilo, on coming to three symbolic doors, freely chooses the one that leads to pleasure. He finds his nymph, Polia, and after an introduction to love's secrets, marries her. The journey is concluded on the island of Venus. The second part focuses on their love story against a background of Treviso mythologised. This fable of initiation, refracted through classical lenses, fascinated readers who knew about romance, and felt flattered at being invited into some kind of far more 'meaningful' illumination. But for whom was it written? The hybrid language requires some knowledge of Latin (early on, an editor had to give a summary of the plot in plain Italian), just as the classical allusions require an acquaintance with antique mythology and religious rites. Was Colonna trying to create a *volgare illustre*, as Dante recommended? Or was he mixing high and low learning and language in another 'macaronic' production? These and many more questions have teased readers and critics for centuries.

Less puzzling, but with an explicit debt to Boccaccio and an implicit one to Colonna, is Jacopo Caviceo's *Libro del Peregrino*, which was composed in the last two decades of the Quattrocento, but not printed until 1508 in Parma. It was dedicated to Lucrezia Borgia, then Duchess of Ferrara. Caviceo relates a dream in which Boccaccio's shade announces that he has become a citizen of Ferrara in order to admire its outstanding ladies. He is then approached by Peregrino (meaning 'pilgrim'), who tells his story. Peregrino, in love with

Ginevra, had been forced to separate from her, and then spends years searching for her near and far. After a joyous reunion and marriage, Ginevra dies after giving birth to a son. Peregrino soon follows, overcome by grief. This novel may not have a tightly knit plot, but it has just about everything else. It was translated into French and Spanish; it may have been the first novel specially written for women. It is full of eloquent, usually deeply melancholic, lovers' set speeches (like Boccaccio's *Filostrato* and *Elegia di Madonna Fiammetta*). It is also in parts an epistolary novel, and has *questioni d'amore*, or love questions with long debating-style speeches, as in Boccaccio's *Filocolo*. Some chapters are nothing but dialogues. Autobiographical elements are present, too, for the travels of the pilgrim to the Near East describe the author's own travels, and place the romance firmly in realistic contemporary settings. Linguistically, the novel adopts a latinate vernacular like Colonna's. Caviceo himself was no stranger to erotic adventures, brawls, exile and wanderings in foreign parts. Like Colonna, he was an unwilling priest. While the novel may seem beyond the pale of accepted literary decorum, its very diversity, and mixture of styles and genres, open up new directions for narrative fiction.

We also have records of Quattrocento prose in a range of writings on various non-fictional subjects: Florentine heads of families often wrote down *ricordi*, or *ricordanze* – noteworthy thoughts and advice about life they wanted passed on, mixed with accounts of family and public events. The wool-merchant Giovanni Morelli, who died after 1441, his contemporary, the magistrate Buonaccorso di Neri Pitti and, later in the century, Alamanno Rinuccini, an anti-Medici republican, penned collections of this sort. A moving example of private letters, striking for their colloquial language and insight into details of arranging marriages, is supplied by Alessandra Macinghi Strozzi (1407–51), of a powerful Florentine family, writing to her sons in political exile; and again by the silk-merchant, Marco Parenti. The state letters (*Commissioni*) of the diplomat Rinaldo degli Albizzi are reports to the Signoria about his fact-finding missions; and Lorenzo's invaluable state letters, only now being edited, afford information not found elsewhere. Sermons, the most important means of basic moral and religious instruction, are a rich genre in the Quattrocento, as, for example, those by the Franciscan Bernardino da Siena (1380–1444). Savonarola's more complex denunciations of political and religious corruption (he was burned at the stake in 1498 mainly for his vituperation of papal Rome) exhibit all the persuasive skill of a studied rhetoric.

Arcadia

The most successful vernacular work of the Quattrocento was one which combined poetry and prose. Sannazaro's *Libro pastorale nominato Arcadia*, of which an incomplete version appeared in the mid 1480s and the final one in 1504, went into over sixty editions in Italian alone and was widely imitated in

France, Spain, Portugal and England, where the vogue for pastoral owed much to Sannazaro's example (see below, pp. 255–6).

For some critics it is hardly a novel, rather a hybrid and ramshackle collection of episodes held together only by the fanciful pastoral setting and central core of shepherds. Sannazaro, however, was developing a new structure out of his Greek and Latin sources (Theocritus and Virgil are specified), transforming the purely poetic eclogue into a mixture of prose narratives and passages of poetry in various vernacular forms: *terza rima*, *sestina* and *frottola*. Some self-conscious statements on the nature of the lyric are in fact interspersed among the narratives. The twelve episodes are linked by interconnecting themes – love, death, friendship – and by an overriding mood of melancholy which gives way by the end to unremitting despair.

Arcadia's action is set in springtime over an uncertain number of days and nights. It opens with Selvaggio trying to humour Ergasto, who is bowed down with his woes: the loss of his beloved as well as of Androgeo, the leader of Arcadia, and of his own mother Massilia. Ergasto's sorrow is offset by a cheerful dialogue between Montano and Uranio about their shepherdesses, and by the introduction of festivities in honour of the goddess Pales – with detailed descriptions of the paintings on her temple doors depicting tales of ancient nymphs and satyrs. At this happy juncture Galizio pleads for a return to the Golden Age, when there was no strife even for lovers. His beloved Amaranta is, like Astraea, bringing back justice on earth. In contrast Logisto and Elpino lament their painful experiences in love, followed by expressions of sorrow over the tomb of Androgeo, and a universal lament at the disappearance of true friends and the spread of spite and avarice. A dirge by Sincero on love's anguish contrasts with a hopeful note supplied by Carino. In Eclogue 8 Eugenio and Clonio engage in a duet on love-sickness, which is followed by the priest Enareto's attempted cure by means of natural and magical ancient rites. One of several links with the Neapolitan court is the description of a vase Sannazaro had acquired from Mantegna; it is here offered as a prize at the games in honour of Massilia. Poussin captured the essence of Sannazaro's sad lyrics in his painting of a metaphorically 'speaking' tomb surrounded by young shepherds poring over the famous inscription *Et in Arcadia ego* ('I too am in Arcadia').

What then is Arcadia? For Sannazaro the ancient Greek scene becomes a metaphor for a genre of poetry about intimate and subjective sentiments, humble and lowly by contrast with the epic sublimity of public poetry on national and heroic subjects. The lyric poems are presented as songs accompanied by the shepherd's *zampogna*, or Pan-pipes, which can give more pleasure than the instruments of professional musicians; as can the tall spreading trees and craggy mountains of the shepherd's world compared with the trimmed gardens and caged birds of the court. At the end of the *Arcadia* Sannazaro addresses his *zampogna*, just as Dante and Petrarch had concluded their *canzoni* with a *commiato* (or envoy in which the poet addresses his poem). His subject-matter may not be grand, but he is proud to have been the first to awaken the sleeping woodlands and show shepherds how to sing forgotten songs. Reinforcing the priest Enareto's words at Pan's shrine (Prose 10), he celebrates the revival of bucolic poetry in Naples after a thousand years of neglect. The values it conveys are by no means trivial: true happiness is enjoyed by those withdrawn from turmoil and satisfied with what they have, unenvious of others' success.

Arcadia is also a metaphor for the community of poets and writers belonging to the Accademia Pontaniana in Naples, most of whom were attached to the Aragonese court. Many of the shepherds are identified as court personalities in the course of the work: Sincero, for example, who signs a mournful Petrarchan *sestina* about night bringing him torment, not peace, is Sannazaro himself. Uranio (Pontano) is elderly and wise and has a dog which guards the flock from wolves, just as the faithful Pontano does the King and his kingdom. Ergasto's lament for Arcadia's leader Androgeo, 'Chi vedrà mai nel mondo / Pastor tanto giocondo?' (Will we ever see such a pleasant shepherd again in the world?) is a tribute to Panormita, founder of the Academy. Meliseo's final lament for his dead and dearly beloved Filli is a transposition into the vernacular of a Latin eclogue by Pontano in honour of his dead wife.

All of this of course reflects the classical pastoral's constant reference back to the real world, while still being a world of the imagination. In some senses Arcadia is a model society, lay and male, in which a common love of letters creates bonds of friendship surpassing social class, titles and, above all, wealth, inherited or earned. The shepherds comfort one another, collaborate in their literary activities and engage in contests in which all prove excellent. In Arcadia there are no hatreds, treacheries or envious rivalries.

Poetry

The forms of poetry

The most respectable metrical forms inherited from the Trecento, with a well-established literary pedigree, remained the sonnet, the lengthier and more metrically complex *canzone*, and to a lesser extent the *ballata*. (The latter, with its associations with music and dance, also had a vast oral repertoire which was recorded in writing in the Quattrocento.) These three forms had, of course, been cultivated by Dante and Boccaccio, and most of all by Petrarch in his *Canzoniere*.

Petrarch's much-admired *Canzoniere* represented a challenge, especially to poets outside Tuscany. By making Petrarch's language their own they were bringing about, willy-nilly, a process of 'Tuscanisation' in the literary vernacular. But shaping a *canzoniere* was not just 'importing' language. Quattrocento poets saw that Petrarch's arrangement of his own 366 poems was anything but haphazard, and that a *canzoniere* had to be a book of sorts, with some unifying principles. Giusto de' Conti, Roman by birth and upbringing, spent his last years at the Rimini court of the Malatesta, and died there in 1449. Completed in 1440, *La bella mano* was printed in 1472 – the 'beautiful hand' in question belonged to Isabetta of Bologna – and contained 150 poems, mostly sonnets. The perceived antithetical effects of Laura on Petrarch's emotions are transferred to Isabetta; and Giusto, like Petrarch, is both happy and tormented in the fire of love. Giusto de' Conti's *canzoniere* remained fashionable up to the eighteenth century. Later in the Quattrocento, Gasparo Visconti (1461–99), a trusted courtier of the Sforza in Milan, composed three *canzonieri*. *Rithimi*, with 246 sonnets, was printed in Milan in 1493, and dedicated to his friend and fellow courtier, the poet Niccolò da Correggio. A second collection was composed for Beatrice d'Este, the cultured wife of Lodovico il Moro; and yet another for Bianca Maria Sforza, whom he accompanied on her way across the Alps to join the Emperor Maximilian, her future husband. Niccolò da Correggio (1450–1508) himself also fashioned a *canzoniere*, entitled *Rime*. Rather than randomly scattering the various metrical forms (other than sonnets), Niccolò divided his *Rime* according to their metre: 312 sonnets, then *canzoni*, then more sonnets, then a group of *capitoli* (see below, p. 163), and so on. Perhaps the most symmetrically structured *canzoniere* was Boiardo's *Amorum libri* (the Latin name recalls Ovid, though the verse was vernacular), whose number symbolism resembles Dante's *Vita Nuova* more than Petrarch's collection. There are three books, each with 60 poems, 50 of which are sonnets (the numbers 3, 10, and 12 seem to govern); and some poems contain acrostics.

In the Kingdom of Naples, the process of 'Tuscanisation' ran up against a vigorous native dialect, as in the *Rime* of Pietro Jacopo de Jennaro (1436–1508). The mixture of sonnets and *canzoni*, and the idealisation of one exclusive lady, in this case 'Bianca', are Petrarchan; but the poems are accompanied by brief explanations, as if the metrical forms and language might be unfamiliar to the reader. Giuliano Perleoni, a contemporary of Jennaro, called his collection, printed in 1492, a *Compendio di sonecti et altre rime de varie texture*. In Naples, one finds the phenomenon of double *canzonieri*. Giovan Francesco Caracciolo devised the *Amori*, and also *Argo*, printed posthumously in 1506. The *canzoniere* of Naples' greatest lyric poet, Sannazaro, *Sonetti e canzoni*, has been shown to be two separate books united by a common dedicatee, Cassandra Marchese. He suggestively describes his poems as 'fragments' which he has saved from a shipwreck and is bringing to port, thereby hinting at a process of deconstruction of former unities, and a perhaps not altogether satisfactory recomposition around Cassandra, his 'port'. (The word 'frammenti' also echoes Petrarch's Latin title for his *canzoniere*: *Rerum vulgarium fragmenta*.) The collection came out only after his death in 1530. Giving one's poems an overall structure seemed to pose too great a constraint for some poets. Tuscans (even Poliziano) were not so drawn to making their own *canzonieri*, and preferred to group their lyrics in less rigid ways. Only recently has Lorenzo's *Libro delle rime* (probably unfinished, containing 166 poems, mainly sonnets, as well as *canzoni, sestine* and *ballate*) been considered a unitary piece, with Lucrezia Donati as his 'donna'.

The *canzoniere*, with its sonnets and *canzoni*, is eminently lyrical. *Terza rima*, Dante's choice for his *Comedy*; and *ottava rima* (octaves) were used for narration, for conceptual matter, and later on in the century, for satirical matter. For the Quattrocento Petrarch, and even more Boccaccio, set the pattern for *terza rima*: Petrarch with his classicising allegories, the *Trionfi*; and Boccaccio with his mythological tales and pastoral allegories like the *Caccia di Diana* and *Amorosa visione* (fifty *canti*, no less). From *terzine* threaded together in thematic units derive *capitoli* (the word means 'chapters'). Five of the entries for Alberti's 1441 poetry contest on friendship were *capitoli*. Leon Battista himself wrote a pastoral *capitolo*, *Tyrsis*, in dialogue form. Later, *capitoli* were written in letter form (a vernacular adaptation of Horace's *Satires*), and brought to new heights by poets born in the Quattrocento, such as Machiavelli and Ariosto (see his *Satire*, below, p. 268)). Lorenzo de' Medici used the *capitolo* for his philosophical poem in the vernacular about the ethical good, *De summo bono*, based on Ficino's letter *De felicitate*. Structured as a debate with two alternating views, it is also called *Altercazione*. Two other important contemporary Florentine poets, Luigi Pulci and Poliziano, used *ottave* for most of their compositions.

Boccaccio was again the source of the *ottava* as an art form for narrative poetry, using it in *Filostrato* (the Troilus and Creseida story) and the long *Teseida*, an epic in the vernacular divided into twelve books like Virgil's *Aeneid*; and most important, in the allegorical pastoral poem *Comedia delle ninfe fiorentine*, also called *Ameto*. It attracted Luigi Pulci in his allegorical pastoral romance, the *Driadeo*; Lorenzo in his parody of it, *Nencia da Barberino* (though doubts have been expressed about the attribution); and Poliziano in his *Stanze per la giostra*, discussed below. Poliziano's *Orfeo*, a classicising pastoral, is also largely in *ottave*. Poliziano, who showed no interest in the metrical forms sanctioned by Petrarch's *Canzoniere* – the sonnet and *canzone* – rejected the collection of lyrics as well, and favoured writing octaves, though they were traditionally 'coarser'.

Lorenzo also used the *ottava* for his earthy account of a partridge hunt, *L'Uccellagione di starne*, as well as *Ambra*, a tale of frustrated love set in harsh winter-time. In the *sacra rappresentazione* (see below, p. 175), it was often used instead of the more traditional popular metrical forms of the *lauda* (which made use of the *ballata* and *sestina* of eight or nine-syllable lines). The *ottava* was also a basic metre for poetry written to be sung or to be accompanied by a musical instrument; and was given emphasis in Florence. When used in short, popular forms, it was called a *strambotto* (which usually had no couplet at the end) or a *rispetto toscano*. Outside of Tuscany Serafino Aquilano (1466–1500), a poet and musician originating from the Abruzzi, but in service for many years at Milan and Mantua, became famous for accompanying his own *strambotti* on the lute. Serafino made *strambotti* the ideal form to be set to music, and also used them for dramatic eclogues and allegorical monologues. The humanist Venetian patrician Leonardo Giustinian (1388–1446) composed tender love songs using *strambotti*, which, it is reputed, were still being sung centuries later. And Poliziano and Lorenzo gave the *strambotto* added prestige.

Another popular form, the *frottola*, with verses of varying length and internal rhyme, was cultivated in the Quattrocento. Leon Battista Alberti wrote a light-hearted one, perhaps for some festivity, inviting lovers to dance: 'Venite in danza, o gente amorosa'. The Florentine *canzoni a ballo*, with their varying metres, are *frottole*, and these seem to have been a basic kind of composition for popular entertainment, as at San Martino. The *frottola* came into its own in Naples, where it was the main metrical ingredient of popular comic sketches with mime, music and *tableaux* in Neapolitan dialect put on at court, called *gliuòmmeri*. Sannazaro, Francesco Galeota, Antonio Caracciolo and Pietro Jacopo de Jennaro lent their talents to these productions. The *sonetto caudato* (sonnet with a tail) was adopted by Burchiello (Domenico di Giovanni) for his comic verse, and later favoured by Francesco Berni (see p. 270).

Lorenzo and Poliziano

Although we now take it for granted that Dante, Petrarch and Boccaccio were the creators of what we now call 'Italian' literature, the view that the Florentine or Tuscan language enjoyed supremacy was studiously nurtured by Florentine humanists like Bruni and Manetti, and became full-blown only in the late Quattrocento. How Florentine, after all, were the three vernacular 'crowns' of literature? Only Boccaccio had spent most of his adult life near Florence, in the village of Certaldo; Dante had written his masterpiece in exile from his beloved Florence; and Petrarch, on his return to Italy from Avignon, his adopted home since youth, had chosen to spend his days at despotic courts like Carrara, Milan and Padua.

It was Lorenzo and Poliziano who made the claim a reality with two anthologies, like manifestos, which provided the new poetics of the vernacular enterprise. The first, the *Raccolta aragonese*, was a collection of Tuscan verse from Dante to Lorenzo himself, sent to Naples in 1476 at the request of the Aragonese royal family. It was preceded by a dedicatory letter of fulsome praise for the excellence of the Tuscan *volgare*, by implication the most advanced in the peninsula because it already had two centuries of illustrious poets behind it. The anthology shows a sense of an unbroken literary tradition unified by geography, by language and by themes.

The second, a collection of Lorenzo's own poems with individual commentaries and an introductory essay or 'Proemio', left unfinished at his death in 1492, has been given the title *Comento de' miei sonetti*. It resembles Dante's

Vita Nuova, or – even more closely, as the sonnets are given a prose philosophical explanation – the *Convivio*. The Proemio, written last, affirms that the vernacular is just as good as Latin for writing 'high' literature, and in some cases better – a daring statement to make in the midst of so many classical scholars. Lorenzo anticipates various objections to a serious statesman like himself writing love poetry in the *volgare*, and refutes them confidently. Against the charge that an important public figure should not be wasting his time writing frivolous and morally suspect love poetry, Lorenzo embarks on a defence of the entire *stilnovo* tradition of love ennobling the soul, and unites it with the latest interpretation of Platonic love by Ficino: 'I believe that human love is not only blameless, but an almost necessary thing, and a true source of refinement and greatness of spirit; and above all it is the reason for moving us to worthy and excellent deeds.' He goes on to defend the appropriateness of the *volgare*, a language for everyday use, spoken by uneducated masses, to deal with noble subject-matter like philosophical love poetry. Lorenzo is adamant that the study of Dante, Petrarch, Boccaccio, Guido Cavalcanti shows that the *volgare* has *copia* – lexical and syntactical richness – and can be used for specialist purposes, to express not only thoughts from all disciplines, but also different linguistic registers – comic, plain and sublime. The dominance of the Florentine/Tuscan language in the peninsula corresponds to Florence's political dominance: and the language can still develop, 'especially if there is added some happy outcomes and increases to the Florentine Empire'. Lorenzo practised what he preached. All his literary compositions were in the *volgare*, which he used for philosophical poems as well as for typically Florentine metrical forms like the *canzoni a ballo*, *rispetti*, and *canti carnascialeschi* (carnival songs).

While Poliziano wrote Latin as well as vernacular poetry, he did not try his hand at sonnets and *canzoni* of a philosophical type. Poliziano's vernacular compositions, while overlapping with Lorenzo's, are marked by hybrid features caused by a mixing and deliberate mis-matching of classical and medieval literary genres and motifs as well as classical and vernacular languages, as in his *Stanze per la giostra di Giuliano*, celebrating the participation of Lorenzo's handsome young brother Giuliano in a jousting tournament in 1475. It was left unfinished after Giuliano's assassination in the Pazzi conspiracy of 1478. The poem was probably meant to rival Luigi Pulci's *Stanze per la giostra di Lorenzo* of 1471.

Greek and Latin myths about Eros are mixed in Poliziano's *Stanze* with the *stilnovo* love tradition. The beginning recalls Boccaccio's *Ameto*: Giulio, an avid hunter free from all sexual attachments – as in the Golden Age – is scornful of women. Love is 'dolce insania ... una ceca peste' (I, 13: sweet madness, a blind plague). But when, in an idyllic flowery meadow, 'sotto un vel candido li apparve / lieta una ninfa' (I, 37: a radiant nymph appeared to him clothed in white – an echo of Beatrice's appearance to Dante in the Terrestrial Paradise), he is struck down by Love. The hunter becomes the prey.

Like Ameto, and Cimone (*Decameron* v, 1), the 'rustic' Giulio is suddenly transformed, and longs only for his nymph.

Following an invocation to Erato, the muse of erotic poetry, the scene changes from Florence and courtly love sentiments to the realm of a pagan Venus. Poliziano turns quotations from classical poets – Ovid, Catullus, Virgil and Lucretius, together with the more arcane Theocritus, Hesiod and (pseudo) Homer (the *Hymn to Aphrodite*) – into vernacular octaves. It was Poliziano who disseminated the Hesiodic myth of the birth of Venus: how she was created from the testicles of castrated Uranus and was wafted by Zephyrs over the foamy waves (her Greek name, Aphrodite, means 'foam-born') to the shores of Cyprus (1, 99–103). The same scene was made famous by Botticelli's painting. The triumph of Venus visualised by Poliziano refers to the ancient goddess of fertility, source of all life in the natural world and the cosmos, and of all pleasure. Many interpretations have been given to the myths of Eros sculpted on the doors of her Palace; Poliziano's comment, 'l'odio antico e 'l natural timore / ne' petti ammorza quando vuole Amore' (1, 88: When Love wishes, He extinguishes ancient hatred and natural suspicion) would seem to provide a unifying thread. Indeed, the final scene of Book I (only a few verses remain of Book II) shows Venus subduing warlike Mars by the pleasures of frenzied love-making: a favourite Renaissance myth about civilisation and the arts taming brutishness.

Studies of Poliziano's vocabulary have revealed that while adopting 'popular' metrical forms, he plucks words directly from Latin and Greek and 'Tuscanises' them, creating neologisms. This love of *varietas* and of an original style following no fixed rules is even more evident in the *Favola di Orfeo*, composed in 1480 on a short visit to the court of Mantua as part of some wedding festivities. Here Poliziano initiated a new genre, the *favola pastorale* or pastoral drama, which was to enjoy immense success in the Cinquecento. The metrical forms are taken over from the *sacra rappresentazione*: octaves, *terzine, canzoni a ballo*; and in the middle there is a long Latin ode in sapphic verse sung by Orpheus to Cardinal Francesco Gonzaga, son of the lord of Mantua, Lodovico Gonzaga.

The play opens with the obliging messenger Mercury delivering the plot in two octaves, just as the announcing angel would do in the *sacra rappresentazione*. Although the story is fundamentally Ovid (*Metam.* x and xi), Poliziano deals with Eurydice's double death by means of two episodes contrasting in genre. The first, a pastoral dramatic eclogue, involves three shepherds. Aristeo, passionately in love with a nymph (and unaware she is Orpheus' wife), laments in *stilnovo* motifs to a more experienced Mopso, who warns him in vain to come to his senses. Tirsi, too, confirms the superlative charms of this 'gentile donzella / che va cogliendo fiori intorno al monte' (gracious young maid gathering flowers on the mountainside). As Aristeo pursues her one day along the riverbank, she is bitten by a snake and dies. In the second part, a scenic representation of the classical myth, Orpheus laments for his dead bride, and softens the hearts of the underworld gods, Pluto, Minos and Proserpina. For a brief moment, as Eurydice nears the daylight, there is triumph – and Orpheus breaks out in Latin verse – followed by defeat as she slips away forever.

The myth of Orpheus, about the poet's power to move wild beasts, trees and stones, and even the gods of the underworld, suggests once again the civilising power of speech and the arts and their ability to overcome barbarity. But Poliziano's version is an odd one for a marriage, for Orpheus, tenderly devoted to his wife Eurydice in life and disconsolate at her second death (which was caused by his own negligence in turning back – interpreted Neoplatonically by Lorenzo de' Medici as a turning back to carnal from spiritual love), in the third episode becomes a misogynist and takes to seducing young boys: 'Conforto e' maritati a far divorzio / e ciascun fugga il femminil consorzio' (I give advice to husbands to leave their wives; let every one flee female company). In revenge, frenzied, drunken Bacchantes beat him to death and dismember his body. The play ends with their chorus, a racy *canzone a ballo* with the refrain 'Ognun segua Bacco, te / Bacco, Bacco, eù oè', a parody of Greek dithyrambs in honour of Dionysus. The entire *favola* is brilliant pastiche: whole sections of Virgil, Ovid and Claudian turned into fifteenth-century *volgare*. Was Poliziano, among other targets, making fun of solemn views about Orpheus, whom Ficino held to be the author of hymns and the founder of a religious movement? Was he providing bawdy but erudite entertainment? Was he profaning the *sacra rappresentazione*? Was he warning husbands to guard their homosexual proclivities lest revenge be taken on them, too? Whatever the case, Poliziano's poetry here, as elsewhere, conjures a remarkable vitality out of the melting-pot of classical poets he knew and loved so well.

Narrative poetry

Peter Marinelli

Pulci and the narrative tradition

Living and writing alongside Lorenzo and Poliziano in Florence was another remarkable poet, who enjoys the distinction of having produced the first in a line of famous chivalric epics which was to include the Cinquecento master-pieces of Ariosto and Tasso. Luigi Pulci, like his friend and master Lorenzo, took up a tradition of popular poetry and adapted it to a local Florentine audience – in this case the tales of Charlemagne and the paladins which minstrels had for centuries recited to fascinated audiences in the Italian squares and halls.

The French poems are thought to have entered Italy principally via minstrels accompanying the bands of pilgrims who made their way over the Alps and along the Po valley on their way to Rome in the thirteenth and fourteenth centuries. Italian *canterini* who heard them wrote down versions in French or a

Franco-Venetian dialect, as for example the two poems preserved in the Marciana Library in Venice, the *Entrée en Espagne* and the *Prise de Pampelune*. The first turns Roland into a knight errant in the manner of the Arthurian heroes, who had simultaneously become famous through the diffusion of the *matière de Bretagne* – Dante's Paolo and Francesca, we remember, were led astray by their reading of *Lancialotto*. The second creates, out of a mere name in the French *chansons*, a character destined to play a major role in Pulci, Boiardo and Ariosto: the zany British prince Astolfo. The Carolingian material was extremely popular in medieval Italy, where literacy was low and oral entertainment highly prized, and it formed the most favoured subject of the *cantari* of the Trecento which, as we noted earlier (see above, p. 119), embraced a wide range of material from legendary, historical and mythological sources and from collections of *novelle* and which were increasingly aimed at a reading as much as a listening public.

The best known of the Quattrocento chivalric romances was probably the prose *Reali di Francia* of Andrea da Barberino (c. 1370–1431), a genealogical treasure-trove which fantastically links the royal house of France with the first Christian Emperor 'Gostantino'. Here we find amply rehearsed the tale of the birth of Charlemagne and his sister, Bertha; the secret love of Bertha and Milo of Anglante; their imprisonment and exile in Italy; the subsequent Christ-like birth of Orlandino (Roland) in a stable near Sutri, outside Rome; the child's youthful prodigies as leader of a troop of boys; his fearless encounter with his uncle when he comes to Rome to be crowned Emperor; and the rediscovery by Charles of his sister and her husband and their return as a family to France. Recognition, reconciliation and restoration are the hallmarks of the tale, in which Roland becomes the fully Italianised Orlando. Hardly less Italianised will be the child Ruggiero (the demi-Saracen destined to become one of the heroes in Boiardo and Ariosto), who comes to life in another of Andrea's works, the sequel to the *Reali*, his *Aspramonte*.

The vigorously vulgarised Charlemagne of the *Reali* is almost a compendium of the indecorous changes wrought upon the Emperor's character since his adoption by the *popolo minuto*. Wrathful and given to domestic violence in this poem, he is just as often depicted as a senile, tearful booby in an Italian tradition that hardened into convention over the centuries. His rehabilitation came about in an aristocratic setting in Florence in the latter part of the fifteenth century. Within four stanzas of the opening of his *Morgante*, Luigi Pulci (1432–84) attributes the origins of his master work to a request by Lorenzo de' Medici's pious mother that he should embark on a literary rehabilitation of the great defender of Christianity, so sadly degenerated into a figure of fun. One wonders what Lucrezia Tornabuoni made of the result, which was published in 1478, but had been read aloud, while in progress, at the dinner-table of her son. For the tale that the jokester Pulci begins to spin involves a Charlemagne all too foolishly susceptible to the traitor Ganelon's calumnies, capable of driving the faithful Orlando into exile and of being beguiled on occasion after occasion. The insulted paladin wanders off alone into the Orient and soon comes upon an abbey full of drolly timorous monks besieged by a trio of murderous giants. Killing two, he subdues the third, Morgante, and takes him into his service. Converted and biddable, and armed with the clapper of a church-bell, Morgante does great execution upon Orlando's foes: militant Christianity with a vengeance. Developed by Pulci from a sparer original in his source, the amiable giant in effect takes over the poem and gives it his name. Not only does Pulci deliberately avoid redeeming Charlemagne, he all but effaces Orlando by making Morgante a gigantic externalisation of the paladin's already prodigious strength.

In the nineteenth century it was discovered that, far from being an original work, the *Morgante* is a free rehandling of two anonymous Tuscan poems, differing widely in tone, texture and artistry, and joined together by something like artistic violence. Its first twenty-three cantos follow a torso called *Orlando*, a rambling and repetitive narrative of vagrant paladins in quest of multiple romantic adventures; its final five cantos are based on a work entitled *La Spagna in rima* (to distinguish it from a similar work in prose), a darkly dramatic and often electrifyingly effective treatment of Ganelon's final treachery and Orlando's noble death. Every writer of a *rifacimento* is more or less at the mercy of the narrative he selects for rehandling, if only because he follows its narrative framework, and the characteristics of its twofold source underlie the *Morgante* from beginning to end – serving repeatedly, however, as a wellspring for Pulci's satire. Unity was never a concern of the popular minstrels, accustomed as they were to recite a canto at a time to an urban populace at a break in their daily business. As a result, the structure of the *Morgante* is of the loosest; its mass of excursions and errancies invariably proceeds from Ganelon's fertility in machination, and the result is an action-filled tangle of events succeeding one another in endless complication, never crystallising into structural or thematic complexity. The search for form will be the concern of other poets in other times and places.

From the old *Orlando* Pulci adopts a gallery of familiar characters and revitalises them in settings invented by the unlearned popular mind. Bambillona, Denmark, Bellamarina and Prussia are all jumbled together in a naive geography that does not allow for distinguishing features. Into these unlocalised landscapes, rich with princesses in danger of being devoured by monsters and rife with giants, lions and dragons, Pulci sets a succession of temperamental paladins. Essentially his poem is determinedly martial and Carolingian, rather than Arthurian and amorous, and the female figures (Chiariella, Luciana, Forisena, Florinetta, Antea, Meridiana) tend to be fairly indistinguishable in action and sentiment. The real interest falls on the males, to the making of whose detailed portraiture a long tradition (absent in the case of the popularly invented females) steadily contributes.

The extraordinary vivacity of some of the episodes is a good indication of the freedom with which Pulci manages his sources and extends the tradition.

While *Morgante* pretends to no structural unity or global organisation, it is infused throughout with an intellectual and stylistic unity deriving from the poet's vision of life as beheld from a very particular angle. That vision of life as impromptu, helter-skelter, bizarre and ever-varying is everywhere on view, in single lines and solitary interjections as much as in extended digressions and lengthy episodes. It is the view of the outsider, and it finds expression in a witty, sceptical, satiric, and ironic poetry that was to touch a very sympathetic chord in Byron, who wrote a lively English version of the first canto.

Born of a noble family himself (but fallen on hard times and compelled to dodge and palter in the shifts of fortune), Pulci appears in his poem in the persona of a simple minstrel in the piazza, cultivating an apartness by assuming that distinct role and at once achieving artistic distance from his material. He comes before his audience – the family-members, scholar-dependents, intimates and table mates of the Medici clan as well as the rough crowd in the piazza – as an impersonator of the naivety, ribaldry, pietism, ignorance and emotionalism of the people; and he ventriloquises the idiom and rhythm of popular utterance: he has them by heart and he voices them to perfection. His sensibility is essentially an innocently malicious one which revels in mimicking the way in which a relatively unlettered mind represents the world of reality in narrative art; hence he brusquely alternates comic and tragic moments, annihilates space and time, begins and ends cantos with pious invocations, utters maxims and proverbs in the reductive folk-wisdom of the streets, even attempts the occasional awkward literary fineness in clusters of anaphoric stanzas. The richness and variability of the Pulcian word-hoard are the essence of the poem and its particular glory. Pulci's diction can be swift and unencumbered in dramatic narratives of action. In certain proems he is capable of a kind of poetic elevation that stands in distinct contrast to his usual level of utterance. Constant fugitive echoes of Dante, Petrarch and the Bible give yet another dimension to his language, complicating the verbal fabric and the persona as well. And the Morgante episodes employ a gross, polysyllabic, cacophonous argot that is one of the poem's wonders. Torrential and seemingly inexhaustible, as grotesque and disproportionate as his eponymous giant, requiring recourse to dictionaries of uncommon words even by natives and scholars in the Italian language, the machine-gun chatter represents the *vox populi* resounding, in amazingly unadulterated form, in the halls of princes. More than any other poem in the tradition, Pulci's is a work requiring to be heard in oral delivery.

The ludicrous provincialism of his sources suffers a severe check when Pulci forcefully asserts his authorial independence and creates three truly remarkable characters from his own imagination – characters who have nothing to do with chivalric romance and indeed divert attention from its repetitive vagaries. Morgante is only the first of the three, and he immediately provides a breakthrough into a world of superhuman activity and strength. In his paradoxical ferociousness and docility, he is a distinct Pulcian original. His essential loveableness is set in high relief when, in canto 18, he picks up a strange companion, a demi-giant only fourteen feet tall called Margutte, who proceeds, in twenty-seven stanzas of outrageous confession, to make a famous profession of faith in lawlessness and self-indulgence. An impenitent creature of monstrous appetites, shameless and self-advertising in the manner of Tutivillus (the scoundrelly devil of the English mystery plays) Margutte drives Morgante into the shadows for a while by his sharper intelligence, though that has the sole aim of filling his belly. Margutte functions, perhaps, as the incarnation of Fraud to Morgante's Force: the two work together to disestablish order and bring on laughable chaos. The pair bring the first part of the poem to its end: Margutte dies of an uncontrollable fit of laughter in canto 19, Morgante of a bite in the heel from a crab in canto 20.

In breakaway individualism the two giants leave even the most famously egomaniacal Arthurian and Carolingian heroes far behind. They represent a Pulcian exploration of subjects not previously amplified into such prominence in chivalric literature (where giants are not unknown), and by dominating the narrative, often to the exclusion of all else, they look ahead to Rabelais and Folengo (see below, p. 273). But they represent only two of the three excrescences of the *Morgante*. Pulci reinforces the tendency of his work to wander into strange mental worlds by introducing yet another of his original creations, the demon Astarotte, in his final five cantos (the addition of which to the *Morgante*, in 1483, created the extended poem to be known for centuries as the *Morgante maggiore*). Discoursing on magic and theology, on predestination and foreknowledge – is this a foreshadowing of the Miltonic devils in Book II of *Paradise Lost*? – Astarotte seems to be familiar with the learned discussions of Pulci's dinner-table companions at the Medici palace. This is an odd departure, for the poet is at pains several times to disclaim erudition and claim indifference to the learned – to Ficino and Landino especially, whose lucubrations on the anagogic, moral and tropological senses of poetry come in for wry dismissal at XXVI, 27.

By its end, something distinctly unsettling has happened to the *Morgante*, further loosening its baggy shapelessness and making it seem more than ever a medley. Pulci abandons his narrative persona, stepping forward in the first person to write an exculpatory digression in rebuttal of allegations of heresy made against him. The introduction of personal biography is intensified by an extreme display of literary self-consciousness in which (in tardy fulfilment of his promise to Lorenzo's mother, now dead) Pulci finally 'redeems' Charlemagne, but does so by writing a long and very dull catalogue of the Emperor's career; only the length and tone of the passage preclude its being taken for a joke. And certainly the stanzas in praise of Poliziano are perfectly sincere, another bewildering excrescence.

In the matter of literary genres, Pulci remains as much a curiosity as the Morgantes, Marguttes and Astarottes who evoked his most characteristic poetry. Denied Christian burial in consecrated ground as an unrepentant heretic, in death he achieved the status of the ultimate outsider, a role he had rehearsed often enough in his life and in his art.

Boiardo

If it seems unlikely that Pulci will ever achieve the status accorded to Ariosto and Tasso by the English-speaking world over four centuries, it is pleasurable to record the growing popularity in recent years of MatteoMaria Boiardo (1441–94) – a partial amends for the oblivion into which he once sank in his native land, an oblivion which affected his reputation elsewhere as well. A prey to linguistic changes that made his language, filled with Lombardisms, seem awkward and provincial in an era of Tuscan sophistication, Boiardo's text ceased to be printed in the middle of the sixteenth century and was supplanted by various *rifacimenti*, works that denatured and misrepresented the original *Orlando innamorato*; in addition, Boiardo suffered the misfortune of never having attracted a translator comparable to Harington and Fairfax, who rendered Ariosto and Tasso into English. His restoration to his rightful place as one of the sovereign Italian poets took place as late as 1830, in England, and then only in consequence of Sir Anthony Panizzi's publication of his text for the first time since the sixteenth century. Since then, modern readers have increasingly discovered in Boiardo a poetic personality of extreme attractiveness and originality, and in his *Orlando innamorato* (two books published in 1483, a third, a fragment, in 1495) a poem of extraordinary beauty and influence.

The Italian chivalric tradition is very distinctly marked by continuity and progression, often deepening into rivalry and desire to supersede. For a poem nearly contemporaneous with *Morgante*, the *Innamorato*, initiated in the 1470s, written fitfully over many years, and cut short by the poet's death in 1494, presents a multitude of contrasts to the earlier poem. In the first place, it was a product of the courtly culture of Ferrara, whose ruling family, the Estensi, were the oldest and most aristocratic dynasty in all of Italy, capable of tracing their lineage back to Carolingian times. For centuries Ferrara had been a city where singers of the 'Matters' of France and Britain (the Carolingian and Arthurian traditions) had been graciously received and where French culture was admired and imitated. The marquis Niccolò II had received the dedication of Niccolò da Verona's *Prise de Pampelune* in the early fourteenth century; a later successor, Niccolò III, ordered French romances to be brought in literally by the cartload, and several scions of the house bore names like Rinaldo, Isotta (Iseult), Leonello (Lionel), Meliaduse and Ginevra (Guinevere). The court appears to have been saturated in the literature of chivalry, and by Boiardo's time, when humanists had been flocking to the city for generations, and French, Latin, and Greek letters were assiduously cultivated, all the conditions were present for a new development of Ferrara's favourite reading material, by now a native possession of both the people and the courtiers.

Fortunate in his historical and cultural circumstances, Boiardo was especially fortunate in the matter of birth and station. He was cousin to Pico della Mirandola, nephew to the Latinist and poet-courtier Tito Vespasiano Strozzi, and a familiar and intimate of Duke Ercole I and his wife Eleanora of Aragon, parents of a young and growing family, the brightest of whom was to become Isabella d'Este, one of the first and greatest admirers of the *Innamorato*. Boiardo spent a lifetime in devoted service to his lord, who had been newly established on his throne in 1471; his affection expressed itself in the dedication of every one of his works to Ercole, and his devotion never wavered – a bright spot in the slippery, treacherous world of Renaissance courts. Writing from within the magic circle of an old culture in a city which was a chief focus for the renewal of classical civilisation, the poet was, one might say, very much the insider, and his consciousness of being part of a privileged world finds expression in two ways: in the persona he adopts to tell his tale, and in the settings in which he imagines himself to be singing. Here he stands in strict contrast to Pulci. Far from appearing as the frowsy market-place minstrel, he comes before his audience in the role of a courtly singer, eager to give pleasure and wholly at one with his hearers, whom he habitually characterises as a troupe of noble damsels and cavaliers enjoying hours of leisure in the halls and garden-enclosures of the palace. The gracious proems and refined farewells in which he greets and dismisses his imagined audience are highly stylised lyrics in the mode of Poliziano, and they represent a world apart from the world, especially the world of historical reality with its grim excursions and alarums. When war with Venice comes to Ferrara in 1482–4, Boiardo shears it of its particularities and metaphorises it into a storm that temporarily interrupts the poet's song. Secure within the magical confines of their youth and station, the audience continues to be beguiled by the poet's tale, which is original with him and not based, like Pulci's, on 'popular follies'.

The *Innamorato* begins with a search for and a delight in novelty, and the novelty is embodied in the almost exclamatory and triumphant title, boldly announcing 'Orlando in love'. Here Boiardo achieves finally and forcefully what Carolingian poetry had been teasingly on the verge of attempting for a long while. Pagan damsels like Dionès in the *Entrée en Espagne* and Chiariella in the old *Orlando* had fallen victim to warm feelings for the great paladin in the time of his errancy, feelings unreciprocated by the chaste warrior. Andrea da Barberino had written solemnly that Orlando died a virgin, but Boiardo seizes the occasion and converts Orlando into an utterly infatuated Arthurian lover within moments of the poem's opening, exploiting obsessive love as a totally transforming passion in a way that Pulci could never have imagined. In one of his extended proems, Boiardo clearly expresses his preference for amorous Arthurian over bellicose Carolingian poetry, though there are noisy combats enough resounding in his pages. What is important, however, is that love is treated comically within his tale, as a madness that unsettles human wits and causes tremendous disorder, whereas the love that is hymned to the audience in the more dignified proems of the frame-story is of an altogether different kind, harmonious and creative in its very essence. This division echoes the Neoplatonic scale of love widely known in the philosophical and literary circles of the society in which the poem was created, and in which love was said to engage either the lower passions or the heart and mind, and was accordingly denominated either Pandemian and vulgar, or Uranian and elevated.

Book 1 of the *Innamorato* presents love as an overmastering passion in which Cupid conquers remorselessly, Ovidian-fashion. Initially, the plot is of the simplest. Charlemagne's realm is invaded by exotic conquerors come with numberless hordes from the furthest ends of the earth – Spain, Tartary, Circassia – and all of them aim to wrest some madly desired thing (a famous horse, a famous sword, a famous helmet) from the Emperor's paladins. It is rather like a fairy-tale, extravagant and enchanting in its sophisticated naivety – and never more so than when the Cathayan enchantress, Angelica, appears at Charlemagne's Whitsuntide feast to destroy the solidarity of his court. Even more powerful than the leaders of invading armies like Gradasso, Ferraguto, Sacripante and Agricane, she immediately prostrates in loving adoration all the assembled warriors, pagan as well as Christian, Charlemagne and Orlando himself not excepted. With one stroke Boiardo attaches Orlando to the triumphal chariot alongside which Petrarch, in his *Trionfi*, had represented Amor dragging his shackled captives; and by making Angelica the focus of universal desire, he raises her into a symbol of all *desiderata*. At this point the poem exfoliates into an interlacing series of narratives. Violent transports of love are succeeded by violent physical transport eastward as her slavish followers determine to follow Angelica home to her native city of Albracca, where the cousins Rinaldo and Orlando find themselves vying for her favours.

The twenty-nine cantos of Book 1 are a sunnily humorous and good-natured rehearsal of the whimsicality and arbitrariness of the passion of love: characters drink from magic fountains that arouse or dampen the passion without rhyme or reason, and the leisurely narrative never sticks to a single story-line for long. Increasingly the poem makes its effect as an entertainment for the young and the young at heart, a feeling that grows upon readers as they encounter yet another of Boiardo's many novelties. Not content with so originally fusing the Matters of France and Britain in presenting Charlemagne's nephew as a romantic lover, Boiardo reaches out also to the third 'Matter', that of Rome or the classical world. Pulci's classicism had been limited to mere scraps of mythological reference used for very occasional embellishment. Boiardo, in contrast, though a serious translator of Greek and Latin works of literature, knew how to utilise the classics for comic and decorative purposes. The use of mythology in allegorical episodes marks him off from Pulci once again. Boiardian allegory can be Ovidian, as when Rinaldo encounters the three Graces, who whip him with flowers for rejecting Angelica's love; it can be emblematic and iconographic, as when Occasion beats Orlando for not taking advantage of Angelica while she sleeps; or it can be clearly moralistic and humanistic, as on the occasion when Astolfo is lured aboard a whale by a Circean Alcina and transported to an unknown fate that Ariosto, in an extended allegory of his own, will render as a descent into lust and self-forgetfulness.

The evidence of Boiardo's classicism is visible throughout his poem, but is never so strongly felt as in his promise, at the end of Book I, to deliver a greater subject ('cosa maggior') in Book II. This takes the form of a new figure to challenge the primacy of the laughable lover who gives the poem its name: it means the introduction of a dynastic hero, Ruggiero, on something like a Virgilian model, who will be used as forefather of the Este dynasty and serve to sing its praises. Working from a story in Andrea da Barberino's *Aspramonte*, Boiardo provides an *enfance* (series of youthful exploits) for the hero, who (born of a Saracen princess and a Christian father, and reared in Africa by the magician Atlante) is destined, after conversion and baptism, to be the ancestor of the Estensi by marriage to Bradamante, the sister of Rinaldo and heiress of Clairmont. The *Innamorato*, begun as a *jeu d'esprit* on Orlando's tribulations in love, now increasingly incorporates a panegyric of the rulers of Ferrara, and the concerns of classical epic begin to infiltrate the medieval romance.

Boiardo never succeeded in unifying the two stories; indeed, he seems deliberately to avoid closure by introducing a new hero, Mandricardo, to open his third book, as he began his first and second by introducing Orlando and Ruggiero: the technique reminds one of Spenser. For whatever reason, he keeps losing the thread of Ruggiero's story, and consequently it is not until Book III that the young hero, who has accompanied his cousin Agramante in his invasion of France, encounters his intended bride. They meet, in a raptly beautiful moment, on the battlefield where Charlemagne's forces have suffered a cruel defeat. Courteous to a defeated enemy, Ruggiero engages in a colloquy with the young warrior whose sex is hidden from him by her armour and helmet, and details his ancestry. Bradamante is captivated, and when she removes her helmet he too falls in love. They are separated in a mêlée, however, and Boiardo's poem breaks off shortly afterwards, leaving this budding romance to be completed by Ariosto. The poem's ending is dramatic in the extreme. The last stanza raises a cry of alarm as the distraught poet registers the descent into Italy of the armies of Charles VIII of France, an invasion that cut off his poem and introduced a long period of warfare into Italy. Few poems can have ended so stunningly, with so brutal an irruption of the world of historical reality into the world of romantic fantasy.

Theatre

The Quattrocento also witnessed the beginnings of Italian theatre in the growth of dramatic entertainments of two kinds: the *sacra rappresentazione* or religious play in the vernacular, and the humanistic comedy in Latin. The origins are to be found in simple proto-dramatic activities of a popular nature, emanating from the churches on the one hand and from secular festivities on the other. As an extension of the liturgy and religious ceremonial comes the enactment of scenes from the Bible, such as the Nativity or the Resurrection, which were presented first in the church and then in the Portico, *piazzale* or cemetery, and developed into fully scripted plays in the Quattrocento. The Umbrian dramatic *laude* evolved as a variant of the lyric form, with several singers, appropriately dressed, performing increasingly complex scenes with more elaborate dialogue and machinery and considerable emphasis on spectacle. A similar embryonic theatre was developed by the *giullari* and *istrioni*, professional entertainers, with realistic and comic farces involving two or more characters in a dialogue or altercation of a crude, often obscene nature, and involving mockery and tricks, often at the expense of rustic characters – such as the *maggi* and *bruscelli* of the Tuscan *contado*. Carnival, with its dressing up, disguise and practical joking, was the time *par excellence* for this popular 'theatre'.

The earliest body of scripted vernacular drama consists of the *sacre rappresentazioni*, considerable numbers of which survive and can be read in modern collections. These are fully scripted plays, based on stories from the Bible and the lives of the saints, and seem fully to have met the intentions of the Church authorities who put them on to instruct and improve, and at the same time entertain, a wide audience. They are in verse (almost entirely *ottava rima*), have numerous *dramatis personae*, and introduce frequent and abrupt changes of scene and time. Elements of realism (everyday details of toilet for example, allusions to local events and scenes) are combined with miraculous and fantastic happenings, and grisly scenes of martyrdom are presented on the stage. Alongside the saints and prophets we find figures from the contemporary world – astrologers, doctors, judges, priests – and there are prominent parts for women, especially the martyrs around whom several of the plays are constructed. The protagonist of the anonymous *Rappresentazione di Sant'Uliva* cuts off her hands (on stage) rather than marry her father, and only regains her hands miraculously after a long and hazardous series of adventures. Impressive stage effects could be achieved, as for example the descent from Heaven of a band of angels singing *laude* in the *Rappresentazione dell'Annunciazione* of Feo Belcari (1410–84), who also wrote the impressive *Rappresentazione di Abramo ed Isaac*, a play making clever use of dramatic irony in setting Abraham's ignorance of God's intention against Isaac's ignorance of his father's – in the context, of course, of the audience's familiarity with the Bible story. And this perhaps was at the root of the decline of the religious plays in the latter Quattrocento, by which time the repetition of the familiar material had begun to pall and the competition of the new humanist theatre began to take effect.

The humanist Latin comedies were inspired by the early Quattrocento discoveries of a number of ancient texts, most importantly twelve hitherto unknown comedies of Plautus (by Nicholas of Cusa in 1429) and of Donatus' commentary on Terence (by Giovanni Aurispa in 1433). This initiated a long process of transcription, editing, printing and translation of the Roman texts, and, significantly, performances by students and teachers in universities, courts and private houses, leading by the beginning of the next century to the first original comedies in the vernacular. Student plays in Latin were often extremely crude, favouring verbal attacks or tricks on teachers and figures of authority, drawing their material frequently from Boccaccio and other *novellieri*, but they became increasingly receptive to the lessons of the Roman playwrights. Aeneas Sylvius Piccolomini, the future Pope Pius II (1405–64), was perhaps the first of the humanists to show the benefit of Roman example in his *Chrysis* (1444) with its restricted stage setting, clearly differentiated characters and lively dialogue, quite close in places to Terence; but others followed, setting the stage for the 'classical' vernacular comedies of Ariosto.

The Cinquecento

Brian Richardson, Peter Marinelli, Anthony Oldcorn,
Richard Andrews

Prose

Brian Richardson

The forms of literary prose

The expansion of the vernacular

In Cinquecento Italy the vernacular finally asserted itself alongside Latin as a widely used medium for literary prose. Confidence in the vernacular grew as it was cultivated by leading literary figures. Its use was further encouraged by the increase in the number and output of printing presses: this development made more easily accessible the texts which were regarded as models of good usage, and it provided new opportunities for writers of widely differing social and geographical origins to gain fame and fortune from work aimed at a readership more varied than that of the age of manuscripts. Vernacular prose was used for all types of subject matter – from fictional narrative to the study of politics, history, social and personal relationships, art, and the vernacular language itself – and for an increasing number of translations from Greek and Latin. As these new horizons were opened up, prose style became more varied. Some writers were indebted to the model of Trecento Tuscan prose; others developed a more agile, informal manner which set out at times to capture the flavour of speech. Prose writing was, however, still by tradition principally the preserve of men, in contrast to lyric poetry, in which women were increasingly finding a voice.

The flourishing of prose was accompanied by a process of standardisation of the literary language during the first half of the century. Around 1500 almost all authors from outside Tuscany were using a type of vernacular which varied to some extent from region to region, indeed from author to author. They owed much to the stable model of the great Trecento Tuscan writers, particularly Boccaccio, but they introduced elements of Latin spelling, syntax and lexis in order to lend greater dignity to the younger language. They were also influenced by the usage of their own region, especially when this usage coincided with Latin spelling. Local influence was certainly much more limited than in prose of a practical nature, and one should not underestimate the degree of uniformity achieved at the start of the century; but the blend of Tuscan, regional and Latin ingredients still varied according to personal choice. Moreover, the introduction of Latin elements betrayed a lack of confidence in the authentic character of the vernacular.

Here, for example, is an extract from a draft dedication of the *De natura de Amore* by Mario Equicola (1470–1525), a native of southern Lazio who subsequently settled at the court of Mantua. Writing probably between about 1505 and 1508, he explains that he refuses to imitate Tuscan when his own vernacular possesses or tolerates an alternative form which is closer to Latin:

Non observo le regule del toscano se non tanto quanto al latino son conforme et le orecchie delectano, però *de* et *di* troverai senza lo articulo, *Dio* non *Iddio* benché sequente vocale; in modo che dove li imitatori de la toscana lingua totalmente ogni studio poneno in lontanarsi dalla lingua latina, io ogni cura et diligentia ho usato in approximarme ad quella: se 'l latino dice *obligatione*, mai non dirrò io *obrigatione*, se 'l latino *homo* non io *huomo*.

(I observe the rules of Tuscan only insofar as they conform with Latin and delight the ears. Thus you will find *de* and *di* without the definite article, *Dio* not *Iddio* even after a vowel; so that where the imitators of the Tuscan language strive to distance themselves from Latin, I have used every effort to get closer to it. If Latin says *obligatione*, I will never say *obrigatione*, if Latin has *homo* I will not use *huomo*.)

This type of language, which refused to restrict itself to any one region and shared the legacy of Latin, was also associated with the language spoken and written in the courts of Italy and was therefore termed by some the *lingua cortigiana*.

But Equicola's passage, with its attack on 'imitators of Tuscan', shows that certain non-Tuscans had begun to reject this hybrid language, which had no firm roots and no great writers, in favour of a Tuscan model. To the exasperation of native Tuscans, this model did not take into account the living language of Tuscany but was that offered by Boccaccio in prose and Petrarch in verse. The polemics on the merits of these different viewpoints form an important part of the Italian *questione della lingua* (language question), and themselves make up a considerable proportion of the prose output of the century.

The fact that so much time and energy were devoted to the *questione* shows that much was at stake. Firstly, the new ideas on Tuscan challenged conventional views on the subordinate status of the vernacular with respect to Latin, the main language of education and of humanist culture. Even if only a few diehards still argued that Latin was inherently superior, it was nonetheless generally assumed that the vernacular was poorer without Latinising traits; but now it was being suggested that the younger language could follow independent rules and yet rival its ancestor. Secondly, the debate touched on the raw nerve of patriotism. Non-Tuscan writers resented the suggestion that they should now remove from their usage the features distinctive of the literary traditions of their own states. Tuscans themselves resented the implication that Tuscan birth no longer conferred a privileged linguistic status. Thirdly, the *questione* threatened to make writing a more difficult business for everyone: if a Trecento model were to be adopted, writers would have to learn a new grammar and vocabulary, often quite different from their own, and then try to re-create a language nearly two centuries old.

The most influential proponent of imitation of the Tuscan Trecento best style was the Venetian nobleman Pietro Bembo (1470–1547). He came to believe that, if the vernacular was to fulfil its potential as a noble and enduring language, writers had to imitate rigorously what were acknowledged to be the most illustrious models, without any contamination from Latin or dialect. He put his Tuscanising principles into practice in his *Asolani* (1505), and justified his doctrine of imitation in the vernacular in his *Prose della volgar lingua*, published in 1525, which mark a watershed in the history of the Italian language. An author, he argued, should write for posterity and should therefore choose the best available language. For Italians, this meant the written model of Boccaccio and Petrarch, which Bembo went on to describe in detail. His analysis complemented the *Regole grammaticali della volgar lingua* by Gian Francesco Fortunio of Pordenone, the first printed grammar of the vernacular (1516). Although the use of Trecento Tuscan was apparently anachronistic, it offered a clearly defined model, unlike the *lingua cortigiana*, and rose above the political instability of the Italian courts, indeed of the whole peninsula.

However, Bembo's principles met at first with strong opposition among non-Tuscans and Tuscans alike. Count Baldesar Castiglione (1478–1529), a Mantuan, eloquently defended in *Il libro del cortegiano* (*The Book of the Courtier*, 1528) his refusal to imitate either Boccaccio or contemporary Tuscan and placed language firmly in a social context. The speakers in his dialogue raise the topic of language in the course of discussing how the courtier must avoid affectation in his behaviour. Unlike Bembo, Castiglione linked writing closely with speech and suggested that it would be affected to use archaic words in either medium. In any case, meaning and clarity of expression were more important than form. One should therefore base one's language on current practice, after having carefully chosen from different sources words which have 'some grace in pronunciation'. The resulting language would be 'Italian, common, copious and varied' (I, 35). Tuscan could be one of the sources used, but Castiglione preferred Latinising forms such as *populo* and *patrone* to the 'corrupt' Tuscan *popolo* and *padrone*.

Giangiorgio Trissino of Vicenza (1478–1550) called his written and spoken language 'courtly', but, like Castiglione, also used the adjectives 'Italian' and 'common', insisting in his dialogue *Il Castellano* (1529) that the language of Dante and Petrarch contained such important contributions from other regions of Italy that it could not properly be termed Tuscan. Trissino was a speaker in the *Dialogo della volgar lingua* written, probably at about the same time, by Pierio Valeriano (Giovanni Pietro Bolzani, 1477–1558) of Belluno. In the *Dialogo* Trissino defends his views on the limits of the contribution which Tuscan should make to the literary language, but is also presented as more balanced in his appreciation of Tuscan than some other northern Italians. Like Castiglione, Valeriano attached importance to speech as well as to writing.

By about 1530 the purist views associated with Bembo had gained wide acceptance throughout most of the peninsula, although Tuscan writers were rather slower to follow Bembo's line. They believed that there was a continuity between Trecento and Cinquecento Tuscan, and that their own knowledge of Tuscan was naturally better than that which outsiders could gain through study. In the 1520s Tuscans had been outraged at the boldness with which northerners were appropriating and even laying down rules for a language which Tuscans regarded as their own heritage. The Florentine Niccolò Machiavelli reacted in his *Discorso intorno alla nostra lingua* (1523 or 1524) to Trissino's adjective 'Italian' and to the way in which the Vicentine was using Dante's *De vulgari eloquentia* to show that the greatest Florentine poet had advocated a poetic language which was not Florentine but 'courtly' (*curialis*). Claudio Tolomei of Siena (c. 1492–1556) argued in favour of the Tuscan (rather than narrowly Florentine) nature of the literary vernacular in *Il Cesano* (drafted by 1529). Tolomei, the first writer to study Italian phonology in any detail, recognised the primacy of verbal over written communication. The importance of their living language was the cornerstone of the approaches to the *questione* of the Florentines Pierfrancesco Giambullari (1495–1555), Giovan Battista Gelli (1498–1563) and Carlo Lenzoni (1501–51).

Thereafter Florentines reconciled patriotism with an acceptance of Bembo's views. Benedetto Varchi (1503–65), in his diffuse dialogue *L'Ercolano*, printed in 1570, defended the literary achievements of Florence since the late Quattrocento and claimed that it was best to learn a language from well-educated native speakers, while reading the best writers as well; yet he acknowledged that it was Bembo who had shown how to write well in Florentine and that one should not write in the same way as one spoke. Vincenzio Borghini (1515–80) and Lionardo Salviati (1539–89) both studied Trecento prose in close detail, as Bembo had done, but also found strong elements of continuity with contemporary usage which, Salviati believed, shared the 'sweetness' (*dolcezza*) of the Trecento language.

These discussions would not have taken place without a widespread confidence in the worthiness of the vernacular in relation to the classical languages. In the 1530s Sperone Speroni of Padua (1500–88) defended, in his influential *Dialogo delle lingue*, the validity of any vernacular for the transmission of knowledge. His ideas were an important source for Du Bellay's *Deffense et illustration de la langue françoise* (1549). Varchi saw the vernacular as more beautiful than Greek and Latin, but had to admit that Greek had more resources and that both Greek and Latin had more famous writers. The belief that the vernacular could surpass the classical languages (even if it had some ground to make up in terms of quantity), and the desire to liberate the vernacular from its long subjection to the older languages, were among the motives behind the large numbers of translations into vernacular prose which were made and printed between about 1540 and 1560, and the corresponding decline in the study of the originals.

The standardisation and spread of vernacular prose were not just dictated by an élite of men of letters: they were also encouraged by the practical needs of the printing industry, particularly that of Venice, easily the major Italian publishing centre. A book printed in an average print run of a thousand copies would need to be saleable as widely as possible, and strongly regional forms would limit its success. At the same time readers expected the language of their texts to conform with what was considered to be correct, even if this correctness conflicted with what the author had originally written. Editors normally revised the language of texts quite freely, especially that of post-Trecento prose works, but on the whole did not slavishly follow purist principles. Among the majority of users of the vernacular there was still a strong prejudice against the wholesale imitation of Trecento Tuscan. In practice, Bembo's rigorous ideals were modified in the course of the century by concessions to contemporary usage of the type for which writers as disparate as Castiglione and Gelli were pleading.

Tedious and hair-splitting though some of the contributions to the *questione della lingua* were, the debate had long-term consequences of the utmost importance for Italy. For the first time, all Italian states shared a literary language which was adopted almost universally (although the use of dialect was preferred in some types of verse and comedy); and since unification this language has become the basis of spoken Italian. But the implications were not just linguistic. Standardisation acted as a stimulus to vernacular literature; only a few authors complained that the new formality was crushing spontaneity and the living contribution of their region. Italian cultural activity as a whole now became more broadly based, taking on a relatively collective character instead of being centred on a court, a city, or at best a region. The shift away from linguistic pluralism mirrored a more general tendency of Cinquecento Italian society and culture to move towards uniformity, a tendency seen especially in the ruthless imposition of religious orthodoxy by the Counter-Reformation and in the dominance of much of a hitherto fragmented but independent peninsula by the Holy Roman Empire.

Rhetoric and form

Humanism influenced the forms of Cinquecento vernacular prose through the study of rhetoric and the flourishing of two genres of classical origin: the dialogue and collections of letters by a single author. One of the reasons for the importance of rhetoric in the Cinquecento was that oratory played an important part in public life, for example in the contexts of political decision-making, diplomacy, the law, civic ceremony, academies and the Church. Many of the leading prose writers wrote to be heard, not just to be read; some were renowned for their oratorical prowess.

But in the course of the century there was increasing study of the means of constructing a stylish and persuasive argument in all types of formal verbal communication, written as well as spoken. Speroni, the leading figure in the Paduan Accademia degli Infiammati, had a strong interest in literary form and wrote several works on rhetoric, including the *Dialogo della retorica* of 1542. His ideas were also disseminated by his Paduan disciple Bernardino Tomitano (1517–76) in his *Ragionamenti della lingua toscana* (Venice, 1545 and 1546; recast and expanded as the *Quattro libri della lingua toscana*, Padua, 1570). Francesco Sansovino (1521–83), of Florentine descent but working in Venice, covered the three classical types of discourse (judicial, deliberative, epideictic) in his *Dell'arte oratoria* (Venice, 1546), but drew the majority of his examples from Petrarch's verse. The substantial *Retorica* (Venice, 1559) of the Florentine Bartolomeo Cavalcanti (1503–62) proved a very popular guide. He made much use of ancient rhetoricians but also drew some of his examples from contemporary writers. Cavalcanti had himself been a public speaker, and he differed from contemporaries in stressing that rhetoric was above all about political persuasion rather than style. However, the philosopher Francesco Patrizi of Cherso (Cres) in Croatia (1529–97) questioned in his *Della retorica* (1562) whether rhetoric any longer had a major part to play in civic life.

The popularity of the dialogue form also reflected the importance which the art of verbal persuasion had in the sophisticated oral culture of the age, particularly in courts and academies. Dialogues were used by all the major Cinquecento prose writers and for every type of subject-matter. They often represented a way of investigating the truth in which a lively but usually harmonious interplay of views might lead to the victory of one speaker representing the author (as in the first book of Bembo's *Prose*), but at other times did not allow any one thesis to prevail. In other dialogues one main speaker dominated proceedings and one or more subsidiary characters merely listened and prompted. The tendency for the dialogue to resemble a treatise became stronger in the second half of the century: another manifestation of the trend, already noted, towards the imposition of a single dominant voice in place of many. The characters were occasionally imaginary, but were often real contemporary figures, frequently drawn from the author's circle of acquaintances. Although Ciceronian dialogues did not include female speakers, these were admitted into some Renaissance dialogues, partly thanks to the precedent of the female narrators in Boccaccio's influential *Decameron* but also as a reflection of women's status in society.

In the Cinquecento the dialogue and the collection of *novelle* came closer together. Just as dialogues often used anecdotes as examples, so the frame-story for *novelle* could give increasingly detailed portraits of social groups and their discussions and entertainments. The *Ragionamenti* of Agnolo Firenzuola (1493–1543) showed how the two genres could even be merged to give a hybrid combination of debate and storytelling.

Much humanist work on rhetoric had concentrated on letter-writing in

Latin, a genre well established since classical times. By the 1530s the need was felt for a collection of vernacular letters which would play the same role of prose model as did the letters of Cicero in the teaching of Latin. The writer who seized this opportunity was not an establishment figure but Pietro Aretino (1492–1556), a hosier's son who had won considerable notoriety for his witty and scurrilous writings and who was now working in Venice. In 1538 he published a collection of his letters, the success of which opened the way to many further books of letters by individuals and to the compilation of anthologies.

Publishing and censorship

The transition from manuscript to print culture was gradual. Although printing had come to Italy in 1465, some well-known prose works of the early Cinquecento were not written for immediate publication via the press, circulating at first in manuscript form. Authors, it is true, would often have to bear some or all of the costs of printing, but hesitation to go into print also reflected the relatively untried nature of vernacular prose and political un- certainties. Works might be composed over a long period, and in any case could be reserved in the first instance for a restricted audience. Machiavelli chose to send only one of his non-literary works to the press, and Castiglione's *Cortegiano*, drafted and revised over several years, was printed only after he had discovered that a pirated edition was about to come out in Naples. None of the works of Francesco Guicciardini was circulated even in manuscript during his lifetime, and only one was printed in Italy during the century. It must be remembered, then, that some prose works which are now regarded as among the most important of the first forty years of the Cinquecento emerged slowly and uncertainly into their final form, or did not have a wide impact until some time after their composition. Later, though, authors increasingly became professionals, writing for the press and hoping to receive financial and other benefits.

   In the first half of the century there was little control over the contents of printed books other than the operation of a system of book-privileges issued by states in order to protect an edition from plagiarism for a limited period. But from the 1540s the Catholic Church and the Italian states began to introduce tighter controls to prevent the circulation of Protestant doctrines and then to repress writings considered harmful to morality, to the reputation of the clergy, or to rulers. Indexes of prohibited books were drawn up, the first to have any wide effect being that authorised by the Council of Trent and published in 1564. Thereafter printers became much warier of offending ecclesiastical or political authorities, and they might have works revised before applying for a licence to print them. Direct or indirect censorship was, then, another factor which could restrict the circulation of certain prose works

(those of Machiavelli and Aretino, for instance) in the form in which we now
know them.

Statecraft and history

Politics and historiography in Florence

In the Cinquecento, as in the previous two centuries, the worlds of politics,
historiography and literature were more closely linked in Florence than in any
other Italian state. The city's turbulent experiences, combined with the
instability of the whole Italian peninsula, were the focal point for most
Florentine prose writing in the first half of the century and inspired a
remarkable series of works, often of great stylistic merit, which analysed recent
history and considered how states, and Florence in particular, should best be
governed and protected.

Since 1434 Florence had been unlike other Italian states in that the city was
poised between republicanism and rule by a single family, the Medici. Their
dominance was based on manipulation of the constitution with the collusion
of supporters among the aristocracy and other recipients of their political
patronage. Republican traditions were threatened but still alive – so much so
that internal opposition, combined with the external pressure of the French
invasion, forced the Medici into exile in 1494. There ensued a struggle
between supporters of a relatively broadly based regime and supporters of one
which was narrower and more aristocratically based. At first the former had
the upper hand, backed by the influential Dominican preacher Girolamo
Savonarola. A new constitution followed the Venetian model, but gave less
power to the upper classes and had no equivalent of the Doge. However,
threats from other powers proved the mechanisms of decision-making to be
cumbersome, and the resentment of the patricians was exacerbated by the
restrictions on their influence. In order to bring Florence closer to the Venetian
constitution, which seemed to offer a social and political stability in strong
contrast with Florence's turmoil, it was decided in 1502 that the head of state
(*gonfaloniere*) was to be appointed for life like the Doge. However, the new
regime was not strong enough to resist the return of the Medici (still private
citizens in theory) in 1512; and, after a briefer period of exile for the family in
1527–30, a Medicean duchy was established in 1532. The defeat of the anti-
Medicean exiles at the battle of Montemurlo in 1537 put an end to any realistic
hopes of seeing a new republic established.

Machiavelli

The most brilliant and original contributor to the political debates of this
fertile period was Niccolò Machiavelli (1469–1527), who emerged into public

life in 1498 when he was elected to a post in the Florentine Chancery. His work there gave him experience of administration of Florentine territory, of diplomacy, and of the problems involved in arming a state. Machiavelli was in principle an apolitical civil servant; but in practice he antagonised and offended the patriciate and came to be seen as closely associated with a regime dedicated to keeping the Medici in exile and to preventing power from falling into the hands of their supporters. When in 1512 the Medici returned and the narrower pre-1494 constitution was restored, he was sacked. The fortunes of the Medici continued to rise in 1513 when Giovanni, a son of Lorenzo il Magnifico, became Pope Leo X and, for the first time ever, the same family controlled two of the major Italian states. This conjunction of events offered a chance to think afresh about what could be done to remedy the Italian weaknesses which foreign armies had exposed ruthlessly over the years since 1494. Frustrated by his enforced leisure and convinced that his practical experience and knowledge of ancient history could benefit the Medici if they were to employ him, Machiavelli took advantage of the new opportunities offered to the Medici and to Italy and wrote the treatise now known as *Il principe* (*The Prince*, first mentioned December 1513, first printed 1532). He contemplated a dedication to the Pope's younger brother Giuliano, but eventually addressed the work to a member of the next generation, Leo's nephew Lorenzo (grandson of il Magnifico).

In chapters 1–11 of his treatise, Machiavelli studied how best to rule different types of principalities, concentrating on newly acquired states. Many readers would have been shocked to find him praising, above all modern Italian princes, Cesare Borgia, bastard son of Pope Alexander VI, who in 1499–1503 had brought under control many towns in the Marche and the Romagna which were nominally part of the Papal States. Cesare was remembered all too well as a ruthless and violent figure who had planned to add Tuscany to his domains. But there was a parallel to be drawn between Cesare's use of his father's position and the way in which one of Pope Leo's younger relatives could profit from the good fortune of the Medici. Machiavelli's analysis of Cesare's career is an example of his proneness to idealise or oversimplify historical evidence in support of a thesis.

Machiavelli then argued (chapters 12–14) that all states had to be based on good arms, which meant one's own troops ('one's own' being a concept only loosely defined) rather than mercenaries or soldiers provided by an ally. A strong army, together with the support of the *popolo* (roughly equivalent to the middle classes) and avoidance of hatred and contempt, were the keys to the prince's independence; he would be able to withstand adversity only if he relied on himself rather than on the support of others.

In chapter 15 Machiavelli began to examine the qualities which bring a prince praise or blame, explicitly leaving aside wishful thinking about imaginary states in favour of genuinely useful advice on the 'effective truth of the matter' ('[la] verità effettuale della cosa'). It would be good, he stressed, to have a reputation for behaviour which traditionally brings praise, such as generosity, kindness and keeping one's word. Indeed, a prince should exploit the gap between what he seems and what he is, cultivating a reputation for virtue and especially for being religious (18, 5). However, some conventional virtues may undermine his power, while qualities which appear to be vices may be essential to his survival. Machiavelli did not remove the distinction between good and evil but argued that 'a prince must, if he wants to keep power, learn to be able not to be good, and use or not use this ability according to need' (15, 1). At the start of chapter 15, Machiavelli drew attention to the radical difference between his own advice and that given by many others who had written on the prince's moral qualities. He was referring to the long tradition of books on the ideal prince which included Xenophon's *Cyropaedia* and Isocrates' oration to Nicocles, a *De regimine principum* by St Thomas Aquinas and another by Egidio Colonna, Petrarch's letter of 1373 to Francesco da Carrara, and recent humanistic treatises such as Pontano's *De principe*. Machiavelli was not the first to draw attention to the difficulty for a ruler of choosing what was truly good rather than what was expedient, but his predecessors had urged that the prince should always be morally irreproachable. Machiavelli's advice on being able 'not to be good' challenged the very basis of traditional treatises addressed to princes, and its impact would have been all the greater for its being presented in the form of just such a treatise rather than as private letter or essay addressed to the Medici.

Wanting to concentrate on giving practical advice, Machiavelli further subverted the conventions of his genre by deliberately omitting to highlight the reasons for which the prince needs to 'maintain his state', in other words the ultimate end which may justify his means. He did not in *Il principe* distinguish between good rule and tyranny, though he did so in other works. Hence the many different interpretations of the purpose of the work. It is, though, no handbook for tyrants; cruelties are held to be justifiable only if used 'for the greatest benefit of one's subjects' (8, 7). The prince should not benefit only the few: it is more important to win the favour of the *popolo* rather than that of the *grandi* or leading citizens (9). He should foster his citizens' skills and the economy of the state (21, 7). Finally, a new Medicean prince could bring about a better future for Italy, as Machiavelli explained in chapters 24–6. Italian princes had neither established good armies nor befriended the *popolo* and controlled the *grandi*, and had thus failed to cope with the upheavals of the previous two decades. Fortune was not to blame. Fortune, Machiavelli acknowledged, is a potent force, but governs perhaps only half of our affairs. We can take precautions against her onslaught while times are favourable; and we could, in theory, enjoy continuous good fortune if we succeeded in adapting our behaviour, proceeding cautiously or impetuously as circumstances required. The fervent final chapter argues that, since the house of Medici had received in 1512–13 such signs of divine favour (their return to Florence, the election of Pope Leo), a Medicean prince who heeded Machiavelli's advice would be strong enough to withstand adverse fortune and could take up arms to liberate Italy from the 'barbarians' oppressing the peninsula. Other Italians, Machiavelli is convinced, would follow the prince's lead in this joint military (rather than political) enterprise.

Il principe, first and most famous of Machiavelli's major works, is remarkable not just for his bold questioning of received ideas but also for its prose, the vigour of which matched his plain speaking. Between the loftier dedication and concluding exhortation, his style is appropriately down to earth, using images and metaphors from building or medicine or nature, echoing the usage of the Florentine chancery and the everyday speech of the city.

Not surprisingly, such an unconventional, at times scandalous, treatise brought him no reward from the Medici. The work to which he devoted his next few years, the *Discorsi sopra la prima deca di Tito Livio* (*Discourses on the First Decade of Livy*, first printed 1531), was dedicated to two young private citizens and probably originated in discussions with a group of younger Florentines in the Orti Oricellari, the gardens of the Rucellai family in Florence. Contemporary problems form a continual subtext, but now Machiavelli studied politics in a broader perspective: the *Discorsi* thus form the most important statement of his political ideas. His discussion was structured rather loosely, sometimes following the chronology of Livy's history of the foundation and rise of Rome, but with the material divided into three books: one on internal matters, a second on the expansion of Rome's territory, and a third on the actions of individuals which made Rome great. This unorthodox scheme was not entirely successful, since it led to a certain loss of coherence in exposition.

In the proem to Book 1 of the *Discorsi* Machiavelli argued that antiquity was being imitated in the fields of art, law and medicine, but that (given the tendency for history to repeat itself) his contemporaries had much to learn from the organisation of the Roman republic and from the behaviour of its citizens. In the consuls, the senate and the tribunes of the plebs, Rome's constitution combined elements of monarchy, aristocracy and democracy. It allowed for the leadership of one man in times of crisis, yet it rightly safeguarded liberty, for tyranny brings in its wake violence, cruelty and immorality. The Roman constitution also protected the interests of the plebs, whose tribunes could veto the action of other magistrates. The price to be paid for this was a continual tension between plebeians and nobles. The alternative would have been a state which, though stable, would have been able to defend only a limited amount of territory, like ancient Sparta or modern Venice. But Machiavelli believed Rome was right to put the 'guardianship of liberty' in the hands of the plebs rather than the nobles. A state such as Rome could use the political involvement of its citizens in order to build a strong army; it would thus be able to expand its territory if necessary, and would avoid the effeminacy and discord which were the fruits of idleness.

Underlying this reasoning was a conviction that citizens should be involved in the state and devoted to its cause. Machiavelli contrasted starkly the sense of political responsibility of republican Romans and the corruption and self-ishness of most modern European countries, especially Italy. This corruption was due partly to social inequality. It could also be combatted by using the power of religion. Machiavelli admired ancient Roman religion because it was used to inspire armies and the plebs and simply 'to keep men good'. Christianity had shown the truth, but its founder's principles had been betrayed by the Church: weakness and passivity had been encouraged in place of glory, strength and patriotism (I, 11–12; II, 2).

After the experiment of the *Discorsi* and for the rest of his life, Machiavelli adopted prose genres descended from classical tradition, conscious of the need to assert firmly and to a wide public the literary superiority of Florence by establishing a presence in the mainstream of contemporary literature. His next major work, the *Arte della guerra* (*Art of War*), printed in Florence in 1521, was structured as a dialogue, a choice which led other Florentines to use this genre in the course of the 1520s. But within this conventional form Machiavelli's message was as uncompromising and uncomfortable as before. The young audience in the Orti Oricellari listening to the main speaker, the soldier Fabrizio Colonna, included the dedicatees of the *Discorsi*. Machiavelli was again teaching the younger generation, and again he was showing how they must learn from the past in order to put right the corruption of the present. In comparison with other works on military matters, Machiavelli's was highly original in not concentrating on warfare alone but in urging the need to integrate civil and military life. In his own age they had grown apart. Soldiers were no longer patriotic, peace-loving, God-fearing citizens. Princes had paid the price of neglecting warfare in favour of elegance and comfort. Turning back to the military practices of ancient Rome, Machiavelli showed how modern methods might be improved; he wanted warfare to become part of the renaissance of things past which Italy had already led in poetry, painting and sculpture. Courageously, at a time when he was hoping to gain the favour of the Medici, he justified the militia of Florentine subjects which he had helped to organise before 1512, and claimed that whoever followed this path would be the first ruler of all Italy.

Machiavelli's *Istorie fiorentine* ('Florentine Histories') also took a polemical stance behind a conventional exterior. He was commissioned to write the work in 1520, after having written an account of the bold rise to political power of the *condottiere* Castruccio Castracani of Lucca (1281–1328) as an exercise in historical style, and dedicated it to Pope Clement VII (nephew of Lorenzo il Magnifico) in 1525. He intended to begin his history in 1434, following on from the Latin histories of Bruni and Bracciolini; but he found that they had dealt inadequately with civil discord, a topic of special importance to him. So he went back to the foundation of the city, concentrating on internal events up to 1434 (Books I–IV) and thereafter bringing in external events as well up to the death of Lorenzo il Magnifico in 1492 (Books V–VIII). The opening chapters of Books II–VIII were used for discourses on general topics. Strife between the nobles and *popolo*, he wrote in III, 1, had had very different effects in ancient Rome and in Florence; yet, while Rome had eventually needed an emperor, at least Florence had now reached a state of relative social equality, so that its government could be reformed by 'a wise lawgiver'. He made it clear, typically pulling no punches, that there should be no return to the way in which the Medici had controlled the city in the Quattrocento. The regime of Cosimo – great-grandfather of the dedicatee – had been 'unbearable and violent' in its last eight years (VII, 4). When the Pazzi family plotted against Clement's father and uncle in 1478, the conspirators failed to find support because the *popolo* was 'made deaf by the fortune and liberality of the Medici' so that liberty was unknown (VIII, 8). Machiavelli expressed the hope in his dedication that he would live long enough to take his history beyond 1492, but this was not to be.

Machiavelli's ideas soon aroused great interest both in Italy and abroad. The *Principe* and the *Discorsi* were not printed in English until 1640, but manuscript translations were circulating in Elizabethan times, and English translations of the *Arte della guerra* and the *Istorie* were printed in 1562 and 1595 respectively. All the major works were printed in London in Italian between 1584 and 1588, and in 1602 there appeared an English translation of Innocent Gentillet's influential *Discours* attacking the *Principe*, which had been published in French in 1576.

Guicciardini

Towards the end of his life Machiavelli became a friend of a younger Florentine with whom he shared a passion for politics, history, and their native city, but who came from an altogether different social and political background, Francesco Guicciardini (1483–1540). As a member of a distinguished patrician family, Guicciardini favoured a narrowly based republic. He was trusted by the Medici, and his career flourished as Machiavelli's languished. After acting as Florentine ambassador to Spain in 1512–13, he moved into the wider orbit of the Medicean papacy and was given difficult posts by Leo X as governor of two faction-ridden cities in the Papal States (1516–24). Clement VII made use of Guicciardini's at times ruthless efficiency by making him President of the Romagna in 1524, and he was also closely involved with the Papal–French alliance against the Emperor Charles V which led to the atrocious Sack of Rome in May 1527 and the renewed exile of the Medici from Florence. He continued to serve Clement and then Alessandro de' Medici, first Duke of Florence, who was assassinated in 1537, but his attempts to restrain the power of Alessandro's successor, Duke Cosimo I, incurred suspicion and he was deprived of an effective voice in Florentine affairs. He withdrew from public life in 1538 to dedicate himself to historical writing.

During his political career Guicciardini wrote works which, in different ways, concerned the government of Florence, but which were composed in order to clarify his ideas rather than for publication. The *Storie fiorentine* ('Florentine Histories', 1508–9) went rapidly over the period from the Ciompi uprising in 1378 to 1454, with the years around 1400 being seen as something of a golden age because the city was ruled by 'decent and wise men', in other words the *grandi*. Then events up to 1509 were described in more detail. Already Guicciardini showed his preference for primary sources by using material from his family's archive, but this was political writing as much as history: he attacked both the regime of Lorenzo il Magnifico and the post-1494 republic. Under Lorenzo, power had been concentrated in the hands of one person; under the popular government it had been put in the hands of incompetent citizens rather than 'men of quality' of his own class (chapter 23).

   The *Discorso del modo di ordinare il governo popolare* ('Discourse on Ordering the Popular Government') was written in 1512 in Logroño, Spain (hence its alternative name, the *Discorso di Logrogno*), before Guicciardini learned of the return of the Medici to Florence. It called for a reform of existing institutions rather than radical change. Both the office of life gonfalonier and the Great Council were to remain, but a crucial stabilising role was to be played by the patricians: exercising their influence through a senate with life membership, they would prevent an ambitious gonfalonier from becoming a tyrant and the ignorant multitude from dragging the state into anarchy. In 1513 and 1516 Guicciardini wrote two *Discorsi* on how the Medici should consolidate their power after their restoration, warning that they should avoid autocracy and rely instead on collaboration with experienced citizens. Guicciardini's major purely political work, the *Dialogo del reggimento di Firenze* ('Dialogue on the Government of Florence', 1521–5), was set in 1494, after the exile of the Medici, and thus allowed him to adopt an apparently more detached stance than in his *Discorsi* while still focusing on ideas and strategies relevant to the present. The first book compares conflicting viewpoints held by Florentine aristocrats: Bernardo del Nero prefers the Medicean regime to the popular republic, while two other speakers favour respectively an oligarchic and a popular government. Del Nero explains that he is not looking for a perfect regime but comparing real ones in order to see which is most law-abiding, just, and respectful of 'the good of all' according to their status. He accepts that the Medicean state was not perfect, but argues that the broadening of the constitution in 1494 would not improve matters. The second book moves on to describe Guicciardini's own programme for the good government of Florence. He amplifies his scheme (already outlined in 1512) of a constitution of checks and balances akin to the Venetian rather than the Roman model, with a popular council, a strong senate with 150 life members which would be in effect the cornerstone of the republic, and a gonfalonier also appointed for life.

   The period after the Sack of Rome brought further disillusionment for Guicciardini. Distrusted by the leaders of the new democratic republic set up after the exile of the Medici in 1527, he entered a period of tension with his own city and of personal introspection. In 1528 he revised and expanded his *Ricordi*, a series of reflections and aphorisms about men and politics on which he had been working since 1512. A final revision was made in 1530. The tone of these *Ricordi* is sceptical but not entirely defeatist. Guicciardini makes it clear that he has no faith in political theory: the future is too unpredictable, fortune too powerful, circumstances too varied. Yet he thought it wiser to be bold than to be timid. The bold man knows the dangers just as well but, instead of expecting the worst, 'taking into consideration how many dangers can be avoided through men's efforts, how many dangers chance eliminates by itself, does not let himself be confounded by all of them, but enters into undertakings on good grounds and with the hope that not all that may be must be' (1530 series, no. 96). One must be guided not by preconceived ideals or rules but by experience, discretion, an ability to compromise and an appreciation of what is in one's own best interests.

Guicciardini clearly differed from Machiavelli both in his approaches to politics and historiography and in his cautious temperament, and his writings form a useful complement and counterbalance to those of his at times over-enthusiastic friend. As we have seen, he believed that it was dangerous to entrust power to the *popolo*, and he was instinctively less inclined to generalise, to have faith in the possibility of a regeneration based on the methods of antiquity, or to see any virtue in civic strife. His *Considerazioni intorno ai Discorsi del Machiavelli* ('Considerations on Machiavelli's Discourses', written probably in 1530) criticised his compatriot's way of putting things 'too absolutely' (I, 3), of seeking universal rules from what Guicciardini considered over-simplifications of historical evidence, and rejected Machiavelli's paradoxical argument that conflict between patricians and plebeians had made Rome great.

Around 1527–8 Guicciardini began another attempt to trace Florentine history from the last quarter of the Trecento onwards, in his *Cose fiorentine* ('Florentine Matters'). He followed a more critical method, using many varied Florentine and non-Florentine sources, among them manuscript ones – an important advance in historical methodology. However, he got no further than 1441. In his last years, he decided to concentrate on the history of the period which he had witnessed himself and in which he had been an actor. Realising that for a true understanding of his times one had to look at the interrelationships between Italian and European powers, he abandoned the narrowly Florentine perspective for a *Storia d'Italia* (Books I–XVI, Florence, 1561; Books XVII–XX, Venice, 1564). About 1535 he began to write on the period after the Battle of Pavia (1525), but then in 1537 he started afresh from 1494, a turning-point not just for Florence but for all Italy. Until that year, he wrote, Italy had enjoyed relative tranquillity, thanks largely to the diplomacy of Lorenzo il Magnifico. But then came the invasion of the French King Charles VIII, only the first of a series of damaging and disruptive incursions by foreign armies. The turmoil of the ensuing four decades (the *Storia* goes up to 1534) was attributed to the rulers of Italy (including the Church), who had proved to be indecisive, corrupt, over-ambitious, and over-confident in a world made unstable by the continual variations of fortune. Guicciardini carefully compared the accounts of earlier historians and drew material from the diplomatic archives of the Florentine state. Yet at the same time he followed classical conventions of historiography, dividing his books into years and using pairs of invented speeches to express opposing views.

Another important innovation in the *Storia* was the way in which Guicciardini delved into the psychological motivation of his main characters, showing how events were moulded by the chance interplay of different personalities. The work was also unprecedented in its breadth. Francesco Vettori had already written a *Sommario* of Italian history between 1511 and 1527 (see below), but Guicciardini's masterpiece was the first major historical work to encompass all the states of the peninsula and to set these states within the still broader framework of European diplomacy. After its publication in Italy it soon won a European reputation, being translated into English by Geoffrey Fenton (1579) and also into Latin, French, Spanish, German and Dutch.

Other Florentine writers on history and politics

The public career of the Florentine patrician Francesco Vettori (1474–1539) was even longer than Guicciardini's. After serving the republic from 1503, he worked closely with the Medici. In 1527 he sided with the popular republic, but then supported the Medici again from 1529 onwards, showing a greater willingness than most of his class to accept dispassionately that political stability could be achieved only by abandoning the city's republican tradition. Vettori's most original work is his *Viaggio in Alamagna* ('Travels in Germany'), in which a description of his diplomatic mission to the Tirol in 1507–8 forms a frame for anecdotes or *novelle* recounted by him or others, and even for a play. Like Machiavelli, Vettori was impressed by the disciplined German way of life. His other works were more strictly historical and political. He wrote a brief biography of the younger Lorenzo de' Medici, with whose apparently autocratic tendencies Vettori had been closely associated in 1515–19, and he criticised the policies of Clement VII vis-à-vis the Emperor Charles V in a *Discorso* of 1525 and a *Dialogo* composed after the Sack of Rome. Vettori's *Sommario della istoria d'Italia (1511–1527)* justified his personal political line as being in Florence's interests, and offered stinging judgements on the papacy and the clergy.

As Vettori's capacity to survive several changes of regime suggests, he had few ideological preconceptions. States imagined by Plato or Thomas More (*Utopia* had appeared in 1516 and had been printed in Florence in 1519) might not be tyrannical, he wrote, but every real state he had read about or seen 'seemed to smell of tyranny' (*Scritti storici e politici*, p. 145). Vettori's cool-headed, sceptical judgements on political reality, and of the reputation of Venice in particular, contrast strongly with the passionate idealism shown by a younger Florentine, Donato Giannotti (1492–1573). Both of his main political works looked to the Venetian republic as the model which would provide stability and civil harmony for Florence. In the dialogue *Della repubblica de' Viniziani* ('On the Republic of the Venetians', written in 1526), Giannotti rejected Machiavelli's pro-Roman bias by pointing out that the Venetian state enjoyed more 'tranquillity and peace' than did Rome. He compared its constitution to a pyramid, at the base of which was the Consiglio Maggiore, surmounted by the senate, the Collegio (which prepared the business of the senate and was responsible for executing its decisions), and at the summit the elected Doge. No single element could gain control; both the patricians and the *popolo* were content, and sedition was thus avoided.

Like Machiavelli, Giannotti was a *popolano*. During the republic of 1527–30 he held one of the chancery posts which Machiavelli had held, and he too lost his post when the Medici returned from exile. From 1531 onwards he wrote his major work, *Della republica fiorentina* ('On the Florentine Republic'), in the belief that the Medicean regime would soon be overthrown and that a republican government would be needed, strong enough to resist external force and acceptable to all. The best constitution should satisfy as far as possible the three classes which would participate in government: *grandi*, *mediocri* and *popolani* (*plebei* were excluded), without allowing any one to dominate absolutely. The *grandi* were particularly to blame for the failure of Florentine republicanism, Giannotti thought, having acted like 'wolves' for the last century in contrast with the lamb-like majority (II, 11–12). His constitution was to have a pyramidal scheme, but his political experience since 1526, and perhaps his reflections on Machiavelli's *Discorsi*, led him towards a more moderate republicanism than that of Venice. The cornerstone of his state would be a Great Council representing all three social groups, though the *grandi* would not be alienated. Like Machiavelli, he proposed a citizen militia.

In 1535 Giannotti argued in a *Discorso delle cose d'Italia* ('Discourse on the Affairs of Italy') that only war against Charles V could prevent the Emperor from extending his power in Italy. But he realised that it was more likely that Italian rulers would passively allow themselves to be 'suffocated' by the imperial army. Giannotti evidently could not share the trust in Italian *virtù* which Machiavelli had expressed at the end of *Il principe* two decades earlier. After the defeat of Montemurlo Giannotti spent the rest of his life in Rome and Venice, still writing occasionally on Tuscan literature and politics. His *Repubblica de' Viniziani* was printed in Rome in 1540 and enjoyed considerable success, helping to build up the image of Venice as a model state. The *Republica fiorentina* was not printed until 1721, but the number of surviving sixteenth-century manuscripts shows that the republican cause lived on even under the Medicean duchy.

Another Florentine who lived most of his life in exile was Antonio Brucioli (1490/1500–66). His case was, however, very different from that of the steadfast Giannotti. He fled the city for the first time in 1522 with other anti-Medicean conspirators, returned in 1527 on the expulsion of the Medici but was banished once more in 1529, this time because of his religious ideas, which were anti-Savonarolan and pro-Lutheran. He became one of the first writers to earn a living through the new opportunities offered by the Venetian printing industry, working as editor, commentator and translator into the vernacular. He also published three editions of his own mediocre philosophical *Dialogi* between 1526 and 1545, revising them in 1537–8 partly because by then he had turned informer to the Medici.

The first book, on moral philosophy, included a group of five political and military dialogues. The *Dialogo della republica* described a state whose stability was based on the Aristotelian concept of 'praiseworthy mediocrity'. Types of government which favour a group or an individual were rejected; the 'middle' class, he considered, must be the best rulers; nearness to the mean must be encouraged by ensuring that all citizens had broadly similar income and expenditure and by preventing individuals from achieving excessive power. Like Machiavelli, from whose works he borrowed freely, Brucioli believed fervently in a citizen militia and in the political importance of religion. However, he was most concerned not with constitutional mechanisms but with the moral, social and physical welfare of the community. Some of his laws regulated personal behaviour; others enforced respect for God and for parents. His just prince was to be a paragon of virtue sent by Heaven, while his military captain should likewise be God-fearing. Tyrants were condemned because they kept power by making their citizens weak, suspicious of one another, and poor.

Discussion of constitutional reform became futile after the failure of the attempt to overthrow Cosimo de' Medici in 1537. However, Florentines born and brought up before then continued to write about the period in which a precarious republicanism had finally collapsed, expressing their views through the medium of the 'Florentine history'. Some of them had been actively involved in public life; others had been on its fringes or mere spectators and could write more impartially. The most strongly anti-Medicean was Iacopo Nardi (1476–1563), exiled in 1530. In Venice he wrote two *Discorsi* (1534) in defence of the opponents of the Medici, condemning this family as tyrannical and corrupt. In 1537–40 he translated Livy's history of republican Rome, and in 1548 he wrote a life of a captain who had served Florence while the Medici were in exile. Around 1553 Nardi began his *Istorie della città di Firenze* (Lyons, 1582, then Florence, 1584), dealing first with the period from 1494 to the suicide in 1538 of the imprisoned rebel leader Filippo Strozzi, and then beginning to narrate another struggle for liberty, Siena's revolt against the Emperor in 1552. His judgements on the Medici were less harsh than in the *Discorsi* of twenty years earlier, and he could contrast Cosimo's qualities with the dissoluteness of his predecessor Alessandro.

Two younger historians whose sympathies were originally pro-republican were Bernardo Segni (1504–58) and Iacopo Pitti (1519–89). After 1530, though, partly because of financial hardship, Segni sided with the Medici. Both he and Pitti were prominent members of the Accademia Fiorentina, the principal cultural organisation of Cosimo's state. Segni's *Istorie*, written in 1553–8, began in 1527 and were left unfinished at the year 1555. He saw Cosimo as gifted but a tyrant; yet in practice he could see no alternative to the principality, because Florentines were not capable of living in freedom. For Pitti, on the other hand, the would-be tyrants of Florence were the *grandi*. His *Apologia de' Cappucci* (1570–5: the 'Cappucci' were the supporters of the popular party) attacks Guicciardini's *Storia d'Italia* for its pro-*grandi* bias and praises the popular regime of 1502–12. Pitti is prepared to see Cosimo as a physician who had restored the state by crushing the *grandi*. His unfinished *Istoria fiorentina* begins by celebrating the glorious defence of Florence in 1529 and by accusing the *grandi* of betraying the city, putting money before liberty and preferring tyranny to laws. It then traces their lack of patriotism back to the fourteenth and fifteenth centuries before concentrating on the period from 1494 to 1529.

The patrician Filippo de' Nerli (1485–1556) also saw Cosimo as a ruler who had ended centuries of discord. He began his *Commentari de' fatti civili occorsi dentro la città di Firenze* ('Commentaries on the Civil Events Occurring within the City of Florence') before 1534 and finished them around 1552. The unusual title was significant: he wanted to show how Florence had been plagued by changes of regime brought about for the benefit of factions (the patricians being as much to blame as other groups), until the exhausted citizens transformed the state into a principality. Peace had been achieved, then; but at a high cost. Nerli concluded with the disturbing comment that, since Cosimo's victory over the rebels had removed any cause for civil disputes and any future malcontents would have to choose exile, 'it seems no longer necessary to record the civil events of our city'.

That past disputes were in effect now irrelevant is shown by the commissions which Cosimo gave to two former opponents to write histories of Florence. The first was Benedetto Varchi (see above, p. 184), who had chosen to join the Florentine exiles after 1530 and had welcomed the assassination of Duke Alessandro in 1537. But Varchi was above all a man of letters, with no interest in politics (his family came from a town outside Florence and he had no class allegiances), and Cosimo recalled him in 1543. The *Storia fiorentina* which he was appointed to write in 1546–7 (published Cologne, 1721) gave a diffuse, unselective account of the decade beginning in 1527, drawing on archive material provided by the Duke. In 1565–6 Cosimo commissioned Giovan Battista Adriani (1511–79) to continue the history of Florence from his accession. Adriani had returned from exile in 1540 and became an influential member of the Florentine Academy. The *Istoria de' suoi tempi* ('History of his Times', Florence, 1583), went up to Cosimo's death in 1574. As the first

Florentine history to begin in the ducal age, it set out not to contrast duchy with republic but to demonstrate how, in a period when almost all Italian states had undergone upheavals, Florence had entrusted herself to Cosimo and had actually extended her territory by annexing Siena. Adriani placed Florentine history in a European context, showing how Cosimo's policies were intended to free the city in the long term from imperial control. With its broad perspective and lack of ideological partiality, Adriani's *Istoria* marked a turning-point in the historiography of Florence.

The last Florentine history commissioned by Cosimo was by Scipione Ammirato (1531–1601), a priest who was born in Lecce and settled in the city only in 1569. Books I–XX of his *Istorie fiorentine* (up to 1434) were printed in Florence in 1600; Books XXI–XXXV followed in 1641. They gave a long and relatively uncritical account of the city from its foundation to the death of Cosimo.

Among Ammirato's numerous other works were his *Discorsi sopra Cornelio Tacito* (Venice, 1594), the title and the structure of which echo Machiavelli's *Discorsi* on Livy. The Florentine's questioning of conventional morality and his anti-clericalism were naturally unacceptable in Counter-Reformation Italy, and his writings had been banned from publication in the Tridentine Index of 1564. Yet his influence remained powerful. This is shown not just by the appearance of works, such as Ammirato's, which set out to refute Machiavelli's thought (even if, as here, he is not named) but also, paradoxically, by the way in which these same attacks adopted a Machiavellian pattern of reasoning. Ammirato pursued the line indicated in 1589 by another priest, Giovanni Botero (see below, p. 201): the 'reason of state' ('ragion di stato') should always have the good of the public as its aim and had to be compatible with religion (XII, 1). Ammirato's proem explained that his purpose was to combat the mistaken opinion 'that states cannot be ruled with the laws of God'. He chose Tacitus, the historian of the early Roman emperors, rather than Livy as his starting-point, one of his reasons being the former's greater relevance to an age in which Florence had passed from republic to principality.

Politics and historiography in other states

The Republic of Venice also had its tradition of official historiography and of political writing, but a much less prolific and less interesting one than that of Florence. In 1530 Pietro Bembo was commissioned to write a Latin history of Venice (*Historiae venetae libri XII*) which went from 1487 to 1513; this was printed in 1551, and Bembo also made a translation into the vernacular, printed in 1552. The *Historia vinetiana* of Paolo Paruta (1540–98), commissioned in 1580 and first printed in 1605, continued the account to 1552. The first four books were written in Latin, but Paruta used the vernacular for the remaining eight books. He had already written *Della perfettione della vita politica* ('On the Perfection of Political Life'): Book 1, *Dialoghi della vita civile*, on man's acquisition of 'civil happiness', came out in 1572; two further books on the virtues and the worldly benefits which adorn them were added in 1579. At the end he quoted the description of a mixed constitution which Gaspare Contarini (1483–1542) had given in his *De magistratibus et republica Venetorum* ('On the Magistracies and Republic of the Venetians'), written about 1523–6 (first edition Paris, 1543). However, Paruta set politics in a broad moral context, first weighing up the claims of the active and the contemplative life; he favoured the former, but the discussion, set in Trento during the Council session of 1562–3, was deeply influenced by religious values. The two books of his later *Discorsi politici* (Venice, 1599), dealt respectively with ancient and modern history. Paruta argued against Machiavelli's preference for the Roman rather than the Venetian republic and defended the role which Venice had played in the Italian context.

The other northern republic, Genoa, was the subject of a work by one of its citizens, Uberto Foglietta (c. 1518–81). His *Della republica di Genova* (the only vernacular work by this defender of the superiority of Latin) is a dialogue, influenced by Machiavelli's ideas on ancient Rome, in which a Genoese citizen tells another who is living in Antwerp of the conflicts between the nobles and the *popolari* which are destroying the city and threatening its freedom. The nobles emerge as the less deserving class, and the publication of these views (Rome, 1559) led to Foglietta's exile. In 1576, however, he was allowed to return to his city and later became its historian (*Historia Genuensium*, Genoa, 1585).

Giovanni Botero (1544–1617) of Bene in Piedmont, a Jesuit for much of his career in the Church, tried to restore moral values to politics in his *Della ragion di stato* ('On the Reason of State', Venice, 1589). 'Why,' he asked, 'should a Christian prince close the door of his secret council-chamber against Christ and the Gospels and set up a reason of State contrary to God's law, as though it were a rival altar?' (II, 15). Botero had a much wider perception than did Machiavelli of the factors underpinning a state's welfare. He attributed considerable importance to the economy, deriving ideas from Jean Bodin, and he included socio-economic considerations in his analysis of the causes of the greatness of cities (*Delle cause della grandezza e magnificenza delle città*), first published in 1588.

The official historiography of Quattrocento Naples was brought to an end by the fall of the Aragonese dynasty and the foreign domination of the Cinquecento. However, among Neapolitan works produced in the second half of the century were the *Istoria del regno di Napoli* by the poet Angelo Di Costanzo (1507–91), which ran from the thirteenth century to 1489 (first version printed 1572, second version 1581), and *La congiura dei baroni del regno di Napoli contra il re Ferdinando I* (first printed Rome, 1566), an account of the barons' conspiracy of 1485–7 by Camillo Porzio (1526/7–80). Porzio had studied in Tuscany and was influenced to some extent by Machiavelli and Guicciardini, but his moralising approach to history was

typical of the second half of the century. He concluded that the catastrophic
outcome of the conspiracy showed God's disapproval both of the barons and
of the cruel Aragonese. Porzio had known the historian Paolo Giovio of Como
(1483–1552), and wrote two books of a *Storia d'Italia* from 1547, where
Giovio's *Historiarum sui temporis libri* (Florence, 1550–2) ended.

Ideal states

Underlying many of the political works described so far was a desire for
reforms which would combat violence, instability and injustice in the imperfect
real world. The same thirst for reform led some writers to describe an ideal,
totally ordered city which could have links with contemporary reality but
which was usually expressly fictional.

Antonio Brucioli must have known of the first Renaissance depiction of an
ideal state, More's *Utopia*. At the end of his *Dialogo della republica*, but only
in its 1526 version, there was a brief description of a distant and immensely
strongly fortified city whose organisation gave due importance to military
training, education in the ancient languages and theology, politics, games and
commerce.

More's work was also known to Anton Francesco Doni (1513–74), son of a
Florentine scissors-maker. He settled in Venice for a few years from 1547, and
in 1548 helped to publish a vernacular translation of *Utopia*. Doni described
in his *Mondi* ('Worlds', 1552–3) a city, seen in a vision, from which all social
evils were absent because their causes were removed; there was complete social
equality and a uniform lifestyle; everyone had to work in order to eat. Free
love and the early separation of children from their mother meant that there
were no family ties. No anguish, therefore, was caused by love or death, and
there were no social rivalries. Equally ruthless was the elimination of disabilities: deformed children were drowned at birth. There was no army nor any
government; a hundred priests oversaw the hundred streets which radiated
outwards from the central temple.

In 1553 appeared Francesco Patrizi's *La città felice* ('Happy City'). This
provided a highly moral environment whose hierarchical social structure
recalled that of Venice, the city in which it was printed. Peasants, artisans and
merchants made up the 'servile and wretched' part of society which existed to
satisfy the needs of the classes of soldiers, magistrates and priests as they strove
for a Platonic perfection.

In the last part of the *Dialoghi dell'Infinito* (1583–90, unpublished until
1957) by Ludovico Agostini of Pesaro (1536–1612), two characters, Infinito
and Finito, representing respectively divine wisdom and limited human reason,
describe an imaginary republic. It will have class divisions, but the aristocratic
regime is to be broadly based, nobility is to be derived from virtue rather than
birth, there are checks on expenditure, the economy is tightly controlled, and
there are measures to combat poverty. The daily routine is ascetic and closely

regulated. Alongside the civil authorities, a parallel religious hierarchy cares for the spiritual welfare of the inhabitants, imposing strict Catholic ritual, for religion is the supreme concern of this state.

Machiavelli had believed that one should not count on men being good, but that unconstrained goodness could be found in well-ordered states. Agostini, however, seems to have had no such faith, and the methods of his republic, as Firpo observed, do not try to persuade its citizens to avoid sin but 'simply make sinning impossible'. Utopianists aimed to shield men from suffering, uncertainty and sin by creating a stable and perfect environment, but the oppressive systems which they devised in order to achieve this end simply made the inhabitants of a state into its servants.

The individual and society

Court life and advice on behaviour: Castiglione

The Cinquecento was fascinated by the question of how individuals should behave. At the root of this interest, or anxiety, lay probably the need of the élite, under threat from political change, to defend and maintain its distinctive character; but the supply of advice must have been stimulated further by demand from an ever-widening reading public, avid for guidance on correct social and professional conduct. The result was an outpouring from Italian presses of a torrent of books of advice on the behaviour of men and women, either within society in general or within a particular framework such as the court or the family. Although the focus was on the individual, authors of such works could express views on the plight of Italy as a whole, sometimes seeing the social and moral standards of the peninsula as menaced by the influences of German Protestantism and Spanish insistence on ceremony. Italian society appeared decadent, too, in the eyes of some foreigners such as Roger Ascham; but to many in the rest of Europe, Italy provided a model of civilised behaviour, and her courtesy books played a major part in the pervasive influence of Italian culture beyond the Alps.

The greatest work in this genre, a vivid record of a crucial phase in Renaissance civilisation as well as a practical manual, was Il libro del Cortegiano (The Book of the Courtier) by Baldesar Castiglione. While carrying out the diplomatic and military responsibilities of a courtier, the author had enjoyed the cultured pleasures of the courtly environment, but he had also suffered from the instability of Italian courts in the face of foreign armies and from the tensions between personal preferences and allegiance to one's master. His service began under the marquis of Mantua, Francesco Gonzaga. In 1504 he moved to the politically less important but culturally more attractive court of Urbino, working first for Duke Guidubaldo da Montefeltro and his wife Elisabetta Gonzaga and then, after the Duke's death in 1508, for Guidubaldo's nephew Francesco Maria della Rovere. However, the new Duke was driven out of Urbino in 1516 by Lorenzo de' Medici, supported by his uncle Pope Leo X, and Francesco Maria sought refuge in Mantua, since he was married to the marquis's daughter. These events and Castiglione's own marriage to a Mantuan in 1516 brought him back into the orbit of the Gonzaga court. However, his wife died in childbirth in 1520, and in 1521 Castiglione became a cleric, the first step towards a new career in the Church. Having accepted Pope Clement VII's offer of the post of papal nuncio to the Spanish court, he arrived in Spain in 1525, in a period of extreme diplomatic tension which culminated in the Sack of Rome. He died in Toledo in 1529.

Two years earlier Castiglione had given instructions for the *Cortegiano* to be printed, and his book appeared in Venice in 1528. It had been composed and rewritten over a long period. Castiglione tells us that he dashed off a first draft in 1508, just after Guidubaldo's death. He chose not to write a treatise and teach through 'distinct precepts' but, 'renewing a pleasant memory' (I, 1), to recount conversations which he says had taken place in Urbino in March 1507. From the start, then, the work was intended as an affectionate tribute to the old Duke and as a memoir of the satisfaction derived from 'the loving company of such excellent people'. The sense of loss would have been even sharper in 1528, not just because of the implications which the Sack of Rome had for Italian courts but, as he went on to point out, because of the deaths of many speakers in the dialogues and of the Duchess Elisabetta. Castiglione's comparison of the work to a 'painted portrait of the court of Urbino' would, according to contemporary aesthetic principles, have implied a certain degree of idealisation. He also explained at the outset that his intention was to describe a 'perfect courtier', the ideal to which all must aspire even if none can fully attain it.

The *Cortegiano* is organised in four books, each describing an evening's conversation, so that the framework for the characters' views itself constitutes a living example of how a courtly society should conduct itself. Each book has either one or two principal speakers who are asked to lead a discussion on a specific topic, and who at times seem to be putting forward Castiglione's own views. But, as we have already seen, he seeks to avoid a didactic tone: the main speakers are almost all frequently interrupted and challenged, the discussions can lead to digressions, the open-endedness of the dialogue form can be used to suggest that there is no clear answer to a thorny question, and Castiglione may allow a consensus reached on a previous day to be contradicted in subsequent discussion.

On the first evening Count Ludovico da Canossa is chosen 'to form in words a perfect courtier'. The first two important qualities which he identifies are noble birth and grace. From the start it has been made clear that the courtier's function is to serve princes 'in every reasonable matter' (I, 1), and these two attributes will help him to achieve his aim by enabling him to make a good first impression. Pressed to explain how one acquires grace, Canossa says that 'good judgement' is necessary. The main rule is to avoid affectation, using what he calls *sprezzatura*: a certain studied negligence, a middle way between casualness and overseriousness, an art which conceals art (I, 26). This leads to the heated debate (mentioned above, p. 183) on affectation in language. Canossa's ideal courtier should be of noble birth. He should have physical accomplishments, particularly military ones: arms must be his principal calling, though his knowledge of this art should not be that of a professional captain and he should shun ostentation (I, 17). He should also have social and artistic talents in the fields of letters, music and the fine arts. The courtier's moral qualities are mentioned briefly (I, 41), but Castiglione's plan is not to develop this topic until later.

On the following evening the discussion is taken a stage further. Federico Fregoso is charged to explain how and when the courtier should make use of the qualities described by Canossa, and he introduces a more pragmatic, even opportunistic note. For instance, the courtier should arrange to do his bold deeds in war under the eyes of his master; he should beware of making a fool of himself when competing with his social inferiors or dancing in public (II, 8–11); and a certain deceit is permissible in cultivating his image (II, 39–40). But Fregoso also brings the discussion closer to the courtier's main purpose by tackling the subject of his relations with the prince. The courtier, says Fregoso, must make himself pleasing to his master and follow his desires, as long as they are honourable. What, though, are the limits to obedience? He argues that one should follow orders in matters beneficial and honourable to the prince and (like Machiavelli) insists that some things which seem good are really evil and vice versa, so that a good end may justify violent means. But, when asked to clarify how one can tell the difference, he declines (II, 23): a disappointing reaction, perhaps, but at least Castiglione had drawn attention to an unconventional line of thought. Fregoso turns the conversation to the courtier's social relations with his equals and to the importance of a good reputation, seen in the context of winning the prince's favour (II, 32). The discussion has raised difficult questions of telling right from wrong and true from false; the best Fregoso can do amidst this uncertainty is implicitly to echo Canossa in Book I by advising courtiers to follow the Aristotelian ideal of behaving with 'a certain honest mediocrity' (i.e. moderation: II, 41). At this point Bernardo Bibbiena takes over the leading role in order to talk at length on how to entertain one's company with wit. He identifies and illustrates three types of *facezia*: the 'urbane and pleasant continuous narration' which is like a *novella*, the quick and sharp witty remark, and the *burla* or clever deceit.

Although the main speakers in the *Cortegiano* are all male, women play an important role in the book: firstly as participants in the discussions (the Duchess Elisabetta and her noble relative Emilia Pia, who are constantly present, maintain a pleasant atmosphere and intervene gently but firmly to move the discussions forward on an even keel) and secondly as objects of discussion in Book III and, indirectly, in Book IV. Castiglione was particularly interested in the status and role of women and had already sketched a study on this question between about 1506 and 1509. At the end of Book II he steers the discussion of jokes and of Boccaccio's *novelle* towards the questions of the respect due to women and of true love. Since these topics are clearly controversial, for the third evening the Duchess allots to Giuliano de' Medici the task of describing a perfect female courtier or 'donna di palazzo'. Giuliano is supported by Cesare Gonzaga. Bitterly anti-feminist arguments are put by Gasparo Pallavicino and Nicolò Frigio, so that both positions in the *querelle des femmes* are represented.

For Giuliano, men and women are equal in their essential qualities; the differences between the sexes are intended by nature to be complementary (III, 12–14). In the context of courts, Gonzaga claims women are essential in order to bring adornment and happiness, and to elicit grace and bravery from the male courtier (III, 3, 51–2). The principal quality required of the 'donna di palazzo' is 'a certain pleasant affability', so that she can entertain men with her talk. Like her male counterpart, she must achieve 'a certain difficult mediocrity' (a middle way), in her case between reticence and outspokenness (III, 5). In the second part of the discussion Giuliano gives advice to women on how to tell true lovers from false and how to return love (he draws the line at extramarital relations even for unloved wives), and then counsels men on how to win and keep a lady's affection.

So far the focus has been on the external accomplishments of the male and female courtier and on their relationships with each other. There has been only passing reference to the question, raised in Book I, 1, of using these accomplishments in the service of the prince, and the courtier's inner life has likewise been practically ignored. Both these omissions are made good on the final evening.

Ottaviano Fregoso, after creating suspense by his late arrival, observes that so far the *aim* of the perfect courtier has not been discussed. The courtier's qualities are not good in themselves but must be used to gain the goodwill of the prince in such a way 'that [the courtier] can and will always speak the truth to [the prince] about any matter he needs to know, without fear or danger of displeasing him' (IV, 5). He must steer the prince away from arrogance and along the 'austere road of virtue' (IV, 10). He will, in effect, be the prince's guide ('institutor del principe', IV, 47). Similarly the 'donna di palazzo' might act as adviser to her mistress (IV, 45). Ottaviano also goes at length (IV, 19–35) into the question of the best constitution, opting naturally for a monarchy rather than a republic but insisting that the ruler must be virtuous and that his regime must avoid aggressive wars and give rise to virtue, unity between classes (via a senate and a popular council), justice and stability (like some utopianists, he saw money and the lack of it as the root of many evils).

The elevated tone is maintained as attention switches to the courtier's own spiritual aspirations. Pietro Bembo, author of the *Asolani* (see below, p. 216), uses Neoplatonic doctrine to show how the more mature courtier can progress upwards from the contemplation of the beauty of one woman towards love of divine beauty. Bembo becomes carried away in a eulogy of divine love, but, typically, Castiglione redresses the balance by making Emilia Pia warn Bembo with gentle wit to beware lest his own soul should leave his body. Dawn is breaking over the countryside of the Marche as the courtiers make their way to their rooms, looking forward to a fifth evening's discussions which would have linked the feminism of Book III with the Neoplatonism of Book IV by taking up the topic of whether women were as capable as men of the divine love described by Bembo. This conclusion, with its suggestion of debates continuing beyond those recorded in Castiglione's text, brilliantly catches the predominant mood of the *Cortegiano*, poised between nostalgia for the past and yet a sense that the ideal courtly society could and should continue into the future.

In modern times the *Cortegiano* has attracted criticism for an alleged lack of commitment and superficiality. It has appeared to some to turn its back on unpleasant, even brutal aspects of contemporary life, in contrast (for instance) with Machiavelli's efforts to find practical solutions to Italy's problems. Indeed, if read without reference to the fourth book, the first two books may seem no more than a shallow courtesy manual in which Castiglione merely teaches the courtier how to conduct a personal public relations exercise, advising him to concentrate on trivial accomplishments, to be insincere and opportunistic and to cultivate his image in order to deceive others out of self-interest.

But, affectionately though the *Cortegiano* portrays a secluded world in the past, Castiglione does not neglect the present. He opens Book II with an unconventional attack on those who praise older courts and blame modern ones, and his belief that past standards can be maintained in the future, implicit in the very writing of the book, is made explicit in the second chapter of Book IV where he expresses the hope that others will be able to find examples of virtue and talent in the current court of Urbino just as he is drawing from the earlier one. Nor does he turn his back on the 'effective truth of the matter', to use Machiavelli's phrase. Not only does Castiglione point to the darker side of court life, to the moral dilemmas of relations with equals and with the prince, but he shares with Machiavelli the aim of putting an end to the degeneracy and political incompetence which has brought shame and destruction to Italy (IV, 4, 8). As for the social skills described in his work, they are not an end in themselves but have a twofold ulterior purpose. Because they make a good impression on others, they will in the first place help contemporaries of his own class hoping to make a successful career in the courts of princes. And then, once the courtier's qualities have won him favour, he will be able to become an effective adviser, a position whose importance for the ruler was acknowledged by Machiavelli in chapters 22 and 23 of *Il principe*.

Castiglione's message is all the more effective for the narrative and dramatic skill with which he uses the dialogue form. A few points now seem unnecessarily laboured, but for the most part he keeps the reader's attention by a series of skilful variations of pace, blending the serious and the light-hearted. He brings his characters to life as individuals while at the same time giving, as he promised, a group portrait which shows us what it meant to belong to the community of a Renaissance court. He is also remarkably good at bringing controversies to life; for example, he gives by far the most readable contemporary account of the issues involved in the *questione della lingua* and of the fierce passions that they aroused.

The range of ideas discussed by Castiglione and his skill in presenting them made the *Cortegiano* one of the best-sellers of the century both in Italy and abroad. Soon after its author's death it circulated in versions in Spanish (1534) and French (1537). London printers brought out translations in English (by Thomas Hoby, 1561) and in Latin and a trilingual edition in Italian, English and French (1588).

Other writers on court life and behaviour

Some later writers were less sure that a courtier's life was preferable to that of a man of letters. Pietro Aretino had experienced life in the court of Rome, where his satirical and erotic verse brought him into conflict with the Church, and in that of Mantua, before settling in the republic of Venice in 1527 and winning great fame for his prose as well as his plays and poetry. His writings were often provocative and iconoclastic, earning him the title of 'scourge of princes', and his prose style was suitably original and often daring. Aretino reacted against Bembo's measured, refined prose, with its select and sometimes archaising vocabulary; instead, he used a much more varied palette, drawing on the resources of everyday contemporary speech as well as using a more eloquent and dignified register. His colloquial style is exemplified by his *Ragionamento de le corti* ('Discussion on Courts', 1538). One of the characters proposes to give up living by his pen and his teaching and move to the papal court. The others persuade him to change his mind by portraying courts as breeding-grounds of hatred, envy, ambition, lies, adulation and other vices; as uncomfortable, squalid, and (in the particular case of Rome) corrupt.

Even a writer who was advising courtiers might feel that there was a gap between reality and Castiglione's portrait of it and that courtiers needed a different kind of advice. Pellegro Grimaldi, in his *Discorsi* on what gentlemen must do to gain their masters' favour (Genoa, 1543), complains that the *Cortegiano* is not of much practical help because nobody could be so perfect, and because it lacks detail. Grimaldi also disapproves of Castiglione's emphasis on what the courtier should *seem* to be, and stresses instead the importance of *being* good and of setting a good example for others. Giovanni Andrea Gilio of Fabriano published in his *Due dialogi* (Camerino, 1564) a *Dialogo de le parti morali appertenenti a' letterati cortigiani et ad ogni altro gentil'huomo*

('Dialogue on the Moral Qualities Appertaining to Courtier-Writers and All Other Gentlemen'). He gives some advice on 'eloquence', including pronunciation and spelling, but most of the work is concerned with the role of the man of letters in guiding and restraining the ruler. He wants his courtier to have social graces, but there is hardly any sense of the court as pleasant and civilised society. Above all the courtier must be virtuous and a devout Catholic. Gilio is more sceptical than Castiglione on the possibility of influencing bad rulers, but he concludes that with the help of such a guide, princes will be loved by their subjects on earth and rewarded in heaven.

Two courtiers who had served the Este of Ferrara gave a somewhat negative picture of court life. One was Giambattista Giraldi Cinzio (1504–73) in his *L'uomo di corte* ('The Man at Court', 1569). The other was Torquato Tasso (1544–95), who had proved unequal to the stress of the court. He acknowledges the timeless beauty and worth of Castiglione's *Cortegiano* in his dialogue *Il Malpiglio overo de la corte* (datable to 1582–3), a colloquy with Giovanlorenzo Malpigli, a young gentleman from the republic of Lucca; the character representing Tasso praises courts as centres of all-round excellence. But, disconcertingly, the same character tends to undermine Castiglione's judgements by giving warning advice to Malpigli, who is uncertain whether to become a courtier or to pursue his studies: courtiers face the dilemma that the very things which win a prince's favour also arouse envy in other courtiers and indeed in the prince himself; they must accept that they are subordinate to the prince; and they must be able to hide their feelings and to dissimulate.

Works counselling courtiers or would-be courtiers were only part of a large body of treatises and dialogues on society (most of which did not restrict their vision to aristocratic environments) and on professional skills. In spite of its title, *Il novo corteggiano de vita cauta et morale* ('The New Courtier, on the Careful and Moral Life') by an unknown author, printed in Venice in about 1535, is a general work on 'honest living'. It contains a miscellany of advice, presented in an inelegant style, on one's relations with others (covering topics such as friendship, love and modesty), on dealing with fortune, on parenthood. Near the end is a series of chapters addressed to various leaders: captains, new princes, the clergy. The tone is at times ascetic and other-worldly, at others cautiously pragmatic: for example, the author concedes that pretence may be morally acceptable if it harms nobody, and he gives advice to women on choosing a lover while preserving modesty.

An important guide to the moral upbringing and education of children up to the age of eighteen, and to friendship, love, marriage, and the duties of parents, was the *Institutione di tutta la vita de l'homo nato nobile e in città libera* ('Disposition of the Whole Life of the Man Born Noble and in a Free City') by Alessandro Piccolomini (1508–79; see also below, p. 219). Born of a distinguished Sienese family, the author studied philosophy in Padua from 1538 to 1542 and was closely involved with Speroni and the Accademia degli Infiammati. The *Institutione* was written in this period and published in Venice in

1542; a revised and expanded version was printed in 1560 as the *Institutione morale*.

Sabba da Castiglione (1480–1554), a Milanese nobleman who joined the Knights of St John of Jerusalem in 1505 but from about 1518 lived apart from the world, wrote a series of austere *Ricordi overo ammaestramenti* ('Things to Remember, or Teachings', Bologna, 1546; longer versions, 1549 and 1554). As befitted a member of his order, Sabba believed in charity towards those in need (the poor, the mentally deficient), but he sternly opposed self-indulgence. One should avoid banquets, for instance, because they can lead to sin. He frowned on the excessive attention paid to Boccaccio (women should read the Bible instead) and to Ariosto. Some of his *ricordi* are addressed to a great-nephew in the same order, but there are also miniature treatises on topics such as the ideal prince, marriage and bringing up children. A *ricordo* on modern courtiers portrays them as not just perfumed fops but also parasitic and dissolute – a scathing attack typical of Sabba's relentless condemnation of the decadence of 'this wretched modern Italy'.

The most famous manual of behaviour of the second half of the century was written by an author who, like Castiglione, chose an ecclesiastical career and had served as papal nuncio. Giovanni Della Casa (1503–56) was a Florentine but spent most of his life outside the city, in Rome and elsewhere. It was at the suggestion of another cleric, Galeazzo Florimonte, himself the author of some *Ragionamenti* on moral philosophy (1554), that he composed, probably in 1551–5, a treatise 'on methods to follow or avoid in everyday social relations', entitled, after Galeazzo, *Galateo overo de' costumi* ('Galateo, or on Manners', published posthumously in his *Rime et prose*, Venice, 1558). Della Casa cleverly adopted the voice of an unlettered old man teaching a youth to 'keep to the straight path for the health of your soul and for the praise and honour of your honourable and noble family'. The style and tone are therefore not excessively formal, and the writer uses snatches of lively direct speech, anecdotes or references to Boccaccio (whose *Decameron* was being increasingly exploited as a fund of examples of behaviour to imitate or, occasionally, to avoid). In spite of the allusion to the youth's soul, the focus is on day-to-day life. Rules of good behaviour are important because, if we break them, we are deprived of 'the company and goodwill of men'. Some of the writer's recommendations are based on the distinction between what is and is not sinful; but, after mentioning briefly that one should avoid vices because they make one 'unpleasant in dealing with others', he hurriedly leaves the subject of vices and virtues with the justification that 'I undertook to show you not the sins but the errors of men' (chapter 28). Getting on well with one's fellows is, in fact, the principle underlying Della Casa's advice. His book starts and ends with detailed explanations of how not to disgust others, at table and elsewhere. It is not a good idea to wash one's hands publicly, except when one is about to eat, or to put one's leg on the table, and one must not show lack of consideration for others by fidgeting or cutting one's fingernails in public. One must not antagonise others by having too sharp a tongue, by being too argumentative, or by using mockery (Della Casa, unlike Castiglione, is extremely cautious about the effects of biting humour). Another potential irritant is excessive ceremony: Della Casa blames the recent trend in this direction on foreign influence, especially that of the Spanish, and there is a feeling elsewhere in the *Galateo* that Italy is losing the battle to keep out corrupting customs from abroad. But, while ceremony based on falsehood and flattery is condemned, one must fit in decorously with what is customary or risk giving offence. Della Casa's use of an uneducated persona does not prevent him from giving rhetorical advice (on storytelling and on the choice of words) and from relating his rules of good behaviour to aesthetic principles. 'One must not be content to do good things,' he argues, 'but one must try to do them prettily too' ('farle anco leggiadre': chapter 28). This *leggiadria* derives from harmony or measure: he shares Castiglione's belief in the principle of avoiding excess.

The *Galateo* was extremely successful, so much so that *galateo* became the Italian word for a book of etiquette or even etiquette in general. The work was reprinted many times in Italy well into the seventeenth century. It was translated into French (1562), English (1576), Latin (1580), Spanish (1585), and German (1597), was paraphrased in several languages, and was adopted as a school textbook by both Jesuits and Protestants.

In 1574 Stefano Guazzo of Casale Monferrato (1530–93) published his popular dialogue on *La civil conversatione*, defined as honest and virtuous living in the world. Guazzo had served the Gonzaga as a courtier, but his advice is addressed to 'every sort of person'. The first book establishes that the company of others makes one virtuous and wise and describes types of behaviour which are less than desirable. Books II and III show how to behave with others, first in general terms and then within specific relationships including marriage and parenthood. In the last book, some of Guazzo's precepts are put into practice at a banquet. The whole work also provided a repertoire of wisdom in the form of proverbs and examples. It has been relatively neglected by Italian criticism, but is a useful source of information on contemporary ideas and attitudes. It was one of the main channels through which knowledge of Italian manners reached the rest of Europe. Two French translations of 1579 were followed by the English version of George Pettie and Bartholomew Young (1581–6), and there were also three translations into Latin and one each into German, Dutch and Spanish.

Alvise Cornaro (c. 1484–1566), a Venetian whose house in Padua became a meeting-place for artists and writers, lamented the recent introduction into Italy of adulation and ceremonies, Protestantism, and a third bad custom: gluttony. His *Trattato della vita sobria* ('Treatise on the Sober Life', 1558) used his own robust health in old age as an example to spur others to abandon excess in favour of 'that divine sobriety [which is] welcome to God, a friend to nature, daughter of reason, sister of the virtues, companion of temperate living'. This was followed by three shorter works on the same theme (1561, 1563, 1565). In spite of its self-righteous tone, the *Trattato* had a remarkable success in English versions until the mid-twentieth century, with titles such as *Sure and Certain Methods of Attaining a Long and Healthful Life*, *The Art of Living Long*, and *How to Live One Hundred Years, by One Who Has Done It*.

If love was a favourite theme of the first half of the Cinquecento, its place was taken in the second half by that of honour. There was a sudden vogue for works on honour and the duel, especially in the 1550s (in 1563 the Council of Trent imposed severe sanctions on duelling): for example, Girolamo Muzio's *Il duello* (1550), Sebastiano Fausto da Longiano's *Il duello regolato* (1551), Giovan Battista Possevino's *Dialogo dell'honore* (printed posthumously in 1553), Giovan Battista Pigna's *Il duello* (1554), and two of Annibale Romei's *Discorsi* (1585). The same rigid insistence on appearance and on codifying behaviour produced books on the gentleman and on the nature and implications of nobility, such as *Il gentil'huomo* by Fausto da Longiano (1542), *Il gentilhuomo* by Muzio (1571), *Il primo libro della nobiltà* (1576) by the Florentine Francesco de' Vieri, Tasso's dialogue *Il Forno overo de la nobiltà* (first version 1578, second version 1585) and *Il perfetto gentil'huomo* by Aldo Manuzio the younger (1584).

Symptomatic in a different way of the attention to practicalities predominant in the second half of the century was the creation of professional manuals. Among these were the dialogue *L'avvocato* ('The Lawyer', Venice, 1554) and the treatise on letter-writing *Del secretario* (Venice, 1564, later expanded) by the prolific Francesco Sansovino, *Il secretario* (Rome, 1589) by Giulio Cesare Capaccio (1552–1634), and *Del buon segretario* (Venice, 1595), by Angelo Ingegneri.

Society and morality

Most of the authors mentioned in the previous sections were giving advice to actual or intending members of an élite society (though the success of some of these works suggests that the readership was wider than this). Those authors who used dialogue form preferred the Ciceronian model so that, by narrating the conversations of real characters in realistic settings, they could commemorate and celebrate a refined way of life. But outside such confines, and in conjunction with the expansion of printing, some authors from the 1530s to the 1550s portrayed the other side of the coin. They were generally from the lower ranks of society and had often left their home towns to seek their fortune elsewhere: on the fringes of minor court society, perhaps, or in Venice, where the printing industry gave new opportunities to earn money as a writer, translator, anthologiser or editor. The versatility of those who lived by the pen in this way earned them the name of *poligrafi*. Their language could be colloquial, their tone comic; their subject-matter could be seamy, even shocking; they often satirised the social and moral corruption of their own times or parodied the fine sentiments of more high-minded men of letters. Their dialogues were anti-Ciceronian, sometimes based on the model of Lucian, with characters who might be fictional or plebeian or both.

An extreme of often exaggeratedly sordid realism, accompanied by verbal fireworks and sharp humour, was marked by two works by Pietro Aretino printed in Venice under false imprints in 1534 and 1536, each containing a three-part dialogue. In the *Ragionamento della Nanna e della Antonia*, Nanna is uncertain whether her sixteen-year-old daughter Pippa should become a nun, a wife or a whore. She recounts to Antonia her own experiences of all three states, giving a catalogue of sexual adventures which illustrates the degradation and hypocrisy of outwardly respectable society. At the end Antonia judges that Pippa would do best to become a whore: nuns betray their vows, wives assassinate holy matrimony, but whores just provide the services for which they are paid. In the first two parts of the second work, the more restrained *Dialogo nel quale la Nanna insegna a la Pippa*, the mother teaches her daughter, still a virgin, about the tricks and the risks of her profession. On the third day they both listen as another woman explains the job of a procuress. Aretino's portrait of male–female relationships was clearly intended to mock the way in which, as we shall see below, Bembo and others had elevated love to a spiritual plane, and it opened the way to a new, irreverent and provocative type of literature.

Nicolò Franco (Benevento 1515–Rome 1570) was Aretino's secretary in the late 1530s until hostility between the two men drove Franco away from Venice. Before his flight, in 1539, he published some vernacular letters (*Pistole vulgari*) to rival Aretino's, a satire of Petrarchism (*Il Petrarchista*), and ten *Dialogi piacevoli* ('Pleasant Dialogues'). Both the letters and the dialogues contain depictions of the miseries of society, as in the Lucianesque fourth dialogue, in which Charon meets five souls (all without any money to offer him) who recount their sordid lives and deaths: a syphilitic whore, a tyrant who was poisoned, a merchant, a pedant, a soldier who lost his money on sex and gambling.

Ortensio Lando (Milan c. 1508/12–c. 1553) used an element of surprise to make his readers reflect on their world. In his *Paradossi* (Lyons, 1543) he amusingly defends thirty paradoxes. Poverty is better than wealth, for example, because it is more conducive to goodness and happiness; blindness is better than sight, because then one would not see such things as the corruption of Italy; women are superior to men; reading Boccaccio's works corrupts both morals and literary style. His *Commentario delle più notabili et mostruose cose d'Italia et altri luoghi* ('Commentary on the Most Notable and Monstrous Things in Italy and Elsewhere', Venice, 1548) reverses the idea of a European visiting Utopia. Here a Utopian is guided on an eye-opening journey through Italy, reputedly the most civilised part of the world – but, as he soon finds out, it is rife with poverty, cruelty and vice, especially in the states controlled by the Spanish.

Doni, like Lando, lived a restless life, much of it outside his native Florence, and from time to time expressed his dissatisfaction with the society in which he lived. With his *Mondi* (which included a description of a utopian state, mentioned above, p. 202) there appeared an *Inferno* whose sinners included an array similar to those ferried by Franco's Charon: scholars, avaricious men, whores, lawyers, soldiers. Doni's rambling but often entertaining *Marmi* (Venice, 1552–3) draw together a series of unrelated open-air dialogues which take their title from their setting on the marble steps of the cathedral of Florence. The characters, who include real people as well as personifications or even talking statues, discuss a miscellany of topics, occasionally protesting about injustices such as the uneven distribution of wealth or the Florentines' lack of appreciation of their fellow citizens' talents.

Giovan Battista Gelli was in a category apart from the *poligrafi*. He led a relatively calm life in Florence, supported the Medici, maintained a high moral tone, and did not become involved in any satire or detailed criticisms of contemporary society. His innovative *Capricci del bottaio* ('The Cooper's Caprices', first complete edition Florence, 1548) has something in common with the works of Della Casa and Cornaro. He advises on how to avoid incurring hatred, he has ascetic views on diet and the conduct of one's life, and he links excessive self-indulgence and sensuality with a general decline in social standards over the previous fifty years. But his concerns in this work are wider and deeper than theirs. Giusto, an old cooper who has neglected his spiritual life, discusses with his soul how he may improve himself. An important theme is the need to use the vernacular in the diffusion of knowledge and in religious devotions (*Ragionamenti* III–VI; here Gelli is developing the ideas of Speroni and his circle mentioned above, p. 184). Gelli's *Circe* (Florence, 1549) depicts conversations between Ulysses and fellow Greeks who have been turned into animals. One by one his former companions explain why they now lead more contented and more virtuous lives. It is not until Ulysses meets a philosopher transformed into an elephant that an animal acknowledges that the gift of reason makes man superior, or at least potentially so: for Gelli's dedication picks up from the *Capricci* the theme of the danger of men neglecting higher things and hence becoming no better than beasts.

Women in society; love and marriage

The Renaissance did not bring new rights or emancipation to the vast majority of women. A very few wielded political power, but only as a temporary measure. Little of the advice on court life and behaviour mentioned above was addressed specifically to women. Yet, although women were seen as subordinate and had far fewer opportunities than men, they could (at least in the upper reaches of society) be seen as deserving of admiration and even of greater independence. Some argued that women were the equals or the superiors of men. The concept of 'Platonic' love was, in the first half of the century, a fashionable way of expressing the refining, civilising influence which women could have on male-dominated society. Some writers stressed the essential contribution of women to the family unit, while others saw marriage as a prison for women and urged them to seek pleasure outside it. One must remember, of course, that almost all the authors who wrote about women were male, and that many of these viewpoints can be interpreted as the result of male self-interest.

The debate between feminists and anti-feminists, to which the third book of the *Cortegiano* belongs, was carried on mainly in the first half of the century. In general, misogyny was rejected. In 1525 the interesting *Della eccellenza et dignità delle donne* by the Milanese nobleman Galeazzo Flavio Capella (1487–1537; his real surname was Capra) was printed in Rome. He shows how women excel in each of the virtues and in attributes such as love, learning and beauty. During the ensuing period of warfare he expanded and recast the work as a dialogue, *L'anthropologia* (Venice, 1533). The defence of woman in Book II is preceded by a defence of the excellence of man; but the gloomier political situation, as the imperial hold on Milan and the rest of Italy tightened, seems to be reflected in the addition of a third part 'on the wretchedness of both [men and women] and the vanity of their studies'. It is this argument which wins the final assent of the men present.

In 1525 Agnolo Firenzuola (1493–1543) wrote an *Epistola in lode delle donne* ('Letter in Praise of Women', first printed 1548) which puts woman's spirit on a par with that of man and provides classical and modern examples of female eloquence, learning and virtue. Sperone Speroni's dialogue *Della dignità delle donne*, published in 1542, discusses whether man is made to serve woman or whether, as is argued by the Paduan speaker who probably represents Speroni, woman is made by nature in such a way that she serves man, though not as a slave. The fifth dialogue of Gelli's *Circe* (see above, p. 214) acknowledges both that women are indispensable in the home and that they are unfairly deprived of opportunities to show their abilities outside it.

It was not until the end of the century that a female voice joined the debate, that of Modesta Pozzo de' Zorzi (Venice 1555–92). Her stimulating dialogue *Il merito delle donne*, published in 1600 under the pseudonym Moderata Fonte, begins with a critical examination by the all-female group of speakers of the behaviour of men towards women, whether daughters, mothers, sisters, wives or lovers. It is pointed out how unjust it is that women should have less authority than men when they are no less meritorious, a situation blamed on men's envy. The shy virgin Corinna rejects the idea of marriage, in which (she says) a woman has nothing to gain but troublesome children and subjection to a husband. However, at the end a wise mother advises her daughter Verginia to overcome her reluctance to marry because the alternative is a drab and lonely spinsterhood.

Works on love were written for the most part by men, but some at least ostensibly took the point of view of women, and it was conventional to have at least one female speaker in dialogues on this subject. They cover a range of approaches, from the philosophical and spiritual to the more realistic and even hedonistic.

Several authors made use of the theory of 'Platonic' love described in the commentary on Plato's *Symposium* which Marsilio Ficino had published in 1474 and which dovetailed conveniently with the contemporary fashion for Petrarchan verse. Also influential was the *De amore* by a Florentine pupil of Ficino, Francesco Cattani da Diacceto, probably written in 1508 and translated by him by 1511 as *I tre libri d'amore*. Castiglione took Ficino's commentary as the basis for Bembo's discourse on love in Book IV of the *Cortegiano*. The Venetian was chosen by Castiglione as the main speaker on spiritual love because he made his public debut as a vernacular author with three dialogues on love, the *Asolani*, probably begun in 1497 and printed in 1505. This work takes its name from the setting at Asolo, near Treviso, in the tiny court of Caterina Cornaro, Queen of Cyprus. Both the language (see above, p. 183) and the framework are strongly influenced by Boccaccio. The speakers are three Venetian youths, who recite their own poems at intervals, and three ladies. On each of the three days one of the men expounds his thoughts on love. The first to speak is the sad Perottino. He attacks love as the source of bitterness (punning on *amare* and *amaro*: I, 9) and of all of life's sufferings. The happy Gismondo then puts the counter-argument that *donne* and *danno* (women and harm: II, 4) are opposed. Love is a natural affection and therefore, if the term is used correctly, it is something good, reasonable and temperate, embracing the whole of creation; women are a source of pleasure to the senses and to the mind alike. On the final day, however, Lavinello disagrees with both his companions. Love is neither all good nor all bad, but a desire whose quality depends on the end which our will gives to it (III, 5). Good love is, as Plato defines it, love of beauty; beauty is a grace born from proportion and harmony which exists in the spirit as well as in the body, and good love should therefore desire both (III, 6). After reciting three *canzoni* on the celestial happiness derived from seeing, hearing and thinking of his beloved, Lavinello recounts a meeting which he has had that morning with a holy hermit. In the second edition of 1530, Bembo makes the hermit begin by arguing on Aristotelian principles against the view that love and desire are the same, before explaining to Lavinello how good love results from following reason rather than the senses. All men, Lavinello included, should try to follow their reason, loving not mortal but divine beauty. Only in this way can one be immune from the turmoil of the world and achieve true happiness.

Another work which proved to be an important model was Firenzuola's ambitious but unfinished *Ragionamenti* ('Discussions'). Of the six days planned, only one was completed, by 1525, when the author was in Rome, and the influence of the work was delayed because it was not printed until 1548. Firenzuola uses a framework like that of the *Decameron* or the *Asolani* in an original way, bringing together the dialogue and the collection of *novelle*. Each day is to begin with philosophical discussion before the midday meal and will then become gradually lighter in tone, moving from the recitation of poems to the recounting of *novelle* and finally to pleasant conversation. Firenzuola uses a group of three men and three women, like that of the *Asolani*; they meet in an idyllic setting in the Florentine countryside. But his women play a much more active role than Bembo's and are relatively outspoken. One of them has no doubt that, just as men have kept women out of positions of authority in public life and religion, so they would probably have driven them out of the world altogether had it not been for sexual attraction. On the first morning the topic for discussion is love. Gostanza Amaretta tells how she married an avaricious and coarse lawyer but then developed a 'Platonic' relationship with a young man. She explains that an earthly and physical love within marriage is compatible with a 'true and holy' spiritual love for another person. This second love derives from attraction to beauty in the opposite sex, but physical beauty is only an initial guide to spiritual beauty, which is the true and lasting object of desire. (On the *novelle* told by the characters, see below, p. 224.)

In 1525 Mario Equicola finally published in Venice his *De natura de Amore* (mentioned above, p. 182). This rambling, clumsily written but encyclopaedic and erudite work does not expound any one theory of love. The first Book describes the opinions on love of writers since the thirteenth century; Books II and III investigate different kinds of love, human and divine, also touching on beauty and friendship; and Book IV condemns 'unnatural' love and looks at the signs and the unhappy effects of love. Contact with Castiglione, who was in Mantua from 1516, seems to have led Equicola to include in Book V a long section on how to attract goodwill through one's personal qualities, skills such as music, and correct use of language. The final book identifies the real aim of love as love of oneself and concludes (in a manner similar to the *Asolani*) that the only truly happy love is that of God.

There is some uncertainty about when and how the three influential *Dialoghi d'amore* by Giuda Abarbanel, better known under his adopted name of Leone Ebreo, began to circulate. The author, born in Lisbon between about 1460 and 1463, had fled first to Spain and then in 1492 to Italy, where he gained fame as a doctor and philosopher. The *Dialoghi* appear to have been written in Latin and were eventually printed in a vernacular translation in Rome in 1535 and frequently thereafter. The two characters, Filone and Sofia, discuss love and desire (suggesting that love of the *onesto* is man's true aim, that union with God is the ultimate happiness, and that perfect human love must unite the sensual and the spiritual), the universal nature of love, and the aims of love (the 'particular' aim being pleasure in union with the object of one's love, the 'universal' aim being to bring greater perfection to what is loved).

Ideal beauty, especially female beauty, was important enough in the context of love to be the main subject of a number of works. Trissino published a short dialogue which describes perfect beauty of body and spirit, drawing on various real women and on literary sources, and combines this with flattery of Isabella d'Este, the embodiment of this ideal (*I ritratti*, 'The Portraits', Rome, 1524). Firenzuola's *Dialogo delle bellezze delle donne* ('Dialogue on Women's Beauty'), written by early 1542, discusses beauty in general and that of individual parts of the body. In *Il libro della bella donna* by Federico Luigini of Udine (Venice, 1554), a group of men describe an imaginary woman of perfect beauty both physical and 'interior' (that is, she is to be of good disposition and accomplished). However, Tasso argues in *Il Minturno overo della bellezza* (written 1592–3 and named after the main speaker, Antonio Minturno) that beauty is perceived by the intellect rather than the senses.

Both Bembo and Castiglione use the dialogue form in order to present spiritual and non-spiritual approaches to the question of love without stating that only one viewpoint is valid. Firenzuola suggested that one person could love both carnally and spiritually. Even Leone Ebreo's dialogues end with Sofia asking Filone to tell her about 'human love'. Nevertheless, all of these works, by their structure or by explicit statements, give most emphasis to the view that love should ideally tend towards the spiritual. In works on love published in Venice from the mid-1530s onwards, after the publication of Aretino's dialogues about the experiences of Nanna (see above, p. 213), the balance tended to tip the other way. Some writers still repeated the conventions of Neoplatonic theory, but there was a parallel interest in the human side of love, in the real as well as or rather than the ideal.

The courtesan Tullia d'Aragona (c. 1510–56) appears as a speaker in two dialogues on love. The first is Speroni's *Dialogo d'amore*, written by 1537 and printed in 1542, in which the discussion never loses sight of reality. It hinges on Tullia's relationship with the poet Bernardo Tasso, and on the pain caused by her jealousy and her resentment of his imminent departure from Venice. Although a third speaker stresses that love must not be separated from reason, which can make us realise our happiness better once we are apart from the beloved, he still depicts love as a centaur in which sense and reason are inseparably combined. Tullia also figures in the *Dialogo dell'infinità di amore* (Venice, 1547) apparently written by her but revised by others. Benedetto Varchi (probably one of the revisers and himself author of lectures and treatises on love) leads a lively Socratic investigation which concludes that love has no bounds. But the discussion is not allowed to become abstract. Tullia observes at the conclusion of the first part that the infinity of love means that lovers can never be satisfied and must always be wretched; and, even though 'vulgar' and 'honest' love are subsequently differentiated with an admiring reference to Leone Ebreo's teaching, Varchi points out that carnal love, being natural, should not be called 'dishonest', and Tullia allows the possibility of a transition in either direction between the two types of love.

Another dialogue which combined philosophy with realism was Giuseppe Betussi's *Raverta* (Venice, 1544; the title derives from the interlocutor

Ottaviano Raverta). The first part is a routine exposition of Neoplatonic ideas, but then the participants move on to a discussion, enlivened by frequent anecdotes and references to the *Decameron*, on some 'doubts of love', such as whether it is harder to pretend to be in love or not to be in love, or how one should declare one's love. The question of whether a man or a woman loves more fervently sparks off a heated discussion between Francesca Baffa and Lodovico Domenichi, whose own *Nobiltà delle donne* (1549) was largely plagiarised from a work by Heinrich Cornelius Agrippa.

Aretino's dialogue, in which Nanna teaches Pippa, was followed by other, but much less licentious works in which an older person teaches a younger one about love. Alessandro Piccolomini's ironically entitled *Dialogo de la bella creanza de le donne* ('Dialogue on Good Manners for Women', better known as *La Raffaella*), written by 1538 and printed in 1540, is easily the best of these, an amusing and colourful work which reflects its author's experience in writing comedy for the stage. Raffaella regrets she did not enjoy herself while young and advises Margarita, neglected by her husband, not to waste her youth: it would be good to deny oneself any pleasure at all, but it is better to commit 'some trivial errors' than to spend old age in bitter regret. Margarita is told how to make herself attractive while maintaining a Castiglionesque lack of affectation and immodesty. Raffaella then deals with the care of the household (Piccolomini, a believer in the diffusion of knowledge through the vernacular, translated Xenophon's *Oeconomica* in the 1530s) and with social behaviour. Her last topic is how to enjoy a successful love affair. But Margarita is not to subvert marriage: she must enjoy herself discreetly while keeping her husband's goodwill and successfully managing the home. Even in his *Institutione* of 1542 (see above, p. 209), Piccolomini advises men that affection for a wife and for a mistress are different in nature.

Relatively mediocre are *Lo specchio d'amore* ('The Mirror of Love', Florence, 1547) by Bartolomeo Gottifredi of Piacenza and the *Ragionamento* which Sansovino published in 1545 (in Mantua, then, with additions, in Venice). Gottifredi begins with advice from an older woman to an unmarried girl on the conduct of a discreet affair with a young man who attracts her. In the second part, by when the affair has begun, the woman distinguishes between attracting someone as a husband or as a lover (one marries out of necessity but one loves for pleasure), and she discusses the progress of the girl's affair. In Sansovino's *Ragionamento* a young man is advised by an experienced one on how to conduct an affair, preferably with a married woman. The older man makes it clear from the start that he does not intend to talk about 'noble love' and dismisses 'Platonic' love as suspect.

While it was accepted that love affairs need not, indeed should not, threaten marriage, which was after all the cornerstone of society, it was also assumed up to the 1540s that love, whether sensual or spiritual, was not an integral part of marriage. One married principally in order to fulfil one's duty. At best, matrimony was seen as a safety valve for sexual desire or a source of comfort, as in the puritanical Brucioli's *Dialogo del matrimonio*. The violent condemnation of all extramarital sexual relations in his *Dialogo di amore* is exceptional. However, in the second half of the century, and especially after the Council of Trent had enacted two decrees on marriage in 1563, the idea of extramarital love became increasingly unacceptable. In the 1560 edition of his *Institutione*, Piccolomini changed his mind and argued that spiritual love should properly be combined in marriage with 'conjugal love'. It is appropriate that Piccolomini should have been chosen by Giovanni Battista Modio to conclude his *Il convito overo del peso della moglie* ('The Banquet, or the Burden of the Wife', Rome, 1554) with eloquent words on the joys of marriage and on the need to choose a wife wisely, for her virtue and manners, and then to treat her well. He urges couples to be like Ulysses and Penelope who 'love each other when present but also remain faithful when apart'. The first of Bernardo Trotto's *Dialoghi del matrimonio e vita vedovile* ('Dialogues on Marriage and Widowhood', Turin, 1578), making the case for remarriage versus widowhood, similarly suggests that 'burning love' for one's husband should develop within marriage. For Torquato Tasso, in his dialogue *Il padre di famiglia*, a wife should be a companion to her husband rather than his servant. Each partner should expect fidelity from the other, but the sort of passion one expects in a lover will only be appropriate in marriage for a brief initial period, before giving way to 'marital love'.

The philosopher Giordano Bruno (1548–1600) used features of Neoplatonic love treatises in his *De gl'heroici furori* (1585), one of the Italian dialogues he published in London during his residence in England (1583–5). These brilliant and controversial works, written in a highly individual and colourful vernacular, concerned both cosmological questions (*La Cena de le Ceneri* – 'The Ash-Wednesday Supper', 1584) and social and moral issues (*Lo Spaccio della bestia trionfante* – 'The Despatch of the Triumphant Beast', 1584), also prominent in his comedy *Il Candelaio* (see below p. 287).

Literature and art

Links between literature and art became particularly close in the Cinquecento. Some of the most prominent figures of the world of letters admired artists greatly and had warm personal relations with them. Castiglione, for instance, wrote modestly in the dedication of the *Cortegiano* that his verbal portrait of Urbino would be less worthy than one by his friend Raphael or by Michelangelo; Titian was an important member of Aretino's circle in Venice; Borghini's links with Vasari and his overseeing of the Accademia del Disegno in Florence were crucial in furthering an integrated cultural policy under Cosimo I. There were perceived similarities between portraits in words and in paint, so that Trissino could describe Petrarch in his *Ritratti* as 'most noble of all painters'. The interest of some writers in art and in art criticism is reflected in

Castiglione's introduction into the *Cortegiano* of advice that the courtier should be able to draw, and of a discussion on the relative superiority of painting and sculpture (I, 49–52). At the same time, artists shared with writers an interest in concepts such as beauty, grace and propriety; and they used the genres of dialogue, biography and autobiography to promote the principles and achievements of their own profession.

The dispute on painting versus sculpture was taken up by Benedetto Varchi in his *Lezzione nella quale si disputa della maggioranza delle arti, e qual sia più nobile, la scultura o la pittura* ('Lecture Discussing the Pre-eminence of the Arts, and Whether Sculpture or Painting is Nobler'), given in Florence in 1547 and printed in 1549/50. He concludes that they have the same aim and are therefore equally noble. He briefly discusses the similarities and differences between poets and painters, comparing Michelangelo with Dante.

The Venetian Paolo Pino naturally takes the side of painting, his own skill, against sculpture in his *Dialogo di pittura* (Venice, 1548). This wide-ranging work provides among other things a defence of painting as a liberal art, a description of the different aspects of painting, and a description of how the ideal artist should behave. He treats the greatest living Florentine and Venetian painters, Michelangelo and Titian, even-handedly: both are like 'gods'.

Giorgio Vasari of Arezzo (1511–74), himself a successful painter and architect, unites theoretical questions, technical information, historical descrip-tion, and critical judgement in his monumental *Vite de' più eccellenti architetti, pittori e scultori italiani da Cimabue insino a' tempi nostri* ('Lives of the Most Eminent Italian Architects, Painters and Sculptors from Cimabue to the Present Day'). After the first edition (Florence, 1550), which culminated in the life of Michelangelo, Vasari published in 1568 a much expanded edition which added lives of contemporaries including Titian. Vasari recounts that one of those who encouraged him to write the work was Paolo Giovio, himself author of Latin biographies, including the *Elogia* (1546 and 1551) of famous men whose portraits hung in his house.

Vasari's lives, written in a lively style often reminiscent of the *novella*, are divided into three groups, according to his interpretation of art history in the previous three centuries. Painting, sculpture and architecture, he explains in the proem, had reached perfection in ancient Greece and Rome but were devastated by the barbarian invasions and the growth of Christianity. These arts began to be revived in Tuscany around 1250. Among his first lives were those of the two Florentine artists who began the revival, Cimabue and Giotto. The proem to Part II outlines his division of art since their time into three periods: one which marked a new beginning but still fell short of the ideal; a second (c. 1400–c. 1500) in which considerable improvement was made in architecture, painting and sculpture, again thanks to Florentines, above all Donatello; and a third in which 'art has done everything which an imitator of nature can do' and has thus reached perfection. The crucial qualities introduced in this last phase, he explains in the proem to Part III, were spontaneity, a judgement which confers grace (a concept found previously in the *Cortegiano*, as is that of the 'excessive study' for which the dryness of the second phase is blamed), and delicacy and charm in design. Inspiration to reject the dryness of previous art came from the unearthing of antique statues, but the originator of the new style was yet again a Florentine, Leonardo da Vinci. Raphael of Urbino is acknowledged as the most graceful of modern painters; but all are transcended by Michelangelo, who has triumphed over modern and even ancient artists, bringing painting, sculpture and architecture to perfection.

Vasari's patriotic admiration for Michelangelo was challenged in the *Dialogo della pittura* by the Venetian *poligrafo* Lodovico Dolce (1508–68). The speaker chosen to represent Dolce's views is Pietro Aretino. He, although born in the same city as Vasari, was a great admirer of Titian and had attacked Michelangelo's *Last Judgement* for impiety. The dialogue, printed in Venice in 1557, also constitutes a homage to Aretino, who died in 1556. Aretino challenges the claim of another Tuscan that Michelangelo is the greatest living painter and sculptor, proposing Raphael in his place. He describes the aim of painting (the imitation of nature), its high status, and its different parts, in a way similar to Pino. He is particularly insistent on the similarities between painters and poets, using Ariosto's portrait of Alcina as his main example; indeed, he claims, all writers are painters. Reviewing the excellence of other sixteenth-century painters, Aretino says that 'our Titian' combines all the gifts found separately in others. Like Pino, he stresses personal qualities: Titian was not only 'divine and without equal' as a painter but also modest, affable, and liked by all who knew him.

That is not a description which could be applied to the character which emerges from the autobiography of the great Florentine goldsmith, medallist and sculptor Benvenuto Cellini (1500–71). During his lifetime he published treatises on the goldsmith's art and on sculpture (1568/9), but his modern reputation as an author derives from the *Vita* begun in 1558. This highly original work is far removed from the manner of Vasari ('Giorgio Vassellario', 'Vase-maker'/'Vassal', as Cellini mockingly called him), and it remained in manuscript until 1728. Cellini sets out from the start to establish his own exceptional status, in life as well as in art. Even his infancy was marked by unusual signs: he picked up a scorpion but was unharmed; his father saw a salamander in the flames, 'something never seen by others' (1, 4). He portrays himself as heroically determined and daring in meeting challenges. During the Sack of Rome, his bravery and resourcefulness as a gunner were crucial in defending Castel Sant'Angelo against the Imperial troops (1, 34–7). When he was imprisoned in the same fortress in 1538, he warned his gaolers to guard him well because he was determined to flee, yet still succeeded in making a spectacular escape. In this and other episodes Cellini cleverly builds up excitement in his narrative by drawing on the tensions which evidently affected his relationships in real life. He was quick to take a dislike to people and often suspected, rightly or wrongly, that his path was blocked by the malevolence or envy of others. His determination not to be thwarted by such opposition, combined with a violent and vindictive streak in his nature, led him continuously into quarrels, duels and even murders. The *Vita* itself was a way of justifying himself and taking revenge over his enemies. But Cellini also had a warm-hearted and generous side, and his praise could be as exaggerated as his blame. Above all, he needed to be appreciated by those whom he respected. His greatest reward was the esteem and understanding of rulers. Even his killing of his brother's murderer is not just recounted as an act of vengeance but is framed by the context of his close relationship with Pope Clement VII (I, 51). The French King Francis I was so pleased with Cellini's skill that he clapped him on the shoulder, calling him 'mon ami', and wondered whether it was a greater pleasure for a king to find a man after his own heart or for a skilled artist to find a prince who enabled him to express his greatness. Cellini said that his own was the greater fortune, but no doubt secretly agreed with the King's response: 'Let us say that [our fortune] is equal' (II, 22).

After Cellini returned from France to Florence in 1545, he failed to strike up a similar rapport with Cosimo de' Medici. He uses the Duke's doubts about whether he could meet the technical challenge of casting his bronze Perseus as the first element in the creation of an atmosphere of suspense surrounding this climactic episode (II, 73–8). He set about the task with confidence and relish, but disaster threatened when his workshop caught fire, rain pouring through the roof started to cool his furnace, and his exertions forced him to bed with a fever. Spurred on by a comment that the work could not be saved, he rose in a fury to see the enterprise to a successful conclusion. Cellini gave thanks to God, who seemed to have guided the project miraculously, nonchalantly turned to a plate of salad and ate and drank heartily before returning to bed 'as if nothing at all had been wrong with me'. But the lack of appreciation shown by Cosimo and his court casts a shadow over the last part of the *Vita*. In 1562, with the artist still uncertain of the favour of the Duke and Duchess, the autobiography breaks off suddenly, as if he had not the heart to continue.

Narrative fiction

The novella

By far the most popular form of fiction in the Cinquecento was the *novella* (short story). Its influence was pervasive. Self-contained stories were often embedded in other works in order to illustrate a point (as in Della Casa's *Galateo*) or simply to entertain (as in Doni's *Marmi*); the same technique was used in epics such as Ariosto's *Orlando furioso*. Stories from the late Duecento onwards were much read and studied, above all those of Boccaccio's *Deca-*

meron. Bembo's *Prose* helped to establish this work as the main stylistic model for artistic prose (see above, p. 183), but it was considered to be within the reach of anyone with basic literacy: for instance, Castiglione, writing to his mother in February 1508, tried to give her an idea of the hopeless inadequacy of a new page of his by complaining that the lad could not even read Pulci's *Morgante* or the *Decameron*. Boccaccio's collection also provided plots which were plundered by authors of comedies, and a repertoire of moral and social situations which was frequently drawn upon in works such as the *Galateo* or Betussi's *Raverta*. The importance of the *novella* in written culture was enhanced by its link with orality in literate circles. The social function of entertaining stories and witty remarks was emphasised by Federico Fregoso in the *Cortegiano* (II, 41) and was considered so important by Castiglione that, as we have seen, he dedicated half of Book II to them. Significantly, framing devices were frequently used in collections of stories in such a way as to provide situations in which tales were recounted to an audience by a *contemporary* narrator. It is not surprising, then, that many new *novelle* were written in the Cinquecento, sometimes as individual stories but also, especially from the 1540s onwards, collected together with others and often set in a frame-story.

Machiavelli wrote only one *novella*, in the period (1518–20) which produced his major literary works; but *Belfagor*, with its hints of political and social satire, was one of the most subtle of the century. The archdevil Belfagor is sent to live as a man for ten years, with a huge sum of money, in order to investigate the claim of most of the damned that their wives had led to their downfall. Machiavelli mocks his fellow citizens' obsession with money and finery by making Belfagor, now known as Roderigo, choose to live in Florence because here he can best live off his wealth through usury, and then by making his Florentine wife proud, overbearing and fond of extravagant expenditure on fashionable clothes. Even his devil-servants prefer to return to hell (where Pluto is a model prince) rather than live under her. Roderigo flees from the city with his creditors at his heels and is sheltered by a peasant, Gianmatteo. In return, he makes Gianmatteo rich as an exorcist: the devil takes possession of the spirit of two rich women and then allows himself to be driven out by the peasant. With a warning to Gianmatteo not to ask any more of him, Roderigo then enters the spirit of the King of France's daughter. Gianmatteo is caught between threats of death from the King if the girl is not cured and from Roderigo if he betrays the agreement to make no further demands on him. The astute peasant puts Roderigo to flight by creating a great noise and convincing him that his wife has come to get him back. Roderigo prefers to return to hell rather than to resubmit to matrimony. Thus an archdevil has found it impossible to rule even a household on earth or to find peace there, and the humblest of Florentines has proved more cunning than he.

We have seen (above, p. 217) that *novelle* played an important part in Firenzuola's *Ragionamenti*. All but the last story of the first afternoon keep to the theme of love, on which the morning's discussion and the company's poems centred. The first story, told by Gostanza, picks up the theme of finding happiness in love outside marriage. The wife of a Tunisian falls in love with a Florentine who had been sold to her husband as a slave; she is persuaded (rather too conveniently) to become a Christian and then to return with her lover to Florence, where they live happily as a married couple. This *novella* is loftier in its themes and style than the subsequent stories, which use a more comic and sometimes colloquial register. All draw on the situations or the language of the *Decameron*. But already in Firenzuola one can see how Cinquecento tastes and attitudes could differ in some respects from those of Boccaccio. Transgressors can be punished with gruesome cruelty: thus the fourth story pays homage to Boccaccio's tale of the Prete da Varlungo (VIII, 2) but ends with the lecherous priest having to castrate himself. The storytellers too are more morally vigilant than in the *Decameron*. After the second tale, for example, they are highly critical of the young man who dresses up as a serving maid in order to win a place in the household of the married woman he loves.

After the first day of the *Ragionamenti*, only the end of Day II, including two stories, survives. About the same time as this work Firenzuola made a free and updated (but incomplete) adaptation of the *Golden Ass* of Apuleius. During the last five years of his life, spent in Prato, he wrote two more *novelle* and *La prima veste dei discorsi degli animali* ('The First [Italian] Version of the Discourses of the Animals'), an elegant adaptation, via a Spanish intermediary, of fables derived from the Indian *Panciatantra*. The *Prima veste* was printed in the posthumous *Prose* of 1548. In 1552 Doni brought out a more complete translation entitled *La moral filosofia*.

Whereas Firenzuola spent most of his life outside Florence and absorbed influences from other regions, the apothecary Anton Francesco Grazzini (1503–84) remained firmly rooted within the city walls and regarded himself as a guardian of the quintessential burlesque and festive Florentine spirit which had flourished in the Quattrocento. This limited the scope of his achievement, but he was nevertheless a complex and interesting figure. He was one of the founders in 1540 of the Accademia degli Umidi, taking the name of 'il Lasca' ('the Dace'), and later strongly resisted its transformation, by colleagues close to Duke Cosimo, into the more serious Accademia Fiorentina. In 1547 he was expelled from this academy and was readmitted only in 1566. But he continued to revive and edit comic verse by other writers and to compose comedies, verse and the *novelle* which he collected as *Le cene* ('The Suppers'). The title derives from the frame-story: five young men and five ladies tell stories while waiting for their evening meal on three successive Thursdays during carnival sometime in the 1540s, which was probably also the period when the collection was written. Grazzini completed the first two *Cene*, but seems to have written only the last story of the third.

An element of originality stems from the decision by Grazzini's narrators to make the stories of each of the last two evenings gradually longer than those of the previous day. Another comes from their preference, no doubt reflecting the author's antagonism towards Medicean authority, for organising themselves on a republican rather than a monarchic pattern (and an even stronger republican note is sounded when a tyrant is stoned to death at the end of II, 5). Compared with the *Decameron*, which Grazzini acknowledges as the loftiest work in the genre, the settings of the stories are narrow in range and municipal. Most take place in Florence, and only one (II, 9) ventures outside Tuscany. Grazzini seems to be writing almost exclusively for readers with an intimate knowledge of the city and of the colourful resources of its spoken language. Another distinctive feature of his stories is his relish for recounting the effects of pain and fear. The *beffe* (tricks) played on those seen as outsiders can be extremely savage. A young man who has endured a joyless adolescence because of a pedagogue takes his revenge with a trick in which the elder man has his penis trapped and is forced to rip it off (I, 2). A pedagogue and a priest are punished violently for falling in love with women (II, 7; II, 8). The *beffa* played by a Sienese priest on a Florentine and the Florentine's revenge in I, 7 both involve the shock provoked by an unexpected confrontation with an exhumed corpse. Another story (I, 9) turns on a fright given to a young Florentine by the madwoman Biliorsa: he finds her one night hanging some pumpkins as if they were men and faints with terror when she tries to hang him too. Pity and horror are two further emotions whose fascination for Grazzini can be seen as he lingers over the 'fearful and most horrible spectacle' of the bodies of Fazio, quartered by the executioner, of his two children, stabbed by his jealous wife, and of the wife herself, all lying in a bloody heap (I, 5), or as he pushes the macabre to its limits in the description of two lovers who have been punished for their illicit liaison, 'without tongue and without eyes, without hands and without feet', groping their way to a last embrace as each bleeds to death from seven wounds (II, 5).

Grazzini is at his best, and achieves more subtle results, when he explores the clash between normality and the improbable in the context of questions of identity. In the first story of the second *Cena* Gabriello, a poor fisherman, achieves wealth and happiness for himself and his wife by pretending to be a rich man who has been drowned. In the long final story (III, 10), Manente, after being kidnapped by Lorenzo de' Medici, is thought to be dead, and when he finally returns to Florence ten months later, he has a hard job to persuade everyone that he is not an apparition. The tale of Manente's courage was admired by D. H. Lawrence, who translated it and intended to go on to turn all the *Cene* into English.

The *novella* was not a popular genre among authors from the Kingdom of Naples, which in the Cinquecento produced only the Latin *Novellae* of Girolamo Morlini (Naples, 1520). But in the central decades of the century it flourished among writers from northern Italy, including those working in Rome, its success encouraged by Bembo's promotion of the *Decameron* as a prose model.

An important but solitary *novella* was written in the mid-1520s by Luigi da Porto of Vicenza (1485–1529), a friend of Bembo and member of the court of Urbino between 1503 and 1505. He used a plot which Masuccio Salernitano had set in Siena at an imprecise date, but moved it to early fourteenth-century Verona and renamed his tragic lovers Romeo and Giulietta (first version Venice [1531]; second version in his *Rime et prosa*, Venice, 1539). Da Porto concentrated the action in a smaller geographical area, brought greater verisimilitude to the characters and setting, and provided a more dramatic ending in which the lovers die together. This was the source used by Bandello (see below), whose version was then adapted by Shakespeare. Da Porto also displayed his narrative skill in the *Lettere storiche* (first published Venice, 1832) which described his experiences while fighting for the Venetian army in 1509–13.

Another friend of Bembo who tried his hand at the *novella* was the Venetian priest Giovanni Brevio. His *Rime et prose volgari* (Rome, 1545) included six independent stories, one of them a plagiarism of Machiavelli's *Belfagor*, and four brief tales linked together as a treatise *De la miseria umana* ('On Human Wretchedness'). A striking story of double incest, for which Brevio drew on Masuccio, is an example of contemporary interest in the human frailty which could lead parents into conceiving an abnormal passion for their children: a mother falls in love with her son, tricks him into sleeping with her, and gives birth to a daughter whom the son later marries, thus becoming at the same time her brother, father and husband.

Francesco Maria Molza of Modena was cited during his lifetime (1489–1544) as one of the most promising of contemporary authors. In spite of his gifts, however, his works, which were mainly poetic, did not prove to be of lasting importance. Most of his adult life was spent in Rome, where the reading public evidently appreciated the *novella*, and he completed five independent stories, four of which were published in Lucca in 1549. Like Brevio's *novelle*, they have no frame-story. But his too self-consciously elegant style prevents his stories from coming to life.

A much less stylish northern writer working in Rome was Marco Cademosto (Marco da Lodi). Six stories were printed with his *Sonetti et altre rime* (Rome, 1544). Cademosto's claim that they were based on real events reflects a concern for verisimilitude which was shared, as we shall see, by Bandello.

Up to the mid-1540s, then, the *novella* was a genre treated respectfully by northern writers, but used only tentatively and sporadically by a handful of them. In 1550–4 the situation changed dramatically with the publication of four substantial and innovative collections. All were by authors born to the west of the Veneto, but the first three were strongly influenced by Venetian culture. The publishing history of the *Decameron* shows that interest in Boccaccio's work reached a peak in the same period, yet authors had the confidence not to imitate it slavishly, keeping their independence in various ways.

Little is known about Giovan Francesco Straparola, who was born in Caravaggio and began his literary career with a volume of courtly poetry (1508). Only in 1550 and 1553 did he publish in Venice *Le piacevoli notti* ('The Pleasant Nights'), in which ten young ladies tell stories on thirteen nights during carnival on the island of Murano (five stories on the first twelve nights and thirteen on the last, when the men join in). Some stories use plots of Boccaccio's, but there are several original features. Two stories are in dialect; the listeners have to try to solve a verse riddle at the end of each story; real men are present (one of them is Bembo); and, most innovatively of all, Straparola uses material from folk-tales, calling his stories *favole* rather than *novelle*. Several stories are set firmly in the realm of fantasy and involve magic or metamorphoses. An example is the tale (II, 1) of the son of the King of England who, because of spells cast by fairies, is born with every virtue but doomed to have the body and habits of a pig until he has been married three times. Only his third wife sees his good qualities, even though he covers their bed in excrement, and thanks to her he returns permanently to human form. The scatological theme is found too in the story (V, 2) of a magic doll which excretes money for its 'mother' Adamantina but, when it is stolen, brings forth instead a 'stinking mess'. Straparola then adds the ingredient of cruelty: when a king tries to wipe himself with the doll, she sinks her teeth into his buttocks and squeezes his testicles, refusing to let go until Adamantina intervenes.

Girolamo Parabosco (Piacenza 1524–Venice 1557), who worked in Venice as a musician, and Silvan Cattaneo (Salò 1514?–1553/64) choose another type of innovation. As Firenzuola had done in the *Ragionamenti* (published in 1548), they make their *novelle* subordinate to a rich and varied frame-story which provides both the kind of discussions and the portrait of a social group associated with the dialogue; but, as in the Ciceronian dialogue but not the *Ragionamenti*, the speakers are identified with real people. In Parabosco's *I diporti* ('The Amusements', Venice, 1550), the patrician poet Domenico Venier and several friends, among them Speroni and Aretino, take shelter from bad weather in a fishermen's hut in the Venetian lagoon. On the first two days they recount sixteen stories which lead to the discussion of six questions of love. Parabosco thus differs from Firenzuola in linking his *novelle* more closely with the company's discussions. His structure is also less rigid, and the third day contains only one *novella* followed by a discussion of *motti* (witty remarks), poetry and praise of contemporary women.

Cattaneo's untitled collection, now called *Le dodici giornate* ('The Twelve Days'), remained unpublished until 1745. Recounting a trip around Lake Garda made by Count Fortunato Martinengo with the author and some students on vacation from Cattaneo's own university, Padua, it intertwines descriptions of the scenery with the group's discussions (for instance, on the topic of women's participation in banquets) and the stories which they narrate to each other.

The restrictions of the *giornata* format were abandoned in the most important collection of the Cinquecento, the *Novelle* of the Dominican friar Matteo Bandello. He was born in 1484 or 1485 in Castelnuovo Scrivia, then part of the Milanese state, and his collection has many links with his experiences of the courts of Lombardy in the early decades of the century. In 1541–2 he followed Costanza Rangone, in whose service he was, into exile near Agen in France, where he died in 1561. During the 1540s Bandello abandoned poetry and, influenced no doubt by his contacts with Margaret of Navarre, then writing her *Heptaméron*, concentrated his efforts on compiling his stories. The first three parts of the *Novelle* (186 stories) were printed in Lucca in 1554, the fourth part (28 stories) in Lyons in 1573.

The open-ended structure adopted by Bandello allowed him to combine the *novella* with features of the courtly *ragionamento* and another fashionable genre, the letter. Adapting a device used in Masuccio Salernitano's *Novellino*, Bandello prefaced each story with a letter of dedication to a contemporary personality. Here he explained the circumstances in which the tale was originally told by some other person, who could be someone as well known as Machiavelli (I, 40). The process of narration was thus placed in a social and cultural context. For example, Bandello's version of the story of Romeo and Juliet (II, 9) was supposedly recounted by a Veronese captain to a group of people, including Bandello, who were taking the waters at a spa, and is dedicated to the celebrated poet and doctor Girolamo Fracastoro. Stories may also be linked with topics of current interest by means of the dedication, the narrator's preamble, or a brief concluding comment. Thus the *novella* of Pantea's fidelity to her husband (III, 9) is told in the course of a discussion on 'excellent women' and begins with the narrator commenting on the need to respect them. The dedication of story 31 of Part II examines the nature of love; the story itself, about the blind passion of a rich Milanese youth for a girl who is his social inferior, opens with a defence by the Milanese narrator of his use of his city's vernacular rather than the 'courtly language'.

Bandello defends himself against accusations that he lacks style by claiming (II, 11, dedication) that 'histories' will always give pleasure, however crudely written, and that his stories are 'not fables but true histories'. It is true that he likes to use historical events as a background in order to lend verisimilitude, and that some of his written sources are historical ones. But Bandello is too good a storyteller to follow sources slavishly. In his version of Giovio's accounts of the wives of Henry VIII of England, for instance (III, 62), he changes details in order to make the story more interesting and persuasive. He also rewrote stories from literary sources, such as the Sienese comedy *Gli ingannati* (II, 36) and *novelle* by other writers.

Although Bandello likes to remind readers of his Lombard background, as in the preface to Part III, the geographical and chronological horizons of his stories are anything but limited. He uses an unusually wide range of registers and subject-matter, which includes the comic, the bawdy, the tragic and horrific, tersely worded historical accounts and sentimental idylls. The *Novelle*

deservedly belong to the select group of Cinquecento prose works which won a
European reputation. Some were translated into French in 1559 and 1565,
then into English by Geoffrey Fenton (1567) and William Painter (1566–7),
and the dramatic qualities of these stories led to their use as a source of plots
by playwrights such as Massinger and Shakespeare.

The principal Tuscan collections of the second half of the century came from
outside Florence. In Siena, Pietro Fortini (c. 1500–62) put together a collection
of bawdy and obscene stories in two parts, *Le giornate delle novelle dei novizi*
('The Days of the Stories of the Novices') and *Le piacevoli et amorose notti dei
novizi* ('The Pleasant and Amorous Nights of the Novices', a title evidently
influenced by Straparola's). These were printed only in the late nineteenth
century. In the first work, five women and two men narrate forty-nine stories
on seven days. In the *Notti*, the number of narrators varies and much of the
time is taken up by activities such as games, discussions, plays and poetry.
Only two stories are included in the first five nights, but then thirty are told in
the final day and night. Fortini came from a *popolare* family and was linked
with the Sienese Congrega dei Rozzi ('Society of the Uncouth'), a group of
artisans proud of their ignorance of Latin. The content of many of the stories is
crude and repetitive and their language deliberately provincial; but Fortini
could at times be an inventive narrator.

However, the Counter-Reformation soon made it impossible to write or
publish such collections in Italy. The edition of Bandello's *Novelle* published in
Milan in 1560 was expurgated. The fourth part appeared, as we have seen,
outside Italy. The last uncensored *Decameron* of the century was printed in
1557, and the work appeared on Indexes of prohibited books from 1559;
thereafter it could be printed only when shorn of anything offensive to the
clergy and religion. The *novella* was too strong not to survive into the rest of
the century, but its nature was changed, particularly in the north, and its
original vigour crushed.

Two new collections published by northern authors in the 1560s were much
more serious in character than Bandello's. The Ferrarese courtier and academic
Giambattista Giraldi Cinzio hoped that the stories of his *Hecatommithi*
('Hundred Stories', Mondovì, 1565) would be of moral benefit to men of all
kinds, from young lovers to those wishing to dedicate themselves to 'the best
form of living'. He returned to a *Decameron*-like frame-story: ten narrators,
fleeing the plague which followed the Sack of Rome by troops who were
'enemies of true religion', tell stories during a sea voyage to Marseilles. Risqué
stories were not proscribed, but there is nothing which could be construed as
disrespectful towards the clergy. Giraldi inserts three dialogues 'on civil life' at
the end of the fifth day and echoed recent teachings of the Council of Trent by
demonstrating the importance of marriage and the wickedness of duels. Two
stories (III, 7 and VIII, 5) provided the subject-matter for Shakespeare's *Othello*
and *Measure for Measure*.

Yet more strongly exemplary were *Le sei giornate* ('The Six Days', Venice,

1567) by the Venetian Sebastiano Erizzo (1525–85), a collection of thirty-six 'avenimenti' (events) intended to contain 'noble and useful teachings of moral philosophy'.

A contrasting world of secluded social refinement is portrayed in works of two members of the Sienese upper class, Girolamo Bargagli (1537–86) and his brother Scipione (1540–1612). Girolamo's *Dialogo de' giuochi che nelle vegghie sanesi si usano di fare* (Siena, 1572) codified the games ('giuochi') played during the characteristic Sienese evening's entertainment (*veglia* or *vegghia*), and included advice on choosing stories. These pastimes formed the theme of a work closely linked with the *Dialogo* but which also looked beyond Siena and back in time to the *Decameron* and Bembo's *Asolani*: Scipione Bargagli's *I trattenimenti* ('The Entertainments', Venice, 1587, but begun in the 1560s). Four noble women and five young men amuse one another during the last three days of carnival in 1553 (while Siena was under siege by a Spanish and Florentine army) with, among other things, debates on questions of love and six stories on the same theme. Girolamo had advised against telling tragic stories in such circumstances, and all but one of Scipione's end happily, including even the first, which is based on a relationship similar to that of Romeo and Juliet. Both these Sienese works show that in Tuscany the *novella* kept its associations with entertainment longer than in northern Italy.

The romanzo

Stories of love could also take the form of the prose romance (*romanzo*). To the genre of stories about tribulations endured by a first-person narrator for the sake of his beloved belonged the *Istoria di Phileto veronese* attributed to Lodovico Corfino (Verona 1497/8–1556), set in 1515–18, written probably during the 1520s. Phileto wins the hand of the woman he loves after a *novella*-type subterfuge, but kills a rival and has to flee his city. After many adventures on land and sea, he returns and is reunited with his wife. Nicolò Franco's *Philena* (Mantua, 1547) tells of a secret love which was not blessed by fortune; we leave the hero Sannio as he decides to renounce the world and turn to God. But Corfino's work was published only in 1899 and the *Philena*, like other *romanzi* of the Cinquecento, enjoyed little popularity. To modern tastes they are too verbose, too prone to erudite digressions, too reliant on conventional sentiments. One might have expected this genre to have attracted more attention. After all, it had well-respected Trecento antecedents in Boccaccio's *Filocolo* and *Fiammetta*, and two of the principal *romanzi* of the late Quattrocento, Sannazaro's *Arcadia* and Caviceo's *Libro del peregrino*, were popular with the reading public, to judge from the number of new editions in the first half of the century. The Hellenistic romances by Achilles Tatius and Heliodorus, and the story of Apollonius of Tyre, were printed in vernacular translations from the 1540s onwards. However, Annibal Caro left his free translation of *Daphnis and Chloe* unpublished, and no leading Cinquecento author composed a *romanzo*. The relative lack of success of *romanzi* can partly be explained by the popularity of two other kinds of narrative fiction, the verse epic and the *novella*. The latter was able to satisfy to some extent the desire for the type of material included in the *romanzo*, since among its range of types it included, as it had done since the *Decameron*, fairly lengthy stories of adventure. The *novella* was also flexible enough to be adapted to serve the moralising spirit of the Counter-Reformation.

Looking back over the history of the *novella* in the Cinquecento, one can see that authors continued to use themes which were well established in the Trecento but that the subject-matter of the genre was developed in new directions, particularly as regards the cruel, the unusual and the fantastic. There were also interesting developments in presentation. Authors used the frame-story or, in Bandello's case, dedicatory letters for discussion of topical issues and introduced real rather than fictitious narrators, so that, in contrast with Boccaccio's *Decameron*, whose stories tended to look back towards earlier generations, the *novella* became more closely involved with contemporary reality. Thanks to such innovations, the genre thrived until the cold hand of the Counter-Reformation altered its character and stifled its growth. But the *novelle* of this period lived on, their skilful depiction of sensuality and violence, bravery and resourcefulness continuing to fascinate and inspire authors from Shakespeare to Lawrence. Italian writers of fiction thus added their own essential contribution, alongside those of Machiavelli, Guicciardini, Castiglione and others, to the rich and varied storehouse of ideas which Cinquecento prose offered to the rest of Europe.

12

Narrative poetry

Peter Marinelli

From Boiardo to Ariosto

Narrative poetry in the Cinquecento essentially builds on the impressive initiatives of Pulci and Boiardo in the late fifteenth century. The truncation of the *Innamorato* in 1494 (see above, pp. 172–5) left dozens of Boiardo's fascinating narrative inventions unresolved and a host of fabulous creatures in a state of suspended animation. To take only the prime players, how, if at all, was the impossible love of Orlando for Angelica to be concluded? What was to be the course of the courtship of Ruggiero and Bradamante, separated as soon as they met, and separated as well by their adherence to different and warring religions? What was to be the result of Agramante's expedition into France? By what means was Charlemagne's empire to be delivered from peril? Lesser characters too had vanished into the unknown: what fate had befallen the always improvident Astolfo, tricked by Alcina? Boiardo's death in the year of invasion deprived his readers of answers, but the intense magnetism of the mystery provoked others to attempt a conclusion. Ariosto was not the only poet to resume the *matière* provided by the *Innamorato*. In 1505, 1514 and 1521 the Venetian Niccolò degli Agostini provided a fourth, fifth and sixth book of continuations to Boiardo's remnant. Raffaele da Verona, known as Valcieco, in 1514 added a fifth book of his own, and in 1518 Pierfrancesco de' Conti da Camerino wrote yet another, sixth book, tracing the life of Ruggiero's and Bradamante's son, Rugino.

These continuations – all the work of poetasters, densely compounding each other's fantasies – are the detritus of Italian romance, belonging to the category of sub- or para-literature. A more independent approach is that of Francesco Bello ('il Cieco') of Ferrara. He shows a certain narrative flair in his *Mambriano*, which takes its name from a new luckless enemy of the paladins who is eventually saved by marrying Carandina, another in the long line of seductive witches. The poem enjoyed a considerable success, with eleven editions between 1509 and 1554. Other developments followed: in 1541 the satirist Francesco Berni (1497–1535) offered a Tuscanised version of Boiardo's poem, wholly revising its original language into something more correct but rather lifeless in comparison, and not refraining from adding stanzas throughout, over 250 in number. This was followed in 1545 by an editorial revision by Ludovico Domenichi, who tended to Venetianise Boiardo's text.

Between them, however, Berni and Domenichi succeeded in usurping Boiardo's original for several hundred years till it was reprinted in England in 1830 by Antonio Panizzi, Librarian of the British Museum. By then, however, the radiance of the *Orlando furioso* itself had long eclipsed the poem from which it originally sprang and in the light of which it could be most fully understood.

Ariosto

A reader coming to Ludovico Ariosto's *Orlando furioso* for the first time is bound to find himself immersed, not to say drowning, in the pell-mell rush and swirl of event and character as the poet (1474–1533) initiates his resumption of Boiardo's *matière*. Undoubtedly there is immense pleasure to be found in surrendering to the rapid flow of the colourful and ever-changing tale. Nevertheless, the reader may also wish to perceive some definition in the landscape, particularly as the poem is so vast, and its narrative method and tonal complexities grow in the course of its forty-six cantos. By way of orientation, we may consider some of the crucial differences between Ariosto on one hand, and the continuators of Boiardo on the other. In the first place, Ariosto stands apart from the versifiers who merely attached their continuations to Boiardo's torso and picked up at the point where he left off. The new poet establishes his independence immediately by breaking chronology and beginning anew at a point of his own choosing; in effect, he begins to dismantle the *Innamorato* and to incorporate various portions of its narrative into his own, recomposing as he proceeds. What immediately distinguishes his work from that of his predecessors is, in essence, an ambition to reshape the entire story before attempting to complete it, to impose form and design upon Boiardo's immensely rich but ultimately shapeless masterpiece.

Ariosto's stance of critical independence is apparent in his selection of a title: his is to be the tale of an Orlando who, once sensually *innamorato*, is (through very long persistence in that unresolved condition) to become *furioso*, a madman. After the title, the opening stanzas compel attention. Here, the three main actions of the *Innamorato* are presented in orderly fashion and emerge as interlocking and interdependent: the wars of the pagans on Charlemagne, the insane love of Orlando for Angelica, and the travails of Ruggiero in his progress to his destiny as Christian dynast. Boiardo's narrative plan had evolved as the poem proceeded, afterthought and modification of original purpose creating an effect of provisional strategies, delightful in every case but ultimately militating against the poem's unity. But though the *Furioso* also changed and grew – from forty cantos in the editions of 1516 and 1521 to forty-six in 1532 – and while there is evidence of afterthought in the *Cinque canti* which Ariosto appears to have excised, its preconceived design is apparent from the first to the last, all the main elements of its framework cooperating as part of a whole to create a complex system of interlace utterly beyond what Pulci or Boiardo might have conceived.

The rupture of the *Innamorato* in mid-story created an opportunity for Ariosto to show his own powers of invention. Boiardo's static portrayal of Orlando as an amusingly incompetent, chastity-ridden lover who, while filled with desire, would never win Angelica is changed to one in which the paladin, initially dignified by Ariosto as a courteous rescuer of damsels in peril (Olimpia and Isabella), soon degenerates into a melancholic, withdrawn hunter of the enchantress, and then into a bestial madman roaming the face of Europe after his intellect crumbles. Equally dynamic is the detailed course of temptation and education through which Ariosto, working from hints in Boiardo, puts Ruggiero, a hero torn between love for Bradamante and his duty to King Agramante. Both Orlando and Ruggiero are propelled by their unruly wills and appetites, and the comparison and contrast between them is pursued to the poem's end.

This contrast in different kinds of love is dramatised in a structural pattern. When (irony of ironies) Angelica elopes in mid-poem with a common foot-soldier, Medoro, and vanishes into a never-never land of romance, the disappointed Orlando succumbs to terrifying insanity in canto 23, the poem's midpoint; in canto 46, the nuptials of Ruggiero and Bradamante, after many vicissitudes, are finally celebrated, and in their marriage the whole future of the Este dynasty is assured. Two kinds of love, destructive and creative, the *insania* and *amore umano* of the Neoplatonists, are quite deliberately poised against each other as balancing points of the large design; and they are Ariosto's expansions and manipulations of a pattern already obvious in Boiardo, though the latter did not exploit them as profoundly as his successor.

The romantic criticism of the nineteenth and a large part of the twentieth centuries had it that the *Furioso* was a poem of 'Harmony' or 'Pure Art,' abstract formulas which made it possible to evade the practical business of examining the work as a complex verbal structure with interior complications expressed in contrast of characters, resonance of episode against episode, or manipulation of rhetoric to differentiate various parts of an extraordinarily changeful narrative. The *Furioso* is far from being an amorphous, haphazard 'dream-poem', and it provides many indications of complex authorial patterning. For instance, the marital banquet that concludes the poem rounds off the immense action begun with Angelica's appearance at Charlemagne's Whitsuntide feast at the beginning of the *Innamorato*, resolving discord into concord. Even more importantly, the poet balances the beginning and end of his own work: the marriage of Bradamante in the liberated city of Paris looks across forty-six cantos to the lustful chase after Angelica by warriors lost in a forest, a 'selva oscura'. In addition, the poet creates a complex system of interrelationships among his three main heroes. These are the two previously mentioned, and (astonishingly, and with a deep sense of Ariostan irony) Astolfo, who emerges in Ariosto's pages as the incarnation of the wise fool, badly burned once by Alcina's untrustworthy love and wary and prudent for the length of the poem thereafter. A character with an extraordinarily long literary life, full of transformations, the Ariostan Astolfo provides the greatest metamorphosis of all. For it is Astolfo who will look down delightedly on the Ariostan landscape of desire and fury from the Moon and the serenity of the Limbo of Lunar Vanities, a perspective afforded no other character in the poem. And Ariosto arranges his narrative so that it is Astolfo who, of all people (after a roundabout voyage of great length, illustrating the old adage *festina lente*) achieves the final overthrow of Agramante, destroying the would-be destroyer and providing the removal of a great obstacle to the union of dynasts. By such magisterial gestures Ariosto gives notice that he has the entire chivalric tradition by heart, feels free to overturn and redirect it, and can achieve a character's redemption by the power of his art. His treatment of Astolfo constitutes a supreme example of his authorial irony, and affirms his belief that the most powerful effects can be achieved by unlikely personalities and comic means.

Like all Ariosto's major characters, Astolfo is constantly on the move, and his voyage is a highly patterned one. It is divided into two parts, of which the first is a circumambulation of the earth on foot, on horseback and by ship; the second is a vertical ascent to heights representative of removal from the turmoil and appetitiveness of the world he leaves behind. He voyages to the Terrestrial Paradise and thence to the moon, which, as the emblem of changefulness and the source of lunacy (his own former lunacy included), is entirely appropriate as a boundary mark for a comic poem that is aware of the limitations of its genre and refrains from following seriously where Dante has already soared. In the first part of his voyage, Astolfo, by recourse to a magic book and an efficacious trumpet given him by the mage Logistilla (a figure for Reason), prudently and forcefully disposes of tyrants and miscreants: he functions as a comic Hercules, achieving victory by witty imaginativeness rather than brute force. In the second part, he contemplates human vanity, foolishness and evil, and cheerfully views the spectacle by participating in the ironic and concentrated wisdom of his creator-poet. This has (need it be said?) nothing whatever to do with contemplation of the divine, and the pietistic allegorisers of Ariosto in the later sixteenth century were never more off the mark than when, failing to understand Ariosto's manipulation of a centuries-old character in accord with a Boethian and Lucianic tradition about the littleness of earth and its incapacity to satisfy human desire, they turned his character into a solemn pilgrim into the heavens, a competitor of Dante. This is to prove utterly insensitive to tone and to reveal oneself ignorant of the comic tradition from which Astolfo derives.

In Astolfo Ariosto had a character with a long lineage. Ruggiero was a relative newcomer, and Ariosto provided him with a highly original and elaborately patterned journey to baptism and marriage. He moves through clearly delineated stages in his passage through a traditional hierarchy of temptations – the flesh, the world, the devil – that keep him from abandoning the pagan for the Christian cause. Presented in the first half of the poem as a young sensualist who is carried aloft by a runaway winged horse to experience unbridled lust in the embraces of Alcina in her island kingdom, he differs very much from the earthbound young warrior of cantos 24–46, for his passion is now for glory and honour, manifested in two ways: in his obsession with the eagle-emblem of Hector and his ruthlessness and avarice in acquiring a kingdom and a throne in eastern Europe. In his fury to possess a kingdom – and Astolfo on the moon has already seen that kingdoms are merely a mass of tumid bladders – Ruggiero becomes a plaything of the Fortune he trusts, and experiences in rapid succession elation and despair; in the end he comes to the nadir of his fortunes in an attempt at suicide when he fears he has lost Bradamante for ever. The fortunate resolution of the plot ensues immediately thereafter with revelations and resolutions, and the *Furioso* terminates with a marriage – as the *Aeneid*, its model throughout, terminated in the versions read in the sixteenth century.

Ruggiero's and Astolfo's careers cross at crucial points, as both of them do (temporally speaking) with that of Orlando: Astolfo liberates Ruggiero immediately before Orlando plunges into madness in canto 23. Nothing, however, links Ruggiero and Astolfo more than the hippogriff, the fantastic winged beast that Ariosto invents to literally transport them from place to place, and simultaneously to figure their various 'transports' of will and passion on one hand, and of bridled and restrained intellect on the other. Whereas the unbridled animal bears Ruggiero to his downfall in a sensual heaven and hellish disillusionment in Alcina's kingdom, Astolfo rides it, bridled and obedient, as low as the depths of hell and as high as the Terrestrial Paradise – where it is humorously stabled and fed grain provided by the Apostles, by long tradition known to be millers who separate the wheat from the chaff. In contrast to these two warriors, differing greatly but both represented as striving upward (though one does so erroneously and with blinded vision), the earthy Orlando demonstrates very little in the way of upward movement. That may explain why, at the height of his madness, he hobbles himself by tying Angelica's dead mare to his foot and dragging it brutally along: an emblematic moment, surely, and one that differentiates him brilliantly from the two riders of the winged horse.

The *Furioso* is occupied by a vast population of characters, the 'ladies and knights' of its first line; there are hundreds of them in the main narrative, while others proliferate in the various *novelle* which Ariosto, availing himself of a penchant for amplification common to Renaissance poets, continually incorporated into his work until its final edition. Here again there is strong evidence of planning and placement. Several of the short tales in the first half of the work are concerned with youthful infidelity in love and reinforce Ruggiero's contemporary dereliction in the arms of Alcina, forgetful, for the moment, of his utterly faithful Bradamante, the maiden who repeatedly attempts to rescue

him from his errors and errancies. In the latter part of the poem, when
Ruggiero's marriage to Bradamante is finally approaching, the *novelle* turn on
the perils of jealousy in marriage; two of the final tales recast material familiar
in *Cefalo*, a mythological play written by Isabella d'Este's cousin, Niccolò da
Correggio, for performance at the wedding festivities of Ferrarese aristocrats.
The action of the poem is continually adjusted to reflect an entire society and
its values, and to achieve decorum in addressing a courtly audience.

A sense of decorum regularly informs Ariosto's poetry, which is the work of
a subtle courtier. He had an eye diplomatically alert for opportunities to bridge
the gap between the world of his imagination and the world of daily reality in
which he moved as panegyrist and celebrator of his city and its society. One of
the most significant aspects of the poet's art is his ambition to classicise the
chivalric romance, thus merging, to an unprecedented degree, the vernacular
and classical cultures, and standing in relation to Ferrara and its history as
Virgil stood in relation to Rome. Ariosto's is essentially a redemptive art, one
which utilises all the resources of Latin literature to recover dignity for the
principal figures of the chivalric tradition by approximating them to archetypes
in the classical tradition. Thus, while Ruggiero is constantly modelled upon
Aeneas, Orlando suggests the Hercules who was *furens*, and Astolfo mimics
the labouring Hercules in romantically remodelled situations that pit him
against monsters, Amazons and Harpies. We first encountered a desire to
rehabilitate the figure of Charlemagne in our discussion of Pulci (see above,
pp. 168–72). But it was Ariosto who finally accomplished the redemption of
the Emperor by re-creating him as the stalwart and pious defender of a Paris
upon which a host of pagans have converged.

Charlemagne's old antagonist, Rinaldo, is similarly redeemed from his
outlaw's habits: he is represented as obediently proceeding (though much
against his will, which is set on pursuing Angelica) to England to raise an
auxiliary force and lead it back to raise the siege of Paris, which is being
savaged by the African warrior Rodomonte. Ariosto remodels him from
Boiardo's attractively headstrong youth to create a romantic-chivalric version
of Virgil's Turnus, chief antagonist in the *Aeneid* to an empire-in-formation.

Ariosto's decorum infuses the chivalric romance with epic qualities not
merely by beginning *in medias res*, or providing the expected statement of epic
purpose at the beginning, or writing catalogues of famous warriors, but, more
crucially, by opening up the perspectives. Ariosto locates his poem in the triple
venues of classical epic – earth, underworld and Heaven – and so achieves a
perspective on the romantic genre that it had not previously possessed. With
Astolfo's flight to the moon, the *Furioso* self-consciously provides a vantage-
point from which to look down upon its sublunary world of passion-ridden
forests. At this point, Astolfo is a surrogate for the poet and stands at the
altitude from which the poet, unbeknown to his readers, has been surveying
the action throughout; for in spite of his initial self-portrayal as a love-stricken
incompetent who says he has trouble in remembering the threads of his story,

he is really the clear-sighted supervisor of his world-as-forest. The persona Ariosto devises for himself in the *Furioso* is mobile in the extreme: its many-sided complexity challenges the relative simplicity of Pulci's and Boiardo's self-dramatisations and surpasses them to a remarkable degree. In one phase the poet is an Ovidian lover whose wits are in danger of being as volatile as Orlando's and who sympathetically makes excuses for Ruggiero's youthful derelictions in love. In another, almost immediately succeeding, he is the Virgilian celebrator of the men and women of a great and famous House, and of the creative spirits whom the magnificence and munificence of the Este court attract to its splendour. In yet another, he is the castigator of the 'Most Christian' and 'Most Catholic' monarchs of France and Spain, warring upon each other, to the scandal of Christianity, while Turks and Arabs possess the Holy Land and infest the Mediterranean. Crucially, he is the learned student of history, a prophet who, in his ability to recollect examples from the classical and medieval periods, reveals a memory that governs time in all its phases and joins the past to the present and future.

All these aspects of the persona are subsumed by the comically profound one according to which Ariosto functions as Maker and Mover of his own poetic world. Here the poet plays very seriously indeed with the Neoplatonic equation that Tasso later employed as well: God is to His creation as the poet is to his own poem. Existing in the timeless world of Ideas above the fury and passion of the sublunary world, capable of transcending the linear concept of time and of being able to see, in the blink of an eye, all time collapsed into one eternal instant, the poet represents time past, present and future as simultaneous in his poem. Hence, from a timeless perspective, he can represent actions as having already occurred (Orlando is seen as maddened and bestialised in canto 19) before they have occurred in the order of time in the poem (Orlando goes mad in canto 23). More dramatically, he can repeatedly interrupt his narrative of eighth- or ninth-century action to recall readers to the contemporary world of sixteenth-century Europe, now again subject to Muslim conquests in the time of yet another Holy Roman Emperor, the Habsburg Charles V. The Aeneas who founded the Roman Empire, the Charlemagne who renewed it as the Holy Roman Empire, and the Habsburg Charles who defends it currently in its hour of extremity are all deliberately housed in the same poem and participate in its imperial theme. The poem is therefore Virgilian, Carolingian and modern, and its creator, utilising the unlikely medium of a comic masterpiece ultimately springing from popular sources, aims to make it the most comprehensive exemplar of the genre and to challenge the classical epic as well. Boiardan, Virgilian and Neoplatonic influences, all of them important in the culture of contemporary Ferrara, flow in upon the *Furioso*, which absorbs and reconciles them all.

We should also note that it reflected the great linguistic debate of its age, the quest for a language worthy of Petrarch and Boccaccio, one free from excessive Latinate or contemporary regional influence (see further above, pp. 181–5).

The 1532 edition of the *Furioso* not only extended the poem by a further six cantos, but submitted it to a thorough linguistic revision, largely in line with the new principles proposed by Ariosto's friend and mentor, Pietro Bembo. With its new linguistic refinement and its unrivalled mastery of the octave form, Ariosto's poem was immediately recognised as the consummate achievement of Carolingian poetry in Italy.

From Ariosto to Tasso

The decades following the triumph of the *Furioso* might have provided a time for taking stock and summing up before pushing forward into new directions; but this is definitely the view of academic hindsight after half a millennium, all too prone to seek neat divisions in literary history. The reality is quite different: when the work was already known in its earlier editions, and even as Ariosto was reworking it into its amplified final form, an avalanche of new epics appeared, many (but not all) of them the work of mere hacks who traded on the public's insatiable appetite for romantic diversion and were unwearied in their exhaustion of an already depleted tradition. In the 1520s and 1530s a small squadron of minor poets sought to keep the tradition alive in works whose titles tell their own story: *Astolfo innamorato*, *Rinaldo furioso*, *Mandricardo innamorato*, and suchlike. Surprisingly, the hacks were sometimes joined by respectable men of letters like Ludovico Dolce, the Ariostan commentator and versatile writer on a variety of literary subjects, who produced not only a *Sacripante paladino* in 1535, but *Le prime imprese del conte Orlando* ('First Exploits of Count Orlando'), which was published posthumously in 1572 and which drew its matter from the *Reali di Francia*, by now several hundred years old and still an astonishingly evergreen, if much-belaboured, source.

In their wild proliferation the endless vistas of romance paradoxically provide the perfect example of a literary dead end. It would take a more sophisticated set of writers to choose other avenues for the exercise of their talents, and another manner of proceeding was chosen by two poets as learned as a good many of those mentioned previously were ignorant. No greater difference, in social station as well as in their conception of art, could be imagined than that between Folengo and Trissino, poets who approach epic from a classical angle and who reveal the gravitational pull of the Latin culture operating in wildly diverse fashion, in their antipodal conceptions of epic. We have seen that there had been a precedent for the Matter of Rome to penetrate the chivalric epic: we witnessed it in Pulci's scrappy bits of mythology, in Boiardo's charmingly romanticised assimilations of Ovid and Virgil, and in Ariosto's powerful evocations of the Graeco-Roman world of myth and history (see above, p. 238).

Teofilo Folengo (1491–1544) was an extravagant and erring spirit if ever there was one, living a footloose, precarious existence that might have served for a vignette in one of his own works. Runaway Benedictine monk and satirist *par excellence* of the monkish state, in 1521 (the year of the *Furioso*'s second edition) he produced the extraordinary work known as *Baldus*, named for its hero. This is a comic epic in twenty-five books of macaronic hexameters, a blending of Latin and the author's own coarse Mantuan dialect, in which the vernacular is treated to the inflections of Latin: that is, the poet gives to Italian words the endings that Latin words would have when declined and conjugated. At least in moderate doses, the bathetic effect is exceedingly droll and pleasurable, as in the picture of the morning star appearing in her rosy wagon. In Folengo, manner and matter live in incongruous conjunction. The narrative, heterogeneous and amorphous, turns on the picaresque adventures of the hero, born to French nobles but living in rustic exile in Italy where, in boorish surroundings in the Mantuan hinterland, the boy gives himself over to a life of low adventures as leader of his three companions – the giant Fracassus, the wily Cingar ('praticus ad beffas') and Falchettus. This sounds quite familiar. It comes as no surprise to learn that Folengo once penned an *Orlandino*, retailing familiar stories drawn from Andrea da Barberino, or that Pulci's *Morgante* and *Margutte* provide the model for Baldus' first two companions – though Folengo goes one better than Pulci by making Falchettus half-man, half-dog, thus descending, in a freak of his bizarre imagination, into the truly subhuman.

While Folengo approaches the romantic tradition light-heartedly, there were others who did so with more serious intent. Many of the humanist readers of Pulci, Boiardo and Ariosto were not impressed by the Italian poems which seemed to them to represent such a decline from the great epics of antiquity, and they turned increasingly to the works of the ancient literary theorists in order to discover a formula for the composition of epic poetry. Indeed a preoccupation with literary theory seems to have affected many of the men of letters of the mid-Cinquecento, and in a plethora of *poetiche* they attempted to lay down rules for all serious poetry. Their influence beyond the Alps was considerable, particularly in France. The genres most seriously affected were epic and tragedy (see below, p. 288), and their great master was, of course, Aristotle. The *Poetics* had been translated into Latin by Valla in 1498, but its real vogue came following Alessandro de' Pazzi's Latin version of 1536 and Francesco Robortello's commentary of 1548. This, and the atmosphere of increased religious discipline accompanying the foundation of the Jesuit order (1540) and the reopening of the Council of Trent (1562–3), left their mark on a whole generation of aspiring epic poets.

To Gian Giorgio Trissino (1478–1550) Ariosto's poem was displeasing precisely because it 'pleased the people', and he spent a lifetime attempting to regularise Italian letters in conformity with Aristotelian rules. Twenty long years of study and writing went into the making of the twenty-seven books of his *Italia liberata da' Gothi* ('Italy Liberated from the Goths', 1547–8), which he dedicated to Charles V and in which he imagined himself working to an Homeric model. His narrative was based on the historian Procopius' account of the struggle of the Byzantine general Belisarius against the Gothic occupiers of Italy in the sixth century – a subject that was to defeat Robert Graves as well. The poem was still-born and defies resuscitation. In his pedantic passion for classical correctness Trissino strives to avoid any obvious contamination from the literature of the people. He eschews the traditional and highly successful *ottava rima* for the fatal fluency of unrhymed hendecasyllabics (meant to approximate the stately hexameters of the ancients), and he carefully avoids taking any posture that cannot be matched in classical epic.

Worst of all, perhaps, is Trissino's irremediable solemnity. If anything, Italian epic literature had been supremely a literature of comedy, informed by a whole spectrum of the risible, from punning and rank obscenity to warm-hearted humour, coruscating wit and trenchant irony. In Trissino, comedy and the self-awareness that goes with it are notable by their absence. Witness his mawkish account of the maiden Elpidia, who upon seeing her lover die, begs to be immured as a nun, receives her daily bread on a turntable from pious hands, changes her name to Rigida in testimony of her asceticism, and in time comes to be venerated as Brigida, the saint. Elpidia-Rigida-Brigida: never before had Italian epic literature been so inept and unwary.

Where Trissino had sought to escape the trap of 'Gothic' romancing by recourse to the last flicker of empire in the pages of early medieval historians, two other writers of epic in this period, before Tasso's emergence on the scene, sought escape from the Carolingian-Arthurian morass in works of Spanish and French inspiration. Bernardo Tasso (1493–1569) wrote an *Amadigi* (1560) based on one of the best and most familiar romances of chivalry, *Amadis of Gaul* by Garci Rodríguez de Montalvo, and it was a work that his famous son, perhaps too much influenced by filial piety, exalted over *Orlando furioso*. The father's work was burdened by the same indecisions that later plagued his son, though the latter was more successful in resolving them. Unity of fable was Bernardo's object, but as the work proceeded he decided to vary his Aristotelian plan by interweaving several other plots into the main narrative. The result was an unwieldy poem of a hundred cantos, far too large a vessel for its dilute inspiration and an outrage, surely, to the heroic virtue of *mesure* (moderation). Bernardo's contemporary Luigi Alamanni (1495–1556), a political refugee in France, sought inspiration in the old French tale of *Gyron le courtois*, which provided the basis for his *Girone il cortese* (1548), but by now this kind of work was clearly an anachronism; towards the end of his life he produced an *Avarchide* (1570) in which a futile effort to blend Arthurian and Homeric materials and treatment only called attention to their stubborn incompatibility. Alamanni was an accomplished Virgilian in his *La coltivazione* (inspired by the *Georgics*), and an equally impressive Horatian in his satires, known to Sir Thomas Wyatt, who imitated them. In epic, however, he revealed a fatal lack of awareness and stunning wrong-headedness in choosing his subject: King Arthur's siege of the city of Bourges in northern France (Avaricum is its Latin name) is scarcely interesting enough to support the whole panoply of Homeric epic, and the action verges on the ridiculous when Lancelot plays the part of a sulking Achilles. The poem is obviously a misfire from the first.

The mass of mediocrity between Ariosto and Tasso makes for a melancholy spectacle. Epic is the most unforgiving of forms, and the number of poets' names that a busily hurrying Time throws into the river of oblivion is, as Ariosto well knew, considerable. To have missed greatness by whatever margin of miscalculation is to have failed unconditionally. We know the hard truth in our own tradition: not to be Milton is to be Blackmore or Cowley.

Tasso

By the time two-thirds of the sixteenth century had elapsed, Italian epic had had a single indubitable triumph in Ariosto, two flawed but beloved successes in Pulci and Boiardo, and a plethora of near misses and outright failures. At this point we must imagine the situation of the young Torquato Tasso (1544–93), driven, both through his filial relationship to a courtier-poet and through education and inclination, by epic ambitions. As a youth of fifteen or sixteen he had conceived an epic poem on a historical subject, the siege and liberation of Jerusalem by the Crusaders in 1096–9, and he had drafted over a hundred octaves, some of them fine enough to find a place in the completed poem. He had put this work aside, perhaps sensing that he was not yet ready for so ambitious a project, and instead composed a more conventional poem, a romance entitled *Rinaldo*, which was published a few years later (1562). In this work Orlando's cousin pursues his courtship of Clarice and wins her after a series of romantic adventures; in its twelve cantos, Tasso's first and last exploitation of a Carolingian narrative, he had gathered strength for the enterprise he had attempted earlier but aborted for lack of power to accomplish the task as befitted its dignity.

Returning decisively to his original theme in the *Liberata*, Tasso was faced with a situation different from that confronting the other three poets in the epic pantheon. When they undertook their works, Pulci, Boiardo and Ariosto were responding to purely literary and historical circumstances. All three shared an immersion in the conventions of Carolingian narrative, and all three composed at a time when no critical tradition governed chivalric writing – indeed the romantic epic, perhaps not even recognised as such, was a new form that seemed simply to have arisen with Boiardo's felicitous incorporation of a Virgilian dynastic theme into a romance about Orlando in love. Critics, not yet formed into partisan bands or coalescing into academies, propounded no critical orthodoxy; Bembo's linguistic laws, assiduously observed by Ariosto, are the closest we come to a code of correctness. Problems of unity and multiplicity were inevitably present, but they appear to have been solved in purely practical literary terms, as in Ariosto's adoption of a triadic scheme to provide a unifying framework for his multifarious narrative. If any part was played by theoretical considerations in the composition of the *Morgante*, the *Innamorato* or the *Furioso*, history has not recorded it; it must be deduced from the texts themselves and from the general cultural milieu. The clear danger to be avoided is that of anachronism – judging works by standards of which the poet was clearly unaware.

The case is very different with Tasso, about whose theoretical preoccupations it is possible we know too much. No other Italian Renaissance poet is so self-conscious in his determination to devote himself worthily to the high calling of epic poetry. He had good reason to be prudent and deliberative in his choice of epic subject and manner of proceeding: an interrelated series of political, religious and literary circumstances conspired to create special conditions for the writing of epic in the last third of the sixteenth century. The poet was an extraordinarily precocious fifteen in 1559, the year of the Peace of Cateau-Cambrésis. The treaty closed a long, bloody period initiated by the first French invasion of Italy in 1494 (the one recorded by Boiardo in his last stanza), and it put paid to the murderous Valois–Habsburg rivalry in Italy (against which Ariosto had raged in some remarkable stanzas) by establishing Spanish rule over Milan, Naples, Sicily and Sardinia. For a poet conscious of the altered state of the peninsula and the powerlessness of a people under foreign domination, a return to the natural ebullience of his predecessors in works permeated by the comic spirit was scarcely conceivable: a new solemnity, a new decorum were the fashion for the times. Again, by 1559 the Counter-Reformation was fully embattled, intent upon establishing an orthodoxy in the arts parallel with that in religious practice. Reinforcing these shifts in sensibility, the Aristotelian revival had within two decades induced a new view of classical epic dignity in contrast to the multiplicity of chivalric epic. Finally, by 1559 Europe had long grown accustomed to fleets of Turkish ships striking from North Africa and operating brazenly along the coasts of the Mediterranean. In the 1540s Europe had witnessed the scandalous collusion of the French with the Turks in their mutual struggle against imperial Spain. Closer to home, Bernardo Tasso had participated in Charles V's attack on Tunis; his daughter had narrowly escaped capture in a Turkish raid on Sorrento. This was to bring home in unmistakable fashion the centuries-old antagonism of the two religions and render the notion of crusade as a theme for epic not only viable but urgent. Lepanto was being enacted even as the poet wrote.

In other times and circumstances, a young poet would find his anxieties sharpened merely by the looming shapes of Homer, Virgil, Boiardo and Ariosto: a sufficiency of powerful models. Tasso had not only these to master and challenge, but a whole range of literary criticism to absorb and evaluate – criticism that had already affected the conduct of Trissino, Bernardo Tasso and Alamanni, and was to affect the young Tasso even in the midst of the composition of his *Liberata*, the writing of which he interrupted to deliver his

Discorsi, an explication of his critical principles. All in all, both in his poetry and in his theoretical writings he manifests an acute, sometimes deeply defensive, sense of what had already been achieved. He also gives clear evidence of knowing what was to be done to achieve greatness in epic and (equally important) what was to be avoided, given some recent resounding failures.

By a stroke of good fortune Tasso came to Ferrara in 1565 in the service of Cardinal Luigi d'Este: in that location he must certainly have experienced a sense of standing at the end of a long and glorious tradition. Unlike writers such as Trissino and Alamanni, who fetched their inspiration from distant Homer and rigid Aristotle, Tasso took advantage of the immediate past and the chivalric and Virgilian traditions of his new home. His concern was to preserve continuity by forging links with his predecessors while diverging purposefully and creatively from them; it was the way in which Virgil had responded to Homer, and Ariosto to Boiardo. At this stage it is more profitable to see him as a conscious craftsman working in relation to other poets than as a timid novice overwhelmed by a mass of conflicting critical views and adjusting his sails to the prevailing winds.

Comparison with his nearest models casts Tasso's art into some relief. His first gesture of homage and rivalry is in his title: it courts comparison by acknowledging but challenging Trissino's and asserting his own superiority: his subject is not the unavailing one of Italy liberated from the Goths in the dimly perceived sixth century, but Jerusalem, the city of the Holy Sepulchre, liberated from the infidel in an age of faith. Here, in effect, Tasso confronts the whole epic tradition of the city under siege, beginning with Troy and continuing with Virgil's Rome-in-embryo within the palisade erected along the Tiber, Boiardo's Albracca besieged by Christians, Ariosto's Paris besieged by Saracens, Trissino's Ravenna besieged by Belisarius, and even, perhaps, Alamanni's bathetic Bourges, besieged by Arthur. In this respect, something of Tasso's eagerness to court comparison with the greatest appears in the triple triumphant recognition of Jerusalem when the crusaders first sight the city, a deliberate recollection of the triple cry raised by Aeneas' sailors when they first sight the shores of Italy.

Boiardo and Ariosto had written fabulous narratives, in which Paris stood as the imperial city of Charlemagne and the centre of Christendom, a role it never had in history and that it had usurped in romantic literature from Aachen (Aix-la-Chapelle). From the first Tasso aims to assert the superiority of a subject drawn from history, surpassing Boiardo and Ariosto by writing of true happenings; in returning epic to the time of the Crusades, he turns also to the time of the composition of the *Chanson de Roland* and the first phase of Carolingian poetry. Again, while he is content to be shown the way by Trissino's learned incorporation of realistic military tactics and manoeuvres, Tasso knows the appeal of the fantastic. Knowledgeable writing about the operation of a siege tower may have been necessary to his plan, but the element from which the tower was to be constructed had to come from a wood filled with magic spirits, an allegorical wild wood of the world, abundant in temptation and long domesticated in romantic epic. As a consequence, the poem is never more exciting than when depicting the flashing splendour of an army on the march, nor more alluring than when subtly adumbrating the dim world of enchantment and magic. By achieving these poetic compromises Tasso reveals himself dependent and independent, scholarly and imaginative at one and the same time. Verisimilitude and magic cooperate to make a living poem.

The moment the *Liberata* opens, crucial choices have already been made. Bernardo Tasso's initial choice of blank verse for the *Amadigi* and Trissino's wrong-headed commitment to it are rejected in favour of the traditional octave. But Tasso asserts his independence by his rejection of the minstrel personality, whether popular or courtly, and of the introductory proems to each canto. He represents himself as a pilgrim, fittingly so in a crusader poem centring on a city which is to be the goal of Christian pilgrimage, and his muse is neither a Heliconian pagan nor the haughty mistress who Ariosto claims has deprived him of his wits: Tasso's muse is that of Christian poetry, who will inspire the poet with celestial ardours but who will also (so the poet prays) forgive him if he intertwines pleasurable fantasies with truth.

His head appears to have been filled particularly with the magical fantasies of Boiardo, from the initial dispersal of Goffredo's (Godfrey de Bouillon's) crusaders by the enchantress Armida, based on Angelica's seduction of Charlemagne's knights in the *Innamorato*, to the Fountain of Laughter which traps the Crusaders, as it does the Christians in Book III of Boiardo's poem (and later Guyon in *The Faerie Queene*, II, xii). And if Boiardo supplied Tasso with models for mysterious magic, Ariosto provided spurs to his imagination in a host of other details: the portrait of Armida, for example, which is modelled on that of Alcina. On a more grandiose scale Tasso often reveals his awareness of Ariosto's historical and dynastic themes and places himself in open rivalry. History, romance and epic establish concordant relations in the *Liberata* as in the *Furioso*, never more obviously than in Tasso's handling of Rinaldo, destined to be the forefather of the Estensi, like Ruggiero before him, whom Tasso hereby displaces. In clear reminiscence of Ruggiero, prophecies of Rinaldo's future glory and the fame of his dynasty are made by Peter the Hermit, while (in a balancing passage) the genealogy of his descendants, figured on a shield like that of Aeneas, is presented to him by the Wise Man of Ascalon: revelation and reason join together in anticipating the glorious future.

It was of course impossible for Tasso to undertake an epic at the court of his masters and fail to incorporate the eulogistic matter that had permeated the *Furioso*. But here he had been severely pre-empted by Ariosto who, in his poem-long narration of Ruggiero's difficult progress to marriage and rule, had exhausted that particular vein. Ariosto submits Ruggiero to a hierarchical series of triple temptations and makes his time of probation protracted and painful. Tasso limits Rinaldo to one temptation in his youthful lust for Armida; in effect he gives his reader the Alcina segment of Ruggiero's story only, without advancing further into sins of worldliness and pride. In the *Furioso*, Ruggiero in all his derelictions, rescues, retrogressions and concatenated moral difficulties emerges as a more complicated character, maturing at the end into an heroic model for Christian princes, and as a worthy husband for the always-constant Bradamante. At the end of the *Liberata*, by contrast, we must cope with the problem presented by the final redemption of Armida, who uses the words of the Virgin to Gabriel: a solution as astonishing as it seems distasteful. What are we to make of a converted witch as the ancestress of the Estensi?

The character of Rinaldo is further complicated by the *Allegory* that Tasso wrote after his poem was completed. Here he figures as the irascible power that, at first setting itself in opposition to the contemplative power (figured in Goffredo, the Christian leader) and creating disorder by removing itself from obedience, submits itself in the end and cooperates with it to re-establish order in the conquest of Jerusalem. This seems fairly innocuous as a very general statement about Rinaldo's role as a fractious lover and penitent warrior. But it flattens the complexity of the action, obliterates the interaction of the whole cast of characters, and utterly annihilates the infinity of rich detail of which the narrative is made. The *Allegory* is recognisably Neoplatonic in orientation, based on Plato's conception of the tripartite organisation of the human body, composed of reason, will and passion. In this respect, it has the look of an attempt to rival Ariosto on this ground also, for the *Furioso* had in 1549 been furnished with a voluminous, minutely annotated commentary by Simone Fornari, learned but redactive, and rigidly insensitive to Ariosto's literary tonalities. The *Liberata* gives evidence of no structural plan that could cause a reader to think in terms of a Neoplatonic allegorical design. Episodes like the magic wood and fountain are clearly allegorical in nature, but actions are more often 'realistic', and characters are depicted with careful attention to Aristotelian decorum and function in a manner appropriate to their roles rather than in obedience to some system of symbolic values.

The *Liberata* is at its strongest in depicting external rather than internal warfare; and in the creation of characters, disposed in recurring patterns and relationships, Tasso is unsurpassable. He delights in clearly distinguished and contrasted types: not only the three markedly different pagan heroines, but the two passive lover-martyrs, Sofronia and Olindo, balanced against the actively martial husband and wife, Odoardo and Gildippe; the Wise Man of Ascalon, representing the life of reason, balanced against Peter the Hermit, standing for theology; the self-possessed and mature Goffredo poised against the passionate adolescent, Rinaldo. The pagans are superbly realised: Argante and Alete are paired voices of force and guile in their embassy, an intransigent warrior and a subtle and menacing diplomat. And minor characters, like the spy Vafrino and the eunuch Arsete, emerge in the round through carefully particularised portraiture and behaviour in accordance with their station.

Most of them are superlative speakers, and we may entertain the thought that Tasso's characters are cast in a dramatic rather than symbolic or allegorical mode. The theatrical aspect of the *Liberata* emerges early on in the scene of Olindo tied to the stake with Sophronia to be burned for their faith and only then declaring his love: an extreme situation, rendered by the poet in a deliberately overwrought style: 'O mighty spectacle.' Armida, beseeching Goffredo's help with all the wiles of her seductive nature, is at the centre of another such dramatic moment, a prolonged soliloquy full of rhetorical mastery. Erminia enters upon extended soliloquy when debating whether to remain in Jerusalem or fly to Tancredi: a psychomachia between Honour and Love that divides her character into two warring personalities. Easily the most dramatically (not to say operatically) conceived scene of all is that in which Armida is abandoned by Rinaldo (like Ariadne and Dido and Ariosto's Olimpia before her), and the poet mediates between actor and viewer-reader with sympathy and encouragement: 'You closed your eyes, Armida . . . open your eyes, poor girl' (XVI, 61). Here the poet functions as an orchestrator of emotional responses to a character seen *en tableau*; elsewhere he repeatedly breaks into apostrophe, addressing Tancredi, Argante, Solimano, Clorinda and Goffredo at climactic moments in the narrative, in which he participates as spectator.

The poet is fully conscious of the dramatic aspect of his presentation. Armida's castle is said to be lit up like a theatre decorated for a nightly festivity, and she herself sits in concealment aloft, as in a theatre-box; the night-battle of Tancredi and Clorinda, the poet exclaims, is worthy of a crowded theatre (a possibility later exploited by Monteverdi); the provocative damsels in the fountain are like nymphs or goddesses rising at night from the floor of a stage; the trees of the magic wood produce nymphs just as stage-devices might reveal similar enchantments; Argante and Tancredi fight their last battle in a valley that seems like a theatre; and, in a moment of tragic solemnity, Solimano sees from the heights the pagan defeat being enacted below him, as if in a theatre or stadium.

All of this makes for profound contrasts between Ariosto and Tasso as creators of characters and presenters of actions. Where Ariosto invariably preserves an ironic distance from the creatures of his imagination, Tasso submits them to an emotional proximity. His is the art of the close-up, and he repeatedly assumes the role of *metteur en scène* and choric commentator. He draws his audience into the scene, openly invoking their admiration, compassion, indignation or sympathy for his actors, and he evokes specific emotional effects more often than intellectual ones. He empowers his characters by allowing them to speak in their own voices, at length and with skill; Ariosto most often relays their words and thoughts in indirect speech, filtering them through his ironic perspective. The crucial difference between Ariosto and

Tasso is that for the earlier poet the world was a forest that he oversaw in his
Neoplatonic providential role of the controlling artist. Tasso conceives of the
world as a theatre with many stages. The concept of *theatrum mundi*, of life as
spectacle, occupies a central place in Tasso's thought:

> an excellent poet (who is called divine for no other reason than that, resembling the
> sublime Artificer in his operations, he participates in His divinity) can create a poem
> in which, as in a little world, one can read here of the disposition of armies, there of
> battles by land and sea, the siege of cities, skirmishes and duels; here jousts and
> descriptions of famine and thirst, storms, fires and prodigies; there heavenly and
> infernal councils; here sedition, discord, errors, adventures, enchantments.

(Discorsi del poema eroico, 1594, Book III)

By the time that was written, one of the major literary quarrels of the
sixteenth century, the Ariosto-Tasso controversy had broken out. Beginning in
1549 with Fornari's anachronistic defence of Ariosto in Aristotelian terms, it
swelled into its second and more furious phase with the publication of the
Liberata in 1581: the appearance of a new and differently organised poem
offered unprecedented opportunities for taking sides. There is no need to
rehearse, even in remorselessly abbreviated form, the attacks and counter-
attacks by critics of pro- or anti-Aristotelian bias, as they raised objections
against Ariosto's supposed lack of unity, morality or originality, or pressed
their case against Tasso on grounds equally flimsy or pedantic. This is a vast
subject, admirably digested into well over a hundred pages of detailed analysis
by Bernard Weinberg. All kinds of documents figure in the contest – letters,
treatises, lampoons – and while they are frequently marked by ignorance,
special pleading, chicanery and pure malice, the debate also produced intelligent considerations of the subject by critics like Giraldi Cinthio and Francesco
Bolognetti, while it had the further effect of not so much creating as
determining a place for Ariosto in the literary canon.

Insofar as the debate proceeded under the shadow of an Aristotle made to
look tyrannical and peremptory, it offered little in the way of illumination for
Ariosto, whose concept of form was not unitary but derived from the
manipulation of multiplicities, as in the interlace technique of medieval
narratives. Starting out from mistaken beginnings, therefore, it lost itself in
ever more distant divagations from its supposed subject. Tasso's *Discorsi* of
1587 and 1594 form part of this remarkable episode, one that he afterward
regretted. The regrets were expressed in a document written to demonstrate the
superiority of his *Gerusalemme conquistata* (1593) over his *Liberata*. The
Conquistata is a reconsideration and rewriting of the *Liberata* so complete as
to constitute a wholly new poem, one from which characters in the earlier
work vanish utterly or come equipped with new names, and from which some
of the most ravishing episodes have been entirely expunged. The coincidence of
polemics and rewriting may raise the old spectre of a Tasso frightened by
Aristotelian proprieties and religious censorship, but the view is mistaken: the

Conquistata was the result of revisions already in hand as early as 1581, when Tasso was forced into print by the appearance of piratical and incomplete editions of the *Liberata*.

Tasso's career had been marked by nervousness and indecision, resulting in constant revision of his poetry and a terror of sending it out into the world. He had persuaded himself into some signal errors – that the *Amadigi* was greater than the *Furioso*, that the *Conquistata* was superior to the *Liberata*. But it is the *Liberata* that ensures his worldwide fame and his survival into our own time as one of the four greatest poets of Italy. In the twentieth century, Tasso and Ariosto have continued to be locked together as poets whose images and music are an enduring part of our visual and aural memory. There is every reason to believe that they will continue to flourish in the century that stretches before us.

13

Lyric poetry

Anthony Oldcorn

'Classicism' and 'anti-classicism'

The battle between the *Tassisti* and the *Ariostisti* over the epic does not have an obvious parallel in the case of lyric poetry, a genre about which the surviving fragment of Aristotle's *Poetics* is silent. 'Classicists' and 'anti-classicists' did on occasion exchange blows, but their opposition to one another should not obscure the fact that both – with the possible exception, among the latter, of iconoclast Pietro Aretino – are united in their devotion to antique precedent. Moreover, in spite of increasing literary specialisation, genres were still not airtight exclusive compartments; there was some give and take. We shall not be surprised to find poets who were predominantly 'classicists' engaging in 'anti-classicist' activities, or vice versa.

It is also remarkable, given the variously erotic subject-matter, how many of the poets we shall encounter, in both camps, were ecclesiastics. At first sight, to some modern eyes, an operation like that of Gerolamo Malipiero (1470s–1547), who in his popular *Petrarca spirituale* (1536) rewrote Petrarch's poems, systematically expunging any reference to profane love, might seem more comprehensible than the versified love pangs (heterosexual and homosexual) of canons, bishops and cardinals. We should remember, however, that the paradigmatic love celebrated by the Petrarchan classicists is upliftingly spiritual and Platonic, while the macrotext of the *Canzoniere* was read as the diary of a conscience torn between this world and the next, a conflict ultimately resolved in a renunciatory ascetic penitential direction.

The romantic myth of the 'popular' origins of anti-classicism has long since been exploded. At most we can point to self-consciously popular or vernacular ingredients. But the classicists too combine ancient and vernacular elements. The principle of imitation (*imitatio*) or emulation (*aemulatio*) remains constant: it is the models imitated that differ. There is nothing surprising about this. It is a tautology which bears repetition that the presence of the Latin and Greek classics in the Italian Renaissance (classical culture was after all what was supposed to be being reborn) is everywhere.

We should not forget that the fifteenth was still essentially a century of manuscript culture. It is tempting but misleading to project into the past our modern notion of 'publication'. Before the diffusion of printing, books had a relatively limited and compartmentalised – by modern standards, practically 'underground' – circulation. The widespread introduction of the printing press was an important factor in the modern organisation of literature which was the (some would say dubious) achievement of the sixteenth century. *Pace* the French writer Montaigne, who suggested we skip him entirely ('Laissons là Bembo'), the crucial figure in the consecration of Literature as the noblest activity of the gentleman was Cardinal Pietro Bembo (1470–1547).

Bembo and the classicist tradition

In August 1546 the seventy-six-year-old Venetian patrician Pietro Bembo, at the height of his fame as the undisputed master of Italian Renaissance classicism, addressed what would prove to be his final sonnet to his future biographer and ideal literary successor, a forty-three-year-old Florentine, since 1544 Archbishop of Benevento and Papal Nuncio (or ambassador) to Venice, Monsignor Giovanni Della Casa (1503–56).

Bembo's sonnet begins, as was not infrequent in such epistolary exchanges, with a figure of *interpretatio nominis*, a solemn word-play on the addressee's name: 'Casa, in cui le virtudi han chiaro albergo', 'Casa [= *house*], in whom/which the virtues have their illustrious dwelling'. The attribution of all virtue to a fellow poet was in keeping with Bembo's Ciceronian conception of the poet's role. Cicero's thumb-nail characterisation of the Orator, 'vir bonus dicendi peritus' (a good man skilled in speaking), and the idea that stylistic and ethical elevation are coterminous, underpin the verse of Bembo and of all his followers. Their supreme concern with the weighty style is meant to be read, as it is in Milton, as a guarantee of their inner moral earnestness. More than anything else, it is its public and formal Ciceronian eloquence that distinguishes the enunciation of these poets from the quintessential privacy of their master Petrarch's confidential and urgent soliloquies ('Che fai? che pensi? che pur dietro guardi?' [What dost? what thinkst? why always looking back?], 'Che debb'io far, che mi consigli, Amore?' [What must I do, what do you counsel, Love?]). Bembo's last sonnet, his swan-song, ended (with a poignant unintentional irony, if we consider the imminent disappointment of Della Casa's overreaching ecclesiastical ambitions) by linking the two together, as poets and public figures, in a sodality of well-earned satisfaction with their shared achievement: 'Qual può coppia sperar destin più degno?' (What worthier destiny can a couple hope for?). It was the equivalent for Della Casa of a public investiture as successor to Bembo's poetic crown. The choice was a wise and generous one, for whatever Bembo's indubitable merits as a pathfinder, Della Casa was to prove the greater poet.

Bembo died the following year, after a full and successful career. To someone who has made the effort required to enter the confined and stylised (the epithet 'mannerist' is often bandied, and for several poets, among them Della Casa, it seems a useful label) world of sixteenth-century lyric poetry, which is substantially Bembo's creation, the sonnet to Della Casa is a moving testimonial – 'a masterly farewell', to quote Bembo's modern editor (and alter ego) Carlo Dionisotti, 'to poetry and to life'. Bembo has been alternately exalted and reviled as the chief architect of sixteenth-century classicising Petrarchism, depending on the critic's opinion as to the usefulness of that phenomenon; but as to its *importance*, both within Italy and beyond, of that there can be no doubt.

The culture of the previous century, though bilingual in Latin and Italian, had tended to keep the ancient and modern languages separate, with Latin being reserved for serious writing. Court literature in Italian, when not ingenuously contaminated with regional dialect forms, was 'ennobled' by lexical and morphological transfusions of Latin. Bembo's revolution consisted in attributing no less prestige to the Moderns than to the Ancients and to Italian than to Latin. His merit was to identify, so to speak, the give and take between vernacular *langue* and *parole*, between literary and demotic Italian, and to proceed to 'purify the language of the tribe' by applying to the mother tongue the same grammatical and stylistic rigours, the same 'work of the file' (in Horace's Latin 'labor limae') that the classical authors of antiquity and the neo-Latin authors of the previous century had brought to their Latin compositions. Or, to be more precise, his merit was to recognise that Petrarch had already done so. If a modern Latin humanist was urged to elaborate his prose or poetic style by imitating the best ancient authors, then an Italian stylist also needed a model to follow. After a profound study of the vernacular canon, Bembo decided, with a bow to the exalted subject-matter treated by Dante, that the stylistic and thematic model for Italian verse was essentially Petrarch, the so-called father, paradoxically, of neo-Latin humanism, and himself a staunch proponent of the principle of eclectic imitation, but who in practice modelled his Latin prose style on Cicero and his poetic style on Virgil. Admittedly, Bembo's Petrarch was not exactly the historical Petrarch we know today, but rather a biographically exemplary Augustinian Petrarch reinterpreted in the light of fifteenth-century Florentine Platonism.

Bembo's Petrarchan campaign can be said to begin in 1501. On the threshold of the century, turning the philological skills he had honed on the classics to modern vernacular literature, in a significant alliance with the great humanist printer Aldus Manutius, Bembo made himself responsible for a technological and cultural innovation hardly less far-reaching – though considerably less violent! – in its consequences than Martin Luther's publication in 1532 of his translation of the New Testament into German. The sixteenth century emblematically opened with the publication of the first *petrarchino* – a pocket-sized but critically impeccable edition (based on Petrarch's final fair copy of his Italian works, in large part in the poet's own hand, now in the Vatican Library, but then in Bembo's possession) of *Le cose volgari di messer Francesco Petrarcha* ('The Vernacular Works of Master F.P.'). The elegantly printed bare text of the *Canzoniere*, twenty-nine lines (the equivalent of two spaced sonnets) to the page, unencumbered by the suffocating commentary typical of the manuscripts and incunabula of the previous century, is for the first time divided into two parts: 'Sonnets and songs written during Laura's lifetime' and 'Sonnets and songs written after Laura's death'. The division stressed the model's apparent autobiographical referentiality, at the same time drawing attention to two alternative rhetorical stances: the radical ambivalence of the poems *in praesentia*, and the elegiac grieving and visionary comfort of the poems *in absentia*. The latter mode is familiar to English readers from Milton's 'Methought I saw my late espousèd saint'. Other paradigmatic mourners were Vittoria Colonna and Veronica Gambara, and the Neapolitan Berardino Rota. In the same remarkably slim and eminently portable volume – the prototype of the little books ('the prayer-books of a lay culture,' remarks Dionisotti) which we see clasped in the hands of so many sixteenth-century portrait-sitters with literary pretensions – there follow Petrarch's triple-rhymed *Trionfi*.

To a modern reader, heir to the Romantic cult of the powerful individual personality, the abnegation of the Bembists is difficult to appreciate. Theirs was a collective enterprise with a shared ideal of perfection. There was, however, a built-in ambivalence between conformity to the model and the will to self-affirmation (and in this ambivalence lie the seeds of mannerism). Bembo's avowed ideal is to write poetry as close to Petrarch's as possible, in theme as well as in language; on the other hand, even he is not committed to complete self-effacement. One recent critic has suggested that, in the interplay – of prime importance in Petrarch's original poetic sequence – between microtext and macrotext, between the individual poem and the collection of which it forms an organic part, the macrotext the poets of the sixteenth century continue to hold in mind, more than a new book of their own, is Petrarch's *Canzoniere* itself, to which their works aspire to be a fitting addendum. In that case, it must be admitted that the following sonnet, composed in the intimate register, in which Bembo indulges the Platonic myth of the soul's return to the star whence it came would not be out of place in the elegiac second part of the *Canzoniere*. By mentioning Laura in his text, however, Bembo deliberately undermines the ventriloquial illusion and makes his own independent claim as a masterly recreator:

> Quando, forse per dar loco a le stelle,
> il sol si parte, e 'l nostro cielo imbruna,
> spargendosi di lor, ch'ad una ad una,
> a diece, a cento escon fuor chiare e belle,
>   i' penso e parlo meco: in qual di quelle
> ora splende colei, cui par alcuna
> non fu mai sotto 'l cerchio de la luna,
> benché di Laura il mondo assai favelle?
>   In questa piango, e poi ch'al mio riposo
> torno, più largo fiume gli occhi miei,

e l'imagine sua l'alma riempie,
   trista; la qual mirando fiso in lei
le dice quel, ch'io poi ridir non oso:
o notti amare, o Parche ingiuste et empie.

(When, perhaps to make room for the stars, the sun departs, and our sky grows dark, and is scattered over with them, as, one by one, by the tens, by the hundreds, they come out fair and bright, I think and say to myself: in which of them does she now shine, whose like there never was beneath the circle of the moon, though the world has much to say of Laura? And thinking this I weep, and when I return to my rest, a greater flood fills my eyes, and her image fills my sad soul; my soul which gazing fixedly upon her, says to her what I dare not say: oh bitter nights, oh unjust cruel Fates.)

The inheritance of Sannazaro

It must be seen as a happy coincidence for the fortunes of Petrarchan classicism that in November 1530, eight months after the publication of Bembo's own exemplary *Rime*, there appeared posthumously in Naples the first edition of the *Rime* or collected vernacular poems of the prestigious senior Neapolitan humanist Jacopo Sannazaro (1457–1530). The publication is important, but not because Sannazaro's work in itself really looked towards the future or was in any way intended, like Bembo's, to forge an Italian literary nation. Though the book may have seemed to corroborate Bembo's classicising model, Sannazaro's Italian poems are if anything the refinement and castigation, on the part of a sensitive poet and a philologically severe Latin and vernacular humanist, of the linguistically and metrically exuberant provincial court poetry of the century into which he was born. His literary horizons from his villa at Mergellina were bounded by the tomb of Virgil and the bay of Naples, and his career is fairly neatly divided by his voluntary exile at the age of forty-four in France, whither he followed his friend and feudal overlord the former king of Naples Frederick of Aragon. Leaving the southern capital in September 1501, he returned to reside there permanently at the beginning of 1505, after Frederick's death.

Sannazaro's Italian production – which includes, in addition to his *Rime*, the mixed prose and verse *Arcadia*, the final corrected edition of which goes back to 1504 (see above, p. 159) – belongs for the most part to the period before his exile. After his return, from 1505 till his death in April 1530, his nostalgic *otium* would be devoted almost exclusively to the refined Latin works to which – like Petrarch himself before him, but unlike Bembo – with a significant cultural miscalculation, he commended his posthumous fame: the *De partu virginis*, a brief, much polished epic in three books on the birth of Christ, and the piscatorial eclogues. The political and dynastic crisis of the first three decades of the century led to a protracted eclipse of vernacular literature in the Neapolitan state, just as it did in Milan and, with the exception of the verse of Machiavelli, even Florence. So while Sannazaro's collected *canzoniere* exhibits an austere metrical fidelity to Petrarch, employing only those canonical poetic forms used by the Master, this particular pupil was far from subscribing to the unbending linguistic fidelity of Bembo. In fact the great Neapolitan humanist's Italian *Rime* became a prestigious model for later generations, partly because of his fame as a Latin stylist and partly due to the *ad hoc* linguistic corrections introduced after the author's death by his Roman editors, in conformity with Bembo's new conservative purism, within a month of their first publication, in the Blado edition. The spontaneity and promptness of this pious revision are a measure of Bembo's victory. The language of the *Arcadia*, published considerably before Bembo's codification of the vernacular, was also subsequently modified to conform to the new standards.

The classicising Petrarchism of Bernardo Tasso

In 1531, the year after the simultaneous publication of the first edition of Bembo's collected poems and of Sannazaro's posthumous *Rime*, Bernardo Tasso (1493–1569), twenty-three years younger than Bembo (and ten years older than Della Casa), published the first of three projected books of *Amori*. Bernardo did not refuse the example of Bembo, whose work was already well known in manuscript and whom he had known personally during his decisive formative years in Padua in the early 1520s. The title of his own collection, however, looked back to Boiardo's *Amorum libri* and beyond that to Ovid's *Amores*. In the preface, Bernardo speaks of his imitation of the Provençal and Italian 'moderns' adduced by Bembo in the *Prose della volgar lingua*, but he also stresses his own direct imitation of antique and recent neo-Latin models. The Padua of Bernardo's late twenties, even more than nearby Venice, was an important centre of avant-garde literary speculation. On the vernacular side, besides Bembo and the grey eminence of Trifone Gabriele (c. 1470–1549), Bernardo frequented many of the poets and theorists who would figure in the later dialogues of the Aristotelian Sperone Speroni (1500–1588) (see above, p. 184). Padua was also an important outpost of neo-Latin literary activity and host to a number of important humanist poets who chose to continue writing in Latin (some of them exclusively) and whom Bernardo greatly admired. The five books of Bernardo's collected *Rime*, published thirty years later in 1560, would eventually encompass a large variety of metres, themes and genres: the *Amori*, the *Egloghe*, the *Elegie*, the *Poemetti* and the religious psalms or *Salmi*. As the century progressed and Italy and its organic intellectuals became less and less independent, we find an increasing incidence in their work of encomiastic poems in praise of the innumerable members of Italy's ruling families, their consorts, and their actual or would-be foreign allies.

One of Bernardo's chief claims to fame is as the transplanter into Italian of the classical ode, for which his chief model is Horace and which he reinvents as a variable sequence of five- or six-line stanzas, each made up of regular combinations of seven- and eleven-syllable lines (*settenari* and *endecasillabi*). Long before suburbia, people found other people's grass greener, and, while the peasants themselves were no doubt muttering under their breaths against the idle and irresponsible lifestyle of the upper classes, Bernardo was busy concocting, in revived pastoral verse, an idealised portrait of their own carefree idyllic 'pastoral' existence, blissful compared with the harsh realities of the life he knew as a courtier. In defence of the pastoral or bucolic convention it should be pointed out that, ever since the Greek Theocritus, the shepherd had been represented as an alter ego of the poet. Pastoral poetry is, then, more autobiographical than it looks. What Bernardo is regretting when he compares the poet's condition to the shepherd's is his own lack of leisure for writing.

The georgic and didactic poem

Another literary genre, which reflects a more realistic taste for country life, the didactic georgic *epyllion* and its offshoots, enjoyed considerable popularity in the sixteenth century and is connected with an important metrical innovation: the invention of blank verse, known in Italian as *endecasillabi sciolti*. Historians of Italian prosody point out that unrhymed isometric eleven-syllabic verse was not altogether unknown before it was used by Gian Giorgio Trissino (1478–1550) in his classicising tragedy *Sophonisba* (1524; see below, p. 288) and his epic poem *L'Italia liberata da' Gothi* (see above, p. 241). His invention was contested by the Florentine Luigi Alamanni (1495–1556), a member, like Trissino, of the group of anti-Medici intellectuals identified with their meeting place in the Oricellari gardens in Florence, and himself a tireless translator and experimenter in rendering classical prosodic forms and literary genres in Italian. Alamanni published his elegant (if not always vigorous) six-book *La coltivazione* while in exile in Paris in 1546. Based on Virgil's *Georgics*, and in the tradition of Hesiod's *Works and Days*, it describes in detail the seasonal occupations of the farmer, with topical excursions on the current state of political affairs in Italy and France. The son of the founder of the Florentine group, Giovanni Rucellai (1475–1525), a nephew of Lorenzo de' Medici and the author of two blank-verse tragedies, *Rosmunda* and *Oreste*, is best known for his free adaptation of the fourth book of Virgil's *Georgics*, a didactic poem on bee-keeping entitled *Le Api* (composed 1524). From Alberti in the fifteenth century to Carducci in the nineteenth, classicists have been challenged by the problem of reproducing quantitative Latin prosody in Italian.

Another experimenter was the Sienese Claudio Tolomei (1503–1565), whose idyllic vision of nature still touches us, though his technical manifesto *Versi e regole della nuova poesia toscana* ('Verses and rules of the new Tuscan poetry') (1539) – one of the scores of treatises on poetics and the art of poetry which this Age of Criticism produced – fell in practice upon deaf ears. The prolific Neapolitan Luigi Tansillo (1510–68), a follower of Sannazaro rather than Bembo, has a number of bucolic and georgic poems to his credit, though in rhymed eight-line stanzas or tercets rather than in blank verse. Among them are his bacchic *Vendemmiatore* (1532), one of the first works to be placed on the Catholic Church's Index of Forbidden Books. We would be forgetting the radically changed social and religious climate ushered in by the Counter-Reformation, however, if we were to show surprise at the fact that Tansillo's varied and voluble production – which includes poems on such diverse and homely topics as the desirability of maternal breast-feeding, *La balia* (composed 1552), or advice on buying a farm, *Il podere* (composed 1560), both written in the *terza rima* metre and the conversational Horatian tone used by Ariosto in his *Satires* – could make room at the end for a prolix and didactic religious poem in *ottava rima* like the *Lagrime di San Pietro* (composed in 1559), in which Saint Peter takes a full thirteen cantos to say he's sorry. This new genre, however, soon became extremely fashionable and was widely imitated.

Ariosto's realistic non-alignment

Ludovico Ariosto (1474–1533), the complex (but uncomplexed) author of the *Orlando furioso* (see above, pp. 234–9), was essentially a narrative and dramatic poet – 'dramatic', not in the sense of violent contrasts (he soon abandoned his youthful attempts at tragedy and decided to stick to comedy), but in his ability to evoke the living, speaking voice. After cutting his humanistic teeth on accomplished Latin hexameters, in addition to the seven epistolary *Satires* (see below), he managed between 1494 and 1525 to accumulate a respectable collection of shorter poems in Italian (5 *canzoni*, 41 sonnets, 12 madrigals, 27 triple-rhymed *capitoli* and 2 eclogues). It may be useful for the reader to recall that the first edition of the *Furioso* appeared in 1516, and the third, revised under the linguistic influence of Bembo, in 1532, eight months before Ariosto's death. The narrative *Furioso* was, then, a lifetime in the making, and the poet's minor works were to a large extent, in Gabriele D'Annunzio's later phrase, 'sparks from the anvil'. The variety of metres employed by Ariosto, and in particular the large number of *capitoli* (more than half as many as the sonnets), is the first clue to the persistence of the models of the previous century and his refusal to yield completely to the new Petrarchan dispensation. This versatile (but fundamentally narrative) prosodic form, the metre of Dante's *Comedy*, was much favoured for lyric poetry in the Quattrocento and was, as we saw, still represented, as was the brief pastoral eclogue, in Sannazaro's transitional *Rime*. Both forms were eschewed, however, by the fastidious Bembo and hardly ever used by his serious sixteenth-century followers. (The verse 'love letters' of Veronica Franco

[1546–91] are another notable exception.) Instead, the *capitolo* became, as we shall see, the preferred metre of the subversive parodic opposition, while the dramatic eclogue took on the structures of classical tragedy and blossomed into the new tragi-comic pastoral genre.

Ariosto's refusal to conform to the hieratic new style was a question of literary temperament. The closest he comes to the timeless absolute epiphanic moment to which the Petrarchan classicists aspired is in his madrigals, no longer the isometric compositions we find in Petrarch, but *poesia cantabile*, poetry for music, in which long and short lines are disposed, with frequent internal and external rhyme and other verbal reiteration, in free musical order. Hitherto a minor prosodic form, the madrigal's range was to be greatly extended by later 'mannerists': the prolific Florentine Giovan Battista Strozzi (1505–71); the blind actor, musician and poetic improviser Luigi Groto (1541–85); and the masterful Torquato Tasso (see below). The madrigal, ally and enemy of time, seeks the significant in the apparently insignificant. The ephemeral occasion of this charming madrigal by Ariosto, for example, is the therapeutic shaving of his mistress's hair; the effect lies in Ariosto's exploitation of the 'poetic function' of language and in the music of the words, more than in their meaning:

> Se mai cortese fusti,
> piangi, Amor, piangi meco i bei crin d'oro,
> ch'altri pianti sì iusti – unqua non fôro.
> Come vivace fronde
> tòl da robusti rami aspra tempesta,
> così le chiome bionde,
> di che più volte hai la tua rete intesta,
> tolt'ha necessità rigida e dura
> da la più bella testa
> che mai facessi o possa far Natura.

(If ever you were kind, weep, Love, weep with me for the lovely golden curls, for never was there a juster cause for weeping. As a harsh tempest strips the living leaves from robust branches, so the fair locks, from which you often used to weave your net, inflexible and grim necessity has stripped from the loveliest head that ever Nature made or ever can make.)

Ariosto's lyric *capitoli*, on the other hand, have an epistolary directness and a concreteness of language reminiscent of the *Satires*, as this opening shows:

> Poich'io non posso con mia man toccarte,
> né dirti a bocca il duol che ognor mi accora,
> tel voglio noto far con penna e carte.

(Since I can't touch you with my hand, or tell you with my mouth the grief I constantly suffer, I want to let you know with pen and paper.)

Michelangelo

'Was Michelangelo [Michelangelo Buonarroti, 1475–1564] a poet too?' asked
the critic Mario Fubini in an article in the newspaper *La Stampa* as recently as
1964. Most critics today would agree that this single-minded and rather
intimidating (and, with almost eighty-nine years to his credit, remarkably long-
lived) personality was one of the most important poets of the century; but that
is about all they would agree on. That and the fact that he was anything but a
professional organised for writing. One of the problems is the scattered state of
the surviving texts, jotted down in the margins of drawings, on bills and
contracts, on the backs of letters, wherever he happened to be working at the
time. A lot of what survives does so in the form of striking but enigmatic
fragments or variant redactions of the same poems. They suggest a piecemeal
technique of composition (though it would be going too far to speak of a
deliberate poetics of obscurity or the 'unfinished'), confirmed by the iterative
paratactic litany-like syntax of much of the more finished work.

The selected and revised transcription of his poetry which the seventy-one-
year-old Michelangelo was working on, possibly with a view to publication,
never saw the light of day. It was not in fact until 1623, almost sixty years after
the poet's death, that his poetic works were published by his grand-nephew
Michelangelo Buonarroti il Giovane. Furthermore, the editor's family piety
and consequent censorship were such that, of the 302 pieces known to us
today, only 137 were included. Girardi's current critical edition distinguishes
three fairly obvious periods: apprenticeship, from 1503 to 1532 (poems 1–55);
maturity, from 1532 to the death of Vittoria Colonna in 1547 (56–266); and a
final penitential phase of Petrarchan reconciliation from 1547 to 1560 (267–
302).

Once we have decided he is a poet, the next question is whether Michelangelo is a Petrarchist. And if not, what is he? One of the most lapidary
definitions of Michelangelo's verse, which seems to oppose programmatically
the concrete realism one would expect of a practising painter, sculptor and
architect to the prating and derivative rhetoric of the Petrarchists, 'things' to
'words', is taken from a verse letter sent by the burlesque poet Francesco Berni
(see below, p. 270) to Michelangelo's friend, the Venetian painter Fra Sebastiano del Piombo, probably in September 1534, a few months before Berni's
own death. The words in italics in the text that follows are contemptuous
quotations from the stylised Petrarchan vocabulary:

> tacete *unquanco, pallide vïole*
> e *liquidi cristalli* e *fiere snelle*;
> e' dice cose e voi dite parole.

(Be still *eftsoon, pale violets,* and *liquid crystals* and *nimble hinds*: he has things to
say, while all you say are words.)

Unlike the other poets treated in this chapter, not excluding Berni and his school, Michelangelo was exceptional in having small Latin and less Greek. It is hard to imagine him in his study. His pithy, energetic and down-to-earth letters deal almost exclusively with practical matters and are devoid of intellectual, artistic or literary speculation. It is remarkable how little written evidence he left behind, apart from his verse, of his spiritual life. The poems are practically all we have to go on. In the narrow, decorous, exclusive, hyper-literary context of mid-century Petrarchan humanism, eloquent and elegant, polished and polite, the dogged urgency of Michelangelo's verse, with its stubborn indifference to current fashion, its wilful Shakespearian contrariness (I am thinking of the *Sonnets*), its almost perverse insistence on matter over manner, is absolutely singular. The Petrarchan model had at its best, in a poet like Della Casa, its own oblique, exquisitely literary intensity, but this is something different. It is as if, while the busy hands were occupied, the mind were to return obsessively, abstractedly, almost mechanically, to fathoming the same relationships, turning over the same irreconcilable concepts, mouthing with variations the same rhythmical words and phrases. Against the dominant culture of the single model, Michelangelo displays a bewildering experimental openness to a variety of styles and registers: Petrarch of course, but also Dante – the Dante of the *Comedy* as stylistic *summa*, if not precisely the Dante of the ultra-expressionistic *rime petrose* – and then the pleiad of the Silver Age Florence in which he himself had made his now-distant début – Lorenzo de' Medici, the vernacular Poliziano, the demotic Luigi Pulci, the bizarre surreal Burchiello – in a word, the Florentine canon of a previous generation, now officially repudiated.

Michelangelo's central obsession seems to be a radical polarisation of the Christian Neoplatonic notion of man's intermediate position between the 'brute' and the 'angel', between materiality and spirituality, immanence and transcendence (of the self), wellness and sickness, beauty and deformity, death and eternity, non-existence and existence, nothingness and being. He lacks the ability – perhaps even the desire – to still his grief in song ('perché cantando il duol si disacerba' ['because the pain becomes less acute in singing'] is a cornerstone of Petrarchan poetics). As evidence of the superior moral sensibility we mentioned apropos of Bembo, there is often something complacently self-regarding about Michelangelo's contemporaries' poetic sufferings. It is one more thing they're good at. In their verse, it is the exceptional moral being of the poet, not that of the beloved catalyst, that is foregrounded. Except perhaps in the case of the realist Ariosto, we are not made curious about their existential relationships. Here, however, it is neither the subject nor the object but their clash which is the centre of attention. Michelangelo is less consoled by philosophy, less culturally carapaced, more vulnerable. His infatuations were swift and intractable – witness the desperation of his sonnet to Tommaso Cavalieri, 'Veggio co' be' vostri lumi' ('I see with your fair eyes').

The contrite Christian sonnets of the final period, 'Carico d'anni e di peccati pieno' ('Burdened with years and full of sin'), for example, or 'Di morte certo, ma non già dell'ora' ('Certain of death, uncertain of the time'), or 'Le favole del mondo m'hanno tolto / il tempo dato a contemplar Iddio' ('The fables of the world have taken from me the time I could have given to contemplating God'), are fine variations on an ascetic Petrarchan topos. More typical of the poet's inveterate eclecticism is the way he rises to the artistic challenge of voicing the same despair in the violently hyperbolic mode and vigorous street language of the expressionist *capitolo* 'I' sto rinchiuso come la midolla' ('I'm caged up like the marrow in the bone'):

> Amor, le muse e le fiorite grotte,
> mie scombiccheri, a' cemboli, a' cartocci,
> agli osti, a' cessi, a' chiassi son condotte.
> Che giova voler far tanti bambocci,
> se m'han condotto al fin, come colui
> che passò il mar e poi affogò ne' mocci?
> L'arte pregiata, ov'alcun tempo fui
> di tant'opinïon, mi reca a questo,
> povero, vecchio e servo in forz'altrui,
> ch'i' son disfatto, s'i' non muoio presto.

(Love and the Muses and my flower-grown grottoes, my precious scribblings, gone up in cymbals, screwbags, hashbills, shitwipes, cowshops. What was the point of making all those puppets, if this is where they got me: a man who swam the ocean and drowned in his own snot? The touted art, for which I was a legend in my time, has brought me to this pass: poor and grown old, a slave to other people, I am undone if I do not die soon.)

This, then, was Michelangelo. Out of step with his time. Strung out between desperation and despair. A proper poet.

Della Casa and Magno

In a century of stylists, the century's greatest stylist was also the century's greatest lyric poet. However, to someone who comes to Giovanni Della Casa (1503–56) via his 'filial' relationship with Bembo, and via his sixty-four austere *Rime* (published in 1558, less than two years after his death, by his secretary Erasmo Gemini) it is surprising to learn of his youthful association with the 'bohemians' of the libertine Roman school of Francesco Berni.

Della Casa, the future author of the *Galateo* (1558; first English translation, 1576), a courtesy-book so popular that even today its eponymous title is a small-letter Italian noun signifying 'etiquette', 'good manners', (see above, p. 210), was born in 1503 into a Florentine merchant family with commercial interests in Rome. He was given a solid grounding in Latin and sent to study law at Bologna and Padua, where instead he pursued his literary interests and became proficient in classical Greek. It was in Padua in the late 1520s that he first met Bembo. Back in Rome in the 1530s he decided, like so many intellectuals of the day, on what was in practice a civil service career in the Church. In Rome also he strayed with Berni in the gardens of Priapus – an errancy, one imagines, more literary than physiological. What is important to bear in mind is that the choice of genres and registers was not an either/or: the greatest Petrarchan craftsman of the day saw nothing wrong in stooping to scatology, just as the foremost cultivator of Italian eloquence could continue to polish his Latin. After all, even Berni was the competent author of elegant Latin *carmina*.

With abnegation and extraordinary prescience, this *grand rhétoriqueur* refined his instruments, the Petrarchan *canzone* and especially the sonnet, for the best part of a lifetime, confident, it appears in hindsight, that the new form would evolve, or *become*, a new content. His existential defeat was his poetic victory. Petrarch's sonnets flow, but over divisions: each line tends to be end-stopped, the first quatrain to be divided from the second, while the two quatrains are kept separate from the tercets. Moreover, the syntactical structure mirrors the metric. This regularity and correspondence are deliberately broken down by Della Casa – his chief technical innovation, variously exploited after him by Torquato Tasso, John Milton and Ugo Foscolo, is the sustained use of enjambement – to create a gravity and amplitude of diction, a dramatic tension between phrasing and prosody, that justify his contemporaries' praise for his sublime and magnificent manner. The sixty-fourth and final poem of his brief *canzoniere*, a sonnet, is a solemn meditation on the biblical myth of creation. But, more than anything else, it is an unspoken plea to the omnipotent divinity to introduce the same order he created in space and time into the poet's inner chaos:

> Questa vita mortal, che 'n una o 'n due
> brevi e notturne ore trapassa, oscura
> e fredda, involto avea fin qui la pura
> parte di me, ne l'atre nubi sue.
>   Or a mirar le grazie tante tue
> prendo, ché frutti e fior, gielo e arsura,
> e sì dolce del ciel legge e misura,
> eterno Dio, tuo magisterio fue.
>   Anzi 'l dolce aer puro e questa luce
> chiara, che 'l mondo a gli occhi nostri scopre,
> traesti tu d'abissi oscuri e misti:
>   e tutto quel che 'n terra o 'n ciel riluce
> di tenebre era chiuso, e tu l'apristi;
> e 'l giorno e 'l sol de la tua man son opre.

(This mortal life, which slips by in one or two brief nocturnal hours, dark and cold, had until now engulfed the pure part of me in its black clouds. Now I begin to contemplate Thy many graces, for fruits and flowers, frost and heat, and so sweet a law and measure of the heavens, everlasting God, were of Thy making. Nay, the sweet air and this clear light that discovers the world to our eyes Thou drewest from the dark confused abyss: and all that shines on earth or in heaven was shut in darkness, and Thou openedest it; and daylight and the sun are Thy works.)

Though it extended to all of Italy, indeed all of Europe, nowhere was Bembo's influence more felt than in his native Venice. Indeed the most important poet of the close of the sixteenth century was also a Venetian. It was appropriate that the new sensibility displayed in the meditative *Rime* of Celio Magno (1536–1602), author of the monumental religious *canzone* 'Deus', should inaugurate the new Baroque century, appearing, in a single volume with those of his friend Orsatto Giustinian (1538–1603), in 1600. As Eliot remarked of Magno's younger contemporary John Webster, the Italian too 'was much possessed with death / And saw the skull beneath the skin'. This is clear from his sonnet, 'Trovo dovunque io giro 'l guardo ...' ('I find wherever I turn my gaze') where love as the ruling moral metaphor is finally exorcised by an omnipresent *memento mori*, and Petrarch's urgent insistence on the flight of time is obsessively fixed in an emblematised contemplation of death.

Women poets

Emulation of the Bembist model gave a voice to an utterly unprecedented number of women poets. The 250 pages of Ludovico Domenichi's *Rime diverse d'alcune nobilissime e virtuosissime donne*, which, published in 1559, reflects the situation at mid-century, already contain poems by ninety-three 'most noble and virtuous' women poets, only a handful of whom are included in modern anthologies. The more or less well-known names are only the tip of the iceberg: the noble widows Vittoria Colonna (1490–1547) and Veronica Gambara (1485–1550); the self-made women or 'honest courtesans' Tullia d'Aragona (c. 1508–56), Gaspara Stampa (1523–54) and Veronica Franco (1546–91); the pastoral Laura Battiferri (1523–89), wife of the Florentine sculptor and architect Bartolomeo Ammannati; the recently rediscovered Chiara Matraini (1514–after 1597); the ill-fated Isabella di Morra (1520–46), murdered by her brothers; and Laura Terracina (1510–after 1577), so much a part of the Petrarchan system that she speaks of herself in the masculine gender; and, in the second half of the century, the female humanist Tarquinia Molza (1542–1617) and the actress Isabella Andreini (1562–1604), both celebrated by Torquato Tasso among others.

The widow of the lord of Correggio, Veronica Gambara, and the widow of the marquis of Pescara, Vittoria Colonna, exchanged elegant if rigid consolatory sonnets. The first published book of poetry by a woman was in fact the volume of *Rime della Divina Vittoria Colonna* (1538). Her high-minded grief and Platonic intellectualism won her the admiration of at least two of the greatest poets of the age, Michelangelo and Galeazzo di Tarsia. Spiritually tempted by ascetic reformist ideas, she was saved for Catholicism by the English Cardinal Reginald Pole.

The Romantic critic Luigi Settembrini, who was looking for authentic passion, thought he had found it in the talented singer and instrumentalist

Gaspara Stampa. He went so far as to declare her the only writer of the century, man or woman, worthy of the name of poet. The 311 collected love poems, the *Rime di Madonna Gaspara Stampa*, were published in the year of her death by her sister Cassandra and dedicated to Giovanni Della Casa. Exaggerating her non-conformity, nineteenth-century critics dubbed her the new Sappho; even today male scholars tend to refer to her with the patronising diminutive Gasparina. Though she died early, at thirty, her verse is dedicated to a series of lovers, most importantly to the Friulan count Collaltino di Collalto, who seems to have been less committed to their three-year relationship than she was. His frequent absences are the occasions for many of her poems. The novelty of her *canzoniere*, in the prevailing Petrarchist context of mutually ennobling reciprocal love, is its theme of love unrequited. Given her profession as a musical performer, we are not surprised by the large number of madrigals. Aside from its melic qualities, her poetry is simple and spontaneous, confessionally introspective, dramatic and discursive, diffuse rather than concentrated, but with moments of passionate emotional intensity. In a sensual and mellifluous sonnet in praise of the night, her inspiration is a realistic lyric *capitolo* of Ariosto's. Though it may remind us of the myths of Glaucus and Aesacus existentially rediscovered by Della Casa in his 'tragic' sonnet, 'Già lessi, e or conosco in me, sì come' ('I had read, and now know in myself, how ...') the Ovidian allusion to Alcmene remains an elegant and decorative mannerist conceit:

> O notte, a me più chiara e più beata
> che i più beati giorni ed i più chiari,
> notte degna da' primi e da' più rari
> ingegni esser, non pur da me, lodata;
>   tu de le gioie mie sola sei stata
> fida ministra; tu tutti gli amari
> de la mia vita hai fatti dolci e cari,
> resomi in braccio lui che m'ha legata.
>   Sol mi mancò che non divenni allora
> la fortunata Alcmena, a cui sté tanto
> più de l'usato a ritornar l'aurora.
>   Pur così bene io non potrò mai tanto
> dir di te, notte candida, ch'ancora
> da la materia non sia vinto il canto.

(Oh night, brighter and more blessed to me than the most blissful and the brightest days, night worthy to be praised by the foremost and rarest minds, not just by me; you alone have been the faithful dispenser of my joys; you have made sweet and welcome all my life's bitterness, bringing back to my arms him whose love bound me. The only thing I lacked then was not to become the fortunate Alcmene [whose lover Jove intervened astronomically to prolong their night together], for whom the returning dawn delayed so much longer than its custom. Yet even thus I will never be able to say such good of you, pure night, that my song's theme does not defeat my song.)

Torquato Tasso

Few authors have combined greatness and fragility in the same degree as Torquato Tasso (1544–95). Few have been so precocious or have declined so precipitously. The son of Bernardo Tasso was, on the twin counts of quantity and quality, the fourth major Italian poet in chronological order after Dante, Petrarch and Ariosto. Despite the rigid hierarchy he himself set up among the literary genres, with pride of place being assigned to the epic (see above, p. 244), Tasso's lyric poetry is crucial, indeed pivotal, acting as it does as a fresh recapitulation of the themes and modes of all of previous Western love poetry, from the *Greek Anthology* and the Latin lyricists to Petrarch, Bembo and Della Casa, and as a bridge to the baroque style of Giambattista Marino (1569–1625) and the *marinisti* of the coming century. Remarkably, many of Tasso's most accomplished lyrics go back to his mid-teens. His consummate art hides art, giving the impression of an amazing ease in treating a variety of subjects and situations. Perhaps because they were constantly corrected, the collected poems display no apparent technical or thematic development. At worst the later verse suffers from the self-mortification brought on by Tasso's increasing ideological conformity and waning personal conviction, all too thinly disguised by the mechanical rhetorical facility of this consummate technician.

Not all of his poetry deals with love. The incomplete and no longer satisfactory current editions, all of which derive from Angelo Solerti's positivist labours, gather 1,708 pieces, in approximate order of composition and in the three categories of love poetry (499 poems), occasional and encomiastic verse (the largest group, with 1,132 poems), and sacred verse (75 poems).

Torquato, who had already published, in rivalry with his father Bernardo, the precocious chivalric romance *Rinaldo* (1562), made his public lyric début at twenty-three in the collective miscellany *Rime degli Academici Eterei* (1567) with forty-two poems dedicated to the singer Lucrezia Bendidio. A decade later, during his imprisonment in Sant'Anna, he planned the publication of his collected poems, and after his release more or less approved the 1591 first volume containing his collected *Amori*, as well as a second volume, containing the panegyric *Laudi* and *Encomi* (1593). He died in 1595, and the third volume, of *Cose sacre*, never appeared in his lifetime. An acute and sensitive critic and theorist as well as a practitioner, he expressed his views on the lyric in his *Lezione sopra un sonetto di Monsignor Della Casa* ('Reading of a Sonnet by D.C.') and the *Considerazioni sopra tre canzoni di Messer G.B. Pigna* ('Considerations on Three Canzoni by G.B.P.'), both read before the academy in Ferrara in the early 1560s, and in the late dialogues *La Cavaletta overo della poesia toscana* and *Il Minturno overo della bellezza* ('[Orsina] Cavaletta, or on Tuscan poetry' and '[Antonio] Minturno, or on beauty').

In the *Cavaletta* Tasso declared music to be the soul of poetry, and in practice, though he preferred the sonnet (the modern equivalent of the Greek epigram) to the traditionally prized *canzone*, he favoured most especially the pastoral madrigal, which recalls the fragments of the *Greek Anthology* in its deceptive inconsequentiality and its free musical scheme of sinuously inter-woven long and short lines. The madrigal, whose most assiduous practitioner was the Florentine mannerist Giovan Battista Strozzi the Elder (1505–71), was eminently suited to Tasso's hellenistic bent, to the casual-seeming *sprezzatura* (the 'art of negligence') of his melodic and sensual inspiration; and while it is true that musicians like Gesualdo and Monteverdi were eager to set his unmatched madrigals to music, at their best the poems already evoke their own languid mood, weave their own subtle music, with no need for an *artifex additus*. Set against the ecstatic silence of a restless, evanescent yet absolute, natural landscape of sun, moon, clouds, stars, woods, fields, wind and water – a landscape without figures, idyllic and often broodingly melancholy, remote from the social commerce of the court – they eschew all realism, invoking fleeting sensations and the subtlest of vibrations, trusting all to suggestion, distilling meaning to a minimum. Precise terminology would detract from their evocative music by drawing attention to content (thought or image). Instead, these poems rely upon allusive (and elusive) 'figures of sound': frail words, alliteration, assonance, internal rhymes, repetition, verbal echoes:

> Qual rugiada o qual pianto,
> quai lagrime eran quelle
> che sparger vidi dal notturno manto
> e dal candido volto delle stelle?
> E perché seminò la bianca luna
> di cristalline stelle un puro nembo
> a l'erba fresca in grembo?
> Perché ne l'aria bruna
> s'udian, quasi dolendo, intorno intorno
> gir l'aure insino al giorno?
> Fur segni forse de la tua partita,
> vita de la mia vita?

(What dew or what weeping, what tears were those that I saw scattered from the cloak of night and from the candid faces of the stars? And why did the white moon sow a pure mist of crystalline stars in the bosom of the fresh grass? Why in the umber air were heard, as if in pain, round and around, the winds stirring till daybreak? Could these be signs of your departure, life of my life?)

Tasso's last (unfinished) work is the 9,000-line religious didactic poem in the blank verse tradition of Trissino and his followers, the erudite *Mondo creato*, an amplification of the summary account of creation contained in Genesis. Given its biblical inspiration and its unrhymed prosody, it lies some-where between Du Bartas's *Sepmaine* (1578) and Milton's *Paradise Lost* (1667). Just as he had striven to emulate Homer and Virgil in his epic *Gerusalemme liberata*, and still more closely in the unfortunate revised version *Gerusalemme conquistata* (1593) (see above, p. 249), Plato in his numerous prose dialogues, and Sophocles in the tragedy of *Re Torrismondo* (1587), here his rivals are the philosophical poets, Lucretius and Dante. Unfortunately Tasso was not a philosopher. His sources, which he accepts uncritically, are patristic rather than scientific. We can almost understand why his younger contemporary the scientist Galileo Galilei (1564–1642), a convinced partisan of Ariosto, had so little time for Tasso's poetry. A Catholic critic, Giorgio Petrocchi, once pointed out that the later Tasso, rather than religious or mystical, is an ascetic poet. Meant to celebrate the creation of the world, in its more convincing moments the *Mondo creato* looks forward to its eschatological destruction.

The anti-classicist tradition: parody, satire, burlesque

The reader should not think that because Bembo was virtuous there were no more cakes and ale. Anti-classicism was, however, essentially a Roman and northern Italian phenomenon. In the feudal south, even late in the century and in a dialect poet like the Sicilian Antonio Veneziano (1543–93), not to speak of the magnificent and solitary Galeazzo di Tarsia (1520–53), or of Angelo di Costanzo (1507–91) and Bernardino Rota (1508–75), the Neapolitan fore-runners of the ingenious conceits and imagery of the coming century, aristo-cratic Petrarchan classicism held exclusive sway. As the reader has learned in preceding chapters, there was an Italian comic tradition well before the 1500s, as well as a conspicuous tradition of poetry in the *terza rima* metre. Dante's *Comedy* and Petrarch's *Trionfi* are prestigious cases in point, but in the 1400s the metre was widely used in a variety of thematic contexts. The overlapping system of rhymes ensures narrative or argumentative continuity and gives the text an irresistible onward-moving flow. The innovation of the Cinquecento was to bring the two traditions together and to make *terza rima*, even more than the traditional expressionist sonnet, the privileged vehicle of comic poetry. Indeed, in this age of genre specialisation, the *capitolo in terza rima* (the term *capitolo* [= 'chapter'] derives, paradoxically in light of its new comic specialisation, from the subdivisions of Petrarch's visionary *Trionfi*), which had been excluded in all but a very few cases from collections of 'serious' verse, became the metre *par excellence* of two 'new' poetic genres: the modern revival of ancient poetic satire, and the *stile bernesco*, which derived its name from that of the Florentine 'irregular' Francesco Berni.

Ariosto and other satirists

Ariosto's seven satires, written between 1517 and 1525 but not published until 1534, take the form of wry confidential letters written to real-life addressees from among his family and friends. Together they present an unvarnished but appealing moral self-portrait, of an individual who doesn't want much but knows what he wants, at odds with the envious and flattering environment of the court, to which he is condemned by necessity as he struggles to hold on to his independence and his precious values of sincerity and freedom. Unlike his predecessors, who identified satire with the preachings and invective of an author like Juvenal, Ariosto's model is Horace, particularly (though he uses the title *Satires*), the more whimsical Horace of the *Epistles*, whose moral and literary tone the poet from Ferrara reinvents to subtle perfection. The laid-back wit and pithiness of their expression has made countless lines proverbial. Invariably autobiographical and concrete, the occasions of the *Satire* are more private than public. The author explains his reasons for not accompanying his patron Cardinal Ippolito d'Este to Hungary; he paints an unflattering portrait of the Roman Curia; he praises the unadventurous sedentary life; he deplores his trials and tribulations as governor of the wild Garfagnana district; he weighs the advantages and disadvantages of marriage – all of this in a masterfully flexible, vigorous and colloquial adaptation of the *terza rima* metre borrowed from Dante, a secondary model after Horace, modern and vernacular, whose own moral outrage the apparently affable and easy-going author can draw upon when the occasion calls for it. The overall tone, urbane, conversationally relaxed, but syntactically complex, may be illustrated by the opening lines of the first satire:

> Io desidero intendere da voi,
> Alessandro fratel, compar mio Bagno,
> s'in corte è ricordanza più di noi;
>   se più il signor me accusa; se compagno
> per me si lieva e dice la ragione
> per che, partendo gli altri, io qui rimagno;
>   o, tutti dotti ne la adulazione
> (l'arte che più tra noi si studia e cole),
> l'aiutate a biasmarme oltra ragione.

(I'm anxious to know from you, brother Alessandro, cousin Bagno, whether anyone remembers us at court; whether my master still finds fault with me; whether any of my friends gets up on my behalf to explain why I stayed on here when the others left; or whether the lot of you, with your degrees in adulation (the subject we study best and set most store by), back him up in blaming me beyond all rhyme or reason.)

Though published before those of Ariosto (in 1532), the twelve satires of the Florentine humanist and political exile Luigi Alamanni were actually composed slightly later. More in the self-righteous rhetorical Juvenalian vein than the familiar Horatian, and appealing directly to a powerful sponsor – the volume is dedicated to the French King Francis I – they declare vociferous war on the traditional social evils (war, the court, greed, ambition) and promote a renunciatory virtue-begins-at-home ideal of social good (peace, study, limited ambitions, a retired and productive life in the country). The third major satirist of the century is another writer from Ferrara, Ercole Bentivoglio (1507–73), who takes his lead from Ariosto's Horatian common-sense *aurea mediocritas* and unaffected informality.

Berni and the Berneschi

The black humourist Francesco Berni (1497/8–1535), a Tuscan transplanted
to the court of Rome, is an extremely influential but oddly contradictory and
elusive figure. Though he affects an unlettered persona, he began his literary
career writing sophisticated Latin love lyrics in the manner of Catullus. In the
parodic or violent *ad personam* attacks and caricatures of his sonnets and
open-ended *sonetti caudati* ('sonnets with a tail' – the longest appendage rivals
that of Alice's mouse, producing a 'sonnet' 77 lines long!), as well as in the
burlesque epistolary *capitoli in terza rima* for which he is even more famous,
he speaks in the first person singular, but paradoxically, unlike Ariosto, he is
never really autobiographical. Though the choice of metrical instrument and
the discursive throw-away manner are deceptively similar, the mask of this
enfant terrible, the most consistent anti-Petrarchist of the century – exhibi-
tionist, absurdist, sardonic, witty, bizarre, nonconformist, mocking, unpredictable, *maudit*, irresponsible, misogynistic, scurrilous, perverse – is in many
ways the very opposite of Ariosto's reasonable normalcy. Berni depicts himself
as a homosexual humanist, just the sort of person Ariosto feared as a teacher
for his son. Alongside the mercurial Berni, Ariosto may seem almost stodgy.
Where Ariosto rehearses conscientious choices, Berni invents performative
occasions. His brilliant *capitoli* are pseudo-extemporaneous monologues composed with a view to oral delivery. Enthusiastic accounts of his actual
recitations survive, and at least one poem, the *Capitolo dell'ago* ('On needles'),
survives as it was reconstructed from memory by the members of his
complicitous audience. His modern vernacular models are the fifteenth-century
Tuscan poets: Burchiello, Antonio Cammelli da Pistoia, Luigi Pulci, the 'rustic'
Poliziano, Lorenzo de' Medici's *Canzoni carnascialesche*. The obscene sexual
punning of Lorenzo's carnival songs was licensed by their seasonal performance as part of the pre-Lenten rites. Berni makes the carnival vacation, with
its suspension of all rules and norms, a permanent dimension of his verse.

One of the sub-genres Berni popularised, the paradoxical encomium, had a
venerable classical history and an immediate precedent in Erasmus' *Praise of
Folly* (1511). Berni's brilliantly inventive surreal nonsense poems in praise of
things normally condemned, 'things without honour', 'things of naught',
naughty things, far from being spontaneous artless inventions, are in fact part
of an exquisitely literary, even Alexandrian, tradition. The poet undertakes to
celebrate, with transparent double-entendre, the most unlikely Arcimboldo-
like collection of paraphernalia: chamber pots, needles, meat jelly or aspic,
eels, Aristotle, artichokes, the bubonic plague, gudgeons, young male servants,
peaches, and the card game known as *primiera*. Most of the objects turn out of
course to be phallic or pygal – in any case sexual – symbols. His epideictic
followers were to laud noses, carrots, mosquitos, church bells, syphilis, spit,
salad, spindles, ovens, mud, hard-boiled eggs, famine, thirst, ignorance, blindness, lice, excommunication, rings, kisses, keys, keyholes, broad beans, pea-

pods, figs ... but the list is a long one. Another undertaking of Berni's was to bring Boiardo's *Orlando innamorato* up to date by 'translating' it into hegemonic Tuscan and adding Ariosto-style moralising introductions to each canto (see above, p. 233). It is one more paradox that a poet who claimed to share Ariosto's impatience with dependence and confinement should choose to imprison himself stanza after stanza in such a formidable project.

Some critics see a progression from the freewheeling paradoxical divertissements of his first Roman period, provocatively and gratuitously obscene, to his later work, with its suggestions of a darker, more tragic, crueller vision. In the second *capitolo* on the plague, for instance, which evokes the grandiose physiological metaphor of the world as perpetual anabolism and catabolism, Berni mocks the received wisdom which sees the plague as a fearsomely negative phenomenon, presenting instead a savage pre-Malthusian scatological vision of the plague as salutary purge, an essential element in the hygiene of the universe.

What Bembo was to elevated poetry, Berni was to comic verse. His imitators are myriad and include, in addition to his immediate circle of correspondents, the humanist Francesco Maria Molza and the unfrocked monk Agnolo Firenzuola (1493–1543), author of an elegy 'On the death of an owl' which parodies Bembo's famous 'tragic' canzone on his brother's death ('Alma cortese, che dal mondo errante') – not forgetting otherwise serious poets like Giovanni Della Casa and Annibal Caro, as well as painters like Angelo Bronzino (1503–63) and, on one occasion, in reply to an epistolary *capitolo* from Berni, Michelangelo himself. The founding canon of the genre's creators was definitively established in the retrospective volume, *Primo libro dell'opere burlesche* (Florence, 1548), whose editor, Anton Francesco Grazzini (1503–84), one of the future founders of the conservative Florentine Accademia della Crusca (1582), salutes Berni as 'padre e maestro del burlesco stile'.

Pietro Aretino

It is a significant tribute to Berni's achievement that among his imitators we find his arch-enemy Pietro Aretino (1492–1556). Perhaps it is not surprising, given his future talent as a literary 'ventriloquist', that the colourful, complex and contradictory apprentice painter Aretino should have made his literary début in Perugia in 1512 with the *Opera Nova del Fecundissimo Giovene Pietro Pictore Aretino zoe Strambotti Sonetti Capitoli Epistole Barzellete et una desperata*, a collection of verse whose chief distinctions are its shameless self-advertisement, its prosodic omnivorousness, and the consummate cleverness with which it mimics current taste, which was of course the taste of the late fifteenth-century courtly lyric – the taste, for instance, of the prolific and immensely successful Ferrarese author Antonio Tebaldeo (1463–1537) and the witty and versatile court poet from Abruzzo Serafino de' Ciminelli known as l'Aquilano (1466–1500). Well into the 1500s, it was the poetic taste of the century's greatest prose *novelliere* Matteo Bandello (1485–1561; see above, pp. 228–9)). The very lack of reticence, the exuberance, the effrontery even, of Aretino's title, its tantalising promise of novelty ('opera nova') and of copia ('fecundissimo'), its bargain offer of a wide variety of popular metres (among which the soon-to-be canonical Petrarchan sonnet is merely an also-ran), its brash, non-humanistic provenance (its author identifies himself as an artisan, *pictore*, not an intellectual), and its patent option for linguistic expressionism over linguistic purity, all these are typical both of the backward-looking moment and of the forward-looking man.

A man without family or fortune, using his wits to avoid being dependent for success on the court (the fickle and subjecting court of the powerful, that is, the court of the courtier), Aretino could be said to have set about mastering its language in order to use the court against itself, as well as to stay one step ahead of inflation. This cobbler's son, who took the name by which he would be known throughout Europe from his birthplace Arezzo, repudiating his family name along with his absent father, was destined to achieve such an extraordinary position of national and international power and political influence with his pen that, by the time of the final 1532 redaction of his *Orlando furioso*, Ariosto could place 'the Scourge of princes, the divine Pietro Aretino' in his catalogue of great contemporaries.

Aretino's flair for imitation implied a corresponding gift for parody, and it is often difficult in his work to draw the line in his hyperboles of praise between obeisance and camouflaged aggression, between sincere homage (though the adjective 'sincere' is always suspect) and deflationary caricature. There was much that was opportunistic and much that was culturally (or politically) perceptive in Aretino's readiness, on the publication of Bembo's *Rime* in 1530, to climb aboard the Bembist bandwagon, placing his violent polemical and satirical vein at its service against, for example, a rebellious former member of the Venetian circle of Bembo and Trifon Gabriele, the defenceless, elegant and vaguely nostalgic poet Antonio Brocardo, whom Aretino boasted, Cyrano-like, of having killed with a sonnet.

Aretino has been called a histrionic and the first journalist; he was certainly the first 'celebrity'. His position of power and privilege (after 1527, from the safe haven of the free Venetian Republic, his praise and blame brought monarchs to their knees, or at least their hands to their purses; in 1543 he was sought after by the Emperor Charles V himself) was hard-won, maintained at the cost of prodigious daily industry, and never ceased to be vulnerable. Though fair words could bring welcome gifts, foul words were often met with sticks and stones. Aretino was a savage and inspired satirist. He first made his name in 1521 with a famous series of 'pasquinades', poems ridiculing Pope and Curia, pinned anonymously to the ancient sculpted torso which the Roman people nicknamed Pasquino. The invective of dispraise was no less extreme than the rhetoric of flattery. The butt of the sarcastic litany of this virulent sonnet is the future Paul III, Cardinal Alessandro Farnese, accused among other things

of having prostituted his sister to the Borgia Pope Alexander VI in order to
obtain his cardinal's hat, as well as of being about to rival him in nepotism
(which, when he became Pope, he did):

> Dimmi, o Farnese mio, padre coscritto,
> che con sì grande onor fusti sensale
> del sangue tuo per esser cardinale,
> qual stella t'ha fra noi papa prescritto?
>   Tu piggior sei ch'un Crasso al mondo scritto
> e della fe' nimico capitale,
> superbo e vile inventor d'ogni male,
> che 'n croce hai Cristo mille volte fitto.

(Tell me, my friend Farnese, conscript father, you who to your honour traded your
own flesh and blood to become a cardinal, what star has singled you out among us to
be Pope? Everybody knows you are worse than Crassus and a mortal enemy of the
faith, a proud and cowardly inventor of all evil, who has nailed Christ to the cross a
thousand times.)

Literary pornography and a rebellious attitude almost cost Aretino his life in
1525, when he deliberately provoked the ire of Francesco Berni's protector, the
powerful Papal Datary Giovanni Matteo Giberti, with the *sonetti licenziosi* –
dramatic bawdy placed in the mouths of the couples depicted in Marcantonio
Raimondi's banned etchings after Giulio Romano's series of drawings illustrative of sixteen copulative positions – only to be stabbed by the latter's
emissaries and left for dead (artistic censorship with a vengeance!) on the
banks of the Tiber in Rome. In 1547 Henry VIII's ambassador to Venice had
him bastinadoed but later made peace. Two years after he had died in his bed
of a stroke, Aretino's works were placed on the Index of Forbidden Books and
publicly burned.

It was significant of the growing intolerance of Counter-Reformation Italy
and Reformation Europe that his sometime protégé turned poetic rival and
reviler Niccolò Franco (1517–70) was not allowed to die a natural death. The
uncompromising licentiousness, defiance and scurrility of Franco's writings,
always fiercely contemptuous of the dominant Petrarchan mode, led him to the
Inquisitor's gallows.

Macaronic and Fidentian verse

With everybody taking sides for Latin or Italian, there had to be someone who
couldn't make his mind up. Or someone who had the brilliant – and
uproarious – idea of combining the two, consecrating in a new literary genre
the involuntary lexical errors of the semi-literate. Though he recognised his
chief precursor in the less sophisticated late fifteenth-century Paduan Tifi
Odasi, a trans-Latin versifier of tales in the Boccaccian tradition, the acknowledged master of the so-called 'macaronic' genre is the Benedictine monk
Teofilo Folengo (1491–1544, born Girolamo, the son of a Mantuan notary;

see above, pp. 148, 240), who wrote under the pseudonym Merlin Coccai. 'Ars macaronica a macaronibus derivata', explained Folengo in a pseudo-scholarly gloss: 'The macaronic art derives from macaroni. Macaroni is a dish – crude, coarse and rustic – made from a mixture of flour, cheese and butter.' (From Folengo's ingredients it is evident that he had in mind not flour-and-water maccheroni, but the little dumplings now known as 'gnocchi'.) 'Therefore macaronics should contain nothing but crassness, coarseness and vulgar words.' Macaronic verse in practice looks like Latin – its syntax is Latin, its rhetoric humanistic and literary – but when the reader takes a closer look, much of the vocabulary turns out to be colloquial Italian, even dialect. The result is a deliberately droll, hybrid, incongruous, invented language, whose humour derives from the bathetic collision of the high and low registers.

The interest of Folengo's macaronic production, however, is more than merely linguistic. Far from the social amenities of the court, and program-matically remote from the aristocratic refinement of the official literary genres, the world the outsider Folengo brings to light is the world of the pre-industrial peasant imagination, in whose mythical Land of Cockaigne (a popular variant of the classicist's Golden Age) the chief pleasure is ingurgitation, eating and drinking till you can eat and drink no more. The literary tradition he has most in common with is the subversive 'carnival' tradition of Luigi Pulci's *Morgante*, Rabelais' *Gargantua* and *Pantagruel*, or the Paduan dialect plays of Angelo Beolco known as Ruzante. Though in later life, under the pressure of the Counter-Reformation, Folengo made the gesture of attempting to re-establish his spiritual credentials by publishing a number of unconvincing religious poems in Italian and Latin, he never really abandoned his ongoing commit-ment to his realistic comic muse. He puts her through her paces in parodies of various classical genres. His *magnum opus* is the *Baldus*, a mock-epic chivalric romance with a peasant hero, in macaronic hexameters, honed like Ariosto's *Orlando furioso* over several editions (1517, 1521, 1539–40, and, posthu-mously, 1552), in which the poem grew from seventeen to twenty-five books. The *Zanitonella sive innamoramentum Zaninae et Tonelli* ('The Loves of Giannina and Tonino') is a collection of shorter poems in various metres which follows the courtship of the peasant lad Tonellus and his lass Zanina. In the following lament, against all expectations, the poet's elementary paratactic syntax and the naïve and dogged persona it evokes give new poignancy to a traditional Virgilian, Dantean and Petrarchan literary topos:

> Phoebus abandonat terras cascatque sotacquam,
> Vultque super lectum se colegare suum.
> Zappator zappam, bovarus lassat aratrum,
> cavaque fossator straccus a casa redit.
> Cuncta repossatum redeunt, gallina polarum,
> porcus porcillum, capra caprile petit.
> Fabri martellos ponunt, pennamque nodari,
> installatque asinos iam molinara suos.

Quisque aliquem busum cercat qualcumque ripossum,
solus ego tota nocte travaio miser.

(Phoebus abandons the earth and falls underwater, he wants a lie-down in his bed. The hoesman puts down his hoe, the ploughman his plough, from the sandpit the sand-digger goes home fagged out. They all go back to their roosts, the hen seeks the henhouse, the pig seeks the pigsty, the goat seeks the goat-pen. The smiths lay down their hammers, the notaries their pens, the miller stables his donkeys. Everybody else finds some kind of hole and some rest. Only poor old me here, at it all through the night.)

A small but secure niche in the annals of Italian poetry is that occupied by the Vicentine jurist Camillo Scroffa (c. 1525–65), who placed on the diminutive Petrarchan stage of his *Cantici di Fidenzio* (seventeen sonnets, one *sestina* and two *capitoli*) the unforgettable Fidenzio Glottocrisio Ludimagistro, pedant, pedagogue and paedophile. This self-styled 'Camilliphylo' (desperately enamoured of Camillo, his ravishing pupil) is a sympathetic and dramatic verbal creation, like Mrs Malaprop or Sam Weller, whose droll manner of speaking endears him rather than making him ridiculous. The gentle parody operates on more than one level. The literary vehicle or institution parodied is the Petrarchan or Petrarchist sonnet, the individual caricatured is a 'character' or a recognisable social type. Each paradoxically redeems the other. Petrarch's liminal sonnet (see above p. 96), a sacred cow if ever there was one, imitated with a straight face by every rhymester in Europe, is made new by the fresh content and context. The indifference and untouchability of the beloved, given the generation gap, social convention, and their particular professional relationship, gives new authenticity and poignancy to the passively adoring stance of the Petrarchan lover. Linguistically speaking, the technique inverts the strategies of macaronic poetry: here a normal Italian syntax plays host to Latinate etymological spelling and morphology, as well as fussy lexical items and fossilised phrases from the schoolmaster's professional vocabulary. The Latin terms and phrases have been italicised in this transcription. The first line, for example, contains that old chestnut, the ablative absolute:

Voi, ch'*auribus arrectis*, auscultate
in lingua *hetrusca* il fremito e il rumore
de' miei sospiri, pieni di stupore
forse d'intemperantia m'accusate.
Se vedeste l'*eximia* alta beltate
dell'acerbo *lanista* del mio core,
non sol dareste venia al nostro errore,
ma di me havreste, *ut aequum est*, pietate.

(You who, *auribus arrectis* [with ears pricked], hearken to the rush and rumour of my sighs in the *Etruscan* tongue, filled with amazement, you will perhaps accuse me of intemperance. If you could but behold the *eximious* exalted beauty of the young *inciter* of my heart, not only would you make allowances for our error, you would also, *ut aequum est* [as is only just], have pity on me.)

And so a chapter that began in the sign of a hieratic Petrarch, sole stylistic and spiritual model for the age, ends with a Petrarch debased and radically deflated, a Petrarch, so to speak tuned to a provincial tin ear – a Petrarch nevertheless still capable of genuine poetic surprises.

14

Theatre

Richard Andrews

The full range of theatrical activity in Italy in the sixteenth century was wider, perhaps, than academic scholars are yet in a position to recognise. Popular theatre, particularly in rural areas, was resistant but undocumented. It has been revived in municipal drama festivals such as the Montepulciano *Bruscelli*, where the dramaturgy in its modern version contains features of plot and structure which seem fossilised from the first decades of the Cinquecento, before any humanist input. The development of religious theatre, from the starting point of Quattrocento *Sacre rappresentazioni* (see above, p. 175), is also a separate story from the one we shall tell here. Inevitably conservative in some respects, it emerged in the seventeenth century having absorbed a number of 'classical' features from the more secular genres.

In a single chapter on theatre in the Cinquecento, it is inevitable that we should concentrate on the lasting revolution which took place in dramaturgy and in the very concept of theatre. This was effected by the deliberate resurrection of modes and assumptions of ancient drama – as these were interpreted by Renaissance scholars, and as they were bent to the needs of Renaissance society. The snowballing effect of these changes on all European theatre is generally recognised. By around 1660, in England, France, Spain and northern Europe, the dominance of 'classical' models in drama was unmistakable; and like other aspects of Renaissance culture it was a trend which had begun Italy. There were a number of features of plot structure, setting and characterisation which had sprung from humanist doctrine and humanist analyses of the ancient texts. Arguably more important still was the transformation of theatre into an autonomous cultural and commercial activity. In the Middle Ages, performed plays (both religious and secular) had been supportive adjuncts to specific social rituals and festivities. In the Renaissance they acquired the status of literature (or 'poetry', to use a more contemporary term), to be read and studied as well as performed. Increasingly, also, they were being offered by professionals on the open market, at all or most times of the year, rather than remaining attached to particular occasions mounted and sponsored by the community. These two characteristics of theatre as modern Europe knows it were stimulated (not always intentionally) by the humanistic revolution of Cinquecento Italy. In addition, two spin-off varieties of performance, equally of Italian origin, were transmitted to European culture: the highly formal aristocratic genre of opera, and the informal plebeian *commedia dell'arte*.

The determined adherence to dramatic forms derived (or thought to be derived) from ancient Greece and Rome led eventually to a plethora of theoretical rules imposed by scholars, some of which could threaten the performing qualities of the scripts. In Spain and England such rules were accepted or rejected as taste and practicality dictated. In Italy, and also in France, they tended to be taken more seriously, and often limited the freedom and flexibility of dramatic imagination. Italian drama of the Cinquecento can conveniently be studied under the three major genres which the theorists themselves established and recognised: comedy, tragedy and pastoral. In all three genres, the small ducal state of Ferrara played a pioneering role.

Where written drama is concerned (there will be separate things to say about improvised theatre), humanist plays emerged in a restricted upper-class context, and were initially performed by amateurs to private audiences. They thus spoke to the assumptions and prejudices of an élite public, as it developed over the course of the sixteenth century. Tragedy and pastoral, in their different ways, can be seen as defining and fostering chosen aspects of aristocratic self-image. Comedy, by its nature, was potentially more subversive; but in Italy it arguably conformed in the end (in its scripted form, at least) to the parameters imposed on it by polite society, scholarly precept, and an increasingly watchful Church. Chronologically it was comedy which developed first, and which made most of the running in creating new models and expectations of theatre.

Scripted comedy to 1550

Humanist scholars discovered, or deduced, from the surviving examples of Plautus and Terence that comedy was a strict dramatic genre, serving a particular purpose: in practice it tended to provoke laughter, though curiously no theoretical formulation ever makes that essential. The plays of Terence had been part of the Latin syllabus for some time, though their portrayal of manners and their moral *sententiae* were emphasised more than their status as theatre. The discovery of more Plautine texts in the early Quattrocento boosted further study of the genre (see above, p. 177) and as humanist attitudes took hold, there was increasing interest in the idea of a purely secular drama, with emphasis on the mimetic portrayal of speech and behaviour rather than the symbolic or poetic modes favoured in medieval theatre. The famous 'three Unities' of time, place and action were initially the practical result of copying the Roman models, rather than pieces of formulated theory. During the course of the Cinquecento they came to be considered obligatory precepts: thus Italian theorists set a precedent against which other European dramatists had to struggle. The division of drama into five acts became another badge of classical imitation (though we now know that it was an imposition by scholars in late antiquity on to earlier texts, and not a structure which either Plautus or Terence would have recognised).

For comedy in particular, perhaps the most significant starting point was the definition of which characters and plots were classed as 'comic'. According to Roman theory and practice, comedy had to treat the private affairs of the middle range of urban society, including its servants and dependants: it was also likely to deploy some kind of censorious mockery against selected categories of person. Any representation of the ruling class or of public issues was excluded, and rural settings were at least rare. The approach to characterisation was generic (in the sense that social and psychological types were depicted rather than individuals), and behaviourist (in the sense that speech and action were mimicked from the outside, with few introspective insights). Initially there was little attempt to establish real dramatic sympathy even for those figures who were to be the victors in the comic contest. Laughter, in this hard-surfaced society, was most often of the deriding or punitive kind: much more the comedy of aggression than that of solidarity or self-recognition. This feature more than any other, perhaps, provided Italian Cinquecento comedy with its theatrical energy – but also, as time passed and taste developed, with its limitations and its tendency to date.

After some university performances in Latin, and then court productions of Plautus and Terence in translation, original comedy in the new style was launched in a small number of compositions which appeared before the Sack of Rome (1527). The stimulus for innovation came initially from the Este court of Ferrara, which had taken the lead in mounting translated productions under Duke Ercole I. Ludovico Ariosto (1474–1533), even more famous as an epic poet (see above, pp. 234–9), produced *La cassaria* ('The Play of the Strong-Box', 1508) and *I suppositi* ('The Substitutes', 1509) for private performance at court, after the anonymous *Formicone* (c. 1503) had been offered by schoolboys in Mantua to their Ferrarese Marchioness, Isabella d'Este. In Urbino, the future Cardinal Bernardo Dovizi da Bibbiena (1470–1520) followed with the very influential *Calandra* ('Calandro's Play') in 1513. In Florence the verse comedies of Lorenzo di Filippo Strozzi (1482–1549) are hard to date with precision: we are more certain about the contribution of Niccolò Machiavelli (1469–1527), with his much praised *Mandragola* ('The Mandrake', c. 1518), followed by *Clizia* (1525). In that same year, Pietro Aretino (1492–1556) produced the early manuscript version of his energetic *La cortigiana* ('The Courtiers' Play'), set in Rome, followed by *Il marescalco* ('The Stablemaster') for the court of Mantua in 1527. Except for those of Strozzi, all the plays mentioned were in prose: this set a pattern followed then by the majority of comedies, with certain fairly well-defined exceptions.

From the first performance of *La cassaria*, a pattern was also set in respect of staging. The fixed set of a Roman comedy was in a street or square with front doors belonging to certain characters. From 1508, this was represented by a wide shallow stage with wings and a backcloth: on the latter was painted an illusionistic view of a townscape, either recognisable or generic, using perspective techniques developed by painters in the previous century. This both integrated the new drama into a contemporary cultural and visual atmosphere, and reinforced the self-sufficient fictional space and time which classical dramaturgy aimed to convey. Later in the Cinquecento, when the techniques of complex movable scenery had been developed, the set for Italian comedy remained dogmatically fixed. This became an obstacle, because indoor action and domestic interchanges could not be depicted on stage as they were in English, French and Spanish drama.

Ariosto established a model of Plautine family intrigue, with overtones from Boccaccio especially in the structure of the central sexual relations. He realised in *I suppositi* that the audience would prefer a contemporary setting with opportunities for topical comment and satire. Bibbiena reinforced the overt derivation from Boccaccio, and used a more fragmentary style of dramaturgy, with a series of comic 'numbers' or routine comic scenes linked by an episodic plot. Bibbiena, Machiavelli and Aretino between them developed a hard-hitting scurrilous line of comedy (sometimes with satirical point, and some-times not), with stories which could end in the triumph of adultery or of the anarchic practical joke (*beffa*). After the Sack of Rome, however, a changing moral climate meant that more favour was given to Ariosto's truly classical model, whereby the dénouement re-established social propriety and orthodox relationships. This did not always imply a 'happy ending' for women in the story, whose wishes might not be consulted in a final pairing-off. In fact both Roman models and current social inhibitions impeded the sympathetic devel-opment of female characters in drama, especially in the more realistic mode of comedy. Young 'heroines' might not appear on stage at all (as in Terence's *Hecyra*), and they were often no more than inert prizes contested by various male rivals. Female performers were extremely rare, except in the most private of circumstances: there was a strong prejudice that a woman who 'exhibited herself' must be personally immoral.

It is the limitations imposed on the heroine which set a distance between the modern reader or spectator and Machiavelli's *Mandragola*, the play from this period which has acquired the greatest critical reputation. The comedy is a single-minded story of how Callimaco tricks the virtuous wife Lucrezia into bed with him, with the help of, among others, a corrupt friar. The tone hovers between carnival hedonism (such as is more frankly displayed in Bibbiena's *Calandra*) and a darker vein of aggressive satire. This ambiguity is interesting, and justifies some of the attention paid to the work, which certainly contains some scenes of devastating black comedy. However, other features betray Machiavelli's inexperience in what was after all a brand new style of dramaturgy; and the dismissive attitude to Lucrezia herself seems to be shared by the dramatist as well as most of the characters. It is significant that modern revivals of the play are rarely very successful; and the unadorned economy of both its main plot and its individual scenes does not even make it very typical of *commedia erudita* in the Cinquecento.

Similarly the work of Aretino, imposing itself on a reader by its uninhibited verbal and farcical energy, has performance qualities aimed so specifically at identifiable audiences that his comedies are hard to adapt to later times. He too is unrepresentative of what became the norm – most of all because of his overbearing authorial presence, stamped as firmly on his dramatic works as on all his others (see above, pp. 219, 271).

In general, these early dramatists felt a certain tension between the demands of performance (which led to a more episodic 'cabaret' style, with remnants of the *giullare* figure who had presided in earlier court entertainments) and those of literary respectability (which suggested a more rational, realistic mode of drama, 'overheard' by spectators rather than played directly to them). Plays were written partly with printed diffusion in mind; some performing scripts may have been different from what was eventually published. Moreover audiences, to begin with, had to be wooed into accepting an unfamiliar dramatic mode. In court performances, especially in Ferrara and later in Grand Ducal Florence, lavish interludes full of music, spectacle, dance and allegory were mounted between the acts: and there would always be a section of the aristocratic public which was more impressed by these than by the neo-classical drama.

After the watershed of the Sack of Rome, a large number of comedies were produced and dramatic norms firmly established during the period 1530–50, with Siena, Florence and the Venetian republic making different but equally crucial contributions. The later verse comedies of Ariosto in Ferrara, written between 1528 and his death, continued to be influential for their thoughtful approach to characterisation and to moral satire. *La Lena* ('The Procuress') (1528) involves some penetrating topical attacks, and an eponymous figure of genuine originality, in a plot which might in some respects be considered clumsy by later standards.

In the republic of Siena, the gentlemanly Accademia degli Intronati took firm control of prestigious entertainments in the city, both public and private. The Academy set new standards for classical comedy with only half a dozen plays. Nearly all were written by authorial teams rather than by individuals, though the name of Alessandro Piccolomini (1508–79) is attached to some, and he clearly played a central role. The best of all was *Gli ingannati* ('The Deceived', 1532), a play of cheerful carnival spirit still capable of working for a modern audience, and a source for the main intrigue of Shakespeare's *Twelfth Night*. In general the Intronati brought into classical comedy the wider-ranging and more emotionally demanding stories of hellenistic and medieval romance, and established a model for a sympathetic suffering heroine with a firm stage presence. The effect on comedy as such, within Italy, was spasmodic; but women characters were later given more weight in mixed genres ('serious' comedy, tragi-comedy, pastoral, tragedy), and the Sienese models foreshadow more flexible and relatively more feminist styles of comedy in other European traditions.

In Florence under the Medici Dukes, from the 1530s onwards, plays were generally more conservative than in Siena: resistant to the development of stage heroines and more attached to the Roman models. Some, indeed, are open reworkings of Plautine and Terentian originals, mingling stories from more than one play in a process of *contaminatio* based on what Plautus himself did with the works of his Greek model, Menander. At the same time the contemporary Tuscan setting was stressed, partly by using Florentine vernacular expressions in the dialogue to create a bond of familiarity with the audience. Florentine dramatists were more numerous and collectively more prolific than the Sienese: authors such as Lorenzino de' Medici, Donato Giannotti, Francesco D'Ambra, Giovan Battista Gelli, Benedetto Varchi, Anton Francesco Grazzini (1504–84) and the extremely productive Giovan Maria Cecchi (1518–87) established by repetition a set of norms and expectations in the public as to what comedy should contain. Their tendency to moralistic satire (particularly against misers and avarice) was occasionally broken by a Boccaccesque adultery or *beffa* play, such as Cecchi's *L'assiuolo* (1549). Medici control over cultural production, and court sponsorship of performances, were firmly established under Duke Cosimo I via his creation of the Accademia Fiorentina.

In Venice, the organisation of public and private entertainment was entirely different. It involved a tense and fluctuating relationship with a more anonymous bureaucratic state, but also greater cooperation between different social classes. Before the arrival of classical influences, there was an established taste for buffoonery, especially for mockery of the different languages and dialects to be heard in the cosmopolitan capital of an overseas empire. What is more, in the early decades the Venetians had to contend with a dramatist and performer of awkward but authentic genius, in Angelo Beolco known as 'Ruzante' (c. 1495–1542). Beolco operated chiefly in mainland Padua, for his landowner patron Alvise Cornaro, but his work was known to the Venetian public and followed up by Venetian practitioners. As 'Ruzante' he began with a personal brand of rustic comedy in Paduan country dialect, mingling patronising contempt for peasants with an astonishing subversive sympathy. From the beginning he developed his own recurrent comic figure, which gave him his stage name: 'Ruzante' was a character in the buffoon tradition, an underdog attracting both derision and solidarity. The three one-act farces *Il parlamento de Ruzante che iera vegnú da campo* ('The Speech of Ruzante Just Returned from the Battlefield'), *Bilora* and *Dialogo facetissimo* ('Very Funny Dialogue'), all now dated around 1529, contain touches of a bleak satirical realism unique in Italian Renaissance literature, albeit blended and toned down with slapstick, crudity and carefully judged topical entertainment. There is in fact little in this early work which is 'classical'; but in the 1530s Ruzante (as both dramatist and performer) moved into the five-act format and realised that he could learn real theatrical lessons from Plautus. He retained his talent for writing individual bravura roles and single 'cabaret' scenes, which prefigure the improvising masks and improvised *lazzi* of later *commedia dell'arte*. His near-professionalism as writer and actor points in the same direction: however, his tendency to establish a confidential relationship between the audience and one performer at a time relates just as much to formal rhetorical and academic display as it does to the popular *giullare* tradition. Ruzante never abandoned the use of dialects, though their purpose fluctuates in his later work between simple realism and purely theatrical comic distortion.

In Venice itself there was already a tendency, far in advance of other Italian centres, for performances to be organised on a basis which was only half private and in some cases nearly commercial. Andrea Calmo (1510–71), Gigio Artemio Giancarli (d. before 1561) and Girolamo Parabosco (1524–57) all seem to have written their comedies at least partly in such a context, though the exact composition of their audiences is not known. Pietro Aretino, established in Venice since 1528, was by now (perhaps surprisingly) more academic and literary with *Lo Ipocrito* ('The Hypocrite') and *Talanta* (both 1542), though the latter play also contains components which foreshadow *commedia dell'arte*. The polygraph (*poligrafo*) Lodovico Dolce (1508–68) wavered between two tendencies. At all events one deduces a lively controversy between those who wanted their comedies culturally and morally respectable and classically orthodox, and a contrasting preference for more free-wheeling theatrical farce based on virtuoso buffoonery. Calmo and Giancarli, like Ruzante, were performers as well as dramatists and wrote meaty speeches and scenes, often in caricatured dialects, for themselves and for specific colleagues. Parabosco is more controlled in his dramaturgy and more monolingual, but he still makes use of set-piece scenes and dialogues which could be recycled into more than one plot, and which thus related to growing professional practice. Whereas in Florence a series of fictional *topoi* were emerging, recognisable to the public but still as much literary as dramatic, in Venetian territory the units in the repertoire were increasingly based on performing skills and performing methodology. And while scholarly orthodoxy was insisting on the use of a single literary language, even in stage comedy, Venetian performers and public were unwilling to abandon the use of a range of dialects, as comic badges for characters and as general sources of fun. Dialect is used realistically and without comic intention in the anonymous *La Veniexiana* (1536) which replaces the Roman types with modern characters and disregards the unities of time and place. Thus in Venice a split occurs between professional popular comedy and academic or courtly humanist drama. The Venetian master and his Bergamask servant, both initially based on social reality, became the cartoon fantasy figures of Pantalone and Zani, and accumulated around them a set of other characters who formed a troupe in the genre which we now call *commedia dell'arte*.

Commedia dell'arte

The origins of the 'Italian comedy' which soon swept through Europe are only partly traceable. A contribution from ancient folklore cannot be ruled out, though it has sometimes been exaggerated. Certainly a number of long-standing traditions, gags and methods of popular street theatre, never recorded on paper, played a very strong part. The very fact of improvising on a scenario, rather than using a written script, may be explained by the illiteracy of the actors who first developed and used the technique. And *commedia dell'arte* was indeed a 'popular' form of theatre – in that it was commercial and thus dependent on public taste, enjoyed by every class of society, and open to a number of tendencies which 'official' culture was in the process of rejecting or even suppressing.

However, it must equally be appreciated that this genre would never have taken the particular form which it did take without the innovations and the raw material introduced by the scholarly dramatists of *commedia erudita*. The standard plot formats, and the standard relationships between the characters, are simply constant recyclings of the Plautine–Terentian–Boccaccian units which scripted drama had diffused and made familiar. Pantalone and the Dottore (the *Vecchi*) are the 'old ones' or fathers – miserly, lustful, pedantic – whose intentions are frustrated by the young lovers (*Innamorati*) who are their children, and by the latter-day scheming slaves (the *Servi*) whose myriad names include Zani, Arlecchino, Brighella, Truffaldino, and the female Franceschina and Colombina. A blustering but ultimately cowardly *Capitano* may be a free mover in the plot, usually a 'blocking' character, humiliated together with the *Vecchi* by the servants and lovers. The solution to the intrigue is provided by a mixture of successful trickery and the discovery of lost family relationships. Every one of these elements was first dramatised and made familiar in neo-classical comedy for courts and academies: they simply proved so theatrically successful that the courtly and academic world lost control of them to professional splinter groups, who wanted to perform the same stories in their own unrespectable way.

The singular features of *commedia dell'arte*, as opposed to scripted literary comedy, can be swiftly outlined. The use of facial masks by certain characters (*Vecchi* and *Servi*, but not *Innamorati* and not always *Capitani*) certainly helped to dictate the energetic visual and performing styles of the genre. However, we may never know how much of an innovation this really was: it is possible, though not demonstrable, that early *commedia erudita* also used facial masks, in imitation of Roman comedy.

The signalling of the masked figures by different dialects is important, and a sign that the genre first developed in the Venetian region. It also emphasises that this was verbal comedy as well as visual, and that the actors made people laugh (like Ruzante and Calmo and Giancarli) by saying amusing things in a caricatured dialect or accent. Pantalone had to speak Venetian, the Dottore

Bolognese, the servants usually a Lombard dialect indicating upcountry Bergamo, the land of the original Zani. (The figure of Arlecchino, originally French, became assimilated linguistically to the other servants.) The Capitano was ideally Spanish, sometimes Neapolitan if there were Spanish soldiers in the audience. Other masks speaking central and southern dialects were introduced as the genre moved south, culminating in the seminal figure of Pulcinella. The lovers, on the other hand, spoke high-flown literary 'Tuscan': this may either have been felt in its turn as a caricature, or else marked them off (for upper-class audiences) as more deserving of sympathy than the masked characters. Whereas dialect had started on stage as anti-literary realism, in *commedia dell'arte* it became a highly stylised and purely theatrical badge, like the equally formulaic costumes which were also worn.

A third devastating innovation was that the female lovers were actually played by female performers. It was the *arte* which provided Europe with its first actresses – who were inevitably then its first theatrical sex symbols, soon joined by the female singing stars of opera. This was flying in the face of firm social convention, and also of an increasingly outraged Church: it made the acting profession even less respectable than it would in any case have been. Nevertheless public and patrons must have approved, because the troupes managed to institutionalise the use of actresses everywhere in Italy except the state of the Church itself. France had followed suit by the time of Molière, and England by the time of Congreve and Wycherley.

However, the most important feature of all, which won amazement and admiration and became rooted in Italian theatre for two centuries, was the technique of improvising on an outline scenario instead of memorising a written script. This had little to do with the 'improvisation' known to modern drama students. Rather than a totally free use of the actor's imagination, it involved the creation and deployment of a huge, but not unlimited, series of repertoire numbers, on the large scale and the small. Actors, each of whom usually specialised in one mask, built up in their commonplace books (*libri generici*) collections of speeches, jokes, verbal and physical routines, all capable of being adapted and reused in different plays. This worked because the scenarios themselves, and the plots which they contained, were also permutations of recycled units: there was a limit on the number and type of broad confrontation which could occur on stage between this equally limited number of characters, and therefore the deployment of stock material and stock routines was relatively simple. Naturally a performance was leavened every time by genuine ad-libs, by acknowledgements of the particular place and occasion, and by an increase in the element of danger which always makes theatre exciting. In the classic period of the genre, it was also controlled by the firm discipline of the best actors and troupes, working as an ensemble rather than as a group of competing individuals. The best analogy from recent culture (proposed by more than one scholar) is that of a good band of jazz musicians taking their turn to improvise around one of a series of well-known tunes, often drawing on an existing stock of 'riffs' and other flourishes.

Commedia dell'arte had swept through Italy and Europe well before the end of the century. In Italy, by distinguishing itself from the written theatre which was increasingly controlled by academic rules, it provided a unique outlet for an audience's more carnival instincts. Masks such as Arlecchino/Harlequin, incarnated by a series of actors over many generations, were celebrated in image and in song as the people's foolish but indestructible heroes. The outlet was welcomed just as much by the aristocracy itself as by other classes: very soon the best troupes were being competed for, as prestige prizes, by patrons ranging from the Duke of Mantua to the King of France. Inevitably, this absorption into the power structures led in the end to routine repetition and banality, after an opening period of glorious novelty and invention. In the mean time, the professionals had taken the structures of academic comedy by the scruff of the neck, shaken them into a more fragmentary but more genuinely theatrical form, and created a performing repertoire, tradition and methodology which even the writers of scripted plays subsequently found hard to ignore. Molière in particular, and the French tradition of stage comedy in general, owed an incalculable debt to the Italian *arte* troupes; and their intermittent presence in Paris over a century and a half was perhaps ultimately even more fruitful than their original diffusion in Italy.

Scripted comedy after 1550

From around 1550, or even earlier, the writers of scripted classical comedy were working in a changed environment. On the one hand, the existence of professional troupes performing improvised versions of the same material offered a challenge, a distraction, and an influence perhaps grudgingly accepted. On the other hand dramatists were confronting – or (more often than not) participating in – the steady increase in academic theory. A stream of treatises and debates sought to formulate and impose rules on all forms of respectable literature and drama. Moreover, the rise of literary theory coin-cided with a change in taste and climate. Ever more often, as the century wore on, anxieties were expressed about social, political and religious propriety, and about the need for all forms of art to support the established system and orthodox ideology. Ultimately this can be linked to the Counter-Reformation, the Council of Trent and the Index of Forbidden Books; but it is important to recognise that a desire for conformity and security was felt in ordinary society, as well as being institutionally enforced.

Theories of literature were thus always enmeshed with theories of morality. 'Decorum' was expected in books and plays: and 'decorum' in art meant a constant confusion between purely artistic criteria, such as coherence and realism, and the need to show an exemplary view of the world. Comedy was bound to sit uneasily with such constraints. If some more extreme theories were followed – and they occasionally were – one might end up with a play containing no reprehensible characters at all, and with very little to laugh at. An example of this is Bernardino Pino's apparently influential *Gli ingiusti sdegni* ('Unjustified Rages', 1553). In the 1570s Pino produced a treatise on comedy, attempting to constrain it within impossible boundaries of morality and snobbishness. Comedies increasingly separated their relatively serious upper-class characters from their plebeian ones. The former would agonise over moral dilemmas or become confused by honest misunderstanding; while the latter, on a parallel track in the same play, would make fools of themselves or each other and provide comic relief. In such sub-plots, the influence of *commedia dell'arte* masks and gags became obvious and well established, while the more high-flown intrigue was influenced ever more by tragedy and other dramatic genres.

The pattern was set most of all by Sforza Oddi (1540–1611), a lawyer and amateur dramatist from Perugia. His most influential work, *Erofilomachia* ('The Struggle of Love and Friendship', 1572) provided an efficient mixture of the romantic and the knockabout: he then had to justify this theoretically in his prologue to *La prigione d'amore* ('Love's Prison', 1589), arguing that the dramatic genres should not be too forcibly distinguished, and that a tragic or tragi-comic element could legitimately add weight to comedy. During the latter part of the century these arguments were implicitly accepted by the most successful amateur craftsman in the genre. The Neapolitan gentleman and philosopher Giambattista Della Porta (1535–1615) had a number of comedies of varying tones performed both privately and at the Viceregal court. His balance of themes and moods can arguably be seen to have an 'Elizabethan' feel; though neither he nor any other Italian comic dramatist ever managed to produce the creative flexibility of language which is the hallmark of English drama in the same period. The number of other writers producing comedies in the later Cinquecento is substantial; none has managed to linger much in the memory of more recent critics, but perhaps a revision of the criteria which we adopt in assessing dramatic texts may lead to some rediscoveries.

This leaves the philosopher Giordano Bruno and his *Il candelaio* ('The Candlestick', 1582), which many of those same critics see as the last shot in the locker of Italian Renaissance comedy. It deploys a grotesque, merciless energy, reminiscent of Aretino at his sharpest, against a trio of sordid comic victims. But it never seems to have been performed; and all the features of this play which rightly fascinate modern readers are those which probably made it unperformable, in the new cautious climate of the times.

In 1589, at a Florentine Grand Ducal wedding of legendary splendour, *commedia erudita* and *commedia dell'arte* were performed on the same stage and given the same status. The Compagnia dei Gelosi offered their most popular scenarios featuring their two current leading ladies, and the

Accademia degli Intronati of Siena, in a new generation, mounted a well-written sentimental comedy, *La pellegrina* ('The Pilgrim Woman'), which had remained unperformed in a drawer since the 1560s. The scenarios were larded with complimentary references to the bride and groom; *La pellegrina* had been censored to remove anti-clerical passages which were no longer acceptable. The two genres of comedy were thus both celebrated, but on separate nights. They both, in any case, took second billing to the fabulous 'Florentine *intermedi*' mounted between the acts, which are now recognised as a landmark in stage spectacle and stage music. Altogether, in Italy, the torch of pure comedy was outshone rather often by the lavish candelabra of larger and more mixed spectacle. The Italians had lit the torch none the less, and it was to be taken up gratefully by Molière, who responded equally to its scripted and its improvised models. Even for English drama, so divergent in so many respects, the structural discipline of revived classical models was an essential ingredient. Leo Salingar has written, regarding Shakespeare and his Italian comic sources: 'Without the force of their example, his own broader and freer methods of dramatic composition would have lacked a basis.'

Classical tragedy and tragi-comedy

In a period which paid such reverence to classical culture, and eventually to Aristotle's *Poetics*, attention was bound to be turned sooner or later to the prestigious genre of tragedy. However, the original roots of tragedy in ancient Greek religion and society were far removed from anything which Renaissance Italy, for all its scholarship, could readily conceive. The derivative Roman models of Seneca tended, rightly or wrongly, to seem more comprehensible: they led to an identification of 'tragedy' with bloodthirsty 'horror', which later achievements in tragic theatre show up as very crude and restrictive. But in all cases, even more than for comedy, the relationship of humanist playwrights to their sources was a tentative, theoretical and largely literary one, generating imitations and developments to which live theatre audiences seem to have responded with some caution. Probably only a small proportion of the eighty or more tragedies composed in the Cinquecento were ever actually performed. This did not prevent the recreated genre from feeding important influences into European literature.

A case in point is the pioneering *Sofonisba*, composed as early as 1515 by Gian Giorgio Trissino (1478–1550; see also above, p. 241): it was printed twenty-three times between 1524 and 1620, but not performed in Italy until 1562 (a performance in French translation having occurred six years earlier). Trissino, as was usual for him, offered a mixture of essential insights and other ideas which were seen as too esoteric. The story is a simple one, of a defeated Numidian queen who chooses death rather than subjugation to Roman conquerors. It thus establishes from the start the search, characteristic of

Renaissance tragedy, for images of aristocratic greatness of soul, in which abstract values of honour and consistency outweigh the more plebeian claims of the flesh. Trissino also established the simple 'blank verse' metre (*endecasillabi sciolti*) which most, though not all, of his successors used for normal dialogue. An immixture of shorter lyrical lines, sometimes involving rhyme, was used for moments of heightened emotion. Rhymed lyric forms were also used for the chorus, whose presence was dictated by both Greek and Roman example – even though it was hard to find any theatrical rationale for it in a Renaissance context, at least until it could be sung rather than spoken. Less acceptable to future practitioners was Trissino's preference for Greek over Roman models in terms of style and structure: for example, he rejected the formal five-act division, and the 'external' Prologue borrowed from comedy, both of which subsequently became normal.

A few more tragedies were composed in the 1520s and 1530s, all still as literary exercises. Giovanni Rucellai composed *Rosmunda* in friendly competition with Trissino: it was published in 1525, and was respected as a precedent by later tragedians. It deals with a story of revenge on the part of a princess of the Gepids against her Lombard conqueror, in a semi-legendary sixth century AD.

For the first truly theatrical experiment in tragedy we have to return to Ferrara, where Giambattista Giraldi Cinthio (1504–73) mounted his *Orbecche* in 1541, in his own house but with the presence and patronage of Duke Ercole II d'Este. Giraldi opted firmly for the Senecan model of blood, revenge and doom, with allegedly instructive and uplifting overtones; but his story is an invented one, albeit based clearly on a Boccaccian model (*Decameron* IV, I, Tancredi and Ghismonda, which was staged more openly by other tragedians). The tale of a daughter marrying secretly against her father's wishes, and of his excessive and tyrannical punishment resulting in her killing him, is highly melodramatic. Nevertheless it does relate to real Renaissance dilemmas: the contrasting demands of romantic love and family duty, and the question as to when royal or princely power becomes tyrannical, and therefore illegitimate. It also introduces a comparison, developed theoretically in the choruses, between the claims of carnal and spiritual (Platonic) love – an issue which also then became a commonplace in the genre, easily made to overlap with an exaltation of eternal heavenly values as against impermanent earthly ones.

In the following year there appeared the unfinished, but well diffused and discussed, *Canace* by the Paduan academic Sperone Speroni (1500–88; see also above, p. 184). This also involves excessive revenge by a father against children: this time the father is the mythological Aeolus, god of the winds, and his children are twins who have committed incest and produced a child. The general approach is arguably more lyrical than dramatic, with a preference in dialogue for irregular rhymed metres rather than the plain *endecasillabo*. Despite the fact that the intended choruses were never written, one can detect even at this early stage some tendencies which might eventually lead to opera.

More immediately, the play sparked a major controversy over both aims and methods, which continued at intervals for the rest of the century and brought tragic theory into the centre of academic debate. Against Speroni was ranged the author of an anonymous *Giudizio* (probably Giraldi), who showed distaste for 'irregularities' identified on grounds which range from the soundly theatrical to the purely pedantic. Giraldi himself continued in any case both to write tragedies (a total of nine, of which seven were certainly performed or publicly read) and to prescribe how they should be written. The *Discorsi intorno al comporre dei Romanzi, delle Comedie, e delle Tragedie* ('Discourses on the Composition of Romances, Comedies and Tragedies') were published in 1553. His theory was a mixture of Aristotelian precept and a shrewd, even obstinate, recognition of what his courtly audiences and patrons wanted to see. His practice quite soon involved writing *tragedie a lieto fine* – he preferred this term to *tragicommedia* – in which the serious issues, and threats to life and limb, of tragic stories were resolved in endings where villains were punished and heroes or heroines saved. This is clearly one way in which he responded to the preferences of his public, but it also harmonised with his ultimately didactic view of tragedy: even his interpretation of Aristotelian 'catharsis' was one which involved moral improvement for the spectator. Another way in which the experience was made theatrically palatable was Giraldi's choice of exotic locations for his plots, no doubt giving imaginative opportunities to his set designers. A fixed 'Scena Tragica', with sumptuous buildings in perspective, was proposed and illustrated by Sebastiano Serlio in an architectural treatise of 1545, along with similar prescriptions for comedy and pastoral.

Giraldi and Sperone, in spite of their quarrel, were often used indiscriminately as models throughout the rest of the century, during which it has to be said that efforts at innovation in tragic theatre were modest where they occurred at all. From the 1540s, the tendency of Venice to seize on all forms of theatrical spectacle was shown in tragedy as well as other genres. Pietro Aretino, usually prone to vaunt his anti-classicism, produced a drama based on Roman history and inhuman ideals of civic virtue. Aretino's *Orazia* of 1546, a predecessor of Corneille's *Horace* in the following century, is verbally and psychologically impenetrable and theatrically perplexing, but it seems nevertheless to have inspired respect in its own time and later. More immediate practical success was obtained by Lodovico Dolce, who produced a workmanlike series of tragedies many of which were certainly performed in Venice, though (as in the case of contemporary Venetian comedy) we still know too little about where and to whom they were offered. Most of Dolce's tragedies are openly based on ancient originals, usually Euripides and occasionally Seneca, sometimes with extensive passages of overt translation. However, his *Didone* (1546) and especially *Marianna* (1565) are more original: *Marianna* deals with the unmerited sufferings of the Jewish queen at the hands of Herod, and offers a tyrant figure considerably more humanly plausible than the average. Dolce's writing, relatively transparent and manageable for an actor, tends at the same time to be a mosaic of echoes from other writers, whether Greek, Latin or Italian. However, in the last resort this can be said of most Renaissance tragic dramatists in Italy: the principle of imitation and *contaminatio*, always respectable at this time, was exacerbated in a genre which ultimately owed its very existence to dutiful imitation of sources.

In the 1570s, Torquato Tasso was probably composing his *Torrismondo*, a story of the fatal discovery of unintentional incest, copying Sophocles' *Oedipus Tyrannus* in its structure of slow revelation, but set in exotic Scandinavian kingdoms: the play was eventually printed in 1587. Also in the 1570s, Luigi Groto 'il Cieco di Adria' (1541–85) added two tragedies to his remarkably wide repertoire of writings and activities: the bloodthirsty *Dalida* (1572) and the over-wordy *Adriana* (1578). The latter play is recognisably a version of the Romeo and Juliet story, set in the poet's native Adria in antique times: it boasts a speech 349 lines long (II, 2), in which the hero justifies himself to the heroine for having unwittingly killed her brother. This too is an extreme version of a general tendency: in the end most of these plays are built around declamation, and a great deal of crucial action takes place off stage. Indeed, from Giraldi's *Orbecche* onwards, Messenger roles were often considered as the most important in the play, and given to the most competent actor. Audiences were expected to surrender themselves to the power of oratory rather than to the interplay of dialogue; and to some extent they were prepared to do so.

It has been noted that three-quarters of Italian Renaissance tragedies bore titles which alluded to their chief female characters. Heroines certainly had more prominence at this time in tragedy than in comedy, and were often granted great nobility of soul as well as powerful speeches. When performance was taken over by *arte* professionals, then the actors were female too. However, the dogmatic need in this genre to keep everything on an implacably heroic level limited the emotional and psychological range of all tragic roles, of either sex. Heroines were given status only at the expense of becoming somewhat inhuman, and often also of suffering bloody outrage before the end of the play.

In 1585, Sophocles' *Oedipus* in translation was chosen as the opening production for Palladio's new purpose-built Teatro Olimpico in Vicenza, confirming that for academicians at least tragedy was a real part of cultural life. Ultimately, though, undiluted tragedy was not fully to the taste of most audiences, and dramatists themselves may have found it restricting and repetitive. Diluted tragedy was preferred, and was more fruitful. On the one hand (following Giraldi's early examples), a middle path was created and formally named 'tragi-comedy'. On the other hand, and more importantly, the serious content of tragedy made its contribution to new theatrical forms less constrained by classical precedent. Early Italian opera allowed itself, like English and Spanish theatre but unlike stricter Italian genres, to play off the serious against the light-hearted within the same drama. And in pastoral plays a new mode was created, in which it became permissible to explore painful emotions, conflict, and even serious danger, but to bring everything round to a happy dénouement.

Pastoral drama

The pastoral mode in literature has a complicated history. The ancient models of Virgil and Theocritus had been picked up by medieval Italian writers in the fourteenth century, with Boccaccio as the major innovator (see above, p. 76). From the start it was recognised that idealised shepherds were often masked versions of real contemporary people, and that well-bred satire and polemic, as well as social compliments, could be elegantly and acceptably veiled by the conventional idyllic façade. The use made of the equally conventional, but unmistakable, erotic charge of most pastoral stories was more complex and difficult to analyse.

By 1500 there was a growing number of texts, some for performance and some not, which mingled pastoral fiction and classical myth (most of all stories of Orpheus, Cephalus, Venus and Adonis) in ways which were sometimes sheer autonomous fantasy but often also involved more direct reference to authors, patrons and their circle. By far the most influential was Sannazaro's *Arcadia*, a text for reading rather than performance but couched in the form of verse dialogues linked by prose narrative (see above, pp. 159–61). Another strand was provided by the use of peasant characters as objects of derision: within the 'pastoral' setting there was a firm class distinction between the languishing *pastori e ninfe* (a projection of the upper-class audience) and the entertaining half-bestial *villani*. This reflected the real assumptions of Renaissance society, whereby civilised behaviour belonged to the town, and country life was automatically despised. Such *satira rustica* sometimes appeared as a separate performance genre, but could also be incorporated as light relief into other kinds of script. The most famous example of deliberate clash between the crude rustic and the languishing shepherd is Ruzante's first known composition, *La Pastoral* (1521): Beolco develops the contrast in his own subversive manner, but it was by no means new even then to bring a *pastore* and a *villano* on to the same stage. The pioneering study of Marzia Pieri (*La scena boschereccia*, 1983) makes it clear how in Italian courts of the early Cinquecento the most favoured form of performance text was a brief occasional piece, often never published, involving some permutation of mythological, 'pastoral' and 'rustic' elements. Frequent use was made of songs and dances: it is no accident that the earliest operas, late in the Cinquecento, favoured plots with a pastoral background. As the century proceeded, most Italian aristocrats shifted their roots from urban palaces to neo-feudal estates. The pastoral genre was undoubtedly instrumentalised to support this change of self-image, as well as fulfilling a range of other functions.

Traditional critical accounts tend to concentrate on how pastoral drama became 'regular' and therefore more acceptable by literary criteria. Sometimes this meant little more than the expansion of the action to cover the canonical five acts. However, the introduction of a classical chorus, as in tragedy, was a significant element, and another pointer towards the development of opera. There were also arguments about which metrical forms were acceptable, and whether they could be mixed. (Pastoral drama, like tragedy but unlike comedy, was always composed in verse.) These controversies, and the process of creating formal rules, were important to writers and spectators in the Cinquecento; but Pieri shows that to concentrate exclusively on such 'regular' elements can produce a one-sided picture of real dramatic practice. For the present study, with so many texts still relatively inaccessible, we must concentrate on those which had a demonstrable long-term influence. The supreme importance given at the time to Tasso's *Aminta* and Guarini's *Pastor fido* is indisputable, and shown by their printing history alone. However, it must always be remembered, and one day it may be related in more detail, how often the pastoral/rustic mode was used as a basis for performances which were private, occasional and ephemeral, and which might pay less heed to classical literary rules.

Sannazaro, of course, had written in and for the court of Naples. An early key figure in the development of pastoral theatre also came from the south. He called himself 'Epicuro Napolitano', and is now generally identified with Antonio Marsi (c. 1475–1555). His 'tragicomedia' *Cecaria*, or *Dialogo di tre ciechi* ('Dialogue of Three Blind Men'), was first performed in 1523, and repeatedly reprinted. It consists largely of extensive static laments by a trio of despairing 'blind' lovers: in the second act they go to consult a woodland oracle about their destiny, but the first act was sometimes published alone. The popularity of this work confirms the willingness of Italian audiences simply to listen to, as well as to read, long elaborate speeches, in a way which leaves little distinction between drama and lyric poetry. The number of passages which were actually set to music and sung must remain a matter for speculation. 'Epicuro Napolitano' reworked the same material into the three-act drama *Mirzia*, composed possibly 1523–8. Apparently far less well known, *Mirzia* was a more genuinely theatrical development of themes in *La Cecaria*, with considerable visual effect, movement and greater characterisation added to its continuing theme of love's sufferings. It also turns the rather anonymous, even allegorical, lovers of the first play very firmly into stylised but human shepherds; and introduces a complication whereby one of them falls in love with the goddess Diana, and can only fulfil his desires by being transformed into a fountain in which she will bathe. Another early development out of *La Cecaria* was an opportunistic imitation, also more dramatic than its model: *I due pellegrini* ('The Two Pilgrims') by Luigi Tansillo (1510–68), composed around 1527. Works like this may represent the tip of a lost iceberg, in the period up to 1540. We are still dealing with relatively short pieces, bearing a variety of titles and descriptions of which 'Egloga' ('Eclogue') was the favourite: and some 'Egloghe', of course, were not written for performance.

In 1545 the Duchy of Ferrara once more became the seat of major innovation, first of all through the figure of Giambattista Giraldi Cinzio whose importance in relation to tragedy has already been discussed. Giraldi mounted a performance in his own house, with ducal patronage, of his new satyr-play *Egle*, in a full classical five acts. Eventually, as might be expected from him, he followed this practical project with theoretical precept: the *Lettera overo Discorso sovra il comporre le Satire atte alla Scena* ('Letter or Discourse on the Composition of Satires for the Stage'). This in the end was not published, perhaps because some of Giraldi's proposals had been overtaken or rejected by later developments in pastoral theatre. *Egle* was in fact a satyr-play rather than a pastoral, openly influenced by an Italian version of Euripides' *Cyclops* (translated by Alessandro de' Pazzi in 1525). Its male characters are satyrs, fauns and woodland gods: the nymphs whom they pursue are equally non-human, being the nature-spirits (*Oreadi, Naiadi, Amadriadi*, etc.) of classical rustic legend. To escape the attentions of their bestial pursuers, the nymphs allow themselves in the end to be transformed (off stage) into vegetation: the satyrs and fauns in their turn were trying to combat the amorous rivalry of the gods of Olympus, who never appear but with whom the aristocratic audience must surely have identified themselves.

In subsequent dramas, human nymphs and shepherds were preferred as protagonists; but *Egle* in many other ways sets the theme and the problematic around which most pastoral theatre then revolved. Everything turns, in most of these plots, around the conflict in the young pursued female between two opposite ideals: on one hand the freedom of virginity (often associated with devotion to Diana, to hunting and to other outdoor sports), and on the other hand surrender (pleasurable in a different way) to the love of a pursuing male. The dilemma is overtly explored, in the female characters, as a subjective one giving rise to a range of emotional nuances, developed as delicately and lyrically as the poet-dramatist knows how. The sub-text, arguably, relates to tensions and contradictory values implicit in the strict behaviour codes of the aristocracy. Both in real life and on stage, young women were praised and admired for being chaste, even for resisting sexual assault to the death; at the same time it was recognised that sooner or later they must change course completely and succumb to respectable marriage. Most of all, the issue was complicated by the contrasting rules of elegant 'courtly' love, which set a value on heightened erotic emotion for its own sake, and seemed to demand some generous recognition, rather than 'coldness' and 'cruelty', from a woman to whom court was paid. On the male side, in fiction at least, the individual's worth was proved by obstinate fidelity through thick and thin, despite a series of rejections and obstacles which brought the lover to despair, and which presented the dramatist with more opportunity to express refined lyrical passion. In these plays, shepherds languish after their nymphs because they are too well-bred and too sensitive to overcome rejection by force. Their agonised self-control is often contrasted with the perennial threat of male rape, encapsulated sometimes in the coarse peasant but more often in the satyr who cannot be seen as fully human at all.

The fact that the animal desires of the satyr are frustrated is of central importance for an analysis of Renaissance pastoral. It is true that the myth of the Golden Age is often evoked, and that simple primitive passion seems to be held up as a blessed relief from the complexities of civilisation. ('Quella rozzezza, / quel viver primo de la prima etade' (That roughness, that primitive way of life of the first age) to quote the first Prologue of Beccari's *Sacrificio*.) In Tasso's *Aminta*, the very concept of 'honour' is seen in one of the choruses as a regrettable corrupting force which interferes with natural pleasure. However, Guarino's *Pastor fido* deliberately reacts against such outright hedonism; and closer inspection of most pastoral drama reveals that gentlemanly values count for much more than superficial elements of escapism. However simple and rural the apparent setting, and however often a shepherd's life may be polemically contrasted with the corruption and oversophistication of the court, all these plays depict a clear class structure which mirrors the world of their audience. The shepherds who win their nymphs in marriage always possess more sheep than the others, are as obsessed with their blood lineage as any Renaissance nobleman, and frequently have a lower class of shepherd waiting on them as servants.

Also in Ferrara, but nearly a decade later than the *Egle*, Agostino Beccari produced and published *Il sacrificio* in five acts. Composed around 1554–5, and performed for a princely wedding, it was this play rather than Giraldi's which set the model for subsequent 'regular' pastoral dramas. Most of its features are typical and recurrent. It deals with three pairs of lovers, each with a different obstacle to overcome. Callinome modestly resists the pursuing Erasto; Carpalio's love for Melidia is threatened by her vengeful brother; and Stellinia, after first accepting Turico, now loves Erasto. (This last complication introduces the 'circular' dilemma of plots like that of *A Midsummer Night's Dream*.) There is a lustful satyr whose schemes are frustrated three times by trickery (showing the input of *beffa* structures from comic drama), and a cheerfully drunken *villano* with a single bravura monologue in Act IV. The goddess Diana plays a part in the story, but only in off-stage events. Most of all, the script has been carefully composed with precise scenic properties and action in mind, so that it has a good chance of full theatrical success. A note in the first edition (1555) tells us that some passages were set to music. The writing contains its necessary dose of pure lyricism, but there is also a real dramatic plot with conflicts, intrigues, complications and changes of heart.

Around the same time, in 1553, Andrea Calmo published in Venice his *Egloghe pastorali*, with heavy influences from his own style of farcical comedy and making use of prototypes of *commedia dell'arte* masks.

In the 1560s the genre was slowly established, with contributions from authors such as Luigi Groto (*Calisto*, 1561), Alberto Lollio (*Aretusa*, 1564), Agostino Argenti (*Lo sfortunato*, 'The Unfortunate Man', 1568) and Flamminio Guarnieri (*Mago* and *Nova Arcadia*, 1569). But the play which attracted a host of admirers was the *Aminta* of Torquato Tasso (1544–95), first performed for the Ferrarese court in 1573. This was the work, perhaps, which induced humanist theory to capitulate and accept a third dramatic genre of pastoral alongside comedy and tragedy; though Marzia Pieri, in arguing this, also observes that '*Aminta* remained a model more praised than imitated'.

The runaway success of *Aminta*, together with these reservations, encapsulates the continuing ambiguity of pastoral theatre. The play was first performed by a famous troupe of *commedia dell'arte* professionals, the Gelosi. Yet its appeal through the ages has probably been more lyric and narrative than dramatic, and indeed this is the reason why subsequent play scripts did not imitate it. Audiences for pastoral were never quite sure whether they wanted to watch dramatic action or listen to beautiful words. Many scripts (including Guarini's *Pastor fido*) went through the stages of a shorter performing text and a longer, more verbally ornate one for printing; and in 1625 the critic Ludovico Zuccolo said that pastorals were in the end more for reading than performing, though others such as Angelo Ingegneri (in 1598) had tried to react against this tendency.

Aminta itself has a relatively simple plot, with just one source of suspense: 'Will the nymph Silvia surrender herself to Aminta's love, before Aminta commits suicide?' She does, of course; but it is notorious that the two lovers never once appear on stage together, even for a final tableau. The Golden Age hedonism of 's'ei piace, ei lice' ('if it pleases, it is permitted') in the first chorus is balanced by immense theatrical modesty, and everything really interesting (including Aminta's rescue of Silvia from the obligatory satyr) is lovingly narrated rather than enacted. An excuse for this may have been found in the classical requirement for a fixed setting, in which most of the diverse action could not plausibly take place. But one has also to point to the artistic strengths which Tasso wanted to display: his mastery of verbal narrative, and the highly charged but oblique eroticism which is also a feature of his epic poem. Equally of interest to its first audience, but also entirely verbal rather than scenic, were the passages of barely veiled allusion to the current court of Ferrara, which contain a good deal of predictable flattery but also some elements of personal vendetta. The private nature of Renaissance court theatre is reinforced once again in this example.

With the genre now established as theoretically respectable, as well as popular, the number of texts increased: at least thirty pastoral-mythological dramas were published in the 1580s, some by authors also involved in other genres such as comedy. The actress Isabella Andreini produced *Mirtilla* in 1588; while Alvise Pasqualigo (*Gl'intricati*, 'People in a Predicament', 1581) and Bartolommeo Rossi (*Fiammella*, 1584) were also practitioners. During this decade, and still in Ferrara, came the second text after *Aminta* to acquire a

European reputation over the following century and a half: *Il pastor fido* ('The Faithful Shepherd'), by Battista Guarino, or Guarini (1538–1612). An early performing version may have existed as early as 1581. First published in 1589, it reached a definitive expanded edition in 1602, and continued to be printed and translated for many generations.

The story has a framework of prophecy and doom. A curse is hanging over the realm of Arcadia, resulting from a female infidelity. The stain can only be wiped out by a marriage between two divine families and (more importantly for the plot) by a supreme example of compensatory fidelity on the part of a male shepherd:

> di donna infedel l'antico errore
> l'alta pietà d'un *pastor fido* ammende.

A male Good Shepherd must make amends for a past female error – and, as it turns out, the hero Mirtillo will risk being sacrificed by his own father. As well as parallels with the story of Christian Redemption, we have an allusion to Abraham and Isaac. A Counter-Reformation allegory may therefore underlie, and give moral sanction to, what is in detail just another tale of amorous pastoral fantasy. Is this play, among other things, a part of the process whereby religious drama acquired classical form?

In practice, the fulfilment of prophecy is a rather forced device to ensure a happy ending, after a tangle of intrigue by the villainous nymph Corisca leads the heroine Amarilli to the point of execution for immorality – at which point the law allows the faithful Mirtillo to offer his own life in exchange. A family recognition scene, in the style of comedy, helps the dénouement; and in general the devices of deception and conflict are also reminiscent of comedy, and very different from the purely emotional tensions of *Aminta*. An important secondary plot concerns the virginal huntsman Silvio and his resistance to the love of Dorinda – a reversal of normal dramatic sexual roles, but with precedents such as the mythical Adonis, and Poliziano's Iulio in the *Stanze* (see above, p. 165). The passions of a satyr, in this play, are harnessed and re-directed by the scheming Corisca for her own ends. The happy ending involves Corisca's own repentance. Scene by scene, the play is both dramatically and psychologically absorbing. In its expanded form it is perhaps too large for most performance resources, but as a text for reading it demonstrated finally that pastoral could have all the dramatic power of other genres, that it could borrow at will from tragedy and comedy as well as from lyrical eclogue, and that it offered an emotional accessibility which neither strict tragedy nor strict comedy were able to permit themselves. The genre therefore continued to flourish, and to be more eclectic than other forms. But the next script to have a major influence takes us out of the Cinquecento: it was *Filli di Sciro*, by Guidobaldo Bonarelli della Rovere (performed in 1605, published 1607) (see further below, p. 334). This plot culminates in a tense and pathetic confrontation based on misunderstanding, adapted from Bargagli's sentimental comedy *La pellegrina* of 1589.

Pastoral plays focused on detailed emotion, and frequently allowed the outcome of the plot to depend on the decision of a heroine. They thus helped to give more autonomy to the female presence on stage, in ways which Italian 'regular' comedy often had to abstain from and which tragedy, with its heroic emphasis, could only partly achieve. This was true whether or not the conventions of a particular performance allowed the female parts to be played by actresses. Both Ingegneri in 1598 and Zuccolo in 1625 commented on the relative scope given to women in these dramas. The suggestion in Muzio Manfredi's *Contrasto amoroso* (1602) that the play might be suitable for a private performance by an all-female cast may not therefore indicate a unique case.

From the staging point of view, pastoral invited a scenic and visual variety which again was curtailed in classical comedy and tragedy. The set for a pastoral drama was likely to be more inventive than for other genres, and to make more use of developments in spectacular movable scenery. Such technical display was by now demanded in interludes and court pageants; subsequently it contributed to the flexibility and splendour of opera. And it was opera more than any other theatrical mode, even more than *commedia dell'arte*, which remained an Italian practice to be developed mainly in Italian states during the following century.

The Seicento

Paolo Cherchi, Albert N. Mancini, David Kimbell

POETRY, PHILOSOPHY AND SCIENCE
Paolo Cherchi

15

The Baroque

Traditionally, the term 'Baroque' defines the period from the death of Tasso (1595) to the foundation of the Accademia dell'Arcadia (1690). However, as often occurs with such periodisations, dates must be taken with some flexibility. Indeed, in this specific case it is not always clear when Mannerism ends and the Baroque begins, nor when the Baroque period ends and Rococo begins. Our task would be easier if it were possible to identify clearly the main characteristics of the Baroque; but we are far from such clarity and the debate on what is typical 'Baroque' is still going on. The only certainty we have is that literary historians have systematically considered the Baroque the nadir of Italian literature, and as a result it is its least studied period. The first condemnations came from the historians who promoted the later 'Arcadia', Muratori and Tiraboschi, who found the metaphors of the Baroque utterly extravagant. The historians of the Enlightenment did not disagree with their predecessors: Baroque literature was lacking any decorum that reason could dictate. The Romantics perpetuated the Enlightenment disdain for this period: not only did they consider it too prone to artificiality and insincerity, but above all (as Manzoni demonstrated) they saw the Baroque as the expression of the most humiliating moment of the Italian nation since the peninsula was occupied by foreign forces. The idealistic criticism of Croce was no more generous, although Croce was the scholar who did the most (as critic and editor) to promote the study of seventeenth-century culture. He condemned the artificiality and lack of any moral sense in the Baroque world, but he also judged individual poets, thinkers and historians in a positive way. Today we are less biased by moral and patriotic considerations, and the Seicento (synonymous with the Baroque) does not appear so poor to us: it is, after all, the century that gave birth to modern science with Galileo and created the opera with Monteverdi. Moreover, one should not forget that Marino – who came to epitomise everything bad in the Baroque world – was also the last great Italian poet to have a resounding influence throughout Europe. Today, thanks to the experience of twentieth-century poetry, we are better disposed and prepared to appreciate Baroque poetry.

The term 'Baroque' was first used by nineteenth-century art historians in order to characterise a style, but it had been known since the Middle Ages as a word defining a particular type of far-fetched and specious syllogism, or a type of irregular pearl. Indeed, the main characteristic of Baroque literature is its 'irregularity' with respect to 'regular' Cinquecento literature based on the classical notions of the 'decorum' and morality of art. It is an 'irregularity' with a system, which, when imitating the classics chooses those of the Silver Age (Seneca, Claudian and the like); when using rhetoric privileges *dispositio* over *inventio*; when using mimetic notions pushes them so far as to reach a crude realism; and when using metaphoric language disdains obvious similarities in favour of those which reveal unseen analogies. For all these reasons Baroque literature was unprecedented in the richness of its subject-matter, in its stylistic experimentation, in its hedonistic overtones and linguistic daring. Overall Baroque writing brought to a critical point some fundamental tenets of Renaissance epistemology: truth is not just the equation of man with nature or of the mind with things, but of the mind with the mind itself, of words with their own signs rather than their own referent. The result was one of liberation and frustration at the same time, because it brought about a divorce between life and literature.

16

Lyric poetry

The innovations of the poets of the late Cinquecento (Tasso, Strozzi, Guarini, Rinaldi and others) provide evidence of a culture prone to experimentalism in polemic – more or less openly declared – with the Bembist variety of Renaissance classicism. The novelty is immediately perceived on the formal level: the poetic discourse relies not so much on a system of thematic correlations as on tropes, on the quality of single words (rare, polysemic), similes and metaphors, a new emphasis which will ultimately lead to *concettismo*. And musicality becomes a pre-eminent feature – which explains why the madrigal becomes a favourite poetical form. On the thematic level, we see that the *canzone*, and lyric poetry in general, move away from 'high' themes – considered more appropriate for epic and tragedy – in favour of 'occasional' themes of middling level, including daily and vulgar subjects. On the other hand, new 'high' themes acquire a new and sustained role, above all patriotic, moral and religious themes which were practically unknown to the lyric poems of the previous generations who sang primarily of love. Each of the main trends in the seventeenth-century lyric – the light or 'melic', the extreme Baroque, the moderate and the classicist – can be seen as emphatic forms of features present in poetry at the turn of the century. We will consider them in turn.

Chiabrera and the melic trend

The first poet who chronologically and formally belongs to the seventeenth century is Gabriello Chiabrera (1552–1638). While studying in Rome with the Jesuits he came into contact with Paolo Manuzio and Sperone Speroni, who nurtured his classical tastes. Equally important was his contact with the French poet M. A. Muret, then ambassador in Rome, because it introduced Chiabrera to the poetry of the Pléiade; but in 1581 Chiabrera had to leave Rome after killing a man in a duel. His earliest poetic composition was an heroic poem, *Delle guerre dei Goti* ('The Gothic Wars', 1582), but he soon branched out into other kinds of poetry. His production is as voluminous as it is varied, for he not only cultivated epic poetry – for example, the *Amedeide* (1607) about the King of Piedmont, Amedeo of Savoy, and *Firenze* (third edition 1637) about the founding of the city of the Medici – but also wrote various pastoral pieces, tragedies, melodramas, and even a brief autobiography. However, the genre in which Chiabrera excelled, and through which he exercised a profound influence, was lyric poetry, where he reached the highest level of musicality and brought about a metrical revolution. Chiabrera applied the classical notion of syllabic quantity to Italian verse, and adopted different metres and metrical schemes from the Greek and Latin tradition – among others, the Pindaric ode, the dithyramb, the Alcaic song and the Horatian epode – and he modelled some of his compositions, especially his *canzonetta* with its paroxitonic seven-syllable couplets, on the French lyrics of the Pléiade. In his numerous collections, from the *Canzoni* (1588) to the *Canzonette* (1591) and *Vendemmie del Parnaso* (1605), to name only three, Chiabrera always aimed at the maximum musical effect, whereby words acquired a simple, evocative, almost magical quality highlighted by his metrical and strophic innovations. Paradoxically, such apparent lightness confers intensity on the psychological and moral elements contained in poems which are often very brief; and perhaps it was this combination that made Chiabrera's *odicine* and anacreontic poems so appealing later to the taste of the Arcadians. Chiabrera's influence was pervasive and long-lasting. Suffice it to say that the *canzonetta*, the madrigal and several other strophic combinations that bear his imprint were the compositions Baroque musicians came to prefer. His influence is clear in poets like Antonio Muscettola (1628–79) and even more so in Francesco Lemene (1634–1704), who, towards the end of the century, produced a 'galant' version of Chiabrera's anacreontic poetry, thus preparing Arcadian taste.

The Baroque vanguard

The 'vanguard' of the poetic Baroque, as we may call it, flared up at the beginning of the seventeenth century and did not abate until the beginning of the following one, enlisting in its ranks an endless number of poets, mostly mediocre or frankly bad; today it is hardly remembered. Thematic innovations were part of this trend; but their trade-mark was the use of *concetti* and *acutezze*, that is of dazzling metaphors. One of the earliest representatives is Tommaso Stigliani (1573–1661), whose renown is due to the *Occhiale* (1627) which he wrote attacking Marino's *Adone*, but he was in fact a better poet than critic. His *Rime* (1601) and *Canzoniere* (1605 and 1623) feature watches, bottles, portraits, mirrors, lanterns, hearts of pasta and similar subjects which Renaissance decorum considered as belonging to comic poetry, not serious poetry where Stigliani provocatively included them. His metaphors contain the most far-fetched combinations: the lady's shoes are 'Atlases', her ring and its stone 'the celestial sphere', the dawn 'mills the grain of the stars and cooks the day in the pot of the sky over the embers of stars'. These *concetti* were to enjoy the full approval of the aestheticians, who considered them to be the main feature of poetic discourse.

This kind of language had many imitators (Giuseppe Artale and Bartolomeo

Dotti, to name two of the best known); and it was applied even to religious poetry, as one can see in Angelo Grillo (1550–1629) with his *Poesie sacre* (1608) or *Christo flagellato* (1608), in which the wounds of Christ are compared to the stars, and gory imagery gives an idea of the morbid sensuality of Counter-Reformation spirituality. However easy it might have been to ridicule these stylistic excesses, the fact remains that for a century the poets of the exaggerated Baroque were engaged in creating a poetic language that could reflect a new vision of reality: it was no longer the static world known in the Renaissance, but an illusory one, and only a special type of metaphor seemed to have the magic power to understand it and, to a certain degree, resist it.

Marino and his followers

The moderate Baroque had its champion in Giovan Battista Marino, the greatest poet of the seventeenth century and one of the greatest Italian poets of all time. Born in Naples in 1569 into a lawyer's family, he led an adventurous life punctuated with violent quarrels and spells of imprisonment. He travelled widely in Italy and spent a long time in Paris before returning to die in his native city (1625). Marino's wanderings from one capital to another give an idea of the changes that were occurring in the cultural map: Bologna and Turin, for example, which were relatively unimportant during the Renaissance, had now become cultural capitals, places where literary reputations were built and destroyed.

Marino appeared relatively late in the literary limelight. After an early fame which he won with a *canzone* about kisses, he published his *Rime* (1602) in two parts and republished them later under the new title of *La lira* (1614), containing a third section. This collection of over 400 poems has an original arrangement because it gathers poems in classes which roughly correspond with literary sub-genres. In the first part the *rime* are classified as 'amorose, marittime, boscherecce, heroiche, lugubri, morali, sacre, varie' (amorous, sea-going, rustic, heroic, gloomy, moral, religious, various); the second part is made up of madrigals, *canzoni* and sonnets; the third one contains the following five classes: 'amorose, lodi, lagrime, divozioni, capricci' (amorous, praises, tears, devotions, caprices). The thematic variety of *La lira* is prodigious, and so are the versatility and craft of the author. Marino's style is musical and rich in tropes, but he shuns extravagant metaphors and excessive musicality. The 'meraviglia' (wonder) he seeks is of an aristocratic type, based on conceits which are admirable for the decorum they maintain. Perhaps this moderation was the reason why Marino's lyric was influential for such a long time; but there is no doubt that the same virtue could be a limitation in the eyes of his contemporaries, who did not see the *Lira* as constituting any really great novelty. Indeed Marino had to prove his leadership with other poetic compositions.

Marino's most original and greatest works were published or written during his stay in Paris. The *Epitalami* appeared in 1616: it is a collection of ten 'augural' and encomiastic poems for kings and aristocrats in which Marino celebrates the world of courts, without any trace of the servility customary in this kind of poetry, but rather with a serious celebration of his own worldly success and that of his own select audience. *La galleria* (1620) is a vast collection of ecphrases, that is descriptions of works of art: Marino was a great connoisseur of art (he 'discovered' Poussin), and in *La galleria*, the first modern work of its kind, he is engaged not only in judging art but in translating into words the lines, colours and volumes of the works described. *La Sampogna* (Paris, 1620), is Marino's most mature work before the *Adone*, even though some of the idylls were published many years earlier. In these idylls one appreciates the greatness of Marino's art in his refined use of classical and contemporary sources, his poetics of 'stealing' (not vulgar plagiarism but a highly refined exercise in rewriting, for literature is born from literature), his propensity to create visual poems, the polymetry, the eroticism and musicality, the symphonic construction of his poems, and their mixture of sensual and macabre in a linguistic texture that creates a sense of soft sonority. The mythological materials acquire a new life not seen before in Italian literature.

The *Adone* ('Adonis') is Marino's most famous work. Initially conceived as an idyll divided into two cantos, it was reworked over two decades, to become a poem of twenty cantos comprising more than 8,000 *ottave*. It is thus the longest Italian poem, but also the poorest in narrative elements; and the main story, coming from a classical source, is well known and is repeated twice in the poem. The poet is in fact engaging in a polemic with the epic poem. For Marino love, not war, was the main subject of the Italian poetic tradition, and it deserved treatment on a scale befitting its importance. Never before had a mythological theme furnished the subject of such an extensive composition.

The poem is based on the myth recounted in Ovid's *Metamorphoses*, but with important additions. Lengthy sections are devoted to the visits of the enamoured Venus and Adonis to the goddess's palace of the five senses, the Island of Poetry, the heaven of the moon and so on; others to Adonis' resistance to the witch Falsirena (who at one stage turns him into a parrot). His idyll with Venus ends when he is killed by a boar which has attempted to kiss the handsome youth. Venus stages elaborate funerals for Adonis, transforms his heart into a flower, and convenes public funeral games that last three days.

The *Adone* is rich in colourful digressions and narrative episodes, sections dedicated to science and politics, and endless descriptions of colours, gems, sounds and flowers. It is a poem – as already observed by Marino's most acerbic critic, Stigliani in the *Occhiale* – with two possible conclusions, the wedding and the election as king, both typical 'closures' of stories. We could also add that it has two beginnings, because the structure or sequence of the main story (meeting – falling in love – happy married life – triumph – separation – death) is repeated. This repetition, rather than reinforcing the story, devalues it because one version makes the other superfluous, and one draws the conclusion that there are no absolute values since all is relative. In the *Adone* the traditional sequence of cause and effect, which is at the basis of all narration, is constantly invalidated: the poem is full of stories not concluded, or not concluded in the way the sequence of causes would allow one to predict.

The main characters are unusually weak: Adonis never initiates any action, and Venus is a victim of events. Marino 'weakens' his characters in many subtle ways. Take, for example, the two stories of the judgement of Paris and the loves of Cupid and Psyche, which do not seem to have anything to do with the main plot; what both stories have in common is the presence of Venus, who in the first episode is proclaimed as the highest beauty while in the second she is overshadowed by Psyche. Thus the *dispositio* of the episodes transforms an absolute value into a relative one, and Venus emerges as a weak character. At the root of these irregularities is Marino's intention to write a poem not based on history (he had in mind particularly Tasso's *Gerusalemme liberata*; see above, pp. 243–9) and on the supreme values (justice, religion, etc.), but on the flimsiest of stories (the ephemeral love of a goddess for a mortal) and the most unstable of values, namely sensual love. For Marino, words in their materiality are the content of a poem (hence the numerous instances of visual poetry), and its form is its concept. In other words, Marino conceived his poem as a grandiose metonymy, whereby the ostensible content (the metamorphosis of Adonis) becomes the form of the poem itself. Indeed the *Adone* is a work which transforms itself through its repetitions and symmetries; and its *dispositio* creates a message of relativity, culminating in the final and longest canto which consists only of games to honour the memory of Adonis (who, ironically, is mentioned only once). The first part is repeated in the second one, but in the process a degradation takes place: in her first appearance to Adonis Venus is disguised as Diana, whereas the second time she appears as a gypsy; in the first part she educates Adonis through a visit to the palace of the senses, whereas in the second that grandiose lesson has a parallel in the reading of Adonis' hand; and through many other similar symmetries the degradation (a typical result of all the metamorphoses) is clear. And so is the message: the story of the poem is irrelevant, and the last canto indulges the ultimate freedom from narrative celebrating pure form (descriptions of horses, arms, dances, etc.). However, when the poem's story seems to have been completely forgotten, it re-emerges in the strangest way. The last pair of jousters, duplicating the famous episode of Tancredi and Clorinda in the *Gerusalemme liberata*, gives what must be considered the real metamorphosis of Adonis: their physical features combined, as well as the combined history of their upbringing, bring back to life the androgynous Adonis, metamorphosed into a couple which will provide the origins of the French royal family. Thus the poem ends by linking myth and history, that history it set out to remove from poetry.

The style of *Adone* is high, always very refined, never obscure, metaphoric but not affected, and grandly musical. The poem's success was remarkable, causing long and heated debates started by Stigliani's *Occhiale*. Marino's influence was great, but (we now know) not as much as it was assumed to have been in the past, when 'Marinism' and 'Baroque' or *secentismo*, all meaning bad taste, were synonymous. In any case, there was never a manifesto or a school of 'Marinism', and the best poets who followed Marino certainly worked with a considerable degree of autonomy. The lesson they learned from him was to avoid the extravagance of conceit and insist rather on metaphors which, thanks to their verbal and musical combination, expressed the instability and fluidity of reality; consequently their poetry has a propensity for emblematic images, for representation of concrete objects, including a more varied typology of women than the one imposed by the Petrarchan model. They set a higher value than previous poets on the themes of life's transience and of death.

Among these poets is Girolamo Preti (1582–1626), who published a collection of *Poesie* (1614) in which the influence of Marino is strong, but the spiritual overtones are original. The idyll *Salmace* (1608) is important for its combination of eroticism and mythology. A declared Marinist, in fact a personal friend of Marino, was Claudio Achillini (1574–1640), author of *Rime e prose* (1632). He occasionally lapsed into the excesses of extravagant metaphors, the most famous being 'Sudate fuochi a preparar metalli' (Sweat, fires, in order to forge metal) which was ridiculed by Manzoni; but on the whole Achillini is fairly moderate and decorous. Worthy of mention is Antonio Bruni (1593–1635), author of several collections such as *La selva di Parnaso* (1615) and *Le veneri* (1633), which are dominated by sensual motifs and overtones. Ciro di Pers (1599–1663) wrote some remarkable plays and *Poesie* (1666) in which existential notes on the meaning of life, its fugacity and mystery, resound with an intensity that has no equal in the seventeenth century. One of the best poets of the seventeenth century was the Jesuit Giacomo Lubrano (1619–93), who wrote when the Baroque seemed to have exhausted itself from internal depletion, when the polemics on Marino were over and the poetic tradition of Chiabrera was about to prevail with Arcadia. This great preacher, who travelled throughout Italy, came to poetry very late in life. *Le scintille poetiche o poesie sacre e morali* ('Poetic Sparks, or Sacred and Moral Poems') appeared in 1690, the same year in which Arcadia was born. Lubrano gave to the metaphor, to the objects represented in his poems (sonnets, madrigals and odes) an oneiric quality, a metaphysical dimension in which reality is used as a way to reach the darkest depths of the self.

Classicists

The trend we call 'classicist' opposed 'Marinism' in favour of a poetry which kept up the traditional decorum. Its novelty was its interest in patriotic themes;

its major representative was Fulvio Testi (1593–1646). Born in Ferrara, Testi studied in Bologna and after a brilliant diplomatic career died – or he may have been murdered – in prison. Testi wrote several comedies and some epic poetry, but his fame is due to his lyric poetry. In 1617 he published, in addition to a collection of *Rime*, a poetic composition of 43 *ottave* known as *Pianto d'Italia* ('The Lament of Italy'). The poem was published anonymously and clandestinely, but its attribution to Testi seems certain. The author mourns the decadence of Italy, which he blames on the Spanish domination. Testi, always solemn, avoids frivolous subjects and focuses on 'patriotic' themes; he disdained the 'Marinist' style and extravagant metaphors. The classical authors were his models to such an extent that in a letter dated before the 1644 Modena edition of his *Rime*, he wrote: 'poetic phrasing cannot be learned from anyone except from Greek and Latin writers'. The dignified and magniloquent poetry of this 'seventeenth-century Horace' (as he was called in his own time) appealed to his contemporaries and, not surprisingly, to the leaders of the Risorgimento. Today we look with greater interest at his letters, which constitute an important historical and human testimony of seventeenth-century society, and we admire the lucidity with which he analysed situations and people, his noble disdain for the court. Testi did not live for poetry, as did Marino and Chiabrera, but wrote poetry in order to understand the state of his world, hoping to find in the perfection of poetic form the ideal with which to contrast the present chaos; poetry was for Testi a vehicle to bring himself closer to the great models of antiquity.

In the second half of the century, as Baroque tendencies waned and a call for rationality was voiced in various cultural circles, the classicist trend found new support. Vincenzo da Filicaia (1642–1707) was one of the most influential voices of this trend. He held important political offices and was favoured by Queen Christina of Sweden, the founder of the Arcadian Academy of which he became one of the first members. In his youth he wrote love poems, but later destroyed them and produced only patriotic, moral or civic poetry. In 1684 he published five *Canzoni in occasione dell'assedio e liberazione di Vienna* ('Poems on the Occasion of the Siege and Liberation of Vienna') which were read by later generations (including the Romantics) and were admired for their pathos, their moral content and their classical construction. The complete collection of his *Poesie toscane* was published in the year of his death. Another important classicist poet was Alessandro Guidi (1650–1712). In 1671 he published his *Poesie liriche*, which he later disowned because of their exaggerated Baroque style: his contact with Roman circles, and with the critic Gravina and Christina of Sweden, had converted him to a more rational type of poetry. But although he condemned extravagant Baroque imagery he still kept a highly rhetorical and theatrical tone in his patriotic and moral *Rime* (1704). Guidi is today remembered for his play *Endimione*, which was defended by Gravina.

17

Mock-epic poetry and satire

Heroi-comic poems

Epic poetry, which was so important in the previous century, declined in the Baroque period when heroic ideals had not only waned but were openly ridiculed (one need only think of *Don Quixote* or of Scarron's *Roman comique*). In Italy this anti-heroic attitude gave rise to a series of mock-epic poems. The first, and certainly the greatest, of these is *La secchia rapita* ('The Stolen Bucket') by Alessandro Tassoni (1565–1635). After studying law, Tassoni followed the *iter* typical of many scholars of the time, serving princes and cardinals, and visiting various Italian and European courts. His *Dieci libri di pensieri diversi* ('Ten Books of Diverse Thoughts', 1620) contains observations, meditations and paradoxical statements on all sorts of topics; but the most interesting part is the last, in which Tassoni attacks ancient authors in favour of modern ones. His strong anti-traditionalist statements precede the famous 'querelle des anciens et des modernes' by many decades. This polemical vein inspired his *Considerazioni sulle rime del Petrarca* (1611) in which he attacks the principle of imitation adopted by the *petrarchisti*, whom he blames for decadence in poetry. From this polemical and irreverent background came *La secchia rapita*. Written between 1614 and 1615 – but published in Paris in 1622, and then, in a revised version, in Venice in 1630 – this poem in twelve cantos recounts the war between the Guelfs of Bologna and the Ghibellines of Modena over a bucket which the Modenese stole from their enemies. The basis for the poem is historical, a local war of 1393 between the two communities; but the central episode, the theft of the bucket, is completely fictitious. The epic tradition allowed the mixture of historical and fictitious elements, but in Tassoni's case, the invented part is so completely banal and 'low' that it demeans or ridicules an already insignificant historical event. In this poem there are many elements typical of the epic-chivalric tradition – from the ancient deities who determine the events in the war to spectacular duels and love scenes – chosen to make the parody more convincing. The language, filled with dialect forms, underscores this absence of decorum. The dispersive and rhapsodic plot gives the idea of an 'open' poem, which creates a world of illusion, remote and provincial at the same time.

Tassoni's poem had many imitators, notably Francesco Bracciolini (1566–1645), who wrote *Lo scherno degli dei* ('The Mocking of the Gods') in 1618 –

that is, before *La secchia rapita* was published; but it seems that Bracciolini saw Tassoni's work in manuscript form. His own poem ridicules classical mythology in the same way Tassoni's does the epic. Also noteworthy is *L'asino d'oro* by Carlo de' Dottori (1618–68), author of one of the most important theatrical pieces of the seventeenth century, *Aristodemo*, and of a series of other lyrical works. *L'asino d'oro* (1652) tells the story of the war between Padua and Vicenza for a banner which bears the figure of a golden ass. After ten cantos of hyperbolic battles fought by caricatural soldiers, the banner ends up hanging from a pitchfork. Dottori's predominantly comic intention does not deter him from including a tragic tale of a duel between a lady and her husband, who leaves her to die – an incongruous episode indicative of the mixture of styles typical of this and other comic epic poems of the period.

Satiric poetry

The mock-epic stems from a critical attitude towards the literary tradition; Seicento satire comes from the same attitude, although the satire is usually more focused on contemporary situations. The Baroque period produced some of the best satiric poetry in the Italian tradition. The strongest voice of this trend is undoubtedly the Neapolitan poet Salvator Rosa (1615–1673) who lived in Naples, Rome, and then mostly in Florence, working as a painter, a profession in which he excelled and for which he is still remembered today. He wrote seven long satires dealing with the subject-matter indicated in their titles: *La musica* (against mixing sacred and profane music), *La pittura* (against ignorant painters), *La guerra* ('War': against bad government), *Tirreno* (autobiographical in nature), *La poesia* in which he attacks the exaggerated metaphors of contemporary poetry (against those poets, for example, who call their ladies' lice 'Silver beasts in a golden forest', or who term the sun an executioner because it 'cuts the shadows' neck with the axe of its rays', or who transform the god of the sea, Neptune, into a dried codfish, calling him 'the salty god'). Despite these criticisms, Rosa himself was not exempt from the defects of which he accused his contemporaries: he is often bombastic and pedantic, especially when underlining his moral intentions.

Satirical poetry flowered particularly in Tuscany, a region where Baroque fashions had little success. Among the poets who are still worth reading are Giovanni Battista Ricciardi (1623–86), the Florentines Jacopo Soldani (1579–1641) and Benedetto Menzini (1646–1704), and Ludovico Adimari (1644–1708).

18

Treatises

Treatises on aesthetics

The seventeenth century was a period of literary experimentalism and innovation as well as one of great scientific breakthroughs and of new political systems (the main one being absolute monarchy); and, as one can imagine, there was a flourishing literature on these subjects. As far as poetry is concerned, we find that the discussion on Aristotle's *Poetics*, so intense in the sixteenth century, dies out; the only major exception may be the work of Paolo Beni (1552–1625), which is closely allied to the Aristotelianism of the late sixteenth century. The reason may be that 'mimesis', as a key aesthetic concept, was completely displaced by that of 'meraviglia' (wonder) caused by conceits and *acutezze*. Indeed the most innovative works in the aesthetics of the seventeenth century are those dedicated to clarifying the subtleties of the *concetto* and the *acutezza*.

The pioneer in the area is Matteo Peregrini (1595–1652) with two works, *Delle acutezze che altrimenti spiriti, vivezze e concetti volgarmente si appellano* ('Concerning "Acuities", or Witticisms, Lively Sayings and Conceits As They are Commonly Called', 1639) and *I fonti dell'ingegno ridotti ad arte* ('The Sources of Wit Explained', 1650). For Peregrini, the *concetto* is not the result of logic (reason) but rather of ingenuity (*ingegno*), an aesthetic faculty which draws things together in a new and surprising way. The *concetto* is, in its essence, a daring metaphor which highlights unsuspected similarities among things in a way that shows the 'acumen' of the poet and which pleases the reader, who marvels at the mysteries of reality. However, Peregrini, perhaps because he was the first to write on the *concetto* and because he had the sense of classical decorum, is quite restrained and advises poets to abstain from *concetti* that are empty, exaggerated or lacking in energy.

Very close to Peregrini's interests was Cardinal Sforza Pallavicino (1607–67), whose works *Del bene* ('Concerning the Good', 1644) and *Dello stile e del dialogo* ('On Style and the Dialogue', 1646) focus on the *concetto*. Like Peregrini, Pallavicino considers the *concetto* to be the fruit of imagination or inventiveness and not the intellect. But with greater vigour than Peregrini, the Cardinal underscores the aspect of delight in poetry, thus opening the road to a hedonism which the Aristotelians of the old school would never have accepted. A *concetto* is successful when it presents a 'novità repentina' (a sudden novelty), the 'nervous and clever' force which distinguishes a true and delightful *concetto* from a daring metaphor. The *concetto* brings literature close to science because like science it finds the universals that are in things which appear to be quite different from each other. It is interesting to remember that Sforza Pallavicino found Marino's poetry lacking that quality which causes 'meraviglia' – a proof of the 'moderation' of Marino's Baroque.

The foremost theorist of the *concetto* was the Jesuit Emanuele Tesauro (1592–1675), who is remembered above all for his *Cannocchiale aristotelico* ('Aristotelian Telescope', 1670, definitive edition). This work is divided into several treatises in which various forms of *acutezza* are examined. Tesauro maintains that it is necessary to abandon the idea that the difference between sign and referent is a defect of human language. Indeed only angels have a language in which sign and referent coincide perfectly; and that is why they know 'the truth', but do not write poetry. In fact poetry exists only thanks to the insufficiency of human language, because its goal is not 'the truth' but 'discourse', and its tool is metaphor. All language is metaphor and can draw together an infinite number of referents in an endless number of combinations. *Ingegno* is that faculty which – like a telescope – brings tremendously distant realities nearer, finding in them common elements. A metaphor can contain many, in fact all other, metaphors if it is created with *ingegno*; and the pleasure for the reader is seeing how this occurs. Given this particular interpretative point of view, one understands why Tesauro concerned himself with distinguishing different forms of language (language of the body, of vowels, etc.; see below, p. 333); and why with him the Baroque reached its highest point, for he succeeded in breaking that link between poetic language and metaphysics which was taken for granted in the Middle Ages and in the Renaissance.

Writers on politics, history and morals

The flowering of political writing at this time is certainly due to Italy's political situation. The impossibility of effective resistance against the invaders found a sort of compensation either in utopian evasion, in satire, or in acceptance of the *status quo*, justified by the 'ragion di stato'. The utopian line had its major representative in *La città del sole* ('The City of the Sun') by the Calabrian Tommaso Campanella (1568–1639), who became a Dominican monk. In 1589 he published his first important work, *Philosophia sensibus demonstrata*, which was condemned by the ecclesiastical authorities. Forced to flee, he went first to Naples, then to Rome, Florence and Bologna. In 1594 he was arrested in Padua, and after a period of incarceration and torture, was freed and exiled to Calabria. Here Campanella became the inspiration behind a popular rebellion. He was betrayed by the peasants he sought to liberate, turned over to the Spanish police and again imprisoned. To avoid execution, he pretended to be mad and remained in prison until 1626. Once freed, he again had problems with the Inquisition and was again forced to flee, this time to Paris, where he was received with honour at the court of Louis XIII. He died in Paris in 1639.

Campanella composed the majority of his numerous works in prison. In addition to a remarkable lyrical production – unique in Italian literature for its metaphysical overtones – he wrote treatises on rhetoric, astronomy and theology both in Latin and Italian; he even composed a defence of Galileo. Some of these works managed to reach Italian and foreign readers, and when he was finally set free, Campanella found that his name had become quite famous. *La città del sole*, written in Italian in 1602 (but first published in Germany in 1623), is a brief dialogue in which a sailor describes the life of the inhabitants and the justice that reigns in a utopian city which represents a combination of communist ideals with a monarchical, theocratic organisation.

The satirical weapon against foreign domination made its strongest show with the *Ragguagli di Parnaso* by Traiano Boccalini. Born in 1556 in Loreto, Boccalini embarked on a political career and was governor of Benevento for a brief period. His sudden death in Venice in 1613 created the suspicion that he was poisoned by the Spanish. In 1605 Boccalini began to publish his *ragguagli* ('dispatches'), which numbered more than 300 at the time of his death; an additional thirty *ragguagli* were published posthumously (1615) with the title *Pietra del paragone* ('Touchstone'). The author imagines Parnassus as a city in a continuous state of holiday, where (mostly) poets and politicians meet. He pretends to send reports from this city, concerning a large variety of themes, such as contemporary poetry or current vices, especially hypocrisy and cruelty. But it is mainly the political theme that dominates the *Ragguagli*. The anti-Spanish satire becomes truly ferocious: the Spanish invaders are incapable of good government, and all that they do is the product of ignorance, barbarity and cruelty. For Boccalini, the Venetian republic represented the ideal government; and because of his republican ideas he wrote hostile criticisms of Machiavelli's *Principe*. Boccalini's political views are more immediately evident in a non-fictional and non-satirical treatise, *La bilancia politica di tutte le opere di Traiano Boccalini* ('The Political Scales of All the Works of T.B.'), published in 1678, which contains a two-part commentary on the writings of Tacitus.

It is significant that in the late sixteenth and early seventeenth centuries interest in Tacitus became very intense, replacing the Livian model which had dominated historical writing in the Renaissance. The change responds to the decline of republican ideals and the ascent of the 'ragion di stato' as a justification of despotism. Thus, if the republican Boccalini violently attacked Tacitus, defenders were not lacking. Examples are Ludovico Zuccolo's *Ragion di stato* (1621) and Ludovico Settala's *Della ragion di stato* (1627), in which the relationship between moral law and the practical needs of the state is lucidly examined, following the theories formulated by Botero at the end of the previous century. Along these same lines, but with a more literary tendency, are the works of the Bolognese nobleman Virgilio Malvezzi (1595–1654), who lived at the Spanish court for many years. In his *Discorsi sopra Cornelio Tacito* (1622) Malvezzi used a sententious style, reminiscent of Tacitus and Seneca, which found many admirers even among the Spanish *concettisti*. All these political writers of the seventeenth century depart from the traditional Aristotelian and Thomistic notion of state and power: they find their models in Machiavelli and Tacitus, but their political interests are wider than those of Machiavelli.

Another interesting writer in this connection is Francesco Fulvio Frugoni (1620–84), author of *Il cane di Diogene* (1689), in which the dog Saetta describes his life with his master, the philosopher Diogenes. It is a work in seven 'barks' hovering between picaresque novel and moral treatise, full of digressions and satirical thrusts against the world of courtiers and men of letters, combining both learned and popular elements.

The relation between politics and morality was the concern also of the historians of this period, for whom history was not just the traditional *magistra vitae*, but an indispensable basis of political praxis. The clearest example of this change is to be found in Paolo Sarpi (1552–1623), author of *Istoria del Concilio Tridentino*, published in London in 1619 and soon translated into several languages. In reconstructing the events of the Council of Trent, Sarpi focuses on the Curia's manipulations, which in his view were aimed at saving its temporal power, and had had disastrous consequences for Christianity. The opposition to the Curia on the part of this monk stemmed from an event of great juridical importance: Venice refused to hand two priests accused of common crimes over to the ecclesiastical tribunal; the Curia then issued an interdict against the Venetian Republic. Sarpi wrote a series of works on the legal controversy, the most important being the *Trattato dell'interdetto di Paolo V* (1606). His prose is austere and lucid, modelled on Machiavelli's. A rejoinder came in Cardinal Sforza Pallavicino's *Istoria del Concilio di Trento* (1556–7), a scrupulous work, slowed down not so much by its documentation as by the aim of rebutting Sarpi's assertions point by point.

Daniello Bartoli (1608–85) was a Jesuit whose major work, *Istoria della Compagnia di Gesù* (1650–73), provides another example of *histoire engagée*. The work is very useful for its documentation, but also fascinating for the description of the exotic countries visited by the Jesuitic missions, as well as for its prose. Bartoli, the 'Marino of Baroque prose' according to De Sanctis' definition, is one of the greatest prose-writers of the century: his style is exuberant and emphatic, yet never *concettista*. In his numerous religious and moral works – such as *Torto e diritto del non si può* ('The Right and Wrong of What May Not Be Done', 1655), ridiculing the Accademia della Crusca, or *L'uomo al punto* ('Man at the Turning-Point', 1657) and *La ricreazione del savio* ('The Wise Man's Recreation', 1659) – Bartoli sets the best model of 'moderate Baroque' prose.

Not directly involved with the problems of politics, but reflecting the same atmosphere of deceit, danger and frustration that inspired the political writers, is a moral literature seeking to teach how to behave in this troubled world, how to exercise prudence in order to attain one's own good. Renaissance educational theory concentrated on the formation of the courtier or the prince, a man whose composure would reflect internal beauty; the moral literature of the seventeenth century addressed itself primarily to clergymen or to people who had no heroic aspirations but had to live their lives with caution and even hypocrisy. A treatise which is emblematic of the existential situation just mentioned is Torquato Accetto's *Della dissimulazione onesta* (1641), where dissimulation does not mean hypocrisy or lying but a shutting oneself off from the world in order to meditate quietly on positive values. Real life is found only in the deepest strata of our soul, not in the surface of worldly things. Accetto's ideas may have been influenced by the mystic 'quietism' of the Spaniard Miguel de Molinos.

Mention should also be made of religious literature, especially of sermons, which can be considered moral works, but in fact are primarily works of rhetoric, and contributed, perhaps more than any other, to the diffusion of Baroque taste. The masterpiece of this genre is the *Quaresimale* (1679) by Paolo Segneri (1624–94), whose sermons are inspired by 'the severe purpose of proving a truth of faith which is also practical'. His prose is free from specious erudition and *concetti*, but is both limpid and passionate.

Science writers

Galileo Galilei (1564–1642) was not only the founder of modern science, but also a remarkably talented man of letters. He wrote poetry and critical works on Dante, Petrarch, Ariosto and Tasso; but he was above all a brilliant prose writer. His major scientific essays, *Il Saggiatore* (*The Assayer*, 1623) and *Dialogo sopra i due massimi sistemi del mondo, tolemaico e copernicano* (*Dialogue Concerning the Two Major World Systems, the Ptolemaic and the Copernican*, 1632), are admirable for the lucidity of their prose and for the argumentative power, irony, and anti-rhetorical features they display. Galileo's prose is unique in the Seicento, and it keeps alive the best tradition of Tuscan prose of the previous century.

The students of Galileo did not imitate his style, however. Evangelista Torricelli (1608–47), the inventor of the barometer, is remembered for his *Lezioni accademiche* which were given at the Accademia della Crusca, the academy that defended, to the point of pedantry, the purity of Italian. The destination of these *Lezioni* gives an idea of the style of Torricelli's prose: slightly emphatic and moderately Baroque. Francesco Redi (1626–98) was the scientist who disproved the theory of spontaneous generation (*Esperienze intorno alla generazione degli insetti*, 1668). He too was a member of the Accademia della Crusca, and his prose is decorous but not as energetic as that of Galileo. Redi's literary fame is based on a dithyrambic poem, *Il Bacco in Toscana* (1685), in praise of wine in general and of more than 500 Tuscan wines. The variety of metres, and the use of rare words and neologisms, enliven this poem, which is otherwise simply a tiresome catalogue. Lorenzo Magalotti (1637–1712) (see below, p. 325) wrote the elegant *Lettere sulle terre odorose d'Europa e d'America dette volgarmente buccheri* ('Letters on the Fragrant Vases of Europe and of America Commonly called *Buccheri*', 1695), in which he surveys an endless number of vases to describe the perfume they exhale. His prose has a sensual, hedonistic quality which anticipates the Rococo.

19

Narrative prose

The novel

During the seventeenth and eighteenth centuries the novel developed as a distinct literary genre and began to impress itself on the literary consciousness of Western Europe as the most prestigious narrative mode. As early as 1640, the novelist Luca Assarino could proclaim with pride in his *Almerinda* (Venice, 1640): 'This is the great century of the novel'. More revealing for an understanding of the historical and aesthetic reasons for the favourable reception of the new genre is the statement in Giovan Battista Manzini's preface to *Il Crediteo* (Bologna, 1637): 'This kind of composition which is called by the moderns *romanzo* is the most difficult – when written in accordance with the rules of art – and as a result the most marvellous and glorious construct that human ingenuity can build.'

No fewer than 180 novels were published in Italy between 1600 and 1699. The pace of production quickened in the 1630s, peaked in the 1640s and 1650s, and practically came to a halt in the 1660s. Many of these novels enjoyed a remarkable popularity with their contemporaries, some of them going through more than thirty editions or reprints (while the same period saw only three new editions of the *Divine Comedy*). Moreover, a good number of them were translated into the other major European languages. Unquestionably, the seventeenth-century novel had a clear international character. The Neapolitan book collector Antonio Matina, in a catalogue of his private library compiled in the 1660s, lists ninety-two Seicento titles in Italian, fifteen in Spanish, twenty in French, and some thirty translations from French. By the middle of the century the historian Vincenzo Nolfi could lament the 'deluge of novels' in the preface to his *Elena restituita* (Venice, 1646): 'Honestly, the current century is going mad with the writing and reading of novels.' Yet until thirty years ago very little critical attention was accorded this vast body of fiction. In the eighteenth century, Seicento novels were dismissed as unreadable because of their diffuse, emphatic, often obscure style, while scholars of the nineteenth century tended to approach them with little sympathy because of their biased views of the post-Renaissance period as a time of negligible literary achievement.

In recent years Italian criticism has effectively addressed the main issues – bibliography, definition of the genre, theory, sociological implications, stylistic problems, reception – and has revealed unsuspected riches in this vast unexplored continent. From a strictly aesthetic point of view, modern readers of Seicento novels may continue to be few in number. But so rich an output should have a broad appeal for those concerned with the relationship between literature and the society which produces it; for the novel reflects, perhaps better than other genres, the ideological, ethical and literary climate of seventeenth-century society. Novelists were dependent upon the approval of a wide public and they therefore consciously reflected the ideas and tastes generally held, a tendency consonant with the fundamental tenet of Italian Baroque poetics that the reader's approval, not adherence to a set of abstract aesthetic values, makes for the success of literary efforts.

In Italy, long fictional works were popular with an aristocracy that did not gravitate around the court and the salons of a national capital such as Paris. It was popular also among the professional and mercantile bourgeoisie who looked to the nobility for an expression of their own social aspirations and literary preferences. A reading public of average education, intellectually not too discriminating, incapable of participating actively in shaping a narrative oriented towards greater moral and psychological realism; the lateness and slowness of the formation of a new literary taste and sensibility; and the return to neo-classicism with the Arcadian movement, account in part for the stagnation in the production of fiction during the late seventeenth and the eighteenth centuries in Italy and for the fact that the Baroque novel turned out to be a literary dead-end.

The type of novel most in vogue belonged to what is generally labelled the heroic-gallant genre; the apogee of these long stories of love, war and chivalric adventure occurred between 1620 and 1660. Marvel in content (extraordinary adventures, intrepid heroism, beautiful heroines, conquering knights) is matched by marvel in form (suspense and convoluted plots; rhetorical amplification and great sensitivity to scenery). The Greek romance, the Renaissance epic, the *novella*, the pastoral and the love lyric are among its main sources. The major characters are generally princes and princesses who have met with adverse fortune. The main, and/or the secondary, plot begins with the separation of a pair of lovers and follows each of the two partners on their separate journeys through the ups and downs of an adventurous existence. The stock-in-trade of these wanderings comprises wide-ranging adventures on land and water, attacks by pirates, abductions, battles, duels, jousting matches, palace intrigues and mistaken identities. Invariably, the narrative closes with the reunion of the two lovers and their eventual marriage. The omniscient narrator generally speaks in the third person. Interpolated tales, conversations and monologues are given in direct speech. Another significant formal feature of novel-writing lies in the adherence to the idea that the language of prose fiction should be elevated and ornate, even sententious.

The Italian heroic novel, of which the Dalmatian Giovan Francesco Biondi (1572–1644) was one of the initiators, can be placed in the long tradition of chivalric literature. Biondi lived away from Italy most of his life, converted to Protestantism and was knighted and made a Gentleman of the Bedchamber by James I. His successful trilogy, *Eromena* (Venice, 1624; London, 1632), *La donzella desterrada* ('The Banished Virgin', Venice, 1627; London, 1635) and *Coralbo* (Venice, 1632; London, 1655), is also indebted to the neo-Latin novel *Argenis* (1621) by John Barclay, a Scottish humanist who sought to assimilate contemporary political history into the courtly adventurous novel. (Dates are those of the Italian edition, followed by the contemporary English translation where one is known to exist.) In the two sequels to *Eromena* politics, even more than love, becomes the predominant theme. Yet any attempt to interpret the trilogy as a consistent *roman à clef* is bound to fail, for only a limited number of episodes are based on actual events and characters. The general tone fluctuates between nostalgia for the chivalric world and the demystification of traditional heroic ideals. Biondi's trilogy reflects this never-resolved contradiction between his appreciation of aristocratic values and bourgeois realism.

Aspects of the allegorical romance, like the constant reference to historical reality, or the equally constant concern to unite the romantic and the realistic, are present also in the novels of many other writers, among whom are Pace Pasini (1583–1644), Francesco Pona (1595–1655), Maiolino Bisaccioni (1582–1663) and Girolamo Brusoni (1614–86), all members of the Venetian Academy of the Incogniti founded by Giovan Francesco Loredano (1607–61), an influential political figure, munificent patron and himself a novelist and translator of novels. Loredano's earliest novel, *La Dianea* (Venice, 1635; London, 1654), was enthusiastically received in its own time. Part of the success may be due to the fact that contemporary readers saw within the fiction a reflection of their own age, that of the Thirty Years' War. Quite complex in format, the *Dianea* centres around the stories of four main couples plus a few minor ones.

Whereas Biondi and Loredano bring heroism into the modern world, a more abstract and sublime form of heroism is depicted in Giovan Ambrogio Marini's *Calloandro fedele* (Rome, 1653), the recognised masterpiece of the heroic novel which remained popular in Italy well into the mid-nineteenth century. Part I of the novel first appeared in 1640, Part II in 1641; Marini (c. 1594–c. 1650), a Genoese priest and religious essayist, spent over a decade improving the coherence and structural unity of the narrative and toning down or deleting episodes or details contrary to the idealistic expectations of readers. The influence of the romances of chivalry can be seen in the exotic setting (Constantinople, Trebizond) and the remote time of the action. The protagonists, Calloandro and Leonilda, are superhuman beings exposed to multitudes of trials and concerned more with their reputation than with history or politics. Their principal weapons in the struggle against a harsh fortune are stoic constancy and clear reason. The representation of the relativity of reality, of the instability of all things, and of a world in turmoil, subject to the whims of

Fortune, and the resulting open-ended structure, with a focus on suspense, shift, metamorphosis and masking, are typical of the Baroque novel.

Great love and devotion, among the most important aspects of the traditional heroic ideal, gain a more prominent place vis-à-vis the recounting of heroic deeds of great figures in such heroic sentimental works as Luca Assarino's *Stratonica* (Milan, 1635; London, 1651) and Bernardo Morando's *La Rosalinda* (Piacenza, 1650; London, 1733), which concentrate on the psychology of love. Compared to the *Calloandro*, Assarino's *Stratonica*, which deals with the theme of *aegritudo amoris* and derives from a *novella* by Matteo Bandello and Petrarch's *Trionfo d'Amore*, seems a masterpiece of conciseness and psychological penetration, features which were to be recognised as the distinctive mark of the psychological novel as it developed in the eighteenth century.

No less valuable a reflection of the more typical idealistic heroism of the age is the Seicento devout novel, which played a role in the religious revival of the Counter-Reformation. Anton Giulio Brignole-Sale's *Maria Maddalena, peccatrice e convertita* (Genoa, 1636) stands out as a prototype of the genre because of its characteristic themes and mixture of religious mysticism and sensuality. Mary Magdalen and other biblical characters like Bathsheba and Susanna are the personifications of a heroic ideal offered to the educated minority of the Baroque age as an alternative to the heroes of the heroic-chivalric novels. The same underlying faith in will-power that enables one to be steadfast and to exemplify the standards of religious orthodoxy are present in the novels dealing with contemporary subjects. Noteworthy for their success and longevity are Giovan Battista Rinuccini's *Il cappuccino scozzese* ('The Scottish Capuchin', Macerata, 1644), reissued in a somewhat revised version as late as 1863, and Antonio Lupis's *La Marchesa d' Hunsleij, overo l'Amazone scozzese* ('The Marchioness of Hunsleigh, or the Scottish Amazon', Venice, 1677), which reached nineteen editions between 1677 and 1723.

Moral indignation and religious fervour can hardly be recognised in the works of Girolamo Brusoni (1614–86), historian, short-story writer, novelist and journalist. His best-known work is his trilogy *La gondola a tre remi* ('The Three-Oared Gondola', Venice, 1657), *Il carrozzino alla moda* ('The Fashionable Carriage', Venice, 1658), and *La peota smarrita* ('The Lost Boat', Venice, 1662). It presents no knight-errantry, but a picture of Venetian *dolce vita* in the middle of the seventeenth century. The protagonist Glisomiro, a learned patrician and an irresistible Don Juan, is an autobiographical projection of the author. The narrative is replete with anecdotes, sketches, descriptions, refined conversations and academic discussions which depict a socio-cultural milieu rather than individual characters. The trilogy resolutely turns its back on the codes of martial and erotic heroism so prominent in the heroic-gallant novels and evidences the progressive transformation of the novel in the direction of a realism grounded in a greater situational and psychological truth. Yet, even as it looks forward to several aspects of the eighteenth-century novel, what might pass for realism in Brusoni's trilogy is still invariably heightened by the Baroque taste for sensational attitudes and situations, and by a preference for metaphor and conceits. Also missing from the work is the consciously vindicated intellectual freedom which, along with freedom of morals, characterises the libertinism of some of the Incogniti of Venice and more especially of Brusoni's friend Ferrante Pallavicino (1615–44), who was beheaded at Avignon for his anti-papal writings. Restless and ambitious, this rebellious monk's interests ranged from erotic narratives such as *La pudicitia schernita* ('Modesty Scorned', Venice, 1638) and the *Rete di Vulcano* ('Vulcan's Net', Venice, 1640) and religious novels such as *Il Giuseppe* (Venice, 1637) and *La Susanna* (Venice, 1638) to satirical fiction. In 1641 he published the *Corriere svaligiato*, the basis for *The post-boy rob'd of his mail* (London 1692–3) attributed to Charles Gildon; and in 1643 the *Divorzio celeste* (London, 1679). The term 'novel', which implies a fictionalised content, may be unsuitable to describe these libertine works. Because of the exceptional blending of rationalist anti-authoritarian satire, contemporary history, autobiography and fiction found in them, they could more accurately be referred to as satires.

This same confluence of several literary traditions (the picaresque novel, the Lucianic dialogue, biography, chronicle, etc.) is patent in one of the best-sellers of late seventeenth-century Europe: Gian Paolo Morana's (1642–c. 1692) *Esploratore turco* (or *Espion du Grand Seigneur*, or *Turkish Spy*), which was issued anonymously in Paris (1684) and then in English in London (1687–94), and inaugurated yet another sub-genre of the modern novel, the pseudo-foreign-letter or spy-fiction. The Turkish spy Mahmut, Morana's narrative alter ego, stands out as an emblematic figure, through whose narcissistic and morally sterile behaviour the author projects a starkly pessimistic vision of later seventeenth-century European society.

The *novella*

The triumph of the novel in the first half of the Seicento was not a victory at the expense of a totally different form of prose fiction, the Boccaccian *novella*, but rather part of its development. A measure of the distance the *novella* had travelled since Boccaccio is the absence of anti-clerical stories and the decline of the *beffa* (practical joke) tales once so typical of this narrative form. This development left romance and history as its main subject-matter, and accounts for the shift from comedy to tragedy as the dominant mode of short fiction. Other striking differences can be found in the frame-story and in the length of the *novelle*. Detecting a unified theoretical pattern in seventeenth-century *novelle* is very difficult. What characterises them is their variety, both in technique and structure and in thematic development.

As in the case of the novel, Venice and Genoa provide the most vivid illustrations of *novella* output. The appearance of the first instalment of the collection by the Accademici Incogniti in Venice in 1641 marked the peak of the vogue of the academic *novella* that was to last beyond the publication in 1651 of the *Cento novelle amorose*, to which forty-six authors contributed. This new *Decameron* lacks a structured frame. Love and death, usually in their more elementary forms of lust and murder rather than passion and sentiment, are the themes which dominate these academic *novelle*. Almost all of the texts in the collection are deeply rooted in the literary tradition. The narrators' proclivity for repeatedly astonishing the reader gives another special imprint to these stories. They are of various length, although the general tendency is toward an expansion obtained by the insertion of inner monologues, speeches, letters, descriptions and comments by the authors.

The tradition of witty retorts initiated by Boccaccio and enhanced by the Renaissance *facetia* spills over into the two major *novella* collections by individual writers: *Le instabilità dell'ingegno* ('The Fickleness of Wit', Bologna, 1635) by the Genoese Anton Giulio Brignole Sale (1605–55) and *L'Arcadia in Brenta* ('Arcadia on the Brenta', Cologne/Venice/Bologna, 1667) by the Venetian Giovanni Sagredo (1617–82). What most sets them apart from their models is the swerve in emphasis from narrative to conversation and comedy of manners. In addition to short narratives, we find here lyrics, songs, puzzles, jokes and descriptions of contemporary life and gossip, local customs and amenities. With Brignole Sale especially it is not *news*, the unusual happenings, that count, but the new ways his Baroque style embellishes and relates them. The four young couples who retire to a villa outside Genoa during an outbreak of plague in the *Instabilità* display wit and verbal skill.

The ludic and parodic aspect of Seicento taste is also visible in one of the oldest and most complete Italian fairy-tale collections, the *Cunto de li cunti* of Giambattista Basile (1575–1632), printed posthumously between 1634 and 1636. It is particularly apparent in the subversive choice of the Neapolitan dialect by the author, a learned man of letters thoroughly versed in the current Marinistic manner. The collection of fifty tales told by ten old hags in the course of five days (which explains its commonly used title *Pentamerone*) is set in a frame-narrative: the story of the deceived Princess Zoza's melancholy and her winning of a husband. Most of the stories derive from the oral tradition rather than from the literary canon. Some of the most familiar folk-tales, among them 'Cinderella', 'Puss in boots', 'Beauty and the beast' and 'The three oranges', are included. Basile had a predecessor in Giovan Francesco Straparola (see above, pp. 227–8), who by the middle of the Cinquecento had turned to folklore and fairy-tales as a major source of his *novelle*. But it is Basile's bold approach to folk materials, his blending of the world of magic with the often coarse and sordid realism of the Neapolitan setting, his infusing of literary preciosity with the vulgar, dialectal tone of the folk-tale, that make the *Pentamerone* a model of Baroque art and a milestone in the history of

European narrative. The moral of the fables remains an open question, since Basile's narrative attitude and personality are complex and ambivalent, both courtly and popular.

Another Seicento masterpiece inspired by popular culture is *Le sottilissime astuzie di Bertoldo* ('The Very Clever Tricks of B.') by Giulio Cesare Croce (1550–1609) and its sequel, *Le piacevoli e ridicolose simplicità di Bertoldino* ('The Pleasant and Ridiculous Escapades of B.', Milan, 1606). The author, born near Bologna, was a professional storyteller who composed verse in dialect and earned his living as a blacksmith. The first book, which features the crafty and ugly peasant Bertoldo, consists of reworkings of materials derived from an anonymous work in Latin dealing with the wisdom of King Solomon, the *Dialogus Salamonis et Marcolphi* (1434). The adventures of his son Bertoldino, a simpleton who has to be rescued by his mother Marcolfa, are more original, but still in the literary tradition of portraying the awkward simplicity of peasants. Structurally, the two parts are presented in the form of a series of encounters between the protagonists on the one hand, and their king and masters on the other, in battles of wit and intelligence. Behind Croce's criticism of the arrogance of power and wealth lies the resentment of the powerless class of exploited peasants. Not one to respect ideological consistency, Croce's curious artistic bent led him to an unrestrained mixing of literary modes (folk-tales, popular anecdotes, proverbs), a fanciful moralising, and a progressive slide from an eclectic narrative in *Bertoldo* to a miscellany of aphorisms and fables in *Bertoldino*; from a realistic setting in *Bertoldo* to one of sheer fantasy in *Bertoldino*.

Travel literature and autobiography

Further examples of the diversity of Seicento prose are to be seen in the travel narratives and autobiographies published in this period. A good example is Francesco Carletti's *Ragionamenti sopra le cose da lui vedute ne' suoi viaggi* ('Reflections on What He Has Seen in His Travels'). This Florentine merchant (c. 1573–1636), who circumnavigated the globe, records minute details of almost every place he visited on his lengthy journeys (1591–1606). Climate, landscape, diet, social customs, the hard life of the Amerindians, the dark sides of the Japanese ethos and the beauty of Goa's women, all the rich variety and colour of the world beyond Europe have their place in his dense, two-part report to his patron, the Grand Duke Ferdinando de' Medici. But the charm of his narrative comes more from the seemingly uninhibited mingling of the merchant's private affairs – reasons why he leaves home, the rhythms of oceanic trade, the operations of international financiers, the problems in regaining his fortune, stolen by Dutch pirates – and the broad sweep of description and analysis by the traveller-explorer. Carletti is capable of amusing directness and also of vigorous descriptive effects; his idiomatic

Florentine prose is so lively and fluent that it carries the reader through sustained descriptions without causing boredom.

The *Viaggi* (Venice, 1667–81) of Pietro Della Valle (1586–1652), a well-to-do Roman aristocrat who toured the East for personal reasons, are neither a journal nor a report, but a collection of 'familiar letters' addressed to a friend, a Neapolitan naturalist. This vast travel book purports to be Della Valle's account of his voyages in Turkey, Persia, the Holy Land, Egypt and India between 1614 and 1626. It is in fact an imaginative compound of fact and fiction, at once an autobiographical traveller's tale and an authentic picture of early seventeenth-century Asia by an exceptionally perceptive and learned, albeit biased, Western tourist. Della Valle offers a rich body of data and at the same time raises fascinating questions about self and otherness, and he does so in a style free from affectation and unusually lucid for the times.

By the middle of the seventeenth century a number of Italian travel writers were looking at other European cultures, specially those of northern Europe. Italian intellectuals were going through a serious cultural crisis and were beginning to travel to the north no longer as teachers, diplomats or artists but as observers and tourists, both inspired and hampered by their awesome national legacy. Illustrations of this trend in Italian travel literature are Lorenzo Magalotti's *Relazioni di viaggio in Inghilterra, Francia e Svezia* and Giovanni Francesco Gemelli Careri's *Viaggi per l'Europa* (Naples, 1693), books which already usher in the next century. Yet the proximity of the modern travel book to autobiographical narrative, contrived from a multitude of adventures or encounters in non-causal series, can perhaps be better inferred from the efforts of obscure travel writers from the Italian provinces such as Francesco Negri (1623–98) and Sebastiano Locatelli (c. 1637–c. 1693).

To be sure, Italian autobiography has never received the attention its English, French and German counterparts have enjoyed. Signs of a reassessment of autobiographical writings have come about recently in the wake of the ongoing debate on the emergence of modern autobiography. There are good reasons for the revived interest in some representative Seicento texts, especially the *Vita scritta da lui medesimo* (1625) of Gabriello Chiabrera (1552–1638), the *Della vita* of Secondo Lancellotti (1583–1643), the *Memorie* (1648) of Guido Bentivoglio (1577–1644) and the *Confessioni* (1696) of Carlo de' Dottori (1618–85). The authors were well-known protagonists of the cultural and literary life of their times, and their writings reflect a diversity of narrative forms and autobiographical styles, anticipating the works of Goldoni, Casanova and Alfieri in the next century (see below, pp. 395–6).

20

Theatre

In the annals of the Italian theatre the Seicento has been traditionally considered a low point between the two great seasons of the High Renaissance and the Settecento. Since the 1960s, however, the generation of Torquato Tasso (1544–95) and Battista Guarini (1538–1612), and the dramatists immediately following them have received more serious and fruitful consideration by scholars. The works of these playwrights, who were the contemporaries of Shakespeare, Lope de Vega and Molière, were both read and acted, and Italian acting companies carried them to all the major capitals of Europe, so that their influence was immediately and widely felt.

The theatre system of the Seicento is better understood from the perspective of spectacle, which represented an essential aspect of the cultural and social life of the courts, the academies and the cities. Even the liturgical and devotional life of the post-Tridentine Church took on a visually spectacular character. The social and political history of centres such as Rome, Venice, Naples, Ferrara, Parma and Turin was reflected and transfigured into theatrical spectacle and the fashionable dramatic forms of the moment, from the court *festa* to the religious drama, from the improvised comedy to opera.

Court festivals retained the social and political significance traditionally associated with them in the Cinquecento. What changed were the frequency and the expectations with which they continued to be welcomed by the élite public and the artists involved in their production. The court *festa* held at Mantua in 1608 to celebrate the marriage of Francesco Gonzaga and Margherita of Savoy, and the Parma festivities of 1628, duplicated in magnificence the Medici's 1589 nuptials, but these and similar events had lost some of the ideological relevance and cultural prestige which the late Cinquecento had attached to them. Courts were now expected to provide theatrical entertainment for their members and foreign guests. In the later 1650s, Cardinal Giovanni Carlo de' Medici, brother of the Grand Duke, personally supervised the court theatrical initiatives and patronised those of the Florentine academies. Indeed, by the middle of the century the political and economic dimensions of the theatre had become more conspicuous owing to the patronage accorded the professional companies. Some princely patrons, moreover, formed troupes, and exchanged or loaned players to foreign rulers.

The Church was no less active than the courts. Though it renewed with energy its attacks on the 'corrupting' influence of the theatre, it ended by appropriating the highly social and public art of drama in order to communicate church teachings to audiences of diverse social and educational backgrounds. Understandably, the irreverent and sometimes offensive humour of the *commedia dell'arte* made it a controversial subject with ecclesiastical detractors. Characteristic of much anti-theatrical clerical writing was the distinction between court and academic theatre and theatrical performances given in streets and squares, which were considered more morally pernicious and socially dangerous. Clerical moralists predictably directed much of their hostility against the mountebanks and other itinerant performers rather than the players of the major troupes who enjoyed the support of men of letters and the nobility. Led by the Jesuits, who promoted acting training in their colleges throughout the Christian world, the Church encouraged the writing and staging of sacred drama aimed at treating religious subjects (biblical and hagiographical) traditionally, in the forms of the secular theatre. It is not surprising that the emerging genre of opera found a favourable terrain for growth at the papal court of Urban VIII (1623–44), where Gian Lorenzo Bernini was experimenting with his grandiose stage-sets and Cardinal Giulio Rospigliosi (later to become Pope Clement IX, 1667–9), the best librettist of the day, was producing his successful performances of religious and epic operas.

Although hard pressed by the restraints of censorship and the competition of the professional companies, the academies continued to produce texts of high quality, build theatres and conduct innovative experiments. They must be given credit for bringing together different theatrical practices, and for mediating between public and private performances, the ideologies of the Church and the court. For example, the Sienese Accademia degli Intronati, founded in 1525, published in 1611 a collection of its plays, *Delle commedie degli Intronati di Siena*, and the Congrega dei Rozzi, founded in 1521 by a group of Sienese artisans, was renamed Accademia dei Rozzi in 1665. In the middle decades of the Seicento the Rozzi specialised in pastoral drama, and in the later seventeenth century they staged the satirical comedies of Girolamo Gigli (1660–1722) and the comedies of character of Jacopo Angelo Nelli (1673–1767).

Commedia dell'arte

The period between 1570 and 1630 is considered the Golden Age of the *commedia dell'arte*, now finally recognised as a new theatrical art-form (see also above, pp. 284–6). Troupes of professional actors travelled throughout Italy and Europe, performing in public markets and squares as well as in princely courts and covered theatres. Seicento historians have posited three major issues in recent *commedia* studies: the relations of the professional actors with the holders of political and economic power; the interrelationship between the written theatre and the improvised comedy; and the development of the comedians' aesthetic ideas from an early poetics of 'naturalness' to the mid-century theory of the *arte* as professional organisation and pure spectacle. In response to new public and market pressures during the Seicento, the system of theatrical production was organised into specialised sectors, where people with distinct competences were active: playwrights, actors, singers, impresarios, scenic designers and musicians.

Scholars have further qualified the received wisdom that stresses the distinction between the first and the second generation of *commedianti*. Noble patronage in the early decades of the seventeenth century proved to be valuable to the professional companies, most notably to those under the protection of the great ducal houses of northern Italy (the Este of Ferrara, Gonzaga-Nevers of Mantua, Farnese of Parma): the Gelosi (c. 1571–1604), the Accesi (c. 1590–c. 1628), the Confidenti (c. 1574–c. 1639), the Uniti (c. 1578–c. 1640) and the Fedeli (c. 1601–c. 1640). During this time, which is also the period of the *commedia*'s closest association with written drama, a number of renowned actor-authors set themselves the task of defining the salient characteristics of the profession. Their method was to publish the materials already circulating among the players, such as *scenari* (scenarios – plot-lines of plays to be performed), *lazzi* (verbal and physical comic routines) and *tirate* (lengthy speeches or soliloquies), posing a series of pragmatic questions concerning acting and improvisation in relation to the scripted drama. This practice fostered a heightened consciousness of recurrent patterns, of the changing and changeable intermingling of popular entertainment forms with the styles and materials of the literary theatre. In a tradition that relied so strongly on improvised dialogue and body-language, it was not the quality of the plot that marked success, but rather the skill of the performance. With regard to subject-matter, the scenarios drew heavily on farce, but much was borrowed from classical and neo-classical scripted texts. In the later seventeenth century, public taste for Spanish drama accounted for a larger proportion of melodramatic and sentimental plots. Similarly, literary pastoral was invaded by comic elements and techniques from improvised comedy.

A number of early seventeenth-century collections and essays significantly extend our knowledge of the genre. In 1607 Francesco Andreini (1548–1624), the leader of the Gelosi company, published the fifty-five dialogues of *Le bravure del Capitano Spavento* as a memorial to his acting career. Flaminio Scala's *Il teatro delle favole rappresentative*, the first collection of scenarios ever printed, appeared in 1611. Between 1618 and 1622 the academic amateur Basilio Locatelli gathered over 100 scenarios which are now kept at the Biblioteca Casanatense in Rome. Pier Maria Cecchini (1563–1645), famous for his performance as the Fritellino mask and *capocomico* of the Accesi, wrote learned essays on the social and moral purpose of the comic theatre in his *Brevi discorsi intorno alla commedia, commedianti e spettatori* ('Brief Essays on Comedy, Actors and Spectators', Naples, 1614). Niccolò Barbieri (1576–

1641), the creator of the Beltram mask, provided with his *La supplica* (1634) the most sustained apology in defence of the acting profession. To be sure, the *comici* of the more prestigious troupes were very eager to produce their own scripted texts. Such creative efforts signal a conscious attempt by players to assert the cultural respectability of their profession against the persistent ecclesiastic hostility and scorn of the men of letters. The most interesting, and decidedly the most prolific, actor-author of the time was Giovan Battista Andreini (1576–1654), son of the famous Andreini theatrical couple, Francesco and Isabella.

The second half of the Seicento saw a gradual decline of the *commedia*'s vitality. Paradoxically, the period coincided with the expansion of activities of various Italian acting companies throughout Europe, particularly in France. Extensive travelling and ever-increasing demands for changes required by regional socio-cultural and linguistic preferences led to the weakening of the original *arte* spirit and the worsening of internal feuding among the major actors, which in turn undermined the team spirit necessary for an improvised performance. In Italy itself, as the century passed its mid-point the professional actors, burdened by the need to please spectators of varying social standing and hard-pressed by the tide of the melodrama, brought experimentation to a virtual halt. Thus the *commedia* reached a greater uniformity of standards and practices than at any other time. While this development helped its diffusion and its appropriation among amateur actors it also hastened a retreat into excessive specialisation (e.g. the special emphasis on masked actors and masked roles). By the end of the century, *commedia* performances had become a stereotyped series of comic routines and slapstick physicality, often extremely coarse and appealing to the lowest taste of the spectators. The collection of engravings by Jacques Callot (c. 1592–1635) known as the *Balli di Sfessania*, historically unreliable as they may be, illustrate eloquently the orientation of the *arte* in Naples: greater movement and energy, obscene humour and the fiendish nature of its masks.

Regular comedy

It is not surprising that the hybrid dramatic forms which distinguish the Seicento theatre – the *commedia dell'arte*, the opera, the *festa* and the achievements of scenic artist and architects – have attracted much more attention than the traditional forms of dramatic literature. The history of the regular comedy, tragedy and pastoral drama in the Seicento is chiefly one of repetition of previous forms and contents, albeit with considerable changes and adaptations which show the vitality, breadth, and generally high technical quality of the dramatic production of the time. These modifications were justified only vaguely in the prefatory matter of the texts as the necessary adjustments 'for current use'.

It is difficult to categorise plays in this age of general *contaminatio* of forms and genres. Especially problematic is the distinction between scripted plays and staged plays, plays written for the theatre and plays written as literature. No matter what the dramatic genre, however, contextualising the regular theatre within the broader intellectual and literary horizons of the period can certainly help us to understand better the ways in which genres flourish within a culture, and to account for the inevitable tension between theorists and historians, in search of orderly patterns, and writers, bent on probing all their expressive resources and potentials. Artistically, we have a history with few masterpieces but with a distinguished global record of achievements, reflecting a generally high degree of theatrical craftsmanship and sophistication. One need only consider the strong influence which Italian dramatic forms and theatrical practices exerted on the dramatic structures of the early modern European theatre.

Though it is true that scenarios are often dependent on the literary comedy, the latter is also notably influenced by the *commedia dell'arte*. Conspicuous in this respect are the short-lived and much-maligned *commedie ridicolose*, unpretentious scripted plays in various dialects often staged, especially in Rome, by academies of amateur actors, which drew heavily on the materials and strategies of the improvised theatre. The regular comedy of neo-classical stamp, both erudite and *grave*, which continued to be cultivated in the Seicento by conservative authors and academic *dilettanti* bent on preserving time-honoured situations, characters and formal patterns (e.g. the unities, five acts), allowed for a wide range of experimentation even with features of the improvised comedy.

Changes such as multiple levels of action, moralising plots and high-ranking characters were introduced by literary dramatists as different in their intellectual and social backgrounds as the Bolognese Giovan Battista Manzini (1599–1664) and the Roman Giovanni Andrea Lorenziani (1637–1712), who deliberately set out to improve on regular comedy (compromised by its relationship with the *arte*) and to produce a more serious comedy, *morale* or *civile*, which could provide effective entertainment as well as a moral lesson. Towards the middle of the century, the Golden-Age Spanish comedy of romantic intrigue began to be imitated in Italy, especially in the productions of Iacopo Cicognini (1577–1633) and his son Giacinto Andrea (1606–60). The younger Cicognini was particularly influential in his own time, and even for some decades thereafter, as a versatile assimilator of the latest trends in dramaturgy. His literary output included some fifty titles, among them *La vita è un sogno* ('Life is a Dream'), a version of Calderón's play, and *Il convitato di pietra* ('The Guest of Stone'), an adaptation of Tirso de Molina's play on the Don Juan theme.

Within this overall picture emerge certain local characteristics which suggest a verifiable strand of regional comic theatre. An excellent example of the modernisation of the regular comedy is *La fiera*, a series of five five-act comedies by Michelangelo Buonarroti the Younger (1568–1646), portraying with verve and vivid realism country-market scenes which form the basis for making representatives of diverse social class perform and, above all, speak. Buonarroti also wrote a comedy in *ottava rima*, *Tancia* (1611), in which he similarly mimics the peasants' language much more than their loves and manners, in the tradition of the Tuscan rustic comedy. The author was a member of the Accademia della Crusca and intended his comedies to serve as a record of popular and dialectal speech. In the same category of home-grown comedy a special place must be given to the artistically more successful and stageworthy 'musical drama' *Il potestà di Colognole* ('The Mayor of C.') by the librettist Giovanni Andrea Moniglia (1624–1700), with which the Florentine Teatro della Pergola was inaugurated in 1647. Among the more original comic productions of the Seicento are the comedies written shortly before his death by the famed poet Carlo Maria Maggi (1630–99), professor of classics and secretary of the Milanese Senate: *Il manco male* ('The Lesser Evil', 1695); *Il barone di Birbanza* (1696); *I consigli di Meneghino* ('M.'s Advice', 1697); *Il falso filosofo* (1698), and the one-act dialogue on the reform of comedy, *Il concorso de' Meneghini* ('The Contest of the Meneghini', 1701). In these plays Maggi makes use in varying degrees of the Milanese dialect and of the fun-loving, good-hearted and sententious comic stock character Meneghino. Because of their local settings and middle-class themes these pieces were obviously destined to have very limited success outside Milan, but they set an important precedent for the establishment of a distinct Lombard literary culture. In Bologna Giulio Cesare Croce (see p. 324) was a prolific writer of popular poems and plays.

Tragedy

Literary drama was likewise extensively cultivated in its traditional form of tragedy. In this turbulent age themes of political violence and religious martyrdom, of impermanence and instability, abounded in dramatic literature. However, regular neo-classical tragedy was the type of theatre deliberately created by dramatists at the bidding of cultured patrons, in response to purely literary influences; and its appeal was largely limited to a refined élite. Towards the end of the century, among those who took an active part in the much-needed reform of the genre was Cardinal Giovanni Delfino (1617–99), whose *Dialogo sopra le tragedie* (1733) represented the aspirations and intentions of the advocates of neo-classical tragedy: traditional forms with modern contents and innovations. Delfino wrote three historical tragedies based on the traditional Counter-Reformation conflict between reason of state and love or personal ethics: *Cleopatra*, *Lucrezia*, *Creso*; and a free adaptation from Ariosto, *Medoro*, all printed posthumously in 1730.

The acknowledged masterpiece of Seicento tragedy is *Aristodemo* (1657) by the Paduan Carlo de' Dottori (1618–85), a courtier and diplomat well known as a poet, satirist and dramatist. Rediscovered in 1948 by Benedetto Croce, the play tells the story of the heroic virgin Merope, loved by her mother Amfia and her betrothed Policare, killed for reasons of honour by her own father, Aristodemo, aspirant to the kingdom of Messenia, who believes her to be impure and therefore unable to placate the gods for an old offence. Dottori's chief model was certainly traditional Greek tragedy. In the development of the compactly constructed plot, however, the author reverts to every theatrical device (flight of the lovers, substitution of persons, deceit, multiple deaths, double recognitions) to reverse the initial situation. Moreover, the play leans heavily upon Senecan horror-tragedy materials of revenge, murder, mutilation and carnage to satisfy the audience's appetite for violence and *meraviglia*; and the characterisation of Merope as a virgin martyr owes much to the Christian ethics and symbolism of contemporary sacred tragedy.

Court tragedy is also the province of Federico Della Valle (c. 1560–1628), now recognised as the most gifted Italian tragedian of the century. He held a minor administrative post at the Turin court of Charles Emanuel I of Savoy for most of his life and moved to Milan in 1606, where he enjoyed the patronage of the Spanish nobility. His slight dramatic opus consists of the youthful tragi-comedy, *Adelonda di Frigia*, printed posthumously; two biblical tragedies, *Iudit* (1627) and *Ester* (1627); and *La reina di Scotia*, written in 1591 but revised and published in 1628. Clearly, the poet's aim was to provide the tragic experience through reading or recitation. Only *Adelonda* was actually per-formed during his lifetime. An acute sense of the vanity of all mundane endeavours, especially court life, and of the futility of politics, and a deep concern with God's providence are the salient characteristics of Della Valle's tragic vision of life. He prefers heroines to heroes. Unlike Dottori, who in *Aristodemo* pursued the development of several characters through a variety of events and changes of mood, Della Valle in his tragedies focuses upon two characters, the victim and the persecutor, who confront each other at a moment of crisis. He employs a language which ranges from lyrical to rhetorical, even studiedly sententious. He adhered to the tradition of the prologue and the chorus and made effective use of hendecasyllabic and septenary lines. The best known of his plays is *La reina di Scotia* (1628) which deals with the last hours of Mary Stuart. The play does not make any concessions to the popular taste for the spectacular: the heroine's execution is not shown on stage but narrated by a messenger, and the events leading up to it are represented less by means of spectacle than by evocation and reflection. The members of the chorus are devoted to their queen. Their anxious questions and their comments on events are those of persons who share the hopes and fears of the protagonist, yet who are aware of the unalterable cosmic plan overruling the conflict of human wills. The poet heightens the dramatic effects of the piece by adopting a simple structure without subdivision into acts and scenes; by emphasising spatial constriction (the gaol-cell where all the action takes place); by eliminating proper names for the characters, who are identified only by their dramatic roles; and by focusing on the last hours of the life of the frail and aged ('povera, inferma ed in età cadente') queen, portrayed as a symbol of oppressed regality as well as of Catholic orthodoxy.

Much more popular and more often performed are the tragedies which originate from the other two centres of theatrical activity, the academies and the Church, for the entertainment and edification of a mixed public. Many of the best, written between 1600 and 1630 by famed *litterati* such as Ansaldo Cebà (1565–1623), Francesco Bracciolini (1566–1645) and Prospero Bonarelli (1588–1659), deviate from Greek and historical matter to turn to epic and fictional subjects. The complicated balancing of tragic and esoteric elements, of spectacle and ironic overtones behind the camouflage of neo-classical conventions, make Bonarelli's *Solimano* (Florence, 1620), with seven editions between 1620 and 1660, in many ways exemplary in the history of Seicento tragic theatre.

Understandably, the militantly religious climate of the age prompted Seicento tragedians to venture into sacred drama and to adapt religious subjects to the forms of contemporary profane tragedy. With its focus on a protagonist, often female, who resists adverse circumstances and persecution, and its reaffirmation of the eternal order of divine justice which removes the traditional tragic conflict (suffering is here seen to be not merely arbitrary but objectively necessary; death not expiatory but rewarding), sacred tragedy provided a perfectly viable alternative to secular tragedy, answering the quest of the Tridentine reformers for miracles and martyrdom. By far the most common source of materials for the *tragedia sacra*, already established as an identifiable type of religious drama already by the late 1560s, was the life of saints, especially of martyrs. Among the most interesting examples of the genre based on hagiographic sources is the *Ermenegildo martire* by the Jesuit Pietro Sforza Pallavicino (1607–67), a prominent churchman, literary critic and historian (see also above, p. 312). The play, performed and published in Rome in 1644, tells how the protagonist, the young Gothic King of Seville, is converted to Christianity by his French bride Ingonda, and is martyred by the agent of the heretical Aryan sect, his own father King Leovigildo. The dramatic economy of the simply structured plot manages to touch all the various registers of the pathetic in its representation of the differing conflicts between paternal and conjugal love and the martyr's unwavering faith.

Another play on the same subject was written by Pallavicino's fellow Jesuit, Emanuele Tesauro (1592–1675), the foremost theorist of the witty or Marinist style (see above, p. 313). In Tesauro's *Ermenegildo*, written in 1621 on the basis of a previous Latin version and published in Turin in 1661, the practice of *concettismo* joins with Christian horror in answering the age's demand for *meraviglia* even on the stylistic level. Whereas Pallavicino's modernist style is sober, selective and restrained, Tesauro's style is slow, threaded with refined conceits, antitheses and parallel structures. Tesauro's current reputation as a tragedian rests primarily on a recently unearthed play *Il libero arbitrio*

('Free Will'), an interesting example of Jesuit theatre in the vernacular. The promotion of a spectacular hagiographic dramatic literature culminated in the melodramatic librettos and operatic productions *San Bonifacio* (1641), *Santa Genoinda* (1642), and *Sant' Alessio* (1643), created by Giulio Rospigliosi for the Roman carnival. The drama of victorious faith inspired by the Catholic Reformation was moving toward seventeenth-century opera and oratorio.

Pastoral plays

While literary tragedy was written to be read or recited, rather than staged, pastorals, like comedies, were meant to be performed; an important fact which is still too often forgotten. Most Italian pastorals, like the celebrated *Aminta* (1578) of Torquato Tasso and the *Pastor fido* (1590) of Battista Guarini (see above, pp. 296–7), were tragi-comedies; but some were designated as tragedies, some as comedies, some as *favole* (further distinguished into *pastorali, boschereccie, piscatorie, marittime*). The entrenched opinion about the decline of the pastoral drama after the publication of the *Pastor fido* (1590) is now contested. On the contrary, the acrimonious *querelle* that took place around the play and the successful defence of Guarini's *tragicommedia pastorale* were of great significance in the development of the genre because they guaranteed the dignity of pastoral tragi-comedy alongside the established forms of tragedy and comedy. Moreover, unimpeded by categorical limits of genre, the pastoral was able to exercise a strong influence on the other forms of Seicento drama. Pastoral strains are regularly heard in tragedy and comedy, especially in terms of love entanglements, preciosity and erotic sentimentality. But the popular notion that Seicento dramatists, when not proselytising, indulged in romantic and pastoral escape fiction needs to be refuted. Tragi-comedy and plays of similar inspiration exploited all the themes typical of Baroque literature: violence and suffering; the mutability of fortune; contradiction between appearance and reality; magic and miracle.

Seicento pastoral drama can boast at least one authentic masterpiece, the *Filli di Sciro* of Guidobaldo Bonarelli (1563–1608). Presented at the court of Ferrara in 1605, published in 1607 and reprinted over thirty times in the next two hundred years, the play is a story of star-crossed lovers with a characteristically Baroque, convoluted but well-constructed plot-line. Even more explicitly than Tasso's *Aminta*, the *Filli di Sciro* gives a major role to the cruelties of court life and the critical historical realities which had engulfed the courts of Italy.

With regard to the cultural and literary relevance of the pastoral repertory, another example may be especially valuable: the *Gelopea* (Mondovì, 1604) by Gabriello Chiabrera (1552-1638), Italy's most celebrated lyric poet after Marino but also a very active writer of tragedies and librettos (see also above, pp. 303–4). In his *favola boschereccia* Chiabrera introduced substantial innovations by eliminating the traditional apparatus of moralistic discussion;

by abolishing the chorus; by simplifying the plot with the omission of the duplicate couples of lovers and of the dénouement through recognition; and by emphasising the relation between representation and audience typical of pastoral drama, by explicit allusions to the rivalries among the ruling Genoese aristocracy and by choosing the Ligurian coast as the setting of the piece.

2I

Opera

David Kimbell

The beginnings of opera

With the production of Guarini's *Pastor fido* (see above, p. 297) at Mantua in
1598 we reach one of the most momentous periods in the history of the Italian
theatre. The same year also saw the staging, in Jacopo Corsi's Florence home,
of what is generally accepted as the first 'real' opera, the *Dafne* of Ottavio
Rinuccini (1562–1621), set to music by Jacopo Peri (1561–1633). In 1600
Rinuccini and Peri collaborated on a more ambitious work, *Euridice*, which
was staged in the Pitti Palace during the celebrations for the wedding of Maria
de' Medici and Henry IV of France. A few years later, in Mantua, the first two
operas of Claudio Monteverdi (1567–1643) were produced. One, *Arianna*
(1608), though it seems to have created the deeper impression on his
contemporaries, is lost, except for various versions of its great lament
'Lasciatemi morire'; the other, *Orfeo* (1607), thanks to the fact that it was
published, is preserved in a relatively unproblematic state, and is admired (and
regularly performed) as the first classic in the 300-year tradition of Italian
opera.

Monteverdi's mastery of so complex a medium would not have been
possible if opera had simply been 'invented' ten years earlier by Rinuccini and
Peri. In fact all three men drew on an accumulated wealth of practical
experience relating to the combination of music and dramatic poetry, and –
perhaps even more important – on a wealth of ideals and imaginative visions,
inherited from humanist scholars and poets, which suggested to them what
further and greater things might still be possible in this field.

The most fundamental of these imaginative visions stemmed from the
conviction that Italian civilisation was the privileged heir to the classical
civilisation of the ancient world. Greek drama, as interpreted by Aristotle,
became a particular object of the humanists' reverence, and a particular focus
for their own theatrical ambitions; and since they understood that it had been
not simply spoken but sung, music had a central place in these reflections. To
re-create classical tragedy in the language of modern music was, however, a
daunting prospect. The synthesis of music and drama could better be essayed,
men felt, in a genre where their relationship seemed more natural, more
intimate and spontaneous: hence the importance of the pastoral.

Giovanni Battista Doni, author of one of the most valuable Seicento treatises on music, explained the appeal of the pastoral: its very language, he said, was 'flowery and sweet . . . so that one may even admit that it has melody in its every part, since there are shown deities, nymphs, and shepherds from that most remote age when music was natural and speech like poetry' (trans. Grout, p. 36). Behind the seemingly naive words lies a profound and very ancient nexus of ideas: a great hierarchy of musics: *musica mundana*; *musica humana*; *musica instrumentalis*: the belief that music as it is sung and played by ordinary mortals in this world (*musica instrumentalis*) is simply a terrestrial reflection or local instance of the sublime cosmic harmony created by God when the universe was first made (*musica mundana*); and that if society is ordered in a seemly, harmonious fashion (*musica humana*) then each order of creation will reflect and resonate with the others. Pastoral brings us close to that ideal: lovers' laments are echoed by forests and mountains; groves, streams and hillsides are peopled with singing and dancing nymphs, oreads and dryads sharing the lovers' joys. In this golden world song is natural, even in everyday life; all poets knew that. In early opera the dependence on pastoral themes was part of a strategy to establish verisimilitude in the fusion of music and drama.

As well as the vision one needed the appropriate technical resources. One needed, that is to say, a music in which characters and actions could be represented: a *stile rappresentativo*; and it had to be possible while singing to perform histrionically, as an actor performs: to *recitar cantando*. It was the recitative style and its more affective relative, the *arioso*, that made this possible. Both idioms were outgrowths of the monody, a species of solo song that evolved in the late sixteenth century in deliberate contradistinction to the classic genres of Cinquecento vocal music, the madrigal and the motet.

Many composers contributed to the emergence of monody, but it is particularly associated with the Camerata, a group of musicians, poets and scholars that used to meet in Florence in the 1570s and 1580s under the patronage of Giovanni de' Bardi. Among the humanist musicians of the sixteenth century, the Camerata were ideologically the most extreme. Their manifesto, and the aesthetic framework for monody, was provided by Vincenzo Galilei's *Dialogo della musica antica e della moderna* (1581). Galilei's starting-point was the miraculous powers ascribed to music by ancient philosophers and poets (for example in the stories of Orpheus). This miraculous art had withered away because, in the quest for sensuality and virtuosity, music had lost contact with its roots in language. If that schism could be healed, so that the melody and rhythm of music sprang direct from a lofty declamation of poetry, and if the harmony of instruments could be confined to the modest office of supporting the singing voice, then perhaps the age of miracles might return. Monody evolved with no particular thought for its dramatic potential; but within twenty years it had been transferred to the theatre to become the primary ingredient of the new art of opera.

The principal poet of the earliest operas was Rinuccini, author of libretti for

Peri's *Dafne*, for *Euridice* (set by both Peri and Giulio Caccini c. 1551–1618), and for Monteverdi's *Arianna*. In each, the greater part is written in *versi a selva*, a free intermingling of *settenari* and *endecasillabi* with occasional use of rhyme, which Rinuccini borrowed from contemporary pastoral drama. But for the more formal and rhetorical addresses to the audience he used strophic *endecasillabi*; he made use of strophic *settenari* and *ottonari* too, for choral dance-songs or madrigals. Peri and Caccini, nurtured in Bardi's academy in the creed of 'prima la parola, dopo la musica' (first the words, then the music) observed these metrical characteristics scrupulously. They aimed at a 'syntactical identity' of words and music in which the line of poetry is, as it were, dressed in music, rather than being dissolved into music. Their style is almost entirely free from the word repetitions and the rhythmic refashioning of the text that had been typical of the madrigal and were soon to become typical of the operatic aria. Though composers were rarely again to be so self-effacing, the way in which Rinuccini, by the varied metrical articulation of his dramas, predetermined the musical function of each constituent part – now recitative, now rhetorical apostrophe, now aria, now choral dance – established a principle that survived down to *Aida*.

In the humanist environment in which the first operas were performed, Rinuccini would have been recognised as chief among the collaborators on *Dafne* and *Euridice*. However, Peri's setting of the latter had an eloquence that deeply impressed Monteverdi, the greatest and most versatile musician of the age: his own *Orfeo* imitates and echoes Peri in a dozen details. But once a composer of Monteverdi's range had taken up the new form, it was inevitable that there should occur the first of those swings of authority and priority, backwards and forwards between poet and composer, which have characterised the whole history of opera. No one was more faithful than Monteverdi to the ideal of 'serving the poetry', to quote Gluck's famous phrase. But such was the scope of his musical imagination, so much more ready was he than Peri to dig down deep into the musical riches of the past (pressing into service madrigals, dance-songs, instrumental ritornellos and sinfonias, colourful ensembles of instruments), that the paradoxical outcome of his fidelity to poetry was a theatrical form in which the commanding dramatic intelligence was that of the composer.

With *Orfeo* and *Arianna* the preliminary stages of experimentation and speculation were over. Clearly a new art-form had been born; and it was to dominate the theatre in Italy for 300 years.

Opera for the public theatre

Monteverdi had been in his early forties at the time of *Orfeo* and *Arianna*. In 1613 he moved to Venice; and since his imagination remained astonishingly fertile into his mid-seventies, he became the link between the famous pioneering achievements at the turn of the century in the courts of Florence and Mantua and the flourishing Venetian public opera houses of the mid-seventeenth century. In 1639, *Arianna* was revived to inaugurate the Teatro San Moisè, one of several new theatres that were springing up in the Most Serene Republic. Stimulated by its success, Monteverdi produced three new operas, the last of which, *L'incoronazione di Poppea* (1643), represents the art of the mid-Seicento as magnificently as *Orfeo* had represented opera's Renaissance origins.

From Florence and Mantua opera had spread first to Rome, where there was wealth to support it, and an array of superlative artists (especially singers) to cultivate it. Briefly, during the papacy of Urban VIII, Rome became the most important centre of operatic activity in Italy; in the long run, however, ecclesiastical censorship, which was erratic and often repressive, crippled the development of the new art-form. Roman musicians (modelling their practices on those of the *commedia dell'arte* troupes) therefore formed the backbone of those travelling companies that carried opera to Bologna, Milan, Venice, Naples and eventually much of Western Europe. It was at the Venetian carnival that it first really took root and flourished.

In the public theatres of Venice, which were generally owned by noble families, but in which traditional notions of magnificence had to be tempered by financial prudence, the nature of opera changed rapidly. For some years librettists continued to parade their humanist learning, but rarely without apologising for the fact that, in this new world, the high-mindedness that had brought opera to birth was impossible to sustain. Modern taste did not care for it; the old ideal of 'prima la parola, dopo la musica' had been succeeded by a demand for 'poesia per musica' (poetry for music); what was more, both poet and composer were often at the mercy of the machinist. Impresarios dared not neglect the Venetian love of spectacle; and from time to time it became a veritable cult, as when Giacomo Torelli was transferring his engineering skills from the Arsenal to the Teatro Novissimo in the 1640s.

Most of the first generation of Venetian librettists, including Monteverdi's collaborators Giacomo Badoaro and Giovanni Francesco Busenello, were members of the Accademia degli Incogniti, and their work was deeply affected by its ideals. The intellectual and moral tone – sceptical and sensuous – was set by their mentor, Cesare Cremonini, Professor of Philosophy at Padua, while the primary inspiration for their poetics was an admiration for Marino (see above, pp. 305–8). To emulate his virtuosity and sensuousness, his partiality for witty precepts and didactic generalisations (*precettismo*), was their highest aim.

They tended to pursue this course in a self-deprecating way. Only with Giovanni Faustini, the principal collaborator of Francesco Cavalli (1602–76) between 1643 and his death in 1651, do we come to a writer prepared to admit to a professional pride in being a librettist. Faustini was a diligent acolyte of those new muses of the Venetian theatre, 'Caprice', 'Fancy', 'Bizarrerie'. He revelled in the pretext to escape from the constraints of classical mythology and ancient history, treating both, or a rejection of both, as the starting-point for extravagant fictions in which the traditional genres of tragedy, comedy and pastoral were inextricably mingled. This trend was intensified by Spanish influence, mediated via the Tuscan writer Giacinto Andrea Cicognini. Cicognini's *Giasone*, set by Cavalli, and *Orontea*, set by Pietro Cesti (1623–69), both produced in 1649, proved two of the most popular and influential operas of the whole Seicento.

The elderly Monteverdi could not warm to the fashion for *precettismo*. He continued to insist that the proper business of opera was the passions of the human heart. For him, as for Cavalli, the finest opera composer of the younger generation, the old affective monodic style therefore remained a central feature of the musical language; often, indeed, as in the laments of Octavia in *Poppea*, it still provided the emotional climaxes of the opera. Compared with Monteverdi's Mantuan operas, however, both madrigalian choruses and instrumental movements declined in number and significance. For its musical pleasures Venetian opera looked increasingly to the solo aria.

Some concern was still felt about the dramatic verisimilitude of arias. They were obviously appropriate for gods and allegorical figures; appropriate for comic and low-life characters; appropriate even for the protagonists if they had good convivial reasons to be singing and dancing. But as delight in fine singing became a principal motive for an audience's enthusiasm for opera, and therefore for its financial backing of a theatre, the question how best to arrange things so that more and more of the show was taken over by song, became a burning issue.

Some librettists frankly admitted that he who paid the piper called the tune: if arias, not affective and rhetorical monodies, were what audiences wanted, they should have them, however incongruous the circumstances. But for most poets and composers the pretexts for arias needed to be convincing, their placing apt and dramatically telling. Two observations can perhaps be made. Sometimes arias were perceived as formalisations of the *arioso* of early opera; that is to say, as expressions of overpowering feeling that might break out at any point in the plot. And sometimes they were perceived as musical analogies to the *lazzi* of the *commedia dell'arte*, or to the metaphors, conceits and adages of Marino and his imitators; that is to say, as something which was acknowledged to be 'unreal', but the virtuosity, or wit, or fancifulness of which was its own justification.

Opera in the third quarter of the century found room for a huge increase in the number of arias. When popular operas were revived (a much rarer event in the Seicento than later), extra or substitute arias were introduced to freshen them up. As arias became an increasingly conspicuous and self-justifying element in opera, poets and composers grew more sensitive and imaginative in placing them, learning to play on the different dramatic and psychological possibilities of entrance arias, mid-scene arias and exit arias (*uscite*, *medie* and *ingressi*).

The Settecento

Franco Fido

22

The first half of the Settecento

The Settecento in Italy was characterised by certain trends apparent in varying degrees throughout the peninsula and influenced by events beyond the Alps. There was, for example, a slow but steady increase in population (from thirteen to nearly eighteen million in the course of the century); an upturn in the economy both industrial and commercial; and a further development of the principal urban centres, Naples and Palermo, Rome and Turin, Milan and Florence. These demographic and economic advances are linked to the new political situation brought about in Italy by the so-called Wars of Succession – the Spanish after the extinction of the Habsburg dynasty in Madrid (1700–14), the Polish, and the Austrian caused by Maria Teresa's succession to the Imperial throne following the death of her father Charles VI (1740–8).

After 1715 Spanish hegemony in Italy was replaced by that of Austria, which gained absolute control of Lombardy, now enlarged by the Duchy of Mantua, and then, following the death of the last of the Medici family, Gian Gastone, in 1737, indirectly acquired control of Tuscany via Maria Teresa's husband, Francesco Stefano of Lorraine. Of the earlier states the Venetian republic, the Papal States and the Duchy of Modena under the Estensi remained more or less unchanged, while the House of Savoy, which briefly gained possession of Sicily from 1714 to 1718, was strengthened by the accession of Victor Amedeus II as King of Sardinia in 1720. The Kingdom of Naples, initially annexed to Austria (1707–34) was then given along with Sicily to Philip of Spain's son, Charles VII, and later, when Charles became King of Spain in 1759, to his son Ferdinand.

The benefits to Milan of the well-organised and relatively modern Austrian administration which replaced the old, inept Spanish rule have often been stressed. And the other 'new' states, Tuscany under the Lorraine, the Kingdom of Naples and Sicily, and also, after the Peace of Aquisgraine (1748), the Duchy of Parma under the Bourbons, were also more receptive in the late Seicento and the Settecento to European ideas, especially English, French and Dutch. In Milan and Naples, and to some extent in Florence, the *letterati* (a term used to designate anyone who was seriously concerned and wrote about science and literature), attempted to apply the 'philosophic' spirit of Descartes, Leibniz and Newton to the traditional fields of law, jurisprudence and literary theory, and also to new or nascent disciplines such as political economy. But

the older states and the lesser centres also showed an awareness of the cultural
and scientific activities of the most advanced European countries.

Muratori and historiography

The greatest scholarly undertaking of the century was the vast collection of
Rerum italicarum scriptores ('Sources of Italian History'), conceived, organised
and completed in Modena by the Estense librarian, Ludovico Antonio Muratori (1672–1750), who benefitted from the example of philological rigour and
paleographic skill set by the Benedictine fathers of the Saint-Maur congrega-
tion in Paris, notably Mabillon and Montfaucon.

Muratori, who was born in Vignola, studied in Modena and Milan; after
ordination and a period as librarian of the Biblioteca Ambrosiana he was
recalled to Modena as court librarian and archivist, a post he held until his
death in 1750. A reader and writer of enormous energy, Muratori came under
the influence of his friend and teacher, Carlo Maria Maggi, whose *Vita* and
Rime he published in 1700. Then in a series of works appearing between 1700
and 1708 – *Primi disegni della repubblica letteraria d'Italia* ('Preliminary
Outline of the Italian Literary Republic', 1703), *Della perfetta poesia* ('Concerning Perfect Poetry', 1706), *Riflessioni sopra il buon gusto nelle scienze e
nelle arti* ('Reflections on Good Taste in the Sciences and the Arts', 1708) – his
aesthetic principles are clearly articulated: he is still tied to a decorative
conception of poetry, but is also conscious of the role of fantasy in literary
creation and is a determined upholder of 'good taste' in all kinds of intellectual
and artistic activity.

While the connection, largely lost today, between literature and science was
a distinctive feature of the culture of the Seicento and Settecento – as is clearly
evident in the great *Storia della letteratura italiana* ('History of Italian
Literature' published by Girolamo Tiraboschi (1772–82), Muratori's successor
at the Estense Library) – the idea of literature as a collective activity practised
within a 'republic' of learned men was peculiar to Muratori. His participation
on behalf of the Estensi in the controversies between Church and Empire over
the possession of the Comacchio region, based on various ancient titles and
rights, drew Muratori's attention to the Middle Ages, the great, largely
ignored, crucible of the modern world. Here, in a commitment to record and
revive the evidence of the past in order to enrich the present, the Modenese
librarian discovered a mission which determined the second part of his career,
without exhausting his polygraphic activities.

After a collection of *Antichità Estensi* ('Ancient Records of the Estense
Family'), Muratori conceived the idea of making an organic collection of the
sources of Italian history from 500 to 1500: diplomas, statutes, chronicles,
narratives, poems, etc. This great collection, made possible and published by a
group of rich Lombard noblemen who formed themselves specially into the

Palatine Society, was compiled in collaboration with the most learned men from all over Italy: the Bolognese Filippo Argelati, the Venetian Apostolo Zeno, the Sienese Uberto Benvoglienti, the Florentine Anton Francesco Marmi and others. The last of the twenty-five volumes of the *Rerum italicarum scriptores* was published posthumously in 1751, completing what was the greatest collection of national history in Europe at that date.

As if to illustrate this vast material Muratori undertook a parallel work, the *Antiquitates italicae medii aevi*, seventy-five dissertations published between 1738 and 1743 covering all aspects of Italian life in the Middle Ages – institutions, customs, rites, superstitions – really the beginning of modern Italian historiography. In a characteristic stance midway between the traditional and the new rationalist culture, Muratori retains the idea of *historia magistra vitae* and a Christian or providential vision of the historical process. But respect for facts and the desire to grasp their human and civil significance clearly prevail over apologetic or confessional concerns, anticipating modern methodology and disciplines such as cultural anthropology and the history of ideas.

Muratori's last important works were the *Annali d'Italia* (twelve volumes, Venice 1744–9), a year-by-year chronicle of the Christian era up to 1500, and the treatise *Della pubblica felicità oggetto de' buoni principi* ('On the Welfare of the People Which Is the Aim of Good Princes', Venice–Lucca, 1749). The former are less original than the *Antiquitates*, but are interesting in showing a sharper distinction between the spiritual Church and the Roman Curia, criticised for its temporal ambitions, and also for the clear, elegant style of the narrative, one of the best examples of Settecento prose. In the *Pubblica felicità*, a synthesis of many of his ideas and a sort of spiritual testament, Muratori returns to a problem previously discussed in *Il Cristianesimo felice nelle Missioni dei Padri della Compagnia di Gesù nel Paraguai* ('The Exultant Christianity of the Missionary Fathers of the Company of Jesus in Paraguay', Venice, 1743–9). Here too the welfare of the people is to be entrusted to a government that, for all its competence and humanity, remains ultimately absolute; but the philanthropic and reformist thrust of the work is characteristic of Muratori's whole intellectual career.

Venice: polygraphs, journalists and dramatists

The best Venetian *letterati* of the early Settecento, all noblemen, were scholars and also reformers of literature and the theatre. Apostolo Zeno (1668–1750), together with Scipione Maffei and Antonio Vallisnieri, founded the *Giornale de' Letterati d'Italia* (1710–18 – continued by his brother Pier Caterino until 1740), one of the earliest and most authoritative literary journals, and also wrote numerous libretti (*drammi*), initially on pastoral subjects (*Gli'inganni felici*, 1695; *Tirsi*, 1696), then on ancient history and mythology (*Lucio Vero*,

1700; *Temistocle*, 1701, etc.). He also wrote oratorios (*azioni sacre*) such as
Giuseppe (1722) and *Ezechia* (1737). Zeno's libretti, which earned him the
post of principal poet (*poeta cesareo*) in Vienna from 1718 to 1729, are of
rigorous classical inspiration: unities of time and place, rejection of all the
frivolous or farcical elements hitherto so frequent, clear and elegant language.
They seem cold and magniloquent to us, but at the time they were the first
authoritative model of a 'reformed' melodrama, followed by all successive
librettists from Metastasio onwards.

The Marquis Scipione Maffei (1675–1755) was a more lively and adventurous figure, an enquiring traveller in various parts of Europe, a journalist
(co-founder of the *Giornale de' letterati d'Italia* to which he wrote the Preface),
historian of his native city (*Verona illustrata*, 1732) and a sharp critic of
prejudice and superstition in many fields from duelling (*Della scienza cavaller-
esca*, 1710) to witchcraft (*Dell'arte magica*, 1749–50).

His preferred literary genre was the theatre, the validity of which he
championed against the Dominican rigorist Father Concina. To combat the
idea that Italy compared poorly with France in drama, he published a selection
of Italian tragedies with a valuable *Discorso storico sul teatro italiano* (1713)
and, towards the end of his life, a treatise *De' teatri antichi e moderni* (1753).
His own works for the stage include the comedies *Le cerimonie* (1728) and *Il
Raguet* (1747), a satire on contemporary affectations and fashions. His
melodrama *La fida ninfa* ('The Faithful Nymph', 1730) was presented in 1732
to the music of Vivaldi, and his tragedy *Merope*, in elegant blank verse, was
performed to great acclaim in Modena by the young and brilliant Luigi
Riccoboni and Elena Balletti. Voltaire called it a 'tragédie sans galanterie',
meaning without erotic passions; but it is rich in tender and domestic
sentiments and has a relatively happy ending (the only death is that of the
hated usurper Polifonte), and thus fitted perfectly the taste of the time and was
widely admired, translated and imitated (by Voltaire himself among others),
and was considered the best Italian tragedy before Alfieri.

The Paduan Antonio Conti (1677–1749) was a traveller and tragedian, a
friend of Newton and correspondent of Leibniz. He is considered one of the
most interesting Italian thinkers of the early Settecento on account of the role he
assigns to fantasy in the arts and sciences – for example in 'Il globo di Venere,
sogno', ('The globe of Venus, a dream') in his *Poesie e prose* (1739) – and his
original attempt to reconcile Platonic and Sensistic[1] ideas in his concept of
beauty. He is best known for his translations of classical and foreign poets
(Callimachus, Horace, Ovid, Racine, Pope) and his four tragedies published in
1751 (*Giulio Cesare, Marco Bruto, Giunio Bruto, Druso*). Clearly influenced by
his reading of Shakespeare's history plays and of 'historical' English theatre
generally, his tragedies are motivated by the belief that the public will respond
more readily to subjects from their own history than to mythological plots. In

---

[1] Sensism or Sensualism: the philosophy which regards impressions gathered by the senses as the
ultimate source of all knowledge.

the event, however, Conti's attempts at historical accuracy and the eloquence of his characters fail to bring these episodes from Roman history to life: they are more suitable for reading than for performance.

Intellectual life in Naples: Giannone, Vico, Genovesi

Maffei and Conti, with their vast erudition, their European contacts and their numerous never-completed projects, illustrate very well what might be called a pre-Enlightenment, open to novelty but characterised by a lofty individualism, with touches of dilettantism in the best sense of the word. Very different was the Kingdom of Naples, where the hopes of some sort of reawakening, raised by the arrival first of a Viennese Viceroy, then of Don Carlos of Bourbon, came up against the age-old inertia of a feudal society and a formidable web of ecclesiastical privilege. In this context there was a closer connection between intellectual research and practical application, even involving a radical commitment to the 'public welfare' or 'public happiness' at the risk of life and liberty. A good example of this is the Neapolitan jurist and historian Pietro Giannone (1676-1748), champion of the rights of the state against the abuses of the Roman Curia in his *Istoria civile del Regno di Napoli* (1721-3). His History earned him European fame and applause, but also fierce attacks, which he escaped by settling in Vienna for ten years, supported by a pension granted him by the Emperor Charles VI. With the arrival of Don Carlos in Naples in 1734 Giannone attempted to return, but he was hunted by the police of the entire peninsula, including that of the King of Naples, who was keen to maintain good relations with Rome; he was arrested in Savoy and spent the last twelve years of his life in various gaols, a victim of his views on the abolition of ecclesiastical jurisdictions and of the courageous and effective way he had expressed his convictions.

The two most interesting of his numerous later works remained unedited for many years: *Il Triregno*, mainly written in Vienna, only appeared in a garbled edition in 1895 and a modern one in 1940 – the single complete codex is still inaccessible in the Roman Inquisitorial Archives; the *Vita* similarly received a decent edition only in 1960. *Il Triregno* is a philosophical history of humanity with the emphasis on religious beliefs and their connection with ecclesiastical power: a pre-Christian phase or *Regno terreno* is followed by the evangelical moment of Christ's incarnation, or *Regno celeste*, and the long degeneration of the Christian message brought about by the Church's assumption of temporal power, the *Regno papale*. Giannone's *Vita*, written in the early years of his imprisonment, gives a rapid reconstruction of the author's progress towards enlightenment; only recently has its considerable literary merit been recognised.

In Naples the young anti-curialist priest Antonio Genovesi (1713-69) encountered the same diffidence, suspicion and hostility which had overwhelmed

Giannone. But the fact that he enjoyed a long and fruitful university career (as Professor of Metaphysics, then Ethics, and finally Political Economy – the first Chair of this in Europe) shows that the reforming elements in Carlos of Bourbon's administration had succeeded in improving the political and cultural climate considerably. Genovesi was a keen student of Locke, Newton and especially Montesquieu, and a strong advocate of knowledge based on the natural sciences and directed at improving public welfare through legal and economic reform. His most important work, the *Lezioni di commercio o sia di economia civile* ('Lectures on Commerce or Civil Economics', 1765), is one of the principal contributions to Italian Enlightenment in its mature phase.

Against this background of Neapolitan culture under the Habsburg Viceroy, and then under the Bourbons, battling courageously for the reform of civil society, the isolated figure of Giambattista Vico (1668–1744) stands out for his indifference to the contemporary political situation. He held a minor teaching post in Rhetoric from 1698, but in 1723 he failed to obtain the Chair of Law he wanted and continued on his solitary way, against the mainstream of philosophical thinking. In opposition to the philosophers currently admired and studied in Naples and elsewhere – Descartes, Malebranche, Spinoza and Gassendi – Vico admired the work of writers he had pondered during the nine years he spent as tutor to a nobleman's children: Tacitus, Plato, Francis Bacon and, later, Grotius. He did not consider the mathematical reason of the Cartesians to be true knowledge insofar as the *cogito* (the statement 'I think') can only testify to the existence of thought, not explain its substance and origins. On the other hand all natural science is illusory in that nature, being the creation of God, can be known only to its creator.

In the six *Orazioni inaugurali* or Latin lectures he wrote between 1699 and 1707, and especially in the seventh, *De nostri temporis studiorum ratione* ('On the Principles of the Scholarship of Our Time'), which was too long to be delivered and which he published in 1708, there was already a clear transition from the juridical interests typical of the Neapolitan speculative tradition to historical and epistemological concerns. One can also speak of anthropology *avant la lettre* in the next work, *De antiquissima Italorum sapientia ex linguae latinae originibus eruenda* ('Concerning the Ancient Knowledge of the Italians to be Derived from the Origins of the Latin Language'), of which only the first of the three books announced, *Metaphysicus*, was published in 1710. Here Vico maintains that the presence in Latin of semantic and etymological clues that would be inexplicable otherwise points to the existence of a primitive Italic *sapienza* or knowledge, of a Pythagorean and theological nature and of Egypto-Etruscan origin, which would have preceded by some centuries the modest origins of Roman civilisation. More significant to us than such an outlandish thesis is the methodology that underlies it, and constitutes his original riposte to the pseudo-science of numbers and of nature: *verum est ipsum factum*, whereby man can know only what he himself does, the product of his own activity. It is therefore history, the human domain *par excellence*, which provides the basis for a metaphysic, as Vico calls it: that is, for science.

All the different intellectual experiences of Vico the student of natural law and Latinist, the ancient historian and the philosopher of history, converge in his masterpiece *Principi di una scienza nuova intorno alla natura delle nazioni* ('Principles of a New Science Concerning the Nature of Nations'), which appeared in Naples in 1725, was republished with extensive additions in 1730 (*Scienza nuova seconda*) and with further corrections and additions in 1744. Here the project of an 'ideal, eternal history covering all nations in their origins, development, maturity and decadence' is made possible by the nexus established by Vico between the *certo* (the 'debris', monuments and documents found and classified by 'philology') and the *vero* (the formulation by 'philosophy' of laws of universal validity or axioms deduced from the *certo*, which in its turn is illuminated by them). The possibility of passing from the realm of facts to that of ideas is established by the analogy Vico discovers between the different phases of development of our individual minds and those of humanity as a whole through history, an analogy which allows us to seek in our own psyche the key to the interpretation of history. Like children in the process of growing up, 'men first feel without perceiving, then they perceive with a troubled and agitated spirit, finally they reflect with a clear mind' (I, ii, 53).

In the beginning, therefore, there was an 'age of gods' – or rather not in the beginning, but in the time of the first men after the Great Flood: in this way Vico reconciles Genesis and the divine creation of Adam and Eve with his own embryonic theory of evolution. In this age of gods man, being dominated by his senses and his elemental needs, embodied his own fear in the face of an incomprehensible nature in fetishist and anthropomorphic cults. This age was followed by an 'age of heroes', when men whose imagination had grown very strong gained access to a *sapienza poetica*, that is to myths, and gathered together in elementary social nuclei dominated by the physically strongest individuals; and finally there was an 'age of men', regulated by reason and law, the 'philosophical' reason of adult humanity and of the modern world. Vico also contemplates the possibility that through an excess of refinement and corruption (as in imperial Rome) a mature nation may fall into a new barbarism, and after the *corso* he has just traced may undergo a *ricorso* with the same phases, so that the Middle Ages of the communes and of Dante could be considered a new age of heroes after that of the Homeric poems.

This theory of *corsi* and *ricorsi* is the best-known, almost proverbial element in Vico's thought, but it is certainly not the most important. His genius consists in having shown that the civilisations of the past should be studied and understood *juxta sua principia* (on their own terms). As long as scholars try to explain their justified admiration for Homer on the basis of an erroneous hypothesis of the 'hidden wisdom' of his poems, that is with an allegorical reading which allows them to find in those works what is not really there – a system of knowledge and principles acceptable to themselves – they will be forever excluded from what Vico proudly presents as his 'discovery of the true Homer': a powerful poetic voice of a whole people, still immature and violent, heroic in the *Iliad*, but already seeking more articulate forms of knowledge and social life in the *Odyssey* – the sum of the memories, beliefs and values of that people at a given moment in their history.

Commenting on the law cited above (p. 349: 'Men first feel ...', I, ii, 53) Vico writes:

This axiom is the principle of poetic sentences, which are formed by feelings of passion and emotion, whereas philosophical sentences are formed by reflection and reasoning. The more the latter rise towards universals, the closer they approach the truth; the more the former descend to particulars, the more certain they become.

These lines explain why Croce and modern proponents generally of the intuitive-expressive, pre-logical or irrational nature of art have recognised Vico as their predecessor. Today it is perhaps another aspect of his precocious historicist philosophy that strikes us as anticipating modern thought. With his interest in the genetic phase of language, his intuition of the creative and evocative power of words as the depository of experiences and relations with nature that have become obliterated by centuries of 'civilisation', Vico can be seen as one of the fathers of modern linguistics and of cultural anthropology. Standing as he does at a philosophical watershed, Vico is clearly out of phase with his times: while his sources (Plato, Bacon, Grotius) belong to the past, his message, which seemed obscure to his contemporaries, is aimed at the future and will find disciples in Herder, Michelet and the Romantic and historicist culture generally of the nineteenth century.

Arcadia

On another watershed, that of poetry, the 'Arcadia' group (see also above, p. 309) provides the opposite example of a perfect harmony with the tastes and cultural inclinations of its period, which is the explanation of its extraordinary success. It was founded in Rome by a group of *letterati* accustomed to meet at the house of Christina, the former Queen of Sweden, who had settled in Rome and become a Catholic. When she died in 1689 fourteen of her circle – priests, magistrates and scholars – founded an Academy to perpetuate her memory and promote the artistic ideals of the group. Their prime aim was a return to the simplicity and good taste of the classics in order to cleanse literature of the artifice and excessive ingenuity of Baroque poetry, of which people were becoming tired. However, if their choice of models – Theocritus, Virgil's *Eclogues*, Sannazaro – was dictated by a firm opposition to the 'bad taste' of the Seicento, the form of their activities still had a good deal of Baroque solemnity and disguise about it. The members called themselves shepherds and assumed names from the classical pastoral: Pan's syrinx was their emblem, the infant Christ their protector, and so on. Their sonnets and *canzonette* on religious or pastoral subjects and their academic papers were published in a series of volumes: *Rime degli Arcadi*, I–IX (1716–22), X–XI (1747–9), XII (1759), XIII (1780) and *Prose degli Arcadi* (three volumes, 1718).

In the sonnets and pastoral *canzonette*, their most typical form, shepherds and nymphs engage in chaste love with blushes, sighs and tears (of emotion in the presence, of lament in the absence, of the beloved). The deliberately ingenuous and affected nature of this poetry did not escape the attention of their contemporaries, and there was no lack of critical and ironical comment on the puerilities and *pastorellerie* of these austere Roman prelates and lawyers. But in the middle of the Settecento especially, when Arcadian 'colonies' sprang up all over Italy, there was widespread appreciation of the positive and mildly reformist aspects of the movement; the clarity and (in the best examples) the musicality of the style; the authentic ring of nostalgia for a natural world of innocence as a refuge from the confusion of historical experience.

The leading figure and first *custode generale* was Giovan Mario Crescimbeni (1663–1728), author of a vast *Istoria della volgar poesia* (1698, 1712); and among the members were some of the most popular poets of their day, Felice Zappi (1678–1719), Carlo Innocenzo Frugoni (1692–1768) and later Jacopo Vittorelli (1749–1835). Other distinguished members who deserve mention include Gian Vincenzo Gravina (1664–1718), Paolo Antonio Rolli (1687–1765), Tommaso Crudeli (1703–45) and Pier Jacopo Martello (1665–1727).

Gravina, who taught civil and canon law in Rome, was one of the founders of Arcadia and drafted its ten laws, in Latin, but he left in 1711 because of disagreements with Crescimbeni. His most interesting literary works include his *Discorso delle antiche favole* ('Discourse on the Fables of the Ancients', 1696), *Della ragion poetica* (1708) and *Della tragedia* (1715), which constitute an attempt to found a science of aesthetics, claiming an epistemic role for classical poetry, superior to logic in revealing the truth immanent in 'the labyrinth of confused ideas'. Like Conti and Maffei, Gravina wrote tragedies with Roman subjects on strictly Aristotelian lines, which almost everyone ever since, Vico excepted, have found cold, rhetorical and undramatic.

Rolli was a pupil of Gravina, and resigned from Arcadia in 1714 out of solidarity with him. He lived for many years in London, composing libretti for Handel and Bononcini, publishing worthy editions of Italian classics and making various translations, including a version of *Paradise Lost*. The best of his varied *Poetici componimenti* (Venice, 1753) are his *canzonette*, with their elegant and vivid country scenes and depictions of the changing seasons conveyed with rare musicality: the cream, with Metastasio's lyrics, of Settecento poetry. Martello also wrote works of literary theory, but always referred back to his great passion, the theatre. *L'impostore, dialogo sulla tragedia antica e moderna* (Paris, 1714), for example, makes a strong case for the idea (shared by Gravina, and later by Metastasio) that 'imitation' in art does not mean making an exact, pedestrian copy but actually departing in some respects from the truth, compared with which it has the advantage of conveying pleasure. His imposing dramatic production, including puppet farces, satirical comedies and tragedies, exemplifies his theories on 'imperfect imitation', 'sweetness of style', 'verse for speaking' and so on. He invented a metre for tragedy (rhymed couplets of *settenari doppi*)[2] which was called 'martelliano' and was later adopted by Goldoni, Chiari and others. Being convinced that for pure spectacle or entertainment conventional theatre could not compete with *commedia dell'arte* on the one hand or opera on the other, and without prejudice or scruple with regard to the so-called Aristotelian rules, Martello produced a sort of encyclopaedic catalogue of the old dramatic forms, with the added stimulus provided by modern French theatre. His tragedies, intended mostly for reading, are notable for their psychological realism and the sharpness with which his characters, never all good or all bad, analyse their own and others' weaknesses.

A better poet than these was the Tuscan Tommaso Crudeli who was connected with the Arcadian taste only marginally. His translations from La Fontaine and his Anacreontic compositions are among the wittiest and most refined verse of the century.

---

[2] A *settenario doppio* is a line comprising two *settenari*, i.e. each half-line has seven syllables.

23

The theatre from Metastasio to Goldoni

Metastasio and melodrama

Metastasio's melodrama is a remarkable expression of some of the main aspirations of the Settecento: the ideal of theatre as a social rite and a vehicle of moral instruction; the nostalgia of scholars for classical tragedy following the French precedent; the hedonism of a courtly society devoted to music. Pietro Trapassi was born in Rome in 1698 of humble parents and died in Vienna in 1782. From childhood he showed an extraordinary talent for improvisation, and he was adopted by Gravina, who oversaw his literary and philosophical education and changed his name from the prosaic Trapassi to the poetic Metastasio. After Gravina's death he moved to Naples, capital of the Austrian Viceroyalty, and was initiated into the musical life of the city by the singer Marianna Bulgarelli (la Romanina) and the composer Niccolò Porpora. He was soon producing compositions for the court, for weddings, birthdays and other occasions, including some dramatic pieces which were very successful. The fashionable mythological idyll was well suited to his liking for the *cantabile* and sensual poetry of Tasso and Marino, a taste which the severely classical education given him by Gravina had refined but not obliterated.

In his first melodrama, *Didone abbandonata*, performed in Naples in 1724 (with music by Domenico Sarro), the Virgilian encounter between the Carthaginian Queen and the destined founder of Rome becomes a clash between Dido's unbridled passion and readiness to sacrifice throne and life for the man she loves and Aeneas' anguish as he is torn between love and duty. Typical of Metastasio's lucid and *cantabile* ariettas is the hero's elegant and self-righteous lament:

> Se resto sul lido,
> Se sciolgo le vele,
> Infido, crudele,
> Mi sento chiamar:
> E intanto, confuso
> Nel dubbio funesto,
> Non parto, non resto,
> Ma provo il martire
> Che avrei nel partire,
> Che avrei nel restar.

(Whether I stay on shore, or I unfurl the sails, I shall be called faithless and cruel; and
so, torn in fatal doubt, I neither go nor stay and I suffer the pain I should have if I left,
I should have if I stayed.)

(I, 18)

The rapturous reception of *Didone* and of the accompanying *intermezzo*,
L'impresario delle Canarie, launched Metastasio on a triumphal career as a
librettist in Naples, Rome and Venice, with *Siroe*, *Catone in Utica* and other
works. His texts follow and perfect the norms established by Apostolo Zeno
while avoiding Zeno's austerity in favour of increased pathos: three acts of
serious subject-matter mostly from ancient history and without comic elements; six characters, four of whom are involved in unreciprocated and often
impossible passions and one of whom is a villain and a traitor. The plot
thickens in the second act with various misunderstandings and surprises,
which are resolved in the third act thanks to magnanimous gestures of sacrifice
or forgiveness or acts of repentance and providential recognition scenes. The
dialogue of the recitative is followed at the end of each scene by an arietta,
which may be 'sentenziosa', 'affettuosa' or otherwise.

In 1730 Metastasio accepted an invitation to become principal poet in
Vienna, where he stayed until his death in 1782. His first ten years here were
his most prolific: eleven melodramas, almost as many *feste teatrali* and
numerous oratorios or sacred dramas. His masterpieces are to be found among
the series of 'sentimental' melodramas influenced by French tragedy, especially
Racine, in which the terrible dilemmas of his characters are tinged with a vein
of melancholy which softens and humanises their heroic sacrifices: *Demetrio*
(1731), *L'Olimpiade* and *Demofoonte* (1733), and others. A further series,
emphasising the same kind of heroic virtues which Metastasio attributed,
probably in all sincerity, to the Emperor and his family included some of his
most popular works, *La Clemenza di Tito* (1734, known to present-day opera-
goers in Mozart's setting of a much altered text), *Temistocle* (1736) and *Attilio
Regolo* (completed 1740 but not performed till 1750).

Attilio Regolo, which ends with the edifying departure of the hero towards a
cruel death, represents Metastasio's closest approach to tragedy, the most
prestigious genre of the period. *L'Olimpiade* is the best compromise between
heroic gesturing and melodious elegy. Free of historical restraints, the dialogue
and the lyric passages are better integrated: the tension arising in the recitatives
from clashes between characters more inclined to lament than to act is resolved
in the soft sigh of the aria, which is invariably structured on a careful play of
symmetrical, parallel or antithetical elements and underlined by anaphora and
rhyme.

The prolific production of the first ten years in Vienna slackened progressively
later during a difficult period for the court and for the poet. More interesting
now than the comparatively few melodramas are Metastasio's writings on
poetry and the theatre, in which he uses his excellent classical culture (he had

translated Horace's *Ars poetica*, for example) to justify the new genre of melodrama which the traditionalists branded as hybrid and monstrous. In his *Estratto della poetica di Aristotile e considerazioni sulla medesima* ('Summary of Aristotle's Poetics and Observations on the Same', 1773) and his *Osservazioni sul teatro greco* he sets out the ideas which had guided him in the composition of his libretti. Melodrama is the direct heir of classical tragedy, which was 'recitata cantando' or chanted, as the Camerata dei Bardi had maintained. The real author is not the composer but the poet, who is responsible for the structure of the plot and the 'actual internal melody' which the musical score only supports and underlines. As for the charge so often brought against Metastasio that his melodrama and his mellifluous characters lack verisimilitude, Metastasio's answer is to distinguish between 'copy', or the mechanical reproduction of an original, and 'imitation', or the search for a 'possible' likeness between the original and the image the artist makes from it using a different medium: words, notes, colours, marble or bronze. We should not therefore expect from a melodrama an illusion of reality, or a deceptive and worthless replica trying to pass off as true what is really false, but the pleasure and wonder generated by the truth to life of a fiction labelled and acknowledged as such.

Metastasio wrote a considerable number of poetic compositions, many of them intended for musical performance, like the elegant nuptial odes of his Neapolitan period and the cantatas, almost all of the Viennese period. His *canzonette*, which were also set to music or could have been, were famous in the Settecento, especially *La libertà* (1735), where he rejoices in his escape from his love for the tyrannical and capricious beauty, Nice: 'Grazie agl'inganni tuoi,/Al fin respiro, o Nice,/Al fin d'un infelice/Ebber gli dei pietà' (Thanks to your tricks I breathe at last, o Nice; at last the gods have taken pity on an unhappy wretch).

While Metastasio's melodramas do not strictly belong to the history of Arcadian poetry, being the original creation of a theatrical genius who went well beyond the theory and practice of the Roman Academy – to which of course he belonged, like everyone else – he was truly an Arcadian, a distinguished one but lacking in any real originality, even in his best poems.

Like Metastasio, Giambattista Casti (1724–1803) lived for a time in Vienna where he wrote some good libretti for Paisiello and Salieri. However, unlike him, Casti enjoyed a well-deserved reputation as a freethinker and libertine thanks to his *Novelle galanti* (much admired by Byron) and the sharp satire of contemporary courts and society that distinguish the verse of his *Poema tartaro* (1797) and *Animali parlanti* (1802).

Goldoni and comedy

At the beginning of the Settecento, alongside musical performances (*opera seria* or melodrama, *opera buffa* and the brief and brilliant *intermezzi*), the professional theatre was still represented after nearly two centuries of popularity by the *commedia dell'arte* (see above, pp. 327–9). The survival of the *commedia dell'arte* – or, as it was often called, 'Italian comedy' or 'improvised comedy' or 'clowns' comedy' – depended on its immediate entertainment value, its ability to adapt to the basic tastes of the paying public with comic gesturing and often crude farce.

Early in the century, among the attempts to restore good taste, reason and verisimilitude in literature, there were naturally proposals for the reform of the theatre. In Verona Scipione Maffei, the journalist and polygraph (see above, p. 346), produced fully scripted comedies satirising contemporary custom. In Tuscany particularly, comedies were frequently performed in academies, schools and private houses: for example, the Florentine Giovan Battista Fagiuoli (1660–1742) wrote numerous plays set in the countryside and rich in dialect characters such as the rustic Ciapo, who appears on a number of occasions. The Sienese Girolamo Gigli (1660–1722) and Jacopo Angelo Nelli (1673–1767) were fervent admirers of French comedy. Gigli's *Don Pilone, ovvero il Bacchettone falso* ('Don Pilone, or the Hypocrite') has a Sienese Tartuffe storming about in the bigoted world of Grand-Ducal Tuscany, and in his *Sorellina di Don Pilone* ('D.P.'s Little Sister') the satire on the local *dévots* actually includes the author's wife.

While nearly all the so-called reformers of comedy in the early Settecento were professional men of letters and the performers of their plays were amateurs, the reverse is true of the lawyer Carlo Goldoni (Venice, 1707 – Paris, 1793), who collaborated throughout his long career with companies of professional comic actors. Among the scenarios he provided for the Imer Company, which was active in Venice in the 1730s, the *Momolo cortesan* (1738) has a characteristic evolution. Goldoni wrote out fully only the part of the protagonist, leaving the other actors (including the usual masks of the *Arte*, the Doctor and Truffaldino, who was played by the famous *zanni*, Antonio Sacchi) free to improvise following the outline indicated for them. Goldoni adopted this solution when he saw that the Pantalone of the company, a certain Francesco Golinetti, spoke and behaved in real life like certain spirited and pleasure-loving Venetian youths of the middle class, the so-called *cortesani*, and he got the idea of giving the actor the part of a *cortesan* – a key moment in the development of Goldoni's comic theatre, marking the incursion into the *Arte* tradition of a character and situation taken from contemporary life.

Several years later, when Goldoni was practising law in Pisa and seemed to have forgotten the theatre, Sacchi asked him for two scenarios, one of which, *Il servitore di due padroni* ('The Servant of Two Masters', 1745), the playwright took up again in 1753 in order to include it in an edition of his comedies. Then he wrote out the full dialogue, probably incorporating various *lazzi* or comic incidents and jests used by Sacchi, the brilliant *zanni* of the *Arte*. This comedy thus provides the best evidence we have of what the old improvised comedy could become in the hands of two great men of the theatre in terms of rhythmical precision, rich and witty invention, and freedom of character-acting as in the case of Truffaldino, who retains an anarchic, almost diabolic, element recalling the remote carnival roots of the comic theatre.

However, the way ahead lay through *Momolo* rather than Truffaldino. When he returned to Venice in 1748 Goldoni became a professional play-wright and committed himself to writing for another Company, Girolamo Medebach's at the Teatro di Sant'Angelo, for which he produced in five years some forty comedies from *La Vedova scaltra* ('The Artful Widow', 1748) to *La Locandiera* ('The Mistress of the Inn', 1753). This quantity, representing about a third of his entire output, indicates the importance of this period in his life, when he brought ideology and dramaturgy together in a series of plays expressing the ideals and lifestyle of a specific group, the Venetian mercantile middle class. It was also in this period that he produced most of his libretti, which made such an important contribution to the development of *opera buffa* (see below, p. 364).

Goldoni's theory at this time is explained in the Preface to the first volume of his *Commedie* (Venice, 1750), in which he stresses the twofold inspiration he received from the book of the World (contemporary society) and the book of the Theatre – the dramatic tradition, language, and 'grammar' codified and perpetuated by his work-mates, the actors. Even more revealing is *Il Teatro comico*, a programme-comedy performed at Sant'Angelo as the first of the sixteen new comedies which he had boldly promised the public for the 1750–1 season. Here, in a 'theatre within the theatre' (as in Molière's *Impromptu de Versailles*), the Medebach actors explain their idea of a rational theatre, purified of the absurdities and scurrility of the old comedy, true to life, with characters, plot, delivery taken from nature: a pleasant and edifying mirror of social life, which sanctioned the use of dialect not for farcical effect but as a true reflection of city speech.

These comedies therefore implement an Enlightened theatrical programme better than did its original French proponents, Diderot or Voltaire: the super-iority of the busy merchants to the idle, impoverished and arrogant nobles (*Il cavaliere e la dama*, 'The Gentleman and the Lady') and consequently the folly of trying to imitate the worst side of the patricians (*Le femmine puntigliose, Il frappatore*; 'The Punctilious Ladies', 'The Cheat'); the importance of paternal authority and of filial obedience in family life, and the superiority of a domestic upbringing to one in the convent (*Il padre di famiglia*); the superiority of virtue to noble titles (*Pamela*, based on Richardson and the first comedy without masks, 1750). At the same time the principles of common sense, naturalness and realism led Goldoni to a broad and surprising 'theatrification' of the world so that alongside his satire on the old characters of French origin – *Il bugiardo* ('The Liar'), *Il giocatore* ('The Gambler'), the slanderer in *La bottega del caffè* ('The Coffee-House') – we find 'new' figures, sometimes vaguely autobiographical, such as *L'avvocato veneziano* or *L'avventuriere onorato* ('The Venetian Lawyer', 'The Honourable Adventurer'), sometimes drawn from an as yet undiscovered Venice of the people, such as *La putta onorata* and *La buona moglie* ('A Girl of Honour', 'The Good Wife').

Mirandolina in *La locandiera*, written in 1752 for the soubrette Maddalena Marliani, is certainly one such character. She appears as the proprietress of an inn in Florence, courted by two noble guests, a penniless Marquis and a rich Count of recent and dubious nobility. The affected misogyny of a new guest, the Cavaliere di Ripafratta, leads Mirandolina to bet she can make him fall in love with her – which she does in two acts, thus having to withstand his passionate advances in the third when she marries Fabrizio, her waiter. Two professional actresses lodging at the inn try to seduce the Cavaliere, but fail to match Mirandolina's success. This is brought about by her feigned preoccupation with her work so that the tools of her trade (sheets, dishes of food) become superb instruments of seduction. On the one hand, Mirandolina's successful and 'natural' deception (underlined by the failure of the two actresses) represents the superiority of the new theatre over the old and the triumph of a clear-sighted, unprejudiced (or *borghese*) attitude over the culture of the three noble admirers, which is based on privilege and prejudice ('I am who I am', the Marquis repeats endlessly). On the other hand, this last of Goldoni's heroines at Sant'Angelo has to give up the game and take refuge in the prosaic arms of her waiter; pointing to an increasing difficulty in reconciling in everyday life the requirements of pleasure (or the Theatre) with those of material realities and interests (or the World). In this sense, the comedy initiates a long crisis starting with Goldoni's break with Medebach in 1753.

He then wrote for the Vendramin brothers at the San Luca theatre until 1762, facing various problems including the competition from Sant'Angelo of Pietro Chiari, an able novelist and playwright. Goldoni experimented with 'historical' plays in verse (*Torquato Tasso*), 'exotic' plays (including an oriental trilogy, *La sposa persiana*, etc.), and also popular plays for the end of carnival, easily the best of this period, *Le massere*, *Le donne de casa soa*, *Il campiello* ('The Cook-Maids', 'The Good Housewives', 'The Public Square', 1754–6).

After a disappointing visit to Rome to produce some of his own comedies at the theatre of Tordinona, he returned in 1759 to Venice, and to the dramatisation of the bourgeois world he had so ably depicted in the typical figure of the merchant Pantalone in the 1750s.

The first signs of a great recovery of creativity in the years 1759 to 1762 are apparent in several non-Venetian plays such as *Gl'innamorati* and *La guerra*, a recollection of the Wars of Succession in a part-grim part-cheerful picture that seems to announce Brecht. But in these years Goldoni wrote three masterpieces in dialect: *I rusteghi*, *La casa nova*, and *Sior Todero brontolon* ('The Boors', 'The New House', 'Mr Todero, the Grumbler'). Apart from the language and the bourgeois setting, what these plays have in common is the contrast between, on the one hand, mature and middle-aged men in the closed world of their family and business exercising the virtues dear to merchants – hard work, thrift, punctuality, respect for authority, prudence – and on the other hand their wives and offspring, clamouring for greater liberty and some sort of respectable recreation.

In *I rusteghi* Signora Felice successfully heads a plot to allow an engaged couple to meet at least once before their marriage is arranged. In *Sior Todero* the protagonist's daughter-in-law manages to marry her own daughter to a young man of good family and of her own choice, in opposition to the old tyrant who wants to marry her off to a servant to save the dowry. Here Goldoni is clearly on the side of the young, and certainly on the lips of Todero and the *rusteghi* Pantalone's proverbial saws sound out-dated and ridiculous, based on a totally negative view of social relations when the time is really ripe for the bourgeois to take a more active part in city life, acquiring some culture, going to the theatre (which the *rusteghi* hate) and adopting some of the political (in the broad sense) virtues of the old ruling class now in decline.

But in *La casa nova* a 'modern' bourgeois couple are on the verge of ruin because of overspending, and are only rescued at the last moment by the generosity of Cristofolo, their old uncle, a retired pork-butcher and benevolent version of the *rustego*. Two years before his departure for France Goldoni can denounce the contradictions in the behaviour of his own class, but he no longer feels like offering positive models, let alone solutions – as he did at the time of the reform. But he conveys his uncertainty in some revealing dramatic metaphors: the carnival about to end and which the *rusteghi* feel hemmed in by; the new house which the snobbish occupants can't afford to finish or furnish.

Another good illustration of this phase of Goldoni's dramaturgy, which is both more intense and more delicately shaded, is afforded by the 1761 trilogy *Le smanie per la villeggiatura*, *Le avventure della villeggiatura* and *Il ritorno dalla villeggiatura* ('Off to the Country', 'Adventures in the Country', 'Back From the Country'). Goldoni was often invited to the splendid villas of admiring noblemen, and he was well equipped to record a custom which became increasingly ridiculous the lower it spread down the social scale: the practice of going into the country when it began to get cold, not in order to do some useful work on one's own land but to repeat the leisurely and often harmful activities of the town in the inappropriate context of the country.

Giacinta, the spoilt daughter of a well-to-do bourgeois, promises to marry Leonardo without really loving him; then, in order to assert her independence and discourage her fiancé's unfounded jealousy, she persuades her father to invite the accomplished Guglielmo into the country with them (*Smanie*) and ends by falling in love with him (*Avventure*). In the end she declines to break with Leonardo, whose expenses in the country have nearly ruined him, and marries him, thus repressing her own passion for Guglielmo (*Ritorno*) in order not to break her promise and give satisfaction to those who had declared her weak and fickle like all women and had foreseen her intrigue with Guglielmo. Against a background of widespread extravagance and gossip, Goldoni's comic note becomes more strident as he focuses on the troubles of the middle

classes, trying to ape the aristocracy and caught in a conflict between freedom
and appearances, between defence of their privacy and the need to cut a dash
in public.

Though Giacinta, who is well aware that she will have to pay a heavy price
in order to behave in a more 'manly' way than the men around her, seems
closer to the heroines of Ibsen or Chekhov than those of Marivaux, Goldoni
gets back to a more open and hearty comic note in his last great popular play,
Le baruffe chiozzotte ('Squabbles in Chioggia', 1762), in which the link
between characters and ambience is closer than in any other of his end-of-
carnival pieces. The setting, the streets and the criminal court of Chioggia,
Goldoni knew well from his youthful employment there. The men are away
fishing; sometimes, if there is a storm, they don't come back; their wives, sisters,
sweethearts wait for them, sewing and chatting. The wives' and fiancées' fear of
the sea, the unmarried women's anxiety to find a husband, the jealousy of men
fostered by their long absences, are an explosive mixture for the people of
Chioggia, and their dark and deep passions are reflected in their noisy, violent
quarrels. Goldoni is aware of the scandalised reactions that this free and
unrestrained behaviour may provoke in a 'civilised' audience and he introduces
a character to cushion its effects, the vaguely autobiographical Isidoro, the
Magistrate's assistant, who listens indulgently and with amusement to the
squabbles and in the end settles them. At the same time, Isidoro's bland
hedonism serves as a foil to the Chioggia people's simpler but more motivated
and powerful appetite for happiness, with their pressing hopes and hardships
to which the Venetian official can only be a passing and uninvolved witness.

The democratic and potentially subversive charge of *Le baruffe* explains the
aversion shown to Goldoni's theatre by the Venetian *letterato*, Count Carlo
Gozzi, younger brother of Gasparo (see p. 375). And the great success of the
Fiabe (fables) which Gozzi wrote beginning in 1761 and then had Antonio
Sacchi's company perform, in opposition to Goldoni's realism (see below,
pp. 361–2), was one of the reasons why the latter accepted an invitation he
received in 1762 to join the members of the Comédie italienne in Paris and
settle in France for two years, writing scenarios and plays for them.

Goldoni's working relations with 'the Italians' proved a disappointment,
because when he arrived the actors had just lost much of their independence
following the fusion of their Company with the Opéra comique, and what they
wanted from him above all were *canovacci*, that is new or patched up scenarios
with *Arte*-style humour – partly as an alternative to the 'serious' comedy of the
Comédie française, and partly because the best and most famous of the
company's actors were specialists in the old *Arte* roles. And Goldoni, after the
rather tepid reception of a few comedies, such as *L'amore paterno* (1763), did
in fact produce various scenarios, some of which he adapted as comedies to
send to Venice, as he had promised Vendramin before he left.

While not achieving the originality of his Italian masterpieces, the plays
written in France are of great interest as an illustration of Goldoni's response

to the challenge which a polished, tightly knit society like the French posed to a critic of customs. Many years before, in Pisa, his *Servitore di due padroni* had expressed his reaction to his absence from Venice, from the world he loved and understood the best: he had returned to his masters, the players of the *commedia dell'arte*. Just so, in Paris, he now created some perfect stage pieces where complications and surprises follow each other in a giddy whirl, as in *Gli amanti timidi* ('The Timid Lovers') and *Il ventaglio* ('The Fan') in which certain objects (two portraits, a fan) play diabolical parts in the plot, provoking contretemps and some startling effects.

At the same time, inspired by the versatility of his new performers, Carlin and Camilla, and the Paris fashion of the *comédie larmoyante*, Goldoni went back to some pathetic situations he had tried out in the past: in *Gli amanti timidi*, and especially in the trilogy *Gli amori di Zelinda e Lindoro*, *La gelosia di Lindoro* and *Le inquietudini di Zelinda* ('Zelinda's Anxieties'), he undertakes an enquiry into the psychology of love and its repercussions which is probably the most original outcome of his move to Paris.

In 1765 he left the 'Italians' and earned his living giving Italian lessons, first to the daughter of Louis XV and then, until 1780, to Louis XVI's sisters, mostly in Versailles. From 1780 until his death he lived in Paris with a modest pension, which was withdrawn during the French Revolution. His last comedies were written in French in the 1770s: *Le Bourru bienfaisant* and *L'Avare fastueux*, which show how well he had learned the lessons provided by Molière, whom he always admired. The better-known of the two, *Le Bourru*, which was well received when performed in 1771 by the Comédie francaise, is a decorous version of the theme of *La casa nova* and the *Villeggiature*, a story of frivolous and imprudent young people who are finally rescued by wiser elderly relatives. But now the contradictions are within the characters themselves (as in Molière's *Le Misanthrope*) – the living oxymorons of the *burbero benefico* (grumpy benefactor) and the *avaro fastoso* (miserly show-off) – as though Goldoni recognised a germ of incipient madness beneath the surface of polite French society.

Gozzi and the *Fiabe*

The *Fiabe* of Carlo Gozzi (1720–1806) and his rivalry with Goldoni are a reaction to the popular success of the latter's comedies in the fifties. Gozzi's intention in having *L'amore delle tre melarance* ('The Love of Three Oranges') performed by Antonio Sacchi and his Company was to show how easy it was to please the Venetian public (assuming that his fable was successful, as it was), and thus how irrelevant was its verdict as proof of the play's value; and to mount a direct attack on the vulgar and subversive Goldoni and Chiari, whom he caricatured in the characters of the Magician Celio and the Fairy Morgana respectively. But the great success of the *Three Oranges* induced

Gozzi to take himself seriously as a playwright, and Sacchi performed more of his fables between 1761 and 1765: *Il Corvo* ('The Crow'), *Re Cervo* ('The Stag King'), *Turandot* and others.

These pieces were almost entirely scripted and in verse, and only Sacchi was allowed room to improvise. As a good upholder of the glorious traditions of the past, Gozzi brings in the masks of the *commedia dell'arte* – Pantalone and Brighella, Tartaglia, Truffaldino and Smeraldina – inserting them in a context of magical adventures, enchantments and transformations drawn from children's stories. In fact, the background of the anti-Goldoni reaction is forgotten as the author translates into theatrical terms the perennial delight in the supernatural, and the fascination of marvels and miracles, which not even Settecento rationalism had been able to suppress from the popular imagination. This explains the huge success the *Fiabe* enjoyed with the German Romantics, from the Schlegel brothers to E. T. A. Hoffman (who drew on them in his stories), and with operatic composers such as Puccini and Prokofiev.

Gozzi's skill as a playwright, over and above his idiosyncracies, is apparent in the various brilliant stage-devices he invented for his numerous, over-long and now forgotten *Drammi spagnoleschi*, also written for Sacchi up to the end of the century and based on Spanish Golden Age plays. Neither these nor his *Marfisa bizzarra* ('Marfisa Gone Wild', 1772), a 'playful romance poem' in twelve cantos attacking the Enlightened Century, can compare with the *Fiabe*. (His interesting *Memorie inutili* are discussed below, p. 395).

24

Opera

David Kimbell

Dramma per musica and *opera buffa*

For all its vitality and popularity, seventeenth-century opera had found few articulate apologists and was sustained by little in the way of intellectual or philosophical underpinning. The advent of an era of weighty theorists and historians of literature – Gravina, Muratori, Crescimbeni, Quadrio – all inspired by ideas of renovation and reform, boded ill for those who cherished opera in its Seicento guise. These men, not generally much interested in opera for its own sake, perceived its development largely, if not entirely, through the libretti, and for those of the second half of the seventeenth century they had conceived a profound contempt. Their views are vividly represented in the writings of a theorist, Stefano Arteaga, who did care for opera, and who discerned in that of the seventeenth century nothing but a 'gross chaos, a concoction of sacred and profane, of historical and fabulous, of mythology ancient and modern, of true and allegorical, of natural and fantastic, all gathered together to the perpetual shame of art'. In an age when the Arcadians were aiming, as Muratori suggested, to reform the arts and sciences 'for the benefit of the Catholic religion, for the glory of Italy, and for public and private profit', opera could not escape fresh and fundamental scrutiny. Throughout the eighteenth century its development was to be conditioned by the educative ambitions of the poets and by their determination to reinstate Aristotelian aesthetics. Opera was revisiting its origins (both real and speculative); and once again the Italian composer was being reminded that his art, if divorced from poetry, had no basis in reason and no moral or spiritual power at all.

The poet revered throughout the eighteenth century as the codifier of a new aesthetics for opera was Apostolo Zeno (see above, pp. 345–6). A founder member in 1691 of the Venetian Accademia degli Animosi, which merged with Arcadia in 1698, and imperial poet at the Habsburg court in Vienna from 1718 to 1729, Zeno demonstrated, in Metastasio's words, 'that our melodrama and Reason are not incompatible things'. His libretti, though over the years they underwent increasingly radical modification, were still being set to music in the early nineteenth century, and the aesthetic system he devised conditioned Italian opera for fully a century after his death in 1750.

Zeno's aims were to restrain the chaotic abundance of the Seicento theatre by the application of reason, and to correct its indifference to matters of taste and morals by adopting a lofty, edifying tone. His real interest, it must be said, was drama, not music (to which he was indifferent, and which he – like many *letterati* of the time – blamed for the deplorable state of seventeenth-century literature). Music was therefore to be kept in its place, relegated to the end of the scene (unless it was required as a stage effect), when the action was over. The basic structural unit of the opera became a scene in which dramatic action (set as *recitativo semplice*) alternated with lyrical reflections. Zeno expanded the former hugely, and seems to have entertained the hope that in due course, as mankind became more rational, the *ariette* – concessions to the effeminacy of contemporary taste – could be omitted altogether and his dramas performed as spoken plays. He recognised, however, that music did demand a special style of dramatic organisation: if they were not to become tedious, *ariette* had to express a wide range of emotions; and if they could only be sung as characters left the stage, the plot necessarily had to become more complicated, with a multitude of comings and goings akin to the structure of comedy. Not that there are many laughs in Zeno: indeed, the elimination of comic characters was to prove one of the most momentous of his innovations.

Zeno's reform of opera led, by design, to the creation of the *dramma per musica* (or *opera seria* as it may conveniently be called once it has been set to music). It also led, as it were by default, to the flowering of Italian comic opera, to the *opera buffa*.

During the course of the seventeenth century those comic and low-life scenes which, in *L'incoronazione di Poppea* for example, had once been integral to the drama, tended increasingly to gravitate towards the close of the act. It was therefore a simple matter, when poets eliminated them from the opera altogether, to preserve them in the form of detached, and therefore transferable, *intermezzi*, performed between the acts. In the principal operatic centres, Venice and Naples, an extensive repertory of such *intermezzi* was produced. Many are lost, but the best of the survivors, such pieces as *Pimpinone* (Venice, 1708) by Tomaso Albinoni (1671–1751) and *La serva padrona* (Naples, 1733) by G. B. Pergolesi (1710–36) appeal more strongly to a modern sense of musical theatre than anything in the contemporary *dramma per musica*. From 1735, at the Teatro San Carlo in Naples, *intermezzi* were replaced by ballets, and that precedent was gradually followed in all the grander theatres. But in the meantime the *intermezzo*, which with its tiny cast and modest instrumental and scenic demands had spread all over Western Europe in something like the same way as *commedia dell'arte* had done, taught composers a great deal about the possibilities of musical comedy, musical characterisation and the coordination of music and dramatic action. It continued to flourish in smaller theatres, and as an interlude or afterpiece for spoken plays.

It was a phenomenon unique to the eighteenth century that its prodigious range of operatic activity came most clearly into focus in the work of its greatest literary figures. To see *dramma per musica* in its highest state of perfection we look, not to any particular composer, but to Metastasio (see also above, pp. 353–5). The same is only marginally less true of the *opera buffa*, which came to maturity in the 1750s in the hands of Goldoni and his musical collaborators.

In the history of Italian opera Metastasio's prestige has been unique. Charles Burney was to observe, in the Preface to his *Memoirs of Metastasio*, that 'the lovers of Italian Poetry as well as vocal Music . . . regard Metastasio as the primary source of their most exquisite delight in the union of those arts.' Admired by contemporary *letterati* and intellectuals as a giant of world literature, he was still being held up as a 'model of truth to nature' in the 1820s. His most admired *drammi* were composed and re-composed literally dozens of times by leading musicians, from Vinci and Pergolesi, via Gluck and Mozart, to Mercadante and Meyerbeer.

For Metastasio the kinship between the *dramma per musica* and Greek tragedy was axiomatic: recitative performed the same functions as the ancient 'scenes of action', and 'what else are the AIRS of our musical dramas, but the ancient *strophes*?' (Burney, *Memoirs*, III, 374). To the charge that genuine tragedy, apt to purge pity and terror, rarely fell within the range of eighteenth-century poets and composers, he, like such theorists of the age as Antonio Planelli, would be likely to retort that it was precisely the ability to touch the heart without dwelling on horror and suffering that testified to the progress of humanity since the pre-Christian era. The catalogue of works Burney appended to his *Memoirs of Metastasio* makes it perfectly clear that edification was at least as important as 'purgation'.

Aria texts were therefore not necessarily overflowings of powerful feeling such as the nineteenth century has accustomed us to regard as normal. Maxims and metaphors retained a central role: the former were entirely at home in a medium so convinced of its educative calling; and metaphor texts (something like a quarter of all aria texts are metaphorical in some way) often proved to be the most musically stimulating, prompting in the composer virtuosic and fanciful displays of musical imagery or tone-painting. Metastasio, a music lover who sometimes improvised at the harpsichord to stimulate his poetic imagination, wrote aria texts more mellifluous than his predecessors' and more regular too. For Zeno's placing of the aria so that it stood outside dramatic time had encouraged composers to treat it more expansively, and the profusion of repeated words and phrases largely obliterated such metrical variety or quirkiness as a lyric might have contained; any such qualities no longer served much purpose in terms of stimulating a composer's rhythmic invention.

While Zeno and his colleagues were fashioning the *dramma per musica* and the comic scenes of Seicento opera were evolving into the *intermezzo*, there was emerging in Naples a third branch of operatic activity, the *commedeja pe mmusicca*, of which the most influential specimen was Antonio Orefice's *Patrò Calienno de la Costa*, to a text by 'Agasippo Mercotellis' (?Niccolò Corvo), performed at the Teatro dei Fiorentini in 1709. Sung in dialect, the *commedeja* took its subject matter from the warm, humdrum vitality of contemporary Neapolitan life. There is sketchy evidence – proverbs in the text, the use of such 'folk' instruments as the *colascione* (long-necked lute) – that much use was made of popular song, and, momentously, the musical numbers were not separated off from the action. And so there developed tiny ensemble scenes of confusion or squabbling (*gliuòmmari*, 'tangles'), the earliest manifestation of that 'metasemantic irrationality' that was to flourish, with intoxicating effect, in the mature *opera buffa*. Gradually, and in particular during the 1720s as Neapolitans became aware of the genius of Metastasio in their midst, the *commedeja* and the *dramma per musica* underwent a process of mutual assimilation. The structure of comic opera became more formalised; Neapolitan dialect was now reserved exclusively for the comic characters, and since it was designed to be funny rather than natural, its tone coarsened. However, by the second quarter of the century a group of Neapolitans was emerging – chief among them Leonardo Leo, Gaetano Latilla and Rinaldo di Capua – whose comic operas, less dependent on the local setting than those of their predecessors, could be enjoyed more widely and soon spread to the cities of the north.

In Venice Goldoni took as firm a grip on the development of comic opera as he had a few years earlier on that of the *commedia dell'arte* (see above, pp. 355–61). The Goldonian repertory of operatic texts is substantial – nearly twenty *intermezzi* and more than fifty *opere buffe* (Goldoni preferred the term *dramma giocoso*); as a group they give as comprehensive a picture of mid-eighteenth-century life as his spoken comedies do. His earlier works are close to the farcical and satirical tone of the *intermezzo*; but during the 1750s greater space was given to serious and *mezzo carattere* roles (roles with both serious and *buffo* characteristics), and he widened the range of his themes to include fantasy (*Il mondo della luna*, first set by Baldassare Galuppi, 1706–85) and sentimental comedy. His operatic version of Richardson's *Pamela*, *La buona figliuola*, became, especially in the 1760 setting by Niccolò Piccinni (1728–1800), one of the most admired works of the century.

Nothing Goldoni did was of greater musical consequence than his invention of the ensemble finale, that is, of an ensemble that is not merely a *gliuòmmaro* but, in Lorenzo Da Ponte's phrase, 'a little comedy in itself', in which music and real dramatic action are coordinated. In the first of these finales (in *L'Arcadia in Brenta*, set by Galuppi in 1749) Da Ponte's recipe is perfectly exemplified, for five characters dress up in *commedia dell'arte* costumes and perform a masquerade. The popularity of these finales made them an indispensable feature of *opera buffa*. In fact, the collaboration of Goldoni and Galuppi was giving the genre an altogether irresistible charm, and during the third quarter of the century its cultural prestige came to rival that of the *opera seria*. Back in Naples it received a kind of official recognition during the 1767–8 season when Tanucci, the prime minister, persuaded the court that it really must hear Giovanni Paisiello's *L'idolo cinese*. In Rome too *opera buffa* played an increasingly important role in the repertory, especially after it had been adopted by the dignified Teatro Alibert in the 1770s.

By this time, especially in the collaboration between the young Paisiello (1740–1816) and Giambattista Lorenzi (1721–1807), the *opera buffa* was losing all contact with 'real life' and becoming, quite unashamedly, a dazzling entertainment. In the verve with which it cultivated the grotesque and the farcical it came close to the spirit of the *commedia dell'arte*. Its range of character types legitimised a wide range of singing styles: alongside the 'natural' kind of song, still admired in Piccinni (whom the Abbé Galiani praised for showing that 'nous chantons tous et toujours quand nous parlons'), Paisiello and his contemporaries cultivated an expansive, ornate, virtuoso style modelled on the vocal heroics of the *opera seria*, and what in a more modern repertory would be called the 'patter-song'. To handle these verbal tirades effectively Paisiello (rather primitively in Rossini's judgement), and later Cimarosa and Rossini himself, developed the so-called *parlante* style, in which a fast, sometimes frantic, delivery of the text is set against an orchestral melody repeated, varied and transposed to provide musical continuity. Ensembles became more frequent and dramatically more ambitious. Many were still simply situation pieces (the splendid yawning and sneezing trio in Paisiello's *Barbiere di Siviglia*, for example), but now practised with a studied virtuosity that makes one think of the *lazzi* of the *commedia*. Increasingly, however, the ensembles were taking over extensive tracts of the dramatic action; the *introduzione* began to evolve at the start of the act, on the same lines as the finale at its close.

After Metastasio

Though Metastasio's reputation was to endure for decades, the easy, harmonious relationship he enjoyed with composers in the 1720s and 1730s was already under strain by the 1750s. Zeno's 'rational' separating out of dramatic action and musical expression was proving to be the fatal flaw in the aesthetics of *opera seria*. Since composers were expected to focus all their skills and imagination on setting lyrics which stood outside the dramatic action and therefore outside the natural passing of time, it inevitably followed – especially when the same Metastasio texts were being set again and again – that in the quest for some expressive and rhetorical ideal, arias became longer, more brilliant, more sophisticated in every dimension, straining theatrical plausibility to breaking point, and calling into question the whole matter of the relationship between poetry and music. The dissatisfaction was mutual: while poets and theorists protested at the way composers were distorting the verse, a composer like Nicolò Jommelli (1714–74) found himself resenting the poet's 'parsimony' with words and his tendency to 'want to do all the singing himself'.

Jommelli, the most richly gifted Italian composer of the central decades of the century, escaped from the limitations of the medium by going to Germany. From 1753 to 1768 he was at the Württemberg court in Stuttgart where, under the patronage of his opera-loving prince, he produced one or two operas annually under close-to-ideal conditions. He was typical of his generation in feeling that poetry (that is, in an operatic context, *recitativo semplice*) was not in itself a dramatically compelling medium. And he therefore drew on his knowledge of the resources of French opera, and indeed of *opera buffa*, to enrich the heroic style both structurally and expressively. Most of Jommelli's Stuttgart operas are settings of Metastasio; but, as in the *tragédie lyrique*, chorus and ballet play a central and integral role; the more powerful monologues are likely to be set as orchestrally accompanied recitatives; from comic opera he borrows the dramatic ensemble to bring into musical focus the scenes of greatest theatrical tension.

Jommelli's achievements in Stuttgart were paralleled on Italian soil by Tommaso Traetta (1727–79) at Parma, another francophile court. Here, indeed, the French association was direct and explicit, for the operas Traetta created in 1758–60 to libretti by Carlo Innocenzo Frugoni (1692–1768) were based on French originals, composed in the 1730s by Rameau. Also, of course, Jommelli's achievements were paralleled by a greater composer and a more famous 'reform': that of Christoph Willibald Gluck (1714–87), who worked at Vienna during the 1760s in collaboration with Ranieri de' Calzabigi, and under the influence of Algarotti's *Saggio sopra l'opera* (*An Essay on the Opera*, published in 1755).

There was much irony in the circumstances of Gluck's reform. It can hardly have been aimed at anything if not at Metastasian *opera seria*. Yet its watchword of 'restricting music to its true office of serving poetry' (Preface to *Alceste*) might for all the world be a quotation from Metastasio himself. The problem was surely this: if music had an intrinsic expressive and dramatic potential (which much eighteenth-century theory denied, but which Algarotti must have believed, and which Gluck was to demonstrate), it could 'serve poetry' only if the poetry was in the first place designed to cater to the formal, expressive and dramatic needs of music.

What this meant in practical terms was that an opera needed a simpler story moving at a slower pace; preferably a familiar story, so that the poet could concentrate not on such questions of theatrical intrigue as 'What happens next?', but on the potentially musical questions: 'What is the pervading atmosphere of this drama? What is the cast of mind of this character, and what are the nuances of feeling he experiences?' And if a place had to be found for choral singing and dancing alongside the solo singing, the plot needed to achieve a genuine integration of the private and the social spheres. Operatic poetry was seen to demand on the one hand monologues and dialogues more imbued with lyrical moods, and on the other, arias during which the action (internal, if not external) could somehow be carried on. It was surely no coincidence that Gluck's reforms (and Jommelli's) were accompanied by a transformation of the style of performance in a spirit emanating from Garrick's naturalistic reform of acting in London in the 1740s.

We may stay in Vienna a moment to pursue the story of the *opera buffa*, which, in the hands of Mozart and Lorenzo Da Ponte (1749–1838), was about to achieve so accomplished a fusion of music and drama, of the purely human and the transcendentally beautiful, that it remains the supreme demonstration of the potential of opera as an artistic medium. In some respects – the more 'natural' individualism of the characters, for example, and the profusion of ensemble scenes – Da Ponte was perhaps indebted to Giambattista Casti (see above, p. 355), whose *Re Teodoro in Venezia*, set by Paisiello in 1784, is one of the peaks of the repertory. But his collaboration with Mozart remains the supreme instance in musical history of what has been called that happiest stroke of good fortune, when a composer who really knows his job has the chance to collaborate with a poet who really knows *his*. And it is right to insist that theirs was a collaborative achievement; the breakthrough to what Da Ponte called 'un quasi nuovo genere di spettacolo' ('a virtually new kind of spectacle') came from both sides.

Historically Mozart was the first great composer of opera who was also a complete master of the newish sonata style. The advantage of this for his ensembles is self-evident: he could sustain a fluctuating continuity by 'symphonic' means, by the 'development' of tiny instrumental figures and the deployment of a vast range of harmonic and tonal resources, simply to describe which conventional analytical vocabulary launches into a catalogue of dramatic metaphors: 'conflict', 'tension', 'resolution'. But the sonata style was no less transfiguring in even the most lyrical arias. Mozart had the musical resources not just to sustain a mood in general terms, but to express, and develop into contrasting facets, its lights and shades, its hesitations and changes of direction. He possessed, that is to say, a technique which enabled him to make the aria not a performance or demonstration of feeling, but an expression of feeling as it is actually lived through and experienced.

Da Ponte played up to these accomplishments. His aria texts are uncommonly long, so that the words, instead of being repeated again and again, can be moved through at a virtually 'natural' speed. Often the frontiers between recitative and musical numbers are dissolved. Ensemble texts have the character of animated dialogue rather than formal speech-making. And Da Ponte and Mozart are not afraid to drop them into the most flagrantly unlyrical contexts: the floor-measuring duet at the start of *Le nozze di Figaro*, or the escape-out-of-the-window duet in Act II. Compared with Mozart all other eighteenth-century opera, even the most uproarious Neapolitan *opera buffa*, seems quaintly decorous in its momentum. To singers at the end of the century Mozart seemed a 'paladin of velocity' (Geltrude Righetti-Giorgi), because in his Da Ponte operas music is made to move at the pace of life itself. No one had attempted that particular kind of realism before. And really no one after

Mozart did either – certainly not Rossini, who, for all his reverence for Mozart and for all his scintillating verve, in many respects reverts to a more artificially playful manner.

What of heroic opera – the *opera seria*? Gluck's work was chiefly influential in France and Germany, where it became an important source of romantic attitudes to opera. In Italy he found few followers (though *Orfeo ed Euridice* made enough of a mark in Naples to be worth parodying in Paisiello's *Socrate immaginario* in 1775); well into the nineteenth century he enjoyed a fearsome reputation as an uncompromising seeker after 'truth', in a form not always congenial to Italian taste. The reluctance of Italians to recognise the expressive potential of instrumental music, and their slowness in drawing on the colouristic and symphonic potential of the orchestra, excluded for some decades other vital ingredients of operatic romanticism.

Nevertheless, between c. 1780 and 1815 Italian opera was slowly transformed. An interest was awakened in 'northern' literature, notably via Melchiorre Cesarotti's 'Ossian' translations (see below, p. 394), which held up Macpherson's *Comala* as a model 'for opera in a new style'. The increasingly political tone of many operas gave a new importance to the chorus. The abolition of the practice of castration during the Napoleonic period necessarily led to an unprecedented dependence on the darker colours of the natural male voices. Many composers enjoyed more cosmopolitan careers, particularly careers that gravitated between Italy and France; and Simon Mayr (1763–1845), a distinguished Bavarian who brought with him some of his Germanic habits of thought, became, around the turn of the century, one of the most influential composers in Italy. All these factors encouraged what might be described as proto-Romantic tendencies in opera.

The crucial development, however, which gathered pace during the 1790s and was fully achieved in Rossini's heroic operas from 1813 onwards, was the absorption into *opera seria* of the more dramatically fluid musical language of *opera buffa*. One notable element of this was the two-movement (slow–fast) aria, which introduced a new dynamic, both physical and emotional, into solo scenes. Still more momentous was the adoption of the dramatic ensemble finale. This became the pivotal feature in the architecture of an opera, a pattern of alternating fast and slow movements coordinated with the dramatic fluctuation between action and introspection. In 1791 Caterino Mazzolà revised Metastasio's *La clemenza di Tito* in this spirit for Mozart; it is amusing and instructive to find the composer describing the process as that of 'converting Metastasio into a real opera'.

25

The Enlightenment and Parini

The Enlightenment in Naples

The various reforms undertaken in the Settecento theatre should be seen against the background of the general questioning of traditional thinking and the adoption of more 'enlightened' views in society as a whole. By 'Enlightenment' we mean the movement, which affected all branches of learning and which was more or less explicitly political, of emancipation from ignorance, prejudice and authority based on superstition and the abuse of power, a campaign undertaken by the most original and open-minded thinkers of the first half of the century, but more systematically in the second half, on a basis of reason and freedom of criticism, aiming at a fairer social organisation and (in the last analysis) a better life for all. The works of the main proponents of the new philosophy, the *philosophes* – Locke, Newton and Hume in Britain, Montesquieu, Voltaire and Diderot in France, to mention only a few of the more important – were read and admired in Italy, although their influence varied according to the economic, legal and political situation in the different Italian states.

What has been said about Goldoni would lead one to assign his comedies to the 'progressive' culture of his time or to label them 'enlightened', but if by this term we mean the followers of the French *philosophes* and 'Encyclopaedists' (from the great *Encyclopédie ou Dictionnaire raisonné des sciences, des arts et des métiers* which Diderot and D'Alembert began publishing in 1751), who devoted their lives to the 'spread of light', then we must concentrate on certain states in particular which we earlier labelled 'new' (p. 343): Naples, Florence to some extent, and especially Milan.

We have already noted the decisive role played by Antonio Genovesi in the movement for the reform of civil society in Naples (p. 347). He was followed a generation later by Ferdinando Galiani (1728–87), an economist, student of Vico, and 'Parisian', actually resident in Paris as Secretary of the Neapolitan Embassy from 1759 to 1769. Galiani was widely admired for his intelligence and wit and became a close friend of D'Holbach, and also of Diderot and Mme D'Epinay, who oversaw the publication, the year after he left Paris, of the work to which he owed his fame: *Dialogue sur le commerce des bleds* (1770, false London imprint). He wrote various other works, including the libretto *Socrate immaginario*, which he composed in collaboration with G. B.

Lorenzi and which was set to music in 1775 by Paisiello; a *Dialogue sur les femmes* (1772); a treatise *Del dialetto napoletano* (1779); and after his 'exile' from France, between 1769 and 1782, he engaged in a voluminous correspondence with Mme D'Epinay, which amounts to a sparkling review of the cultural and social life of Naples and Paris.

The 1780s saw the publication of the major works of the Enlightenment in Naples: *La scienza della legislazione* by Gaetano Filangieri, a member of the old princely family of Arianello (1753–88), and the *Saggi politici* ('Political Essays') of Francesco Mario Pagano (1748–99). Filangieri's book is a grandiose project – especially remarkable for a young man – to reform civil society by means of a series of radical initiatives, including the abolition of the monstrous feudal system, leaving the barons in possession only of their estates and assigning public administration and justice to qualified magistrates loyal to the state; it also envisaged reform of the penal law, the abolition of torture and the protection of the rights of the accused, and provision of public education to ensure, if not equality between rich and poor, at least a narrowing of the intellectual and economic gap.

Pagano, who studied under Genovesi and an associate of Vico's, was a lawyer and law-teacher, a friend of Filangieri and a fellow Mason. His *Saggi politici*, explicitly Vichian in origin, are an ambitious 'essay in symbolic sociology' (Venturi), according to which the myths and heroes of the distant past become examples of a socio-anthropological reality which continues up to the present time. Pagano was a forceful writer, and his *Ragione criminale* (posthumously published in 1803) gained international recognition. His relatively brief career exemplifies the course and tragic conclusion of the Neapolitan Enlightenment. His interest in the primitive world and myth derives from Vico; his commitment to translate the lessons of philosophy and history into political action comes from the Encyclopaedists and the French Revolution. He was one of the most active and influential members of the republican government in Naples in 1799, was arrested with the return of the Bourbons and was hanged – with the shameful acquiescence of Nelson, who allowed Ferdinand IV to ignore the guarantees given to the republicans in the capitulation agreement. His fate was shared by Admiral Francesco Caracciolo, the journalist Eleonora Fonseca Pimentel, the physician and scientist Domenico Cirillo and many others.

The breadth and diversity of reformist thought in Naples is revealed by the work of Giuseppe Maria Galanti (Molise, 1743–1806), the most active and faithful of Genovesi's pupils. Finding the ideas of Vico, Giannone, Filangieri and Pagano too abstract and 'metaphysical', he embarked on a study of the geography and economy of the south, gaining official recognition and support as 'visitatore del Regno' for an analysis of the condition of the peasants, until the French Revolution alarmed the Bourbons into an explicitly reactionary policy. The solidity and originality of his research, based on precise statistics, and the clarity of his proposed reforms are apparent in his masterly *Nova descrizione storica e geografica delle Sicilie* (1786–90). His *Elogio di Niccolò Machiavelli ... con un Discorso intorno alla costituzione della società ed al governo politico* ('Eulogy of N.M. ... With a Discourse on the Constitution of Society and on Government', 1779), which he had to publish anonymously in view of clerical opposition to his proposed edition of Machiavelli, is the most definitive tribute paid by the Enlightenment in the south to the Florentine's 'sentimenti generosi e liberi'. Galanti's youthful interest in English and French narrative stimulated his *Osservazioni intorno a' romanzi, alla morale e a' diversi generi di sentimento* ('Observations on the Novel, on Morals and on the Various Kinds of Emotions', 1780), pre-Romantic in flavour and equipped with an interesting 'feminist' appendix in the later 1786 edition: 'Saggio intorno alla condizione delle donne nello stato civile ed alle leggi coniugali' ('Essay on the position of women in the state and on marriage laws').

The Enlightenment in the north

While university teaching and public office were the best platforms in Naples for Enlightenment programmes to destroy or weaken the *ancien régime*, elsewhere, and especially in the north, there was a more varied culture and a new range of intellectuals: the cosmopolitan traveller, the professional journalist etc. Among those leaving the old paternalistic states such as Piedmont or Venice and keen to savour the new Europe was Alberto Radicati, Torinese author of the Deist and anti-clerical *Discours moraux, historiques et politiques* (1736). Another was Francesco Algarotti (Venice, 1712–64) who travelled in France, England, Germany and Russia, became a friend of Voltaire and chamberlain to Frederick II of Prussia, and quickly attracted attention with his timely and readable *Newtonianismo per le dame* ('Newtonianism for Ladies', 1737). His was a happy, typically Settecento combination of good taste and classical and encyclopaedic culture. He was a master of a form particularly suited to his versatile, but not very original or profound talent: the essay, of medium length (*Sopra la pittura*, *Sopra l'Opera in musica*), or short (*Sopra la necessità di scrivere nella propria lingua*, *Sopra l'imperio degl'Incas*: 'On Painting', 'On the Opera', 'On the Need to Write in One's Own Language', 'On the Inca Empire'), etc., almost all of them collected in his *Opere varie* (Venice, 1757). His *Viaggi di Russia* ('Travels in Russia'), consisting of letters written in 1739 (with an additional four to Scipione Maffei in 1751–2), again show him to be a keen observer of the contemporary world and a perceptive and agreeable writer.

In 1757 Algarotti joined with Frugoni (see above, p. 351) and the Mantuan Jesuit Saverio Bettinelli (1718–1808) to publish *Versi sciolti di tre eccellenti moderni autori* ('Poems in Blank Verse by Three Excellent Modern Authors') which immediately became famous because of Bettinelli's introductory *Dieci lettere di Publio Virgilio Marone scritte dagli Elisi all'Arcadia di Roma sopra gli abusi introdotti nella poesia italiana* ('Ten Letters by P.V.M. Written from the Elysian Fields to the Roman Arcadia Concerning the Malpractices That Have Been Introduced into Italian Poetry'). The *Lettere virgiliane* (Bettinelli's own abbreviation) launched a trenchant attack on the Italian poetic tradition, and particularly on the obscure and extravagant *Divine Comedy*, appealing to an ideal of 'modernity' (or rationality and naturalness) familiar to the Greeks and Romans and brilliantly illustrated in the writings of 'modern' English and French writers – as Bettinelli demonstrated subsequently in his *Lettere sopra vari argomenti di letteratura scritte da un Inglese ad un Veneziano* ('Letters on Various Literary Matters Written by an Englishman to a Venetian') or *Lettere inglesi* (1766). His treatise *Dell'entusiasmo delle belle arti* ('On Enthusiasm in the Fine Arts', 1769), with its insistence on the power of 'nature' and 'feeling', would seem to set Bettinelli in the forefront of Enlightenment thinking; but his later *Risorgimento d'Italia negli studi, nelle arti e ne' costumi dopo il mille* ('The Revival of Italy in Scholarship, Arts and Customs After 1000', 1773) shows that his modern classicism was still tied to a Jesuit cultural programme, careful not to lose contact with the élites. It is closely linked on the one hand to the historical writing of Voltaire (*Essai sur les mœurs*) and on the other to the educational practice of the Jesuits in their various colleges and churches. Even though Bettinelli did not actually edit or contribute to periodicals, the form and style of his best and most enduring work, the *Lettere Virgiliane* and *Inglesi*, is reminiscent of journalism, the type of publication Settecento intellectuals found most effective to reach and teach their readers, the Enlightenment genre par excellence.

To be more precise, intellectual activity in the different Italian centres in the Settecento was focused in the academies and the journals, the former still operating with the name, often the ritual, of the old Renaissance academies, but now reflecting the commitment – cultural, but also sometimes economic and political – to *projects* or proposals, more or less advanced, for reform. And the periodicals (*gazzette* or *fogli*) were the most obvious and convenient vehicles for this purpose.

In Tuscany, where the new Lorraine dynasty of Francesco Stefano, Maria Teresa's future husband, was much more favourably disposed than the Medici towards the intellectuals, the Accademia dei Georgofili, founded by Pompeo Neri in 1753, engaged in research on economics and agriculture, and Giovanni Lami founded and directed, from 1740 to 1769, the weekly *Novelle letterarie* ('Literary News').

The political and cultural climate of Venice, with a declining oligarchy jealously guarding its privileges and suspicious of novelty, was much less liberal than the Florentine, but the city was still a major centre of the printing industry and book trade: hence the plethora of periodicals, many of them produced by the booksellers with an eye to the market. The most active writer and journalist in eighteenth-century Venice was Gasparo Gozzi (1713–86), Carlo's elder brother and one of the impoverished noble class effectively excluded from power (see also above, pp. 361–2). His solid classical culture and refined taste are apparent in his collection of *Lettere diverse* (I: 1750; II: 1752) to friends and *letterati* in Venice, perpetuating a Cinquecento tradition; they provide an urbane and perceptive commentary on a range of subjects: the benefits of the printing press, the pleasures of the countryside, day-to-day events in the city, and so on.

His personality is characterised by a keen but not bigoted devotion to the Italian literary heritage and a satirical, somewhat detached and disenchanted attitude to contemporary customs. His fidelity to the classics is evident in his *Difesa di Dante (Giudizio degli antichi poeti sopra la moderna censura di Dante attribuita ingiustamente a Virgilio)* ('Defence of Dante: Verdict of the Ancient Poets on the Modern Criticism of Dante Unjustly Attributed to Virgil', 1758), a reasoned and polemical reply to Bettinelli's *Lettere virgiliane*. His *Sermoni* in blank verse (the first twelve published in 1763, the other six posthumously) provide a lively picture of the foibles and fashions of contemporary polite society, but they also reveal a deeper and more original vein when he reflects on his own austere principles of conduct and a sense of isolation resulting from this: an existential confession on a sad, even bitter note from a poet forced to take on gloomy tasks in order to survive:

> Tutto attonito miro: ampio deserto
> Mi sembra il mondo e solitario orrore.

(I gaze around me in astonishment: the world appears to me like a vast desert, a dreaded solitude)

(XIII, A Marco Foscarini)

One of his tasks was journalism, the publication, at the beginning of the 1760s, of three periodicals. One, *Il mondo morale*, published in instalments in 1760, was really a kind of allegorical novel, with a frame (like that in the *Decameron* or *Canterbury Tales*), for the various fables, translations, poems and so on. The other two, *La Gazzetta veneta* (1760–1) and *L'Osservatore veneto* (1761–2), published twice a week, were more strictly journalistic in the modern sense of purveying news. Gozzi was motivated by the need for a city chronicle providing practical information (arrival of ships, articles for sale, lottery numbers etc.), but he also had in mind the great model of all Settecento journals with any literary or philosophical pretensions, Addison and Steele's *Spectator*. This twin motivation and the quality of Gozzi's prose, which is both simple and elegant, give an unmistakable flavour to these vivid documents of the life of his day, with their touches of drama reminiscent of Goldoni (whom Gozzi admired and praised) and that mixture of wonder and tolerance with which the classical essayists and moralists record the conduct of their fellow mortals.

The dissident Baretti

Also in Venice at this time was a Piedmontese friend and admirer of Gozzi,
who between 1763 and 1765 edited, virtually single-handed, the fortnightly
Frusta letteraria ('The Literary Scourge'). The young Giuseppe Baretti (1719–
89) had produced a string of humorous poems, attacks on pedantic professors,
translations from the French and other works before spending nine years in
London as a teacher of Italian and publishing various works connected with
his teaching, including a very successful *Dictionary of the English and Italian
Languages* (1760), the proceeds from which allowed him to return to Italy,
travelling through Portugal, Spain and southern France. On the advice of his
friend Samuel Johnson he recorded his experiences and observations in his
Lettere familiari a' suoi tre fratelli Filippo, Giovanni e Amedeo ('Familiar
Letters to his Three Brothers, F., G. and A.'), the first two volumes of which
appeared in Milan and Venice respectively in 1762 and 1763; the final two
volumes were never published owing to the intervention of the diplomatic
representatives of the countries he visited with the censors in Lombardy and
Venice.

Baretti was too impulsive and impatient to provide a clear and detailed
account of these countries in the style of contemporary French travel-memoirs.
His work is essentially autobiographical, using the short and congenial format
of the letter to his brothers to record 'a chaotic jumble' of impressions and
reflections aroused by his lively curiosity but always centred on the compelling
subject of his own mobile self. The most varied, unforeseen or trying situations
become 'interesting' (in Settecento parlance) as soon as they involve the
author: compare, for example, his elaborate and solemn letter on the Lisbon
earthquake of 1755 (I, 19), or his many descriptions of awful Portuguese inns
(consciously rivalling Berni's poems on the subject two hundred years previously), and the account of his meeting with two English Misses on the coach
from London; or his comic thumbnail sketches of truculent soldiers and
officials in Portugal.

For the *Frusta* Baretti cleverly invented a 'double', the irascible old soldier
Aristarco Scannabue, who has retired to the country to read the new books
handed on to him by a friend, a neighbouring priest: the mostly idiosyncratic
reactions of Aristarco to current literary fashions are recorded in articles for
the journal, three or four for each issue. The *Frusta* is clearly reminiscent not
only of the best English journals – the *Tatler*, the *Spectator*, Johnson's
Rambler – with their 'philosophy for everyday' and their didactic aims; but
also of Zeno and Maffei's *Giornale dei letterati d'Italia* ('Journal of Italian
Men of Letters'), and Lami's *Novelle letterarie*, for example, with their
bibliographical material; also of Gozzi's publications with their penchant for
brief articles and sketches and lively prose. But the *Frusta* does not really
belong together with the other Italian journals we have mentioned, because of
the strong impression made on Baretti during his residence in England by

English journalism as a whole, and especially by the long lists of subscribers to the English journals, the influence they exerted on their readers and their great commercial success. Hence his choice of Venice with its wealth of printers and booksellers and flourishing book trade.

We must reckon the balance of Baretti's journalistic adventure as respectably positive when we consider the lively style of his polemics (against the frivolous and effeminate poetry of the Arcadians, the short-sighted and bigoted cult of the past of the antiquaries, and against the Italian Enlightenment and Francomania generally). Also on the credit side we should place his gruff insistence on literature being 'useful' and his well-judged interventions in the linguistic debate, resulting in his discovery of a model of lively, natural and anti-academic prose in the *Vita* of Benvenuto Cellini. On the negative side is Baretti's failure to identify (and therefore to attract and keep) a specific readership. He was a practical soul, essentially conservative, and the targets of his sarcasm include not only the desiccated devotees of the old culture (whom he views from the perspective of his own experience of the infinitely more modern English society), but also other writers fighting more effectively than he did for the renewal of Italian letters, such as Goldoni, whom he attacks bitterly in at least four articles for the alleged immorality of his comedies. Baretti is like his spokesman, Aristarco, a voice crying in what he thought was a wilderness (but wasn't); but Aristarco, with his robust and colourful prose, was still a happy and effective vehicle for turning to artistic advantage, at least, what were really serious limitations, from the journalistic viewpoint, in Baretti's culture.

In January 1766, after twenty-five numbers, the *Frusta* was prohibited by the Venetian authorities. Baretti brought out eight more issues in Ancona – really one continuous attack on Father Appiano Buonafede, who had ridiculed him and his journal in *Il bue pedagogo* ('The Pedagogue Ox', 1764) – and in 1766 he returned to London, where, apart from various journeys to France, Spain and Italy, he remained until his death in 1789. In this second English period he produced several important works: *An Account of the Manners and Customs of Italy* (1768), a defence of his country against the attacks of an impatient English traveller, Dr Samuel Sharp; *A Journey from London to Genoa, through England, Portugal, Spain and France* (1770), a translation of the two volumes of letters to his brothers with the addition of the second part that he had not been able to publish in Italy; and a *de luxe* edition in three volumes of the works of Machiavelli, with a preface in which he criticises Machiavelli for having deliberately tried to undermine Princes by divulging their vices (an Enlightenment thesis which Alfieri was to adopt and use in Machiavelli's favour).

Most typical of the works of this second London period are the *Discours sur Shakespeare et sur Monsieur de Voltaire* (1777) and the *Scelta di lettere familiari fatta per uso degli studiosi di lingua italiana* ('Selection of Familiar Letters for the Use of Students of the Italian Language', 1779). In the former,

Baretti, an admirer of Shakespeare and friend of Garrick, charges Voltaire (in French!) with petty, classicist prejudices and a substantial ignorance of foreign languages which prevents him from appreciating the English dramatist. In its insistence on the earthy and passionate nature of Shakespeare's imagination, and its brilliant demonstration of the artificiality of the pseudo-Aristotelian unities, the *Discours* is often considered pre-Romantic, which it perhaps is in the Italian context, but far less so in the context of French and English culture where criticism of the unities was well established.

The letters in the *Scelta*, almost all really by Baretti under assumed names, are intended as models for students of Italian and provide a broad panorama of Baretti's ideas, rather more open-minded on various political and literary questions and more modern than those of Aristarco fifteen years earlier. But this comparative accommodation to Enlightened thinking is counterbalanced by a return to a literary, Tuscanising prose which is much less lively and 'modern' than in the *Frusta* – a typical example of Baretti's never being in harmony with his time or, basically, with himself. The frequent autobiographical touches (nostalgia for the country he has abandoned, the family he has never had) are a further attraction of the collection.

Milan: *Il Caffè*, the Verri brothers, Beccaria

One of Aristarco's best-known targets in the *Frusta* (apart from Goldoni's comedies, which were condemned for their coarse language and their satire of the nobles and sympathetic treatment of popular characters), was the periodical *Il Caffè, ossia brevi e vari discorsi distribuiti in fogli periodici*, ('The Coffee-House, or Various Short Articles Distributed in Periodical Sheets'), which came out every ten days from June 1764 to May 1766. Although printed in Venetian territory (in Brescia), it is really an example of Milanese Enlightened thought at its most articulate and mature. For a comparatively brief period in the 1760s the reformist policy of Maria Teresa and her Minister, Kaunitz, carried out in Lombardy by her plenipotentiary, the Austrian Count Firmian, encouraged the Milanese intellectuals to collaborate, at least with proposals, discussions and comments, in the development of a more modern administrative and economic structure; it was not fortuitous, therefore, that the founder and effective director of *Il Caffè*, Count Pietro Verri (1728–92) and one of his senior collaborators, Count Gian Rinaldo Carli of Capodistria, were invited to participate in the Lombard administration and help implement some of the reforms they had proposed.

Again it was the *Spectator* which inspired the idea of setting the articles of *Il Caffè* in the framework of conversations supposed to have taken place in the Milanese coffee-house of a certain wise Greek, Demetrius. The youthful contributors, members of the Accademia dei Pugni (the fists), which met in Pietro Verri's house (his younger brother, Alessandro, the economists Carlo

Sebastiano Franci and Alfonso Longo, the mathematician Paolo Frisi, and, most important of all as we shall see, the versatile Cesare Beccaria) concerned themselves with a wide range of subjects from commerce and agriculture to meteorology, medicine and the theatre, always in accordance with Enlightened principles: promotion of public welfare, war on prejudice, concern for the practical problems of life in society. They were Sensist in philosophy (see above, p. 346, note), and in politics advocates of a strong and competent central government; and they were opposed to any feudal relics (privileges, onerous taxes and exemptions) which obstructed the modernisation of the state.

In literature they advocated a clear, up-to-date language, containing (if necessary) neologisms and gallicisms, and they favoured content – concrete facts and useful, original ideas – rather than the Tuscan 'form' which the purists defended so jealously: 'things and not words'. Some of the most important linguistic articles were written by the young Marquis Cesare Beccaria (1738–94) whose famous *Dei delitti e delle pene* ('Of Crime and Punishment') was composed with the encouragement and advice of Pietro Verri: it was published in Livorno in the summer of 1764, just when the first numbers of *Il Caffè* were appearing.

The great originality of Beccaria's little book, and one of the reasons for its extraordinary European success, is the fact that it addresses the thorniest problems of criminal law and the contemporary Italian penal system from a point of view combining the logical rigour of the *philosophes* with the compassion of Rousseau; also the way it bases its demand for the abolition of torture and the death penalty on a belief in the equality of all men which only Rousseau and Diderot (in some of his then still unpublished works) had articulated equally forcefully and explicitly. Beccaria's ideas were received with enthusiasm and horror; significantly, the term 'socialist' appeared here for the very first time, with a negative connotation, from the pen of Beccaria's Venetian opponent, Father Ferdinando Facchinei (*Note ed osservazioni sul libro intitolato Dei delitti e delle pene*, 1765). Beccaria's work was admired by Voltaire and D'Alembert, and praised by Jeremy Bentham as the source of his ideas on society and justice. It was translated into various languages (the French version by André Morellet being particularly influential), and was the most important Italian contribution to the European Enlightenment.

Although the *Caffè* circle broke up in 1766, Pietro Verri, now a government official, continued to write various important works perpetuating the philosophical, historical and legal interests of the journal: *Meditazioni sull'economia politica* (1771), *Discorso sull'indole del piacere e del dolore* ('Discourse on the Nature of Pleasure and Pain', 1773) and *Osservazioni sulla tortura* (1777), etc. His *Storia di Milano* was to be one of Manzoni's sources for *I Promessi Sposi*. His *Ricordi a mia figlia* ('Advice to My Daughter', 1777) shows us Verri the loving and enlightened father, profoundly interested in the physical and intellectual development of his daughter, more feminist, one could say, not only than his contemporaries but than many later intellectuals.

Alessandro Verri (1741–1816), after a long journey in France and England where he was warmly received and honoured, on his own account and that of his brother and Beccaria (who had been with him in Paris for a while), settled in Rome in 1767, where he adopted the conservative and classicising tastes of the Roman *letterati*. This radical cultural and political conversion is reflected in his novels, which were written in a literary, Tuscanising language remote from the lively and (according to the purists) slovenly diction of *Il Caffè*, and were inspired by the scholarly archaeological interests he had newly acquired: *Le avventure di Saffo poetessa di Mitilene* (1780) and especially *Le notti romane* ('Roman Nights', 1782–90), which were enormously successful, and mark a significant transition from neo-classical ideals to the pre-Romantic taste for ruins.

Parini: from Sensism to neo-classicism

Before founding the Accademia dei Pugni and *Il Caffè*, Verri and some of his colleagues had been members of the more moderate and traditional Accademia dei Trasformati, which dated back to the Cinquecento and had been revived in 1743 by the rich Count Giuseppe Maria Imbonati, in whose house the members met to recite their compositions on prearranged topics. To this Academy was admitted in 1753 a young penniless seminarist from Brianza, a certain Giuseppe Parini (1722–99), who was to become the greatest Italian poet of his day and the most complete representative of Enlightenment literature in the country.

Parini's main qualification for admission to the socially prestigious Trasformati was a little book he had published the previous year, *Alcune poesie di Ripano Eupilino* ('Some Poems by R.E.'), a collection including serious poems in which the obviously Arcadian inspiration (nymphs, woods and shepherds) was fortified by a background of Latin culture (Horace and the elegiac poets), of Cinquecento lyric poetry and jocular verse in the currently fashionable style of Francesco Berni. Parini was ordained in 1754 and became tutor to the children of the Duke and Duchess Serbelloni, only leaving their service in 1762 after a disagreement with the Duchess, with whom however he remained on friendly terms. The background to his poetry thus consists of the bland and prudent reformism of the Trasformati on the one hand, and on the other the fascinating, and to him irritating, spectacle of the elegant, sumptuous and frivolous life of the Milanese aristocracy. In the prose pieces, verse epistles and odes read to his Academy colleagues in the 1750s and 1760s the ideological and poetic programme of the young Parini emerges clearly: his goal is a peaceful, hard-working and frugal society, still close to its agricultural origins and remote from the ideals of commerce, luxury and constant struggle for progress upheld by the cosmopolitan *Caffè* (*Sopra la guerra*, *La vita rustica*, 'On War', 'Country Life'); literature is to have a civil and educative function

(*Discorso sopra la poesia*). The most important works of this period are the *Dialogo sopra la nobiltà* and especially the ode *La salubrità dell'aria* (1759). The former features a conversation between two corpses, a poet and a nobleman still arrogantly contemptuous of the people, and proclaims the vanity of noble titles, the equality of all men and the need for the nobles to justify their privileges by their contribution to society. *La salubrità dell'aria*, a seemingly innocuous subject suggested by the Trasformati, launches into an attack on the pollution around and within Milan caused by 'il lusso, l'avarizia, la stolta pigrizia', the greed, ignorance and idleness of private speculators and public bodies.

La salubrità dell'aria is a good example of Sensist theories of poetry where the emphasis is on precise terminology and epithets carrying sensual suggestions in order to convey the physical presence of objects. But Parini does not in fact abandon the traditional language of his beloved classical poets: he aims to enrich it by embracing and filtering subject-matter generally considered unpoetical (rice-fields, stable manure, animal corpses, dung-carts), and he discovers how well they support his idea of poetry. The sound and images of the poet's allusions to the thyme, crocuses and wild mint of the Milanese countryside do raise the stylistic tone, but these faded remnants of a tired-out pastoral tradition acquire new life and colour alongside and because of the 'aria lenta' (heavy air), 'sali malvagi' (the poisonous salt), the 'umor fracidi e rei' (the harmful putrid water), the 'aliti corrotti' (polluted air). So what seems a straight quotation from Horace acquires a totally modern meaning:

> Va per negletta via
> Ognor l'util cercando
> La calda fantasia
> Che sol felice è quando
> L'utile unir può al vanto
> Di lusinghevol canto.

(Through neglected paths, always in search of the useful, goes the fertile imagination which is only happy when it can unite the useful with the quality of pleasurable song.)

It is here that the Christian Parini and the Encyclopaedists of *Il Caffè*, philosophically so different, can join hands, as we see in the odes contemporary with Parini's *Il giorno* ('The Day'), to which we will come shortly: in *L'educazione*, for example, where the convalescence of his pupil Carlo Imbonati provokes a eulogy of the marriage of nature and reason; and in *L'innesto del vaiuolo* in praise of the campaign for inoculation against smallpox by his friend and protector Doctor Bicetti; in *Il bisogno* ('Need') where the preventive, rather than punitive, approach of a Swiss magistrate inspires a description of a man driven to violence by hunger, recalling Beccaria's impassioned arguments; and finally, in *La musica*, an eloquent denunciation of the practice of operating on boys to produce *castrati*.

In 1763 and 1765 respectively there appeared in Milan two poems, *Il mattino* and *Il mezzogiorno* ('Morning' and 'Midday'), published anonymously but immediately recognised as the work of Parini. They were intended, together with *La sera* ('Evening') which never materialised, to form a single poem illustrating the daily life of a young Milanese nobleman, idle, frivolous, proud and depraved, through the lips of a fictitious tutor ('precettor d'amabil rito') who respectfully describes and prescribes the various rites which make up his pupil's day: awakening, breakfast, toilet etc. The tone is elevated and solemn, as though the Young Gentleman's silly and effeminate activities were sublime enterprises, fit material for heroic verse; and the metre chosen is, appropriately, blank verse, which had been used in heroic poems since the Cinquecento (Annibale Caro's version of the *Aeneid* for example), and had become fashionable again for the rational or 'scientific' verse of the Settecento.

Il giorno harks back to the satirical tradition of ancient Rome (Horace, Juvenal, Persius) and of modern Italy (from Tassoni to Martello), but its 'serious' and declamatory treatment of ordinary or frivolous material is closer to Boileau's *Le Lutrin* and Pope's *Rape of the Lock*, which Parini, who knew no English, could read only in translation. However, his poems are characterised by an original combination of two elements: on the one hand, a fascination with the most refined aspects of the polite world which appealed to the humanist's aesthetic sense and to his Sensist interest in the lights and colours, scents, flavours and tactile impressions of fine objects and materials; and on the other, the genuine indignation felt by a humble countryman, convinced of the necessity and dignity of work and the sanctity of the family, at the idle, arrogant and cynical lifestyle he is depicting.

Il mattino presents us with a rapid succession of visits by various teachers during the hero's 'petit lever': the dancing, French and singing masters (whose instruction he dispenses with thanks to his innate ability, so that he merely engages them in salacious gossip). This is followed by the important 'performance' of his *parrucchiere* (wigmaker), his ablutions and dressing – minute descriptions which might become tedious without the introduction of other themes, like the comparison of this highly civilised young man with his coarse ancestors, whose violence and abuses probably created the family fortune but who could at least work and fight, and who therefore are preferred by the poet to their offspring despite the tutor's abhorrence of their crudity. A further counterpoint is provided by the allusions to the peasants, craftsmen and workmen who are breaking their backs to support the *Giovin Signore* (Young Gentleman) while he is asleep or idling; and the picture is further varied by the fables and brief explanations of the origins of objects and ceremonies so important to the world the poet describes: powder, *cicisbeismo* (the result of a quarrel between Love and Hymen, which Venus settled by assigning the days with the lady to the one and the nights to the other: *Il mattino*, 313ff.).

Parini's criticism is directed not at the nobility as a whole but at those who abuse their privileges and live like parasites, showing nothing but contempt for the people. It is at its most effective in *Il mezzogiorno*, which is set in the home of the *Dama* or married lady to whom the *Giovin Signore* is 'cavalier servente', the gentleman chosen by the lady to accompany her on her social round, following a custom well established in the polite society of Settecento Italy, and condemned by Goldoni, but even more vehemently by Parini, as a serious threat to social stability and the sanctity of the family. New figures now appear at the table of the lady and her complaisant husband (so different in this respect from his jealous ancestors, and so often absent because he is attending on another lady whose husband in turn is away attending on yet another lady): parasites, travellers, *petits maîtres*, pseudo-intellectual know-alls peddling foreign ideas and fashions. If Parini's ironical treatment of the superficial advocates of commerce and luxury is aimed at the Accademia dei Pugni and Pietro Verri in particular (who had been the Duchess Serbelloni's lover), it means that between the *Mattino* of 1763 and the *Mezzogiorno* of 1765 Parini has opened a new front against what he sees as the élitist and libertine version of Enlightened thinking proposed by Verri and his aristocratic friends.

Parini's ideological and poetic commitment is at its peak in his 'Fable of Pleasure', in which the tutor provides his pupil with an incontrovertible justification of social inequality: men were once all equal, which the gods found boring; so they sent down Pleasure, a handsome winged figure to which men reacted differently: some proved capable of receiving its influence and distinguishing beauty and goodness from ugliness and thus deserving to enjoy the most exquisite sensations, while the others were obtuse individuals, incapable of raising themselves above brute necessity, who

> ... quasi bovi, al suol curvati, ancor
> Dinanzi al pungolo del bisogno andaro:
> E tra la servitude e la viltade
> E 'l travaglio e l'inopia a viver nati
> Ebber nome di plebe.

(... went like oxen, bent to the ground before the lash of necessity; mean and servile from birth, subject to toil and want these were called plebs.)

(ll. 324–8)

Equally famous is the account of the servant who kicked a pet dog of the Lady which had bitten him, and was promptly discharged and reduced to beggary with his unhappy family. From time to time, as in the conclusion of this story, and also at the end of *Il mattino*, where he turns his attention to the crowd that risked being trampled by the Giovin Signore's carriage in his anxiety to reach his lady, Parini seems to abandon the Tutor's respectful and adulatory note and reveal his true feelings. This is particularly apparent in a magnificent passage at the end of *Il mezzogiorno*. As the carriages of the Milanese nobility parade along the Corso, the evening shadows momentarily establish equality between men:

> Ma la notte segue
> sue leggi inviolabili, e declina
> con tacit'ombra sopra l'emispero;
> e il rugiadoso piè lenta movendo
> rimescola i color varii infiniti,
> e via gli spazza con l'immenso lembo
> di cosa in cosa: e suora de la morte
> un aspetto indistinto, un solo volto
> al suolo, ai vegetanti, agli animali,
> ai grandi ed a la plebe equa permette;
> e i nudi insieme ed i dipinti visi
> de le belle confonde, e i cenci e l'oro.

(But night follows its inevitable laws, and sinks over the globe with silent shadows, gently stirring a varied range of colours with its dewy foot, then brushing them away with its broad mantle: and like a sister of death grants only a vague shape, a single visage to earth and plants and living creatures alike, confusing the bare and the painted faces of beauties, rags and riches.)

Il mattino and *Il mezzogiorno* proved acceptable not only to Enlightened readers, but also to the Austrian administration, which was trying to modernise the Lombard economy and legal system and limit the privileges of the feudal aristocracy. This rapprochement of interests between poet and government in the 1770s brought Parini various honours and commissions: he directed the official *Gazzetta di Milano* for a year in 1769; he was appointed Professor of Eloquence and Letters at the Scuole Palatine and, after the suppression of the Jesuits in 1773, at the Brera Academy; and he was invited to write various dramatic pieces for the court, including a script set to music by the young Mozart, *Ascanio in Alba*.

However, after the death of Maria Teresa in 1780 her son and successor, Joseph II, adopted a strong centralising policy which drastically reduced the role of the local élites. Pietro Verri, and Parini too, felt isolated and betrayed by this new policy, although Parini kept his Chair and his lodgings at the Brera Academy. His disappointment at the scant regard paid to his support of the régime is reflected in various of the poems he wrote at this time: the blank verse *Al consigliere barone De Martini* ('To Councillor Baron D.M.'), the odes *La recita dei versi*, *La tempesta* ('The Storm') and especially *La caduta* ('The Fall', 1785), in which his isolation, discomfort and poverty, which might be thought the result of intransigence and lack of diplomacy, are represented as evidence of a profound moral conscience.

The most serious consequence of this isolation was his failure to complete *Il giorno*. At some point, probably towards the end of the seventies, the third and concluding part of his poem, *La sera*, split into two distinct parts, *Il vespro* and *La notte* ('Evening' and 'Night'), which Parini worked on until almost the end of his life but never completed or published; but he continued to correct *Il mattino*, and rewrite *Il mezzogiorno* with the new title of *Il meriggio*

('Afternoon'). The fragmentary and unfinished text of the *Vespro* and the *Notte* is to be found in a series of autographs in the Biblioteca Ambrosiana in Milan – on the basis of which scholars have made a conjectural edition of this second *Giorno*.

European affairs between the accession of Joseph II and the French Revolution probably made Parini's campaign against the behaviour of the Lombard nobility less urgent, and as he tried to complete his poem this may have contributed to his change of focus from 'message' to form. He seems increasingly dedicated to neo-classical ideals of simplicity and tranquillity in the *Vespro* and especially in the *Notte*, which contains some of his best verse, as for example his lines on the absurd pastimes of the young titled imbeciles, such as cracking a coachman's whip or blowing a postilion's horn or unravelling tapestries and carpets. But these are just fragments, lacking the organic structure of *Il mattino* or *Il mezzogiorno*, these latter having been written at a time when the poet felt in harmony with current cultural developments, with the movement of history.

The exquisitely elegant odes of his maturity and old age signal a departure from what we would now call militant poetry and a search for refuge and compensation in perennial values: the company of a few chosen friends and the admiration of the loveliest noble ladies in Milan and Venice (*Il pericolo*, 'Danger', 1787?, for Cecilia Tron; *Il dono*, "The Gift", 1789–90, for Paola Castiglioni; *La gratitudine*, 1790, for Cardinal Durini). His belief in the necessary connection between beauty and moral integrity, which had been the motivating force behind his aesthetics from the time of the *Discorso sopra la poesia* (1761) and his *Principi generali delle belle lettere applicati alle belle arti* ('General Principles of Literature Applied to the Fine Arts', 1773–7), now becomes his main criterion for the interpretation of history. *A Silvia, o sul vestire alla ghigliottina* ('To Sylvia, or on Dressing for the Guillotine', 1795), deploring an immodest female fashion, is one manifestation of his horror at the excesses of the Revolution, that were partly responsible for his resignation from the municipal administration which he had agreed to join at the beginning of the French occupation.

Two of his final odes, *Il messaggio*, a tribute to the beauty of Maria di Castelbarco, ('inclita Nice'), and *Alla Musa* (1796) for the wedding of a disciple, bring his poetic career to a close: testimony still to his dedication to 'truth' and 'innocent beauty', but also to his remoteness from the world of history and politics. The first odes and poems of *Il giorno* had really grown out of a happy equivocation: at an exceptionally favourable moment, historically and culturally, Parini had been able to ignore, partly to overcome, the limitations of his intellectual situation and his own background as priest, citified provincial, humanist teacher, servant of the great and faithful subject of the Emperor – limitations which, when he had outlived that moment, were to push him towards the chaste and delicate poetry of his ivory tower: but it is the first Parini whom the men of the Ottocento, from Foscolo to De Sanctis, understood and loved and made a symbol of the new civil and patriotic spirit of Italy. His later evaluation of his options was only too accurate: it led him to narrow his field of action and to be more in harmony with himself, without grandiose ambitions but also without damage to his inner self; and his later poetry is refined without being frivolous, lucid, moderate: the reminiscences of Horace serve not merely to justify his isolation (*odi profanum vulgus* ...; *integer vitae scelerisque purus* ...), but seem like a becalmed echo of experiences with which he has now come to terms. In this sense there is no better incarnation of the clarity of vision and moderation of the Lombard Enlightenment than the author of *Il giorno*, and no one whose life so closely mirrors the course of its history.

26

Alfieri and pre-Romanticism

Alfieri

Together with Parini, the writer most admired by the Risorgimento patriots as the man who restored a civil and political conscience to Italian culture was Vittorio Alfieri (Asti, 1749 – Florence, 1803). After a period of restless and inconclusive study at the military academy in Turin, the favoured place of education of northern aristocrats, Alfieri visited various parts of Italy and Europe between 1766 and 1775, 'about ten years of travel and dissolute conduct' as he was to write in his autobiography: in other words, not the usual Grand Tour of young Settecento travellers but a continual flight from his own anxiety and discontent in a search for serenity and peace within himself which continued to elude him.

The third part of his *Vita* ('Giovinezza', 'Youth') provides some fleeting and revealing glimpses of his headlong dash across Europe: occasional encounters that would prove decisive for his intellectual development, as with Tomaso Valperga di Caluso in Lisbon; stormy love affairs that drag him into dangerous situations, like the duel with Penelope Pitt's husband in London; his disgust and contempt for the various courts of the *ancien régime* and their fawning, powdered courtiers; desultory reading, especially of French writers and *philosophes*; his liking for the desolate and stormy landscapes of Scandinavia and the bleak countryside and proud people of Spain.

He returned to Turin where he wrote a tragedy, *Cleopatra*, performed at the Carignano Theatre in 1775. He hit on the subject by chance from seeing various tapestries in his mistress's anteroom which suggested to him an analogy between his own enslavement to this lady and Antony's passion for the Egyptian queen. The 'existential' genesis of this modest, rather raw *Cleopatra* (especially by comparison with so many Settecento tragedies written to implement some literary theory), and its unexpected success at its first performance, are more significant than the play itself, because it was this experience that induced Alfieri to persist in a literary career and diverted his ambitions to tragedy from satire, which had inspired his best writing before this, as in his *Esquisse du jugement universel*, 1773.

He stays faithful to a single method of composition from the time of *Filippo*, the first of his mature tragedies. The 'idea' or 'invention' arises originally from what is often a flash of recognition of some event or character that is 'tragediabile'; the 'stesura' or prose drafting of a succession of scenes follows, and finally, often after months or years, the 'versification', as slow and painstaking a process as the preceding phases had been fast. From this drafting process emerges the inevitable and, on the poet's own admission, uniform 'ossatura' (structure) of his tragedies: 'five full acts, a single subject ... the dialogue involving only the main characters, no consultants or spectators ... as violent and harsh as nature allows' (letter to Calzabigi). The hardest art is the versification. The myth which Alfieri puts out in his autobiography – a writer desperate for glory but ignorant and used to writing in French, not Italian, struggling for years to acquire first a language, and then a style – is only his dramatisation of his long pursuit of a 'verso tragico', a poetic style different from the more or less 'cantabile' verse of the lyric or epic, using the *endecasillabo sciolto* (blank verse) to achieve what he regards as the indispensable effect of a spoken language that is both energetic and noble. This would be something new in the Italian theatrical tradition.

The characteristics of his verse style are well known: the splitting up of the eleven-syllable line so as to include as many as five changes of speaker in one line; frequent use of monosyllables, especially personal pronouns and adverbs; systematic use of enclitic forms. The result is an 'un-real' language, very intense, mirroring the exceptional greatness of his characters (normally four) and the extremes of virtue or vice which they represent.

Filippo, conceived and drafted in 1775, and versified three times between 1776 and 1781, is archetypal in the emphasis given to the *furor regnandi* of the implacable Spanish king who slaughters his wife and son. The threatening giant, the tyrant, who will dominate Alfieri's tragedies to the end, embodies the author's intolerance of all forms of absolute authority, which is as strong as the unquenchable thirst for power of his terrifying protagonists.

Alfieri published his first ten tragedies in Siena in 1783. The most notable, apart from *Filippo*, are those taken from the Greek tragic repertoire – not directly, because Alfieri did not know Greek yet, but via Father Brumoy's *Théâtre des Grecs* or other modern versions: *Polinice* and *Antigone* (conceived and drafted 1775–6, versified 1777–8); *Agamennone* and *Oreste* (conceived 1776, drafted 1777, versified 1777–81); *Merope* (conceived and written 1782) and *Timoleone* (1779–82). The cycle formed by the first two, on the bloody Theban myth of the Labdacides, culminates with the deaths of the brothers Eteocles and Polynices, each at the hands of the other, and of their sister Antigone, judged guilty of giving a proper funeral to Polynices, who had been left unburied on the orders of the tyrant Creon. In the two plays forming the Argive cycle, which end respectively with the murder of Agamemnon by his wife Clytemnestra and her lover Aegisthus and with Orestes' revenge on the adulterers with the aid of his sister Electra, Alfieri had in mind not only Brumoy's versions but also the tragedies of Seneca and Voltaire's *Oreste*. But in each case the outcome is totally original. Alfieri approaches the Greek myths, with their grim picture of the cruelty and mysterious justice of Fate, with the intention of exploring the elemental drives of the characters in ways that will be comprehensible to his contemporaries; and, to apply a Freudian terminology (which is certainly less anachronistic in the context of Alfieri's tragedies than in that of any other great Italian writer), he searches in their unconscious, rather than in the workings of Fate, for the origins of their neuroses, which he portrays by means of obsessive images and metaphors: a brother's blood for Eteocles' hatred of Polynices; the shades of night for the murder of husband and mother in the palace at Mycenae.

Historically the most important of the four is *Antigone*, which was performed in Rome in the Spanish Embassy with the author taking the part of Creon; and after this Alfieri draws on his experience as an actor as well as a poet and becomes increasingly conscious of the specifically theatrical qualities of his works for the stage, intended to be seen as well as heard. *Timoleone* is also significant: it is closer to *Virginia*, his play based on Roman history (1777–81) than the other Greek plays, forming part of the so-called 'tragedies of liberty' where the action is polarised in a clash between tyrant and anti-tyrant, ending in tyrannicide (as in *Timoleone*) or more often with the sacrifice of his opponent, whose death is his only way of asserting his liberty, as an increasingly pessimistic poet came to believe.

Alfieri was dissatisfied with the Sienese edition of his tragedies and super-vised personally the second, definitive edition (six volumes, Paris, Didot, 1787–9), which contained the ten already published and nine new ones. Of these four are 'tragedies of liberty': *La congiura de' Pazzi* ('The Pazzi Conspiracy', conceived 1777), *Agide* (1784–6), *Bruto primo* and *Bruto secondo* (1786–7). *La congiura de' Pazzi*, like his treatise *Della tirannide*, was suggested to him by his reading of Machiavelli, and makes an interesting contrast with *Virginia*. While the Roman father's sacrifice of his daughter in order to save her honour provokes a promising popular reaction against the over-powerful decemvirs, Raimondo de' Pazzi's conflict with Lorenzo de' Medici in Quattrocento Florence fails to rouse the people and he has to die. But *La congiura* is the best demonstration of the subtle relationship and secret affinity between tyrant and anti-tyrant, each of whom feels and understands perfectly the mind and thoughts of the other.

Saul and *Mirra*, by common consent Alfieri's tragic masterpieces, were first published in the Didot edition. *Saul*, which was inspired by Alfieri's reading of the Bible, was conceived, drafted and versified in 1782 in the space of a few months. The implacable God of the Old Testament, a personification of absolute authority far more concrete and no less mysterious than the Greek Fate, allows the author to combine the roles of persecutor and persecuted in the Israelite king, caught between the divine wrath and his own lust for power. At one level, therefore, Saul is both tyrant and victim; his is the tragedy of tyranny lived and depicted from the inside, an absorbing interiorisation of the conflicts that underlie so much of Alfieri's theatre. But at another level Saul realises very well, in his lucid moments, that the real danger comes not from

God or the Philistines or David and the priests, but from the need that he has, being no longer young and strong as he once was, for the support and affection of David, the new 'anointed of the Lord' who is venerated by Saul's own children, his daughter Micol (David's wife) and Jonas. In this sense *Saul* is also a tragedy of old age, of the tormenting uncertainty by which we are assailed when our powers decline but our desires and ambitions are as strong as ever.

Here, as elsewhere in his tragedies, Alfieri anticipates an idea very much alive today: others, by their very existence, constitute a restriction on the affirmation of one's self, which cannot, however, do without them. This intolerance-dependence is all the more painful in view of the old king's past greatness. So Saul's rapid journey towards the death that awaits him on the battlefield is matched by a journey into the depths of his own character, to the dried-out roots of his very being. The 'tragic' and the 'sublime', to which Alfieri refers so often in the *Pareri* (judgements) on his tragedies, are more intimately fused here than in any other of his plays – with one possible exception.

That exception is *Mirra*, conceived, drafted and versified between 1784 and 1786. Alfieri read the story in the *Metamorphoses*; but Ovid's Mirra, in a series of long monologues, is capable of confronting the heart-rending conflict between her love for her father and her horror of incest, and becomes Ciniro's lover. What Alfieri keeps from the *Metamorphoses* is Mirra's incestuous desire, while her interior struggle and the death she suffers as a result of her hesitant confession of impure love, even though not consummated, come from another source, Racine's *Phèdre* – another story of unconsummated love, that of Theseus' wife for her stepson Hippolytus. But there is an important difference between the two plays. Mirra's attempt to conceal her love lasts much longer, as late as the second scene of Act v, where her confession is a free translation of Ovid:

> ... da te morir io lungi? ...
> O madre mia felice! ... almen concesso
> a lei sarà ... di morire ... al tuo fianco

(Must I die far from you? ... O my lucky mother! at least she will be able ... to die ... at your side)

– a half-confession which comes as a terrible revelation to Ciniro and which, late and reluctant as it is, justifies the dying Mirra's lament for her lost innocence:

> Quand'io ... tel ... chiesi
> Darmi allora ... Euriclea, dovevi il ferro ...
> Io moriva innocente; empia ... ora ... muoio.

(When I asked you, you should have given me the knife, Euriclea ... Then I should have died an innocent; ... now I die an impious wretch.)

(v, 4)

This story of a daughter who tries in vain to repress her passion for her father and, when her secret is exposed, kills herself with her father's sword has inevitably provoked some obvious psycho-analytic readings. Certainly nowhere so intensely as in Mirra does Alfieri probe and articulate the conflict between duty and desire. And the youthfulness of this poor girl engaged in a pathetic, rather than heroic, struggle against the demons at the edges of her conscience intensifies the desolation of her death.

From Antigone, who faces death in order to fulfil her duty, to Virginia, killed by her father to save her honour, to the innocent and dishonoured Mirra, who kills herself, Alfieri's pessimism deepens to the point of denying freedom of choice and personal initiative. The other tragedies in the Didot edition (*Maria Stuarda, Don Garzia, Sofonisba*) as well as the posthumous dramas of the late 1780s, such as *Alceste seconda* (inspired by Euripides) and the 'melotragedia' ('melotragedy' or 'tragedy of intrigue') *Abele*, all confirm this trend and, in different ways, the general exhaustion of Alfieri's tragic vein.

The rest of his impressive literary production presents us with a marked *chiaroscuro* between decidedly mediocre works, where the outcome fails to meet the author's intentions, and other texts of considerable ideological and artistic interest. The clearly 'minor' works, whose interest for us is mainly historical, can be divided into two groups, before and after his precipitous 1792 departure from Paris where he had been living with Luisa Stolberg, the Countess of Albany, estranged wife (and from 1786 widow) of Charles Edward Stuart, the Pretender to the English throne. So we have on the one hand *Etruria vendicata* ('Etruria Avenged'), four laboured cantos in octave rhyme on the assassination of Alessandro de' Medici by his cousin Lorenzino (1778–86); the five odes on *America libera*, inspired by the American War of Independence (1781–83); the ode *Parigi sbastigliato* ('Paris Freed of the Bastille'), composed hot on the heels of the events of 1789 and in support of the French Revolution, and the little fable, *Le mosche e l'api* ('The Flies and the Bees').

In the last decade of his life, spent in Florence after his flight from France, which now seemed to him prey to the vices and follies of an unrestrained mob, he wrote the Second Part of his brief and biting epigrams (the First Part belongs to the period before 1786). He also composed his sixteen satires in tercets, in which he castigates the vulgarity and pseudo-democracy of contemporary society with an eye on the great satirists of the past, from Juvenal to Parini. *Il misogallo* ('The Francophobe') is a violent attack on the France of the Revolution and Terror, while four of his six *Commedie* (1800–3) combine attacks on tyranny, oligarchy and so-called democracy with a vague model of constitutional equilibrium between the three.

There is no lack of energetic, successful writing in these works (all published posthumously), particularly in the Satires (*L'educazione, I viaggi*) or the most original and least polemical of the comedies, *La finestrina* ('The Little Window'); but as a whole they reflect the disappointment of the old champion of liberty at what seem to him the monstrous aberrations of modern politics, and a frankly reactionary and obsessive resentment against the stupid and coarse middle classes, the greedy uncontrolled mob, the French in general and the *philosophes* in particular. But the political treatises of the years 1777–87 are quite another story: *Della tirannide*, *Del principe e delle lettere*, *Panegirico di Plinio a Traiano* and *Della virtù sconosciuta* ('On Virtue Unrecognised'), a moving evocation of his dead friend Francesco Gori Gandellini – published together in Kiel in 1788–9 and then in a pirate edition in Paris, 1800–1.

The two books of *Della tirannide*, conceived in 1777, discuss an idea frequently expressed in the tragedies and with epigrammatic clarity in *Virginia*: power concentrated in the hands of a single man is always tyrannical; even the most 'enlightened' monarch who can make or ignore laws is a despot; the test of tyranny is not the prince's cruelty but the freedom he has to exercise such cruelty whenever he wants to, and thus the very existence of absolute power. And the glue that holds such a monstrous system together and makes it so difficult to break is fear: the sovereign's distrust and suspicion of his subjects and their passive awe and cowardly terror before authority.

In the three books of *Del principe e delle lettere*, which are stylistically less lively but more original than *Della tirannide*, Alfieri illustrates the antithetical nature and radical incompatibility of tyrant and writer: the former can survive only by destroying freedom, which is an indispensable condition for the activities of the latter. The prince is therefore obliged to reduce the intellectuals to silence, either by suppressing them physically or by making them courtiers. The honest writer, for his part, when his country falls under a despot, can only go into exile, and fight the enemy with his impassioned writings from outside his country (and here obviously the author is representing himself as a martyr of liberty in his self-banishment from his native Piedmont). In the conviction that 'il dire altamente alte cose, è un farle in gran parte' (to speak noble things nobly is, in large measure, to do them) Alfieri identifies the *letterato* as the true enemy of tyranny and the modern champion of the freedom which the heroes of the past defended with the sword: he is the one hope for a better future, if only his voice is heeded by those citizens in whom 'the plant, man' is still living.

Of his other two treatises, the *Panegirico* makes the paradoxical suggestion that a just prince (if such a being could exist) would renounce his power and hand it back to his subjects; *Della virtù sconosciuta*, perhaps Alfieri's best literary prose work before the *Vita*, is a dialogue with his friend Gori, who had died two years previously, in which Alfieri, confronted by Gori's shrewd detachment, is induced to examine his conscience and temper the heroic prosopopoeia of the sublime writer he has just outlined in the treatise *Del principe*.

Compared with his incursions into other 'genres' or sub-genres – political poems, satires, and comedies, following a more or less conscious programme of experimentation – Alfieri's *Rime* (more than 300 compositions, mostly sonnets, published partly by the author in 1789 and partly posthumously by his secretary Tassi in 1804), are a significant success. They consist of a substantial *canzoniere* for the Countess of Albany with the insertion of poems on everyday events, typical of the genre since Petrarch – and indeed Alfieri acknowledges Petrarch and Dante's *Vita Nuova* as his models, Petrarch in particular, the supreme master of poetic language, whose treatment of the theme of love frustrated by the absence of the beloved inspires Alfieri's poems for the Countess, redeeming the triteness of the subject with the dignity and polish of the master's stylistic example; at the same time we have the diary of his perpetual travelling across Europe matching the fluctuations in his feelings. At the centre of this dual landscape two images stand out: the radiant (and to the modern reader tedious) figure of the incomparable Countess of Albany, obliged to live apart from her lover to observe the proprieties, and the other far more compelling image of the poet riding backwards and forwards between Tuscany and Alsace, accompanied by the obsessions of love and glory, anger and gloom, time and death. So Alfieri is right when, admitting his inferiority to his great Petrarchan model, he claims for his 'sighs of love' the dignity and interest of an authentic psychological and sentimental document in which the gentleness and melancholy of the *Canzoniere* are clouded and overlaid by the tempestuous and declamatory voice of the pre-Romantic poet.

Between neo-classicism and pre-Romanticism

Certain contrasting features of Settecento culture appear in Alfieri in a dramatic form, from the cult of harmony and simplicity, and of the heroic ideals of the Graeco-Roman models, to a keen and anxious exploration of the ego which brings us very close to the pre-Romantic sensibility. The latter part of the century, with the decline of reformist illusions in Lombardy and Naples, the initial enthusiasm for the Revolution followed by indignation at the excesses of the Terror, and the incipient rise of Napoleon, is characterised by a series of traumas and crises to which writers respond in conflicting ways which it is difficult to describe without resorting to simplistic antitheses.

While a national conscience is beginning to develop, as in Gian Rinaldo Carli's article *Della patria degli Italiani* in *Il Caffè*, and in Alfieri's writings, the most concrete geopolitical entities for Italians are still their own region, and Europe. This perhaps explains the outburst of dialect poetry: among the Trasformati in Milan (Domenico Balestrieri, Carl'Antonio Tanzi and even Parini) and in Venice (Anton Maria Lamberti, Francesco Gritti). The Sicilian Giovanni Meli (1740–1815) is the best, but the least 'dialectal', of these poets in that he uses Sicilian as a 'variant', no less literary and more musical than the Tuscan employed by the late Arcadian poets: for example, his exquisite compositions in the *Favuli murali* ('Moral Tales') and *Buccolica* (a pastoral idyll structured on the popular Settecento scheme of the four seasons).

At the opposite extreme to the region was Europe, the Europe of the courts, the *philosophes*, of travel, of literary works remote from the Italian tradition and hence more exciting. Of these none was more influential than the 'Ossianic' poems invented by the Scot James Macpherson and passed off as original poems by Ossian, a Gaelic bard of the third century. Among the European writers who were tired of useful and rational poetry, and who were seduced by the elemental intensity and apparent primitiveness of the Ossianic poems, was the Paduan scholar Melchiorre Cesarotti (1730–1808), author among other works of a *Saggio sulla filosofia delle lingue* (1785) which represented the most advanced thinking of the embryonic linguistics of the Settecento with its insistence on the legitimacy and mobility of all languages, which are never 'pure' but constantly adapt to the evolution and needs of the 'spirito nazionale'. The *Poesie di Ossian*, an excellent translation into Italian blank verse of Macpherson's compositions, published by Cesarotti in 1763 and later enlarged, introduced into Italy a taste for 'primitive' poetry, for misty and stormy northern landscapes, laments for dead heroes, gloomy nights spent beside the camp-fire and religious awe before a wild and grandiose nature, which was to recur in varying shapes in the poetry of the early Ottocento. Thus just as the label of 'neo-classical' is appropriate for the late odes of Parini and the Roman novels of Alessandro Verri, not least because of their obvious analogies with the visual arts, so the adjective 'pre-Romantic' is often used for Cesarotti's experiment and its sequel in Alfieri and Monti.

However, other authors writing towards the end of the century, indeed some of the more interesting, escape this dichotomy, or rather they lend themselves, at different times, to the use of both terms – in the same way as it will be possible, one generation later, to talk of Leopardi's classicism *and* Romanticism. This is the case of the Veronese nobleman Ippolito Pindemonte (1753–1828), a self-styled 'provinciale' after a journey to England in his youth, who made a translation of the *Odyssey* but was also the author of some feeling, pre-Romantically pensive *Prose e poesie campestri* ('Prose and Poetry of the Countryside'), written between 1784 and 1788. It is also the case of the Rimini abbot Aurelio de' Giorgi Bertola, a professor first at Naples and then Pavia, who travelled in Germany and Switzerland, wrote a history of German literature and translated the *Idylls* of Gessner. In what is probably his most successful work, his *Viaggio sul Reno e ne' suoi contorni* ('Travels on the Rhine and its Banks', 1795) the picturesque impressions of the sentimental traveller are framed by regular references to classical, Palladian canons and filtered through a concept of *grazia* (the subject of a lecture course given by Bertola in Pavia and published posthumously as *Saggio sopra la grazia nelle lettere e nelle arti*, 'Essays on Grace in Literature and Art').

In these travel-books, whether true accounts of actual travels, like Bertola's on the Rhine, or fictions incorporated in novels, as in his friend Pindemonte's *Abaritte*, we find a new tone compared with what we have seen in the travel literature of the early and mid Settecento, in Algarotti or even Baretti. Now the traveller is looking inside himself as much as, or more than, he looks at the landscape; or rather he translates his impressions of the changing scenes around him into a sentimental history of his travelling self. We have moved, in other words, on to the terrain of autobiography, the rise of which, together with that of the theatre and journalism, constitutes one of the most character-istic innovations of the Settecento.

The late Settecento autobiographies

Various factors undoubtedly contributed to the proliferation of memoirs in the Settecento: the great English and French novels written in the first person, connected in turn to the vogue among middle-class readers for stories of exemplary characters who build their own careers and then write about them; the attempt to thread together a string of reminiscences up to the present day so as to reconstruct in some way the coherent identity which the English empiricists, particularly Hume, had tried to convert into a series of perceptions; and, last but not least, the strong influence exerted by Rousseau's *Confessions* when they first appeared (the first six books posthumously in 1782, the second part in 1789): the first attempt to trace at first hand 'le seul portrait d'homme, peint exactement d'après nature et dans toute sa vérité qui existe et qui probablement existera jamais'. (The only portrait existing and which probably will ever exist of a man depicted exactly after nature and in all his truth.)

Of the numerous late Settecento autobiographies that we might mention to conclude this chapter, four stand out for their historical and human interest and their literary quality. Between 1789–90 and the eve of his death Giacomo Casanova (1725–98) composed his *Histoire de ma vie*, above all in order to relive in writing the vivid sensations and intense pleasures of his vagabond, libertine life and thus compensate for his gloomy and solitary existence as librarian in a remote castle in Bohemia; and indeed his *Histoire*, written in fluent French and, as the Verri brothers would say, all 'cose' (all 'content'), constitutes one of the most entertaining and exciting tales of the century. Only recently have we been able to read the original unbowdlerised text, in the Brockhous–Plon edition of 1960.

In 1797–9 there appeared in Venice the three volumes of the *Memorie inutili della vita di Carlo Gozzi scritte da lui medesimo e pubblicate per umiltà* ('Useless Memoirs of the Life of Carlo Gozzi Written by Himself and Published out of Humility'), which the author of the *Fiabe* had begun to draft many years previously as a defence against the accusations and calumnies of his enemies, real and imaginary. These reminiscences slowly evolved into the idiosyncratic story of his life, still chronologically and structurally disordered but with a compelling ring of authenticity.

Gibbon, who knew a lot about autobiography, once observed that Goldoni's best comedy was his *Mémoires de M. Goldoni, pour servir à l'histoire de sa vie, et a celle de son théâtre* (three parts, Paris, 1787). The theatre does in fact feature prominently in the Memoirs, the second part being a *catalogue raisonné* of Goldoni's comedies, and from beginning to end we find the story of a vocation, that of the playwright and his progressive, irresistible triumph. And many of the scenes do in fact smack of the theatre, or of comedy as Gibbon thought, the protagonist appearing in a halo of good humour and modesty but also of unshakeable faith in his mission, which helps him to overcome all sorts of difficulties and obstacles in his reform of the theatre. But behind this cheery picture of a serene and phlegmatic playwright we catch glimpses of the worries and 'vapeurs noires' of a much more complex and vulnerable character, artfully exposed in these superficially straight reminiscences.

Alfieri began to write his *Vita* in Paris, after reading the autobiographies of Cellini, Rousseau and Goldoni, but his first draft was interrupted by his departure from France in 1792. The definitive version, carefully written out between 1798 and 1803 and published posthumously in 1804, is divided into four Epochs. The first three, *Puerizia. Abbraccia nove anni di vegetazione*; *Adolescenza. Abbraccia otto anni d'ineducazione*; and *Giovinezza. Abbraccia circa dieci anni di viaggi, e dissolutezze* ('Childhood. Covers Nine Years of Vegetation'; 'Adolescence. Covers Eight Years of Lack of Education'; 'Youth. Covers About Ten Years of Travels and Dissoluteness'), prepare the gestation and epiphany of the tyrant-hating tragedian, the faithful lover and the patient and determined student, up to his conversion in 1775-7. The fourth, *Virilità. Abbraccia trenta e più anni di composizioni, traduzioni, e studi diversi* ('Manhood. Covers Thirty and More Years of Compositions, Translations and Diverse Studies'), illustrates the concrete results following that great turning-point. Thus on the one hand, Alfieri, like other autobiographers of the Settecento, tries in his *Vita* to find something which will provide a meaning and justification for his existence. On the other, like Rousseau, he discovers in his childhood-memories the causes and the premonitions of his adult destiny. The result is a portrait, written in a strikingly original style, of a passionate and restless man, capable however of facing his own egotism, without concealing it from himself and without taking satisfaction in it. In this sense, as it has been justly observed, the whole of Italian *Sturm und Drang* is represented by this one remarkable work.

The age of Romanticism
(1800–1870)

Giovanni Carsaniga

27

The Romantic controversy

Writers and cultural policy

In January 1816 the Milan journal *Biblioteca italiana* published an article *Sulla maniera e l'utilità delle traduzioni* ('On the manner and usefulness of translations'), suggesting that Italian writers would benefit from a knowledge of foreign literature. This apparently unexceptional proposition triggered off a fiery debate which raged on and off for a long time, eventually outliving its own usefulness, and is emblematic of the whole period this chapter attempts to survey. Napoleon's invasion of Italy in 1796 and his eventual conquest of the peninsula had led to the establishment of a Kingdom of Italy in the north of the country which was seen by many patriots as a first step towards national unity and independence. With the collapse of the Kingdom in 1814 Milan, the capital of Lombardy, had returned under Austrian domination. It was without doubt the most advanced city in the most developed area of a woefully underdeveloped country. The Austrian plenipotentiary, Count Josef Heinrich von Bellegarde, soon realised that, besides the old aristocracy, traditional supporters of the Habsburgs who had ennobled their ancestors, he might also enlist the support of many radical intellectuals sorely disappointed by Napoleonic totalitarianism, who therefore would not appear as stooges of the new government. Among these were the doyen of Italian poets, Vincenzo Monti, then aged sixty-three; Pietro Giordani (1774–1848), who had become well known eight years earlier for his *Panegirico di Napoleone legislatore* ('Panegyric of Napoleon the Law-giver'), and the geologist Scipione Breislak (1750–1826). One of the prickliest, most radical and most disappointed intellectuals was the thirty-eight-year old Ugo Foscolo (1778–1827), at that time a captain in the former Napoleonic army, which the Austrian army was preparing to absorb. He was well known for his short-lived and controversial professorship at Pavia University, his poems and his novel, *Le ultime lettere di Jacopo Ortis* ('The Last Letters of Jacopo Ortis'), which was to become at least as famous in Italy as Goethe's *Die Leiden des jungen Werthers* had been in the rest of Europe (see further below, p. 412).

Bellegarde intended to set up a showpiece literary journal, a propaganda medium to organise the consensus of the cultured classes around the policies of the Austrian government, and a rallying point for many intellectuals who would eagerly seize the chance to earn some money by writing. This opportunity was fairly rare at the time, even in Milan. Although by the late eighteenth century the figure of the writer as courtly retainer had practically ceased to exist in Italy, the new structures of patronage, such as paid contributions to journals, sinecures in the civil service and teaching posts, were still scarce and unreliable. Alfieri (see above, pp. 387–93) could afford to put forward in his essay *Del principe e delle lettere* ('On Princes and Literature', 1778–89, published in 1801) the idea that literature, if it was to spur society to moral regeneration, should be absolutely independent of princely patronage: his own income was so large that, even after divesting himself of most of his estates to cut his links with the Turin Court, he had still enough to live comfortably on. In his 1809 inaugural lecture at Pavia, Foscolo appeared firmly committed to Alfieri's theory. He pointedly turned down Monti's recommendation that he should make an ingratiating token gesture towards the Ruler, and inserted instead a barbed note against writers who flattered those in power. However, in February 1815, with a volte-face even his contemporaries found difficult to swallow, Foscolo, at Bellegarde's request, dutifully prepared the editorial plan for the new journal, accepting without reservation the principle that rulers have the right to instil in their subjects, through literature, the principles of moderation and subservience. Faced, however, with the practical implications of becoming the journal's editor, and with the obligation, as an officer, to swear allegiance to Austria precisely when the Empire was once more being challenged by Napoleon (March 1815), Foscolo went into exile (see below, p. 416). By the time the article on the usefulness of translations was published, the travel-writer and diplomat Giuseppe Acerbi (1773-1846) was in charge of *Biblioteca italiana*, and Monti, Giordani and Breislak were a few months away from their resignation.

Perhaps Foscolo initially thought he could remain ideologically independent from the rulers and have a purely commercial relationship with them. Independence might have been possible had literature really been able to discharge the ethical and inspirational task Alfieri and Foscolo wished it to perform, because then it would have had an autonomous function. But the idea that Italian society would or could be led to moral regeneration by literature was total nonsense when about ninety per cent of the population was illiterate, and only a tiny proportion of the rest ever bought or read any books. This fact did not escape a young intellectual living in a quiet cultural backwater, Count Giacomo Leopardi of Recanati (1798–1837) (see below, pp. 418–26). How could Italian literature be popular, he noted in a diary he had begun to keep in 1817, if books were in the hands of only one social class, and poets confined themselves to following the ideas of a cultural establishment insensitive to such universally inspiring ideas as glory, freedom and love? The regeneration of society would bring about the regeneration of literature, not the other way round. Leopardi had clearly perceived, and he was to confirm in *Discorso di un italiano intorno alla poesia romantica* ('An Italian's

Discourse about Romantic Poetry', 1818, published only in 1906), that the real danger was not so much economic dependence as ideological conformity.

The controversy over translations

The author of the article on the usefulness of translations was Anne-Louise-Germaine Necker de Staël-Holstein (1766–1817), already well known in Italy for her novel *Corinne* (1807) and her essay *De l'Allemagne* (1810) through which Italian intellectuals, very few among whom knew any German or English, derived their partial and often distorted view of European Romanticism and German idealistic philosophy. Acerbi did not publish a perceptive letter by Leopardi which radically sidestepped the question of translations to focus on the central problem of the nature and function of poetry and poetic inspiration; and he entrusted Giordani with the official reply, which he wrote with his usual wisdom and moderation, accepting some of Madame de Staël's criticisms of the state of Italian literature, while remaining confident of the values of established tradition. Other replies were not only unintelligent (affirming, for instance, that the heirs to the great classical tradition had no need to read foreign rubbish) but also scurrilous and abusive. The level of literary controversy and debate in Italy was then, and remained for some time, deplorably low: a fact not unrelated to the precarious economic status of writers, who saw any criticism of themselves or the ideas they professed as an attack on their position and income, which they acrimoniously defended.

One of the positive outcomes of the debate was that the best contributions to it provided models of how to argue cultural questions. That was also one of the intentions of *Il conciliatore*, a short-lived journal (September 1818–October 1819) founded and funded by Count Luigi Porro Lambertenghi, and published twice a week by a group including Giovanni Berchet (1783–1851), Pietro Borsieri (1788–1852), Lodovico di Breme (1780–1820), Federico Confalonieri (1785–1846), Silvio Pellico (1789–1854) and Ermes Visconti (1784–1841). As its title implied, it aimed at, and achieved, a style of debate in which the opponents' positions were taken into account as worth discussing, not dismissed as the ravings of self-serving lunatics. It did not seek superficial consensus but informed opinions. It tried to be a forum open not only to Romantics and classicists but also to non-aligned intellectuals from different regions (Lombardy and Piedmont in the first instance) and different social classes. It brought together literature, economics and applied sciences, the tradition of the Enlightenment so brilliantly represented in Milan by one of the leading journals of the previous generation, *Il Caffè*, edited by Pietro and Alessandro Verri (see above, pp. 378–80), and the less intransigent among the Catholic intellectuals, who were amenable to a more liberal interpretation of religious dogma. It did all that not by hugging the middle of the road but from its own very distinctive standpoint, which got it into repeated trouble with police censorship in spite of the fact that it was not promoting mayhem and subversion but an alternative, more flexible Establishment ideology. *Il conciliatore* left to the journals of the following generation, such as Vieusseux's *Antologia* (1821–33) (see below, p. 424), an enduring legacy whose importance was inversely proportional to its short duration.

On the surface there appeared to be two opposing parties, the classicist, upholding the values of tradition, and the Romantic, opting for experimentation and innovation, which included embracing some of the ideas and techniques found in contemporary foreign literatures (including the term *romantic*). In fact, even writers who never made a profession of Romanticism were already heavily dependent on translations. Monti read Goethe's *Werther* and Shakespeare's works in French translations before 1783. Foscolo's work before 1816 echoes a number of little-known translators, not to mention the better-known ones like Melchiorre Cesarotti and Aurelio Bertòla. Leopardi read everything he could lay his hands on, including large amounts of foreign literature. Of course, the debate was substantially about how to break the cultural monopoly of the ruling classes in a pre-industrial age when middle- and working-class education was becoming increasingly important. The most intelligent opponents of the Romantics (like Carlo Giuseppe Londonio) were aware of, and deplored, their attempt to democratise the consumption of literature. There was a political dimension to the debate, not only because all cultural questions have such a dimension, but also because in an age of rampant censorship and repression literature was the only forum where political questions could be cautiously aired in disguise. That accounts for Pellico's inaccurate statement, coloured by the political persecution which shortened the life of *Il conciliatore*, that Romantic meant 'liberal' and that classicist was a synonym of 'reactionary' and 'spy of the Austrians'. The first equation can perhaps be granted, and created problems for the Austrian propagandists, who could encourage the diffusion of contemporary literature in the German language only at the cost of supporting the literary tastes of their political opponents. To disprove the second it is enough to look at Giordani and Leopardi, who, while refusing to have anything to do with Romanticism, were the object of persistent police harassment because of their political radicalism. Even the distinction between upholders of the classical tradition and writers open to modern influences is inapplicable when considering poets like Foscolo or Leopardi, who expressed the modern sensibility in impeccably traditional form.

Did Italian Romanticism exist?

Faced with these, and other contradictions and complexities, an Italian student of German Romanticism, Gina Martegiani, proclaimed in 1908 that 'Italian Romanticism does not exist'. Statements such as this raise the intractable logical problem whether in order to say that X does not exist one must first have some idea of what X would be like if it existed. According to Martegiani, Italian Romanticism, had it existed, ought to have shared many of the features (such as individualism, intellectual cosmopolitanism, cult of the imagination) of the Romantic movements in the rest of Europe. Instead it exhibited patriotism (essentially non-individualistic), cultural nationalism, historicism. But, we may ask, how can that 'it' which is *not* Romanticism be identified by the characterising traits it does not have?

Another problem is that most of the characteristics Romanticism is supposed to possess can be found somewhere at any time in history. One looks therefore for their concentration at some particular time and place. That seems reasonable enough, but does not explain why that particular combination of traits should have been chosen, why a period should be characterised by new and untraditional traits and trends which are by definition displayed by a minority, however influential (there is hardly any doubt that during Romanticism the majority of those entitled to express an opinion were against it). One way out of all these difficulties is to use 'Romanticism' as a conventional label for a specific historical period; but by doing so one includes within it all those who would have hated to be so labelled, and one must then sort things out by one of the previous doubtful criteria. Perhaps the best policy is to define as 'Romantics' those who called themselves such, leave it at that, and not pursue a controversy on labels which already seemed pointless at the time to a few perceptive minds such as Leopardi's, or Byron's.

Women writers and the literary canon

The final strand in this complex web centring on Madame de Staël's article is that the latter was written by a highly respected woman writer nearing the end of her long productive life. Much of the acrimony it aroused was due to the fact that the Italian literary establishment was, or (more accurately) considered itself to be, nearly exclusively male. If women expressed any opinions on the controversy, none achieved any prominence or diffusion. In fact the number of women mentioned in current literary histories can be counted on the fingers of one hand – some say because Italy's political, economic and cultural backwardness in the first half of the nineteenth century allowed no women to emerge. That is debatable, because outstanding intellectuals can flourish, albeit in small numbers, in conditions of extreme backwardness; in fact, many develop their skills partly as a reaction against those conditions (one thinks of Vico, Giannone, Genovesi, Filangieri, Cuoco, all from the least favoured and worst-governed parts of Italy). One might expect a few equally gifted women to establish themselves against similar odds.

The reason why they did not is that the emergence of people canonisable as outstanding by contemporaries and posterity is not a fact of history or a natural phenomenon but a cultural construct. One accepts the given literary canon, as we do on the whole in this history, not necessarily because the authors included in it are 'great' (though they may well be judged so for a number of different reasons), or because their works are still read for pleasure (those who read them today do so mostly because they are prescribed), but because the formation of the canon is itself a part of Italian cultural history worth investigating, indeed the only thing that can be profitably investigated in the limited space available. To include in the canon a token handful of women because they are deemed to be (nearly) as good as their male counterparts presupposes the acceptance of the very criteria by which the male-dominated canon has been established, which, again to give women their due, should be seriously questioned.

Various people, interestingly enough, were trying to give women their due in the first half of the nineteenth century. In 1821-2 Ambrogio Levati began his unfinished biographical dictionary with its fifth class, reserved to famous women. Two years later Ginevra Canonici-Fachini (1779–1870), a writer, biographer and feminist from Ferrara, published a list of famous women in Italian literature, from the fourteenth century to her own age. In 1836–8 a group of Italian writers, including women, translated and supplemented with Italian names *Les Vies des femmes célèbres* (1834) by the Duchess d'Abrantès. In 1842 the library of a specialist collector and bibliographer, Count Pietro Leopoldo Ferri, contained works by over 145 Italian women active in literature between 1800 and 1840. The combined total in these, and other, repertories for that period, with some overlaps, approaches two hundred names. Furthermore, Ferri mentions at least six early nineteenth-century editorial initiatives specifically reserved to women's writings.

All this interest in women obviously had its roots in Enlightenment feminism, but also points to the fact that they were considered important to literature in some way. The fact that about 200 reputable women are not mentioned in the canon may suggest that, judging them as if they were men, their published work was not of the same standard; but it surely points to the fact that their real importance cannot be judged by that standard. A quick browse through the biographical and bibliographical data shows that they excelled in areas marginal to the literary canon, like translation and letter-writing. The presence among them of many extemporaneous poets and improvisers, like Teresa Bandettini (1763–1837), Fortunata Sulgher Fantastici (1755–1824) and her daughter Massimina (1788–1846), continuing a tradition well established at least since the seventeenth century but certainly with earlier roots, points to the preference given by women to the oral code, confirmed by the presence among them of storytellers (like Ernesta Monari and Anna Puoti) and in general by women's dominant role in society as oral transmitters of culture. It comes therefore as no surprise when we are told that so many of them were friends, correspondents, hostesses, sometimes even lovers, of their more celebrated male counterparts. This information is obviously provided with the intention of bathing them in reflected glory, but, looked at in a different perspective, it means that by their correspondence, conversations, invitations to their salons or boudoirs, hospitality, and in some cases concrete offers of help they formed a supportive connecting network, bringing many of their more famous male colleagues together in fruitful contact, and positively nurturing canonic literature. Its history cannot be fully understood without studying literary salons such as those of Cornelia Rossi-Martinetti, Giustina Renier-Michiel, Clara Maffei and Maria Giuseppina Guacci; noting the large amounts of money Quirina Magiotti Mocenni invested in maintaining Foscolo; reading the correspondence of Isabella Teotochi Albrizzi and Fanny Targioni-Tozzetti with the most distinguished writers of their day; assessing the work in publishing and translating of women like Carolina Arienti who in 1804 founded, and largely wrote and compiled, *Il corriere delle dame*; or Edvige de Battisti Scolari, Marianna Bacinetti-Florenzi, and Concetta Ramondetta Fileti, who made available to Italian readers works by Schiller, Goethe, Schelling, Cousins and Poe; remembering Emilia Luti, who gave a most intelligent collaboration to Manzoni's revision of *I promessi sposi*, and Giuseppa Catelli Papi, who sweetened Tommaseo's work with 'nobili sentimenti e . . . elegante linguaggio' (noble feelings and elegant language), both contributing at the same time a great deal of ill-paid housework. Future historians may throw light on the significance of women in literature not merely by studying the published poems, dramas and novels which many of them wrote to emulate men and prove their worth according to heteronomous criteria, but also by reconstructing the non-literary, oral, social component of their contribution to literature.

28

Monti

Changing sides: the Bassville affair

In July 1825, nearly a decade after the appearance of Madame de Staël's article, Vincenzo Monti (1754–1828) reopened the whole debate on classicism and Romanticism, which had been quiescent for some time, with *Sulla mitologia*, a poetic discourse (*sermone*) defending the use of mythology in poetry. Monti's leading position in the Italian Parnassus was by then unassailable, though in an age when writers were not above trading insults with one another, he had received his share of obloquy. He had made enemies by surviving and prospering through an age of revolutions and reversals, witnessing the collapse of the old order, the Napoleonic wars, the various political changes from Republic to Empire under French rule, and the restoration of the old order after Napoleon's final defeat. None of these changes had been radical and complete. Napoleon had not made the old social structure obsolete. The Restoration could not undo much of what Napoleon had achieved. True, some of the most persistent and dangerous opponents of each régime had been persecuted, imprisoned or executed; yet many members of the ruling and cultured classes had, by necessity, been left in place or allowed to re-emerge after a short period of obscurity, in order to ensure reasonably efficient administration and transfer of powers. Many proto-industrialists, landowners, lawyers, booksellers, printers, army officers, politicians, and even a few artists and writers besides Monti had been able to live through the changes reasonably unscathed, and had adapted to each new master's demands without necessarily attracting the reputation of spineless turncoats or creating a critical or historical 'problem'.

Monti's apparent political inconsistency has traditionally been seen as a moral question, to be tackled by focusing on the poet himself. One should look instead at the reception of his work, which influenced and shaped his poetic activity. At the same time as Alfieri was loftily theorising his opposition to princely patronage, Monti, only five years younger, without a private income but with the keen appreciation of the importance of money typical of his smallholder milieu, was busy convincing his family, and himself, that the only way to success for an aspiring middle-class writer was to sell himself to his potential readers. His early correspondence is full of references to the promised remuneration for his poems or the actual gifts received from one or the other patron. Thus his poetic career was largely moulded by his readers' evaluation of his work. Unlike that of his older or younger contemporaries, it straddled a period when the quick pace of technological change was making printed matter available more cheaply to a wider readership who previously could not afford it. With the collapse of book prices and the better organisation of their distribution, the potential paying readership expanded way beyond a few private patrons. Writers had to attract the attention of unknown people whose interest, ability to understand and willingness to submit to their authority could not be assumed as a matter of course. The choice between writing for the chosen few or for the common herd no longer had the same meaning as in the previous century, when the common herd of those who could read books was also exceedingly small. Authors who had long targeted a small group as suitable recipients of their work now stood to be selected or ignored by the new reading and paying public. Monti's initial reputation was made by the occasional poems (like *La bellezza dell'universo*, 'The Beauty of the Universe', or *A S. E. Il Principe Sigismondo Chigi*, 'To H. E. Prince Sigismondo Chigi') he offered to a restricted wealthy private market in the late 1770s and early 1780s. When the dying private-patronage system was shattered by the French Revolution he turned to public patronage, and ended with his fame solidly bolstered by the new publishing industry which had developed in Northern Italy for the mass market largely through government intervention.

Just before the French Revolution Monti was living in Rome as secretary to the Pope's nephew, Prince Luigi Braschi. Ideological backwardness was so deeply entrenched in the notion of the universal mission of the Holy See and the old imperial tradition that a few bright members of the papal establishment could safely play around with new ideas, and in 1792 could be ready to welcome Nicolas Joseph Hugou, known as Bassville, who had moved up from Naples as an unofficial French emissary. Regrettably Bassville misjudged the climate, behaved arrogantly and tried to have Bourbon coats of arms replaced by new revolutionary emblems. Someone engineered an affray near the Via del Corso during which he was stabbed to death (13 January 1793). Monti, who had met him and feared that compromising documents bearing his name might be found among Bassville's papers, wrote a long poem, *In morte di Ugo Bassville* ('On Ugo Bassville's Death', usually known as *Bassvilliana*) confessing to his friendship with the deceased, while at the same time endearing himself to his enemies by painting a gory picture of the French Revolution. The poem was a runaway success, with fourteen editions and reprints in six months, and over a hundred by Monti's death in 1828. The penalty of success was the difficulty of retaining control over his work, and the danger that other people would use it for their own ideological ends. When the French appeared to gain the upper hand, Monti began to distance himself from *Bassvilliana* in his private correspondence, and in 1797 he fled from Rome to Milan, then the capital of the Cisalpine Republic. There he promptly wrote a Hymn, sung at La Scala on 21 January 1799, to celebrate the sixth anniversary of Louis XVI's execution, which he had compared in *Bassvilliana* to Christ's passion. Accused of being an untrustworthy turncoat, he was defended by Foscolo, who said an artist could not be blamed if his work, written without flattering intentions, gave support to those in power; furthermore, the creation of a literary master-piece did not necessarily imply assent to the ideas expressed therein.

That may also have been Monti's sincere belief. The words 'Servirò e canterò per chi mi comanda' (I will serve and write poems for whoever pays me) are often quoted from one of his early letters as evidence of his lack of moral fibre, but the quotation usually stops short of the following important three words, 'ma carta bianca' (but no strings attached). This yearning for independence is repeatedly confirmed in Monti's letters and poems: he is not concerned with politics, he regrets that he is obliged to write occasional poems, the only battles he is interested in are those of Achilles and Aeneas. *Carte blanche* could readily be granted by private patrons, only interested, if at all, in the dedicatory letter bearing their name. Monti wrongly believed he could enjoy the same freedom when the work was meant for a wider public, and he often complained of being given official commissions he could not refuse; but he could easily switch from being Napoleon's official bard to praising Archduke Johann of Austria because he was using the same poetic medium steeped in centuries of poetic tradition; and, as is often the case, the medium was the message, hallowing a stable tradition whose political foundation was the divine rule of kings and the changelessness of the power structure. The occasional content was less important: 'We poets', Monti is rumoured to have said, 'are at our best when we are pretending.'

The language of classicism

The medium of poetry had not significantly changed since the Renaissance, when the Italian literary language was standardised on that of fourteenth-century Tuscan writers (see above, pp. 181–5). It was a dogma of some classicists like Antonio Cesari (1760–1828) that only that archaic language was acceptable in literature. Monti, like many Milanese intellectuals, refused to submit to Tuscan dictatorship in linguistic matters and disagreed with Cesari's extreme view that recent words should be banned from official dictionaries, even if he agreed to avoid them in formal poetry. As a rule ordinary words could not be used in poetry: not *bicchiere, peso, andare* (glass, weight, to go) but the more elevated *nappo, pondo, gire*. Other common concepts (say, *caffé*, coffee, or *leone*, lion) had to be disguised by metaphors (*il legume d'Aleppo* or *di Mocca*, the bean from Aleppo or Mocha, *il biondo imperator della foresta*, the blond emperor of the forest), or expressed by reference to classical tradition, particularly mythology.

That does not mean that the average aristocrat was proficient in the literary language. Alfieri had shown in his satire *L'educazione* ('On Education', 1796) how poor their schooling was, and Carlo Porta had given in his Milanese dialect poem *La nomina del cappellan* ('The Appointment of the House-Chaplain', 1819) a brilliantly funny example of the Italianised dialect spoken by the gentry. Nor does it mean that mythology was popular: by the end of the eighteenth century it was already deemed by some (like Vincenzo Lancetti, prefacing his *Areostiade*) 'esausta' and 'stucchevole' (worn out and tiresome). It means that they were both emblems of privilege: the literary language as the symbol of, and vehicle for, a backward-looking political and educational system which stuck to obsolete ideas together with the obsolete words which conveyed them in order to protect the interests of a minority; mythology as part of the mainstay (classical studies) of an educational curriculum open only to those whose parents had the means to send them to school, or who received their education through being committed to the priesthood. As early as 1816, defence of it was less a homage to literary tradition than an affirmation of conservatism. Mythology had been used to 'embellish' raw science and technology (a bit like the incongruous arabesques and wrought-iron lacing found on early sewing-machines) in the didactic poems published in consider-able numbers towards the end of the eighteenth century and at the beginning of the nineteenth. This genre wavered between the desire not to remain insensitive to modern progress, and the tendency to represent it in the abstract, as if it had nothing to do with real social development. When Monti celebrated the first flight of a hot-air balloon (*Al Signor di Montgolfier*, 'To M. de Montgolfier', 1784), the progressive significance of technology was neutralised by his backward glance to Jason's voyage. Two other well-known Italian examples of the genre, in which the potential impact of the new discoveries on the existing social order is removed to the sphere of poetic imagination, are *Invito a Lesbia Cidonia* ('Invitation to Lesbia Cidonia', 1793), a description by Lorenzo Mascheroni, one of Monti's older friends and mentors, of the botanical gardens of the University of Pavia; and *L'elettrico* ('Electricity'), by Cesare Arici, one of Monti's younger imitators, posthumously published in 1838. Didacticism was at the same time affirmed by the traditional language of classical education, and denied by the fact that the latter could not possibly function as an effective means of communication.

The uses of mythology

Classicism enabled Monti and his school to write for those in power *and* have *carte blanche* at the same time, since the imaginative use of mythology seemed to remove poetry from the contingencies of the political arena to a sphere of ideal beauty (as if 'pure' literature was not a political choice). It is therefore not surprising that Monti at the end of his career sang once more the praises of mythology, which he had made the substance of nearly all his poetry, at a time when the original classicism-versus-Romanticism controversy had already abated and Romanticism was gradually establishing itself as the alternative establishment ideology. That is why Monti wished to keep alive one of the options in the alternative. And, as conservatives usually do, he claimed the middle ground: 'I am not at all against the style of poetry you call Romantic and I call classical', he protested: 'I am against excess on either side.' He may have drawn some comfort from the young Leopardi, who had just expressed his nostalgia for ancient myth in *Alla Primavera, o delle favole antiche* ('Spring, or About Ancient Fables', 1822), although Leopardi's position, as we shall see, was totally different. Monti might have remembered what he had written nearly twenty years earlier, dedicating to Napoleon *Il bardo della Selva Nera* ('The Bard of the Black Forest'). What was mythology if not the story of ancient heroes told by poets for the generations to come? Indeed, Monti fancied his own celebratory poetry might form the core of some future mythology.

His most durable achievement is the 'translation', more exactly the rewriting in the Italian blank verse of which he was the acknowledged master, of the very embodiment of classical mythology, Homer's *Iliad*, of which four editions appeared between 1810 and 1825. Monti knew little Greek and translated from Latin, helped by his friend Andrea Mustoxidi and other consultants whenever he wished to refer to the original text (hence Foscolo's biting epigram 'Questi è Vincenzo Monti cavaliero, / gran traduttor dei traduttor d'Omero', 'Here's Vincenzo Monti, knight, great translator of Homer's translators'). But accuracy was not his main concern. He outlined it in *Considerazioni sulla difficoltà di ben tradurre la protasi dell'Iliade* ('Considerations on the Difficulty of Translating Well the Protasis of the Iliad', 1807): to remain faithful to the ideal of poetic perfection represented by the Italian poetic tradition, into which the ancient Greek original had to be reborn. 'When one translates,' he wrote, 'one should show due consideration not to the language of what is being translated, but to that of the translator.' Philologically sounder versions have been produced since, but none has so far matched his. The miracle of the perfect conjunction between ancient myth and a unique, semi-dead poetic language is probably unrepeatable. Monti knew it: in one of his last poems, written for the name-day of his wife (*Pel giorno onomastico della mia donna Teresa Pikler*, 1826), he said she could be proud of having been loved by the author of *Bassvilliana* and the Italian version of the *Iliad*, the two works by which he wished to be remembered.

The intervening decade had placed the revival of the debate on mythology in a different perspective. The emphasis had gradually been shifting from what writers should be doing in principle to how they should make their work acceptable to their readership, whether or not they needed its financial support. No one, obviously, wanted to do away with fantasy and imagination in poetry. The question was no longer which myths should be used by poets, but which myths were part of the consciousness of the reading public. Clearly Graeco-Latin mythology, preferred by Monti, was known only to a small minority with a specialised education, and its scope, however noble, was therefore limited. The times demanded a broadening of the range of poetic content for a wider public, a revitalisation of tradition. Other possibilities remained open: the replacement of mythology with history, whose recent developments (as Foscolo noted in his inaugural lecture) had touched most ordinary people; the replacement of pagan with Christian mythology, known to all; the use of universal emotions inherent in the very biological and physiological nature of human beings (love, death, the nostalgia of youth, hope and disillusionment, the dialectics of finiteness and infinity). The choice between them was largely to shape the work of Foscolo, Manzoni and Leopardi.

29

Foscolo

Love and politics: *Ultime lettere di Jacopo Ortis*

Ugo Foscolo became famous with *Ultime lettere di Jacopo Ortis* ('The Last Letters of Jacopo Ortis'), bringing together fiction, history and autobiography in an epistolary novel which derived its structure and motifs from three of the previous century's best-sellers: Rousseau's *Les rêveries du promeneur solitaire* and *La Nouvelle Héloïse*, and Goethe's *Die Leiden des jungen Werthers* (apart from a host of other sources, including the Bible, Alfieri, Sterne, Gray, Young, and earlier writings by Foscolo himself). The first unfinished draft was completed by a hack, and appeared in three garbled versions (one in 1798, and two in 1799) which were justifiably disowned by Foscolo in 1801. In October 1802 Bodoni published the complete edition as far as Jacopo's suicide. This was subsequently revised and augmented in 1816 and 1817. It dealt, far more clearly than Goethe's *Werther*, with the contrast between social conformity and individual emotions, which Foscolo clearly described as a political contrast. It suggested, at least a century before Wilhelm Reich, Marcuse and other writers on sexual politics, that political, economic and sexual repression go together. Jacopo cannot marry Teresa because, after Napoleon's cession of Venice to Austria with the Treaty of Campoformio (1797), he has to seek political asylum elsewhere. Her father, already under suspicion, would be further compromised and financially ruined by the match. The unhappy love affair ends with Jacopo's suicide. Foscolo boasted that it was 'the first book that induced females and the mass of readers to interest themselves in public affairs' (*Essay on the Present Literature of Italy*, 1818).

There is a close relationship between *Ortis* and other partly autobiographical works by Foscolo, particularly the contemporary *Sonnets* (Pisa, 1802: here numbered as in Gavazzeni's edition). One finds in both the defence of the teaching of Latin (Son. III, *Ortis* 11 Nov.); the Petrarchan description of the beloved's beauty (Son. IV, *Ortis* 20 Nov.); the protagonist's despair projected against a stormy romantic landscape (Son. V, *Ortis* 7 Sept.); the praises of Florence (Son. VIII, *Ortis* 25 Sept.). The 'yearning for glory and filial love' (from Son. I, better known as *Alla sera*, of 1803) preventing the poet's suicide is echoed in Ortis's letter dated Ferrara 20 July, evening. The beginning of *Dei sepolcri* (1806–7) repeats ideas contained in *Ortis* 25 May. Yet, to develop as a poet, Foscolo had to transcend autobiography through a fundamental reassessment of the function of poetry, ultimately leading to his Pavia lectures, with their stress on the civilising influence of the arts, and to the remainder of his poetic and critical activity. In the fourth section of his introduction to his translation of Callimachus' (and Catullus') 'The Locks of Berenice', *La chioma di Berenice* (1803), he set poetry the task of 'celebrating memorable stories, famous deeds and heroes; of firing souls with the love of valour, cities with the love of independence, minds with that of truth and beauty'. Therefore poets must strike minds with the *meraviglioso* (what induces wonderment because it is at once wonderful and miraculous) and hearts with *passioni* (a word denoting strong emotions leading to action). Both are cultural phenomena: *passioni* are rooted in society, the *meraviglioso* is dependent upon human inclinations and notions (otherwise it is merely ridiculous or unbelievable). Thus sensitivity to the *meraviglioso* is akin to religion, but less to Christianity than to polytheism, which creates divine myths for every natural event. And poets must be theologians, creators of supernatural myths, deriving from human experience their power to amaze and inspire wonderment. Through myth poetry becomes the memory of civilisation, with the power to confer eternity upon heroic deeds, images of beauty, lofty ideas: a sort of antidote against the poisoning disillusionments to which human beings are subjected. Foscolo's classicism therefore mediates between Monti's and Leopardi's. Monti believed in traditional unchanging models, capable of fixing into perfect and closed forms what is mutable and open-ended in nature, perhaps because his basic conservatism made him shun change and describe even his changing age by reference to classical myths. Foscolo, on the contrary, posited myth as one of the forms of the real world, representing, as Vico might have put it, the ideal eternal history of the human spirit. Leopardi was to neglect mythology altogether in his poetry, inspired by basic psychological concepts and emotions which he was to term *illusioni*, a word probably derived from Foscolo's *Ortis* (letters of 4 and 15 May).

A new mythology: *Le Grazie*

In this context the autobiographical nature of Foscolo's four major sonnets known by the titles *Alla sera*, *A Zacinto*, *Alla madre* and *Alla Musa* (the first three in the collection of *Poesie* published by Destefanis in 1803, the fourth added in the Nobile edition of *Poesie* later the same year) acquires a new and more mature dimension. The poet's personal experience seems to derive its significance no longer from contingent facts, like the political events of 1797–8 in *Ortis*, but from a wider, almost mythical background, alluded to by references to the universality of death, the birth of Venus and the journeys of Odysseus, the inspirational presence of the poetic Muse accompanied but also led away by the Hours. New events require new myths, or at least a new and fresher look at old ones. In celebrating Luigia Pallavicini's survival of the riding accident which left her disfigured (*A Luigia Pallavicini caduta da cavallo*, 1800, 1803), and Antonietta Fagnani Arese's recovery from an illness (*Alla Amica risanata*, 1803) Foscolo used classical tradition merely as a starting-point (inventing, for instance, the story of Diana's fall from her golden coach), and made several deliberate allusions to a more recent model, the Odes of Parini, who had first used classical tradition as the foundation of his contemporary mythopoeia: the exploits of the *Giovin Signore*, the Young Gentleman, described in *Il giorno* (see above, pp. 382–5).

The highest achievement of Foscolo's new mythology is his celebration of the civilising function of literature and art in general in a poem he intended to dedicate to the sculptor Antonio Canova, *Le Grazie*. He began developing the idea in some poetic fragments on the Graces, alleged in *La chioma di Berenice* (1803) to be translations from a Greek hymn, and continued working on it until shortly before his flight from Italy and eventual arrival in England, where he spent the rest of his life in exile. In 1822 he added some 200 lines from the still unfinished poem to a *Dissertation on an Ancient Hymn to the Graces* contained in a volume of *Outline Engravings and Descriptions of the Woburn Abbey Marbles*, which reproduces among other sculptures Canova's group *The Three Graces*, which had been acquired by the Duke of Bedford. *Le Grazie* is what the Greeks called an *aition* ('cause'), that is, a narrative poem explaining through a myth some aspect of nature; of which the contemporary examples Foscolo knew best were Monti's *Musogonia* ('The Generation of the Muses', 1793), and Manzoni's *Urania* (1809), both presenting the idea that the Muses and the Graces brought civilisation to primitive men. Various editors have attempted to order the various, occasionally overlapping parts of the unfinished poem into a coherent whole: the most convincing reconstruction of the order of composition so far is Vincenzo Di Benedetto's (1990). It may be argued, however, that *Le Grazie* cannot be reconstructed precisely because the material Foscolo elaborated was not yet capable of being given a final structure: otherwise the poet would have found the time to do it himself. The order of composition, though extremely illuminating, cannot in itself show what shape the finished poem would have had, since the poet might have preferred not to place the various fragments in chronological order. Claudio Varese perceptively pointed out that *Le Grazie* was allegedly inspired by Greek poetic fragments; that it was begun soon after *Ortis*, itself structured like a series of epistolary fragments; that artistic sensibility had been for some time influenced by archaeological discoveries leading to the appreciation of the aesthetic possibilities not merely of incomplete works found as fragments, but of art, even criticism, initially conceived or offered as fragmentary. Thus *Le Grazie* turns out to be a neo-mythological creation not only in its content but also in its form, its incompleteness being a structural metaphor for the archaeological myth of the newly unearthed fragment, evidence of a pristine unrecoverable perfection.

One of the themes of the introductory remarks to *La chioma di Berenice*,

and of the contemporary cultural debate moving from the theoretical elaboration of neo-classicism to the Romantic controversy of the next decade, was the
substantial difference between the ancient and the modern world, raising all
manner of issues, concerning not only the function of poetry and literature in
either, or both, but also the possibility of transposing poetic forms and
contents from the distant past to the present, as well as from one language to
another. That is why the art of translating occupied Foscolo as it had occupied
his older friends Cesarotti and Monti. Besides his version of Catullus' poem
Foscolo wrote an 'experiment of translation from the *Iliad*' (*Esperimento di
traduzione dell'Iliade*, 1807, begun in 1804), and the Italian version of
Laurence Sterne's *Sentimental Journey* (*Viaggio sentimentale di Yorick lungo
la Francia e l'Italia*, 1813), begun with the help of an English lady friend in
1804 when he was in France on army duties. It is possible that his attempt to
rival Monti, who was also translating Homer, lies at the origin of the break
between the two in April 1810. While Monti's main concern was the language
of translation (see above, p. 410), Foscolo believed in the translator's duty to
penetrate and express as much as possible the spirit of the original, a task in
which he believed he had the edge over Monti because of the latter's ignorance
of Greek. But other things, chief among them their radically different attitude
to the power structure, separated the two poets, the break between whom was
allegedly triggered by Monti's disparaging remarks about one of Foscolo's
idols, Alfieri, and Foscolo's professed dislike for a poem by Monti's protégé
Cesare Arici.

Dei sepolcri: a 'smoky enigma'

The *Esperimento* was published almost at the same time as *Dei sepolcri*, the
poem for which Foscolo is deservedly famous. One of Homer's translators,
Ippolito Pindemonte (1753–1828), had attracted Foscolo's interest by publishing (in 1805) the beginning of what would become the standard Italian
version of the *Odyssey* (1822), and was planning a piece of sepulchral poetry
entitled *I cimiteri* which he left unfinished on receiving Foscolo's *Dei sepolcri*
dedicated to him. The occasion was a decree extending to Italy the French
legislation prohibiting burial outside cemeteries, and consequently the inter-
ment inside churches of the corpses of famous people. Foscolo called his poem
carme, a Latinism with connotations of ritual and ceremonial utterance,
prophecy, oracle, even riddle of difficult interpretation (as indeed the poem
appeared to the prejudiced Giordani, who called it a 'smoky enigma'). Its
central idea is often superficially linked to the 'graveyard tradition' represented
by such poets as Gray, Young, Campbell and Legouvé – which is surprising,
considering its clear rejection of sentimental spiritualism and religious inspiration. To Foscolo funereal rites are a means whereby the culture of the living
perpetuates the memory of the deceased, who do not profit from it or survive

death in any other-worldly sense. What is left of the dead, namely the recollection of their thoughts and actions, may inspire the living to 'egregie cose' (noble deeds) only if society is not decaying and dulled by corruption, and a few strong spirits are present to leaven its mass. Many other ideas and images link up with this central proposition (such as the danger that the new decree might cause great people to die unhonoured; the impact on the poet's imagination of the tombs of great Italians in Florence; the contrast between the garden-like appearance of English cemeteries and the macabre aspect of ossuaries in Italian churches; the vision of the battle of Marathon; the concluding prophecy of Cassandra), but not in any strictly logical order which might allow one to analyse the poem into consequent parts. In a sense *Dei sepolcri* is as strongly influenced by the aesthetic of the 'fragment' as *Le Grazie*. That does not mean that either poem, whether finished or unfinished, should be read as if it lacked unity; only that the 'fragments', whether real (as in *Le Grazie*) or ideal, should be taken as forming or presupposing a virtual whole (which is indeed true of archaeological fragments). Foscolo himself declared that he did not wish to appeal to the 'sillogismo dei lettori', meaning his readers' analytical faculty, but to their imagination and heart. Once again (and this lesson was fully learned by Leopardi in his early *canzoni*), he avoided using the present as a pretext to recollect the classical past: the classical tradition was a means to a better understanding of the present. The message of *Dei sepolcri* is so powerfully directed to Foscolo's own time that its enormous wealth of Greek and Latin quotations, allusions, reminiscences and cross-references comes almost as a surprise when it is revealed by scholars such as O'Neill and Di Benedetto. This was the last significant poetic work by Foscolo, apart from his two tragedies: *Ajace*, which failed (also for political reasons) when it was staged in Milan at the end of 1811, and *Ricciarda*, which fared no better in 1813.

Exile

By the time the debate on classicism was reopened by Madame de Staël, Foscolo had left Italy. He had identified himself with his character, Jacopo Ortis, to the extent of transcribing into the novel excerpts from his personal letters and vice versa. The identification with the character, short of suicide, would become closer if Jacopo's creator, too, went into exile. With the collapse of the Italic Kingdom his position as an officer of the former Napoleonic army had become untenable; and he had many enemies and had lost many influential friends. He was not an endearing person. He was rather ugly, shrill of voice, given to theatrical gestures, a gambler who borrowed money he did not always pay back, a persistent womaniser whose many loves (as he himself put it in a letter to Antonietta Fagnani Arese) were made up of 'great risks, short and desultory pleasures, late repentance and endless tears'. He was not averse to bending the truth to suit his ends. Nevertheless, many people who affected to dislike him because of his vices really hated him because he did not suffer fools gladly.

Foscolo spent a year and a half in Switzerland, whither he had escaped on 30 March 1816, and then repaired to London. There he was to embark on a prodigious literary activity, also spurred by his constant financial needs, even more pressing because of his unremitting extravagance. Perhaps as a reward for helping Foscolo with his translation of Sterne, a Miss Fanny Hamilton had been left around 1804 with a daughter by him. In 1821 the girl discovered her father in London and came to live with him, bearing a not insignificant inheritance received from the grandmother who had brought her up. Foscolo, unconcerned about the girl's future, immediately dissipated her money in building an elegant cottage, which he could not afford and had to sell off at a loss to appease his many creditors barely two years later. Amidst love affairs with ladies and housemaids, quarrels with friends and enemies, bouts of well-being and high living alternating with illness and malnutrition, he found the energy to write for various influential journals like *The Edinburgh Review* and *The Quarterly Review* many essays which were to prove a significant contribution to the knowledge of Italian literature and history in nineteenth-century Britain. Much of his final months was spent in sickness, often living in hovels under an assumed name to escape his creditors. Death from dropsy came as a merciful, though untimely, release on 10 September 1827. His mortal remains were moved in 1871 to Santa Croce in Florence and laid to rest with those of the great Italians he had commemorated in *Dei sepolcri*.

30

Leopardi

'Mad and desperate study'

One of the would-be participants in the debate around Mme de Staël's views was Giacomo Leopardi, who in 1815 was a sickly seventeen-year-old from Recanati, a small hill town in the papal province of Marche. Deemed unsuitable for a sanctuary by the angels who had winged the house of the Virgin Mary all the way from Nazareth to its territory (they moved it after only one year to its final resting place at nearby Loreto), Recanati nevertheless ended up with something at least as important. It was a library of over 15,000 books collected in an informed and systematic way by Count Monaldo Leopardi (1776–1845), taking advantage of the sale of books from the religious houses abolished during French rule. Monaldo was one of those conservatives who believed the world was being swamped by a tide of pernicious liberalism, and was therefore prepared to swim against the tide, even when that meant falling foul of established authority. He was passionately committed to education. He opened his library to his fellow citizens (who seem to have ignored the opportunity) and obtained for his first-born, Giacomo, a dispensation to read banned books when the boy was only fifteen. Giacomo was often openly bitter in his letters about his father's narrow-minded and rigid attitude and beliefs, and grew up to dislike nearly everything he stood for; yet he knew he was sincere, had for him a trust and affection as deep and lasting as the ideological chasm that divided them, and, within Monaldo's limitations, received from him unfailing support. But Giacomo needed a father figure who could share his ideas and aspirations, and found him in Pietro Giordani (see above, p. 399), with whom he remained in close and affectionate correspondence from 1817 to 1832.

Giacomo took so much advantage of the free use of the library, the only freedom and relaxation he had, that by the time he sent the *Biblioteca italiana* his reply to Mme de Staël's article he had permanently ruined his health. The amount of reading and writing he did in seven years of 'mad and desperate study' was prodigious. He learned Latin, Greek, Hebrew, French, probably Spanish (he studied English later on while waiting for the ink to dry on whatever he was writing). Thus he formed a lasting interest in the theory of language, and became one of the most accomplished and perceptive philologists of his time. He read, translated and wrote critical studies of many Greek and Latin authors, trying to keep up with the latest developments (such as Monsignor Angelo Mai's discovery of fragments by Fronto and Dionysius of Halicarnassus). He read extensively most Italian poets of the previous three centuries, together with some of the earlier classics and some minor poets from his own region. He had a remarkable memory which enabled him to retain things he had only superficially studied: one of his early poems, *Appressamento della morte* ('Death Approaching', 1816) contains a large number of references to Dante's *Divina Commedia*, which he had read only once. His memory, however, was not a mere mental accomplishment, but became one of the most significant elements of his emotional and intellectual life, as he himself noted in *Zibaldone*, the lengthy diary (4526 pages) he compiled from 1817 to 1832 (mostly written from 1821 to 1823), which its first editor, Carducci, defined as the 'organic encyclopaedia' of his thought. The recollection of the past was an abiding source of pleasure for Leopardi, to whom most physical pleasures were denied by ill health and cramped lifestyle, and became an essential ingredient of his poetry. 'Memories' is the title of two of his poems, *Le rimembranze* (1816) and *Le ricordanze* (1829), and the opening motif of *A Silvia* ('To Sylvia', 1828), one of his best-loved *canti*.

While learning about the past Giacomo kept a close watch on contemporary events. He welcomed the French defeat at Tolentino (2 May 1815) with a discourse clearly influenced by Foscolo's *Ortis* in its attack on Napoleonic despotism, but well founded in its criticism of the mismanagement and rapacity of the French administration. His first two *canzoni*, *All'Italia* ('To Italy'), deploring his country's political and moral decadence, and *Sopra il monumento di Dante* (1818), taking the planned erection in Florence of a monument to Dante as a pretext for lamenting present corruption, were read by his contemporaries as poems in the Petrarchan or Foscolian mould exhorting patriots to heroic deeds; and Risorgimento conspirators formed the impression that the poet was one of them ('our father froze with fear', wrote his brother Carlo). When in 1858 De Sanctis voiced the opinion that if Leopardi had lived until 1848, he would have sided 'as a comforter and co-fighter' with the patriots, he certainly reflected the general consensus, even if both he and the patriots would have found it difficult to explain why or how exactly the poet was 'on their side'. Those who disliked his poetry, like Niccolò Tommaseo and Gino Capponi, had at least a clear target in his philosophy, which they construed as one of despair, born, they believed, of his physical afflictions and lack of religious belief. Leopardi would have disagreed with both groups. He declared, in a letter of 24 May 1832 to Louis De Sinner, that his ideas were not the by-product of his personal conditions. He was, however, fully aware of their subversive and radical potential. In fact the various Restoration police forces assessed Leopardi as politically dangerous, and took appropriate measures by keeping him under surveillance throughout his life and banning his works until well after his death.

The first two *canti* escaped the attention of the police, perhaps because their rhetoric appeared traditional and their contents predictable to unsubtle readers. Soon afterwards Leopardi composed two poems on contemporary events. The very title of the first one, 'On the death of a woman whom her debaucher had had murdered by a surgeon together with her unborn child', aroused Monaldo's disapproval. The third one, however, *Ad Angelo Mai*, was dedicated to the respected prelate who had not long before discovered Cicero's *De republica*, and Monaldo allowed Giacomo to send it for publication to a friend, Pietro Brighenti. Neither knew that Brighenti was an informer of the Austrian police, and that he had duly reported that *Ad Angelo Mai* was tainted with 'deadly liberalism'. Giacomo himself, in a letter to Brighenti (28 April 1820), had defined the poem 'full of frightening fanaticism, dealing with anything but ancient manuscripts'. In fact it rejected the very notion which many readers have lazily seen as its overall meaning: that literature and the memories of past glories are the necessary inspiration for action and could be the spur to the moral and political regeneration of Italy. If that were really the case, the poem suggests, the present time would not be so corrupt, soul-deadening and hopeless. Such views undermined the Austrian government's cultural policy, which used the controversy between Romantics and classicists as a diversion from, or a substitute for, more important social and political debates, and pursued the programme of de-mystification Leopardi had begun in 1816 with his two unpublished letters to *Biblioteca italiana*. Though seemingly in agreement with the journal's classicist stance, they vigorously advocated the rejection of traditional models, whether in translations or in imitations, and the need for new literary forms. Leopardi believed that modern poets, like the ancient ones, should turn for inspiration directly to 'nature', which in this case meant what lies around us, the real world, perhaps excluding human artefacts but certainly including human society. This was a truly subversive programme, because it implied that the debate about books should become a debate about real issues and problems.

Leopardi's education was based on the syllabus then current in the Jesuit schools, in which 'Philosophy' embraced science. He came into contact not only with seminal authors like Spinoza, Hobbes, Maupertuis, Rousseau, Bayle, Helvétius and Voltaire (even if they were studied only to be refuted), but also with the progressive tradition of the Catholic scientific Enlightenment. The Church condemned Enlightenment philosophy because it might lead to a weakening of its conservative influence, but accepted new scientific ideas because it could not stop their advancement or ignore technological discoveries. In fact some of the best contemporary scientists and writers on science were in holy orders, men such as François Jacquier, Aimé-Henri Paulian, Jean Saury and the brilliant Rudjer Boscovic. Leopardi was acquainted with their work. Out of the five notebooks of *Dissertazioni filosofiche* written by him between the ages of thirteen and fourteen, two contain scientific dissertations. Next he wrote a *Storia dell'astronomia* ('History of Astronomy', 1813) from its origins in classical and eastern antiquity to the latest discoveries and researches, touching upon its implications for religion, comparative traditions and scientific methodology, and concluding with a bibliography of primary sources of over 300 works by 230 authors or editors. A similar wealth of references is appended to the essay *Sopra gli errori popolari degli antichi* ('On the Popular Errors of the Ancients', 1815), on the history of myths and popular traditions, containing many ideas later developed in his poetry. Leopardi's interest in scientific matters continued throughout his life, sustained by his friendship with some noted scientists who in 1829 thought him suitably qualified to apply for the Chair of Natural History at Parma University.

Science and the idea of Nature: the evolution of the *Canti*

It is important to stress Leopardi's interest in science because it underpins his idea of Nature, which is not merely a poetic contemplation of beautiful landscapes or a wistful imagination of the pristine human condition, but the very focus of his poetry and thought, leading him to meditate further on the problem of human happiness and its social and political implications. Scholars have argued at length about the development of the concept of Nature in Leopardi's *Canti*, and have taken the history of their publication as a critical metaphor for the structured development of his thought. Ten *canzoni*, adding to the three already mentioned, *Nelle nozze della sorella Paolina* ('For his Sister Paolina's Marriage'), *A un vincitore nel pallone* ('To a Football Champion'), *Bruto minore* ('Brutus Minor'), *Alla primavera o delle favole antiche* ('To Spring, or about Ancient Fables': see above, p. 410), *Inno ai Patriarchi* ('Hymn to the Patriarchs'), *L'ultimo canto di Saffo* ('Sappho's Last Song') and *Alla sua donna* ('To his Lady'), all written between 1818 and 1823, were published in 1824. They are said to be evidence of a stage in the poet's development when his pessimism was tempered by his trust in a motherly Nature and his hope for a re-awakening of consciences. A number of *Idilli* followed in 1825: a title Leopardi derived from the Greek root *eid-* meaning 'vision', with the diminutive suffix carrying connotations of sharpness and concentration. The most famous among them is *L'infinito* (1819), in which cosmic infinity is powerfully implied by contrast: a nearby hedge blocking the view suggests distant limitless vistas. Life's limitations thus become (as indeed they did for Leopardi) a powerful emotional and imaginative stimulus, and the short compass of the poem (fifteen lines) comes to symbolise, by contrast, the limitless possibilities of poetry. A longer poem in this group, *La vita solitaria* ('Solitary Life', 1821), can best be seen as a collection of four shorter *idilli* relating the various times and sensations of the day to the ages and vicissitudes of human life.

The next edition of the *Canti* (Florence, 1831) included what critics termed *grandi idilli*, as if by then Leopardi's meditation on the unhappiness of the human condition necessarily caused by Nature had reached a greater range and depth (*A Silvia*, 1828; *Le ricordanze*, 1829; *La quiete dopo la tempesta*, 'Quiet After a Storm', 1829; *Il sabato del villaggio*, 'Saturday in the Village', 1829; *Canto notturno di un pastore errante dell'Asia*, 'Night Song of a Wandering Shepherd in Asia', 1830). Finally we witness a gradual downturn towards the desperate celebration of unhappy love in the so-called 'cycle' of Aspasia, the name he used to celebrate Fanny Targioni-Tozzetti (see above, p. 405), which was added to the 1835 Naples edition: *Il pensiero dominante* ('The Uppermost Thought', 1831?); *Amore e Morte* ('Love and Death', 1831); *A se stesso* ('To Himself', 1833?); *Aspasia* (1834); to which may be added the cosmic pessimism of *La ginestra o il fiore del deserto* ('The Broom, or the Desert Flower', 1836) posthumously published in the Florence edition of 1845.

There is, of course, development: but is that the same as growing, unremitting pessimism? In his 1832 letter to De Sinner, Leopardi said he had fully expressed his feelings about the human condition eleven years earlier in *Bruto minore* (where we read what Brutus might have thought before committing suicide at Philippi). As a poet he needed Nature to be alive, sentient, endowed with human attributes, someone one can speak to regardless of whether she is responsive or aloof, mother or stepmother. In *La sera del dì di festa* ('Holiday Eve', 1820), Nature appears actively antagonistic, yet the poet's feelings towards her are warm. *La vita solitaria* opens on a masterly sequence of natural images: the early morning rain drumming gently on the roof, the hen fluttering in the coop, the uncertain light of the rising sun, the clouds in the sky, the first chirping of birds. At the end of its first section Nature is described as contemptuous of individual misery and anguish, while taking care of the general good: thus the poet can at the same time contemplate both suicide and the manifold beauties of the surrounding environment. Nature is holy, attractive and with a motherly voice in *Alla primavera*. She is described as both mother and stepmother in his last major poem, *La ginestra*, in which the idea Leopardi had inherited from seventeenth-century science, that Nature was a machine which human beings would eventually master and control, 'breaking all opposition' (exemplified in *Ad Angelo Mai* by Columbus' great voyage of discovery), culminates in the image of humankind linked together to oppose Nature's destructive power symbolised by Vesuvius.

Leopardi's religious education led him to reflect on the idea of God in *Zibaldone*. He thought it logically untenable that God should be an absolutely good, pure spirit, since the Absolute Being must necessarily include all possible manners of being, including evil or material ones. Given that 'Nature is the same as God' (*Zibaldone*, 393), and is *all* there is, Nature, which often takes on a positively value-loaded sense (as in the adjective 'natural') must be value-free. Its good and bad aspects are relative to human vision. Nature is in fact neither good nor bad, perhaps merely indifferent: that is the message of *Dialogo della Natura e di un islandese*, 'Dialogue between Nature and an Icelander', one of the *Operette morali* ('Short Moral Treatises', written in 1826–7, published in 1827 and, in augmented editions, in 1834 and 1845), a series of elegant meditations in dialogue form, mostly about the distorted perspective whereby humans see themselves as the most important beings in the universe, whereas they are actually insignificant in the natural scheme of things.

Nature and society

Leopardi's speculation on Nature overflows, like his scientific interests, into many reflections on human culture and society, extensively developed in *Zibaldone* and the *Discorso sopra lo stato presente dei costumi degli italiani* ('Discourse on the Present State of Italian Society', 1824). The relationship between Nature and society is central to his poems. His landscapes are always peopled with living beings, described not as shapes or figures but mostly through the noises they make because of the things they do. This may well be a consequence of Leopardi's poor eyesight, but it is also a reflection of his overriding concern with the human condition. A description of living beings as shapes or outlines, even when painted in colour, is not as effective in capturing life as a description of them in action. We catch only a glimpse of the eyes of Silvia (*A Silvia*) but continuously hear her song and the clatter of her loom. *La quiete dopo la tempesta* and *Il sabato del villaggio* are peopled with human beings making various noises. Then there are the animals. The evening scene at the beginning of *Le ricordanze* is brought to life by the croaking of the frogs in the field and the noises of the servants nearby, quietly working in the house. The opening of *Il passero solitario* ('The Lonely Sparrow', 1830?) is full of birdsong, bleating of sheep and lowing of cattle. Even the apocalyptic visions of the end of civilisation in *A un vincitore nel pallone* and *La sera del dì di festa* get their poignancy from the cautious movements of the fox and the noise of the wind through the dark forest covering the ruins of the former Italian towns, and from the memory of a past conceived in acoustic terms (the *noise* of ancient peoples, the *cry* of our famous ancestors, the *clangour* of the Roman Empire). Though empty of people, the landscapes in *L'infinito* and the second section of *La vita solitaria* come alive in the mind of the observer, whose presence is stressed by the repeated use of the personal pronoun *io*.

The relationship between Nature and human beings and their groupings into societies raise a number of questions relevant to individual and social happiness, the subject of innumerable treatises during the Enlightenment, and Leopardi's pivotal concern. He believed that human life is necessarily unhappy, because happiness is bound up with pleasure, but pleasure proceeds from the cessation of anguish – and yet leads to anguish because one's potentially infinite desire for pleasure is bound to remain unsatisfied. If human life is unhappy why do we care to perpetuate it? Why are there human beings in the cosmos? What are they there for? asks the shepherd in *Canto notturno*. Are human societies perfectible? How can the masses be happy when individuals

are not? Does progress lead to more or less happiness? Leopardi flatly denied
(*Zibaldone* of 13 July 1826) that he was against progress as such; but he was
not convinced that happiness could come to humankind from its headlong
rush into industrial and technological development. His concern was not
abstractly philosophical: it led him to reflect on such concrete matters as public
health in an increasingly urbanised society, industrial diseases, the unequal
ratio of educational provisions and benefits across social classes, even the
possible extinction of the human race due to the fact that we human beings are
the only living creatures capable of fighting Nature and creating large-scale
changes in the environment. Hence we, unlike most animals, also have the
unique ability to do harm to ourselves and other members of our own species.
In the fragment *Dialogo tra due bestie* (1820: part of the preparatory work for
Operette morali) a bull and a horse discuss the various causes of human
extinction, among them the fact that human beings did not live according to
nature, developed science and technology and 'believed the world had been
made for their benefit'.

The notion that the poet was somehow *progressivo*, in the sense of caring for
the well-being and happiness of the common people, long antedates Luporini's
famous 1947 essay. Leopardi stubbornly rejected the most advanced bourgeois
ideology of his time not because he was an obscurantist unable to grasp it, but
precisely because he fully understood it. He did not spend an equal amount of
energy in combating reactionary ideas like his father's (from which nevertheless
he vehemently dissociated himself) because by then they had lost much of their
credibility and appeal. But it was worth dissenting from his Tuscan friends Gino
Capponi and Giovan Pietro Vieusseux because they had considerable social
prestige and political authority. Vieusseux edited *Antologia*, perhaps the most
influential Italian journal of the time. The Italian Romantic intellectuals of the
first half of the century, who, according to Giuseppe Montani's review of
Monti's poem on mythology (*Antologia*, October 1825), pledged their support
to the development of factories and shops, and, contemplating the hustle and
bustle of merchant ships in the harbour, paid homage to free trade and the
steam engine, were moving along the mainstream of historical development. If
one calls *them* 'progressive' Leopardi most definitely was not *progressivo*. But
moving forward in time, as history does by definition, is not in itself a guarantee
of 'progress' in the sense of better quality of life or increased general happiness
and well-being, of which Leopardi, who was very observant, did not see much
around. He died nearly a quarter of a century before the political unification of
the country fulfilled the hopes of the liberal-conservative intellectuals whose
beliefs he had satirised (*Paralipomeni della Batracomiomachia*, 'A Supplement
to the Battle of the Mice and the Frogs', 1830–1; *Palinodia al Marchese Gino
Capponi*, 'To Marquess Gino Capponi: A Recantation', 1835), but one doubts
whether the outcome would have led him to change his mind. Political and
administrative change did little to stop the age-old exploitation of the working
masses, or to abate the fear the ruling classes had of their legitimate aspirations,

which justified their continued repression. In the very year united Italy reverently celebrated the centenary of Leopardi's birth, a few hundred demonstrators clamouring for cheaper bread were massacred in Milan by the artillery of General Fiorenzo Bava Beccaris: a heroic feat for which he was immediately rewarded by King Umberto I with a seat in the Senate and the title of Commander of the Order of the Military Cross of Savoy.

Leopardi and his readers

Leopardi's contemporaries formed an opinion of his reprehensible (or inspiring) radicalism only from the small proportion of his writings current in his lifetime, that is (if one excepts a few erudite works), his collected *Canti* and *Operette morali*. *Zibaldone* was first published in 1898–1900 as an offshoot of the centenary celebrations. His letters, an equally important source to us, were obviously known only to their recipients until they were traced, collected and published, a work culminating in the 1934–41 edition by Francesco Moroncini and others. If those who read Leopardi's published writings thought them, for whatever reason, as important as we do who can read the rest of his work, that can only mean that those relatively few poems and prose works are a unique distillation of experience, a concentration of poetic wisdom, and that they were meant to be the full expression of their author's 'message'. But there is more to Leopardi's work than its message. Poised between classicism and Romanticism, Leopardi used his mastery of rhetorical tradition, from classical to Italian literature and from Petrarch through the Renaissance and seventeenth-century poetic mannerism down to Monti and Foscolo, to fashion an economical poetic language in which words and quotations acquire a new and original meaning. To give but one example of *callida junctura* ('clever juxtaposition' as Horace defined it): in 'vago errore' (Petrarch) and 'dilettosi errori' (Bernardo Tasso) the word *errore* meant 'wavering motion, wandering'. Leopardi applied the adjective *dilettoso* ('pleasant, delectable') to *errore* in its other meaning of 'misapprehension'. Thus 'beautiful mistakes' was his poetic alternative to Foscolo's *illusioni*, the lovely myths of happy youth, blissful love, beautiful and motherly Nature, shared by all human beings. They replaced the old Greek and Roman fables dear to Monti, his predecessors and followers, and known only to a few.

Since reality is nothingness, illusions, which are insubstantial, are the only real thing (*Zibaldone*, December 1819). Infinity becomes almost perceptible when one is hedged in by visible boundaries, and its perception leads to a clearer vision of one's finiteness and limitation before Nature. In this circularity, harking back to the cycles of ancient philosophy, there is an almost dialectic tension between the pleasure and inspiration illusions give to humankind, and the fact that they are destined to remain unrealised and unfulfilled. Leopardi questioned the Aristotelian principle of non-contradiction in 1824, long before Bertrando Spaventa, Augusto Vera and Angelo Camillo De Meis introduced Hegel's dialectics to Italy in the 1860s. The oppositions between Being and Non-being, Ancients and Moderns, imagination and reason, thought and action, motherly and unmotherly Nature, love and death, and many other dichotomies, remained unresolved not so much because of Leopardi's ignorance of Hegel's philosophy, as because a forward-looking synthesis reconciling the opposition between thesis and antithesis would have seemed to him too easy a way out.

Italian culture, however, was not ready for Leopardi's uncompromising clarity of vision. His idylls were seen as idealised and charming, but narrow, descriptions of rural life, with craftsmen merrily singing at night, lonely sparrows chirping on top of isolated towers, meditative shepherds looking at the moon, little girls carrying impossible posies of roses and violets (they do not blossom at the same time, as Pascoli pedantically pointed out). This reductive interpretation was more successful in neutralising Leopardi's radicalism than the combined efforts of Church and police. His striking love poetry, always celebrating 'a woman who cannot be found' even when inspired by identifiable women, was too intellectual and reflective to be popular. The rising middle classes engaged in their nation-building work needed a charismatic writer to embody their ideology in a successful literary work, and found him in Alessandro Manzoni.

31

Manzoni and the novel

Early life and works

Cesare Beccaria, famous in the 1760s throughout the civilised world for advocating the abolition of torture and capital punishment, wished to stop the affair between his lively and beautiful daughter, Giulia, and Giovanni Verri, the playboy brother of his friends Pietro and Alessandro (renowned editors of *Il Caffè*, one of the most influential journals of the Italian Enlightenment; see above, pp. 378–80). Pietro arranged Giulia's marriage to the obscure Count Pietro Manzoni, twenty-six years her senior, as if that could stop the affair. In 1785 she gave birth to Alessandro, whom her husband acknowledged although he was (presumably) Giovanni Verri's son. After seven years in a steadily worsening relationship, Giulia went to live with Carlo Imbonati, a wealthy merchant banker, and Alessandro was farmed out to various religious boarding schools which gave him very unpleasant memories but a good classical education. By reaction he became a confirmed anti-clerical and challenger of established authority, ready to join the Romantic movement, and make friends with some of its acknowledged leaders, like Ermes Visconti and Federigo Confalonieri. His nationalism and love of history were stimulated by his contacts with the Neapolitan historian Vincenzo Cuoco, while his enthusiasm for poetry was kindled by sympathetic advice from Monti and Foscolo.

Imbonati, who had never met Alessandro, invited him to Paris early in 1805, but died suddenly before his arrival, making Giulia his heiress and laying the foundations of her son's future financial well-being (a fact that later on must have seriously troubled his conscience). Through his mother's circle of friends Alessandro came into contact with a group of intellectuals known as *les idéologues*, from the views of one of them, the philosopher Antoine Destutt de Tracy, who believed that the philosopher's task was chiefly to analyse the origins and mechanism of mental processes: philosophy was to become 'ideology' in the special sense of 'enquiry into the development of ideas'. Manzoni's closest friend among them was Claude Fauriel, a former follower of Robespierre who had retired from politics in 1802, at thirty years of age, to devote himself to literary studies, becoming in due course an authority on Romance and particularly Provençal literature.

The *idéologues* continued to further the ideals of the Enlightenment while Napoleon and the ruling class which had emerged from the French revolution were busy promoting bourgeois conservatism, and restoring religion as the natural ally of a hierarchically structured society. Neo-classicism, by its traditional mythological imagery, flattered the imperialistic ambitions of the new rich. Romanticism projected itself as the new Restoration ideology, capable of applying its fresh energies and youthful imagination even to the promotion of good old middle-class virtues, such as political moderation, social order, aesthetic harmony and Christian morality. That may explain why many intellectuals of this age (such as Monti, La Harpe, De Gérando and Chateaubriand) could move from one extreme to the other of the cultural and political spectrum, or go through religious conversions, without appearing to lose their ideological coherence: they continued to serve their class interests, however radical the change might appear from the outside. Conversion is an ambivalent phenomenon: on the one hand it is a 'turning upside-down' of one's life; and as such it has almost revolutionary connotations. On the other it is a call to order, a return to tradition, revelation and long-established teaching, the supreme act of obedience to a divine Lord. The theme of conversion has therefore multiple and ambiguous resonances and lends itself to representing as a radical change what is merely a shift within the boundaries of one's ideology. Manzoni too went through a series of interrelated and complementary 'conversions'. From being a Deist (he was never an atheist) he accepted Catholicism. Over a period of about twenty years he moved from literary classicism to Romanticism, from poetry to prose-writing, and from democratic radicalism to enlightened conservatism.

His first move was from bachelorhood to married life. His wife was Henriette Blondel, the younger daughter of a Swiss banker friend of Imbonati's. The marriage was blessed in Milan on 6 February 1808 by a Swiss Protestant minister, no Catholic priest being willing to perform the marriage of a Calvinist with an anti-clerical whose mother was known to have lived in sin. In June the Manzonis were back in Paris, where they met Eustachio Degola, a priest from Genoa belonging to that deviant strain of Catholic theology, rather similar to Calvinism in its emphasis on Divine Grace and the need for uncompromising moral rigour, known as Jansenism from its founder, the Dutch bishop Cornelis Janssen (1585–1638). Degola was thus ideally suited to cater for the spiritual needs of both Henriette and Alessandro, without pressing them to disown the substance of their respective Protestant and *idéologue* ethics. He became their spiritual counsellor, and eventually accepted Henriette into the Catholic Church (the Manzonis had already gone through a Catholic marriage ceremony on 15 February 1810).

Like most young men with literary ambitions, Manzoni began by writing poetry. He found it easier to innovate by replacing traditional content (eroticism with moralism, respect for established authority with revolutionary Jacobinism, reverence for the Church with anti-clericalism, mythology and hero-worship with realism, and so forth) than by challenging the old medium of classicist poetry. When he ended up proclaiming his rejection of neo-classicism in impeccably neo-classical verse (*A G. B. Pagani*, 1803), he found himself in an impasse. *Urania* (1809), a brave attempt to celebrate the civilising influence of poetry, derived its ideas more from Vico than from the classical tradition (and contributed something to Foscolo's *Le Grazie*, see above, p. 414), but Manzoni confessed his dissatisfaction to Fauriel (6 September 1809): 'One should not write poetry like that. I may possibly write worse poems, but I shall never write anything like that any more.' By 1812, after a few more unfinished poems on social and political subjects, Manzoni had exhausted most of the subject-matters he could find in the lay culture of the Enlightenment. His religious conversion, opening up a rich store of biblical and sacred themes, was almost an artistic necessity. He set out to write a cycle of twelve religious hymns for the main Christian festivals. The first, *La Risurrezione*, was composed between April and June 1812. In three years he managed to write three more hymns. He had kept the promise made earlier to Fauriel. The *Inni sacri* had nothing to do with neo-classicism: they were based on themes known to all people, whatever their education and social class, and were therefore a significant step towards a more popular poetry. But were they also better poems? Religious and devotional concepts were hammered out in strongly rhythmical verse, through images of rigorous theological orthodoxy and admirable lexical ingenuity. They were incomparable because there was nothing to compare them to. Italian criticism has since lavished praise on the *Inni sacri*, but Manzoni himself must have been intimately dissatisfied, since it took him about five years to write *La Pentecoste*, his fifth and last complete hymn. After 1822, while religious inspiration was as strong as ever in his prose writing, religious verse occurred only in unfinished fragments.

Since content, however worthy, could not in itself furnish Manzoni with a set of formal criteria, he resorted to morality as the foundation of critical judgement. Thus Beauty would be judged in terms of Truth and Goodness: a formulation bringing together again the three persons of the old philosophical trinity. Where else, apart from Religion, could Truth be found? To the avid reader of Walter Scott's historical novels, friend of distinguished historians like Cuoco, Fauriel and Augustin Thierry, born and brought up in an exciting age when common people (whether in Napoleon's army or on the barricades) were seen to be shaping the events of the world, the answer was easy: in History. A writer, argued Manzoni in his *Lettre à M. Ch[auvet]* (1823), does not acquire merit by inventing fictitious tales, but by choosing among the many documented facts those susceptible of poetic and dramatic treatment, and linking them together in such a way as to portray what history often neglects: the humanity of its protagonists, their sorrows, their joys; so that dramatic invention should accord not only with history but also with what is always true of all people at all times. Thus he came to reject the old-fashioned military and dynastic history in favour of popular history, but he nevertheless continued to assess large-scale events as the outcome of individual actions, even when he presented them otherwise. Hence he explained social injustice by individual corruption: and his recipe for social change could only be the demonstrably inadequate remedy of personal conversion and total adherence to the Church's teaching.

Manzoni reversed the old Aristotelian principle – that artists should imagine what sort of things could possibly happen in order that their creation might have the ring of truth – and instead maintained that writers should concentrate on truth, so that they may be able to imagine what sort of things could possibly happen. This led him to refute the pseudo-Aristotelian rules of dramatic unity. His rebuttal (*Lettre à M. Ch[auvet]*) was based not on philology, like Schlegel's, but on a moralistic and philosophical argument. A playwright wishing to keep the action within the limits prescribed by those rules must either alter the course of events or precipitate a dramatic climax. In the former case truth is compromised. In the latter the events appear to arise out of the whim of blind fate, or the vagaries of chance, not out of human passions and emotions. If, rejecting *coups de théâtre*, the playwright relies too heavily on sudden psychological changes, and on love as being the only emotion capable of producing them, nobler and more important sentiments are neglected, and the writer's moral standards are lowered. The traditional conflict between love and duty, emotions and rationality, arouses the interest of the audience more for the manner in which protagonists solve their dilemmas than for the ethical substance of the conflict itself. The advantage of choosing historical subjects for one's tragedies is that the reader already knows which decision will be taken; and the analysis of the conflict is freed from the distracting element of suspense.

Manzoni's application of these ideas was not without problems. In his tragedy *Il Conte di Carmagnola* ('The Count of Carmagnola', 1820) Marco, a Venetian Senator, contrasts in a long monologue his devotion to his country and his love for his friend Carmagnola – after he has already decided to betray him. That inevitably weakens the dramatic impact of the speech, which sounds too much like crocodile tears. To avoid this kind of pitfall in his next tragedy Manzoni had to transform the dilemma of an individual like Marco, torn between two equally defensible and contingent choices, into the universal dilemma of the human condition, always hesitating between the reasons of the world and the precepts of God. In *Adelchi* (1822), the protagonist, son of Desiderio King of the Longobards, has to fight at his father's side in a war he believes to be unjust and bound to be lost; but the conflict between fealty and righteousness is already resolved, both in Adelchi's mind and from a superior viewpoint (shared, of course, only by God and by writers who choose a position of omniscience) which takes into account the whole course of events and their justification. *Il Conte di Carmagnola* and *Adelchi* were undoubtedly better than most contemporary tragedies and received Goethe's praise. Their style was more mature and their verse less stilted than in the *Inni sacri* or indeed most verse drama of the period, yet they were still remote from the spoken language. In moving from poetic monologue to dramatic dialogue Manzoni had come nearer the language of social communication. However, the fact that he did not wish his tragedies to be staged is an implicit admission of his failure to tackle the language problem successfully. Plans for a third tragedy, *Spartaco*, never came to fruition. The next step (after 1822) was to cease using verse altogether as a medium for imaginative literature and try prose fiction.

The novel

At the beginning of the nineteenth century Hegel could salute the novel as the modern bourgeois epic. In the more developed countries of Europe, like Britain and France, the rapid increase in education required by the Industrial Revolution went hand in hand with a rise in the number of novels written for the developing middle- and lower-class market. In Italy the novel market lagged behind, given the much lower levels of literacy. Whatever readership existed was satisfied by translators: native writers were in any case reluctant to write novels because of the low status of the genre. Historical novels were considered particularly objectionable, because they blurred the distinction between what was real and what was not and usurped some of the functions of history proper, which, from classical times to the Renaissance and beyond, had traditionally included fictitious 'reconstructions' of what historical figures were supposed to have said. Novels were the plague of youth, corrupting their morals. The fact that, in spite of these and other objections, they sold well was taken as evidence of their evil influence. The moral argument was nevertheless important because it broadened a controversy traditionally confined to literary *production* (conformity to accepted rules, formal features, admissible content) to include at least one important aspect of *consumption*, namely whether and under what conditions a work would prove acceptable to readers. Romantic apologists of the novel, including Manzoni, also took to the moral ground, granting their opponents' premise that novels affected their readers emotionally, but for very different reasons: novels could fulfil a socially useful moralising and ideologising function.

Manzoni tried to understand not only the needs of his actual and potential readership, but also the future directions in which it might develop. The fact that most people had no access to literature robbed a writer's work of much of what today would be called 'relevance' – what artists at the time saw in terms of social function, meaning and dignity. It was tempting to compensate for that loss by theorising the *de facto* separation between art and life as if it was *de jure*, and believing that art stood above and outside the flux of human reality, which it 'imitated' or reflected. Hence the main criterion for artistic appreciation was how truthful the reflection was. Literary beauty should be judged in terms of its historical truth and moral goodness. Manzoni, who accepted these ideas, left himself no other option than to believe that fiction was untrue, therefore morally wrong; and that future, and more mature, readers would reject historical novels. He began to mull over this question in an essay *Del romanzo storico e in genere dei componimenti misti di storia e d'invenzione* ('On the Historical Novel and in General on Works in which History is Mixed with Fiction') when he was still writing the first draft of *I promessi sposi*; and completed it probably in 1849 after the last rewriting and revision of his novel. This essay has often been seen only as a condemnation of the genre, when in fact it is also a very early specimen of *Rezeptiontheorie*, the branch, that is, of literary history dealing with the relationship between authors and their public.

The strength of Manzoni's religious and moral beliefs helped him to be an extremely perceptive observer of people and events, but ultimately prevented him from forming an accurate view of their historical context. His essays, on the Longobardic domination of Italy (*Discorso sopra alcuni punti della storia longobardica in Italia*, of which the final version appeared in 1847), on the French Revolution compared to the Italian 1859 uprising (*La rivoluzione francese del 1789 e la rivoluzione italiana del 1859*, 1860–9) and the atrocious 'trial' of a Milanese barber and his alleged accomplices accused of having caused the 1630 plague (*Storia della Colonna infame*, 1842), are notable mainly as evidence of his prejudiced ideas. The same can be said of *Osserva-zioni sulla morale cattolica* ('Observations on Catholic Morality', 1819), which otherwise marks a vital stage in his development as a lucid and persuasive prose-writer. In attempting to refute the *History of the Medieval Italian Republics* by the Swiss historian Jean-Charles-Léonard Simonde de Sismondi, in which the Catholic Church was criticised for its corrupting influence on Italian social and political life, Manzoni failed to see that he could not refute Sismondi merely by assuming what he should have attempted to prove: that Catholic morality is perfect and that all corruption comes from transgressing the moral code. That appears to be unassailably true only because it is tautological, given that morality is defined as embodying an ideal of perfection, and corruption as a transgression of the moral code. For Manzoni 'it is unnecessary to use any evidence to justify the Church: its doctrines are enough': in other words, the test of Catholic doctrine is theological and *a priori*, not historical. To support this proposition, however, he had to keep stressing the distinction between Religion, as a perfect moral system, and the Church, as an institution admittedly including fallible men; which was, of course, implicitly conceding Sismondi's point.

The ideological programme

Manzoni's many physical and psychological disabilities only strengthened his resolve to pour into writing, the only pursuit of which he modestly felt capable, all the intellectual energies and spiritual resources he could not devote to other tasks. Writing became his ideological, and in a sense his political, project, from his early poems to his mature work. Given that poetry must set itself Truth as its object (*Lettera sul Romanticismo al Marchese Cesare d'Azeglio*, 1823); that literature must be a branch of moral philosophy, and that any poetry not tending to a moral end was 'a plague, a vituperation, a calamity' (*Materiali estetici*, 1816–20); that moral questions must be subordinated to the teaching of the Gospel (*Della moralità delle opere tragiche*, 1845?), it follows that all literature must be subservient to the teaching of the Gospel. That a reasonably wealthy member of the upper class should undertake this project over a period of twenty years responded to a deeply felt belief that his class had a heavy responsibility in the moral guidance of the poorer strata of society, and a Christian duty to exercise it: what is now called paternalism.

Paternalism is undoubtedly preferable to exploitation, but that does not make it a forward-looking attitude. One of its components was the fear that people of Manzoni's social standing (indeed he had it himself, as can be argued from his treatment of crowds in *I promessi sposi*) had of the 'dangerous classes' (as the French called them), the rabble who in 1814 had killed Giuseppe Prina, the Finance Minister of the Italian Republic, a short distance from Manzoni's house, and had shown themselves capable of bloody uprisings in various parts of Europe throughout the 1820s and 1830s. An important component of the project was therefore the spreading of a message attributing the sufferings of the oppressed and exploited not to unjust social structures but to the sinful failings of individuals within them, and offering as a remedy to the various evils of society not economic re-structuring and the reform of institutions, which would have been against established interests, but the conversion of individual evildoers. Many authoritative voices (including Gino Capponi's) spoke against the education of the poorer classes, because it would give them the dangerous urge to better themselves. If the poor had to learn to read, they must be given books telling them they could improve their condition within the existing social system by listening to the advice of their betters, working hard, saving and staying away from political 'trouble'; where all this failed, they could count on Providence and Christian charity, which, in Manzoni's own words (*Morale cattolica* II, 5), 'orders the rich to give their surplus, without giving the poor the right to ask for it ... which would cause most serious harm'.

Manzoni's project may appear progressive and enlightened in the context of the largely post-feudal and pre-industrial Italy, where the notion of *popolo*, 'people', often did not include the working classes; the bourgeoisie was effectively hamstrung by economic underdevelopment and foreign domination; and many intellectuals denounced the evils of industrialism in the name of the mythical values of Italy's rural civilisation, making a virtue of the country's backwardness. But views such as his had already been impugned during the Enlightenment by Jacobin theorists, and were being widely refuted by 'socialist' thought (the word had been in use since 1827). After all, his age was one of intense and far-reaching social transformations culminating in the revolutions of 1848, the Communist Manifesto and the Paris Commune of 1871. Some younger contemporaries, like Carlo Pisacane, Carlo Cattaneo, Luigi Settembrini (who condemned the ideology of *I promessi sposi* in his lessons on the history of Italian literature), or Ippolito Nievo (see below, p. 441) were politically far more radical and long-sighted. One need not go far to demonstrate the ideological limitations of *I promessi sposi*; it is enough to compare it to its first version, which was never published in its author's lifetime.

From *Fermo e Lucia* to *I promessi sposi*

Manzoni began working on what was to become *I promessi sposi* (*The Betrothed*; henceforth *PS*) not long after returning from a second stay in Paris (1819–20). His attention was caught by the seventeenth-century *gride* (edicts) quoted in *Sul commercio de' commestibili e caro prezzo del vitto* ('On the Trade in Foodstuffs and the High Cost of Provisions', 1802) by the economist Melchiorre Gioia; and by one edict, in particular, concerning the prevention of lawful marriages. He thought, as he told his stepson Stefano Stampa years later, that a thwarted marriage 'would be a good subject for a novel, with the plague as a grand finale sorting everything out'. In the story, set in and near Milan in 1628–30, a betrothed couple are separated by the lust of the village squire, Don Rodrigo, who bets his cousin that he will seduce the girl (Lucia) and forbids the local priest (Don Abbondio) to marry them. When the young pair, protected by a good friar (Padre Cristoforo), seek refuge elsewhere, Rodrigo has Lucia abducted and the friar removed to a distant convent. But the abductor, the powerful Innominato, goes through a religious crisis, frees Lucia and is converted by Cardinal Federigo Borromeo. The reunion of the betrothed is further delayed by the plague, but they both survive it and finally find security and happiness, and a greater wisdom and maturity, through their experiences.

Manzoni had initially chosen as his title *Fermo e Lucia* (hereafter *FL*), the protagonists' original names, following the example of Scott (*Ivanhoe*), Richardson (*Pamela*), Bernardin de Saint-Pierre (*Paul et Virginie*) and Goethe (*Hermann und Dorothea*). However, he decided that Fermo Spolino (something like 'Firmin Shuttley') was too obvious a name for a silk weaver: he became Renzo Tramaglino, a less transparent allusion both to his trade (*trama* means 'weft') and to Lake Como where the story begins (the *tramaglio* is a net used by local fishermen). The crime-laden Conte del Sagrato became the Innominato ('Un-named'). Lucia Zarella was also renamed. Reading Rivola's biography (1656) of Cardinal Borromeo, Manzoni found the name Lucia Mantella among the first fourteen members of an Ursuline Convent founded by the cardinal in Cannobio in 1605: the slight change, to 'Mondella', added a symbolic association with the idea of purity (Latin *mundus*, 'pure').

Manzoni and his closest friends soon began such an extensive revision of *FL* that it became necessary to write a second version from scratch, which was published in three volumes in 1827 as *I promessi sposi*. Unlike *The Betrothed* in English (another Scott title, incidentally), or *Les Fiancés* in French, *two* words – 'promised spouses' – were used to refer to the couple, signifying the gap between the marriage promise and its fulfilment, eventually bridged by the grace of God, which helps the couple to overcome the harrowing experiences in between. The process of turning an 'untidy heap of paper' into a polished piece of work was also a process of self-censorship which, as Claudio Varese has convincingly shown, blunted the novel's radical and provocative edge. For instance, where *PS*, in describing the bread riots, paints a bleak picture of an irrational and violent mob, *FL* warns in the same context: 'Heaven forbid that anyone should aggressively blame for their ignorance or their fanatical resentment a class of people who never had education or leisure and could never earn bread by their labours.' Another area in which Manzoni exercised self-censorship was love. Lucia is far less idealised in *FL*: one can even begin to understand Don Rodrigo's infatuation with her. When she tries to dissuade Fermo from his violent intentions she 'nearly [throws] her arms around his neck': a very natural gesture towards a man who would have been her legal husband within the next hour or so, yet removed from *PS*. The corrections resulted in outstanding narrative and formal improvements in the first published version, which, after further fine linguistic tuning, became the masterpiece it is; but they also paved the way for a relentless process of ideologisation of the novel, mainly in a conservative and reactionary sense, well into the following century. As early as 1828 Father Cesari defined it as 'the most efficacious and fruitful Lenten sermon, compared to which the strongest sermons are like lukewarm water'.

The *questione della lingua*

Many of those who deny that *PS* was an ideological novel have no difficulty in accepting that it was a most powerful and successful propaganda instrument for a national language, an effective medium of practical spoken and written communication far beyond the needs of literary prose. The *questione della lingua*, which agitated Italian intellectuals from Dante down to Pasolini (see above, pp. 49, 181 etc.), had occupied Manzoni as early as 1806, when he wrote to Fauriel (9 February) that 'the state of Italy, fragmented, with widespread inertia and lack of education, has widened the gap between the spoken and the written language so much that the latter can almost be considered a dead language'. He immediately, and significantly, linked this fact to the moral inefficacy of a semi-dead literary language, noting that Parini's *Il giorno* had been no more effective in reforming society than Virgil's *Georgics* in reforming agriculture. In announcing his novel to Fauriel (3 November 1821), he made a perceptive and accurate analysis of the socio-linguistic differences between France, where writers used a language actually spoken and

understood throughout the nation, and Italy, where they used the literary form
of a minority regional language (Tuscan), on the standards of which there was
no agreement even among the few who understood it. This problem was closely
discussed in the second, and longer, of the two draft introductions to *FL*.

A possible practical solution for Manzoni might have been to use a language
grammatically identical to the literary language, and therefore understandable
to all its users, but lexically open to all Italian-based spoken languages and
Italianised dialects. But where could this language be found? If a writer
proceeded to invent it there was no guarantee that a hybrid so constructed
would be universally acceptable. It was therefore better to look for an existing
language, already endowed with sufficient cultural prestige, actually used by a
living community, and strive to have it accepted by all: the obvious choice was
Tuscan, more specifically, 'the language spoken and written in Florence'. In
mid-July 1827 Manzoni's large family travelled to Florence, where he began
the second-stage revision bringing the text closer to the Tuscan written and
spoken standard, with the help of local friends and, later on, of Emilia Luti, the
Florentine governess employed by his son-in-law Massimo D'Azeglio. The
final version was published between 1840 and 1842. Great effort was
expended on the illustrations, which were designed not only to give it popular
appeal but also, at a time when copyright laws were weak, to prevent others
from pirating it, in the mistaken belief that the original woodcuts could not be
copied (they could be, and were easily, by a lithographic process). Largely
because of the additional expense involved Manzoni made a financial loss of
some 40,000 lire (then about twenty times the yearly salary of a secondary
schoolteacher). The print run was meant to be 10,000 copies (best-seller level,
at the time) but it actually reached only 4,600. For the sake of comparison, the
good cultural journals and magazines of the day all had under 1000 subscribers.

The language question was not only one of the theoretical issues central to
the composition of the novel, but also one of its internal themes. Renzo's
education is also a linguistic education. Language is shown as a vehicle of
manipulation. The *gride* create the illusion that justice may be safeguarded by
legal formulae. Latin is used to obfuscate and repress, Spanish words enable
Chancellor Ferrer to reassure the supply Commissioner without being understood by the rioters. Highly placed characters show particular skill in using
language: the Prince in persuading his daughter Gertrude of her conventual
destiny, the Conte Zio and the Provincial of the Capuchin Order in skirmishing
about the fate of Padre Cristoforo (an admirable piece of dialogue in which
what is unsaid counts more than what is spoken). On a metalinguistic level the
novel begins with the Narrator's deliberate refusal to adopt an outdated model
of language. It offers nomenclatures that did not yet exist in any literary text
destined for mass consumption, such as the taxonomy of geographical features
at the opening of Chapter 1, or of the weeds in Renzo's vineyard in Chapter
33. The freshness of Manzoni's prose can best be appreciated in comparison

with the works of Carlo Varese, Giovan Battista Bazzoni, Vincenzo Lancetti or Francesco Domenico Guerrazzi, all of whom published in 1827 mediocre and today unreadable novels.

I promessi sposi marked one of the last stages in the long-standing *questione della lingua*. Granted that a common national language could not evolve in a situation of political and social division, economic backwardness and rampant illiteracy, many people strangely deduced from this premiss that those evils could be remedied by a concerted act of linguistic engineering, as if by putting the Italian language right Italian society could be put right too. Manzoni did, of course, perceive the priority of the social over the linguistic question, but even he maintained that it was possible, through linguistic propaganda and organised governmental and educational pressure, to nurture a small Florentine-speaking embryo into an Italian-speaking national body. He was right in believing that a viable national language had to have its roots in real, practical linguistic usage and not in dusty old books or even dustier Academies. But, of course, his choice of Florence as the cradle of the new language was based on the cultural prestige Florentine usage had acquired in the fourteenth century, not on its standing in the nineteenth, which among the majority of non-Tuscan speakers was actually negligible. As Isaia Graziadio Ascoli, the father of Italian linguistics, predicted as early as 1873, the Florentine solution was bound to fail, and the national language emerged out of the growing linguistic contribution of all Italian regions to the national culture, fostered by educational and social improvements, and, in the present century, the spread of the mass media. Yet, while Manzoni's linguistic engineering project failed, his novel was the greatest single contribution to the formation of a viable national language, the model for generations of educated Italians. That was because it paradoxically conformed more to Ascoli's eclectic view than to Manzoni's own normative position. After all it was not the work of a Florentine, but of a Milanese dialect speaker, whose second language was French, his third what he called *parlar finito* (a sort of Italianised Milanese), and his fourth a constantly evolving literary Italian, adapted almost day by day to its writer's cultural needs. The power, beauty, luminous perfection of the definitive version are just as much the result of all the previous cultural and linguistic influences as of the final Florentinisation process.

Room to dissent

Any piece of literature which, like *I promessi sposi*, raises a wealth of important issues would be extremely rewarding to read even if it was not full of delights which a few pages in a literary history cannot hope to reveal. Perhaps one of its lasting attractions is its satisfying interaction between simplicity and complexity. It has a simple plot, dealing with ordinary people, written in clear language. It carries a simple (some would say simplistic) message of faith in divine Providence. On the other hand it has a many-layered structure. Manzoni knew perfectly well the properties of the multiple framing device, used by Boccaccio (whose *Decameron* he had in mind in describing the plague); and the function and effect of pretending to be simply 'editor' of a manuscript, used by Cervantes, Defoe, Scott, Goethe and Foscolo. On the *outer frame* we glimpse the text by the (fictitious) seventeenth-century anonymous writer. The *inner frame* contains the story of the wise first reader of his manuscript, then re-writer of the story, whom we are asked to identify with the real Alessandro Manzoni but is in fact a character in a piece of fiction describing how he became the Narrator, and involving his son, his son's guinea-pigs, various friends, and 'twenty-five readers' whom he directs, cajoles, persuades, humours, allows to skip over boring bits, amuses with witty remarks, amazes with wise psychological insights, educates by his remarkable knowledge and understanding of history, inspires with his profound humanity. Inside this frame there is the *story* of the thwarted marriage of the *promessi sposi*, meshing from time to time with seventeenth-century *history*, particularly the plague and the Italian offshoots of the Thirty Years' War. As we open the novel we join the select group of readers Manzoni has implied. We are therefore drawn into the inner frame, becoming deeply involved in the task of comparing the original text with its much better re-writing, and the seventeenth-century historical background with the history of the Narrator's times and our own. Free to move between and outside the various narrative frames, we not only learn the stories, but also learn about their telling, and the implications of both. Manzoni thus created so much intellectual 'space' within the limited confines of the novel, further expanded by the twin published versions of the text, as to compensate for its own ideological conditioning (though that may not have been his conscious purpose). Ultimately dissenting readers owe him their freedom to dissent, for which they have not always been grateful.

In the context of the overall cultural backwardness of Italian intellectual life, disguised here and there by peaks of intellectual excellence whose influence was felt only in cultured circles, Manzoni's work had a liberating effect. Those who deny or minimise his ideological intent *because* his novel is a masterpiece, as well as those who declare it a masterpiece *in spite of* his ideology, are guilty of faulty logic and do him a disservice. Manzoni's project was demonstrably narrow and arguably deficient; but so was Leopardi's contention that human beings are necessarily unhappy. Only if one considers its full import (of which plenty more evidence is available in his writings and letters) in the context of the specific Italian situation for which it was designed (which may account for his novel's comparative neglect outside Italy) can one understand why his novel turned out to be so much more than mere propaganda, unlike those written during his lifetime and afterwards by many imitators who claimed to follow in his footsteps, as if that was easy or enough. His classicist poetry was an indictment of classicism. His tragedies polemically disregarded accepted rules and were influential in repealing them. His treatise on Catholic morals shunned the ornate rhetorical prose favoured by religious apologists. His *Inni sacri* were unconventional, to say the least. He was the first Italian to write a novel in a language which literate readers could enjoy, and he gave classicist literature a blow from which it never recovered. His realism, however moderate, was a source of inspiration for the *veristi* writers in the second half of the century. The outstanding value of his contribution to Italian culture can be fully appreciated without pretending, as far too many have done, that he was also the supreme repository of all social, political, moral and religious wisdom in nineteenth-century Italy. He would most certainly have disagreed, and not out of false modesty. The doubts he always felt (particularly at the end of his long life), the unresolved contradictions in his own thought, his attempts to overcome them through successive 'conversions', his sensitivity to other people's problems, prevented him from becoming smug and self-satisfied in his outwardly unshakeable beliefs. Whether one agrees with his conclusions or not, the intellectual rigour he applied to scrutinising his own motives and understanding those of others was rare in the Italian culture of his age, perhaps unique in imaginative writers; and was an undeniably positive fact in a society afflicted by empty verse-mongers, flatulent rhetors, superficial intellectuals and corrupt ideologists.

32

Other novelists and poets of the Risorgimento

Novelists

Manzoni's novel, a skilful blend of traditional values and new perspectives, pleased everybody, except a few ultra-conservatives and advanced radicals. Thus he could be the holy patron of traditionalists, and at the same time be claimed by some as the ideal forerunner of the new *veristi*, who, in the latter half of the century, inspired by French naturalism, aimed to make their fiction an even closer reflection of true life. Conservatives and innovators both acknowledged him as their master, in a controversy reproducing much of the theoretical weakness, and cultural and political pointlessness, of the classicism-versus-Romanticism battle. The real divide was between a literature which, in its forms and contents, was still a middle-class monopoly, and the largely oral culture of the illiterate or semi-literate masses which the educated minority did little to enfranchise and empower. The fact that many of the authors mentioned in this section (and others not mentioned) are hardly if ever read today is both a sign of their failure to anticipate the needs and aspirations of the new politically emancipated and educated readership which the Risorgimento would inevitably produce, and of their success in expressing the intellectual narrow-mindedness and political conservatism of their peers, who accorded them a fame which from our vantage point it would be simplistic to judge undeserved.

Many novelists tried to 'educate' the lower classes: for example, Giulio Carcano (1812–84), or the Jesuit Antonio Bresciani Borsa (1798–1862), who polemically followed not in Manzoni's but in Cesari's footsteps. Others continued to cultivate the historical novel, among them two of Manzoni's closest friends, Tommaso Grossi (1790–1853) and Massimo Taparelli, Marquess D'Azeglio (1798–1867), husband of Manzoni's first daughter Giulia, and President of the Council of Ministers in the Kingdom of Piedmont and Sardinia before the better-known Count Cavour. Grossi, warmly encouraged by Manzoni, wrote narrative poems (*La fuggitiva*, 'The Fugitive', first in Milanese dialect, then in Italian; *Ildegonda*, *I Lombardi alla prima crociata*, 'The Lombards on the First Crusade') and a novel, *Marco Visconti*. D'Azeglio's novels, among them *La disfida di Barletta* ('The Challenge at Barletta') and *Niccolò de' Lapi*, enjoyed a greater notoriety, though today he is perhaps better known as a memorialist. The passage from his posthumous autobiographical reminiscences *I miei ricordi*, where he tells how as a child he broke an arm while on a country walk with his father, and (at his bidding) kept quiet about it so as not to worry his nervous mother, was a favourite with school anthologies. Many of the main actors of the Risorgimento, such as Silvio Pellico, Federico Confalonieri, Gino Capponi, Luigi Settembrini, Carlo Bini and Giuseppe Cesare Abba, left memoirs which can still be read with interest. Pellico's memoirs (*Le mie prigioni*, 'My Prisons', 1832) were said 'to have harmed Austria more than a lost battle' because of their successful promotion of the aims of moderate Italian nationalism, particularly with foreign readers. Francesco Domenico Guerrazzi (1804–73) also shared his recollections with his readers, first in an autobiographical novel *Il buco nel muro* ('The Hole in the Wall'), then in the posthumous *Il secolo che muore* ('The Dying Century'), a searing indictment of post-unification Italian politics. Unlike Manzoni, Guerrazzi went on the barricades in 1848 and poured much revolutionary zeal into his fiction, but couched it in archaic and bombastic language. Thus his novels, such as *La battaglia di Benevento* ('The Battle of Benevento'), *L'assedio di Firenze* ('The Siege of Florence') and *Beatrice Cenci*, are rather reminiscent of modern heaters disguised as period log fireplaces: one does not know whether to deplore their phony style or their ineffectiveness.

While many of these writers followed Manzoni's example in choosing stories from the past in order to make their points about the present, others turned to their own time for inspiration. Giovanni Domenico Ruffini (1807–81), a friend and disciple of Mazzini, wrote in English *Lorenzo Benoni, or Passages in the Life of an Italian* and *Doctor Antonio* in order to popularise in Britain the cause of the Risorgimento patriots. Giuseppe Rovani (1818–74) wrote *Cento anni* ('One Hundred Years'), a fresco of Milanese society, as if it had been narrated by a ninety-year-old man, although this device is almost forgotten as the story goes on through twenty-six parts and over 1000 pages. The novel is uneven and occasionally weak, because it suffers from a lack of credible characterisation of the various famous characters who appear in it. It is, however, the first Italian example of the kind of extended novel which will be later called 'saga', pursuing the tendency towards increasingly larger tableaux initiated by Sir Walter Scott's *Waverley* cycle and Balzac's *Comédie humaine*. It is also one of the first Italian examples of serialised fiction.

Nievo

Ippolito Nievo (1831–61) visited Milan in 1857, soon after the publication of the first instalments of *Cento anni*: this may have inspired him to attempt something similar. The narrator of *Le confessioni di un italiano* ('Confessions of an Italian') is Carlo Altoviti, a Venetian gentleman who commits his memoirs to posterity in his eighty-third year of age. Nievo wrote and prepared the long novel for publication in only eight months, finishing it as the meeting between Cavour and Napoleon III at Plombières (1858) was laying the grounds for what Italian historians call the Second War of Independence (1859), followed by Garibaldi's expedition to Sicily (1860). Nievo took part in both, becoming one of the General's administrators. The old steamer *Ercole* which was bringing him from Palermo to Naples together with all the expedition's accounts – but fortunately without the manuscript of the novel – sank without trace on 6 or 7 March 1861, barely ten days before united Italy came officially into being (minus Venetia and Rome, still held respectively by the Austrians and the Pope). The novel was posthumously published in 1867, a year after the new Kingdom, allied with France and Prussia in the third war against Austria, had been soundly defeated because of top-brass incompetence, and the annexation of Venetia had been procured indirectly through the Prussian victory at Sadowa. Thus the atmosphere was not propitious to the reception of a novel spanning the history of Venetia and Italy from 1775 to the 'eve of the great defeat' of Piedmont by Austria at Novara (23 March 1849) which ended the first war of independence. To allay the suspicion that the book might contain or inspire political recriminations the word *italiano* in the title was replaced with *ottuagenario* (eighty-year-old) by reference to the narrator's age. The real author, however, was in his late twenties, and he managed to infuse his creation with a youthful vigour which makes it a most interesting piece of fiction, and one of the best Italian novels ever written. It contains the only really credible female character to emerge from the literature of this period, compared to whom Manzoni's Lucia is, in the words of her own parish priest (chapter 38), 'this Miss Still-Waters-Run-Deep, this holier-than-thou girl, this little plaster Our-Lady-of-Dolours who would make you feel a sinner if you didn't trust her.'

'La Pisana', thus called from the name of her maternal grandmother's family, is the daughter of the Count and Countess of Fratta who have adopted Carlo, born of the mésalliance of the Countess's sister with a gentleman from Torcello. Pisana is the only true love of Carlo's life, from his childhood mostly spent in the cavernous kitchen of Fratta castle, through his peregrinations across Italy, to his imprisonment in Naples and his final exile in London. Her sudden appearances brighten Carlo's existence like flashes of light. With astonishing maturity Nievo oversteps the romantic fad for unrequited and misunderstood love. What we find in the novel is not sentimental posturing but an emotion genuinely arising out of shared hopes and aspirations. Carlo and Pisana's love is spontaneous, sincere, untainted by hypocrisy, free from obligations and conditions of any sort, undemanding, unhoped-for. Pisana's character, therefore, cannot be bound by conventional morality but must be capable of both indifference and tenderness, fickleness and unpredictable devotion, chastity and impurity, violent and opposed emotions. After twenty-three long chapters, full of daring adventures, vivid descriptions and deep reflections, and peopled with a variety of principal characters and colourful personages reflecting life in Italy through three generations, Pisana dies; but the 'correspondence of amorous feelings' between the protagonists (to use Foscolo's words in *Dei sepolcri*) ensures her survival in Carlo's and in the readers' memory.

Being the only Italian romantic novel that could stand up to *I promessi sposi*, *Le confessioni* suffered unjustly from the comparison. The first ten chapters, describing Carlo's childhood in the castle and his adolescence in Venice, were often seen as the pleasing work of a *manzoniano*, schooled in the fine humour, delicate touch, subtle moralism and narrative style of his great model, down to the quotation in the original language of ancient statutes and laws of the Venetian Republic. These chapters were often reprinted separately, as if they were an autonomous novel, spoiled by the irrelevance or lack of appeal of the remaining thirteen chapters, which Nievo might have polished had he lived longer. This view misrepresents both the status of the manuscript, fully revised and ready for the press, and the structure of the novel. The difference between the two parts is not due to authorial neglect but to a deliberate and significant contrast between childhood memories, clustered around colourful images and powerful impressions without any precise chronology, like a mythical golden age outside time, and the more mature recollections of the adult Carlo, whose life unfolds dynamically alongside the main events of Italian history. The content of the second half was also less palatable, not only because, after the defeats of Lissa and Custoza, the Italian readership was rather disillusioned with Risorgimento myths, but also because Nievo's ideology was uncomfortably radical, far removed from Manzoni's soothingly providential view of events.

The novel was unpopular also because it reflected Nievo's belief (better developed in his posthumous political writings) that the new Italy could not be made simply by replacing one government with another, without restructuring society to bring justice and better living conditions not only to the social class to which most readers belonged but to all, including the peasantry which had been hitherto rather neglected by political theorists. 'One cannot begin to improve the condition of the peasants as if they were a breed of horse', he wrote in the short story *La nostra famiglia di campagna* ('Our Country Family', 1855). The upper classes could not redeem the lower classes by shedding their blood in wars and various conspiracies: they should first of all redeem them through justice and education – in that order, because one cannot teach people who are kept in hunger and need by economic exploitation. These ideas were confirmed by Nievo's experience as a member of Garibaldi's expedition, which he reported in his letters to his cousin Bice Melzi d'Eril. He found in Sicily a primitive and cruel society, with an archaic economy based on barter, where peasants and shepherds went around dressed in animal skins, and those who had become outlaws in order to survive joined Garibaldi's Thousand because they naïvely believed he would free them from their oppressive landlords. But Garibaldi could not dispense with the existing ruling class, whose support he needed to consolidate his victory. In fact when peasants rose in Bronte (Catania), killing some landowners and their families and invading the land granted to Nelson in 1799 and still owned by his absentee heirs, Garibaldi's lieutenant, Nino Bixio, had their leaders lined up against a wall and shot. Had Nievo lived a few more years he would have seen the peasant revolt in southern Italy ferociously repressed by the new government, with more casualties than in all the wars of independence, and episodes of unspeakable savagery on both sides.

Political literature and literary criticism

Insofar as it fed on and fostered the ideals of national liberty and independence, the literature of Romanticism coincided in Italy with the literature of the Risorgimento; even in its major works of imagination, such as Foscolo's *Sepolcri*, Leopardi's *Canti* and Manzoni's *Promessi sposi*, it displayed social and political preoccupations that were peculiar to the historical situation of the country. In addition, however, there was in Italy a vast political production which can only be mentioned here, and yet has considerable literary merits. In his writings (collected in the one-hundred-volume National Edition) Giuseppe Mazzini (1805–72), the Genoese founder of the *Giovine Italia* (1831) and apostle of the Risorgimento, developed a religious, quasi missionary, conception of literature as the embodiment in time of universal values (such as country, freedom, destiny) and an indispensable vehicle for the civil and political education of the people – a concept that was fundamental in forming such politically committed critics as Carlo Tenca (1816–83). Carlo Cattaneo (1801–69), a Milanese economist, journalist and historian, brought to maturity the distinctly secular tradition of Lombard Enlightenment. His rational and lucid analysis of Italian affairs provided a healthy antidote to Mazzini's rhetorical manners. Among his many achievements is the founding of *Il Politecnico* (1839–44, restarted in 1860), a monthly magazine 'of studies applied to culture and social prosperity', which was to become a source of strength and inspiration for all progressive intellectuals in the twentieth, as well as the nineteenth, century in Italy (see p. 543). The Piedmontese priest Vincenzo Gioberti (1801–52) gave expression to the hopes of educated Catholics by attempting to reconcile the patriots' progressive aspirations with the notion of the supremacy of the Italian papacy. His *Del primato morale e civile degl'Italiani* ('Of the moral and civil primacy of the Italians', Brussels 1843) affirms the historical superiority of Italians, calling for the expulsion of all foreign powers from the peninsula and the establishment of a federation of Italian free states presided over by the Roman Pontiff.

As the first writer who evaluated literature by specifically relating it to the times and places in which it was produced, Ugo Foscolo was the true initiator of Romantic literary criticism and aesthetics in Italy. However, it was Francesco De Sanctis (1817–83) who, as Italy achieved unity and independence, gave her an organic and enduring system of aesthetics. A professor of literature from the Naples region, De Sanctis was actively involved in politics as Minister of Education in the first Italian government and for two more periods in the 1870s. His masterpiece, and the masterpiece of Italian Idealism, was his *Storia della letteratura italiana* ('History of Italian Literature', 1870–1), which he conceived as a history of the 'Italian spirit' starting with the Sicilian School in the Duecento and culminating in the present with the achievement of national unity. The idea of nationhood is for him the fundamental value, and literature is the mirror that reflects it across the ages. Thus, despite his original idea of a transcendent 'form' in which the traditionally separate concepts of form and content are synthesised, De Sanctis identified the autonomy of the literary work with the exemplarity of its moral discourse. As we will see, this position was to have enormous influence later on both idealist (Croce) and Marxist (Gramsci) aesthetics in Italy.

'Popular' poetry

The peasant revolt, significantly dubbed *brigantaggio* in official histories, was practically ignored by canonic literature which, on the whole, tended to reflect the concerns of the Risorgimento establishment, hovering between the need for some form of social and economic change, and the fear that things might get out of hand if the downtrodden masses really claimed their rights. Aleardo Aleardi (1812–78) and Giovanni Prati (1815–84), who lived long enough to see Rome become the capital of the united Kingdom, were appointed members of Senate not only for their fashionable languid Romanticism but also because they had been effective interpreters of this fear. Aleardi's *Per un giuoco di palla nella valle di Fumane* ('A Ball Game in Fumane Valley') begins by commemorating the onetime peaceful concord between the lord in his manor and the peasant at his gate, and closes on a vision of bloody peasant revolt, possibly a memory of the 1849 uprisings said to have been stirred up by the Austrians. The Austrians were a convenient scapegoat for all political evils, but in this case they were not uninvolved: they hoped that the fear of peasant anarchy would induce the landowning class to remain faithful to their traditional protector, the Imperial and Royal Majesty in Vienna. Many landowners, on the contrary, favoured the Kingdom of Piedmont-Sardinia because they knew it to be even more conservative than Austria, and hoped that by shifting their allegiance from a far-away power, known to have serious problems in central Europe, to a nearby kingdom which needed their support, they would more effectively safeguard their interests. The works of Claude-Frédéric Bastiat, a French free-trader who defended the notion of private property against the attacks of Proudhon, inspired Aleardi to write an ode against Communism (*Il comunismo e Federico Bastiat*), seriously putting forward the view that the wretchedness of the lower orders, however pitiful, was 'irremissibile' (unalterable) because it had been sanctioned by God. Prati was even more successful than Aleardi in becoming the semi-official poet of the new Italian court, which he followed in its moves from Turin to Florence (1865) and then Rome (1871). He achieved notoriety fairly early in life with a poem, *Edmenegarda* (1841), which caused scandal because it was a transparent description of the adultery of a well-known lady, whose lover had then deserted her; but it was otherwise quite traditional in language and outlook. A year later he published *Canti lirici* and *Canti per il popolo*, whose reactionary message was satirised by Nievo (*Versi*, 1854):

> Listen, o nations,
> to an arcane spell.
> The poor are happy,
> the rich in hell.
> Blessed be the wretches
> who skimp and suffer
> to fill the bellies
> of their bloodsuckers.

Perhaps the only fruitful aspects of Prati's inability to understand the real world around him was his choice, as the subject of his late poetry, of the wonderland revealed to him by a kind fairy, Azzarelina, who helps him to become so small as to move freely, meeting insects and small animals amongst the grass and the flowers (*Iside*, 1878). Neither Prati nor Aleardi was able to produce anything comparable to what was written beyond the Alps by their near-contemporaries Heine, Uhland, Lamartine, Hugo, Vigny, Musset, Gérard de Nerval, Baudelaire, to mention but a few. They transported to Italy a few themes of European poetry that would be acceptable to their public. They did not, therefore, 'Europeanise' Italian literature, but provincialised European literature, and they had a visible influence on the least cosmopolitan but most innovative poet of the following generation, Giovanni Pascoli (see below, pp. 476-9).

It was not impossible, however, to write truly 'popular' verse, capable of giving pleasure even to the less literate members of society. Many patriotic poems were on everybody's lips: Goffredo Mameli's *Inno di Garibaldi* still survives as the official anthem of the Italian republic. Giuseppe Giusti (1809-50), one of Manzoni's Tuscan friends, wrote political satire based not on abstract moral figments but on contemporary events. His *Scherzi* ('Jests'), at first circulated in eagerly sought-after manuscript copies and later just as eagerly pirated all over Italy, ridiculed and pilloried the miserable little tyrants placed by Austria on the tottering thrones of the minor Italian states, together with the police informers, the reactionary noblemen ready to kowtow to their Imperial and Royal Majesties, the turncoats. Giusti's satire was mostly concerned with what was wrong – on which everybody agreed – and did not aim to suggest solutions, about which no agreement would have been possible: that is perhaps why it was so successful. His poems, written in simple language, with catchy rhythms, exude common sense and basic honest morality. However, the very virtues that made them so popular when they were written dated them and made them much less appealing to subsequent generations.

Some of the best literature of the Romantic period (and of other periods) was written in a dialect and would deserve more than a marginal mention in a history necessarily focussing on works written in Italian, and (in this chapter) on the concerted effort by Manzoni and others to hasten the development and diffusion of a national language across all dialect boundaries as an instrument of cultural and political unification. Dialect poets, however popular in their own town or region, could rarely hope to achieve fame and reputation outside it where their language might prove incomprehensible. Yet they had a great advantage over mainstream poets: they were free from the shackles of the classicist literary tradition allowing in verse only those concepts which could be expressed through a disused lexicon; and, writing in their spoken language, they could break through the thickets of metaphors hedging such topics as sexual love, ordinary everyday acts and objects, 'unpoetic' images and ideas (see above, p. 408). Their language had great stylistic homogeneity and did not suffer from the main fault of Italian versifiers, who often mixed in the same line archaic words and colloquialisms. Carlo Porta (1775-1821), another of Manzoni's friends, wrote in Milanese dialect not merely biting satire (see above, p. 409), but also poems reaching the kind of emotional depth and range (*La Ninetta del Verzee* – 'Ninetta of the vegetable market'; *Lament del Marchionn di gamb avert* – 'Lament of bow-legged Mark') that one finds only rarely even in Italian or European literature of later periods. He deserves to be rated among the great European Romantic poets. Porta's verse had a deep influence on Giuseppe Gioachino Belli (1791-1863) who came to know it during a visit to Milan in 1827, and was inspired by it to write over 2000 sonnets in Roman dialect giving fascinating insights into popular life in the Rome of the Popes.

Tommaseo

Niccolò Tommaseo (1802-74) is mainly remembered today for his monumental dictionaries *Nuovo Dizionario de' sinonimi* (1830) and *Dizionario della lingua italiana* (1858-79, with Bernardo Bellini, completed by Giuseppe Meini) which are still useful tools for the study of pre-twentieth-century Italian; and still of interest are his studies on Dante's *Divina Commedia* and his collections of popular poems and songs (*Canti toscani, corsi, illirici, greci*, 1841-2). Like Foscolo, he was born in a former Venetian territory (Sibenik, in Dalmatia), received a good classical education and was very bright, proud, touchy, unrefined, unappealing and oversexed. Unlike Foscolo, he had an unquestioning religious faith with which his libido was constantly in conflict. He documented every phase of the struggle in his personal journal (*Diario intimo*, posthumously published in 1938), where he also obsessively recorded the names of the people he saw, the titles of the books he read, what he ate, when and how much (from fifty to sixty-seven mouthfuls of food), how long he chewed it, how frequently he washed behind his ears or had his toenails cut. When *Antologia* was suppressed in 1833, allegedly because of one of his articles, Tommaseo went to France, where he published political writings and a book of poems, *Confessioni* (1836), whose finicky linguistic elaboration, of which later poets were to be mindful, somewhat stunts their emotional impact. His real 'confessions', the kind where baring one's soul comes, as in Rousseau, perilously close to exhibitionism, are found in the novel *Fede e bellezza* ('Faith and Beauty', 1840), which Manzoni wittily defined 'half carnival, half Lent' because of its peculiar mixture of eroticism and religious repression. Giovanni, the protagonist of the novel, an obvious projection of its author with all his frustrations, hang-ups and (in today's parlance) sexist ideas, meets in France Maria, who, in spite of being a 'fallen woman', has qualities that make her worthy of his love. They narrate to each other their life stories and help each other to overcome temptations, mostly Giovanni's (he is obsessed by women). He challenges a Frenchman who had said disparaging things about Italy, hoping to avenge his country's honour through his own likely death in the ensuing duel, with scant sense of responsibility towards Maria whom he has just married. But he only manages to get himself seriously wounded. Maria nurses him back to health and dies of TB: a couple of *promessi sposi* of sorts, then, but how different from Manzoni's. To begin with, Tommaseo's attempt to achieve a simple and incisive language is painfully overdone. Setting out emotions on a page, choosing his words carefully with true lexicographer's fastidiousness, almost as if he could best describe the psychology of his characters through the study of imaginary textual variants, must have seemed to him a way of purging his own passions and distancing himself from them. His characters all speak as if they were reading a sixteenth-century translation from Latin, a style unsuited to the ordinariness of the story and to the many descriptions of the women by whom Giovanni is constantly attracted, which he jots down in his journal and (unbelievably) inflicts on Maria, discussing with her how he could improve them: ' "Her visage was like a flower in bud" ... What do you think?' ' "In bud" sounds awkward.' 'Perhaps "just about to blossom".' 'Perhaps.' 'Oh, but I've got "blossom" a bit further on ...'.

For all its festering, repressed eroticism *Fede e bellezza* has many fascinating pointers to the fiction of more liberated times yet to come. It is perhaps the first Italian example of the middle-class novel, without heroes or adventures. It has an untidy but complex structure combining autobiography, journal, letter-writing, and framing devices such as the 'story within the story'. Its almost morbid interest in psychology, the reciprocal titillation of religion and eroticism, spiced with the infringement of taboos (talking about other women to one's beloved or even thinking of them during love-making; imagining one's lover as a sibling with whom to enjoy a near-incestuous pleasure; making love to a sick woman; seducing a celibate), the theme of the redemption of the fallen woman and her death through consumption, will all be dear to future generations. One finds interesting anticipations also in Tommaseo's later poems, particularly those written after the fall of the Venetian republic in 1848–9, when the author (who had taken part in its foundation and defence) was obliged to escape to Corfu. They are inspired by the amazing discoveries of contemporary astronomers and imbued with the mystical awe of cosmic infinity which had already fired Leopardi's imagination; but, unlike Leopardi's *canti*, they express an unwavering certainty that everything in nature operates according to the will of God. For Tommaseo (who wrote a paper opposing Darwin's theories) science must be illuminated by faith. Tommaseo helps one to understand how religion, which prompted Manzoni to expunge sex from his novel, could become one of the main ingredients of eroticism in Catholic-inspired narrative, from Fogazzaro to Bacchelli and Piovene; how the questions put to the moon by Leopardi's wandering shepherd expanded into Pascoli's cosmic visions; how the neat and restrained descriptions of Romantic narrators turned into the morbid and flamboyant pictures on D'Annunzio's easel.

33

Opera since 1800

David Kimbell

Romantic opera

During the Risorgimento opera played a more central part in national life than at any time before or since. When Felice Romani described Donizetti as 'a patriot of the intellect and the imagination' and when Carducci exclaimed of Verdi's early operas, 'Oh songs unforgettable and sacred to anyone born before the '48 [the 1848 risings]!', they were paying the tribute of several generations to a whole repertory of Italian opera from Rossini to Verdi. From the theatre which was its proper home this music overflowed into the streets (ground out on barrel-organs), into the divine service (as organ voluntaries), into soirées, receptions and other social gatherings, grand or modest. It became a kind of folk music, through which people – as long as they were not completely isolated from civic life – could express themselves, and to which they turned for consolation or inspiration in times of crisis.

More than at any time since the late seventeenth century, opera owed this esteem almost entirely to the music, scarcely at all to the poetry. For fifty years the craft of writing words for opera had been in decline. There is a barbed observation in Mme de Staël's essay on translation to the effect that listening to the words of Italian opera 'for five hours every day must necessarily make the nation's intellect obtuse for want of exercise'. But Manzoni was to define Italian Romanticism as a cultural movement that aspired to take 'the useful as its aim, the true as its subject, the interesting as its means'; and Mazzini in his *Filosofia della musica* was to urge composers to involve themselves in the progress of civilisation and become 'its spirit, its soul, its sacred perfume'. In an age whose artistic and intellectual leaders were thus preoccupied with serious matters, an inane opera would hardly do.

The Roman librettist Jacopo Ferretti, lecturing to the Accademia Tiberina in 1834, expressed his confidence that matters were improving. Between about 1780 and about 1810 a troop of mediocrities had, he felt, come close to 'extinguishing the divine fire lit by Metastasio'; but now *castrati* had disappeared from the opera house, the scenographer was learning to take instruction from the poet, new Romantic and liberal ideals were beginning to leave their mark. Amelioration was not achieved without difficulty, however. Traditionally opera houses had been regarded as adjuncts of the ruling dynasty or government; and this perception came increasingly into conflict with what librettists and composers really wanted to write about, making the Romantic period a critical one in the practice of theatre censorship. While working on *I Puritani*, an opera composed for Paris, Bellini wrote an ironic commendation of it to a Neapolitan friend, remarking that it would be ideal for production in Naples 'since it contains no religion, no nefarious love affairs, no politics whatsoever'. But it was precisely the attempt to enlarge or redirect the ethical and social thrust of opera into such areas that, for Bellini and his more serious-minded contemporaries, was the critical issue.

The translation controversy and the classic-versus-Romantic controversy that in large part stemmed from it (see above, pp. 401–2) suggested a new repertory of operatic subjects. Briskly on the heels of Mme de Staël's essay, Rossini produced the first Italian 'Shakespeare opera', *Otello* (Naples, 1816). (One puts the term in inverted commas because its indebtedness to the English original is slight; the full inspirational potential of Shakespeare, or indeed of any other great dramatist working in a different tradition, was revealed only by Verdi.) Another Rossini opera, *La donna del lago* ('The Lady of the Lake', Naples, 1819) anticipated the enthusiasm for Sir Walter Scott which was to climax in the late 1820s. His historical romances were attractive both for their pictur-esque qualities (they exerted a profound influence on operatic scenography) and for the extreme emotional and ethical juxtapositions which they facilitated: the confrontation of chivalry and barbarism; the 'superimposition of sensational-ism on Alfierian nobility'. 'Gothic horror', which few of the better Italian poets much cared for, was introduced into opera by Gaetano Rossi and found itself thoroughly at home there. Dreams, nightmares and visions made excellent set-pieces; a condition of emotional or psychological derangement seemed to suit opera singers well. Two of the foundation stones of Romantic melodrama, the great ensemble finales and the tragic close – the 'tableau of terror' as Romani called it – depended upon the quenching of reason by passion.

If Rossini opened up a new range of subjects in fashionable taste, it was not until Vincenzo Bellini (1801–35) that a musical language evolved which was really in tune with their tragic and violent atmosphere. Casting off completely any Rossinian elements of graceful and sparkling 'play', Bellini adopted a style of *cantabile* lyricism which in its simplicity and directness was redolent of popular song (of which he was something of a connoisseur), but enormously intensified by the burden of dissonant appoggiaturas which it so often carried. Above all Bellini's relationship with his librettist, Felice Romani (1788–1865), was distinguished by what contemporaries liked to describe as his 'philoso-phical' fidelity to the poetry. An unexpected tribute comes from Wagner, who declared Bellini to be 'one of my predilections: his music is all heart, closely, intimately linked with the words.' Romani remarked on the new qualities he and Bellini demanded of performers: 'in this opera [*La straniera*, Milan, 1828] it is not just a matter of singing, it is a matter of passion, of soul, of imagination; here is love in all its transports, sorrow with all its sighs, mis-chance in all its pallor.'

In the works of the young Giuseppe Verdi (1813–1901) all the ingredients of Italian Romanticism come together, directed by an imagination of rare boldness and an intense seriousness matching Manzoni's or Mazzini's own. *Macbeth* (Florence, 1847) even finds room for those elements of the 'fantastic' which generally played small part in the Italian Romantic movement. But above all Verdi was a social composer: social in the superficial sense that his idea of a successful opera was an opera well performed to enthusiastic audiences in packed theatres throughout Italy; social in the creative sense that his operas seriously engage with the question of how people live together in society. Verdi was obsessively fascinated by the family, especially by fathers and daughters; and he liked to set these familial relationships in a vividly evoked community, which, in his early works up to and including *La battaglia di Legnano* ('The Battle of Legnano', Rome, 1849), often expressed itself in a thrillingly aspirational or hortatory style with 'Risorgimental' overtones.

After the triumph of his third opera *Nabucco* (Milan, 1842), Verdi found himself, particularly through his association with the Maffei salon, in the thick of Milanese cultural life. He enjoyed friendships with leading men of letters in the Lombard capital, particularly with two translators, Andrea Maffei himself (translator of, besides much else, the dramatic works of Schiller), and Giulio Carcano (translator of Shakespeare). Stimulated by them, he read widely in the dramatic literature of Western Europe, searching out the startling confrontations and idiosyncratic characters on which his melodramatic imagination thrived. Verdi far surpassed his predecessors in his ideal of fidelity to his literary models, not as a sterile gesture of piety, but because his imagination took fire so directly from the works he read and because he found in them theatrical and poetic qualities that helped him give a unique *tinta* to each of his own operas.

The musical design of a Romantic 'Melodrama' (to use the preferred generic term) depended upon a scheme that came to be known as the 'Code Rossini'. A scene whose principal function was, say, the presentation of the prima donna in a *cavatina* would normally comprise an instrumental prelude (to evoke the atmosphere), a recitative (to explain the situation), a *cantabile* (a slow reflective aria), a linking passage (during which some motive would be supplied for a change of mood), and a *cabaletta* (a fast brilliant aria, sung twice). In ensemble scenes a number of additional movements tended to accrue round this basic framework, and of course, for dramatic purposes, elements of it could be omitted or fused together. Both musically (because of its variety) and theatrically (because of the thrilling momentum it gradually built up) the 'Code Rossini' recommended itself to composers, performers and audiences alike. Established at about the time of the Restoration, it wore well, and was still the basis for the great majority of numbers in Verdi's *Il trovatore* (1851) and *La traviata* (1853).

The long-established link between poetic metre and musical form made even so bold an innovator as Verdi curiously cautious in some respects. In principle his quest for unconventional plots was matched by a desire to create new formal structures, and while at work on *Il trovatore* he speculated about an operatic ideal 'in which there were neither cavatinas, nor duets, nor trios, nor choruses ... and in which the whole opera was (if I might express it this way) one single piece'. In practice his powers of musical invention were as deeply beholden to the structural qualities of a libretto as to its qualities of plot and characterisation. Recitative continued to be written in *versi a selva* (an irregular succession of *settenari* and *endecasillabi* generally without rhyme), aria and ensemble texts in the relatively small range of metres inherited from the eighteenth century. However, Manzoni's choral dramas had given a new popularity, and a new emotional incandescence, to such relatively under-used metres as the *decasillabo* and the *dodecasillabo* (the *senario doppio*), a quality that proved stimulating when transferred to the choral scenes of opera ('Va pensiero, sull' ali dorate', 'O Signore dal tetto natio', for example). Altogether 'parisyllabic' verse found a more conspicuous place in romantic opera: its more rigid pattern of stress and articulation was well calculated to support the vehement rhythmic energy of the new lyrical style of Bellini, Donizetti and Verdi.

Opera since unification

During the 1860s, as Verdi led Italian opera to the supreme achievements of *Don Carlos* (Paris, 1867) and *Aida* (Cairo, 1871), a younger generation was emerging whose attitude to Verdi, initially at least, was ambiguous. Of these *scapigliati* (see below, p. 460), Arrigo Boito (1842–1918) – cosmopolitan intellectual; poet, composer and critic; lapsed Wagnerian and ultimately Verdi's most noble-minded collaborator – was, as far as opera is concerned, the important figure. And *Mefistofele* (original version Milan, 1868; revised version Bologna, 1875), for which, in the approved Wagnerian style, Boito wrote both words and music, is the work on which his early reputation was made. For high-mindedness and sheer vaulting ambition the opera has no parallels in nineteenth-century Italy: begun when Boito was barely out of his teens, it aspired to recreate the whole vast panorama of both parts of Goethe's *Faust*. In its original version it discarded the formal conventions of traditional opera with polemical zest, ignoring all Goethe's cues for song, except the tomcat's song from the *Hexenküche* scene, the model for Mefistofele's, 'Ecco il mondo / vuoto e tondo'. The preface to the printed score and libretto emphasised the importance of its metrical innovations, and Boito (who as a music critic had often deplored the rhythmic poverty of nineteenth-century Italian music) does indeed introduce to opera an unprecedented range and flexibility of metre. In the hands of librettists like Giuseppe Giacosa and Luigi Illica this quality became a standard requisite, and was certainly one of the enabling sources of Puccini's incomparably lissom *cantabile*. Finally, *Mefistofele* provided the most comprehensive demonstration of the *scapigliato* fascination with evil, perceived as 'the embodiment of the everlasting "No!" addressed to the True, the Beautiful, the Good'. The Mephistophelian villain returns in later Boito libretti, in Ponchielli's *La Gioconda* and in Verdi's *Otello*.

The phenomenon of Wagnerism (the first Wagner production in Italy was that of *Lohengrin* at Bologna in 1875), and the turning away of the younger generation of Italian composers from the native traditions of opera saddened Verdi in the 1870s, and Boito, the very embodiment of cosmopolitan iconoclasm, became something of a *bête noire* to him. Ironically the three operas *Simon Boccanegra II* (Milan, 1881), *Otello* (Milan, 1887) and *Falstaff* (Milan, 1893), in which a mellower Boito served as Verdi's librettist and which survive as his own finest monument, are supreme embodiments of operatic *italianità*.

The *italianità* takes very different forms in each. But as an artistic idea it surely finds its most glorious vindication in *Falstaff*. The composer insisted that this, his last opera, was 'not an *opera buffa* but a depiction of character', primarily of Falstaff himself, a much-loved example of Shakespeare's genius for what Verdi liked to call 'inventing truth'. Because of this interest in character, Boito's libretto, the most brilliant of all operatic adaptations of Shakespeare, simplifies the farcical plot of *The Merry Wives of Windsor* while at the same time drawing on *Henry IV*, Parts I and II, for many of its richly human details. Nevertheless, in everything he said and wrote about *Falstaff*, it is the 'Latin spirit', not the Englishness, that Boito consistently emphasises; and he packs his text with Boccaccian echoes (the refrain in the love music, for example), with archaic and recondite vocabulary, and with a scintillating virtuosity of metrical contrivance designed to proclaim that Latin spirit. The text of the opera's one set aria, Fenton's 'Nel canto estasiato', is a Petrarchan sonnet. Verdi's music, too, for all its manifest originality and ostensible strangeness, embodies the values of traditional Italian opera. Song is supreme, and the vocal melodies arise from the heightened declamation of poetry; the emotions are human, elemental and universal; the freedom of form and the virtuosity of orchestration may be unprecedented in Verdi's work, but their unmistakable aim remains clarity of design and luminosity of sound.

Before the end of Verdi's career another literary movement left its mark on opera. *Cavalleria rusticana*, by Pietro Mascagni (1863–1945), a sensational triumph at its Roman première in 1890, was ostensibly modelled on one of Verga's Sicilian short stories. It created a vogue for what is commonly called operatic *verismo*, though in truth it has little enough in common with the real article (see below, pp. 463ff.). Its picturesque idealisation of Sicilian peasant life is as close to the pastoral convention as to Verga; and Mascagni's music, far from being understated or informal or 'lifelike' (whatever that may mean in an operatic context) reasserts the values of old-fashioned aria-based melodrama with a brazenness that is almost operetta-like. Rural *verismo* is also attempted in *I pagliacci* (Milan, 1892) by Ruggiero Leoncavallo (1857–1919); and several composers, most notoriously Umberto Giordano (1867–1948) in

Mala vita (Rome, 1892), followed the French naturalists in trying to transplant opera to the milieu of the urban proletariat, usually in Naples.

The element of operatic *verismo* that had the most interesting musical consequences was its concern with the setting or ambience in which the drama took place; it encouraged the habit of what we might describe as musical documentation (anticipated in Verdi's *Aida*), for composers sought to evoke these settings not only as vividly, but also as authentically as possible. Giacomo Puccini (1858–1924) was the supreme exponent of this *ambientismo*, taking enormous trouble to make the setting an integral part of his opera, in some cases almost a character in it, like the river in *Il tabarro*. He made field trips to inhale the appropriate atmosphere (*Suor Angelica*); studied the available printed sources of unfamiliar musical worlds (*La fanciulla del West*; *Turandot*); even filled his ears with the sounds of a language of which he didn't understand a word (*Madama Butterfly*).

But in general, though the 'disgusting realism' of *La Bohème* appalled an old idealist critic like Eduard Hanslick, and although Puccini certainly was not shy of squalor and brutality, the term *verismo* sits uncomfortably on art of such exquisite and languorous refinement. Puccini was rather a decadent: and the motor force that inspired his work was what he frankly described as his 'Neronic instinct'. Much of the substance of his scores is taken up with the celebration of suffering; the celebration of the senses is not less important. The quintessence of Puccini is to be found in 'E lucevan le stelle', the aria sung by the condemned Cavaradossi in Act III of *Tosca*, a recollection of an erotic encounter with Tosca which evokes in turn memories of sight, hearing, smell, taste and touch. What is particularly telling is that the text of this aria was written at Puccini's insistence, to replace an idealistic 'Farewell to Life and Art' which he found impossible to compose (though the elderly Verdi had thought it deeply moving).

The tawdriness of so many of Puccini's chosen subjects, the apparent lack of spirituality in his treatment of them, the sadism that breaks out in so many scenes, were qualities which, for most listeners, were more than compensated for by his prodigious musical and theatrical gifts; perhaps they were even 'redeemed' by his genius for suggesting the existence of 'grandi dolori in piccole anime' ('great sufferings in little souls'). But they were an affront to the aspirations of the emergent *generazione dell'ottanta*, Alfredo Casella (1883–1947), Ildebrando Pizzetti (1880–1968) and Gian Francesco Malipiero (1882–1973). In principle the *generazione dell'ottanta* aspired to get away from the national obsession with opera altogether, especially from the 'melodismo canzonettistico' (Pizzetti) of its more recent manifestations, because they believed that in the process of becoming an international commodity, it had sacrificed its spiritual idealism. In fact, even Casella was to compose three operas, while for Pizzetti and Malipiero opera was soon to become absolutely central to their life's work.

Italian opera as a flourishing, institutionalised tradition – that is, with an ordered system of commissioning, collaboration (between composer, poet, designer and others) and production – died with Puccini. And since the craft of libretto-writing died with it, younger composers tended to look to real poets for collaborators. The most notable case is clearly D'Annunzio (see below, p. 473), author of a crop of operas produced in the second decade of the century: Mascagni's *Parisina* (1913), Malipiero's *Sogno d'un tramonto d'autunno* (1913); Riccardo Zandonai's *Francesca da Rimini* (1914); Pizzetti's *Fedra* (1915) (which for a time became an inspirational paradigm for a new style of opera that abandoned 'melodismo canzonettistico' to gravitate between a flexible arioso, scrupulously deferential to the poetry, and choral song); *La nave* (1918) by Italo Montemezzi (1875–1952). All but the first of these were settings of pre-existent plays, abbreviated and occasionally slightly adapted, an avant-garde notion which Richard Strauss had made fashionable with *Salomè*. Since then Italian composers have regularly drawn on the particular gifts of the finest contemporary writers in the attempt to revivify operatic convention: Malipiero and Pirandello; Giorgio Ghedini and Quasimodo; Goffredo Petrassi and Montale; Luciano Berio and Calvino.

No one has been more resourceful in his quest to rediscover the roots of operatic *italianità* than Malipiero, whom Dallapiccola repeatedly declared to be the most important artistic personality in Italian music since Verdi. His *Sette canzoni* (Paris, 1920) may be cited as an example. It is a work comprising seven miniature operas which together add up to about forty-five minutes of music, and its 'libretto' is an anthology of early Italian poetry: Jacopone da Todi, Alamanni, and especially Poliziano. Malipiero's motive for this seemingly eccentric choice is absolutely typical for that post-Puccinian generation: 'in it one rediscovers the rhythm of our music, that is to say that truly Italian rhythm which, little by little during three centuries, was becoming corrupted in operatic melodrama.'

The literature of united Italy
(1870–1910)

Robert Dombroski, Felicity Firth

34

Writer and society in the new Italy

Robert Dombroski

With the creation of a unified national state, Italy entered a new cultural dimension, as the pace of industry and modernisation quickened and the nation's cultural institutions embarked on a course of extensive renewal. The unification could not be complete without the development of a national culture, which necessitated not only the general distribution of literacy (in 1861, 75% of the populace could not read or write Italian), but also the creation of a cultural tradition in which the contemporary liberal and anti-authoritarian ideologies that had fuelled the Risorgimento and supported industrial expansion could prosper. To these ends, state schools at all levels were reorganised, learned academies replenished, and new national libraries, museums and archives created. Liberal legislation guaranteed secondary schools and universities freedom of teaching and research; their structures were made uniform and their teaching staff expanded to incorporate prominent writers, scientists and intellectuals. But in spite of this new impetus to cultural activity, the project of a homogeneous national culture met with unsurmountable obstacles. The contradictions and disparities of an essentially impoverished and backward nation full of regionalisms, where traditional social, cultural and intellectual forms persisted, coupled with the ideological fragmentation among and within the various groups that fought the battles of the Risorgimento, made Italian cultural unification a difficult goal to realize.

For intellectuals, and for writers in particular, the age-old problems of identity, support and recognition were ever more crucial in the new Italy. While modernised state schools and universities became the workplace of some men of letters (Carducci and Pascoli are good examples of writers with university chairs) which guaranteed them a life of study and research, the great majority of writers who were not supported by family trusts (meaning mostly those from the lower or middle strata of the bourgeoisie) had to face the problem of subsistence according to the rules of the cultural marketplace, which appeared more severe than ever before, as literature was now produced on a national scale to meet the demands of an expanding reading public. The new, nationally oriented, publishing houses, newspapers and magazines all favoured the development of professional writers whom they could commission to write for specific readerships. The decision as to what was to be published was made almost wholly by the publishing houses and editors of serial publications.

Although writers facing this new situation assumed different positions which varied according to class origin and political convictions, they all displayed a general intolerance for what they perceived as the more materialistic attitude to life in the new society. In effect, the position of the writer changed markedly the moment he passed from his socio-political role as the voice of liberal, Risorgimento ideals to that of being a producer of literary texts for a book-buying public. An exemplary case in point is that of Giovanni Verga, whose development as a writer from his early patriotic and explicitly romantic novels to the mature pessimism of the *Novelle rusticane* and *Mastro-don Gesualdo* clearly parallels his experience as an artist in society, forced to subordinate his personal beliefs to the demands of a public indifferent to traditional values.

This new socio-economic context also had a positive side to it. It afforded writers the opportunity to detach themselves from traditional literary models and from the constraints of established institutions. With no social tasks to carry out, writers were free to develop their own capabilities; in some cases, this meant expanding their literary horizon, looking for inspiration not to Italy's cultural past, but beyond their nation's geographical boundaries, to the literature of more advanced societies. So the liabilities and instabilities of the cultural market can be seen to have caused forces motivating different forms of expression to transcend regional boundaries and aesthetic orientations and converge in acknowledging the essential uncertainty of life under capitalism: an indispensable presupposition to the perspectives and practices of literary modernism. The literature of united Italy emerges therefore from the strains and pressures of modernity. It attempts to work through the negative conditions of modern life, transforming the loss of values, and of cultural and artistic identity, into a source of creative material and energy.

It is not by chance that the first negative reactions to the new rhythms that a unified capitalist system imparted to Italian social life should in the 1860s come from Milan, the Italian city in which the spirit of the bourgeoisie was most pervasive and industrial growth the strongest. From Milan the *scapigliati*, a loosely knit group of self-styled bohemians, opposed the politically moderate and sentimental strains of Italian Romanticism, foregrounding the dark side of social and psychological realities. Drawing on the genius of Baudelaire and the brilliant visions of Hoffmann and Poe, such writers as Emilio Praga (1839–75) and Igino Ugo Tarchetti (1839–69) assailed the bourgeois aesthetic fixations that dominated Italian culture: principally the cult of classic beauty, which they opposed with images of horror and decay. The *scapigliati* thus presented their vision of the modern environment, while producing allegories of their own condition as displaced intellectuals involved in the menacing, yet magical, quality of modern life. The eccentric style, irregular syntax and vocabulary of Carlo Dossi (1849–1910), his intermixing of Tuscan and Lombard speech, his parody of conventional narrative perspectives, and his ironic confusion of reality and fantasy were all ways of portraying and denouncing simultaneously the contradictions and polyphony characteristic of modern society.

Carducci and classicism

In the poetry of Giosuè Carducci (1835–1907), the theme of the alienated or displaced intellectual is dramatised, paradoxically, from positions secured within the boundaries of official culture: in fact, from the Italian Academy, an institution built on tradition, which more than any other opposed the demands of modernisation. Carducci, Italy's first poet laureate (Nobel Prize for Literature, 1906) was Professor of Italian Eloquence at the University of Bologna. Regarded by Benedetto Croce as Italy's greatest modern poet, he, like the *scapigliati*, contested Romantic sentimentalism, but in the name of classical ideals of harmony and balance, which he posited as the essential prerequisites of a healthy and progressive humanity. All of Carducci's poetry, in every phase of its evolution, resonates with a desire to make past and present agree. Most of his poems depend on the assumption that the poet is the artificer of such a correspondence, and that he alone can transmit it to a collective consciousness assailed by the materialism and decadence of the present. If we impose the classical order upon ordinary reality, thereby showing that there is order and harmony in reality – that it is not uncertain and fragmentary as the true modernists will claim – poetry can bring us to an understanding of the power of stability and the serenity of order. Carducci's way of expressing his own passionate and volatile nature, his fondness for the rugged landscape of his native Maremma, as well as his distaste for bourgeois city life, was to filter it through classical metres and poetic theory.

The first phase of Carducci's poetry is animated by a distinctly republican and Jacobin sensibility and characterised by a virulent anti-clericalism. The fullest dramatisation of this secularism is the 'Inno a Satana' ('Hymn to Satan', 1863), a poem that envisages modernity in the image of Satan who, as the avenging force of reason, embodies all that is rebellious and progressive. A major aspect of Carducci's poetry, which becomes most evident in the collection of political verse *Giambi e epodi* ('Iambics and Epodes', 1867–79) is the attempt to adapt contemporary subject-matter to the laws of classical prosody. But there is a contradiction in Carducci's early poetic technique, which he will never succeed in truly resolving. His republican fury confers a certain recklessness with respect to his classical ideal, undermining its very premises with dissonant references to immediate experience and familiar objects and events. The general effect is one of realism, but of a realism circumscribed and weighed down by classical rhetoric. Carducci's poetry is concerned ultimately not with things themselves, nor even with their essences, but rather with their expression in a language of classical beauty.

With the destruction of the Papal States and their absorption into Italy in 1870, Carducci's poetry entered into a distinctly conservative phase. Less involved with glorifying patriotic deeds, his poems were now concerned mainly with capturing the elegance of images and phrases inherited from the past. The collection *Rime nuove* ('New Rhymes', 1887) displays the more intimate side of Carducci's inspiration: his youthful aspirations, recollections, melancholic nostalgia for an irrecoverable past – themes, however, that are all more or less burdened by the literature they seek to emulate, as for example the sonnet 'Funere mersit acerbo' ('Plunged in bitter death') in which the poet, like Virgil's Aeneas listening to the lament of children who died prematurely, summons his dead brother to welcome the soul of his own child, Dante, who had recently passed away.

The *Odi barbare* ('Barbarian Odes', 1877–9) are so entitled because they represent a 'rude' attempt to reproduce classical metres in modern verse, which consists in transposing a metre based on the length of syllables into one dependent on rhythmic accentuation – a procedure which, according to Carducci, the ancients would have considered 'barbarous'. This collection contains some of Carducci's more memorable lyrics and is representative at once of his most intense classicism and of his Romantic disillusionment: the discrepancy between the unique grandeur of Roman civilisation and the misery of the present, as in 'Dinanzi alle Terme di Caracalla' ('Before the Baths of Caracalla'), a poem in sapphic stanzas, in which the poet invokes the numen Febris (Fever) to prevent the 'uomini novelli' (new men) and 'lor picciole cose' (their petty concerns) from desecrating the ruins of antiquity; or in the elegiac distichs of 'Nella piazza di San Petronio' ('In the Square of San Petronio') that passionately mourn the passing of a heroic medieval civilisation of irrecoverable beauty. More original and contemporary are poems that accentuate the despondency of modern existence, such as 'Alla stazione in una mattina d'autunno' ('At the Station on an Autumn Morning'), in which Carducci transcribes in alcaic stanzas the departure of his beloved in the grey, rainy dawn of the Bologna railway station; or 'Nevicata' ('Snowfall'), where the premonition of death is underlined in the cold silence of a winter storm.

The poet's disenchantment with the new social order is a familiar theme in Italian Romantic poetry that can be traced back to Foscolo and Leopardi. In Carducci, however, it produces different and even opposite effects. The past for him is not a refuge of eternal beauty and harmony which the poet himself creates, fully aware that it is nothing but a beautiful illusion – either to be cherished as in Foscolo or dissolved as in Leopardi. Rather it is a veritable repository of virtue and idealism, a model that, juxtaposed to the negativity of the present, can be revived poetically. In contrast to his great Romantic predecessors, Carducci believed that the forms and conventions of classical poetry had not been exhausted, that they existed as a universal touchstone, and that all the poet had to do was to summon them into existence, identify with them, and re-exhibit them in relation to contemporary events and personal experience.

Naturalism and *verismo*

At the opposite end of the peninsula, in Sicily, the unification laid bare a backward, underdeveloped, archaic culture: an alien land, with its own customs and language, just as distant and different in time as in geography from the northern cities and the unfolding process of modernisation. Yet it was from Sicily that the Italian modern narrative tradition, begun by Manzoni, gained its greatest impetus.

In the new Italy, the Sicilian writer was doubly trapped, in the ambiguities of writing in a market economy and in social conditions unfamiliar to his northern counterparts, with whom he had to communicate. His principal concern was how to express the realities of a regional, archaic culture in a language appropriate to both characters and author which could be understood by a large and diversified reading public. French naturalism, particularly the work of Zola, provided a general methodological blueprint which, however, was destined to undergo considerable revision in the Sicilian context. Capuana, Verga and De Roberto all made the cornerstone of their literary aesthetics the dispassionate observation of reality. They were also careful to establish with scientific precision the social context of their characters' actions. But although the Sicilian novelists thought they too were participating in the scientific process, and that their fiction was a means of psychological and sociological understanding, they lacked Zola's belief in the power of science to change existing social conditions. Once the strong beliefs they held in liberal Risorgimento ideals were shattered, their politics became deeply conservative. However, their pessimistic belief that nothing in Sicily could ever change, while justifying their conservatism, enabled them to focus on the age-old truths of an a-historical, peasant society, destined, they thought, to exist for ever on the fringes of the capitalist social order. From the works of the Sicilian *veristi*, an entirely new literary landscape emerged: one devastated by nature and dominated by the blind passions and voracious instincts of characters for whom economic survival is the one and only motive force of existence.

Capuana

Luigi Capuana (1839–1915), an advocate of French naturalism, circulated in Italy Emile Zola's conception of the 'experimental' novelist who, like a scientist working in his laboratory, gathers and analyses the documents of human reality. His objective is to produce a fiction that is true to reality by virtue of its form. Capuana's first novel, *Giacinta* (1879), dedicated to Zola, is the case history of a young woman who challenges bourgeois morality by rejecting the man she really loves, then taking him back as a lover after she has married an aristocrat whom she detests. She thus avenges the injustice of a moral code that makes her an outcast simply because, as a child, she was the victim of rape. Giacinta's act of defiance is fatal, for it leads to madness and suicide.

Capuana's purpose is to write at once a psychological study of Giacinta and a sociological study of the community that oppresses her.

Capuana's attitude toward Zola and the experimental novel changed markedly during the course of his literary development, as he distanced himself from positivism and the hopes associated with its progressive social philosophy. In his essay 'La crisi del romanzo' ('The Crisis of the Novel', 1898), he claims that Zola could never have taken seriously his own formula for 'experimental' fiction. Dispassionate observation must be subjected to the demands of literary art. The novel, rather than being a scientific programme that examines cause-and-effect relations, must give characters and events the liberty to be what they naturally are. The novelist must be true to the intimate nature of what he represents. Capuana's last novel, *Il marchese di Roccaverdina* ('The Marquis of Roccaverdina', 1901), is based on a situation quite as eccentric as that of *Giacinta*. The Marquis is an egotistical, solitary individual who conveniently marries off his peasant mistress to his most devoted employee, whom he then murders out of jealousy. The guilt he suffers for the crime gradually drives him mad. But the novel differs from *Giacinta* in that its emphasis falls on the irrational and violent side of the Marquis's behaviour rather than on the effects of social prejudice on human psychology.

Verga

The dispassionate neutrality of the artist was also at the centre of the literary aesthetics of Giovanni Verga (1840–1922). Consistent with the naturalists' programme, Verga too championed scientific precision in the creation of an autogenous art that was an objective, unbiased investigation of human life and upheld the priority of real, demonstrable human events, particularly of the 'mysterious' and 'contradictory' processes of human psychology. Verga's major aesthetic concern was how to express the thoughts and feelings that people of a particular social stratum experience in their minds, and to do so in a language that could be conveyed to a large and diversified reading public without any apparent mediation. His great achievement, unparalleled among Italian naturalists, was to fashion a language and a style that reproduced (actually mimicked) specific mental and behavioural events. Accordingly, he strove to capture the essence of what he saw to be a process of living by focusing on one or more of the parts of a cultural whole – components which bear the names of their re-creation as texts, for example *I Malavoglia* (*The House by the Medlar Tree*, 1881) and *Mastro-don Gesualdo* (1889).

Before his conversion to *verismo*, Verga tried to work out some then current assumptions about the vanity of bourgeois life and, especially, the perilous charms of wealthy, sophisticated women. In *Una peccatrice* ('A Sinner', 1866), a young Sicilian playwright loses his creative spirit at the hands of a seductive countess. *Eva* (1869) recounts the self-destructive love of a Sicilian painter for a Florentine ballerina. In *Tigre reale* ('Royal Tigress', 1875) the Sicilian protagonist, after savouring the ephemeral pleasures of high society and witnessing at first hand the death of his Russian mistress, returns home to his wife and family. Of this group of works, which includes *Storia d'una capinera* ('Story of a Blackcap', 1870, an epistolary novel against forced religious vocations), *Eros* (1875) stands out as being Verga's first success at creating an inherently objective narrative perspective, devoid of self-reference and authorial intrusion, while at the same time remaining faithful to the theme of how intelligence and creativity fall prey to erotic pleasure. Sentimental rhetoric and autobiography aside, this group of narratives can usefully be viewed as an attempt by the young Verga to deal with the experience of meaninglessness and despair in a civilisation now strengthened by the capitalist development of business and industry. Verga altogether rejects the valuelessness of bourgeois existence, transforming his melancholy into a perspective designed to foreground allegorically both his nostalgia for wholeness and his alienation as an artist. He will develop this new perspective – which takes the reader away from modern civilisation to an alien land of unique pre-industrial societies – by degrees, from a position that juxtaposes the comforts of bourgeois life to primitive otherness: from *Nedda* (1874) and *Fantasticheria* ('Rêverie', 1879) to *I Malavoglia* and *Mastro don Gesualdo*.

'The novel,' Verga explains in his letter-preface to *L'amante di Gramigna* ('Gramigna's Mistress', 1880), 'will have the imprint of a real event, and the work of art will appear *to have made itself*, to have matured to the point where it gives the impression of being a spontaneous, natural product, wholly detached from its author'. Although Verga claims that his stories will speak for themselves, it is not to be inferred from this that he believed that the plain facts of peasant life would speak for themselves. As is clear from his Introduction to *I Malavoglia*, his 'sincere and dispassionate' study presupposed hypotheses based in values; it also assumed that the enquiry itself was a strategy aimed at achieving knowledge about human social life in a large cross-section of society, extending from the lowest to the most privileged classes.

Under the general title of *I vinti* ('The Vanquished'), Verga planned a cycle of five novels – *I Malavoglia*, *Mastro-don Gesualdo*, *La duchessa di Leyra* ('The Duchess of Leyra'), *L'onorevole Scipioni* ('The Honourable Scipioni'), and *L'uomo di lusso* ('The Man of Luxury') – of which he completed only the first two. The struggle for existence was for Verga the motivating force of human activity, which he equated with progress. Seen from a distance, the course of mankind towards progress appears grandiose, but, as we focus in on it, we see the anxieties, the greed and selfishness it encompasses. Like a great tide, the movement of progress sweeps everyone away (the cycle of novels originally was to bear the title of 'La marea', 'The Tide'). All the novelist can do is observe the weak who have fallen by the wayside, victims of mankind's forward march. The tide spares no one; there are no victors in Verga's world; those who appear to come out ahead today will be overtaken tomorrow.

Verga's guiding principle held that humanity, in its desire to move forward, was engaged at various levels in a struggle displaying a complex range of human emotion, and that the higher one went on the social ladder the more intricate the language of desire became. The writer's task was to be true to his subject-matter, which in effect meant creating a narrative voice that belonged to the world being represented and one in which all its constituent parts were condensed.

While working on his project, Verga wrote a large number of short stories, most of which are contained in the collections *Vita dei campi* ('Life in the Fields', 1880) and *Novelle rusticane* ('Country Tales', 1883). The form of the *novella* is particularly suitable to Verga's pessimistic vision of subaltern individuals oppressed by both nature and culture. These stories are all based on a single, extreme situation and focus on figures whose struggle either to live out their passions or merely to survive ends in tragic defeat. Within this general structure, Verga highlights the distinct otherness of his characters and the deeply alien character of their world, one removed as much as is realistically possible from the bourgeois reader's conception of human society. The heroes of these tales all succumb to the violence of the social world which either intrudes on their natural innocence, as in *Jeli il pastore* ('Jeli the Shepherd'), or curbs irrational, female passion, as in *La lupa* ('The She Wolf').

Two *novelle* in particular illustrate the force of Verga's vision of the cruelty and inhumanity of social and human institutions, and the power of material interests. In *Rosso Malpelo* – the name given to a boy working in a sulphur mine – every detail, every object, every gesture and word, are indispensable effects of the inexorable movement of fate and the heroic existence of a protagonist who never surrenders or gives up his primitiveness. In *La roba* ('Possessions'), the forces that shape moral personality are distilled into an austere narrative rhythm intent on capturing the irony of an existence governed uniquely by the compulsion to possess property and the intransigent logic of avarice.

I Malavoglia is the story of the Toscano family (the Malavoglias, as they are known to the community of Aci Trezza) and of their struggle to survive amid the pressures generated by the unification of Italy and the expansion of capitalist enterprise. The Malavoglias own a house, which they refer to as 'la casa del nespolo' (the house by the medlar tree, hence the title of the English translation) and a fishing-boat called 'La Provvidenza', repositories of value on which the family bases its living and activity in the fishing trade. The novel recounts the end of the Malavoglias' way of life. The family's dissolution begins with the conscription of young 'Ntoni into the military (thus depriving it of the strongest segment of its work-force) and Padron 'Ntoni's decision, on account of an unproductive yield of fish the preceding year, to buy a shipment of 'lupini' (lupins, used for fodder) on credit and to use the fishing-boat to transport them to market. The 'Provvidenza' is shipwrecked and in the storm Padron 'Ntoni's son Bastianazzo drowns. The Malavoglias in turn lose their house and their honour, as 'Ntoni is jailed on charges of smuggling and Lia, dishonoured by Don Michele, becomes a prostitute.

The novel's principal theme is that individual creeds and private conscience do not ensure the survival of a way of life in a society governed by materialistic self-interest. Pressures exerted by the ruling classes on politically and economically subordinate groups or individuals, combined with the demands of social progress, will ultimately force changes in the latter's behaviour and cognitive orientations. But adaptation to change summoned by the lure of material progress does not guarantee either the continuance of past subsistence or a change for the better. The logic of the capitalist market economy justifies, for the sake of majority interest, the sacrifice not only of the weak and those unable to cope but also of the strong and resourceful. In society, the battle-lines are drawn; from the conflict the vanquished will emerge either to die in isolation (as does Padron 'Ntoni) or to begin once again the process of survival (as do Alessi and Nunziata).

The opposing ideologies and narrative functions of Padron 'Ntoni and his grandson 'Ntoni make up a large part of the novel's thematic nucleus, for both of them, albeit in different ways, are victims of social progress. Padron 'Ntoni defends the moral compactness of the family: its mythical space as well as the immanence of meaning on which its concrete existence depends. 'Ntoni, the patriarch's realistic counterpart, represents a dissonance crucial to the work's inner form. In his rebellious desire for new experiences, he regards the family's world as imperfect. The outside world he has visited causes him to question the ideal of inherited value, to which he opposes a concept of life as interested activity. While there is nothing the Malavoglias can do to resist the economic logic of their subaltern existence, 'Ntoni's primitive awareness of a secularised world provides no compensation for the loss of the centre. As an outcast, he will never return to the comforts of home. Once the process of disintegration and alienation begins, 'Ntoni – like Verga – will realise that the good life he yearns for is a romantic myth: a dream of wholeness, necessary to compensate for the harsh realities of competition and survival in the market system.

Verga's disbelief in human progress may also be viewed from the standpoint of the novel's style. In attempting to picture the life of a Sicilian fishing village in the most complete way possible, Verga invents a world of literally too many voices, indicative of the numerous roles played within the social community. His use of free indirect style allows him to assert his control over the composite interplay of voices embodied by the subject-matter. By inhabiting the minds of his characters, he uses their thoughts and feelings as vehicles for transcribing his own anxieties as an uprooted and isolated author, forced to compete in a world of material determinants.

Mastro-don Gesualdo builds on the thematic of *I Malavoglia*. The soothing intellectual refuge provided by the Malavoglias' archaic, rural world has been thoroughly eclipsed by the reality of material interests. We move ahead from a pre-modern to a modern society where different cultures and class interests intersect. The new protagonist is not a family and a way of life, but rather an individual, Don Gesualdo Motta, who employs all of his intelligence and physical endurance to make good in a fiercely competitive world. The perspective adopted in *I Malavoglia* gives way to a narrative space in which the distance between author, subject-matter and reader is dramatically fore-shortened. The rhetoric of impersonality still holds sway, but now the narrator has assimilated into his authorial voice a diversity of social perspectives, modulating them with his own insights and judgement, while allowing the more complex inner world of his characters to speak for itself.

The novel centres on the life of Mastro Gesualdo, an ambitious stone-mason from a small town near Catania who, because of his wealth, is given entry into the circles of a decadent provincial nobility. Through hard work, Gesualdo apparently succeeds in moving up the social ladder. He abandons the simple country life of a tradesman, his family and his illiterate mistress Diodata to marry into the penniless and downfallen Trao family. But the protagonist's desire to move ahead effectively spells his defeat. The nobility regards him as an intruder; there is no basis for communication with his wife Bianca, or with their daughter Isabella who – the reader learns early on – is not really his child. Gesualdo lives out his life alone as an unwanted guest in his daughter's home in Palermo, alienated both from his daughter, who is ashamed of his humble origins, and from the peasant masses, who regard him as their enemy.

A significant feature of *Mastro-don Gesualdo* is the chronological time in which its action takes place: 1820–48. Thus Verga captures the struggle for life, in a historical moment prior to the unification, as a crude and violent, naturally economic phenomenon, yet about to be subjected to the justificatory ideology of a national market-system which equates social and economic progress. Gesualdo brings into that time-frame his modern desire to change his social status, and is thoroughly defeated. While his zest for material property exhibits a heroic resolve to dominate nature and competitors alike, it prevents him from understanding the cultural logic that underwrites his alienation, and which operates with the same indifference to pain and with the same material certainty as govern his own compulsion to succeed. Verga provides no refuge from the struggle for life: his sentences are stark and incisive, as dry and as mercilessly objective as the landscape. Style now becomes a means to desecrate any and all tendencies toward mythical recomposition; rarely are we afforded time to rest, but, with Gesualdo, must move frantically through the convulsive space of his entrepreneurial strategies. The cyclical time of *I Malavoglia*, which supported the myth of origin and plenitude, is replaced by a linear narrative time that obeys only rules dictated by the author's desolate vision. The work's episodic structure reflects the fragmentation of Gesualdo's psyche, his natural blindness to everything except what he owns and what he wants. Verga's narrative logic excludes Gesualdo from his social community; in so doing the author prepares him for his ultimate exclusion from historical time, which is his death. His 'death-in-life', his existence as a self-consumed monadic entity, produces the reverse image of liberal development and self-understanding that dominates in the nineteenth-century bourgeois novel.

The power and depth of Verga's narrative art was not fully appreciated until after the Second World War when, after the defeat of Fascism, the renewed workers' movement and democratic political debate drew attention once again to the harsh social realities of the Mezzogiorno, depicted in Verga's narratives. Neo-realism drew on Verga's example in its creation of a politically committed fiction, founded on the objectivist principles of direct observation and reproduction of customs and language.

De Roberto and other veristi

Although there are no mirages of wholeness in *Mastro-don Gesualdo*, there is a trace of the faith that was defeated: the value of self-sacrifice and hard work – Gesualdo's secular religion. In the naturalist perspective of Federico De Roberto, such a faith in human powers has no basis of expression whatsoever. The youngest of the Sicilian *veristi*, De Roberto (1861–1927) lived most of his life in Catania. Unlike Capuana and Verga, his approach to naturalism accentuated scientific induction, and the determinism of physiological and environmental factors. In his masterpiece *I Viceré (The Viceroys*, 1894) De Roberto's fatalism is disguised as the objectivity of a chronicler who records the history of the Uzeda family, descendants of the Spanish viceroys. The Uzedas, like all of the landed Sicilian aristocracy, are natural enemies of the Risorgimento, intent on perpetuating their rule in the new Italy. *I Viceré* is the story of how they work to quell the Risorgimento's revolutionary impetus by bringing it under their control and exploiting it to further their own survival as a ruling class. Following the basic tenets of naturalism, De Roberto positions his narrator on the outside of his subject with an eye on the numerous family members and how they relate among themselves and with the public. There is no one perspective which he favours; instead his purpose is to present a polyphony of individual voices, each a variation on the novel's general themes of violence, cruelty and insanity. The family is seen as a repository not of value and tradition, but rather of desperate, instinctual conflict. Its members, a veritable gallery of grotesque figures, are consumed with envy and anger for each other, and unite only to repel outsiders or to protect the family's interests. They represent a race that has degenerated into madness. Yet, although blind to reality and delirious, this ancient nobility is capable of adapting in order to preserve itself from extinction as a ruling class. De Roberto's political message can hardly go unnoticed: history is monotonous repetition; although external conditions change, the nobility's prestige will never die.

With *I Viceré* De Roberto pushes naturalism to its outer limits. The intensity of his polemic forces a distortion in the object of his analysis, causing his emphasis to fall, in the final instance, not on the historical existence of the Sicilian aristocracy but rather on madness and paradox – themes which tend to abandon the closed space of linear narrative so well defined by Verga for the open-ended world of possibility. For if history is indeed paradoxical, then the form in which history is written may itself be contradictory and ambiguous.

The borders of naturalism

Within the boundaries of Naturalism are to be located the works of numerous other writers of the time whose literary fortunes are linked to more regional rather than national concerns. In Tuscany, the tendency is to highlight the violence and hardships of country life, as in the stories of Renato Fucini's (1843–1921) *Le veglie di Neri* ('Evenings with Neri', 1884) or in the novels of Mario Pratesi (1842–1921) such as *L'eredità* ('The Inheritance', 1889) and *Il mondo di Dolcetta* ('Dolcetta's World', 1895). Most of the Neapolitan narratives focus on the struggle for survival in the midst of the poverty and misfortunes of city life. In the work of the journalist and novelist Matilde Serao (1857–1927), Naples is represented in all its colour and eccentricity, from the misery of its squalid alleys, as in *Il ventre di Napoli* ('The Belly of Naples', 1884) to the bourgeois and aristocratic interiors of *Il paese della cuccagna* ('The Land of Cockayne', 1890), a masterful novel depicting a wide range of Neapolitan figures who hope to hold the winning number in a lottery destined to change their lives. A more poetic image of the Neapolitan character issues from the work of Salvatore Di Giacomo (1860–1934). In his fiction, plays, and, above all, his dialect verse, Di Giacomo captures a popular world of spectacle and moral expediency, echoing the city's voice in all of its nuances and emotional vibrations. Among his best-known plays is *'O voto* ('The Vow', 1889), the story of an ailing dye-worker who makes a vow to the Madonna promising to marry a prostitute if he is brought back to health.

In contrast to the central and southern narratives, the fiction produced in the north appears much less regional in tone, as it tends to focus on bourgeois or upper-class existence. Camillo Boito (1836–1914), brother of the *scapigliato* Arrigo, was attracted by the cowardice and deceit that lay behind the façade of good manners and appearance. *Senso* ('A Thing Apart', 1882), one of his finest stories, was adapted into a feature film in 1954 by Luchino Visconti. Luigi Gualdo (1847–1898) wrote *Decadenza* ('Decadence', 1892), the first Italian novel to centre on the theme of *ennui*. Anna Zuccari Neera (1845–1918) examines bourgeois existence from the standpoint of women who, for the sake of love, are forced to live tormented and lonely lives. The most popular of the Milanese writers of the time was Emilio De Marchi (1851–1901), a novelist who, in the tradition of Manzoni, wrote morally uplifting stories that spotlighted honest people victims of a corrupt society. His best-known novels are *Demetrio Pianelli* (1889) and *Arabella* (1892).

Cuore *and* Pinocchio

The writer and journalist Edmondo De Amicis (1846–1908) is known primarily for his famed *Cuore* ('Heart: A Schoolboy's Journal', 1886) written for children, which, after *I promessi sposi*, was at the time the most widely read book of prose in Italy. Instrumental in the formation of the moral consciousness of several generations of Italians, the work's popularity extended well into the 1950s. Human dignity, self-sacrifice, civil responsibility, family values are the book's recurring themes, developed within the structure of a diary kept by Enrico, a primary-school child, which includes letters from the boy's parents and stories dictated by his teachers involving children from the country's different regions. Everything recounted is from the heart (whence the book's title) and designed to teach and inspire; every experience harbours a moral lesson in right conduct for the good citizen. Taking elementary education as his base, De Amicis hoped to solidify the national character and thus extend the moral values of secularism to all children, rich and poor alike.

While *Cuore* appealed primarily to Italians, *Le avventure di Pinocchio* (*The Adventures of Pinocchio*, 1883) was destined to gain universal acclaim as one of the greatest children's stories of all time. Its author, Carlo Collodi (penname of Carlo Lorenzetti, 1826–1890), a public official and journalist, became interested in children's literature during the 1870s, translating from Perrault (*I racconti delle Fate*, 1875) and publishing several pedagogically inspired books for school use. *Pinocchio*, written at the end of Collodi's career, also makes clear its educational objectives, as it teaches its young readers to be obedient, study, work hard, save money, avoid bad company, and so on. Critics agree that *Pinocchio* may be read as a kind of *Bildungsroman*, aimed at showing that for a child to grow into a good citizen he must abandon the puppet within him and become trustworthy, dependable and respectful of society's rules. But whatever pedagogical intentions underlie the narration, the book's great charm consists in Pinocchio's adventures, in the life, not of the boy, but of the puppet. Pinocchio is a kind of picaresque hero who learns little if anything from his misfortunes. Thrown into the maelstrom of modern life, he suffers abandonment and loss, and experiences the cruelty and violence of a society in which people struggle just to keep alive. If there is anything that Pinocchio's adventures teach him, it is the true nature of the social world. But the fantastic perspective governing the novel contradicts the harsh realities it describes, opening the text to a host of interpretations, from Freudian to Marxist, all of which are to some degree legitimate.

Fogazzaro *and* Deledda

The most European of the Italian novelists of the 1880s in terms of culture and education was no doubt Antonio Fogazzaro (1842–1911). Born into a wealthy

Catholic family of Vicenza, he learned several foreign languages at an early age, which enabled him to read widely in German, French and English literature. His intellectual concerns, unique among his contemporaries, become apparent in his novels which, although still largely naturalistic in perspective, are concerned mostly with psychology, dream and mystery. *Malombra* (1881), his first novel, is the story of Marina, an ambiguously charming and beautiful noblewoman who believes she is the reincarnation of a former lady of the manor who died under mysterious circumstances, and Corrado Silla, an unsuccessful writer, whom Marina sees as the reincarnation of the Lady's former lover. Although his first, *Malombra* is Fogazzaro's most interesting novel by virtue of its attempt to unite a naturalistic concreteness of description, inspired by a democratic sensibility with respect to the popular masses, with the vagaries and fascination of mystery.

From the disquieting yearnings of *Malombra*, Fogazzaro moves to political intrigue and sublime love in *Daniele Cortis* (1885), a novel about a Catholic lawmaker's struggle to realise his ideal of a truly Christian democracy, and the sublimation of physical passion in art in *Il mistero del poeta* ('The Mystery of the Poet', 1888), the melodramatic story of a poet's love for an emotionally fragile woman. Distinctly more sedate in tone, while more ambitious in scope, is Fogazzaro's best-known novel, *Piccolo mondo antico* (*Little World of the Past*, 1896) a work centred on the peculiarities of northern Italian provincial life during the ten years preceding the unification. The narration revolves around daily life in a bourgeois household and takes as its focus the marriage of Franco and Luisa: the difference in their characters, the difficulties they have in communicating with one another, the death of their child, and finally their separation. *Piccolo mondo antico* reconstructs from memory the life and values of a world on the edge of modernity, capturing in simple narrative rhythms the commonplace truths it was seen to encompass. With *Piccolo mondo moderno* (*The Man of the World*, 1901) Fogazzaro returns to the present to foreground again the problems of a Catholic intellectual, Piero Maironi, son of Franco and Luisa of *Piccolo mondo antico*, condemned to a life of both sensuality and idealism. *Il Santo* (*The Saint*, 1905) continues the life of Piero, who, having now become a monk, leads, unsuccessfully, a movement aimed at reforming the Church. By comparison, distinctly social are the concerns of Sibilla Aleramo's (pseud. Rina Faccio, 1876–1960) first novel *Una donna* (*A Woman*, 1906), which paints a portrait of female oppression, speaking out against the institutions of marriage and the family. Aleramo's subsequent narrative production can best be summed up in *Amo dunque sono* ('I Love, Therefore I Am', 1927), a novel that places the emphasis on its author's need to love and be desired.

The emphasis Fogazzaro placed on spiritual conflict, sin, remorse and expiation is equally prominent in the work of the Sardinian novelist Grazia Deledda (1871–1936). Deledda, who was awarded the Nobel Prize for literature in 1926, belongs to a more recent generation of naturalists. Her numerous novels are set for the most part in the primitive world of her island homeland, guarded by tradition and ancestral values. They all take as their focus the transgression of some ancestral law and revolve around the conflicts which ensue, as seen from the perspective of a young girl whose vision of life is deeply affected by her own roots in that world. Like Verga's primitives, Deledda's protagonists are all victims, but the author, in recounting their fates, makes no claim to either objectivity or impersonality. Rather, her point of view endeavours to arouse compassion and sorrow for predicaments seen to be more spiritual than social.

D'Annunzio

Whereas the purpose of naturalism was to make unfamiliar realities accessible by means of art, the symbolism and decadence which developed at the turn of the century sprang from the belief that the reality of the outside world is in itself unknowable; that its objects are nothing but material signs of some hidden and mysterious essence of life. For many European writers of the time, the inaccessibility of reality was a characteristic effect of modern life. The interior world of the artist was thus considered a place of refuge; the artwork it produced, a means of safeguarding, however minimally, a besieged individuality. The artist's predicament consisted in the need to create, knowing fully well that the objects of his creative talent would be subjected to the rules of the market place, which would mean the 'death' of true art.

Gabriele D'Annunzio (1863–1938) had no doubts whatsoever that Art, which he identified with Beauty and Tradition, was alive and well. In fact, he dedicated his entire life as poet, playwright, novelist and military hero to its defence, as well as to its production, that is to say, to the production of Beauty. Like the protagonists of his novels, D'Annunzio bears the full weight of an overpowering aesthetic impulse to go beyond the degraded and valueless world of industrial capitalism in search of a new vitality in old hierarchies: in a sacred, mysterious and mythical substance that literature can never truly capture. Art is produced by reproducing in the rhythm of the word the language of Beauty. In so doing, the problematic subjectivity of the modern artist, described above, fuses with the artefact to the point where it ceases to exist altogether. As a result, the Beauty produced can refer only to itself and not to the interior world of the artist, which has been sealed off, referred to only indirectly by means of poetic emblems. D'Annunzio's art, as it issues from his faith in the regenerative power of myth, is an attempt to re-harmonise the world. The fragmented subject having been removed from the scene, the poet is free to evoke the space of myth, sing the sacred charms of Mystery and Tradition, and make Beauty live again in the sensual correspondences he creates.

D'Annunzio's major poetry is vibrant with the sensuous physicality of the natural world. The *Laudi* ('Praises', 1903), chiefly *Alcyone*, are among D'Annunzio's greatest achievements, and celebrate the return to myth: the victory of a new pagan humanity over a degraded modern age. In the *Laus vitae* ('Praise of Life'), the poet, who in the guise of a new Ulysses is the poem's hero and *Übermensch*, exalts Life and the power of desire and possession. The poet's itinerary sweeps him through the heart of ancient Greece and Renaissance Italy, the grandeur of which he juxtaposes to the squalor of modern life in the 'terrible' cities overrun by the popular masses who, although brutalised by capitalism, contain a reserve of vitality and new energies. The poet-*Übermensch*, becoming a natural element, dominates the world through instinct and sensation. In *Alcyone* D'Annunzio diminishes the heroic impetus of the poet's inspiration in order to evoke through phonosymbolic imagery a form of pagan baptism by submerging the reader's senses in the sultry warmth of summer. 'La sera fiesolana' ('Fiesole in the evening') and 'La pioggia nel pineto' ('The rain in the pine forest') reflect perhaps better than any other of the lyrics D'Annunzio's capacity to reveal secret analogies and hidden relationships through instantaneous, musical perception. Like all of *Alcyone*, they may be read as the songs of a pagan fertility ritual, as they evoke the joy of being united to the sun and the sea, and to the fragrance and vigour of the natural landscape. In 'Stabat nuda aestas' ('Summer stood naked'), Summer is a beautiful naked woman whom the poet hunts and captures; in 'Versilia' and 'Meriggio' ('Midday') it is the poet who is caught by desirous wood nymphs in the heat of August, on the threshold of summer's waning; autumn stalks the poet with melancholic foreboding of loss and decay. *Alcyone* concludes with the autumn and the poet left alone, abandoned by the ripeness of a season past.

D'Annunzio's early stories, from *Terra vergine* ('Virgin Land', 1882) to *San Pantaleone* (1886), draw on naturalism for their setting and general thematic. But the struggle for survival among the peasants in the author's native Abruzzi is largely decontextualised: its purpose is to represent brutality and ritual violence as elements of the sacred substance of blood and race. Everything that is archaic and regressive in these stories, the blood rituals, sacrifice and religious fanaticism, has a distinct libidinal function: it evokes principles of wholeness and hierarchy counterpoised to the relativist values of the fragmented modern world. Hence D'Annunzio reinvents a primitive consciousness in order to transfer it to a time and existence that he and his readers share.

D'Annunzio's first novel, *Il piacere* (*The Child of Pleasure*, 1888), recounts the emblematic moments in the life of Andrea Sperelli, the author's alter ego, whose goal is to 'make his life into a work of art'. But Sperelli, like all of D'Annunzio's aesthete heroes, necessarily fails in his desire for perfection, for more powerful than the artist are the corruption and vulgarity of a society dominated by the petty middle-class interests of the shopkeepers and the kind of spiritual rabble that, at the novel's close, eagerly wait to take hold of the spoils of a defeated aristocracy. The perfection he aspires to exists in another time and place, just as the story's theme of sensual love is nothing other than the acting out of a desire for fullness that can never be completely satisfied.

Giorgio Aurispa in *Il trionfo della morte* ('The Triumph of Death', 1894) is another typical D'Annunzian intellectual, out of place in the crass materiality of the city, and seeking a fulfilment that only death will provide. None of D'Annunzio's exceptional protagonists is truly capable of dominating, not even the *Übermensch* heroes of *Il fuoco* ('The Fire', 1900) and *Forse che sì forse che no* ('Perhaps Yes Perhaps No', 1910), who are also defeated in their desire for wholeness. They aspire to a past which is irremediably lost. The elegant upper social class of D'Annunzio's heroes, its conventions, moral virtues and inestimable values, all belong to a social mythology, devoid of pragmatic impulses and objectives. It constitutes the figurative dimension of the hero's experience, inserted into a narrative system which employs naturalistic form to suggest the possibility of regeneration through myth. D'Annunzio's protagonists lose their battle to attain perfection because they exist in history; their thought and actions are placed within the confines of literal meaning. It is only in *Le vergini delle rocce* (*The Virgins of the Rocks*, 1895) that D'Annunzio effaces the distinction between the literal and the figurative, as the impulse towards organic wholeness dominates at the formal as well as at the thematic level. Narration gives way to oratory; the plot sheds every residue of tension between the real and the ideal. There is nothing the reader can recognise as belonging to his own world of prose, as he is thrown without any mediation whatsoever into an alien reality, beyond history, into the realm of the Imaginary, where life begins and everything is possible. But even the protagonist Claudio is in the end defeated. His objective of initiating a new race through his mythical coupling with one of the Virgins of Trigento is never realised. For if Claudio were to bring about the ideal of the *Übermensch* and begin a new cosmic cycle, he would actually be sowing the seed of his own destruction. In a society of regenerated men, there would be no need for a religion of beauty. Art, in D'Annunzio's novels, can exist only in the form of an absent object, the thing possessed by the subject that has disappeared into nature to become myth, sensation, music and legend.

The sphere of the archaic and the Dionysian force of the poetical are also the focal point in D'Annunzio's theatrical works, including his operas (see above, p. 456). Influenced by Nietzsche and Wagner, D'Annunzio aspires to a new kind of tragedy, one which reactivates Dionysian fury for the purpose of giving a new vigour, and thus a new future, to the Nation. The new tragedy is an heroic gesture that feeds on obscure, atavistic violence. The playwright, as Stelio Effrena explains in *Il fuoco*, is like a new Perseus who, having slain Medusa, displays her severed head. The play, like Medusa's head, will transfix the audience in such a way that it will never be forgotten.

The plays incorporate a wide range of typically D'Annunzian themes (blood rituals, madness, incest, tragic heroism, violent passion), all conceived in ways to bring the audience into direct contact with the sacred substance and regenerative power of myth. Most acclaimed by critics are *La città morta*

('The Dead City', 1896) and *La figlia di Iorio* (*The Daughter of Iorio*, 1907). The former is a drama of incest meant to resemble Greek tragedy, set in modern Greece at the site of an archaeological excavation. The archaeologist Leonardo is in love with his sister Bianca Maria, whom he kills when he learns that she is in love with their mutual friend Alessandro. For Leonardo, the murder is an act of purification, while for his blind wife Anna, it miraculously restores her sight. *La figlia di Iorio*, written in verse, is set in the ancestral, legendary world of the Abruzzi, a sensuous and violent land, bound by age-old rituals and superstitions. It tells the story of Mila di Codro, the outcast daughter of Iorio, who takes refuge from a drunken mob in the home of Aligi. In giving her sanctuary, Aligi defiles the patriarchal code, is forced to leave, and, with Mila, hides away in a cave. Aligi, in defence of Mila, slays her father and is about to be executed for parricide when Mila confesses that it was she who murdered him and that she had bewitched his son. Mila walks heroically into the flames of Lazzaro's funeral pyre, an act which restores order, purifying the tribe of Aligi's transgressions.

A markedly different orientation in D'Annunzio's writing can be seen in several works written from 1910 on, beginning with the short prose narratives of the *Faville del maglio* ('Sparks from the Hammer', 1911–14) and culminating in the doleful reflections of *Notturno* ('Nocturne', 1921) and *Cento e cento e cento pagine dal libro segreto di Gabriele D'Annunzio* ('One Hundred, One Hundred and One Hundred Pages from the Secret Book of Gabriele D'Annunzio', 1935). These are works which, rather than exhibiting the world as Beauty and Spectacle, are devoted to meditation and self-analysis, and to thoughtful reflection on the meaning of myth and symbol. Yet it would be inaccurate to characterise D'Annunzio's later phase as a genuine departure from his early fantasy literature. For even if these writings foreground, to a certain degree, the discontinuity and isolation that defined individuality in the age of capitalist expansion, they retain the mythical categories of D'Annunzio's previous production. The poet is still the supreme artificer, the *Übermensch* capable of initiating the process leading to utopian fulfilment.

Pascoli

The poetry of Giovanni Pascoli (1855–1912) represents the other side of Italian aestheticism, the roots of which reach back not to Tradition but to what the poet sees as the essences of small things and to the desires associated with their perception and knowledge. Pascoli's 'fanciullino' (the child-like, poetic sensibility existing potentially in everyone, but that only children and poets have in abundance) is the notion that sets a dichotomy between poet and society, children and adults, the world of simple, country life and the industrialised city. Instead of D'Annunzio's Tradition and arcane lineages, it is the secret life of childhood and the rural landscape that exists beyond history and is one and the same with poetry. The spiritual substance of mysterious essences is embedded in commonplace reality; the poet's task is one of discovering these hidden essences. The child-like poet, however, is not everyman; but like the D'Annunzian aesthete, he too possesses a unique consciousness and perception, he too is capable of insights and knowledge that penetrate where reason and science cannot, and he too unites poetic expression with the absolute purity of being. But in contrast to D'Annunzio, there is a strong democratic vein in Pascoli, which runs counter to the stated uniqueness of child-like perception and takes as its focus objects associated with modest, unpretentious origins which the poet constructs in a simple and unassuming language and style.

Pascoli's first and most original collection of poems, *Myricae* (1891), takes its title from the Vergilian verse 'arbusta iuvant humilesque myricae' (I am fond of the small trees and the humble tamarisks) which stands as the work's epigraph. The *Myricae* at once draw on the classical tradition so revered by Carducci and, with the fidelity they display toward the world of objects, on naturalism. Their distinguishing mark, however, is the fragmentary character of their imagery. The poet possesses the sensible world by capturing its mysterious essences. The images are stitched together as in a rhapsody; their purpose is not to represent but to illuminate, by means of sounds and silences, the mysterious features of human existence that objects conceal. The humble object is foregrounded by means of precise definition. Flowers, plants, birds, objects emblematic of agrarian living, names and places, referred to with a scientific precision unprecedented in Italian poetry, are summoned as figures of the poet's modest reality. The phonosymbolic quality of the diction, the ample use of onomatopoeia, a-grammatical syntax, sudden transitions in focus, recondite analogies, all contribute to highlight fleeting, dream-like moments of perception. The effect is a disquieting sense of the obscure nature of being, as it is hidden in the simplest of things. The thematic substance of the *Myricae* revolves around the family hearth, the homestead, the memory of which emits a haunting presence of childhood and of the child's sense of bewilderment as well as his fears: of abandonment and death. In his preface to the collection, Pascoli describes the sense impressions of his rhymes as the 'fluttering of birds, the rustling of cypresses, and the distant chant of bells', all reminders of the life of the poet's extinct family; and from the first, *Il giorno dei morti* ('The Day of the Dead') to the last, *Ultimo sogno* ('The Last Dream'), the *Myricae* are a meditation on loss. In each poem the mind confronts an image (a plough left abandoned in an open field, a solitary country church, the cry of a child in the night), designed to haunt the reader as if the whole world were reduced to these signs.

Death is also an obsession in some of the finest verse of Pascoli's second collection, *Poemetti* (1897), but here it is more the exception than the rule. While such poems as *I due fanciulli* ('The Two Children') and *L'aquilone* ('The Kite') combine images of splendour and emptiness into ambiguous, disquieting visions reminiscent of the *Myricae*, the *Poemetti* are largely an apology for country life, intent on transmitting the joy of taking refuge in a world that resists the evil of modern society. Country life fosters intimacy and solidarity; it protects against the new subjectivity of individualism, against wholly private spheres of activity, against the meaninglessness and existential despair that comes from the man-dominated environments which have eliminated nature. It is only in this perspective that we can grasp the ideological meaning of Pascoli's religion of country life, embodied in the industrious peasant who, in intimate contact with nature, performs tasks that are always the same, in harmony with the rhythmic passing and return of the seasons. The ideological fable he constructs in the *Poemetti* in relation to the Barga family is the poet's nostalgia for wholeness of which only traces remain (memories, mementos, objects). Unlike Verga, whose naturalism destroys the myth of the good society, Pascoli retains his faith in the spontaneity and purity, the unity of social life, and in the sacred figures that have passed away.

In the *Canti di Castelvecchio* ('Songs from Castelvecchio', 1903), Pascoli's anguish over the deaths in his family (his father was murdered in August of 1867 and his oldest sister, mother and brother Luigi died shortly after) takes on a more pervasive form than in the *Myricae*. Death is inescapable and ever present as the new country landscape of Castelvecchio di Barga, where he took residence in 1895, interacts with the past of his childhood in San Mauro, reactivating a host of desperate memories. The peace attained in the *Poemetti* is no longer possible; the reader is invited to enter and participate in the poet's inner world of sounds and colours, and in the flow of images which make up a lyrical narrative of the seasons as they unfold. It is a universal or cosmic death that such poems as *La cavalla storna* ('The Grey Mare'), and *Il ciocco* ('The Log') evoke: the death of poetry at the hands of technological civilisation which expresses the desire to possess and transform. Pascoli's strategy is to name things as they are and to return to the elemental forms of experience present in the soul of a child. The reader is thus made to see the world with the candour of a child's vision, in its original freshness: to feel death as irrecoverable loss and to experience desire without knowledge, as the sweet but undefined affirmation of need.

In the *Poemi conviviali* ('Banquet Songs', 1904), the richness of Pascoli's cultural background appears in full light. His conception of poetry as childlike meditation is applied to subjects of history and myth that represent crucial stages in mankind's development. In contrast to Carducci, however, Pascoli makes no attempt to capture the uniqueness of the classical world and juxtapose it to the present; instead he transforms it into an arena of poetic meditation (an historical analogue to the 'fanciullino') from which the poet voices his own decadent sensibilities: the shadow between idea and reality, the vagueness of desire and the mysteries of existence, as, for example, in 'Solon', where the Athenian poet and lawmaker conceives of poetry as a doleful chant that transcends death, or in 'Alexandros', the great conqueror Alexander the

Great who, having no more peoples to subdue, acknowledges the emptiness of fame and limits of human knowledge.

It is easy to see why Pascoli has contributed more than any other poet of the time, including D'Annunzio, to the renewal of Italian poetry in the twentieth century. Pascoli's 'fanciullino' theory of poetry achieves in practice the creation of a new language of poetry which replaces the heritage of ideas and images of the past with the recognition of a new poetic field of object-reality. Especially in the *Myricae*, the poems contain a small group of images which in their simple and uncommon referentiality take hold of the reader's mind. The world is reduced to these images which become universal symbols, captured not only visually but also in their sound. The mind that shifts from image to image produces a fragmented and suspended syntactical rhythm which matches, thematically, the loss of equilibrium that can only be compensated for in fresh combinations of words and, thus, new revelations of reality.

Popular fiction

At the opposite extreme from the poetic and rhetorical complexities of D'Annunzio and Pascoli, and at the outermost boundaries of naturalism and realism can be set a large assortment of narratives that fall within the category of 'popular fiction'. Advancing no claim to literary quality, these novels seek only to provide the common reader with scenes of adventure, romance and horror and to excite pity for the ills of society. Among such writers Emilio Salgari (1863–1911) was, and remained throughout the twentieth century, the most popular. He wrote numerous stories set on the sea and in the perilous jungles of the Far East, such as *Il corsaro nero* (1889) and *Le tigri di Mompracem* (1911). One of Salgari's fictional characters, the Malayan pirate Sandokan, is still universally known in Italy. Just as prolific were Carolina Invernizio (1851–1916), author of *La sepolta viva* ('The Woman Buried Alive' – 1889), *Il treno della morte* (1906), and many other terrifying and pathetic stories of love and hardship, and the Neapolitan Francesco Mastriani (1819–91), whose more than one hundred novels (including the immensely popular *La cieca di Sorrento* ('The Blind Woman of Sorrento' – 1852) and *I Misteri di Napoli* (1875)) describe the miserable living conditions of the populace of his native city.

35
Pirandello

Felicity Firth

The world-wide reputation of Luigi Pirandello (1867–1936) rests largely upon his plays. His name is associated with theatrical innovation, the representation on the stage of shifting levels of reality, masks, role-playing, and the relationship between art and life. His acknowledged masterpiece *Sei personaggi in cerca d'autore* (*Six Characters in Search of an Author*) is perennially discussed by critics and theatre historians, and he ranks with Ibsen, Chekhov, Brecht, Shaw and Beckett as a colossus of twentieth-century theatre.

His contribution to world literature ought, however, to be assessed in the light of his mastery of two genres, the play and the short story. Some of the plays were based on the stories, with varying success, but the stories cannot be seen simply as the store-house from which the plays are drawn. They outnumber them by five to one in any case, and deserve to be studied in their own right for a fair picture of Pirandello's creative achievement. For an understanding of his philosophic stance, and of his work as a whole, there are essays and novels too which have to be considered. The volumes of poetry, which belong to his earliest period, mark his literary apprenticeship, and while they are of interest, poetry is clearly not Pirandello's natural medium.

His entire oeuvre seems to have been 'fashioned out of pain', to echo his own appraisal of *Don Quixote*. His dramatic protagonists, from Enrico IV to the unnamed self-portrait, the grand old man of letters in *Quando si è qualcuno* (*When One Is Somebody*), are all motivated by the need to accommodate themselves within an intolerable condition. Those, like Leone Gala in *Il giuoco delle parti* (*The Rules of the Game*) or Baldovino in *Il piacere dell'onestà* (*The Pleasure of Honesty*), who seek to abstract themselves, are merely suppressing beneath their chilling exteriors what Pirandello calls a 'cry of despair' or an Erinys, a fury-song, a scream of rage or protest at the human lot. A comprehensive reading of the short stories reinforces this impression, epitomised in the title of one: 'Pena di vivere così' ('The pain of living like this').

Pirandello was very much the product of his milieu and his moment. He spent the first twenty years of his life in Sicily, moving eventually to study philology at the University of Bonn, and settling in Rome in 1892. Although he never lived continuously in Sicily as an adult, his inheritance remained that of his not wholly European early environment, a blend of Latin passion and Arab isolation and concentration, mixed with the paradoxical Sicilian mania for cerebration, analysis and argument. The volcanic, earthquake-ridden land-scape also provided him with a constantly recurring image of life as a seething luminous flow which hardens gradually into solid masses of petrified rock. This substratum of turbulence, which erupts in violence and disaster, he found echoed in Sicilian society, barely kept under by the crust of bourgeois formality coagulating above it. Cavusù, the name of the village near Agrigento where he was born, is the Sicilian word for chaos, and Pirandello delighted in referring to himself as a 'child of chaos'.

Early essays and novels

In the world of ideas too, Pirandello felt the ground to be shifting beneath his feet. This is clear from his important early essay of 1893, *Arte e coscienza d'oggi* (*Contemporary Art and Conscience*), a statement of his intellectual starting-point which demonstrates his awareness of living in an age of transition. He describes the modern spirit as profoundly sick, and deplores all the contemporary materialistic explanations of the universe and the inade-quacy of current modes of thought and artistic expression – determinism, symbolism, naturalism, decadentism and so on. 'Coscienza', by which he means both conscience and consciousness, is at crisis-point. 'We can have no knowledge, no precise notion of life; only a feeling, inevitably changeable and changing.' He was already using the word 'relativity': 'Now that all the old standards have crumbled . . . our awareness of the relativity of all things is so all-embracing that it has become impossible to form judgements.' While here he is clearly referring to moral and scientific judgements and not to the principle of cognition itself, the seeds of popular relativism, later to become his hallmark, are palpably present.

The most important works in the period up to 1910 are the essay on humour, *L'umorismo* (*Humour*, 1908), two novels, *L'esclusa* (*The Outcast*, 1893) and *Il fu Mattia Pascal* (*The Late M. P.*, 1904), and a hundred or more short stories. *L'umorismo*, originally devised as a series of lectures, is an exposition, backed up by lengthy illustrations from literature, of Pirandello's idiosyncratic definition of 'humour', that ironic dual perspective, entirely distinct from the comic spirit, which enables one to see both sides of an ambiguous situation. According to Leonardo Sciascia it is yet another reminder of Pirandello's Sicilian provenance, deriving from the Arab incapacity to separate, as the Greeks do, the tragic from the comic. In a frequently quoted passage Pirandello describes a bedaubed and bedizened old lady in girlish garments, the antithesis of what an old lady should be. The immediate response, laughter, accompanies what Pirandello calls the 'avvertimento del contrario', the intellectual recognition of the contradiction. Later, with know-ledge of her tragic history, comes a second response: laughter is checked and mockery turns to pity as the 'sentimento del contrario' takes over, once the incongruity is apprehended by the heart as well as the head. There is a good deal of graphically illustrated anti-rationalist argument in *L'umorismo*: the image of life as a mighty river which human beings vainly try to control and channel into pathetic little irrigation systems; the mind seen as an infernal little machine which refines every warm impulse from the heart and makes of it a poisonous abstract concept; the human race hurtling *en masse* towards the tomb, glass eyes, wooden legs and all, adjusting their masks in their headlong flight in a desperate attempt to project a favourable outward image of non-existent inner selves.

The novel *L'esclusa* also deals with the gap that exists between a person's outer face and inner reality. Marta Ajala is the innocent victim of public opinion. Mistakenly she is thought to be an adulteress and is hounded by family, potential employers and her local community (recognisably Agrigento) from one desperate remedy to another, until finally, in an access of self-doubt, she turns to her putative lover and becomes the adulteress she has long been thought to be. Ironically it is only after she has transgressed that her husband relents and takes her back. The novel establishes the principle, to be found everywhere in Pirandello's writing, that life is tolerable only if one can see one's worth reaffirmed in the minds of other people.

Il fu Mattia Pascal (1904) was written initially to rescue Pirandello's family finances after the flooding of his father's sulphur mines near Agrigento, the main source of his income. He was by now married with three children; the disaster proved a turning-point in his personal history in that it triggered the mental illness from which his wife Antonietta was to suffer for the rest of her life. Of his seven novels, *Il fu Mattia Pascal* is the most widely read. It is the story of a man who by a twist of chance is given the opportunity to start life again and construct for himself an entirely new personality. In its exploration of the nature of identity it foreshadows notions of the self as illusory and fragmented that were to be a major feature of Pirandello's theatre in the 1920s. Mattia Pascal finds that the past is not a disposable commodity; the existential vacuum does not sustain life. In his case he needs to see his very existence reflected in the minds of others. It is a sharp philosophical book laced with anti-rational argument. In a central chapter the case is made that it is our very anxiety to understand life that cuts us off from it. Instinct prompts Mattia, in his new life, to reach out to Adriana, his landlord's daughter, and offer her his love. But without a past and a persona, he has no one to offer her to love in return; he can only hope to see an empty space reflected in her eyes. Defeated, he returns to his home town to find that life has gone on without him. Thought to be dead, he is not recognised. All the people see is a man who looks remarkably like the dead Mattia. He concludes that he does not know who he is but only who he has been in the past. The existential parable seems very modern. There is no essential self to function as a guide; one can only speak with any certainty of what has been.

The novel *Uno, nessuno e centomila* (*One, No-one and a Hundred*

Thousand), first projected in 1912 but not completed until 1926, again explodes the myth of single identity. Written in a deliberately alienated, mock-naïve tone well suited to questioning philosophic assumptions, it opens with the protagonist Vitangelo Moscarda's discovery that he has a crooked nose, and that consequently the perception of him by others differs from his own perception of himself. Appalled by the thought of the hundred thousand botched and partial versions that his contemporaries must receive of him, he sets out to destroy these images with a deliberate programme of disconcerting actions. Ultimately he frees himself even of the burden of self-awareness and, bereft of self, is absorbed into the cosmos, having taken leave of his reason. One *punto vivo* or live spot remains, the ability to suffer. He suffers and so he is; the book is a study in the pain of human consciousness, and at the same time a compendium of *pirandellismo*, essential reading for anyone seeking to understand the author's basic reasoning. It has a curious authority deriving both from the honesty of its despair and from the clarity of its organisation.

Short stories

Pirandello produced short stories continuously throughout his adult life, from 1894 until his death in 1936. The greatest concentration of good stories belongs to the early period before the First World War. A division is discernible between stories written before and after (roughly) 1910. The earlier stories are purely pessimistic, expressing a sombre acceptance of an incomprehensible universe governed by chance, brief accounts of the momentary reversals which occur when chance interferes with human lives. Typical of the period are 'Marsina stretta' ('The tight jacket'), 'La mosca' ('The fly'), 'Va bene' ('Very well') and 'La toccatina' ('The greeting'). After 1910 Pirandello's horizon widens and a metaphysical dimension creeps in. Life is still a trap as in 'La trappola' of 1912, but occasionally it offers the consolation of a visionary glimpse of some other dimension of being as in 'Canta l'epistola' ('Reciting the epistle'), 'Notte' ('Night'), 'Ciaula scopre la luna' ('Ciaula discovers the moon') and 'La carriola' ('The wheelbarrow'), brief episodes suited to an episodic form.

Around 1910 the stories bear witness to Pirandello's growing concern with relativism. The world becomes not merely incomprehensible but unknowable, a principle which works against the authority of the omniscient narrator and against narrative itself. He now casts his stories increasingly in the form of monologues, using various devices to establish the single subjective standpoint. He may either use 'free indirect speech', or first-person narrative addressed direct to the reader, framed within a reported dialogue, or attributed to a fictive observer concerned in some way with the story.

Plot and character are not primary concerns of Pirandello's. For him there is no such thing as character, and a world ruled by chance is not story-shaped. His stories break in upon crisis points in individual lives when affliction or constraint has built up to such a pitch that the tension snaps, producing confession, tragedy, hilarity or bleak philosophising.

On the whole the stories evince a deeper pessimism than the plays. 'La trappola', already mentioned, is possibly Pirandello's darkest statement. Humanity is portrayed as a doomed race, segregated from the flow of life, slowly solidifying, 'fixed for death'. 'We couple, corpse with corpse, and in our couplings think we are bestowing life . . . in fact we are bestowing death: one more for the trap!' In similar nihilistic vein are stories like the early 'In silenzio' ('In silence') and 'Il libretto rosso' ('The little red book') or the later 'Niente' ('Nothing') and 'La distruzione dell'uomo' ('The destruction of man'). Numerous stories are set in Sicily, and in these the suffering is well-rooted in poverty and its attendant vices, greed, dishonesty, cruelty and disregard for the value of human life. Animals figure as emblems of the irrational and the instinctive, 'la bestia', the wayward beast which foils human delusions of control. The appealing black kid in 'Il capretto nero' which turns into a rank and ruttish billy-goat is the story of all our loves; a stray bat in 'Il pipistrello' disrupts a theatrical performance; elsewhere a dying horse distracts a bride from her wedding night, and indeed horses, dogs, cats, flies and crows are all unwitting agents of death.

All this darkness is conveyed with a light touch, shot through with paradox, wit, irony and a sense of absurdity. The figures who claim Pirandello's attention are often contradictions in themselves: the visionary lawyer, the euphoric prisoner, the murderous child, and repeatedly the lucid madman. Marriages are entered into in despair and death is frequently courted, with grim success or with comical anti-climax. Relationships are dislocated; nothing fits. Outward appearance is constantly misleading. The caricatural element is strong, for grotesque ugliness is seen as one more illustration of the work of chance. There is also an abundance of absurdist detail, for in a meaningless world random objects can assume disproportionate importance, like the blade of grass worth dying for in 'Canta l'epistola' or the shiny wrapping-paper which is a reason for living in 'La morte addosso'.

Theatre

This was a time when the Italian theatre was attempting to assimilate, albeit in a toned-down form, the subversive innovations of the Futurists (see below, pp. 495-7), mixing the symbolic with the real, breaking down the coherence of characters and privileging gesture and action over dialogue. This produced the so-called 'grotesque' theatre of, among others, Luigi Chiarelli (1884-1947), Luigi Antonelli (1882-1942) and Rosso di San Secondo (1887-1956). Pirandello never abandoned short fiction as a medium, but his output of stories decreased sharply when he began writing seriously for the theatre from 1917 onwards.

When relativism became his major preoccupation it was a natural progression that he should complete his abandonment of the authorial position and allow his characters to engage in autonomous confrontation on the stage (relegating his own voice to the stage directions). The initial inspiration for his plays before the great relativistic works were conceived, was Sicily. After long expressing reluctance to write for the theatre he had collaborated with the Sicilian dialect dramatist and director Nino Martoglio in the staging of two one-acters, *La morsa* (*The Vice*) and *Lumíe di Sicilia* (*Sicilian Limes*), in 1910, and in 1916 was persuaded by the Sicilian actor Angelo Musco to write for him a purely comic play. He produced *Pensaci, Giacomino!* (*Think About It, Giacomino*) and *Liolà* (1917), followed closely by *Il berretto a sonagli* (*The Cap with Bells*, 1918), all written in the native dialect of Agrigento (Pirandello's mother tongue and the subject of his doctoral thesis at the University of Bonn). The protagonists of all three are subversives, advocates of an independent morality: Professor Toti, who deliberately plans his own cuckolding; Liolà, who fathers babies to settle old scores, and the very Sicilian Ciampa in *Il berretto a sonagli*, whose complaisance in his wife's adultery is itself a costly protest against the prevailing code of vengeance and justice. The Sicilian ethos itself gives rise to the conflict, provoking the individual's rebellion against the oppressive rule of public opinion. In this respect these first plays resemble Luigi Chiarelli's *La maschera e il volto* ('The Mask and the Face', 1916), sometimes acclaimed as 'Pirandellian' although it also deals with purely social pressures and not existential ones.

Cosí è (se vi pare) (*Right You Are (If You Think So)*, 1917) is Pirandello's first dramatic statement of relativism. The realist theatre of his predecessors, Ibsen, Chekhov, Verga and all writers of traditional domestic drama, was based on belief in the existence of a world whose absolute truth was accessible, and the merit of the realist play was measured by the faithfulness with which it represented 'reality'. The central thesis of Pirandello's 'new theatre' is that since no such verifiable world exists, each individual has to create a truth of his own to live with. Sometimes these 'truths' conflict, a situation made for theatre, and classically embodied in *Cosí è (se vi pare)*. Alternately Signor Ponza and Signora Frola hold the stage, carrying their audiences with them (the one on the stage and the one in the auditorium). The veiled figure of Signora Ponza, summoned in vain at the end to resolve the mystery, constitutes a salutary warning to those who would trespass across the boundaries of private truth.

The implications of relativism for the theatre were immense; they included the loss of belief in the concept of character, and loss of faith in the competence of language to convey meaning, doubts which had been embodied in Pirandello's thinking as far back as *L'umorismo* and *Il fu Mattia Pascal*. But his relationship with traditional bourgeois realist theatre was ambivalent; in many of his plays he continued to borrow its techniques while undermining its assumptions with his vision. Contrary to popular belief, he tended to avoid technical innovation except in his four plays on the theatre. He had witnessed the experiments of Expressionists and Futurists and his theatre owes little to these innovators. He felt some affinity with Rosso di San Secondo and the self-styled 'grotesque' theatre with its non-naturalistic vision of human beings as tormented puppets, but on the whole his contribution to the demise of realism had more to do with vision than with technique. His legacy was perhaps that he freed the stage from triviality; in the words of Nicola Chiaromonte, 'with him the theatre becomes again what it was in its earliest beginning: an empty space where one plays at questioning the meaning of human deeds and passions'.

Pirandello, like his contemporary Evreinov whom he greatly admired, saw all life as theatre. Performance is humanity's only means of expression. There is a gulf between inwardness and outwardness, between inspiration and expression, which humans constantly struggle to bridge in life and in art, and which is perhaps most nearly bridged in the theatre itself. Theatre, as Dr Hinkfuss says in *Questa sera si recita a soggetto* (*Tonight We Improvise*), is 'art, yes, but life as well. Creation, yes, but not durable creation: it is of the moment. A miracle: form which moves.' The theatre came to be for Pirandello an emblem of all forms of communication, and his growing preoccupation with it was both practical and philosophical; the actor was the exemplar of humanity, struggling to make his inner life known through masks and roles and mimicry.

Inevitably the theatre is fallible. The process of conveying inspiration from author, via script, director and actors, to an audience is full of pitfalls. The failure of theatre is the failure of communication as a whole. This was a theme Pirandello could never leave alone and which he was still grappling with when he died. At this point it becomes logical to deal with the plays thematically.

Theatrical procedures are taken to pieces and found wanting in four of Pirandello's plays, in the so-called theatrical trilogy: *Sei personaggi in cerca d'autore* (1921), *Ciascuno a suo modo* (*Each In His Own Way*, 1924) and *Questa sera si recita a soggetto* (1930); and in *I giganti della montagna*, (*The Mountain Giants*), begun in 1928 and still unfinished, its questions unanswered, when he died. In all four a group of actors is seen performing, or trying to perform, a play, based on events which are either fictional or fixed by having happened in the past. The primary concern in each case is not the sequence of events in the story to be told, but the manner of the telling. The inner stories in the trilogy are fairly lurid melodramas: in *Sei personaggi* a tale of adultery, prostitution and incest; in *Ciascuno a suo modo* one of betrayal, suicide and whirlwind passion; while *Questa sera si recita a soggetto* deals with a story of primitive obsessional jealousy.

All three transcend the banality of their subject-matter. In *Sei personaggi* six ghostly figments, the supposed rejects of some author's imagination, interrupt a rehearsal in a theatre and demand to be given expression. They are searching for an author to tell them their meaning. They exist as partial beings in the context of a few contingent episodes, as raw consciousness lacking any kind of social presence. To be complete they need bodies, voices, direction and a fair hearing; above all, a look at the non-existent text. What they find is not an author but a stage; performance is their only option. Conflict and confusion ensue as each tries to hold the stage and impose his or her version of events on the others. The play's formlessness, its lack of a sequential plot, its complete break with the patterns and structures of traditional theatre, caused fighting in the streets of Rome on its first night. The disturbing existential image of a bunch of lost souls clamouring for definition dominates the play, accounting for its perennial appeal to theatre directors. Pitoëff and Reinhardt recognised the profundity of its symbolism and staged influential productions in Paris and Berlin. It is now seen to have constituted a turning-point in theatrical history, both as a statement of twentieth-century *angst* and as a searing analysis of the limitations of realist theatre.

In Pirandello's scheme of things human beings have to write their own scripts. He shares the existentialist premiss: there are no essences; there is no 'character'; as Donata Genzi says in *Trovarsi* (*To Find Oneself*), 'There is no such thing as being, being is making yourself.' Drama arises when what you are for others is outside your control. This is demonstrated in *Ciascuno a suo modo*. Delia Morello is seen as 'good' in Act I and as 'bad' in Act II. The tenor of the play is that of a debate or inquest. Delia listens to her attackers and defenders and accepts their versions in turn. Between the acts the play itself is discussed by a supposed 'audience' on stage, fiercely divided in their verdicts. In the inner play the mouthpiece character, Diego Cinci, recommends the only tenable philosophic stance: recognition of human fallibility and limitation, and acceptance that the only certainties are the 'little certainties of today', names, addresses and little sums of money. The theatrical trickery of the rigged interval discussions, and the planted characters of Nuti and Moreno in the audience who are finally mesmerised into mimicking in 'reality' the fictional dénouement, provide an entertaining element of surprise as well as reinforcing the play's message of uncertainty and its suggestion that life, for want of a pattern, will sometimes copy art.

There is more theatrical trickery in *Questa sera si recita a soggetto*. This was the fruit of Pirandello's practical experience as a theatre director of his own Teatro d'Arte (1925–8). When Mussolini withdrew his support for this venture, Pirandello lived for two years in Berlin, where the flourishing producers' theatre led by Max Reinhardt inspired in him both scepticism and admiration. *Questa sera*, in which the actors rebel against the director, Dr Hinkfuss, was dedicated to Reinhardt. The basic scenario is based on the story 'Leonora, Addio!' of 1910, in which the ex-opera singer Mommina is destroyed by her Sicilian husband's possessiveness. To achieve the miracle of living theatre the actors decide to rid themselves of both text and director, and improvise. Mommina, overcome by emotion, all but dies on stage as a result. The actor cannot afford to jettison discipline and technique (we discover anyway that Hinkfuss, like some theatrical Wizard of Oz, has remained in control of the lighting); and perhaps in life too, if we are to survive we should stand back from ourselves and give the actor's version. The idea goes back to *L'umorismo*: let the mask slip and you look upon the face of death or madness.

In *Questa sera* the extremes of theatrical practice are explored: the Reinhardtian indulgence in lavish spectacle, in the noisy religious procession trooping through the auditorium, in the garish village night-club with its jazz, bright lights and trashy prostitutes, and above all in the spectacular airfield by night with which Hinkfuss-Reinhardt demonstrates his virtuosity; and at the other extreme we have the bare stage, the imaginary prison walls, the fateful 'two boards and a passion' of the final scene. Actors interrupt with scripted heckling from the auditorium, while the actors in the play continue the action in the intervals, bickering in all the theatre's public spaces. Pirandello may have a name for breaking the barrier of the proscenium arch, but there is never any real improvisation or confrontation. In the theatre he seems merely to flirt with the idea of fluidity, clinging – perhaps in trepidation – to a strict and total control.

In the plays of the trilogy, the imperfections of theatre are laid bare. Directors, scripts, scenery and actors fail to communicate. In the case of *I giganti della montagna*, Pirandello himself failed to complete the script, perhaps because in it he had posed a vital irreducible question which he had found unanswerable: what is art for? Is the intention of the creative artist to realise his vision, in itself and for its own sake, or is it to communicate whatever he can muster of his vision, however incompletely, to an uncomprehending public? The action takes place in a kind of magical no-mans-land 'on the borders between fable and reality', and Pirandello, in the guise of Cotrone the magician, offers to a bedraggled bunch of actors the crucial choice between the conflicting states of make-believe and real life. Either they may stay in Cotrone's enchanted villa and realise their dream of poetic drama to perfection but in isolation, or they may take their inadequate talent and exhausted resources up the mountain, to where the Giants (of industry and materialism) will provide them with an audience of mindless and brutish underlings who may very well destroy them. At the point where they are offered the choice Pirandello stopped writing, but his son Stefano has written an account of his father's intentions for the final act. The actors were indeed to stage their fable, and be torn to pieces by hooligans. The question is whether Pirandello perceived this outcome as defeat, emblematic of the death of poetry in the twentieth century, or as a bid for life, a valiant stand for art in a philistine age. Stefano Pirandello's notes are inconclusive, and directors have interpreted them in conflicting ways.

In *I giganti*, with its apparitions and miracles, Pirandello breaks new ground, venturing into the realm of the supernatural. He grouped it with two other plays, *La nuova colonia* (*The New Colony*, 1928) and *Lazzaro* (1929), and called the three his 'myths'. *I giganti* is the most successful. In the other two Pirandello seems less sure of his subject-matter: social justice, regeneration, life after death and the power of faith. They are problematical plays with immense themes, but remain minor works.

Trovarsi (1932) provides another illuminating exploration of the principle of performance. The symbolic actress/protagonist, Donata Genzi, in her search for herself, attempts to live authentically, without 'performing', in her love affair with Eli, an instinctive, unself-conscious child of nature. She covers every mirror in their cabin by the sea, but self-awareness is not so easily routed. Only on the stage is she free of herself, finding her only authenticity in the constant metamorphosis afforded by performance.

The most concentrated and tragic treatment of this theme is found in Pirandello's masterpiece of 1922, *Enrico IV* (*Henry IV*). The assumed madness of the unnamed twentieth-century individual referred to as Enrico is a metaphor for all human refuges from chaos. In his own words it is 'the self-evident and deliberate caricature of that other ongoing masquerade of all time in which we all, unwittingly, play the fool; masking ourselves with whatever it is we think that we are'. The acting-space itself appears as a metaphor for consciousness, a fragile circle of fantasy to be protected at all costs against invasion by outside predators. The grotesque unreality of Enrico's pantomime, his clumsy paint, dye and fancy dress, serve to underline his pathos and vulnerability. The play has an emotional charge which raises it from philosophic demonstration to the status of classic tragedy. Enrico is an intensely theatrical figure of Lear-like stature, lucid in madness, and the embodiment of human isolation, 'il grande Mascherato', who in darkness contemplates 'the misery which is not his alone but that of all humanity'.

Enrico feels he is the prisoner of his portrait, which hangs at the back of his throne-room; the Unknown Woman in *Come tu mi vuoi* (*As You Desire Me*) strives to resemble the portrait of the person she hopes she is; Baldovino in *Il piacere dell'onestà* follows a notional picture of an imaginary man of integrity; Martino Lori in *Tutto per bene* (*All For the Best*) believes he is one person and discovers he is another. The multiple and fragmented personality and the unsuccessful search for self eventually became axioms of twentieth-century European theatre. Pirandello's contribution was to point out the dramatic possibilities of this modernist motif, and he must have exercised an incalculable influence when he enjoyed a brief but decisive vogue in Paris in the 1920s. His view of personality is palpably present in the plays of Crommelynck, Salacrou, Giraudoux, Anouilh, and later in those of Camus, Sartre, Beckett and Ionesco.

There are even Absurdist traits to be detected in Pirandello's work, long before the notion of Absurdism had been formulated. Such tendencies are to be observed in the novels, in *Così è (se vi pare)* and outstandingly in *L'uomo dal fiore in bocca* (*The Man with the Flower in His Mouth*, 1926). This is almost an anti-play in that there is no story and the words do not arise from or lead to action. The dialogue is virtually a monologue; no exchange is hoped for. Words and random images tumble over each other and, like Beckett's *Krapp's Last Tape* or Ionesco's *Le Roi se meurt*, the play comes over as the representation of a state of mind, one man's protest against the dying of the light. Two men sit at a café table at the side of a road in a halo of light shed by a single street-lamp. A voice in the night speaks with quiet insistence about the heightened love of life which comes with knowledge of mortality. The flower in the man's mouth is cancer. The play consists of a single act, a bare half-hour upon the stage, and its brevity is part of its message. It leaves its audience with the ineluctable impression that life itself is a terminal disease.

The Rise and Fall of Fascism
(1910–45)

Robert Dombroski

36

Poetry and the avant-garde

The turn of the twentieth century in Italy was a time of great upheaval. Modernisation and expanding industry, while producing unprecedented prosperity, had disrupted the existing political and social institutions and alienated the popular masses. The modern, industrial society formed by economic liberalism was blamed for leading the country to the brink of collapse. Thanks to the parliamentary system, a once 'well-knit' and 'vital' human community had been replaced by the self-interest of political parties; the 'people' – the grandiose concept that galvanised the forces of Italian national unity – had been degraded, thanks to socialism, into the reality of 'social classes'; an organic world, supported by tradition and moral values, had been turned into one dominated by political economy and materialism. The ways of reacting to this imaginary state of affairs combined age-old conservatism with vitalism and mysticism, and relied on myth and intuition as an antidote to positive knowledge. Philosophical vitalism at the turn of the century held that there existed in all living things a 'primary finality' or 'vital flux' which could not be reduced, as Darwinian science maintained, to environmental variables. The vitalistic philosophy which influenced Italian thought most in this period was that of Henri Bergson (1859–1941), who emphasised the cognitive power of intuition: its capacity to penetrate to the heart of objects and reveal what is unique and rationally inexpressible in them.

Although positivism was in itself believed to be a-political, its appeal to 'scientific' facts and its rejection of all spiritual and metaphysical doctrines, as well as its interest in the then developing social sciences, made it a strong ally of the socialist movement, whose appeal in this period had grown considerably, to the extent that in some quarters positivism was identified with socialism. The attacks against positivism issued from all quarters, some of the more substantial coming, in the footsteps of Marx, from the left (e.g. Antonio Labriola, 1843–1904). Croce headed the liberal assault in the name of neo-idealism (see below), and the young militants who congregated around the cultural reviews of the time united the most disparate of ideological forces to combat what was regarded as the true intellectual and spiritual menace of the time.

A major factor in this reaction to industrialisation, science and democracy was the new social condition of the intellectuals. The first two decades of the twentieth century witnessed in Italy an intensification of the change, begun with the unification, in the position of intellectuals in society. Once a privileged, economically independent caste, the intellectuals gradually became salaried workers, employed for the most part in education or, to much lesser degree, in the then nascent cultural industry. In other words, the democratisation of culture widened the ranks of the literate and educated, creating intellectual groups that had to compete for recognition. Like their Risorgimento predecessors, they too attempted to bridge the gap separating High Culture and the concrete politico-economic processes of social change. But unlike their forebears, they had no predetermined role to play in the fashioning of society, no channels of social mobility which would guarantee success in the real world. The government, moreover, was regarded as promoting solely the interests of Big Business and the urban proletariat at the expense of the middle and lower-middle strata of society. As a result, the intellectuals felt displaced to the margins of the social system. Bereft of traditional privileges and having no collective mandate to further, they became increasingly more politicised, mounting, from the right to the left of the political spectrum, projects for subversive action. The many intellectual currents of social activism which flourished between 1900 and 1915 (Futurism, Nationalism, Irredentism, Interventionism, etc.) were designed to restore a human and social dignity believed to be lost, and at the same time to improve the lot of particular class and group formations in relation to others.

These tendencies find their most forceful expression in the first three Florentine reviews of the century. *Il Regno* (1903–6), under the direction of Enrico Corradini (1865–1935), diffused the ideology of nationalism, while *Hermes* (1904–6), edited by the novelist and critic Giuseppe Antonio Borgese (1882–1952), was largely D'Annunzian in orientation. *Leonardo* (1903–7) represented the aspirations of a group of young intellectuals, led by Giovanni Papini (1881–1956) and Giuseppe Prezzolini (1882–1982), who in their profound dislike of bourgeois passivity espoused a kind of pagan individualism, founded in irrationalism, vitalism and intuitionism. Papini and Prezzolini, who went on to found *La Voce* (1908–16), continued in their role as intellectual provocateurs throughout the first half of the century.

The impact of rapid modernisation was felt most strongly by the writers born between 1875 and 1890, who reached maturity during the first decade of the new century at the height of industrial expansion. This generation, which comprised several of the most prominent literary intellectuals of the century, experienced at first hand what Walter Benjamin has called the decline of the 'aura'. The feeling of a colourless existence within the masses elicited a host of aesthetic responses, from rebellion to doleful meditation on mankind's common fate. But there was no doubt that the beginning of the age of commodity production had signalled a turn away from Italy's classical past and from the notion of art as the exclusive property of the humanist élite. In the modern capitalist world, art is part of the fluctuations and ambiguities of life as regulated by the market economy; it thus relates to the entire social fabric.

Futurism

'Death to the past' was the rallying cry of Futurism, a movement launched in 1909 by Filippo Tommaso Marinetti (1876–1944) with the first of several manifestos attacking the age-old institutions of Italy's Catholic-humanistic legacy while exalting the rule of technology and the beauty of industrial civilisation. Marinetti and his Futurist associates promote the new relationship between art and social reality under capitalism. The artist becomes an integral part of society; his genius is a commodity whose value depends solely on the laws of the market system. In proclaiming the beginning of a new and active alliance between man and the machine, Futurism demonstrated the need for all people of every social class to realise their dependence on the process of industrialisation. Futurists had to eliminate from within themselves and from their world all traces of the traditional notions of nature, man and human productivity. Their attack on society involved not only written manifestos such as *Contro la Venezia Passatista*, *Contro la Montmartre* or *Contro la Spagna Passatista* ('Against Venice "Passatista"', 'Against Montmartre', 'Against Spain "Passatista"' – *passatista* meaning *passé*) but physical assaults and riots as well. They opened headquarters in various cities from which to move forth on their enemies, publish newspapers and gain publicity. Their art and lifestyle fostered the search for a new aesthetic based on the beauty of the machine, its violence and velocity. Many Futurist documents insist on the ritualised destruction of the architectural signs of the past; museums, for example, were not merely to be shut down, but blown up. Individuals too had to eradicate the *passé* components of their existence, to peel away the external layers of socialisation in order to get to their sensual and machine-like inner core. The new Futurist individual is a metallised composite of flesh and interchangeable mechanical parts, a human engine designed to generate speed. Similarly, the machine has human qualities: a personality, a soul, will-power. When metallised man and humanised machine become one, the result is a constant interchange of intuition, rhythm, instinct and metallic discipline. The highest – in the sense of most revolutionary – form of man–machine intercourse is war. War is a purifying process for the ongoing eradication of *passé* trends and tendencies in both the individual and the social structure. In war, the machines best express their power to 'renovate': they destroy existing bonds between people and thus promote the development of an entirely different, goal-oriented, material-producing social system – the wartime political economy. Man's role changes in wartime: he becomes a cog in a giant mechanism, a parameter in a massive logistical calculation, an extension of destructive devices as well as one himself. His bodily makeup neither has nor contains any inherent, transcendent source of value: consisting of replaceable parts, his very brain may be programmed to maximise efficiency and output. By humanist standards, he loses his identity and becomes standardised; but at the same time, as the Futurists are quick to emphasise, his experience becomes vividly visceral and personal. Combat and conflict take on a sexual value: the turbulence and chaos of battle are linked to sexual intercourse in a very blatant way. War is a 'furious coitus'. The Futurist goal is to maximise the frequency and intensity of orgasms. All life builds to the ultimate orgasm, the climax of the life-and-death struggle. From the standpoint of aesthetics, Futurism's revolutionary programme stressed the coherent simultaneity of experience and the interpenetration of objects, in contrast to the static representation of reality in which a high premium was placed on linear causality and the historical determining of experience. In poetry, the technique of agrammatical writing is a correlative to life's state of perpetual strife and aggression. It confuses multiple levels of reality, while at the same time, by emulating graphically and sonorically the unwinding of physical and psychic energies, it resolves the cognitive dilemma which such a mixing of things proposes. For Marinetti, Futurist poetry, in exhibiting the force of carnal violence, destroys both the classical principles of harmony and decorum and the romantic, bourgeois ideal of the subject's psychic and moral integrity.

Of the Futurist poets, Ardengo Soffici (1879–1965) produced some of the best experimental verse of the time. Painter, art and literary critic, Soffici was an active mediator between Italy and the French avant-garde. He introduced Italian artistic culture to Impressionist and Cubist painting, and wrote a seminal essay on Rimbaud (1911). *Bif & ZF+18 – Simultaneità e chimismi lirici* ('Bif & ZF+18 – Simultaneity, Lyric Chemisms', 1915), his collection of Futurist poems, is a collage of visual and auditory impressions that combine memory and sensation to give the effect of poetry in motion. The simultaneous amalgamation of everything the poetic self has experienced generates a plurilingual text in which classical terminology is combined with foreign and dialectal utterances. Soffici's experimental poems are complemented by his attempt to be part of a political vanguard, as is evidenced in his picaresque novel *Lemmonio Boreo: l'allegro giustiziere* ('Lemmonio Boreo, the Happy Executioner', 1912), in which the protagonist, a kind of Tuscan Don Quixote who prefigures in thought and deed the Fascist *squadrista*, roams the countryside in search of wrongs to put right. In the 1930s, Soffici was to embrace Fascism wholeheartedly, writing propaganda poems that exhibited the order and decorum he had so rigorously denounced.

Diametrically opposite to Futurism's enthusiasm for the age of machines is the compelling, albeit short-lived, work of Carlo Michelstaedter (1887–1910). In *La persuasione e la rettorica* ('Persuasion and Rhetoric', 1913), Michelstaedter advances, in the wake of Leopardi and Nietzsche, one of the period's most devastating attacks on philosophical optimism and progress. The central idea of his 150-page tract, written as a doctoral thesis, is that human life is founded on illusion, its sole purpose being to forestall death. Technical progress cannot stop the inevitable. The fate of humankind is to suffer, no matter what the rhetoric of science preaches. Its 'illusory persuasion' must be replaced by 'authentic persuasion', which consists in the acceptance of man as a biological entity destined for extinction. Only by taking hold of the present and accepting the negativity of life can one avoid the trappings of rhetoric and illusion. Thus Michelstaedter stands in stark opposition to the various 'isms' of his time which sought to counter the breakdown of the old order by advancing new forms of spirituality.

Poetry

The crepuscolari

Another kind of response to the machine era and to the social conflicts it generated are the lyrics of the so-called 'crepuscular' poets. The metaphor, coined by the critic and novelist Giuseppe Antonio Borgese to refer to a condition of consumption and decline, describes a group of poets whose melancholic verse was a sign of their living as survivors in the wake of modernisation. Unlike D'Annunzio and Pascoli they could neither revivify the past or evoke its glory; nor did they believe in the power of poetry to compensate for the loss of traditional values. In marked contrast to the Futurists, the *crepuscolari* desired to flee the alienating effects of industrialisation and the cultural marketplace by taking refuge in a monotonous world of commonplace realities, among simple, unattractive things which inspire an equally simple, unheroic and delyricised verse, often indistinguishable from ordinary speech. By far the most prominent of the *crepuscolari* was Guido Gozzano (1883–1916), author of the collections *La via del rifugio* ('Road of the Shelter', 1907) and *I colloqui* ('Conversations', 1911). Gozzano stands out from other notable representatives of the movement, such as Sergio Corazzini (1886–1907) and Marino Moretti (1885–1979), for the intensity and range of his verse, and ultimately, for his ironic indifference to the subject-matter of his poems. In recounting the poet's own unvaried, banal life in the provinces amid the 'buone cose di pessimo gusto' (good things in bad taste), Gozzano's poetry centres on the impossibility of being a genuine poet; it tells of a dreamless life devoid of hope and emotions in which nothing – not even the simple things – has meaning.

In capturing the dullness of ordinary existence, the *crepuscolari* not only extended the poet's field of vision, but also marked a new course for Italian poetry that would be characterised by a greater openness, more intricate correspondences, and a general dismantling of traditional poetic unities in favour of loosely articulated, fragmentary utterances. The work of Corrado Govoni (1884–1965) and Aldo Palazzeschi (1885–1974), poets associated with the *crepuscolari* early in their careers, represents a definite turn in such a direction. Govoni's lyrics attempt to enliven a dead social reality by expressing the disconnected, atomised fragments of the world and of human experience in their distinct colours and vibrations. Palazzeschi's voice regresses to its infancy, becomes the sound of child at play with the verbal and social props of adulthood. His nonsense verses mock the poetic culture of his day, from such naturalistic conventions as onomatopoeia to the phantasmagorical imagery of modern life celebrated by the Futurists. Both Govoni and Palazzeschi write from an avant-garde perspective, clearing the decks of tradition and seizing on the dislocation of structures in modern society to fashion unique poetic styles. Palazzeschi, moreover, extended his experimentalism to narrative fiction with novels including *Il codice di Perelà* ('Perelà's Code', 1911), and *Le sorelle Materassi* (1934).

If the new poetry was the mirror-image of a disintegrated reality and of the random and solitary life of the human subject, it was also capable of generating its own antithesis. Piero Jahier (1884–1966) translated into the stylistic austerity of his war-diary (*Con me e con gli alpini*, 1919) the quest for moral commitment that distinguished the milieu of the Florentine periodical *La Voce*. In the work of Camillo Sbarbaro (1888–1967), the heightened consciousness the poet shows of his predicament produces a hallucinatory vision of displaced objects and deformed individual features. The poetry of Clemente Rèbora (1885–1959), by contrast, aspires toward totality and moral voluntarism, while in Arturo Onofri (1885–1928) poetry becomes a means of celebrating the presence of God in nature. Vincenzo Cardarelli (1887–1959), founder of *La Ronda* (see p. 509), sought a return to a classical purity of style, harking back to Leopardi and Manzoni.

Campana

The poet who captures most distinctly, and also transcends, the chaotic existence of the subject in industrialised society is Dino Campana (1885–1932), Italy's own *poète maudit*, who spent the last twelve years of his life confined to a mental hospital. Campana sought to unleash the potentially destructive force of poetry by creating dizzying visions of commonplace reality. His poems are meant to excite. Familiar places and things explode in a myriad of analogies; they appear in highlighted proximity and instantaneity, as in a confused, schizophrenic vision. The delirium is meant to redeem reality of its meaninglessness at the same time as it exhibits the subversiveness of poetic language. In the *Canti orfici* ('Orphic Songs', 1914), Campana converts the hazard and chance of his universe into the mystery and magic of a journey back to a Mediterranean homeland, towards nothingness and death. Campana's poetic vision is an expressionistic *tour de force*. His world cries out viscerally in despair; it has lost every sense of orientation. The poet can mirror life only in the form of pain; he writes with 'sangue alle dita' (blood on his fingers).

Saba

In contrast to the avant-garde, Umberto Saba (pseudonym of Umberto Poli, 1883–1957) regarded poetry much less as a means of transcending the insecurity and instability of daily life than as an occasion for self-analysis. While the experimentalists demanded originality of the poet, Saba believed his sole responsibility was to be forthright. Honesty, accountability to one's self, conscience, were in his view the essentials on which poetry depended. The poet's self-discovery leads back to roots deeply embedded in tradition and in the collective consciousness of his people. To return to, rather than repudiate, tradition was for Saba synonymous with being original: it provided access to his 'origins', thus to the uniqueness of his life and its poetic expression. Through self-knowledge the poet could arrive at an unimpaired quality of being, establish an internal harmony of emotion, partake of the collective consciousness and unite with nature. Such an ideal of plenitude conflicts, however, with the reality of alienation. To link up poetically with a community is to partake of its grief and misfortunes, to experience its pain and suffering, while at the same time taking pleasure in the aesthetic consolation it offers. The imagination seeks to understand the world completely, to integrate mind and reality, but knows that torments will persist and that peace is not at hand. What the poet seeks can be had only at the expense of knowledge. Self-examination and consolation are irreconcilable processes. This contradiction is at the heart of Saba's poetry. It is a vision that holds no illusion of innocence, no escape either into mystery or tradition, no aestheticist nostalgia for 'ripeness'. It prescribes only a response in the form of a face-to-face confrontation with the vacuity of existence. Poetry prevents poet and reader from falling into the existential void; it extracts beauty and pleasure from what is negative and intolerable in life.

Early on in his career, Saba decided to incorporate all of his poetry into a book designed to capture the development of his life as in a novel. He gave the book the title of *Canzoniere* ('Songbook', 1900–45) evoking primarily Petrarch, but also a collection of poems by Heinrich Heine, entitled *Canzoniere* in an Italian translation of 1866. Saba intended his poetic autobiography to be a wholly modern *canzoniere* which, while paying homage to the classical lyrical tradition and its idealisation of human experience, represented life concretely in all its variegated and fragmented impurity. Saba devoted most of his life to ordering, revising and editing his *Canzoniere*, the definitive version being published posthumously in 1961. He went as far as documenting its evolution in *Storia e cronistoria del 'Canzoniere'* ('History and Chronicle of the Songbook', 1948), a detailed assessment of the book which he himself wrote in the years between 1944 and 1947. In its final form, the *Canzoniere* is divided into three volumes, the first two containing eight books each, the third, nine. The three-part division is meant to correspond roughly to the development of the poet's life and poetry from youth to old age.

Taken in its entirety, the *Canzoniere* is indeed a kind of autobiographical 'novel', organised around a number of significant themes all united by the need to recover some undefinable locus of plenitude. The early poems, *Poesie dell'adolescenza e giovanili* ('Poems from Adolescence and Childhood', 1900–7), focus on the feelings and sensations of the poet in his youth, on the world seen through the eyes of innocence, and in general attempt to paint a portrait of the poet as a young man. They work mainly with more traditional and conventional poetic forms, such as the *endecasillabo*, and their stanzaic patterns and poetic vocabulary are mostly modelled after the classics studied at school, particularly Petrarch and Leopardi. In the *Versi militari* ('Military Verses', 1908) Saba's voice begins to take on its peculiar intimacy and simplicity of tone and diction. The experience of brotherhood and community, themes that resonate throughout the *Canzoniere*, also begin to emerge, as does the poet's fondness for animals, which he sees in the 'simplicity and nakedness of their lives' as being close to God.

The themes of shared suffering and the saintliness of animals are disclosed in two of Saba's best-known poems, contained in the collection *Casa e campagna* ('Home and Countryside', 1909–10): 'La capra' ('The Goat') and 'A mia moglie' ('To my Wife'). The first of these is about a captive goat which reminds the poet of his own sadness and pain. The goat's condition of being alone and tethered, satiated, and drenched by the rain is voiced in a doleful bleating which the poem echoes in its chant. In 'A mia moglie', Saba compares his wife Lina to a series of barnyard animals, 'le femmine di tutti / i sereni animali / che avvicinano a Dio' (the females of all / the serene animals / who draw closer to God). As in all the poems in this collection, the graceful simplicity of the images conceals adolescent fantasies and fears. Lina's qualities which liken her to a white pullet, a pregnant heifer, a faithful and protective bitch, as well as a graceful swallow and a prudent ant, are the materialised feelings of a child for his mother whose link to him is just as precarious as the life of the animals she resembles. *Trieste e una donna* ('Trieste and a Woman', 1910–12), Saba's largest single collection (forty-five poems in all), is the story of the poet's love for Lina, set against the background of Trieste. It is a troubled love, beleaguered by suspicions of betrayal and by the anguish and despair the poet suffers on account of his complexes. The city in its 'tristezze molte / e bellezze di cielo e di contrada' (many sorrows / and beauties of sky and land) provides solace. It is there in the *osterie*, on the street corners of the old city, among the crowds in the market places, on the docks or in the cemetery, that the poet discovers he is not alone in his tormented existence and that the city and its people make his personal traumas acceptable.

In Saba's later collections, it is the lightness of things that holds the poet's attention. Happy apparitions that wander through his life in the form of young girls, his daughter in 'Cose leggere e vaganti' ('Light and drifting things'), his young love Chiaretta to whom he dedicates 'L'amorosa spina' ('The loving thorn') and the host of *fanciulle* (girls) that populate 'Preludio e canzonette' and 'Fanciulle'. But even here the poet's joy is tempered by the realisation that the sensuous and desirable children of his fantasy, for whom 'la vita è solo ancora un gioco / generoso' (life is still an unselfish game) and who are 'con levità connesse / con gli déi, tutte simili un poco' (joined in levity / like the gods / all somewhat alike) will some day feel the weightiness of life.

From *Autobiografia* ('Autobiography', 1924) to *Il piccolo Berto* ('Little Berto', 1929–31), the life the poet loves and detests at the same time is embodied in echoes from the past, which become the voices of his psyche. In *Cuor morituro* ('The Moribund Heart', 1925–30), the places and people of his youth are reinvoked from a position close to death. The paradise of youth returns in dream-sequences that cannot be transformed into reality. The sweetness of youth cannot be renewed, for the poet has lost hope; the only prospect left is for him to join his dead mother in her grave. The most compelling poem of this collection, however, is 'Il borgo', a *canzonetta* that announces the only positive solution to the poet's malaise: 'd'essere come tutti / gli uomini di tutti / i giorni' (to be like all everyday men). The poet's dying heart can be revitalised if he comes out of himself to get a clearer, more objective knowledge of his predicament. Saba's experience of psychoanalysis will contribute to a greater clarity of self-understanding. It also marks the beginning of a more intense simplicity which from *Cuor morituro* on moves towards a bareness of style where words are cut down to a minimum and rhyme schemes abandoned altogether. The ultimate source of measure and harmony is no longer tradition. It is a presence in the things themselves which the word makes resonate. In *Parole* ('Words', 1933–4), *Ultime cose* ('Last Things', 1935–43) and *Mediterranee* ('Mediterranean Scenes', 1946), Saba's verses are directed toward an unspecified 'tu': a boyhood friend, himself, or a Jew, like himself, living at the time of the racial edicts. In these later collections that are part of the final volume of the *Canzoniere*, the poems incorporate multiple elements of tension, addressing themselves to his and his times' 'unbearable ills'. Having reached such depths of despair and anguish, he implicitly asks, 'How is poetry possible?' He puts some hope in myth and music, has attachment to his Mediterranean origins, but it is the feeble attachment of an old man whose life was anything but extraordinary.

The birds of Saba's last poems are an appropriate metaphor for the poet's lifelong aspiration towards a paradise on earth. Like the canaries imprisoned in their cages who dream of their native habitat, the poet realises that his happiness is a dream that will never come true. Suffering is one and the same with living, an effect of existence just as natural as the impulse to escape. But Saba, following Leopardi rather than his older contemporaries, realises in the final analysis that no compensation is possible, there is no way of exiting from his wretchedness, no aesthetic pleasure, no community of listeners, no means whatsoever of acquiring the sought-after ripeness: 'Parlavo vivo a un popolo di morti. / Morto alloro rifiuto e chiedo oblio' (Alive I used to speak to a dead people. / I reject the dead laurel and ask to be forgotten). (See further below, pp. 554–5.)

Ungaretti

The poetry of Giuseppe Ungaretti (1888–1970) is also largely autobiographical. But in contrast to the modest intentions of Saba's project, Ungaretti's embodies from its very beginning a myth of renewal. Ungaretti's art is nothing less than a programme for reclaiming a lost innocence which is at once the beginning and the end of history. His conception of poetry is inextricably linked to the idea of miraculous creation. The negative term 'history', which in Saba holds sway over aesthetic pleasure and compensation, is repressed altogether, dismissed with one sweep of the poetic word. Like Vico's primitives, the modern poet in Ungaretti's canon turns to the magic of words. The linguistic tradition is a repository of lyrical resonances which the poet collects and integrates into his own sensations. In this way he gains access to the deep emotional core of his race, its collective psyche, which tradition safeguards and nourishes. Poetic imagery is mythical by virtue of the mysterious power it wields. Its scope is to attain a unique moment of fullness devoid of any and all logical connections.

In itself, Ungaretti's desire to revive poetic tradition through the mysterious power of words can be considered as just another variant of the decadent or Romantic desire to regain, in the era of advanced industrialisation, a supposedly lost 'freedom' by proving the superiority of intuition over logic and of 'experience' over technology. These general modernist characteristics aside, Ungaretti's poetic subversiveness is never an end in itself, but rather a cognitive process aimed at realising new unities of being which in his first collection *L'allegria*, originally *Allegria di naufragi* ('The Joy of Shipwrecks', 1914–19), is signalled by absence, by a poetic space at once dilated and empty. Against the backdrop of war, this extraordinary collection of poems recreates the silence to which the modern age has condemned poetry. The loss of language, or muteness, represents the poet's resignation to an existence perceived as the destruction of being. The poet responds not by total silence, but by lunging into the substance of things in such a way as to unleash the force of poetic meaning from the fragments of words left within him:

> Ecco il mio cuore
> che s'incaverna
> e schianta e rintrona
> come un proiettile.

(Here is my heart, become a cavern, and bursting and thundering like a projectile.)

In *Sentimento del tempo* ('Sentiment of Time', 1933) and later books, especially *Il dolore* ('Grief', 1947) and *Un grido e paesaggi* ('A Cry and

Landscapes', 1952), the void of *L'allegria* has been expanded and filled out. Subversiveness and order are interdependent parts of a new mode of poetic consciousness that depends on the definitive end of a tradition from which it draws its vital energy.

The poetic situation begins when the poet, in a moment of existential uncertainty, starts to understand himself in relation to absolute existence. The ontological problem which Ungaretti resolves with the poetics of 'allegria' is that of uniting into one single dimension the atemporality of being and events experienced within the flux of time. Thus the concrete existence of the foot-soldier on the front line is dematerialised into *Life*. Harmony is attained at the moment when the negative conditions of existence are effaced, when the perception of truth translates into lived truth. At that point, poetry ceases being an illumination and becomes *Life*. In sharp contrast to Saba, for whom life contained in equal measure harmony and fragmentation, Ungaretti's phenomenological notion of *Life* consisted in the subject's domination of reality. The fusion of the subjective and the objective in *Life* produces the *raptus* ('l'allegria'). In this sudden transition from history to *Life* the subject reclaims the purity and innocence it was lacking:

> Questo è l'Isonzo
> e qui meglio
> mi sono riconosciuto
> una dolce fibra
> dell'universo.

(This is the Isonzo, and here best I recognised myself, a sweet fibre of the universe.)

The poet's spirit has been liberated from all of its impurities; it achieves the condition of being 'full'. This dissolution of the materiality of lived experience into a phenomenological quest for authenticity, this epiphanic leap into Being, makes possible the poet's communion with the Absolute. Poetry is for Ungaretti literally a means of redemption. But what is more important is that he regards the achieved totality not as the by-product of his own, personal desire, but rather as an objective dimension. Between poetry and reality there is no disjunction.

Il sentimento del tempo gives figure and substance to the dematerialised impulses of *L'allegria*. There is a return to order, reflected in the use of punctuation and traditional metrics, which in the first collection had been discarded. The precariousness of individual life is no longer expressed in images of self-abandonment or in anarchic cries into the emptiness of the blank page, but has evolved into a well-defined attitude which centres on myth, tradition and the sublime as mirrors of the Absolute. This collection, assembled mainly during the years of Fascist rule, invites the reader to share in the poet's experience of Time and to become resolute in the quest for a *canto italiano*, the essence of a distinctively Italian poetic voice. To put it another way, fullness or authenticity are no longer predicated on poetic desire, as in *Allegria*. Rather they become realities in time that must be subdued aggressively. Thus the classical world Ungaretti reclaims becomes the content of an extreme form of Romanticism, unknown in Italy:

> Mi presero per mano nuvole.
> Brucio sul colle spazio e tempo,
> Come un tuo messaggero,
> Come il sogno, divina morte

(Clouds took me by the hand. I burn time and space on the hill, Like your messenger, Like dream, divine death.)

(Canto Quarto)

Such is the desire for communion with the Absolute that the poet in his plunge into the emptiness of illusion feels not even the slightest remorse or fear. From the standpoint of technique, the Baroque – especially of the Gongorean and Shakespearean variety – becomes the medium of Ungaretti's experience of present time expressed through complex analogies and arcane metaphors. Paradoxically, the Baroque, embodied in the figuration of Rome, is the poet's vehicle for attaining the 'innocence' of the classic vision in which – to complicate things further – religion is a necessary component. The most representative poems of this collection are 'Sirene' ('Sirens') and 'L'isola' ('The island'), in which the poet achieves his union with the cosmos through the sensuous mirage of illusion. In the second half of *Sentimento del tempo*, Ungaretti's preoccupation with the absolute brings him to confront the existence of God and the crises and torments of the dynamics of belief, dramatically expressed in the hymns 'La Pietà', 'Caino', and the seven cantos of *La morte meditata* ('The Meditated Death').

The collections *Il dolore*, *La terra promessa* ('The Promised Land', 1950), *Un grido e paesaggi* and *Il taccuino del vecchio* ('The Old Man's Notebook', 1960), develop the Baroque complexities of *Sentimento del tempo* and employ them (especially in *Il dolore*) to convey dramatically such moments of personal catastrophe as the death of the poet's son Antonietto ('Amaro accordo', 'Bitter agreement' and 'Tu ti spezzasti', 'You shattered yourself'), or the tragedy of war as reflected in the ruins of Rome ('Folli i miei passi', 'Mad are my steps'). These poems are written in what Ungaretti calls the 'Baroque style of titanic suffering'. In their oblique syntax and polysyllabic diction, they display again the poet's search for firm foundations and permanence, expressed in his contemplation of both the frailty of his dead son and the ruins of ancient Rome.

Quasimodo

Salvatore Quasimodo (1901–68, Nobel prize for literature 1959) is the poet whose lyrics best illustrate what was then referred to as 'hermetic' poetry: a verse sealed in impenetrable imagery where nuances of sound and colour take precedence over subject-matter. In his books *Oboe sommerso* ('Sunken Oboe', 1932), *Erato e Apollion* ('Aerato and Apollyon', 1936) both contained in *Ed è subito sera* ('And It Is Suddenly Evening', 1942), the poet is absorbed in the vagaries of the landscape, nature's mysteries and the substance of the un-fathomable, arcane past of his Sicilian homeland. Poetry moves away from reality toward the lyrical world of the poem. A sense of external reality is conveyed through sounds and cadences, as in the verses:

> Ognuno sta solo sul cuor della terra
> trafitto da un raggio di sole:
> ed è subito sera.

(Everyone stands alone in the heart of the world, transfixed by a ray of sun, and it is suddenly evening.)

This poem, meant to echo the austere voice of the solitary poet amid the silence and emptiness of the world, illustrates well the paradoxical operational principle of Quasimodo's poetry, if not that of the hermetic lyric in general: that after the destruction of all illusions the poet's music can still help us forget.

Montale

The fundamental difference between Eugenio Montale (1896–1981) and his major contemporaries consists in his rejection of the assumption that, despite the negative conditions of human existence, poetry carried out a largely positive function, whether it be that of expressing the fantasies of a collective consciousness, bringing the hidden self out from the depths, fusing the disparate elements of consciousness into a harmonious totality, or linking the poet entrapped in historical contingency with the mysterious substance of origins, race, people or nature. If there is any one thing Montale assimilated from the poets of his time it was the belief, held by Gozzano and the *crepuscolari*, that poetry was a failed enterprise devoid of all legitimacy. 'Codesto solo oggi possiamo dirti, / Ciò che *non* siamo, ciò che *non* vogliamo' (We can only tell you today, / what we are *not*, what we do *not* want).

These lines conclude the prefatory poem to *Ossi di seppia* ('Cuttlefish Bones', 1925). The title of the book denotes the lifeless, dried-out remains washed ashore by the waves, which poetry drags out into the clean light of day. The elementary nakedness of these verses is the only thing capable of transcending the situation which seems to make poetry impossible. Out of the anguish and malaise can come only negation and the 'Divine indifference' which is both defiance and self-affirmation. If poetry is to be reborn, it must be reborn into history, de-formed and desiccated ('qualche storta sillaba e secca come un ramo', some crooked syllable and dry like a branch), skeleton-like and impotent. For it to reappear the materiality of the world must be given back. Montale's intention in writing *Ossi di seppia* was to achieve some kind of absolute expression. To capture in words the substance of things was of course impossible, but the desire to do so persisted none the less. Montale's starting-point is with the realisation that poetry in its aspiration toward essentiality must abandon the poet's conceptualised perceptions of the world. Adhering to reality involves a fresh act of naming. Through naming, things are captured in all their actuality, beyond any relationship with the subject; the object-world is called into being, forced into the open by the resolute desire of the poet to be clear. As a result of naming, the subject loses its centrality, becoming one among other objects to be named.

Furthermore, the subject-matter of the poems carries the burden of a new moral commitment, as is apparent from 'I limoni' (the first poem in the book), where Montale sets himself apart from the poets laureate who 'si muovono soltanto fra le piante / dai nomi poco usati' (move only among plants / with little-used names). His poetic terrain is more familiar, although less trodden: 'strade che riescono agli erbosi / fossi' (streets that turn into grassy / ditches) and 'viuzze che seguono i ciglioni ... e mettono negli orti, tra gli alberi dei limoni' (little paths that follow the banks ... and end up in kitchen gardens, among lemon trees). Even the poor can enjoy the scent of lemons; their colour brightens up the wintry landscape; but this is small compensation for a world which escapes our understanding, leaving us with the vain hope that one day, through some weak link in the system ('l'anello che non tiene'), truth will emerge. Thus Montale marks the distance setting him apart from both D'Annunzio and Pascoli, on the one hand, and Ungaretti and Saba, on the other.

The thematic nucleus of the *Ossi di seppia* consists in negativity, its principal theme being 'il male di vivere', a wholly objective condition which has little resemblance to Romantic or aestheticist malaise. Life's evils are present in the ordinary things of this earth: in 'il rivo strozzato che gorgoglia' (the hoarse voice of a strangled brook), 'l'incartocciarsi della foglia' (the shrivelling of leaves), 'il cavallo stramazzato' (the fallen horse) – and are all effects of a destructive necessity permeating the world. The world of the *Ossi* is mainly Liguria, Montale's native region, a land parched by the sun, immobile, essential in its sounds and colours, and intimately involved with the sea that bathes its shores. From within this landscape the poet confronts the naked truth of life. Dismantling common illusions of meaning and purpose, he searches out every possible exit from the material necessity governing the world. Like Pascoli and Saba, he entertains momentarily the fantasy of childhood harmony and peace. But instead of recovering the child's spontaneity and oneness with things, he is more reflective and detached than ever, a child grown old. Nature too holds a potential for relieving the poet's anguish. He desires its essentiality, hopes to achieve its manifest balance, and perhaps savour its ripeness and permanence. He would have liked to have been 'rough and elemental', as well-honed as a pebble turned over by the sea; but instead, he is introspective, slow to act, intent on finding the reason for the world's ills, following his mind instead of his heart. The sea, on the other hand, in its strong rhythms and elemental movements, in its power to clean and transform, in its capacity to purge itself of the waste deposited in its depths, is a paradigm for the poet's style.

In *Le occasioni* ('The Occasions', 1939) the search for a deeper stratum of reality produces concrete moments in which the object reveals its unfathomable secret of being in a sudden burst of radiance. The poems of this collection focus exclusively on objective reality; each is an 'occasion' for redeeming the negativity of history; but they do so by conveying difficult, largely undecipherable messages.

The sub-text of *Le occasioni* is the tumultuous history of the late 1920s and 1930s: the consolidation of Fascist dictatorial rule, the rise of Nazism, the purges, the Spanish Civil War, the invasion of Ethiopia – events that strike to the heart of Montale's liberal ideology. In such a climate, the search for some measure of objective truth loses its urgency. The more brutal reality becomes, the greater the need to safeguard whatever values still remain uncontaminated, above all poetry. The poet as a servant of truth has been thoroughly defeated by historical reality. The autobiographical self, removed from the lyrical narrative, appears now only intermittently, in flashes that energise the mind, directing it to other places and events. The subject of the *Ossi* has been transformed into a transcendental self, crystallised in the myth of Clizia, the angel with 'steel-like eyes' whose sacred message is summoned to save the poet from the barbarism that threatens the world. Clizia is not the only female figure Montale invokes in the *Occasioni*. Real women from his past, all engaged in surviving life's onslaught, constitute 'occasions' for salvation. Insignificant objects and moments from the past break into the poet's conscious mind as revelations that briefly counter the brutal realities of present time.

La bufera e altro ('The Storm and Other Things', 1956) contains poems written between 1940 and 1954. As in *Le occasioni*, the female figures, the cognitive and inspirational forces behind Montale's vision, move effortlessly in and out of the verses, leaving no stability of meaning. In 'Finisterre', the section composed during the Second World War, Clizia prevails. Later on, the poet calls on 'Mosca' and 'Volpe' (Fly and Fox), nicknames assigned to less beatific presences in the poet's life. Thus, *La bufera* reinstates a line of personal narrative, abandoned in the previous book, which covers two distinct historical moments: the war years alluded to in the book's title, and their aftermath leading into the 1950s and the Cold War. The first moment is characterised by the poet's dream of a better world for everyone, the second by his disillusionment: the realisation that the death and destruction have led not to the restoration of values, but rather to their complete effacement in a society governed wholly by personal economic interests. It might have been better to live during Fascism, when the lines of battle were clearly drawn: 'It was easier to use oneself up, to die / at the first beating of wings, at the first / encounter /

with the enemy; that was child's play.' These are lines from 'L'ombra della magnolia' ('The shade of the magnolia'), the poem in which Montale bids farewell to his divine mistress Clizia, for now amid the vulgarity of the masses he can no longer find reason to believe in the existence of a higher sphere.

37

Philosophy and literature from Croce to Gramsci

The literary and ideological quarrels of this period were disputed in numerous reviews and literary magazines. By far the most important of these was *La critica* (1903–44), edited and directed by Benedetto Croce. In its pages, Croce carried forward his struggle against positivism and empiricism, establishing his reputation as Italy's greatest modern philosopher and as the intellectual and moral rallying point for anti-Fascist intellectuals. In spite of *La critica*'s vast influence, however, Crocian neo-idealism, with its foundation of reason and hierarchy and its staunch defence of liberal democracy, did not satisfy the needs of younger intellectuals, who, removed as they were from the sources of political power, sought more radical answers. *Leonardo* (1903–7) and *La Voce* (1908–16), the reviews which best reflect the climate of turbulent intellectual upheaval that characterised Italian society in the period prior to the Great War, provided a forum for the dissemination of several varieties of European irrationalism. The Triestine Scipio Slataper (1888–1915) was one of the contributors to *La Voce* whose idealism cost him his life at the front. From the pages of *La Ronda* (1919–23), Riccardo Bacchelli (1891–1985), called for a return to classical ideals in literature and art, in opposition to the vanguardism of *Lacerba* (1913–15); while Piero Gobetti's *Energie nove* (1918–20) and *La rivoluzione liberale* (1922–5) championed a working-class revolution based on liberal-democratic principles, and *L'ordine nuovo* (1919–25), founded by Antonio Gramsci, appealed to Marxist notions of class struggle in an attempt to unite intellectuals and proletariat in the battle against capitalism.

All in all, the culture in which Fascism took root was one in search of moral and intellectual direction. Its many currents of thought were both a sign of its heterogeneity and a symptom of the deep socio-economic crisis at its base. The leaders of the Fascist movement, as well as their constituents, experienced the same displacement from the operative channels of social mobility as did the new intellectual groups. But unlike other radical groups of the time, they provided a large-scale political and organisational solution to the problem. Fascism came to power as a response to the disintegration of society; it drew on the irrationalism of the age to equate a new totality of existence with a vitalistic process; it consolidated its power by force but also, culturally, by formalising the totality to which it aspired in the construction of myths.

The principal philosophical legacy which early twentieth-century Italian thought drew on and developed was German idealism, particularly its Hegelian and Fichtian variants. Its major exponents were Benedetto Croce and Giovanni Gentile. Their espousal of idealism involved the rejection of all positivist modes of thought (the scientific and deterministic conceptions of reality which then governed Italian socialism) in favour of reality, considered to be the free, self-expression of the 'spirit'.

Croce

The philosophy of Benedetto Croce (1866–1952) – originally referred to as 'absolute idealism', (the only reality is the spirit), subsequently as 'absolute historicism' (the only reality is history) – was an explicit attempt to reform Hegelian dialectics. It was formulated in four distinct parts corresponding to as many activities of the human spirit: aesthetics (*Estetica come scienza dell'espressione e linguistica generale*, 'Aesthetics as the Science of Expression and General Linguistics', 1902), logic (*Logica come scienza del concetto puro*, 'Logic as the Science of the Pure Concept', 1905), economics and ethics (*Filosofia della pratica*, 'Philosophy of the Practical', 1909). In contrast to the Hegelian notion of 'contradiction' as the determining factor in the movement of ideas, Croce argued that the forms of the spirit are based on reciprocal 'distinctions' between the theoretical and the practical, on the one hand, and the particular and the universal, on the other. Art (pure intuition) has for its object knowledge of the particular, while logic (i.e. philosophy) is knowledge of pure concepts (universals); economics is volition of the particular, while ethics is volition of the universal. For Croce, the term 'economics' includes all human activity having a practical objective (e.g. law and politics). These forms of the mind's activity are dynamically interrelated, each presupposing the other. Just as no practical activity is possible without knowledge, no conceptual thought is possible without intuition, for thought is expressed in language and language is of its very nature intuitive. Art, however, enjoys in Croce's system an autonomy all its own, lest it be confused with allegory or didactics.

The relationship between these four distinct forms of knowledge can never be categorically determined. Beauty, Truth, Utility and the Good are qualities of reality that are historically variable, and as such constitute the criteria of historical judgement. History is, for Croce, nothing but the circular movement of these cognitive forms; since history is the only reality, historical knowledge is the only theoretically valid form of knowledge. Philosophy, therefore, combines with historiography in the study of the forms that the human spirit from time to time assumes, and since it is the spirit that seeks to know itself over time, all history is contemporary; that is to say, history is the awareness that the spirit has of its own historicity. To the raw factuality of history (the struggles and conflicts that make up the course of history, as opposed to our knowledge of them) Croce assigned a kind of Hegelian providentialism: human history is the history of the spirit's struggle to free itself from oppression and ignorance; it is therefore the history of freedom. The concrete suppression of human liberties by oppressive political régimes amounts to nothing but temporary pauses in the march of freedom.

In the area of aesthetics, Croce's influence was deep and widespread, particularly among academic critics, and this is why his presence looms so large in the history of twentieth-century Italian literature and culture. For Croce art was a primordial force, the original, cognitive link between the human spirit and the world. In a conception developed from Vico, Croce argued that poetic knowledge (art) precedes rational thought and is at once intuition, expression, language and representation. Its principal quality is purity, for it is in no way conditioned by practical need or historical circumstance. As a lyrical intuition that combines form and feeling in a-priori synthesis, art – Croce maintained – is not to be confused with the art-object, because the concrete realisation of intuition-expression in any one specific technique, literary genre or form is a practical operation, guided by reason and utility. Art, therefore, is disinterested and self-sufficient, a universal, cosmic form transcending all that is practical, including the art-object itself. It follows that literary criticism has as its primary function the acknowledgement or confirmation that the work of art is 'a work of art', that poetry is 'poetry' or, if contaminated by other cognitive forms, 'non-poetry'. In defence of his aesthetics, Croce published numerous volumes of practical criticism, as for example: *La poesia di Dante* (*The Poetry of Dante*, 1921); *Ariosto, Shakespeare e Corneille*, 1920; *Poesia e non poesia* ('Poetry and Non-Poetry', 1923); *Poesia popolare e poesia d'arte* ('Popular Poetry and Art-Poetry', 1932).

Present in all of Croce's criticism is the classical ideal of poetic harmony, identified principally with Ariosto and Goethe and reflective of a sense of order and organicity. The ambiguity and contradictions associated with literary modernism were for him signs of aesthetic degeneration. Of his Italian contemporaries, Croce gave positive consideration only to Carducci and the Neapolitan poet Francesco Gaeta, while in regard to such major figures as Pirandello and D'Annunzio, as well as the entire modern French tradition from Mallarmé to Valéry, he showed nothing but a total lack of understanding.

Gentile

During the first decade of the century, Croce's strongest ally was Giovanni Gentile (1875–1944), the Sicilian philosopher who under Fascism became Minister of Education and President of the Accademia d'Italia. United in the battle against positivism, Croce and Gentile worked closely together in disseminating Hegelian categories of thought. Their collaboration was, however, short-lived, as Gentile developed positions incompatible with Croce's elaborate four-part system of thought; and later, when Gentile joined the Fascist party, the relationship between the two came to a definitive end.

Gentile's more radical brand of Idealism became evident with the publication in 1912 of *L'atto del pensiero come atto puro* ('Thought as Pure Act'), followed by *Teoria generale dello spirito come atto puro* ('General Theory of the Mind as Pure Act', 1916) and *Sistema di logica come teoria del conoscere* ('Logic as Theory of Knowledge', 1917–22). While Croce's philosophy emphasised distinct forms of spiritual activity, Gentile maintained that the only existing reality is thought: thought in the act of thinking, hence the denomination 'Actualism'. Such a conception assigns to the thinking subject the power to absorb history and culture into a process internal to itself. History, which for Croce was the Spirit's awareness of its own historicity, for Gentile was one and the same with the mind's account of it. Since there is nothing outside the act of thought, the thinking subject incorporates both history and tradition; the national past becomes then the present and, thus, the basis for political action (Nationalism).

The thinking subject of Gentile's philosophy is the pure, transcendental, universal Self which assimilates, and thus unifies within itself, the multitude of discrete individual subjects. Following Fichte, Gentile believed that the natural world studied by the empirical sciences was also a product of thought. Nevertheless, the subject imagines nature as having an independent existence; it creates, therefore, an artificial, abstract entity for the purpose of giving an objective status to its subjectivity, but knowing well that objectification is nothing but another act of thought.

Gentile's 'Actualism' has its most decisive consequences in the realms of politics and law, for the universal subject finds its concrete identity in the State as the embodiment of absolute morality. It is therefore not hard to understand how his philosophy lent itself to the aspirations of Fascist totalitarianism. As Fascism's official philosopher, Gentile applauded Mussolini's régime as the ultimate synthesis of Italian culture (*Che cos'è il fascismo. Discorsi e polemiche*, 'What Fascism Is. Speeches and Polemics', 1925).

In the field of aesthetics, Gentile opposed the Crocean theory of art as an autonomous, intuitive form of knowledge, arguing that the work of art comprised a totality of intellectual, moral and imaginative elements, bound in an indivisible, organic whole. He thus emphasised the unity of cultural and aesthetic elements in poetry and – also in contrast to Croce – promoted the kind of criticism which focused on the integral personality of the author. His aesthetic treatise (*Filosofia dell'arte*, 'Philosophy of Art', 1931), as well as his studies of specific authors (*Manzoni e Leopardi*, 1928), exerted an influence almost as widespread as Croce's. Gentilian positions are clearly recognisable in, for example, the writings of Luigi Russo (1892–1961), the academic critic and polemicist who, with Mario Fubini (1900–78), carried on the neo-idealist legacy in the field of literary studies.

Gramsci

Although the philosophies of Croce and Gentile had their greatest resonance on the Right, they also provided the impetus for the renewal of Marxism which in Italy was begun by Rodolfo Mondolfo (1877–1976) and carried on by Antonio Gramsci (1891–1937). Gramsci belonged to a group of intellectuals in Turin around the time of the Great War who aligned themselves with the workers' movement in establishing a revolutionary perspective. Jailed by the Fascists in 1926, he spent the rest of his life in prison, where he compiled a long series of diversified reflections on politics and culture, known as the *Quaderni del carcere* (*Prison Notebooks*, 1949, 1975). Gramsci's great importance and originality consists in his reformulation of the conceptual basis of Marxism. His theory opposed the official doctrine of historical materialism in the emphasis it put on the role of human subjectivity and culture in the development of society. In contrast to the determinism of 'scientific' Marxism, Gramsci accentuated the interaction of objective reality with human thought and creativity, focusing on the moral and cultural basis of political rule. The essential idea of his doctrine of 'hegemony' is that a ruling social group exercises its hold over society by means of the socio-cultural institutions it creates. It becomes 'hegemonic' because through education and leadership it has established its own values as universal norms of political and moral behaviour. Such a social and ideological unity leads to the creation of a 'historic bloc' in which the interests of all the groups comprising the social body coincide as a result of the acceptance of the ruling class's world view as 'common sense'. The collective will that derives from hegemony unites the disparate and often discordant components of society into a 'people-nation', expressive of a 'national-popular' culture. The identity of the ruling social group is made possible through the work of its intellectuals. Intellectuals, organically linked to a particular social group, promote its values through the cultural apparatuses they influence; and they supply the foundation and sustenance for artistic culture.

In the area of aesthetics and criticism, Gramsci opposed Crocean idealism with a materialistic conception of technique as the process by which poetic 'intuition' becomes a work of art by virtue of its relationship to history. Aesthetic values are conditioned by the social and material practices of a given society that grants a particular work of art its subject-matter and the logical basis of its specific form. By and large, the criticism that Gramsci fosters in the *Quaderni del carcere* emphasises the organic value of literature. It is an attempt to bring together the struggle to form a new culture and the critique of literary form. It therefore demands that the critic focus on the social uses of literature and on the activity of criticism itself as a means of promoting and safeguarding hegemony.

Fascism and culture

Although it is true that Fascism failed to develop a culture which could be called specifically fascistic, it accommodated a host of viewpoints that shared a general tendency toward mythic thinking and vitalism. It was thus possible for Fascism to satisfy the irrational impulses of different social groups and cultural orientations. Nationalists, classicists, traditionalists, conservative élitists and religious moralists, on the one hand, Futurists, modernists (*novecentisti*), anti-bourgeois populists and D'Annunzian-type aesthetes, on the other, came together to form a coalition within Fascism, held together by a common hatred for socialism and the pluralism characteristic of liberal democracy. Prominent thinkers who held important positions in the Fascist government include, besides Gentile, the jurist and theoretician of Nationalism, Alfredo Rocco (1875–1938), the historian Gioacchino Volpe (1876–1971) and Giuseppe Bottai (1895–1959), spokesman for technocratic Fascism and editor in chief of *Critica fascista* and *Primato*, the two major Fascist reviews. Fascist policy did not significantly disrupt the Italian cultural tradition.

With the exception of Communism, it tolerated many forms of opposition and competing models of socio-cultural organisation (for example, Catholicism and liberalism), as well as an entire generation of young writers and intellectuals, such as Cesare Pavese and Elio Vittorini, who looked towards America for inspiration.

Indeed throughout the 1930s Italy was a major consumer of American fiction in translation, and Italian writers contributed significantly to the making of 'the American myth'. In 1935 Mario Soldati (b. 1906) published *America, primo amore* ('America, my first love') in which he looked with eyes full of wonder at the daily life of ordinary Americans, and even during the war it was possible to read *America amara* ('Bitter America'), a fascinating and discriminating reportage by Emilio Cecchi (1884–1966) on America's new industrial civilisation. On the whole, Italian literary culture adjusted well to a régime that ensured its 'relative' autonomy, while involving many writers directly in its political and cultural policies (Pirandello, Ungaretti and Gadda being the most important) and creating institutions that gave recognition as well as material compensation for their work. The *Enciclopedia italiana*, founded by Gentile in 1925 and published between 1929 and 1939, enlisted the contributions of numerous literary intellectuals, and the 'Reale Accademia d'Italia' included among its fellows such prominent figures as Pirandello, Marinetti and Bontempelli. So, in spite of the kind of liberal anti-Fascism espoused by Croce and his followers, which was tolerated by Mussolini, and the exile or imprisonment of a handful of dissident intellectuals (Gramsci, but also the conservative, Giuseppe Antonio Borgese), Italian culture was not affected significantly by Fascism.

38

The novel

Compared to poetry, the Italian novel of the early twentieth century appears relatively underdeveloped. This weakness can be attributed mainly to the relative absence in modern Italian history of a strong middle-class culture within which the novel, as in France and England, could have evolved. The work of Italy's greatest nineteenth-century novelists, Manzoni and Verga, was affected to a notable degree by foreign writers (Scott and Zola respectively) and, with very few exceptions (Svevo and Gadda), the same is true throughout the first half of the twentieth century: Italian novelists are significantly influenced by imported fiction, particularly British and American.

The most important direction which the modern Italian novel took after Verga was toward greater subjectivity. The total social world of the naturalist perspective was replaced, in the best novelistic production of the time, by the totality of the individual subject. In Pirandello's novels (see above, pp. 481–3) a single commonplace event enclosed a lifetime's experience, while with D'Annunzio (above, pp. 473–6) the life encapsulated in an object or set of memories harboured the spiritual substance of mysterious essences. For both these writers, the individual stood at odds with an external reality of anarchic forces, taking refuge beyond the borders of reason in some rarefied ontological space. By means of literature, D'Annunzio transformed life into art and spectacle; whereas Pirandello demonstrated that true life was realisable outside the self, either in nature or in madness.

Svevo

The uniqueness of Italo Svevo (pseudonym of Ettore Schmitz, 1861–1928) consisted in his discovery of life as being one and the same with the self, as being, in all its ambiguity and contradictory situations, the effect of will and desire. Literature, instead of furnishing a means of escape, becomes with Svevo a medium of self-analysis and introspection. Its purpose is not to produce a work of art, but rather to 'write' in order to safeguard life from the pressures and hostilities of society and history.

Svevo's particular genius was influenced by his native Trieste, a Middle European city of bourgeois entrepreneurs, and by the fact that he was neither an academic nor a professional writer, but rather a businessman for whom literature was no more than a pastime. His first novel, *Una vita* (*A Life*, 1892) is a study in weakness or ineptitude (its original title was *Un inetto*), a theme that is also the principal focus of *Senilità* (*As a Man Grows Older*, 1898) and *La coscienza di Zeno* (*Confessions of Zeno*, 1923). *Una vita* is the story of Alfonso Nitti, a young intellectual from the country outside Trieste who comes to the city to work in a bank. His idealism and undefined dreams of intellectual success are at odds with the crude reality of the business world. Alfonso is clearly aware of his inferiority with respect to the decisive and practical-minded bourgeois whose moral health, capacity for work and sound judge-ment he cannot emulate. Alfonso's intellectual qualities gain him entry into the bank manager's house. He has an affair with Annetta, the manager's daughter, who harbours vague desires of escape from the grey, material world of her father. But Alfonso cannot seriously engage with reality. He welcomes the prospect of marrying Annetta, but cannot get himself around to accepting a move up the social ladder. He renounces Annetta and returns to the country in search of his roots, quits his job, sends Annetta a letter which is interpreted by the family as an attempt at blackmail, is invited to a duel by Annetta's brother, and finally, seeing no way out of his hopeless predicament, commits suicide.

Alfonso's role as an alienated intellectual finds several analogues in the works of the early Verga, Fogazzaro and D'Annunzio. But in contrast to characters who represent distinct authorial ideals, Alfonso has nothing to oppose to his discontents except his own malaise, self-deception and contra-dictions. His life, distant as it is from any romantic desire for authenticity or aesthetic valorisation, has no redeeming qualities whatsoever. 'Alfonso', says Svevo, 'was conceived as the very personification of the Schopenhauerian affirmation of life which is so close to its negation.' But unlike the decadents for whom being alone and anti-social was a way of emphasising the superiority of the intellectual hero, Svevo employs Alfonso's negations to underline both the degeneracy of his character and the prosaic quality of life under capitalism from which his neurotic aberrations derive.

Alfonso Nitti's suicide marks the death of the petty bourgeois intellectual who, on account of his own ineptitude, is unable to find an ideological alternative to the society he opposes. It also indicates Svevo's rejection of the narrative paradigm associated with Naturalism according to which the prota-gonist's life is recounted in chronological time as a case history set within a specific milieu. With *Senilità* the naturalist perspective is notably diminished, as Svevo takes as his focus not the relationship between character and society, but the unconscious motivations that determine the character's survival. The novel's protagonist, Emilio Brentani, is a writer who suffers from the same infection of the will, which generates daydreaming and wish-fulfilling fantasies. He differs from Alfonso Nitti in that his 'senility' is one and the same as the acceptance of bourgeois normality. The grey, monotonous life he leads as an insurance broker is for Emilio a small price to pay for the stability and protection it provides. The narrative begins with the possibility of his life changing as he has started an affair with Angiolina, a working-class young woman who embodies all the energy and health that he lacks. The novel is largely the story of this unsuccessful relationship. Emilio guards against his own passion for Angiolina. His aim is to limit her influence on him: to have an affair without running any risks, while continuing to meet his responsibilities toward his family (meaning his sister Amalia, who will eventually die from her ether-drinking habit) and his career. The fact of the matter is that he has no grasp of actuality. His plan to be aloof is very much at odds with the seriousness of his passion and so he is unable to plan his conduct: he cannot decide how to act, although he deceives himself continually in thinking he has. At the end of Emilio's story, the narrator seals the protagonist's history with a final ironic commentary meant to mirror Emilio's own senile consciousness. He would like to think that losing Angiolina and Amalia was like being deprived of an important part of his own body, but as time passes his peace and sense of security return, as his instinct of self-preservation again takes over, censoring any and all disruptive desires. But if desire cannot be suppressed totally, it can be reformed by reason. The book ends with a poignant account of this adjustment. Svevo evokes Angiolina as some distant, unattainable reality, at once exhilarating and banal. From the perspective of 'senility', her charm and fascination consists in the fact that she is undecipherable, a free-floating narrative object, reconstructed after the event.

In contrast to Svevo's two previous novels, *La coscienza di Zeno*, written twenty-five years after *Senilità*, is a first-person narrative. Zeno Cosini, a Triestine businessman, has decided in his old age to tell the story of his experience with psychoanalysis. His psychoanalyst, Doctor S., has instructed him to write down his memories as a prelude to the actual therapy. Zeno recounts therefore selective episodes from his life (his attempts to give up smoking, his father's death, his marriage, his infidelity, and finally his business partnership) and in so doing produces the text of the novel which the Doctor, vindictively, publishes when Zeno suddenly decides to break off the analysis.

Zeno is firmly installed in a world of dull, yet gratifying bourgeois values (conscience, duty, truth, legality, etc.) which he both admires for the sense of well-being they foster, and at the same time exposes as façades, manufactured to give an air of respectability to human needs and drives. Zeno's unique gift is an unrelenting consciousness that discloses, at every turn of the narrative, the modes of deception he himself creates in order to safeguard desires he can never thoroughly satisfy. Zeno's neurosis is his means of knowledge, while writing helps him convert his handicap into a powerful hermeneutic that exposes in a clear light all his contradictions and fictions. Yet at the same time, writing too – Zeno tells us – is deceptive, language being the false colouring people give to their thoughts and feelings. There is nothing in Zeno's account of himself that is 'true'; what is 'true' is only his desire and its offspring: contradiction and equivocation.

Compared to Alfonso and Emilio, Zeno is an inherently comic character. In fact, he is often referred to as a kind of Charlie Chaplin, constantly bumping into things but capable of escaping unscathed from the most difficult of situations. His fascination as a character consists in his comic fallibility, which is an effect of the basic incongruity between his conscious and unconscious selves. By composing his own autobiography, Zeno can regulate totally its events, while simultaneously giving himself over to his other self, which operates in him as a second nature. The incongruities of his being are glaring, but, as Zeno himself realises, they are natural to being a subject in the world of monopoly capitalism – a commodity that continually exchanges itself for itself, that differentiates among its many roles and postures (patient, son, husband, lover, rival, businessman, writer), while elaborating with slight variations the same story.

Zeno's story is about a typically bourgeois sickness: alienation from external reality. The medication of self-analysis reveals how the patient has internalised the logic of commodity exchange that regulates, as on the stock market, the index of his desire. In other words, he relates to things and people in a purely functional manner; their existence is an effect of his needs. It is thus not an accident that his return to health is prompted by an act of speculation on the market. Zeno is cured of his bourgeois malady because, paradoxically, he becomes part of it. Accepting sickness as the rule, he is finally free. Life, he writes in the final note of his diary, is ultimately a terminal illness that admits of no cure. The social order in the age of machines, he concludes, is immutable. All that is left is the hope of annihilation which will free the world of 'parasites and disease'. His fatalism derives from a first-hand knowledge of the logic of capitalist production. Exchange value has invaded; it spreads its lethal disease beyond the façade of convention and respectability to the point where its human products, weak, bespectacled men, will fashion mankind's ultimate destruction. It is senseless for Zeno to rebel against it, for machine-age technology has become omnipotent and the natural world which it has poisoned has succumbed to its rule. *La coscienza di Zeno* ends with Svevo's prediction of a cataclysm for the modern world, which will spring from man's chronic ineptitude. Only after the ultimate explosion, 'when the earth returns to its nebulous state', will civilisation be free of sickness and life begin anew.

In the last years of his life, Svevo wrote several stories and plays, mainly on the theme of old age, the subject-matter also of what was to become his fourth novel. Svevo's perspective on ageing is just as ironic and comic as that taken on his younger protagonists' 'senility', which now has become a physical as well as a moral handicap. *La novella del buon vecchio e della bella fanciulla* ('The Nice Old Man and the Pretty Girl', 1927) tells the story of a widowed old man who masks his desire by giving his love affair with his young mistress an educational pretext. The play *Rigenerazione* ('Regeneration', 1926), which Svevo wrote in the last year of his life, is a farcical treatment of the pressures of modernity on old age.

The fragments of *Un contratto* ('The Contract'), *Le confessioni del vegliardo*

('The Confessions of an Old Man'), *Umbertino*, *Il mio ozio* ('My Leisure') and *Il vecchione* ('The Old Old Man') centre on the life of an older, retired Zeno. Ten years have passed since he abandoned his course of psychoanalysis and now, after an operation which he hoped would restore his virility (but of course doesn't), he returns to writing which takes on the function of purifying his past life. In *Le confessioni del vegliardo* Svevo refers to writing as a kind of personal moral hygiene which he attends to every night before going to bed. The historical originality of this conception of literature cannot be overstated, for with it the Italian novel loses its public function as a vehicle for ideology and becomes a writing practice geared to recovering the private sphere of life in its most intimate psychological detail.

Italian literary culture, however, was not moving in the direction mapped out in Svevo's works. It still had a large ideological axe to grind, as is evidenced by the subversive attitudes toward culture and society that characterised the *Voce* milieu in the first quarter of the century. The novel, which was often equated with consumer-oriented production or a return to nineteenth-century models, was left out of the experimentalist programs of the time. As a result, the early twentieth century produced few truly original novelists. If there was no wholly new basis for reinventing the novel (Freud, for example, was largely unknown until the 1950s), the only reasonable approach to innovation was to build on the great achievements of naturalism: in particular on the Verghian practice of dispassionate narration. Pirandello, Tozzi and Borgese regarded Verga's art as an approach to reality without ideological mediation. For Pirandello, Verga provided mainly a stage of modernist paradox, and not at all a narrative formula, while in Borgese the return to Verga amounted to little more than the acceptance of his objectivist perspective.

Borgese

Giuseppe Antonio Borgese was a distinguished literary critic and professor of German and aesthetics at the universities of Turin, Rome and Milan; during the 1930s, while in political exile in the United States, he taught at the universities of California and Chicago and at Smith College. Borgese's reputation as a writer is linked primarily to *Rubé* (1921), a novel which offers an intense account of the ideological habits of the petty bourgeoisie in the period of the transition from interventionism to the post-war social conflicts and the birth of Fascism. Filippo Rubé seeks to compensate for his ineptitude and problematic personal identity through the mystique of vitalism and irrationality. Wounded in the war, he cannot forget the heightened experience of combat, has difficulty readjusting to normal life, leaves his wife and takes a Parisian mistress who drowns in a boating accident. Suspected of killing her, Rubé spends a brief time in gaol; when released, he begins a search for his own personal identity. His investigation confirms the crisis and fragmentation of his identity, his passivity and ineptitude. His life comes to an abrupt end when, caught by chance in the midst of a socialist demonstration, he is trampled to death by the mounted police. The ambiguity of Rubé's protest against the reified experience of an alienated social life is presented as a metaphor for an entire social class which, in spite of its rebellious spirit, remains ideologically locked to the forces that oppress it.

Tozzi

In the work of Federico Tozzi (1883–1920) Verga's legacy is recovered in an expressionist key as a means of representing a world on the verge of disintegration. The characteristic features of Tozzi's expressionism – his fragmented syntax, crafted to mirror the discontinuity of thought and action, and his dynamic use of imagery – are present in the *Ricordi di un impiegato* ('Diary of a Clerk', 1920), his first important work, which recounts, in the form of memoirs, the author's own experience as a clerk employed by the railways.

We find the same theme of isolation in a hostile world in *Con gli occhi chiusi* ('With Closed Eyes', 1919), a novel considered by many to be Tozzi's masterpiece. The title refers to a condition of 'blindness': the protagonist's inner life of dream and fantasy obstructs his vision of reality so completely that his actions and feelings are impossible to understand. At the level of narration, the 'blindness' again makes it difficult to distinguish between the narrating voice and the things narrated. Like Leopoldo, protagonist of the *Ricordi*, Pietro Rosi is weak and ineffective in relating to others: a typical Tozzian character, living through his illusions on the brink of self-destruction, in a dog-eat-dog world.

In Tozzi's third novel, *Il podere* ('The Farm', 1921), Pietro's character-structure is reflected in Remigio Selmi, a railway employee who upon his father's death quits his job in order to manage the country farm he has inherited. Once again, a weak and passive protagonist is victim of the ill-will and antagonism of the others around him. Everyone from his stepmother to the servants holds him responsible for not being the master his father was. His ineffectiveness as a 'padrone' is seen as a threat to a system of clearly defined class relations. The ineptitude, which in Svevo was a powerful means of understanding, in Tozzi's repressive country world is regarded as a disease that must be eradicated. The resentment against Remigio is so strong that he is forced into solitude, until he meets his death at the hands of an enraged farmhand, Berto, who slays him with an axe.

The predicament for all of Tozzi's heroes consists in their inability to offer an alternative to patriarchal rule. In fact, against their own will to the contrary they try unsuccessfully to be like their fathers, but because they lack belief in the social function of power, because they are trapped in their dreams of brotherhood and love, they exert their will ineffectively. In *Il podere*, Tozzi's realism does not permit any bond of solidarity between the outcast Remigio and the peasant Berto who, like his victim, is not at home in his world. The objectivity of economic and cultural determinism, inherited from Verga, coupled with Tozzi's own sense of inveterate human malice, prevents any attempt at reciprocal understanding. But in *Il podere* the passions and values of a particular social formation are not only seen against the unrelenting logic of economic life. The farm is not simply an object of study, as in the Verghian perspective, but rather a place where the perversity and corruptness in human nature are exhibited in deliberately distorted images. Compared to *Con gli occhi chiusi*, the style of *Il podere* is more dispassionate, and suggests a greater assimilation by the author of the dynamics of his brutal community and of the language of its violence and alienation. He thus refrains from commenting on the action of his characters, but only records their conscious feelings and impressions. As a result the text ceases to appear as a kind of antagonistic dialogue between an autobiographical persona and society and becomes a larger symbolic system in which all the weak, regardless of class affiliation, share the same negative fate.

Tre croci (*Three Crosses*, 1920) is Tozzi's most dramatic portrayal of human degradation. Constructed entirely of dialogue and soliloquy, the novel gives a rapid account of the moral and economic ruin of three brothers, owners of an antiquarian bookshop inherited from their father. For reasons of ineptitude and withdrawal, their financial difficulties spiral to the point where they forge a promissory note, an action which seals their fate and plunges them headlong to a disastrous end. Their drama consists, however, less in their inability to avoid bankruptcy than in their moral blindness which, on account of Tozzi's dramatic style, is offered as a spectacle of universal significance. The brothers' deaths (by suicide and from the effects of apoplexy and gout) take on the appearance of a sacrificial rite, aimed at expiating the sin and guilt inherent in all human existence.

The originality of Tozzi's novels lies in the way they register the contradiction between the activities of a traditional agrarian society and the development of petty-bourgeois interests. His characters all occupy the middle ground between these two radically different worlds. Their existential despair appears in relation to their inability to belong to the past and their unwillingness to take control of the future. What sets Tozzi's narratives apart from strictly existential works is their inner dynamism, which compensates for the 'deadness' of a world on the brink of disintegration. Thus, through his expressionistic style, he energises both the brutality of the oppressors and the genuinely degraded experience of their victims.

Bontempelli and Alvaro

Tozzi's expressionistic version of provincial reality had few if any followers during the 1920s, as the novel turned away from naturalism in its attempt to create new and different forms of realism. Massimo Bontempelli (1878–1960) was founder and director of the review *900*, and leader of the *stracittà* movement, to which he assigned the task of de-provincialising Italian culture by formulating an aesthetic response to the intellectual and emotional needs of the modern masses. Bontempelli, who joined the Fascist party in 1924 and was secretary of the Fascist Union of Writers in 1928–9, believed that the prime function of a properly modern literature was to act on the collective consciousness by opening new mythical and magical perspectives on reality. In contrast to naturalism and to the neo-naturalist position of the *strapaese* movement headed by Mino Maccari (1898–1981) which defended the myths of rural Italy, Bontempelli fostered the poetics of 'magic realism', which was an appeal to the mysterious and fantastic quality of reality. His own novels and plays, the best known of which are *La scacchiera davanti allo specchio* ('The Chessboard Before the Mirror', 1922), *Minnie la candida* ('Candid Minnie', 1928), *Il figlio di due madri* ('The Son of Two Mothers', 1929), in spite of their aesthetic shortcomings, are good examples of one kind of experimentalism that could respond to the modern temperament. These works also illustrate the contradiction at the base of the magic-realist project: the desire for a fantastic literature tempered by the equally present need, after Futurism, for a return to order and a new rationality. Hence the aims of fantasy, non-conformism, and unconscious creation, proposed by Bontempelli, could never translate into a truly radical change of perspective.

Bontempelli's *900* project also involved the Calabrian journalist Corrado Alvaro (1895–1956), who for a short time acted as secretary of the review. Alvaro's novels recount the drama of his Calabrian homeland and its suffering inhabitants. They combine the hard reality of Verghian naturalism with the fantasy and irreality characteristic of Pirandello's later production. Their general theme, not uncommon among southern writers, is man's need to free himself from the social and moral bonds of his origins and upbringing and risk the hazards of modern existence. But the myths of a timeless peasant society remain in the writer's imagination, generating a perspective on life, at once epic and lyrical, that affects the entire texture of the narrative. *Gente in Aspromonte* ('People in Aspromonte', 1930), Alvaro's best-known novel, tells the story of Antonello Argirò, a young shepherd who, out of poverty and humiliation, becomes a bandit. The social theme of exploitation and rebellion loses its force of conviction, however, as the narrator, identifying with the victim, reveals his nostalgia for the supposed authenticity of peasant life. In *L'uomo è forte* (*Man Is Strong*, 1938), written after his visit to the Soviet Union, Alvaro creates a surreal atmosphere of fear and suspicion to illustrate life in a totalitarian state. The tradition of the historical novel was valiantly upheld by Riccardo Bacchelli (see p. 509) with, among many others, *Il diavolo al Pontelungo* (*The Devil at Long Bridge*, 1929) and the three-volume saga of peasant life in the Po valley *Il mulino del Po* (*The Mill on the Po*, 1938–40).

Savinio and Buzzati

The aim of a fantastic literature proposed by Bontempelli finds its best expression during the 1920s in the works of Alberto Savinio (pseudonym of Andrea De Chirico, 1891–1952). Savinio was born in Greece and spent a large portion of his life outside Italy, especially in Paris, where he associated with the major exponents of the European avant-garde. His works exhibit the surrealist concept of writing as uninterrupted fantasy or endless melody and colour, yet they are rather controlled efforts at free association, in no way comparable to the 'automatic' texts of the more radical French surrealists. Their distinguishing mark is their playful irony, which contradicts the narrative preconceptions of the extra-textual worlds they represent. Savinio's predilection for the classical world as a kind of emotional homeland, capable of inspiring the free play of the imagination, is at the basis of a varied narrative and dramatic production in which mythology is playfully combined to create incongruous analogies with ordinary bourgeois life, as, for example, in *Hermaphrodito* (1918) and *La partenza dell'Argonauta* ('The Departure of the Argonaut', 1920). In *Angelica o la notte di maggio* (1927) Savinio depicts the encounter of Greek popular life with international finance, playfully setting Eros (Cupid) as mythical analogue to the heroine who however is unknowable because behind her beauty and charm there is absolutely nothing to know. The space of childhood, full of enchantment and illusion, becomes in *Tragedia dell'infanzia* (1937) and *Infanzia di Nivasio Dolcemare* (1941) a metaphor for Savinio's poetic game of analogies. The child's tragedy consists in the fact that he has been imprisoned by adults in an oppressive world of meaning, forced to abandon his fantasy and therefore begin his movement towards death.

In contrast to the relatively playful attitude toward the fantastic adopted by Savinio (and later by Delfini and Landolfi – see below, pp. 549–50) stands the work of Dino Buzzati (1906–72). In *Bàrnabo delle montagne* ('Bàrnabo of the Mountains', 1933) and *Il deserto dei Tartari* (*The Tartar Steppe*, 1940) Buzzati constructs his narratives in a series of outwardly realistic frames, meant to evoke and chart simultaneously a sense of apprehension and anticipation. While the earlier of the two novels harbours the prospect that the protagonist, a forest ranger accused of cowardice in a former confrontation with a band of thieves, will be given the opportunity to regain his lost dignity as he waits in vain for the thieves' return, *Il deserto dei Tartari* makes clear that although the hero should not despair, he deceives himself in waiting, and that his existence is a senseless prison of anguish. Giovanni Drogo, an army lieutenant, spends practically his entire life in a fortress at the edge of a desert in anticipation of an attack by the Tartars, which would give meaning to his life. But the Tartars never come, and Drogo grows old and dies in solitude. *Il deserto dei Tartari*, Buzzati's best-known work, has been praised for its fable-like, quasi surreal mood and landscapes, reminiscent of Kafka's *The Trial* and *The Castle*.

Solaria

The late 1920s and early 1930s witnessed the resurgence of prose fiction in Italy. Alberto Moravia (see below, pp. 551–2) published his masterpiece, *Gli indifferenti* (*The Time of Indifference*), in 1929. Firmly grounded in the daily life of an upper middle-class Roman family of the time, the novel paints a cruel, distinctly realistic, picture of bourgeois life during Fascism, its base appetites and self-interest, while focusing mainly on the passivity and ineptitude of the intellectually minded son in revolt, Michele, who fails in his every attempt to move beyond the empty world of his family's indifference. In the same year an entire number dedicated to the memory of Italo Svevo appeared in the literary monthly *Solaria*. *Solaria* (1926–33) was a point of intersection for some of the significant literary intellectuals of the time. It published poems by Ungaretti, Saba and Montale, some early fiction of Gadda and Vittorini, and set as its primary task the Europeanisation of Italian culture, while at the same time establishing as models for contemporary Italian narrative, together with Svevo and Tozzi, such European contemporaries as Kafka, Proust, Joyce and Gide. Its collective objective was to realise a literature at once respectful of classical form and sensitive to the new directions charted by the international avant-garde. Creating a European literature entailed bringing together the kind of deep historical and moral sense of life found in the novels of Manzoni, Balzac and Dostoevski with the sense of deep human structure owed to the modern discovery of the unconscious. For the *solariani* this mission was more a sense of direction than a blueprint: a call for experimentation that involved writers of different temperaments and ideological orientations. In essence, it was a difficult if not impossible project to realise, since many of the leading contributors – Gadda and Vittorini in particular – moved in directions that were largely irreconcilable with classical realism.

At first most of *Solaria*'s prose writers tested their ability with the form of the short story. Giovanni Comisso (1895–1969) wrote *racconti* aimed at capturing in simple, everyday speech elementary sensations deriving from the narrator's unmediated contact with physical reality. His stories, from *Porto dell'amore* ('Port of Love', 1925) to *Gente di mare* ('People of the Sea', 1929) and the novels *Il delitto di Fausto Diamante* ('Fausto Diamante's Crime', 1926) and *Storia di un patrimonio* ('Story of an Inheritance', 1929) all seek to recover an authenticity of emotion and sensual experience that has been suffocated by bourgeois institutions. With the same purpose of juxtaposing literature and society, Arturo Loria (1902–57) centred his interest on the picaresque lives of social misfits. Thieves, escaped prisoners, prostitutes, as well as bourgeois outcasts and anti-conformists, make up the diversified cast of the *novelle* contained in his collections *Fannias Ventosca* (1929) and *La scuola di ballo* (1932).

While Comisso and Loria attempted to create by means of the imagination what they believed could not be created in society, Alessandro Bonsanti (1904–

83) regarded literature as a place for psychological analysis. With the exception of his early narratives which, in the spirit of Loria, focus on life as adventure and rebellion, Bonsanti's mature production abandons completely any meaningful identification between the individual and social dimensions. Instead, he takes as the object of his narratives the inner world of his characters, abandoning plot altogether in favour of an interior monologue into which, from time to time, he inserts his own thoughts. *Racconto militare* ('Military Story', 1937) is one day in the life of its main character De Luca, fragmented into minute episodes that attempt to probe the most intimate recesses of the character's mind. But compared to that of Svevo, or Proust whom he imitates in *La vipera e il toro* ('The Viper and the Bull', 1955) and *I cavalli di bronzo* ('The Bronze Horses', 1956), Bonsanti's psychological realism is undercut by a fundamental moralism that prevents his characters from being left alone and speaking their own minds. In all of his narratives, Bonsanti remains within the realm of philosophical judgement; his inner plots are only the effect of *his* analysis, and therefore fail to constitute, as in Svevo and Proust, a hermeneutic.

Bilenchi

Solaria's European outlook, as we have mentioned, accommodated several different perspectives, including forms of existentialist realism that took as their object of study the complex of reified relationships in terms of the working class. The Tuscan Romano Bilenchi (1909–89) stands out in this respect. Born into the tradition of populism, Bilenchi was committed early on to the revolutionary ideals of left-wing Fascism, but soon turned to anti-Fascism, fought in the Resistance, and after the war became a leader in the Communist intelligentsia. The thematic nucleus of his stories is alienation and oppression. Reality for his characters is always unknowable, hostile and indeterminate. They all suffer from a weakness which is both ontological and socio-economic. Their real poverty and exploitation is subsumed into a dread of some unknown, maleficent force that looms over their individual lives. Bilenchi often chooses children or adolescents as protagonists so as to capture the formative stages of an individual's relation to society and focus on a world of innocence and fantasy continually under threat. *Anna e Bruno* (1938), *Mio cugino Andrea* ('My Cousin Andrew', 1943), and the novel *Conservatorio di Santa Teresa* ('Conservatory of Saint Theresa', 1940) depict the bliss of childhood ignorance and the disenchantment and alienation that growing up fosters. *La miseria* ('Misery', 1941) and *La siccità* ('Drought', 1941) are stories that best express Bilenchi's sense of the inexplicable forces at work within the subaltern lives of his characters. In both there is an insistence on the existential fact of oppression and solitude, whether it is in the context of one family's struggle for material survival in the face of brutal exploitation by another, or before the violence of nature itself. Implied in both stories is the need for collective existence, the building of a human community on the basis of need and solidarity. In Bilenchi's post-war writings, such as *Il bottone di Stalingrado* ('The Stalingrad Button', 1972), the passage from existentialism to Marxism is highly visible in the formation of a collective consciousness that suffers the disillusionment of political failure.

Vittorini

With the exception of Carlo Emilio Gadda, the most original writer to emerge from the *Solaria* milieu was Elio Vittorini (1908–66). His first novel, *Il garofano rosso* (*The Red Carnation*, 1933-6) – banned by Fascist censors for what was thought to be excessive sex and violence – roughly charts, in the character of the hero Alessio, the author's own youthful enthusiasm for Fascism, an affiliation he was quick to abandon upon realising that his anti-bourgeois and socialist positions were incompatible with the régime's politics. Other themes in the novel include the adolescent protagonist's search for truth, selfishness which leads to the failure of noble ideals, and the renovating potential of the worker. *Erica e i suoi fratelli* ('Erica and Her Brothers'), an unfinished novel written in 1936, is the story of a young girl from a working-class family who became a prostitute at thirteen in order not to become a servant of the bourgeoisie.

Conversazione in Sicilia ('Conversation in Sicily', 1938–9), Vittorini's most important novel, marks a sharp turn away from the naturalist-inspired realism of the writer's first two books, as well as from the dominant fictional trends of the time. Written in the first person as the voice of a collective subject, the novel records a journey backward into the mythical past in search of a lost humanity and an ancient wisdom capable of vindicating a world that has been brutally offended by history. The protagonist, Silvestro, is a bourgeois intellectual caught in a web of 'abstract furies'. Depressed, ashamed, unable to talk, he lives in the 'quietude of hopelessness'. Prompted by a letter from his father, he takes a train south to his native Sicily to visit his mother. The stops along the way and his conversations with fellow travellers are all symbolic events that place the hero squarely facing some basic truth about human life. That humanity has been offended, and that one must fulfil 'other obligations', is a theme recurring on almost every page. Through Silvestro's return to his mountain town, to his mother, and to the core of his land and culture he relives the myths of a crude and essential reality before the news of his brother's death in the war brings him back to the political world of the present.

The fascination the novel inspires is due primarily to its allusive, lyrical style. The narrative reads somewhat like a musical score. Its modulated harmony, counterpoint and refrain, indeterminate grammatical forms, formulaic syntax, as well as its sometimes biblical language, are all techniques that suspend the reality of everyday events within a deeper poetic dimension, the purpose being to convey the sense of prophecy associated with messianic narratives.

In *Uomini e no* (*Men and Not Men*, 1945; discussed further below, p. 543) Vittorini comes to grips with the central problem raised in *Conversazione*, namely how to free the world from evil, an evil within and outside man. Vittorini's answer is formulated in the juxtaposition of 'men' (anti-Fascists) and 'not-men' (Fascists). The regeneration of Italian society will come about only when the old, bourgeois civilisation is replaced by a society of simple and serious workers.

Gadda

The recognition of Carlo Emilio Gadda (1893–1973) as perhaps the greatest Italian novelist of the twentieth century derives from the uniqueness of his literary language and style. His writings employ numerous styles and lexical modes, from the arduous structures of classical Latin to the austere language of modern science and the spontaneous automatism of the surrealists. Gadda's plurilingualism depends largely on the notion of the identity of historical and linguistic realities. Language embraces all forms of conscious and unconscious expression, equalling the vast number of ways one can perceive the world. This assertion of the legitimacy of all linguistic codes accounts only in part for the striking originality of Gadda's work. The diverse linguistic contributions offered by the various literary traditions and social environments taken in themselves serve only to extend the range of what can be regarded as Gadda's naturalist-positivist viewpoint, regulated by the need for concrete under-standing and by an impulse toward systematic analysis. Gadda's technical and scientific training as a civil engineer left him with a concept of exterior reality as the rational interaction of discrete units, a network of channels and structures to which everything somehow belonged. At the same time, Gadda's personal experience told him that traditional rationality and morals fail to account for the incomplete, dark side of human cognition which does not operate according to the rules of causal necessity or logic. Rather than a functionally structured system, reality appeared to Gadda as an entanglement: a psychological and metaphysical knot which becomes more and more involved the more one tries to unravel it. Gadda refers to such a condition of being and of existence as 'grotesque' or 'baroque'; it is an 'objective' condition which generates its own principle of expression, namely the 'macaronic', a form of writing designed to subvert conventional forms of cultural and literary knowledge. Gadda's numerous reflections on the nature of the world and of writing, on the interrelationship of cognitive and literary systems, and on the limitless expressive capacity of the written word have no equal in twentieth-century Italian literature. Each of his texts is metalinguistic and metanarrative in the most rigorous sense of the terms. They all submit language and literature to a merciless tribunal; all are eager to prosecute the most cherished of idols, including the integrity and the juridical identity of the author himself.

The importance of the *Giornale di guerra e di prigionia* ('War and Prison Diary', 1950), which comprises the war diaries Gadda wrote from 1915 to 1919, consists in its being a spontaneous transcription of experience that documents the attitude toward reality which forms the basis of his literary and philosophical outlook. Gadda's aim in the *Giornale* is to record with precision the real world of encampments, battles and military strategy, as well as his personal activities, even as far as indicating changes in timetables and in lodgings, or describing the contents of a meal. He seeks to present an objective portrait of himself, of his ideals and shortcomings and – insistently – of his keen sensitivity and neurotic temperament. But as his diary progresses, the impossibility of any sort of detached observation of the external world becomes apparent. The tension between Gadda and the disquieting features of his environment is the *Giornale*'s principal theme. Disorder and selfishness disturb him the most, inciting aggressive diatribes against his fellow combatants, their trivialisation of military life, lack of commitment and discipline, ignorance and inefficiency. Gadda enjoys seeing himself as the antithesis of such a temperament, as a stranger to a race which has rendered Italy throughout the centuries a place unfit to inhabit.

Gadda's early fiction returns to many of the themes of his war journal. The narrator of these prose pieces is almost always an outsider whose ideals and heightened sensitivity are violated by the realities of his society and by the base attitudes and values of its ruling class. In *La Madonna dei filosofi* ('The Madonna of the Philosophers', 1931) we get our first glimpse at a characteristically Gaddian double, 'l'ingeniere Baronfo', who, like all of Gadda's fictional counterparts, is forced unmercifully to live in a chaotic world devoid of rational and moral foundations. *La meccanica* ('Mechanics'), an unfinished short novel, partially published in *Solaria* in 1932 and in book form in 1970, satirises the different attitudes of the Milanese social classes with respect to the war, while *Il castello d'Udine* ('The Castle at Udine', 1934) comprises autobiographical fragments and memoirs of the war and its aftermath.

Throughout the 1930s Gadda continued his anti-bourgeois polemics in a number of 'Milanese sketches' which he incorporated in the volume entitled *L'Adalgisa. Disegni milanesi* (1940). Striking in this collection is Gadda's use of dialect, which he weaves into the fabric of a well-modulated Tuscan prose in order to unmask the pretentions of a class for whom appearance is paramount. The sketches are replete with grotesque images of baseness and filth; they exude the noise and confusion of a social life of deceit and illusion, all of which Gadda transcribes in a mixture of fierce contempt and amusing condescension.

La cognizione del dolore (*Acquainted With Grief*), which was serialised in the literary magazine *Letteratura* (1938–41, final book version 1970) consists of nine fragments or 'tracts', four of which appear also in other collections.

The novel's setting is an imaginary South American country called Maradagàl (which is a caricature of Lombardy, although Gadda spent several years working in Argentina): specifically, Lukones, a town located in the region of Neá Keltiké. In one of Lukones's stately villas the middle-aged protagonist, Gonzalo Pirobutirro d'Altino, lives with his mother. A neurotic and melancholic engineer and literato *manqué*, Gonzalo lives the life of a recluse in terrible contempt for anyone and anything that intrudes on his solitude. He treats his mother with hostility for her attachment to the outside world, and aggressively refuses to enlist the protection of an association of night watchmen. One night, while Gonzalo is away, the señora is found dead – slain, the reader is left to believe, either by the watchmen or by Gonzalo himself.

The difficulty one confronts in reading *La cognizione del dolore* is establishing the distance that separates the narrator from the author and his major characters. In the figure of Gonzalo, Gadda produces an external image of himself, projected in the form of impulses and instincts, contained and determined by a specific history. He extends this self-image to include its presence in the minds of others as it has been perceived, reflected on, and systematised by his ego. This latter mode of self-projection is the novel's narrating voice, which functions as a screen between the instinctual world of Gonzalo/Gadda and the reader. The degree to which the psychological distance can be maintained depends on the gravity of the impulse. The narration is determined wholly by the forces of passion and not by any predetermined schema. The novel's styles, therefore, hinge on the degrees of difference that separate the narrator from Gonzalo's relations with the external world. The geographical and social setting and the episodes relatively extraneous to Gonzalo's inner world are written with various kinds of humour, ranging from ironic understatement to more direct and engaging forms of comic incongruity. As we are brought closer to Gonzalo's personal world, in the social context of the country villa, grotesque caricature and derision predominate. The narrator produces these deformations as the expression of Gonzalo's perspective, just as the deformed perspectives of the others generate the caricature of Gonzalo. At the centre of this world of perverted images the tragedy of mother and son is played out: their isolation, loneliness and frightful dependence on one another.

Gadda's second, and perhaps most important, novel, *Quer pasticciaccio brutto de via Merulana* (*That Awful Mess on Via Merulana*), was also serialised in *Letteratura* (1946) before it came out in book form in 1957. Its roots are found in *La cognizione del dolore*, which ends with a murder and the beginning of an investigation. As Gadda himself defined it, *Quer pasticciaccio* is a detective story and thus employs the structure and many of the strategies common to that genre: two crimes, a burglary and a murder, set into motion an investigation headed by a detective. The process of detection and interrogation lead the reader into a world without boundaries, where everything and everyone is to some degree suspect. The principle of suspicion generates an overriding sense of causal ramification. As the scheme of things is disentangled, we learn not to dismiss any detail; everything is potentially relevant and meaningful, nothing is safe, nothing can be spared scrutiny, everyone is vulnerable, everyone is guilty.

Gadda criticism has agreed that the meaning of *Quer pasticciaccio* is to be found in its detailed reproduction of chaos, in its representation of the evil of everyday life during Fascism and in its all-inclusive indictment and condemnation, from which only the murdered Roman lady, Liliana Balducci, and a few lower-class female characters are saved. From the very beginning, the reader enters a twisted, snarled reality. The entanglements on which Gadda founds his investigation are mainly emotional or sexual in character: the relationship between Liliana and her young domestics, between Liliana and her husband, between Liliana and her cousin Giuliano. In contrast to the traditional detective story, *Quer pasticciaccio* gives no illusion that the social community is fundamentally healthy; its entire system of culture and civilisation must be subjected to interrogation; its Fascist rule of law must be toppled. In a manner consistent with Freud's teaching, Gadda portrays the law, grotesquely embodied in Mussolini's regime, as no more than a manifestation of desire. He ruthlessly attacks its ever-present hedonistic pathology, its terrorism and despotism. In terms of literary style, Gadda's Freudian struggle against the law turns into a battle against the aesthetic ideals of bourgeois realism and its veristic and neo-realistic variants. The writing, as in all of Gadda's works, is meant to provoke rather than represent. His images do not imitate any form of objective reality, but exhibit objects already culturalised by use and convention, lodged as ideal constructs within the collective psyche.

Gadda's virulent diatribe against Fascism becomes the exclusive subject-matter of *Eros e Priapo*, a pamphlet also written in 1945–6. The linguistically spectacular, Freudian-inspired argument is that Fascism marks the victory of Eros over Logos. It has thus perverted human collective life, transforming it into demented, unbridled aggressiveness, twisting an ideally healthy narcissism into pathological identification with (and subordination to) the phallus-leader Mussolini, whose rhetoric appeals particularly to an aroused female population eager to comply with his advances.

The destabilising power of Gadda's prose has changed the course of Italian fiction in our time. The naturalist and neo-realist traditions his writings undermine have now all but disappeared, their reality shattered under the yoke of his parody and linguistic violence. Upon this destruction the best Italian writers of the 1980s and 1990s have continued to build, employing the tools that Gadda honed to perfection: polyphony and pastiche, tempered by an unrelenting self-consciousness.

The aftermath of the
Second World War
(1945–56)

John Gatt-Rutter

39

After the Liberation

The end of political censorship in post-Liberation Italy enabled Italians to take a good look at themselves, to explore Italy stripped of Fascist rhetoric and come to terms with the barbarity of the war and the concentration camps in a supposedly civilised Europe, and to seek political renewal for the Italy that was taking shape out of the ruins of war.

The coalition of anti-Fascist parties soon started falling apart after the war, and the 1948 elections saw a Christian Democrat majority in government and other parties excluded from power. Church influence waxed strong, not only with the threat of excommunication wielded as an electoral stick, especially against the strong Communist Party, but also with the mobilisation of mass piety during the Holy Year of 1950 followed by the Marian Year of 1951. The Republican constitution of 1947, many of whose most important democratising provisions were for decades to remain a dead letter, had marked the high point of radical change. Redistribution of land, however, and abolition of the iniquitous share-cropping system of *mezzadria*, led to the transformation of the peasantry into modern small farmers, and to the disappearance of the peasant novel by about the mid-1950s, after some of its last and finest instances in the work of Jovine, Silone, Pavese and Fenoglio. Likewise, the mechanisation of agriculture eventually made it impossible for poetry to return to the exquisite nature lyricism of much hermetic poetry from the 1930s to the 1950s.

Italian writing of the later 1940s on the whole failed to operate a decisive renewal of literary culture, and the amorphous enterprise that went under the loose label of *neorealismo* gradually fell apart. One of the key issues in the literary debates of the immediate post-war years was the question of continuity or discontinuity with the Fascist era. Most writers in Italy, even early opponents of Fascism, had unavoidably had some truck with the régime, which, after all, long enjoyed very widespread support from anti-leftists across the world. For many Italians, not only intellectuals, it was Nazi occupation in 1943 that forced an often painful political choice; and though some had made their choice earlier than that, others left it till even later. Several writers were thus subsequently involved in a less than dignified covering of tracks or salving of consciences.

Against those who dismissed the literature of the Fascist era indiscriminately, many writers and critics who had been active under Fascism were able to justify their stance as implicitly critical and oppositional to the regime. The Catholic critic Carlo Bo, in his essay 'Che cos'era l'assenza', republished in his volume *Scandalo della speranza* ('The Scandal of Hope', 1957), championed hermeticism as having been opposed not only to Fascism but also to false values in general, and thus tendentially to any politics, which the hermetics saw as inimical to the essentially spiritual values of literary culture. Guido Piovene's *La coda di paglia* (1962), on the other hand, is a startlingly detailed confession of one Catholic writer's moral capitulation to Fascism.

This debate thus merged into the debate over whether writing necessarily had to engage politically with the present; and, in that case, whether political considerations took precedence over literary creativity, or whether the latter itself generated political insights of its own; how to conceptualise the relationship between writers and the Italian people (the ambiguous word 'popolo' generally implying the masses of workers and as yet largely illiterate peasants). The debate reached a high point in the pages of *Il Politecnico* (1945–7), leading to the editor Vittorini's dramatic break with the Communist Party. With the political polarisation of the Cold War, from 1948 onwards, and the concomitant pressure towards cultural, ideological and social conformity under the Christian Democrat government in Italy, many non-Communist writers and intellectuals were driven (if only briefly) leftwards, pressing their concerns in the Alleanza della Cultura and in the international grouping of Intellectuals for Peace.

In 1950 a group of anti-Communists, headed by Benedetto Croce and including political personalities like Ferruccio Parri, leader of the now defunct Partito d'Azione, and writers like Ignazio Silone created the international, pro-Western Congress for Cultural Freedom (financially supported by the United States Central Intelligence Agency, as the opposing bodies were by Moscow). Silone contributed his 'Emergency exit' to Richard Crossman's volume of testimonials by ex-Communists, *The God That Failed* (1950). Political issues fossilised into geopolitical and ideological confrontation and contributed to inhibiting literary innovation until the complex international crisis of 1956.

40

Neo-realism

Italian neo-realism, though notoriously difficult to define, does present a recognisable set of features of which any individual work may provide its own sub-set. It was part of the atmosphere of the time, rather than a school or a programme. Calvino, in his well-known preface to the 1964 edition of his novel *Il sentiero dei nidi di ragno* ('The Path to the Nests of Spiders'), stressed the compulsive storytelling of the Resistance and the uncoordinated, unprofessional spontaneity of the new writers who emerged from the war-time experience. Most outstanding 'neo-realist' works in fact present non-neo-realist features, while works which were not realist at all in technique, such as the highly experimental novels of Vittorini, appeared deceptively at home within the cultural ambience of neo-realism thanks to their contemporary relevance.

All neo-realist works directly engage with history, with the present moment seen as one in which individuals participate in collective destinies. The experience by many of Resistance, civil war or internment explains both the sense of individual responsibility in the making of history and the counter-vailing sense of the individual's impotence in the grand historical process, the sheer struggle to survive amid the cataclysm. This often problematical public engagement impelled writers to escape from the ivory tower of self-centred or aesthetic contemplation in which they had sought refuge from the impositions of Fascism, and tempted them in the direction of popular epic. Typically, these works take the form of memoirs or more or less fictionalised documentaries or chronicles of the recent past, from the rise of Fascism in the early 1920s to the Resistance and right up to the present. Though the social need for the retelling of a hitherto censored past is undeniable, perhaps the most interesting of these works are those that treat post-Liberation Italy and the present moment itself, even up to and beyond the 1948 Christian Democrat election victory. Two very different works in this category are Pavese's *La luna e i falò* (*The Moon and the Bonfires*, 1950) and Silone's *Una manciata di more* (*A Handful of Blackberries*, 1952). The attempted fusion of *scrittori* with *popolo*, however, rarely if at all comes off on the page, as it did not on the stage of Italian society, and few neo-realist novelists showed the self-critical ability to confront this populist delusion, as Saba had done decades earlier in the poem 'Il borgo' ('Township').

The term *neorealismo* was first coined in the 1940s to describe the objectivist and epic perspective of film-makers like Visconti and Rossellini, who had taken their cameras out of the studio and on to the streets and squares and fields of contemporary Italy and resorted largely to non-professional actors, ordinary Italians who more or less acted themselves. Certainly, much neo-realist narrative literature is cast in that filmic mode, but it also draws on earlier models of literary realism: Verga and other late nineteenth-century *veristi*; the great European realists, from Balzac to Tolstoy and Zola; and the novelists of the 'American Renaissance', from Mark Twain and Herman Melville to Ernest Hemingway and Sinclair Lewis, familiar to Italians from Vittorini and Cecchi's anthology *Americana* (1941).

Theoretical support for this backward-looking model of realism was derived from the Hungarian Marxist critic Gyorgy Lukács and, less legitimately, from Gramsci's analysis of the reasons for the lack of an Italian 'national popular' literature in his prison notebooks, *Quaderni del carcere* (see above, p. 513). These began appearing in the late 1940s in an arrangement that suited the Italian Communist Party's strategy of achieving an anti-Fascist hegemony through a coalition of all progressive forces. The most schematic model was the 'socialist realism' of the Soviet theorist Zhdanov and his Italian mediator Emilio Sereni: a positive, forward-looking narrative, in which revolutionary proletarian heroes and heroines overcome the legacy of the past and the forces of reaction, liberating the new productive forces of socialism.

Renata Viganò (1900–76), in her typically neo-realist *L'Agnese va a morire* ('Agnese Goes to Die', 1949), sees the Resistance in epic terms as the struggle of a whole population, the peasants of the lower Po valley, against the occupying Germans. Agnese's elderly husband is killed by the Germans; she in turn leaves a German soldier for dead and works with the partisans until she is found out and shot. Viganò presents major set-pieces, such as that in which a partisan group, lost in a blizzard, wanders the causeways and waterways. In contrast, the stories and novels of Beppe Fenoglio (1922–63) develop Resistance and peasant themes against the setting of his native Piedmont with a highly individualistic, even idiosyncratic, rather than a populist inflexion. His *I ventitre giorni della città di Alba* ('The Twenty-Three Days of the City of Alba', 1952) draws on autobiographical experience with an intense sense of actuality. Death – even outside the context of war and Resistance, as in *La malora* (*Ruin*, 1952) – is felt as an ever-present possibility, yet the language is alive with humour and word-play. In the posthumous, unfinished and massive *Il partigiano Johnny* (*Johnny the Partisan*, 1968), English plays a powerful part in the text's linguistic, psychological and, ultimately, political stance.

A distinctive strand of Italian literary neorealism was that elaborated in the Florentine journal *Società* in 1945 by Romano Bilenchi and Gianfranco Piazzesi, who argued for reportage (*cronaca*) as the essential mode of literary commitment to reality in a historical situation too huge and complex for the individual participant-observer to grasp fully. This theorising tallied closely with the real conditions of much writing of the war and post-war period. Straightforward eye-witness or autobiographical accounts, diaries, letters, documentary writing predominated in the mid-1940s, much of it by non-professional writers, including Gramsci's *Lettere dal carcere* (*Letters from Prison*, 1947). One of the least 'literary' and most austere monuments is the 1952 collection of *Lettere di condannati a morte della Resistenza italiana* ('Letters of the Italian Resistance Fighters Sentenced to Death'). Many such documentary works were late in appearing: Paolo Emilio Taviani's *Pittaluga racconta – romanzo di fatti veri (1943–45)* ('Pittaluga Relates: A Novel of True Facts'), though written in 1945, came out in 1988. Piero Caleffi's memoirs of the German labour camps, *Si fa presto a dire fame* ('It's Easy Enough to Say "Hunger"'), did not appear until 1955, while Ada Gobetti's *Diario partigiano* came out in 1956.

Cronaca was presented in *Società* as being also a traditional literary form native to Florence, and indeed in all the work of the Florentine Vasco Pratolini (1913–91) the local chronicle is a determinant dimension and appears in two titles of 1947, *Cronache di poveri amanti* (*A Tale of Poor Lovers*) and *Cronaca familiare*. Affective involvement with characters and subject-matter is prominent. The first weaves a mesh of social, sexual and political relations in a predominantly working-class street in Florence during the second wave of Fascist violence in the 1920s, highlighted by the self-sacrifice in folk-hero style of an anti-Fascist worker nicknamed Maciste. The second is addressed throughout in the second person by the narrator to his deceased younger brother, who had been orphaned and adopted by an English butler in Florence during the final years of Fascism. As such, it is an extremely intimate presentation of the alienating effects of poverty.

The 'chronicle' mode was already evident in Pratolini's *Il Quartiere* (*The Naked Streets*, 1944), an affectionate portrayal of a bunch of Florentine working lads, to which Pasolini's devastating *Ragazzi di vita* (*The 'Ragazzi'*, 1955) on Rome's non-working lads might appear a sardonic riposte. The weaknesses of Pratolini's vision appear in the trilogy *Una storia italiana*, whose title construes chronicle as history and Florence as Italy. The first work of this trilogy, *Metello*, which appeared in the same year as *Ragazzi di vita*, helped fuel the controversy over neo-realism and hastened its demise.

Peasant novels

The local or regional focus in neo-realist works betokens the pressing need to recognise Italy's bewildering diversity underlying the Fascist image of national unity. But this fostered a contrary weakness: the failure to see the interconnectedness at the national and global level of local and regional destinies, particularly the foundational pact between northern industrialists and southern landowners – what Gramsci had called the 'blocco storico' of Italian unification.

This alliance enshrined both the class divide and the subservience of the south as a backward colony of the north, held in place by systems of patronage and corruption and the repressive apparatus of the state, and ultimately, after 1945, by the military balance of the greater powers on the European chequerboard. Few works until Sciascia's *Gli zii di Sicilia* ('Sicilian Uncles', 1958) make this connection between the local and the global which neo-realists for over ten years virtually censored from consciousness, leaving it to be addressed by the enormously and internationally popular Giovanni Guareschi (1908–68).

Guareschi's Don Camillo books read like a parody of neo-realism. Beginning with *Don Camillo – Mondo Piccolo* (*The Little World of Don Camillo*, 1948), they recreate with swashbuckling verve the local atmosphere of a small rural town in the lower Po valley as a microcosm of Cold War Italy. The parish priest of the title is continually engaged in apparently bitter but actually playful sparring (often in the literal physical sense) with his political adversary, the Communist mayor Peppone. This neo-realist scenario is undercut by the comic tone and the up-to-the-minute, snappy, flippant style, as also by the impact of national and international politics at local level. The talking Christ on the cross establishes a religious discourse transcending (or subtly transforming) the political wrangling. In their progression to *Don Camillo e i giovani d'oggi* (*Don Camillo Meets Hell's Angels*, 1969), the Don Camillo books acutely chart the conversion of the peasant into a modern agribusiness entrepreneur.

What was seriously taken as neo-realism can be seen in the post-war stories of Francesco Jovine (1902–50) and above all his novel *Le terre del Sacramento* (*The Estate in the Abruzzi*), completed just before his death in 1950. The setting is the writer's native Molise. The subject-matter – the bloody repression under Fascism of peasants in revolt after being cheated of access to land – echoes Silone's pre-war *Fontamara*. But the perspective, language and omniscient style of narration are literary, not popular. A historical novel not too unlike De Roberto's *I Viceré* of 1894 (see above, p. 469), it combines Jovine's two recurrent themes: the demoralising futility of life in the country towns of the south (with compensatory sexual behaviour); and the grievances of the peasantry. The focus gradually fixes upon Luca Marana. A young law student of peasant family, he takes the side of the peasants whom he has unwittingly helped to dupe and is killed along with many of them by the Fascists.

A landmark text on the grievances of the southern peasantry is *Cristo si è fermato a Eboli* (*Christ Stopped at Eboli*, 1945) by Carlo Levi (1902–75). Based on the Turinese author's detention in Lucania in 1936 for anti-Fascist activities, it vividly represents, against a gaunt landscape of man-made despoliation, degradation and despair, a rare encounter between north and south, between modernity and age-old fatalism. Levi the painter and medical doctor interacts not only with the poverty-stricken peasants, but also with the scarcely less indigent and hopeless petty bourgeoisie – the mayor, the doctors, the pharmacist, the tax-collector, the wretched parish priest – of whom he paints memorable portraits. Levi dwells on the peasants' belief in magic and the supernatural, on their belonging to a submerged, archaic civilisation. He proffers the utopian political solution of an autonomous peasant state, but more effectively conveys the peasants' awareness of being excluded from history and the modern polity.

Ignazio Silone (pseud. of Secondino Tranquilli, 1900–78) also pursued the mirage of a peasant polity. A high-ranking Communist who left the Party in horror of Stalin's crimes, Silone described himself as 'a Socialist without a party and a Christian without a church'. He was indeed persecuted by the Fascists and despised by the Communists. His early novels, published in Switzerland where he lived in exile until 1945, enjoyed remarkable popularity abroad while being totally ignored in Italy. The most important of these is *Fontamara* (Zurich, 1933; Milan, 1949), the quasi-oral story of how the destitute peasants of an Abruzzi village become aware of being exploited by the Fascist-supported landowners. Silone returned to Italy in 1945 and his *Una manciata di more* (*A Handful of Blackberries*, 1952), about Abruzzi peasants who occupy the land and declare a Soviet, has something of the epic tone of *Fontamara*, only the enemy now is the Communist Party, out to capture the peasant movement for its own political ends. *Il segreto di Luca* (*The Secret of Luca*, 1956) presents the peasant at the private level, as capable of the highest nobility and self-sacrifice in defence of the honour of the woman he loves.

Levi and Silone thus go beyond the moralistic stance common in neo-realism; and in the meagre but diverse and telling oeuvre of Rocco Scotellaro (1923–53) the historic awareness of the Italian peasantry finds its sharpest expression – not only in his unfinished autobiographical novel, *L'uva puttanella* ('The Bloody Grapes', 1955), and in the poems of *È fatto giorno* ('Day Has Come', 1954), but also in his precocious work of oral history drawn from his peasant interlocutors, *Contadini del Sud* ('Southern Peasants', 1954).

Pavese

The life, writings and suicide of Cesare Pavese (1908–50) bring to crisis point both the temporarily dominant neo-realist paradigm and also the broader tensions within Fascist and post-Fascist Italian society and culture, the imperatives of political responsibility and courage: to comply, or resist? To rethink social arrangements radically? To embrace class war and revolution? The political could also be personal, particularly in relationships between the sexes, but also in terms of the individual's loyalties or personal inadequacies in relation to persons, places, the past, institutions – to existence itself.

The increasingly rapid submersion of Italy's age-old peasant society often appears in Pavese as a contrast between *città* (the rational, the civilised, the world of historical progress) and *campagna*, or *collina*, the hills (the instinctual, the primitive, the mythic timeless world attuned to the rhythms of nature, which Pavese called *il selvaggio*). This amounts to a profound problematisation of the affray of the late 1920s between *stracittà* and *strapaese* (see above, p. 522), rendered intimate by Pavese's own division between his native Langhe hills near Turin and the ancient yet modern industrial city itself. Especially as a spectator of war and Resistance, he strove to capture the tragic essence of all these conflicts by lifting the meticulously observed realities of the here-and-now to an absolute and timeless mythic level, clinging to a faith in artistic creation as the privileged site for the establishment of ultimate meanings, the transcendence of the real, or its essential revelation. The real remains always Pavese's obligatory point of departure and of return – in effect, his critical arena, his corrective to the lure of *il voluttuoso*, aestheticism. Moreover reality is not presented simply as objectively given, but as mediated, in each of his works, through an individual consciousness, which (despite the variety of protagonists thus focalised) is always recognisably a facet or *alter ego* of the writer himself, whether as narrating subject (usually male) or in the third person (for most of the female protagonists).

Pavese began and ended as a poet, having published the precociously neo-realist collection *Lavorare stanca* ('Work is Tiring') in 1936 and enlarged it in 1941. This *poesia-racconto* matter-of-factly renders the here and now in a speaking voice far removed from the meditative tones and evanescent images of the then dominant hermetic poets, using a long-limbed line approximating free-verse metrics which blends echoes of Whitman and of the Latin hexameter. Many later poems obsessively play on repeated images, words, phrases, building a mythic fixity in which human figures appear to be part of a rite played out through them by the world of nature.

The writer's counterbalancing interests in reality and myth were elaborated, with preponderant emphasis on subject-mediated realism, in the numerous short stories which Pavese wrote from 1936 onwards, and particularly in the essays of *Feria d'agosto* (*The Harvesters*, 1946), leading to the novels on which his reputation mainly rests. These can be divided in two interlocking series, both of them very concretely engaging the individual's participation in society, seen in precise historical and geographical terms – those of contemporary Piedmont.

The first series deals with social mores and the psychic mechanisms of the individual, and begins with *Paesi tuoi* ('Your People', 1941), in which the Turin mechanic, Berto, becomes the half-aghast and half-complicit witness of a murderously incestuous relationship between the peasant Talino and his sister Gisella. The mythic overtones of *il selvaggio* invade Berto's urban consciousness, and recur in an appropriately different guise in the rites of the rural middle class in *Il diavolo sulle colline* (*The Devil in the Hills*). Written in 1948, this appeared the following year along with two other short novels, *La bella estate* (*The Beautiful Summer*), begun in 1940 (which gave its name to the trilogy), and *Tra donne sole* ('Among Women Alone'), which was written in 1949. The latter two have female protagonists and are Turin-based, presenting the alienation of town life very much in terms of women's lack of civic goals and their sexual exploitation by men. *La bella estate* focuses on the unwary victim, the working-class girl Ginia, blindly falling into the trap, while conversely *Tra donne sole* is a first-person narrative by the self-made working woman, Clelia, who, as she sets up her fashion boutique, surveys with hard-won detachment the frivolity and futility that surround her. The narrative opens with the attempted suicide of the young Rosetta, and closes with her actual suicide. Clelia discovers that Rosetta, like herself, had been used by her lover for rote sex.

The perspective on survival as being determined by character emerges even more strongly in the second series of novels, which explicitly take within their scope the political history of Italy and the political responsibilities of the individual, and in which Pavese's fiction more closely shadows autobiography. *Il carcere* (*The Prison*, written in 1938–9) and *La casa in collina* (*The House on the Hill*, written in 1947–8) appeared in 1948 under the joint title *Prima che il gallo canti* (*Before the Cock Crows*), which, with the contents of the two novels, constitutes a remarkably honest and harsh self-accusation of betrayal and guilt, almost unique in literature, conducted partly through the protagonists' own awareness, but also, more damningly, over their heads, leaving the reader to deduce their lack of awareness.

This is done baldly in the first novel, an interesting contrast to Carlo Levi's *Cristo si è fermato a Eboli*. Here Stefano, an engineer, is, like Pavese and Levi, a northerner in political detention in Italy's far south. The imprisonment of the title, however, is far less a political than an existential, psychic and mythic matter. Stefano is imprisoned by his desire for the inaccessible female and his impatience with the subservient one, as he is imprisoned by the empty sea and the harsh Calabrian mountains. He avoids engagement either with local dissidents or with the left-wing detainee held in the same township.

In *La casa in collina*, the most pointed, but much less obviously implied, index of bad faith on the part of the narrator-protagonist, a Turin high-school science master called Corrado, is his advice to his colleague Castelli not to sign the oath of allegiance to Mussolini's short-lived Nazi puppet regime, the Italian Social Republic. Castelli is jailed, transported and never heard of again. Corrado, on the other hand, is left alone (for the time being at least), but his account never refers to his own taking of the Fascist oath. This is one instance of Pavese's meticulous chronicling, in *La casa in collina*, of political issues and attitudes and moves by individuals across a wide gamut of situations during 1943 and 1944, from the Allied bombings to the fall of Mussolini, then the armistice, and on to the German occupation of the north and the armed Resistance.

All is rigorously mediated through Corrado, who consistently retreats from political responsibility, as from personal responsibility to a former girl-friend, Cate, though he is probably the father of her young boy Dino. When Cate and her anti-Fascist friends are rounded up, Corrado hides in a monastery (as Pavese himself did) with Dino. Dino runs away to join the partisans, while Corrado seeks a safer haven in the hills. The world of nature, a seeming Eden in which Corrado had long sought refuge from others, and in which warfare seemed a boyish game, is sickeningly revealed as the blood-drenched scene of *il selvaggio*, no less than political centres such as Turin.

These two books may be seen as Pavese's confession of political guilt (confirmed in his diary, *Il mestiere di vivere* (*The Business of Living*), in which political issues impinge rarely but crucially), as well as documents of the paralysis or perplexity of many Italians. The intervening novel, *Il compagno* ('The Comrade', 1947), may be seen as a compensatory gesture. Here the working-class guitarist, nicknamed Pablo, moves towards active anti-Fascism in the late 1930s, as Pavese did not until after the fall of Mussolini. However, this positive movement is less convincing than the typically Pavesian negatives: Pablo's jealousy of his morally superior friend, Amelio; his desire for the *femme fatale*, Linda; his lack of self-reliance.

Pavese's culminating narrative achievement, *La luna e i falò*, carries on the history of Italy in a rural Piedmontese microcosm to the post-war Catholic dominance through the narrating consciousness of the foundling identified only as Anguilla (Eel), who had left for America before the war on the run from Fascism, but mostly in pursuit of opportunity. He returns to the village where he grew up in poverty, in search of his roots and of the three dazzling daughters of the gentleman farmer for whom he used to work, but discovers that he has irremediably lost his past and that the three girls are dead – the youngest, Santa, executed by partisans as a Fascist double agent. Peasant life now is even harsher than under Fascism, and the hopes raised by the Liberation appear to have come to nothing. The real, through recurrent, imagery takes on a mythic nature, as in *La casa in collina*. Memory and dialogue create an interplay of different time systems – the serial time of history, the memorial time of autobiography, the cyclical time of mythicised nature (the moon and the bonfires of the title) – ending with the final revelation, the negative epiphany, of the ritual hilltop bonfire, a kind of sacrificial holocaust, in which Santa's body was consumed.

Pavese left behind, among discursive and other writings, the intense, gem-like poems of *Verrà la morte e avrà i tuoi occhi* ('Death Will Come and It Will Have Your Eyes', 1951), centred on his last unsuccessful love affair, but his favourite book, possibly his most original, was *Dialoghi con Leucò* (*Dialogues With Leucò*, 1947). Its mythic mode, of dialogues between Greek deities (with the Mother-Goddess signalled in the title as the central presence), mostly about the tragic grandeur of mortal human beings, makes the here-and-now seem shadowy and remote.

Vittorini

Elio Vittorini (1908–66) signposts the route from the writing of the Fascist period (see above, pp. 526–7) towards a recognisably post-modern stance. His *Uomini e no* (*Men and Not Men*, 1945), the most self-consciously literary elaboration of the Resistance theme, does not present the author's own experience in the Resistance in Tuscany. Summarising this novel's plot gives little idea of its quality. Set in Milan, it flouts neo-realist transparency by its stylised, repetitive, quasi-operatic dialogue and by the complexity of its three tiers of narrative. These centre on Enne 2, an intellectual who has turned to action rather than submit to a cruelly oppressive system but shares little else with the working-class resistance fighters. His dangerous quest to eliminate the brutal Cane Nero torments him less than that for his childhood sweetheart Berta. His stream of consciousness is shadowed by a counter-narrative, conducted by his mysterious 'spectre' and printed in italics. The third narrative strand is closer to neo-realist impersonality, and weaves among a number of participants in the clandestine struggle. Much of the attention centres on the vicious mastiffs kept by Kapitan Clemm, who, with cold-blooded deliberation and relish, makes them devour alive the beggar, Giulaj, after he has killed one of them in self-defence with a file.

The dogs are thematised within the argument about 'men and not-men' prompted in the book by the bewilderingly ferocious phenomenon of Nazism. The muscular turns and moves of this narrative argument are enhanced by Vittorini's very explicit play with the very mechanisms of narrative – a feature more calculated to appeal half a century later than in the neo-realist climate of the time. Vittorini himself remained dissatisfied with the unresolved tensions within his works, especially their tendency to look nostalgically backwards rather than forwards.

Vittorini's restless, questing vitality characterises both his subsequent novels and his role as one of Italy's leading literary intellectuals until his death in 1966. Between 1945 and 1947 he published the Milan journal *Il Politecnico*, which led debate in Italy particularly with regard to the relationship between the literary and the political. Communist critics such as Mario Alicata, Carlo Salinari, Carlo Muscetta and Gaetano Trombatore took issue as much with radical writers and critics to the left of the Party as with those to the right of it. Vittorini, a non-Party pro-Communist during most of the 1940s, nevertheless hosted a sharp controversy in *Il Politecnico*, in which he argued, against the Communist leader, Togliatti, that literature could perform its revolutionary role better if *not* trammelled by political directives. He reopened the controversy in his 1951 essay 'Le vie degli ex-comunisti', which, with a carefully tailored selection of his essays and articles from the Fascist era and afterwards, appeared in his *Diario in pubblico* in 1957. *Il Politecnico*, echoing Carlo Cattaneo's project of a century earlier (see above p. 444), entertained an international and encyclopaedic medley of new thinking and writing, addressing both cultural and more strictly scientific, even technical, as well as sociological and other issues, and aimed at informing and educating the working class, as well as addressing a more intellectual readership; but it failed to bridge the contemporary socio-cultural divide.

From 1951 to 1958, Vittorini directed Einaudi's narrative series, 'I Gettoni', presenting many new kinds of writing both from home and abroad, though prolonging the neo-realist ethos that combined a strong moral commitment to actuality and the progressive stance with the hermetic tendency towards poetic prose and self-contemplation. Many representative works of the period appeared under that imprint, including Mario Tobino's quizzical account of Italy's military campaign in North Africa, *Il deserto della Libia* (1952), and Mario Rigoni Stern's *Il sergente nella neve* (*The Sergeant in the Snow*, 1953), on the Russian campaign, Carlo Cassola's *Fausto e Anna* (1952) and Beppe Fenoglio's peasant novel, *La malora* (1954). On the other hand, Giuseppe Tomasi di Lampedusa's *Il gattopardo* (*The Leopard*) was turned down for what Vittorini considered to be its fatalistic rejection of historical progress and apparent nostalgia for the old aristocracy.

Vittorini's own novels continued to display his experimentalism and his uncertainties. A new version of his early *Il garofano rosso*, with a revealing – and evasive – preface, was published in 1948. *Erica e i suoi fratelli*, also written in the 1930s but serialised in 1954, appeared with the post-war *La garibaldina* (serialised in 1950) in 1956. Of this diptych of contrasting models of Sicilian womanhood, the latter centres on a grand old lady who had been a heroine of the Risorgimento but now domineers her lowlier fellow-Sicilians of a later epoch, while the former presents a young girl who defies the pious conventions and provides for her parentless younger brothers and sisters by resorting to prostitution and the joyousness of group companionship – a pathetic sort of alternative society.

These two short novels are the most coherent of Vittorini's narrative works. His other post-war works – *Il Sempione strizza l'occhio al Fréjus* (*The Twilight of the Elephant*, 1947); *Le donne di Messina* (*The Women of M.*, 1949, extensively revised in 1964); and *Le città del mondo* ('The Cities of the World', abandoned in the mid-1950s and published posthumously in 1959) – display multiple tensions. The plight of the poor in post-war Italy is foregrounded – northern construction workers in the first, southerners trying to build a rural commune out of the ruins of war in the second, assorted casualties of the common fate wandering across Sicily in the third – but complicated by multiple plots, transhistorical or emblematic characters and narrative modes. The reader is admitted into the literary laboratory, and 'l'autoritarismo dello scrittore che si crede Dio' ('the authoritarianism of the writer who thinks he is God', as Vittorini puts it in his intriguing notes posthumously published as *Le due tensioni* in 1967, p. 34) is tacitly abolished. Yet this strikingly modern aspect of the writing was undercut, in Vittorini's mind, by his being trapped thematically in an archaic model of society and work, which ultimately constrains the writing itself. These are precisely his 'due tensioni' – the 'affective' pull towards the past, the familiar, counteracting the 'rational' urge towards the new, towards a liberating technology and new processes of literary production.

Naples and the urban south

The tension between affection for enduring traits and revulsion against an intolerable social situation is marked in other southern writers of the period, especially those based in Naples. Carlo Bernari (whose *Tre operai*, 'Three Workers', of 1934, together with another southern work, Corrado Alvaro's *Gente in Aspromonte*, of 1930, foreshadowed neo-realism – see above, p. 522) chronicles and castigates conditions in war-time and post-war Naples in *Napoli guerra e pace* (1945), *Prologo alle tenebre* ('Prologue to Darkness', 1947), *Speranzella* (1949), and *Vesuvio e pane* ('Vesuvius and Bread', 1952); while Giuseppe Marotta's *L'oro di Napoli* (*Neapolitan Gold*, 1947), *San Gennaro non dice mai no* (*Return to Naples, 1948*), and *Gli alunni del sole* ('The Pupils of the Sun', 1952) take a light-hearted view of the Neapolitans' traditional resourcefulness in adversity.

The comic dramas of Eduardo De Filippo of this period present the triumph of Neapolitan kindliness over the hard of heart, as in *Napoli milionaria!* (1945), in which the hapless yet invincibly happy Gennaro returns home from a Nazi labour camp to save his ruthless racketeering wife Amalia from herself. The moral calculus (if not the dramatic action) is more dubious, and thereby more convincing, in *Filumena Marturano* (1946), in which the protagonist, a 'kept woman', at last manoeuvres her keeper into marrying her and recognising her three sons as legitimate – a remarkable analogy to Italy's post-Liberation shift from Fascist to Catholic norms.

Domenico Rea (1921–93), in his stories and sketches of *Spaccanapoli* (1947), *Gesú, fate luce* ('Jesus, Make Light', 1950), *Ritratto di maggio* ('May Portrait', 1953) and *Quel che vide Cummeo* ('What C. Saw', 1955), is equally exuberant but far more deadly, and goes straight for the aching nerve as uncompromisingly as Pasolini in *Ragazzi di vita* and *Alí dagli occhi azzurri* ('Blue-Eyed Ali'), with no pious hopes or visible judgemental perspectives. Rea progressively moves towards an absolute simplicity of language – shedding his initial abrupt shifts of sociolect between snatches of Neapolitan speech and literary phraseology – and towards a broader perspective in which individual gestures find a fuller explanation; but, even in his novel *Una vampata di rossore* ('A Ruddy Blaze', 1959), he withholds the sense of narrative completeness, as if no story can ever be fully told. The external rationale for his narratives can be read in the essays collected in *Il re e il lustrascarpe* ('The King and the Shoe-Shine Boy', 1960), and especially in 'Le due Napoli', of 1950, later appended to *Quel che vide Cummeo*, contesting the sentimental image of the Neapolitan underclass surviving by their gaiety and wits with an historical analysis of poverty in the southern capital.

The post-war works of the Tuscan Curzio Malaparte (=Kurt Suckert, 1898–1957, born in Prato) are close to neo-realism in the unnerving immediacy of his reportage of the horrors of war, but distant from it in the visibility of his personality and highly coloured literary style. After his internationally celebrated first-person account of Poland and the Ukraine under the Nazi onslaught in *Kaputt* (1944), he turned in *La pelle* ('The Skin', which he published himself in 1949) to the degradation of Naples and Italy under American occupation in 1944, with even more shocking results.

The starving Neapolitans stage a Dutch auction to hand over their German prisoners to the Allied authorities; for the first time in their history, mothers sell their boys to the Moroccans among the Allied forces; a father makes a tourist attraction of his daughter as Naples' one remaining virgin. The whores affect blonde pubic wigs for the pleasure of their new black clients among the occupying US troops. There is a ritual accouchement among the homosexuals who have flocked to liberated Naples from all over Europe. Air-raid casualties and an eruption of Vesuvius add to the cataclysmic effect wrought by the writer, who threads the work with a discourse on the undoing of Christ's sacrifice. This includes hardly bearable memorial forays to the scene of an avenue of dying Jews crucified in the Ukraine and to the Christ-like death of his own dog Febo under vivisection in Pisa. The very speciousness of the authorial voice, the documentary stance, and the morality and metaphysics of the book, as well as its high-handed model of narrative discourse, distinguish *La pelle* from Malaparte's other works.

The death camps

The need to bear witness and strive to understand was of course most categorical with regard to genocide, involving as it did the systematic dehumanisation – first the moral and then the physical annihilation – of millions of Jews and other victims of Nazism. Primo Levi's *Se questo è un uomo* (*Survival in Auschwitz*, 1947), an account of over a year spent by its author in Auschwitz under perpetual threat of the gas chamber, is one of the outstanding testimonies by a death-camp survivor, forcing the issue of neo-realism and of literary values. Levi was an industrial chemist, and not a professional writer. His book flaunted no fashionable literary pretensions and remained virtually unnoticed until republished by Einaudi in 1958, keeping alive one of the recurring nightmares which afflicted many in Auschwitz – that of telling their story to people who would not listen.

Reality in its most awful guise fills *Se questo è un uomo*, but the discourse is fashioned by Levi's stance as a partly Jewish scientific rationalist who believed not in a transcendent God, but in humanity. At Auschwitz he found an infernal system, a Utopia in reverse, based on perfect scientific rationality combined with perfect anti-humanity. His captors had turned themselves into machine-like brutes and their victims into unpersons. The meticulous description of the Auschwitz system of exploitation of human labour and of industrialised genocide is carefully articulated in its narrative progression from experiential incomprehension to a scientific account of the Nazis' social and biological experiment and the inmates' struggle to retain both life and dignity. The most explicit point in this process comes when Levi tries to recall, for a fellow prisoner, the Ulysses episode in Dante's *Inferno* ('fatti non foste a viver come bruti', 'You were not made to live like beasts'), interpreting it self-redemptively, only to end despairingly ('infin che 'l mar fu sopra noi rinchiuso', 'until the sea had closed over us').

Levi's title recalls Vittorini's *Uomini e no*, and the humanist logic in the two otherwise dissimilar books operates consistently. Neither work has much, if any, explicit political content, beyond the revulsion against Nazi-Fascism, though Vittorini was a Communist when he wrote his. Both operate at a broader moral level, facing the horror of Nazi brutishness as a *human* product, no less than the degradation of its victims. The morality of resistance is not without its ambiguities. Resistance to Nazi-like acts commits one to apparently similar acts (tenfold reprisals against active Nazis or Fascists to counter the latter's indiscriminate reprisals against the civilian population). Yet resist one must, as the formerly pacifist American Martha Gellhorn had already found in her well-meaning encounters with young Nazis between 1934 and 1936. For this reason, accusations of manicheism levelled at much literature presenting Nazi-Fascism are beside the point. Just as it is historically and epistemologically impossible for anyone on the Resistance side to 'see' the humanity of the Nazi-Fascist enemy as subject, Resistance writing can judge the actions of those on the side of the Resistance only in terms of the values of the Resistance itself. Thus the compassion for the Fascist dead felt by the conformist Corrado in the finale of Pavese's *La casa in collina* is functional to the character's own moral ambiguity.

The female subject

Pavese's *Tra donne sole* and *La bella estate* were remarkable for two specific reasons. First, in projecting the female subject, whether in first-person or third-person narration. And second, in treating the alienation of everyday living with subtle matter-of-factness and without the metaphysical pretensions of existentialism. This overlapping territory was to be explored with a subtle penetration (which the hullaballoo of literary debate long overlooked) by women writers in particular. They subjected matrimonial and family relations to withering examination, anticipating the feminist watchword that 'the personal is political', and helping to form the awareness that brought about extensive reforms in the rights and status of women from the 1970s onwards. Here we have, for Italy, a genuinely new realism without the 'neo', a severely disciplined realism which draws on the tradition of bourgeois realism from Flaubert to Chekhov and many English-language women novelists (and also perhaps on Svevo) and which establishes a corpus of increasingly self-conscious and self-confident feminist writing in Italy.

Yet it would not be legitimate to corral Italian women writers into a simple category. The stories and novels of Anna Banti (pseud. Lucia Lopresti, 1895–1985) present female subjugation and the drive towards self-determination not with low-key realism but in a richly florid and musical style. Her *Artemisia* (1947) is a transhistorical dialogue between the author and the seventeenth-century female painter Artemisia Gentileschi. Other works range from the late Roman Empire to the distant future, including contemporary Italy in *Il bastardo* (1953; revised version, *La casa piccola*, 1961).

Alba De Céspedes (born in 1911) and Natalia Ginzburg (1916–91), on the other hand, make the everyday texture of women's lives in their own time speak authoritatively for a pervasive and oppressive nullity not only in women's subordinate condition, but in male privilege also. De Céspedes, despite her wide readership, waited long for recognition. Her novel *Dalla parte di lei* (*The Best of Husbands*, 1949), like Ginzburg's *E' stato così* (*The Dry Heart*, 1947), deals with a woman who has murdered her husband. The former is set against the last years of Fascism and the Resistance struggle, while the latter involves characters seemingly incapable of conceiving any sort of serious commitment, even at the private level; yet both convey with inexorable finesse the husband's overwhelming disinclination to allow the wife an autonomous personality. In De Céspedes, the traditional matrimonial and familial conventions of polite society appear intrinsically hollow and alienating, whereas the early Ginzburg presents tragic individual casualties of those conventions.

De Céspedes's novel *Prima e dopo* (*Between Then and Now*, 1955) also traverses the Resistance period through a female consciousness, while the stories of *Invito a pranzo* ('Invitation to Lunch', 1955), often imply the context of a precise historical situation. *Quaderno proibito* (1952) takes the form of a secret diary kept by the forty-three-year-old Valeria Cossati and precisely dated to 1950–1. But the stifling atmosphere of cold war and of Rome's conformist Catholicism is felt rather than stated, as are the subtle generational shifts in familial mores which structure the novel. Rather as in Svevo's *La coscienza di Zeno* (see above, p. 517), Valeria's diary reaches towards self-realisation and wholeness only to recoil into conventional role-playing, no longer unthinkingly, but in bad faith.

The same fragility of the self, particularly female, belying the apparent solidity of middle-class living, is also the subject of Ginzburg's works. In these, outcomes are more often tragic, though the tone is dictated by the flat dialogue of characters who cannot see beyond their situation or escape it. This mental prison is presented in the *novella* 'La madre', included in *Cinque romanzi brevi* (1964): the obliteration of a pitifully young widowed mother, largely at the hands of her own insensitive parents, is narrated from the point of view of her two uncomprehending little boys. The silences in the narration create the space where understanding is established between writer and reader. In Ginzburg's early works the historical moment is perceived sharply, but far less through reference to public events than in terms of what kinds of relationships are available to women. *Tutti i nostri ieri* (*All Our Yesterdays*, 1952) extends Ginzburg's method to a wider array of characters across three generations and confirms Calvino's judgement on Natalia Ginzburg as escaping the bounds of neo-realism by her focus on middle-class living.

The 'deceit and sorcery' of the title of the first novel by Elsa Morante, *Menzogna e sortilegio* (*The House of Liars*, 1948) also apply to disastrous family relationships, as recalled by the reminiscing young Elisa: the powerfully ambiguous forces of fantasy and love, of dream and desire, which rule the characters take the narrative even further away from neo-realism.

Beyond the fringe of neo-realism

Other writers also operated outside the pieties of neo-realism. Gadda remained for the time being a coterie influence, albeit of prime importance. Dino Buzzati (see above, p. 523) continued to tap his fantastic vein with the play *Un caso clinico* (1953) and *Sessanta racconti* (1958), while Antonio Delfini (1907–63) and Tommaso Landolfi (1908–79) had as far back as the 1930s started writing works which playfully challenged the conception of a verifiable reality, blending elements of fantasy, magic realism, surrealism, metaphysics, parody and autobiography. Such were Delfini's provincial stories from *Ritorno in città* (1931) to *Il ricordo della Basca* (1938) and *La Rosina perduta* (1957). His *Diari*, a compelling 'autobiographical novel' of the years 1927–61, published only in 1982, has contributed significantly to his recent revival. Landolfi's tales, from *La pietra lunare* and *Il mar delle blatte* ('Moonrock' and 'Cockroach Sea', 1939) to *Le due zittelle* ('The Two Old Maids', 1945), are often tongue-in-cheek and have an air of pastiche. *La bière du pêcheur* (1953), *Rien va* (1963) and *Dès mois* (1967) are couched as diaries, but the incoherence of reality still does not break through in these, any more than in his previous writings, with sufficient intensity or narrative urgency to disrupt convincingly the assumptions of normality or to problematise 'reality' in any radical way.

The Sardinian Giuseppe Dessí (1909–77), subordinating the external world to subjective experience in *Racconti vecchi e nuovi* ('Tales Old and New', 1945), and in the novel *Introduzione alla vita di Giacomo Scarbo* ('Introduction to the Life of G.S.', 1948), takes the subjective to the point of fantasy in *Storia del principe Lui* ('Story of Prince Him', 1949), but then reconstitutes a verifiable referential universe, closer to that of neo-realism, through the dimension of memory, in the novel *I passeri* ('The Sparrows', 1955).

The Milanese Luigi Santucci (b. 1918), began, with *Misteri gaudiosi* ('Joyful Mysteries', 1946), a series of affectionately comic stories, sketches and novels satirising the quirks and dogmatism of free-thinkers and religious alike (including the clergy), leading up to the more far-reaching deployment of his Christian values in the historical novel of post-Risorgimento provincial life, *Il velocifero* (1965). He also wrote two religious plays, latter-day *sacre rappresentazioni* (see above, p. 175) – *Chiara* (1955) and *L'angelo di Caino* (1956) – and indeed, apart from De Filippo, Italy's few dramatists of this period incline towards the religious and the existential and away from neo-realism.

From *Spiritismo nell'antica casa* (*Spirit-Raising in the Old House*, written in 1944 and first performed and published in 1950) until his death in 1953, Ugo Betti (b. 1892) wrote eleven tense dramas in which the protagonists are forced to face their own guilt – sexual, social or political, but always existential – and somehow redeem or transcend it. Settings are always emblematic or archetypal rather than naturalistic, as often indicated in the very titles – *Corruzione al Palazzo di Giustizia* (*Corruption in the Palace of Justice*, written in 1944–5), *Delitto all'isola delle capre* (*Crime on Goat-Island*, written in 1946), *Acque turbate* (*Troubled Waters*, written in 1948). Betti (a high court judge under Fascism) pitches at the universal and avoids politics, yet several plays clearly allude to issues of the moment: *Corruzione* touches on the guilt of the judiciary when anti-Fascist purges were on the agenda; *La regina e gli insorti* (*The Queen and the Rebels*, written in 1949) reverses the roles of whore and queen not long after the Italian monarchy had been abolished by referendum; *L'aiuola bruciata* (*The Burnt Flowerbed*, completed in 1952) presents an analogy to the Cold War, with one side invoking historical determinism. Every issue, however, is pinned down to individual conscience, and Betti's theatrical skill lies precisely in stripping away one self-deception after another to reveal the self naked.

For Diego Fabbri (1911–80) also, conscience is the stage and guilt the substance of the drama, but more explicitly in Catholic terms, which proves a liability in the daring *Processo a Gesú* (*The Trial of Jesus*, written 1952–4), a metadrama in which the trial is the play and the audience is the jury. It is not so much Jesus who is on trial, but a group of post-Holocaust Jews who in effect attempt, and fail, to clear themselves of deicide. The divine vocation of the individual is revealed with more convincing surprises and psychological finesse when the frame of reference is Catholic, as in *Inquisizione* (written in 1946).

Novelists on the whole eschewed a religious standpoint. In *Tempo di uccidere* ('Time for Killing' – 1947) Ennio Flaiano (1910–72) gave a subtly ironical portrayal of an anguished Italian officer who fights in and survives the Ethiopian war (1935–36). Flaiano's gentle, half-sad, half-satirical vein runs through his extensive writing for the cinema, which includes the script for Fellini's *La dolce vita*. Vitaliano Brancati (1907–54) further refined his satirical treatment of Sicilian middle-class mores, especially sexual, in his last works – the stories of *Il vecchio con gli stivali* ('The Old Man With the Boots', 1945); and the novels *Il bell'Antonio* (1949) and *Paolo il caldo* ('Randy Paolo', 1955). However, it is with Alberto Moravia (pseudonym of Alberto Pincherle (1907–90)) that the exploration of sexual behaviour and sexual experience goes beyond social satire to question the existential basis of the upper-middle-class condition, at its most rarefied in the political and religious capital, Rome.

The brilliant short novel *Agostino*, of 1944, centred on an immature male, was followed by a second, *La disubbidienza* (*Disobedience*, 1948), written, like all Moravia's works, as the exhaustive and compelling narrative of a consciousness. The male protagonist, Luca, is entering upon sexual maturity when he is overcome by an existential crisis indistinguishable from a rejection of bourgeois family living, largely triggered by his discovery that the domestic shrine to the Madonna conceals a safe containing cash and valuables. The novel hinges on the male-centred contrast between the sexual avidity of the governess who attempts to seduce him and the generous warmth of the nurse who heals him through sexual initiation. The ambitious *La Romana* (*The Woman of Rome*, 1947) updates and develops the Carla of *Gli indifferenti* (see above, p. 524) in Adriana, who finds herself emblematically caught between the police chief Astarita and an anti-Fascist student, progressing, through one of Moravia's more intricate plots, towards moral and political virtue, if not exactly autonomy.

Post-war existential crisis and writer's block are explored within the matrimonial relationship in *L'amore coniugale* (*Conjugal Love*, 1949) and *Il disprezzo* (*A Ghost at Noon*, 1954), while other works move closer to the neorealist mode. *Il conformista* (*The Conformist*, 1951) is an ironic account of Marcello's desperate and invariably fruitless endeavours to conform with authoritarian norms, climaxing with his mission as a Fascist secret agent to kill a prominent anti-Fascist exile in Paris, recalling the real-life murder of Carlo Rosselli. Moravia's analysis of Marcello's Fascism as fear of homoeroticism, or fear of eros as such, is consonant with the theories of Wilhelm Reich, but found little favour in Italy, though Bertolucci's film brilliantly brought out the book's even more than usually marked oneiric quality. The conformism of the title may indeed have had more to do with post-war Catholic hegemony than with Fascism. Feminist criticism has blasted Moravia, but *Il conformista*, though male-centred, credits autonomy, and especially sexual autonomy in a lesbian relationship, to two very different female victims of male power, and consistently annihilates the male protagonist.

Moravia drew close to neo-realism in the *Racconti romani* (*Roman Tales*, 1954) and *Nuovi racconti romani* (1959). These tales still focus on the individual consciousness, usually with a moral irony that goes over the heads of the characters, now drawn from the petty bourgeoisie or the underclass of Rome in the 1950s, with the cash nexus, as always, determinant. *La Ciociara* (*Two Women*, 1957), Moravia's avowed tribute to the Resistance, goes beyond these limits. Here, in a relatively uncontrived plot, Cesira, seeking refuge in her native hills from war-time Rome, overcomes her shopkeeper mentality and achieves civic consciousness through the cathartic experience of war, liberation and rape.

It is this typically neo-realist cathartic effect that Italo Calvino (1923–85) side-steps in *Il sentiero dei nidi di ragno* ('The Path to the Nests of Spiders', 1947), focusing the Resistance through a twelve-year-old Genoese street-boy, Pin, as an adventure involving a ragged partisan band on whose lack of political consciousness the commissar Kim ponders in philosophical vein. The vivid actuality remains indecipherable, and largely ludic. Life, even war, appears as play, both in the living and in the writing, which draws out the curious geometries and the multifarious sense-impressions of what is observed.

These characteristics mark Calvino's works, from the short stories about the war, the Resistance and after (*Ultimo viene il corvo*, 'The Crow Comes Last', 1949, and *L'entrata in guerra*, 'Beginning of War', 1954) to his novels written in a realist mode (*La speculazione edilizia*, *A Plunge Into Real Estate*, 1957, and *La giornata di uno scrutatore*, 'A Day in the Life of a Scrutineer', 1963). Yet these, and the stories grouped together as *Gli amori difficili* (*Difficult Loves*) in the *Racconti* volume of 1958, are also acute, strictly focused, chronicles of history experienced without being understood. Calvino more boldly pursued new modes of signification and new approaches to the real through his collection of fairy-tales selected from various Italian dialects, *Fiabe italiane* (*Italian Folk Tales*, 1956), and especially through the light-heartedly moral and historical fantasies of his three novels *Il visconte dimezzato* (*The Cloven Viscount*, 1952), *Il barone rampante* (*The Baron in the Trees*, 1957) and *Il cavaliere inesistente* (*The Non-Existent Knight*, 1959), published together in 1960 as *I nostri antenati* (*Our Ancestors*). A baroque viscount split into two halves – one good, one evil – by a cannonball; an eighteenth-century baron's son, who, at twelve years of age, takes to the trees for the rest of his life; an empty suit of armour in Charlemagne's army, a 'man' who doesn't exist and knows it, accompanied by his utterly physical squire who all too palpably exists but doesn't know it: these figures gave free rein to Calvino's remarkable talent for literary play with ingenious narrative geometries and tactile sensations in a multifaceted yet always crystalline style, and were to lead him to ever new 'cosmi-comic' and metachronic adventures in the 1960s and 1970s (see below, pp. 594–5).

41

History and the poets

Calvino explores the interface between the two sides of writing – the shared
referential domain of lived life and the discursive artefact of the writing on the
page. His fiction progresses from the first towards the second, converging with
Italy's literary transformation during the 1960s. The hermetic generation of
poets, dominant since the 1930s (see above, pp. 502ff.), were concerned with
the metaphysics of absence, of a barely apprehensible 'I' and 'thou', and the
metaphysics of language, rather than the contingency of things or events. The
pressure of history – the events of the 1940s – did not immediately reverse this
abstentionist stance.

Formidably austere, but also disarmingly quotidian, Eugenio Montale's war-
time and post-war poems collected in the symbolically titled *La bufera* ('The
Storm', 1956; see also above, p. 507) metaphysically confront the cataclysm of
the Second World War. Epiphanic glimpses or 'flashes', they embrace the
Western world from the road to Damascus as far as New England while
remaining firmly anchored in Montale's war-time home, Florence, and tied to
his parental Liguria. The poet's consternation links personal fates, lost loved
ones, with the general fate, connecting or conflating life, death and possible
after-lives or other lives. *La bufera* is dominated by the presences and absences
of female figures, loved at once humanly and transcendentally: Clizia in the
major fifth section, 'Silvae', and Volpe (Fox) in the sixth, 'Madrigali privati'.
These are visiting angels, apparent victims, but also *stilnovo* or even Christo-
logical redeemers, as in 'L'ombra della magnolia' and in 'Iride' ('Rainbow').
The cunningly elusive play of rhyme – including internal and near-rhymes –
and line-length and syntax, varying from deceptively limpid brevity to
labyrinthine structures with multiple embeddings and lengthy parentheses is all
contained within an arduously coherent discourse. The exceptionally confident
and transparent tour-de-force, 'L'anguilla', is composed of a single, sinuous,
threshing, eel-like, thirty-line sentence in which the eel is the vital 'torch,
whiplash, / arrow of Love on earth'.

Elsewhere, the obscurity of *La bufera* is that of the perceived world.
Montale's language imperiously absorbs the most unpoetic lexis, as the poetry
transfigures mundane objects, especially small living creatures, into elusive
signals, so that the poet's bewildered gnostic stance is as animistic as it is
mystic, interrogating an anguishingly enigmatic phenomenal universe, and
more manicheistic than that of most Resistance novels, defining earthly powers

as 'iddii pestilenziali' or 'iddio taurino' or 'mostro cornuto' ('taurine deity', 'horned monster'). In a lower key, the impeccably prosaic reportage of *La farfalla di Dinard* ('The Butterfly of Dinard'), which appeared in the same year as *La bufera*, likewise conveys inklings of a reality beyond the conventionally accepted one.

For Ungaretti, too (see above, pp. 502–4), personal griefs – the loss of his brother and of his nine-year-old son – combined with the anguish for his country in war and under German occupation in the volume *Il dolore* ('Grief', 1947) with a dramatic quality rare in contemporary Italian poetry. Autobiography becomes more than ever the prominent element, justifying the collective title, *Vita d'un uomo* ('The Life of a Man', 1969) which the poet was to give to his works before his death in 1970. In brief bursts, the 'Giorno per giorno' sequence chronicles the pain of paternal bereavement, but also the continued communication with his dead child. 'Tu ti spezzasti' more elaborately recreates a memoried exotic landscape (anticipating *Un grido e paesaggi*, 'A Cry and Landscapes', of 1952). The 'Roma occupata' sequence adds the liturgical component 'Santo, santo che soffri' (Holy, holy you suffer), in 'Mio fiume anche tu' ('You too my river'), with its insistent 'Ora che ... Ora che ... Ora ora ...' (Now that ...) evoking Nazi horrors (see also above, pp. 502–4).

Ungaretti never completed the ambitious *La terra promessa* ('The Promised Land'), which produced the 'Ultimi cori' ('Final choruses') invoking a transcendent goal, and the 'Cori descrittivi di stati d'animo di Didone' ('Choruses descriptive of states of mind of Dido'), whose rarefied atmosphere is far removed from the contingent self. *Un grido*, on the other hand, also contains the ironically, even humorously, prosaic travelogue through memory, 'Monologhetto', which begins as a car ride into southern Italy, and takes in the carnival in Pernambuco and an Egyptian Shiite festival in Alexandria, to end with a stripping off of poetic masks: 'Poeti, poeti, ci siamo messi / Tutte le maschere; / Ma ognuno non è che la propria persona.' (Poets, poets, we have put on every mask, but each of us is only his own persona.)

Italy's trauma does not figure in Mario Luzi's post-war production, from the love-sequence of *Quaderno gotico* ('Gothic Notebook', 1947), until *Onore del vero* ('Respect for the Truth', 1957), an exquisite hermetic arcadia of vague metaphors and vague pieties, of a metaphysical time and place impervious to historical contingency until the sea-change of *Nel magma* ('In the Magma', 1963). On the other hand, Corrado Govoni's *Aladino* (1946) expresses anguish and outrage at German atrocities in Rome, including the shooting of the poet's son as a hostage, in characteristically vivid colours and rhythms, but brings no permanent change to this prolific poet's otherwise festive and always sharply sensory style (see above, pp. 497–8).

Saba's poetry also presents a purely personal reaction in 1944, and particularly the poem 'Avevo', which complains about the Fascists and Germans who have deprived him of his life in Trieste. Otherwise, it adds mostly light minimalist pieces, such as his moralities about birds (*Uccelli* –

quasi un racconto, 'Birds, Almost a Story', 1948), and brief dialogues with his daughter Linuccia and his assistant Carletto: graceful pieces, and prosier than ever, yet different from the brief reminiscing prose pieces of *Ricordi-Racconti*, published shortly before the author's death in 1957, and the even briefer apophthegms and observations of *Scorciatoie e raccontini* ('Short Cuts and Short Stories', 1946). All these are more or less explicitly cast in engaging dialogue form, founded on Saba's belief in instinctual understanding shared by all living things, but the prose works go beyond a sympathetic understanding of individuals to touch on themes in culture and even politics with the same sympathetic wisdom. Saba also busied himself with the management of his own fame: first by repeated editions of the *Canzoniere* of his collected poems, and second by his disarming self-exegesis, *Storia e cronistoria del Canzoniere* (1948; see above, p. 499). His posthumous autobiographically based novel *Ernesto* (1975) unblinkingly narrates a transient love that unself-consciously speaks its name, ushering the sixteen-year-old protagonist into adult sexuality through a liaison with an adult male in the Trieste of 1898. The Triestine speech of 1898 alternates with the now of the elderly narrator's Italian.

None of these poets investigated the everyday phenomenology of dictatorship and war or Cold War and the human experience, the sweets and sores, the pressures of Italy's fast-changing society – the ground occupied by the novel and by neo-realism. Neo-realist and Resistance poetry was disappointing: pseudo-populist balladry, quasi-heroic or quasi-epic narrative, rousing rhetoric. It failed to rise to the challenge of events. 'Pure' poetry, as it was called, like Luzi's, looked away from the historical and the social to metaphysical contemplation of love, landscape, time, memory, death, producing brief lyrics usually well under a page long in a highly stylised and rarefied idiom. Thus in Attilio Bertolucci's *Lettera da casa* ('Letter from Home', 1951) the loss of loved ones is absorbed into the modulation of the verse and the seasons. Vittorio Sereni's *Diario d'Algeria* (1947) forces the issue already suggested in his *Frontiera* (1941): the contingencies of history impinge directly on the poetic self – Sereni as army officer, then prisoner of war – in titles or images as concrete as that of 'Pin-up girl' or the first D-Day casualty (in 'Non sa piú nulla ...'), but cannot change the poet's 'music' of absence, of alienation from history as such, of death-in-life ('Non sanno d'essere morti / i morti come noi' – They don't know they're dead those who are dead like us).

Quasimodo's poems on the Milan air-raids and Nazi occupation in *Giorno dopo giorno* ('Day after Day', 1947) accommodate the new subject-matter into the allusive poetic discourse of hermeticism with the change from first-person singular to plural. *La vita non è sogno* ('Life Is Not a Dream', 1949) extends this bardic voice and stance and the theme of *patria* with addresses to God and mentions of Buchenwald and Stalingrad, while *Il falso e vero verde* ('The True and the False Green', 1954) climbs out of the hermetic mode into a more concretely historical discourse of civic poetry. Likewise, Sergio Solmi (1899–1982), in his works up to *Levania* (1956), was to move towards a prosaic contemporary discourse still implicitly undercut by the negative dialectic of metaphysics. Franco Fortini (pseudonym for Lattes, b. 1917), especially in the war and Resistance poetry of *Foglio di via* ('Waybill', 1946), came close to bridging the 'neo-realist' and 'hermetic' modes at the beginning of his long career as both poet and militant intellectual, which included working with Vittorini on *Il Politecnico*.

Sandro Penna (1906–77), always outside hermeticism, in his *Appunti* ('Notes', 1950) and *Una strana gioia di vivere* ('A Strange Joy in Living', 1956) and *Croce e delizia* ('Torment and Delight', 1958), sharply captures the present moment with paradoxical *joie-de-vivre* in exquisitely epigrammatic lyrics mostly on homoerotic love. Equally direct, yet not unsophisticated, lyricism is to be found in several dialect poets, especially from the Tre Venezie: Virgilio Giotti, from Trieste (1885–1957), who assembled his previous collections of lively scenes and sensations in *Colori*; the sharp Giacomo Noventa (Ca' Zorzi, 1898–1960); the wistful Biagio Marin (1891–1985), from Grado, who wrote a multitude of brief, musically rhymed, short-lined poetic gems.

Pasolini

Gem-like, musically rhymed poems in the dialect of Friuli (also in the Tre Venezie), were the first published works of Pier Paolo Pasolini (1922–75) in *Poesie a Casarsa* (1942) and in *La meglio gioventú* ('The Best of Youth', 1954). Reviewing the former, Gianfranco Contini observed that Pasolini was using dialect not so as to strike, as traditionally, a 'lower', more popular, but a more exquisite register than that available in standard literary Italian. Pasolini used dialect as a means of escaping from the prefabricated discourse of hermeticism into an even more private world of sweet, sinful innocence, echoing the lyric tradition from the medieval Provençal to the French Decadents, with images of boyhood death and God as an almost magical presence in nature.

He flaunts his virtuosity in his first Italian collection, *L'usignolo della Chiesa Cattolica* ('The Nightingale of the Catholic Church'), written in the 1940s but published in 1948, which runs through a startling variety of styles, subject-matters and poetic modes or genres, including genuinely prosaic prose-poems, liturgical and evangelical poems, sex, statuary, panoramic vistas, and more. Before he was hounded out of his maternal Casarsa to Rome, on an unproven charge of seducing minors, he wrote a novel on fresh Friulan peasant youth, *Il sogno di una cosa* (*A Dream of Something*, 1962), and two even more tongue-in-cheek homoerotic novels, *Amado mio* ('Lover') and *Atti impuri* ('Impure Acts', published posthumously in 1982). By 1954 he had grasped the contradictions of his own person, his culture and his times in the long poem 'Le ceneri di Gramsci' (*The Ashes of Gramsci*), republished in the volume of the same title. Here, in super-sophisticated *terza rima* with decadent-realist *coloritura*, he addresses the dead Gramsci and confesses his own, and Italy's, inability to live up to Gramsci's historic vision of proletarian revolution.

The following year, Pasolini published his ultra-realist quasi-novel, *Ragazzi di vita* (revised edition 1979), which became the target of a politico-literary hullabaloo and also an obscenity trial, and hastened the death of neo-realism by its presentation, largely in their own raw slang, of the hopelessness of the underclass of the youths of the Rome slums. An inexorable determinism dictates the appalling deaths that seal each of the connected stories, from the first chapter, in which Riccetto saves a drowning bird, to the last, where he nonchalantly allows his young friend Genesio to drown. But Pasolini waged war on his own and other people's irrationalism, founding in 1955 the Bologna journal *Officina*, as co-editor with Francesco Leonetti and Roberto Roversi (and, from 1958, with Franco Fortini and others). *Officina*, keeping a neo-Marxian faith, championed neo-experimentalism – tendentially rational, scientific and objective – against the newborn neo-avantgarde, presumptively anti-rational, anti-scientific and anti-objective.

In retrospect, what the two rival movements had in common was greater than what divided them, and both can be seen as part and parcel of the radical transformation of Italian intellectual culture which was getting under way. In this transformation, no single individual was to play a greater part than Pasolini. He was not the only intellectual to combine the roles of poet, fiction-writer, theorist, critical essayist and journal editor – to which he was soon to add those of screenplay writer, film-maker, playwright, and public polemicist; but, defining himself as a 'style-horse' ('bestia da stile'), he was alone in striving to bring to bear all his available literary and intellectual resources to define and meet head-on what many saw as the central problem of Italian and world society: not this or that political issue or cause, but the problem of Power itself. Others in Italy and elsewhere – especially France and Germany – saw things the same way. For them, the objective became, not to perfect this or that literary genre, this or that literary style, but to attack, with whatever means, through whatever medium, the discourse of Power itself, its false rationale. Language, communication, representation – all forms of discourse came to be seen as the arena of cultural engagement. Their structures, their meanings, their modes of production and consumption were to be laid bare and under-mined from within or converted into forces for human betterment. Such, within their diversity, were the projects of *Officina* and of other journals and movements that appeared from the late 1950s onwards, given greater urgency by the dramatic international events of 1956 (see below, pp. 564–5).

Contemporary Italy (since 1956)

Michael Caesar

42

The late 1950s and the 1960s

Like '1945', the emblematic date of '1956' is seen as heralding the start of a new period in Italian literary history, and for broadly similar non-literary reasons. But it would be some time before the true extent of the broad cultural changes which began to be felt in the mid-1950s could be gauged. It is true that the political events of 1956 itself in Eastern Europe did register promptly with an influential portion of the Italian intelligentsia. Khruschev's partially leaked denunciation of Stalin at the Twentieth Congress of the Communist Party of the Soviet Union and Soviet military intervention in Hungary and Poland in the same year delivered a profound shock to the intellectual left, caused many sympathisers among the educated classes to abandon their support for the Italian Communist Party, and initiated a period of reassessment of the relations between literature and politics. But this was less important in the long run than the very rapid expansion of the Italian economy in the 'boom years' (1958–63), the new levels of prosperity and choice offered by the triumph of consumerism from the 1960s onwards, and the effect which these had on the social and material conditions of literature, both at the point of production and at that of consumption. At this broad level, the period under consideration in this chapter is distinguished from its predecessors by three factors in particular: the extension of educational and cultural opportunities to a greatly increased number of people; an unprecedented degree of commercial concentration and rationalisation in the production of the printed word; and the insertion of publishing in a complex web of 'cultural industries', amongst which there are media and technologies which seem to present a direct challenge to literature.

The period since 1956, however, is not itself all of a piece and the sections into which this chapter is divided try to give some account of the differences in emphasis insofar as these are visible from so distortingly close a perspective. The first, covering the years from 1956 to 1969, examines a span of years in which cultural militancy enjoyed a potency which was not to be repeated in the subsequent decades.

The older poets

Among the poets born before the First World War whose collections published in the 1950s and 1960s confirmed their reputation are Carlo Betocchi (1899–

1986), Sandro Penna (see above, p. 556), and Alfonso Gatto (1909–76). Gatto's painterly eye for landscape and still-life is everywhere present in the poems of *Osteria flegrea* ('The Phlegrean Inn', 1962) and, especially, *Rime di viaggio per la terra dipinta* ('Poems From a Journey Through the Painted Land', 1969). During the same period, a number of younger poets, who are sometimes rather slightingly referred to as the 'middle generation', were establishing a firm literary identity of their own. I shall be concerned in this section particularly with Mario Luzi (b. 1914; see also above, p. 554), Giorgio Caproni (1912–90), and Vittorio Sereni (1913–83 – see above, p. 555).

The poems from the late 1950s published in *Dal fondo delle campagne* ('From the Depths of the Country', 1965) underline Luzi's confidence in the control of the reasoning word and in the possibility of knowing the 'spiritual essence of the universe'. The thing is seen, reflected upon, weighed in the balance, and given definitive linguistic form; a dignified, at times austere, moral sententiousness is often the outcome. The poems of *Nel magma*, written between 1961 and 1963, reveal the Eliotean streak in Luzi's poetic talent, a combination of Catholic spiritual and moral themes and the registration of pointed conversations between adults in a naturalistic narrative and dialogue which is quite close to the spoken word, but appears tense: provocative, even aggressive, questioning which awaits or demands an answer. But the articulation of the dialogue points to a relativisation of values and a decentring of the replying self, features which are further defined, with complete metrical and rhythmical assurance, in the 'purgatorial' poems of *Su fondamenti invisibili* ('On Invisible Foundations', 1971) and in the remarkable later collections *Al fuoco della controversia* ('By the Fire of the Debate', 1978), *Per il battesimo dei nostri frammenti* ('For the Baptism of Our Fragments', 1985) and *Frasi e incisi di un canto salutare* ('Phrases and Interpolations of a Song of Health and Greeting', 1990).

Caproni's diction could not be more different from that of Luzi, with its short, incisive, lines playing extensively on variations of the *canzonetta* to produce a poetry that is phonically and metrically memorable. It is notable also for the modest, self-effacing figure of a poet who seems to laugh at himself at the moment that he is addressing difficult themes: the loss of his mother, the 'death of God', the uncertainty of life, seen often as a journey, with the anxiety to arrive and the fear of doing so, most famously in *Congedo del viaggiatore cerimonioso* ('The Polite Traveller Takes His Leave', published in 1965). Caproni's poetry shares with Sereni's a down-to-earth commonsensical quality which, however, takes off in a different direction in the latter. While Caproni hangs on to the remnants of his subjectivity, Sereni in *Gli strumenti umani* ('Human Instruments', 1965) is alert to the small doubts and questions, the making, unmaking and remaking of the self, the interplay of self and others. He combines the weariness of a generation pressurised and unwilling to make ideological statements with a practical 'let's get on with it' approach to life. Sereni is also subject to visions, to sudden flashes of insight, and the poem becomes an attempt to put this fleeting yet implicitly totalising apprehension down on paper, particularly in the returns to childhood loss and historical destruction in the last section of *Gli strumenti umani* and in parts of the poet's last collection, *Stella variabile* ('Variable Star', 1981).

Novels of memory

The time of personal or collective memory which is the dimension of some of Sereni's most powerful poetry also provides the setting for a number of novels written, or published, between 1956 and the early 1960s. The recent past, which extends to the years between the wars, to the war itself and to the immediate post-war period, is seen from a particular social angle, that of a region or town or family or group, and is often imbued with nostalgia. The trend which I am describing was discussed by Calvino, in an essay written at the time, as 'epic yielding to elegy', a 'sentimentalisation', one might say, of a historical material whose political and ideological implications have been rendered inaccessible by the crisis of neo-realism. The first part of *La brace dei Biassoli* ('Embers of the B.', 1956), by Mario Tobino (1910–91), is a fine example of the childhood memory of rural family life, recounted in a series of thumbnail sketches by an autobiographical narrator who reappears as an adult in the second half of the book. Tobino was for many years director of the psychiatric hospital at Lucca, and some of his later novels are a direct account of that experience; *Gli ultimi giorni di Magliano* ('The Last Days of M.', 1982) is a protest against the closing of mental hospitals in Italy.

In *Lessico famigliare* (*Family Sayings*, 1963), Natalia Ginzburg (1916–91; see also above, p. 548) writes an autobiographical account of growing up in a Jewish-Catholic family in inter-war Turin which she invites us to read 'as if it were a novel', thereby pointing up the ambivalent interplay of memory and fiction which also runs through Tobino's book. Perhaps the most intriguing feature of *Lessico famigliare* is precisely the 'family sayings' or 'language' of the title, a private idiom which yet provides a kind of oral history of the social milieu and period as well as of the family itself, in a way comparable to that in which Ginzburg was to use letters (real or fictional) in some of her later books.

The Resistance is the subject of *La ragazza di Bube* (*Bube's Girl*, 1959), a novel in which Carlo Cassola (1917–87) passes judgement on his war-time experience, articulating the discomfort of that 'middle generation' which was not responsible for Fascism but had to live with its consequences. His subsequent, prolific, writing concentrated on a poetic rendering of the day-to-day, eschewing any concern with political or ethical questions (although privately he was in later life to become active in the campaign for unilateral disarmament and peace). Cassola's fiction appealed to the same broad readership as the many novels of the journalist, script-writer and film-director Mario Soldati (see above, p. 514). The early fiction of Giorgio Bassani (b. 1916) speaks likewise of disappointment and renunciation, but his is a fiction from which all judgement has been drained. Here the incommensurability between the consciousness of the historical actors and what is about to happen (as in *Il giardino dei Finzi-Contini, The Garden of the F-Cs*, 1962) or what has happened (as in the story of the concentration camp survivor in 'Una lapide in Via Mazzini', in *Cinque storie ferraresi, A Prospect of Ferrara*, 1956) is suspended before the reader in the all-reflecting, impenetrable crystal of memory. The drama of stigmatisation and victimhood is played out in the setting of a provincial city (Ferrara) whose profound inertia is only seldom, and momentarily, disturbed.

It was Bassani, acting on behalf of the publishers Feltrinelli, who decided to accept *Il gattopardo* (*The Leopard*), the novel by the virtually unknown Sicilian writer Giuseppe Tomasi di Lampedusa (1896–1957) that was to become an unexpected best-seller in the years after its publication in 1958. The novel opens in May 1860, the date of Garibaldi's landing in Sicily. The political unification of Italy and the emergence of new political leaders and a new social order are in the air. But the social-realist emphasis on the transition of power from one class to another is less important than the moral climate of accommodation – the expectation that everything will change just to remain the same and that it makes little difference anyway – which seems to be both actively encouraged in the book and melancholically accepted; Bassani was probably right when he spoke of the novel expressing the 'pessimism' of Italian readers. The words with which the author judges the expectations of the lovers Angelica and Tancredi, in their 'pursuit of a future which they thought would be more real, but which then proved to be only smoke and wind' (chapter 4), apply equally to the hopes engendered by political unification and, by an extension clearly endorsed by the author, to those of the Resistance as well. The long view of a history which leads nowhere is as congenial to the protagonist, Don Fabrizio, as it is to his disenchanted author.

Reviews

Part of Lampedusa's *cachet* came from his very isolation, but the emphasis of these years was increasingly on the collective. In particular, the importance of the role played by the literary magazines in the promotion of new writing and new ideas about literature during the late 1950s and the 1960s cannot be overestimated. It was comparable to that of *La Voce* and the other reviews published during the decade-and-a-half before the First World War (see above, pp. 509–10). Of the four discussed here (*Officina, Il Menabò, Il Verri* in this section and *Quindici* below (p. 579)), the earliest was *Officina*, edited in two series between 1955 and 1959 by Francesco Leonetti (b. 1924), Pier Paolo Pasolini (1922–75) and Roberto Roversi (b. 1923), with significant contributions in particular from the critics Angelo Romanò (1920–89) and Gianni Scalia (b. 1928) and the poet and essayist Franco Fortini (1917–94). *Officina* mounted a vigorous polemic against decadentism in general, and Italian decadentism in particular. Its principal target was the *novecentista* line in poetry from *La Ronda* to hermeticism, with hermeticism being seen as the main expression of the Fascist period and interpreted as non-political, evasive, intimist and fearful of or rejecting any contact with reality. It was also seen as instilling a mystical attitude towards form and poetry. At the same time, the magazine polemicised, in a less systematic way, against neo-realism. Thus it managed to come out against both a supposedly hermeticist 'autonomy' of art and a realist notion of artistic 'engagement'. *Officina* was vague about what the 'new commitment' of the intellectual should be. Pasolini argued for a recuperation of late nineteenth- and early twentieth-century civic poetry – Carducci, *La Voce*, and especially Pascoli's *Poemetti* – as the way to a true contemporary experimentalism. Other important contributions to this revision of the canon were Scalia's essays on De Sanctis and Serra, and Romanò's on Manzoni and the *scapigliatura* (see above, p. 460).

After the closure of *Officina*, Roberto Roversi went on to found and edit *Rendiconti* (1961–77, in two series). The title of his first collection of poems (or 'one poem in several *canti*'), *Dopo Campoformio* ('After C.', 1962), alludes both to the despair of defeat and the grim determination to hang on, which will be apparent in an even more exasperated form in his 1976 novel *I diecimila cavalli*, ('The Ten Thousand Horses'). Francesco Leonetti was the only one of the *Officina* group who was able to strike up a dialogue with the neo-avant-garde (and also with *Il menabò*). Despite his considerable output of poetry and experimental novels throughout our period, notably *Conoscenza per errore* ('Knowledge by Mistake', 1961), *L'incompleto* (1964), *Tappeto volante* ('Flying Carpet', 1967), *Percorso logico del 1960–75, poema* ('Logical Route from 1960 to 1975: a Poem', 1976), *In uno scacco (nel settantotto)* ('Setback (In Seventy-Eight)', 1979) and *Palla di filo* ('Ball of Thread', 1986), Leonetti's political militancy has acted as a barrier to identification with any purely literary project.

The two most considerable writers associated with *Officina* were undoubt-edly Pier Paolo Pasolini (see also above, p. 556) and Franco Fortini. Although Pasolini devoted increasing amounts of time in the 1960s to his career as script-writer and film-maker (see *Alì dagli occhi azzurri*, translated as *Roman Nights and Other Stories*, 1965) and, in the middle of the decade, to his writing for the theatre too, he continued to exploit the poetic vein developed in *Le ceneri di Gramsci* (*The Ashes of Gramsci*) in his subsequent collections, *La religione del mio tempo* ('The Religion of My Time', 1961) and *Poesia in forma di rosa* ('Poem in the Form of a Rose', 1964). By the time of *Trasumanar e organizzar* ('Transhumanise and Organise', 1971), however, Pasolini was writing a kind of anti-poetry, very direct and polemical in tone, foreshadowing the campaigns he was to unleash shortly afterwards in the Italian press against the revival of

Fascism and the 'anthropological mutation' signalled by the final collapse of peasant (and Third World) culture in the face of global consumerism (*Scritti corsari*, 'Piratical Writings', 1975 and *Lettere luterane*, *Lutheran Letters*, 1976). There is a profound disgust, and a sense of exhaustion, in the late poems which is felt also in the extraordinary unfinished novel of the same period, *Petrolio* ('Oil', 1992). But in all his many-sided, energising, cultural activism, Pasolini remained the same person, and despite his posthumous sanctification as a prophet without honour, he continues in reality to be reviled. The reasons are essentially social, for Pasolini 'represents' the dangerous classes (equally remote from the honest toilers of neo-realism and the variously alienated cyphers of 1960s 'industrial literature'). His was a populist decadentism at daggers drawn with its aestheticising cousin, which already in the 1950s was the real target of his polemical interventions in *Officina*.

In *I poeti del Novecento*, Fortini accuses Pasolini of not playing fair with the reader, demanding the latter's trust and then taking refuge in what he calls 'lyrical extra-territoriality'. What Fortini means by this is that Pasolini speaks always 'as a poet', thus arranging things so that he can never be challenged on the grounds of argument. Fortini, on the other hand, always maintained a clear distinction between his work as a poet and his work as an essayist and polemicist, even though he may sometimes address the same issues in the two modes: the 'error' signalled in the title *Poesia e errore* (1959) includes the political and ideological mistakes acknowledged in the essays of *Dieci inverni* ('Ten Winters', 1957) for example. Speaking of his lyrical identity, Fortini underlines the insecurity and challenge of the role: 'Poetry / changes nothing. Nothing is certain, but write', he says in 'Traducendo Brecht' (*Una volta per sempre*, 'Once and For All', 1963). The injunction to write has a biblical ring about it, even though it is delivered in a world where nobody asks or can ask the writer to speak on their behalf. Nevertheless, Fortini in his verse often does speak with a prophetic voice, and his most sympathetic critic, P. V. Mengaldo, has drawn attention to the pre-eminence of parable and allegory in his poetry. In fact, Fortini is particularly conscious of the imagined community to which he is speaking, and the shifting patterns of relationship with that community (interaction with and separation from it) are important to him as a writer. He might perhaps best be described as 'watchful', adopting an attitude of both expectation (*attesa*) and attention (*attenzione*), and this is a quality that is particularly apparent in his essays. It enables him to adopt a position of true independence and acute perspicacity on the political and cultural realities of his time, but it also leads him almost inevitably into a radical cultural pessimism. It will therefore be no surprise to find Fortini both adopting a critical attitude towards the ideas developed in *Il menabò*, which we will consider next, and remaining fundamentally hostile to the neo-avant-garde.

Il Menabò was founded by Elio Vittorini and Italo Calvino in 1959; its tenth and last issue, published in 1967, was dedicated to the work of Vittorini, who had died the previous year. From the beginning it was conceived as something more than a simple review, and each number contained both critical essays and substantial original works. The focus of the magazine was on the new and the contemporary, not only in creative writing, but also in social, cultural and literary theory, and from the mid-1960s its contributors included such non-Italian names as Roland Barthes, Maurice Blanchot, Jean Genet and Hans Magnus Enzensberger. But it began, in the first three numbers, by reviewing the literary production of the decade since the war, concentrating on themes which might initially have suggested a retrospective stance: dialect literature, southern writing, war literature and post-war poetry (the latter contributed by Fortini). Vittorini had made it clear in the first issue, however, that there was a crisis in literature which arose from deep and serious causes, amongst which he recalled such 'well-known contemporary torments' as the impact of mass culture on the experience of humanistic culture, the rise of science and technology, and the decline of the individual as the subject of ideological self-determination, 'in short, as hero'. Not only the threats themselves, but also the defensively jokey way in which Vittorini lists these 'torments' (*strazi*), indicate that what is at issue, in a phase of rapid neo-capitalist expansion, is the status of the humanist intellectual as traditionally understood. It was in this context that the debate on 'literature and industry', initiated by Vittorini in number 4 (1961), took off.

What was meant by 'industry' was defined by Gianni Scalia in his only, but fundamental, contribution to *Il Menabò*, an essay entitled 'Dalla natura all'industria':

[Industry] is no longer simply an aspect of economic reality, but the given *totality* of present reality; and it has an impact on all aspects of social and individual life in the 'post-modern' world. Industry is to be understood as scientific and technological decision-making, the planning of production and consumption, the organisation of the means of cultural communication, the creation of new kinds of work, new institutions, new models of behaviour.

(No. 4, 1961, p. 100)

In these terms, the word 'industry' is something of a misnomer. It has to do with the organisation of work in general (not just in the factory), the specific forms which that takes in modern capitalism (rational, specialised, proletarian) and its consequences at an individual and social level (analysed particularly in terms of 'alienation'). All of this is of concern to writers not only because it is new, or at any rate newly obvious in the years of the 'economic miracle' (and Vittorini is urging them to take the new on board), but also because many writers are themselves in the thick of the social transformation going on, either themselves working in industry (generally as copywriters, or in personnel or public relations, occasionally at more senior managerial levels), or are at least becoming aware of the contradictions and limitations of their humanistic self-image.

The different positions taken up in the wake of *Il Menabò*'s special number on literature and industry may be described in terms of the distinction between *apocalittici* and *integrati* which Umberto Eco (b. 1932) worked out in relation to one aspect of the debate, the attitude, positive or negative, to be adopted towards the perceived encroachment of the mass media. Amongst the 'integrated', those who considered the process described to be irresistible and indeed a new challenge for those intellectuals who at first might feel threatened by it, we might include Vittorini himself, at least to the extent that he envisages a renewal of humanism through scientific culture (but ultimately to the benefit of the humanists). The 'apocalyptic' position was identified by Eco with the novelist and critic Elémire Zolla (b. 1926), and more specifically with Zolla's book *Eclissi dell'intellettuale* ('Eclipse of the Intellectual', 1959), in which he states that 'the new society underlines the process of commodification of life; the only horizon which it opens is that which leads to the increase of production; its human ideal is the efficient specialist and the conspicuous consumer who does not possess his own range of differentiated preferences, but adapts meekly to the trends of production.' The most common position shares features of both of these, denouncing the ubiquity and totalising effect of 'industry' while looking for pockets of resistance or freedom. For Scalia, an industry whose reach is global can – must – still be 'comprehended' and 'transformed' by reason. Calvino, in his essay 'La sfida al labirinto' (1962), thinks that literature must 'do more' than simply report what is around us. Only Fortini, in a typically pugnacious intervention ('Astuti come colombe', in *Il Menabò* 5, 1962), denounces the 'literariness' of the whole debate, and calls for some modest self-awareness on the part of the *letterati* ('a sociology of the literati as professionals': p. 32).

'Industrial' novels

Vittorini insisted that the 'new' literature was not to be *about* 'industry', but was to be 'on an industrial level'. He had in mind particularly the French *nouveau roman*, but his rallying-call was generic enough to find an echo in practically the whole subsequent history of Italian writing with which this chapter is concerned. Nevertheless, there was in the late 1950s and the 1960s a spate of writing about industry, or more broadly, contemporary industrial society, directly inspired, it would seem, by the economic boom and the vast social transformations taking place in its wake. Calvino himself, at the same time as completing the trilogy published as *I nostri antenati* (*Our Ancestors*) in 1960, turned his attention to such themes as the speculative destruction of the Ligurian coastline in *La speculazione edilizia* (*Plunge Into Real Estate*, 1957; but the theme was also adumbrated in *Il barone rampante* published in the same year, on which see above, p. 552). He also concerned himself with industrial pollution and the manipulation of information in *La nuvola di smog* (*Smog*, 1958), and with the contrast between the city and nature, conformism and anti-conformism, standardisation and individualism in the urban fables based on the figure of the alienated labourer Marcovaldo, many of which, written in the early 1950s, appeared in *Racconti* (1958) and then in *Marcovaldo ovvero Le stagioni in città* (*Marcovaldo or the Seasons in the City*, 1963).

In addition to this strain of Calvino's writing, a number of authors and texts became, rightly or wrongly, associated with 'industrial literature' in this period. They included Luciano Bianciardi (1922–71), author of *Il lavoro culturale* ('Cultural Work', 1957), *L'integrazione* (1960), *La vita agra* (*It's a Hard Life*, 1962); Lucio Mastronardi's (1930–79) Vigevano novels; *Tempi stretti* ('Time Is Short', 1957) and *Donnarumma all'assalto* (*The Men at the Gate*, 1959) by Ottiero Ottieri (b. 1924); *Il padrone* (*The Boss*, 1965) by Goffredo Parise (1929–86), a savage satire which marks a radical shift from the subject-matter and style of his earlier novels; and the first two novels published by Paolo Volponi (1924–94), *Memoriale* (*The Memorandum*, 1962) and *La macchina mondiale* (*The Worldwide Machine*, 1965). Different though these novels are in style and narrative technique, a composite picture may be drawn from them. Both space and time are depicted as highly and, it would appear, rationally organised. The order of city streets, of apartment blocks and office blocks, often gives a momentary uplift to the provincial newcomer before he familiarises himself with the bleak interiors which are their counterpart – cramped, featureless, anonymous. The factory model of the patterning of time in shifts – an important theme in one of the few novelists who actually write about the production-line from direct experience, Luigi Davi (b. 1929) – is internalised by the urban worker into strict demarcations between day and night, working week and weekend: for the first time, the weekend, perceived as no less organised than the rest of the week, with its endless traffic jams and Monday morning anti-climax, emerges as a distinct time in fiction (Bianciardi, Calvino). The experience and techniques of social control receive particular attention: how the personnel manager will select the most suitable workers (Ottieri); how the individuality of the industrial worker – Albino Saluggia in Volponi's *Memoriale* – which is complex and stratified at both the social and the psychological level, clashes with the need of management to standardise the worker.

One further feature of the industrial novel should be mentioned which is less directly concerned with the representation of the sociologically verifiable world, namely the emphasis on neurosis and what might be called the 'infantilisation' of the subject. Memorable examples include Calvino's Marcovaldo, mentioned above (p. 568), Mastronardi's teacher Antonio Mombelli in his 1962 novel *Il maestro di Vigevano* ('The Teacher from V.') ('the consciousness of being useless . . . Ada lets me have a little money each day for my personal expenses'), and Bianciardi's first-person narrator in *La vita agra* (the terror of crossing the road because not only are the cars going to mow you down, but their insurance won't pay up if they do). The most striking of these diminished selves is the first-person narrator of Parise's *Il padrone*. This unnamed individual is made to exist in a nursery world of comic-strip names and fantasy situations, whose origins seem to be attributable in equal measure to his own disingenuousness, to the diabolical malevolence of the 'boss' of the title, and to the author's simultaneous polemic against both industrial organisation and popular culture.

All of these features, however, point to questions already being taken up elsewhere and are drawn into the mill of the neo-avant-garde and its principal arm, the Gruppo 63. But, in order to understand what these were saying, we must take a step back in time and redirect our focus, once again, to poetry.

Poets of the neo-avant-garde

Luciano Anceschi (1911–95) founded *Il Verri* in Milan in 1956, and continued to edit the review, which comes out quarterly, until his death: it is now, at the time of writing, in its ninth series. Its guiding principle has been a phenomenological approach to literature which supposes an integration of the 'autonomous' and the 'heteronomous' aspects of art already signalled by Anceschi in his 1936 book *Autonomia ed eteronomia dell'arte*. On the one hand, what we have in literature is a work that is always 'in progress', open, provisional and tentative; on the other, it is necessarily responsive to and interactive with all aspects of reality and culture. This vision of a literature which is both self-regulated and conditioned by other systems proved attractive to a generation of young poets and philosophers who rejected any idea of literature following a political lead, but were not attracted either by isolation in a formalist ghetto. That *Il Verri* was actively present at the birth and during the relatively short life of the neo-avant-garde is certain; its subsequent flourishing has shown that the review was not confined to that experience.

Before examining in detail the work of the poets associated with *Il Verri*, and particularly those who appeared in the 1961 anthology *I novissimi* which in many ways can be seen as the launch of the neo-avant-garde, it may be helpful to trace briefly the story of the Gruppo 63 and the outlines of the debate about language and the status of the self in poetry which took place within it; the no less exhaustive debate about the experimental novel will be addressed later. The Gruppo 63 officially came into being during a series of seminars, readings, lectures and theatrical performances organised by Nanni Balestrini on the fringe of the fourth 'Settimana internazionale della nuova musica' held in Palermo in October 1963. The Gruppo was more a loose network than a formal organisation. The process of inclusion or exclusion, acceptance or rejection, could be a painful one and contributed to a widespread, sometimes frankly envious view of the Gruppo as inward-looking. Those who 'belonged' saw themselves in part as rebuilding bridges with the 'historic', modernist avant-gardes. They also wanted to bring up to date both the technical and the theoretical tools of literary research in Italy by keeping in touch with what was going on elsewhere in Europe (particularly, in the mid-1960s, through contacts with the *Tel quel* group in Paris), and, very significantly, to overcome what were perceived as artificial barriers between the arts.

At the heart of the poetics of the neo-avant-garde lies a radical distrust of language. This manifests itself as a critique of the tasks of 'reflecting' or 'expressing' objective and subjective reality which literary language allegedly sets itself, and at the same time a commitment to 'demystifying' the everyday uses to which language is put, particularly in the sphere of mass communications. The claims of language to represent truth or essence, including the 'true feelings' of the poet, are contested by a programmatic de-semanticisation of language. Syntax may be disregarded, words wrenched out of context or deformed, different linguistic levels (or different natural languages) run together, to produce a hybrid effect in which sense is difficult or impossible to establish in terms of the 'normal' code. Alongside the negation, or disintegration, of language, there is a more ironic approach to the codes of the mass media. This approach relies principally on the technique of collage or montage, and exposes semantically untouched fragments of public discourse by placing them alongside others in unexpected and often disturbing combinations. A principal exponent of the latter kind of experiment, particularly in the form of visual poetry, is Lamberto Pignotti (b. 1926).

The critical attitude towards language is closely entwined with what was to become the best-known formula or slogan of the neo-avant-garde, the 'reduction of the self' (*riduzione dell'io*). There are a number of different strands to this concept. For the poet, there is the fundamental, preliminary understanding that the content of poetry is not what it says, but what it does. In his introduction to *I novissimi*, Alfredo Giuliani states: 'What poetry does is precisely its "content" . . . its way of doing coincides almost entirely with its meaning.' Poetry is demystified: it cannot save mankind or change the world, but neither is it a means of consolation or escape; it is a specific form of experience of reality, a critical experience (the phenomenological background to this is in Husserl, mediated via Sartre). Thus, the importance given to 'things' and to 'experience' in the poetry of the neo-avant-garde is partly in opposition to what Antonio Porta called the 'ostentation' of the self. The ideal is a 'poeta-oggettivo' rather than a 'poeta-io'. The poet 'descends' into reality, with an attitude of openness, engaged upon discovery or research, establishing a contact which may at first be difficult or painful. The idea is to get reality to reveal itself, beyond the deception of appearances. Thus, as Lucio Vetri explains, at the same time as the poet 'enters into' reality, s/he brackets it through a double process of estrangement: a distancing of the world, and a refusal on the poet's own part to be taken in by its appearances. The reader, meantime, encounters a 'reduction' of his or her own self. Poetry is not to seduce but to shock or disquiet the reader; forced to estrange his or her self, the reader is not to be satisfied with given meanings. There is, nevertheless, no other place, away from here; poetry is not an elsewhere or an outside into which to escape.

The important anthology of new poets *I novissimi* (1961, reissued with a new preface in 1965) was edited and introduced by Alfredo Giuliani (b. 1924), who was at the time poetry editor of *Il Verri*. Giuliani was probably the most cogent exponent of the theories of objectivity, but his own poetry (collected in *Versi e nonversi*, 1986) has proved less convincing, for he has not been able to find what Giovanni Raboni (b. 1932, himself a distinguished poet and an indefatigable critic and promoter of other poets' work) calls a 'stylistic identity' to fill the gap left by the renunciation of syntactic or lexical order. The case of Elio Pagliarani (b. 1927), the first of the poets anthologised in *I novissimi*, is rather different. Although the lengthy extracts from 'La ragazza Carla' ('The girl Carla'), a naturalistic narrative poem about the experiences and perceptions of a Milanese office-girl first published in *Il Menabò* in 1960, might seem to have more to do with the 'literature and industry' tendency than with the neo-avant-garde, the point has been made that Pagliarani shared with the neo-avant-garde the conviction that the attack on contemporary society should begin with a critical and demystifying representation of its languages and the ideological functions which they performed. It is now clear, in retrospect, that 'La ragazza Carla' was only one moment in Pagliarani's development. From the experimentation with the long, 'Majakovskian', line in *Lezione di fisica* ('Physics Lesson', 1964) to the percussive repetitions of *Rosso Corpo Lingua* ('Red Body Tongue', 1977) and the, quite different, restraint of *Esercizi platonici* ('Platonic Exercises', 1985), Pagliarani has constantly renewed and refreshed himself.

Nanni Balestrini (b. 1935) and Antonio Porta (1935–89) were the two youngest of the poets represented in *I novissimi*. Balestrini is a man of many parts. As well as a poet and novelist, he has been an indefatigable cultural organiser and a political activist whose involvement with the autonomous far-left movements in the 1970s drove him into a prolonged political exile in France. Most of Balestrini's novels – *Vogliamo tutto* ('We Want Everything', 1971), *La violenza illustrata*, (1976), *Gli invisibili* (*The Unseen* 1987), *L'editore* (1989) – have been vehicles for his political convictions at the same time as being markedly experimental in form, using 'ready-made' discourses, written or spoken (tape recordings, newspaper extracts, parts of other novels), suppressing punctuation, changing point of view and upsetting the normal patterns of narrative sequence. These are techniques which Balestrini also made use of in his poetry; he was closer than the other *novissimi* to an idea of random, automatic or computer writing, fascinated as he was by the possibilities offered by the unconscious, and certainly unliterary, uses of language itself. Hostile to the 'inertia' of language, he set out to 'lay a trap' for it and to distance the reader (*Poesie pratiche*, 'Practical Poems', 1976). In his later collections, especially in *Le ballate della signorina Richmond* ('The Ballads of Miss R.', 1977), Balestrini allows the lighter, more humorous side of his poetic personality (always implicit in his irreverent approach to poetic language and forms) to emerge explicitly, as in the thirteenth of the 1977 *ballate*, in which the language of the mayor of Siena's campaign to eradicate the town's pigeons is adapted to a plan to snare and decapitate the unemployed.

Porta was the most substantial poet to emerge from the neo-avant-garde. His 'upturned eyelid' (the title of his first collection, *La palpebra rovesciata*, 1960) permitted a deliberately estranged and anti-ironic gaze upon reality. This rejection of irony is a blessing, because it allows space to those features which make Porta a very strong poet. The impression of strength is made all the sharper by the marked rhythms of his poetry, the 'percussive' quality to which Fortini, and Porta himself, have drawn attention. Often the poems will consist of segments (and may themselves form segments of a larger sequence, as in *Invasioni*, 1984), but they are given a sense, a kind of direction, and a communicativeness by the beat. Thematically too, Porta is a flesh-and-blood poet, at the root of whose poetry many critics have seen an existential trauma which he himself has spoken of as 'tragic'. Porta writes of sex, other people, personal relations (see especially *I rapporti*, 'Relations', 1966), and he confronts difficult subjects: the sadism of the concentration camps ('Come se fosse un ritmo', 'As if it were a rhythm', 1966–7, is one of the most chillingly compelling poems on this subject ever written), and later, violence against women (in some of the *Brevi lettere* of the mid-1970s) or the ambiguities of (his own) sexual identity (for example, in 'Amleto', 1978). The *Brevi lettere* mark a turn towards greater communicability and comprehensibility, and this is confirmed by the use of a diary form in 'Come può un poeta essere amato?' (*Diario '81–'82*) ('How can a poet be loved?' . . .), or the increasing tendency to date the poems, precisely to the day. The very project of *Nel fare poesia* ('Poetry in the Making', 1985), which was a sort of guided tour of his poetry, was a particularly interesting and successful attempt to create an autobiographical macro-text out of the fragments of a poetic career that was brought to a close all too quickly.

Edoardo Sanguineti (b. 1930) was already an established poet (and critic) when *I novissimi* was published. He was represented in the anthology mainly by extracts from the two poetic cycles *Laborintus* (1956) and *Erotopaegnia* (1960). *Laborintus* is a descent into a psychic hell which draws extensively on Jungian imagery and interests such as alchemy in long incantatory sweeps where boundaries are quickly blurred. The opening lines:

composte terre in strutturali complessioni sono Palus Putredinis/ripose tenue Ellie e tu mio corpo tu infatti tenue Ellie eri il mio corpo/immaginoso

('compound earths in structural compositions are [or 'I am'] Palus Putredinis slender Ellie rests [or 'rest slender Ellie'] and you my body you slender Ellie were really my imaginative body')

(trans. Smith, 1981, p. 373)

set up homologies between swamp, womb, body and Jungian *anima* which will reverberate throughout the twenty-seven poems which make up the cycle.

As in the seventeen poems of *Erotopaegnia*, many of the sequences appear to be hallucinatory or dream-like. In both cycles, Sanguineti characteristically uses a very long line, with the line-ending generally signalling a breathing space (rather than a break in sense), although sometimes there is a clear enjambement. The effect is of a flow of words, quite strongly marked rhythmically, as though it were a narrative poem, but without an obvious narrative. 'Foreign' languages are incorporated, both natural (here mainly Latin and Greek) and the jargon of academic or professional specialisms. The impression is created of a cut-up language; the effect, paradoxically, is of great communicativeness. There is no reticence or concealment on the part of the speaker, but it is for the reader to make the connections, to make sense.

It would be wrong to conclude our survey of the *novissimi* poets without considering the work of a poet who was never a part of the neo-avant-garde, but whose similarities and differences with his younger contemporaries have somehow helped to define his own literary identity. Andrea Zanzotto (b. 1921) has spent most of his life in the Veneto village of Pieve di Soligo, and much of his early poetry alludes in a hermetic way to that landscape. With *La beltà* ('Beauty', 1968), Zanzotto's focus changed, and language itself became the object of his poetic enquiry. This is not to say that the 'real' world was suddenly excluded from his verse; the people and the places of his region remained recognisably present, in some ways more so than before, given Zanzotto's renewed interest in the sounds and cadences of the dialect. But Zanzotto's *petèl* (baby-talk) is largely invented, and – here the affinity with the neo-avant-garde is apparent – the status of language itself as a meaning-giving system is called into fundamental question. Zanzotto, who by some critics is seen as the most important Italian poet since Montale, explores in his poetry from *La beltà* on the means of opening to the reader the possibility of establishing at least a provisional meaning. This may come about, not when the reader recognises some hypothetically perfect match between language and reality which the writer spends all his stylistic effort in trying to achieve, but in the opposite way, when the reader participates in the disintegration of words, in a centrifugal movement away from apparent meaning:

> Quante perfezioni, quante
> quante totalità. Pungendo aggiunge.
> E poi astrazioni astrificazioni formulazione d'astri
> assideramento, attraverso sidera e coelos
> assideramenti assimilazioni

(So many perfections, o so many totalities. It adds, stinging. And then abstractions starfactions the making of stars frost-bite across sidera and coelos frost-bites assimilations)

> (Opening lines of 'La perfezione della neve', trans. Smith 1981, p. 213)

But one important difference between Zanzotto and the neo-avant-garde is that Zanzotto is both less politicised and, more importantly, far less dogmatic than his experimentalist cousins. There is in his poetry room for doubts about his own doubts; if all language is questionable, that includes the language of the questioning itself.

Experimental novels

The neo-avant-garde was relatively slow in turning its collective mind to prose fiction, but by the mid-1960s the question of experimentalism in the novel was commanding attention. The argument about the novel was in certain respects more bitter, and more personalised, than those which had to do with poetry. This may have been in part because of the sense that there was no serious tradition of the novel, still less of the experimental novel, in Italy, and that one therefore had to be created. The names of Svevo and Pirandello (as novelist) were invoked from early twentieth-century modernism, and that of Carlo Emilio Gadda (see above, pp. 527–30) provided a more immediate antecedent to the experimentation of the 1960s. In the process, other reputations were savagely attacked, particularly those of Bassani, Cassola and the Pasolini of the Roman novels, all seen as embodying in their prose, though in different ways, the sentimentalism, provincialism, and misguided narrative realism attributed by the neo-avant-garde to the fiction of the 1950s. This denigration was given a sharp political spin by the Marxist critic Alberto Asor Rosa in his influential polemic against Gramscian populism, *Scrittori e popolo* ('Writers and People', 1965). In the early stages of the discussion about the novel at least, there was considerable anxiety to emerge from the 'backwardness' supposedly characterising Italian fiction and to reforge the links both with European modernism (Proust, Kafka, Musil, and Joyce, to whom Eco devoted an extensive study included in his *Opera aperta, The Open Work*, 1962) and with contemporary artists abroad, particularly the proponents of the *nouveau roman*.

The debate about the novel went through two successive phases. In the first, there was general agreement on the non-mimetic function of fictional prose, but participants were exercised nevertheless by the problem of what the novel does in society. On this central issue, there was profound disagreement between those like Angelo Guglielmi who denied any functional value to literature whatsoever (while failing to explain how a falsely neutral term like *fruizione*, 'use', was *not* valorised), and a writer-critic like Sanguineti, who took it for granted that the literary product is autonomous, but wanted to interpret that fact in ideological terms: the challenge to the reader on the aesthetic level, or at the level of interpretation, also acts paradigmatically as a challenge to political or institutional authority. Between these two, Renato Barilli occupied a more purely phenomenological position, arguing that contemporary experimentalism constitutes a 'normalisation' and a 'lowering' (*abbassamento*) of the sense of anguish and alienation generally portrayed as exceptional in modernist authors. Barilli further assimilated these procedures to a new kind of twentieth-century rationality, tending to free itself of ideology and to suspend judgement, which is characteristic also of other disciplines. The neo-avant-garde was already beginning to map out the territory that would later be given the name of post-modernity. This predominantly existential and phenomenological emphasis of the debate, which proved attractive to the Moravia of *La noia* (*The Empty Canvas*, 1960) and *L'uomo come fine* ('Man As End', 1963), gave way, however, to a more internal, meta-narrative focus. This second phase drew on the languages of formalism and structuralism, and subsequently, of semiotics. It was precisely in the late 1960s and in something of a rush, that many of the most important thinkers in these fields, from Saussure to Barthes, from the Russian Formalists and Jakobson to Greimas and Hjemslev, were first translated into Italian (extensive details may be found in Corti and Segre's *I metodi attuali della critica in Italia*, 1970, itself a landmark book).

There were a number of writers who in the 1960s identified strongly with the experimentalist project, where 'experiment' implies an expectation of combinatory freedom and open-endedness rather than any suggestion of verifiability. All of the *novissimi* except for Pagliarani tried their hand at the prose novel, sometimes very successfully. Balestrini's expertise and his interest in 'found' languages (random excerpts from already published sources) are to the fore in *Tristano* (1966), while the two novels which Sanguineti published in 1963 (*Capriccio italiano*) and 1967 (*Il giuoco dell'oca*, 'The Goose Game') are enriched by his use of multilingualism and his marvellous evocation of dreamscapes. What is often lacking is the narrative drive forwards which makes the reader want to keep on turning the pages. But this is something that threatens the work of many of the experimental novelists. Alberto Arbasino (b. 1930), for example, was seen at the time as the most *outré* of the young critics and novelists on the scene. *Fratelli d'Italia* ('Brothers of Italy', 1963, revised in 1976 and again in 1993), Arbasino's most ambitious work, tracks the movements of a number of writers, artists and film-makers in and around Rome as they discuss the problem of the novel, try to create, drop names and acid, in what is ultimately a triumph of death. The whole thing is vaguely reminiscent of Fellini's *La dolce vita*, which of course is mentioned, like everything else. The novel is voracious, being itself a rewrite or an absorption of many other novels and novelists; and it is bulimically regurgitative, spewing out its own meta- (or meta-meta-?) literary commentary in *Certi romanzi* ('Certain Novels', 1964, itself rewritten and reissued in 1977 and 1993). There is an Arbasinesque promiscuity also in the later writings of Germano Lombardi (1925–93) who, after practising a tightly disciplined rhetoric of precise observation in the manner of the *nouveau roman* in the novels from *Barcelona* (1963) to *Il confine* ('The Border', 1971), moves towards a deliberate plotlessness and a readiness to move characters and events backwards and forwards in time from one text to another in such faintly Lowryesque tales as *Cercando*

Beatrix ('Looking for B.', 1976), *China il vecchio* ('Old China', 1987) and *L'instabile Atlantico* (1993).

The problem of readability, whether in the sense of deciphering the words on the page, or in that of getting from one page to the next, recurs in the work of two other 'difficult' writers whose reputation was made at this time, in the wake of the recuperation of Gadda and the vogue for experimentation. Antonio Pizzuto (1893–1976) began to publish relatively late in life, strongly encouraged by such critics as Contini and Segre and by writers like Bilenchi and Luzi. His most accessible novel remains his first, *Signorina Rosina* (1959), even though that already shows features, such as a constantly shifting grammatical subject and a fragmentary paratactic style, which made critics think, misleadingly, of a surrealistic 'automatic writing'. *Hilarotragoedia*, the first novel of Giorgio Manganelli (1922–90), was published in 1964, followed by the influential collection of essays *Letteratura come menzogna* ('Literature as Lie') in 1967 and *Nuovo commento* in 1969. Together with *Centuria* (1979), a book of 'possible' stories which has some affinities with Calvino's *Se una notte d'inverno un viaggiatore* (*If on a Winter's Night a Traveller*) published in the same year, these constitute Manganelli's most distinctive contribution to the work of the avant-garde. The title-essay of the 1967 book seems oddly misnamed: 'letteratura come cerimonia' might have been a better choice for this smug celebration of the purely rhetorical joys of literature, its social uselessness and scandalous immoralism, its predilection for the cruel, the sadistic and the corrupt, its irreverence and cynicism, and the buffoonery of its practitioners. The two early novels ransack and parody the literary tradition to construct a baroque meditation on death and decay. The laughter which it generates not infrequently moves up a gear precisely into that 'hilarity' which is on the verge of panic.

Calvino, reviewing *Hilarotragoedia* in 1965, made the point that Manganelli was part of the first generation of writers since Carducci to be connected with the universities (Manganelli was a professor of English, Sanguineti is an Italianist, and so on). Manganelli's choice of a parodistic treatise-form is a negative comment on the traditional novel, but also, I would add, a rather obvious move for an academic to make. Calvino went on to question the value of novel-experimentation in Italy, as opposed to France, because the tradition itself did not amount to much: Italy's tradition, like England's (*sic*), is one of prose rather than of the novel. These observations are characteristic of the sympathetic but rather detached view of the experimental novel which Calvino took in the pages of *Il Menabò* and elsewhere. Calvino's own experiments with the possibilities of narrative prose beyond the realist and historical-fantastic modes of the 1950s and early 1960s will be examined in the next section. But mention should be made here of three other writers who, while never part of any formal or informal movement, contributed with one or more of their writings to that sense of renewal of the novel which characterised the 1960s in Italy: Anna Maria Ortese (b. 1914), Giuseppe Berto (1914–78), and Luigi Malerba (b. 1927).

Alongside a lyrical-realist style of storytelling, perfected in the 1950s, and some very successful pieces of journalism, especially travel-writing, Ortese is best-known for the 'Romantic fable', as she called it, published in 1965, *L'iguana* (*The Iguana*), centred on the figures of the rich young Milanese Aleardo, who buys up islands, and the iguana-woman-servant who awaits him on his newest acquisition, and who 'like the prime matter of alchemical writings is everything that is oldest and freshest in the substance of the world, the very nature of the world's ever-renewed invitation to "strike a fraternal pact with horror"' (from the dust-jacket, presumably written by the author herself, of the Adelphi 1986 edition of the novel). The purely fantastic side of this fable is a reminder of the continuing, late, presence on the Italian scene of the consummate fantasist Dino Buzzati (see, *inter alia*, *Un amore*, *A Love Affair*, 1963, and *La boutique del mistero*, 'The Mystery Shop', 1968) and of Calvino in 'cosmi-comic' mode. Ortese's fascination with a kind of magical horror will recur, in darker and more emphatically psychopathological tones, in her remarkable late stories, *In sonno e in veglia* ('Sleeping Waking', 1986), and in the novel *Il cardillo addolorato* ('The Grieving Finch', 1993). The interest in altered states of consciousness, finally, and the hallucinatory quality of the novel connect both with a number of the neo-avant-garde fictions already mentioned and with contemporaneous novels such as Berto's *Il male oscuro* (*Incubus*, 1964), a semi-autobiographical account of a psychoanalytical therapy, and Malerba's *Il serpente* (*The Serpent*, 1966).

While most critics limit their appreciation of Berto (who also wrote some successful screen-plays) to parts of *Il male oscuro*, especially the death of the father and the meeting with the child-bride, and the first half of *La cosa buffa* (*Antonio in Love*, 1966), Malerba has acquired a far more solid reputation. The stories of *La scoperta dell'alfabeto* ('The Discovery of the Alphabet', 1963) set the scene for the total dissociation of 'language' from 'reality' which underlies *Il serpente* and *Salto mortale* ('Somersault', 1968), the first the bewildered 'confession' of a Roman stamp-dealer who claims to have eaten his lover, the second a *giallo* (detective story) within a *giallo* where it is left to the reader to decide whether what is written is true or false. The almost limitless possibilities of writing and at the same time its 'ultra-difficoltà' are stressed. The implicit theme of power, or rather its appearance, comes to the surface in *Il protagonista* (1973), a novel about sexual impotence, and in the stories of *Le rose imperiali* ('The Imperial Roses', 1974) devoted to tyrannical display (the allusion is to China; see also *Cina Cina*, 'China China' 1985). Malerba maintains his interest in what might be called remote states of consciousness, whether these are linguistic (as in *Il pataffio*, 'Epitaph', 1978, and the related study, *Le parole abbandonate* ('Abandoned Words', 1977) or psychological (*Diario di un sognatore*, 'Diary of a Dreamer', 1981), and will alternate stories with a recognisably contemporary setting with novels whose very titles allude to a distance, from which the here and now is visible in a different perspective: *Il pianeta azzurro* ('The Blue Planet', 1986: the colour of the Earth seen from space), or *Il fuoco greco* ('Greek Fire', 1990), a novel set in Byzantium around the first millennium. Malerba is a totally original writer; associated for a time with the Gruppo 63, he has never allowed himself to be captured by any single tendency or set of problems. His characters are frequently obsessives, and much of the reader's pleasure consists in the satisfaction of following through these horrendously logical obsessions. But their author is far too canny to allow himself to be stuck on any one track.

The richly varied literary debates and experiments which took place in Italy during the 1960s, and whose impact reached beyond the cliques and *groupuscules* who provided the emotional and intellectual energy of the neo-avant-garde, were underpinned by broadly shared assumptions about the relations between politics and culture. The writers, artists and scholars who identified with the avant-garde were not themselves outsiders, as Umberto Eco has pointed out. They were already part of the establishment, fighting their battles from within. They nevertheless tended to see themselves as pursuing a revolutionary politics as well as wanting to revolutionise literature, even though the former objective took on specifically cultural forms. These were, firstly, the perceived need to convince the political leadership of the left – essentially the Italian Communist Party, which was regarded as secretly aristocratic and élitist in its attitude towards culture – that new developments in cultural theory and literary practice, as well as the emergence of the mass media, should not be dismissed as 'irrationalist', but could make their own contribution to changing consciousness and behaviour; and secondly, the conviction that while political revolution remained a long-term possibility, it was feasible to act on the cultural front more immediately and more effectively; indeed, it was necessary to do so, given the 'mystificatory' role of conventional forms of literary discourse and of the means of mass communication in society at large.

All this was abruptly challenged by the events that took place on the streets in Italy between 1967 and 1969, from the early agitation in the universities, through the French troubles of May 1968 and their reverberations in Italy, to the factory strikes and occupations during the 'hot autumn' of 1969 with its termination in the Milan bomb attack in December of that year. Not only did political revolution, to some at least, seem possible, but the researches conducted within the self-enclosed laboratories of literary and critical experimentation suddenly appeared cold and fruitless. The months of *contestazione* coincided almost exactly with the brief life of *Quindici*, a journal set up by the Gruppo 63 in 1967 under the editorship of first Giuliani and then Balestrini, and it was in the pages of this severe publication, with the format of a Chinese wall-newspaper and challengingly lengthy articles, that the politico-cultural crisis of the neo-avant-garde was played out. Increasingly, the space was monopolised by purely political essays drafted by writers and critics who were attempting to carve out a specifically political space for themselves; the delicate balance between cultural and political innovation was broken; the old Gramscian charge against the intellectuals of busybodying themselves with everything was suddenly relevant again, and *Quindici* closed (paradoxically at the moment when it was achieving its greatest commercial success) with the members of its editorial board scattering in different directions. It was the emblematic ending, what Eco proudly called the 'suicide', of a remarkable literary decade.

43

The 1970s

Poetry

Many people in Italy lived the 1970s as an anticlimax, in some respects a frightening one as economic recession and political violence crept up the agenda. It was seen as a period of 'riflusso', both of reaction and of withdrawal, on the part of many intellectuals, from the social and above all political activism of the late 1960s. It was a period of widespread cynicism about politics in general and revolutionary politics (including cultural politics) in particular, and one in which it became necessary, if not inevitable, that priority should be given to private rather than public concerns, individual rather than historical issues.

There are indeed a number of symptoms of such a trend in the poetry written and published during the decade. It is not only in relation to poetry, however, that it is probably more accurate to speak of a redefinition of the relationship between the personal and the political, the individual and the historical, and of each one of these terms, rather than to imagine a cut-and-dried antithesis between predetermined entities. In many cases, indeed, there is a politicisation of the (hitherto) personal domain. In the brief space available, I shall mention three aspects of this trend of poetic writing in the 1970s: the re-emergence of a concern with the everyday, the mundane and neglected, which in its more 'crepuscular' vein owes much to the gentle ghost of Guido Gozzano, but which also inspires some notable narrative poetry; the impact of feminism, in part continuing a political tradition of interventionist poetry, in part providing a space for women to make themselves heard in a strikingly male-dominated environment, and in part offering new perspectives on subjectivity; this last connecting immediately with the third aspect of the 1970s trend: a profound renewal of thought about the self and about language, away from the 'depersonalisation' of much Sixties poetry and prose, particularly under the pressure of new psychoanalytical writing and with the immediate example, in Italian poetry, of Zanzotto's *La beltà* and *Pasque* ('Easters', 1973).

Eugenio Montale had published no new volumes of poetry since *La bufera e altro* in 1956 (see above, p. 553); now in the 1970s he published no fewer than three (*Satura*, 1971, *Diario del '71 e del '72*, 1973, and *Quaderno di quattro anni*, 'Notebook of Four Years', 1977), in addition to verse translations, prose pieces and a collected volume *L'opera in versi* ('Works in Verse', 1980), which included poems written after 1977. Not only does this late flowering constitute a distinctive 'fourth phase' in the work of Italy's major twentieth-century poet, but it also contributed in no small way to the agenda of the years in which the poems appeared. The poems of the 'Xenia' section in *Satura* (1971), dedicated to the memory of his wife, recall her in terms of affectionate intimacy, focusing on small details of their domestic life together and of his daily routine without her. What saves them from sentimentality is a radical pessimism which, if anything, will become even more acute in the subsequent collections, and a marvellously supple diction, at times almost conversational in tone, which will often acquire a colloquial, satirical, sometimes querulous and vulgar edge. With its frequently dismissive references back to earlier poems and their readers, Montale's poetry of the 1970s often reads as a deliberate undermining of the *poeta laureato* which, with the conferment of the Nobel prize in 1975, he duly became. His denunciation of the consumerisation of poetry in his acceptance speech ('Poetry is not a commodity, it is an utterly useless product') confirms the aristocratic view of poetry on which this dismissal is based.

Montale's 'lowering' of the tone, his deployment of the domestic and the colloquial, and his use of the 'diary' or 'notebook' as the structural model of his later collections connect with significant parts of other poets' work in the 1970s. Examples might include the diary and travel-notes favoured by Sanguineti from *Reisebilder* on ('Travel Sketches', 1971; for this development, see the volume of collected poems, *Segnalibri*, 'Bookmark', 1982), or the extraordinarily courteous and deadly barbs fired off by Aldo Palazzeschi (1885–1974) in *Via delle cento stelle* ('Street of the Hundred Stars', 1972). In some respects it also recalls the work of some of those poets who together are seen as having an affinity with Sereni and constituting the 'linea lombarda' of Italian poetry, though each of them has a distinct poetic personality: Nelo Risi (b. 1920), perhaps the most traditionally 'political' of these poets; the Ticinese writer Giorgio Orelli (b. 1921); Luciano Erba (b. 1922); and Bartolo Cattafi (1922–79), who, though born near Messina in Sicily, came in the Milanese phase of his life to share a characteristic attention to the world of objects and the small, intimate detail, and a propensity to irony and self-irony (exactly what Porta had objected to). The use of anecdote or remembered incident as the basis of the poem could also give rise to full-blown verse narratives, as in the case of Giancarlo Majorino (b. 1928).

These varied characteristics are not, however, confined to Lombardy, nor indeed to the generations born before the war. Three other poets should be mentioned in this context. Giovanni Giudici (b. 1924), whose complete poems were published by Garzanti in 1991, presents himself as a paragon of both effability and affability, self-narrational, ironic, confessional in a worldly-wise though not cynical way, his thoughts of conjugal infidelity and other peccadilloes both haunted and indulged by his 'educazione cattolica' (the title of his first collection, 1963). The late work of Attilio Bertolucci (b. 1911) puts us in mind of Montale's statement that his separate collections should be read as a 'single work'. Bertolucci's *La camera da letto* ('The Bedroom', published in two parts, then as a whole in 1988) is an autobiographical narrative poem, steeped in the contours and colours of his native region which Bertolucci has made the centre of all his poetry: the landscape of Casarola, the Po valley, the backdrop of the nearby Appennines and of the city of Parma. He has called the poem a 'family romance' and referred to himself, punningly, as an 'annalista'. It is a kind of diary in verse, with precise references to dates and family events, the whole history 'outside' always present but rarely foregrounded. The strength of the poetry, as Giuliano Manacorda has rightly observed, is in its consistency and dependability. The discursive and familiar tone, the attention to small things, and the sense of loss and vulnerability which accompanies such attention continues, finally, in the early work of one of the most considerable young poets to emerge in the 1970s, Maurizio Cucchi (b. 1945), notably in 'Le briciole nel taschino' ('Crumbs in the pocket', in *Il disperso*, 'The Lost', 1976). But there is already in Cucchi a tendency to let the narrative 'run away', to destabilise the speaking voice, in a way which makes him less immediately communicative than the other poets discussed here, and which takes him towards a kind of research to which we shall return shortly.

Feminism and poetry

Feminism drew attention to 'the private' in entirely different ways. In the first place, the movement insisted, in many cases, on the active presence and role of women in society, thus immediately problematising traditional associations between the feminine, the internal, the domestic and the private. The most determined and creative personality in this reclaiming of public territory is Dacia Maraini (b. 1936), whose novels – most notably the semi-documentary *Memorie di una ladra* ('Memoirs of a Female Thief', 1972), *Donna in guerra* (*Woman at War*, 1975) and *Storia di Piera* ('Story of P.', 1980), followed by *Isolina, la donna tagliata a pezzi* (*Isolina*, 1985) and *La Lunga vita di Marianna Ucría* (*The Silent Duchess*, 1990) – essays, plays and poetry are direct and forceful in their appeal – even if they do not always have to spell things out quite so painstakingly as in these lines to 'a nice critic' from 'Le poesie delle donne':

> Una donna che scrive poesie e sa di
> essere donna, non può che tenersi attaccata
> stretta ai contenuti perché la sofisticazione
> delle forme è una cosa che riguarda il potere
> e il potere che ha la donna è sempre un
> non-potere, una eredità scottante e mai del tutto sua.

(A woman who writes poetry and knows that she is a woman, cannot but stick closely to the content because the sophistication of form is something that concerns power and the power which women have is always a non-power, a difficult inheritance, never entirely their own.)

(In *Donne mie*, 'Women', 1974).

Maraini contributed a critical note to the anthology *Donne in poesia*, ('Women in Poetry'), edited by Biancamaria Frabotta (b. 1947) in 1976. This anthology, together with Laura Di Nola's *Poesia femminista italiana* (1978), to some extent corrected the obvious failure by male critics even to recognise women's poetry, let alone to comment on it intelligently. The formation of women's cultural centres in the late 1970s, most famously the Centro Virginia Woolf in Rome, the creation of the feminist publishing houses Edizioni delle Donne and La Tartaruga in the same period, and the emergence of a number of magazines and journals, were likewise indications of a new female activism in the public domain.

But the impact of feminist thought, particularly in its French variants, was also more indirect and in some ways more problematic. It was not just a question of challenging, or even conquering, male space, but, more fundamentally, of defining the space from which women speak. This meant that since the language of the emotions and of the body had already been structured in a certain way by men (certain things were spoken of in certain ways, others not), the starting-point is often a silence, which may be both a denial of speech (as in Maraini's *Marianna Ucría*) and the entirely new, or rediscovered, vantage point from which to recreate the world. Silence is both suffering and strength, as in the figure of Frabotta's Héloïse, reproaching Abelard for a fluency which is also a cheapness of speech ('Eloisa', in *Il rumore bianco*, 'White Noise', 1982). In questioning both the identity of the subject of history and the nature of subjectivity itself, feminist thought brought into focus two of the crucial questions for writing in the 1970s and 1980s.

Problems of the self and language

The psychological subject is both omnipresent and fragmented in the poetry of the 1970s. In some respects, it makes a startling comeback from the 'reduction of the self' celebrated by the previous decade. Reduction does not give way to plenitude, however – telling one's own story, autobiography, are not possible in any straightforward sense – but rather to a dispersal of the self. The self is constantly alluded to, but the confessional or enunciatory language of the lyric poem comes out as a stuttering or stammering. It is difficult to complete the line or make the connection between one thought and the other; a new phrase or image grows on the body of the old, and another on that; alternatively, the process takes place within the phrase, as though within a series of brackets. Fabio Doplicher (b. 1938), who is also a playwright, writes a narrative, like Cucchi in places, carried forward by flashes and fragments (see *I giorni dell'esilio*, 'Days of Exile', 1975, and *Cronaca del terzo stato*, 'Report from the Third Estate', 1977). In *I Segni* ('Signs', 1972), Gregorio Scalise (b. 1909) uses the end-stop no less effectively to interrupt the flow of meaning (a device also used by Porta in the 1970s). With analogy the preferred form of expression, considerable demands are made on the reader of poetry in the 1970s who is invited to reconstruct the connections, or to recognise the impossibility of doing so. The poetic performance becomes a kind of 'speaktease', in which language seems to promise to deliver and does not. A degree of conflict with the reader is made explicit in the loudly proclaimed autonomy of the word (*parola*), autonomy from what is thought of as reality and from coerced meanings, both in the anthology *La parola innamorata* ('The Word in Love', 1978: 'Poetry uses its readers, it is not used') and in the magazine *Niebo*, published in Milan from 1977 to 1980 and edited by the poet Milo De Angelis (b. 1951). De Angelis's first collection in particular, *Somiglianze* ('Likenesses', 1976), made critics talk of a return to the Orphic strain in Italian poetry (for example, in the manner of Campana, see above, p. 498) or even of a new hermeticism.

Poems which so often seem to hang on the edge of meaning may owe their paradoxically communicative power to this hidden conflict with the reader, or to the 'unspeakability' of the traumatic relationships at their heart (as is frequently the case with Porta, who becomes an increasingly important presence through the 1970s and 1980s, not least with his impressive and influential anthology *Poesia italiana degli anni Settanta*, 1979), or to that 'vocation to the transgressive sign' which Lorenzini attributes to one of the finest poets of her generation, Amelia Rosselli (1930–96). Drawing on all her three languages (Italian, French, English), as well as her musical education, Rosselli traced in a succession of fine books (from which the author made her own selection in *Antologia poetica*, 1987, which also contains an essay by Giovanni Giudici and an interview with Giacinto Spagnoletti) the experiencing of a 'breakdown' of language, its inability either to represent or even illusorily to reconstruct the real world. Out of the remains of an extensive culture, through a technique of word-manipulation inherited from a predominantly English tradition of pun, nonsense and aggressive assonance à la Hopkins, Rosselli fashioned an alternative, entirely convincing, hallucinating discourse: the sign is transgressed within, and perhaps in function of, a circuit of human need and desire, which is recognisable, however painful. But in some poets a real aphasia is threatened by the practice of what might be called dis-phasia, a willed language-disorder, and the redirection of attention away from the poem, the phrase, or even the word to ever smaller units, the morpheme or the phoneme. Examples of this may be seen in the poetry of Angelo Lumelli (b. 1944) with his indicatively titled 'Esempi di afasia' in *Cosa bella cosa* ('Examples of aphasia', in 'Lovely Thing', 1977), or in that of Cesare Viviani (b. 1947), beginning with *L'ostrabismo cara* ('Squint', 1973).

It is, however, impossible to do justice to the many individual talents which came to the fore or were confirmed during the 1970s, not least with the help of a series of excellent (if sometimes partisan) anthologies, including, beyond those already mentioned, *Il pubblico della poesia*, edited by Alfonso Berardinelli and Franco Cordelli in 1975, and *Poesia italiana oggi*, edited by Mario Lunetta in 1981. Mariella Bettarini (b. 1942) was editor of the magazine *Salvo imprevisti* ('Barring Unforeseen Circumstances', 1973–) and has also written on women and sexuality in *Felice di essere* ('Happy to Exist', 1978). Nanni Cagnone (b. 1939) is the author of *What's Hecuba to him or he to Hecuba?* (1976; title in the original), while Patrizia Cavalli (b. 1947) was one of the strongest individual talents to emerge in the 1970s (see *Poesie 1974–92*, 1992). Tomaso Kemeny (b. 1939), in addition to his poetry, was also responsible with Cesare Viviani for organising two controversial poetry conferences at the end of the 1970s (proceedings in *Il movimento della poesia italiana negli anni Settanta*, 1979, and *I percorsi della nuova poesia italiana*, 'The Paths of the New Italian Poetry', 1980). Special attention should also be drawn to those poets who work, in a sense laterally, in the area of concrete and/or visual poetry. The name of Lamberto Pignotti has already been mentioned, and to it should be added that of Adriano Spatola (1941–88), founder and director with Giulia Niccolai (b. 1934) of the magazine *Tam tam* (founded 1971) and of the publishing house Geiger, which were two of the principal vehicles of experimental poetry in the 1970s, but just part of Spatola's indefatigable efforts on behalf of what he described as 'total poetry'. Niccolai's strength lies in a particularly humorous use of multilingual wordplay and nonsense (*Harry's bar, e altre poesie 1969–1980*, 1981). What Spatola will be remembered for above all, over and beyond the novel (*Oblò*, 'Porthole', 1964) and the poetry (notably *Diversi accorgimenti, Diverse Devices*, 1975, translated by Paul Vangelisti in 1978) which he published between the mid-1960s and his death, are his many poetry performances in Europe and America, his sheer physical bulk and the rich voice becoming part of the meaning of a poet who, unlike many of his fellows, was an artist to his fingertips.

It was, however, a paradox of the 1970s that alongside an apparent proliferation of poets, there was ever less confidence amongst them that what they were writing was being read (except by other poets), or even could be read, inasmuch as the institution of poetry itself seemed anachronistic or redundant. Both aspects of this paradox are apparent in the reluctance to practise 'poetics' compared with the 1960s, that is, to make resounding statements about poetry and the world, and in the conviction that one should simply be getting on with 'doing' poetry, however impossible it might be. The contradictoriness of the situation is visible also in the multiplication of small publishing-houses and magazines, as well as in the search for alternative circuits of communication. Part of the lack of confidence, indeed, was an acute awareness of the limited range of the printed word, and especially of the printed poetic word, in a consumer-led cultural market. One advantage of the small magazine was that it had, by and large, a self-selecting, targetable, clientèle; but there was also the parallel desire to reach out to a wider, and anonymous, audience. Poetry readings gained in frequency and popularity, as did poetry festivals. Barely had such circuits been activated, however, than they were perceived as being threatened with appropriation by the culture industry.

Theatre

Some poets embraced enthusiastically, others not at all, the possibilities of public performance. In the theatre itself there were some points of contact with the experience of poetry in the 1960s and 1970s, most notably, perhaps, the subordination of the written word to the performance. For much of our period, and until the spectacular successes of Dario Fo and Franca Rame in the late 1970s and 1980s, the best-known representatives of Italian theatre abroad were Giorgio Strehler (b. 1921) and Eduardo De Filippo (1900–84). The Piccolo Teatro di Milano, under the direction of Strehler, was the most successful embodiment of a certain idea of public theatre, though one that came under increasing attack from a variety of sources: from private companies who thought it received too much subsidy, from political radicals in the late 1960s who thought it did not reach out to a wide enough public, or to new publics, and from new authors who felt their work was neglected. Most of Eduardo's best-known work was written before 1956 (see above, p. 545), but the performances continued, often with the veteran actor-writer in one of his own roles. In London, he earned special affection during the 1970s partly through his own appearances and partly through the patronage, and the interpretations, of Laurence Olivier.

The 1960s and the 1970s saw the steady encroachment on what had hitherto been the writer's space by the other components of the theatrical world, despite the reiteration in extreme form of the primacy of the word by an author such as Pasolini with the various pieces that he conceived originally in the mid-1960s, the confessional recitations of the Catholic writer Giovanni Testori (1923–92), and the steady production for the stage of a number of professional playwrights and others, such as Ginzburg and Moravia, who turned their attention to the theatre from other genres. Director's theatre (in which the director à la Strehler casts himself as the privileged interpreter of the author's words) began to run out of steam at this time. Other factors which contributed to a weakening of the authored script were the crisis of idealist criticism and the development of new university departments (notably the Dipartimento Arte Musica Spettacolo at Bologna) devoted to 'lo spettacolo' and drawing on semiotics, the creation by the mass media of a market of images, the new ideas coming from the anarchic utopianism and body-centred mysticism of such 'alternative' groups as The Living Theatre, as well as the proliferation of the protest movements and the worsening of social conflict around 1968. Renewed attention was given to mime and to choreography, to gestural technique and to theatrical traditions in which the spoken word plays a limited, stylised or non-existent role, from Noh to the commedia dell'arte. At the same time, the invasion of the auditorium by the action had already been met with acclaim in Luca Ronconi's famous 1968 production of the Orlando furioso adapted by Sanguineti. In the years that followed audiences found themselves participating with greater or lesser enthusiasm, especially in some

of the happenings and events of the so-called 'Roman school', mainly played in
small and precarious theatre clubs in the late 1960s and early 1970s.

Out of this theatrical mix which somehow managed to combine carnival and
high seriousness, clowning and didacticism, at least two star acts, very different
one from the other, emerged in the 1960s and 1970s. Carmelo Bene (b. 1937)
is a performer above all of monologues and one-man shows, a great declaimer
in the tradition of Marinetti, contemptuous or indifferent towards the audience, unrelenting in his portrayal of the artist as victim. More substantial by
far is the controversial figure of Dario Fo (b. 1926) who, in a career which
now spans nearly fifty years, has sought progressively to harness the classic
resources of the Italian theatre (especially in its hidden, 'popular' forms) to a
leftist political agenda. His subjects have ranged from the condemnation of
establishment Catholic (read Christian Democrat) hypocrisy and corruption in
the faux-medieval virtuoso one-man performance *Mistero buffo* (*Comic
Mysteries*, 1969) to the exposure of Communist reformism and the Party's
supposed abandonment of the industrial workers in a series of 1970s productions, the denunciation of state-inspired terrorism (notably in *Morte acciden-
tale di un anarchico*, *Accidental Death of an Anarchist*, 1970), and, with his
wife Franca Rame (b. 1929), the espousal of feminism. Rame's *Tutta casa,
letto e chiesa* (*A Woman Alone and Other Plays*, 1977) was a particularly
powerful statement at one of the high points of the women's movement.

Fiction

The difficulty of defining a role for themselves as writers after the challenges of
the 1960s was one that was faced by novelists as well as poets. The fiction of
the 1970s tends to fall between a working-through of problems left over from
the experimentation (and the resistance to it) of the previous decade and the
return to a generally more circumspect and circumscribed kind of fiction-
writing which will characterise the Eighties. These years, however, also provide
a vantage-point from which to survey the work of some of the most significant
narrators of the post-war period. In the following pages, I shall pay particular
attention to Elsa Morante, Primo Levi, Leonardo Sciascia, Italo Calvino, and
to the particular case of Umberto Eco.

Morante and other women writers

In her first two novels, *Menzogna e sortilegio* (*The House of Liars*, 1948) and
L'isola di Arturo (*Arturo's Island*, 1957), Elsa Morante (1912–85) created
liminal worlds in which the repeated traumas of childhood loss and rejection,
adolescent generosity and betrayal, adult failure and sadism, were enacted in a
stately, measured language that barely contained the madness of reason.
Morante liked to think of the artist, that is of herself, as a 'protagonista solare',

the 'sun-figure who in myth confronts the dragon of the night, to liberate the frightened city', as she wrote in 1959. But as her career progressed the nocturnal side of her writing came increasingly to the fore, and when the sun shone, as in the figure of the Pazzariello (Neapolitan term for street-vendor) in the title-poem of her 1968 collection *Il mondo salvato dai ragazzini*, ('The World Saved by Children'), it did so with the force of a kind of post-meridian panic, a kind of terror; it is, after all, the worship of the sun which determines Laius to kill Oedipus in the remarkable variation on Sophocles in this collection, 'La serata a Colono'. Thus, while in *L'isola di Arturo*, the island itself, suspended in the first-person narrator's memory, provides some focus, an anchor almost, to Arturo's endless, and endlessly frustrated, waiting, in *La Storia* (*History: a Novel*, 1974), an epic novel of the last years of the Second World War and its aftermath set in Rome, the equivalent character, the child Useppe, not only never reaches adolescence, but is from the outset designated as an angelic figure, already touched by death. The note of despair, not only personal, but also political and historical, was sounded more deeply still in Morante's last novel, *Aracoeli* (*Aracoeli*, 1982). If *La Storia* recounts the slaughter of innocence, the subsequent novel maps the self-destruction wrought by experience.

The intensity of Morante's language, her expertise in narrative structuring (on a nineteenth-century model, a choice which earned her much opprobrium, particularly for *La Storia*), her absorption of deeply felt parts of the biblical and classical tradition within a culture that was Jungian and surrealist in formation, above all her capacity to create from these elements a personal mythology that was still communicable and meaningful to others, combined to make hers a uniquely powerful voice in post-war Italian writing. Despite the extremely personal (and to some unacceptably sentimental or overwrought) quality of her work, she emerged as an important point of reference, though not a model to be followed, for the newly conscious and questioning young women writers who began to publish from the mid 1970s on and whose work will be considered along with that of their male contemporaries in the next section.

Certain other senior women writers either produced new work, or were republished, or were afforded new critical attention at this time. Anna Banti's *Artemisia* (1947) was republished in 1970, and repeatedly thereafter, to much acclaim, thus ensuring an audience for her later work, notably the autobiographical novel *Un grido lacerante* ('A Scream', 1981). Fausta Cialente (1898–1994), who had established her reputation in the 1930s as a writer of novels with exotic Eastern settings, returned to notice in 1976 with *Le quattro ragazze Wieselberger* ('The Four W. Girls'), narrated by one of the surviving daughters of a well-to-do Triestine family of the late nineteenth century. Gianna Manzini (1896–1974) with the autobiographical *Ritratto in piedi* ('Full-Length Portrait', 1971) and Lalla Romano (b. 1906) with a number of works in which fiction and autobiography interweave in the narration of often painful family relations (between mother and son in *Le parole tra noi leggère*, 'Light Words Between Us', 1969, between grandmother and grandchild in *L'ospite*, 'The Guest', 1973) also contributed, along with Natalia Ginzburg (see above, pp. 548–9), to the retrospective construction of a tradition of women's writing. This canon emphasised the themes of family, history and memory, but did not, generally speaking, mount a strong critique of the patriarchy. It tended to be regarded with both gratitude and some wariness by younger women writers.

Primo Levi

Primo Levi (1919–87; see also above pp. 546–7) owes his pre-eminence to the clarity of his moral vision, which is accompanied and enhanced by a crystalline prose style. The chemical metaphor is perhaps too obvious to describe the writing of a research scientist who both celebrated the very bible of his art, the periodic table, and adapted it to the demands of autobiographical memory in *Il sistema periodico* (*The Periodic Table*, 1975), and who made use of his scientific knowledge in many of his short stories. Levi also drew on the world of work to create the memorable figure of Tino Faussone, the Piedmontese rigger and raconteur of *La chiave a stella* (*The Wrench*, 1978). Levi, like Morante, wrote a historical novel *sui generis*: *Se non ora, quando?* (*If Not Now, When?*, 1982) followed the fortunes of a scratch partisan formation of Jewish escapees which operated in Western Russia towards the end of the war, a theme of great fascination and emotional power in itself, but one which also raises, for Levi and for the reader, questions about the whole history of Jewish suffering across the centuries, the nature of identity and the price of survival. But it is above all as a moralist of profound insight that Levi will be remembered. This side of his reputation is linked to the two early books which recounted the author's experiences as a prisoner in Auschwitz and their immediate aftermath, *Se questo è un uomo* (1947; new edition, 1956) and *La tregua* (*The Truce*, 1963), and to the exceptionally fine essays which were published as a volume shortly before his death, *I sommersi e i salvati* (*The Drowned and the Saved*, 1986). In these essays, he explores not only the nature of the Jewish experience, but also and above all the psychology of survival, the difficulty of remembering, and the moral need to do so. In particular, the argument and the rhythm of the writing make it clear how survivors and their children alike must develop the ability to judge without sentimentality or self-indulgence the demands for allegiance of the powerful and the pleas for forgiveness of the guilty.

Sciascia and other Sicilian writers

Although Leonardo Sciascia (1921–89) shares with Levi what has been described as a 'moral intransigence', there is a substantial difference between the two writers that goes beyond their geographical location at opposite ends of the country, with the profound historical differences between their two regions (Levi was from Turin, Sciascia from Racalmuto, in the extreme southwest of Sicily). Levi, even at the height of his despair (as a writer, at least), looks instinctively for dialogue, for interaction, for correspondence and communication. Sciascia seems a much more lonely figure (again, as a writer). His favoured *modus operandi* is that of investigation, an attitude towards the world which came to assume different, but more or less regularly alternated, patterns in his published work. The figure of the detective who attempts, against the odds, and often against the active opposition of others, to reconstruct the circumstances of the crime and to identify the guilty, without success, first appears in the two novels of the 1960s which deal with Mafia themes: *Il giorno della civetta* (*The Day of the Owl*, 1961) and *A ciascuno il suo* (*To Each his Own*, 1966). It is then taken up again in the political fables of the Seventies, *Il contesto* (*Equal Danger*, 1971) and, indirectly, *Todo modo* (*One Way or the Other*, 1974), and reappears in such late fictions as *Porte aperte* (*Open Doors*, 1987) and *Il cavaliere e la morte* (*The Knight and Death*, 1988). The detective may be read as an alter ego of the first-person researcher who appears in other works, in which, on the basis of scanty and often incomplete documents, and of usually not more than circumstantial evidence, Sciascia seeks to put together again a long-neglected historical event or chain of events, involving a mystery (for example, *Atti relativi alla morte di Raymond Roussel*, 'Documents Concerning the Death of R.R.', 1971, or *La scomparsa di Majorana*, *The Mystery of M.*, 1975) or an injustice (for example, *Dalla parte degli infedeli* 'Among the Infidels', 1979). The characteristic situation in Sciascia is the conflict, or more exactly the simple noncommunication, between the patient research, conjecture, deduction, speculation and reconstruction of the investigator, and the 'wall of silence', *omertà* or blankness which faces him. The mystery will never be unravelled, the truth will not out. But, on the other hand, what is known, what is recoverable, is enough to ensure that things cannot be taken at face value: never was there a more practical application of the adage 'pessimism of the intelligence, optimism of the will' than in Sciascia's denunciation of state complicity and corruption in the aftermath of the abduction and murder of Aldo Moro (*L'affaire Moro*, 1978). A year earlier, in *Candido, ovvero un sogno fatto in Sicilia* (*Candido, or A Dream Dreamed in Sicily*, 1977), Sciascia had invented a Voltairean (but contemporary) hero who ends by freeing himself from Enlightenment rationalism and from all fathers, including Voltaire. In the author's own writing, Candido's gesture seems an empty one. The lonely task of the investigator continues, even while history pursues its own, quite separate, path.

The Sicily of Sciascia's work (most directly represented in a documentary-realist way in his first two books, but ever-present in his subsequent work, from historical fictions such as *Il consiglio d'Egitto*, *The Council of Egypt*, 1963, to essays, critical writings and occasional pieces) is seen pessimistically, within a tradition of Sicilian writing about Sicily which tends to perceive the island as 'oppressed from without and corrupted from within'. While not all Sicilian writers take any particular view of Sicilian history, there is a strong sense of regional self-awareness, and even identification, among them. A narrative line that stretches from De Roberto, Verga, Capuana and Pirandello through Vittorini and Brancati, continues in the post-war years to a number of interesting writers in addition to Tomasi di Lampedusa and Sciascia. Giuseppe Bonaviri (b. 1924) moved away from neo-realism in the late 1950s towards a narrative in which science and fantasy play an increasing part, especially in the 'triptych' comprising *Il fiume di pietra* ('The Stone River', 1964), *La divina foresta* ('The Divine Forest', 1969) and *Notti sull'altura* ('Nights in the Hills', 1971); this links him at least thematically, and in some respects stylistically too, with both Levi and Calvino. Stefano D'Arrigo (b. 1919) was initially, like Bonaviri, a protégé of Vittorini's, and long extracts from his work in progress appeared in *Il Menabò* 3 (1960). But the huge novel *Horcynus Orca* did not appear as a whole until 1975, to a very mixed reception. While some saw it as stylistically and narratologically anachronistic, others have appreciated both its immense mythopoeic sweep and the inventiveness of its language. It is probably truer to say, however, that it remains one of the great unread works of post-war Italian writing.

Two other Sicilian writers may be mentioned here, even though the bulk of their work belongs to the 1980s. Vincenzo Consolo (b. 1933) came to prominence with *Il sorriso dell'ignoto marinaio* (*The Smile of the Unknown Mariner*, 1976). Like a number of important Sicilian novels, it deals with one of the traumatic moments of the impact of the Risorgimento in Sicily, in this case the peasant revolt at Alcara Li Fusi (near Cefalù) set off by the landing of Garibaldi's Thousand. Consolo's peculiarly expressive (but difficult) language, his frequently nocturnal settings and atmosphere, and his mixing of fiction, reportage, document and invention, are particularly effective in the short stories and other pieces gathered in *Le pietre di Pantalica* ('The Stones of P.', 1988) and in a fictional return to Cefalù in the early 1920s in *Nottetempo, casa per casa* ('Night Time, House By House', 1992). Gesualdo Bufalino (b. 1920) had published hardly anything before the appearance of *Diceria dell'untore* (*The Plague-Sower*) in 1981 and *Argo il cieco* (*Blind Argus*) in 1984, both of them highly successful experiments in self-conscious, and self-critical, autobiography. The stories of *L'uomo invaso* (*The Keeper of Ruins*, 1986) and those that go to make up what is nevertheless a self-contained novel, *Le menzogne della notte* (*Night's Lies*, 1988), are less theatrical, but perhaps for that reason their knowing inconsequentiality becomes more grating on the reader. Bufalino has also published a number of volumes of short pieces, somewhat in the manner of Sciascia, on the customs and peculiarities of Sicily (especially *Museo d'ombre*, 'Museum of Shadows', 1982).

Other 'regional' writers

There is perhaps less regional literary self-consciousness elsewhere in Italy than there is in Sicily, though it is not lacking in Sardinia thanks to Giuseppe Dessí (1909–77) and Salvatore Satta (1902–75) who achieved posthumous fame with *Il giorno del giudizio* (*The Day of Judgement*, 1979), and in Naples with Raffaele La Capria (b. 1922) and Michele Prisco (b. 1920), in addition to Bernari and Rea (see above, pp. 545–6). Moving to the north-east of the country, the Veneto, Friuli and the areas bordering on or within the former Yugoslavia, another group of writers suggests itself as having at least a 'family resemblance', even though individually they are very different from each other. Ferdinando Camon (b. 1935), like many of the writers of this region, has a deeply religious undercurrent in his work, and has also written interesting novels on the background to far-right terrorism in the area in the 1970s (notably *Occidente*, 'West', 1975, and *Storia di Sirio* 'Story of Sirius', 1981). *Il complesso dell'Imperatore* ('Everything About the Emperor', 1972), by the Triestine writer Carolus Cergoly (b. 1908), caught the imagination of a public fascinated by 'Mitteleuropa' which a few years later would provide an audience for the writings of the Germanist Claudio Magris (b. 1939; his *Danubio*, *Danube* was published in 1986). Luigi Meneghello (b. 1922), in the books dedicated to his native Malo, near Vicenza (*Libera nos a malo*, 'Deliver Us From Evil', 1963, *Pomo pero*, 'Apple Tree Pear Tree', 1974), to the Resistance (*I piccoli maestri*, *The Outlaws*, 1964), and to the Italian road to education (*Fiori italiani*, 'Italian Gems', 1976), evokes the dialect, rather than reproducing it at length, in order, by ironic counterpoint, to suggest the blind spots and concealments of official Italian. The Friulan writer Carlo Sgorlon (b. 1930) has written movingly about the dying peasant culture of the region, but his best book (after *Il trono di legno*, *The Wooden Throne*, 1973) is probably his account of the Friulan contingent which took part in the building of the Trans-Siberian railway, *La conchiglia di Anatai* ('Anatay's Shell', 1983). Fulvio Tomizza (b. 1935) left his family home in Istria after the border settlement with Yugoslavia in 1952. In a prolific output, his most successful work is the 'Materada' trilogy: *Materada* (1960), *La ragazza di Petrovia* ('The Girl From P.', 1963) and *La quinta stagione* ('The Fifth Season', 1965); though *La miglior vita* ('The Better Life', 1977), based on the Materada parish records, and *L'amicizia* ('Friendship', 1980) are also notable. Finally, Goffredo Parise, who, like Meneghello, is from the Vicenza area, is mentioned here for the second time, simply because with *Sillabario n. 1* (*The Abecedar*, 1972) and *Sillabario n. 2* (*Solitudes. Short Stories*, 1982) he produced his finest work, short, distilled *exempla* of moral or psychological behaviour, organised under the heading of an affective quality ('Friendship', 'Goodness') or generic indication ('Cinema', 'Family') which, like Manganelli's *Centuria* or Calvino's *Palomar*, seem merely to suggest the outlines of a story, and yet to require no further elaboration.

Calvino

There is a real sense of place even in the imaginary cities of memory and desire, of exchange and the dead, which are described in Calvino's *Le città invisibili* (*Invisible Cities*, 1972), for, just as (so we are told) from all of Marco Polo's reports in that novel there emerges the memory of Venice, so beneath many of these constructions of the mind lie the ground plan and architecture of the hill villages of Calvino's Western Liguria, their canals and *carrugi*, their arcades and tunnels, buttresses and balustrades, their 'thin' houses stretching to the sky, one pushed against the other in continuous ribbons above the valley-beds. Calvino's later writing combines and explores many different spaces: the intergalactic voids and subatomic matter present in *Cosmicomiche* (*Cosmicomics*, 1965) and in some of the stories of *Ti con zero* (*Time and the Hunter*, 1967), far-flung corners of the terrestrial globe whose names still retain a kind of childish magic, Tula, Palenque, Kyoto (*Palomar*, 1983, and *Sotto il sole giaguaro*, *Under the Jaguar Sun*, 1986), the invented South Americas and Japans of *Se una notte d'inverno un viaggiatore* (1979), geometric and labyrinthine structures, city-scapes, the neat little bits and bobs of suburban living (in both *Se una notte* and *Palomar*). That these entirely different spaces coalesce without strain, sometimes in the same book, is perhaps due in part to Calvino's ability to convince the reader, even in those texts which have a generically 'historical' setting (such as the 'medieval' forest and tavern of *Il castello dei destini incrociati*, *The Castle of Crossed Destinies*, 1973), that these spaces are entirely in the present, that the space of the text is fully autonomous, that text and reader are fully present to each other. In other words, Calvino achieves the oldest ambition of the art of storytelling which he studied so closely: to make the story 'come alive', in an entirely personal and modern idiom.

This idiom is often thought of as cerebral and resolutely theoretical. Calvino was fascinated with patterns, sequences, repetitions, diagrams, and musical, mathematical or architectural structures, anything which serves to give shape to a fundamentally disorderly universe (but also which serves to make things happen; only when the rhythm is established can the writing 'flow'). He was also a careful student of those currents in structuralism and semiotics which contributed in the 1960s and 1970s to the reflowering of narratology. The coexistence of these traits made Calvino the paradigmatic 'experimenter' of post-war Italian fiction. He combined an attitude of interrogation and speculation towards the universe, the natural world, and the world of human actions and emotions with a commitment to understanding and refining his technique as a narrator, particularly in *Il castello dei destini incrociati*, which is almost a guided tour to the making of stories, and in the (not always quite so convincing) analysis of the process of reading which is (in part) *Se una notte d'inverno un viaggiatore*. 'Scientific' observation and the kind of technical 'exercise' familiar to one who during his Paris years collaborated with

Raymond Queneau's OuLiPo group contribute undoubtedly to the quiet self-confidence which Calvino displays in all his later writing. From self-confidence and the gently mocking humour that goes with it comes that quality of 'lightness' which Calvino celebrated in his *Lezioni americane* (*Six Memos for the Next Millennium*, 1988). 'Lightness' is not irresponsibility, nor mere playfulness, but is something like an illusion of which we (readers) are totally, and joyfully, convinced. It is a figment.

Morselli, Volponi and others

For much of the decade there continues to be an implicit division between two kinds of fiction-writing. Some authors of course work along quite individualistic paths, and among them I would mention (in addition to Luigi Malerba, see above, pp. 578–9) the particular cases of Guido Morselli (1912–73) and Paolo Volponi (1924–94). Morselli became something of a *cause célèbre* when in the space of four years the Milanese publishing house Adelphi brought out six novels, none of which the author had succeeded in having published before his death by suicide in 1973. The first three, *Roma senza papa* ('Rome Without a Pope', 1974), *Contropassato prossimo* (*Past Conditional: a Retrospective*) and *Divertimento 1889* (both 1975), all in different ways manipulate historical characters and historical events to produce a kind of counter-history, a narrative of the rulers of Italy cast in the subjunctive mood. The other novels, *Il comunista* ('The Communist', 1976), *Dissipatio H.G.* (1977) and *Un dramma borghese* ('A Bourgeois Drama', 1978), focus on the recent past and on a post-nuclear future through the reflections of a narrating consciousness that feels itself inadequate to the events and choices with which it has been faced, and are altogether bleaker in tone. Nuclear catastrophe figures largely also in two of Paolo Volponi's novels, *Corporale* ('Corporal', 1974) and *Il pianeta irritabile* ('The Irritable Planet', 1978). In the first, it is part of the terror that not only confronts contemporary man, but also blocks him psychologically, recounted in a 'neurotic', fragmented prose that recalls the voices of Albino Saluggia in *Memoriale* and Anteo Crocioni in *La macchina mondiale*. In the second novel, which is written instead as a kind of fairy-tale, nuclear disaster is seen as something that has already occurred and has been survived (with distinct echoes of Latin American fabulation à la Carlos Fuentes) by a monkey, an elephant, a goose and a dwarf. Two other novels, *Il sipario ducale* (*Last Act in Urbino*, 1975) and *Il lanciatore di giavellotto* ('The Javelin Thrower', 1981), take Volponi's native Urbino as their setting, and like the others explore the themes of political violence, neurotic sex, dependency and the desperate search for some residual decency and political coherence in a language that is frequently 'irritable' and can be vituperative, but which can never simply be taken for granted. These same qualities are evident in Volponi's return to the 'industrial' theme in *Le mosche del capitale* ('The Flies of Capitalism', 1989) and in his continuing meditation on the fortunes and failings both of Italian capitalism and the Italian left in *La strada per Roma* ('The Road to Rome', 1991).

Writers such as Malerba, Morselli and Volponi do not fit easily on either side of the implicit division which I have mentioned, and which exists for much of the 1970s, between, on the one side, those writers who seem to write principally 'for themselves' or 'for literature', writers for whom the act of writing is part of a continuing process of linguistic or metaphysical research; and, on the other, those who write 'for the reader', in general a pre-conceived reader who is familiar with the conventions of narrative realism, is not keen to have his or her expectations disappointed, and is unlikely to welcome much formal experimentation. The bitterness of avant-garde polemics, such as those directed against Bassani and Cassola, may have abated since the late 1950s and early 1960s, but there is often a complete lack of interest among 'serious' writers, and especially critics, in the 'well-made novel' or the 'romanzo medio', the work of such writers as Piero Chiara (1913–86), Gina Lagorio (b. 1922), Giovanni Arpino (1927–87) and Alberto Bevilacqua (b. 1924). There is somewhat more indulgence, however, for the four-handed detective stories penned by Carlo Fruttero (b. 1926) and Franco Lucentini (b. 1920), starting with *La donna della domenica* (*The Sunday Woman*, 1976). To some degree this division hides others. There is, for example, a metropolitan intolerance of what are perceived as the nostalgic values of the provinces which continues a town–country divide that has been an undercurrent of all twentieth-century Italian literature. But the role of 'la provincia' requires a separate essay to itself: from the strength derived from their 'provincial' setting by such writers as Bufalino and Zanzotto, to the reassessment of provincial values in Volponi or, obliquely, in the novels of Giuseppe Pontiggia (b. 1934).

What is noteworthy, however, is that towards the end of the decade even those writers who might regard themselves as 'experimental' are asking themselves serious questions about the reader, under the multiple impact of research in narratology (which by enquiring into the mechanisms of narrative communication puts the reader firmly in the frame), the development of the sociology of literature, and a burgeoning specialist and journalistic bibliography which makes everyone aware that the nature of the cultural market is changing rapidly and that readers ('consumers') are coming to literature differently educated and with different expectations. The scientific analysis of these phenomena in Umberto Eco's *Lector in fabula* (*The Role of the Reader*, 1979) is matched on the literary front by Calvino's anxiety-ridden quest for the reader in *Se una notte d'inverno un viaggiatore* of the same year, with its magical squaring of the circle at the end.

Celati and Vassalli

The careers of two of the younger and most talented writers who had associated with the neo-avant-garde towards the end of the 1960s, Gianni

Celati (b. 1937) and Sebastiano Vassalli (b. 1941), are emblematic in this regard. Celati's four novels of the 1970s – *Comiche* ('Silent Movies', 1971), *Le avventure di Guizzardi* ('G.'s Adventures', 1973), *La banda dei sospiri* ('The Gang of Sighs', 1976) and *Lunario del paradiso* ('Paradise Almanac', 1978), the last three of them republished, with revisions, as *I parlamenti buffi*, 'Funny Talk', 1989 – are steeped in the knockabout comedy of the silent films, and use a disjointed, often ungrammatical or semantically unstable language to attempt a verbal equivalent of those visual representations of the anarchic behaviour of the body. The characters are socially marginalised, often victimised, and are on the edge equally of identity (names are impermanent or twisted) and of language. What changed most dramatically in the three titles published, after a long silence, in the 1980s – *Narratori delle pianure* (*Voices From the Plains*, 1985), *Quattro novelle sulle apparenze* (*Appearances*, 1987) and *Verso la foce* ('Journey to the Mouth of the Po', 1989) – was the language, which, from having been exuberant and mocking, now becomes restrained and almost minimalist. The intensity and pain of Celati's personal search, his impatience with the falsity of institutions, particularly 'literary' institutions, the despairing conviction that we are out of touch with ourselves, all these are undiminished. But they are conveyed in a language which tries to be faithful to what is there (inspired by the landscape photograph rather than by the slapstick movie) and at the same time to allow the reader to make an imaginative and a moral response. As Antonio Tabucchi observed in a review of *Narratori* (in *Il manifesto*, 22 June 1985), Celati 'puts himself forward first as listener, and then as storyteller'; he is part now of an *exchange* of stories.

Sebastiano Vassalli shares with Celati a profound distrust of literary institutions in general, and has repeatedly made public abjurations of his time with the avant-garde in particular (see especially his 1983 pamphlet *Arkadia* and, with Attilio Lolini, *Belle lettere*, 'Literary Letters', 1991). Even if there runs through nearly all his work a deep desire to understand Italy and its history, Vassalli's writing has become increasingly 'narrative' and linguistically communicative. Part of his resentment against the neo-avant-garde is based on its inhibition of storytelling in himself and others, and he has abandoned the experimentalist deployment of a kind of anti-language as a way of exposing the ideological mystifications of capitalism in favour of an explorative, probing, reflective historical narrative. This process began with the novels of the late 1970s and early 1980s, and is fully realised in his exploration of the life of Dino Campana (with whom Vassalli strongly identifies) in *La notte della cometa* (*The Night of the Comet*, 1984) and in the marvellous reconstruction of a seventeenth-century Lombard witch-trial in *La chimera* (*The Chimera*, 1990). This novel is both a homage to Manzoni and an alternative history to his.

Eco

If Celati and Vassalli have both achieved a successful, albeit tormented, 'life after the avant-garde', the biggest splash into the narrative mainstream was undoubtedly achieved by Umberto Eco with his novel *Il nome della rosa* (*The Name of the Rose*), published in 1980, and within a few years a global best-seller. Eco had been an active participant in the debates of the Gruppo 63, had built up a brilliantly successful academic career as Professor of Semiotics at the University of Bologna (*Trattato di semiotica generale*, *A Theory of Semiotics*, 1975), and had an active role as a columnist and *maître à penser*. Eco has been throughout his career in the best sense of the words a mediator and a synthesiser. His fascination with the homologies between the scholasticism of Thomas Aquinas and the modernist concerns of James Joyce led him to write on each of them and to seek a unified language that could adequately speak of both. Similarly, when considering contemporary culture, Eco rejected the idealist distinctions, at any rate as absolutes, between high and low, popular and learned; again, he looked for a language that was capable of speaking of culture as a whole. The language which he found – and which at a technical level he has done so much to elaborate – was that of semiotics: the notion, on the one hand, of a code by which meaning is structured, and on the other, of a Peircean idea of the sign not as referential but as cumulative (the meaning of a sign is understood by reference to another and so on potentially *ad infinitum*). *Il nome della rosa* is a semiotic triumph, not just because much of its content is devoted to various and sometimes conflicting strategies for the interpretation of signs, but because it is in its own way a *summa*, the representation within a single system of the medieval and the modern, the popular and the learned, the philosophical treatise and the detective story, in a unity which refuses exclusive categorisations, which insists on the continuities between the words of the Bible and sexual initiation, between technical practicality and doubt, between laughter and death. However, the uncertainty which runs through it as to whether there is any order in the universe, and as to how far the process of interpretation may go, is addressed theoretically in *I limiti dell'interpretazione* (*The Limits of Interpretation*, 1990) and fictionally in *Il pendolo di Foucault* (*Foucault's Pendulum*, 1988). This second novel may be interpreted as a sombre warning against the potential perversions of a semiotic universe in which, it seems, anything could, if someone so desired, be made to mean anything else.

44

The 1980s

The 1980s were, if not a golden, at least a silver age for Italian fiction. That was certainly the view which many reviewers and publicists, and some novelists themselves, took of the matter, particularly in the first half of the decade. There was a substantial element of market hype in this evaluation, and indeed one of the most striking features of the literary scene from the late 1970s on has been the extent to which commercial criteria have become part of the public (and not just professional) discourse on literature. Quite explicit market pressures drive on the search for the 'best-seller' (on the model of the most recent exemplar, *Il nome della rosa*; the phenomenon is pored over by the *literati* as though it were some exotic beast, like Dürer's rhinoceros) or that for 'new' or 'young' writers, in a bid to oxygenate the waters of the literary pond. These are sustained, or demanded, by changes in the structure of the culture industry itself, including a concentration of ownership of publishing houses, an internationalisation of the market through take-overs or cooperation deals, and an ever more complex intertwining of interests in publishing, the printed media and television, all of which provide opportunities both for extending the interface between publisher and public and for promoting particular products and targeting specific groups of readers.

But this 'triumph of narrative' was also real, at least for a time. A larger number of books were published, sold and, presumably, read. There was also probably an improvement in the overall quality of fiction-writing. What the commercial expansion of the market ensured was that there was more space and greater visibility for writers for whom it might otherwise have been just that bit more difficult to make a mark. The new writers of the 1980s included some relative late-comers. As well as the customary 'old beginners' (in addition to Bufalino, one should mention Carmelo Samonà, 1926–90, whose moving first novel, *Fratelli* ('Brothers') about the relationship with a mentally ill brother, and the need to invent new languages to communicate with him, was published in 1981), there were also some women writers whose late breakthrough into writing had been preceded by years of personal and/or political struggle. The search was for new favoured young writers in particular, and some were undoubtedly promoted too rapidly or beyond their real capacity; but a number, as we shall see, have survived. What is more difficult to pin down, certainly from the perspective of only a few years' distance, is the kind, or kinds, of writing that the 1980s produced, and I shall just mention, at this stage, one apparent divergence. Both Calvino by the mid-1970s and then Eco, were enjoying considerable international success, and at the same time many young writers were looking abroad, particularly to the English-speaking world, for their cultural reference-points. There was, as a consequence, in the 1980s a certain 'internationalisation' of Italian fiction, in both subject-matter and language, a trend which was accelerated by a tendency to make the written language itself less literary. But at the same time, there was much interest in 'roots', personal, family, regional or ethnic. This need was also expressed in poetry in the remarkable expansion in the writing of dialect poetry in the 1970s and 1980s and the revival of interest in those who had been writing earlier (such as the Veneto poet Biagio Marin, 1891–1985, and the Lucanian Albino Pierro, b. 1916). This unexpected renewal coincided with an accelerating decline in the use of dialect for everyday purposes, and thus mirrored in some respects the situation of poetry as a whole: more poets writing for fewer readers. But in addition to the dialect work of leading poets in Italian such as Pasolini and Zanzotto, others such as Tonino Guerra (b. 1920), Franco Loi (b. 1930) and Franco Scataglini (1930–94) achieved major reputations in this period for a purely dialect output.

Taken in the round, Italian fiction of the 1980s combined the awareness, and sometimes acceptance, of the global dimensions of contemporary mass culture (of which the literary novel or poem is also in some sense a part) with the need to preserve at least on paper the memory of where we have come from, but also, generally speaking, to question it. The turn to origins is one of the themes that sustains the later writing of Celati and Vassalli, and it is associated with a rediscovery, and a reinterpretation, of the art of 'plain' storytelling. On the other hand, the struggle both to give expression to a fictional past self and to understand, and make apparent to the reader, the interconnections between an individual and a historical past – the struggle, in short, to 'tell my story' (once it has been decided what that story is), is evident in the early fiction of a number of writers, all of them women, who in the 1980s produced a body of work that consolidated their reputations.

Women writers

Francesca Sanvitale (b. 1928) has written three novels which take women protagonists at various stages of their lives through a chronological progression roughly corresponding with the author's own lifespan: *Il cuore borghese* ('The Bourgeois Heart', 1972), *Madre e figlia* ('Mother and Daughter', 1980), *L'uomo del parco* ('The Man in the Park', 1982). More recently, *Verso Paola* ('Journey to Paola', 1991) has underlined Sanvitale's pessimistic sense of the loss of memory and judgement in contemporary 'post-modernity', while *Il figlio dell'Impero* ('The Son of the Empire', 1993) is an ambitious historical fiction set in nineteenth-century France. The appeal to the same Napoleonic and post-Napoleonic history, but a history seen in a different way, more as a collective imaginary memory than as a documented past, is a move made also by Rosetta Loy (b. 1931) in *Le strade di polvere* (*The Dust Roads of Monferrato*, 1987), after a series of novels set in more recent historical times in Italy. *Sogni d'inverno* ('Winter Dreams', 1992) returns to the years after the war first adumbrated in *La bicicletta* ('The Bicycle', 1974), and addresses a theme already present in Sanvitale, and frequently returned to by women writers elsewhere in Europe and America, the relationship between mothers and daughters; history again rumbles in the background and occasionally intrudes. The description of a relatively privileged childhood and the growing awareness of the world outside, characteristic of the early Loy, is also the subject of *La bambina* ('The Girl', 1976), the first novel by Francesca Duranti (b. 1935). The novel is unusual in its high degree of autobiographical explicitness (for example, the protagonist is referred to by the author's own name, while being described in the third person).

In both Loy and Duranti, it is (so they have stated) a particular house that has triggered the memory from which narrative will flow, and it is a house that features prominently in Duranti's much-acclaimed *La casa sul lago della luna* (*The House on Moon Lake*, 1984). In this case the narrative is very different. With a male protagonist and an invented plot, the novel enters into a depiction of fantasy and wish-fulfilment. Another strand of Duranti's writing, that of social criticism, comes to the fore in her subsequent novels, *Lieto fine* (*Happy Ending*, 1987) and *Effetti personali* ('Personal Effects', 1988), while the relation between life and art returns in *Ultima stesura* ('Last Draft', 1991). In a writer such as Fabrizia Ramondino (b. 1936), both linguistic invention and stylistic and structural complication play a larger part than in some other writers, but her two novels to date, *Althénopis* (1981) and *Un giorno e mezzo* ('A Day and a Half', 1988) and her collection of stories, *Storie di patio* ('Patio Stories', 1983), are also concerned with the recuperation of memory, from childhood and from the most recent past, and the difficulties of remembering. Time is dilated or contracted through the differential uses of narrative voices, the 'sincerity' of recollection is both authenticated and undermined by the extensive use of footnotes in the first novel, and so much of memory seems consigned to intimate, disposable, signs whose very specificity marks them out, and the writing too, for rapid obsolescence. In Ramondino, indeed, history, in its 'essence', is even more tantalisingly ungraspable than it is in Loy, while in the novels of the Triestine writer Giuliana Morandini, history is more confidently relied upon as an interlocutor with the personal destinies of the subject: the German occupation of Vienna in *I cristalli di Vienna* (*Blood Stains*, 1978), the unreal quality of modern Trieste in *Caffé Specchi* ('Mirror Café', 1983), the still-divided city in *Angelo a Berlino* ('Angel in Berlin', 1987). She too takes a leap into the distant past, sixteenth-century Germany (and, like a number of her contemporaries, adopts a painter and painting as her subject) in *Sogno a Herrenberg* ('Dream at H.', 1991). It is perhaps not too fanciful to suggest that

Morandini's more autobiographical writing is entrusted to the anthologies through which she has explored the 'marginal' states of female madness, earlier women's writing and *triestinità*: . . . *e allora mi hanno rinchiusa* ('. . . and then they locked me up', 1977), *La voce che è in lei* ('The Voice Which Is in Her', 1980), *Da te lontano* ('Far from You', 1989).

Tabucchi

The best writing of all of the novelists discussed so far displays a narrative maturity which comes not only from long familiarity with the craft of writing, but also from extensive reflection on personal and historical experience, and from the ability to envisage a reader who might respond to the narrating voice. The one other writer who attained a similar degree of narrative power during the 1980s is Antonio Tabucchi (b. 1943), author of a dozen novels, collections of stories and theatrical dialogues. Tabucchi's is a haunted imagination. His protagonists have a pervasive sense of anxiety and guilt, but, unlike Kafka's for example, they carry their imprisoning horizon with them. This is the sense of the title of *Il filo dell'orizzonte* (*Vanishing Point*, 1986): a horizon that is neither waiting to be crossed nor crowding in on the protagonist, but always there, at the same distance, always unreachable. Tabucchi furthermore is assailed by an anxiety that engenders a different hell from Kafka's: not the doubt as to how one's action will be judged, but the uncertainty as to whether it matters, or what matters and how. It is a peculiarly semiotic anxiety: the world is full of signs, and we do not know how to interpret even the ones which we have put there ourselves. The first preoccupation of the haunted imagination is the desire for something or someone which, or who, will answer a need or a question. The search for the other is foregrounded both in *Notturno indiano* (*Indian Nocturne*, 1984; an archive-researcher unknowingly pursues his alter ego in a fascinatingly observed journey through the subcontinent) and in *Il filo dell'orizzonte*, which is a 'sort of detective story', just as *Donna di Porto Pim* ('Woman of P.P.', 1983) is a 'sort of travel book', made up of the flotsam and jetsam of adventurous reading, as well as adventurous journeys. The imagination is also haunted by what we have done and where it is taking us, our collective past and future, or what we may call 'history'; the anxieties of history are particularly evident in Tabucchi's third collection of stories, *L'angelo nero* ('The Black Angel', 1991; earlier recollections are *Il gioco del rovescio*, 'The Game of Reversal', 1981, and *Piccoli equivoci senza importanza*, *Little Misunderstandings of No Importance*, 1985), and in his novel *Sostiene Pereira* (1993). Finally, the imagination is seen to haunt, not only be haunted, in the (re)creation of other artists' dreams in *Sogni di sogni* ('Dreams of Dreams', 1992), in the proliferation of 'voices', and the ease with which characters can enter the dreams and fantasies of others elsewhere in Tabucchi's fiction, for example in *Requiem* (1992).

A new generation of writers

At the same time as narrative fiction was reasserting itself as the dominant literary form, and as the medium through which new voices could make themselves heard, there were other developments in the world of the novel. One of the most arresting has been the further weakening of the traditionally rigid demarcations between 'high' and 'low', 'cultivated' and 'popular' in Italian culture. Here again, Eco's best-seller helped to bring about a change of gear. The knowing use of the conventions of the detective story to write something that is not quite a detective story not only follows a well-established practice in post-war Italian writing, of which the novels of Gadda and Sciascia are the best-known examples, but is part of a more recent trend on the part of 'serious' fiction to incorporate what hitherto tended to be regarded as 'popular' genres, the detective story itself in *Comici spaventati guerrieri* ('Comic Frightened Warriors', 1986) by the Bologna-born writer Stefano Benni (b. 1948), or the two novels by Gianfranco Manfredi (b. 1948), *Magia rossa* ('Red Magic', 1983) and *Cromantica* (1985), or the thriller in *Uccelli da gabbia e da voliera* ('Caged Birds', 1982) by Andrea De Carlo (b. 1952), and in Eco's second novel, as well as (though in a form largely hidden by the luxuriance of the language) in Aldo Busi's *La delfina bizantina* ('The Byzantine Dauphine', 1987). Busi (b. 1948) combines in his novels a linguistic exuberance which for some is reminiscent of Gadda, an inability to stop talking, vanity, an urge to provoke and to please at the same time, sexual athleticism, a gift for acute social satire across the classes, and a rather melancholic sense of the loss of the Italian *provincia*. Constantly reinventing himself in public, Busi is a frequent TV performer, and personifies the current *dérèglement de tous les genres* if not *de tous les sens*.

The Gothic is an important component in the work of the exceptionally talented Paola Capriolo (b. 1962): for example, *La grande Eulalia* ('The Great E.', 1988), *Il nocchiero* ('The Helmsman', 1989), *Il doppio regno* ('The Double Kingdom', 1991) and *Vissi d'amore* ('I Lived for Love', 1992). Science fiction appears in Benni's *Terra!* (1983). (Benni probably shares with Busi the distinction of being Italy's funniest contemporary writer; both writers seem to have been to the school of Vonnegut, or perhaps Coover.) The fantastic and the mystery-tale are widely drawn on; an example might be Laura Mancinelli's *I dodici abati di Challant* ('The Twelve abbots of C.', 1981) and *Il fantasma di Mozart* ('M.'s Ghost', 1986), the first of which displays the fascination with a real or imagined historical past and its literary manipulability which characterises much fiction of the 1980s. One of the most successful examples of this pseudo-historical writing was the first novel by the poet Roberto Pazzi (b. 1946), *Cercando l'imperatore* (*Searching for the Emperor*, 1985), and to a lesser extent his second, *La principessa e il drago* (*The Princess and the Dragon*, 1986), both of them set in the last years of Tsarist Russia and combining, in the first case at least, what Raboni in his preface called the 'claustrophobic fascination of imprisonment, exile' (the last days of the

Romanovs) and 'the adventurous-picaresque fascination of the journey, of a search across hostile and uncertain spaces' (the hopeless expedition of the Preobrajensky regiment to rescue them). Pazzi's most interesting work since then has been his *Vangelo di Giuda* ('The Gospel According to Judas', 1989), a complicated tale of intrigue, forgery, pastiche and apocryphal writing. The subject-matter at least, if not the style or narrative technique, is not unexpected in a decade which explored at length, in these and other writings, the meta-narrative potentialities of pastiche, montage, paraphrase, parody, allusion and quotation. It all reflects a situation in which the traditional, if untheorised, distinction between serious literature and 'rubbish' has broken down. As Franco Fortini has said, the occasional slummings of the aristocratic writer of the past have given way to a situation in which we all live off the 'guano' which our society produces day by day (and of which the finest metaphorical description is in Calvino's 1977 story 'La poubelle agréée', now in *La strada di San Giovanni*, 'The Road to S.G.', 1990).

There are nevertheless some younger writers, poets as well as novelists, for whom the representation of personal and/or collective experience remains, or has again become, a primary concern. Andrea De Carlo, after a successful start with two novels in which American minimalist writers seem to have been his principal inspiration, and a very shaky 'middle' period, appears to have opted for a generational novel in *Due di due* ('Two'), where two young men growing up in the rebellious 1960s choose diverging but ultimately intersecting paths. Both Claudio Piersanti (b. 1954) and Enrico Palandri (b. 1956) began their precocious writing careers from another rebellion, that of 1977 at the University of Bologna where they were both students. Indeed, Palandri's *Boccalone* (1979), a skilfully narrated love story in a student setting, was widely seen at the time as a kind of chronicle of those events, at least in their more communitarian and libertarian guise (the novel steers well clear of *autonomia* and the armed movement), and the most successful literary work to come out of them. Both writers (Piersanti's equivalent novel was *Casa di nessuno*, 'No Man's House', 1981) have settled in their subsequent work for careful notations of contemporary life, interlaced with autobiographical reminiscence and a concentration, in an intimist way, on small things, with a markedly melancholic turn in Piersanti, rather more fantastical and, at times, light-hearted in Palandri. Sandra Petrignani (b. 1952) belongs to what is perhaps the last generation of writers to be affected directly by the feminism of the 1970s, and this experience is reflected in her journalistic work (*Le signore della scrittura*, 'The Ladies of Writing', 1984, contains some valuable interviews with women writers) and, less directly, in her first two novels, *La navigazione di Circe* ('The Voyage of C.', 1987) and *Il catalogo dei giocattoli* (*The Toy Catalogue*, 1988), in both of which the nature of writing and the nature of time are mediated through a finely poised style condensed into very brief chapters or sections.

But the disillusionment with politics, certainly with the 'grand politics' of the Communist Party and the whole Communist world (the universal disgust with the corruption of the old ruling parties in Italy came a little later), is widespread throughout the younger generation: in Gianni D'Elia (b. 1953) for example, whose collections of poems, *Non per chi va* ('Not for Who Goes', 1980) and *Febbraio* ('February', 1985) are characteristic of a poetry which tries to re-establish contact with the 'essentials' that politics have left out. In Valerio Magrelli (b. 1957), the most accomplished poet of his generation, the focus is on the strangeness and unexplainability of objects, not in a romantic vein, but in a way which interacts with the lucid consciousness of the speaking subject. Magrelli, the author of three collections to date – *Ora serrata retinae* (1980), *Nature e venature* ('Natures and Veinings', 1987) and *Esercizi di tiptologia* ('Exercises in Typtology', 1992) – belongs no less than Palandri, say, to a generation of writers, or to a kind of writer, that continues to interrogate the world in the expectation of transforming it in the light of intelligence.

There is a difference of emphasis in the work of some of these writers' contemporaries. Daniele Del Giudice (b. 1949) has written two novels, *Lo stadio di Wimbledon* ('Centre Court', 1983) and *Atlante occidentale* (*Lines of Light*, 1985), and some shorter pieces which may be compared with Magrelli's poetry for their lucidity, but which are distinctly more ascetic, even astringent, in tone. This is in spite of the fact that the central project of the fictions – the attempt to enter the mind of another – is essential both to friendship, a value that is discreetly celebrated in *Atlante*, and to narration. Del Giudice has not felt the need to go on writing fictions come what may, and it is possible that his preoccupation with the very act of seeing, with vision and with insight, will in due course demand another, non-narrative, form of expression. Another sparing writer is Elisabetta Rasy (b. 1947), who, since contributing to the debate on women, language and writing with *La lingua della nutrice* ('The Nurse's Tongue', 1978) and *Le donne e la letteratura* ('Women and Literature', 1984), has published three short novels and a collection of stories. Here 'sparingness' is almost a metaphor for the disembodiment of characters whose every word seems to reach out to define the body, its desires and limits. The body and the languages available to describe it, and the culture in which it is both celebrated and despised, are foremost in the writings of Pier Vittorio Tondelli (1955–91), who, starting from the mimesis of the youth and street jargon of the 1970s, conducted with the 'philological fervour' of a Pasolini, in *Altri libertini* ('Other Libertines', 1980), progressed through satirical sketches of military life in *Pao Pao* ('Bang Bang', 1982) and of the sin-drenched beaches of *Rimini* (1985) to the post-AIDS love story of *Camere separate* (*Separate Rooms*, 1989). Tondelli's narrative drive comes from his mastery of the vernacular, thus from his excellent ear for dialogue. He too was a listener, and that is evident in his journalistic and occasional pieces, as it is in his promotion of young 'under twenty-five' writers in the three anthologies he edited between 1986 and 1990: *Giovani blues* ('Young Blues'), *Belli e perversi* ('Beautiful and Perverse') and *Papergang*.

What these three writers have in common – despite their quite different pre-occupations and styles – is a certain willingness or desire to suppress the first-person singular voice, to minimise the individuality of the author in favour of a plurality of voices, an interleaving of sounds. A similar (relative) lack of interest in foregrounding the self and in trying to match the personal with the historical is evident in prose writers like Nico Orengo (b. 1944), who is also a poet, Giampiero Comolli (b. 1950), with his interests in anthropology and ethnography, and Marco Lodoli (b. 1956) whose work to date – from his first novel *Diario di un millennio che fugge* ('Diary of a Millennium in Flight', 1986) to the stories of *Grande raccordo* ('Outer Ring Road', 1989) and two rather whimsical *novellas, I fannulloni* ('The Idlers', 1990) and *Crampi* ('Cramp', 1992) – shows him to be a novelist and storyteller of very consider-able versatility. Mario Fortunato (b. 1956), author of a well-received collection of stories, *Luoghi naturali* ('Natural Places', 1988), then made an interesting move by tapping (he was not the only one to do so) what might become a rich vein in the future, that of immigrant literature, with his transcription of *Immigrato* ('Immigrant', 1990), the story of the Tunisian Salah Methnani. In fact, it is characteristic of the younger generation of Italian writers that they are alert to the complex political and cultural interrelations that now exist between Italy's different identities both beyond and within its borders, in a way that neither the national and regional concerns of neo-realism, nor the literary internationalism of a Calvino, could envisage. This particular sensi-bility, whose formation was crystallised by the events in Europe of 1989, is particularly apparent in writers of the calibre of Sandro Veronesi (b. 1959), particularly in his second novel, *Gli sfiorati* ('Glancing Blow', 1990), after *Per dove parte questo treno allegro*, ('Where This Happy Train Is Heading', 1988), and Susanna Tamaro (b. 1957) in the stories of *Per voce sola* ('For Solo Voice', 1990).

These writers of fiction have something in common with those tendencies in late 1970s and 1980s poetry which have aligned themselves against the lyric, thought of primarily as a dominance of the subjective, and in favour of what has sometimes been called an 'allegorical' (as opposed to symbolic) writing, one in which the otherness of the poetic discourse is stressed without there being a necessary logical or psychological ('symbolic') relation between the elements involved. The lessons of Cagnone, Lumelli and Luigi Ballerini (b. 1940), as well as much older masters such as Edoardo Cacciatore (b. 1912) and Emilio Villa (b. 1914), are not lost on a younger generation of poets, particularly those who constituted themselves (in the late 1980s) as the 'Gruppo 93'. These writers are both profoundly hostile to what is seen as the overheated self-exaltation of the 'parola innamorata' poets, and committed to the presence of thought in poetry.

Somewhere amongst these names, and amongst the many more which there has not been space to mention, are those with which the literary history of the next decade, and the next century, will begin.

Bibliography

The following bibliographies are intended as a guide to the principal primary and secondary sources which readers may wish to consult in connection with the various chapters. For reasons of space they are highly selective and are not intended to provide the detail and precision of specialist bibliographies such as are indicated in the General Introductory Bibliography which follows, and to which readers requiring more detailed information are referred. The structure of the whole and the arrangement of entries are aimed to take account of the span and diversity of the material and to simplify as far as possible the reader's task in searching for the relevant volumes.

General

Listed below are some of the most up-to-date histories, dictionaries and manuals of Italian literature along with reference works useful for Italian, and an indication of those periodicals which provide bibliographical surveys:

Bibliographical studies

Cudini, Piero (ed.), *Letteratura italiana*, Milan, 1988.
Pasquini, Emilio (ed.), *Guida allo studio della letteratura italiana*, Bologna, 1985.
Puppo, Mario and Baroni, Giorgio, *Manuale critico bibliografico per lo studio della letteratura italiana*, 4th edn, 1994.

Periodicals etc. with bibliographical reviews of Italian literature

The Year's Work in Modern Language Studies, London, Modern Humanities Research Association (annual).
MLA International Bibliography of Books and Articles on the Modern Languages and Literatures, New York, Modern Language Association of America (annual); available on CD-Rom through Silver Platter; on line through OCLC FirstSearch.
Rassegna della letteratura italiana.
Studi e problemi di critica testuale.

Reference works

Bondanella, Peter and Bondanella, Julia Conway (eds.), *The Macmillan Dictionary of Italian Literature*, London, 1979.

Bonora, Ettore (ed.), *Dizionario della letteratura italiana*, 2 vols., Milan, 1977.

Branca, Vittore (ed.), *Dizionario critico della letteratura italiana*, 4 vols., Turin, 1986.

Contini, Gianfranco, *Schedario di scrittori italiani moderni e contemporanei*, Florence, 1978.

Cosenza, Mario E., *Biographical and Bibliographical Dictionary of the Italian Humanists and of the World of Classical Scholarship in Italy 1300–1800*, Boston, MA, 1962.

Dizionario biografico degli italiani, Rome, 1960 (in progress). (DBI)

Migliorini, Bruno, *Cronologia della lingua italiana*, Florence, 1975 (essential dates in literature and language).

Petronio, Giuseppe (ed.), *Dizionario enciclopedico della letteratura italiana*, 6 vols., Bari–Rome, 1966–70.

Russell, Rinaldina (ed.), *Italian Women Writers: A Bio-Bibliographical Sourcebook*, Westport, CT–London, 1994.

Bio-bibliographical dictionaries of Italian writers are included in the Histories of Italian Literature edited by Asor Rosa, Barberi Squarotti, and Cecchi and Sapegno listed in the section below.

Recent histories of Italian literature

Asor Rosa, Alberto (ed.), *Letteratura italiana*, 10 vols., Turin, Einaudi, 1982–90.

Balduino, Armando (ed.), *Storia letteraria d'Italia*, Padua, Piccin, 1991–3 (completely revised edition of *Storia letteraria*, formerly published by Vallardi).

Barberi Squarotti, Giorgio (ed.), *Storia della civiltà letteraria italiana*, 6 vols., Turin, UTET, 1990–5.

Cecchi, Emilio and Sapegno, Natalino (eds.), *Storia della letteratura italiana*, 9 vols., Milan, Garzanti, 1987.

Ceserani, Remo and De Federicis, Lidia, *Il materiale e l'immaginario*, 5 vols., Turin, Loescher, 1991–3.

Ferroni, Giulio, *Storia della letteratura italiana*, 4 vols., Turin, Einaudi, 1991.

Letteratura italiana Zanichelli, ed. P. Stoppelli and E. Picchi, Bologna, Zanichelli, 1993 (CD-Rom anthology of major authors to 1900, with search tools).

Muscetta, Carlo (ed.), *La letteratura italiana. Storia e testi*, 10 vols., Rome–Bari, Laterza, 1970–80.

Prosody and metrics

Borromeo, Beatrice, 'Storia della metrica e storia della poesia. Rassegna di studi', *Lettere italiane* 47 (1995) 290–311 (extensive bibliography of recent studies).

Elwert, W. Theodor, *Versificazione italiana dalle origini ai nostri giorni*, Florence, 1973.

Orlando, Sandro, *Manuale di metrica italiana*, Milan, 1994.

Pazzaglia, Mario, *Manuale di metrica italiana*, Bologna, 1991.

ORIGINS AND DUECENTO

Texts

ANTHOLOGIES

Arese, Felice (ed.), *Prose di romanzi*, Turin, 1976.
Castellani, Arrigo (ed.), *I più antichi testi italiani*, 2nd edn, Bologna, 1976.
Contini, Gianfranco (ed.), *Poeti del Duecento*, 2 vols., Milan–Naples, 1960 (best anthology and commentary for poetry).
Dionisotti, Carlo and Grayson, Cecil (eds.), *Early Italian Texts*, 2nd edn, Oxford, 1965.
Marti, Mario (ed.), *Poeti del Dolce stil novo*, Florence, 1969.
Marti, Mario (ed.), *Poeti giocosi del tempo di Dante*, Milan, 1956.
Monaci, Ernesto (ed.), *Crestomazia italiana dei primi secoli*, Rome–Naples, 1955 (new edn by Felice Arese).
Monteverdi, Angelo (ed.), *Testi volgari italiani dei primi tempi*, Modena, 1941.
Panvini, Bruno (ed.), *Poeti italiani della corte di Federico II*, Catania, 1989.
Segre, Cesare and Marti, Mario (eds.), *La prosa del Duecento*, Milan–Naples, 1959 (best anthology and commentary for prose).
Ulivi, Ferruccio and Savini, Marta (eds.), *Poesia religiosa italiana dalle origini al '900*, Casale Monferrato, 1994.
Varanini, Giorgio and Baldassari, Guido (eds.), *Racconti esemplari del Due e Trecento*, Rome, 1993.
Viscardi, Antonio, Nardi, Bruno *et al.* (eds.), *Le origini: Testi latini, italiani, provenzali e franco-italiani*, Milan–Naples, 1956.
Vitale, Maurizio (ed.), *Rimatori comico-realistici del Due e Trecento*, Turin, 1976.

INDIVIDUAL AUTHORS

Bonvesin de la Riva, *Opere volgari*, ed. G. Contini, Rome, 1941.
Cavalcanti, Guido, *Rime*, ed. D. De Robertis, Turin, 1986.
Cavalcanti, Guido, *Rime*, ed. L. Cassata, Anzio, 1993.
Cino da Pistoia, *Rime*, ed. G. Zaccagnini, Pistoia, 1936.
Conti di antichi cavalieri, ed. A. Del Monte, in *Studi mediolatini e volgari* 10 (1962) 161–207.
Faba, Guido, *Gemma purpurea*, in A. Castellani, 'Le formule volgari di Guido Faba', *Studi di filologia italiana* 13 (1955) 5–78.
Fiore e Detto d'amore, ed. G. Contini, Milan, 1984.
Fiori e vita di filosafi ed altri savi ed imperatori, ed. A. D'Agostino, Florence, 1979.
Francesco d'Assisi (St Francis), *Gli scritti e la leggenda*, ed. G. Petrocchi and I. Di Guardo, Milan, 1983.
Giacomo da Lentini, *Poesie*, ed. R. Antonelli, Rome, 1979.
Giamboni, Bono, *Libro de' vizi e delle virtudi e Trattato di virtù e di vizi*, ed. C. Segre, Turin, 1968.
Giovanni da Vignano, *Flore de parlare*, in C. Frati, 'Flore de parlare o Somma d'arengare attribuita a ser Giovanni Fiorentino da Vignano in un codice marciano', *Giornale storico della letteratura italiana* 61 (1913), 1–31, 228–65.
Guinizzelli, Guido, *Poesie*, ed. E. Sanguineti, Milan, 1986.
Guittone d'Arezzo, *Rime*, ed. F. Egidi, Bari, 1940

Jacopone da Todi, *Laude*, ed. F. Mancini, Bari, 1974.
Latini, Brunetto, *Li livres dou Tresor*, ed. F. J. Carmody, Berkeley–Los Angeles, 1948.
   Rettorica, ed. F. Maggini, Florence, 1915.
   Tesoretto, ed. M. Ciccuto, Milan, 1985.
Novellino, ed. G. Favati, Genoa, 1970.
Onesto da Bologna, *Rime*, ed. S. Orlando, Florence, 1974.
Polo, Marco, *Milione*, ed. V. Bertolucci Pizzorusso, Milan, 1975.
Ristoro d'Arezzo, *Composizione del mondo colle sue cascioni*, ed. A. Morino, Florence, 1976.
Rustico di Filippo, *Sonetti*, ed. P. V. Mengaldo, Turin, 1971.
Sordello, *Poesie*, ed. M. Boni, Bologna, 1954.

TEXTS IN ENGLISH TRANSLATION

Guido Cavalcanti, *Complete Poems*, trans. M. A. Cirigliano, New York, 1992.
Novellino, trans. E. Storer, London, 1925.
Marco Polo, *Travels*, trans. A. Ricci, London, 1931.

Studies

GENERAL, INCLUDING LANGUAGE

Battaglia, Salvatore, *La coscienza letteraria del Medioevo*, Naples, 1965.
Bruni, Francesco, *L'Italiano. Elementi di storia della lingua e della cultura*, Turin, 1984.
Dardano, Maurizio, *Lingua e tecnica narrativa nel Duecento*, Rome, 1969.
Devoto, Giacomo, *Profilo di storia linguistica italiana*, Florence, 1953.
Dronke, Peter, *The Medieval Lyric*, New York, 1969.
Kleinhenz, Christopher, *The Early Italian Sonnet*, Lecce, 1986.
Migliorini, Bruno, *Storia della lingua italiana*, Florence, 1960 (trans. and abridged by T. G. Griffith as *History of the Italian Language*, London, 1966).
Schiaffini, Alfredo, *Tradizione e poesia nella prosa d'arte italiana dalla latinità medievale a G. Boccaccio*, Rome, 1943.
Segre, Cesare, *Lingua stile e società. Studi sulla storia della prosa italiana*, Milan, 1963.
Storey, H. Wayne, *Transcription and Visual Poetics in the Early Italian Lyric*, New York–London, 1993.
Tagliavini, Carlo, *Le origini delle lingue neolatine*, 4th edn, Bologna, 1964.

Individual authors and topics

OCCITAN INFLUENCE

Bertoni, Giulio, *I trovatori d'Italia*, Modena, 1915.
Crescini, Vincenzo, 'Il discordo plurilingue di Rambaldo di Vaqueiras', *Nuovi studi medievali* 1 (1923) 73–106.
Ugolini, Francesco, *La poesia provenzale in Italia*, 2nd edn, Modena, 1949.
Viscardi, Antonio, *Problemi e orientamenti critici di lingua e di letteratura italiana*, vol. 4, Milan, 1948, pp. 1–39.

SICILIANS

Folena, Gianfranco, 'Siciliani', in *Dizionario critico della letteratura italiana*, vol. 3, ed. V. Branca, 2nd edn., Turin, 1986

Marti, Mario, 'Iacopo da Lentini', *Enciclopedia dantesca*, vol. 3, pp. 334–6.

Quaglio, Antonio Enzo, 'I poeti della "Magna Curia" siciliana', in *Letteratura italiana. Storia e testi*, vol. 1/1, Bari, 1970, pp. 171–240.

Santangelo, Salvatore, *Il volgare illustre e la poesia siciliana del secolo XIII*, Palermo, 1923.

Schiaffini, Alfredo, *Momenti di storia della lingua italiana*, 2nd edn, Rome, 1953, pp. 7–42.

SICULO-TUSCANS AND GUITTONE

Folena, Gianfranco, 'Cultura poetica dei primi Fiorentini', *Giornale storico della letteratura italiana* 147 (1970) 1–42.

Margueron, Claude, *Recherches sur Guittone d'Arezzo*, Paris, 1966.

Marti, Mario, 'Guittone d'Arezzo', in *Dizionario critico della letteratura italiana*, ed. V. Branca, vol. 2, Turin, 2nd edn, 1986.

Moleta, Vincent, *The Early Poetry of Guittone d'Arezzo*, London, 1976.

Schiaffini, Alfredo, *Tradizione e poesia nella prosa d'arte italiana*, Rome, 1943, pp. 39–70 (for Guittone's epistolary).

STILNOVO

Bertelli, Italo, *La poesia di Guido Guinizzelli e la poetica del 'Dolce Stil Nuovo'*, Florence, 1983.

Corti, Maria, *La felicità mentale. Nuove prospettive per Cavalcanti e Dante*, Turin, 1993.

Favati, Guido, *Inchiesta sul Dolce Stil Nuovo*, Florence, 1975.

Gorni, Guglielmo, *Il nodo della lingua e il verbo d'amore*, Florence, 1981.

Marti, Mario, *Storia dello Stil Nuovo*, Lecce, 1973.

Moleta, Vincent, *Guinizzelli in Dante*, Rome, 1980.

Nardi, Bruno, 'Filosofia dell'amore nei rimatori italiani del Duecento e in Dante', in *Dante e la cultura medievale. Nuovi saggi di filosofia dantesca*, 2nd edn, Bari, 1949, pp. 1–92.

Pertile, Lino, 'Il nodo di Bonagiunta, le penne di Dante e il Dolce Stil Novo'. *Lettere Italiane* 46 (1994) 44–75.

Shaw, James E., *Guido Cavalcanti's Theory of Love*, Toronto, 1949.

PROSE

Battaglia Ricci, Lucia, 'Introduction', in *Novelle italiane: Il Duecento. Il Trecento*, Milan, 1982, pp. xix–xxix.

Branca, Daniela, *I romanzi italiani di Tristano e la Tavola Rotonda*, Florence, 1968.

D'Ancona, Alessandro, *Studi di critica e storia letteraria*, 2nd edn, vol. 2, Bologna, 1912, pp. 1–163.

Del Monte, Alberto, 'La fisionomia dei "Conti di antichi cavalieri" ', in *Romania: Scritti offerti a F. Piccolo*, Naples, 1962, pp. 251–70.

Di Francia, Letterio, *La novellistica*, vol. 1, Milan, 1924.

Genot, Gérard and Larivaille, Paul, *Etude du Novellino*, vol. 1, *Répertoire des structures*, Nanterre, 1987.

Hall, Joan, ' "Bel parlare" and Authorial Narration in the *Novellino*', *Italian Studies* 44 (1989), 1–18.

Monteverdi, Angelo, *Studi e saggi sulla letteratura italiana dei primi secoli*, Milan–Naples, 1954, pp. 127–65.

Segre, Cesare, 'Le forme e le tradizioni didattiche', in *La littérature didactique allégorique et satyrique*, ed. H. R. Jauss, Heidelberg, 1968, pp. 58–145.

Segre, Cesare, 'Sull'ordine delle novelle nel "Novellino" ' in *Miscellanea di studi in onore di Vittore Branca*, vol. 1, *Dal Medioevo al Petrarca*, Florence, 1983, pp. 129–39.

TRECENTO

Dante

Texts

Vita Nuova, ed. D. De Robertis; *Rime, Il Fiore e Il Detto d'Amore*, ed. G. Contini, in *Opere minori*, 1/1, Milan–Naples, 1984.

De vulgari eloquentia, ed. P. V. Mengaldo; *Monarchia*, ed. B. Nardi; *Epistole*, ed. A. Frugoni and G. Brugnoli; *Egloge*, ed. E. Cecchini; *Questio de aqua et terra*, ed. F. Mazzoni, in *Opere minori*, vol. 2, Milan–Naples, 1979.

Convivio, ed. C. Vasoli and D. De Robertis, in *Opere minori*, 1/2, Milan–Naples, 1988.

La Commedia secondo l'antica vulgata, ed. G. Petrocchi, 4 vols., Florence, 1994.

TEXTS IN TRANSLATION

Vita Nuova, trans. B. Reynolds, Penguin Classics, Harmondsworth, 1969; trans. M. Musa, Oxford, 1992.

Rime, text and trans. by K. Foster and P. Boyde, *Dante's Lyric Poetry*, 2 vols., Oxford, 1967.

Convivio, trans. C. Ryan as *The Banquet*, Saratoga, Cal., 1989; trans. R. Lansing, *Dante's 'Il Convivio'*, New York, 1990.

De vulgari eloquentia, ed. and trans. S. Botterill, Cambridge, 1996; trans. S. Purcell as *Literature in the Vernacular*, Manchester, 1981.

Monarchia, text and trans. by P. Shaw, Cambridge, 1995.

Epistole, text and trans. by P. Toynbee, 2nd edn, Oxford, 1966.

Commedia, text, trans. and commentary by J. D. Sinclair, 3 vols., Oxford, 1946; Ch. S. Singleton, 6 vols., Princeton, NJ, 1970–5. Trans. and commentary by M. Musa, 3 vols., Penguin Classics, Harmondsworth, 1984–6.

Studies

GENERAL

Enciclopedia dantesca, 6 vols., ed. U. Bosco, Rome, 1970–8.

The Cambridge Companion to Dante, ed. R. Jacoff, Cambridge, 1993.

Dante: An Encyclopaedia, ed. R. Lansing, New York (2000)

DANTE'S LIFE

Barbi, Michele, *Life of Dante*, trans. P. Ruggiers, Los Angeles, 1960.

Padoan, Giorgio, *Introduzione a Dante*, Florence, 1975.

Petrocchi, Giorgio, *Vita di Dante*, Bari, 1989.

MINOR WORKS

Took, John F., *Dante, Lyric Poet and Philosopher: An Introduction to the Minor Works*, Oxford, 1990.

FIORE

Barański, Z. G., Boyde, P. and Pertile, L. (eds.), *Lettura del 'Fiore'*, Letture Classensi 22, Ravenna, 1993.

VITA NUOVA

Branca, Vittore, 'Poetics of Renewal and Hagiography Tradition in the *Vita nuova*', in *Lectura Dantis Newberriana*, ed. P. Cherchi and A. C. Mastrobuono, vol. 1 (1988) 123–52.

Picone, Michelangelo, *Vita nuova e tradizione romanza*, Padua, 1979.

Singleton, Charles S., *An Essay on the 'Vita Nuova'*, Cambridge, MA, 1949 and Baltimore, 1977.

RIME

Barolini, Teodolinda, 'Dante and the Lyric Past', in *The Cambridge Companion to Dante*, pp. 14–33.

Boyde, Patrick, *Dante's Style in his Lyric Poetry*, Cambridge, 1971.

Durling, Robert M. and Martinez, Ronald L., *Time and the Crystal: Studies in Dante's 'Rime petrose'*, Berkeley, CA, 1990.

CONVIVIO AND DE VULGARI ELOQUENTIA

Barański, Zygmunt G., 'Dante's Biblical Linguistics', *Lectura Dantis* 5 (1989) 105–43.

Corti, Maria, *La felicità mentale. Nuove prospettive per Cavalcanti e Dante*, Turin, 1983.

Leo, Ulrich, 'The unfinished *Convivio* and Dante's Rereading of the *Aeneid*', *Medieval Studies* 13 (1951) 41–64.

Mengaldo, Pier Vincenzo, *Linguistica e retorica di Dante*, Pisa, 1978.

Shapiro, Marianne, *De vulgari eloquentia: Dante's Book of Exile*, Lincoln, NE, 1990.

MONARCHIA

Davis, Charles T., *Dante and the Idea of Rome*, Oxford, 1957.

Passerin d'Entrèves, Alessandro, *Dante as a Political Thinker*, Oxford, 1952.

COMMEDIA

Commentaries by:

Bosco, Umberto and Reggio, Giovanni, Florence, 1979.

Mattalia, Daniele, Milan, 1984.

Pasquini, Emilio and Quaglio, Antonio, Milan, 1982–6.

Sapegno, Natalino, Florence, 1985.

Chiavacci Leonardi, Anna Maria, Milan, 1991–7.

An electronic *concordance* to past and present commentaries is available on line in the *Dante Dartmouth Database*, ed. Robert Hollander.

General studies

Auerbach, Erich, *Dante, Poet of the Secular World* [1929], Chicago, 1961.
Barolini, Teodolinda, *The Undivine Comedy: Detheologizing Dante*, Princeton, NJ, 1992.
Boyde, Patrick, *Perception and Passion in Dante's Comedy*, Cambridge, 1993.
Contini, Gianfranco, *Un'idea di Dante*, Turin, 1976.
Croce, Benedetto, *The Poetry of Dante* [1921], trans. D. Ainslie, New York, 1922.
Foster, Kenelm, *The Two Dantes and Other Studies*, London, 1977.
Freccero, John, *Dante: The Poetics of Conversion*, ed. R. Jacoff, Cambridge, MA, 1986.
Gilson, Etienne, *Dante and Philosophy*, trans. D. Moore, New York, 1963.
Mazzotta, Giuseppe, *Dante's Vision and the Circle of Knowledge*, Princeton, NJ, 1993.
Nardi, Bruno, *Dante e la cultura medievale*, ed. P. Mazzacurati, Bari, 1983.
   Nel mondo di Dante, Rome, 1944.
Singleton, Charles S., *Dante Studies 1: Elements of Structure*, Cambridge, MA, 1954.
   Dante Studies 2: Journey to Beatrice, Cambridge, MA, 1958.

Particular aspects

Armour, Peter, *Dante's Griffin and the History of the World*, Oxford, 1989.
Auerbach, Erich, 'Figura', in *Scenes from the Drama of European Literature*, trans. R. Manheim, New York, 1959.
Barański, Zygmunt G., 'La Commedia', in *Manuale di letteratura italiana: storia per generi e problemi*, ed. F. Brioschi and C. Di Girolamo, vol. 1, Turin, 1993, pp. 492–560.
Boyde, Patrick, *Dante Philomythes and Philosopher: Man in the Cosmos*, Cambridge, 1981.
Chydenius, Johan, *The Typological Problem in Dante*, Helsingfors, 1958.
Davis, Charles T., *Dante's Italy and Other Essays*, Philadelphia, 1984.
Hollander, Robert, *Allegory in Dante's Commedia*, Princeton, NJ, 1969.
   Studies in Dante, Ravenna, 1980 (pp. 131–218 on Virgil).
Iannucci, Amilcare A. (ed.), *Dante e la 'bella scola' della poesia*, Ravenna, 1993.
Pertile, Lino, 'Dante's *Comedy* beyond the "Stilnovo"', *Lectura Dantis* 13 (1993) 47–77.
   '*Paradiso*: A Drama of Desire', in *Word and Drama in Dante*, ed. John C. Barnes and Jennifer Petrie, Dublin, 1993, pp. 143–80.
Picone, Michelangelo (ed.), *Dante e le forme dell'allegoresi*, Ravenna, 1987.
Scott, John A. *Dante's Political Purgatory*, Philadelphia, 1996.

LECTURAE (collections of individual readings of each of the 100 cantos):

Lectura Dantis scaligera, 3 vols., Florence, 1967–8.
Nuove letture dantesche, 8 vols., Florence, 1966–76.
Wlassics, Tibor (ed.), *Lectura Dantis Virginiana: Introductory Readings*, 3 vols, Charlottesville, VA, 1990–5.

PERIODICALS entirely devoted to Dante studies:

Studi danteschi
Dante Studies
Lectura Dantis
L'Alighieri

Boccaccio

Texts

Tutte le opere di Giovanni Boccaccio, general ed. V. Branca, 10 vols. (vols. 7–8 still to appear), Milan, 1964– .
Corbaccio, ed. P. G. Ricci, Turin, 1977.
Decameron, ed. and intro. V. Branca, 6th edn, Turin, 1991 (contains an extensive and up-to-date bibliography; the text of the *Decameron* reproduces Branca's 1976 critical edition based on the Hamilton 90 holograph).
Elegia di madonna Fiammetta, in *Opere di Giovanni Boccaccio*, ed. C. Segre, Milan, 1963.
Genealogie deorum gentilium, ed. V. Romano, 2 vols., Bari, 1951.

TEXTS IN TRANSLATION

L'Ameto (Comedia delle ninfe fiorentine), trans. J. Serafini-Sauli, New York–London, 1985.
Amorosa visione, trans. R. Hollander, T. Hampton, M. Frankel, intro. V. Branca, Hanover–London, 1986.
Boccaccio on Poetry: Being the Preface and Fourteenth and Fifteenth books of Boccaccio's 'Genealogia deorum gentilium', trans., ed. and intro. C. G. Osgood, Princeton, NJ, 1930; rpt Indianapolis, 1956.
Concerning Famous Women, trans. and intro. G. A. Guarino, Rutgers, NJ, 1963.
The Corbaccio, trans., ed. and intro. A. K. Cassell, Urbana–Chicago–London, 1975.
The Decameron, trans. and intro. G. H. McWilliam, Penguin Classics, Harmonds-worth, 1995.
Diana's Hunt, ed., trans. and intro. A. K. Cassell and V. Kirkham, Philadelphia, 1991.
The Eclogues, trans and intro. J. Levarie Smarr, New York–London, 1987.
The Elegy of Lady Fiammetta, trans. and ed. M. Causa-Steidler and T. Mauch; intro. M. Causa-Steidler, Chicago, 1990.
The Fates of Illustrious Men, trans. and abridged L. Brewer Hall, New York, 1965.
Il Filocolo, trans. D. Cheney with T. G. Bergin, New York–London, 1985.
Il Filostrato, trans. R. P. apRoberts and A. B. Seldis, New York–London, 1986.
Nymphs of Fiesole (Ninfale fiesolano), trans. J. Tusiani, Rutherford, NJ, 1971.
The Book of Theseus (Teseida), trans. B. M. McCoy, Sea Cliff, NY, 1974.
Life of Dante (Trattatello in laude di Dante), trans. V. Z. Bollettino, New York–London, 1990.

Studies

GENERAL

Billanovich, Giuseppe, *Restauri boccacceschi*, Rome, 1945.
Branca, Vittore, 'Giovanni Boccaccio rinnovatore dei generi letterari', in *Atti del Convegno di Nimega*, ed. C. Ballerini, Bologna, 1976, pp. 13–35.
  Boccaccio medievale e nuovi studi sul 'Decameron', 7th edn, Florence, 1991.
  Boccaccio: The Man and his Work, trans. R. Monges and D. J. McAuliffe, New York, 1976.
Hollander, Robert, *Boccaccio's Two Venuses*, New York, 1977.

Kirkham, Victoria, *The Sign of Reason in Boccaccio's Fiction*, Florence, 1993.
Muscetta, Carlo, *Giovanni Boccaccio*, Bari, 1972.
Padoan, Giorgio, *Il Boccaccio, le Muse, il Parnaso e l'Arno*, Florence, 1978.
Smarr, Janet Levarie, *Boccaccio and Fiammetta: The Narrator as Lover*, Urbana–Chicago, 1986.
Studi sul Boccaccio, a periodical, directed by V. Branca and founded by him in 1963, entirely devoted to the study of Boccaccio.

DECAMERON

Almansi, Guido, *The Writer as Liar: Narrative Technique in the 'Decameron'*, London–Boston, 1975.
Asor Rosa, Alberto, '*Decameron* di Giovanni Boccaccio', in Asor Rosa, vol. 1, pp. 473–591 (see p. 608).
Auerbach, Erich, 'Frate Alberto', in *Mimesis*, trans. W. Trask, Garden City, NY, 1957, pp. 177–203.
Baratto, Mario, *Realtà e stile nel 'Decameron'*, Vicenza, 1970.
Barbina, Alfredo (ed.), *Concordanze del 'Decameron'*, 2 vols., Florence, 1969.
Bosco, Umberto, *Il 'Decameron'*, Rieti, 1929.
Cottino-Jones, Marga, *Order from Chaos: Social and Aesthetic Harmonies in Boccaccio's 'Decameron'*, Washington, DC, 1982.
D'Andrea, Antonio, *Il nome della storia*, Naples, 1982, pp. 86–134.
Strutture inquiete, Florence, 1993, 127–45.
Fido, Franco, *Il regime delle simmetrie imperfette*, Milan, 1988.
Getto, Giovanni, *Vita di forme e forme di vita nel 'Decameron'*, 1957; new edn Turin, 1986.
Lee, Alfred Collingwood, *The 'Decameron': its Sources and Analogues*, 1909; rprt Haverston, PA, 1973.
Marcus, Millicent Joy, *An Allegory of Form*, Saratoga, CA, 1979.
Mazzotta, Giuseppe, *The World at Play in Boccaccio's 'Decameron'*, Princeton, NJ, 1986.
Neri, Ferdinando, *Storia e poesia*, Turin, 1936, pp. 53–60.
O'Cuilleanáin, Cormac, *Religion and the Clergy in Boccaccio's 'Decameron'*, Rome, 1984.
Stewart, Pamela D., *Retorica e mimica nel 'Decameron' e nella commedia del Cinquecento*, Florence, 1986.
'Narrazione e ideologia nella novella di Melchisedech', in *Omaggio a Gianfranco Folena*, ed. M. Cortelazzo and G. Peron, Padua, 1993.
Wallace, David, *Giovanni Boccaccio: 'Decameron'*, Cambridge, 1991.

MINOR WORKS

Grossvogel, Steven, *Ambiguity and Allusion in Boccaccio's 'Filocolo'*, Florence, 1992.
Hollander, Robert, *Boccaccio's Last Fiction: 'Il Corbaccio'*, Philadelphia, 1988.
McGregor, James H., *The Shades of Aeneas: The Imitation of Virgil and the History of Paganism in Boccaccio's 'Filostrato', 'Filocolo', and 'Teseida'*, Athens–London, 1991.

Padoan, Giorgio, 'Il *Corbaccio* tra spunti autobiografici e filtri letterari', *Revue des Études Italiennes* n.s. 37 (1991) 1–4, 21–37.

FORTUNE

Boitani, Piero (ed.), *Chaucer and the Italian Trecento*, 2nd edn, Cambridge, 1987.

Cole, Howard C., *The 'All's Well' Story from Boccaccio to Shakespeare*, Urbana–Chicago, 1981.

Cummings, Hubertis Maurice, *The Indebtedness of Chaucer's Work to the Italian Works of Boccaccio: A Review and Summary*, 1916; rprt New York, 1965.

Stewart, Pamela, D., 'How to get to a happy ending: *Decameron* III 9 and Shakespeare's *All's Well*', *Studi sul Boccaccio* 20 (1991–2) 325–39.

Wright, Herbert Gladstone, *Boccaccio in England from Chaucer to Tennyson*, London, 1957.

Petrarch

Texts

Opera quae extant omnia, Basle, 1554 (repr. 1581).

Rime, trionfi e poesie latine, ed. F. Neri *et al.*, Milan–Naples, 1951.

Prose, ed. G. Martellotti *et al.*, Milan–Naples, 1955.

Opere latine, ed. A. Bufano, 2 vols., Turin, 1975.

Canzoniere, ed. G. Contini (with important introd. essay), Turin, 1964.

Africa, ed. N. Festa, Florence, 1926.

Bucolicum carmen (with facing Italian trans.), ed. T. Mattucci, Pisa, 1970.

Epistolae familiares, ed. V. Rossi and U. Bosco, 4 vols., Florence 1933–42.

Epistolae 'sine nomine', with Italian trans., ed. U. Dotti, Bari, 1974.

De viris illustribus, ed. G. Martellotti, Florence, 1964.

Rerum memorandarum libri, ed. G. Billanovich, Florence, 1943.

TEXTS IN TRANSLATION

Petrarch's Lyric Poems: the 'Rime sparse' and Other Lyrics, trans. and ed. R. M. Durling, Cambridge, MA, 1976.

The Triumphs of Petrarch, trans. E. H. Wilkins, Chicago, 1962.

Petrarch's 'Africa', trans. T. G. Bergin and A. S. Wilson, New Haven and London, 1977.

Bucolicum carmen, trans. T. G. Bergin, New Haven and London, 1974.

Petrarch's Secret, or The Soul's Conflict with Passion, trans. W. H. Draper, London, 1911.

The Life of Solitude, trans. J. Zeitlin, Urbana, IL, 1924.

Letters on Familiar Matters I–VIII, trans. A. S. Bernardo, New York, 1975; *IX–XVI*, Baltimore and London, 1982.

De remediis, trans. C. H. Rawski, Bloomington, IN, 1991; *Four Dialogues for Scholars*, trans. C. H. Rawski, Cleveland, OH, 1967.

The Renaissance Philosophy of Man, ed. E. Cassirer *et al.*, Chicago, 1948 (trans. by H. Nachod of *De suis ipsius*).

Selections from the 'Canzoniere' and Other Works, trans. M. Musa, Oxford, 1985 (contains trans. of *Posteritati* and Mont Ventoux letter).

Studies

GENERAL

Amaturo, Raffaele, *Petrarca*, in the series Letteratura italiana Laterza, Bari, 1971.
Bergin, Thomas G., *Petrarch*, New York, 1970.
Bloom, Harold (ed. and intro.), *Petrarch* (Modern Critical Views series), New York, 1988.
Bosco, Umberto, *Francesco Petrarca*, 3rd edn, Bari, 1965.
Dotti, Ugo, *Vita di Petrarca*, Bari, 1987.
Foster, Kenelm, *Petrarch: Poet and Humanist*, Edinburgh, 1984 (rprt 1987).
Mann, Nicholas, *Petrarch* (Oxford Past Masters series), Oxford, 1984 (rprt 1987).
Mazzotta, Giuseppe, *The Worlds of Petrarch*, Durham and London, 1993.
Quaglio, Antonio E., *Francesco Petrarca*, Milan, 1967.
Sapegno, Natalino, *Storia della letteratura italiana*, vol. 2, Milan, 1965, pp. 187–313.
Scaglione, Aldo (ed.), *Francis Petrarch Six Centuries Later*, Chapel Hill, NC, 1975.
Whitfield, John H., *Petrarch and the Renascence*, Oxford, 1943.
Wilkins, Ernest H., *Life of Petrarch*, Chicago, 1961.
    Studies in the Life and Works of Petrarch, Cambridge, MA, 1955.

VERNACULAR WORKS

Barberi Squarotti, Giorgio, 'Le poetiche del Trecento in Italia', in *Momenti e problemi di storia dell'estetica. Parte prima. Dall'antichità classica al barocco*, vol. 5, Milan, 1959, pp. 255–324.
Bernardo, Aldo S., *Petrarch, Laura, and the Triumphs*, Albany, NY, 1974.
Billanovich, Giuseppe, 'Tra Dante e Petrarca', *Italia medioevale e umanistica* 8 (1965) 1–45.
Durling, Robert M., 'Petrarch', in *The Figure of the Poet in Renaissance Epic*, Cambridge, MA, 1965, pp. 67–87.
Eisenbichler, K. and Iannucci, A. A. (eds.), *Petrarch's 'Triumphs': Allegory and Spectacle*, University of Toronto Italian Studies 4, Ottawa, 1990.
Foster, Kenelm, 'Beatrice or Medusa: The Penitential Element in Petrarch's *Canzoniere*', in *Italian Studies presented to E. R. Vincent*, ed. C. P. Brand and U. Limentani, Cambridge, 1962, pp. 41–56.
Hainsworth, Peter, 'The Myth of Apollo and Daphne in the *Rerum vulgarium fragmenta*', *Italian Studies* 34 (1979) 28–44.
    Petrarch the Poet: An Introduction to the 'Rerum vulgarium fragmenta', London–New York, 1988.
Jones, Frederick J., 'Laura's Date of Birth and the Calendrical System Implicit in the *Canzoniere*', *Italianistica* 1 (1983) 13–33.
    'Arguments in Favour of a Calendrical Structure for Petrarch's *Canzoniere*', *Modern Language Review* 79 (1984) 579–88.
Petrie, Jennifer, *Petrarch: The Italian Tradition and the 'Canzoniere'*, Dublin, 1983.
Rico, Francisco, ' "Rime sparse", "Rerum Vulgarium Fragmenta". Para el título y el primer soneto del "Canzoniere" ', *Medioevo romanzo* 3 (1976) 101–38.

Roche, Thomas P., Jr, 'The Calendrical Structure of Petrarch's *Canzoniere*', *Studies in Philology* 71 (1974) 152–72.

Santagata, Marco, *I frammenti dell'anima: storia e racconto nel 'Canzoniere' di Petrarca*, Bologna, 1992.

Sturm-Maddox, Sarah, 'Petrarch's Siren: "dolce parlar" and "dolce canto" in the *Rime sparse*', *Italian Quarterly* 27 (1986) 5–19.

Waller, Margaret, *Petrarch's Poetics and Literary History*, Amherst, MA, 1980.

Wilkins, Ernest H., *The Making of the 'Canzoniere' and other Petrarchan Studies*, Rome, 1951.

LATIN WORKS AND HUMANISM

Baron, Hans, *From Petrarch to Leonardo Bruni*, Chicago, 1968.

'Petrarch: His Inner Struggles and the Humanistic Discovery of Man's Nature', in *Florilegium Historiale. Essays presented to W. K. Ferguson*, Toronto, 1971, pp. 18–51.

Billanovich, Giuseppe, *Petrarca letterato. I. Lo scrittoio del Petrarca*, Rome, 1947.

Bouwsma, W. J., 'The Two Faces of Humanism. Stoicism and Augustinianism in Renaissance Thought', in *Itinerarium Italicum. The Profile of the Italian Renaissance in the Mirror of its European Transformations*, ed. H. A. Oberman *et al.*, Leiden, 1975, pp. 3–60.

De Nolhac, Pierre, *Pétrarque et l'humanisme*, 2nd edn, Paris, 1907.

Durling, Robert M., 'The Ascent of Mt. Ventoux and the Crisis of Allegory', *Italian Quarterly* 18 (1974) 7–28.

Kristeller, Paul O., 'Petrarch's Averroists', *Bibliothèque d'Humanisme et Renaissance* 14 (1952) 59–65.

Eight Philosophers of the Italian Renaissance, Stanford, CA, 1966.

Rico, Francisco, *Vida u obra de Petrarca. I. Lectura del 'Secretum'*, Padua, 1974.

Seigel, Jerrold E., *Rhetoric and Philosophy in Renaissance Humanism. The Union of Eloquence and Wisdom. Petrarch to Valla*, Princeton, NJ, 1968.

'Eloquence and Silence in Petrarch', *Journal of the History of Ideas* 26 (1965) 147–74.

Trinkhaus, Charles, *Petrarch and the Formation of Renaissance Consciousness*, New Haven–London, 1979.

Tripet, Arnaut, *Pétrarque ou la connaissance de soi*, Geneva, 1967.

Ullmann, B. L., 'Petrarch's Favourite Books', in *Studies in the Italian Renaissance*, 2nd edn, Rome, 1973, pp. 113–33.

Weiss, Roberto, *The Spread of Italian Humanism*, London, 1964.

Minor writers of the Trecento

General studies

Asor Rosa, vol. 1 (see above, p. 608).

Getto, Giovanni, *Letteratura religiosa del Trecento*, Florence, 1967.

Muscetta, Carlo and Tartaro, Achille (eds.), *Il Trecento: dalla crisi dell'età comunale all'Umanesimo*, 2 vols., Bari, 1971.

Sapegno, Natalino, *Storia letteraria del Trecento*, Milan and Naples, 1963.

Tartaro, Achille, *Forme poetiche del Trecento*, Bari, 1971.

Varanini, Giorgio, *Lingua e letteratura italiana dei primi secoli*, 2 vols., Pisa, 1994.

Verse

TEXTS

The Age of Dante: An Anthology of Early Italian Poetry, ed. J. Tusiani, New York, 1974.
Cantari del Trecento, ed. A. Balduino, Milan, 1970.
Poemi cavallereschi del Trecento, ed. G. G. Ferrero, Turin, 1965.
Poesia italiana: il Trecento, ed. P. Cudini, Milan, 1978.
Poeti giocosi del tempo di Dante, ed. M. Marti, Milan, 1956.
Poeti minori del Trecento, ed. N. Sapegno, Milan and Naples, 1952.
Rimatori del Trecento, ed. G. Corsi, Turin, 1969.

STUDIES

Botterill, Steven, 'Autobiography and artifice in the medieval lyric: the case of Cecco Nuccoli', *Italian Studies* 46 (1991) 35–57.
Petrocchi, Giorgio, *Scrittori religiosi del Trecento*, Florence, 1974.
Picone, Michelangelo and Bendinelli Predelli, Maria (eds.), *I cantari: struttura e tradizione*, Florence, 1984.

Prose

TEXTS

Anthologies

Mistici del Duecento e del Trecento, ed. A. Levasti, 2nd edn, Milan–Rome, 1960.
Novelle italiane, I: Il Due–Trecento, ed. L. Battaglia Ricci, Milan, 1982.
Prosatori italiani del Trecento, I: Scrittori di religione, ed. G. De Luca, Milan–Naples, 1954.
Prose di romanzi: il romanzo cortese in Italia nei secoli XIII e XIV, ed. F. Arese, Turin, 1962.
Volgarizzamenti del Due e Trecento, ed. C. Segre, Turin, 1964.

History

Compagni, Dino, *Cronica*, ed. G. Luzzatto, Turin, 1968.
Dino Compagni's Chronicle of Florence, ed. D. E. Bornstein, Philadelphia, 1986.
Villani, Giovanni, *Cronica: con le continuazioni di Matteo e Filippo*, ed. G. Aquilecchia, Turin, 1979 (selection).
   Croniche di Giovanni, Matteo e Filippo Villani, Trieste, 1857–8 (complete).
Villani's Chronicle: Being Selections from the First Nine Books of the 'Croniche fiorentine', ed. R. Selfe and P. Wicksteed, London, 1906.

The novella

Il Pecorone, ed. E. Esposito, Ravenna, 1974.
Sacchetti, Franco, *Trecentonovelle*, ed. E. Faccioli, Turin, 1970.
   Opere, ed. A. Borlenghi, Milan, 1957.
Tales from Sacchetti, ed. M. Steegmann, London, 1908; Westport, CT, 1978.
Sercambi, Giovanni, *Novelle*, ed. G. Sinicropi, 2 vols., Bari, 1972.

Devotional literature

Catherine of Siena, *Dialogo della divina Provvidenza*, ed. A. Puccetti, Siena, 1980.
Il Libro, ed. U. Meattini, Alba, 1975.
Le lettere, ed. U. Meattini, Rome, 1987.
Le lettere di santa Caterina da Siena, ed. P. Misciattelli, 6 vols., Florence, 1939–47.
Libro della divina dottrina, ed. M. Fiorilli, Bari, 1928.
I, Catherine: selected writings of St. Catherine of Siena, ed. K. Foster and M. J. Ronayne, London, 1980.
Catherine of Siena, *The Dialogue*, trans. and ed. S. Noffke, New York, 1980.
The Letters of Catherine of Siena, ed. S. Noffke, Binghamton, NY, 1988–
The Prayers of Catherine of Siena, ed. S. Noffke, New York, 1983.
I Fioretti di S. Francesco, ed. G. Davico Bonino, Turin, 1983.

Dante commentaries

Alighieri, Jacopo, *Chiose all''Inferno'*, ed. S. Bellomo, Padua, 1990.
Alighieri, Pietro, *Il 'Commentarium' all''Inferno'*, ed. R. Della Vedova and M. T. Silvotti, Florence, 1978.
Petri Allegherii super Dantis ipsius genitoris Comoediam Commentarium, ed. V. Nannucci, Florence, 1845.
'Anonimo Fiorentino', *Commento alla 'Divina Commedia'*, ed. P. Fanfani, 3 vols., Bologna, 1866–74.
Le antiche chiose anonime all''Inferno' di Dante secondo il testo marciano, ed. G. Avalle, Città di Castello, 1900.
Barzizza, Guiniforte, *Lo 'Inferno' della 'Comedia' di Dante Alighieri*, ed. G. Zaccheroni, Marseille–Florence, 1838.
Benevenuto de Rambaldis de Imola, *Comentum super Dantis Aldigherii Comoediam*, ed. J. P. Lacaita, 5 vols., Florence, 1887.
Boccaccio, Giovanni, *Esposizioni sopra la 'Comedia' di Dante*, ed. G. Padoan, Verona, 1965.
Buti, Francesco da, *Commento sopra la 'Divina Commedia' di Dante Alighieri*, ed. C. Giannini, 3 vols., Pisa, 1858–62.
Chiose anonime alla prima cantica della 'Divina Commedia', ed. F. Selmi, Turin, 1865.
Le chiose cagliaritane, ed. E. Carrara, Città di Castello, 1902.
Chiose sopra Dante: testo inedito ('Falso Boccaccio'), Florence, 1846.
Giovanni Bertoldi da Serravalle, *Translatio et comentum totius libri Dantis Aldigherii*, ed. M. da Civezza and T. Domenichelli, Prato, 1891.
Jacopo, della Lana, *'Comedia' di Dante degli Allegherii col commento di Jacopo della Lana bolognese*, ed. L. Scarabelli, 3 vols., Bologna, 1866.
L'Ottimo Commento della 'Divina Commedia', ed. A. Torri, Pisa, 1827–9.

STUDIES

Botterill, Steven, 'The Trecento Commentaries on Dante's *Commedia*', in *The Cambridge History of Literary Criticism, II: The Middle Ages*, ed. A. J. Minnis, Cambridge, 1994.
Green, Louis, *Chronicle into History: An Essay on the Interpretation of History in Florentine Fourteenth-Century Chronicles*, Cambridge, 1972.

Jenaro-MacLennan, L., *The Trecento Commentators on the 'Divina Commedia' and the Epistle to Cangrande*, Oxford, 1974.

QUATTROCENTO

Humanism

TEXTS

Poeti latini del Quattrocento, ed. F. Arnaldi and L. Gualdo Rosa, Milan–Naples, 1964 (*PLQ*).
Prosatori latini del Quattrocento, ed. E. Garin, Milan–Naples, 1952 (*PrLQ*).
Renaissance Latin Verse: An Anthology, ed. A. Perosa and J. Sparrow, London, 1979.

STUDIES

See, in general, entries in Asor Rosa, *DBI* (see above p. 608).

Burke, Peter, *The Italian Renaissance: Culture and Society in Italy*, Cambridge, 1986.
Cassirer, Ernst, Kristeller, Paul O. and Randall, John H., *The Renaissance Philosophy of Man*, Chicago, 1948.
Cole, Alison, *Art of the Italian Renaissance Courts*, London, 1995.
Grafton, Anthony and Jardine, Lisa, *From Humanism to the Humanities*, Cambridge, MA, 1986.
Hankins, James, *Plato in the Italian Renaissance (Milan, Rome, Florence)*, vol. 1, Leiden, 1990.
Kohl, Benjamin and Witt, Ronald, *The Earthly Republic: Italian Humanists on Government and Society*, Manchester, 1978.
Kraye, Jill (ed.), *The Cambridge Companion to Renaissance Humanism*, Cambridge, 1996.
Kristeller, Paul O., *Renaissance Thought and its Sources*, New York, 1979.
Marsh, David, *The Quattrocento Dialogue*, Cambridge, MA, 1980.
Panizza, Letizia (ed.), *Philosophical and Scientific Poetry in the Renaissance* (*Renaissance Studies* 5, 1991).
Rabil, Albert (ed.), *Renaissance Humanism: Foundations, Forms, and Legacy*, 3 vols., Philadelphia, 1988.
Schmitt, Charles, Skinner, Quentin and Kessler, Eckhard, *The Cambridge History of Renaissance Philosophy*, Cambridge, 1988 (*CHRP*).

Education, libraries, translations

Copenhaver, Brian, 'Translation, terminology and style', in *CHRP*, pp. 77–110.
Garin, Eugenio (ed.), *Il pensiero pedagogico dell'Umanesimo*, Florence, 1958.
Grendler, Paul, *Schooling in Renaissance Italy: Literacy and Learning 1300–1600*, Baltimore, 1989.
Mercer, R. G. G., *The Teaching of Gasparino Barzizza*, London, 1979.
Reynolds, Leighton D. and Wilson, Nigel G., *Scribes and Scholars*, Oxford, 1991.
Ullman, Berthold, *The Origin and Development of Humanistic Script*, Rome, 1960.
Wilson, Nigel, *From Byzantium to Italy: Greek Studies in the Italian Renaissance*, London, 1992.

Humanist profiles

BRUNI, LEONARDO

Bruni, Leonardo, 'Panegyric to the City of Florence', in Kohl and Witt, *Earthly Republic*.
Baron, Hans, *From Petrarch to Leonardo Bruni*, Chicago, 1968.
Griffiths, G., Hankins, James and Witt, Ronald, *The Humanism of L. Bruni: Selected Texts* (English trans.), Binghamton, NY, 1987.

ALBERTI, LEON BATTISTA

Opere volgari, ed. C. Grayson, 3 vols, Bari, 1960–73.
I libri della famiglia, Turin, 1969 (trans. in Watkins, R. N., *The Family in Renaissance Florence*, Columbia, SC, 1969; also by Guarino, Guido, *The Albertis of Florence: L. B. Alberti's 'Della Famiglia'*, Lewisburg, NJ, 1971).
Marsh, David (ed. and trans.), *Leon Battista's Dinner Pieces: A Translation of the Intercenales*, Binghamton, NY, 1987.
Gadol, Joan, *L. B. Alberti: Universal Man of the Early Renaissance*, Chicago, 1969.
Robinson, Christopher, *Lucian and his Influence in Europe*, London, 1979.

VALLA, LORENZO

De vero falsoque bono, ed. M. Lorch, Bari, 1970 (English trans. with facing Latin by A. K. Hieatt and M. Lorch, *On Pleasure*, New York, 1977).
De libero arbitrio in *PLQ* (English trans. in Cassirer, Kristeller and Randall, *The Renaissance Philosophy of Man* (see above, p. 622).
The Treatise on the Donation of Constantine, trans. C. B. Coleman, New Haven, CT, 1922; reprint Toronto, 1971.
Lorch, Maristella, *A Defense of Life: Valla's Theory of Pleasure*, Munich, 1985.
Panizza, Letizia, 'L. Valla's *De vero falsoque bono*, Lactantius and Oratorical Scepticism', *Journal of the Warburg and Courtauld Institutes* 41 (1978) 76–107.
Trinkaus, Charles, *In Our Image and Likeness*, 2 vols., London, 1970.

WOMEN HUMANISTS

King, Margaret and Rabil, Albert (eds.), *Her Immaculate Hand. Selected Works by and about the Women Humanists of Quattrocento Italy*, Binghamton, NY, 1983.
King, Margaret, 'Book-lined Cells: Women and Humanism in the Early Italian Renaissance' in Rabil, *Renaissance Humanism* (see above, p. 622).
Kristeller, Paul O., 'Learned women of Early Modern Italy: Humanists and university scholars', in Labalme, P. (ed.), *Beyond their sex: Learned Women of the European Past*, New York, 1980.
Rabil, A., *Laura Cereta, Quattrocento Humanist*, Binghamton, NY, 1981.

Power, patronage and literary associations

See entries in Rabil, *Renaissance Humanism*, and Asor Rosa, (see p. 608) (particularly valuable for this section).

FLORENCE

Ames-Lewis, Frances (ed.), *Cosimo 'il Vecchio' de' Medici, 1389–1464*, Oxford, 1992.

Brucker, Gene, *Renaissance Florence*, Berkeley, 1983.
Field, Arthur, *The Origins of the Platonic Academy of Florence*, Princeton, NJ 1988.
Mallett, Michael and Mann, N., *Lorenzo the Magnificent*, London, 1966.
Martines, Lauro, *The Social World of the Florentine Humanists, 1390–1460*, London, 1963.

ROME

Piccolomini, Enea Silvio, *Commentarii* (Latin and Italian trans.), ed. L. Totaro, Milan, 1984.
   Memoirs of a Renaissance Pope. An Abridgement, trans. F. A. Gragg, London, 1960.
D'Amico, John F., *Renaissance Humanism in Papal Rome: Humanists and Churchmen on the Eve of the Reformation*, Baltimore, MD, 1983.
Stinger, Charles L., *The Renaissance in Rome: Ideology and Culture in the City of the Popes, 1443–1527*, Bloomington, IN, 1983.

VENICE

Folena, Gianfranco (ed.), *Storia della cultura veneta dal primo Quattrocento al Concilio di Trento*, Vicenza, 1981.
King, Margaret, *Venetian Humanism in an Age of Patrician Dominance*, Princeton, NJ, 1986.
Milanesi, M. (ed.), *G. B. Ramusio: Navigazioni e viaggi*, Turin, 1980.
Stocchi, Manlio Pastore (ed.), *Una famiglia veneziana nella storia: I Barbaro*, Venice, 1996.

NAPLES

Costa, Gustavo, *La leggenda dei secoli d'oro nella letteratura italiana*, Bari, 1972.
Kidwell, Carol, *Pontano: Poet and Prime Minister*, London, 1991.
Ryder, Alan, *Alfonso the Magnanimous (1396–1458)*, Oxford, 1990.

FERRARA

Gundersheimer, Werner L., *Ferrara: The Style of a Renaissance Despotism*, Princeton, NJ, 1972.
Longhi, Roberto, *Officina ferrarese*, Rome, 1957.
Pasquazi, Silvio, *Rinascimento ferrarese*, Rome, 1957.
Salmons, J. and Moretti, W., *The Renaissance in Ferrara*, Cardiff-Ravenna, 1984.

Vernacular literature

LATIN AND THE VERNACULAR

Grayson, Cecil, *A Renaissance Controversy: Latin or Italian*, Oxford, 1960.
Hainsworth Peter *et al.* (ed.), *The Languages of Literature in Renaissance Italy*, Oxford, 1988.
McLaughlin, Martin, *Literary Imitation in the Italian Renaissance*, Oxford, 1995.
Tavoni, Mirko, *Latino, grammatica, volgare. Storia di una questione umanistica*, Padua, 1984.

Vernacular prose

Prosatori volgari del Quattrocento, ed. C. Varese, Milan–Naples, 1955.
Novelle del Quattrocento, ed. G. G. Ferrero and M. L. Doglio, Turin, 1975.
Motti e facezie di Piovano Arlotto, ed. G. Folena, Milan–Naples, 1953.
Colonna, Francesco, *Hypnerotomachia Polifili*, ed. G. Pozzi and L. A. Ciapponi, Padua, 1980.
Leonardo, Da Vinci, *Scritti scelti*, ed. A. M. Brizio, Turin, 1966.
The Literary Works of Leonardo da Vinci, trans. J. P. Richter, Oxford, 1970.
Masuccio Salernitano (Tommaso Guardati), *Il novellino*, ed. S. Nigro, Bari, 1975.
Clements, Robert and Gibaldi, Joseph, *An Anatomy of the Novella*, New York, 1977.

Vernacular poetry

See the articles by A. Battistini and G. Gorni in Asor Rosa, and by D. De Robertis in Cecchi and Sapegno, *Il Quattrocento* (see above, p. 608).

LYRIC POETRY

Lorenzo de' Medici

Opere, ed. M. Martelli, Turin, 1965.
Canzoniere, ed. T. Zanato, Florence, 1991.
Comento de' miei sonetti, ed. T. Zanato, Florence, 1991.
Selected Writings, ed. C. Salvadori, Dublin, 1992.
Hook, Judith, *Lorenzo de' Medici*, London, 1984.

Poliziano, Angelo

Poesie italiane, ed. S. Orlandi, Milan, 1976.
Rime, ed. D. Delcorno Branca, Florence, 1986.
L'Orfeo, ed. A. Tissoni Benvenuti, Padua, 1986.
Stanze cominciate per la giostra di Giuliano de' Medici, ed. V. Pernicone, Turin, 1954.
The Stanze of Angelo Poliziano, trans. D. Quint, Amherst, MA, 1979.
Branca, Vittore, *Poliziano e l'umanesimo della parola*, Turin, 1983.
Ghinassi, Ghino, *Il volgare letterario nel Quattrocento e le 'Stanze' del Poliziano*, Florence, 1957.
Maier, Ida, *Politien. La formation d'un poète humaniste*, Geneva, 1966.

Sannazaro and pastoral

Opere volgari, ed. E. Carrara, Turin, 1952; reprint 1970.
De partu virginis, ed. C. Fantazzi and A. Perosa, Florence, 1988.
Arcadia and Piscatorial Eclogues, English trans. by Ralph Nash, Detroit and Toronto, 1966.
Cooper, Helen, *Pastoral: Medieval into Renaissance*, Ipswich, 1977.
Kidwell, Carol, *Sannazaro and Arcadia*, London, 1993.
Levin, Harry, *The Myth of the Golden Age in the Renaissance*, Bloomington, IN, 1969.
Marinelli, Peter, *Pastoral*, London, 1971.
Poggioli, Renato, *The Oaten Flute: Essays on Pastoral Poetry*, Cambridge, MA, 1975.

NARRATIVE POETRY

Origins

Le Chanson d'Aspremont, d'après un poème du XIIIe siècle, ed. J. Bédier, Paris, 1925.
L'Entrée en Espagne: chanson de geste franco-italienne, ed. A. Thomas, 2 vols., Paris, 1913.
La Prise de Pampelune, ed. A. Mussafia, Vienna, 1864.
Andrea da Barberino, *I Reali di Francia*, ed. G. Vandelli and G. Gambarin, Bari, 1947.
Andrea da Barberino, *Aspramonte*, ed. L. Cavalli, Naples, 1972.

Pulci, Luigi

Morgante, ed. D. Puccini, 2 vols., Milan, 1989. There are only partial English translations of the *Morgante*: Canto 1 by Byron (*Poetical Works*, ed. J. Jump, London, 1970); Canto 3 by Joseph Tusiani, *Annali d'Italianistica* 1 (1983) 3–18.
De Robertis, Domenico, *Storia del 'Morgante'*, Florence, 1958.
Getto, Giovanni, *Studio sul 'Morgante'*, Florence, 1967.
Jordan, Constance, *Pulci's 'Morgante': Poetry and History in Fifteenth-century Florence*, Washingon, 1986.
Lebano, Edoardo A., 'Luigi Pulci and Late Fifteenth-Century Humanism in Florence', *Renaissance Quarterly* 27 (1974) 489–98.

Boiardo, Matteo

Orlando innamorato, ed. G. Anceschi, 2 vols., Milan, 1978.
 English translation by C. S. Ross, Berkeley, CA, 1989.
 For continuations of Boiardo see Neil Harris, *Bibliografia dell'"Orlando Innamorato'*, 2 vols., Ferrara, 1988–91.
Di Tommaso, Andrea, *Structure and Ideology in Boiardo's 'Orlando Innamorato'*, Chapel Hill, NC, 1972.
Franceschetti, Antonio, *L'"Orlando Innamorato' e le sue componenti tematiche e strutturali*, Florence, 1975.
Marinelli, Peter V., *Ariosto and Boiardo: the Origins of 'Orlando Furioso'*, Columbia, MO, 1987.
Il Boiardo e la critica contemporanea: Atti del Convegno di 1969, Florence, 1970.

Theatre

TEXTS

Sacre rappresentazioni del Quattrocento, ed. L. Banfi, Turin, 1963.
Teatro umanistico, ed. A. Perosa, Milan, 1965.
Teatro latino medievale, ed. E. Franceschini, Milan, 1960.
Teatro goliardico dell'umanesimo, ed. V. Pandolfi and E. Artese, Milan, 1965.

STUDIES

D'Ancona, Alessandro, *Origini del teatro italiano*, 3 vols., Turin, 1891.
Faccioli, Emilio, *Il teatro italiano: Vol. I: Le origini e il Quattrocento*, Turin, 1975.
Radcliff-Umstead, Douglas, *The Birth of Modern Comedy in Renaissance Italy*, Chicago, 1969.
Staüble, Antonio, *La commedia umanistica del Quattrocento*, Florence, 1968.

CINQUECENTO

Prose

GENERAL

Forms of literary prose

Basso, Jeannine, *Le genre épistolaire en langue italienne (1538–1622): répertoire chronologique et analytique*, 2 vols., Rome, 1990.

Cox, Virginia, *The Renaissance Dialogue: Literary Dialogue in its Social and Political Contexts, Castiglione to Galileo*, Cambridge, 1992.

Dionisotti, Carlo, 'Tradizione classica e volgarizzamenti', in *Geografia e storia della letteratura italiana*, Turin, 1967, pp. 125–78.

Grendler, Paul F., *The Roman Inquisition and the Venetian Press 1540–1605*, Princeton, NJ, 1977.

Guthmüller, Bodo, 'Fausto da Longiano e il problema del tradurre', *Quaderni veneti* 12 (1990) 9–152.

Marazzini, Claudio, *Il secondo Cinquecento e il Seicento*, Bologna, 1993.

Migliorini, Bruno, *Storia della lingua italiana*, 5th edn, Florence, 1978.

Murphy, James J. (ed.), *Renaissance Eloquence: Studies in the Theory and Practice of Renaissance Rhetoric*, Berkeley, CA, 1983.

Pozzi, Mario (ed.), *Discussioni linguistiche del Cinquecento*, Turin, 1988.

Quondam, Amedeo (ed.), *Le 'carte messaggiere': retorica e modelli di comunicazione epistolare*, Rome, 1981.

Richardson, Brian, *Print Culture in Renaissance Italy*, Cambridge, 1994.

Snyder, Jon R., *Writing the Scene of Speaking: Theories of Dialogue in the Late Italian Renaissance*, Stanford, CA, 1989.

Sorrentino, Andrea, *La letteratura italiana e il Sant'Uffizio*, Naples, 1935.

Trovato, Paolo, *Con ogni diligenza corretto: la stampa e le revisioni editoriali dei testi letterari italiani (1470–1570)*, Bologna, 1991.

Trovato, Paolo, *Il primo Cinquecento*, Bologna, 1994.

Vitale, Maurizio, *La questione della lingua*, 2nd edn, Palermo, 1978.

Statecraft and history

Albertini, Rudolf von, *Firenze dalla repubblica al principato*, Turin, 1970.

Eliav-Feldon, Miriam, *Realistic Utopias: The Ideal Imaginary Societies of the Renaissance 1516–1630*, Oxford, 1982.

Gilbert, Felix, 'The Venetian Constitution in Florentine Political Thought', in *History: Choice and Commitment*, Cambridge, MA, 1977, pp. 179–214.

The individual and society

Aguzzi Barbagli, Danilo, 'La difesa di valori etici nella trattatistica sulla nobiltà del secondo Cinquecento', *Rinascimento*, 2nd series 29 (1989) 377–427.

Donati, Claudio, *L'idea di nobiltà in Italia: secoli XIV–XVIII*, Bari, 1988.

Erspamer, Francesco, *La biblioteca di don Ferrante: duello e onore nella cultura del Cinquecento*, Rome, 1982.

Fahy, Conor, 'Three Early Renaissance Treatises on Women', *Italian Studies* 11 (1956) 31–55.

Grendler, Paul F., *Critics of the Italian World (1530–1560): Anton Francesco Doni Nicolò Franco and Ortensio Lando*, Madison, WI, 1969.
King, Margaret L., *Women of the Renaissance*, Chicago and London, 1991.
Nelson, John Charles, *Renaissance Theory of Love: the Context of Giordano Bruno's 'Eroici furori'*, New York, 1958.
Panizza, Letizia (ed.), *Women in Italian Renaissance Culture and Society*, Oxford (European Humanities Research Centre), 1998.
Robb, Nesca A., *Neoplatonism of the Italian Renaissance*, London, 1935.
Zonta, Giuseppe (ed.), *Trattati d'amore del Cinquecento*, Bari, 1912; rprt 1975 with an introduction by Mario Pozzi.

Literature and art

Barocchi, Paola (ed.), *Trattati d'arte del Cinquecento fra manierismo e controriforma*, 3 vols., Bari, 1960–2.
Blunt, Anthony F., *Artistic Theory in Italy 1450–1600*, Oxford, 1940.

Narrative fiction

Albertazzi, Adolfo, *Il romanzo*, Milan, 1902.
Di Francia, Letterio, *La novellistica*, 2 vols., Milan, 1924–5.
Guglielminetti, Marziano (ed.), *Novellieri del Cinquecento*, vol. 1, Milan–Naples, 1972.
Salinari, Giambattista (ed.), *Novelle del Cinquecento*, 2 vols., Turin, 1955.

Individual authors

Abarbanel, Giuda, *see* Ebreo, Leone

Adriani, Giovan Battista
Istoria de' suoi tempi, 8 vols., Prato, 1822–3.

Agostini, Ludovico
La repubblica immaginaria, ed. L. Firpo, Turin, 1957.

Aretino, Pietro
Opere di Folengo, Aretino, Doni, ed. C. Cordié, vol. 2, Milan–Naples, 1976, pp. 1–567.
Aretino, Pietro, *Sei giornate*, ed. G. Aquilecchia, Bari, 1969.
Larivaille, Paul, *Pietro Aretino fra Rinascimento e Manierismo*, Rome, 1980.
Petrocchi, Giorgio, *Pietro Aretino tra Rinascimento e Controriforma*, Milan, 1948.

Bandello, Matteo
Tutte le opere, ed. F. Flora, second edn, 2 vols., Milan, 1942–3.
Fiorato, Adelin Charles, *Bandello entre l'histoire et l'écriture*, Florence, 1979.
Griffith, T. Gwynfor, *Bandello's Fiction: An Examination of the 'Novelle'*, Oxford, 1955.
Rozzo, Ugo (ed.), *Matteo Bandello novelliere europeo*, Tortona, 1982.

Bargagli, Girolamo
Dialogo de' giuochi, ed. P. D'Incalci Ermini, Siena, 1982.

Bargagli, Scipione
I trattenimenti, ed. L. Riccò, Rome, 1989.

Bartoli, Cosimo
Bryce, Judith, *Cosimo Bartoli*, Geneva, 1983.

Bembo, Pietro
Opere in volgare, ed. M. Marti, Florence, 1961.
Prose e rime, ed. C. Dionisotti, 2nd edn, Turin, 1966.
Lettere, ed. E. Travi, vols 1–4, Bologna, 1987–93.

Borghini, Vincenzo
Scritti inediti o rari sulla lingua, ed. J. R. Woodhouse, Bologna, 1971.

Botero, Giovanni
Della ragion di stato, ed. L. Firpo, Turin, 1948.

Brucioli, Antonio
Dialogi, ed. A. Landi, Naples, 1983.
Spini, Giorgio, *Tra Rinascimento e Riforma: Antonio Brucioli*, Florence, 1940.

Bruno, Giordano
Dialoghi italiani, ed. G. Gentile and G. Aquilecchia, Florence, 1958.
De gl'heroici furori, ed. P.-H. Michel, Paris, 1954.
Ciliberto, Michele, *Giordano Bruno*, Bari, 1990.
Spampanato, Vincenzo, *Vita di Giordano Bruno*, Messina, 1921.

Capella, Galeazzo Flavio
Della eccellenza e dignità delle donne, ed. M. L. Doglio, Rome, 1988.

Castiglione, Baldesar
Castiglione, B., Della Casa, G. and Cellini, B., *Opere*, ed. C. Cordié, Milan–Naples, 1960.
Il libro del Cortegiano con una scelta delle Opere minori, ed. B. Maier, 3rd edn, Turin, 1981.
Il libro del Cortegiano, ed. V. Cian, 4th edn, Florence, 1947.
The Book of the Courtier, trans. G. Bull, Penguin Classics, Harmondsworth, 1967.
Le lettere, ed. G. La Rocca, vol. 1, Milan, 1978.
Cian, Vittorio, *Un illustre nunzio pontificio del Rinascimento: Baldassar Castiglione*, Città del Vaticano, 1951.
Hanning, R. W. and Rosand, D. (eds.), *Castiglione: the Ideal and the Real in Renaissance Culture*, New Haven–London, 1983.
Ossola, Carlo and Prosperi, Adriano (eds.), *La corte e il 'Cortegiano'*, 2 vols., Rome, 1980.
Rebhorn, Wayne, *Courtly Performances: Masking and Festivity in Castiglione's 'Book of the Courtier'*, Detroit, 1978.
Woodhouse, John R., *Baldesar Castiglione: A Reassessment of 'The Courtier'*, Edinburgh, 1978.

Cattaneo, Silvan
Caccia, Ettore, *Silvan Cattaneo e la novella del Cinquecento*, Salò, 1966.

Cattaneo, Silvan and Grattarolo, Bongianni, *Salò e sua riviera*, Venice, 1745; rprt Bologna, 1970.

Cavalcanti, Bartolomeo
Lettere edite e inedite, ed. C. Roaf, Bologna, 1967.

Cellini, Benvenuto
Opere, ed. G. G. Ferrero, Turin, 1972.
Castiglione, Della Casa, Cellini, *Opere*, see under Castiglione.
Vita, ed. O. Bacci, Florence, 1901.
Autobiography, trans. G. Bull, Penguin Classics, Harmondsworth, 1969.

Cornaro, Alvise
Scritti della vita sobria, ed. M. Milani, Venice, 1983.
Fiocco, Giuseppe, *Alvise Cornaro: il suo tempo e le sue opere*, Vicenza, 1965.

Della Casa, Giovanni
Castiglione, Della Casa, Cellini, *Opere*, see under Castiglione.
Prose di Giovanni della Casa e altri trattatisti cinquecenteschi del comportamento, ed. A. Di Benedetto, 2nd edn, Turin, 1991.
Il Galateo, ed. E. Scarpa, Modena, 1990.
Il Galateo, ed. G. Barbarisi, Venice, 1991.
Santosuosso, Antonio, *Vita di Giovanni Della Casa*, Rome, 1979.

Dolce, Lodovico
Cicogna, E. A., 'Memoria intorno la vita e gli scritti di messer Lodovico Dolce letterato veneziano del secolo XVI', *Memorie dell'I. R. Istituto veneto di scienze, lettere ed arti* 11 (1862) 93–200.
Roskill, Mark W., *Dolce's 'Aretino' and Venetian Art Theory of the Cinquecento*, New York, 1968.

Doni, Anton Francesco
Opere di Folengo, Aretino, Doni, ed. C. Cordié, vol. 2, Milan–Naples, 1976, pp. 569–971.
I Marmi, ed. E. Chiòrboli, 2 vols., Bari, 1928.
I mondi e gli inferni, ed. P. Pellizzari, Turin, 1994.

Ebreo, Leone
Dialoghi d'amore, ed. S. Caramella, Bari, 1929.

Equicola, Mario
Kolsky, Stephen, *Mario Equicola: the Real Courtier*, Geneva, 1991.

Erizzo, Sebastiano
Le sei giornate, ed. R. Bragantini, Rome, 1977.

Firenzuola, Agnolo
Opere, ed. D. Maestri, Turin, 1977.
Le novelle, ed. E. Ragni, Rome, 1971.

Fonte, Moderata, see Pozzo, Modesta.

Fortini, Pietro
Novelle, 4 vols., Bologna, 1967 (rprt of Florence, 1888–1905 edn).
Le giornate delle novelle dei novizi, ed. A. Mauriello, 2 vols., Rome, 1988.

Franco, Nicolò
Il Petrarchista, ed. R. L. Bruni, Exeter, 1979.
Le pistole vulgari, ed. F. R. De Angelis, Sala Bolognese, 1987 (rprt of 1542 edn).

Gelli, Giovan Battista
Opere, ed. D. Maestri, Turin, 1976.
Pozzi, Mario (ed.), *Trattatisti del Cinquecento*, vol. 1, Milan–Naples, 1978, pp. 851–1158.
De Gaetano, Armand L., *Giambattista Gelli and the Florentine Academy*, Florence, 1976.

Giannotti, Donato
Opere politiche and *Lettere italiane*, ed. F. Diaz, 2 vols., Milan, 1974.
Republica fiorentina, ed. G. Silvano, Geneva, 1990.
Ridolfi, Roberto, 'Sommario della vita di Donato Giannotti', in *Opuscoli di storia letteraria e di erudizione*, Florence, 1942, pp. 55–164.
Starn, Randolph, *Donato Giannotti and his 'Epistolae'*, Geneva, 1968.

Giovio, Paolo
Lettere, ed. G. G. Ferrero, 2 vols., Rome, 1956–8.
Historiae sui temporis, ed. D. Visconti and T. C. P. Zimmerman, 2 vols. Rome, 1957–85.

Giraldi Cinzio, Giambattista
Gli ecatommiti, ovvero Cento novelle, 3 vols., Turin, 1853–4.
Villari, Susanna, *Per l'edizione critica degli 'Ecatommiti'*, Messina, 1988.
L'uomo di corte, ed. W. Moretti, Modena, 1989.
Schifanoia, 12 (1992) (papers from conference held in 1989).

Grazzini, Anton Francesco
Le cene, ed. R. Bruscagli, Rome, 1976.
Le cene, ed. E. Mazzali, Milan, 1989.
Rodini, R. J., *Antonfrancesco Grazzini*, Madison–Milwaukee–London, 1970.

Guazzo, Stefano
Lievsay, John L., *Stefano Guazzo and the English Renaissance 1575–1675*, Chapel Hill, NC, 1961.
Patrizi, Giorgio (ed.), *Stefano Guazzo e la 'Civil conversazione'*, Rome, 1990.

Guicciardini, Francesco
Opere, ed. E. Scarano, 3 vols., Turin, 1970–81.
Storie fiorentine, ed. R. Palmarocchi, Bari, 1931.
Cose fiorentine, ed. R. Ridolfi, Florence, 1945.

Storia d'Italia, ed. S. S. Menchi, Turin, 1971.
Dialogo e discorsi del reggimento di Firenze, ed. R. Palmarocchi, Bari, 1932.
Scritti politici e ricordi, ed. R. Palmarocchi, Bari, 1933.
Ricordi, ed. R. Spongano, Florence, 1951.
Lettere, ed. P. Jodogne, Rome, 1986– .
Gilbert, Felix, *Machiavelli and Guicciardini*, Princeton, NJ, 1965.
Phillips, M., *Francesco Guicciardini: the Historian's Craft*, Toronto, 1977.
Ridolfi, Roberto, *Vita di Francesco Guicciardini*, revised edition, Milan, 1982 (*Life of Francesco Guicciardini*, trans. Cecil Grayson, London, 1967).
Francesco Guicciardini nel V centenario della nascita, 1483–1983, Florence, 1984.

Machiavelli, Niccolò
Tutte le opere, ed. M. Martelli, Florence, 1971.
De principatibus, ed. Giorgio Inglese, Rome: Istituto storico italiano per il Medio Evo, 1994.
Legazioni, commissarie, scritti di governo, ed. F. Chiappelli *et al.*, Bari, 1971– .
La vita di Castruccio Castracani, ed. R. Brakkee, Naples, 1986.
Discorso intorno alla nostra lingua, ed. P. Trovato, Padua, 1982.
The Chief Works and Others, trans. by A. H. Gilbert, 3 vols., Durham–London, 1989.
The Discourses of Niccolò Machiavelli, ed. and trans. L. J. Walker, with new introd. and appendices by C. H. Clough, 2 vols., London, 1975.
Florentine Histories, trans L. F. Banfield and H. C. Mansfield, Jr, Princeton, NJ, 1988.
Bock, Gisela *et al.* (eds.), *Machiavelli and Republicanism*, Cambridge, 1990.
Coyle, Martin (ed.), *Niccolò Machiavelli's 'The Prince': New Interdisciplinary Essays*, Manchester, 1995.
Dionisotti, Carlo, *Machiavellerie*, Turin, 1980.
Gilbert, Allan H., *Machiavelli's 'Prince' and its Forerunners*, Durham, NC, 1938.
Gilbert, Felix, *Machiavelli and Guicciardini*, see Guicciardini.
Gilmore, Myron P. (ed.), *Studies on Machiavelli*, Florence, 1972.
Hale, John R., *Machiavelli and Renaissance Italy*, Harmondsworth, 1972.
Raab, Felix, *The English Face of Machiavelli: A Changing Interpretation 1500–1700*, London, 1964.
Ridolfi, Roberto, *Vita di Niccolò Machiavelli*, rev. edn, Florence, 1981 (*Life of Niccolò Machiavelli*, trans. Cecil Grayson, London, 1963).
Ruffo Fiore, Silvia, *Niccolò Machiavelli: An Annotated Bibliography of Modern Criticism and Scholarship*, New York, 1990.
Whitfield, J. H., *Machiavelli*, Oxford, 1947.
Discourses on Machiavelli, Cambridge, 1969.

Nardi, Iacopo
Istorie della città di Firenze, ed. L. Arbib, 2 vols., Florence, 1842.
Pieralli, Alfredo, *La vita e le opere di Iacopo Nardi*, vol. 1, Florence, 1901.
Montevecchi, Alessandro, *Storici di Firenze: studi su Nardi, Nerli, Varchi*, Bologna, 1989.

Nerli, Filippo de'
Commentari de' fatti civili occorsi dentro la città di Firenze, Augusta, 1728.
Niccolai, Alberto, *Filippo de' Nerli, 1485–1556*, Pisa, 1906.
Montevecchi, *Storici di Firenze*, see under Nardi, Iacopo.

Parabosco, Girolamo
I diporti, in *Novellieri minori del Cinquecento*, ed. G. Gigli and F. Nicolini, Bari, 1912, pp. 1–199.

Patrizi, Francesco
Vasoli, Cesare, *Francesco Patrizi da Cherso*, Rome, 1989.

Piccolomini, Alessandro
Dialogo de la bella creanza de le donne, in *Prose di Giovanni della Casa e altri trattatisti* (see Della Casa), pp. 431–506.
Cerreta, Florindo, *Alessandro Piccolomini letterato e filosofo senese del Cinquecento*, Siena, 1960.

Pitti, Iacopo
Istoria fiorentina, ed. F. L. Polidori, in *Archivio storico italiano*, 1 (1842) 1–208.

Porto, Luigi da
Lettere storiche, ed. B. Bressan, Florence, 1857.
Brognoligo, Gioachino, 'La vita e le opere di Luigi da Porto', *Studi di storia letteraria*, Rome, 1903, pp. 7–117.

Porzio, Camillo
La congiura de' baroni del Regno di Napoli contra il re Ferdinando primo e gli altri scritti, ed. E. Pontieri, 2nd edn, Naples, 1964.

Pozzo, Modesta (Moderata Fonte)
Il merito delle donne, ed. A. Chemello, Mirano (Venice), 1988.
Kolsky, Stephen, 'Wells of Knowledge: Moderata Fonte's *Il merito delle donne*', *The Italianist* 13 (1993) 57–96.

Romei, Annibale
Solerti, Angelo, *Ferrara e la corte estense nella seconda metà del secolo decimosesto. I Discorsi di Annibale Romei, gentiluomo ferrarese*, 2nd edn, Città di Castello, 1900.

Salviati, Lionardo
Brown, Peter M., *Lionardo Salviati: A Critical Biography*, London, 1974.

Sansovino, Francesco
Ragionamento nel quale brevemente s'insegna a' giovani uomini la bella arte d'amore, in *Prose di Giovanni della Casa e altri trattatisti* (see under Della Casa above).
Bonora, Elena, *Ricerche su Francesco Sansovino imprenditore libraio e letterato*, Venice: Istituto veneto di scienze, lettere ed arti, 1994.
Cicogna, E. A., *Delle inscrizioni veneziane*, 6 vols., Venice, 1824–53, vol. 4, pp. 32–91.
Roaf, Christina, 'Francesco Sansovino e le sue *Lettere sopra le diece giornate del Decamerone*', *Quaderni di retorica e poetica* 1 (1985) 91–8.

Segni, Bernardo
Storie fiorentine ... colla vita di Niccolò Capponi, Augusta, 1723.

Speroni, Sperone
Opere, 5 vols., Manziana (Rome), 1989 (rprt of 1740 Venice edn).
Pozzi (ed.), *Trattatisti del Cinquecento* (see under Gelli, Giovan Battista), pp. 469–850.
Canace e scritti in sua difesa, ed. C. Roaf, Bologna, 1982.
Lettere familiari, ed. M. R. Loi and M. Pozzi, vols 1– , Alessandria, 1993– .
Fournel, Jean-Louis, *Les Dialogues de S. Speroni*, Marburg, 1990.

Straparola, Giovan Francesco
Le piacevoli notti, ed. G. Rua, 2 vols., Bari, 1927; rprt 1975 with introduction by M. Pastore Stocchi.

Tasso, Torquato
Dialoghi, ed. E. Raimondi, 2 vols., Florence, 1958.
Il conte, overo De l'imprese, ed. B. Basile, Rome, 1993.
Brand, Charles Peter, *Torquato Tasso*, see under Tasso below, p. 635.

Tolomei, Claudio
Sbaragli, Luigi, *Claudio Tolomei umanista senese del Cinquecento: la vita e le opere*, Siena, 1939.

Trissino, Giangiorgio
Scritti linguistici, ed. A. Castelvecchi, Rome, 1986.
Morsolin, Bernardo, *Giangiorgio Trissino*, 2nd edn, Florence, 1894.

Varchi, Benedetto
Opere, Trieste, 1858.
Pirotti, Umberto, *Benedetto Varchi e la cultura del suo tempo*, Florence, 1971.
Montevecchi, *Storici di Firenze*, see under Nardi, Iacopo.

Vasari, Giorgio
Le vite ... nelle redazioni del 1550 e 1568, ed. P. Barocchi and R. Bettarini, 8 vols., Florence, 1966–87.
Boase, Thomas S. R., *Giorgio Vasari: The Man and the Book*, Princeton, NJ, 1979.

Vettori, Francesco
Scritti storici e politici, ed. E. Niccolini, Bari, 1972.
Devonshire Jones, Rosemary, *Francesco Vettori: Florentine Citizen and Medici Servant*, London, 1972.

Narrative poetry

GENERAL

Bowra, Cecil M., *From Virgil to Milton*, New York, 1963.
Durling, Robert, *The Figure of the Poet in Renaissance Epic*, Cambridge, MA, 1965.
Gardner, Edmund G., *Dukes and Poets in Ferrara*, New York, 1968.
Giamatti, A. Bartlett, *The Earthly Paradise and the Renaissance Epic*, Princeton, NJ, 1966.

Greene, Thomas M., *The Descent from Heaven: a Study in Epic Continuity*, New Haven, CT, 1963.

Hathaway, Baxter, *The Age of Criticism: the Late Renaissance in Italy*, Ithaca, NY, 1962.

Murrin, Michael, *The Allegorical Epic: Essays in its Rise and Decline*, Chicago, 1980.

Weinberg, Bernard, *A History of Literary Criticism in the Italian Renaissance*, Chicago, 1961.

ARIOSTO

Orlando Furioso, ed. C. Segre, Milan, 1976.

Orlando furioso secondo l'edizione del 1532 e con le varianti delle edizioni del 1516 e del 1521, ed. S. Debenedetti and C. Segre, Bologna, 1960. Modern English trans. by Barbara Reynolds (2 vols., Penguin Classics, Harmondsworth, 1975–7), and Guido Waldman (London, 1974).

Ascoli, Albert Russell, *Ariosto's Bitter Harmony: Crisis and Evasion in the Italian Renaissance*, Princeton, NJ, 1987.

Binni, Walter, *Metodo e poesia di Ludovico Ariosto*, Florence, 1961.

Brand, Charles Peter, *Ludovico Ariosto: a Preface to the 'Orlando Furioso'*, Edinburgh, 1974.

Gardner, Edmund G., *The King of Court Poets: a Study of the Work, Life and Times of Ludovico Ariosto*, New York, 1968.

Javitch, Daniel, *Proclaiming a Classic: the Canonisation of 'Orlando Furioso'*, Princeton, NJ, 1991.

Marinelli, Peter, *see under* Boiardo above, p. 626.

Rodini, Robert J. and Di Maria, Salvatore, *Ludovico Ariosto: An Annotated Bibliography of Criticism, 1956–80*, Columbia, MO, 1984.

Wiggins, Peter DeSa, *Figures in Ariosto's Tapestry: Character and Design in the 'Orlando Furioso'*, Baltimore–London, 1986.

TASSO

Gerusalemme liberata and *Gerusalemme conquistata* in *Opere*, ed. B. T. Sozzi, 2 vols., Turin, 1974.

Rinaldo, ed. Michael Sherberg, Ravenna, 1990.

Modern English trans. of the *Liberata* by Ralph Nash (Detroit, 1987), and Joseph Tusiani (Cranbury, NJ, 1970).

Brand, Charles Peter, *Torquato Tasso: a Study of the Poet and of his Contribution to English literature*, Cambridge, 1965.

Chiappelli, Fredi, *Studi sul linguaggio del Tasso epico*, Florence, 1957.

Fichter, Andrew, *Poets Historical: Dynastic Epic in the Renaissance*, New Haven, CT, 1982.

Getto, Giovanni, *Interpretazione del Tasso*, Naples, 1951.

Quint, David, 'Political Allegory in the *Gerusalemme Liberata*', *Renaissance Quarterly* 43 (1990) 1–29.

Ramat, Raffaello, *Per la storia dello stile rinascimentale*, Florence, 1953.

OTHER WRITERS

Alamanni, Luigi, *Girone il cortese*, Paris, 1548.

L'Avarchide, Florence, 1570.

Bello, Francesco (il Cieco), *Mambriano*, 2 vols., Turin, 1926.
Berni, Francesco, *Orlando Innamorato di M. M. Boiardo, rifatto da F. Berni*, Florence, 1971.
Folengo, Teofilo, *Baldus*, ed. Emilio Faccioli (with facing translation in Italian), Turin, 1989.
Tasso, Bernardo, *Amadigi*, Venice, 1560.
Trissino, Giangiorgio, *L'Italia liberata dai Goti*, Venice, 1835.

Lyric poetry

TEXTS

Modern anthologies

Lirici del Cinquecento, ed. C. Bo, Milan, 1945.
Lyric Poetry of the Italian Renaissance: An Anthology with Verse Translations, ed. L. R. Lind, New Haven, CT, 1954.
Lirici del Cinquecento, ed. L. Baldacci, Florence, 1957 (updated by G. Nicoletti, Milan, 1975).
Lirici del Cinquecento, ed. D. Ponchiroli, Turin, 1958 (updated by G. Davico Bonino, Turin, 1968).
Poesia italiana: Il Cinquecento, ed. G. Ferroni, Milan, 1978.
Pasquinate romane del Cinquecento, 2 vols., ed. V. Marucci, A. Marzo and A. Romano, Rome, 1983.

Individual poets

Aretino, Pietro, *Poesie varie*, ed. G. Aquilecchia and A. Romano, vol. 1, Rome, 1992.
Ariosto, Ludovico, *Satire*, ed. C. Segre, Turin, 1987.
Bembo, Pietro, *Prose e rime*, ed. C. Dionisotti, Turin, 1966.
Berni, Francesco, *Rime*, ed. D. Romei, Milan, 1985.
　Rime burlesche, ed. G. Barberi Squarotti, Milan, 1991.
Buonarroti, Michelangelo, *Rime*, ed. E. N. Girardi, Bari, 1967.
Colonna, Vittoria, *Rime*, ed. A. Bullock, Rome–Bari, 1982.
Della Casa, Giovanni, *Rime*, ed. R. Fedi, 2 vols., Rome, 1978, rprt Milan, 1993.
Matraini, Chiara, *Rime e lettere*, ed. G. Rabitti, Bologna, 1989.
Sannazaro, Iacobo, *Opere volgari*, ed. A. Mauro, Bari, 1961.
Stampa, Gaspara, *Rime*, ed. M. Bellonci and R. Ceriello, Milan, 1994.
Strozzi, Giovan Battista, *Madrigali inediti*, ed. M. Ariani, Urbino, 1975.
Tarsia, Galeazzo di, *Rime*, ed. C. Bozzetti, Milan, 1980.
Tasso, Torquato, *Rime 'eteree'*, ed. L. Caretti, Parma, 1990.
　Rime, 2 vols., ed. B. Basile, Rome, 1994.
Tebaldeo, Antonio, *Rime*, ed. T. Basile and J.-J. Marchand, 3 vols., Modena, 1989–92.
Trissino, Giovan Giorgio, *Rime 1529*, ed. A. Quondam, Vicenza, 1981.

STUDIES

General

Croce, Benedetto, *Poeti e scrittori del pieno e del tardo rinascimento*, 3 vols., Bari, 1945–8.

Daniele, Antonio, *Linguaggi e metri del cinquecento*, Rovito, 1994.

Dionisotti, Carlo, *Geografia e storia della letteratura italiana*, Turin, 1967.

Gli umanisti e il volgare tra quattro e cinquecento, Florence, 1968.

Erspamer, Francesco, 'La lirica', in *Manuale di letteratura italiana: storia per generi e problemi*, ed. F. Brioschi and C. Di Girolamo, vol. 2, Turin, 1994, pp. 183–270.

Fedi, Roberto, *La memoria della poesia: canzonieri, lirici e libri di rime nel Rinascimento*, Rome, 1990.

Friedrich, Hugo, *Epoche della lirica italiana: il Cinquecento*, 2nd edn, Milan, 1975.

Guglielminetti, Marziano, *Manierismo e barocco*, Turin, 1990.

Quondam, Amedeo, *Il naso di Laura: lingua e poesia lirica nella tradizione del classicismo*, Modena, 1991.

Rossi, Aldo, 'Lirica volgare del primo cinquecento', in *Forme e vicende, Per Giovanni Pozzi*, ed. O. Besomi, Padua, 1988, pp. 123–57.

Santagata, Marco and Quondam, Amedeo (eds.), *Il libro di poesia dal copista al tipografo*, Modena, 1989.

Weinberg, Bernard, *A History of Literary Criticism in the Italian Renaissance*, 2 vols., Chicago, 1961.

Petrarca e il petrarchismo. Atti del terzo congresso dell'Associazione per gli studi di lingua e letteratura italiana, Bologna, 1961.

Petrarchism

Baldacci, Luigi, *Il petrarchismo italiano del Cinquecento*, Padua, 1974.

Calcaterra, Carlo, 'Il Petrarca e il petrarchismo', in *Questioni e correnti di storia letteraria*, Milan, 1949, pp. 167–273 (vol. 3 of Momigliano, Attilio, ed., *Problemi e orientamenti critici di lingua e letteratura italiana*).

Forster, Leonard, *The Icy Fire. Five Studies in European Petrarchism*, Cambridge, 1969.

Guglielminetti, Marziano (ed.), *Petrarca e il petrarchismo: un'ideologia della letteratura*, 2nd edn, Alessandria, 1994.

Hempfer, Klaus W. and Regn, G. (eds.), *Der Petrarkistische Diskurs*, Stuttgart, 1993.

Petrie, Jennifer, *Petrarch: The Augustan Poets, the Italian Tradition and the Canzoniere*, Dublin, 1983.

Quondam, Amedeo, *Petrarchismo mediato: per una critica della forma 'antologia'*, Rome, 1974.

Wilkins, Ernest Hatch, 'A General Survey of Renaissance Petrarchism', *Comparative Literature* 2 (1950) 327–41.

Specialist studies

Bonora, Ettore, 'Il classicismo dal Bembo al Guarini', in *Storia della letteratura italiana: il Cinquecento*, ed. E. Cecchi and N. Sapegno, Milan, 1988, pp. 165–746.

Della Terza, Dante, 'Imitatio: teoria e pratica: l'esempio del Bembo poeta', in *Forma e memoria*, Rome, 1979, pp. 115–47.

Ferroni, Giulio and Quondam, Amedeo, *La 'locuzione artificiosa': teoria ed esperienza della lirica a Napoli nell'età del manierismo*, Rome, 1973.

Jones, Ann Rosalind, *The Currency of Eros. Women's Love Lyric in Europe, 1540–1620*, Bloomington, IN, 1990.

Longhi, Silvia, *Lusus: il capitolo burlesco nel Cinquecento*, Padua, 1983.

Martini, Alessandro, 'Ritratto del madrigale poetico fra Cinque e Seicento', *Lettere italiane* 33 (1981) 529–48.
Mirollo, James V., *Mannerism and Renaissance Poetry: Concept, Mode, Inner Design*, New Haven, CT, 1984.
Romei, Danilo, *Berni e berneschi nel Cinquecento*, Florence, 1984.
Santangelo, Giorgio, *Il Bembo critico e il principio dell'imitazione*, Florence, 1950.
   Il petrarchismo del Bembo e di altri poeti del Cinquecento, Rome–Palermo, 1967.
Taddeo, Edoardo, *Il manierismo letterario e i lirici veneziani del tardo cinquecento*, Rome, 1974.
Vecchi Galli, Paola, 'La poesia cortegiana tra XV e XVI secolo: rassegna di testi e studi (1969–1981)', *Lettere italiane* 34 (1982) 95–141.

Theatre

GENERAL

Texts

Ingegneri, Angelo, *Della poesia rappresentativa e del modo di rappresentare le favole sceniche* (1598), reproduced in Marotti, *Storia* (see next entry).
Marotti, Ferruccio (ed.), *Storia documentaria del teatro italiano. Lo spettacolo dall'Umanesimo al Manierismo. Teorica e tecnica.* Milan, 1974.
Serlio, Sebastiano, *I sette libri dell'architettura*, ed. Fulvio Irace, Bologna, 1978 (anastatic rprt of 1584 edition).

Studies

Attolini, Giovanni, *Teatro e spettacolo nel Rinascimento*, Bari, 1988.
Clubb, Louise George, *Italian Drama in Shakespeare's Time*, New Haven and London, 1989.
D'Ancona, Alessandro, *Origini del teatro italiano*, Turin, 1891.
De Panizza Lorch, Maristella (ed.), *Il teatro italiano del Rinascimento*, Milan, 1980.
Enciclopedia dello Spettacolo, Rome, 1954–62 (supplements 1966, 1968).
Jacquot, Jean (ed.), *Le Lieu théâtral à la Renaissance*, Paris, 1964.
Kenyon, Nicholas and Keyte, Hugh, *Una Stravaganza dei Medici. The Florentine Intermedi of 1589* (BBC Channel 4 Television 1990: booklet to accompany broadcast performance).
Mamone, Sara, *Il teatro nella Firenze medicea*, Milan, 1981.
Pieri, Marzia, *La nascita del teatro moderno in Italia tra XV e XVI secolo*, Turin, 1989.
Pirrotta, Nino, *Li due Orfei*, Turin, 1969 (trans. by Karen Eales as *Music and Theatre from Poliziano to Monteverdi*, Cambridge, 1982; includes article by Elena Povoledo on Italian scenography in the sixteenth century).
Zorzi, Ludovico, *Il teatro e la città. Saggi sulla scena italiana*, Turin, 1977.

COMEDY

Anthologies

Commedie del Cinquecento, ed. A. Borlenghi, 2 vols., Milan, 1959.
Commedie del Cinquecento, ed. N. Borsellino, 2 vols., Milan, 1962–7.
Il teatro italiano: II, La commedia del Cinquecento (plays and documents), ed. G. Davico Bonino, 3 vols., Turin, 1977–8.

Commedie bresciane del Cinquecento, ed. N. Messora, Bergamo, 1978.

Teatro veneto, ed. G. A. Cibotto, Parma, 1960.

Five Italian Renaissance Comedies (Mandragola, Lena, Marescalco, Ingannati, Pastor fido), ed. B. Penman, Harmondsworth, 1978.

Three Renaissance Comedies (Moscheta, Lena, Talanta) ed. C. Cairns, Lampeter, 1991 (more vols. to follow).

Individual authors

Accademia degli Intronati, *Gli ingannati*, ed. F. Cerreta, Florence, 1980.

Il Sacrificio degli Intronati and *Gli ingannati* (rprt of 1537 edn), ed. N. Newbegin, Bologna, 1984.

Aretino, Pietro, *Opere, vol. II – Teatro*, ed. G. Petrocchi, Milan, 1971.

Ariosto, Ludovico, *Tutte le Opere, vol. IV: Commedie*, ed. A. Casella, G. Ronchi and E. Varasi, Milan, 1974.

The Comedies of Ariosto, trans. and ed. E. M. Beame and L. S. Brocchi, Chicago, 1975.

Bibbiena, Cardinal (Bernardo Dovizi), *La Calandra*, ed. G. Padoan, Padua, 1985.

Bruno, Giordano, *Il candelaio*, ed. G. Barberi Squarotti, Turin, 1973.

Della Porta, Giambattista, *Commedie*, ed. V. Spampanato, Bari, 1911.

Teatro, vol. II: Commedie, ed. R. Sirri, Naples, 1980.

Grasso, Nicola, *Eutichia*, ed. L. Stefani, Messina–Florence, 1978.

Grazzini, Anton Francesco, *Teatro*, ed. G. Grazzini, Bari, 1953.

Machiavelli, Niccolò, *Mandragola e Clizia*, ed. E. Raimondi, Milan, 1984.

Parabosco, Girolamo, *La notte & Il viluppo; L'Hermafrodito & I contenti; Il pellegrino & Il marinaio* (rprts of 1560 edn), ed. G. Vecchi, 3 vols., Bologna, 1977.

'Publio Philippo Mantovano', *Formicone*, ed. L. Stefani, Ferrara, 1980.

'Ruzante' (Angelo Beolco), *Teatro*, ed. L. Zorzi, Turin, 1967.

I Dialoghi; La seconda orazione; I Prologhi alla Moschetta, ed. G. Padoan, Padua, 1981.

Strozzi, Lorenzo, *Commedie*, ed. A. Gareffi, Ravenna, 1980.

Studies

Andrews, Richard, *Scripts and Scenarios: the Performance of Comedy in Renaissance Italy*, Cambridge, 1993.

Baratto, Mario, *Tre studi sul teatro: Ruzante, Aretino, Goldoni*, Venice, 1964.

La commedia del Cinquecento: aspetti e problemi, Vicenza, 1975.

Clubb, Louise George, *Giambattista Della Porta, Dramatist*, Princeton, NJ, 1965.

Herrick, Marvin T., *Comic Theory in the Sixteenth Century*, Urbana, IL, 1950.

Italian Comedy in the Renaissance, Urbana, IL, 1960.

Howarth, William D., *Comic Drama: The European Heritage*, London, 1978.

Mango, Achille, *La commedia in lingua nel Cinquecento*, Milan, 1966 (bibliography).

Mariti, Luciano, *Commedia ridicolosa: Storia e testi*, Rome, 1978.

Padoan, Giorgio, *La commedia rinascimentale veneta (1433–1565)*, Vicenza, 1982.

Radcliff-Umstead, Douglas, *The Birth of Modern Comedy in Renaissance Italy*, Chicago, 1969.

Salingar, Leo, *Shakespeare and the Traditions of Comedy*, Cambridge, 1974.

Sanesi, Ireneo, *La Commedia (Storia dei generi letterari italiani)*, 2 vols., Milan, 1954.

Seragnoli, Daniele, *Il teatro a Siena nel Cinquecento*, Rome, 1980.

COMMEDIA DELL'ARTE

Texts

Falavolti, Laura (ed.), *Commedie dei Comici dell'arte*, Turin, 1982.
Ferrone, Siro (ed.), *Commedie dell'arte*, 2 vols., Milan, 1985–6.
Pandolfi, Vito, *La Commedia dell'arte, storia e testo*, 6 vols., Florence, 1957.
Richards, Kenneth and Richards, Laura, *The Commedia dell'arte: a Documentary History*, Oxford, 1990.
Scala, Flamminio, *Il teatro delle favole rappresentative* (1611), ed. F. Marotti, 2 vols., Milan, 1976 (scenarios).

Studies

Cairns, Christopher (ed.), *The 'Commedia dell'arte' from the Renaissance to Dario Fo*, Lampeter and Newiston, NY, 1989.
Duchartre, Pierre Louis, *The Italian Comedy*, trans. R. T. Weaver, New York, 1966.
Ferrone, Siro, *Attori, mercanti, corsari*, see below, p. 645.
Lea, Kathleen M., *Italian Popular Comedy*, 2 vols., Oxford, 1934.
Molinari, Cesare, *La commedia dell'arte*, Milan, 1985.
Taviani, Ferdinando and Schino, Mirella, *Il segreto della commedia dell'arte*, Florence, 1982.
Tessari, Roberto, *La commedia dell'arte nel Seicento. Industria e arte giocosa nella società barocca*, Florence, 1969.
Commedia dell'arte: la maschera e l'ombra, Milan, 1984.

TRAGEDY

Texts

Il teatro italiano, II: La tragedia del Cinquecento, ed. M. Ariani, 2 vols., Turin, 1977 (plays and documents – includes Tasso's *Aminta* and Guarini's *Pastor fido*).
Teatro del Cinquecento, I: La tragedia, ed. R. Cremante, Milan–Naples, 1988 (includes Giraldi's *Egle*).
Aretino, Pietro, *Orazia* – see his *Teatro*, above, p. 639.
Della Porta, Giambattista, *Teatro*, ed. R. Sirri, vol. 1, *Tragedie*, Naples, 1978.
Giraldi Cinthio, Giovan Battista, *Cleopatra*, ed. M. Morrison and P. Osborn, Exeter, 1985.
Scritti contro la 'Canace', ed. Christina Roaf, Bologna, 1982.
Osborn, Peggy, *G. B. Giraldi's 'Altile'. The Birth of a New Dramatic Genre in Renaissance Ferrara*, Lampeter and Newiston, NY, 1992 (text and introduction).
Speroni, Sperone, *Canace e scritti in sua difesa*, ed. C. Roaf, Bologna, 1982.

Studies

Herrick, Marvin T., *Italian Tragedy in the Renaissance*, Urbana, IL, 1965.
Tragicomedy. Its Origin and Development in Italy, France and England, Urbana, IL, 1955.
Horne, Philip R., *The Tragedies of Giambattista Cinthio Giraldi*, Oxford, 1962.

PASTORAL

Texts

Beccari, Agostino, *Il Sacrificio*, in *Parnaso Italiano*, ed. A. Rubbi, vol. 17, Venice, 1784–90.

'Epicuro Napolitano' (Antonio Marsi?), *Drammi pastorali*, ed. Italo Palmarini, 2 vols., Bologna, 1969.

Giraldi Cinthio, Giovan Battista, *Egle*, see *Teatro del Cinquecento*, ed. Cremante, above, p. 640.

Guarini, Battista, *Il pastor fido*, see *Il teatro italiano*, ed. Ariani, above, p. 640.

Sannazaro, Jacopo, *Opere volgari*, ed. A. Mauro, Bari, 1961.

Tansillo, Luigi, *L'Egloga e i poemetti*, ed. F. Flamini, Naples, 1893.

Tasso, Torquato, *Aminta*, see *Il teatro italiano*, ed. Ariani, above, p. 640.

Zuccolo, Ludovico, *Della eminenza del pastorale*, in *Dialoghi*, Venice, 1625.

Studies

Bigi, Emilio, 'Il dramma pastorale nel Cinquecento', *Atti del Convegno sul tema 'Il teatro classico nel '500'*, Rome, 1971.

Greg, Walter W., *Pastoral Poetry and Pastoral Drama*, London, 1906.

Pieri, Marzia, *La scena boschereccia nel Rinascimento italiano*, Padua, 1983.

THE SEICENTO

General works on the Seicento

Calcaterra, Carlo, *Il Parnaso in rivolta. Barocco e antibarocco nella poesia italiana*, Milan, 1940 and Bologna, 1961.

Croce, Benedetto, *Storia dell'età barocca in Italia*, Bari, 1929.

Elwert, Theodore, *La poesia lirica italiana del Seicento*, Florence, 1967.

Jannaco, Carmine and Capucci, Martino, *Il Seicento* (*Storia della letteratura d'Italia*), Vallardi, Milan, 1986.

Raimondi, Ezio, *La letteratura barocca*, Florence, 1961.

Poetry (texts and studies)

GENERAL

Lirici marinisti, ed. B. Croce, Bari, 1910.

Lirici del Seicento e dell'Arcadia, ed. C. Calcaterra, Milan–Rome, 1936.

Opere scelte di G. B. Marino e dei Marinisti, ed. G. Getto, 2 vols., Turin, 1949.

Marino e i Marinisti, ed. G. G. Ferrero, Milan–Naples, 1956.

La poesia del Seicento, ed. C. Muscetta and P. P. Ferrante, Turin, 1964 (vol. 7, in 2 parts, of *Il Parnaso Italiano*).

La satira, ed. V. Cian, Milan, 1945.

La satira nel Seicento, ed. U. Limentani, Milan–Naples, 1961.

INDIVIDUAL POETS

Chiabrera, G., *Canzonette, rime varie, dialoghi*, ed. L. Negri, Turin, 1952 and 1968.
  Opere di G. Chiabrera e lirici del classicismo barocco, ed. M. Turchi, Turin, 1974.
  P. L. Cerisola, *L'arte dello stile: poesia e letterarietà in G. Chiabrera*, Milan, 1990.
Guidi, Alessandro, *Poesie approvate*, ed. B. Maier, Ravenna, 1981.
Marino, Giovan Battista, *L'Adone*, ed. G. Pozzi, Milan, 1976 (rprt Milan, 1990), with
  a fundamental introductory study.
  La galleria, ed. M. Pieri, Padua, 1979.
  La sampogna, ed. V. De Valdé, Parma, 1993.
  La lira, ed. O. Besomi and A. Martini (thus far only *Rime amorose, Rime marittime,*
  Rime boscherecce, Ferrara, 1987–91).
  Lectura Marini, ed. F. Guardiani, Ottawa, 1989, vol. 1, *The sense of Marino*, ed.
  F. Guardiani, New York–Ottawa–Toronto, 1994.
Rosa, Salvator
Limentani, Uberto, *Bibliografia della vita e delle opere di Salvator Rosa*, Florence, 1955.
  'Salvator Rosa: Supplemento alla bibliografia', *Forum Italicum* 7 (1973), 268–79.
Tassoni, Alessandro, *Opere*, ed. L. Fassò, Milan, 1942.
  La secchia rapita, ed. O. Besomi, Padua, 1987–90.
  Puliatti, Pietro, *Bibliografia di Alessandro Tassoni*, Florence, 1969.
Testi, Fulvio, *Lettere*, ed. M. L. Doglio, 3 vols., Bari, 1967.

Prose: non-fiction

GENERAL

Texts

Trattatisti e narratori del Seicento, ed. E. Raimondi, Milan–Naples, 1960.
Politici e moralisti del Seicento, ed. B. Croce and S. Caramella, Bari, 1930.
Scritti politici del '500 e del '600, ed. B. Widmar, Milan, 1964.
Scienziati del Seicento, ed. M. L. Altieri Biagi and B. Basile, Milan–Naples, 1980.

Studies

Anceschi, Luciano, *Le poetiche del Barocco*, Bologna, 1963.
Costanzo, Mario, *Critica e poetica del primo Seicento*, 3 vols., Rome, 1969–71.
Diffley, Paul, *Paolo Beni – A Biographical and Critical Study*, Oxford, 1988.
De Mattei, Rudolfo, *Il problema della Ragion di Stato nell'età della Controriforma*,
  Milan–Naples, 1979.
Morpurgo Tagliabue, G., 'Aristotelismo e Barocco', in *Retorica e Barocco – Atti del III*
  Congresso Internazionale di Studi Umanistici, Rome, 1954, pp. 119–95.

INDIVIDUAL AUTHORS (TEXTS AND STUDIES)

Accetto, Torquato, *Della dissimulazione onesta*, ed. S. S. Nigro and G. Manganelli,
  Genoa, 1983.
Bartoli, Daniello, *Scritti vari*, ed. M. Regillo, Milan, 1939.
  Scotti, M., *D. Bartoli – P. Segneri, Prose scelte*, Turin, 1967.
  Renaldo, John J., *Daniello Bartoli: A Letterato of the Seicento*, Naples, 1979.
Boccalini, Traiano, *Ragguagli di Parnaso e scritti minori*, 3 vols., ed. L. Firpo, Bari, 1948.

Campanella, Tomaso, *Tutte le opere*, ed. L. Firpo, Milan, 1954 (only 1 vol. has appeared).
Opere letterarie, ed. L. Bolzoni, Turin, 1977.
Scritti scelti, ed. L. Firpo, Turin, 1949.
Galilei, Galileo, *Edizione Nazionale delle Opere*, 20 vols., Florence, 1929–39.
Scritti letterari, ed. A. Chiari, Florence, 1943 and 1970.
Battistini, Andrea, *Introduzione a Galileo*, Bari, 1989.
Magalotti, Lorenzo, *Lettere sopra i buccheri, con l'aggiunta di lettere contro l'ateismo scientifiche, erudite e di relazioni varie*, ed. M. Praz, Florence, 1945.
Pallavicino, Pietro Sforza, *Storia del Concilio di Trento e altri scritti*, ed. M. Scotti, Turin, 1968.
Redi, Francesco, *Lettere e Consulti, Bacco in Toscana, Naturali osservazioni ed esperienze*, ed. V. Osimo, 2 vols., Milan, 1927.
Sarpi, Paolo, *Opere*, ed. G. and L. Cozzi, Milan–Naples, 1969.
Istoria del Concilio Tridentino, ed. G. Gambarin, 3 vols., Bari, 1930, and by R. Pecchioli, Florence, 1966.
L'istoria dell'interdetto e altri scritti editi e inediti, ed. M. D. Busnelli and G. Gambarin, 3 vols., Bari, 1940.
Cozzi, Gaetano, *Paolo Sarpi tra Venezia e l'Europa*, Turin, 1979.
Lievsay, John L., *Venetian Phoenix and some of his English Friends (1606–1700)*, Lawrence, KS, 1973.
Wooton, David, *Paolo Sarpi Between Renaissance and Enlightenment*, Cambridge, 1983.

Prose: narrative

TEXTS

General

Romanzieri del Seicento, ed. M. Capucci, Turin, 1974.
Novelle italiane. Seicento e Settecento, ed. D. Conrieri, Milan, 1982.
Viaggiatori del Seicento, ed. M. Guglielminetti, Turin, 1967.
Trattatisti e narratori del Seicento, ed. E. Raimondi, Milan–Naples, 1960.

Individual authors

Basile, Giovan Battista, *Lo cunto de li cunti, overo lo trattenimento de peccerille*, ed. and trans. M. Rax, Milan, 1987.
The Pentamerone of Giambattista Basile, trans. N. M. Penzer, 1932 (rprt Westport, CT, 1975).
Bentivoglio, Guido, *Memorie e lettere*, ed. C. Panigada, Bari, 1934.
Brignole Sale, Anton Giulio, *Le instabilità dell'ingegno*, ed. G. Formichetti, Rome, 1984.
Brusoni, Girolamo, *La gondola a tre remi*, ed. F. Lanza, Milan, 1971.
Carletti, Francesco, *Ragionamenti del mio viaggio intorno al mondo*, ed. P. Collo, Turin, 1989.
Croce, Giulio Cesare, *Le sottilissime astuzie di Bertoldo. Le piacevoli e ridicolose simplicità di Bertoldino*, ed. P. Camporesi, Turin, 1978.
De' Dottori, Carlo, *Confessioni*, ed. A. Daniele, Padua, 1987.

Della Valle, Pietro, *The Journeys of Pietro della Valle the Pilgrim*, trans. G. Bull, London, 1989.

Lancellotti, Secondo, *Vita in prosa e in versi*, ed. M. Savini, Rome, 1971.

Locatelli, Sebastiano, *Viaggio di Francia (1664–1665)*, ed. L. Monga, Moncalieri, 1990.

Magalotti, Lorenzo, *Relazioni di viaggio in Inghilterra, Francia e Svezia*, ed. W. Moretti, Bari, 1968.

   Lorenzo Magalotti at the Court of Charles II: his 'Relazione d'Inghilterra' of 1668, trans. W. E. Knowles, Middleton, Waterloo, Ontario, 1980.

Pallavicino, Ferrante, *Il corriere svaligiato*, ed. A. Marchi, Parma, 1984.

Studies

Almansi, Guido, 'L'esploratore e la genesi del romanzo epistolare pseudo-orientale', *Studi secenteschi* 7 (1966) 35–65.

Asor Rosa, Alberto, 'La narrativa italiana del Seicento', in *Letteratura italiana, III. Le forme del testo, 2. La prosa*, Turin, 1984, pp. 715–57.

Camporesi, Piero, *La maschera di Bertoldo*, 2nd edn, Milan, 1993.

Capucci, Martino, 'Fiaba, novella, romanzo', in *Il Seicento*, ed. C. Jannaco and M. Capucci, 3rd edn, Padua, 1986, pp. 591–686.

Chlodowski, Ruffo, 'Il mondo della fiaba e il *Pentamerone* di Giambattista Basile: Dai sistemi narrativi del Rinascimento al sistema narrativo del barocco nazionale italiano', in *Cultura meridionale e letteratura italiana. I modelli narrativi dell'età moderna*, Naples, 1985, 191–252.

Conrieri, Davide, 'Il romanzo ligure dell'età ligure', *Annali della Scuola Normale Superiore di Pisa* 4.3 (1974) 925–1038.

Cultura meridionale e letteratura italiana: Atti XI Congresso AISLLI, Napoli, 1982, ed. P. Giannantonio, Naples, 1985.

Jones, W. McKendry, *Protestant Romances; Pattern of Reality in the Prose of Sir Giovanni Francesco Biondi*, Lawrence, KS, 1980.

Mancini, Albert N., 'Il romanzo nel Seicento. Saggio di bibliografia', *Studi secenteschi* 11 (1970) 205–74; 12 (1971) 443–98.

   'Il romanzo italiano nel Seicento. Saggio di bibliografia delle traduzioni in lingua straniera', *Studi secenteschi* 16 (1975) 183–217.

   Romanzi e romanzieri del Seicento, Naples, 1981.

Porcelli, Bruno, 'Le novelle degli Incogniti', *Studi secenteschi* 26 (1985) 101–39.

Rizzo, Gino (ed.), *Sul romanzo secentesco*, Galatina (Lecce), 1987.

Santoro, Marco (ed.), *La più stupenda e gloriosa macchina. Il romanzo italiano del sec. XVII*, Naples, 1981.

Varese, Claudio, 'Momenti e implicazioni del romanzo libertino del Seicento', in *Scena, linguaggio e ideologia dal Seicento al Settecento*, Rome, 1985, 69–100.

Theatre

COMMEDIA DELL'ARTE

Texts

Barbieri, Nicolò, *La supplica*, ed. F. Taviani, Milan, 1971.

Cecchini, Pier Maria, *Un commediante e il suo mestiere*, ed. C. Molinari, Florence, 1983.

Commedie dei comici dell'arte, ed. L. Falavolti, Turin, 1982.
Commedie dell'arte, ed. S. Ferrone, 2 vols., Milan, 1985–6.
Perrucci, Andrea, *Dell'arte rappresentativa, premeditata e all'improvviso*, ed. A. G. Bragaglia, Florence, 1961.
Scala, Flaminio, *Il teatro delle favole rappresentative*, ed. F. Marotti, 2 vols., Milan, 1976.
Scenarios of the Commedia dell'arte: Flaminio Scala's Il teatro delle favole rappresentative, trans. H. F. Salerno, New York, 1967.

Studies

Apollonio, Mario, *Storia della commedia dell'arte*, Florence, 1982.
Ferrone, Siro, *Attori, mercanti, corsari. La Commedia dell'arte in Europa tra Cinque e Seicento*, Turin, 1993.
Heck, Thomas F., *Commedia dell'arte. A Guide to the Primary and Secondary Literature*, New York–London, 1988.
Marotti, Ferruccio and Romei, Giovanna, *La commedia dell'arte e la società barocca*, Rome, 1991.
Nicoll, Allardyce, *The World of Harlequin*, Cambridge, 1963.
Pietropaolo, Domenico (ed.), *The Science of Buffoonery: Theory and History of the Commedia dell'arte*, Ottawa, 1989.
Richards, Kenneth and Richards, Laura, *The Commedia dell'arte. A Documentary History*, see above, p. 640.
Taviani, Ferdinando, *La commedia dell'arte e la società barocca*, Rome, 1969.
Taviani, Ferdinando and Schino, Mirella, *Il segreto della commedia dell'arte*, see above, p. 640.
Tessari, Roberto, *La commedia dell'arte nel Seicento*, see above, p. 640.

COMEDY, TRAGEDY, PASTORAL

Texts

Drammi per musica dal Rinuccini allo Zeno, ed. A. Della Corte, 2 vols., Turin, 1958.
Il teatro tragico italiano, ed. F. Doglio, Bologna, 1960.
Teatro del Seicento, ed. L. Fassò, Milan–Naples, 1956.
Maggi, Carlo Maria, *Il teatro milanese*, ed. D. Isella, Turin, 1964.
Bonarelli, Guidobaldo, *Filli di Sciro, discorsi ed appendici*, ed. G. Gambarin, Bari, 1941.
Buonarroti, Michelangelo, Il Giovane, *La Fiera. Redazione originaria 1619*, ed. U. Limentani, Florence, 1984.
De' Dottori, Carlo, *Aristodemo*, ed. L. Fassò, Turin, 1976.
Della Valle, Federico, *Tragedie*, ed. A. Gareffi, Milan, 1988.

Studies

Alonge, Roberto, 'Tensione tematica e tensione formale in alcune commedie del Seicento', *Studi secenteschi* 12 (1971) 29–99.
Angelini, Franca, *Il teatro barocco*, Bari, 1975.
Apollonio, Mario, *Storia del teatro italiano*, 2nd edn, vol. 2, Florence, 1981.
Carandini, Silvia, *Teatro e spettacolo nel Seicento*, Bari, 1990.
Clubb, Louise George, *Italian Drama in Shakespeare's Time*, Princeton, NJ, 1989.

Getto, Giovanni, *Barocco in prosa e poesia*, Milan, 1969.

Isella, Dante, *I lombardi in rivolta, da C. M. Maggi a C. E. Gadda*, Turin, 1984.

Mariti, Luciano, *Commedia ridicolosa: comici di professione, dilettanti, editoria teatrale nel seicento*, Rome, 1979.

Pieri, Marzia, *La scena boschereccia nel Rinascimento italiano*, Padua, 1983.

Pierce Palen, Glen, *The Caratterista and Comic Reform from Maggi to Goldoni*, Naples, 1986.

Sanesi, Ireneo, *La commedia*, 2 vols., 2nd edn, Milan, 1954.

Individual authors

Croce, Franco, *Carlo de'Dottori*, Florence, 1957.

Federico della Valle, Florence, 1965.

Daniele, Antonio, *Carlo de'Dottori. Lingua, cultura e aneddoti*, Padua, 1986.

Godard, Alain, 'La Filli di Sciro de Guidubaldo Bonarelli: Précédents littéraires et nouveaux impératifs idéologiques', in *Réécritures: commentaires, parodies, variations dans la littérature italienne de la Renaissance*, Centre interuniversitaire de recherche de la Renaissance italienne, Equipe de recherche associée, 3 vols., Paris, Université de la Sorbonne Nouvelle, 1983–7, vol. 2, 1984, pp. 141–225.

Perella, Nicholas J., *The critical fortunes of Battista Guarini's 'Il pastor fido'*, Florence, 1973.

'Heroic virtue and love in the *Pastor fido*', *Atti dell'Istituto Veneto di Scienze, Lettere ed Arti* 132 (1974) 653–706.

Sanguineti White, Laura, *Dal detto alla figura. Le tragedie di Federico della Valle*, Florence, 1992.

SETTECENTO

General

Binni, Walter, *Classicismo e Neoclassicismo nella letteratura del Settecento*, Florence, 1963.

Preromanticismo italiano, Bari, 1974.

Carpinetto, Dino and Ricuperati, Giuseppe, *Italy in the Age of Reason (1685–1789)*, trans. C. Higgit, London–New York, 1987.

Folena, Gianfranco, *L'italiano in Europa. Esperienze linguistiche del Settecento*, Turin, 1983.

Fubini, Mario, *Dal Muratori al Baretti. Studi sulla critica e sulla cultura del Settecento*, Bari, 1954.

Graf, Arturo, *L'Anglomania e l'influsso inglese in Italia nel secolo XVIII*, Turin, 1911.

Lee, Vernon (Paget, Violet), *Studies in the XVIIIth Century in Italy*, Chicago, 1908.

Robertson, J. G., *Studies in the Genesis of Romantic Theory in the Eighteenth Century*, New York, 1962.

Venturi, Franco, *Settecento Riformatore*, vol. 1, *Da Muratori a Beccaria*, 1969; vol. 2, *La chiesa e la repubblica dentro i loro confini, 1758–1774*, Turin, 1976.

Muratori, Ludovico

Rerum italicarum scriptores, 27 vols., Milan, 1723–38.

Opere (*Dal Muratori al Cesarotti*, vol. 1), ed. G. Falco and F. Forti, Milan–Naples, 1964.
Tiraboschi, Girolamo, *Storia della letteratura italiana*, 9 vols., Modena, 1787–94.
Bertelli, Sergio, *Erudizione e storia in L. A. Muratori*, Naples, 1960.

Venice

TEXTS

Maffei, Scipione, *Opere drammatiche e poesie varie*, ed. A. Avena, Bari, 1928.
  De' teatri antichi e moderni e altri scritti teatrali, ed. L. Sannia Nowe, Modena, 1988.
Conti, Antonio, *Le quattro tragedie*, Florence, 1751.
  Prose e poesie, vol. 1, Venice, 1739; vol. 2, Venice, 1756.
  Versioni poetiche, ed. G. Gronda, Bari, 1966.
Zeno, Apostolo, *Drammi scelti*, ed. M. Fehr, Bari, 1929.

STUDIES

Mattioda, Enrico, *Teorie della tragedia nel Settecento*, Modena, 1994.
Silvestri, Giovanni, *Scipione Maffei europeo del Settecento*, Modena, 1994.
Badaloni, Nicola, *Antonio Conti. Un abate libero pensatore tra Newton e Voltaire*, Milan, 1968.

Naples

TEXTS

Genovesi, Antonio, selected writings in *Riformatori napoletani* (*Illuministi italiani*, vol. 5), ed. F. Venturi, Milan–Naples, 1962.
  Autobiografia, lettere e altri scritti, ed. G. Savarese, Milan, 1962.
Giannone, Pietro, *Opere* (*Illuministi italiani*, vol. 1), ed. S. Bertelli and G. Ricuperati, Milan–Naples, 1971.
  Il Triregno, ed. A. Parente, Bari, 1940.
Vico, Giambattista, *Opere*, ed. F. Nicolini, 8 vols., Bari, 1911–41.
  Opere (selections), ed. F. Nicolini, Milan–Naples, 1953.
  The New Science, trans. and ed. Th. C. Bergin and M. H. Fish, Ithaca–London, 1948.
  The Autobiography, trans. and ed. M. H. Fish and Th. G. Bergin, Ithaca–London, 1975.

STUDIES

Badaloni, Nicola, *Introduzione a Giambattista Vico*, Milan, 1961.
Caponigri, A. Robert, *Time and Idea; the Theory of History in Giambattista Vico*, Chicago–London, 1953.
Croce, Benedetto, *The Philosophy of Giambattista Vico*, trans. R. G. Collingwood, London, 1913.
Fubini, Mario, *Stile e umanità di G. B. Vico*, Bari, 1946.
Pompa, Leon, *Vico: A Study of the 'New Science'*, London, 1975.
Ricuperati, Giuseppe, *L'esperienza civile e religiosa di Pietro Giannone*, Milan–Naples, 1970.

Vaughan, Frederick, *The Political Philosophy of Giambattista Vico: An Introduction to 'La Scienza Nuova'*, The Hague, 1972.
Villari, Lucio, *Il pensiero economico di Antonio Genovesi*, Florence, 1958.

Arcadia

TEXTS

Poeti minori del Settecento, ed. A. Donati, 2 vols., Bari, 1912–13.
Lirici del Settecento, ed. B. Maier, Milan–Naples, 1959.
Gravina, Gian Vincenzo, *Tragedie cinque*, Naples, 1715.
  Scritti critici e teorici, ed. A. Quondam, Bari, 1973.
Martello, Pier Jacopo, *Scritti critici e satirici*, ed. H. S. Noce, Bari, 1963.
  Teatro, ed. H. S. Noce, 3 vols., Bari, 1981.
Rolli, Paolo, *Liriche*, ed. C. Calcaterra, Turin, 1926.

STUDIES

Dorris, George E., *Paolo Rolli and the Italian Circle in London*, The Hague–Paris, 1967.
Fido, Franco, 'Il teatro parallelo di P. J. Martello', in *Le Muse perdute e ritrovate*, Florence, 1989.
Quondam, Amedeo, *Cultura e ideologia di Gian Vincenzo Gravina*, Milan, 1968.

Metastasio

TEXTS

Tutte le opere, ed. B. Brunelli, 5 vols., Milan, 1953–4.

STUDIES

Binni, Walter, *L'Arcadia e il Metastasio*, Florence, 1963.
Russo, Luigi, *Metastasio*, Bari, 1943.
Sala di Felice, Elena, *Metastasio. Ideologia, drammaturgia, spettacolo*, Milan, 1983.
Varese, Claudio, *Saggio sul Metastasio*, Florence, 1950.

Goldoni and comedy

TEXTS

La commedia del Settecento (*Il teatro italiano*, vol. 4), ed. R. Turchi, 2 vols., Turin, 1987.
Goldoni, Carlo, *Tutte le opere*, ed. G. Ortolani, 14 vols., Milan, 1936–56.
  Opere, con appendice del teatro comico del Settecento, ed. F. Zampieri, Milan–Naples, 1954.
  Le opere. Edizione nazionale, Venice, 1993 – (published to date: *La bottega del caffè, La baruffe chiozzotte, Il bugiardo, La Castalda, Pamela fanciulla-Pamela maritata, I pettegolezzi delle donne, L'uomo prudente, Una delle ultime sere di carnevale*).
  Memoirs of C. Goldoni Written by Himself, trans. J. Black, ed. W. A. Drake, Westport, CT, 1976.

Three Comedies (*Mine Hostess, Three Boors, The Fan*), trans. Clifford Bax *et al.*, Westport, CT, 1979.
The Holiday Trilogy, trans. A. Oldcorn, New York, 1994.

STUDIES

Sanesi, Ireneo, *La commedia*, 2 vols., Milan, 1911.
Turchi, Roberta, *La commedia italiana del Settecento*, Florence, 1985.
Angelini, Franca, *Vita di Goldoni*, Bari, 1993.
Anglani, Bartolo, *Goldoni: il mercato, la scena, l'utopia*, Naples, 1983.
Baratto, Mario, *La letteratura teatrale del Settecento in Italia* (*Studi e letture su C. Goldoni*), Vicenza, 1985.
Fido, Franco, *Guida a Goldoni. Teatro e società nel Settecento*, Turin, 1993.
    Da Venezia all'Europa. Prospettive sull'ultimo Goldoni, Rome, 1984.
Folena, Gianfranco, *Vocabolario del veneziano di Carlo Goldoni*, Rome, 1993.
Holme, Timothy, *A Servant of Many Masters. The Life and Times of C. Goldoni*, London, 1976.
Taylor, Hobart Chatfield, *Goldoni. A Biography*, New York, 1913.

Gozzi, Carlo

TEXTS

Le Fiabe, ed. E. Masi, 2 vols., Bologna, 1884–5.
Opere. Teatro e polemiche teatrali, ed. G. Petronio, Milan, 1962.
La Marfisa bizzarra, ed. C. Ortiz, Bari, 1911.

STUDIES

Luciani, G., *Carlo Gozzi (1720–1806). L'homme et l'œuvre*, 2 vols., Lille–Paris, 1977.

The Enlightenment

TEXTS

Algarotti, Francesco, *Saggi*, ed. G. Da Pozzo, Bari, 1963.
Bettinelli, Saverio, *Lettere virgiliane e inglesi e altri scritti critici*, ed. V. E. Alfieri, Bari, 1930.
    Risorgimento d'Italia negli studi nelle arti e ne' costumi dopo il mille, ed. S. Rossi, Ravenna, 1976.
Filangieri, Gaetano; Pagano, Mario; Galanti, G. Maria, selected writings in *Riformatori napoletani* (*Illuministi italiani*, vol. 5), ed. F. Venturi, Milan–Naples, 1962.
Galiani, Ferdinando, *Opere*, ed. F. Diaz and L. Guerci, Milan–Naples, 1975.
Giornalismo letterario del Settecento, ed. L. Piccioni, Turin, 1949.
Letterati, memorialisti e viaggiatori del Settecento, ed. E. Bonora, Milan–Naples, 1951.

STUDIES

La cultura illuministica in Italia, ed. M. Fubini, Turin, 1964.

GOZZI, GASPARO

Texts

Opere scelte, ed. E. Falqui, Milan, 1939.
Scritti scelti, ed. N. Mangini, Turin, 1960.
La 'Gazzetta veneta' per la prima volta riprodotta nella sua letteraria integrità, ed. A. Zardo, Florence, 1957.
L'Osservatore veneto, ed. E. Spagni, Florence, 1914.

Studies

Il lavoro di un intellettuale nel Settecento veneziano, ed. I. Crotti and R. Ricorda, Padua, 1989.

BARETTI, GIUSEPPE

Texts

La frusta letteraria, ed. L. Piccioni, 2 vols., Bari, 1932.
Epistolario, ed. L. Piccioni, 2 vols., Bari, 1936.
Prefazioni e polemiche, ed. L. Piccioni, Bari, 1933.
La scelta delle lettere familiari, ed. L. Piccioni, 2 vols., Bari, 1912.
Opere, ed. F. Fido, Milan, 1967.

Studies

Collison-Morley, Lacy, *Giuseppe Baretti, with an Account of his Literary Friendships and Feuds in Italy and in England in the Days of Dr Johnson*, London, 1909.
Jonard, Norbert, *G. Baretti (1719–89). L'homme et l'oeuvre*, Clermont-Ferrand, 1963.
Lubbers-Van der Brugge, Catharina Johanna, *Johnson and Baretti. Some Aspects of Eighteenth-century Literary Life in England and Italy*, Groningen–Djakarta, 1951.
Giuseppe Baretti: un piemontese in Europa, ed. M. Cerruti and P. Trivero, Alessandria, 1993.

'IL CAFFÈ', BECCARIA AND THE VERRI BROTHERS

Texts

'Il Caffè' 1764–66, ed. G. Francioni and S. Romagnoli, Turin, 1993.
Riformatori lombardi piemontesi e toscani, ed. F. Venturi, Milan–Naples, 1958.
Beccaria, Cesare, *Opere*, ed. S. Romagnoli, 2 vols., Florence, 1958.
  Opere, Edizione nazionale, ed. L. Firpo and F. Francioni, Milan, 1984– (4 vols. published to date).
  Dei delitti e delle pene, ed. F. Venturi, Turin, 1970.
Verri, Alessandro, *I romanzi*, ed. L. Martinelli, Ravenna, 1975.
Verri, Pietro, *Opere varie*, vol. 1 only, ed. N. Valeri, Florence, 1947.
  'Manoscritto' per Teresa, ed. G. Barbarisi, Milan, 1983.
Verri, Pietro and Verri, Alessandro, *Viaggio a Parigi e Londra (1766–76): Carteggio*, ed. G. Gaspari, Milan, 1980.

Studies

Atti del Convegno Internazionale su Cesare Beccaria, Accademia delle Scienze di Torino, Turin, 1966.

Cerruti, Marco, *Neoclassici e giacobini*, Milan, 1969.
Maestro, Marcello T., *Voltaire and Beccaria as Reformers of Criminal Law*, New York, 1942.
Romagnoli, Sergio, *La buona compagnia. Studi sulla letteratura italiana del Settecento*, Milan, 1983.
Valeri, Nino, *Pietro Verri*, Milan, 1937.

PARINI, GIUSEPPE

Texts

Tutte le opere, ed. G. Mazzoni, Florence, 1925.
Prose, ed. E. Bellorini, 2 vols., Bari, 1915.
Poesie, ed. E. Bellorini, 2 vols., Bari, 1929.
Poesie e prose. Con appendice di poeti satirici e didascalici del Settecento, ed. L. Caretti, Milan–Naples, 1951.
Il Giorno, ed. D. Isella, Milan–Naples, 1969.
Le odi, ed. D. Isella, Milan–Naples, 1975.

Studies

Bonora, Ettore, *Parini e altro Settecento*, Milan, 1982.
Fido, Franco, *Le metamorfosi del centauro*, Rome, 1977.
Isella, Dante, *L'officina della 'Notte' e altri studi pariniani*, Milan–Naples, 1968.
Petrini, Domenico, *La poesia e l'arte di Giuseppe Parini*, Bari, 1930.
Petronio, Giuseppe, *Parini e l'Illuminismo lombardo*, Bari, 1972.
Savarese, Gennaro, *Iconologia pariniana. Ricerche sulla poetica del figurativo in Parini*, Florence, 1973.
Spongano, Raffaele, *La poetica del sensismo e la poesia del Parini*, Messina–Milan, 1934.

ALFIERI, VITTORIO

Texts

Opere, ed. by the Centro Nazionale di Studi Alfieriani, Asti, 1951– (40 vols. published to date).
Opere, ed. A. Di Benedetto, Milan–Naples, 1977 (one vol. only to date).
Tragedie, ed. P. Cazzani, Milan, 1957.
Vita, ed. G. Dossena, Turin, 1981.
Le commedie, ed. S. Costa, 2 vols., Milan, 1988–90.

Studies

Binni, Walter, *Saggi alfieriani*, Rome, 1981.
Branca, Vittore, *Alfieri e la ricerca dello stile con cinque nuovi studi*, Bologna, 1981.
Di Benedetto, Arnaldo, *Le passioni e il limite. Un'interpretazione di Vittorio Alfieri*, Naples, 1994.
Fubini, Mario, *Vittorio Alfieri. Il pensiero, La tragedia*, 2nd edn, Florence, 1953.
Ritratto dell'Alfieri e altri studi alfieriani, 2nd edn, Florence, 1963.
Joly, Jacques, *Le désir et l'utopie. Études sur le théâtre d'Alfieri et de Goldoni*, Clermont-Ferrand, 1978.
Miller, Charles R. D., *Alfieri. A Biography*, Williamsport, PA, 1936.

Raimondi, Ezio, *Il concerto interrotto*, Pisa, 1979.
Russo, Luigi, 'Alfieri politico', in *Ritratti e disegni storici, serie iii*, Florence, 1963.
Sapegno, Natalino, 'Alfieri politico', in *Ritratto di Manzoni e altri saggi*, Bari, 1966.
Scrivano, Riccardo, *La natura teatrale dell'ispirazione alfieriana*, Milan–Messina, 1962.
  Biografia e autobiografia. Il modello alfieriano, Rome, 1976.
Sirven, Paul, *Vittorio Alfieri*, 8 vols., Paris, 1934–51.

PRE-ROMANTICISM

Texts

Bertola de' Giorgi, Aurelio, *Viaggio pittorico e sentimentale sul Reno*, ed. A. Baldini, Florence, 1942.
  Selected writings in *Lirici del Settecento* and *Viaggiatori del Settecento* (see above, pp. 648, 649).
Cesarotti, Melchiorre, *Opere scelte*, ed. G. Ortolani, 2 vols., Florence, 1945.
Critici e storici della poesia e delle arti nel secondo Settecento (Dal Muratori al Cesarotti, vol. 4), ed. E. Bigi, Milan–Naples, 1960.
Discussioni linguistiche del Settecento, ed. M. Puppo, Turin, 1966.
Il fiore della lirica veneziana, ed. M. Dazzi, 4 vols., Venice, 1956–9 (vol. 2).
Meli, Giovanni, *Opere*, ed. G. Santangelo, Milan, 1965–8.
Pindemonte, Ippolito, *Opere*, 4 vols., Milan, 1832–3.

Studies

Ceserani, Remo, 'Ippolito Pindemonte', in *Letteratura italiana. I Minori*, vol. 3, Milan, 1961.
Marzot, Giulio, *Il gran Cesarotti. Saggio sul preromanticismo italiano*, Florence, 1949.

AUTOBIOGRAPHIES

Texts

Casanova, Giacomo, *Histoire de ma vie*, 6 vols., Wiesbaden–Paris, 1960.
  Histoire de ma vie, ed. F. Lacassin, H. Watzlawick and A. Stroev, 3 vols., Paris, 1992.
Gozzi, Carlo, *Memorie inutili*, ed. G. Prezzolini, 2 vols., Bari, 1910.
The Memoirs of Count Carlo Gozzi, trans. J. A. Symonds, 2 vols., London, 1890

Studies

L'Autobiografia. Il vissuto e il narrato. Issue of *Quaderni di Retorica e poetica* 1, Padua, 1986.
Autobiography. Issue of *Annali d'italianistica* 4, 1986.
Casanova. Issue of *Europe* 64 no. 697, May 1987.
Childs, James Rives, *Casanova. A Biography Based on New Documents*, London, 1961.

THE AGE OF ROMANTICISM (1800–1870)

The Romantic controversy

TEXTS

Discussioni e polemiche sul Romanticismo, ed. E. Bellorini, 2 vols., Bari, 1975.

I manifesti romantici, ed. C. Calcaterra, Turin, 1951.
Il Conciliatore, ed. V. Branca, Florence, 1948–54.

STUDIES

Abrantès, Duchesse d' (Laura Saint-Martin Permon Junot), *Vite e ritratti delle donne celebri d'ogni paese continuata per cura di letterati italiani*, Milan, 1836–8.
Bandini-Buti, Maria, *Donne d'Italia. Poetesse e scrittrici*, 2 vols., Rome, 1946.
Bizzocchi, Roberto, *La Biblioteca italiana e la cultura della restaurazione* (1816–1825), Milan, 1979.
Bollati, Giulio, *L'Italiano*, Turin, 1983.
Cadioli, Alberto, *Introduzione a Berchet*, Bari, 1991.
Canonici Fachini, Ginevra, *Prospetto biografico delle Donne Italiane rinomate in Letteratura dal Secolo decimoquarto fino a' giorni nostri*, Alvisopoli, 1824.
Carsaniga, Giovanni, 'Italian Language and the Intellectual, 1750–1850', in *Literature and Western Civilisation*, ed. D. Daiches and A. K. Thorlby, vol. 4, London, 1975, pp. 351–76.
'Realism in Italy', in *The Age of Realism*, ed. F. W. J. Hemmings, Harmondsworth, 1974, pp. 323–55.
Costa-Zalessow, Natalia, *Scrittrici italiane dal XIII al XX secolo. Testi e critica*, Ravenna, 1982.
Ferri, Pietro Leopoldo, *Biblioteca femminile italiana*, Padua, 1842.
Fubini, Mario, *Romanticismo italiano*, Bari, 1971.
Greco, Oscar, *Biobibliografia femminile italiana del XIX secolo*, Venice, 1875.
Levati, Ambrogio, *Dizionario biografico cronologico diviso per classi*, Milan, 1821–2 (only the section on women published).
Martegiani, Gina, *Il Romanticismo italiano non esiste*, Florence, 1908.
Petronio, Giuseppe, *L'autore e il pubblico*, Padua, 1981.
Politica ed economia in Alessandro Manzoni, Atti del Convegno 22–24 febbraio 1985, Comune di Bergamo, 1985.
Problemi del Romanticismo, ed. U. Cardinale, 2 vols., Milan, 1983.
Rasy, Elisabetta, *Le donne e la letteratura*, Rome, 1984.
Ricuperati, Giuseppe, 'Periodici eruditi, riviste e giornali di varia umanità dalle origini a metà Ottocento', in Asor Rosa, vol. 1, see above, p. 608.
Spaggiari, William, *Il ritorno di Astrea. Civiltà letteraria della Restaurazione*, Rome, 1990.

Monti, Vincenzo

TEXTS

Opere, ed. M. Valgimigli and C. Muscetta, Milan–Naples, 1953.
Opere scelte, ed. G. Barbarisi, G. Chiodaroli and G. Bettola, 2 vols., Turin, 1971–4.
Epistolario, ed. A. Bertoldi, Florence, 1928–31.
Gli scritti di Vincenzo Monti sulla lingua italiana, ed. A. Dardi, Florence, 1990.

STUDIES

Barbarisi, Gennaro *et al.*, *Vincenzo Monti fra magistero e apostasia*, Ravenna, 1982.
Binni, Walter, *Monti, poeta del consenso*, Florence, 1981.

Kerbaker, Michele, *Shakespeare e Goethe nei versi di Vincenzo Monti*, Florence, 1897.
Masson, Frédéric, *Les diplomates de la Révolution. Hugo de Bassville à Rome, Bernadotte à Vienne*, Paris, 1882.

Foscolo

TEXTS

Opere, Edizione Nazionale, Florence, 1933–   (23 vols. to date).
Opere, ed. F. Gavazzeni, Milan–Naples, 1974–81.
Lettera apologetica, ed. G. Nicoletti, Turin, 1978.

STUDIES

Berengo, Marino *et al.*, *Lezioni sul Foscolo*, Florence, 1961.
Cambon, Glauco, *Ugo Foscolo, Poet of Exile*, Guildford, 1980.
Cavallini, Giorgio, *Studi e note su Foscolo e Leopardi*, Rome, 1990.
Cerruti, Marco, *Introduzione a Foscolo*, Bari, 1990.
Derla, Luigi, *L'isola, il velo, l'ara. Allegoria e mito nella poesia di Ugo Foscolo*, Genoa, 1984.
Di Benedetto, Vincenzo, *Lo scrittoio di Ugo Foscolo*, Turin, 1990.
Dionisotti, Carlo, *Appunti sui moderni. Foscolo, Leopardi, Manzoni e altri*, Bologna, 1988.
Lindon, John, *Studi sul Foscolo 'inglese'*, Pisa, 1987.
O'Neill, Tom, *Of Virgin Muses and of Love. A study of Foscolo's 'I sepolcri'*, Dublin, 1981.
Radcliff Umstead, Douglas R., *Ugo Foscolo*, New York, 1970.
Varese, Claudio (ed.), *Ugo Foscolo. Autobiografia dalle lettere*, Rome, 1979.
    Foscolo: sternismo, tempo e persona, Ravenna, 1982.
Vincent, Eric R., *Ugo Foscolo: An Italian in Regency England*, Cambridge, 1953.

Leopardi

TEXTS

Tutte le opere, ed. W. Binni and E. Ghidetti, Florence, 1969.
Dissertazioni filosofiche (1811–12), ed. M. De Poli, Montepulciano, 1983.
'*Entro dipinta gabbia*': *Tutti gli scritti inediti, rari e editi 1809–1810*, ed. M. Corti, Milan, 1972.
Zibaldone, ed. G. Pacella, 2 vols, Milan, 1991.
Leopardi, Monaldo, *Dialoghetti sulle materie occorrenti nell'anno 1831*, ed. C. Grabher and A. Briganti, Bologna, 1972.
I Canti nelle traduzioni inglesi, ed. G. Singh, Recanati, 1990.
Canti of Giacomo Leopardi with a Selection of his Prose, trans. J. G. Nichols, Manchester, 1994.
Moral Tales, trans. P. Creagh, Manchester, 1983.
Pensieri, trans. W. S. Di Piero, New York–Oxford, 1984 (bi-lingual edition).

STUDIES

Bini, Daniela, *A Fragrance from the Desert. Poetry and Philosophy in Giacomo Leopardi*, Saratoga, CA, 1983.

Binni, Walter, *La protesta di Leopardi*, Florence, 1982.

Carducci, Giosué, 'Le tre canzoni patriottiche di Giacomo Leopardi' in *Opere*, Edizione Nazionale, vol. 20, Bologna, 1937, pp. 153–4.

Carpi, Umberto, *Il poeta e la politica: Leopardi, Belli, Montale*, Naples, 1978.

Letteratura e società nella Toscana del Risorgimento, Bari, 1974.

Carrannante, Antonio, *I diletti del vero. Percorsi della poesia leopardiana fra filosofia e filologia*, Pisa, 1987.

Carsaniga, Giovanni, *Giacomo Leopardi: The Unheeded Voice*, Edinburgh, 1977.

De Sanctis, Francesco, 'Schopenhauer e Leopardi', in *Saggi critici*: now in *Leopardi*, ed. C. Muscetta and A. Perna, Turin, 1960, pp. 417–67.

Gioanola, Elio, 'Considerazioni inattuali sullo "storicismo" leopardiano', in *Il pensiero storico e politico di Giacomo Leopardi*, Florence, 1989.

Luporini, Cesare, *Leopardi progressivo*, Rome, 1981.

Manacorda, Giuliano, *Materialismo e masochismo: il 'Werther', Foscolo e Leopardi*, Florence, 1973.

Marti, Mario, *I tempi dell'ultimo Leopardi (con una 'Giunta' su Leopardi e Virgilio)*, Galatina, 1988.

Il pensiero storico e politico di Giacomo Leopardi, Atti del VI Convegno internazionale di studi Leopardiani, Recanati, 9–11 settembre, 1984. Florence, 1989.

Perella, Nicholas J., *Night and the Sublime in Giacomo Leopardi*, Berkeley, CA, 1970.

Timpanaro, Sebastiano, *Antileopardiani e neomoderati nella sinistra italiana*, Pisa, 1982.

Classicismo e illuminismo nell'Ottocento italiano, Pisa, 1988.

Whitfield, John H., *Giacomo Leopardi*, Oxford, 1954.

Manzoni and the novel

TEXTS

Tutte le opere, ed. A. Chiari and F. Ghisalberti, 10 vols., Milan, 1957–74.

I promessi sposi, ed. L. Caretti, Turin, 1971, 2 vols.; *The Betrothed*, trans. B. Penman, Penguin Classics, Harmondsworth, 1983.

Lettere sui Promessi sposi, ed. G. A. Amoretti, Milan, 1985.

Tommaseo, Niccolò, *Colloqui col Manzoni*, ed. T. Lodi, Florence, 1928.

On the Historical Novel, trans. S. Bermann, Lincoln, NE–London, 1984.

STUDIES

Bàrberi Squarotti, Giorgio (ed.), *Prospettive sui 'Promessi sposi'*, Turin, 1991.

Barberis, Carlo et al., *Tra Manzoni e Jacini. La cultura rurale e lombarda dell'Ottocento*, Milan, 1985.

Berengo, Marino, *Intellettuali e librai nella Milano della Restaurazione*, Turin, 1980.

Borlenghi, Aldo, *Il successo contrastato dei "Promessi sposi" e altri studi sull'Ottocento italiano*, Milan–Naples, 1980.

Bruscagli, Riccardo, Turchi, Roberta (eds.), *Teorie del romanzo nel primo Ottocento*, Rome, 1991.

Carsaniga, Giovanni, 'Manzoni and his Twenty-five Readers', in *The Shared Horizon*, ed. T. O'Neill, Dublin, 1990, pp. 123–40.

'Questo matrimonio non s'ha da fare', *Italian Studies* 42 (1987) 56–68.

Colummi Camerino, Marinella, *Idillio e propaganda nella letteratura sociale del Risorgimento*, Naples, 1975.

Dombroski, Robert S., *L'apologia del vero. Lettura ed interpretazione dei 'Promessi sposi'*, Padua, 1984.

Getto, Giovanni, *Manzoni europeo*, Milan, 1971.

Leone De Castris, Arcangelo, *La polemica sul romanzo storico*, Bari, 1959.

Leri, Clara, *Oscura prosa rimata. Studi sugli Inni sacri manzoniani*, Pisa, 1989.

Mazzocca, Fernando, *Quale Manzoni? Vicende figurative dei 'Promessi sposi'*, Milan, 1985.

Meier-Brügger, Elisabeth, *'Fermo e Lucia' e 'I promessi sposi' come situazione comunicativa*, Frankfurt–Bern–New York–Paris, 1987.

Pavan, Massimiliano, *Manzoni e la storiografia risorgimentale*, Treviso, 1973.

Raimondi, Ezio, *Il romanzo senza idillio. Saggio sui 'Promessi sposi'*, Turin, 1974.

Sala Di Felice, Elena, *Il punto su Manzoni*, Rome–Bari, 1989.

Spinazzola, Vittorio, 'I Promessi sposi: l'io narrante e il suo doppio', in *Studi di lingua e letteratura lombarda offerti a Maurizio Vitale*, vol. 2, Pisa, 1983, pp. 841–59.

Spongano, Raffaele, *Le prime interpretazioni dei 'Promessi sposi'*, Bologna, 1967.

Studi sulla cultura lombarda in memoria di Mario Apollonio, by various authors, Milan, 1972.

Varese, Claudio, *Fermo e Lucia: un'esperienza manzoniana interrotta*, Florence, 1964.

L'originale e il ritratto: Manzoni secondo Manzoni, Florence, 1975.

Other novelists and poets of the Risorgimento

TEXTS

Aleardi, Aleardo, *Canti italiani e patrii – Idillio – Canti spirituali – La campagna di Roma*, ed. G. Battista Pigi, Verona, 1975.

D'Azeglio, Massimo, *Ettore Fieramosca (o la disfida di Barletta)*, Pordenone, 1992.

I miei ricordi, ed. A. Pompeati, Turin, 1972.

Giusti, Giuseppe, *Opere*, ed. N. Sabbatucci, Turin, 1976.

Poesie, Milan, 1982.

Guerrazzi, Francesco Domenico and Bini, Carlo, *Scritti scelti*, ed. A. Cajumi, Turin, 1955.

Nievo, Ippolito, *Opere*, ed. S. Romagnoli, Milan–Naples, 1952.

Due scritti politici, ed. M. Gorra, Padua, 1988.

Le confessioni di un italiano, ed. P. Ruffilli, Milan, 1982.

The castle of Fratta, trans. L. F. Edwards, London, 1957 (abridged).

Pellico, Silvio, *Le mie prigioni*, Milan, 1990.

Prati, Giovanni, *Poesie varie*, ed. O. Malagoli, 2 vols., Bari, 1929–33.

Tommaseo, Niccolò, *Fede e Bellezza*, ed. L. Baldacci, Milan, 1990.

Poesie e prose, ed. P. P. Trompeo and P. Ciureanu, Turin, 1973.

STUDIES

Baldi, Guido, *Giuseppe Rovani e il problema del romanzo nell'Ottocento*, Florence, 1967.
Bozzetti, Cesare, *La formazione del Nievo*, Padua, 1959.
Branca, Vittore and Petrocchi, Giorgio (eds.), *Niccolò Tommaseo nel centenario della morte*, Florence, 1977.
Colummi Camerino, Marinella, *Introduzione a Nievo*, Bari, 1991.
Gorra, Marcella, *Nievo fra noi*, Florence, 1970.
Haller, Herman W. (ed.) *The Hidden Italy. A Bilingual Edition of Italian Dialect Poetry*, Detroit, 1986.
Teodonio, Marcello, *Introduzione a Belli*, Bari, 1992.

OPERA

GENERAL

Algarotti, Francesco, 'Saggio sopra l'opera in musica, 1755', in *Illuministi italiani*, vol. 2: *Opere di Francesco Algarotti e di Saverio Bettinelli*, ed. E. Bonora, Milan–Naples, 1969. (Originally published 1755; English edn Glasgow, 1768.)
Bianconi, Lorenzo and Pestelli, Giorgio (eds.), *Storia dell'opera italiana* (6 vols.), Turin, 1987 (continuing).
Di Stefano, Carlo, *La censura teatrale in Italia (1600–1962)*, Bologna, 1964.
Gronda, Giovanni and Fabbri, Paolo, *Libretti d'opera italiani dal Seicento al Novecento*, Milan, 1997.
Kerman, Joseph, *Opera as Drama*, New York, 1956.
Kimbell, David R. B., *Italian Opera* (National Traditions of Opera), Cambridge, 1991.
Parker, Roger (ed.), *The Oxford Illustrated History of Opera*, Oxford, 1994.
Rinaldi, Mario, *Felice Romani: dal melodramma classico al melodramma romantico*, Rome, 1965.
Robinson, Michael F., *Naples and Neapolitan Opera*, Oxford, 1972.
Sadie, Stanley (ed.), *History of Opera* (The New Grove Handbooks in Music), Basingstoke, 1989.
The New Grove Dictionary of Opera, 4 vols., London, 1992.
Schmidgall, Gary, *Literature as Opera*, New York, 1977.

SEICENTO

Bjurström, Per, *Giacomo Torelli and Baroque Stage Design*, Stockholm, 1961.
Doni, Giovanni Battista, *Compendio del trattato de' generi e de' modi della musica*, Rome, 1635 (passages trans. in D. J. Grout, *A Short History of Opera*, New York, 1947).
Donington, Robert, *The Rise of Opera*, London, 1981.
Fenlon, Iain and Millet, P. N., *The Song of the Soul: Understanding 'Poppea'* (Royal Musical Association Monographs 5), London, 1992.
Glover, Jane, *Cavalli*, London, 1978.
Muraro, Maria Teresa (ed.), *Venezia e il melodramma nel Seicento*, Florence, 1976.
Pirrotta, Nino, *Music and Theatre from Poliziano to Monteverdi*, trans. K. Eales, Cambridge, 1982.
Rosand, Ellen, *Opera in Seventeenth-Century Venice: The Creation of a Genre*, Berkeley, CA, 1991.

Sternfeld, Frederick William, *The Birth of Opera*, Oxford, 1993.
Tomlinson, Gary, *Monteverdi and the End of the Renaissance*, Oxford, 1987.
Whenham, John (ed.), *Claudio Monteverdi: 'L'Orfeo'* (Cambridge Opera Handbooks), Cambridge, 1986.
Worsthorne, Simon Towneley, *Venetian Opera in the Seventeenth Century*, Oxford, 1954.

SETTECENTO

Burney, Charles, *Memoirs of the Life and Writings of the Abate Metastasio*, London, 1796.
Dean, Winton and Knapp, John Merrill, *Handel's Operas: 1704–1726*, Oxford, 1987.
Gallarati, Paolo, *Musica e maschera: il libretto italiano del settecento*, Turin, 1984.
Heartz, Daniel, *Mozart's Operas*, Berkeley, CA, 1990.
Muraro, Maria Teresa (ed.), *Venezia e il melodramma nel settecento*, Florence, 1978.
Steptoe, Andrew, *The Mozart–Da Ponte Operas*, Oxford, 1988.
Strohm, Reinhard, *Essays on Handel and Italian Opera*, Cambridge, 1985.
Yorke-Long, Alan, *Opera at Court: Four Eighteenth-century Studies*, London, 1954.

SINCE 1800

Abbiati, Franco, *Giuseppe Verdi*, 2 vols., Milan, 1959.
Adamo, Maria Rosaria and Lippmann, Friedrich, *Vincenzo Bellini*, Turin, 1981.
Ashbrook, William, *Donizetti and his Operas*, Cambridge, 1982.
Budden, Julien, *The Operas of Verdi*, 3 vols., London, 1973, 1978, 1981.
    Verdi (The Master Musicians), London, 1985.
Carner, Mosco, *Puccini, A Critical Biography*, 2nd edn, London, 1974.
Conati, Marcello (ed.), *Interviews and Encounters with Verdi*, trans. R. Stokes, London, 1984.
Groos, Arthur and Parker, Roger, *Giacomo Puccini: 'La Bohème'* (Cambridge Opera Handbooks), Cambridge, 1986.
Hepokoski, James, *Giuseppe Verdi: 'Falstaff'* (Cambridge Opera Handbooks), Cambridge, 1983.
    Giuseppe Verdi: 'Otello' (Cambridge Opera Handbooks), Cambridge, 1987.
Kimbell, David R. B., *Verdi in the Age of Italian Romanticism*, Cambridge, 1981.
Large, David Clay and Weber, William (eds.), *Wagnerism in European Culture and Politics*, Ithaca, NY, 1984.
Martin, George, *Verdi: His Music, Life and Times*, London, 1965.
Mazzini, Giuseppe, 'Filosofia della musica (1836)', in *Edizione Nazionale degli scritti di Giuseppe Mazzini*, vol. 8, Imola, 1910.
Osborne, Richard, *Rossini* (The Master Musicians), London, 1986.
Stendhal (H. Beyle), *The Life of Rossini*, trans. R. N. Coe, 2nd edn, London, 1985.
Walker, Frank, *The Man Verdi*, London, 1962.
Weaver, William and Chusid, Martin (eds.), *The Verdi Companion*, London, 1980.
Weaver, William and Puccini, Simonetta (eds.), *The Puccini Companion*, New York, 1994.
Weinstock, Herbert, *Donizetti and the World of Opera in Italy, Paris and Vienna in the First Half of the Nineteenth Century*, London, 1964.
    Rossini: a Biography, London, 1986.
    Vincenzo Bellini: His Life and His Operas, New York, 1972.

LITERATURE OF UNITED ITALY (1870–1910)

General

TEXTS

Capuana, Luigi, *Saggi sulla letteratura contemporanea*, 2 vols., Catania, 1882.
Verga, Giovanni, *Lettere a Luigi Capuana*, Florence, 1975.

STUDIES

Bolzoni, Lina, 'Le tendenze della Scapigliatura e la poesia fra tardo-romanticismo e realismo', in *Letteratura italiana: storia e testi* 7, 2, Bari, 1970–80.
Carsaniga, Giovanni, 'Scapigliatura', in *The Age of Realism*, ed. F. W. J. Hemmings, Baltimore, 1974.
Clerici, Luca, *Invito a conoscere il Verismo*, Milan, 1977.
Dombroski, Robert S., *Properties of Writing: Ideological Discourse in Modern Italian Fiction*, Baltimore–London,1994.
Mariani, Gaetano, *Storia della Scapigliatura*, Caltanissetta, 1971.
Spinazzola, Vittorio, *Verismo e positivismo*, Milan, 1977.

Individual authors

ALERAMO, SIBILLA

A Woman, trans. Rosalind Delmar, London, 1979.
De Ceccatty, Rene, *Sibilla: vita artistica e amorosa di S. A.*, Milan, 1992.

CAPUANA, LUIGI

Antologia degli scritti critici, ed. W. Mauro, Bologna, 1971.
Il Marchese di Roccaverdina, Milan, 1969.
Racconti, ed. E. Ghidetti, 3 vols., Rome, 1973–4.
Madrignani, Carlo Alberto, *Capuana e il naturalismo*, Bari, 1970.
Pacifici, Sergio, *The Modern Italian Novel from Capuana to Tozzi*, Carbondale, IL, 1973.
Traversa, Vincenzo P., *Luigi Capuana, Critic and Novelist*, The Hague, 1968.

CARDUCCI, GIOSUÈ

Edizione Nazionale delle opere di Giosuè Carducci, Bologna, 1935–40.
Giosuè Carducci: A Selection from the Poems, trans. E. A. Tribe, London, 1921.
Carpi, Umberto (ed.), *Carducci poeta*, Pisa, 1985.
Mattesini, Francesco, *Per una lettura storica di Carducci*, Milan, 1975.
Scalia, Eugène, *Carducci: His Critics and Translators in England and America 1881–1932*, New York, 1937.
Williams, Orlando C., *Giosuè Carducci*, London, 1914.

COLLODI, CARLO

Tutto Collodi per i piccoli e per i grandi, ed. P. Pancrazi, Florence, 1948.
Pinocchio, ed. F. Tempesti, Milan, 1972.
The Adventures of Pinocchio, trans. C. Della Chiesa, New York, 1972.

Bertacchini, Renato, *Collodi narratore*, Pisa, 1961.
Garroni, Emilio, *Pinocchio uno e bino*, Bari, 1975.
Genot, Gérard, *L'Analyse structurelle de Pinocchio*, Florence, 1970.

D'ANNUNZIO, GABRIELE

Tutte le opere, ed. E. Bianchetti, 10 vols., Milan, 1939–50.
The Child of Pleasure, trans. G. Harding, New York, 1898.
The Daughter of Jorio, trans. C. Porter, 1907; rpt Westport, CT, 1969.
The Triumph of Death, trans. G. Harding, 1896; rpt New York, 1975.
Cervigni, Dino (ed.), *D'Annunzio*, special number of *Annali d'Italianistica*, 1977.
Dombroski, Robert, 'D'Annunzio's mythical narratives', *The Italianist* 10 (1990) 41–70.
Felice, Angela, *Introduzione a D'Annunzio*, Bari, 1991.
Gibellini, Pietro, *Logos e mythos: Studi su D'Annunzio*, Florence, 1985.
Jacomuzzi, Angelo, *Una poetica strumentale: Gabriele D'Annunzio*, Turin, 1974.
Jullian, Philippe, *D'Annunzio*, New York, 1973.
Klopp, Charles, *Gabriele D'Annunzio*, Boston, 1988.
Lorenzini, Niva, *Il segno del corpo (Saggio su D'Annunzio)*, Rome, 1984.
Mariano, Emilio (ed.), *D'Annunzio e il simbolismo europeo*, Milan, 1976.
Raimondi, Ezio, *Il silenzio della Gorgone*, Bologna, 1980.
Ricciardi, Mario, *Coscienza e struttura nella prosa di D'Annunzio*, Turin, 1970.
Roda, Vittorio, *Il soggetto centrifugo*, Bologna, 1984.
Valesio, Paolo, *Gabriele D'Annunzio: The Dark Flame*, New Haven–London, 1992.

DE AMICIS, EDMONDO

De Amicis, ed. A. Baldini, 2 vols., Milan, 1948.
Heart: A School Boy's Journal, trans. I. Hapgood, New York, 1922.
Timpanaro, Sebastiano, *Il socialismo di Edmondo De Amicis*, Verona, 1983.

DELEDDA, GRAZIA

Romanzi e novelle, ed. N. Sapegno, Milan, 1971.
The Mother, trans. M. Steegman, 1923; rpt Dunwoody, GA, 1974.
Balducci, Carolyn, *A Self-Made Woman*, Boston, 1975.
Dolfi, Anna, *Grazia Deledda*, Milan, 1979.
Lombardi, Olga, *Invito alla lettura di G.D.*, Milan, 1989.

DE MARCHI, EMILIO

Opere complete, ed. G. Ferrata, 4 vols., Milan, 1959–63.
Demetrio Pianelli, trans. M. Nowett, 1905; rpt New York, 1977.
Spinazzola, Vittorio, *Emilio De Marchi romanziere popolare*, Milan, 1971.

DE ROBERTO, FEDERICO

I Vicerè, Milan, 1962.
The Viceroys, trans. A. Colquhoun, New York, 1962.
Madrignani, Carlo Alberto, *Illusione e realtà nell'opera di Federico de Roberto*, Bari, 1972.
O'Neill, Thomas, 'Lampedusa e De Roberto', *Italica* 42 (1970) 170–82.
Spinazzola, Vittorio, *Federico De Roberto e il Verismo*, Milan, 1961.
Tedesco, Natale, *La norma del negativo: De Roberto e il realismo critico*, Palermo, 1981.

FOGAZZARO, ANTONIO

Tutte le opere, ed. P. Nardi, 15 vols., Milan, 1931–45.
Daniele Cortis, trans. J. R. Tilton, New York, 1887.
Little World of the Past, trans. W. J. Strachan, London, 1962.
The Saint, trans. M. Prichard-Agnetti, New York, 1907.
Gallarati-Scotti, Tommaso, *The Life of Antonio Fogazzaro*, 1922, rpt Port Washington, NY, 1972.
Ghidetti, Enrico, *Le idee e le virtù di Antonio Fogazzaro*, Padua, 1974.
Tellini, Gino, *L'avventura di 'Malombra' e altri saggi*, Rome, 1973.

PASCOLI, GIOVANNI

Myricae, ed. G. Nava, Rome, 1991.
Tutte le opere, 6 vols., Milan, 1939–52.
Poems of Giovanni Pascoli, trans. A. Abbott, New York, 1927.
Poems, trans. E. Stein, New Haven, CT, 1923.
Bàrberi-Squarotti, Giorgio, *Simboli e strutture delle poesie di Pascoli*, Messina–Florence, 1966.
Capovilla, Guido, *La formazione letteraria del Pascoli*, Bologna, 1988.
Ferri, Teresa, *Miti e percorsi della poesia pascoliana*, Rome, 1988.
Ukas, M., 'Nature in the Poetry of Giovanni Pascoli', *Kentucky Foreign Language Quarterly* 13 (1966) 51–9.
Varese, Claudio, *Pascoli decadente*, Florence, 1965.

PIRANDELLO, LUIGI

Texts

The standard edition of Pirandello's works is the seven-volume *Opere di Luigi Pirandello*, Milan, consisting of:
Novelle per un anno, 2 vols., 1969; new edn, 3 vols. 1985–90.
Tutti i romanzi, 2 vols., 1973.
Maschere nude (the plays), 2 vols., 1958; new edn, 1986– .
Saggi, poesie e scritti varii, 1973.

Principal translations include:
Collected Plays, 7 vols, ed. R. Rietty, Paris, London, New York, 1987 (4 vols published to date).
Three plays, London, 1985.
Naked Masks, New York, 1952.
Pirandello Short Stories, trans. F. May, New York and London, 1965 (paperback edn 1975).
The Late Mattia Pascal, trans. W. Weaver, New York, 1964.
One, No One and One Hundred Thousand, trans. W. Weaver, New York, 1990.
Notebooks of Serafino Gubbio, trans. C. K. Scott-Moncrieff, London, 1990.
On Humor (*L'umorismo*), trans. A. Iliano and D. P. Testa, Chapel Hill, NC, 1974.

Studies

Alonge, Roberto, *Pirandello tra realismo e mistificazione*, Naples, 1972.

Angelini, Franca, *Il teatro del Novecento da Pirandello a Fo*, Bari, 1976.
Bassnet-McGuire, Susan, *Luigi Pirandello*, London–Basingstoke, 1983.
Büdel, Oscar, *Pirandello*, London, 1966.
Cambon, Glauco (ed.), *Pirandello*, Englewood Cliffs, NJ, 1967. (Collection of important critical essays.)
Chiaromonte, Nicola, 'Pirandello and the Contemporary Theatre', *World Theatre* 26 (1967).
D'Amico, Alessandro and Tinterri, Alessandro, *Pirandello capocomico*, Palermo, 1987.
Firth, Felicity, *Pirandello in Performance*, Cambridge, 1990.
Giudice, Giovanni, *Pirandello*, Turin, 1963; English trans. (slightly abridged) *Pirandello: a Biography*, Oxford, 1975.
Leone De Castris, Arcangelo, *Storia di Pirandello*, Bari, 1962.
Livio, Gigi, *Il teatro in rivolta. Futurismo, grottesco, Pirandello e pirandellismo*, Milan, 1976.
Maclintock, Lander, *The Age of Pirandello*, Bloomington, IN, 1962.
Mirmina, Emilia, *Pirandello novelliere*, Ravenna, 1973.
Moestrup, Jørn, *The Structural Patterns of Pirandello's Work*, Odense, 1972.
Ragusa, Olga, *Luigi Pirandello: An Approach to his Theatre*, Edinburgh, 1980.
Sciascia, Leonardo, *Pirandello e la Sicilia*, Caltanissetta–Rome, 1961.
Stone, Jennifer, *Pirandello's Naked Prompt: The Structure of Repetition in Modernism*, Ravenna, 1989.
Vicentini, Claudio, *L'estetica di Pirandello*, Milan, 1970.
Vittorini, Domenico, *The Drama of Luigi Pirandello*, New York, 1957.
See also the *Atti* of the annual conferences held in Agrigento since 1974 and published by the Centro Nazionale di Studi Pirandelliani, Agrigento, Sicily; and the Yearbook of the Society for Pirandello Studies (formerly the British Pirandello Society) 1980–   .

VERGA, GIOVANNI

Opere, Milan, 1965.
Cavalleria Rusticana, and Other Stories, trans. D. H. Lawrence, London, 1926; rpt Westport, CT, 1975.
The House by the Medlar Tree, trans. R. Rosenthal, Berkeley and Los Angeles, 1964.
Little Novels of Sicily, trans. D. H. Lawrence, Oxford, 1925; rpt Westport, CT, 1975.
Mastro don Gesualdo, trans. D. H. Lawrence, New York, 1923; rpt Westport, CT, 1976.
The She-Wolf and Other Stories, trans. G. Cecchetti, Berkeley–Los Angeles, 1973.
Alexander, Alfred, *Giovanni Verga*, London, 1972.
Baldi, Guido, *L'artificio della regressione: tecnica narrativa e ideologia nel Verga verista*, Naples, 1980.
Bigazzi, Roberto, *Verga novelliere*, Pisa, 1975.
Cattaneo, Giulio, *Giovanni Verga*, Turin, 1963.
Cecchetti, Giovanni, *Il Verga maggiore*, Florence, 1968.
Debenedetti, Giacomo, *Verga e il naturalismo*, Milan, 1976.
Dombroski, Robert, *Properties of Writing: Ideological Discourse in Modern Italian Fiction*, Baltimore–London, 1994.
Lucente, Gregory L., *The Narrative of Reality and Myth*, Baltimore–London, 1979.
Luperini, Romano, *Simbolo e costruzione allegorica in Verga*, Bologna, 1988.
Ragusa, Olga, *Verga's Milanese Tales*, New York, 1964.

THE NOVECENTO (SINCE 1910)

Futurism

De Maria, L. (ed.), *Per conoscere Marinetti e il futurismo*, Milan, 1981.

Dombroski, Robert and Sharkey, S., 'Revolution, Myth and Mythological Politics: The Futurist Revolution', *Journal of European Studies* 6 (1976) 231–47.

Futurist Manifestos, ed. U. Apollonio, New York, 1973.

Kirby, Michael, *Futurist Performances*, New York, 1971.

Manifesti, proclami, interventi e documenti teorici del futurismo, ed. L. Caruso, Florence, 1980.

Martin, Marianne, *Futurist Art and Theory, 1909–1915*, Oxford, 1969.

Salaris, Claudia, *Storia del futurismo*, Rome, 1985.

Anthologies of poetry

Ballerini, Luigi (ed.), *Shearsmen of Sorts: Italian Poetry 1975–93*, published as 'Italian Poetry Supplement 1992' of *Forum Italicum*.

Brevini, Franco (ed.), *Poeti dialettali del Novecento*, Turin, 1987.

Di Nola, Laura (ed.), *Poesia femminista italiana*, Rome, 1978.

Gentili, Alessandro and O'Brien, Catherine (eds.), *The Green Flame. Contemporary Italian Poetry with English Translation*, Dublin, 1987.

Golino, Carlo (ed.), *Contemporary Italian Poetry*, Berkeley–Los Angeles, 1962.

Mengaldo, Pier Vincenzo (ed.), *Poeti italiani del Novecento*, Milan, 1978.

Raboni, Giovanni (ed.), *Poesia italiana contemporanea*, Florence, 1981.

Sanguineti, E. (ed.), *Poesia italiana del Novecento*, 2 vols., Turin, 1969.

Smith, Lawrence R. (ed. and trans.), *The New Italian Poetry: 1945 to the Present*, Berkeley–Los Angeles–London, 1981.

General studies and studies on more than one writer

Aricò, Santo L., *Contemporary Women Writers in Italy: A Modern Renaissance*, Amherst, MA, 1990.

Asor Rosa, Alberto, *Scrittori e popolo*, Rome, 1991.

Baranski, Zygmunt G. and Pertile, Lino (eds.), *The New Italian Novel*, Edinburgh, 1993.

Bàrberi Squarotti, Giorgio, *La forma e la vita: il romanzo del Novecento*, Milan, 1989.

Caesar, Michael and Hainsworth, Peter (eds.), *Writers and Society in Contemporary Italy*, Leamington Spa, 1984.

Corti, Maria and Segre, Cesare (eds.), *I metodi attuali della critica in Italia*, Turin, 1970.

Debenedetti, Giacomo, *Poesia italiana del Novecento*, Milan, 1980.

Dizionario della letteratura italiana del Novecento, ed. A. Asor Rosa, Milan, 1992.

Dombroski, Robert, *L'esistenza ubbidiente: intellettuali e fascismo*, Naples, 1984.
    Properties of Writing: Ideological Discourse in Modern Italian Fiction, Baltimore–London, 1994.

Falcetto, Bruno, *Storia della narrativa realista*, Milan, 1992.

Fortini, Franco, *I poeti del Novecento*, Bari, 1977.

Gatt-Rutter, John, *Writers and Politics in Modern Italy*, London, 1978.

Grana, Gianni (ed.), *Letteratura italiana, Novecento*, 10 vols., Milan, 1979–80.

Jones, Frederick, *The Modern Italian Lyric*, Cardiff, 1986.

Leonelli, Giuseppe, *La critica letteraria in Italia (1945–1994)*, Milan, 1994.

Lorenzini, Niva, *Il presente della poesia*, Bologna, 1991.

Lucente, Gregory, *Beautiful Fables: Self-consciousness in Italian Narrative from Manzoni to Calvino*, Baltimore–London, 1986.

Luperini, Romano, *Il Novecento*, 2 vols., Turin, 1981.

Luti, Giorgio, *Introduzione alla letteratura italiana del Novecento*, Rome, 1985.

Manacorda, Giuliano, *Storia della letteratura italiana fra le due guerre (1919–1943)*, Rome, 1980.

Storia della letteratura italiana contemporanea (1940–1975), Rome, 1977.

Letteratura italiana d'oggi (1965–1985), Rome, 1987.

Mariani, Gaetano and Petrucciani, Mario, *Letteratura italiana contemporanea*, 4 vols., Rome, 1979–87.

Merry, Bruce, *Women in Modern Italian Literature*, Townsville, Queensland, 1990.

Muscetta, Carlo, *Realismo, neorealismo, controrealismo*, Milan, 1976.

Pacifici, Sergio (ed.), *From 'Verismo' to Experimentalism: Essays on the Modern Italian Novel*, Bloomington, IN, 1969.

The Modern Italian Novel from Capuana to Tozzi, Carbondale, IL, 1973.

Pozzi, Giovanni, *La poesia italiana del Novecento*, Turin, 1965.

Pullini, Giorgio, *Il romanzo italiano del dopoguerra*, Milan, 1961.

Cinquant'anni di teatro in Italia, Rocca San Casciano, 1960.

Puppa, Paolo, 'Itinerari nella drammaturgia del Novecento', in *Storia della letteratura italiana. Il Novecento*, vol. 2, pp. 713–864 (Garzanti – see above p. 608).

Ramat, Silvio, *Storia della poesia italiana del Novecento*, Milan, 1976.

Salinari, Carlo, *Preludio e fine del neorealismo*, Naples, 1968.

Spagnoletti, Giacinto, *Storia della letteratura italiana del Novecento*, Rome, 1994.

Turconi, Sergio, *La poesia neorealista italiana*, Naples, 1968.

Vetri, Lucio, *Letteratura e caos. Poetiche della 'neoavanguardia' italiana degli anni Sessanta*, Milan, 1992.

Wood, Sharon, *Italian Women's Writing, 1860–1994*, London and Atlantic Highlands, NJ, 1995.

Periodicals devoted to twentieth-century literature are:

Otto/Novecento, Letteratura italiana contemporanea, Autografo, Studi novecenteschi

Individual authors

ALVARO, CORRADO

Man is Strong, trans. F. Frenaye, New York, 1948.

Revolt in Aspromonte, trans. F. Frenaye, New York, 1962.

Reina, Luigi, *Cultura e storia di Alvaro*, Naples, 1973.

BASSANI, GIORGIO

The Garden of the Finzi-Contini, trans. I. Quigley, London, 1974.

The Heron, trans. W. Weaver, London, 1993.
The Smell of Hay, trans. W. Weaver, London, 1975.
Dolfi, Anna, *Le forme del sentimento. Prosa e poesia in Giorgio Bassani*, Padua, 1981.
Neiger, Ada, *Bassani e il mondo ebraico*, Naples, 1983.
Sempoux, André, ed., *Il romanzo di Ferrara. Contributi su Giorgio Bassani*, Louvain, 1983.

BETTI, UGO

Three Plays on Justice, trans. G. H. McWilliam, San Francisco, 1964.
Three Plays (The Queen and the Rebels, The Burnt Flower-Bed, Summertime), trans. H. Reed, London, 1956.
Crime on Goat Island, trans. H. Reed, London, 1960.
Licastro, Emanuele, *Ugo Betti: An Introduction*, Jefferson, NC, 1985.

BONTEMPELLI, MASSIMO

L'avventura novecentesca, Florence, 1974.
Racconti e romanzi, ed. P. Masino, 2 vols., Milan, 1961.
Baldacci, Luigi, *Massimo Bontempelli*, Turin, 1966.
Saccone, Antonio, *Massimo Bontempelli: il mito del 900*, Naples, 1979.

BORGESE, GIUSEPPE ANTONIO

Rubè, trans. I. Goldberg, New York, 1923.
Licata, Vincenzo, *L'invenzione critica: Giuseppe Antonio Borgese*, Palermo, 1982.
Santangelo, Giorgio, ed., *Giuseppe Antonio Borgese: la figura e l'opera*, Palermo, 1985.

BRANCATI, VITALIANO

The Lost Years, trans. P. Creagh, London, 1992.
Amoroso, Giuseppe, *Vitaliano Brancati*, Florence, 1978.
Lauretta, Enzo, *Invito alla lettura di Brancati*, Milan, 1973.

BUZZATI, DINO

Romanzi e racconti, Milan, 1975.
Teatro, ed. G. Davico Bonino, Milan, 1980.
A Love Affair, trans. J. Green, London, 1965.
Restless Nights: selected stories, trans. Lawrence Venuti, Manchester, 1984.
The Tartar Steppe, trans. Stuart Hood, Manchester, 1952; Boston, 1995.
Crotti, Ilaria, *Buzzati*, Florence, 1977.
Giannetto, Nella, *Il coraggio della fantasia: studi e ricerche intorno a Dino Buzzati*, Milan, 1989.
Ioli, Giovanna, *Dino Buzzati*, Milan, 1988.

CALVINO, ITALO

Our Ancestors, trans. A. Colquhoun, London, 1980.
The Baron in the Trees, trans. A. Colquhoun, New York, 1977.
Difficult Loves, trans. W. Weaver, New York, 1985.
If on a Winter's Night, trans. W. Weaver, London, 1993.
Italian Folktales, trans. G. Martin, Harmondsworth, 1982.
Cannon, Joann, *Italo Calvino: Writer and Critic*, Ravenna, 1981.

Girelli Carasi, Fabio, *Guida alla lettura di Italo Calvino*, Milan, 1991.
Hume, Kathryn, *Calvino's Fictions: Cogito and Cosmos*, Oxford, 1992.
Quaderni d'italianistica 5 (1984): issue devoted to Calvino.
Re, Lucia, *Calvino and the Age of Neo-realism: Fables of Estrangement*, Stanford, CA, 1991.

CAMPANA, DINO

Opere e contributi, ed. E. Falqui, 2 vols., Florence, 1973.
Dino Campana: Orphic Songs, trans. I. L. Solomon, New York, 1968.
Bonaffini, Luigi, *La poesia visionaria di Dino Campana*, Isernia, 1980.
Bonifazi, Neuro, *Dino Campana*, Rome, 1978.
Ferri, Teresa, *Dino Campana: l'infinito del sogno*, Rome, 1985.
Li Vigni, Ida, *Orfismo e poesia in Dino Campana*, Genoa, 1983.

CARDARELLI, VINCENZO

Opere, ed. C. Martignon, Milan, 1981.
Di Biase, Carmine, *Invito alla lettura di Cardarelli*, Milan, 1975.
Dei, Adele, *La speranza è nell'opera: saggio sulle poesie di V.C.*, Milan, 1979.

CROCE, BENEDETTO

Aesthetics as Science of Expression and General Linguistics, trans. D. Ainslie (rev. edn. 1922; rpt New York, 1965).
'Aesthetics', *Encyclopedia Britannica*, 14th edn, 1929.
Philosophy–Poetry–History: An Anthology of Essays, trans. C. Sprigge, London, 1965.
Bonetti, Paolo, *Introduzione a Croce*, Bari, 1989.
Caponigri, A. Robert, *History and Liberty: The Historical Writings of Benedetto Croce*, London, 1955.
Galasso, Giuseppe, *Croce e lo spirito del suo tempo*, Bari, 1990.
Giammattei, Emma, *Retorica e idealismo: Croce nel primo Novecento*, Bologna, 1987.
Orsini, Gian Napoleone Giordano, *Benedetto Croce: Philosopher of Art and Literary Critic*, Carbondale, IL, 1961.
Piccoli, Raffaello, *Benedetto Croce*, London, 1922.
Sasso, Gennaro, *Benedetto Croce: la ricerca della dialettica*, Naples, 1976.

DE FILIPPO, EDUARDO

Four Plays (The Local Authority, Grand Magic, Filumena Marturano, Napoli Milionaria), trans. C. Ardito and P. Tinniswood, London, 1992.
Di Franco, Fiorenza, *Le commedie di E. De Filippo*, Bari, 1984.
Mignone, Mario B., *Eduardo De Filippo*, Boston, 1984.

DELFINI, ANTONIO

Opere, Turin, 1982– .
Marchetti, Giuseppe, *Delfini*, Florence, 1975.
Paolazzi, Andrea and Belpoliti, Marco, eds, *Antonio Delfini*, Milan, 1994.

FENOGLIO, BEPPE

Johnny the Partisan, trans. S. Hood, London, 1995.
A Private Matter, trans. M. Grazia di Paolo, New York, 1988.

Ruin (La malora), trans. J. Shepley, New York, 1992.
De Nicola, Francesco, *Introduzione a Fenoglio*, Rome–Bari, 1989.
Grignani, Maria Antonietta, *Beppe Fenoglio*, Florence, 1981.
Soletti, Elisabetta, *Beppe Fenoglio*, Milan, 1987.

GADDA, CARLO EMILIO

Acquainted With Grief, trans. W. Weaver, London, 1969.
That Awful Mess on Via Merulana, trans. W. Weaver, London, 1965.
Adams, Robert Martin, *After Joyce: Studies in Fiction After Ulysses*, New York, 1977.
Carlino, Marcello (ed.), *Gadda: progettualità e scrittura*, Rome, 1987.
Contini, Gianfranco, *Quarant'anni di amicizia. Scritti su Carlo Emilio Gadda*, Turin, 1989.
Dombroski, Robert, *Introduzione allo studio di Carlo Emilio Gadda*, Florence, 1975.
Ferretti, Gian Carlo, *Ritratto di Gadda*, Bari, 1987.
Flores, Enrico, *Accessioni gaddiane*, Naples, 1973.
Gioanola, Elio, *L'uomo dei topazi: saggio psicanalitico su Gadda*, Genoa, 1977.
Roscioni, Gian Carlo, *La disarmonia prestabilita: saggio su Carlo Emilio Gadda*, Turin, 1975.

GENTILE, GIOVANNI

The Philosophy of Art, trans. G. Gullace, Urbana, IL, 1960.
The Theory of Mind as Pure Act, trans. H. W. Carr, London, 1922.
Brown, Merle Elliott, *Neo-Idealistic Aesthetics: Croce–Gentile–Collingwood*, Detroit, 1966.
Del Noce, Augusto, *Giovanni Gentile: per una interpretazione filosofica della storia contemporanea*, Bologna, 1990.
Harris, Henry Silton, *The Social Philosophy of Giovanni Gentile*, Urbana, IL, 1960.

GINZBURG, NATALIA

The City and the House, trans. D. Davis, London, 1990.
Dear Michael, trans. S. Cudahy, London, 1975.
The Little Virtues, trans. D. Davis, Manchester, 1985.
Bullock, Alan, *Natalia Ginzburg: Human Relationships in a Changing World*, New York and Oxford, 1991.
Clementelli, Elena, *Invito alla lettura di Natalia Ginzburg*, Milan, 1986.

GOZZANO, GUIDO

Poesie e prose, ed. A. De Marchi, Milan, 1961.
De Rienzo, Giorgio, *Guido Gozzano: vita di un rispettabile bugiardo*, Milan, 1983.
Martin, Henriette, *Guido Gozzano (1883–1916)*, Paris, 1968.
Sanguineti, Eduardo, *Guido Gozzano: indagini e letture*, Turin, 1966.
Stäuble, Antonio, *Sincerità e artificio in Gozzano*, Ravenna, 1972.
Vallone, Aldo, *I crepuscolari*, Palermo, 1970.

GRAMSCI, ANTONIO

Quaderni dal carcere, ed. V. Gerratana, 4 vols., Turin, 1975.
Lettere dal carcere, ed. S. Caprioglio and E. Fubini, Turin, 1965.
Cronache torinesi: 1913–1917, ed. S. Caprioglio, Turin, 1980.

Prison Notebooks, vol. 1, trans. J. Buttigieg, New York, 1992.
Selections from the Prison Notebooks, trans. Q. Hoare and G. N. Smith, New York, 1971.
Letters from Prison, ed. F. Rosengarten, trans. R. Rosenthal, New York, 1993.
Selections from Cultural Writings, ed. D. Forgacs and G. N. Smith, trans. W. Boelhower, Cambridge, MA, 1985.
Badaloni, Nicola, *Il marxismo di Gramsci dal mito alla ricomposizione politica*, Turin, 1975.
Bobbio, Norberto, *Saggi su Gramsci*, Milan, 1990.
Cammett, John McKay, *Antonio Gramsci and the Origins of Italian Communism*, Stanford, CA, 1967.
Clark, Martin, *Antonio Gramsci and the Revolution That Failed*, New Haven, CT, 1977.
Davidson, Alastair, *Antonio Gramsci: Toward an Intellectual Biography*, London, 1977.
Dombroski, Robert, *Antonio Gramsci*, Boston, 1989.
Femia, Joseph V., *Gramsci's Political Thought*, Oxford, 1981.
Holub, Robert, *Antonio Gramsci: Beyond Marxism and Postmodernism*, London, 1992.
Lo Piparo, Franco, *Lingua, intellettuali, egemonia in Gramsci*, Bari, 1979.
Mazzotta, Giuseppe, *Gramsci: la modernità compiuta*, Cosenza, 1988.

GUARESCHI, GIOVANNI

Comrade Don Camillo, trans. Frances Frenaye, London, 1964.
Don Camillo's Dilemma, trans. Frances Frenaye, London, 1954.
The Little World of Don Camillo, trans. Una V. Troubridge, London, 1951.
The World of Don Camillo, trans. Una V. Troubridge and Frances Frenaye, London, 1980.
Vené, Gianfranco, *Don Camillo, Peppone e il compromesso storico*, Milan, 1977.

LAMPEDUSA, TOMASI DI

The Leopard, trans. A. Colquhoun, London, 1961.
Buzzi, Giancarlo, *Invito alla lettura di Giuseppe Tomasi di Lampedusa*, Milan, 1972.
Gilmour, David, *The Last Leopard: A Life of Giuseppe di Lampedusa*, London, 1988.

LANDOLFI, TOMMASO

Opere, ed. Idolina Landolfi, Milan, 1991–4.
An Autumn Story, trans. J. Neugroschel, New York, 1989.
Cancerqueen, and Other Stories, trans. and ed. K. Jason, New York, 1986.
Capek-Habekovic, Romana, *Tommaso Landolfi's Grotesque Images*, New York, 1986.
Macrì, Oreste, *Tommaso Landolfi: narratore, poeta, critico*, Florence, 1990.

LEVI, CARLO

Christ Stopped at Eboli, trans. F. Frenaye, New York, 1947.
Napolillo, Vincenzo, *Carlo Levi: Dall'antifascismo al mito contadino*, Cosenza, 1986.

LEVI, PRIMO

Collected Poems, trans. R. Feldman and B. Swann, London, 1992.
The Drowned and the Saved, trans. R. Rosenthal, London, 1988.
If Not Now, When?, trans. W. Weaver, London, 1987.
If This Is a Man; The Truce, trans. S. Woolf, London, 1987.
The Mirror Makers: Stories and Essays, trans. R. Rosenthal, New York, 1990.

Moments of Reprieve, trans. R. Feldman, London, 1987.
Cicioni, Mirna, *Primo Levi: Bridges of Knowledge*, Oxford, 1995.
Tarrow, Susan, ed., *Reason and Light: Essays on Primo Levi*, Ithaca, NY, 1990.
Vincenti, Fiora, *Invito alla lettura di Primo Levi*, Milan, 1973.

MALAPARTE, CURZIO

The Skin, trans. D. Moore, Boston, 1952.
Cancogni, Manlio, *Malaparte. Invito alla lettura*, Florence, 1976.
Guerri, Giordano Bruno, *L'arcitaliano: vita di Curzio Malaparte*, Milan, 1980.

MICHELSTAEDTER, CARLO

Bini, Daniela, *Carlo Michelstaedter and the Failure of Language*, Tallahassee, FL, 1992.
Campailla Sergio, *Pensiero e poesia di Michelstaedter*, Bologna, 1973.

MONTALE, EUGENIO

New Poems, trans. G. Singh, New York, 1976.
Poesie/Poems, trans. G. Kay, Edinburgh, 1964.
Provisional Conclusions, trans. E. Farnsworth, Chicago, 1970.
The Storm and Other Poems, trans. C. Wright, Oberlin College, OH, 1978.
Selected Poems, New York, 1966.
The Butterfly of Dinard, trans. G. Singh, London, 1971.
Almansi, Guido and Merry, Bruce, *Eugenio Montale: The Private Language of Poetry*, Edinburgh, 1977.
Avalle, D'Arco Silvio, *Tre saggi su Montale*, Turin, 1970.
Biasin, Gian Paolo, *Il vento di Debussy: la poesia di Montale nella cultura del Novecento*, Bologna, 1982.
Cambon, Glauco, *Montale's Poetry: A Dream in Reason's Presence*, Princeton, NJ, 1982.
Carpi, Umberto, *Montale dopo il fascismo: dalla 'Bufera'a 'Satura'*, Padua, 1971.
Cary, Joseph, *Three Modern Italian Poets*, New York, 1992.
Cataldi, Pietro, *Montale*, Palermo, 1992.
Contini, Gianfranco, *Una lunga fedeltà: saggi su Montale*, Turin, 1982.
Forti, Marco, ed., *Montale*, Milan, 1976.
Jacomuzzi, Angelo, *La poesia di Montale dagli 'Ossi' ai 'Diari'*, Turin, 1978.
Huffman, Claire, *Montale and the Occasions of Poetry*, Princeton, NJ, 1983.
Luperini, Romano, *Montale e l'identità negata*, Naples, 1984.
	Storia di Montale, Bari, 1986.
Singh, G., *Eugenio Montale: A critical study*, New Haven, CT, 1973.
West, Rebecca, *Eugenio Montale: Poet on the Edge*, Cambridge–London, 1981.

MORANTE, ELSA

Opere, ed. C. Cecchi and C. Garboli, 2 vols., Milan, 1988–90.
Aracoeli, trans. W. Weaver, New York, 1984.
Arturo's Island, trans. Isabel Quigly, Manchester, 1988.
History: a Novel, trans. W. Weaver, New York, 1977.
Agamben, Giorgio et al., *Per Elsa Morante*, Milan, 1993.
Ravanello, Donatella, *Scrittura e follia nei romanzi di E.M.*, Venice, 1980.
Venturi, Gianni, *Morante*, Florence, 1977.

MORAVIA, ALBERTO

The Time of Indifference, trans. A. Davidson, St Albans, 1975.
The Conformist, trans. A. Davidson, Harmondsworth, 1976.
Two Women (La Ciociara), trans. A. Davidson, Harmondsworth, 1982.
The Woman of Rome, trans. L. Holland, London, 1984.
Heiney, Donald, *Three Italian Novelists: Moravia, Pavese, Vittorini*, Ann Arbor, MI, 1968.
Sanguineti, Eduardo, *Alberto Moravia*, Milan, 1962.
Wood, Sharon, *Woman as Object: Language and Gender in the Work of Alberto Moravia*, London, 1990.

PALAZZESCHI, ALDO

Man of Smoke, trans. N. J. Perella and R. Stefanini, New York, 1992.
The Sisters Materassi, trans. A. Davidson, New York, 1953.
Guglielmi, Guido, *L'udienza del poeta: saggi su P. e il futurismo*, Turin, 1979.
Tamburri, Anthony J., *Of saltimbanchi and incendiari: A. P. and avant-gardism in Italy*, Rutherford and London, 1990.

PASOLINI, PIER PAOLO

The Letters of Pier Paolo Pasolini, trans. S. Hood, London, 1992.
Selected Poems, trans. N. MacAfee, London, 1984.
The Ragazzi, trans. E. Capouya, London, 1989.
Theorem, trans. S. Hood, London, 1992.
A Violent Life, trans. W. Weaver, London, 1968.
Golino, Enzo, *Pasolini: il sogno di una cosa*, Bologna, 1985.
Martellini, Luigi, *Introduzione a Pasolini*, Rome–Bari, 1989.
Rinaldi, Rinaldo, *Pier Paolo Pasolini*, Milan, 1982.

PAVESE, CESARE

Devil in the Hills, trans. P. Owen, London, 1990.
Dialogues with Leucò, trans. W. Arrowsmith, New York, 1989.
The House on the Hill, trans. W. J. Strachan, 1977.
The Leather-Jacket Stories, trans. A. Mirch, London, 1980.
The Moon and the Bonfires, trans. L. Sinclair, London, 1978.
Guiducci, Armanda, *Il mito Pavese*, Florence, 1967.
Heiney, Donald, *Three Italian Novelists: Moravia, Pavese, Vittorini*, Ann Arbor, MI, 1968.
Thompson, Doug, *Cesare Pavese*, Cambridge, 1982.
Venturi, Gianni, *Pavese*, Florence, 1970.
Wlassics, Tibor, *Pavese falso e vero. Vita, poetica, narrativa*, Turin, 1985.

PENNA, SANDRO

Remember Me, God of Love, trans. B. Robinson, Manchester, 1993.
This Strange Joy: Selected Poems of Sandro Penna, trans. W. S. Di Pietro, Cleveland, OH, 1982.
Garboli, Cesare, *Penna Papers*, Milan, 1986.

PRATOLINI, VASCO

Family Chronicle, trans. M. King, London, 1991.
Metello, trans. R. Rosenthal, London, 1968.
Bertoncini, Giancarlo, *Vasco Pratolini*, Rome, 1987.
Russo, Fabio, *Vasco Pratolini: introduzione e guida allo studio*, Florence, 1989.

QUASIMODO, SALVATORE

Selected Writings, trans. A. Mandelbaum, New York, 1960.
To Give and To Have, and Other Poems, trans. E. Farnsworth, Chicago, 1975.
Beall, Chandler, 'Quasimodo and Modern Italian Poetry', *Northwest Review* 4 (1961) 41–8.
Cambon, Glauco, 'Quasimodo', *Chelsea* 6, 1960.
Rossi, Louis, 'Salvatore Quasimodo: A Presentation', *Chicago Review* 14 (Spring 1960) 1–27.
Stone, Bernard, *Quasimodo House*, New York, 1987.
Tedesco, Natale, *L'isola impareggiabile: significati e forme del mito di Quasimodo*, Florence, 1977.
Tondo, Michele, *Salvatore Quasimodo*, Milan, 1976.

REA, DOMENICO

Naples and Pompei, trans. P. Garvin, London, 1977.
Prina, Serena, *Invito alla lettura di Domenico Rea*, Milan, 1980.
Romeo, Vincenzo, *Domenico Rea lo stilista plebeo*, Naples, 1989.

REBORA, CLEMENTE

Le poesie (1913–1957), Milan, 1961.
Clemente Rebora nella cultura italiana ed europea. Atti...1991, Rome, 1993.
Marchione, Margherita, *Clemente Rebora*, Boston, 1990.

SABA, UMBERTO

Italian Sampler: An Anthology of Italian Verse, trans. T. Bergin, Montreal, 1964.
Cary, Joseph, *Three Modern Italian Poets*, New York, 1992.
Cecchi, Ottavio, *L'aspro vino di Saba*, Rome, 1988.
Guagnini, Elvio, *Il punto su Saba*, Bari, 1987.
Lavagetto, Mario, *La gallina di Saba*, Turin, 1974.
Tordi, Rosita (ed.), *Umberto Saba: Trieste e la cultura mitteleuropea*, Trieste, 1985.

SAVINIO, ALBERTO

Bramanti, Vanni, *Gli dei e gli eroi di Savinio*, Palermo, 1983.
Carlino, Marcello, *Savinio: La scrittura in stato d'assedio*, Rome, 1979.

SBARBARO, CAMILLO

Contemporary Italian Poetry: An Anthology, ed. C. Golino, Berkeley–Los Angeles, 1962.
Guglielminetti, Marziano, *Sbarbaro poeta ed altri liguri*, Palermo, 1983.
Lagorio, Gina, *Sbarbaro: un modo spoglio d'esistere*, Milan, 1981.

SCIASCIA, LEONARDO

Candido or A Dream Dreamed in Sicily, trans. A. Foulke, Manchester, 1985.
The Day of the Owl, trans. A. Colquhoun, Manchester, 1984.
Equal Danger (Il contesto), trans. A. Foulke, London, 1974.
The Moro Affair: The Mystery of Majorana, trans. S. Rabinovitch, Manchester, 1987.
One Way or Another (Todo modo), trans. S. Rabinovitch, Manchester, 1987.
Ambroise, Claude, *Invito alla lettura di Leonardo Sciascia*, Milan, 1974.
Farrell, Joseph, *Leonardo Sciascia*, Edinburgh, 1995.
Jackson, Giovanna, *Leonardo Sciascia, 1956–76: A Thematic and Structural Study*, Ravenna, 1981.
Onofri, Massimo, *Storia di Sciascia*, Rome, 1994.

SCOTELLARO, ROCCO

The Dawn is Always New: Selected Poetry of Rocco Scotellaro, trans. R. Feldman and B. Swann, Princeton, NJ, 1980.
Giannantonio, Pompeo, *Rocco Scotellaro*, Milan, 1986.

SERENI, VITTORIO

Tutte le poesie, ed. M. T. Sereni, Milan, 1986.
Selected Poems, trans. M. Perryman and P. Robinson, London, 1990.
Luzi, Alfredo, *Introduzione a Sereni*, Rome, 1990.

SILONE, IGNAZIO

Bread and Wine, trans. H. Fergusson II, London, 1964.
Fontamara, trans. E. Mosbacher, London, 1985.
The School for Dictators, trans. W. Weaver, London, 1964.
The Story of a Humble Christian, trans. W. Weaver, London, 1970.
D'Eramo, Luce, *L'opera d'Ignazio Silone*, Milan, 1971.
Martelli, Sebastiano and Di Pasqua, Salvatore, *Guida alla lettura di Silone*, Milan, 1988.

SLATAPER, SCIPIO

Opere, 6 vols., Milan, 1950–58.
Luperini, Romano, *Scipio Slataper*, Florence, 1977.

SVEVO, ITALO

A Life, trans. A. Colquhoun, New York, 1963.
As a Man Grows Older, trans. B. de Zoete, New York, 1962.
Confessions of Zeno, trans. B. de Zoete, New York, 1958.
Camerino, Giuseppe, *Svevo*, Turin, 1981.
De Lauretis, Teresa, *La sintassi del desiderio: struttura e forma del romanzo sveviano*, Ravenna, 1976.
Furbank, Philip Nicholas, *Italo Svevo: The Man and the Writer*, Berkeley–Los Angeles, 1966.
Fusco, Mario, *Italo Svevo: coscienza e realtà*, Palermo, 1984.
Gatt-Rutter, John, *Italo Svevo: A Double Life*, Oxford, 1988.

Ghidetti, Enrico, *Italo Svevo: la coscienza di un borghese triestino*, Rome, 1992.

Lavagetto, Mario, *L'impiegato Schmitz e altri saggi su Svevo*, Turin, 1975.

Lebowitz, Naomi, *Italo Svevo*, New Brunswick, ME, 1977.

Moloney, Brian, *Italo Svevo: A Critical Introduction*, Edinburgh, 1974.

Saccone, Eduardo, *Commento a 'Zeno'*, Bologna, 1973.

Staley, Thomas, ed., *Essays on Italo Svevo*, Tulsa, OK, 1969.

TOZZI, FEDERICO

Three Crosses, trans. R. Capellero, New York, 1921.

Cavalli-Passini, Anna Maria, *Il 'mistero' retorico della scrittura: saggi su Tozzi narratore*, Bologna, 1984.

Maxia, Sandro, *Uomini e bestie nella narrativa di Federico Tozzi*, Padua, 1971.

Rimanelli, Gioe, 'Federico Tozzi: Misfit and Master', *Italian Quarterly* 14, 1971.

Voza, Pasquale, *La narrativa di Federico Tozzi*, Bari, 1974.

UNGARETTI, GIUSEPPE

Selected Poems of Giuseppe Ungaretti, trans. A. Mandelbaum, Ithaca–London, 1975.

Cambon, Glauco, *Giuseppe Ungaretti*, New York, 1967.

   La poesia di Ungaretti, Turin, 1975.

Cary, Joseph, *Three Modern Italian Poets*, New York, 1992.

Dombroski, Robert, *L'esistenza ubbidiente: intellettuali e fascismo*, Naples, 1984.

Guglielmi, Guido, *Interpretazione di Ungaretti*, Bologna, 1989.

Jones, Frederick J., *Ungaretti*, Edinburgh, 1977.

Rebay, Luciano, *Le origini della poesia di Ungaretti*, Rome, 1962.

VITTORINI, ELIO

The Dark and the Light, New York, 1960.

Men and Not Men, trans. H. Sarah, New York, 1987.

The Red Carnation, trans. A. Bowyer (1952; rpt Westport, CT, 1972).

The Twilight of the Elephant and Other Novels: A Vittorini Omnibus, trans. C. Brescia, New York, 1973.

Women of Messina, trans. F. Frenaye and F. Keene, New York, 1973.

Briosi, Sandro, *Vittorini*, Florence, 1970.

Catalano, Ettore, *Le forme della coscienza*, Bari, 1977.

Heiney, Donald, *Three Italian Novelists: Moravia, Pavese, Vittorini*, Ann Arbor, MI, 1968.

Potter, Joy Hambeuchen, *Elio Vittorini*, Boston, 1979.

VOLPONI, PAOLO

Last act in Urbino, trans. Peter N. Pedroni, New York, 1995.

My troubles began, trans. Belen Sevareid, New York, 1964.

Baldise, Enrico, *Invito alla lettura di P.V.*, Milan, 1982.

ZANZOTTO, ANDREA

Selected Poetry, text and trans. R. Feldman and B. Swann, Princeton, NJ, 1975.

Hand, Vivienne, *Zanzotto*, Edinburgh, 1994.

Welle, John P., *The Poetry of Andrea Zanzotto*, Rome, 1987.

Index

Abarbanel, Giuda (Leone Ebreo) 217
Abba, Giuseppe Cesare 441
Abbracciavacca, Meo 18
Abrantès, Duchess d' (Laura Saint-Martin Permon Junot) 404
Accademia degli Animosi 363
Accademia dell'Arcadia 301
Accademia della Crusca 271, 315, 316
Accademia del Disegno (Florence) 220
Accademia Fiorentina 199, 225
Accademia dei Giorgofili 374
Accademia degli Incogniti 320, 323, 339
Accademia degli Infiammati 186, 209
Accademia degli Intronati 281, 288, 327
Accademia d'Italia 511
Accademia Pontaniana 149, 161
Accademia dei Pugni 378
Accademia dei Rozzi 327
Accademia Tiberina 450
Accademia dei Trasformati 380, 381, 393
Accademia degli Umidi 225
Accetto, Torquato 316
Acciaiuoli, Donato 138
Acciaiuoli, Niccolò 86
Acerbi, Giuseppe 400, 401
Achilles Tatius 231
Achillini, Claudio 308
actor-authors 328
actors
    amateur 330
    female 285
    professional companies 296, 327–9
Actualism 512
acutezza (dazzling metaphor) 304, 312, 313
Adimari, Ludovico 311
Adriani, Giovan Battista 199

aesthetics 312–13, 363, 445
    Croce 511
    D'Annunzio 473
    Gentile 512
    Gramsci 513
    Parini 385
    Sicilian writers 463
    Verga 464
Agostini, Ludovico 202–3
Agostini, Niccolò degli 233
Agrippa, Heinrich Cornelius 219
Aimeric de Peguilhan 8
Alamanni, Luigi 242, 257, 269, 456
Albert the Great 48
Albertano da Brescia 31
Alberti, Leon Battista 138–40, 147, 150, 152–3, 156, 163, 164
Albinoni, Tommaso 364
Alcaic song 304
Aleardi, Aleardo 445
Aleramo, Sibilla 472
Alfani, Gianni 25
Alfieri, Vittorio 346, 387–96, 400, 408–9
Alfonso the Magnanimous of Aragon 149
Algarotti, Francesco 368, 373
Alicata, Mario 543
Alighieri, Antonia (daughter of Dante) 41
Alighieri, Dante see Dante
Alighieri, Gemma (wife) 41
Alighieri, Jacopo (son) 41, 112, 126
Alighieri, Pietro (son) 41, 126
allegory 59–60, 72, 163, 174–5, 297
Alvaro, Corrado 522, 545
Amicis, Edmondo De see De Amicis
Ammirato, Scipione 200
amplificatio technique in storytelling 84
Anceschi, Luciano 570
Andalò del Negro 71

Andrea da Barberino 168
Andreas *see* Capellanus, Andreas
Andreini, Francesco 264, 328
Andreini, Giovan Battista 329
Andreini, Isabella 164, 264, 296
Angiolieri, Cecco 6, 116
Anonimo fiorentino 127
Antologia journal 424
Antonelli, Luigi 484
Antonio da Ferrara 112, 115
Antonio da Tempo 109
Antonio degli Alberti 115
Apollonius of Tyre 231
Apuleius, Lucius *see* Golden Ass
Aquilano, Serafino *see* Serafino de'
    Ciminelli
Aquinas, St Thomas 47, 48, 190, 598
Aragona, Tullia d' 218, 264
Arbasino, Alberto 576
Arcadia group 350–2, 363, 377
Arcadia (Sannazaro) 159–61
Archimedes 137
Aretino, Pietro 187, 208, 213, 219, 222,
    251, 280
    comedies 279, 281, 283
    lyric poetry 271–3
    tragedy 290
    see also 'pasquinades'
Argelati, Filippo 345
Argenti, Agostino 296
Argyropoulos, Giovanni 145
Arici, Cesare 409, 415
Arienti, Carolina 405
Ariosto, Ludovico 163, 245, 270, 316
    comedies 279–81
    lyric poetry 258–9
    Orlando furioso 223, 233–40, 587
    satire 268–9
Aristotle 24–5, 141, 312, 336
    Economics 139
    Ethics 134
    lectures on and translations of 145
    original texts preserved 137
    Poetics 241, 312, 355
    revival 244
Arnaut, Daniel 13, 27
Arpino, Giovanni 596
ars amandi (love doctrine) 16

art and literature, links between 220–3
Artale, Giuseppe 304
Arthurian tradition 121, 172, 173, 242
Ascham, Roger 203
Ascoli, Isaia Graziadio 437
Asor Rosa, Alberto, 575
Assarino, Luca 318, 321
Augustine, St 47
    influence on Petrarch 99, 104, 134
Aurispa, Giorgio 475
autobiography 378, 412, 500, 502
    late Settecento 395–6
    post-war 537, 554
    in Seicento 324–5
    see also memoirs
Averroës (Ibn Rushd) 24–5, 48, 91

Bacchelli, Riccardo 449, 509, 522
Bacinetti-Florenzi, Marianna 405
Bacon, Francis 348, 350
Badoaro, Giacomo 339
Bagno, Panuccio dal *see* Panuccio
Balestrieri, Domenico 393
Balestrini, Nanni 570, 572–3, 576, 579
ballata (ballad) 17, 95, 119, 161, 163
Ballerini, Luigi 606
ballet 364, 368
Balletti, Elena 346
Balzac, Honoré de 441
Bandello, Matteo 227, 228–9, 272, 321
Bandettini, Teresa 404
Banti, Anna 548, 589
Barbaro, Ermolao The Younger 148
Barbato di Sulmona, Marco 106
Barbieri, Niccolò 328–9
Barclay, John 320
Bardi, Giovanni de' 337, 338
Baretti, Giuseppe 376–8
Bargagli, Girolamo 231, 298
Bargagli, Scipione 231
Barilli, Renato 575–6
Barlaam 71
Baroque 301–2, 304–9, 311, 323
    in Ungaretti 504
Barthes, Roland 567, 576
Bartoli, Daniello 315
Bartolomeo da San Concordio 121, 124
Barzizza, Gasparino 135, 147

Barzizza, Guiniforte 126, 127
Basile, Giambattista 323
Bassani, Giorgio 563–4, 575
Bassville (Nicolas Joseph Hugou) 407
Battiferri, Laura 264
Bazzoni, G. B. 437
Beatrice d'Este 156, 162
Beccadelli, Antonio (Panormita) 149
Beccari, Agostino 295
Beccaria, Cesare 379, 427
beffe (tricks) 156–7, 226, 280, 282, 295, 322
Belcari, Feo 176
Bellay, Joachim Du *see* Du Bellay, Joachim
Bellegarde, Joseph Heinrich von 399–400
Belli, Giuseppe Gioachino 447
Bellini, Bernardo 447
Bellini, Vincenzo 451
Bello, Francesco ('il Cieco') 233
Bembo, Bernardo 134
Bembo, Pietro 134, 154, 183–5, 207, 252–6
    Asolani 183, 216
    history of Venice 200
    influence of 240, 243, 263–4
    Petrarchan campaign 253–5
    Prose della volgar lingua 154, 183, 223
    sonnets 252
Bene, Carmelo 588
Beni, Paolo 312
Benjamin, Walter 494
Benni, Stefano 603
Benoit de Sainte Maure 9
Bentham, Jeremy 379
Bentivoglio, Ercole 269
Bentivoglio, Guido 325
Benvenuto (Rambaldi) da Imola 126
Benvoglienti, Uberto 345
Beolco, Angelo *see* Ruzante
Berardinelli, Alfonso 585
Berchet, Giovanni 401
Bergson, Henri 493
Berio, Luciano 456
Bernardino da Siena 159
Bernari, Carlo 545
Berni, Francesco 233–4, 260, 263, 268, 270–1

Bernini, Gian Lorenzo 327
Beroaldo, Filippo 156
Berto, Giuseppe 578
Bertola, Aurelio de' Giorgi 394
Bertoldi da Serravalle, Giovanni 110, 126
Bertolucci, Attilio 555, 582–3
Bessarion, Cardinal Giovanni 146, 147
Betocchi, Carlo 561–2
Bettarini, Mariella 585
Betti, Ugo 550
Bettinelli, Saverio 373–4, 375
Betussi, Giuseppe 218–19
Bevilacqua, Alberto 596
Bianciardi, Luciano 569
Bianco da Siena 118
Bibbiena, *see* Dovizi, Bernardo
Bible
    as Dante's source 47, 52, 53, 56, 60
    interpretation of 137, 141, 142, 176
    see also sacra rappresentazione
    volgarizzamento in Trecento 121
Biblioteca italiana 399–400, 418
Bilenchi, Romano 525–6, 536, 577
Bini, Carlo 441
Biondi, Giovan Francesco 319–20
Biondo, Flavio 149, 152
Bisaccioni, Maiolino 320
Black Death 76, 81, 90
Blanchot, Maurice, 567
blank verse (*endecasillabi sciolti*) 257, 289, 382, 410, 500
Blondel (later Manzoni), Henriette 428
Bo, Carlo 534
Boccaccio, Giovanni 22, 70–88, 164, 438
    Amorosa visione 71, 75, 105
    Bucolicum carmen 75
    Caccia di Diana 72–3
    Commedia delle ninfe fiorentine 72, 75, 163
    Corbaccio 81, 85
    Decameron 22, 34, 36, 72, 73–4, 76–85, 113
        De casibus virorum 87
    Elegia di Madonna Fiammetta 76
    Esposizioni sopra la Commedia 86, 126
    Filocolo 73–4, 158, 159
    Filostrato 74–5, 163
    Genealogie deorum gentilium 87

influence 112, 158, 163, 181, 183, 186, 216, 223–7, 280, 323, 438, 454
Ninfale fiesolano 76
and Petrarch 70
public lectures on *Inferno* 126
Rime 72
Teseida delle nozze d'Emilia 74–5, 163
Trattatello in laude di Dante 86
Zibaldone laurenziano 85
Boccalini, Traiano 314
Bodin, Jean 201
Bodoni, Giambattista 412
Boethius, Anisius Manlius Severinus 31
influence on Dante 41
vernacular translation of 121
Boiardo, MatteoMaria 162, 245
Orlando innamorato 151, 172–5, 233, 271
see also Ariosto, *Orlando furioso*
Boito, Arrigo 453, 454
Boito, Camillo 470
Bolognetti, Francesco 249
Bolzani, Giovanni Pietro 183
Bonagiunta Orbicciani da Lucca 15, 17–19, 27
Bonarelli, Guidobaldo 297, 334
Bonarelli, Prospero 333
Bonaviri, Giuseppe 592
Bonsanti, Alessandro 524–5
Bontempelli, Massimo 514, 521–3
Bonvesin de la Riva 6, 31
Borgese, Giuseppe Antonio 494, 497, 519–20
Borghini, Vincenzio 184, 220
Borgia, Lucrezia 151
Borsieri, Pietro 401
Botero, Giovanni 200, 201, 314
Bottai, Giuseppe 514
Bracciolini, Francesco 310–11, 333
Bracciolini, Poggio 146, 148, 152, 157
Brancati, Vitaliano 551
Brasca, Santo 148
Breislak, Scipione 399
Breme, Ludovico di 401
Bresciani Borsa, Antonio 440
Brevio, Giovanni 227
Brignole-Sale, Anton Giulio 321, 323

Brocardo, Antonio 272
Bronzino, Angelo 271
Browning, Robert 8
Brucioli, Antonio 198, 202, 220
Brunetto Latini 7, 30, 32, 40, 64
Bruni, Antonio 308
Bruni, Leonardo 133, 137–8, 145, 146, 152–3
novelle 156
Bruno, Giordano 219, 287
Brusoni, Girolamo 320, 321–2
Bufalino, Gesualdo 592, 599
Bulgarelli, Marianna 353
Buonafede, Appiano 377
Buonaiuti, Marchionne di Coppo di Stefano di 122
Burchiello, Il (Domenico de Giovanni) 164
Burney, Charles 365
Busenello, Giovanni Francesco 339
Busi, Aldo 603
Buti, Francesco da 126–7
Buvalelli, Lambertino 8
Buzzati, Dino 523, 549–50, 578
Byron, George Gordon, Lord 170, 403

caccia genre 72, 119
Cacciatore, Edoardo 606
Caccini, Giulio 338
Cademosto, Marco (Marco da Lodi) 227
Caffè, Il, periodical and group 378–80, 401
Cagnone, Nanni 586
Calderón de la Barca, Pedro 330
Caleffi, Piero 537
Callot, Jacques 329
Calmo, Andrea 283, 295
Calvino, Italo 329, 456, 535, 549, 552, 553, 563, 568–9, 577–8, 594–5, 596, 600, 604, 606
Camerata group of musicians 337
Cammelli ('il Pistoia'), Antonio 151, 270
Camon, Ferdinando 593
Campana, Dino 498, 585, 597
Campanella, Tommaso 313–14
Canonici-Fachini, Ginevra 404
Canova, Antonio 414
cantare genre 119, 123, 168

canti carnascialeschi (carnival songs) 165, 270
Cantico delle creature see *Laudes Creaturarum*
canzone verse form 11, 12, 13
　a ballo 119, 164
　Convivio (Dante) 47
　Della Casa 263
　palinodic 15
　religious 16–17
　in Seicento 303
　Vita Nuova (Dante) 45
canzonette 304, 355
　pastoral 351
Canzoniere see Petrarch
Capaccio, Giulio Cesare 212
Capella, Galeazzo Flavio 215
Capellanus, Andreas 8, 21
capitoli 162, 163, 258–9
　in *terza rima* 268, 270
Capodilista, Gabriele 148
Capponi, Gino 419, 424, 433, 441
Capriolo, Paola 603
Caproni, Giorgio 562
Capua, Rinaldo di 366
Capuana, Luigi 463–4
Caracciolo, Admiral Francesco 372
Caracciolo, Antonio 164
Caracciolo, Giovan Francesco 162
Carbone, Ludovico 157
Carcano, Giulio 440, 452
Cardarelli, Vincenzo 498
Carducci, Giosuè 459, 461–2, 478, 511
Carletti, Francesco 324–5
Carli, Gian Rinaldo 378, 393
carnival
　opera at Venetian 339
　(theatre) 176, 280, 281, 588
　tradition in literature 274
Caro, Annibale 271
　Daphnis and Chloe 231
Carolingian tradition 24, 121, 168, 172–3, 175, 234, 242, 243–6
Casa, Giovanni della 210–11, 223, 252–3, 262–3, 265, 271
Casanova, Giacomo 325, 395
Casella, Alfredo 455
Cassola, Carlo 544, 563, 575

Casti, Giambattista 355, 369
Castiglione, Baldesar 183, 187, 209, 220, 223–4
　Il libro del Cortegiano (*The Courtier*) 203–8
Catelli Papi, Giuseppa 405
Catherine of Siena, St 124–5
Cattafi, Bartolo 582
Cattaneo, Carlo 434, 444
Cattaneo, Silvan 228
Cattani da Diacceto, Francesco 216
Catullus, Gaius Valerius 150, 166, 270, 415
Cavalca, Domenico 124
Cavalcanti, Bartolomeo 186
Cavalcanti circle 25
Cavalcanti, Guido 18, 22–5, 27, 68, 126
　influence on Dante 40, 41–2, 43, 44–5
Cavalli, Francesco 339–40
Cavalli, Patrizia 586
Caviceo, Jacopo 158
Cebà, Ansaldo 333
Cecchi, Emilio 514, 536
Cecchi, Giovan Maria 282
Cecchini, Pier Maria 328
Cecco d'Ascoli 112–13
Ceccoli, Marino, 116
Celati, Gianni 596–7, 600
Cellini, Benvenuto 222–3
censorship 187, 230, 327, 526, 533
Cento novelle amorose 323
Cereta, Laura 143
Cergoli, Carolus 593
Certame Coronario 139
Cesari, Antonio 408, 435, 440
Cesarotti, Melchiorre 370, 394
Cesti, Pietro 340
Chanson de Roland 245
Chaucer, Geoffrey 31, 75, 87
Chekhov, Anton 548
Chiabrera, Gabriello 35, 303–4, 308, 325, 334–5
Chiara, Piero 596
Chiarelli, Luigi 484, 485
Chiari, Pietro 358
Chiaromonte, Nicola 486
Chiose Cagliaritane (anonymous glosses on *Commedia*) 126

Chiose Selmiane (or *Marciane*)
(anonymous glosses on *Inferno*)
126
chivalrous epic/romance
in Duecento 32–4
in Trecento 119
in Quattrocento 167–75
in Cinquecento 238–240
Christina, Queen 309, 350
Chrysoloras, Manuel 136
Chrysostom, St John 137
Cialente, Fausta 589
Ciampolo degli Ugurgieri 121
Cicero 7, 30, 90, 92, 104, 121, 133–6,
138, 141, 154, 252, 420
Cicognini, Giacinto Andrea 330, 340
Cicognini, Iacopo 330
Cielo d'Alcamo 11
Cigala, Lanfranco 8
Ciminelli *see* Serafino Aquilano
Cino da Pistoia 3, 25–6, 27, 71, 95, 110
Cinthio/Cinzio, Giambattista Giraldi *see*
Giraldi Cinzio, Giambattista
Cirillo, Domenico 372
Clareno, Angelo 124
classicism
and Carducci 461–2
language of 408–9
classicism versus Romanticism
controversy 399–405, 406, 409–10
classicists, in Seicento lyric poetry 308–9
cobbola verse form 11
Coccai, Merlin *see* Folengo, Teofilo
Cola di Rienzo 122
Collodi, Carlo (Carlo Lorenzetti) 471
Colombini, Giovanni 124
Colonna, Egidio 190
Colonna, Francesco 148, 158
Colonna, Giovanni 89, 90, 95, 133
Colonna, Vittoria 254, 264
comedy
in Quattrocento 176–7
in Cinquecento 273–89, 286–8
in Seicento 329–31
in Settecento 355–62
comic tradition 58, 155, 156–7, 268, 271,
274
Comisso, Giovanni 524

Commedia see Dante
commedia dell'arte
Cinquecento 283–8
Seicento 327–9, 330
Settecento 356
commedia erudita 284, 287
commedia ridicolosa 330
commiato (Provençal *tornada*) 15
Communism 514, 533–4, 536, 538,
543–4, 561, 579, 588, 605
Communist critics 543
Comolli, Giampiero 606
Compagni, Dino 22, 122
Compagnia dei Gelosi 287
concentration camps *see* death camps
concetto 303, 304, 312–13
Conciliatore, Il journal 401–2
Confalonieri, Federico 401, 427, 441
Confessions (St Augustine) 47, 104, 134
Consolo, Vincenzo 592
consuetudo (Latin usage) 152
Contarini family of Venice 148
Contarini, Gaspare 201
Conti, Antonio 346
Conti di antichi cavalieri 34
Conti, Giusto de' 162
Conti, Nicolò di 148
Conti, Pier Francesco de' 233
Contini, Gianfranco 556, 577
contrapasso (retributive principle) in
Dante's *Commedia* 63–4
Convenevole da Prato 89
copia (lexical and syntactical richness)
165, 272
copyists, medieval 10–11
Corazzini, Sergio 497
Cordelli, Franco 585
Corfino, Lodovico 231
Cornaro, Alvise 211
Cornazzano, Antonio 151, 157
corone see sonnet, cycles
Corradini, Enrico 494
Il Corriere delle dame 405
Cortese, Paolo 154
Corti, Maria 576
Corvo, Niccolò (?'Agasippo Mercotellis')
365
court festivals 326

court life and courtier's behaviour
203–12
courtier, female (*donna di palazzo*) 206
Cremonini, Cesare 339
crepuscolari poets 497–8, 505
Crescimbeni, Giovan Mario 351
Critica, La review 509
Critica fascista review 514
Croce, Benedetto 301, 331, 350, 445,
461, 509–11, 534
Croce, Giulio Cesare 324
Crocioni, Anteo 595
Crossman, Richard 534
Crudeli, Tommaso 351, 352
Cucchi, Maurizio 583
cultural policy in Romantic period
399–400, 401
culture and Fascism 514
Cuoco, Vincenzo 403, 427, 429
Cusa, Nicholas of *see* Nicholas of Cusa
(Cusanus)
D'Alembert, Jean 371
Dallapiccola, Luigi 456
D'Ambra, Francesco 282
Dandolo, Andrea (Doge of Venice) 122
Daniel, Arnaut *see* Arnaut, Daniel
D'Annunzio, Gabriele 449, 456, 473–6,
511, 515
Dante 3, 7, 18, 39–69, 103, 164, 316
Commedia 16, 18, 49, 54–68, 100,
105, 112, 318, 419
Inferno 13–14, 22, 39, 57, 58, 64–5,
126
Purgatorio 8, 57, 58, 61–2, 65
Paradiso 57, 58, 62, 65–6, 68
commentaries on 110, 125–7
Convivio 45, 46–50
De vulgari eloquentia 11, 26, 36, 47,
48, 101, 109, 184
Detto d'amore 7, 41
Ecloge 68
Epistle to Cangrande della Scala 57
Epistolae 51–4
Il fiore 41
influence on minor literature of
Trecento 112
influence on Petrarch 104–6
letters *see* Epistolae

Monarchia, 50–1, 112
Questio de aqua et terra 68
in *Raccolta aragonese* 164
Rime 44–6, 50
and the Sicilian school 14
and the vernacular 153
Vita Nuova 3, 11, 25, 36, 41–4, 72,
92–3
Da Ponte, Lorenzo 366, 369
Da Ponte, Luigi 226–7
D'Arrigo, Stefano 592
Darwin, Charles 429
Davanzati, Chiaro 17, 18–19
Davi, Luigi 569
D'Azeglio, Marquess Massimo Taparelli
436, 440–1
De Amicis, Edmondo 471
death camps, post-war writing on 546–7,
555, 564, 573, 590
De Angelis, Milo 585
De Carlo, Andrea 603, 604
De Céspedes, Alba 548–9
De Chirico, Andrea *see* Savinio, Alberto
De Chirico, Giorgio 523
decorum (linguistic) 153, 238, 244, 304,
312
De Filippo, Eduardo 545, 587
De Gerando, Joseph Marie 428
Defoe, Daniel 438
Degola, Eustachio 428
Dei, Andrea 122
Del Giudice, Daniele 605
Deledda, Grazia 472–3
Delfini, Antonio 523, 549
Delfino, Giovanni 331
D'Elia, Gianni 605
Della Porta, Giambattista 287
Della Valle, Federico 332
Della Valle, Pietro 325
De Marchi, Emilio 470
De Meis, Angelo 426
D'Epinay, Madame Louise Florence
371–2
De Roberto, Federico 469–70, 538
De Sanctis, Francesco 419, 444–5
Descartes, René 343, 348
Dessí, Giuseppe 549, 593
Destutt de Tracy, Antoine 427

De Vega, Lope 326
devotional poetry in Trecento 118–19
devotional prose in Trecento minor
    literature 123–5
dialect
    in Boccaccio's *Decameron* 82
    in comedy 282–3
    in *commedia dell'arte* 284–5
    in Dante's *Commedia* 58
    in Folengo 274
    in Goldoni 358
    and 'invented' languages 148
    novella in 228
    in Pasolini 556
    in Pirandello 485
    pre-Romantic outburst of (in poetry)
        393
    regional 152, 323
    in Tassoni 310
dialectic
    importance of Latin and Greek 132–3
dialogue
    anti-Ciceronian 213
    Castiglione's use of 208
    Ciceronian 139, 186, 212, 228
    Latin prose 138
    in the novel 159
    and *novelle* 217
    popularity of (Cinquecento) 186
    used by Bembo and Castiglione 218
    Valla's use of 141
Di Benedetto, Vincenzo 414, 416
Di Costanzo, Angelo 201, 268
dictamen (ornamented prose) 17, 29
Diderot, Denis 371, 379
Di Giacomo, Salvatore 470
diglossia 152
    see also dialects, regional
Di Nola, Laura 584
Dionigi da Borgo San Sepolcro 71
Dionisotti, Carlo 108, 253
Disticha Catonis 31
dithyramb 304
documentary writing
    post-war 537
    post-war fictionalised 535
Dolce, Ludovico 222, 240, 283, 290
dolce stil novo see stilnovo

Dolopathos 34
Domenichi, Ludovico 219, 233–4, 264
Domenico di Giovanni *see* Burchiello, Il
Donà family of Venice 148
Donati, Corso 22
Donati, Forese, and Dante 6, 45
Donati, Gemma 41
Donation of Constantine 51, 141
Doni, Anton Francesco 202, 214
Doni, Giovanni Battista 336–7
Donizetti, Gaetano 453
Doplicher, Fabio 584
Dossi, Carlo (Alberto Pisani) 460
Dotti, Bartolomeo 305
Dottori, Carlo de' 311, 325, 331–2
Dovizi, Bernardo (Bibbiena) 79, 279
dream-vision formula, Boccaccio 85
Du Bartas, Guillaume 267
Du Bellay, Joachim 184
Duranti, Francesca 601

eclogues 150, 164, 258
Eco, Umberto 567–8, 575, 579–80, 596,
    598, 599, 603
Edinburgh Review, The 417
education
    Petrarch on 133–4
    in Quattrocento 135–7
    women's 143
Einaudi, Luigi 544, 546
Eleanora of Aragon 151
empiricism 509, 512
Enciclopedia italiana 514
Encyclopaedists (in Enlightenment) 370,
    381
endecasillabi 7, 75, 101–2, 338
endecasillabi sciolti see blank verse
Energie nove review 509
Enlightenment 347, 427
    condemned by Church 420
    Milan 378–86
    Naples 371–3
    in the north 373–5
    in Venice 374–5
Entrée en Espagne 168
Enzensberger, Hans Magnus 567
epic
    in Trecento 119, 121

in Quattrocento 167–72
in Cinquecento 231, 240, 243, 245, 310
Epicuro Napolitano 293
epode, Horatian 304
epyllion, didactic georgic 257
Equicola, Mario 151, 182, 217
Erasmus, Desiderius 142, 150, 270
Erba, Luciano 582
Erizzo, Sebastiano 230
erotic writing
	poetry 208, 251
	poetry (Petrarch) 95–7
	prose 448–9
Este family of Ferrara 135, 150–1, 156, 162
ethics, Valla and reform of Christian 140–2
etiquette 210–11
Euclid 137
Euripides 290, 294
exempla 33–4, 59, 123
existentialism 526, 548
	in theatre 486–7
experimentalism in the novel 575–80, 596

Faba, Guido 29
Fabbri, Diego 550–1
fabliaux 85
Facchinei, Ferdinando 379
Facio, Bartolomeo 149, 152
Fagiuoli, Giovan Battista 356
Fairfax, Edward 172
Faitinelli, Pietro dei 117
'Falso Boccaccio' (anonymous set of glosses) 126
fanciullino theory of poetry (Pascoli) 476, 479
Fantastici, Fortunata Sulgher 404
Fantastici, Massimina 404
farce 176, 282
Fascism 537
	collapse of 565
	and culture 509, 514
	and philosophy 509–14
	and poetry 493–508
	post-war 533–4, 539–40

as subject-matter 538
and Vittorini's novels 526–7
Fatti di Cesare 34
Fauriel, Claude 427, 429, 435
Faustini, Giovanni 339
Fausto da Longiano, Sebastiano 212
favole (stories from folk-tales) 166, 228, 334
Fedele, Cassandra 143
Fellini, Federico 551, 576
female subject in writing 547–9
	see also women
female vanity, in Boccaccio 81, 85
feminism
	1970s 581
	and anti-feminism 85, 215
	Enlightenment 404
	and Moravia 551
	and poetry 583–4
	post-war 548
	publishing houses 584
	see also women
Fenoglio, Beppe 533, 536, 544
Fenton, Geoffrey 196, 229
Ferrara 150–1, 172, 278, 294
Ferretti, Jacopo 450
Ferri, Pietro 404
Fichte, Johann 512
Ficino, Marsilio 25, 145, 163, 165, 216
Filangieri, Gaetano 372
Fileti, Concetta Ramondetta 405
Filicaia, Vincenzo da 309
films 535–6
	novels based on silent 597
	see also Pasolini
fin'amors 9, 11, 12, 17, 18
Fiore (anon.) 7, 41
Fiorentino, Giovanni 123
Firenzuola, Agnolo 186, 215, 218, 224–5, 271
Flaiano, Ennio 551
Flaubert, Gustave 548
Florence
	Black Death (1348) 76
	and Boccaccio 75, 86
	in Cinquecento 282
	in Dante's *Commedia* 67–8
	in Dante's *Epistole* 53

humanists under the Medici 144–5
politics and Dante 46, 53
politics and historiography 188–200
Florimonte, Galeazzo 210
Fo, Dario 587, 588
Fogazzaro, Antonio 471–2
Foglietta, Uberto 201
Folengo, Teofilo 171, 240–1, 273–4
Baldus 241, 274
Folquet de Marselha 12
Fonte, Moderata (pseud. Pozzo de' Zorzi)
215
formalism 576
Formicone (anon.) 279
Fortini, Franco (Lattes) 556, 557, 564,
565–6, 604
Fortini, Pietro 230
Fortunato, Mario 606
Fortunio, Gian Francesco 183
Foscarini family of Venice 148
Foscarini, Lodovico 142
Foscolo, Ugo 263, 399–400, 408, 411,
412–17, 429, 438, 444, 462
Dei sepolcri 415–16
Le Grazie 413–15, 416, 429
Ultime lettere di Jacopo Ortis 412–13,
416
Frabotta, Biancamaria 584
frame-story in *novelle* 228, 232
Francesco da Barberino 126
Francesco di Vannozzo 115
Franci, Carlo Sebastiano 378–9
Francis of Assisi (St) 5–6, 124
Franciscan prose in Trecento 124
Franco, Niccolò 213, 231, 273
Franco, Veronica 258–9, 264
Frederick II (Emperor) 9–10, 21, 35, 50
French Revolution *see* Revolution, French
Frescobaldi, Dino 25
Frescobaldi, Matteo 115
Frezzi, Federico 112
Frisi, Paolo 379
frottola 160, 164
Frugoni, Carlo Innocenzo 351, 368, 373
Frugoni, Francesco Fulvio 315
Frusta letteraria periodical 376, 378
Fruttero, Carlo 596
Fubini, Mario 260, 512

Fucini, Renato 470
Futurism 495–7

Gabriele, Trifone 256, 272
Gadda, Carlo Emilio 514, 515, 524,
527–30, 549, 575, 577, 603
Gaeta, Francesco 511
Galanti, Giuseppe Maria 372
Galen 137
Galeota, Francesco 164
Galiani, Ferdinando 371
Galilei, Galileo 268, 316–17
Galilei, Vincenzo 337
Galuppi, Baldassare 366
Gambara, Veronica 254, 264
Garbo, Dino del 25, 126
Garibaldi, Giuseppe 442–4
Garrick, David 369
Gassendi, Pierre 348
Gatto, Alfonso 562
Gaza, Theodore 146
Gazzetta veneta periodical 375
Gellhorn, Martha 547
Gelli, Giovan Battista 184–5, 214–15,
282
Gelosi *see* Compagnia dei Gelosi
Gemelli Careri, Giovanni Francesco 325
Genet, Jean 567
Genovesi, Antonio 347–8, 371
Gentile, Giovanni 510, 511–12, 514
Gentillet, Innocent 193
gentilezza in Duecento love poetry 24
George of Trebizond 146
georgic poetry 257
Georgics (Virgil) 103
Ghedini, Giorgio 456
Giacomo da Lentini 11–12, 15, 17, 21
Giacomo Pugliese 13
Giacosa, Giuseppe 453
Giamboni, Bono 31
Giambullari, Pierfrancesco 184
Giancarli, Gigio Artemio 283
Giannone, Pietro 347
Giannotti, Donato 197, 282
Gigli, Girolamo 327, 356
Gildon, Charles 322
Gilio, Giovanni Andrea 208–9
Ginzburg, Natalia 548–9, 563, 587, 590

Gioberti, Vincenzo 444
Gioia, Melchiorre 434
Giordani, Pietro 399, 401, 415, 418
Giordano da Pisa 124
Giordano, Umberto 454–5
Giornale de'Letterati d'Italia 345–6, 376
Giotti, Virgilio 556
Giotto, Boccaccio on 88
Giovanni da Vignano 29–30
Giovine Italia 444
Giovio, Paolo 202, 221
Giraldi Cinzio, Gianbattista 209, 230, 249, 289, 294
Girolamo da Siena 124
Giudici, Giovanni 582, 585
Giuliani, Alfredo 571, 572, 579
giullari (professional entertainers) 176
Giusti, Giuseppe 446–7
Giustinian family of Venice 148
Giustinian, Leonardo 164
Giustinian, Orsatto 264
gliuòmmeri 164
Gluck, Christoph Willibald 368–70
Gobetti, Ada 537
Gobetti, Piero 509
Goethe, Johann Wolfgang von 412, 430, 434, 438, 453
Golden Ass, The (Apuleius) 151, 225
Goldoni, Carlo 356–61
  in France 360–1
  Memoirs 325, 395–6
  operatic texts 366
Gonzaga family 203
Gonzaga, Francesco 151, 326
Gottifredi, Bartolomeo 219
Govoni, Corrado 497, 554
Gozzano, Guido 497, 581
Gozzi, Carlo 360, 361–2, 395
Gozzi, Gasparo 375
grammatica see Latin
Gramsci, Antonio 445, 509, 513, 536, 537, 556–7
Graves, Robert 242
Gravina, Gian Vincenzo 309, 351, 353
Grazzini, Antonio Francesco (il Lasca) 225–6, 271, 282
Greek
  literature in 132, 145, 147

in Quattrocento 136–7, 148
Gregory the Great 124
Grillo, Angelo 305
Grimaldi, Pellegro 208
Gritti, Francesco 393
Grossi, Tommaso 440
Grotius (Hugo de Groot) 350
Groto, Luigi 259, 291, 296
Gruppo 63: 570–1, 579, 598
Gruppo 93: 606
Guacci, Maria Giuseppina 405
Gualdo, Luigi 470
Guardati, Tommaso (of Salerno) *see* Masuccio, Salernitano
Guareschi, Giovanni 538
Guarini (or Guarino), Battista (1538–1612) 293, 295, 296, 297, 326, 334, 336
Guarino, Battista (1425–1503) 135, 151
Guarino Veronese (1374–1460) 135, 142, 147, 150, 152
Guarnieri, Flamminio 296
Guazzo, Stefano 211
Guerra, Tonino 600
Guerrazzi, Francesco Domenico 437, 441
Guglielmi, Angelo 575
Guicciardini, Francesco 187, 193–6, 199
Guidi, Alessandro 309
Guido delle Colonne 9, 13, 20
Guidotto da Bologna 30
Guinizzelli, Guido 13, 18, 19–22, 43
Guittone d'Arezzo 15–17, 18–22, 27

Hanslick, Eduard 455
Harington, John 172
Hawkwood, John 119
Hegel, Georg 426, 431, 509, 510, 511
hegemony, Gramsci's doctrine of 513
Heine, Heinrich 499
Heliodorus 231
Hemingway, Ernest 536
hendecasyllables *see endecasillabi*
Henry of Sardinia *see* 'Re Enzo'
Henry VII, Emperor 51–3, 68
Heptameron (Margaret of Navarre) 229
heptasyllables, rhyming 7
Herder, Johann 350
Hermes review 494

hermetics in poetry 504–5, 534, 553–6, 565, 574
Herodotus 137
heroi-comic poems 310–11
Hesiod 166, 257
Hippocrates 137
historicism, absolute 510
historicist culture *see* Vico, Giambattista
historiography 188–202
 Muratori and 344–5
history
 in Dante's *Commedia* 62–3
 and neo-realism 535
 and post-war poets 553–7
 in Trecento prose literature 121–3
 writing of
  in Trecento minor literature 121–3
  in Cinquecento 188–203
  in Seicento 313–17
 see also historiography
Hoby, Thomas 208
Hoffman, E. T. A. 362
Homer 137, 350, 410, 415
Homer (pseudo) 166
Horace
 influence on later writers 163, 253, 257, 269, 355
 influence on Petrarch 103, 134
Hugou, Nicolas Joseph *see* Bassville
humanism
 civic 137–8
 in Quattrocento 131–43
 Roman 146–7
Hume, David 371, 395
Husserl, Edmund 571
hypostases in Duecento love poetry 23

idealism, absolute 510
idéologues 427
Idyll 421–2
Illica, Luigi 453
Imbonati, Carlo 427
imitation in art 351–2
improvisation in theatre 285–6, 328, 353
Index of Forbidden Books (Catholic Church) 258, 273
Indovinello veronese 4

industrial society, problems of 493, 498, 502
Ingannati, Gli (anonymous) 281
Ingegneri, Angelo 212, 298
ingegno 312, 313
intellectuals in modern Italy 493–4
introspection and grief in Duecento love poetry 23
'invented' languages 148, 274
Invernizio, Carolina 479
Isidore of Seville 36
Isocrates 190
istrioni (professional entertainers) 176
Italian language, debate on, *see* language

Jacopo della Lana 126
Jacopone (Iacopone) da Todi 6, 118, 456
Jahier, Piero 498
Janssen, Cornelis 428
Jennaro, Pietro Jacopo di 162, 164
Jerome, St 85, 135
Johnson, Samuel 376
Jommelli, Nicolò 367–8
journalism 345–7, 375–80, 399–401, 417, 424, 444
 in modern Italy 494, 495, 509, 514, 524–5
 in post-war Italy 536, 543, 549, 557, 564–8, 578, 584
Jovine, Francesco 533, 538
Joyce, James 575
Juvenal 85, 269

Kafka, Franz 523, 575, 602
Kemeny, Tomaso 586

La Capria, Raffaele 593
Labriola, Antonio 493
Lacerba review 509
Lactantius 135
Lagorio, Gina 596
Lambertenghi, Luigi Porro 401
Lamberti, Anton Maria 393
Lami, Giovanni 374
Lampedusa, Giuseppe Tomasi di 544, 564, 592
Lancellotti, Secondo 325
Lancetti, Vincenzo 409, 437

Lancia, Andrea 126
Landino, Cristoforo 127, 153
Lando, Ortensio 213
Landolfi, Tommaso 523, 549, 550
language
  evolution of vernacular language 3–36,
    113, 127, 139, 145, 148, 164–5
  Latin and the vernacular
    in Duecento 3–4, 28, 31–3
    in Trecento 48–9, 89, 121–2
    in Quattrocento 140–1, 152–4,
      181–2
    in Cinquecento 181–2, 273–5
  questione della lingua
    in Trecento 48–50, 108–9
    in Quattrocento 164
    in Cinquecento 181–5, 208, 239–40,
      253
    in Settecento 379
    in Ottocento 435–7
  Tuscan 148, 161, 166, 378, 380, 408
  see also literary language, translations,
    vernacular, Volgare
Lapo, Gianni 25
Lasca *see* Grazzini, Antonio Francesco
Latini Brunetto *see* Brunetto Latini
lauda drammatica genre in Trecento 118
laude 163, 176
Laura
  Petrarch's 89–90, 91, 94, 95, 100
  in Bembo's poetry 254–5
Lawrence, D. H. 226
Leibnitz, Gottfried 343, 346
Lemene, Francesco 304
Lenzoni, Carlo 184
Leo, Leonardo 366
Leonardo da Vinci 157
Leonardo review 494, 509
Leoncavallo, Ruggiero 454
Leone Ebreo *see* Abarbanel, Giuda
Leonetti, Francesco 557, 564, 565
Leopardi, Giacomo 400–1, 410, 411,
  413, 416, 418–26, 449, 462, 501
  Canti 419–20, 421, 422, 423–5
  Idilli 421
  letters 425
  Operette morali 425
  satire 424

  scientific interest 420–1
  Zibaldone 419, 422–3, 425–6
Leopardi, Monaldo 418
Lessing, Gotthold 80
Levati, Ambrogio 404
Levi, Carlo 538–9, 541
Levi, Primo 546, 590, 591
Lewis, Sinclair 536
Li fet des Romains 34
libraries, private 135–7, 147, 318, 344,
  404, 418
Libro dei sette savi 34
literacy in the Trecento 110–11
literary language *see* language
literary magazines *see* reviews
literature
  and art 220–3
  children's 471
  and independence in Romantic period
    400
  and industry 567–8
  political (Risorgimento) 444–5
  and science 344
  sociology of 596
Living Theatre, The 587
Livy
  and Petrarch 133
  vernacular translation of 121, 198
Locatelli, Basilio 328
Locatelli, Sebastiano 325
Locke, John 371
Lodi, Marco da *see* Cademosto, Marco
Lodoli, Marco 606
Loi, Franco 600
Lolini, Attilio 597
Lollio, Alberto 296
Lombardi, Germano 576–7
Longo, Alfonso 379
Loredano, Giovan Francesco 320
Lorenzetti, Carlo (pen-name: Carlo
  Collodi) 471
Lorenzi, Giambattista 367, 372
Lorenziani, Giovanni Andrea 330
Lorenzo, il Magnifico *see* Medici, Lorenzo
  de'
Loria, Arturo 524
Lorris, Guillaume de 7, 85, 105
Loy, Rosetta 601

Lubrano, Giacomo 308
Lucan 135
Lucentini, Franco 596
Lucian 140
Lucretius 166
Luigini, Federico 218
Lukács, Gyorgy 536
Lumelli, Angelo 585
Lunetta, Mario 585
Lupis, Antonio 321
Luti, Emilia 405, 436
Luzi, Mario 554, 555, 562
Lydgate, John 87

macaronic language 148, 154, 158, 241,
    273–5, 527
Maccari, Mino 522
Machiavelli, Niccolò 163, 184, 187,
    188–93, 203
    Arte della guerra 192
    Belfagor 224, 227
    Discorsi 191, 192, 193
    Discorso intorno alla nostra lingua 184
    Il Principe (The Prince) 189–91
    Istorie fiorentine 192–3
    Mandragola 279, 280
    reception and influence 195, 197, 201,
        314, 373, 377
Macinghi Strozzi, Alessandra 159
Macpherson, James ('Ossian') 370, 394
madrigal 95, 119, 259, 267, 337
Maffei, Andrea 452
Maffei, Clara 405
Maffei, Scipione 345, 346, 356
Magalotti, Lorenzo 317, 325
Maggi, Carlo Maria 331, 344
Magna curia (Great Court) of Emperor
    Frederick II 9–10, 14, 15, 18
Magno, Celio 264
Magrelli, Valerio 605
Magris, Claudio 593
Mainardi, Arlotto 157
Majorino, Giancarlo 582
Malaparte, Curzio (Kurt Suckert) 546
Malatesta, Battista da Montefeltro 142
Malebranche, Nicolas 348
Malerba, Luigi 578–9
Malipiero, Gerolamo 251

Malipiero, Gian Francesco 455, 456
Mallarmé, Stephane 511
Malpaghini, Giovanni 95
Malvezzi, Virgilio 315
Mameli, Goffredo 446
Manacorda, Giuliano 583
Mancinelli, Laura 603
Manetti, Giannozzo 145, 149
Manfredi, Gianfranco 603
Manfredi, Muzio 298
Manganelli, Giorgio 577
Manganello (anonymous poem) 151
Manifesto, Il, newspaper 597
'mannerists' 259
Manutius (Manuzio), Aldo 136–7, 148,
    158, 212, 253
Manuzio, Paolo 303
Manzini, Gianna 589
Manzini, Giovan Battista 318, 330
Manzoni, Alessandro 379, 414, 427–39,
    448, 450, 515
    essays 429–30 432
    Fermo e Lucia 434–5
    I promessi sposi 432, 433, 434–9, 440–1
    language debate 435–7
    religious hymns 429
    tragedies 430
Maraini, Dacia 583–4
Marchionne di Coppo 122
Margaret of Navarre 229
Marin, Biagio 556, 600
Marinetti, Filippo Tommaso 495–6, 514
Marini, Giovan Ambrogio 320
Marino, Giovan Battista 266, 301, 305–8,
    339, 340
Marmi, Anton Francesco 345
Marotta, Giuseppe 545
Marsi, Antonio 293
Martegiani, Gina 402–3
Martello, Pier Jacopo 351
Martino da Canale 32
Marxism 509, 513, 526
Mascagni, Pietro 454, 456
Mascheroni,Lorenzo 409
masks, in theatre 285, 286, 287, 329,
    357, 362
Massinger, Philip 230
Mastriani, Francesco 479

Mastronardi, Lucio 569
Masuccio Salernitano 150, 155, 229
Matina, Antonio 318
Matraini, Chiara 264
Mayr, Simon 370
Mazzeo di Ricco 18, 21
Mazzini, Giuseppe 444, 450
Mazzolà, Caterino 370
media, mass 568, 571, 587
Medici family 136, 144–5, 188–90, 193,
    196–200, 326, 343
Medici, Lorenzino de' 282
Medici, Lorenzo de' 17, 145, 153, 159,
    163, 164–7, 204, 261
Meini, Giuseppe 447
Meli, Giovanni 393
melodrama *see* theatre
Melville, Herman 536
memoirs, post-war 535
Menabò, Il periodical 566–8, 577, 592
Meneghello, Luigi 593
Mengaldo, Pier Vincenzo 566
Menzini, Benedetto 311
meraviglia 312, 413
merchants, role in travel writing 148
Mercotellis, Agasippo (?Niccolò Corvo)
    365
Metastasio, Pietro (Pietro Trapassi) 351,
    353–5, 365, 367–8, 370, 450
Meung, Jean de 7n, 105
Michelangelo Buonarroti the Younger
    330–1
Michelangelo (Michelangelo Buonarroti)
    220, 221, 222, 260–2, 271
Michelet, Jules 350
Michelstaedter, Carlo 496–7
Mico da Siena 18
Milan
    in the Enlightenment 378–86
    in newly unified Italy 460
Mirandola *see* Pico della Mirandola
Mocati, Bartolomeo 18
Mocenni Magiotti, Quirina 405
mock epic 310–11, *see also* epic;
    parody
Moderata Fonte *see* Pozzo de' Zorzi,
    Modesta
Modio, Giovanni Battista 220

Molière, Jean-Baptiste Poquelin 285, 286,
    326
Molina, Tirso de 330
Molinos, Miguel de 316
Molza, Francesco Maria 227, 271
Molza, Tarquinia 264
Monari, Ernesta 404
Mondolfo, Rodolfo 513
Mondo morale, Il periodical 375
Moniglia, Giovanni Andrea 331
monody 337
Montemezzi, Italo 456
Montaigne, Michel de 252
Montale, Eugenio 456, 505–8, 553–4,
    581–2
Montefeltro, Battista Malatesta da 142
Montefeltro, Duke Federigo da 136
Monteverdi, Claudio 336, 338–40, 364
Monti, Vincenzo 399, 406–11, 413
Morana, Gian Paolo 322
Morandini, Giuliana 601–2
Morando, Bernardo 321
Morante, Elsa 549, 588–9
Moravia, Alberto 524, 551–2, 576, 587
More, Thomas 196, 202
Morelli, Giovanni di Pagolo 159
Moretti, Marino 497
Morlini, Girolamo 226
Morra, Isabella di 264
Morselli, Guido 595
Morte di Giovanni Aguto (anonymous)
    119
motet, in Seicento 337
Motti e facezie del Piovano Arlotto
    (anonymous) 157
Mozart, Wolfgang Amadeus 369–70
Muratori, Ludovico Antonio 301, 344–5
Muret, Marc Antoine 303
Muscetta, Carlo 543
Muscettola, Antonio 304
Musil, Robert 575
Mustoxidi, Andrea 410
Muzio, Girolamo 212
mythology
    Christian replacing pagan 411
    classical 72, 75, 76, 87, 151, 165–7
        Trecento narrative poetry 110
        Quattrocento novels 158

Quattrocento poetry 174
Seicento 306
idyll 353
new (*Le Grazie* of Foscolo) 413–15
uses of (age of Romanticism) 409

Naples 149–50, 347–50, 371–3
post-war writers 545–6
Napoleon Bonaparte 410, 427–8
invasion of Italy 399–400, 406
Nardi, Jacopo 198
Nationalism 512
naturalism and *verismo* in newly unified
Italy 463, 464–79
Nazism 543, 547
Neera, Anna Zuccari *see* Zuccari Neera
Negri, Francesco 325
Nelli, Francesco 86
Nelli, Jacopo Angelo 327, 356
neo-avant-garde
poetry 557, 570–5
prose fiction 575–80
neo-classicism in Enlightenment 382–6,
428, 429
neo-experimentalism 557
neo-realism
and Calvino 552
and Moravia 552
post-war 469, 535–7, 546, 555
Neoplatonism
and Duecento love poetry 24–5
and Quattrocento love poetry 174
in Cinquecento 207, 219, 235, 239
and Michelangelo 261–2
Neri, Pompeo 374
Nerli, Filippo de' 199
Nero, Bernardo del 194
Newton, Isaac 343, 346, 371
Niccolai, Giulia 586
Niccolò da Correggio, 151, 162, 238
Niccolò da Verona 172
Niccolò de' Rossi 126
Nicholas of Cusa 134, 146, 177
Niebo poetry magazine 585
Nietzsche, Friedrich 475
Nievo, Ippolito 441–4
Nogarola, Angela 142
Nogarola, Ginevra 142

Nogarola, Isotta 142, 143
Nolfi, Vincenzo 318
notaries in Duecento, unique position of
28–9
novecentista line in poetry 565
900 522
novel
(1910–45) 515–30
demarcations of modern 603, 604
detective 603
devout 321
epistolary 159
experimental 575–80
fiction since 1956: 588–98
Gothic 603
heroic-gallant genre 319
'industrial' 568–70
of memory 563–4
modern debate on the 575–6
nineteenth century 431–2, 440–5
peasant 533, 537–9
picaresque 315, 471, 524
in Quattrocento 158–9
in Seicento 318–22
see also romanzo, individual novelists
novella 33–6
Boccaccio 83, 85, 154–5
Trecento minor literature 123
Quattrocento 154–8
Cinquecento 223–311
combined with the letter 229
and dialogue in Cinquecento 186
subordinate to frame-story 228
Seicento 322–4
Novella del grasso legnaiuolo
(anonymous) 156
Novelle letterarie journal 376
Novellino 34–6
Novello da Polenta, Guido 68
Noventa, Giacomo 556
Novissimi poets and anthology 570–5,
576
Novo corteggiano, Il (anonymous) 209
Nuccoli, Cecco 116

Occitanic (*langue d'oc*) poetry 8
Odasi, Corrado 148
Odasi, Tifi 148, 273

Oddi, Sforza 287
ode
  in Carducci 462
  classical 257
  nuptial 355
  in Parini 385–6, 414
  Pindaric 304
Officina magazine 557, 564–6
Olivier, Laurence 587
O'Neill, Tom 416
Onesto da Bologna 18, 26, 27
Onofri, Arturo 498
opera 298, 327
  aria texts 365
  buffa 355, 357, 364, 366–7
  commedeja pe musica 365–6
  dramma per musica 363–6
  intermezzi 355, 364, 366
  libretti 339–40, 345–6, 351, 354, 453
  parlante style 367
  for public theatre 338–40
  realism in 369–70
  recitativo semplice 368
  romantic (Risorgimento) 450–53
  Seicento 336–40
  seria 355, 364, 367, 370
  in Settecento 363–70
  since unification of Italy 453–6
  Spanish influence 340
  travelling companies 339
  verismo 454–5
  see also theatre, melodrama
oratorio 354
oratory
  in Cinquecento 185
  in Duecento (political) 29–30
Ordine Nuovo review 509
Orefice, Antonio 365
Orelli, Giorgio 582
Orengo, Nico 606
Origen 137
Orlandi, Guido 23–4
ornamented prose *see dictamen*
Ortese, Anna Maria 578
Osservatore veneto periodical 375
'Ossianic' poems (James Macpherson)
  394
ottava rima 74–5, 119, 163, 176, 258, 331

Ottieri, Ottiero 569
Ottimo Commento 126
ottonari 338
Ovid 74, 151, 166
  Ars amatoria 103
  influence
    on Dante 41
    on Petrarch 99, 103
    on Masuccio Salernitano 150
  Metamorphoses 103, 104, 121, 306

Pagano, Francesco Mario 372
Pagliarani, Elio 572
Painter, William 81, 229
painting versus sculpture, dispute on 221
Paisiello, Giovanni 355, 367, 372
Palandri, Enrico 604, 605
Palazzeschi, Aldo 497–8, 582
Pallavicino, Ferrante 322
Pallavicino, Pietro Sforza 312, 315, 333
Palmieri, Matteo 138
Pandolfini, Agnolo 140
Panizzi, Anthony 172, 234
Panormita (Antonio Beccadelli) 149
Panuccio dal Bagno 18
Panziera, Ugo 124
Paolino, Minorita 71
Paolo da Perugia 71
Paolo dell'Abaco 71
Papi, Giuseppa Catelli 405
Papini, Giovanni 494
Parabosco, Girolamo 228, 283
Parenti, Marco 159
Parini, Giuseppe 380–6, 414, 435
Parise, Goffredo 569, 593
Parker, John 87
parody 148, 153, 167, 268, 270
  Aretino 272
  Dossi 460
  Scroffa 275
  Seicento 310–11, 323
Paruta, Paolo 200
Pascoli, Giovanni 426, 446, 449, 459,
  476–9
Pasini, Pace 320
Pasolini, Pier Paolo 537, 545, 556–7,
  564–6, 575, 587
Pasqualigo, Alvise 296

'pasquinades' (of Aretino) 272
Passavanti, Jacopo 124
pastoral drama 166, 292–8, 329, 334–5
pastoral romance 150, 159–61, 163
Pateg (or Patecchio), Girard 6
Patrizi, Francesco 186, 202
patronage
    end of private 407
    Laurence Olivier 587
    new structures in nineteenth century
        400
    in Quattrocento 136–7, 144–51
        Ferrara 150–1
        Florence 144–5
        Naples 149–50
        Rome 145–6
        Venice 147–8
    in unified Italy 459–60
Paul the Deacon (Paolo Diacono) 76
Paul, St, influence on Petrarch 99, 134
Pavese, Cesare 514, 533, 535, 539,
    539–43, 547–8
Pazzi, Alessandro de' 241, 294
Pazzi, Roberto 603–4
peasant novel *see* novel, peasant
peasant society, post-war 540, 542, 565
Peire d'Alvernhe 3
Peire Vidal 17
Pellegrina, La (anonymous) 288
Pellico, Silvio 401, 441
Penna, Sandro 556, 562
Peregrini, Matteo 312
Pergolesi, Giovanni Battista 364
Peri, Jacopo 336, 338
Perleoni,Giuliano (Rustico Romano) 162
Pers, Ciro de 308
Petrarch (Francesco Petrarca) 89–107
    Africa 90, 106
    Bucolicum carmen 106
    Canzoniere 92–104
    cultural and moral context 91–2
    De otio religioso 90, 107, 133
    De remediis utriusque fortunae 90–1,
        107, 133
    De sui ipsius et multorum ignorantia
        91, 107, 134
    De viris illustribus 90, 107
    De vita solitaria 90, 107, 133

Epistolae metricae 106
Familiares 90
    as humanist 132–5
    influence on Boccaccio 87–8
        on minor literature of Trecento 112
        on Quattrocentro 132–6, 148, 156,
            160–5
        on Cinquecento 183, 251–68, 275–6
        on Seicento 310, 321
        on Ottocento 412, 419, 425
    letters 133–4
    Mont Ventoux letter 98, 134
    Posteritati 107
    programmed sequences of poems 16,
        27, 73
    Rerum memorandarum libri 90, 107
    Rerum vulgarium fragmenta see
        Canzoniere
    Rime see *Canzoniere*
    Secretum 90, 107, 133
    Seniles 90
    Trionfi 90, 104–6, 254, 268, 321
    and Umberto Saba 499–500
petrarchino (pocket-sized works of
    Petrarch) 253–4
Petrarchism, sixteenth-century classicising
    253–7
Petrassi, Goffredo 456
Petrignani, Sandra 604
Petrocchi, Giorgio 268
Pettie, George 211
philosophers of the Enlightenment 371,
    379
philosophy (1910–45) 509–14
phonology, Italian 184
Piazzesi, Gianfranco 536
Piccini, Niccolò 366
Piccolo, Pietro 72
Piccolomini, Aeneas Sylvius (Pope Pius II)
    146, 177
Piccolomini, Alessandro 209, 219, 281
Pico della Mirandola 144, 145, 173
Pier della Vigna 13, 17
Pieri, Marzia 292–3
Pierro, Albino 600
Piersanti, Claudio 604
Pietro da Bescapè 6
Pigna, Giovan Battista Nicolucci 212

Pignotti, Lamberto 571, 586
Pilato, Leonzio 71
Pimentel, Eleonora Fonseca 372
Pindemonte, Ippolito 394, 415
Pino, Bernardino 287
Pino, Paolo 221
Piovene, Guido 449, 534
Pirandello, Luigi 456, 480–90, 511, 514, 515, 519, 575
Pisacane, Carlo 434
Pitti, Buonaccorso di Neri 159
Pitti, Iacopo 199
Pius II, Pope *see* Piccolomini
Pizzetti, Ildebrando 455, 456
Pizzuto, Antonio 577
placiti (sworn statements) on land disputes 4
Planelli, Antonio 365
planh (complaint) 16
Platina 136
Plato 25, 134, 137, 145, 216, 348, 350
Platonic love 214, 216
Plautus 151, 177, 278, 279, 282–3
plays, scripted versus staged 330
plazer (enumeration of satisfactions) 16
Pliny 148
Plotinus 137
poesia aulica in Trecento 114–15
poesia cantabile 259
poesia giocosa in Trecento 115–16
Poli, Umberto *see* Saba, Umberto
poligrafi (polygraphs) 212, 283
   in Venice 345–7
Politecnico, Il (journal) 444, 534, 543, 556
politics
   and culture (1960s) 579
   geography and economy (Galanti) 372–3
   and historiography
      Florence 188–200
      Genoa 201
      Naples 201–2
      Venice 200–1
   ideal states in Cinquecento 202–3
   and love 412–13
   modern disillusionment with 604–5
   and morality, relationship between 315

Seicento writers on 313–17
   and society reflected in Dante's *Commedia* 66–8
Poliziano, Angelo 133, 134, 145, 154, 157, 163, 164–7, 261, 456
Polo, Marco 32, 147
polysyndeton, in Petrarch 103
Pona, Francesco 320
Pontano, Giovanni 149, 150, 190
Pontiggia, Giuseppe 596
populism 525
Porpora, Niccolò 353
Porta, Antonio 571, 572–3, 582, 585
Porta, Carlo 409, 447
Portinari, Bice (?Dante's Beatrice) 41
Porto, Luigi da *see* Da Porto, Luigi
Porzio, Camillo 201–2
positivism in modern Italy 493–4, 509, 511
Possevino, Giovan Battista 212
Pound, Ezra 25
Pozzo de' Zorzi, Modesta (Moderata Fonte) 215
Praga, Emilio 460
Pratesi, Mario 470
Prati, Giovanni 445–6
Pratolini, Vasco 537
pre-Enlightenment 347
Preti, Girolamo 308
Prezzolini, Giuseppe 494
Primato review 514
Prina, Giuseppe 433
printing 144, 147, 148, 185, 187–8, 198, 203, 212, 251–2, 407
Prisco, Michele 593
Prise de Pampelune 168
professional manuals 212
Propertius, Sextus 150
prosimetron (alternation of poetry and prose) 41
Protonotaro *see* Stefano Protonotaro 10
Proust, Marcel 525, 575
Provençal influence 8–11, 15, 28
Ptolemy 137
publishing
   in Cinquecento 187–8, 203, 251–2
   in Seicento 318
   in Ottocento 407, 412, 459–60

in 1980s 596, 599
Pucci, Antonio 119
Puccini, Giacomo 453, 455–6
Pugliese, Giacomo 13
Pulci, Luigi 145, 163, 165, 167–72, 241, 274
Puoti, Anna 404

Quarterly Review, The 417
Quasimodo, Salvatore 456, 504–5, 555
Queneau, Raymond 595
questione della lingua see language
Quindici magazine 579–80
Quintilian 141
Quirini, Giovanni 115
Quirini, Niccolò 115

Rabelais, François 171, 274
Raboni, Giovanni 572
Racine, Jean 354
Radicati, Alberto 373
Raimbautz de Vaqueiras 8, 11
Raimondi, Marcantonio 273
Raimondo da Capua 125
Rainerio (notary) 4
Rame, Franca 587
Ramondetta Fileti, Concetta 405
Ramondino, Fabrizia 601
Raphael (Raffaello Santi) 220
Rappresentazione di Sant' Uliva (anonymous) 176
rappresentazioni, sacre 277, 550
Rasy, Elisabetta 605
'Re Enzo' 11
Rea, Domenico 545–6
Reale Accademia d'Italia 514
realism
    bourgeois 548
    in Dante's *Commedia* 59–60
    exaggerated 213
    socialist 536
    see also neo-realism
Rebora, Clemente 498
recitativo semplice 368
Redi, Francesco 316–17
reflexivity in Petrarch 92
reformist thought 372
'regional' writers of 1970s 593

Regno, Il periodical 494
Reich, Wilhelm 412, 551
Reinhardt, Max 487
relativism 483–6
religious plays 175–6, 550
Rendiconti review 565
Renier-Michiel, Giustina 405
Resistance, and literature 535, 540, 542, 543, 547, 555–6, 563
reviews 564–8, 586, 599
    see also journalism in post-war Italy
Revolution, French 393, 407
Rezeptiontheorie (relationship between authors and public) 432
rhetoric
    in Cinquecento 185–7
    devices in Petrarch's *Canzoniere* 103
    enhanced study of 152
    importance of Latin and Greek 132
    in the lyric 17
    Valla and 141
Ricci, Pier Giorgio 86
Ricciardi, Giovanni Battista 311
Ricco *see* Mazzeo di Ricco
Riccoboni, Luigi 346
Richardson, Samuel 357, 366
ricordi/ricordanze (thoughts and advice) 159, 195, 210
Rienzo, Cola di 122
rifacimenti 169, 172
Righetti-Giorgi, Geltrude 369
rime see also *ottava rima, terza rima*
Rinaldo d'Aquino 13
Rinaldo degli Albizzi 159
Rinuccini, Alamanno 159
Rinuccini, Cino 115
Rinuccini, Giovan Battista 321
Rinuccini, Ottavio 336, 337
Risi, Nelo 582
rispetto toscano 163
Ristoro d'Arezzo 30
Ritmo cassinese 4
Ritmo di S.Alessio 4
Ritmo laurenziano 4
Rivoluzione liberale review 509
Roberti, Ercole de' 151
Robortello, Francesco 241
Rocco, Alfredo 514

Rococo 317
Rodriguez de Montalvo, Garci 242
Rolli, Paolo Antonio 351
Roman de la Rose (Guillaume de Lorris and Jean de Meung) 7, 85, 105
Roman de Troie (Sainte Maure) 9, 13, 75
romance
  allegorical 320
  chivalric 154
  prose *see romanzo*
romance material in Trecento vernacular translation 121
Romani, Felice 451
Romanò, Angelo 564
Romano, Giulio 273
Romano, Lalla 589
Romanticism 399–457, 504
Romanticism versus classicism, controversy 399–405, 406, 409–10
romanzo (prose romance) 231–2
Romei, Annibale 212
'Romeo and Juliet' stories 155, 156, 227, 229, 291
Ronconi, Luca 587
Ronda, La review 498, 509, 565
Rosa, Salvatore 311
Rospigliosi, Giulio 327, 334
Rosselli, Amelia 585
Rossellini, Roberto 536
Rossi, Bartolommeo 296
Rossi, Gaetano 451
Rossi, *see* Niccolò de' Rossi
Rossi-Martinetti, Cornelia 405
Rossini, Gioacchino Antonio 370, 451, 452
Rosso di San Secondo *see* San Secondo, Rosso di
Rota, Bernardino 254, 268
Rousseau, Jean Jacques 379, 395, 412
Rovani, Giuseppe 441
Rovere, Guidobaldo Bonarelli della 297
Roversi, Roberto 557, 564–5
Rucellai, Giovanni 257, 289
Ruffini, Giovanni Domenico 441
Russo, Luigi 512
Rustichello da Pisa 32
Rustico di Filippo 6

Ruzante (Beolco, Angelo) 274, 282, 292

Saba, Umberto (Umberto Poli) 499–502, 535, 554–5
Sabadino degli Arienti, Giovanni 156
Sabba da Castiglione 210
Sacchetti, Franco 113, 123
Sacchi, Antonio 356, 361
sacra rappresentazione (religious play in vernacular) 163, 166, 175–6, 277
sacred drama 354
Sagredo, Giovanni 323
Sale, Anton Giulio Brignole *see* Brignole Sale
Salernitano, Masuccio *see* Masuccio
Salgari, Emilio 479
Salieri, Antonio 355
Salinari, Carlo 543
Salingar, Leo 288
Sallust, vernacular translation of 121
Salutati, Coluccio 110, 136
Salviati, Lionardo 184
Salvo imprevisti magazine 585–6
Samonà, Carmelo 599
San Secondo, Rosso di 484, 486
Sanguineti, Edoardo 573–6, 577, 582
Sannazaro, Jacopo 149, 150, 162, 164
  Arcadia 159–61, 255–6, 292, 293
  De partu virginis 150, 255
  Eclogae piscatorie 150, 255
  Rime 255–6
Sansovino, Francesco 186, 212, 219
Santucci, Luigi 550
Sant'Uliva, Rappresentazione di 176
Sanvitale, Francesca 600–1
Sapegno, Natalino 108, 119
Sarpi, Paolo 315
Sartre, Jean-Paul 571
satire
  Alamanni 242
  Alberti 139, 140
  Aretino 208
  Ariosto 258, 268–9
  Cinquecento 268
    Cinquecento theatre 282
  Folengo 241
  Giusti 446
  Goldoni 357–8

Leopardi 424
Machiavelli 224
ottava rima used in 163
Parini 382
Parise 569
political (Seicento) 314
Pulci 169
satira rustica 292
satiric poetry 311
satirical comedy 352
Satta, Salvatore 593
satyr-plays 294–5
Savinio, Alberto (Andrea De Chirico) 523
Savonarola, Gerolamo 159
Sbarbaro, Camillo 498
Scala, Flaminio 328
Scalia, Gianni 564, 567, 568
Scalise, Gregorio 584
scapigliatura 460, 461, 470, 565
Scarron, Paul 310
Scataglini, Franco 600
Schmitz, Ettore *see* Svevo, Italo
schools
    in Quattrocento 135–6
    role of Venetian 147–8
Sciascia, Leonardo 481, 538, 590–2, 603
science
    breakthrough of (Seicento) 312, 316–17
    and literature 344
    natural 348–50
scientific thought in Duecento 30–1
Scolari, Edvige de Battisti 405
Scotellaro, Rocco 539
Scott, Walter 429, 434, 435, 438, 441, 451
Scroffa, Camillo 275
sculpture versus painting, dispute on 221
Sebastiano del Piombo 260
Segneri, Paolo 316
Segni, Bernardo 199
Segre, Cesare 576, 577
semiotics 576, 587, 598
Seneca 92, 104, 121, 133–5, 288, 290–1
Sennuccio del Bene 95, 115
Sensism 379, 380–2

Serafino Aquilano (Serafino de' Ciminelli) 151, 163–4, 271
Serao, Matilde 470
Sercambi, Giovanni 113, 123
Sereni, Emilio 536
Sereni, Vittorio 555, 562–3, 582
Serlio, Sebastiano 290
Sermini, Gentile 155
sermons in Duecento, importance of 33
Serravalle *see* Bertoldi, Giovanni da
serventese 16, 72
    in Trecento narrative poetry 119
sestine 95, 160, 163
Settala, Ludovico 314
Settembrini, Luigi 264, 434, 441
settenari
    in opera 338
    in poetry 257
settenari doppi 352
Sforza, Bianca Maria 162
Sforza, Ludovico 151
Sgorlon, Carlo 593
Shakespeare, William 75, 288, 326, 378
    All's Well That Ends Well 81
    Cymbeline 81
    Measure for Measure 230
    Midsummer Night's Dream, A 295
    Othello 230
    Romeo and Juliet 227
    Twelfth Night 281
    and Verdi 452, 454
Sharp, Samuel 377
Sicilian poetry centres in Italy 18–19
Sicilian school
    in Duecento 9–14
    poesia aulica in Trecento 114–15
Sicilian writers
    1970s 590–2
    in newly unified Italy 463
    see also Pirandello
Siculo-Tuscan group of imitators 14
Silone, Ignazio 533, 534, 535, 539
Simone da Cascia 124
Sismondi, Simonde de 432
Slataper, Scipio 509
Società (Journal) 636
sodalitas (personal friendship) 25
Soffici, Ardengo 496

Solaria (literary monthly journal) 524, 525, 526, 528

Soldani, Jacopo 311

Soldanieri, Niccolò 120

Soldati, Mario 514

Solerti, Angelo 266

Solmi, Sergio 555–6

Song of Songs' influence on Dante 41, 42

sonnets
  augmented 16
  cycles of 16
  Della Casa 263
  Guinizzelli 19
  invention of 11–12, 15–16
  Petrarch 95
  Rustico di Filippo 6
  sonetti caudati 164, 270
  sonetti licenziosi 273

Sophocles 267, 291

Sordello da Goito 8

La Spagna in rima 169

Spagnoletti, Giacinto 585

Spanish influence on Italian theatre 340, 362

Spatola, Adriano 586

Spaventa, Bertrando 426

spectacle, theatrical 326–7

speech
  closely linked with writing 183–4
  superior to writing 184

Speroni, Sperone 184, 186, 215, 218, 289, 303

Spinoza, Baruch 348

spirit in Duecento poetry 23

Staël (Staël-Holstein), Anne-Louise Germaine Necker de 401, 403, 418, 450

Stampa, Gaspara 264–5

Stampa, Stefano 434

Statius 75, 103

Stefano Protonotaro 10

Stern, Mario Rigoni 544

Sterne, Laurence 415

Stigliani, Tommaso 304

stile bernesco 268

stilnovo 18, 25, 26–7, 110, 114, 553
  in Boccaccio 72

Lorenzo de' Medici's defence of 165
  in Petrarch 102, 103–4, 106
  in *Vita Nuova* 42, 44, 94

La storia di Merlino 121

Storie pistoresi (anonymous) 122

strambotto 119, 163–4

Straparola, Giovan Francesco 227–8
  influence on Pietro Fortini 230

Strauss, Richard 456

Strehler, Giorgio 587

Strozzi, Alessandra Macinghi 159

Strozzi, Giovan Battista 259, 267

Strozzi, Lorenzo di Filippo 279

structuralism 576

studia humanitatis (liberal arts) in Quattrocento 136

Sturm und Drang (Italian) and Alfieri's *Vita* 396

Suckert, Kurt *see* Malaparte, Curzio

Suriano, Francesco 148

Svevo, Italo 515–19, 520, 548, 575
  La coscienza di Zeno 517–18
  Senilità 516–17
  and *Solaria* journal 524
  Una vita 516–17

symbolism in newly united Italy 473

synaeresis 102

synaloepha 102

synecdoche 103

Tabucchi, Antonio 597, 602

Tacitus, Publius 200, 314, 348

Tam tam magazine 586

Tamaro, Susanna 606

Tansillo, Luigi 258, 293

Tanzi, Carl' Antonio 393

Tarchetti, Ugo 460

Targioni Tozzetti, Fanny 405

Tarsia, Galeazzo di 264, 268

Tasso, Bernardo 218, 242, 244, 256–7

Tasso, Torquato 209, 243–50, 259, 263, 295, 316, 326
  Allegory 247
  Aminta 293, 296, 297, 334
  contrast with Ariosto 248–9
  Discorsi 245, 249
  Gerusalemme Conquistata 249–50, 267

Gerusalemme Liberata 243, 244–7, 250, 307
Il Forno overo de la nobilità 212
Il Malpiglio overo de la corte 209
Il Minturno overo della bellezza 218
Il padre di famiglia 220
lyric poetry 266–8
Rinaldo 243
Torrismondo 291
Tassoni, Alessandro 310–11
Taviani, Paolo Emilio 537
La Tavola Ritonda 121
Tebaldeo, Antonio 151, 271
Tel quel 571
Tenca, Carlo 444
tenzone (poetic exchange) 11, 16, 45
Teotochi Albrizzi, Isabella 405
Terence 151, 177, 278, 279, 282
Terracina, Laura 264
terza rima
   Boccaccio 72, 75, 105
   capitolo in 268
   Dante 163
   Pasolini 556
   Sannazaro 160
Tesauro, Emanuele 313, 333
Testi, Fulvio 309
Testori, Giovanni, 587
theatre
   1970s 587–8
   academic theory increase 286–7
   acting 283
   audience participation 587–8
   in Cinquecento 277–98
   commedia dell'arte 283–6
   commedia erudita 284, 287
   effects of Renaissance on 277–8
   improvising on outline scenario 285
   Living Theatre 587
   in Medici Florence 282
   melodrama 329, 353–5
   Metastasio to Goldoni 353–62
   pastoral drama 166, 291–8
   in Quattrocento 175–7
   Roman school 588
   scripted comedy 278–83, 328
   in Seicento 326–35
   in Venice 282

   see also acting; actors; comedy; tragedy
theatrum mundi (life as theatre) in Tasso 249
Theocritus 160, 166, 292, 350
Theophrastus 85
Thierry, Augustin 429
Thomas (author of French romances) 3
Thucydides 137
Tiraboschi, Girolamo 301, 344
Titian (Tiziano Vecellio) 220
Tobino, Mario 544, 563
Tolomei, Claudio 184, 257
Tolstoy, Leo 536
Tomasi di Lampedusa, Giuseppe *see* Lampedusa
Tomitano, Bernardino 186
Tomizza, Fulvio 593
Tommaseo, Niccolò 419, 447–9
Tondelli, Pier Vittorio 605
Torelli, Giacomo 339
Tornabuoni, Lucrezia 168
Torricelli, Evangelista 316
Tozzi, Federico 519, 520–1
Traetta, Tommaso 368
tragedia a lieto fine see tragi-comedy
tragedy
   affected by rules 241
   classical 288–91, 355
      see also theatre, melodrama
   (Greek) and *dramma per musica* 365
   Seicento 329, 331–4
      sacred 333
   Settecento 346, 352
tragi-comedy 290, 291–2, 334
tragi-comic pastoral genre 259
tragic tales 155
translation
   controversy over 399–402
   from Greek and Latin, increasing 181
   Greek into Latin 136–7, 241
   into other European languages 172, 193, 196, 202, 208, 211–12
   of the novel (Seicento) 318
   see also vernacular
Trapassi, Pietro *see* Metastasio
travel writing 147, 148, 324–5, 373, 578
   pre-Romantic period 394–5
   within the novel 159

treatises
  on aesthetics 312–13
  in Seicento 312–17
Trissino, Gian Giorgio 183, 217–18, 220
  Italia liberata da' Gothi 241–2
  Sofonisba 257, 288–9
Tristano Corsiniano 33
Tristano Riccardiano 32–3
Tristano Veneto 33
trobar clus verse form 9, 16, 18
trobar ric verse form 9, 12, 16
Trombatore, Gaetano 543
Trotto, Bernardo 220
troubadors *see* Provençal influence in
  Duecento
Troyes, Chrétien de 3
Tuscan imitators in Duecento 14–15
Tuscan language *see* language
Tuscan lyric 145
'Tuscanisation' of literary vernacular *see*
  language
Twain, Mark 536

Uberti, Fazio degli 112
Ungaretti, Giuseppe 502–4, 514, 554
unification of Italy 459–60
Utopia, set in Italy by Ortensio Lando 213
Utopia (More) 196, 202

Valcieco (Raffaele da Verona) 233
Valeriano, Pierio *see* Bolzani, Giovanni
  Pietro
Valerius Maximus, vernacular translation
  of 121
Valéry, Paul 511
Valla, Lorenzo 133, 137, 140–2, 146,
  149, 152–3
Vallisnieri, Antonio 345
Vangelisti, Paul 586
Vaqueiras *see* Raimbautz de Vaqueiras
Varano, Costanza 142
Varchi, Benedetto 184–5, 199, 218, 221,
  282
Varese, Carlo 437
Varese, Claudio 414, 435
varietas 166
Vasari, Giorgio 220, 221–2
Vassalli, Sebastiano 597, 600

Veneziano, Antonio 268
Venice 147–8, 346–7
Vera, Augusto 426
Verdi, Giuseppe 452–4
Verga, Giovanni 454, 460, 464–9, 478,
  515, 521, 536
  I Malavoglia 464–5, 466–8
  Mastro don Gesualdo 464, 467–9
  novelle 466
Vergerio, Pier Paolo 106, 136, 138
verismo 439–40
  and naturalism 463–70
  in opera 454–5
vernacular
  blended with Latin 241
  Catherine of Siena 125
  Dante's *Commedia* 58, 126
  debate over 181–5
  'ennobled' 139, 253
vernacular (*cont.*)
  expansion of (Cinquecento) 181–5,
    200–1
  in Ferrara 150
  Florentine (Boccaccio) 81
  Francis of Assisi 5–6
  and Latin 152–4, 181–2
  Leonardo da Vinci's *novelle* 157
  letters in (Cinquecento) 187
  literature in 152–177
    Duecento 28–9
    women and 146
  and Lorenzo de' Medici 165
  Medici patronage of the 145
  Petrarch 89, 112
  prose translations (Duecento) 31–3
  Pulci's argot 170–1
  religious plays in the 175–6
  role and status of 109
  standardisation and spread of 185
  superiority over Latin (Dante) 48–9
  translations into (Quattrocento) 131–2,
    135–7
  translations of minor literature
    (Trecento) 120–1
  in Trecento Italy 113, 120–1
  see also translation
vernacular glosses (*chiose*) 126
Verona, Niccolò da *see* Niccolò da Verona

Veronese, Battista Guarino 135, 142, 147, 152
Veronesi, Sandro 606
Verri, Il magazine 570, 572
Verri, Alessandro 378, 380
Verri, Pietro 378–9, 384, 401
versi a selva 338
Vespasiano da Bisticci 136
Vettori, Francesco 196
Il Viaggio di Carlomagno 121
Vico, Giambattista 348–50, 371–2, 403, 413, 429, 502, 511
Vieri, Francesco de' 212
Vieusseux, Pietro 402, 424
Viganò, Renata 536
Vignano *see* Giovanni da Vignano
Villa, Emilio 606
Villani, Filippo 122
Villani, Giovanni 22, 30, 122
Villani, Matteo 122
Vincent of Beauvais 7, 33
Vinci, Leonardo da *see* Leonardo da Vinci
Virgil 47, 103, 107, 121, 135, 160, 166, 238, 257, 292, 350
Visconti, Ermes 401, 427
Visconti, Gasparo 162
Visconti, Giovanni 90
Visconti, Luchino 470, 536
Vittorelli, Jacopo 351
Vittorini, Elio 514, 524, 526–7, 534, 536, 543–5, 547, 556, 566–8
Vittorino da Feltre 135
Vivaldi, Antonio 346
Viviani, Cesare 585, 586
Voce, La (review) 494, 498, 509, 519, 564–5
volgare
    Dante's praise for Tuscan 164
    first evidence of Italian 4, 9
    illustre 158
    see also vernacular
volgarizzamento 31–3, 120–1, 124, 131–2, 135–7
Volpe, Gioacchino 514
Volponi, Paolo 569, 595–6
Voltaire 346, 374, 379
vowel systems, Sicilian and Tuscan 10–11
Wagner, Richard 454, 475

Webster, John 264
Weinberg, Bernard 249
Wilkins, Ernest Hatch 94
wit, verbal (*motti e facezie*) 157
women
    acting in comedy 281–2, 285
    Boccaccio's biographies of 87
    in Cinquecento society 186, 206, 214–20
    female subject (post-war) 547–9
    first novel for 159
    as humanists in Quattrocento 142–3
    and lyric poetry in Cinquecento 181
    and need for vernacular 154
    Pietro Verri on 379
    poets of Cinquecento 264–5
    and reading Boccaccio 210
    shortage of (as readers of vernacular literature) 146
    see also feminism
women writers
    Trecento 124–5
    Quattrocento 142–3
    Cinquecento 264–5
    Ottocento 403–5
    Novecento 472–3, 547–9, 588–90, 599, 600–2, 605
World War II and literature 555, 556, 590
    see also death camps, post-war writing on
writing
    closely linked with speech 183–4
    inferior to speech 184
Wyatt, Thomas 242

Xenophon 139, 190, 219

Young, Bartholomew 211

Zandonai, Riccardo 456
Zanzotto, Andrea 574–5, 581, 596
Zappi, Felice 351
Zeno, Apostolo 345–6, 354, 363–5, 367
Zeno, Pier Caterino 345
Zhdanov, Andrej 536
Zola, Emile 463–4, 536
Zolla, Elémire 568
Zuccari Neera, Anna 470
Zuccolo, Ludovico 298, 314